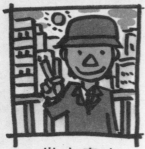

岸本斉史

Uh... Oh! Right! I wanted to let you all know that with this volume begins Part Two, so I look forward to your patronage. To those who have not yet read Part One, please read from volume 1. Then again, feel free to read it from the middle as well... (laughs).

—*Masashi Kishimoto, 2005*

Author/artist Masashi Kishimoto was born in 1974 in rural Okayama Prefecture, Japan. After spending time in art college, he won the Hop Step Award for new manga artists with his manga **Karakuri** (Mechanism). Kishimoto decided to base his next story on traditional Japanese culture. His first version of **Naruto**, drawn in 1997, was a one-shot story about fox spirits; his final version, which debuted in **Weekly Shonen Jump** in 1999, quickly became the most popular ninja manga in Japan.

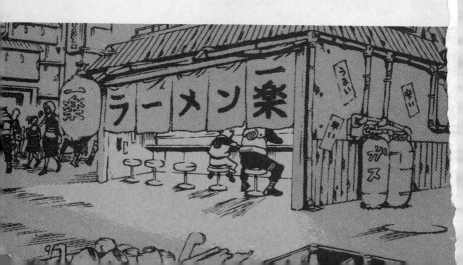

NARUTO

3-in-1 Edition
Volume 10
SHONEN JUMP Manga Omnibus Edition
A compilation of the graphic novel volumes 28–30

STORY AND ART BY MASASHI KISHIMOTO

Translation & English Adaptation/Naomi Kokubo, Mari Morimoto, Kyoko Shapiro, HC Language Solutions, Inc., Eric-Jon Rössel Waugh
English Adaptation/Deric A. Hughes, Naomi Kokubo, Benjamin Raab, Ian Reid, HC Language Solutions, Inc., Eric-Jon Rössel Waugh
Touch-up Art & Lettering/Sabrina Heep, Gia Cam Luc, Mark McMurray, Inori Fukuda Trant
Design/Sean Lee (Original Series)
Design/Sam Elzway (Omnibus Edition)
Editor/Joel Enos (Manga Edition)
Managing Editor/Erica Yee (Omnibus Edition)

Printed in Canada

Published by VIZ Media, LLC
P.O. Box 77010
San Francisco, CA 94107

10 9 8 7 6 5 4
Omnibus edition first printing, January 2015
Fourth printing, May 2022

VIZ MEDIA
viz.com

ratings.viz.com
RATED T TEEN

PARENTAL ADVISORY
NARUTO is rated T for Teen and is recommended for ages 13 and up. This volume contains realistic and fantasy violence.

SHONEN JUMP

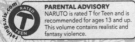

SHONEN JUMP MANGA EDITION

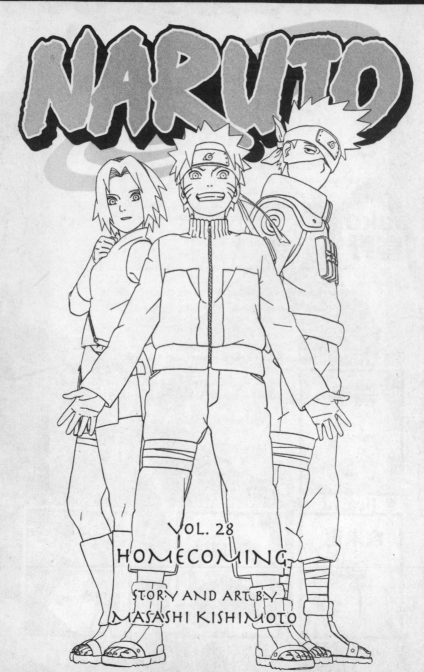

NARUTO

VOL. 28

HOMECOMING

STORY AND ART BY

MASASHI KISHIMOTO

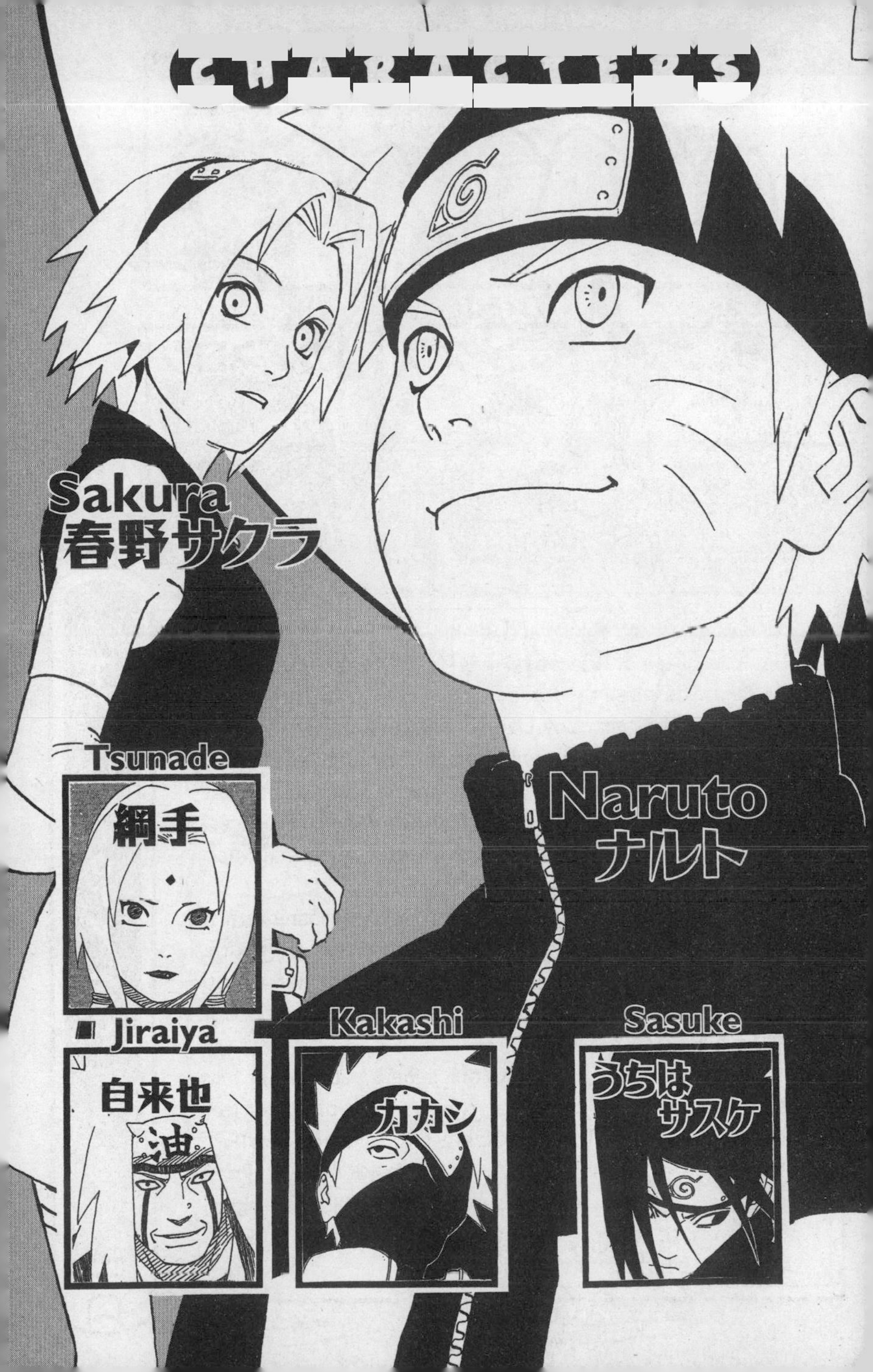
CHARACTERS
Naruto
ナルト
Sakura
春野サクラ
Tsunade
綱手
Sasuke
うちはサスケ
Kakashi
カカシ
Jiraiya
自来也
油

Ebizo

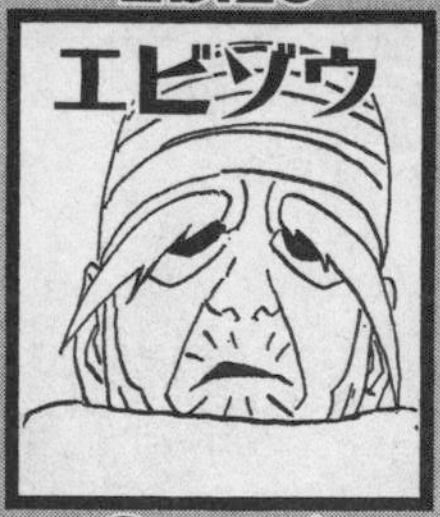
エビゾウ

Granny Chiyo

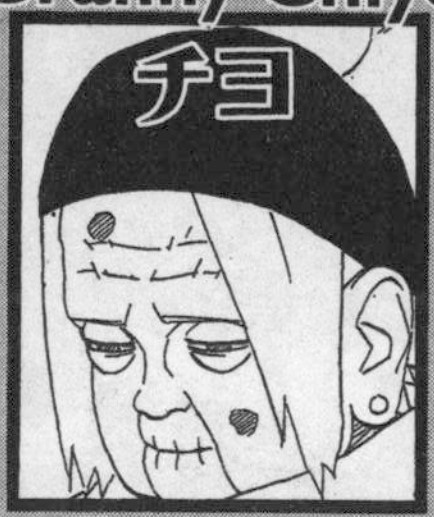
チヨ

Gaara

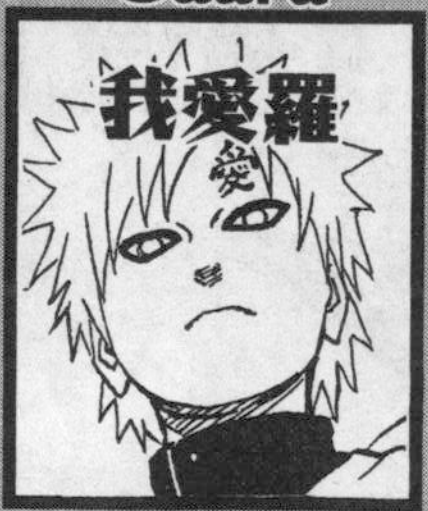
我愛羅

Sasori

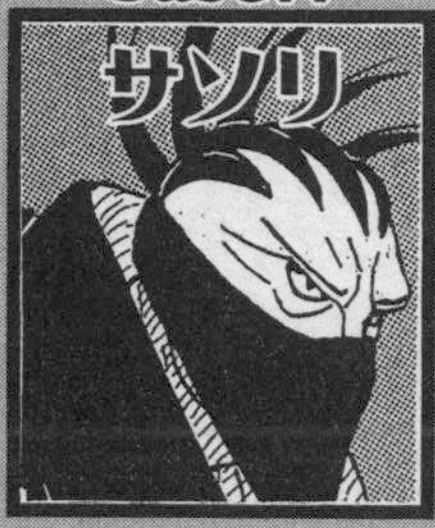
サソリ

Deidara

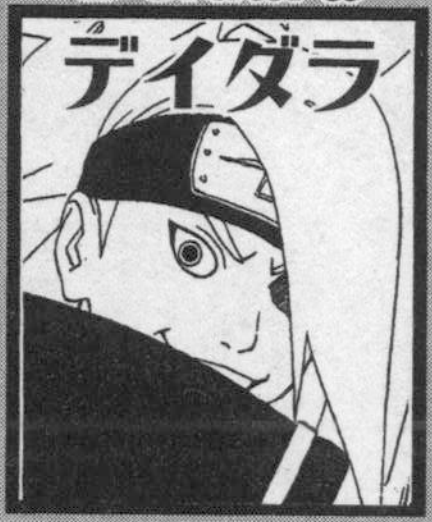
デイダラ

Kankuro

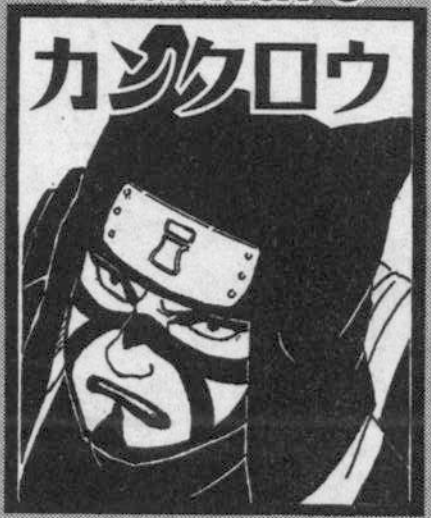
カンクロウ

The Story So Far...

Twelve years ago a destructive nine-tailed fox spirit attacked the ninja village of Konohagakure. The Hokage, or village champion, defeated the fox by sealing its soul into the body of a baby boy. Now that boy, Uzumaki Naruto, has grown up to be a ninja-in-training, learning the art of ninjutsu with his teammates Sakura and Sasuke. During the Second Chûnin Exam, Orochimaru, a former student of the Third Hokage, attacks Naruto and the others. He leaves a curse mark upon Sasuke and then vanishes.

During the Third Exam, Orochimaru and company return to launch *Operation Destroy Konoha*, a campaign that ends with the sacrifice of Lord Hokage's life. Following the fierce battle against Orochimaru and Kabuto, Lady Tsunade then becomes the Fifth Hokage.

In the wake of the battle, Konoha suffers yet another loss when Sasuke, tempted by Orochimaru's offer of power, leaves with the Sound Ninja Four. Desperate to save his friend, Naruto enters into a bitter fight with Sasuke, but is ultimately unable to stop him. Amid movement by both Orochimaru and the mysterious organization the Akatsuki, Naruto and the others begin further training!!

NARUTO

VOL. 28
HOMECOMING

CONTENTS

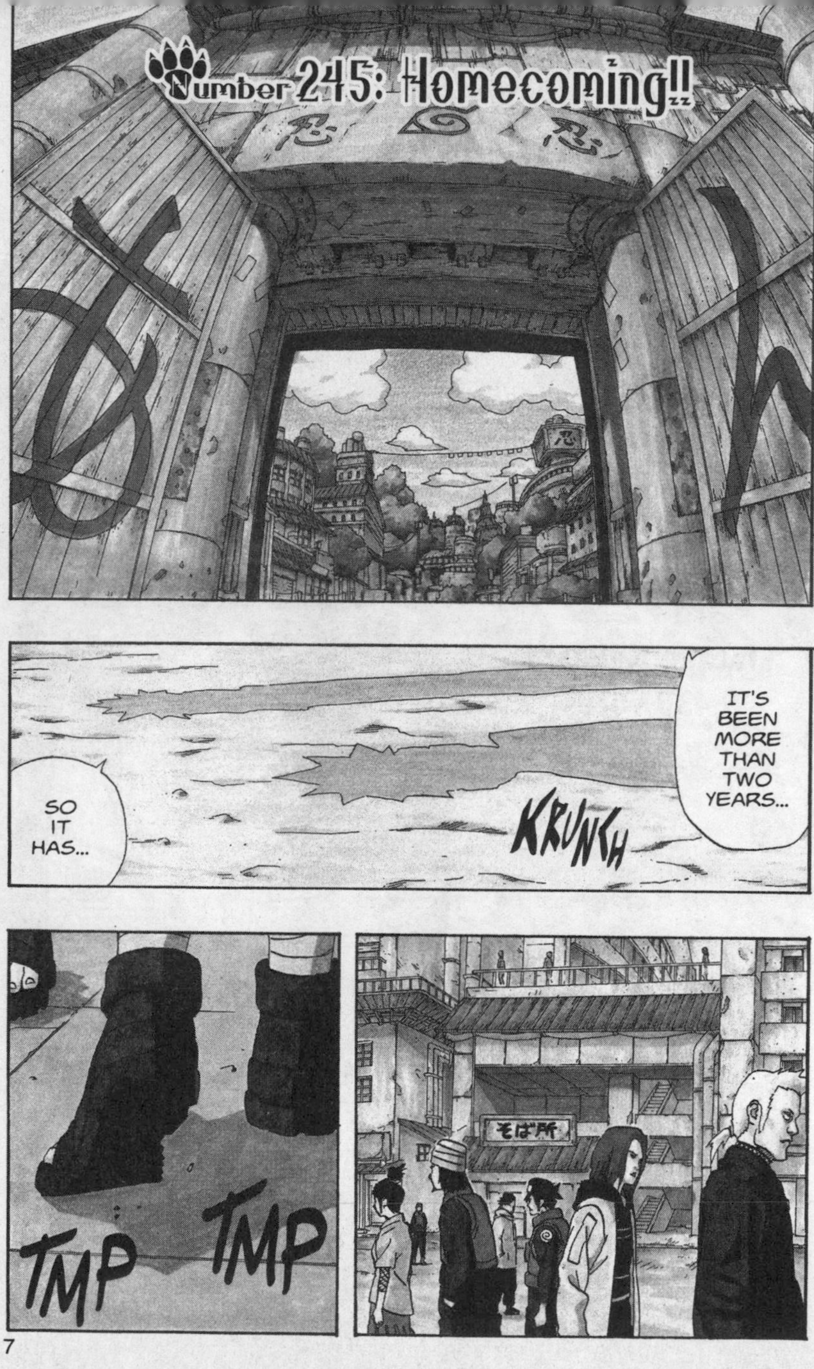
Number 245: Homecoming!!
IT'S BEEN MORE THAN TWO YEARS...
KRUNCH
SO IT HAS...
そば所
TMP
TMP

SECOND JUTSU POPULARITY SURVEY!!

10th Place/
Gaara
1,383 votes

6th Place/
Uchiha Itachi
2,997 votes

5th Place/
Nara Shikamaru
3,003 votes

3rd Place/
Hatake Kakashi
5,430 votes

1st Place/
Uchiha Sasuke
6,647 votes

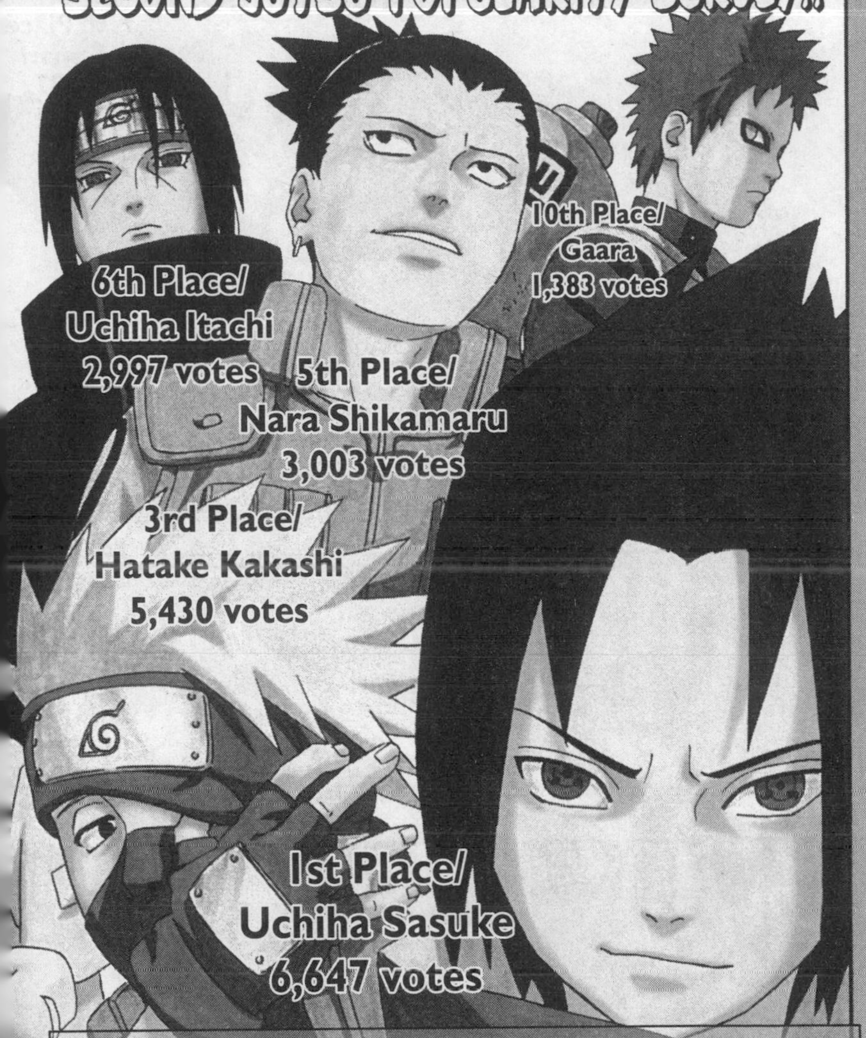

● The Jutsu Popularity Survey Results ●

1st Place/Rasengan 6,354 votes	8th Place/Sharingan 1,531 votes	15th Place/Mind Transfer Technique 535 votes
2nd Place/Chidori 5,665 votes	9th Place/Byakugan 1,197 votes	16th Place/Reverse Lotus 513 votes
3rd Place/Lightning Blade 5,188 votes	10th Place/Mangekyo Sharingan 670 votes	17th Place/Sakura Blizzard* 511 votes
4th Place/Tsukuyomi 3,447 votes	11th Place/Art of Suffocating Darkness 653 votes	18th Place/Ninja Harem 509 votes
5th Place/8 Trigrams 64 Palms 1,624 votes	12th Place/Ninja Centerfold 617 votes	19th Place/Shadow Doppelganger 499 votes
6th Place/Summoning 1,611 votes	13th Place/Lions Barrage 616 votes	20th Place/One Thousand Years of Death 490 votes
7th Place/Shadow Possession 1,575 votes	14th Place/Summoning: Blade Dance 576 votes	

*Sakura's Jutsu from the movie Ninja Clash in the Land of Snow

Number 245: Homecoming!!

8th Place/ Haruno Sakura 2,394 votes

11th Place Temari 1,037 votes

9th Place/ Hyuga Hinata 1,598 votes

7th Place/ Hyuga Neji 2,497 votes

2nd Place/ Uzumaki Naruto 5,614 votes

4th Place/ Umino Iruka 4,128 votes

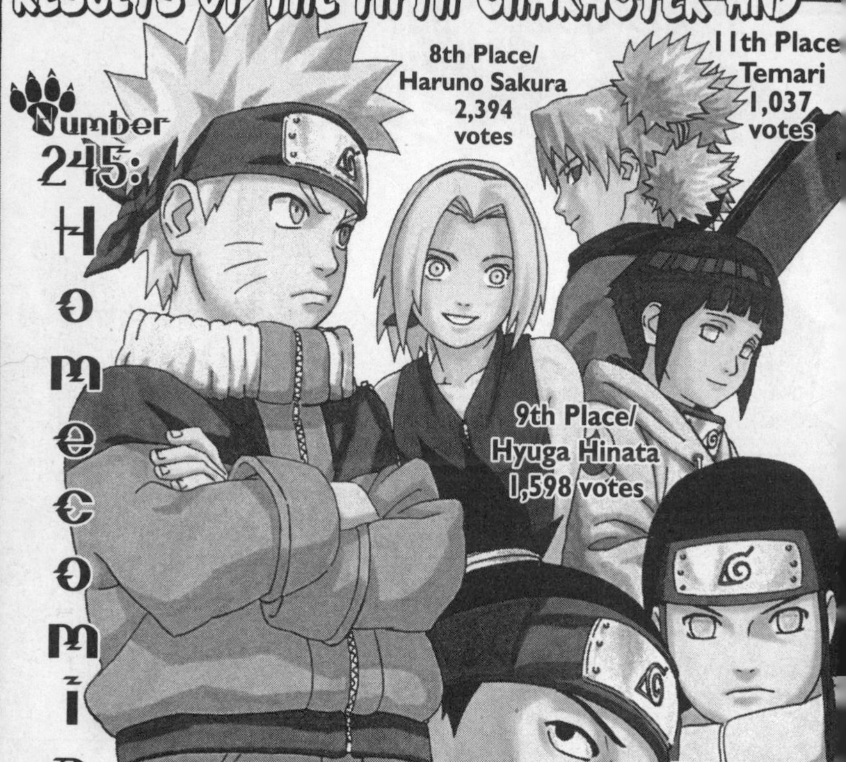

● **More of the Character Popularity Survey Results** ●

12th Place/Inuzuka Kiba 788 votes	18th Place/Kimimaro 478 votes	24th Place/Tenten 280 votes
13th Place/Rock Lee 722 votes	19th Place/Yakushi Kabuto 473 votes	25th Place/Tayuya 225 votes
14th Place/Yamanaka Ino 717 votes	20th Place/Gekko Hayate 434 votes	26th Place/Sarutobi Asuma 221 votes
15th Place/Haku 706 votes	21st Place/Aburame Shino 377 votes	27th Place/Orochimaru 211 votes
16th Place/Tsunade 595 votes	22nd Place/Fourth Hokage 345 votes	28th Place/Hoshigaki Kisame 202 votes
17th Place/Might Guy 559 votes	23rd Place/Jiraiya 317 votes	29th Place/Shizune 163 votes
		30th Place/Kankuro 117 votes

This poll was conducted in Japan.

NARUTO -ナルト-

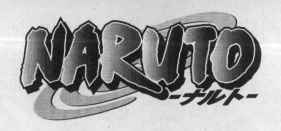

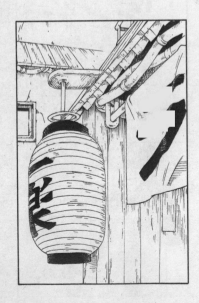

READ THIS WAY

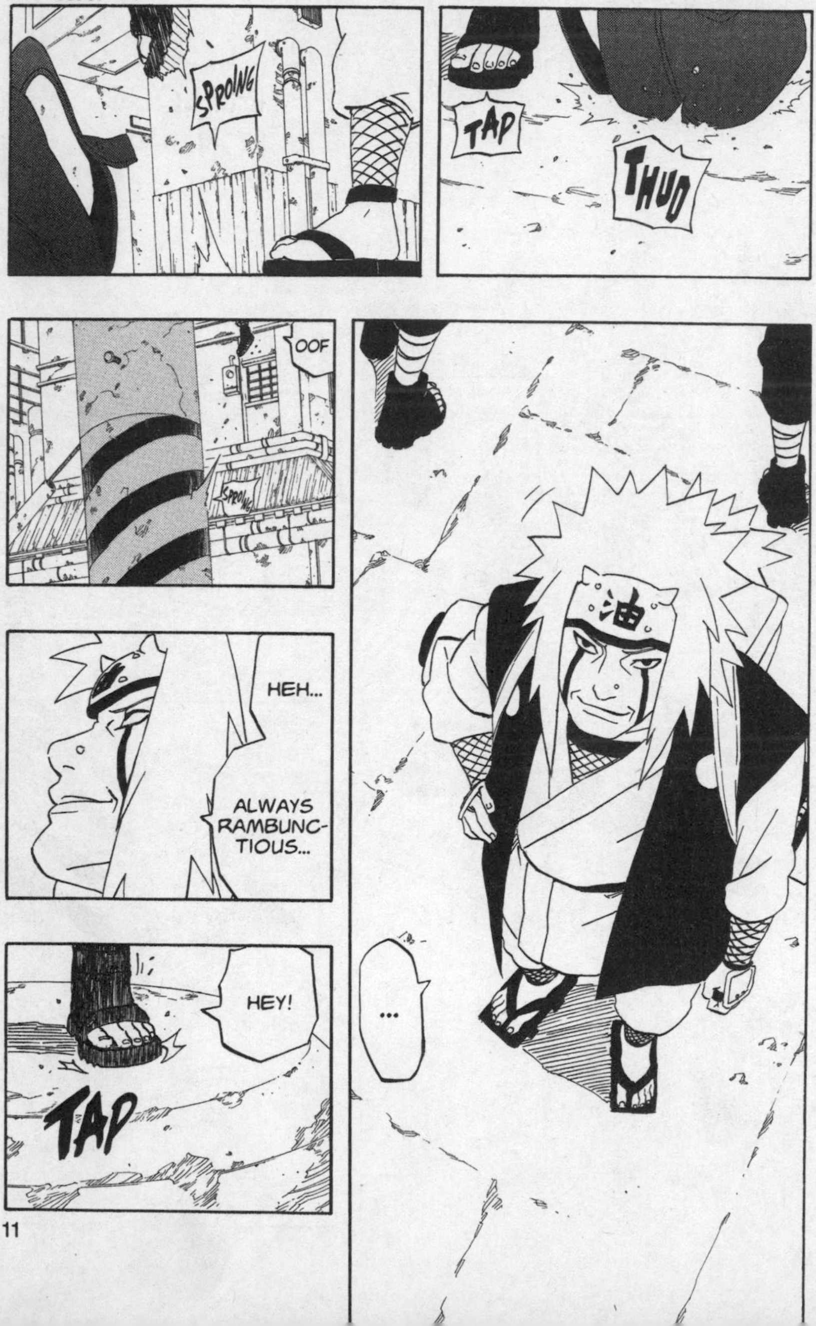

TAP
THUD
SPROING
...
OOF
SPROING
HEH...
ALWAYS RAMBUNC-TIOUS...
HEY!
TAP

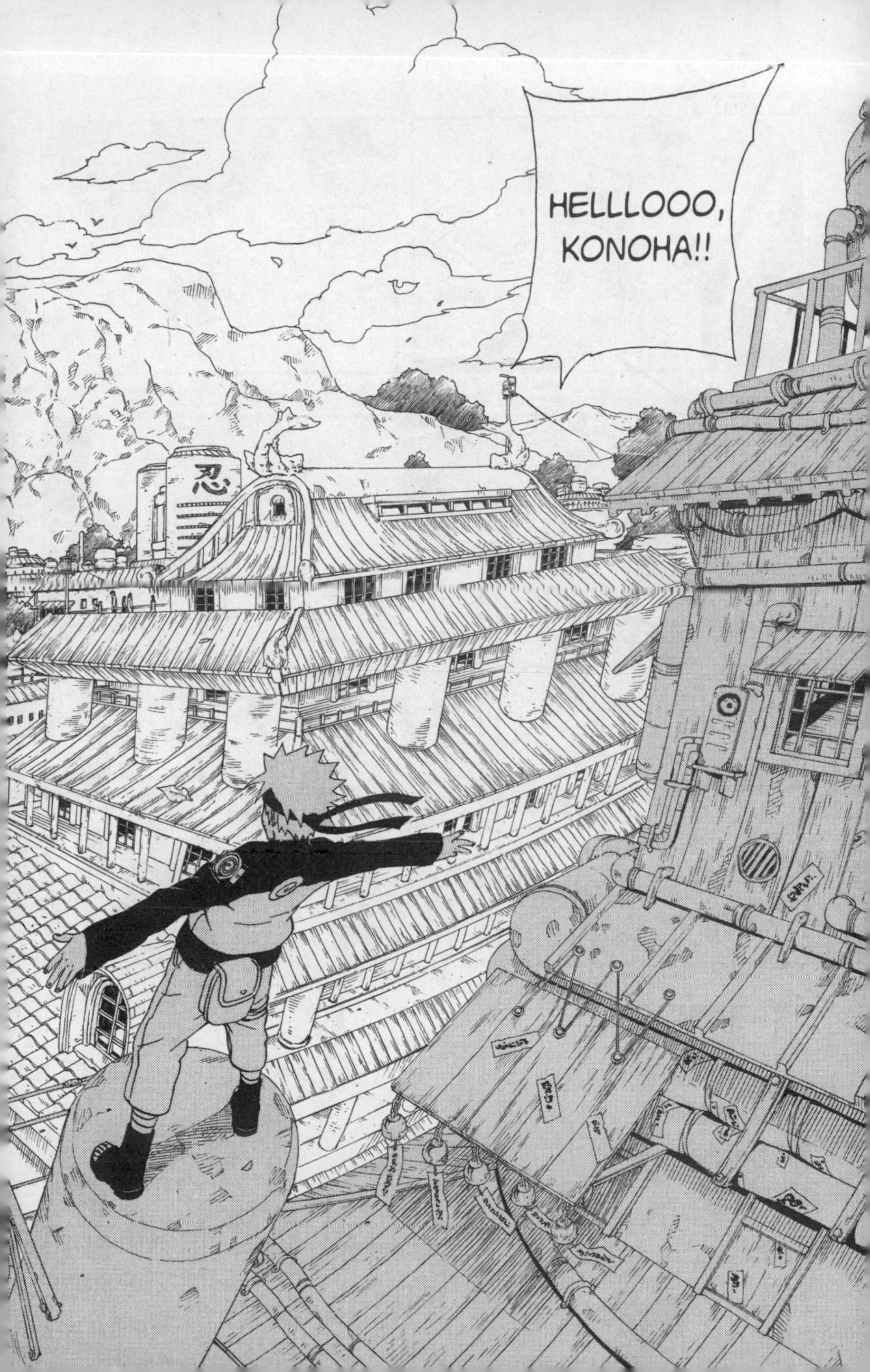
HELLLOOO, KONOHA!!

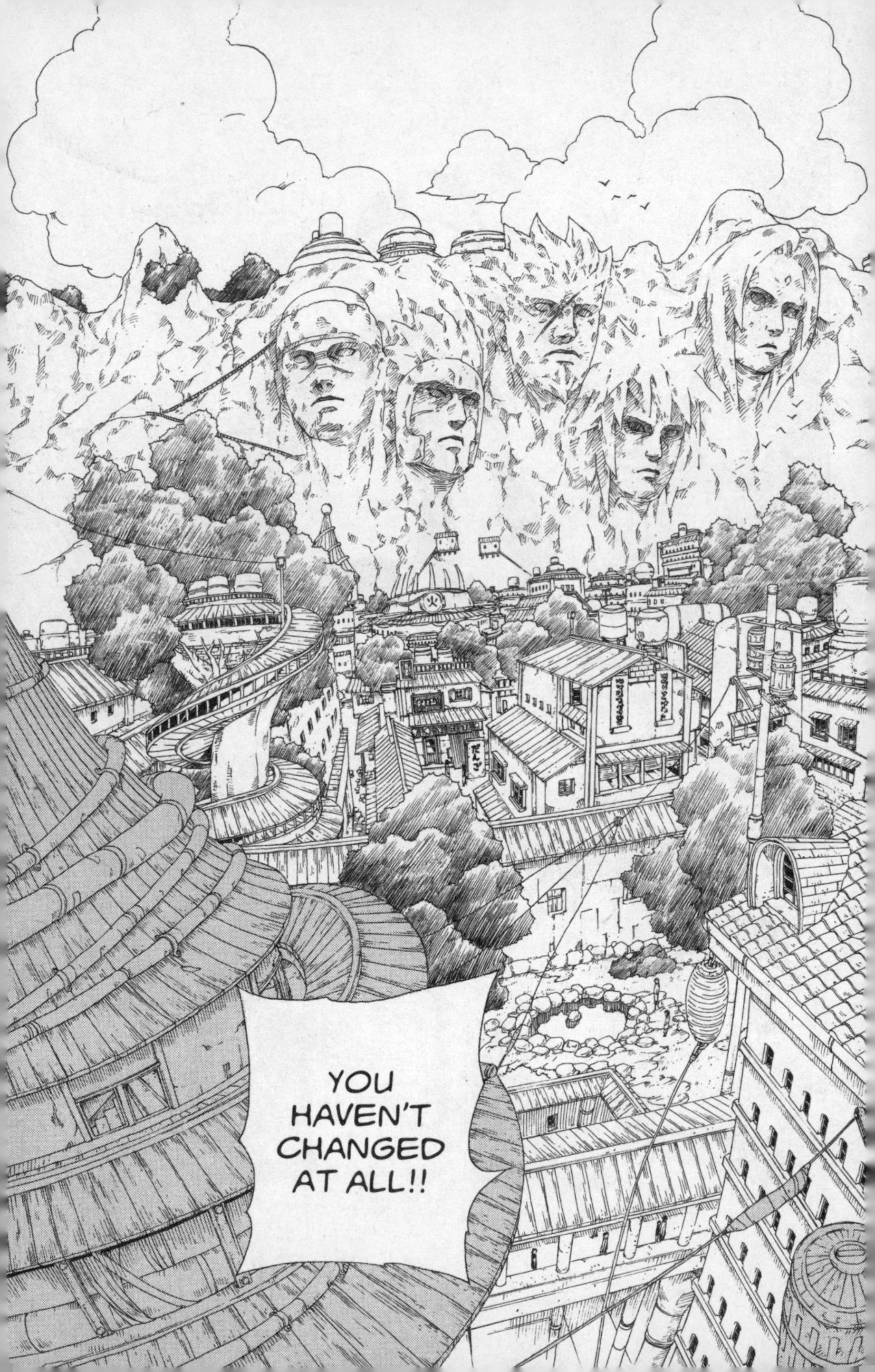
YOU HAVEN'T CHANGED AT ALL!!

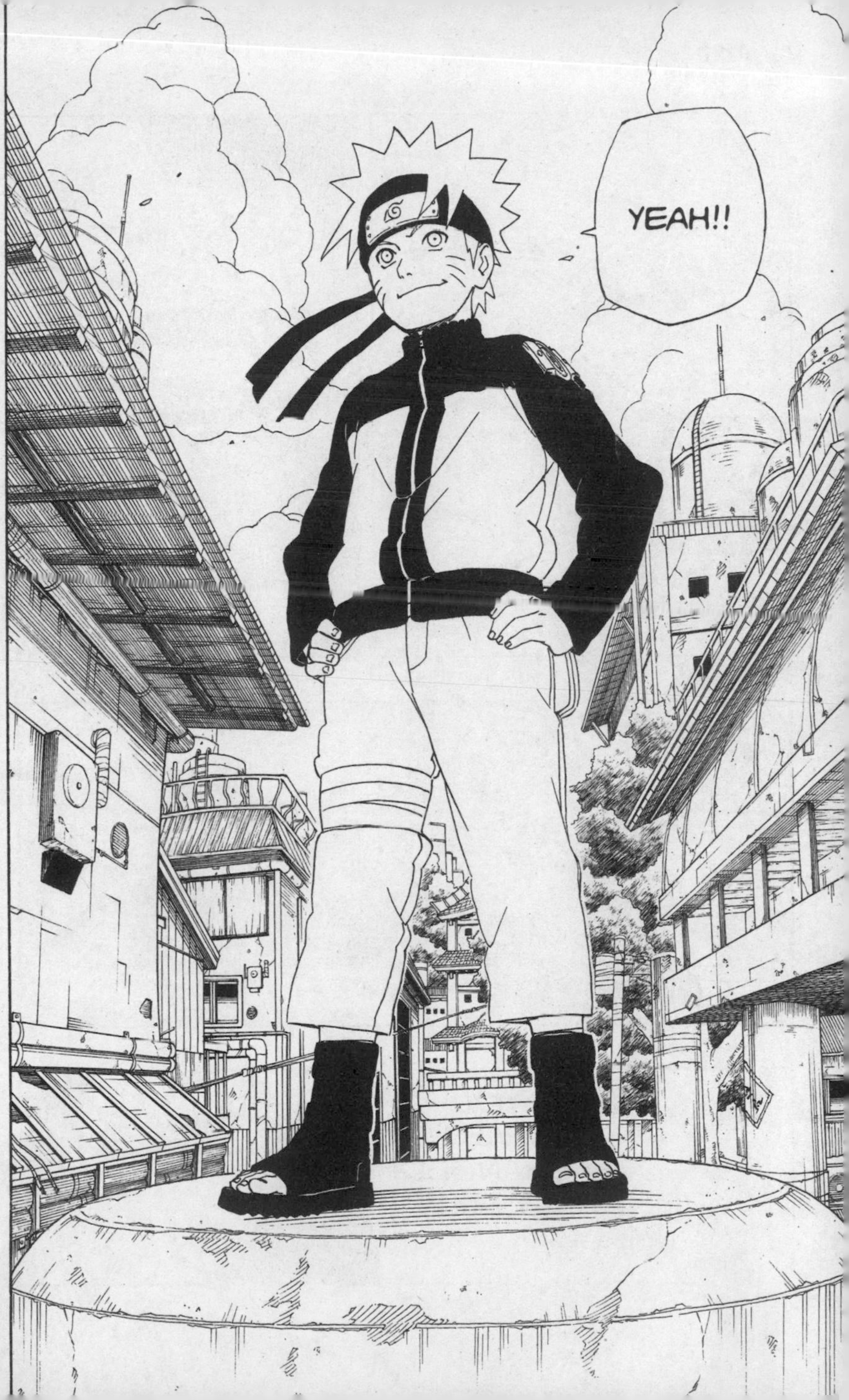
YEAH!!

READ THIS WAY

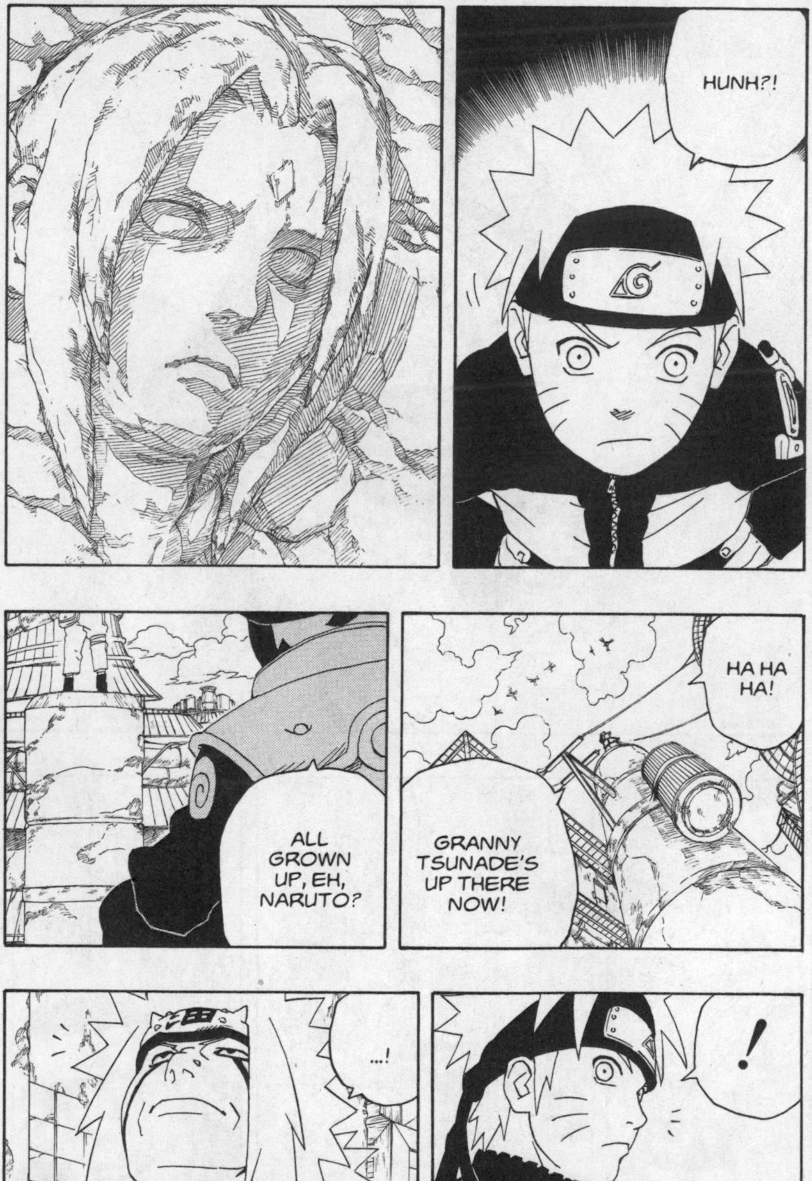
HUNH?!
HA HA HA!
GRANNY TSUNADE'S UP THERE NOW!
ALL GROWN UP, EH, NARUTO?
!
...!

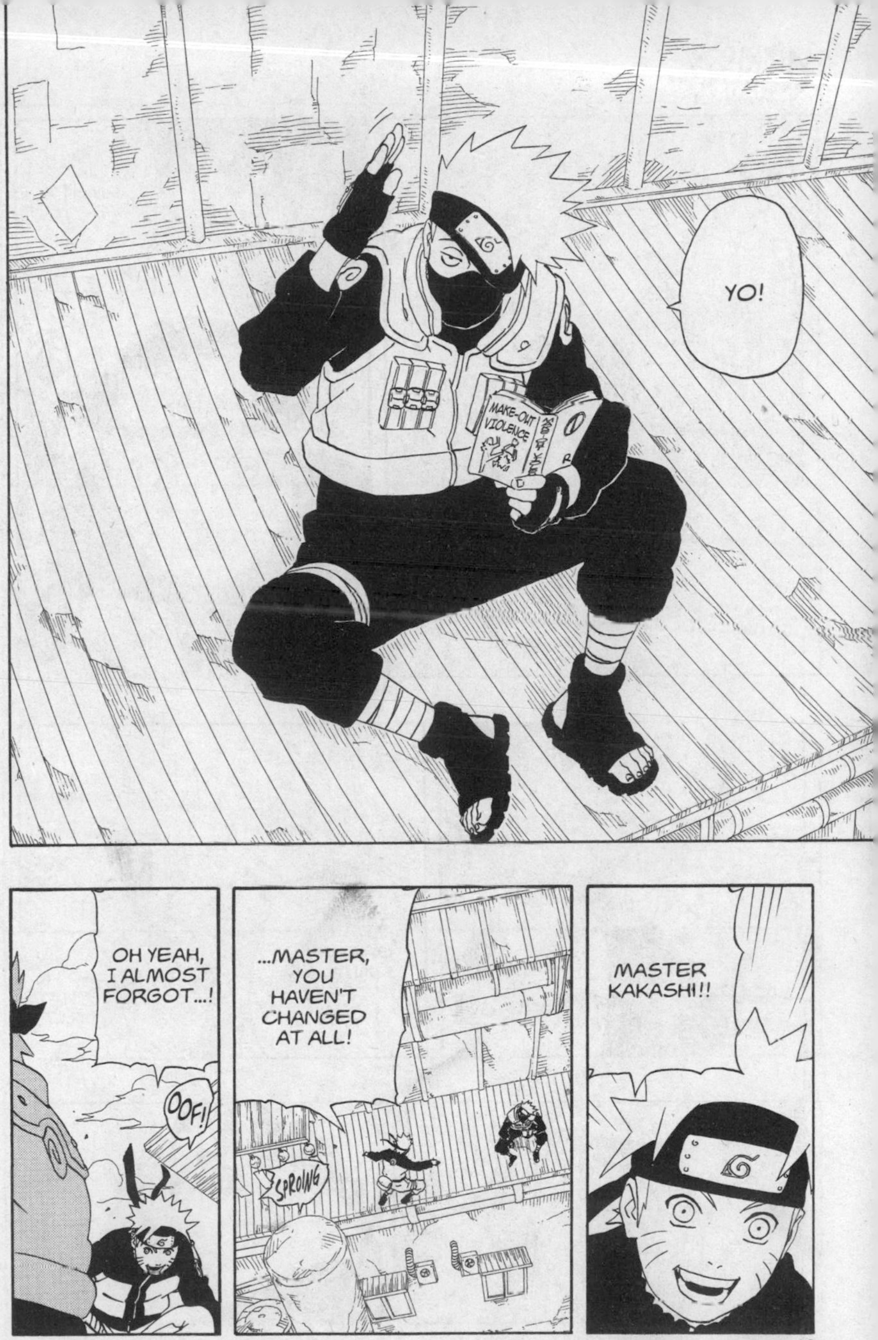
YO!
MAKE-OUT VIOLENCE
MASTER KAKASHI!!
...MASTER, YOU HAVEN'T CHANGED AT ALL!
SPROING
OH YEAH, I ALMOST FORGOT...!
OOF!

READ THIS WAY

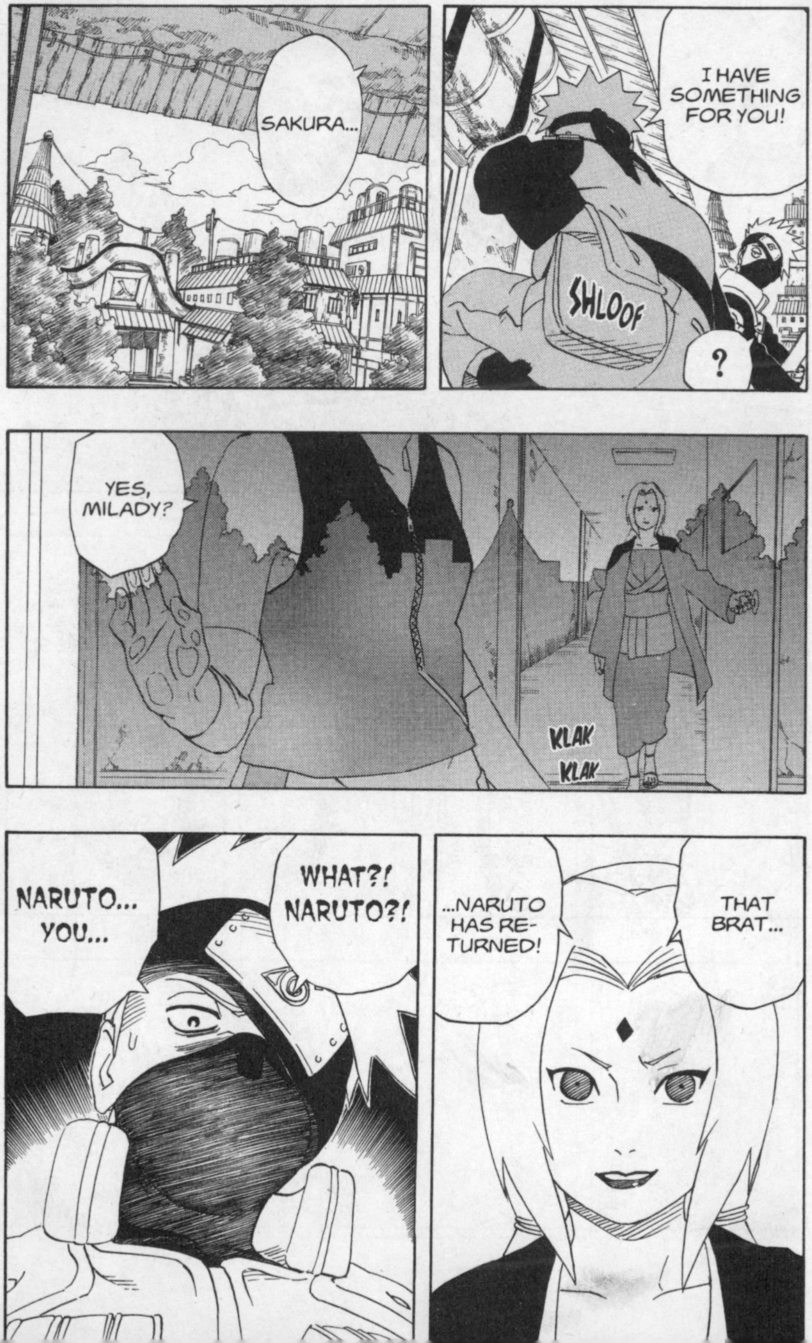
I HAVE SOMETHING FOR YOU!
SHLOOF
?
SAKURA...
YES, MILADY?
KLAK
KLAK
THAT BRAT...
...NARUTO HAS RE-TURNED!
WHAT?! NARUTO?!
NARUTO... YOU...

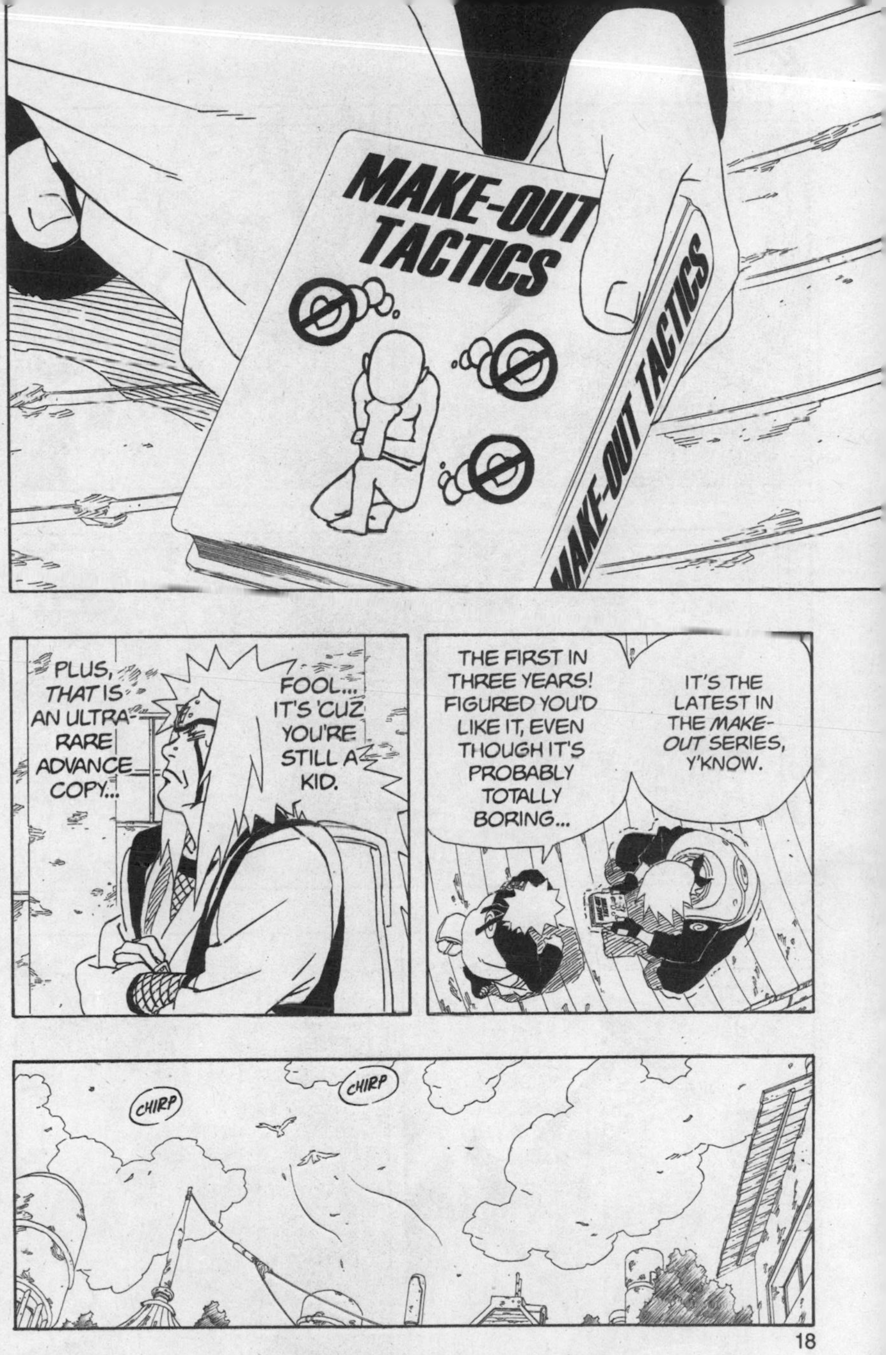
MAKE-OUT TACTICS
MAKE-OUT TACTICS
IT'S THE LATEST IN THE *MAKE-OUT* SERIES, Y'KNOW.
THE FIRST IN THREE YEARS! FIGURED YOU'D LIKE IT, EVEN THOUGH IT'S PROBABLY TOTALLY BORING...
FOOL... IT'S 'CUZ YOU'RE STILL A KID.
PLUS, *THAT* IS AN ULTRA-RARE ADVANCE COPY...
CHIRP
CHIRP

READ THIS WAY

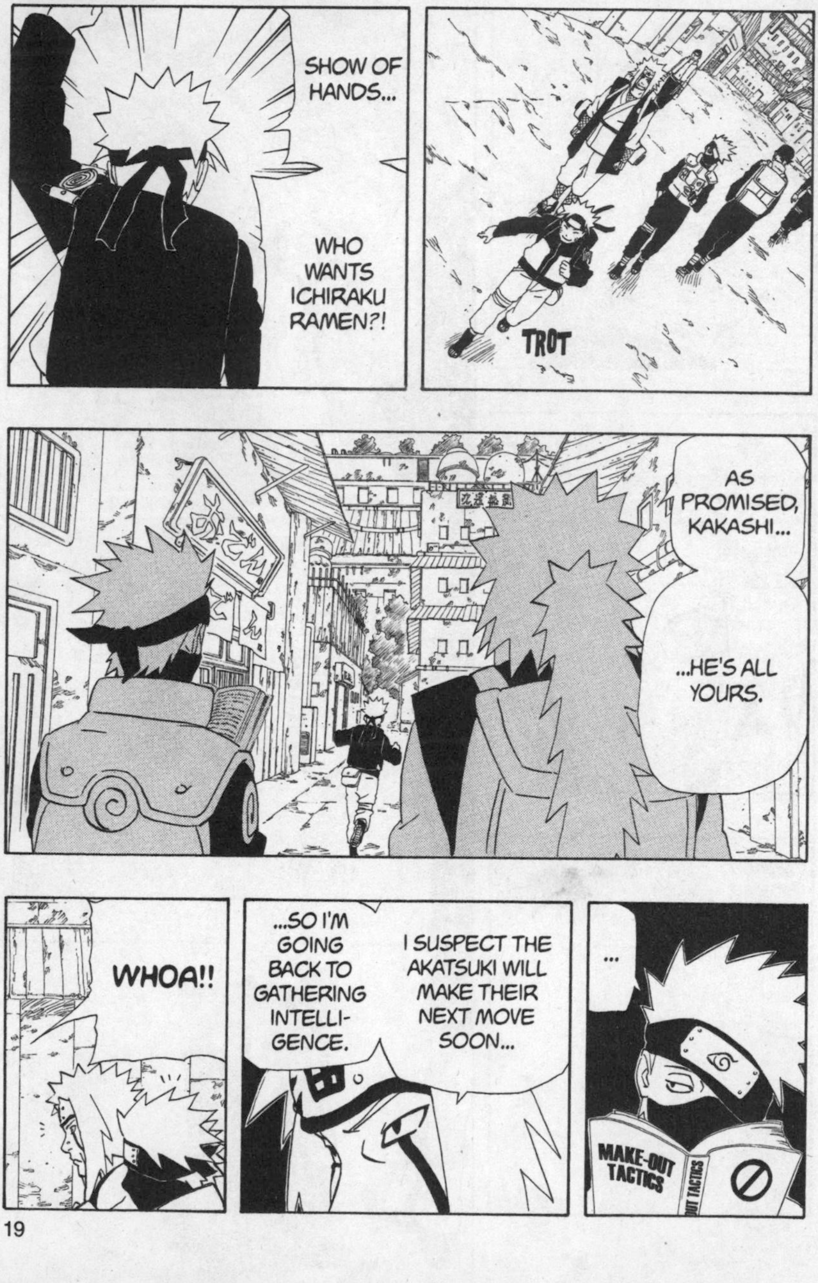
TROT
SHOW OF HANDS...
WHO WANTS ICHIRAKU RAMEN?!
AS PROMISED, KAKASHI...
...HE'S ALL YOURS.
...
MAKE-OUT TACTICS
I SUSPECT THE AKATSUKI WILL MAKE THEIR NEXT MOVE SOON...
...SO I'M GOING BACK TO GATHERING INTELLI-GENCE.
WHOA!!

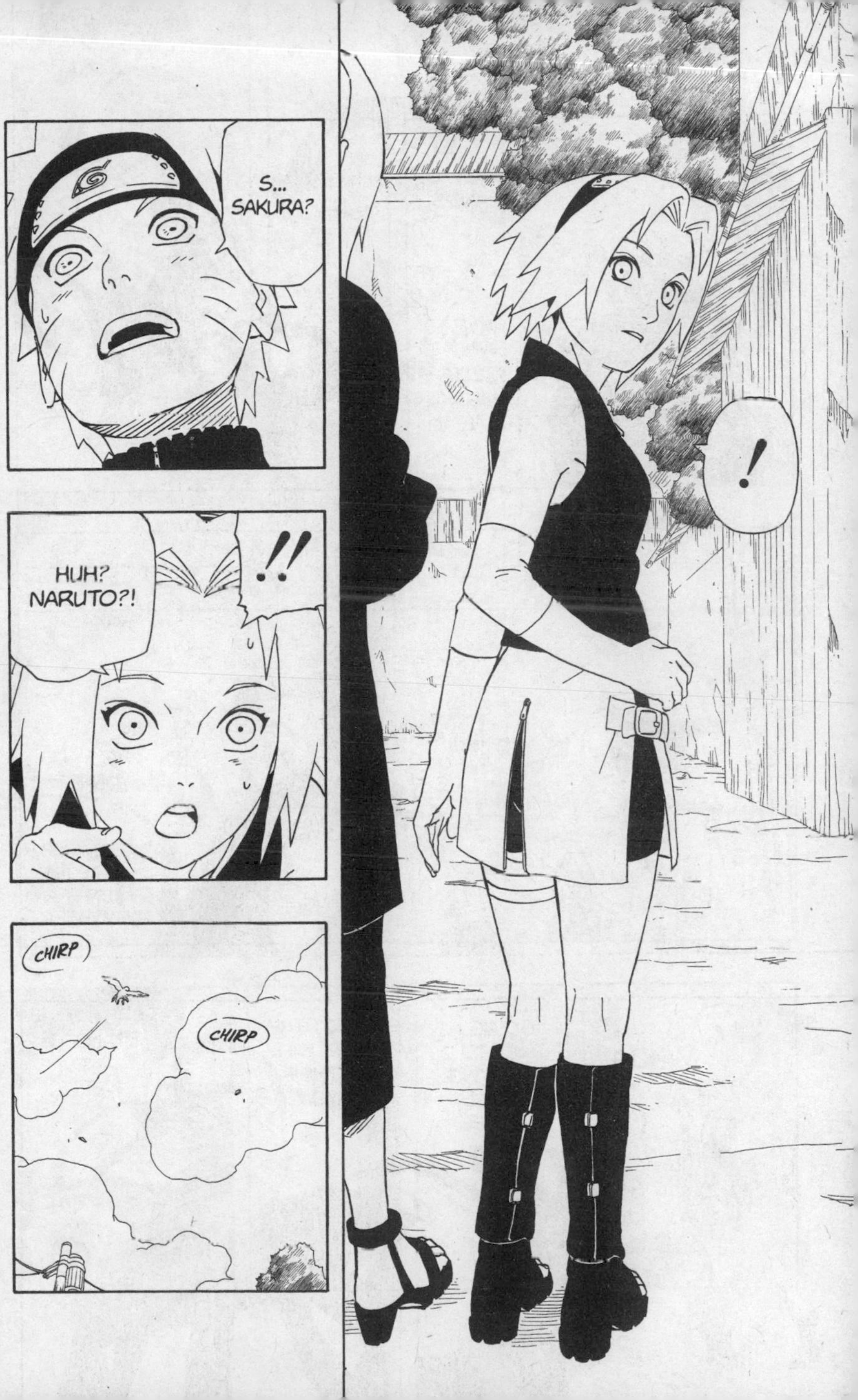
!
S...
SAKURA?
!!
HUH?
NARUTO?!
CHIRP
CHIRP

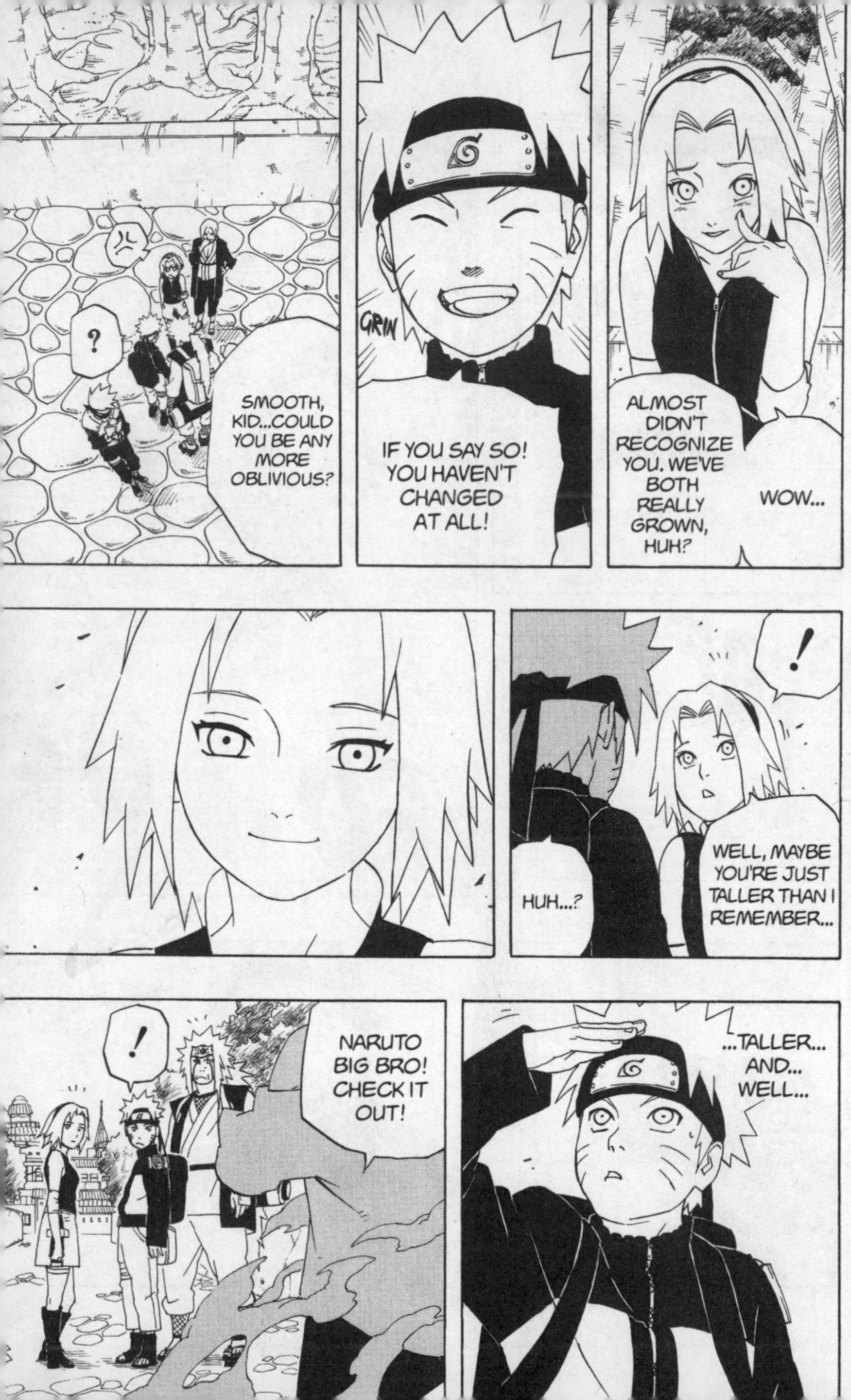
WOW...
ALMOST DIDN'T RECOGNIZE YOU. WE'VE BOTH REALLY GROWN, HUH?
GRIN
IF YOU SAY SO! YOU HAVEN'T CHANGED AT ALL!
SMOOTH, KID...COULD YOU BE ANY MORE OBLIVIOUS?
?
!
WELL, MAYBE YOU'RE JUST TALLER THAN I REMEMBER...
HUH...?
...TALLER... AND... WELL...
NARUTO BIG BRO! CHECK IT OUT!
!

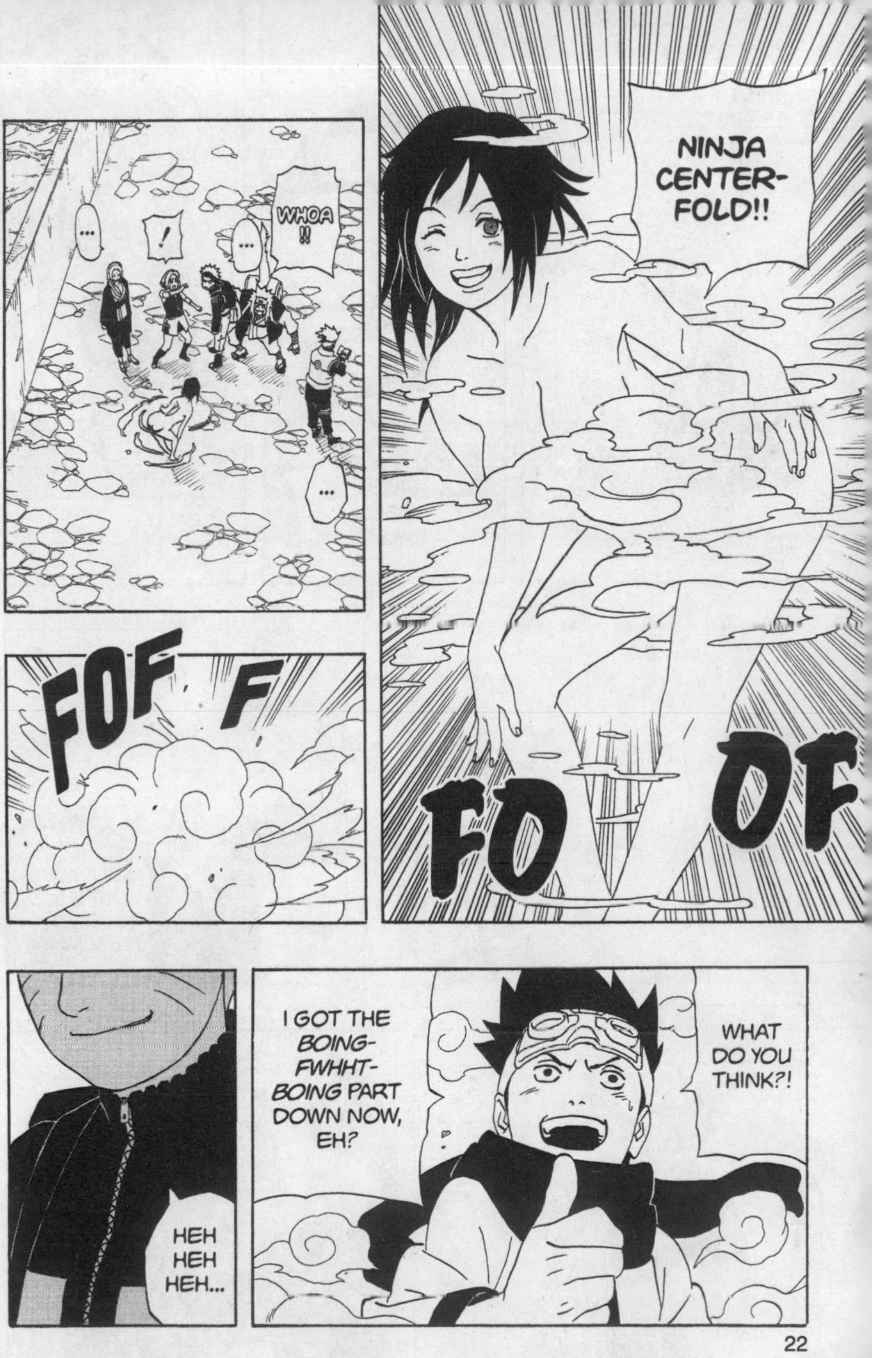
NINJA CENTER-FOLD!!
FO OF
WHOA !!
...
!
...
...
...
FOF F
I GOT THE BOING-FWHHT-BOING PART DOWN NOW, EH?
WHAT DO YOU THINK?!
HEH HEH HEH...

READ THIS WAY

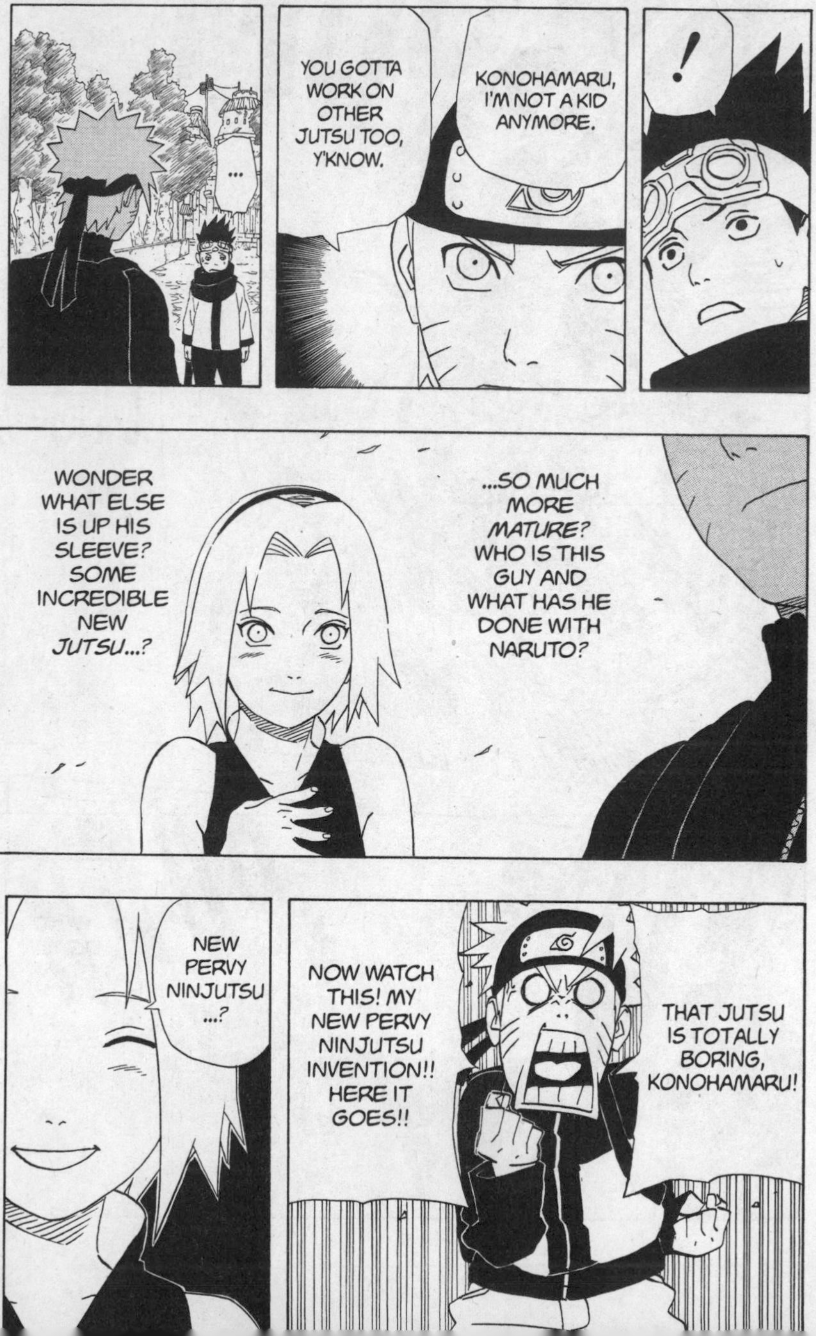
!
KONOHAMARU, I'M NOT A KID ANYMORE.
YOU GOTTA WORK ON OTHER JUTSU TOO, Y'KNOW.
...
...SO MUCH MORE *MATURE*? WHO IS THIS GUY AND WHAT HAS HE DONE WITH NARUTO?
WONDER WHAT ELSE IS UP HIS SLEEVE? SOME INCREDIBLE NEW *JUTSU*...?
THAT JUTSU IS TOTALLY BORING, KONOHAMARU!
NOW WATCH THIS! MY NEW PERVY NINJUTSU INVENTION!! HERE IT GOES!!
NEW PERVY NINJUTSU ...?

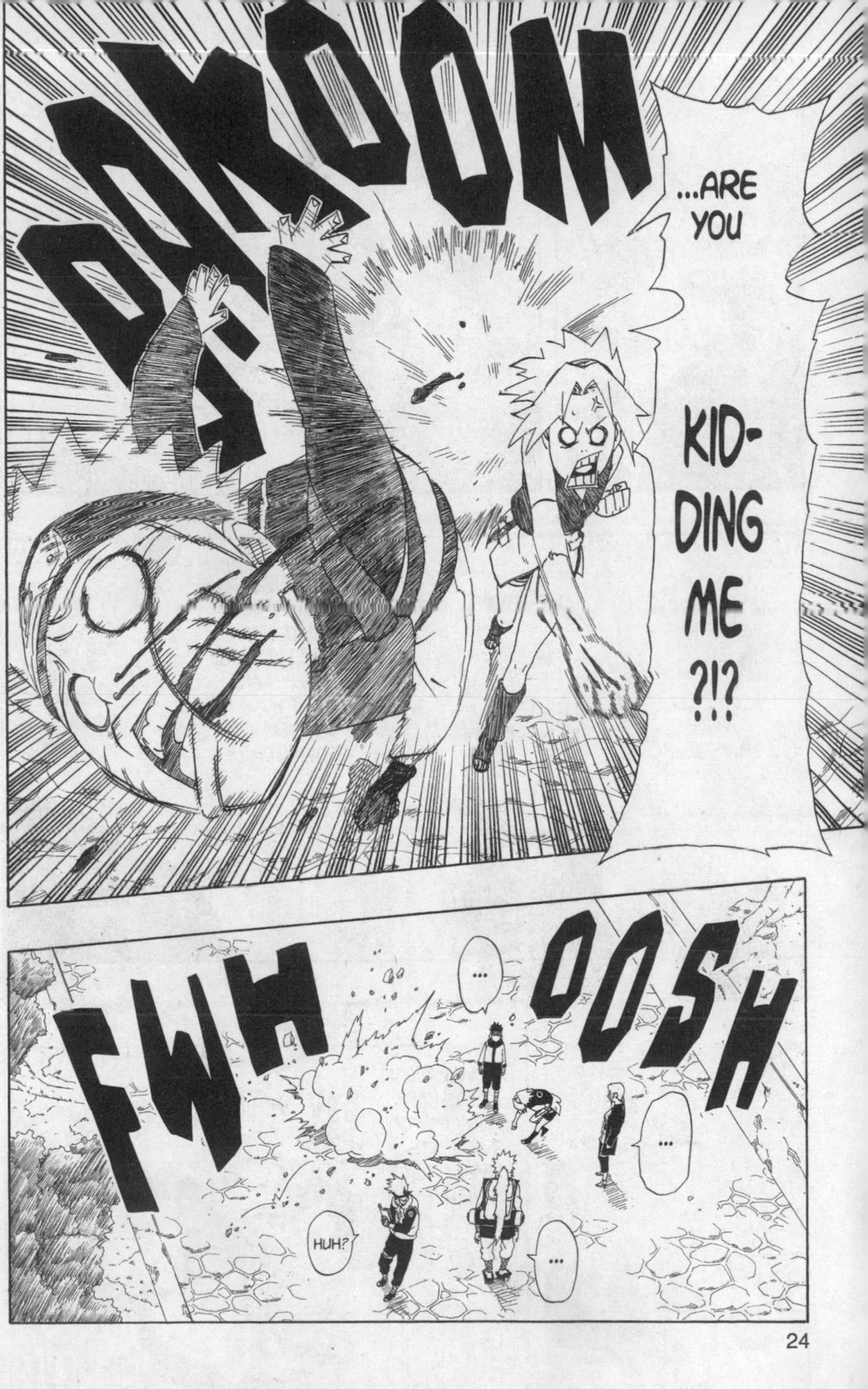
...ARE YOU KIDDING ME ?!?
FWHOOSH
...
...
...
HUH?

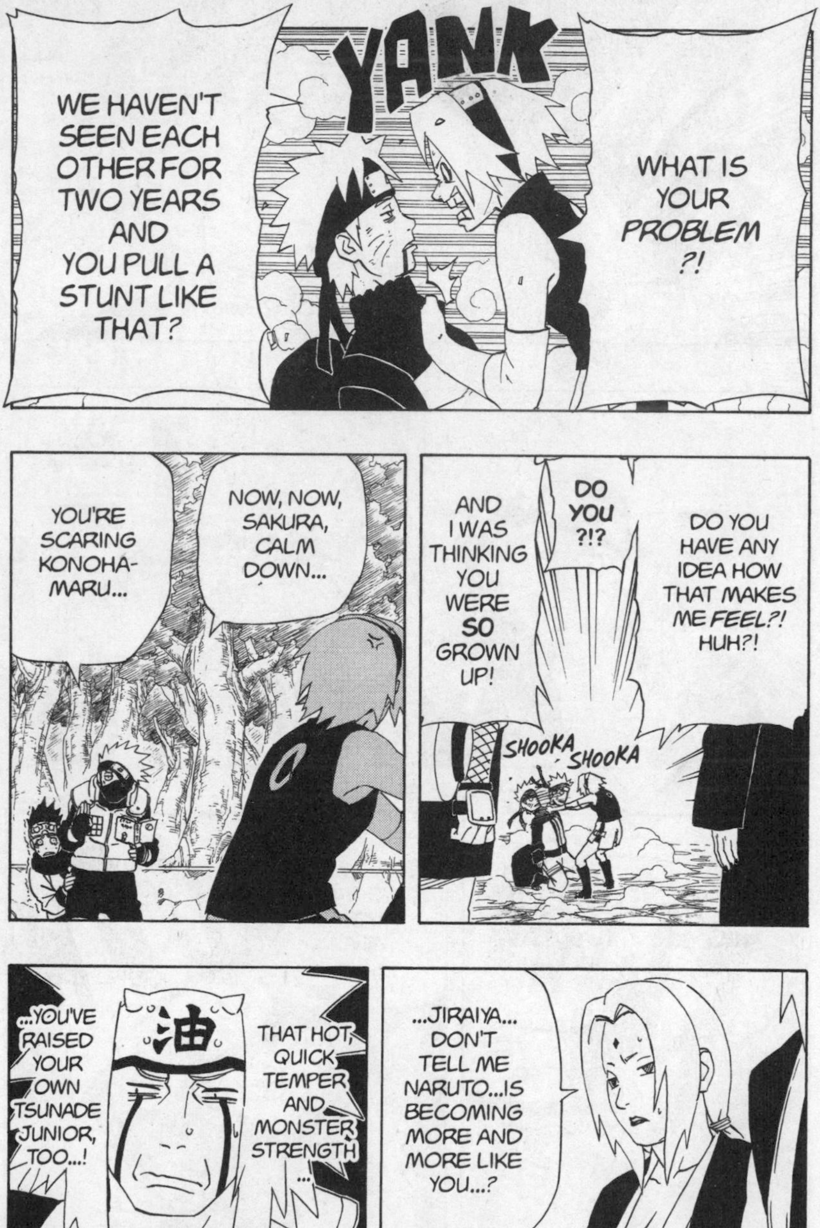
YANK
WHAT IS YOUR PROBLEM ?!
WE HAVEN'T SEEN EACH OTHER FOR TWO YEARS AND YOU PULL A STUNT LIKE THAT?
DO YOU HAVE ANY IDEA HOW THAT MAKES ME FEEL?! HUH?!
DO YOU ?!?
AND I WAS THINKING YOU WERE SO GROWN UP!
SHOOKA SHOOKA
NOW, NOW, SAKURA, CALM DOWN...
YOU'RE SCARING KONOHA-MARU...
...JIRAIYA... DON'T TELL ME NARUTO...IS BECOMING MORE AND MORE LIKE YOU...?
油
THAT HOT, QUICK TEMPER AND MONSTER STRENGTH...
...YOU'VE RAISED YOUR OWN TSUNADE JUNIOR, TOO...!

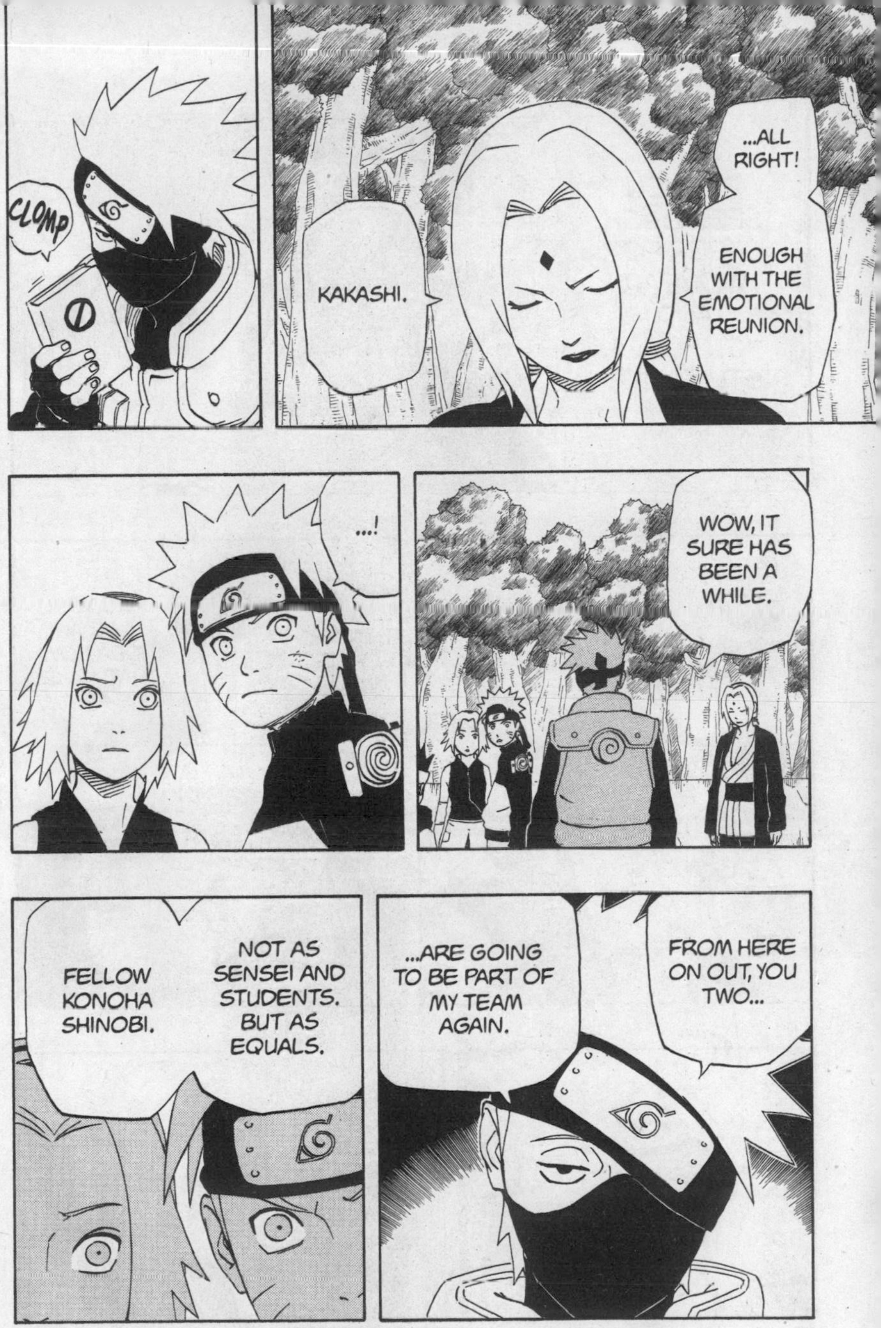
...ALL RIGHT!
ENOUGH WITH THE EMOTIONAL REUNION.
KAKASHI.
CLOMP
WOW, IT SURE HAS BEEN A WHILE.
...!
FROM HERE ON OUT, YOU TWO...
...ARE GOING TO BE PART OF MY TEAM AGAIN.
NOT AS SENSEI AND STUDENTS. BUT AS EQUALS.
FELLOW KONOHA SHINOBI.

READ THIS WAY

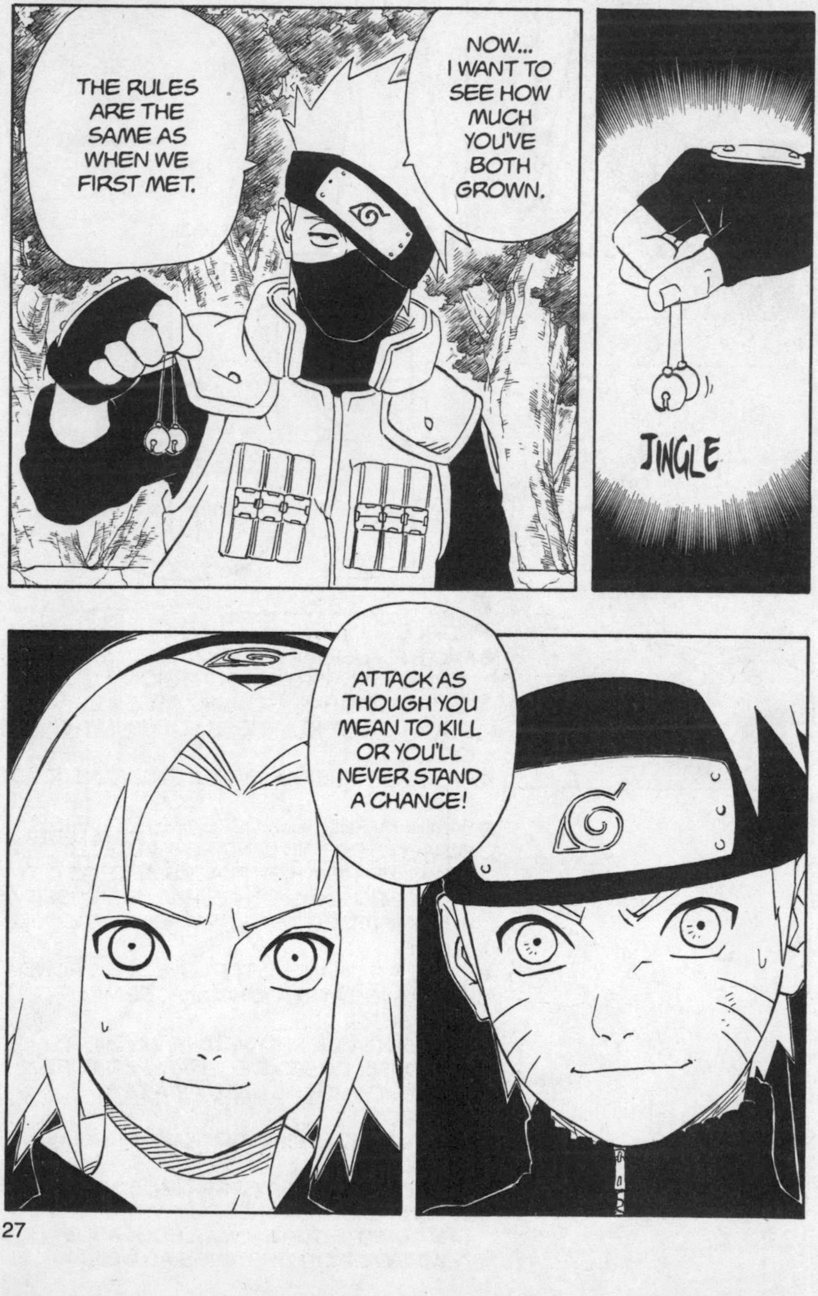
JINGLE
NOW... I WANT TO SEE HOW MUCH YOU'VE BOTH GROWN.
THE RULES ARE THE SAME AS WHEN WE FIRST MET.
ATTACK AS THOUGH YOU MEAN TO KILL OR YOU'LL NEVER STAND A CHANCE!

MEET MASASHI KISHIMOTO'S ASSISTANTS, PART 9

ASSISTANT NO. 9 MURAKAMI MASAKI

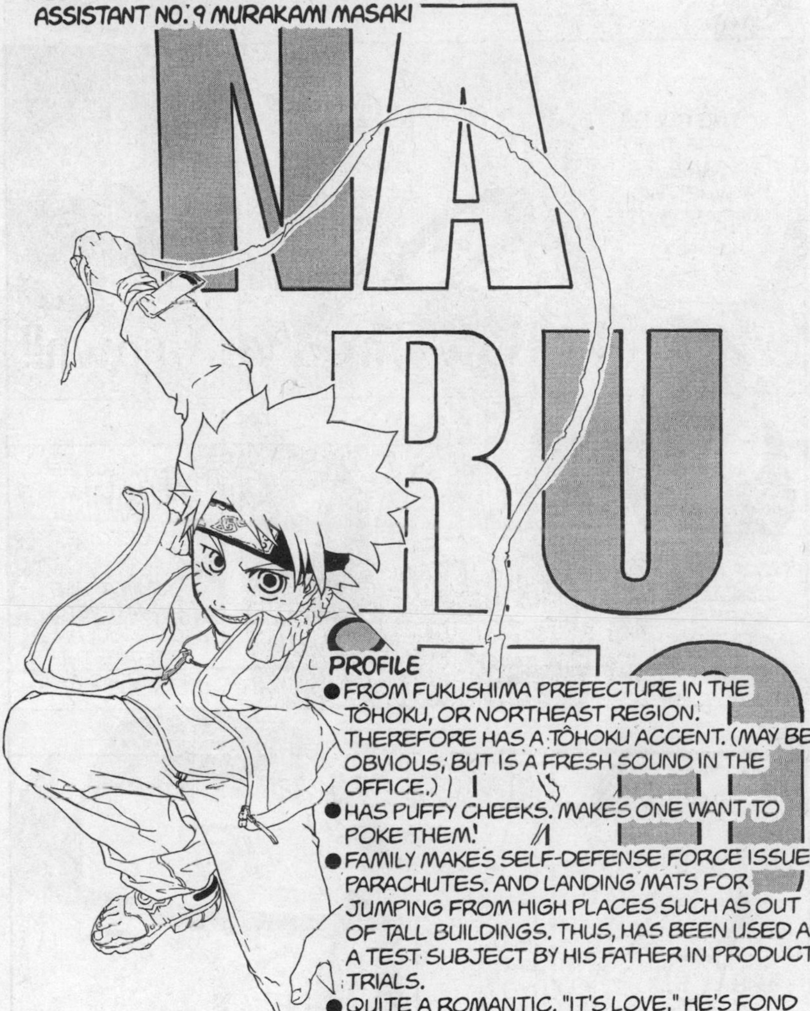
NARUTO
2005.5.6
村上正樹

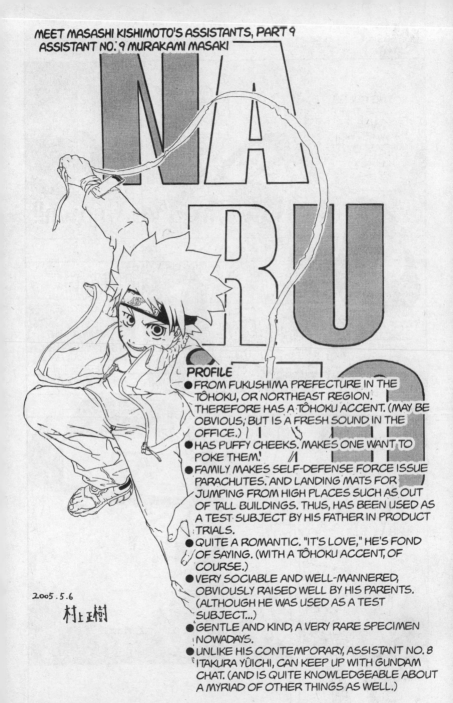

PROFILE

- FROM FUKUSHIMA PREFECTURE IN THE TÔHOKU, OR NORTHEAST REGION. THEREFORE HAS A TÔHOKU ACCENT. (MAY BE OBVIOUS, BUT IS A FRESH SOUND IN THE OFFICE.)
- HAS PUFFY CHEEKS. MAKES ONE WANT TO POKE THEM!
- FAMILY MAKES SELF-DEFENSE FORCE ISSUE PARACHUTES. AND LANDING MATS FOR JUMPING FROM HIGH PLACES SUCH AS OUT OF TALL BUILDINGS. THUS, HAS BEEN USED AS A TEST SUBJECT BY HIS FATHER IN PRODUCT TRIALS.
- QUITE A ROMANTIC. "IT'S LOVE," HE'S FOND OF SAYING. (WITH A TÔHOKU ACCENT, OF COURSE.)
- VERY SOCIABLE AND WELL-MANNERED, OBVIOUSLY RAISED WELL BY HIS PARENTS. (ALTHOUGH HE WAS USED AS A TEST SUBJECT...)
- GENTLE AND KIND, A VERY RARE SPECIMEN NOWADAYS.
- UNLIKE HIS CONTEMPORARY, ASSISTANT NO. 8 ITAKURA YÛICHI, CAN KEEP UP WITH GUNDAM CHAT. (AND IS QUITE KNOWLEDGEABLE ABOUT A MYRIAD OF OTHER THINGS AS WELL.)

Number 246:

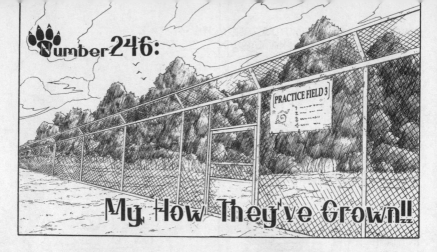

My How They've Grown!!

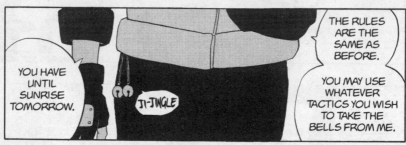

THE RULES ARE THE SAME AS BEFORE.

YOU MAY USE WHATEVER TACTICS YOU WISH TO TAKE THE BELLS FROM ME.

YOU HAVE UNTIL SUNRISE TOMORROW.

JI-JINGLE

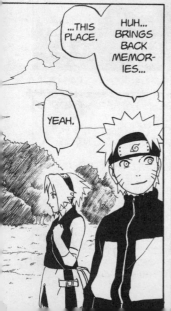

...THIS PLACE.

HUH... BRINGS BACK MEMORIES...

YEAH.

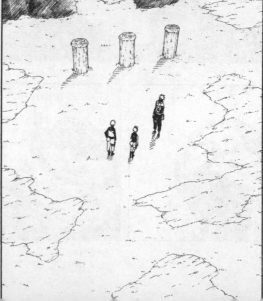

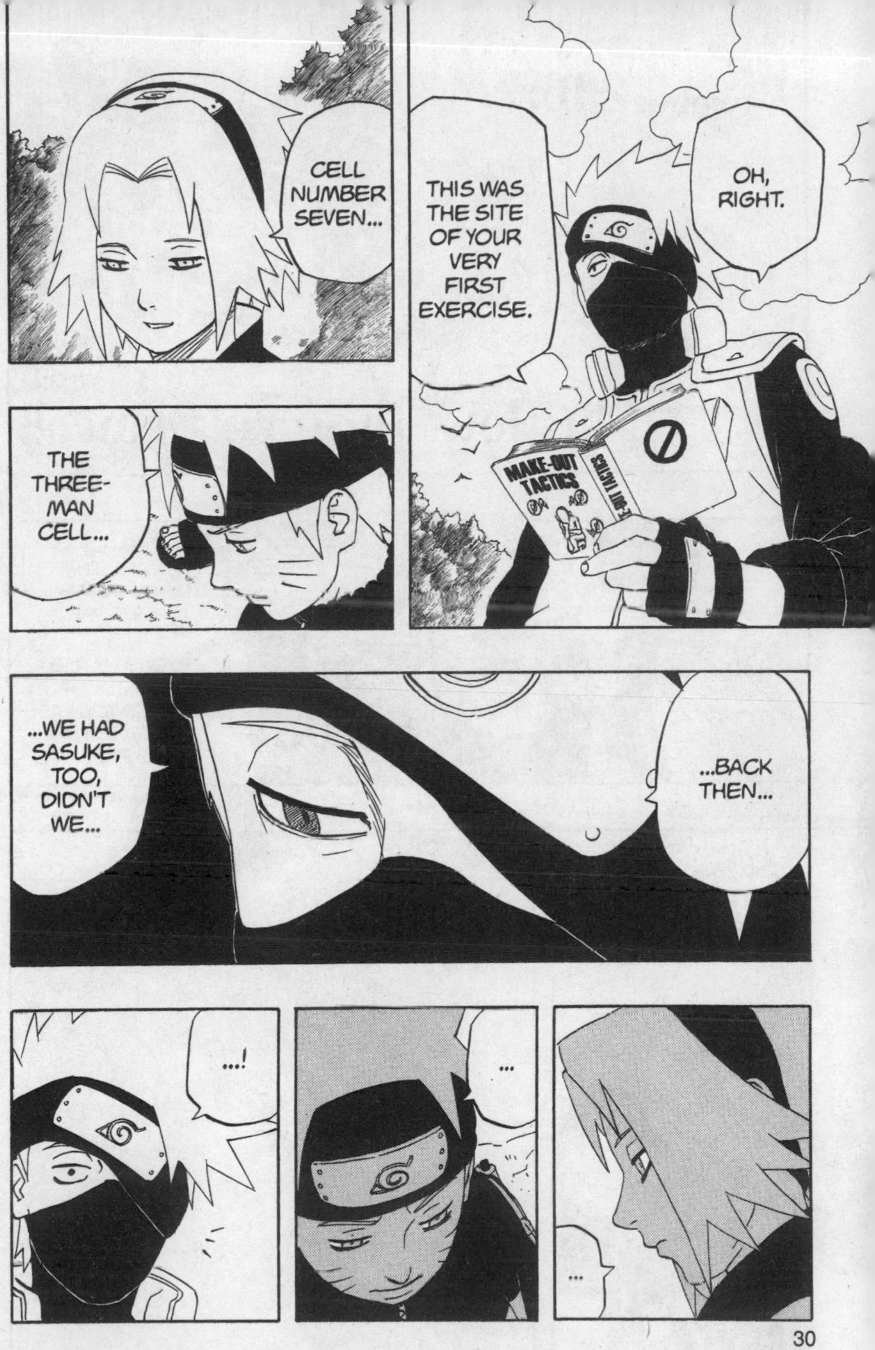
OH, RIGHT.
THIS WAS THE SITE OF YOUR VERY FIRST EXERCISE.
MAKE-OUT TACTICS
CELL NUMBER SEVEN...
THE THREE-MAN CELL...
...BACK THEN...
...WE HAD SASUKE, TOO, DIDN'T WE...
...
...
....!

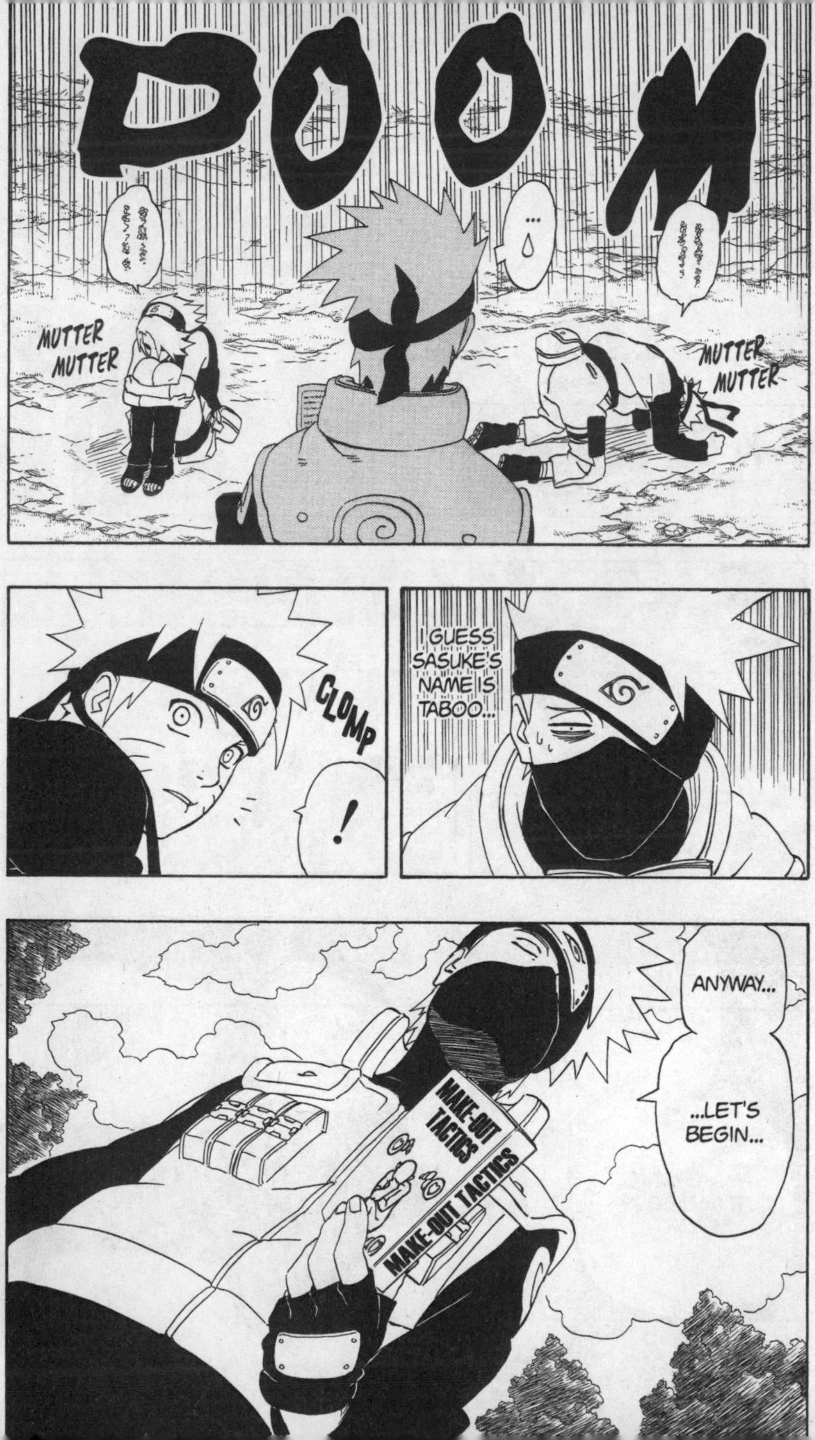
DOOM
MUTTER MUTTER
...
MUTTER MUTTER
I GUESS SASUKE'S NAME IS TABOO...
CLOMP
!
ANYWAY...
...LET'S BEGIN...
MAKE-OUT TACTICS
MAKE-OUT TACTICS
MAKE-OUT TACTICS

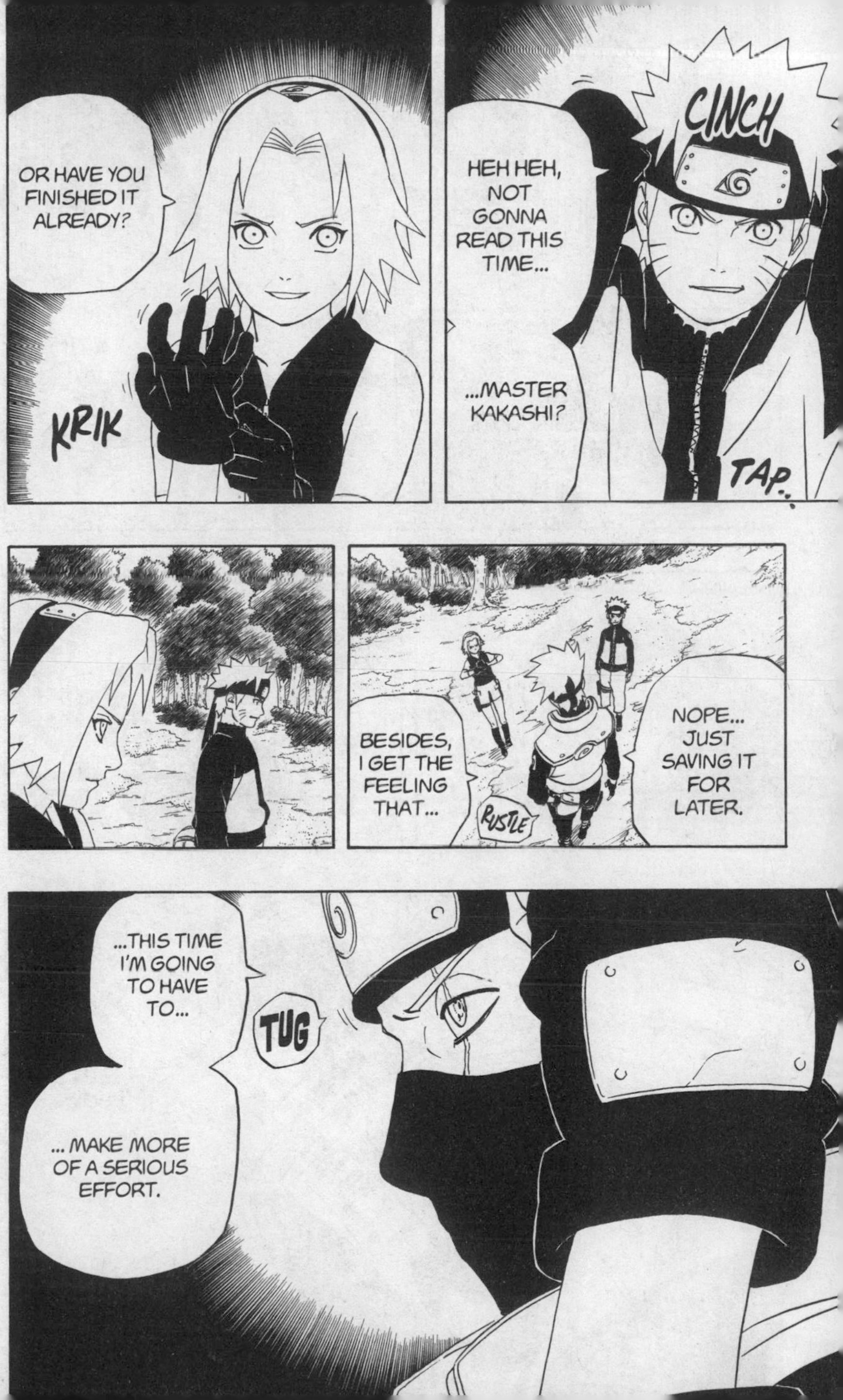
CINCH
HEH HEH, NOT GONNA READ THIS TIME...
...MASTER KAKASHI?
TAP...
OR HAVE YOU FINISHED IT ALREADY?
KRIK
NOPE... JUST SAVING IT FOR LATER.
BESIDES, I GET THE FEELING THAT...
RUSTLE
...THIS TIME I'M GOING TO HAVE TO...
TUG
... MAKE MORE OF A SERIOUS EFFORT.

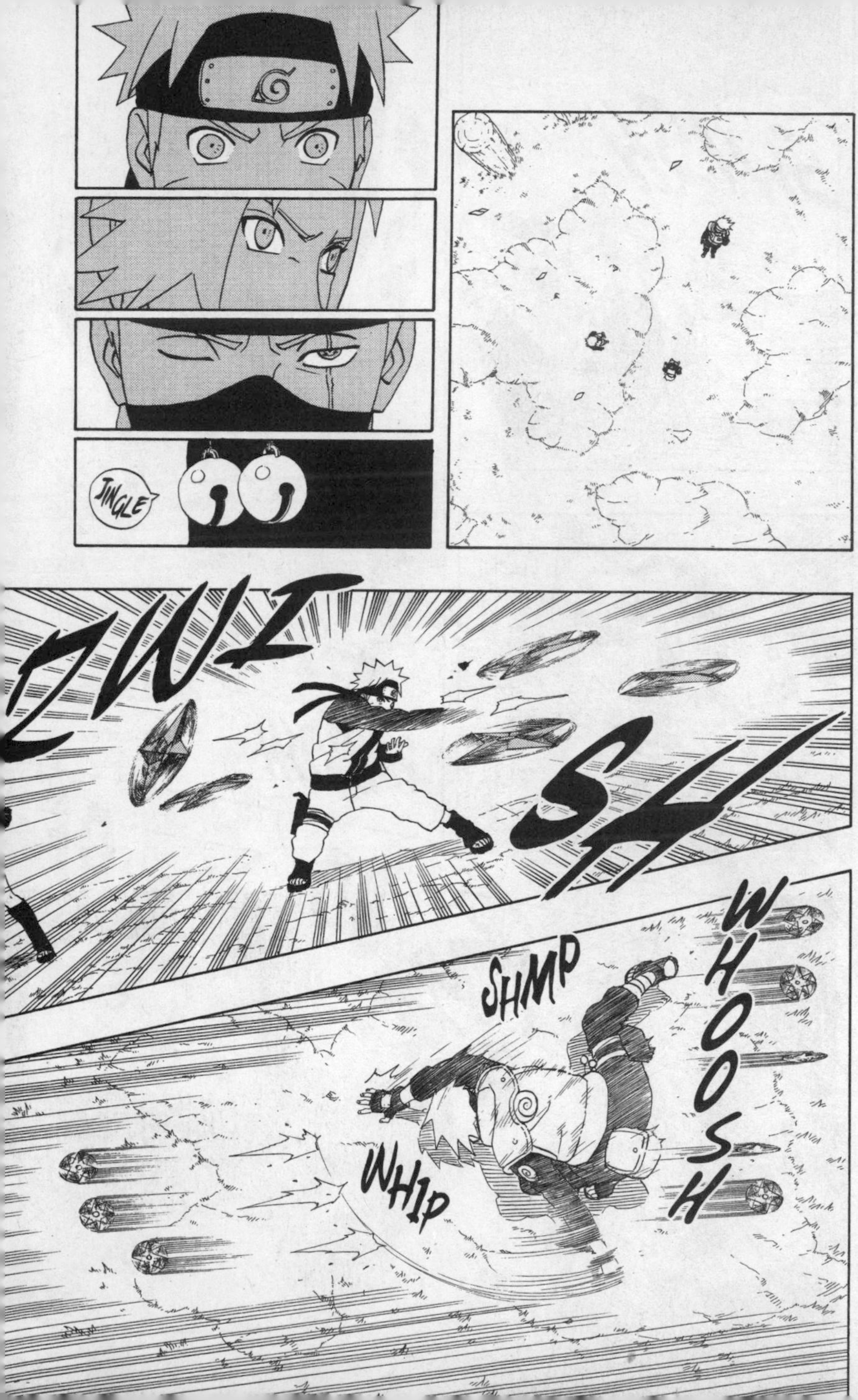
JINGLE
ZWISH
WHOOSH
SHMP
WHIP

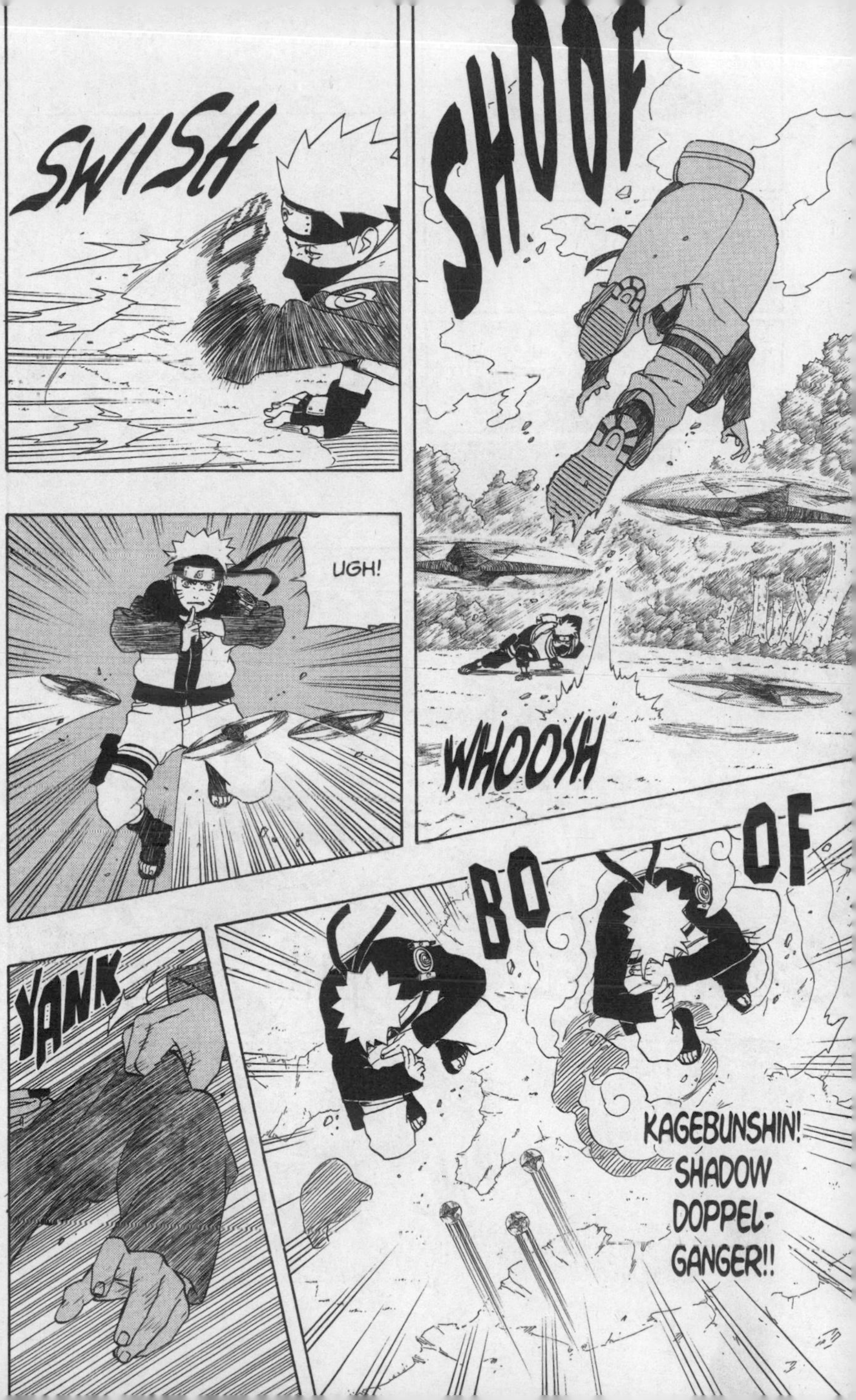
SHOOF
WHOOSH
SWISH
UGH!
BOOF
KAGEBUNSHIN! SHADOW DOPPEL-GANGER!!
YANK

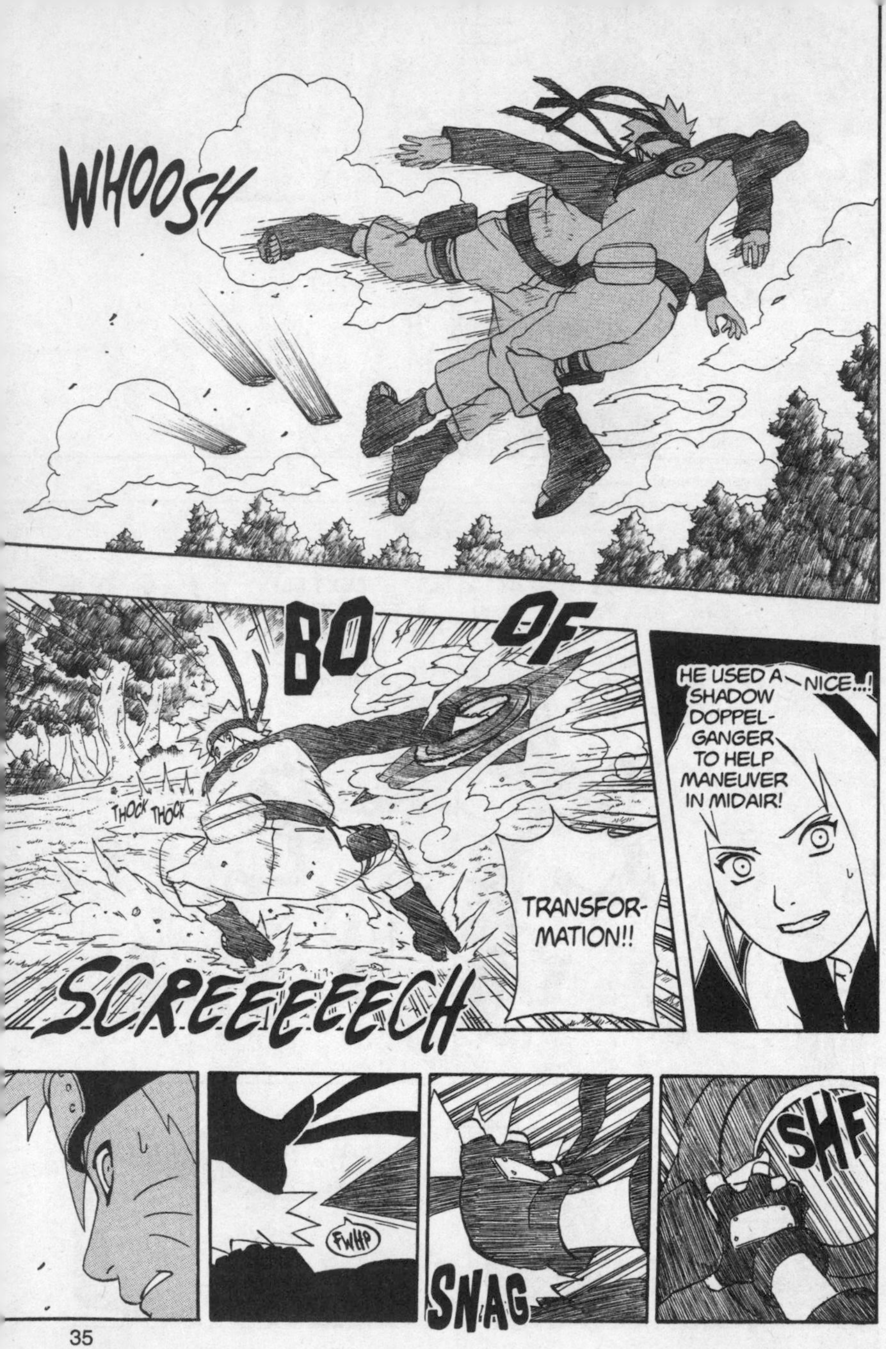
WHOOSH
NICE...!
HE USED A SHADOW DOPPEL-GANGER TO HELP MANEUVER IN MIDAIR!
BOOF
TRANSFOR-MATION!!
THOCK THOCK
SCREEEEECH
SHF
SNAG
FWHP

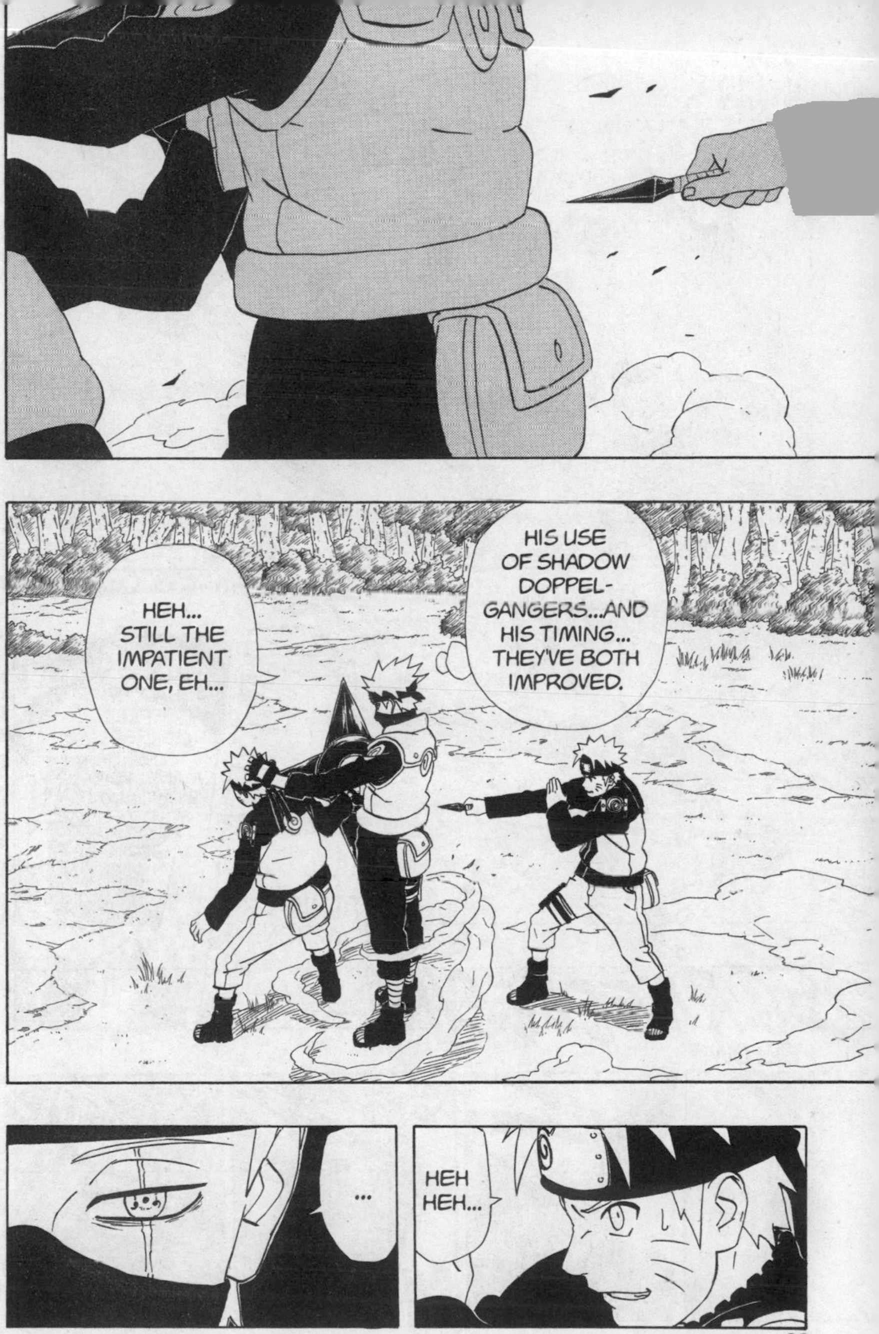
HIS USE OF SHADOW DOPPEL-GANGERS...AND HIS TIMING... THEY'VE BOTH IMPROVED.
HEH... STILL THE IMPATIENT ONE, EH...
HEH HEH...
...

READ THIS WAY

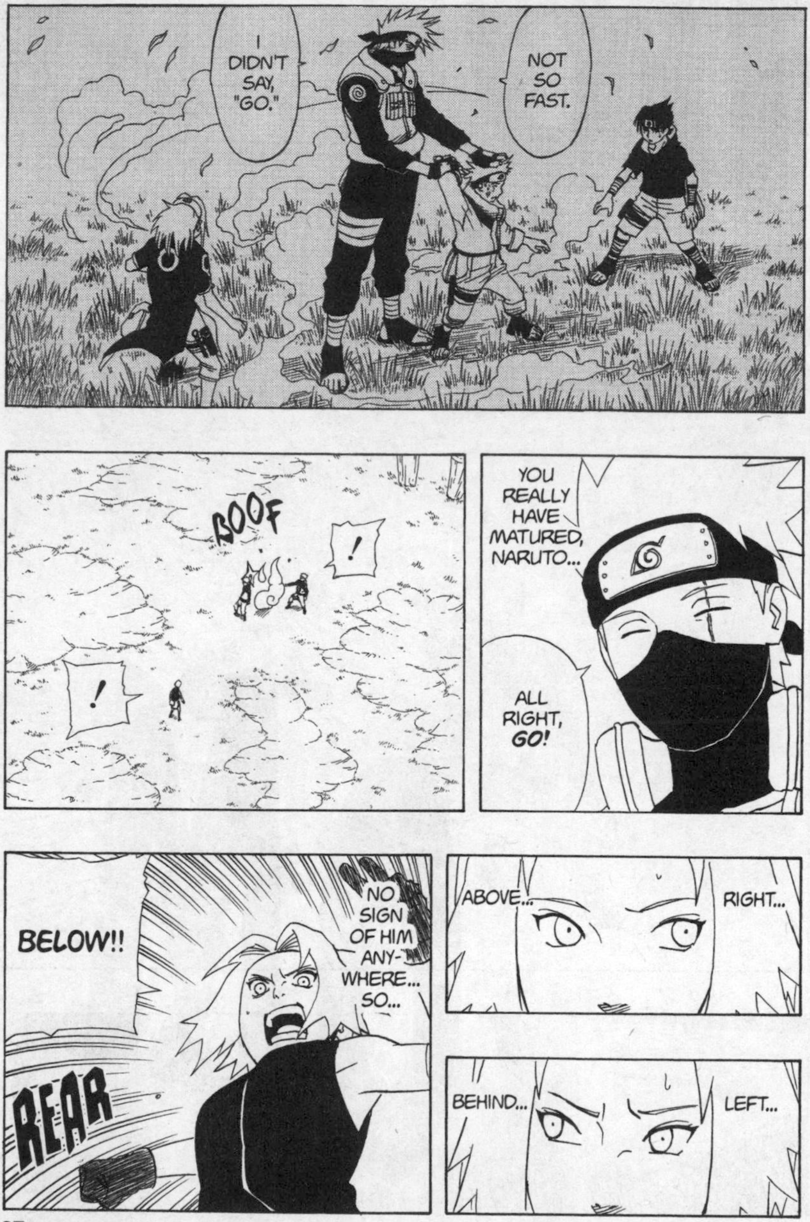

NOT SO FAST.
I DIDN'T SAY, "GO."
YOU REALLY HAVE MATURED, NARUTO...
ALL RIGHT, GO!
BOOF
!
!
RIGHT...
ABOVE...
LEFT...
BEHIND...
NO SIGN OF HIM ANY-WHERE... SO...
BELOW!!
REAR

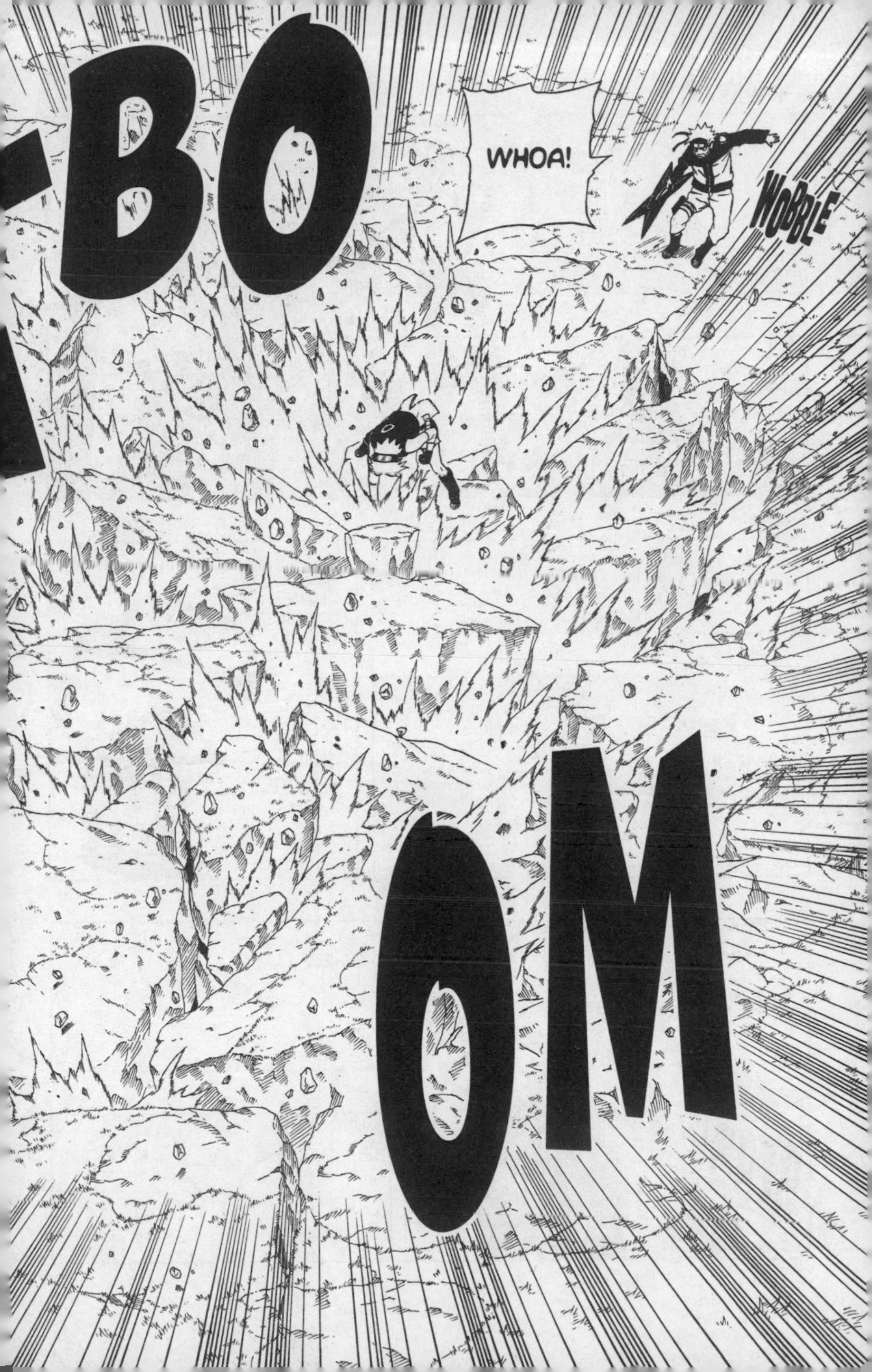
WHOA!
WOBBLE
BOOM

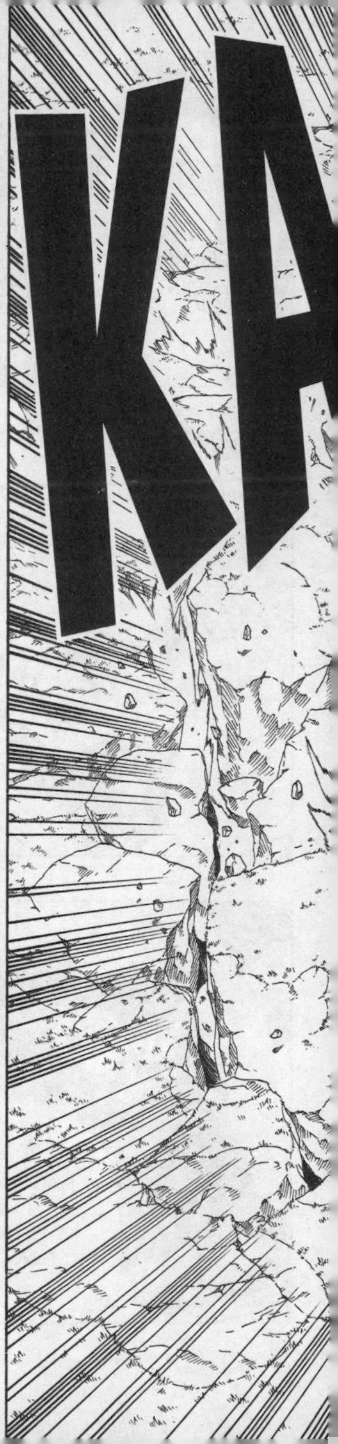
KA

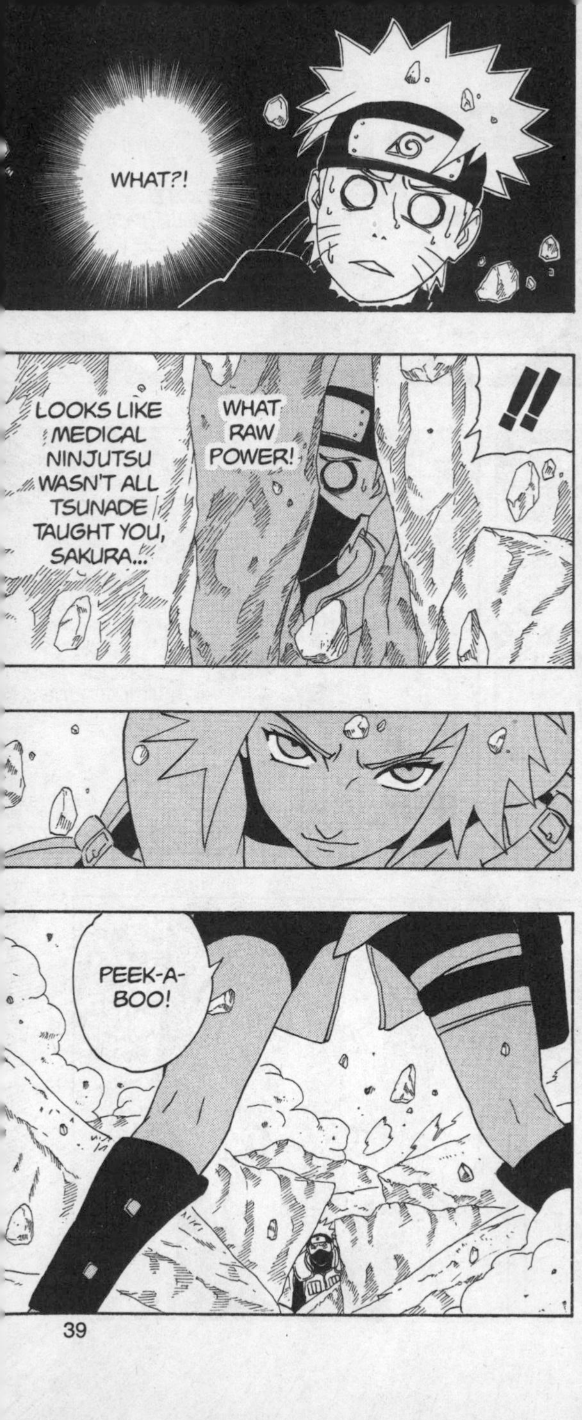
WHAT?!
!!
WHAT RAW POWER!
LOOKS LIKE MEDICAL NINJUTSU WASN'T ALL TSUNADE TAUGHT YOU, SAKURA...
PEEK-A-BOO!

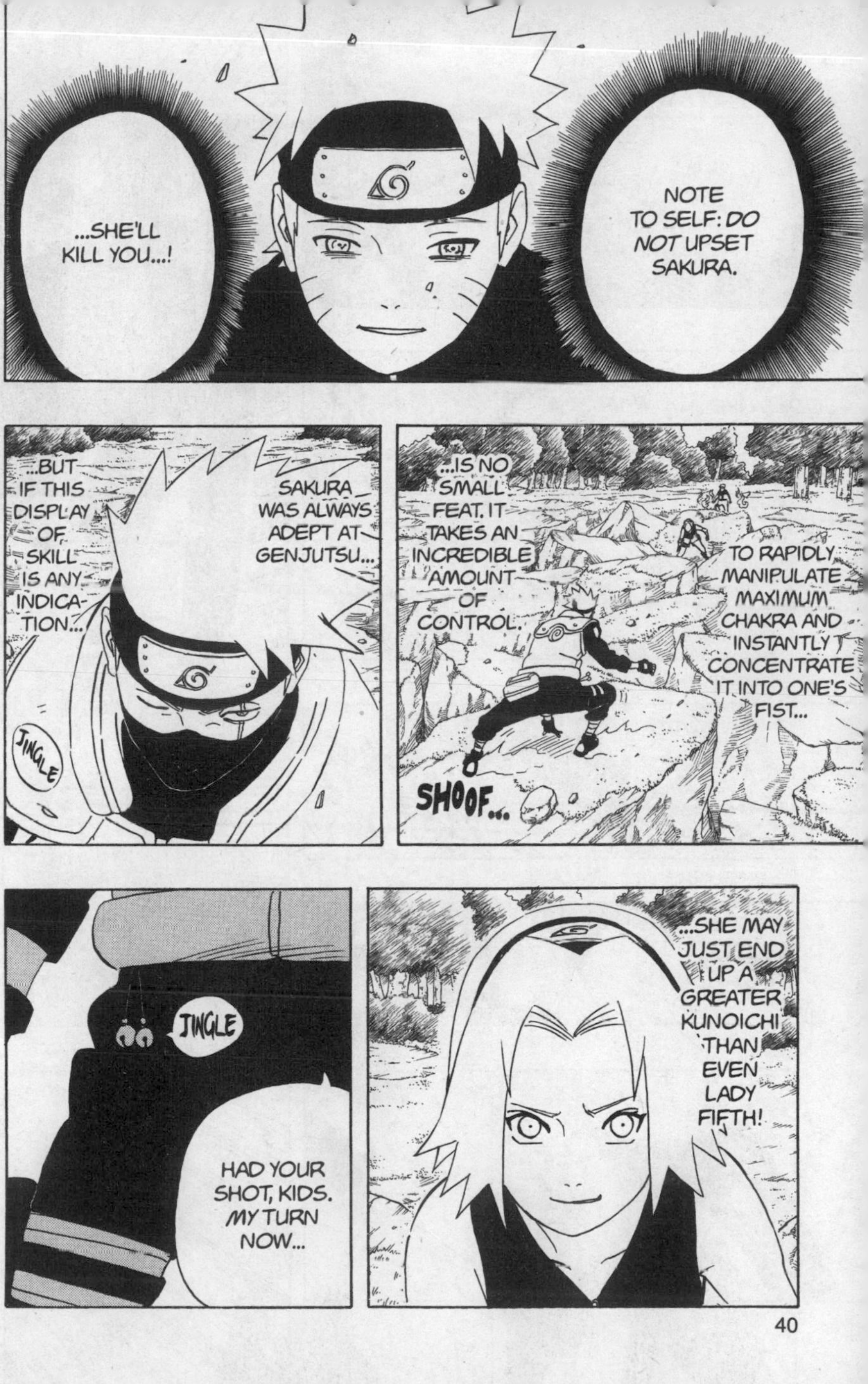
NOTE TO SELF: *DO NOT* UPSET SAKURA.
...SHE'LL KILL YOU...!
TO RAPIDLY MANIPULATE MAXIMUM CHAKRA AND INSTANTLY CONCENTRATE IT INTO ONE'S FIST...
...IS NO SMALL FEAT. IT TAKES AN INCREDIBLE AMOUNT OF CONTROL.
SHOOF...
SAKURA WAS ALWAYS ADEPT AT GENJUTSU...
...BUT IF THIS DISPLAY OF SKILL IS ANY INDICATION...
JINGLE
...SHE MAY JUST END UP A GREATER KUNOICHI THAN EVEN LADY FIFTH!
JINGLE
HAD YOUR SHOT, KIDS. *MY* TURN NOW...

READ THIS WAY

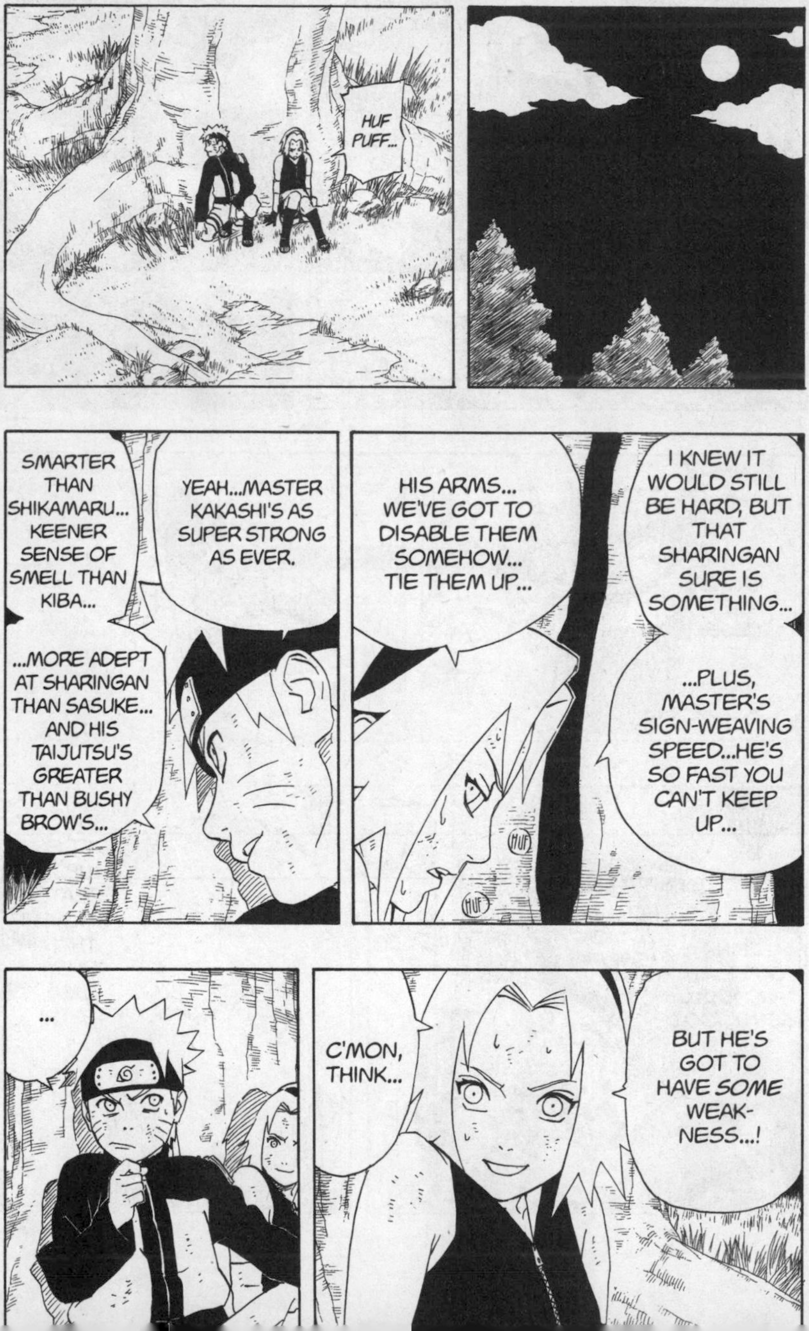
HUF PUFF...
I KNEW IT WOULD STILL BE HARD, BUT THAT SHARINGAN SURE IS SOMETHING...
...PLUS, MASTER'S SIGN-WEAVING SPEED...HE'S SO FAST YOU CAN'T KEEP UP...
HIS ARMS... WE'VE GOT TO DISABLE THEM SOMEHOW... TIE THEM UP...
HUF
HUF
YEAH...MASTER KAKASHI'S AS SUPER STRONG AS EVER.
SMARTER THAN SHIKAMARU... KEENER SENSE OF SMELL THAN KIBA...
...MORE ADEPT AT SHARINGAN THAN SASUKE... AND HIS TAIJUTSU'S GREATER THAN BUSHY BROW'S...
BUT HE'S GOT TO HAVE *SOME* WEAKNESS...!
C'MON, THINK...
...

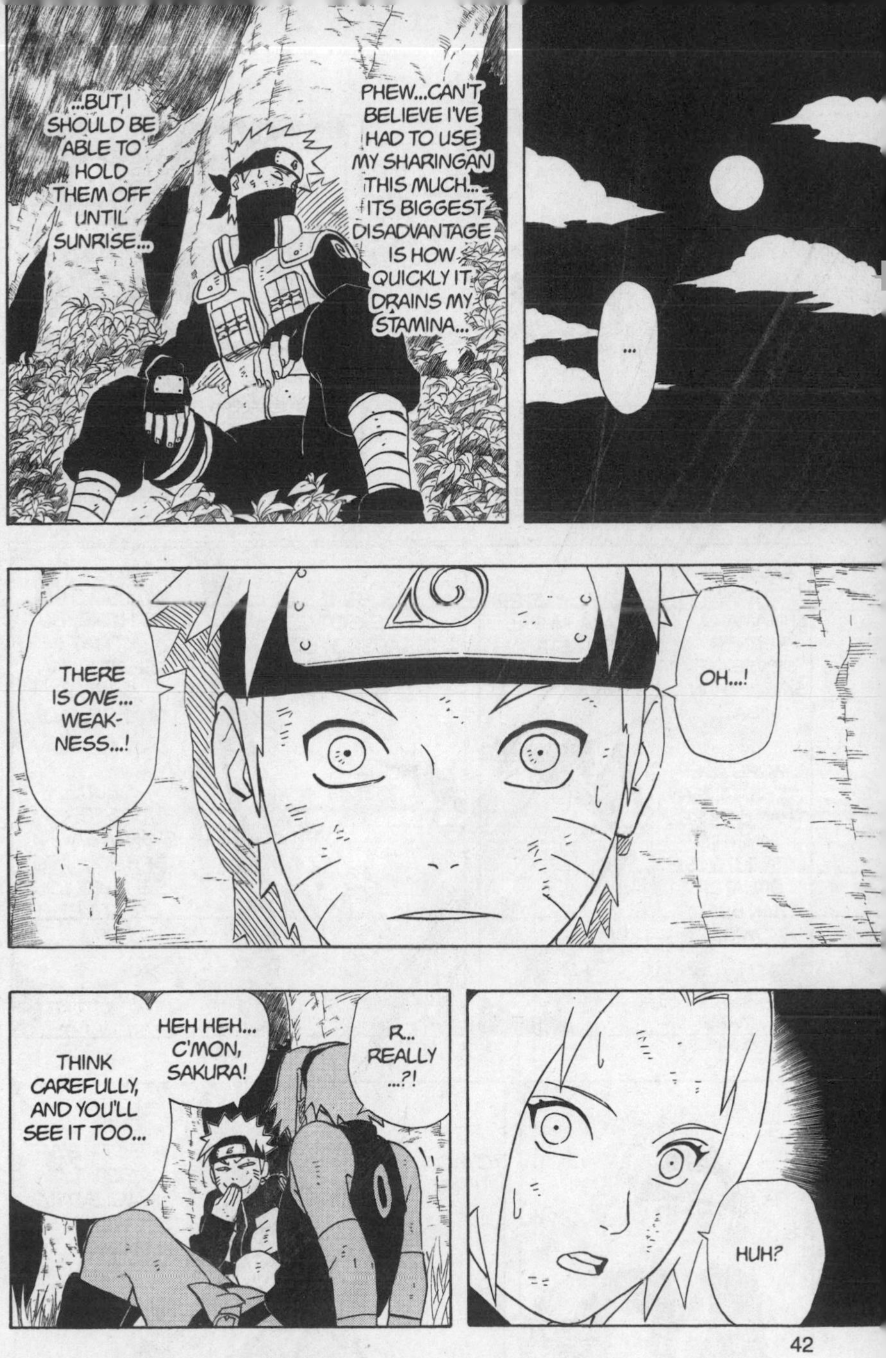
...
PHEW...CAN'T BELIEVE I'VE HAD TO USE MY SHARINGAN THIS MUCH... ITS BIGGEST DISADVANTAGE IS HOW QUICKLY IT DRAINS MY STAMINA...
...BUT, I SHOULD BE ABLE TO HOLD THEM OFF UNTIL SUNRISE...
OH...!
THERE IS *ONE*... WEAKNESS...!
HUH?
R... REALLY ...?!
HEH HEH... C'MON, SAKURA!
THINK CAREFULLY, AND YOU'LL SEE IT TOO...

READ THIS WAY

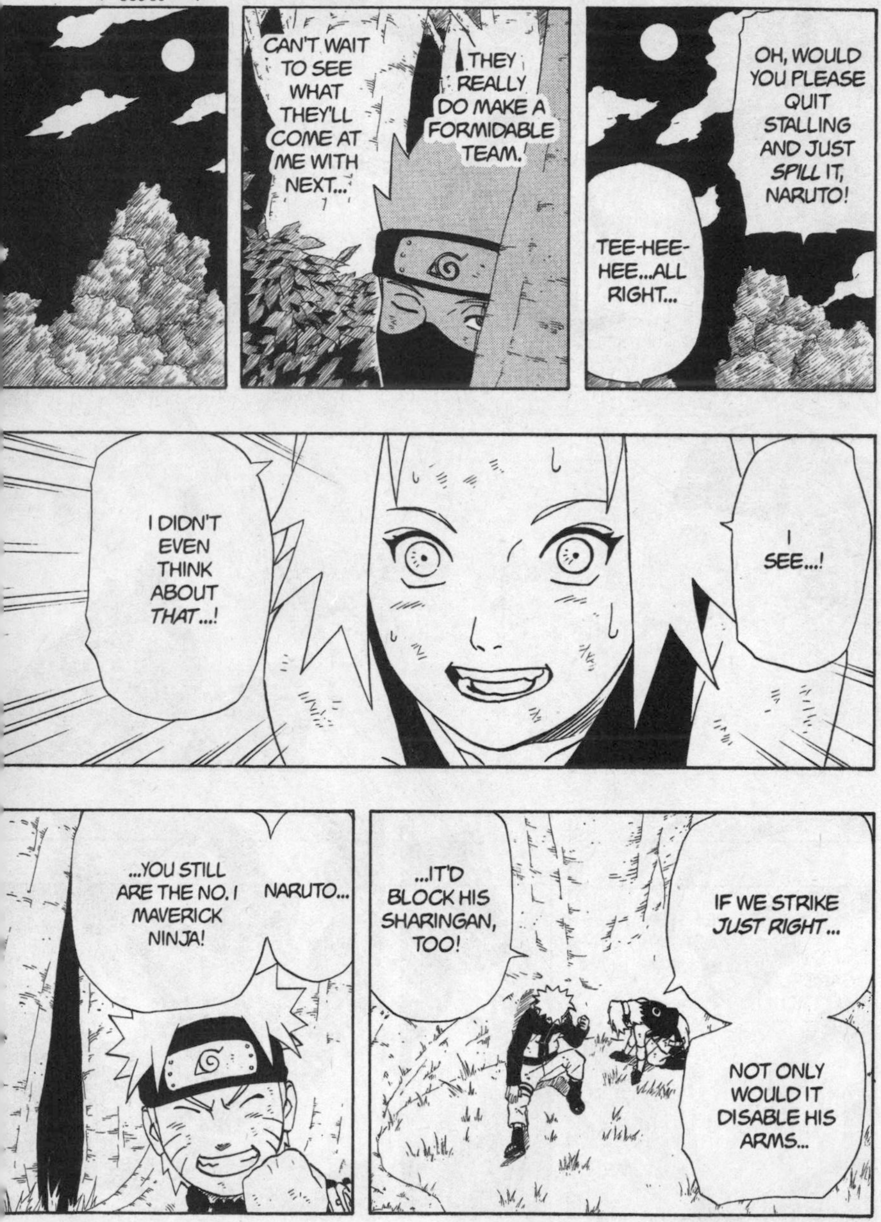
OH, WOULD YOU PLEASE QUIT STALLING AND JUST *SPILL* IT, NARUTO!
TEE-HEE-HEE...ALL RIGHT...
THEY REALLY DO MAKE A FORMIDABLE TEAM.
CAN'T WAIT TO SEE WHAT THEY'LL COME AT ME WITH NEXT...
I SEE...!
I DIDN'T EVEN THINK ABOUT *THAT*...!
IF WE STRIKE *JUST RIGHT*...
NOT ONLY WOULD IT DISABLE HIS ARMS...
...IT'D BLOCK HIS SHARINGAN, TOO!
NARUTO...
...YOU STILL ARE THE NO. 1 MAVERICK NINJA!

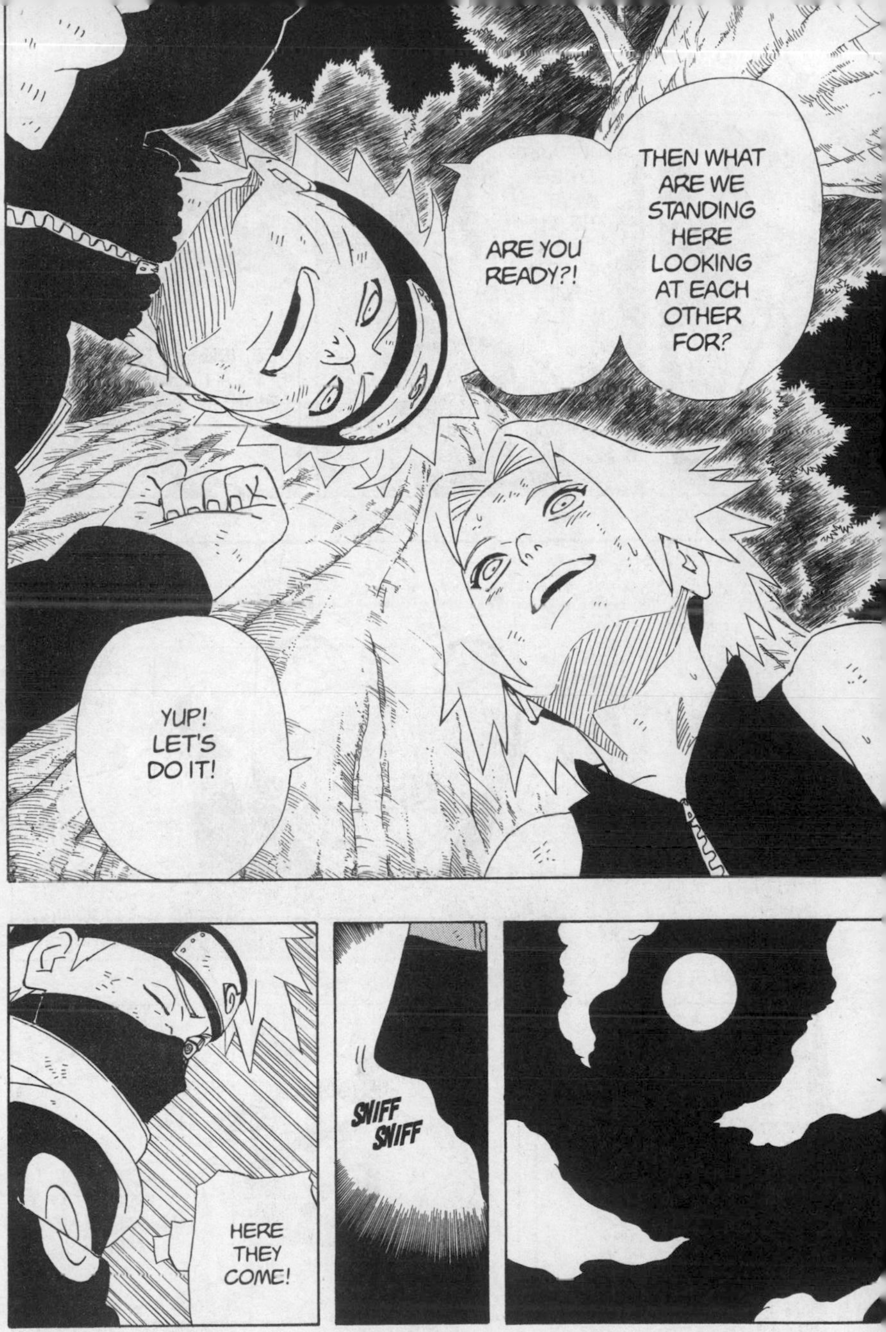
THEN WHAT ARE WE STANDING HERE LOOKING AT EACH OTHER FOR?
ARE YOU READY?!
YUP! LET'S DO IT!
SNIFF SNIFF
HERE THEY COME!

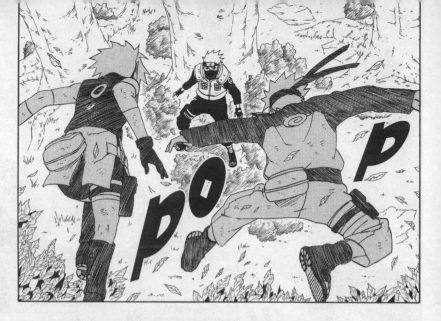

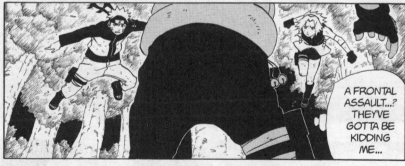

A FRONTAL ASSAULT...? THEY'VE GOTTA BE KIDDING ME...

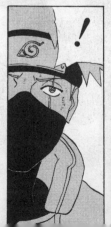

!

HERE I GO! HEY, MASTER KAKASHI...

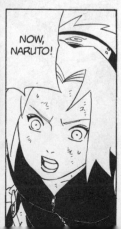

NOW, NARUTO!

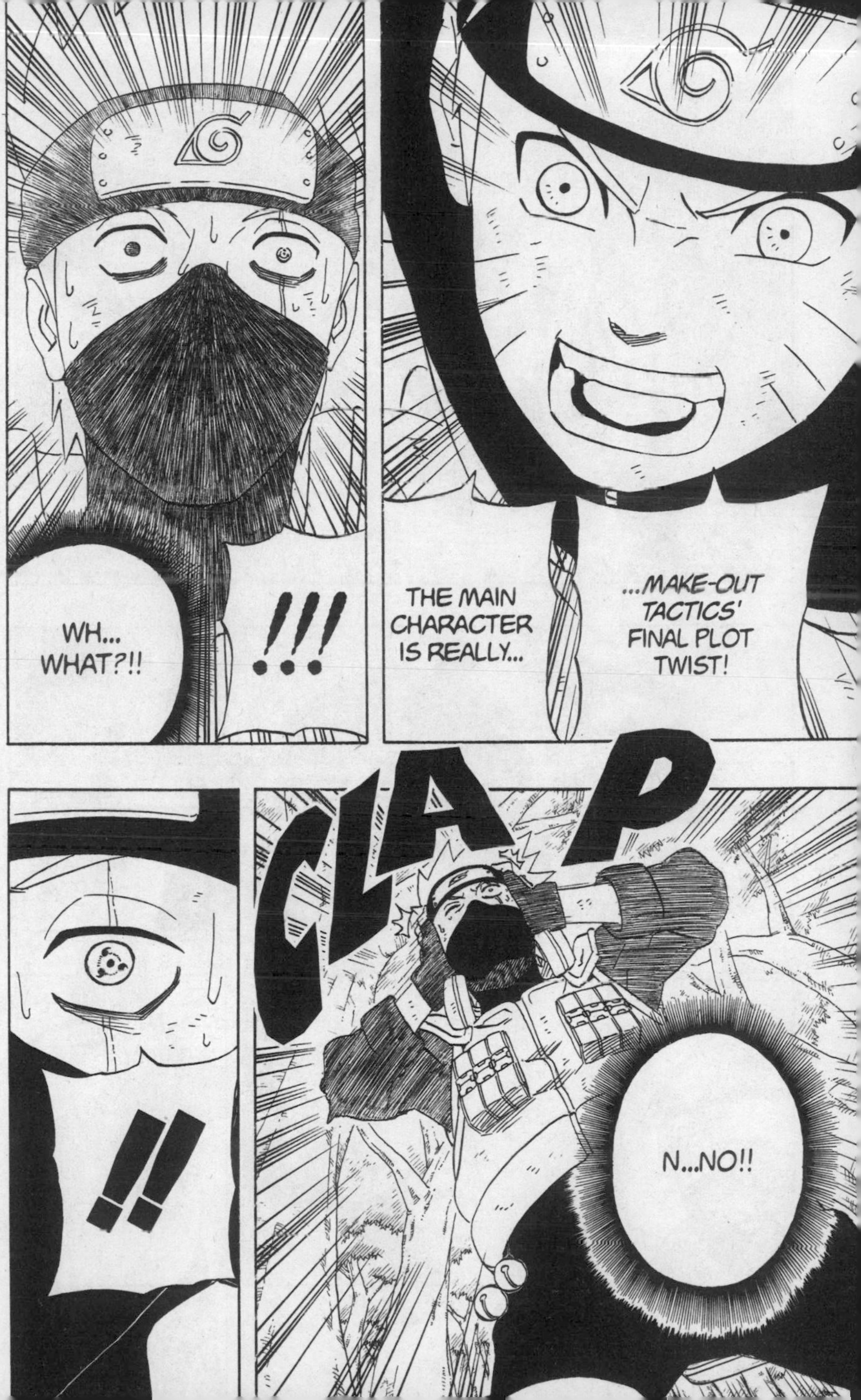
...MAKE-OUT TACTICS' FINAL PLOT TWIST!
THE MAIN CHARACTER IS REALLY...
!!!
WH... WHAT?!!
CLAP
N...NO!!
!!

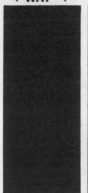

READ THIS WAY

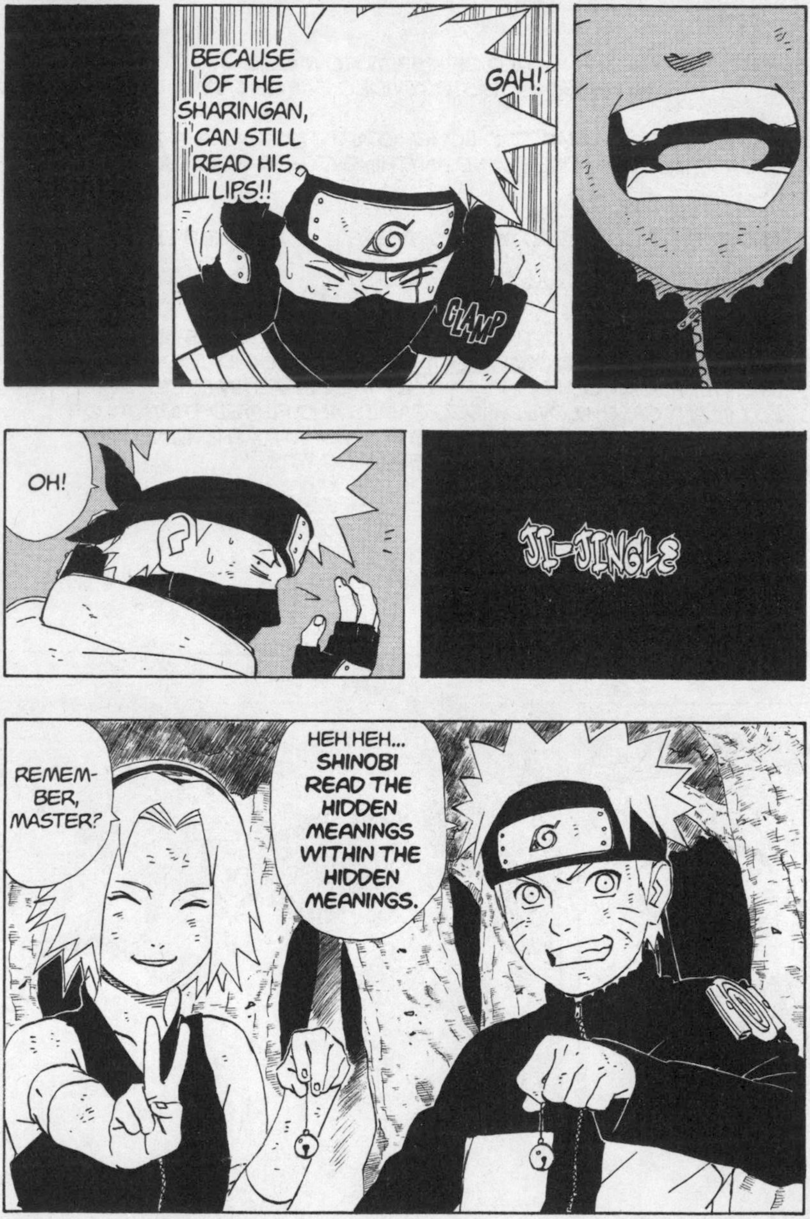
GAH!
BECAUSE OF THE SHARINGAN, I CAN STILL READ HIS LIPS!!
CLAMP
JI-JINGLE
OH!
HEH HEH... SHINOBI READ THE HIDDEN MEANINGS WITHIN THE HIDDEN MEANINGS.
REMEMBER, MASTER?

THE WORLD OF KISHIMOTO MASASHI
MY PERSONAL HISTORY, VIDEO GAMES PART 1

SOMETIMES, IF I DRAW TOO LONG, I START THINKING, "HAVE I EVER SPENT TIME IN MY LIFE DOING ANYTHING OTHER THAN DRAWING PICTURES?"

AND THEN IT COMES TO ME. YES, THERE IS ONE OTHER THING.

WHICH IS...VIDEO GAMES.

EVER SINCE I WAS A KID, I LOVED PLAYING VIDEO GAMES ALMOST AS MUCH AS I LOVED DRAWING. MY FRIENDS ALL DID, TOO... AND EVEN MY FOLKS, SO I DON'T THINK OF MYSELF AS AN EXCEPTION... BUT IN ANY CASE, I LOVED VIDEO GAMES AND PLAYED THEM A LOT. OF COURSE, THE STANDARD GAME PLATFORM AT THE TIME WAS THE FAMILY COMPUTER, A.K.A. THE FAMICOM.

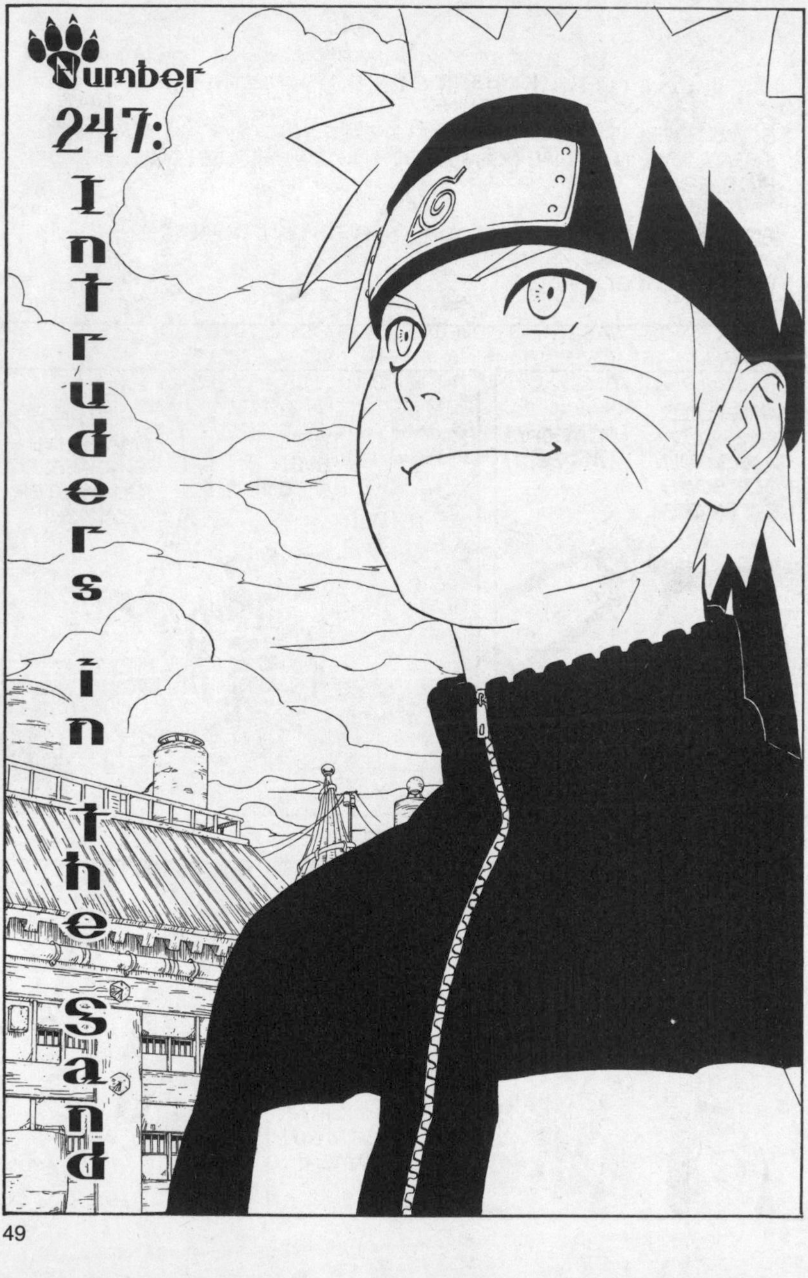
Number 247: Intruders in the Sand

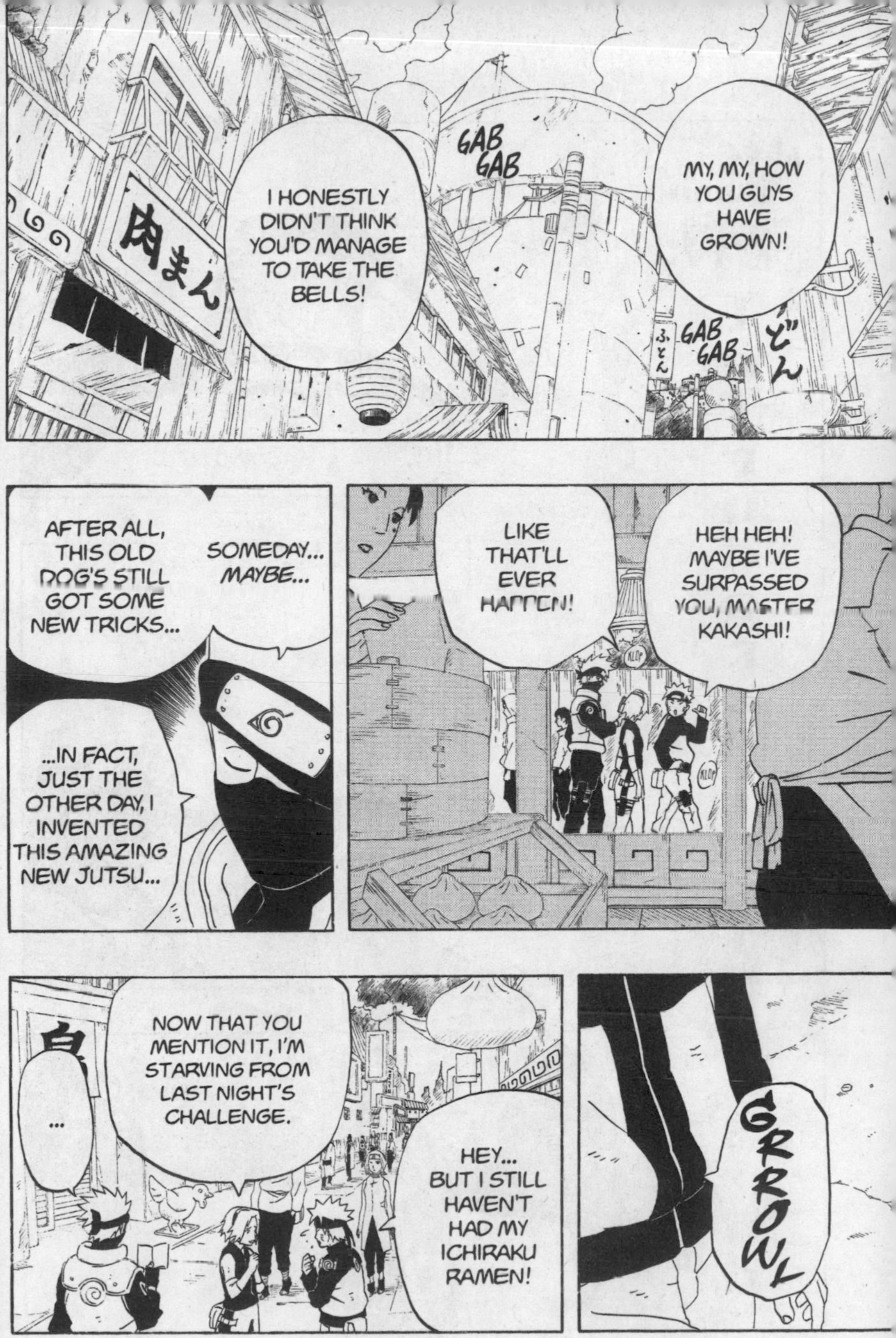
MY, MY, HOW YOU GUYS HAVE GROWN!
GAB GAB
GAB GAB
I HONESTLY DIDN'T THINK YOU'D MANAGE TO TAKE THE BELLS!
肉まん
ふとん
どん
HEH HEH! MAYBE I'VE SURPASSED YOU, MASTER KAKASHI!
LIKE THAT'LL EVER HAPPEN!
KLOP
KLOP
SOMEDAY... MAYBE...
AFTER ALL, THIS OLD DOG'S STILL GOT SOME NEW TRICKS...
...IN FACT, JUST THE OTHER DAY, I INVENTED THIS AMAZING NEW JUTSU...
GRROWL
HEY... BUT I STILL HAVEN'T HAD MY ICHIRAKU RAMEN!
NOW THAT YOU MENTION IT, I'M STARVING FROM LAST NIGHT'S CHALLENGE.
...

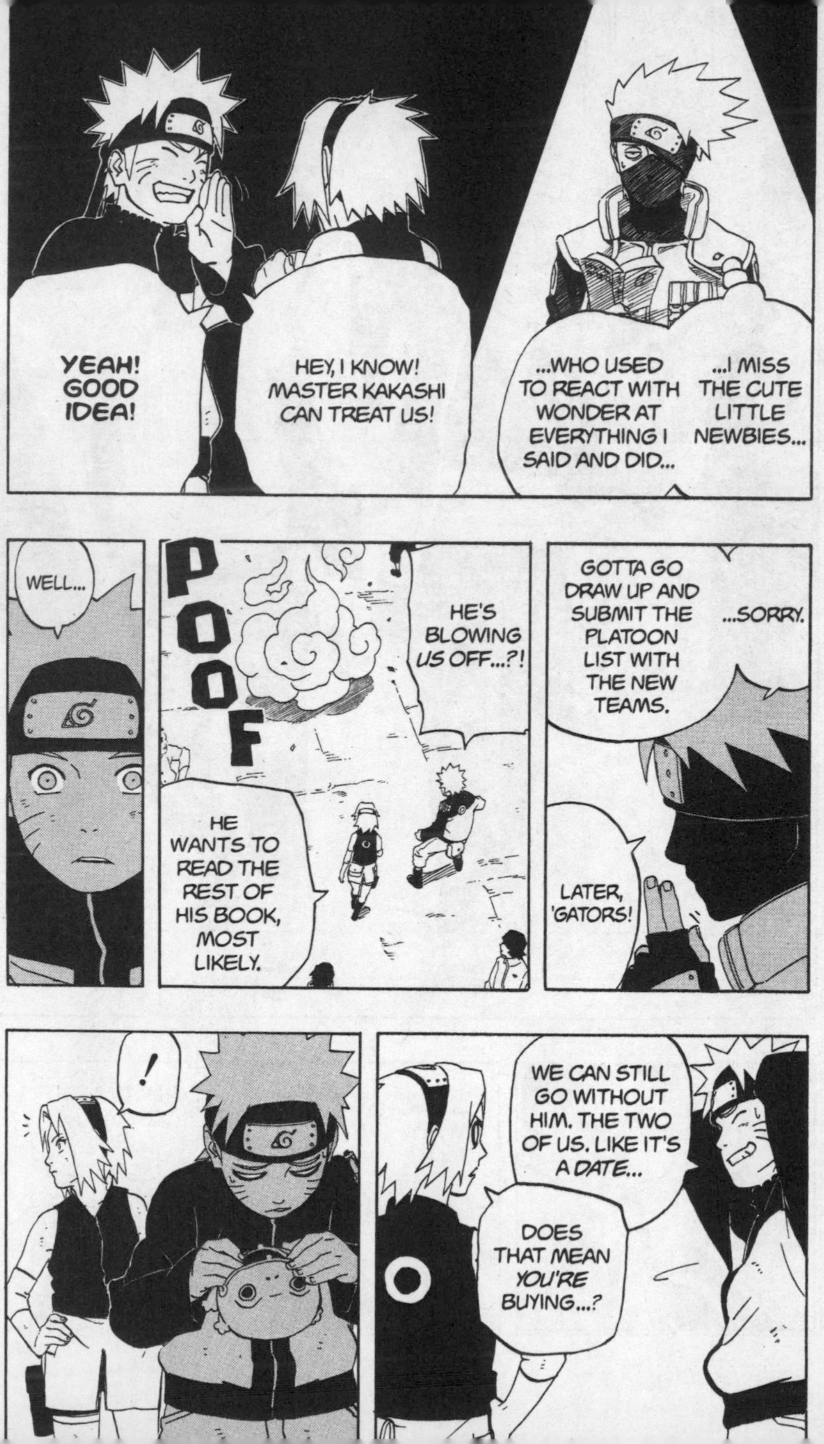
...I MISS THE CUTE LITTLE NEWBIES...
...WHO USED TO REACT WITH WONDER AT EVERYTHING I SAID AND DID...
HEY, I KNOW! MASTER KAKASHI CAN TREAT US!
YEAH! GOOD IDEA!
...SORRY.
GOTTA GO DRAW UP AND SUBMIT THE PLATOON LIST WITH THE NEW TEAMS.
LATER, 'GATORS!
POOF
HE'S BLOWING US OFF...?!
HE WANTS TO READ THE REST OF HIS BOOK, MOST LIKELY.
WELL...
WE CAN STILL GO WITHOUT HIM. THE TWO OF US. LIKE IT'S A DATE...
DOES THAT MEAN YOU'RE BUYING...?
!

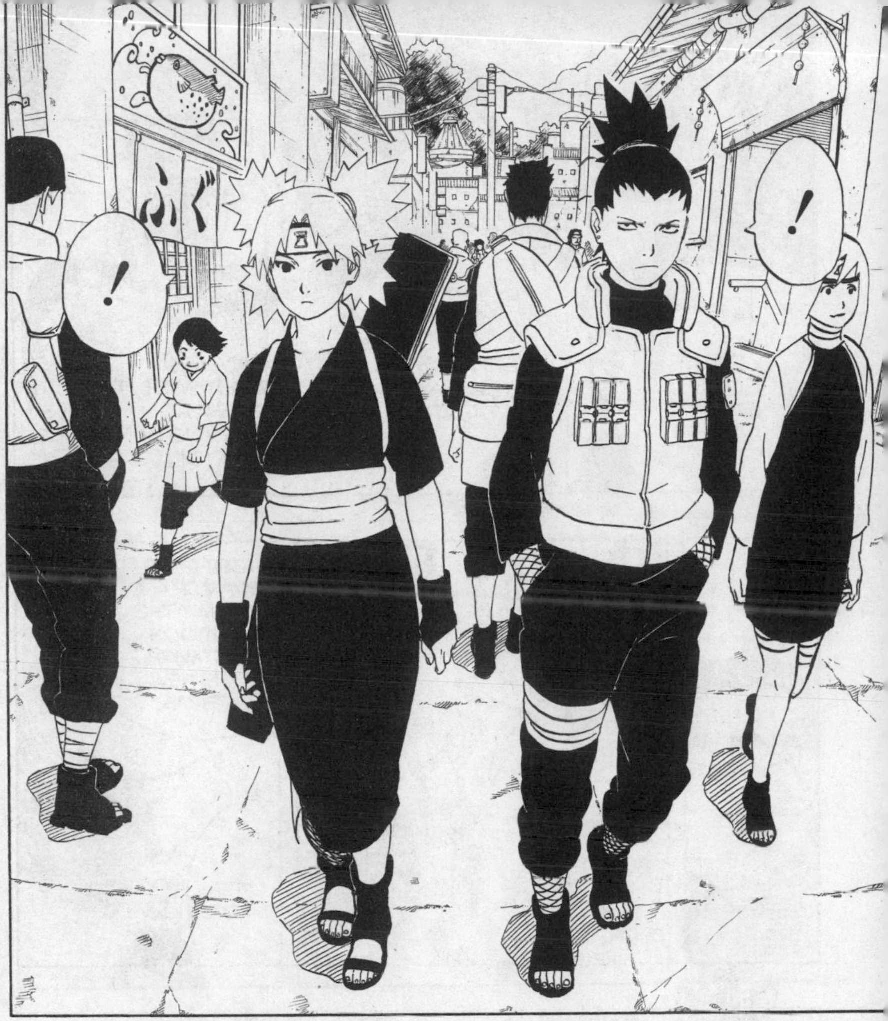
!
!

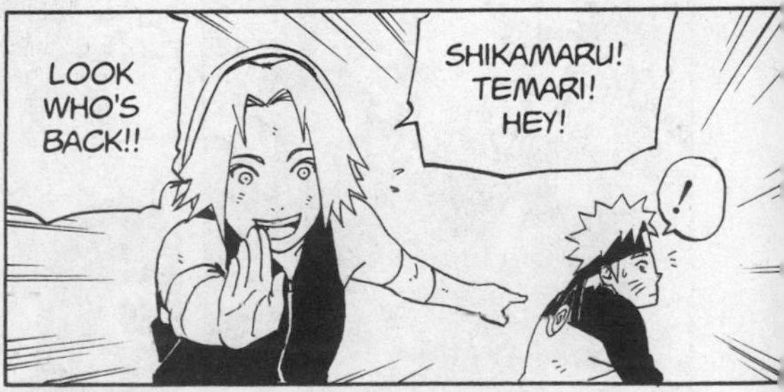
SHIKAMARU! TEMARI! HEY!
LOOK WHO'S BACK!!
!

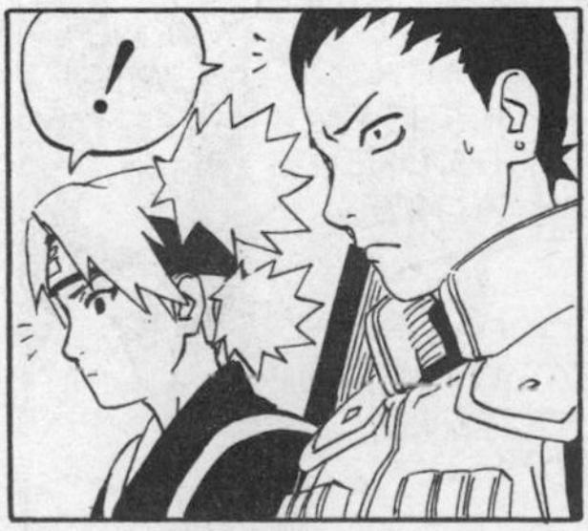
!

READ THIS WAY

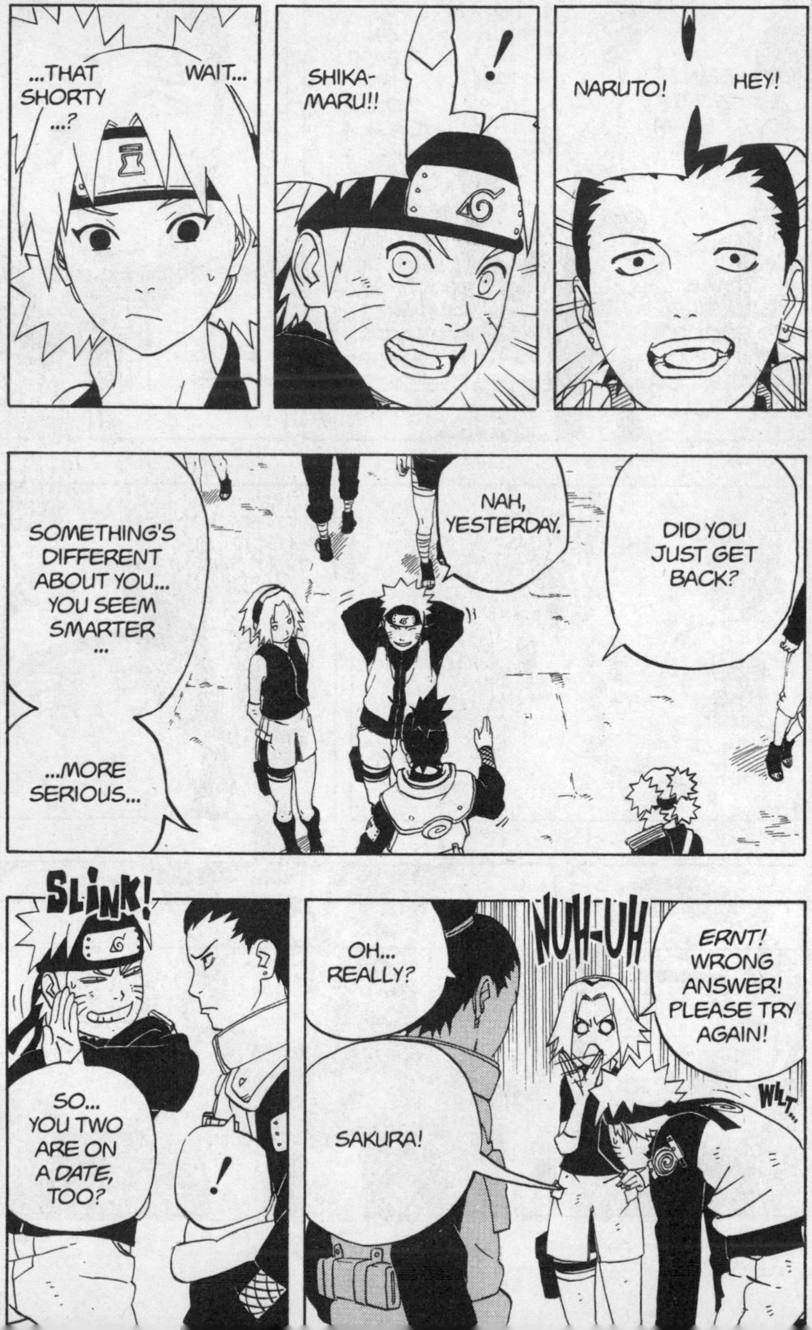
HEY!
NARUTO!
!
SHIKA-MARU!!
WAIT...
...THAT SHORTY ...?
DID YOU JUST GET BACK?
NAH, YESTERDAY.
SOMETHING'S DIFFERENT ABOUT YOU... YOU SEEM SMARTER ...
...MORE SERIOUS...
NUH-UH
ERNT! WRONG ANSWER! PLEASE TRY AGAIN!
OH... REALLY?
WILT...
SAKURA!
SLINK!
SO... YOU TWO ARE ON A DATE, TOO?
!

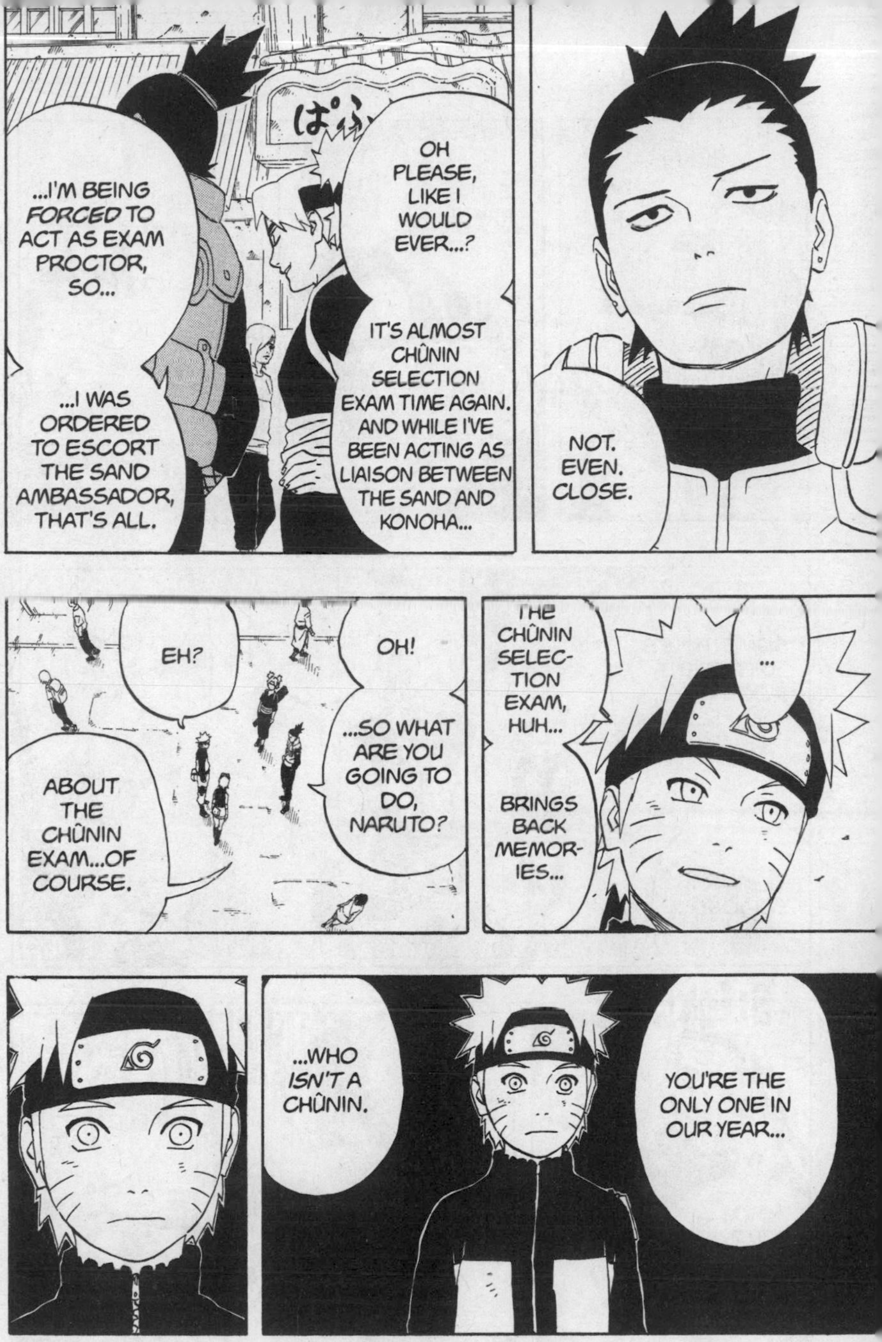
NOT. EVEN. CLOSE.
OH PLEASE, LIKE I WOULD EVER...?
IT'S ALMOST CHÛNIN SELECTION EXAM TIME AGAIN. AND WHILE I'VE BEEN ACTING AS LIAISON BETWEEN THE SAND AND KONOHA...
...I'M BEING *FORCED* TO ACT AS EXAM PROCTOR, SO...
...I WAS ORDERED TO ESCORT THE SAND AMBASSADOR, THAT'S ALL.
...
THE CHÛNIN SELEC-TION EXAM, HUH...
BRINGS BACK MEMOR-IES...
OH!
...SO WHAT ARE YOU GOING TO DO, NARUTO?
EH?
ABOUT THE CHÛNIN EXAM...OF COURSE.
YOU'RE THE ONLY ONE IN OUR YEAR...
...WHO *ISN'T* A CHÛNIN.

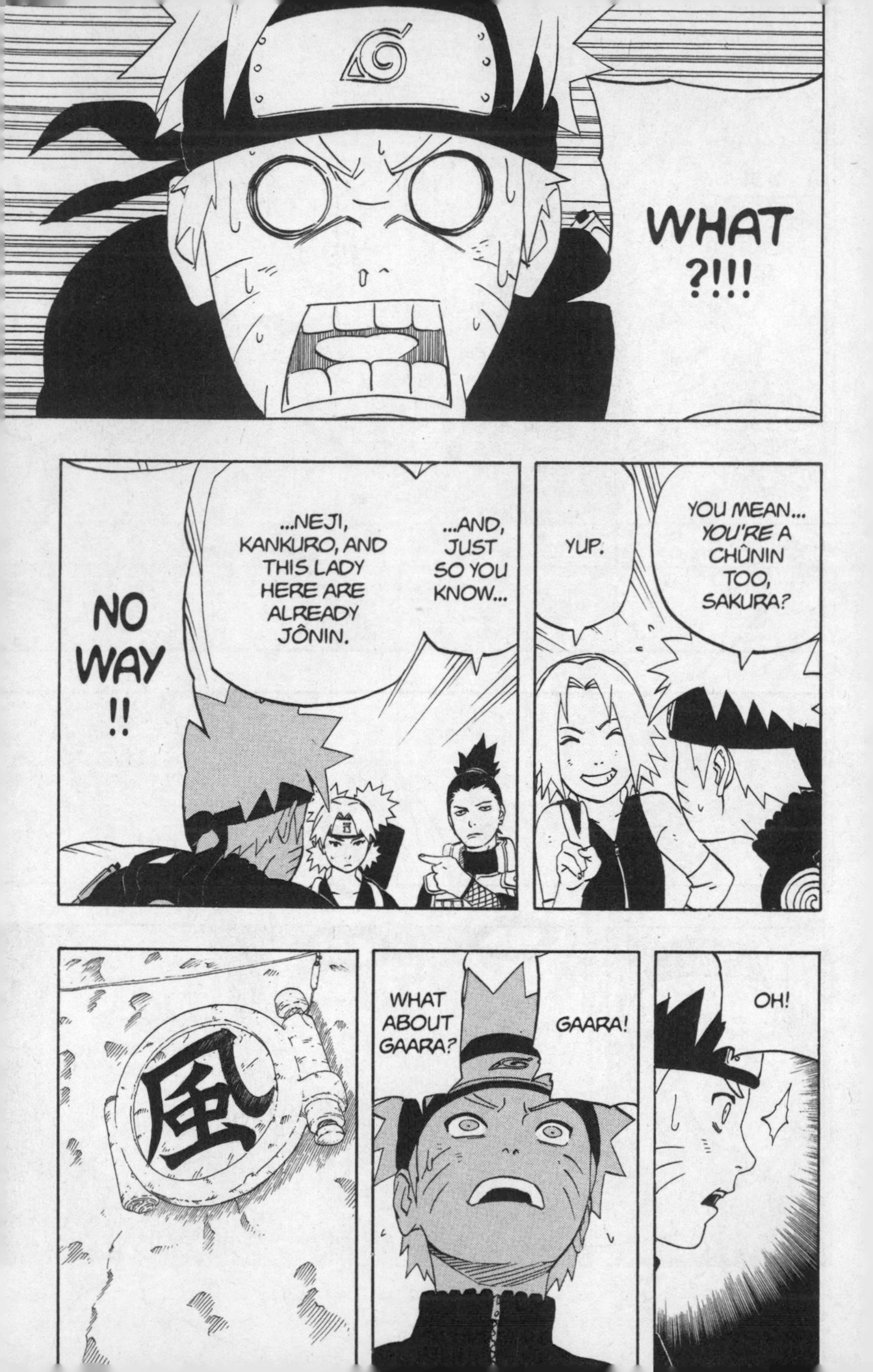
WHAT ?!!!
YOU MEAN... *YOU'RE* A CHÛNIN TOO, SAKURA?
YUP.
...AND, JUST SO YOU KNOW...
...NEJI, KANKURO, AND THIS LADY HERE ARE ALREADY JÔNIN.
NO WAY !!
OH!
GAARA!
WHAT ABOUT GAARA?
風

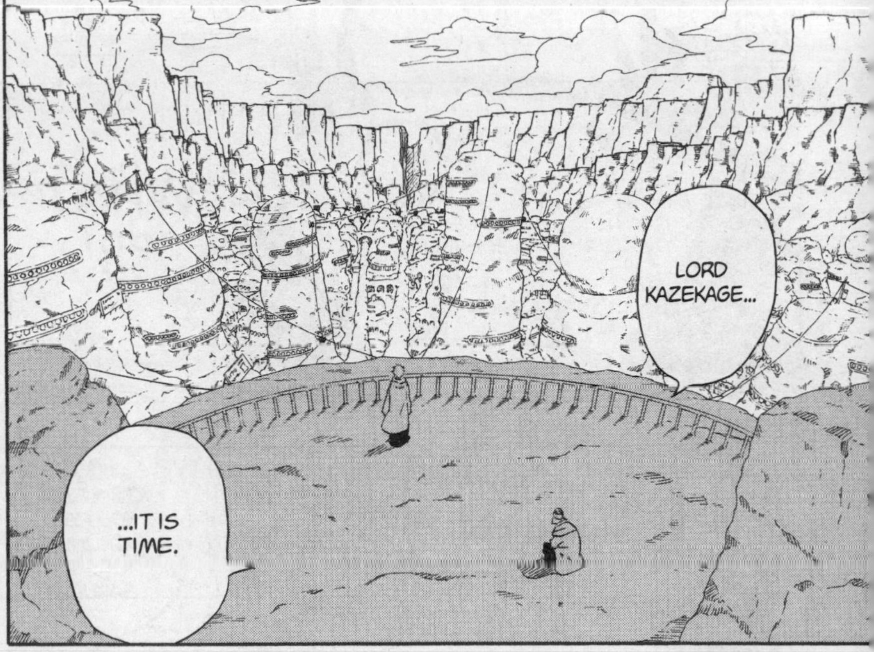
LORD KAZEKAGE...
...IT IS TIME.
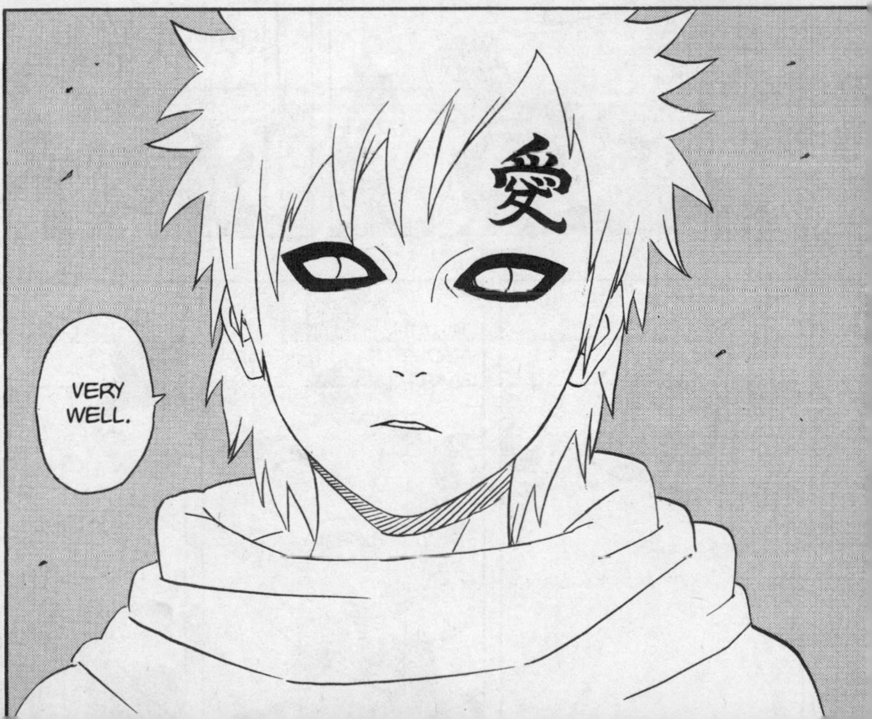
VERY WELL.

READ THIS WAY

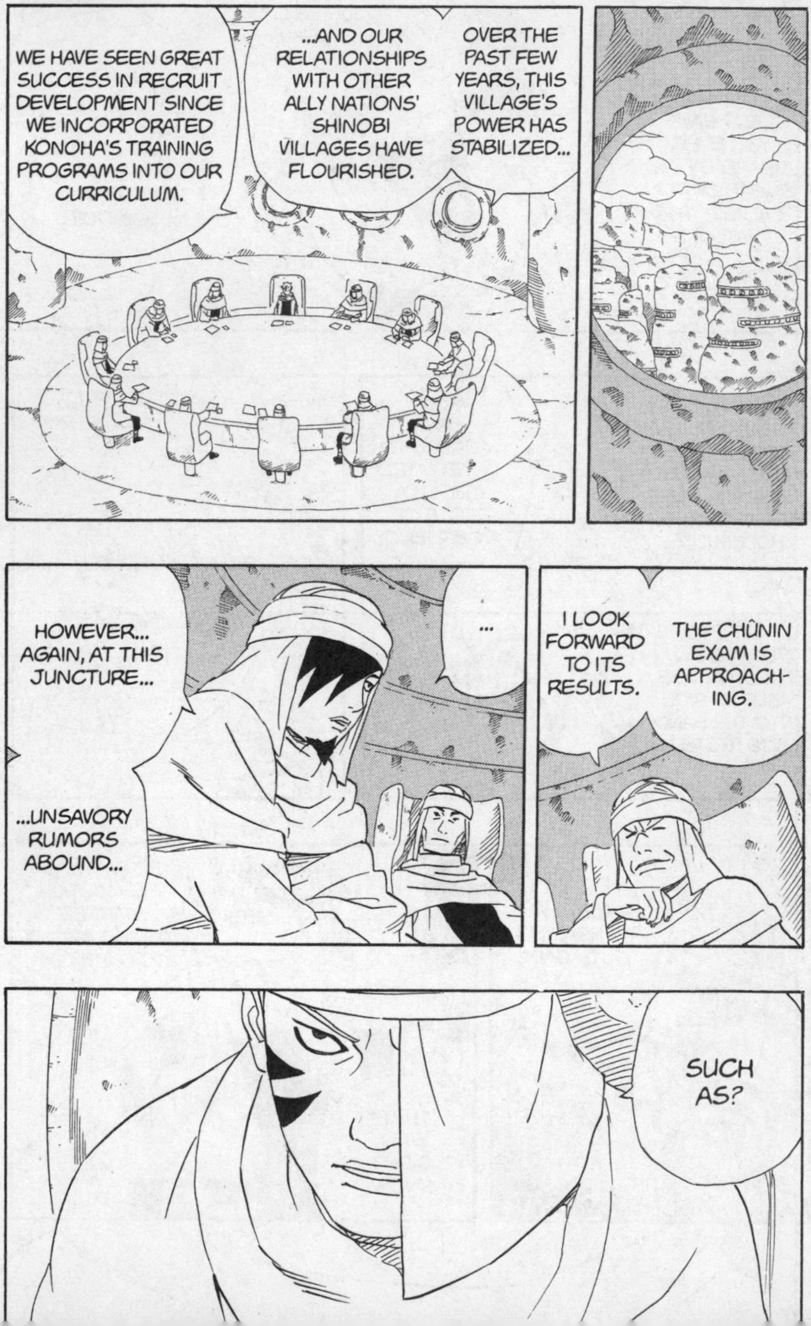
OVER THE PAST FEW YEARS, THIS VILLAGE'S POWER HAS STABILIZED...
...AND OUR RELATIONSHIPS WITH OTHER ALLY NATIONS' SHINOBI VILLAGES HAVE FLOURISHED.
WE HAVE SEEN GREAT SUCCESS IN RECRUIT DEVELOPMENT SINCE WE INCORPORATED KONOHA'S TRAINING PROGRAMS INTO OUR CURRICULUM.
THE CHÛNIN EXAM IS APPROACH-ING.
I LOOK FORWARD TO ITS RESULTS.
...
HOWEVER... AGAIN, AT THIS JUNCTURE...
...UNSAVORY RUMORS ABOUND...
SUCH AS?

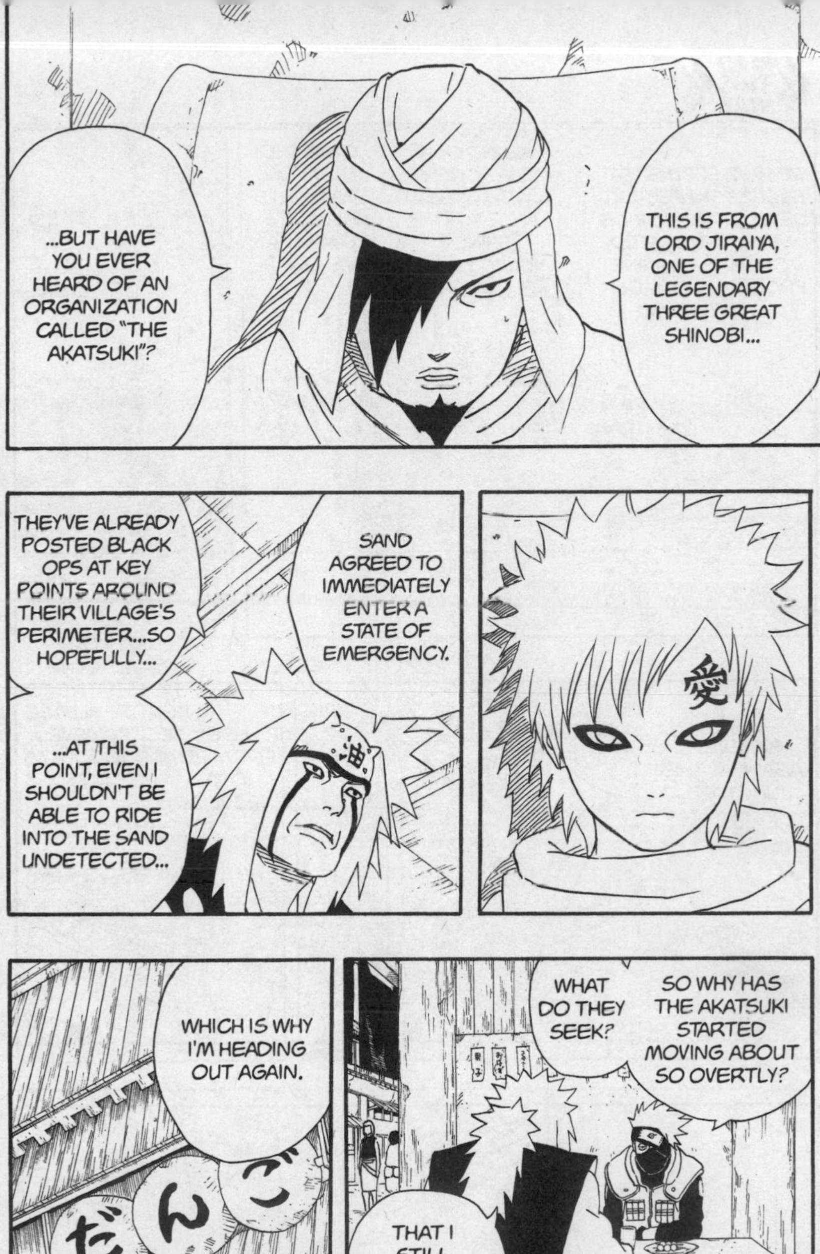
THIS IS FROM LORD JIRAIYA, ONE OF THE LEGENDARY THREE GREAT SHINOBI...
...BUT HAVE YOU EVER HEARD OF AN ORGANIZATION CALLED "THE AKATSUKI"?
SAND AGREED TO IMMEDIATELY ENTER A STATE OF EMERGENCY.
THEY'VE ALREADY POSTED BLACK OPS AT KEY POINTS AROUND THEIR VILLAGE'S PERIMETER...SO HOPEFULLY...
...AT THIS POINT, EVEN I SHOULDN'T BE ABLE TO RIDE INTO THE SAND UNDETECTED...
SO WHY HAS THE AKATSUKI STARTED MOVING ABOUT SO OVERTLY?
WHAT DO THEY SEEK?
THAT I STILL DON'T KNOW.
WHICH IS WHY I'M HEADING OUT AGAIN.
だんご

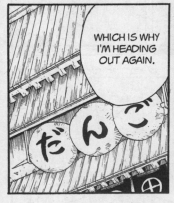

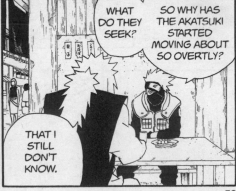

READ THIS WAY

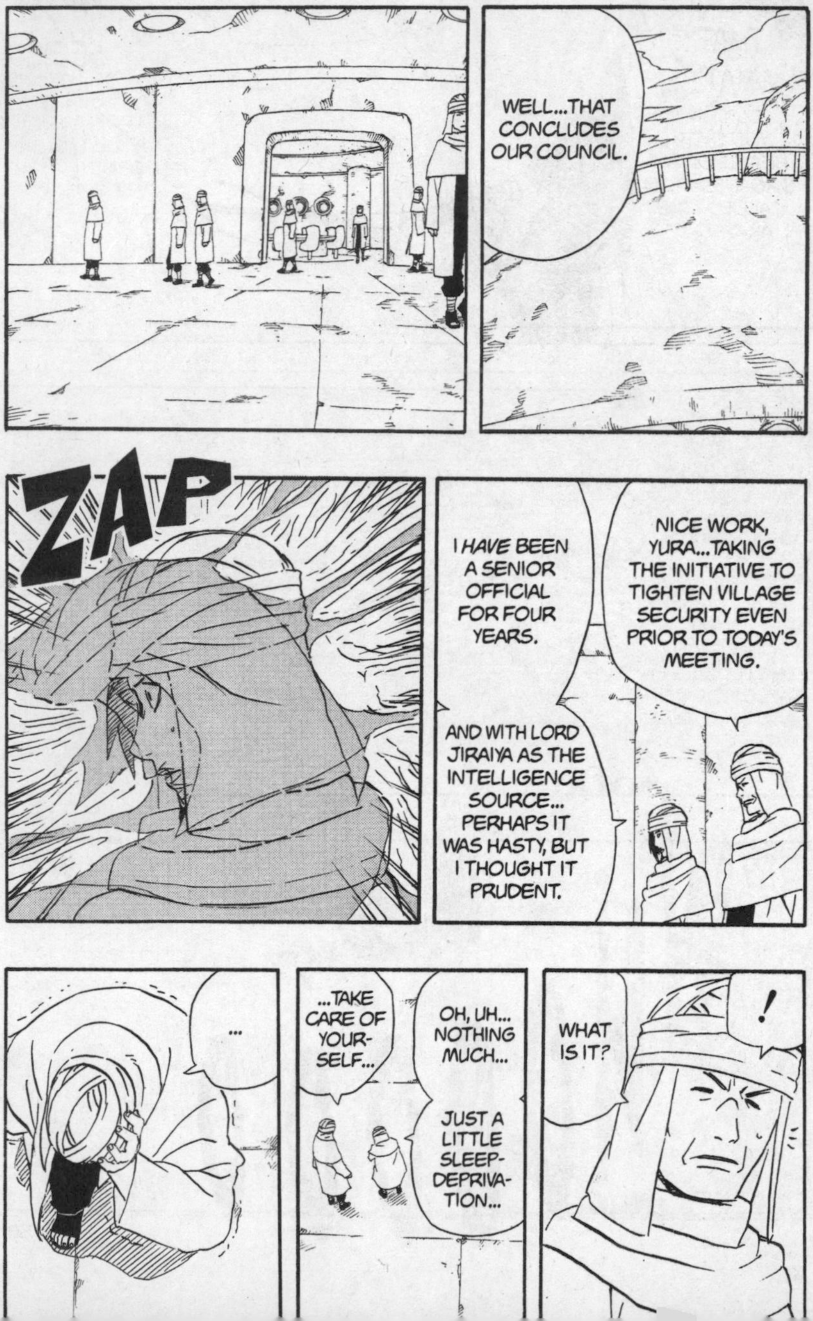
WELL...THAT CONCLUDES OUR COUNCIL.
NICE WORK, YURA...TAKING THE INITIATIVE TO TIGHTEN VILLAGE SECURITY EVEN PRIOR TO TODAY'S MEETING.
I *HAVE* BEEN A SENIOR OFFICIAL FOR FOUR YEARS.
AND WITH LORD JIRAIYA AS THE INTELLIGENCE SOURCE... PERHAPS IT WAS HASTY, BUT I THOUGHT IT PRUDENT.
ZAP
!
WHAT IS IT?
OH, UH... NOTHING MUCH...
JUST A LITTLE SLEEP-DEPRIVATION...
...TAKE CARE OF YOURSELF...
...

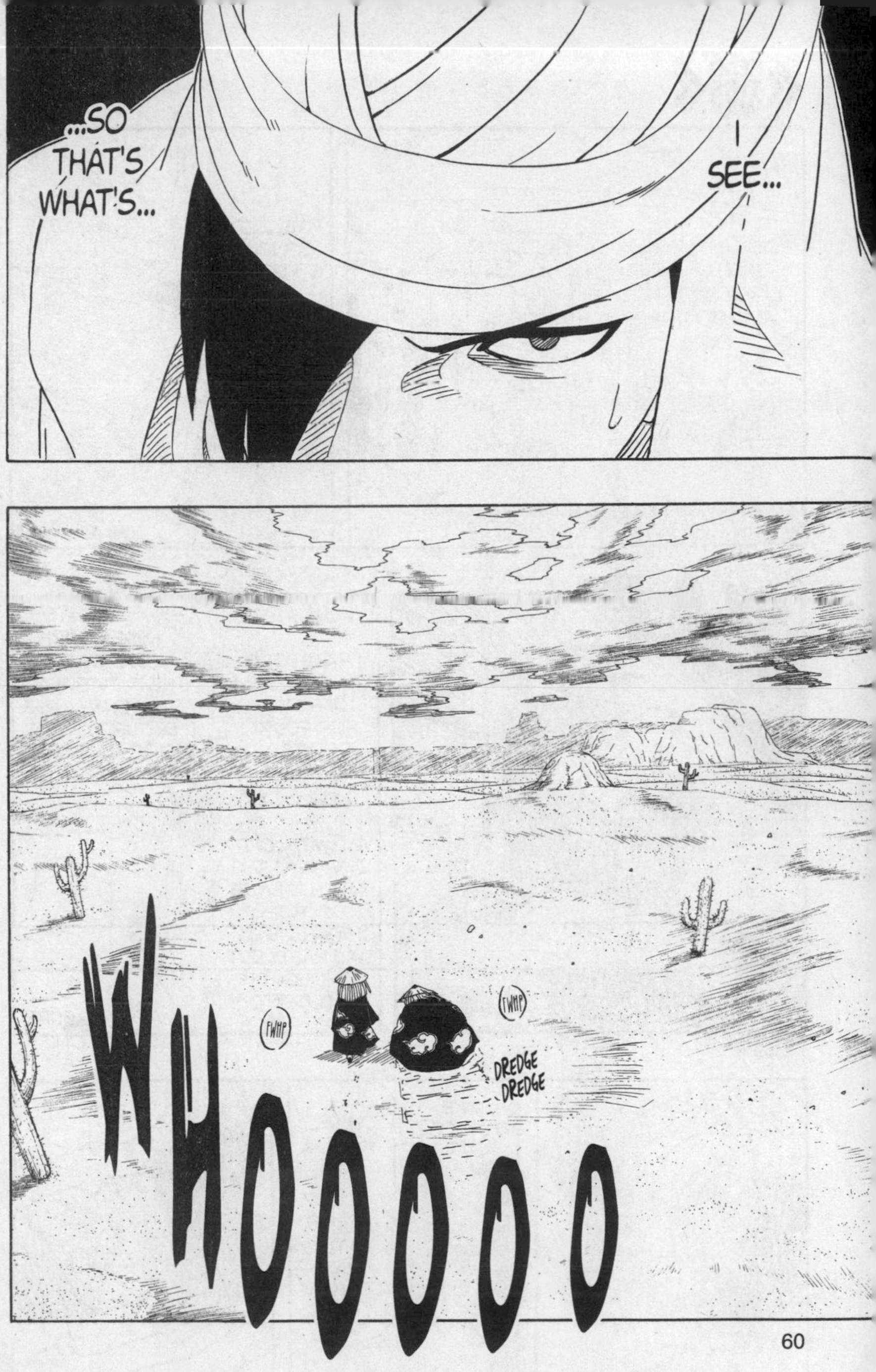
I SEE...
...SO THAT'S WHAT'S...
FWHP
FWHP
DREDGE DREDGE
WHOOOOO

READ THIS WAY

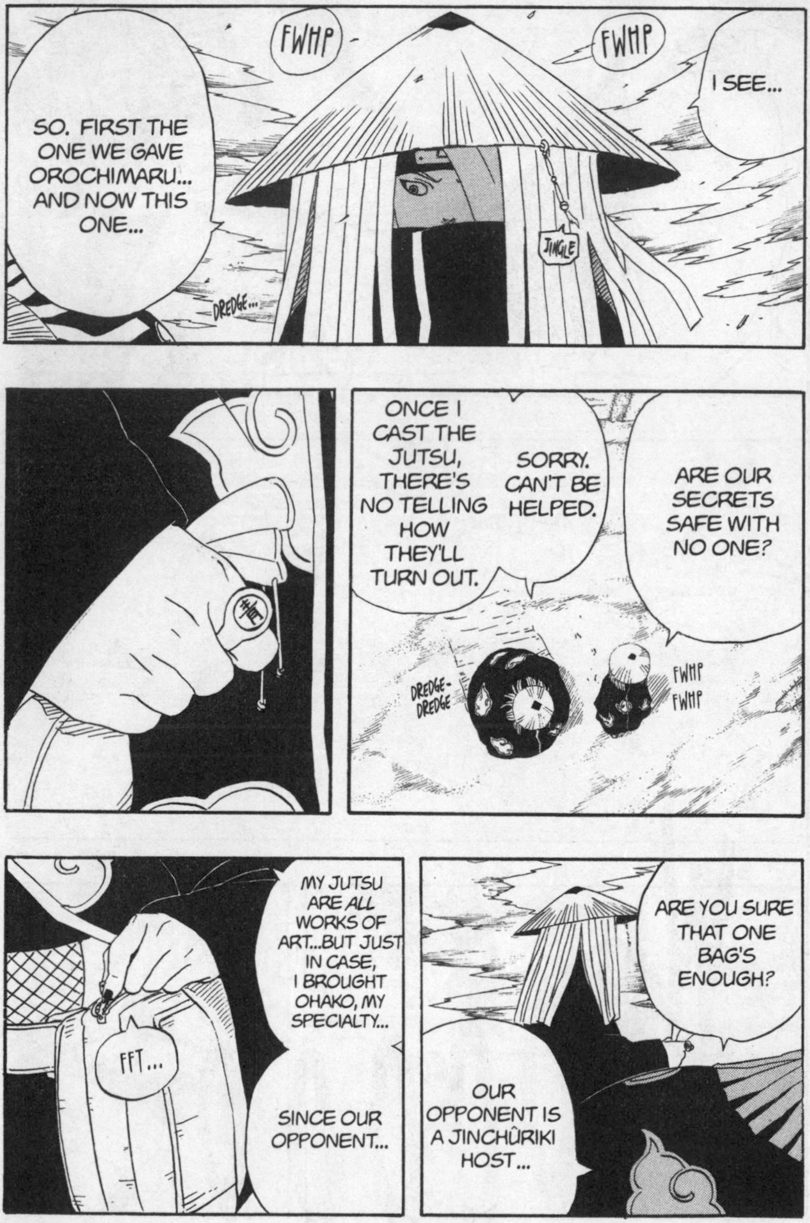
I SEE...
FWHP
FWHP
SO. FIRST THE ONE WE GAVE OROCHIMARU... AND NOW THIS ONE...
JINGLE
DREDGE...
ARE OUR SECRETS SAFE WITH NO ONE?
SORRY. CAN'T BE HELPED.
ONCE I CAST THE JUTSU, THERE'S NO TELLING HOW THEY'LL TURN OUT.
FWHP
FWHP
DREDGE-DREDGE
ARE YOU SURE THAT ONE BAG'S ENOUGH?
OUR OPPONENT IS A JINCHÛRIKI HOST...
MY JUTSU ARE ALL WORKS OF ART...BUT JUST IN CASE, I BROUGHT OHAKO, MY SPECIALTY...
SINCE OUR OPPONENT...
FFT...

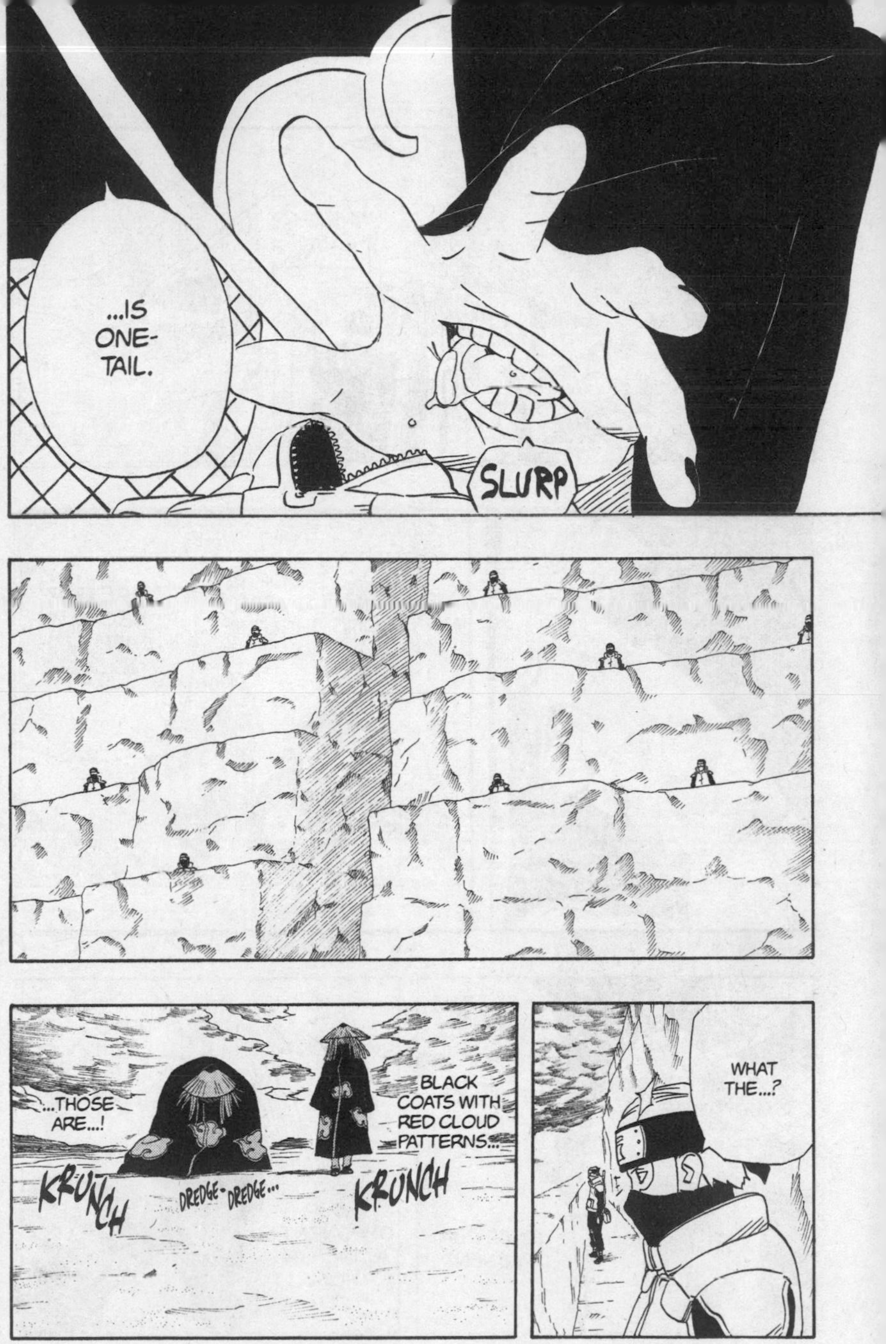
...IS ONE-TAIL.
SLURP
WHAT THE...?
BLACK COATS WITH RED CLOUD PATTERNS...
...THOSE ARE...!
KRUNCH
DREDGE-DREDGE...
KRUNCH

READ THIS WAY

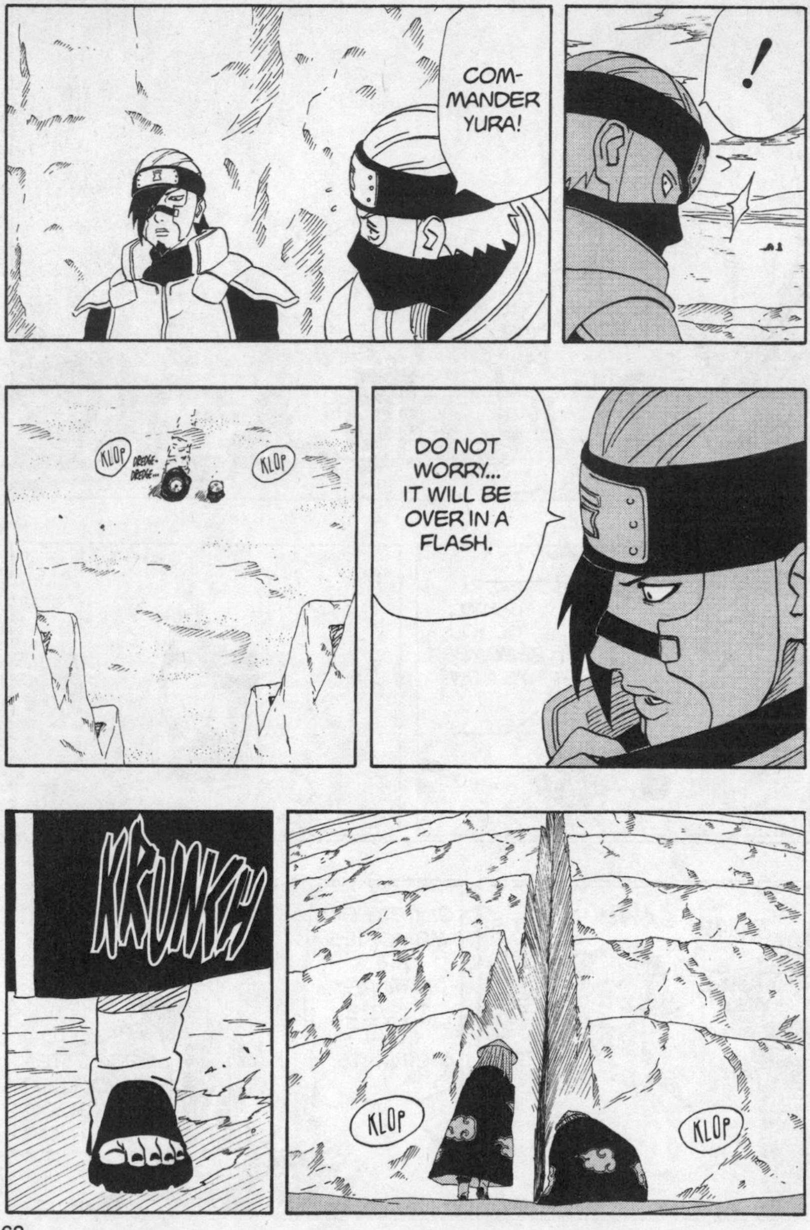
!
COM-
MANDER
YURA!
DO NOT
WORRY...
IT WILL BE
OVER IN A
FLASH.
KLOP
DREDGE-
DREDGE...
KLOP
KLOP
KLOP
KRUNCH

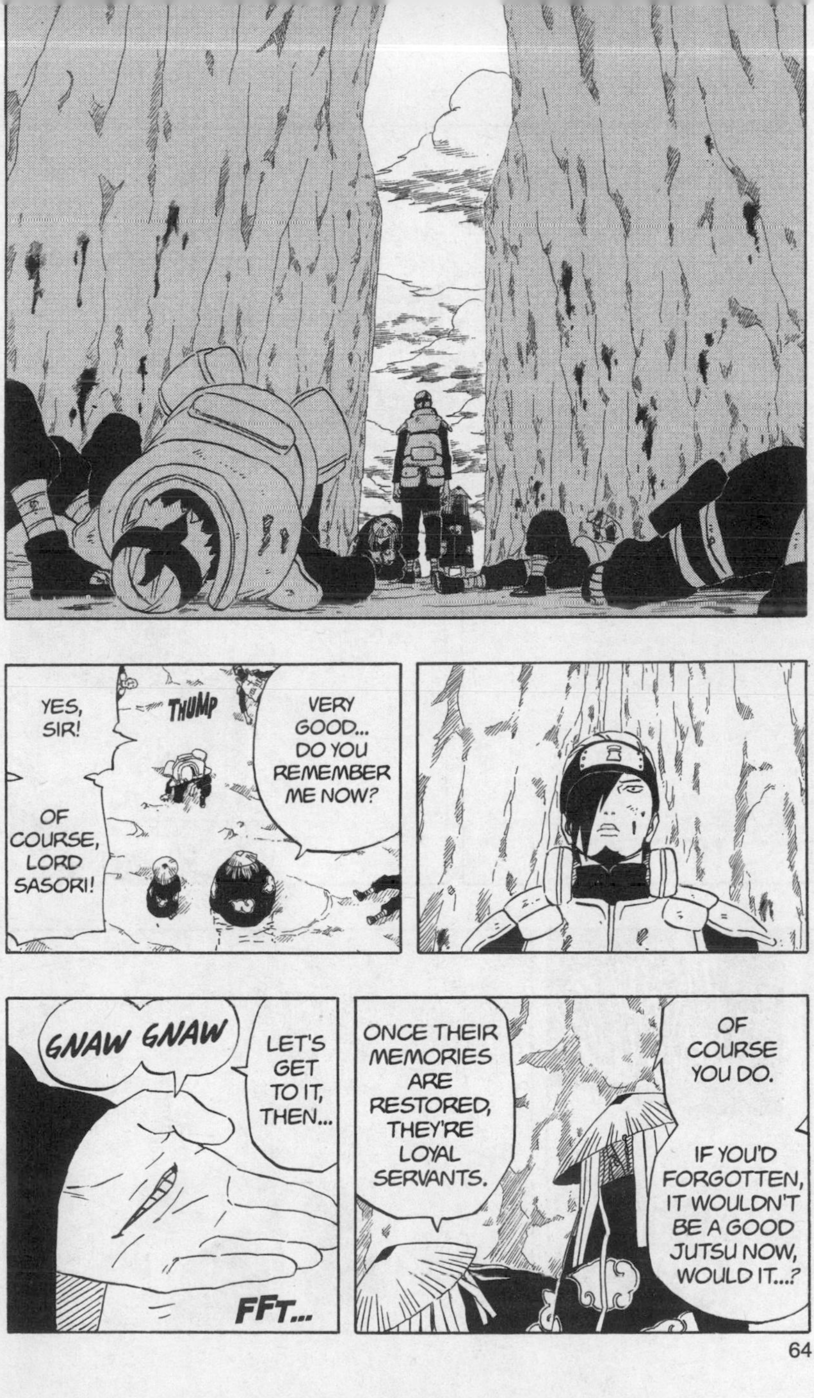
VERY GOOD... DO YOU REMEMBER ME NOW?
THUMP
YES, SIR!
OF COURSE, LORD SASORI!
OF COURSE YOU DO.
IF YOU'D FORGOTTEN, IT WOULDN'T BE A GOOD JUTSU NOW, WOULD IT...?
ONCE THEIR MEMORIES ARE RESTORED, THEY'RE LOYAL SERVANTS.
LET'S GET TO IT, THEN...
GNAW GNAW
FFT...

READ THIS WAY

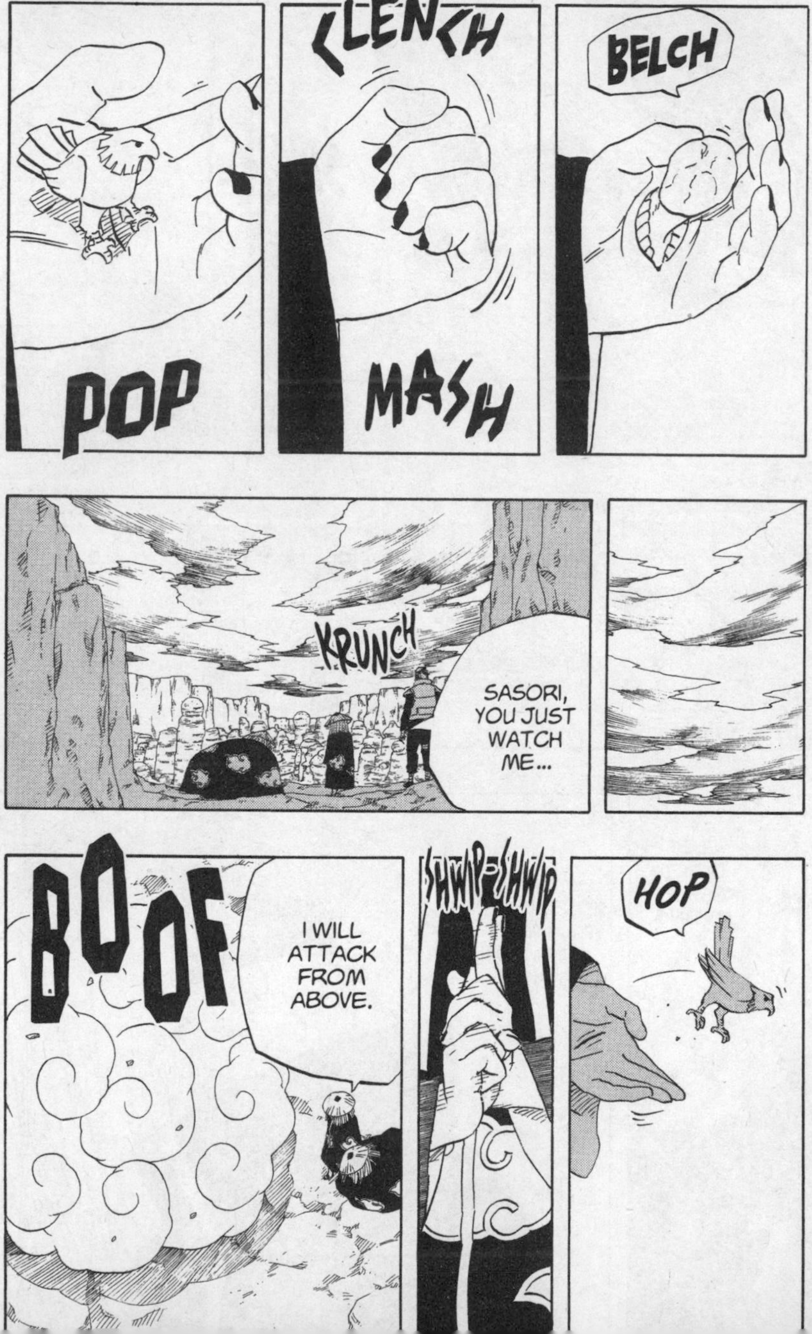
BELCH
CLENCH
MASH
POP
KRUNCH
SASORI, YOU JUST WATCH ME...
HOP
SHWIP-SHWIP
I WILL ATTACK FROM ABOVE.
BOOF

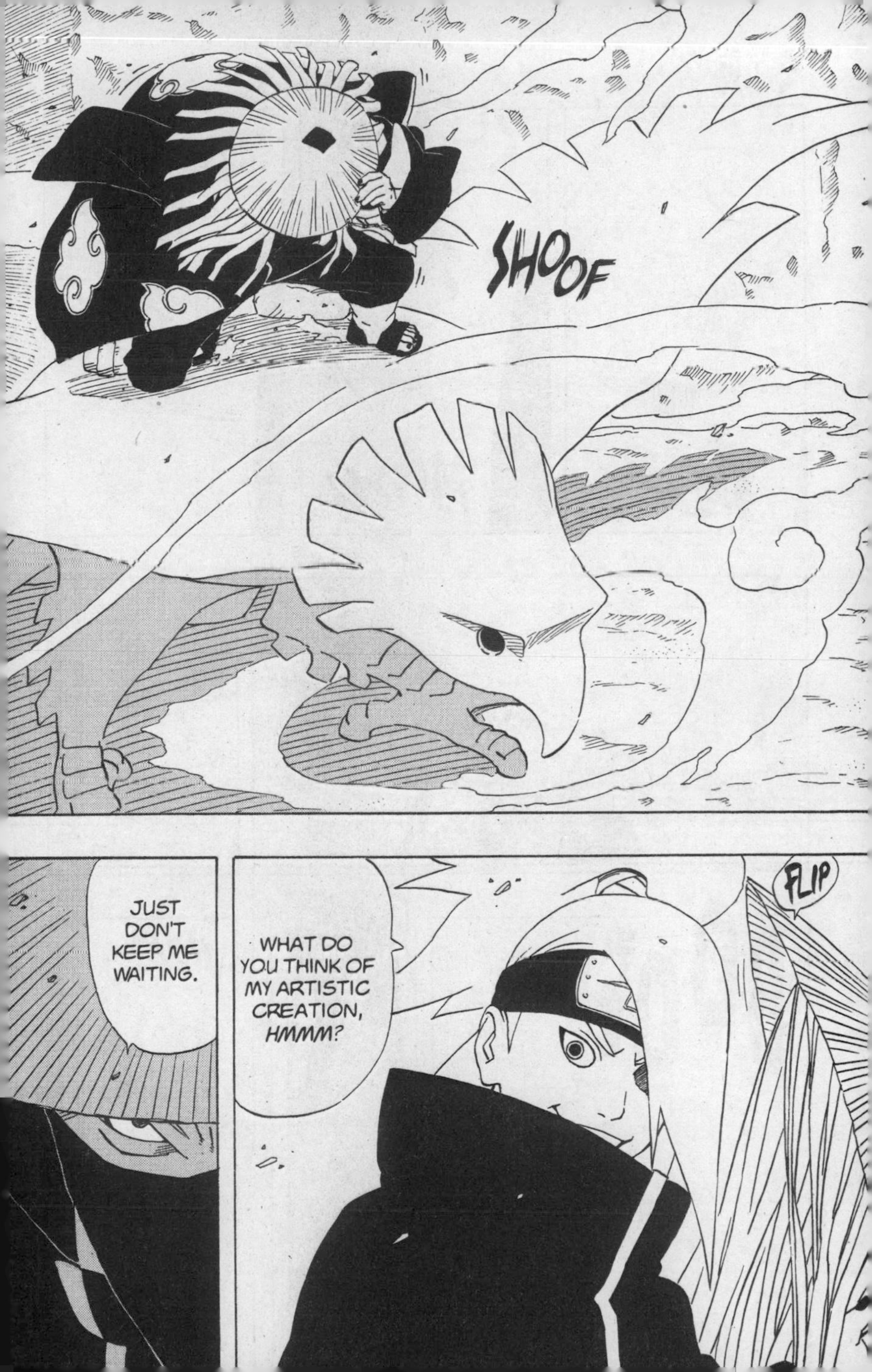
SHOOF
FLIP
WHAT DO YOU THINK OF MY ARTISTIC CREATION, HMMM?
JUST DON'T KEEP ME WAITING.

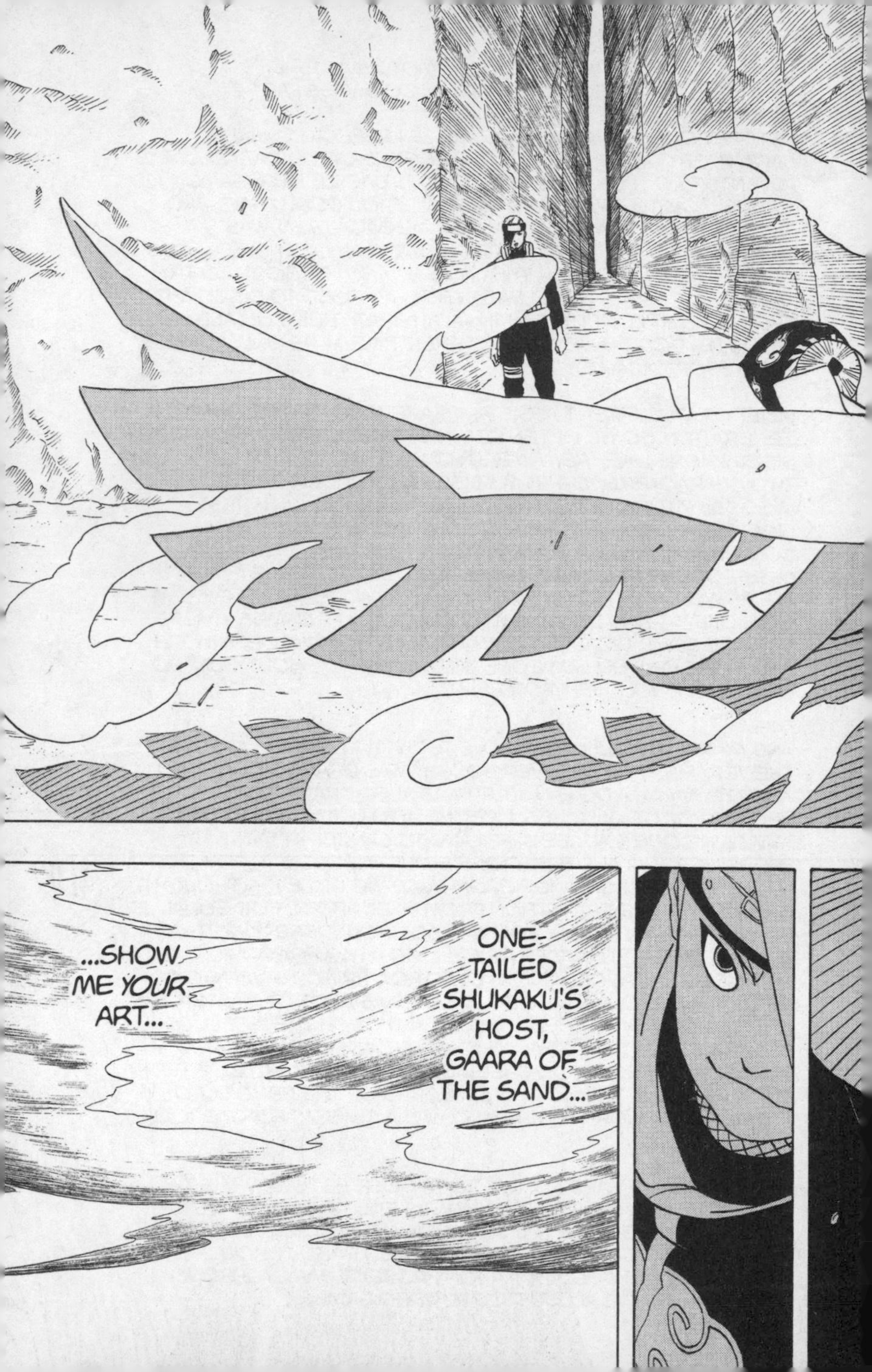
ONE-TAILED SHUKAKU'S HOST, GAARA OF THE SAND...
...SHOW ME YOUR ART...

THE WORLD OF KISHIMOTO MASASHI
MY PERSONAL HISTORY, VIDEO GAMES PART 2

AS I PREVIOUSLY WROTE IN VOLUME 25, I ESPECIALLY LIKED CARTRIDGE GAMES, SUCH AS "THE LEGEND OF ZELDA," "ZELDA 2: ADVENTURE OF LINK," "THE MYSTERIOUS CASTLE MURASAME," "KID ICARUS," "CASTLEVANIA," AND "METROID." YOU COULD SAVE AND RELOAD THESE GAMES, WHICH, FOR ME BACK THEN, WAS TREMENDOUSLY APPEALING. RECENTLY, MANY OF THESE GAMES WERE RE-RELEASED FOR THE GAME BOY, SO I DECIDED TO TRY THEM OUT AGAIN... I WAS PLEASANTLY SURPRISED TO DISCOVER THEY WERE STILL QUITE FUN. IN FACT, I BEAT THEM ALL (ALTHOUGH BECAUSE I DON'T HAVE A LOT OF FREE TIME, I WAS ONLY PLAYING THEM SPORADICALLY).

MOST OF MY CURRENT ASSISTANTS ARE ALSO OF THE FAMICOM GENERATION, SO WE OFTEN REMINISCE ABOUT THAT ERA, HAVING DISCUSSIONS LIKE, "REMEMBER HOW WE HAD TO 'RIOT' WITH JUST TWO CHARACTERS," OR "IN MISSISSIPPI ["MURDER ON THE MISSISSIPPI"], REMEMBER HOW YOU COULD KILL WITH JUST A SINGLE KNIFE THRUST," AND SO ON. AT SOME POINT, THE CONVERSATION WOULD ALWAYS TURN TO EITHER TO *DRAGON QUEST* OR THE *FINAL FANTASY* SERIES (I BET IT'S TRUE FOR YOU ALL AS WELL). WITH ONLY PARTIAL ALLEGIANCES--I.E. FF FANS WHO STILL LIKE DQ AND DQ FANS WHO STILL OWN FF GAMES--THERE EMERGE SOME BIZARRE COMMENTS. AS THE TALK GETS MORE AND MORE HEATED, SOMEONE WILL INVARIABLY SHOUT OUT, "SO WHAT ABOUT YOU, KISHIMOTO-SAN?"

AND MY REPLY WOULD BE, "I LOVE TORIYAMA-SENSEI'S ART, AND THE VERY FIRST GAME I EVER BOUGHT WAS DRAGON QUEST, SO I WANT TO SAY I'M A DQ FAN... BUT I WAS ALSO DRAWN TO FF BECAUSE OF ITS GLITCHES, LIKE THE ABILITY TO LEVEL-UP BY ATTACKING ONE'S ALLIES IN FFII AND TO CANCEL ATTACKS BY PRESSING THE A AND B BUTTONS SIMULTANEOUSLY. IN FFIV, THE LITTLE TWINS PALOM AND POROM MADE ME CRY EVEN THOUGH IT WAS A GAME. THE TRANSITION FROM PIXEL ART TO POLYGONAL 3D COMPUTER GRAPHICS IN FFVII WAS SO GROUNDBREAKING THAT I CAN'T DENY THAT I LOVE FF AS WELL. SO AM I A FF MANIAC? ...YET DQ WAS SO BALANCED TOO. I LOVED HOW PRINCE SAMANTORIA OF DQII--WHO ALWAYS DIED SO EASILY--WAS ABLE TO MASTER THE ZAORIKU, OR REVIVE SPELL. AND EVEN THOUGH THE "SPELL OF RESURRECTION" WAS REALLY LONG, THE MUSIC THAT PLAYED DURING THE PASSWORD SCREEN BECAME MY FAVORITE OF THE DQ SERIES. BUT THEN, DQI~III'S "LEGEND OF THE HERO LOTO", IS A THREE-PART WORK THAT REALLY WAS A CLASSIC FOR ME TOO.

...SO IT'S REALLY HARD FOR ME TO CHOOSE BETWEEN THE TWO. AND MY ASSISTANTS, TOO, THEY ALWAYS END UP GIVING VAGUE ANSWERS AS WELL. SO THE DEBATE IS USUALLY SETTLED WITH MUTUAL ADMIRATION FOR AND AGREEMENT ABOUT HOW INCREDIBLE THE COLLABORATION PROJECT GAME "CHRONO TRIGGER" WAS. WE ALL JUST LOVE VIDEO GAMES.

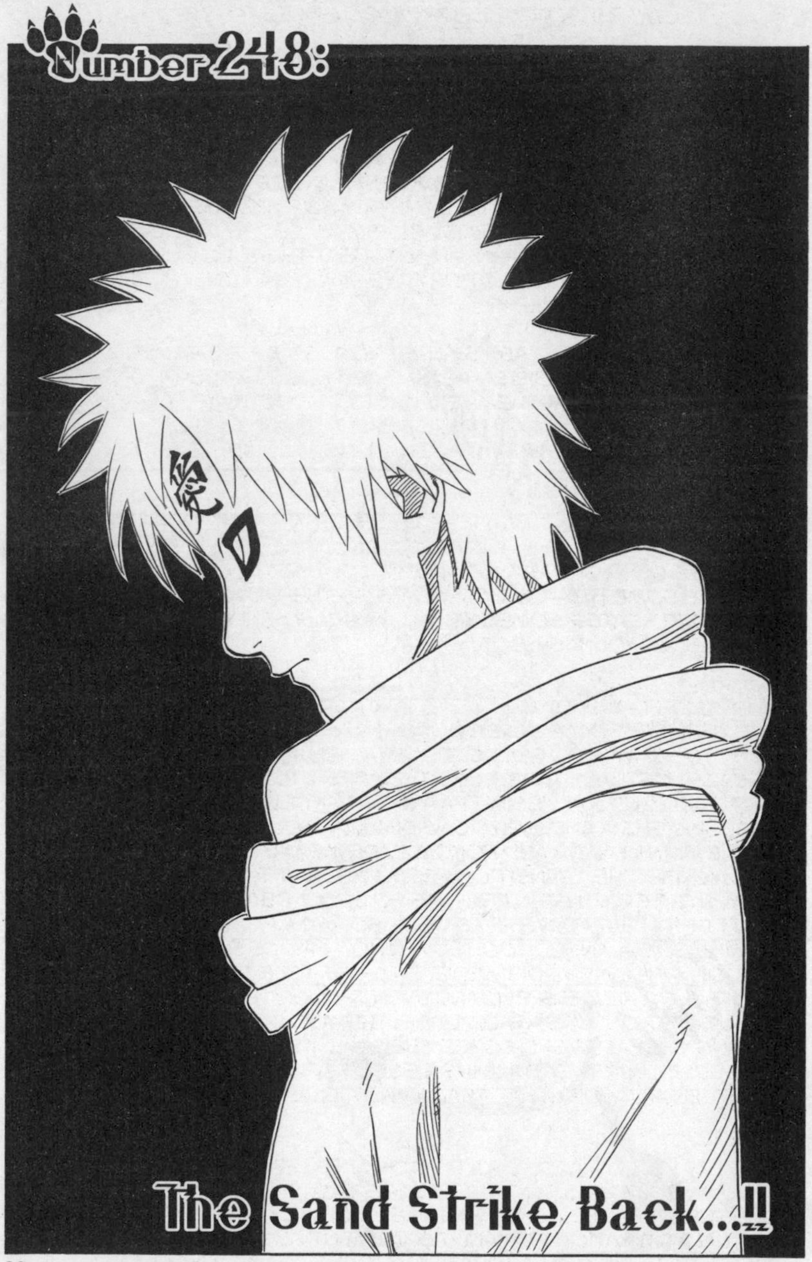
Number 248:
The Sand Strike Back...!!

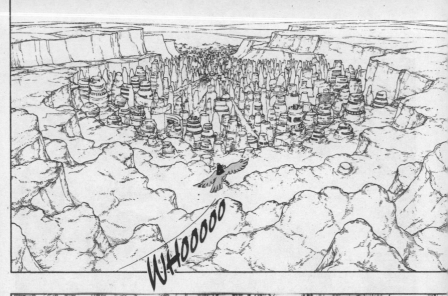

WHOOOOO

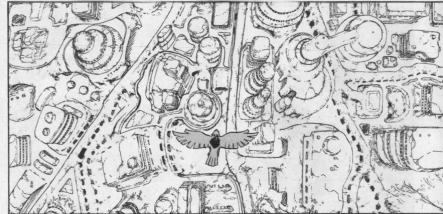

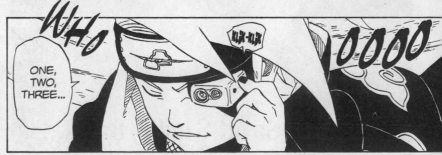

WHO

ONE,
TWO,
THREE...

KLIK-KLIK

OOOOO

READ THIS WAY

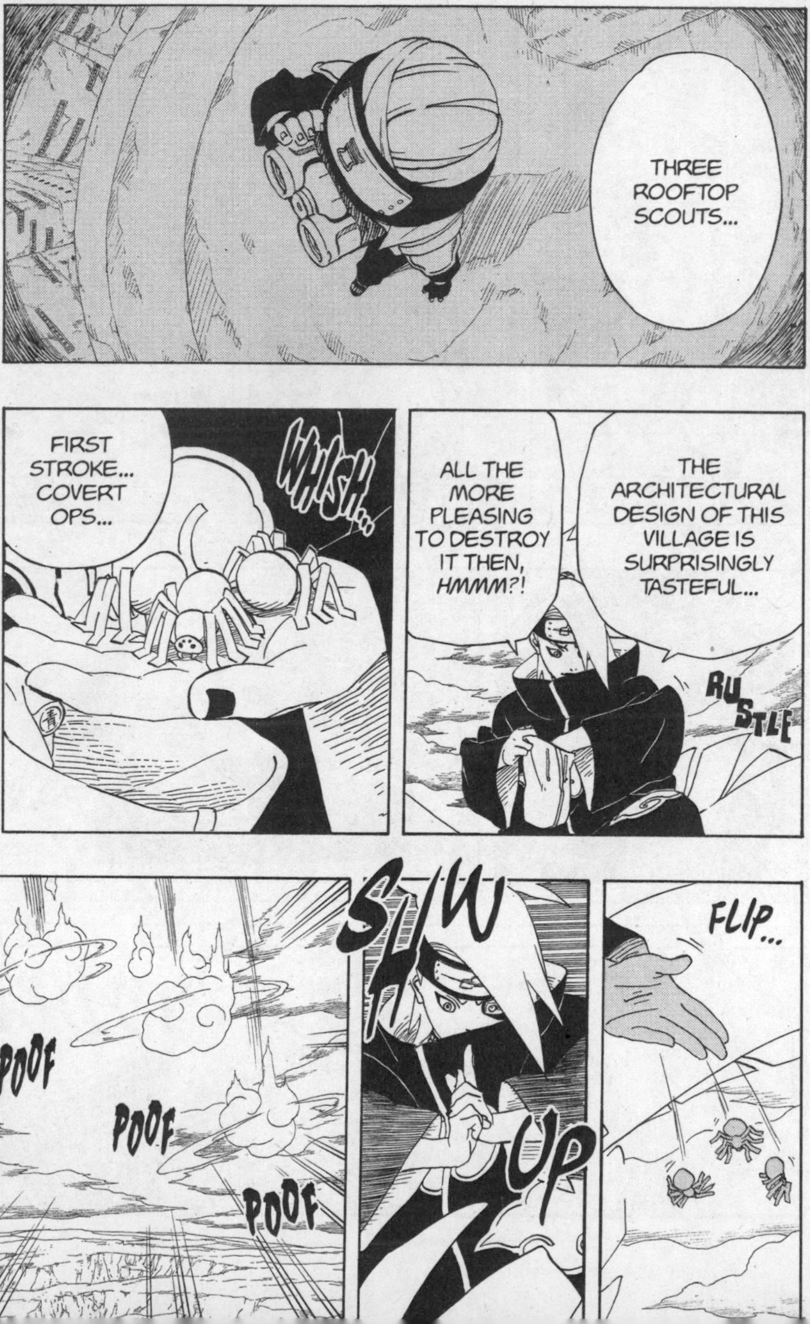
THREE ROOFTOP SCOUTS...
THE ARCHITECTURAL DESIGN OF THIS VILLAGE IS SURPRISINGLY TASTEFUL...
ALL THE MORE PLEASING TO DESTROY IT THEN, *HMMM?!*
RUSTLE
WHISH...
FIRST STROKE... COVERT OPS...
FLIP...
SHWUP
POOF
POOF
POOF

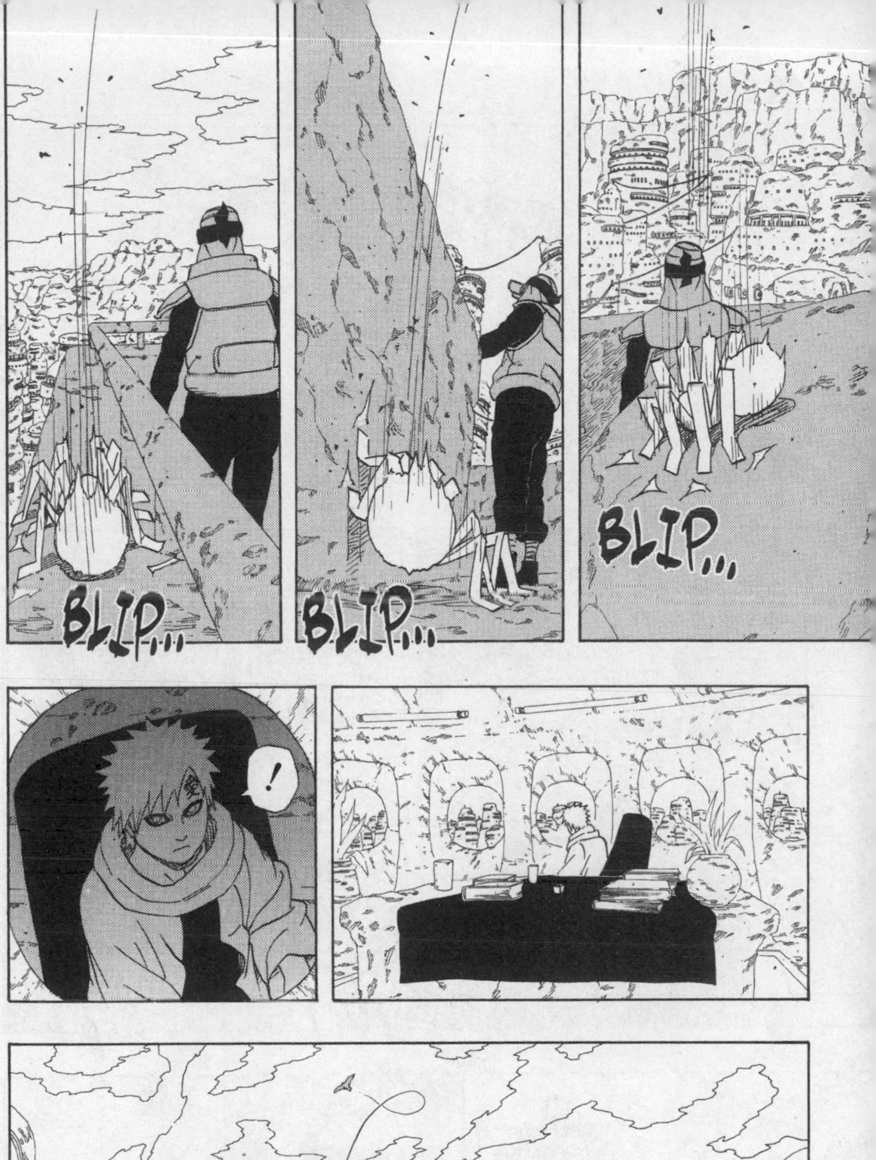
BLIP...
BLIP...
BLIP...
!

READ THIS WAY

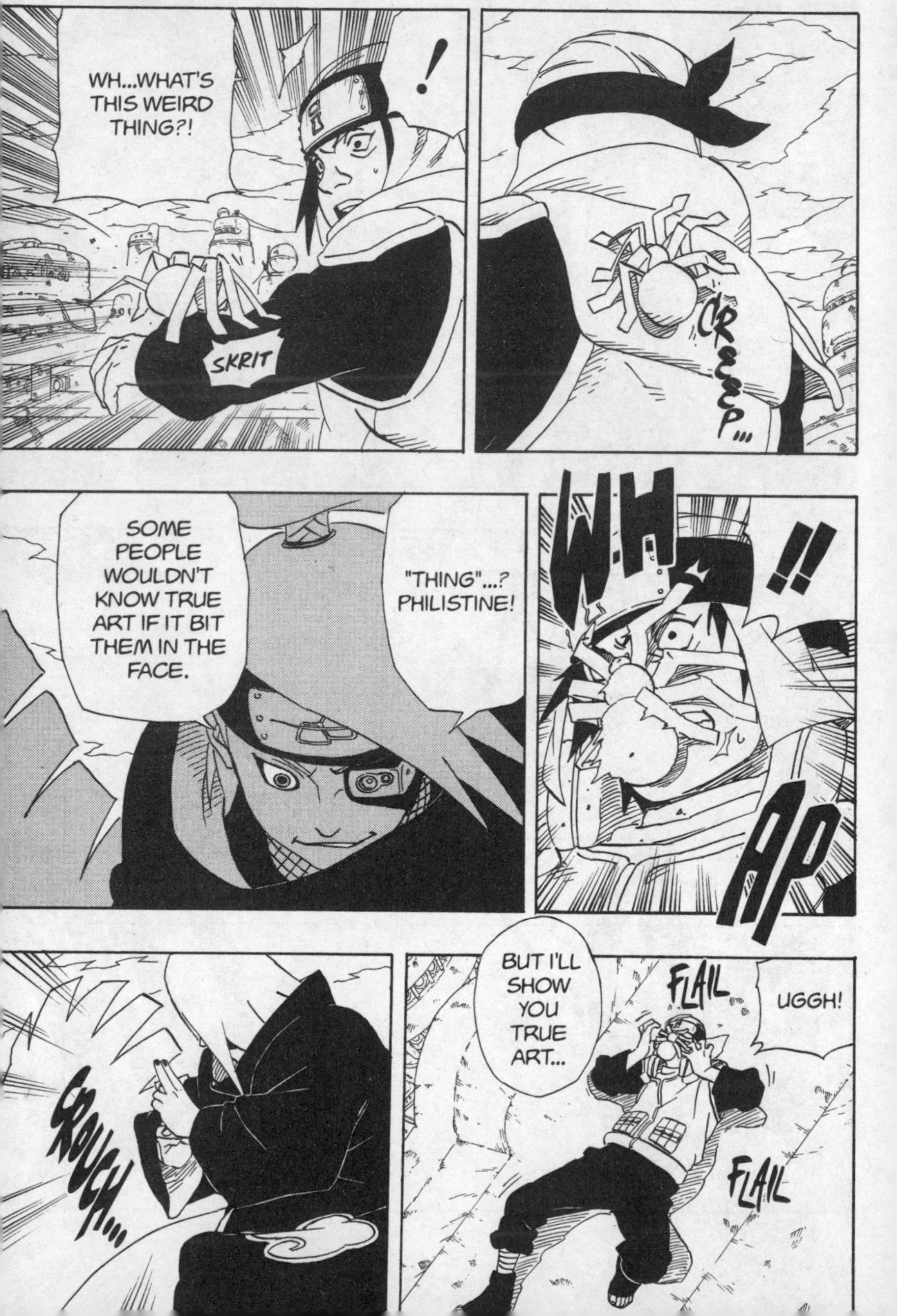
CREEEP...
!
WH...WHAT'S THIS WEIRD THING?!
SKRIT
WHAP!!
"THING"...? PHILISTINE!
SOME PEOPLE WOULDN'T KNOW TRUE ART IF IT BIT THEM IN THE FACE.
UGGH!
FLAIL
BUT I'LL SHOW YOU TRUE ART...
FLAIL
CROUCH...

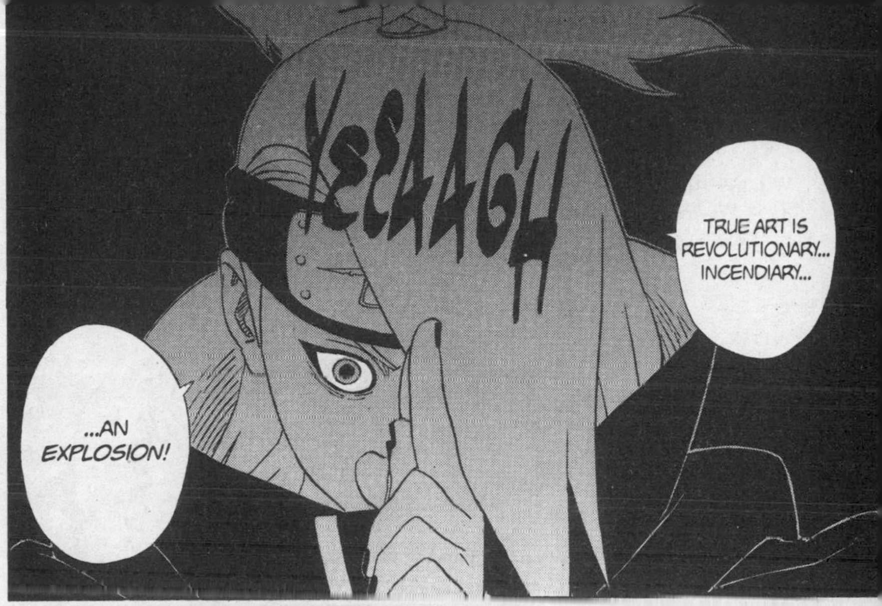
YEEAAGH
TRUE ART IS REVOLUTIONARY... INCENDIARY...
...AN EXPLOSION!

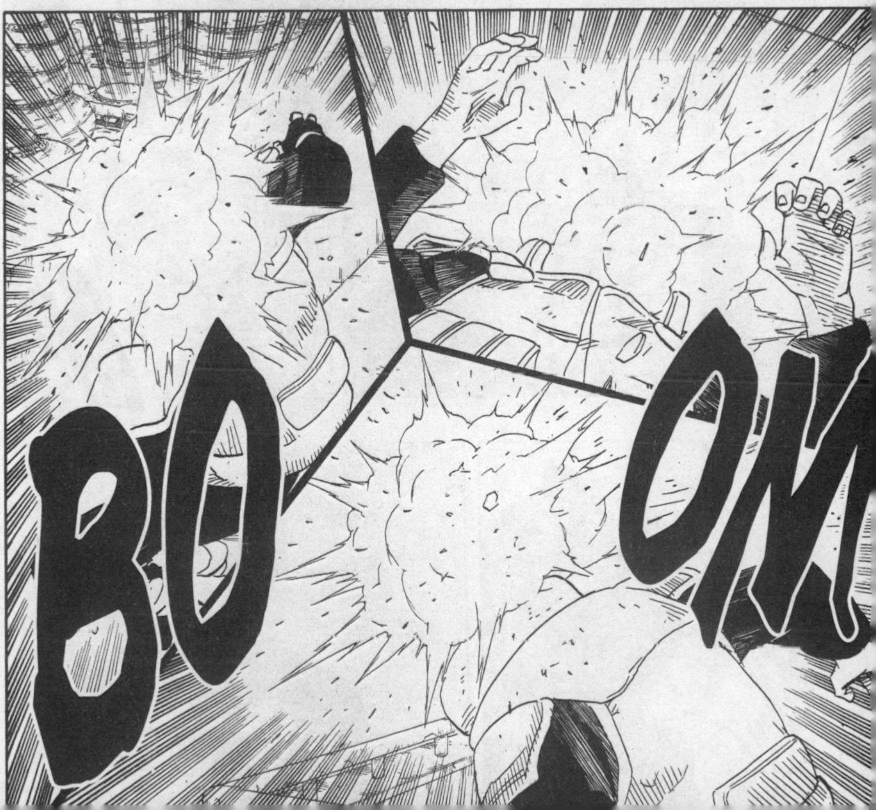
BOOM

READ THIS WAY

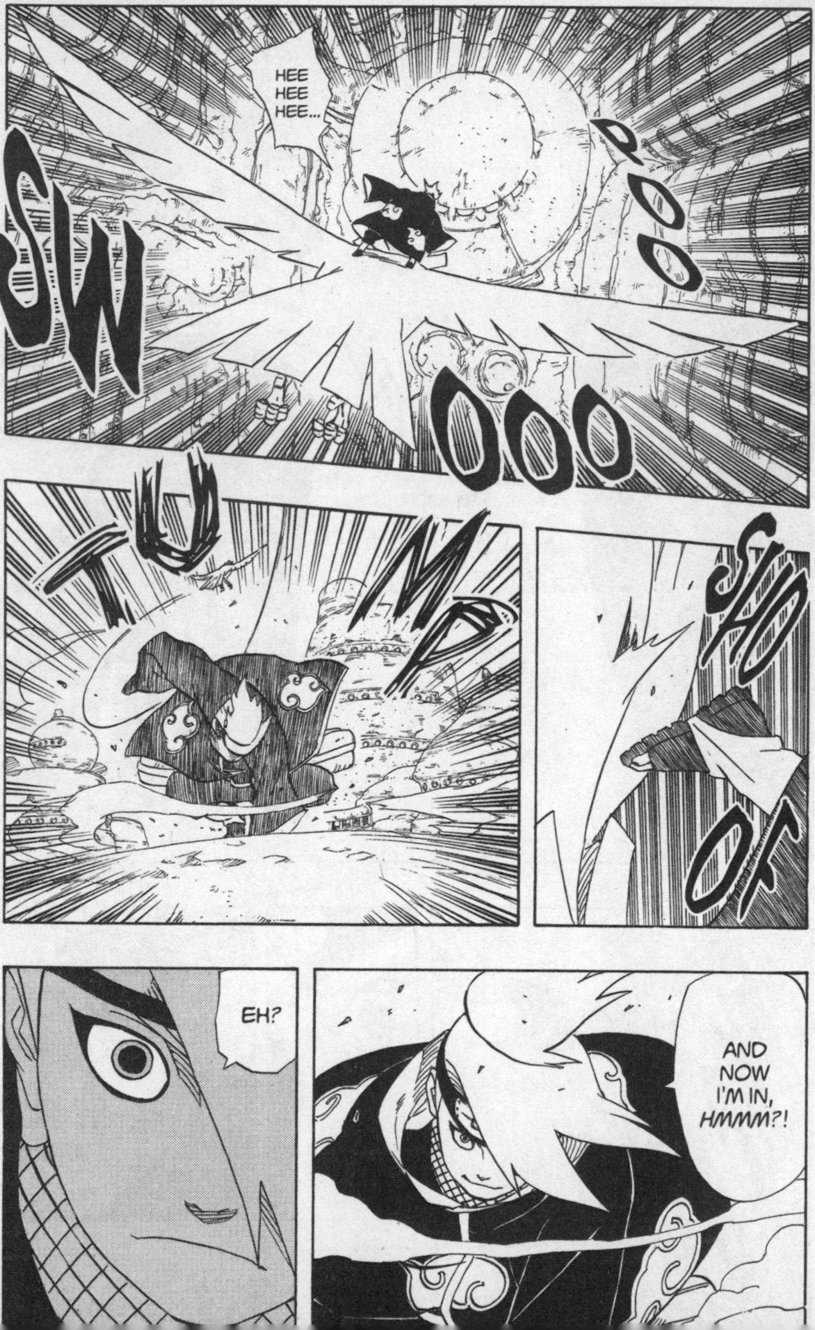
HEE HEE HEE...
SWOOOOOP
SHOOF
THUMP
AND NOW I'M IN, HMMM?!
EH?

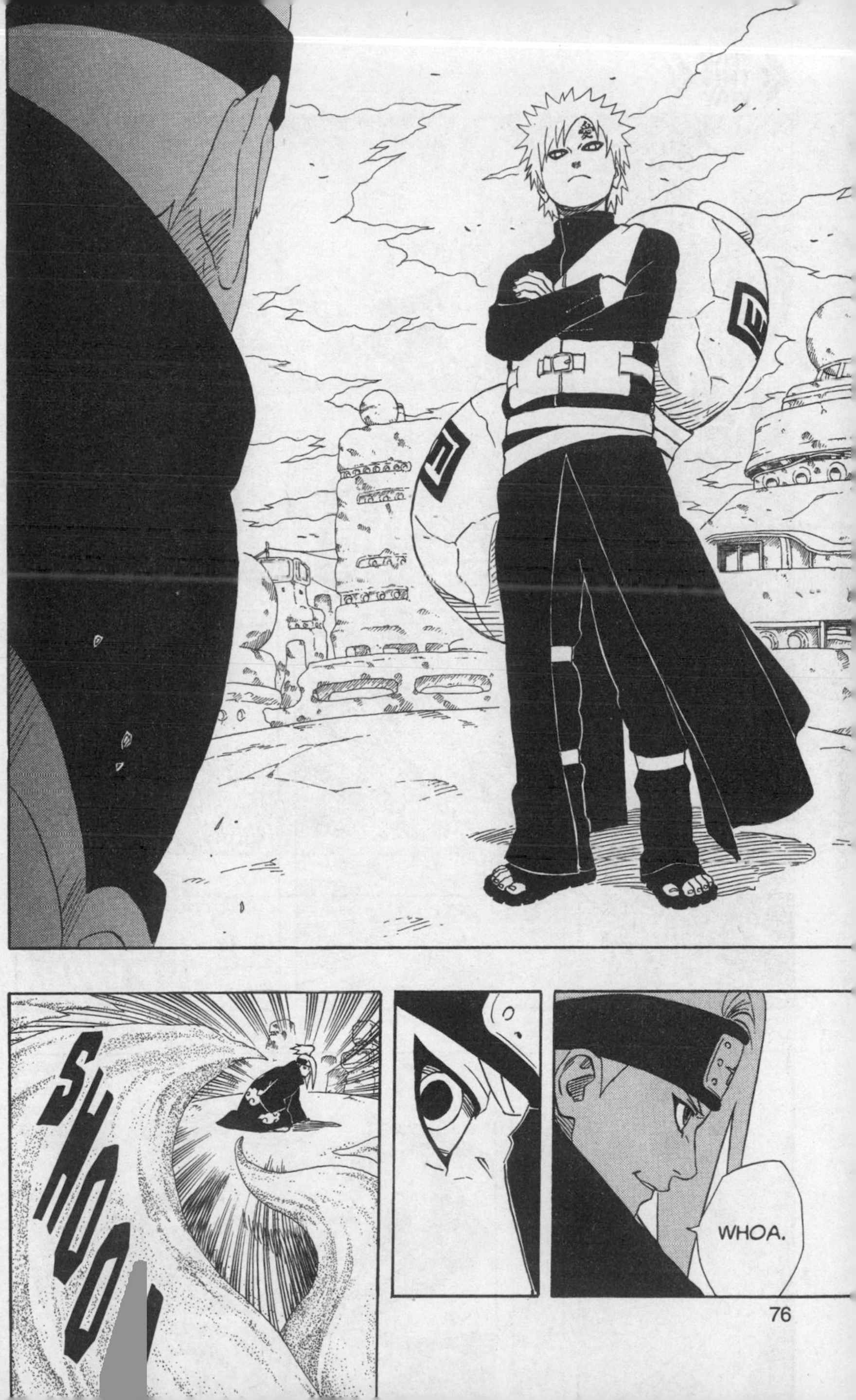
WHOA.
SHOO

READ THIS WAY

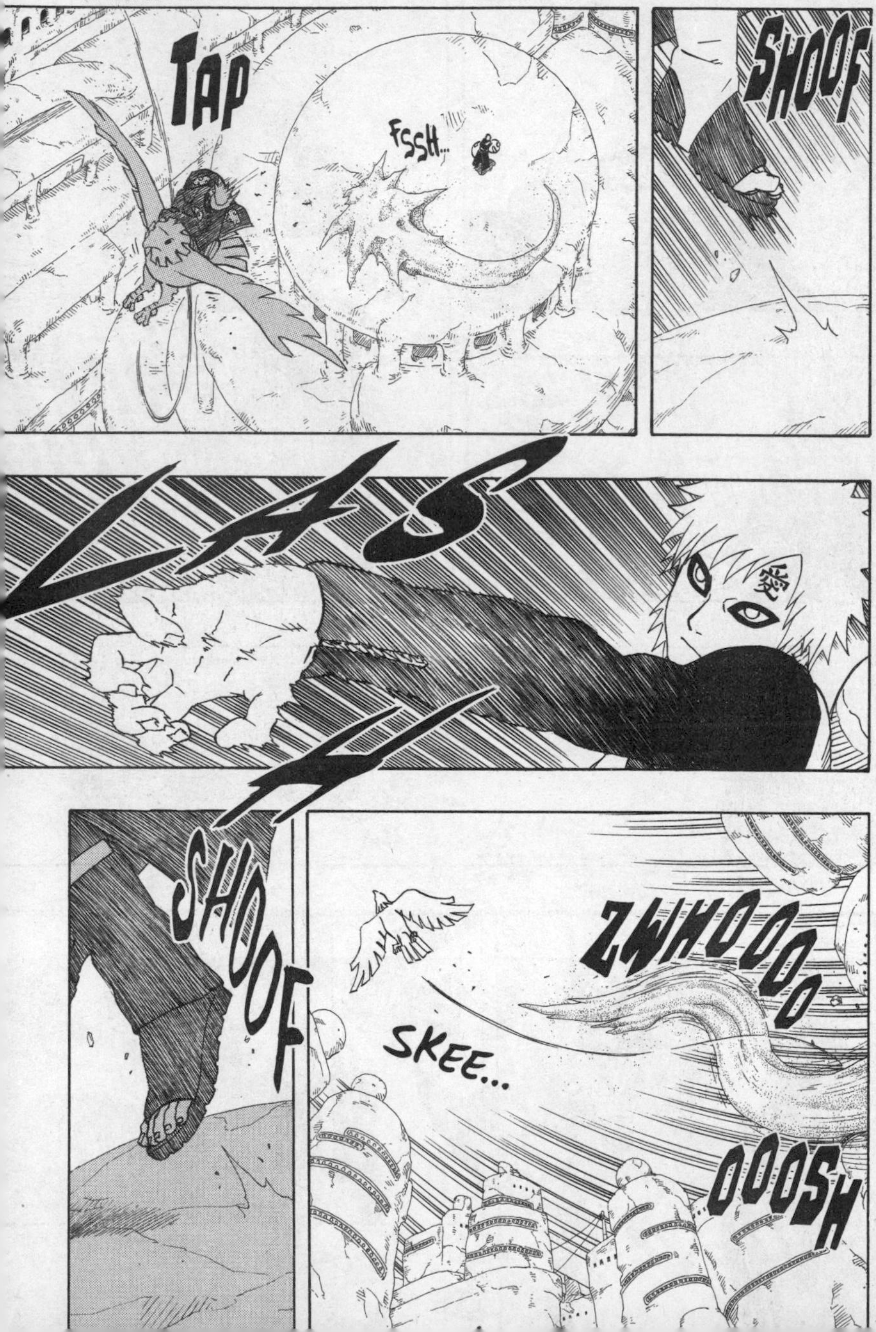
SHOOF
TAP
FSSH...
VASH
ZWHOOOOO
OOOSH
SKEE...
SHOOF

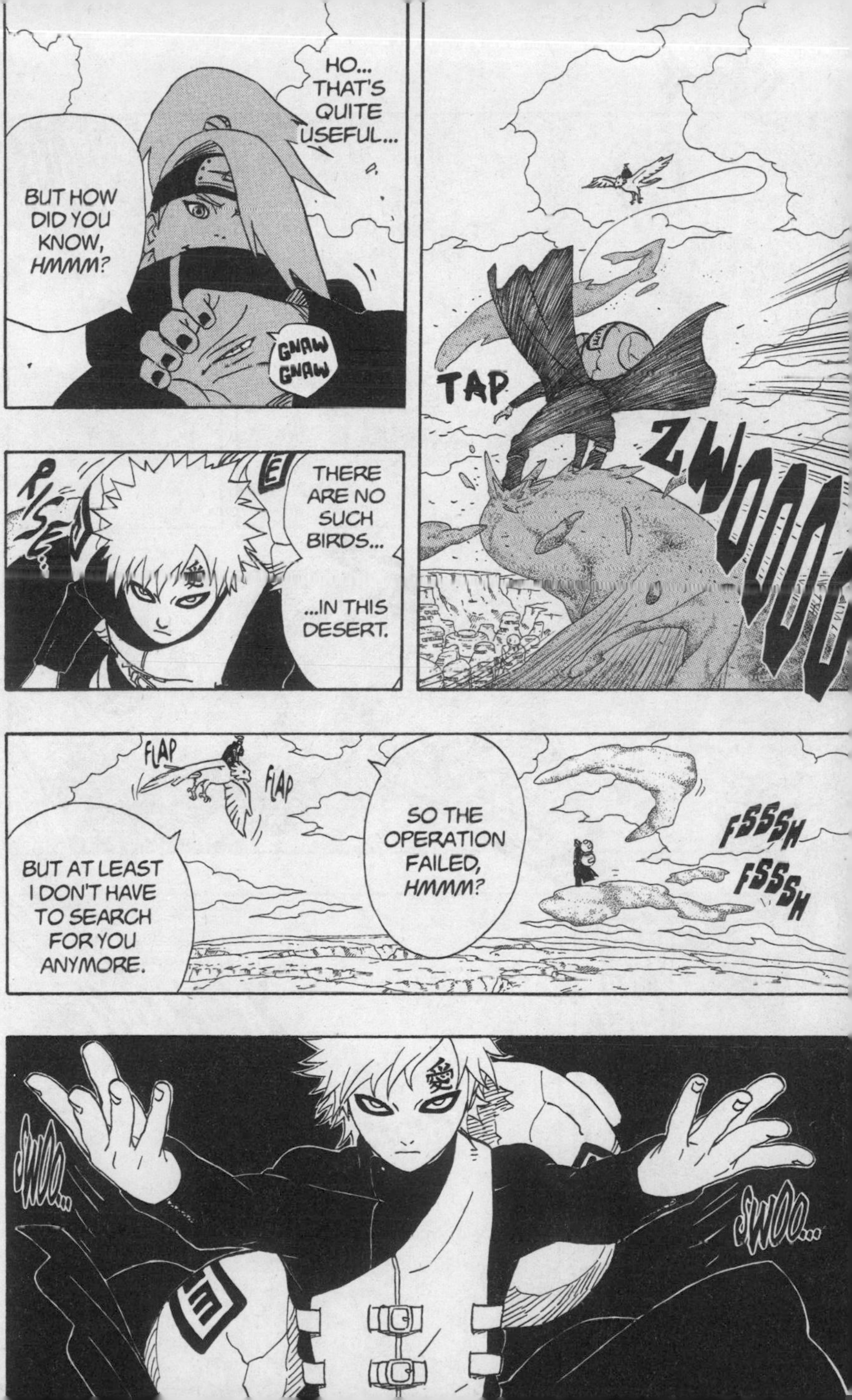
TAP
ZWOOOO
HO... THAT'S QUITE USEFUL...
BUT HOW DID YOU KNOW, HMMM?
GNAW GNAW
THERE ARE NO SUCH BIRDS...
...IN THIS DESERT.
RISE...
FSSSH
FSSSH
SO THE OPERATION FAILED, HMMM?
FLAP
FLAP
BUT AT LEAST I DON'T HAVE TO SEARCH FOR YOU ANYMORE.
SWOO...
SWOO...

READ THIS WAY

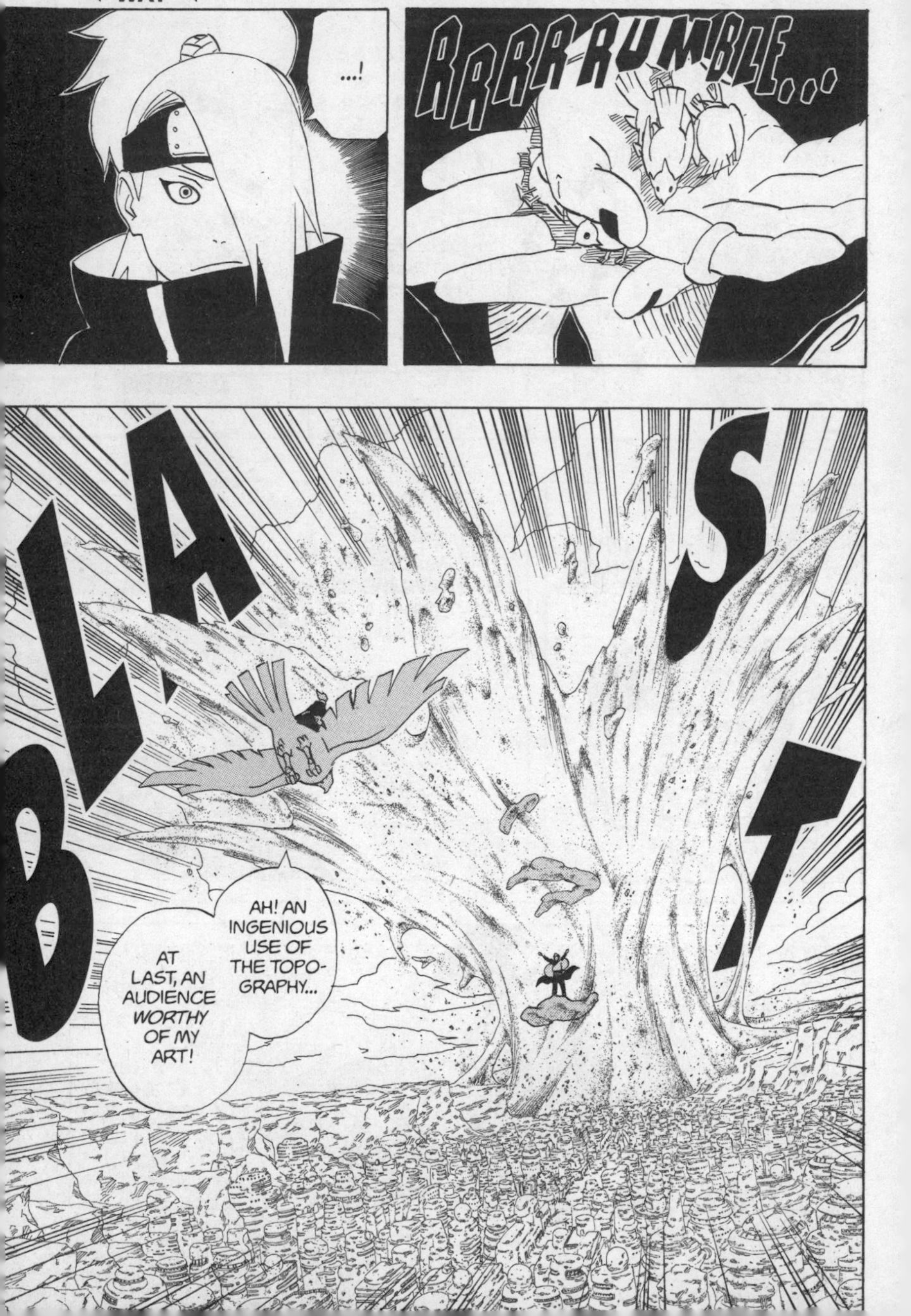
RRRRUMBLE...
...!
BLAST
AH! AN INGENIOUS USE OF THE TOPOGRAPHY...
AT LAST, AN AUDIENCE WORTHY OF MY ART!

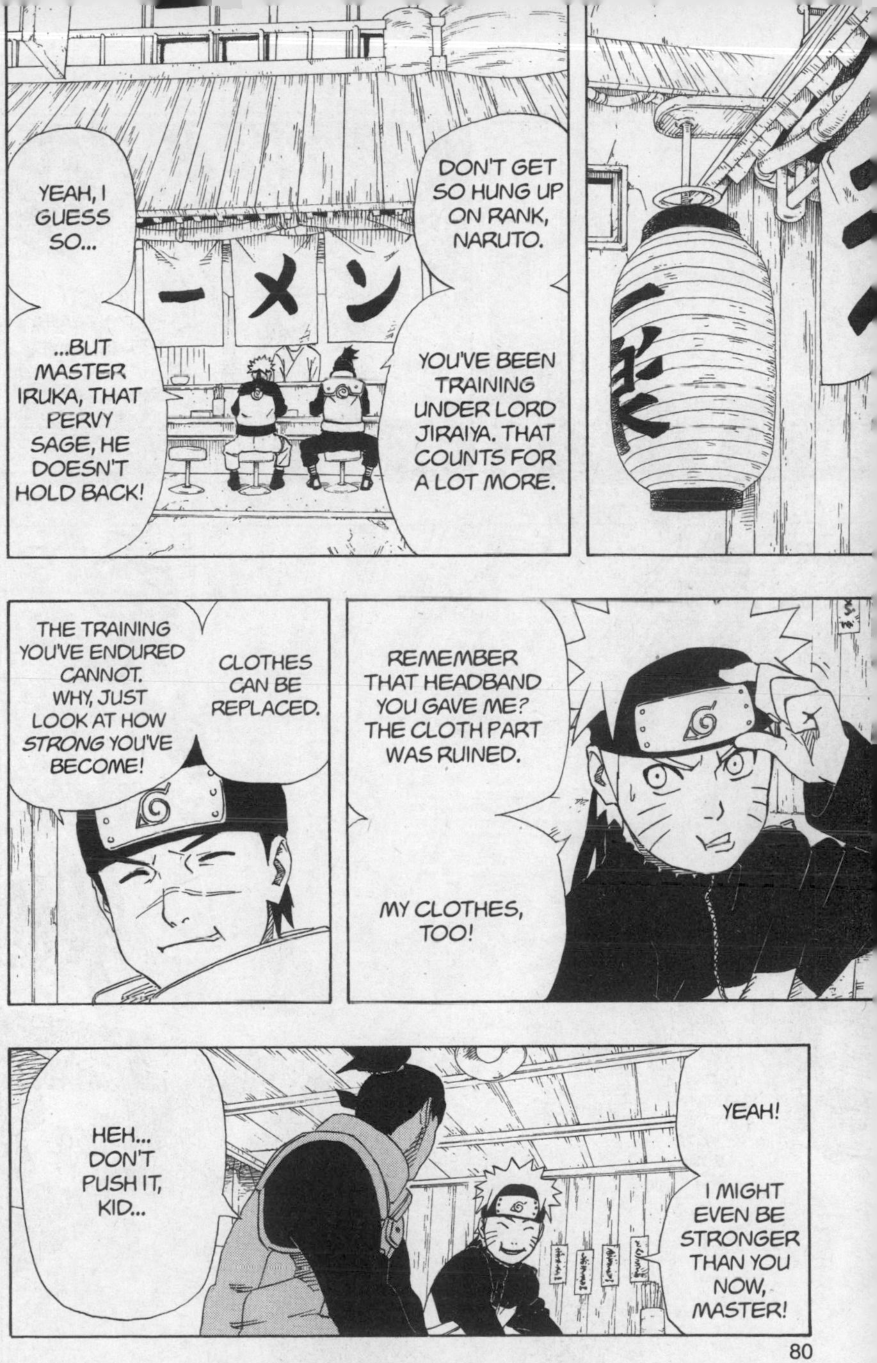
DON'T GET SO HUNG UP ON RANK, NARUTO.
YEAH, I GUESS SO...
...BUT MASTER IRUKA, THAT PERVY SAGE, HE DOESN'T HOLD BACK!
YOU'VE BEEN TRAINING UNDER LORD JIRAIYA. THAT COUNTS FOR A LOT MORE.
REMEMBER THAT HEADBAND YOU GAVE ME? THE CLOTH PART WAS RUINED.
MY CLOTHES, TOO!
CLOTHES CAN BE REPLACED.
THE TRAINING YOU'VE ENDURED CANNOT. WHY, JUST LOOK AT HOW *STRONG* YOU'VE BECOME!
YEAH!
I MIGHT EVEN BE STRONGER THAN YOU NOW, MASTER!
HEH... DON'T PUSH IT, KID...

READ THIS WAY

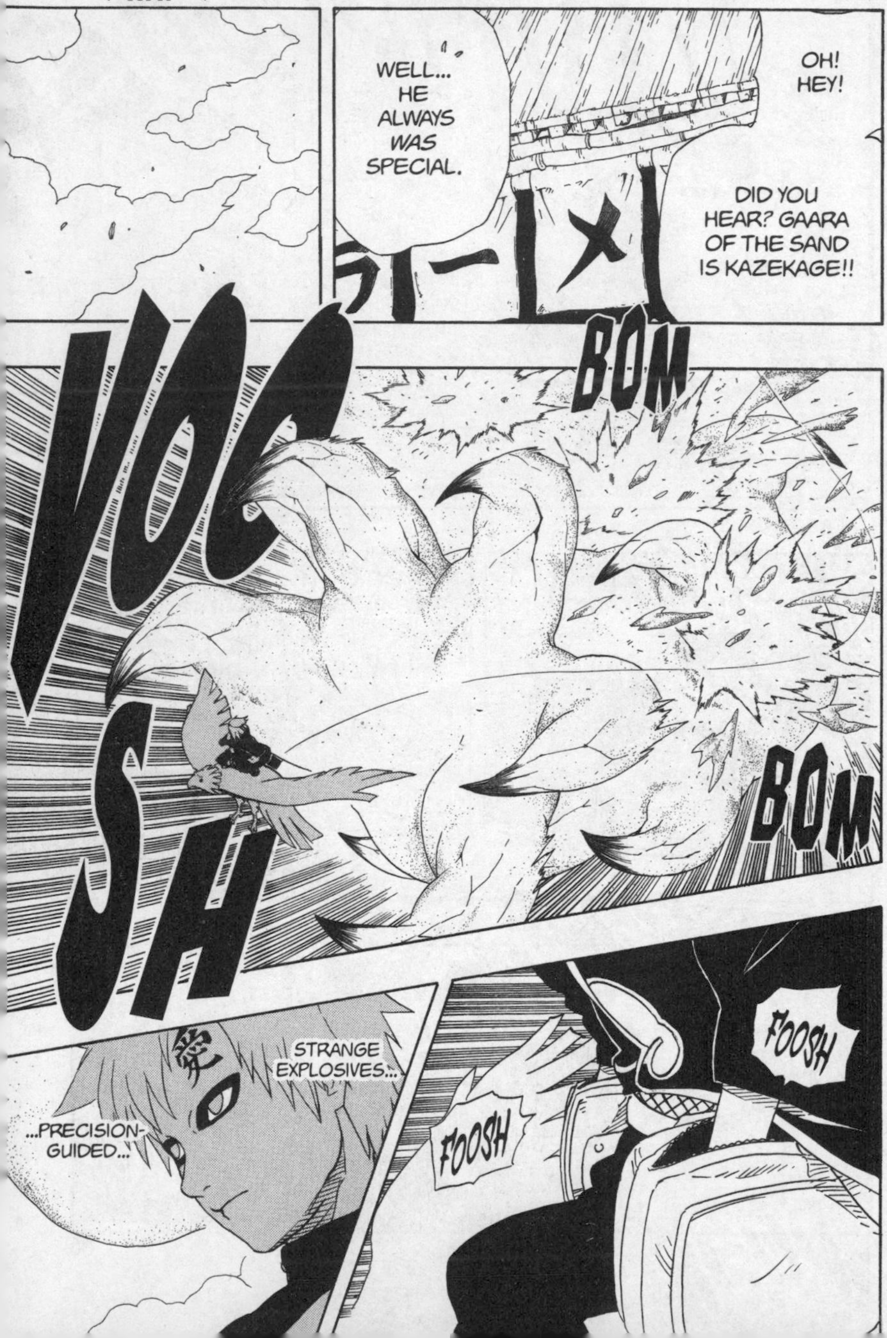
OH! HEY!
DID YOU HEAR? GAARA OF THE SAND IS KAZEKAGE!!
WELL... HE ALWAYS WAS SPECIAL.
BOM
BOM
VOOSH
FOOSH
FOOSH
STRANGE EXPLOSIVES...
...PRECISION-GUIDED...

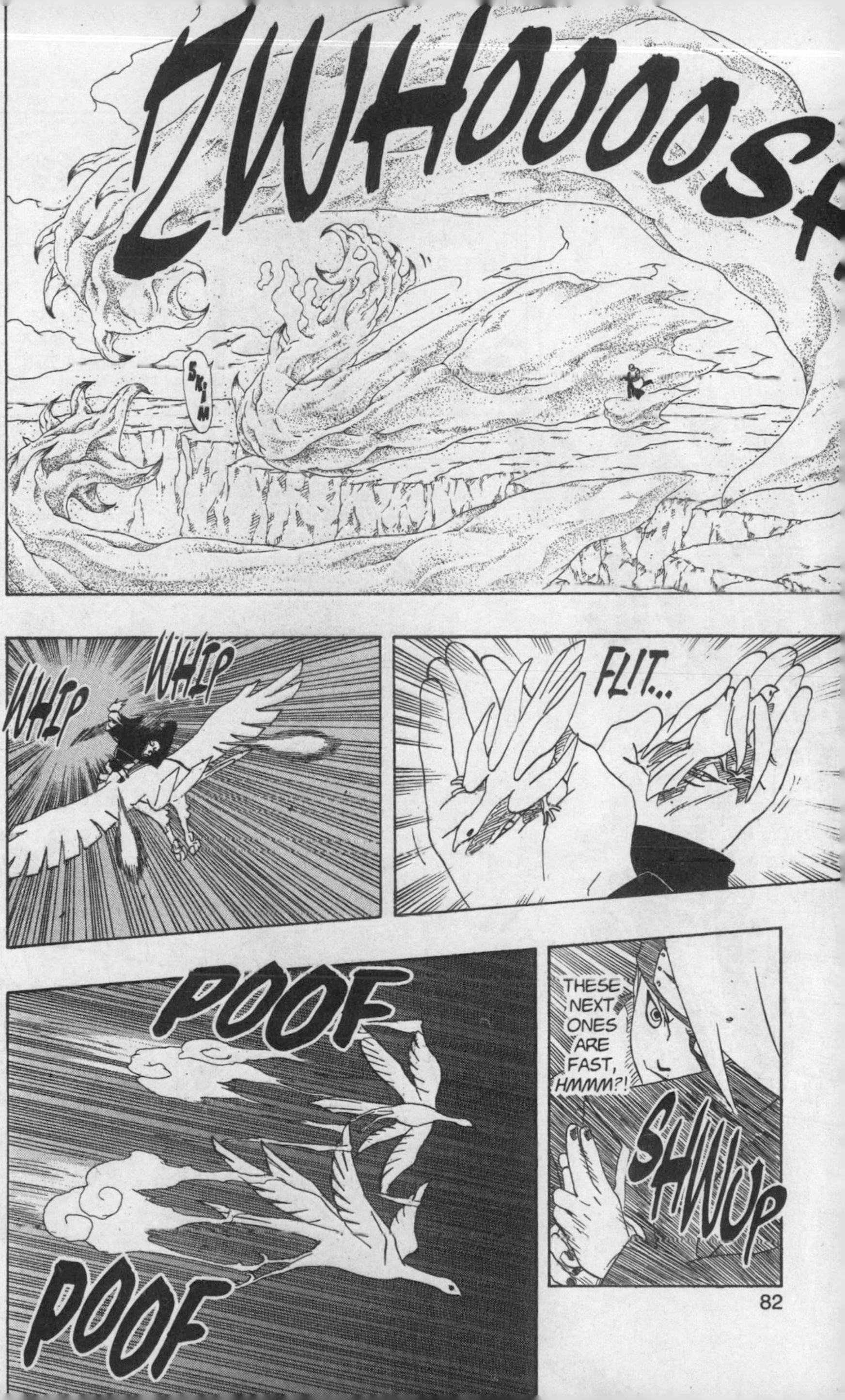
ZWHOOOOOSH
SKIM
FLIT...
WHIP
WHIP
THESE NEXT ONES ARE FAST, HMMM?!
SHWOP
POOF
POOF

READ THIS WAY

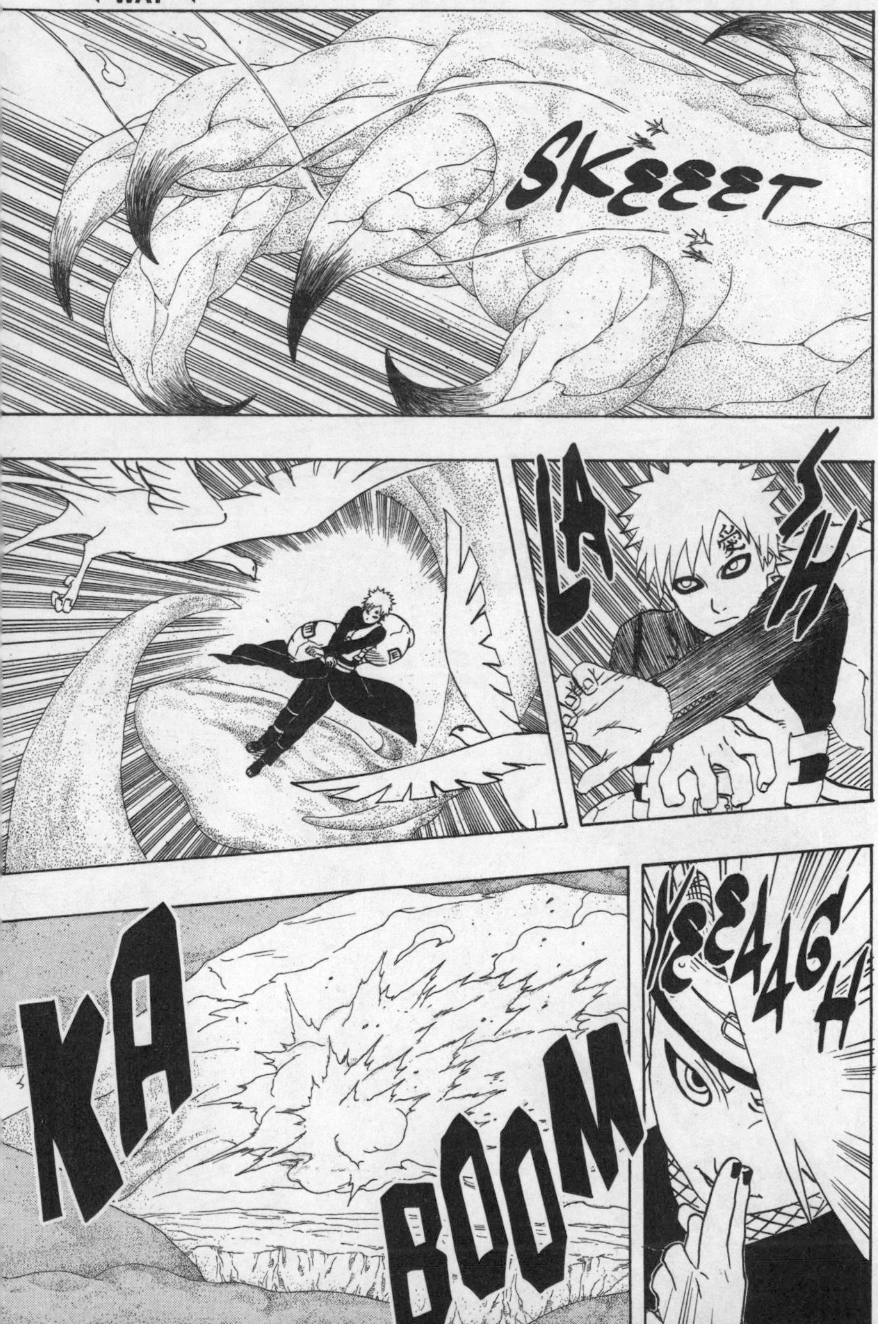
SKEEET
LASH
YEEAAGH
KA
BOOM

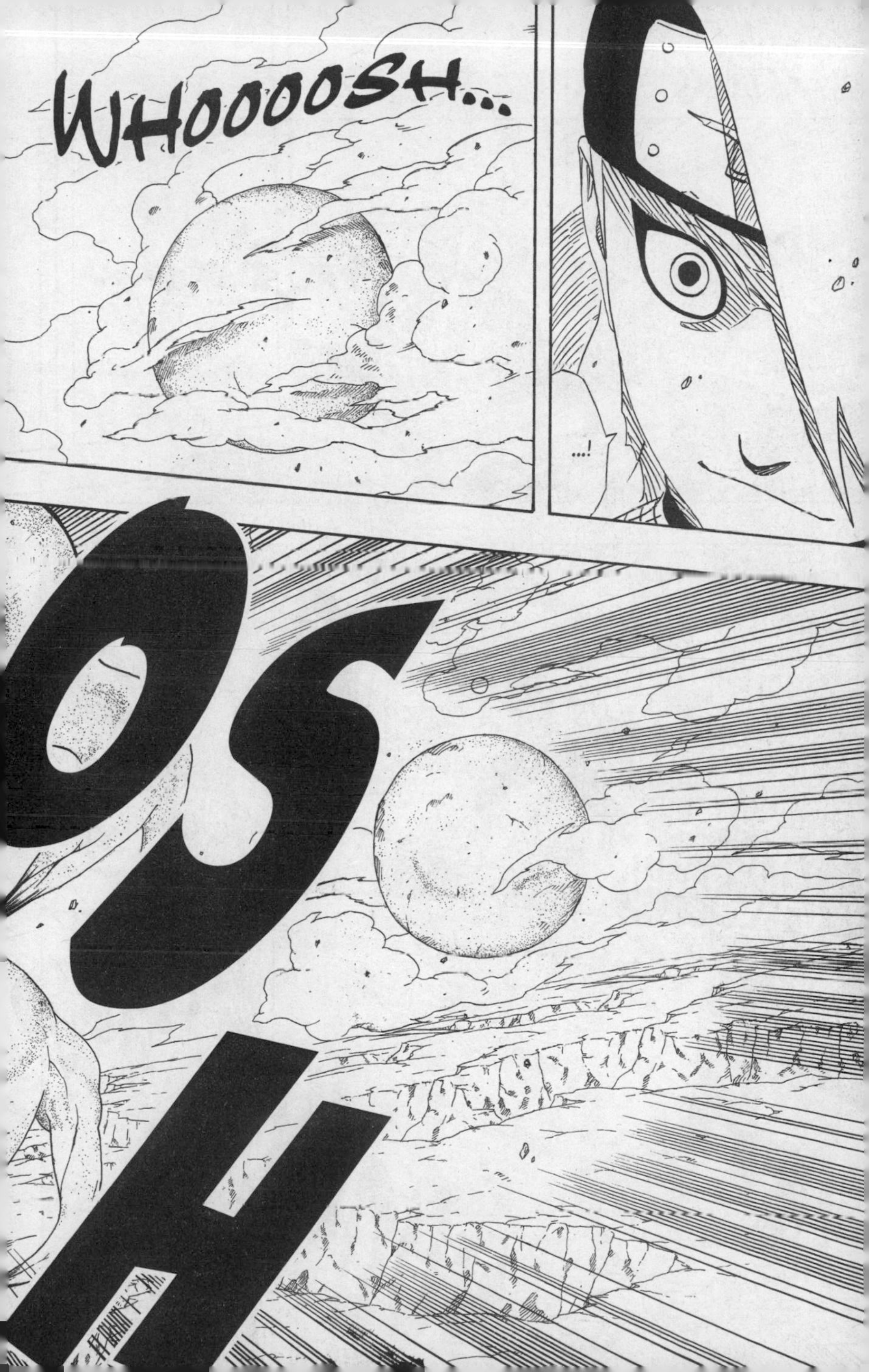

...!
WHOOOOSH...
OSH

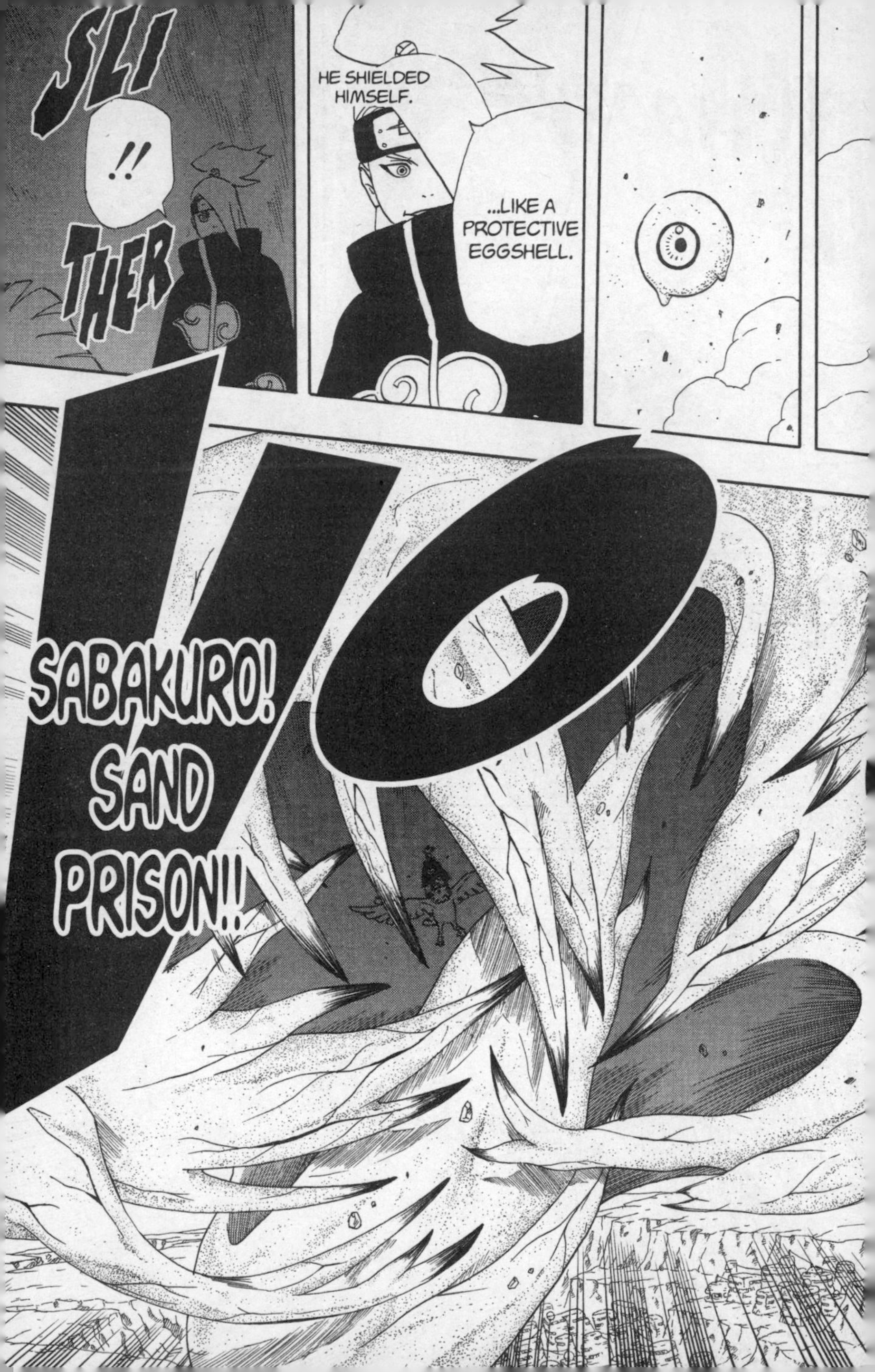
HE SHIELDED HIMSELF.
...LIKE A PROTECTIVE EGGSHELL.
SLI
!!
THER
SABAKURO! SAND PRISON!!

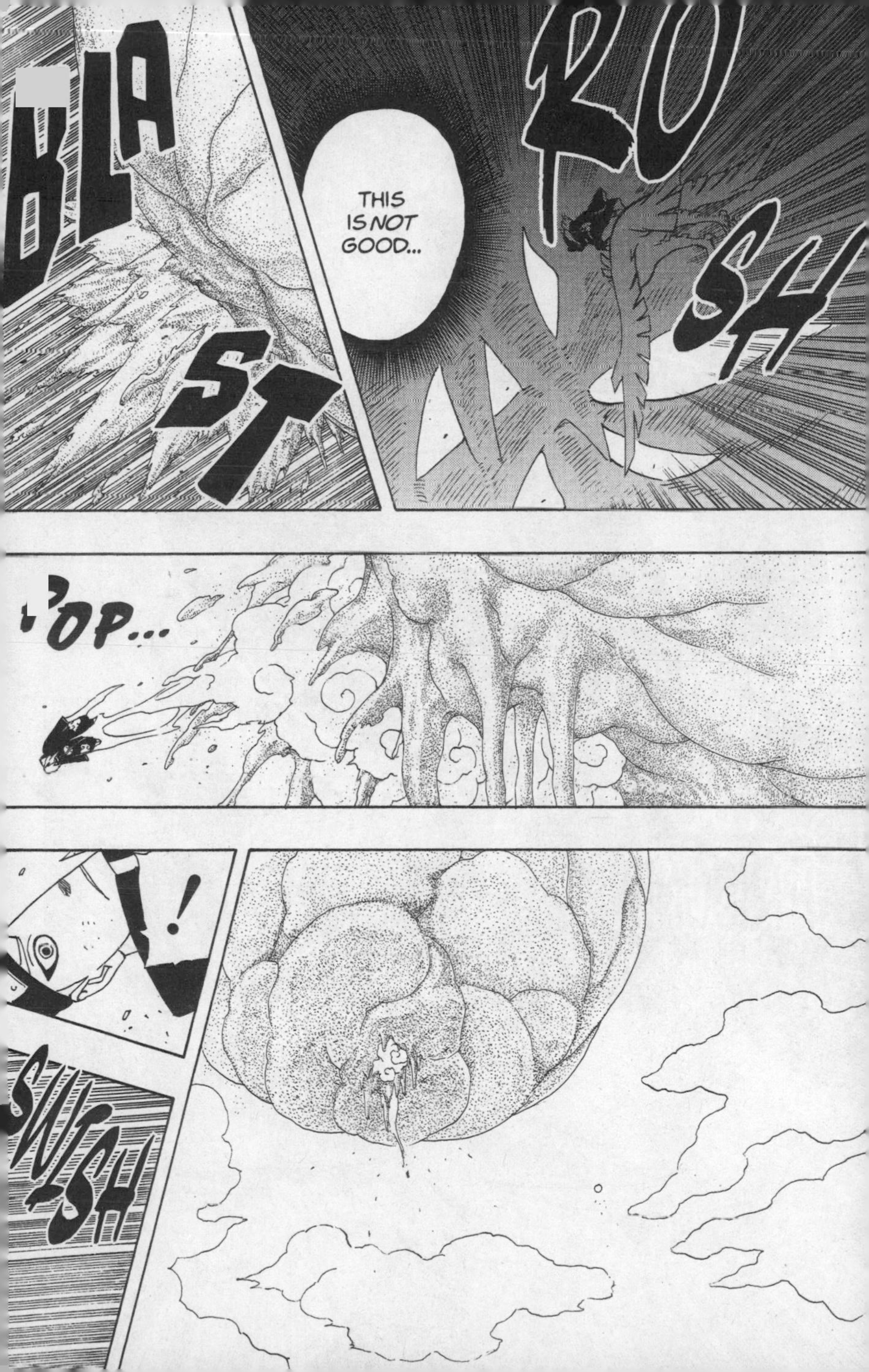
ROSH
THIS IS NOT GOOD...
BLAST
POP...
!
SWISH

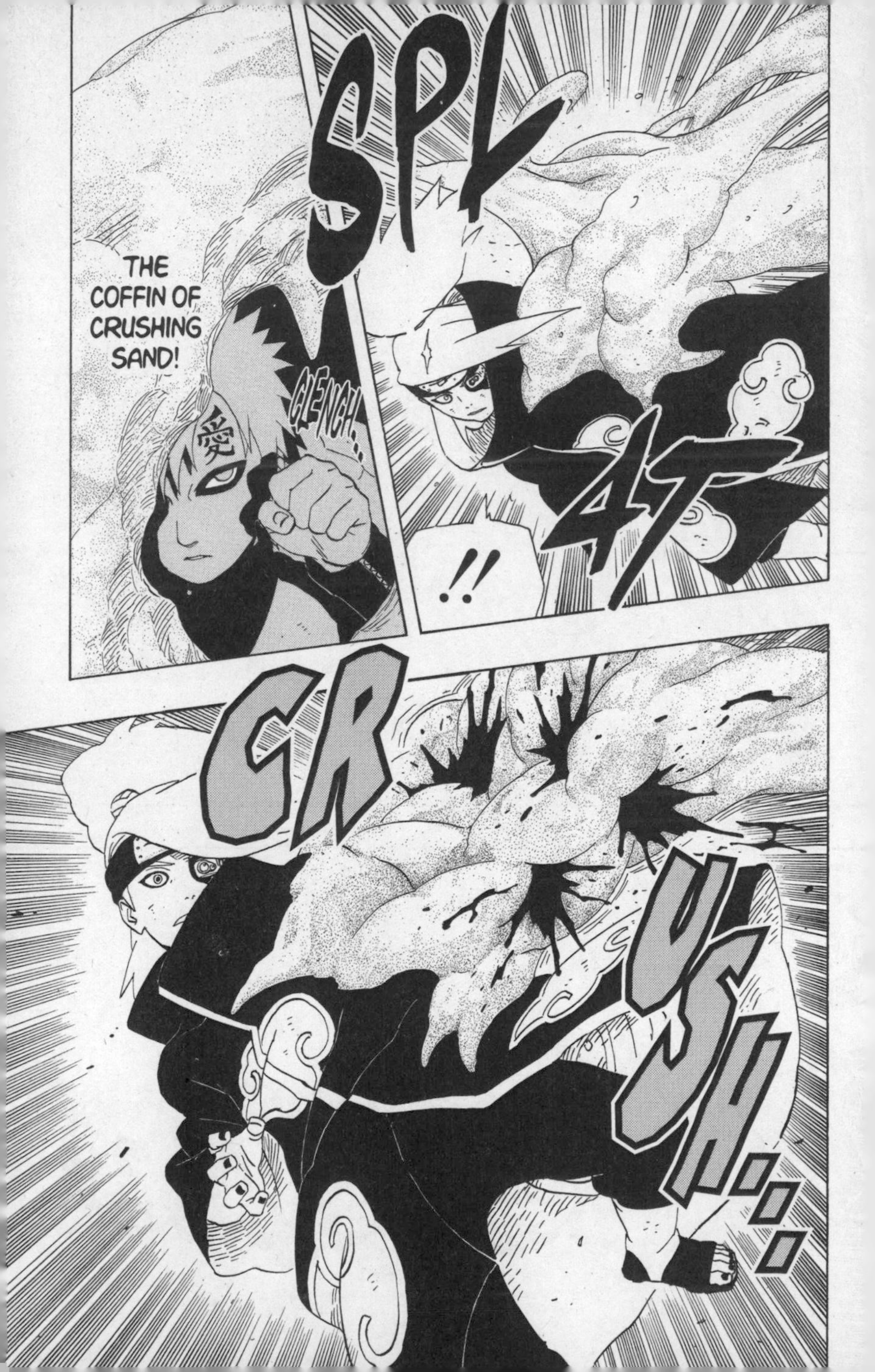
SPL
AT
!!
THE COFFIN OF CRUSHING SAND!
CLENCH...
CR
USH...

NARUTO

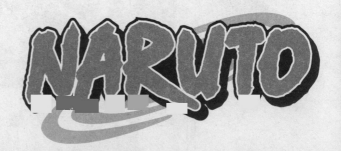

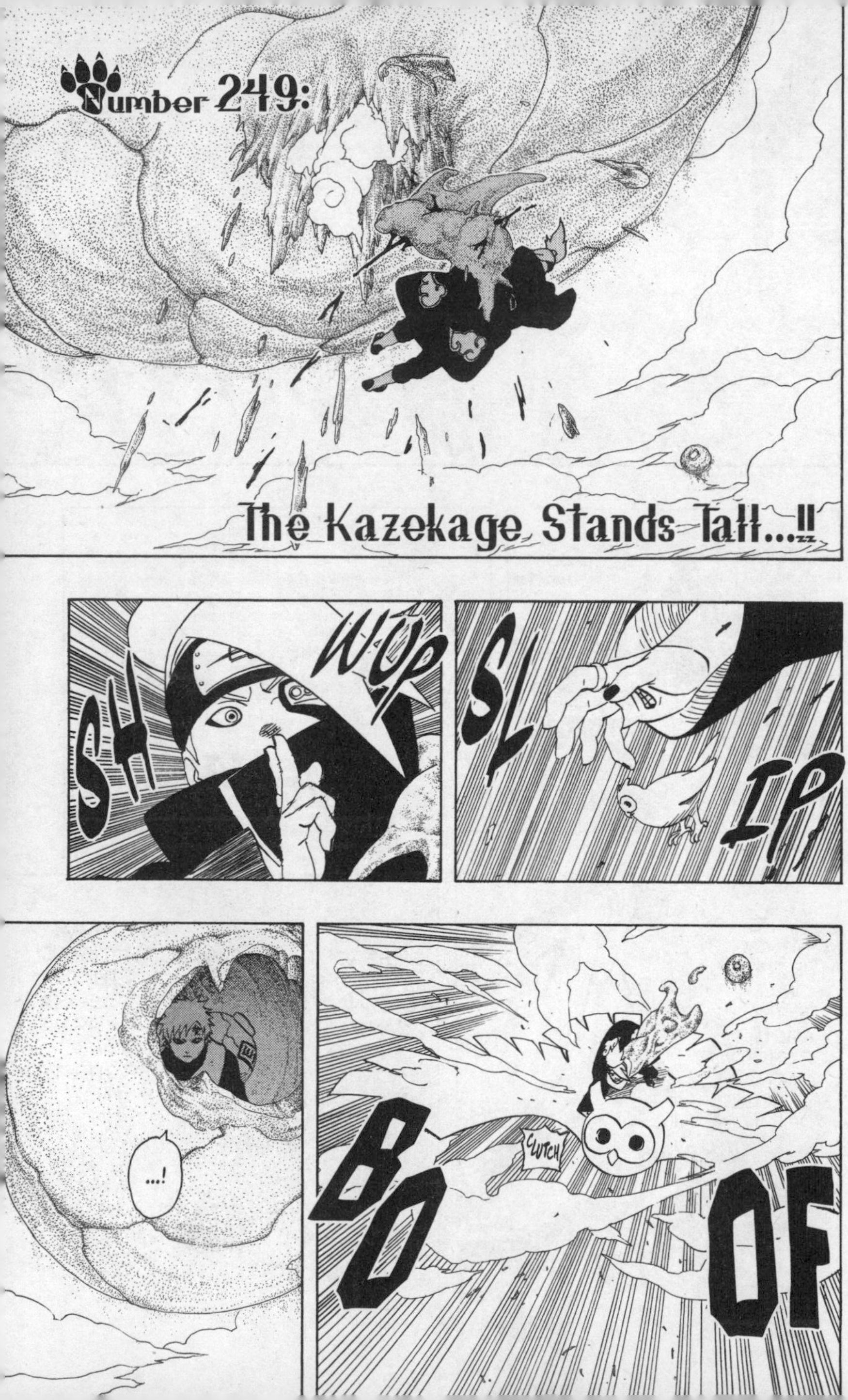
Number 249:
The Kazekage Stands Tall...!!
SLIP
SH
WOP
CLUTCH
BOOF
...!

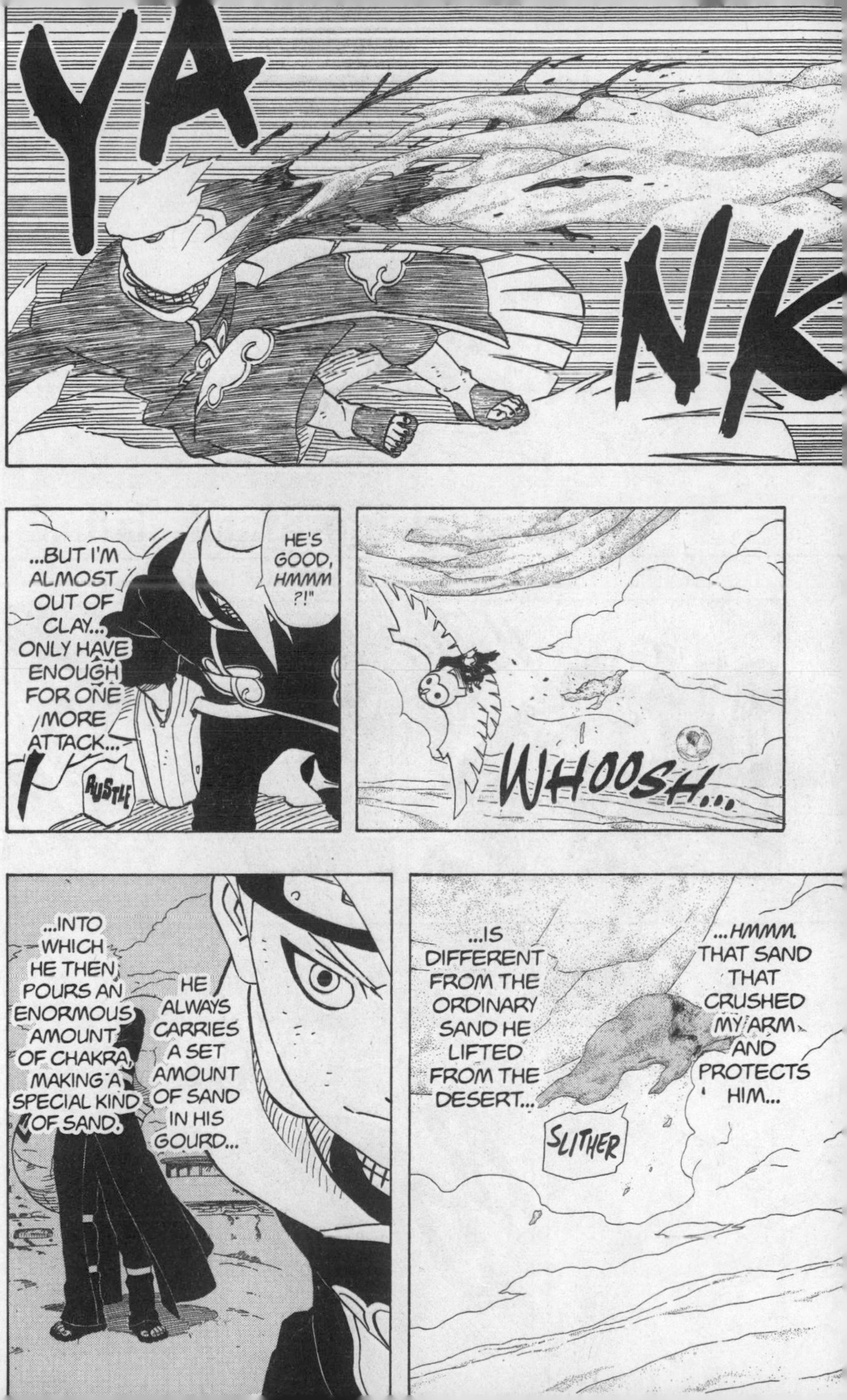
YANK
WHOOSH...
HE'S GOOD, HMMM?!"
...BUT I'M ALMOST OUT OF CLAY... ONLY HAVE ENOUGH FOR ONE MORE ATTACK...
RUSTLE
...HMMM. THAT SAND THAT CRUSHED MY ARM AND PROTECTS HIM...
...IS DIFFERENT FROM THE ORDINARY SAND HE LIFTED FROM THE DESERT...
SLITHER
HE ALWAYS CARRIES A SET AMOUNT OF SAND IN HIS GOURD...
...INTO WHICH HE THEN POURS AN ENORMOUS AMOUNT OF CHAKRA, MAKING A SPECIAL KIND OF SAND.

READ THIS WAY

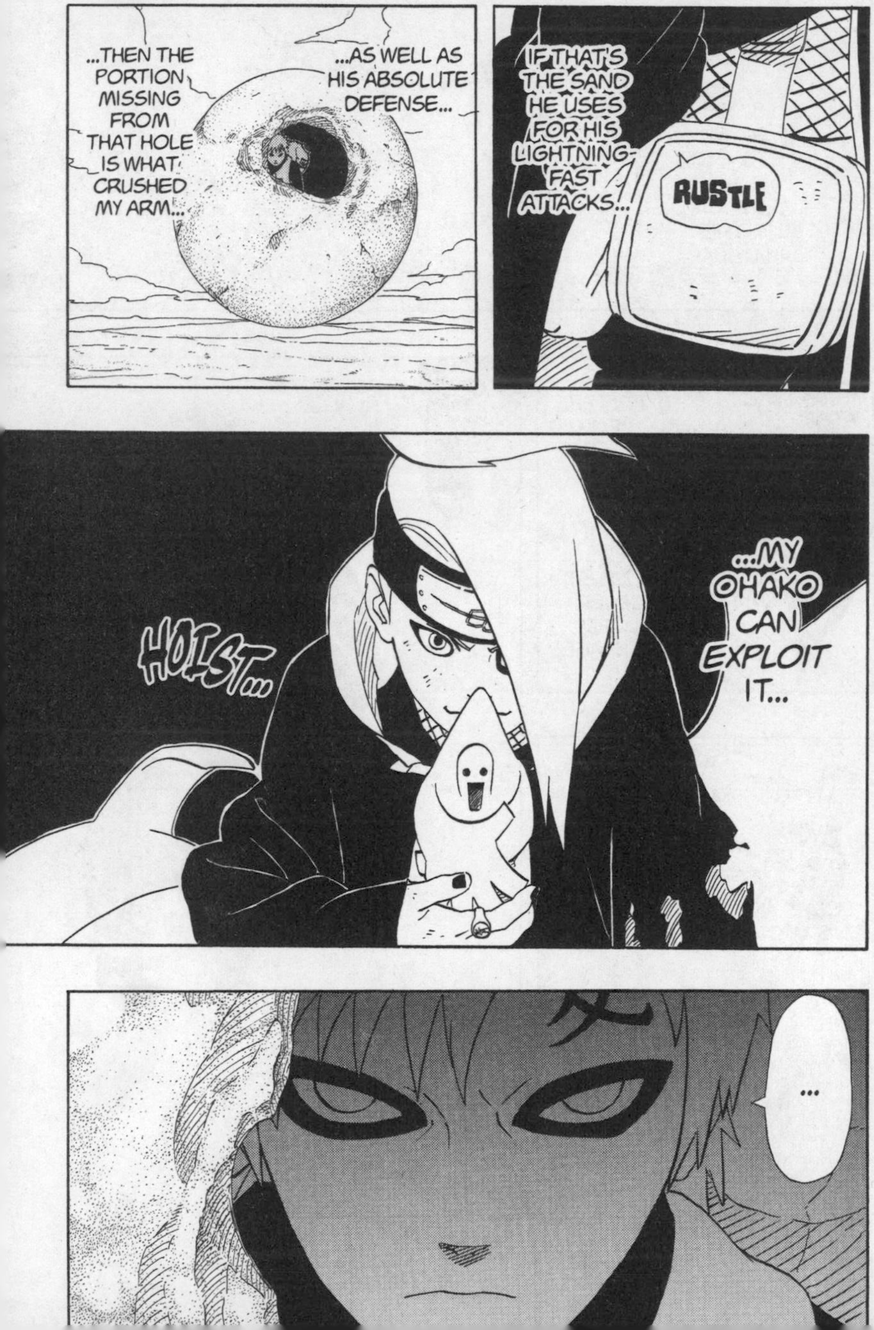
IF THAT'S THE SAND HE USES FOR HIS LIGHTNING-FAST ATTACKS...
RUSTLE
...AS WELL AS HIS ABSOLUTE DEFENSE...
...THEN THE PORTION MISSING FROM THAT HOLE IS WHAT CRUSHED MY ARM...
...MY OHAKO CAN EXPLOIT IT...
HOIST...
...

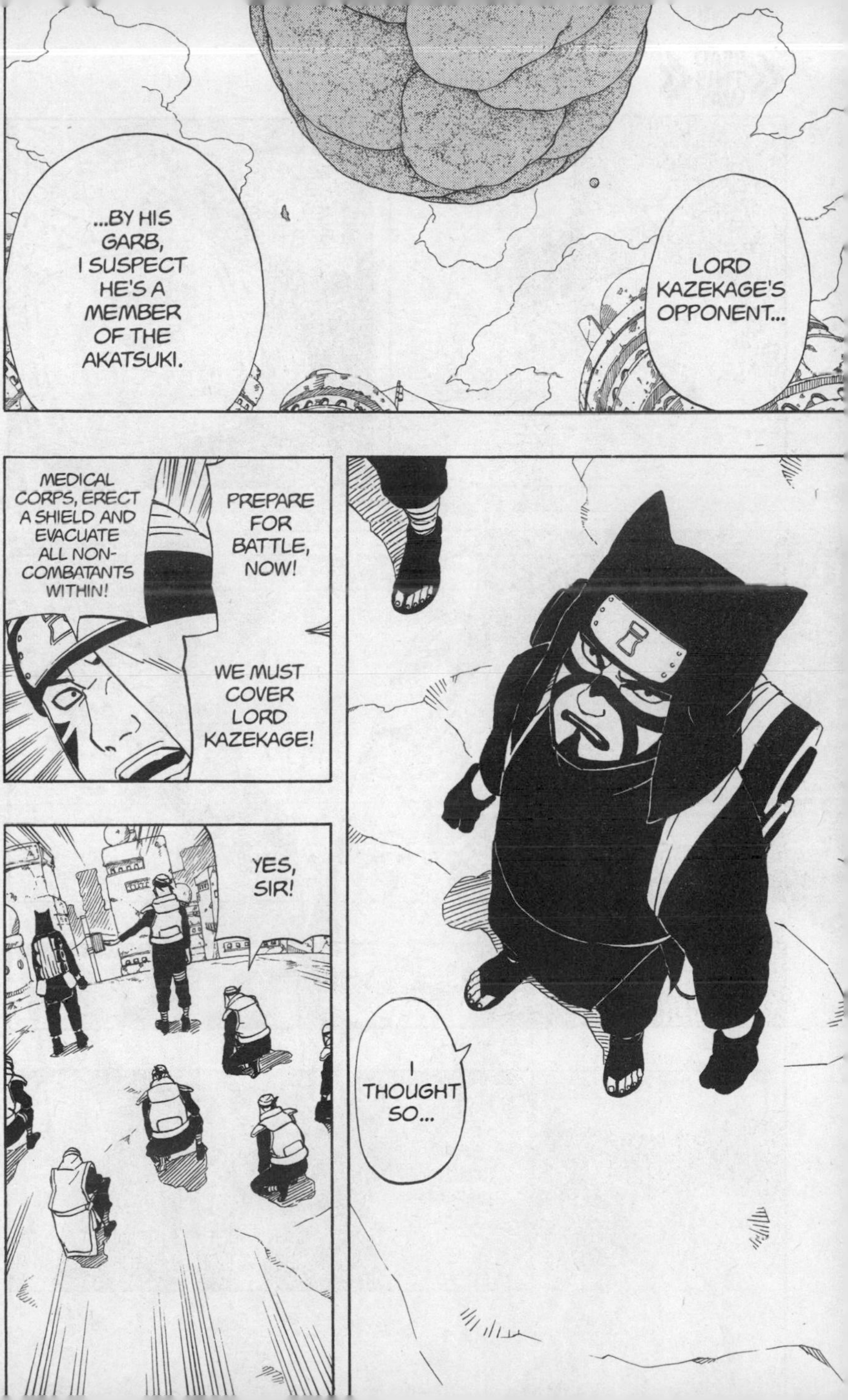
LORD KAZEKAGE'S OPPONENT...
...BY HIS GARB, I SUSPECT HE'S A MEMBER OF THE AKATSUKI.
I THOUGHT SO...
PREPARE FOR BATTLE, NOW!
MEDICAL CORPS, ERECT A SHIELD AND EVACUATE ALL NON-COMBATANTS WITHIN!
WE MUST COVER LORD KAZEKAGE!
YES, SIR!

READ THIS WAY

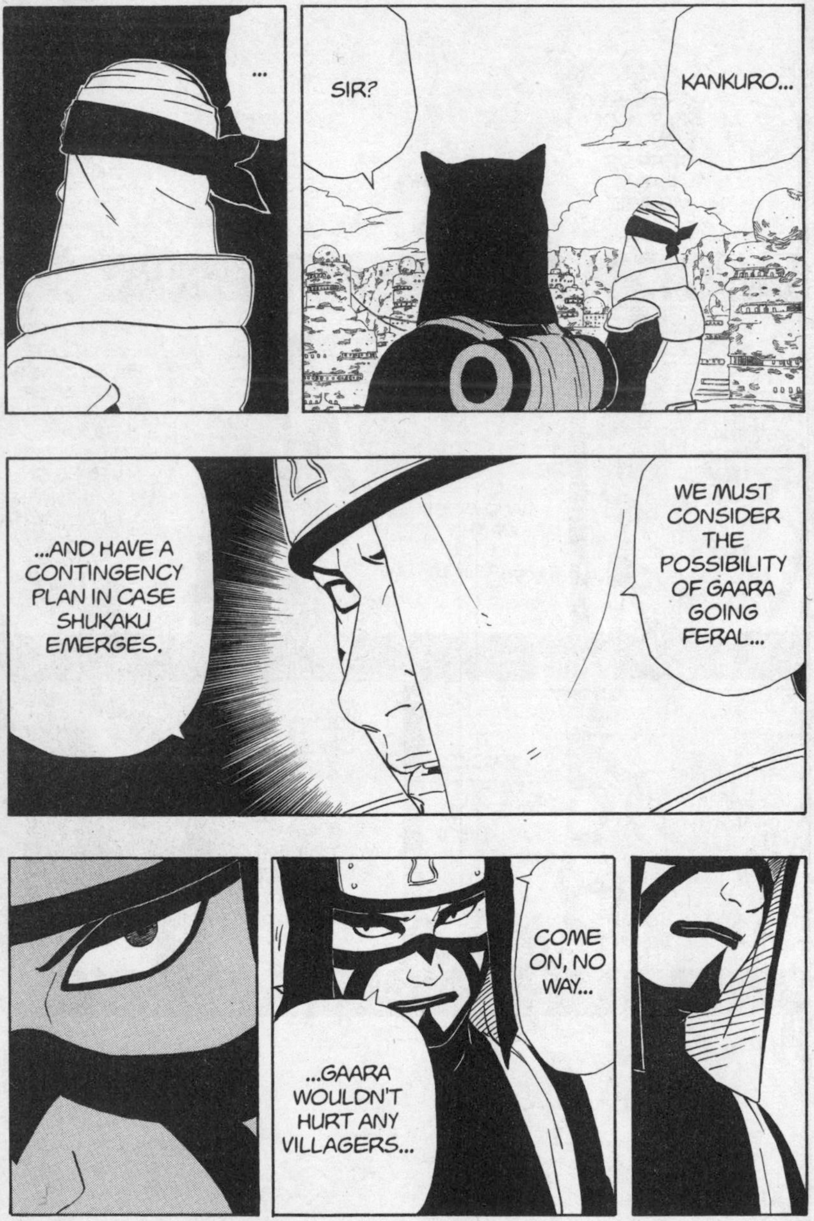
KANKURO...
SIR?
...
WE MUST CONSIDER THE POSSIBILITY OF GAARA GOING FERAL...
...AND HAVE A CONTINGENCY PLAN IN CASE SHUKAKU EMERGES.
COME ON, NO WAY...
...GAARA WOULDN'T HURT ANY VILLAGERS...

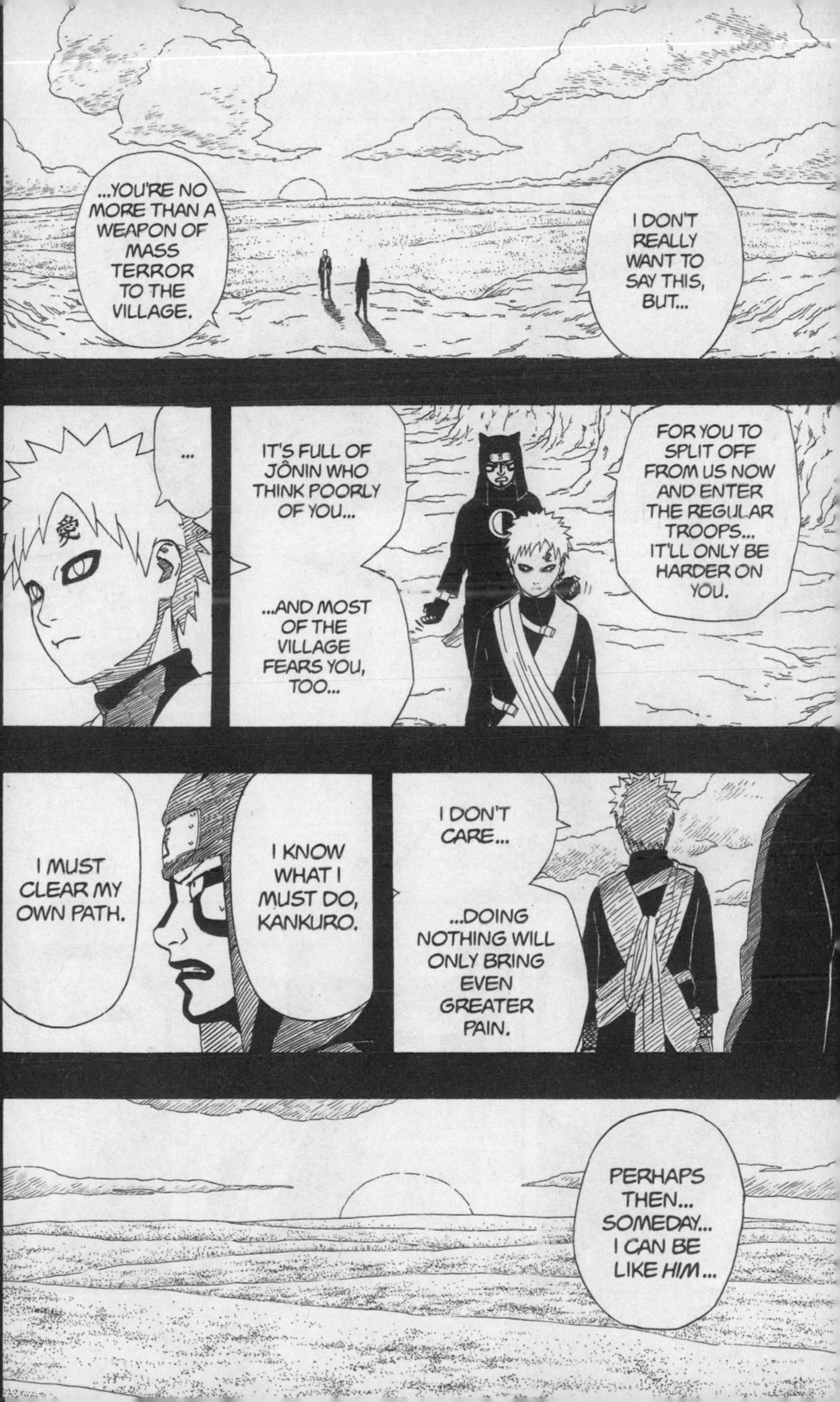

I DON'T REALLY WANT TO SAY THIS, BUT...
...YOU'RE NO MORE THAN A WEAPON OF MASS TERROR TO THE VILLAGE.
FOR YOU TO SPLIT OFF FROM US NOW AND ENTER THE REGULAR TROOPS... IT'LL ONLY BE HARDER ON YOU.
IT'S FULL OF JÔNIN WHO THINK POORLY OF YOU...
...AND MOST OF THE VILLAGE FEARS YOU, TOO...
...
I DON'T CARE...
...DOING NOTHING WILL ONLY BRING EVEN GREATER PAIN.
I KNOW WHAT I MUST DO, KANKURO.
I MUST CLEAR MY OWN PATH.
PERHAPS THEN... SOMEDAY... I CAN BE LIKE *HIM*...

READ THIS WAY

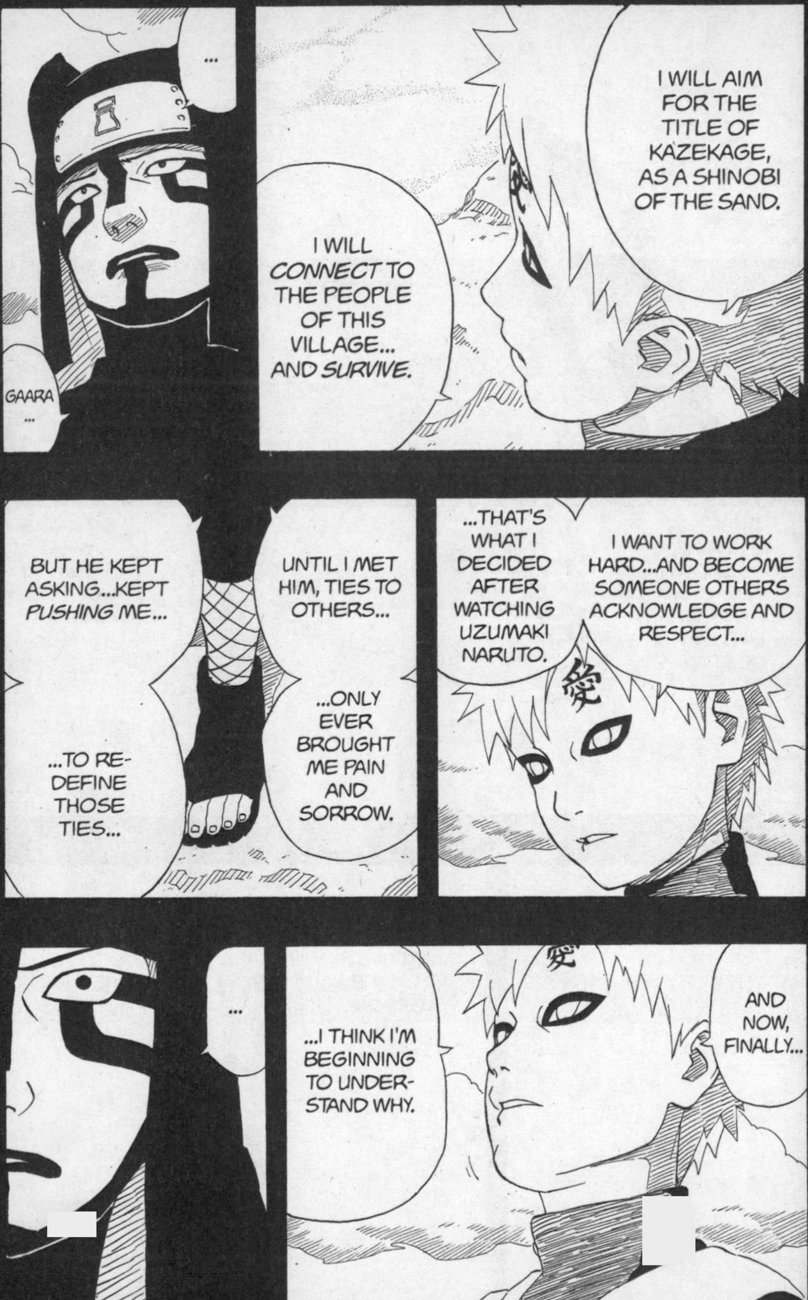
I WILL AIM FOR THE TITLE OF KAZEKAGE, AS A SHINOBI OF THE SAND.
I WILL *CONNECT* TO THE PEOPLE OF THIS VILLAGE... AND *SURVIVE.*
...
GAARA ...
I WANT TO WORK HARD...AND BECOME SOMEONE OTHERS ACKNOWLEDGE AND RESPECT...
...THAT'S WHAT I DECIDED AFTER WATCHING UZUMAKI NARUTO.
UNTIL I MET HIM, TIES TO OTHERS...
...ONLY EVER BROUGHT ME PAIN AND SORROW.
BUT HE KEPT ASKING...KEPT *PUSHING* ME...
...TO RE-DEFINE THOSE TIES...
AND NOW, FINALLY...
...I THINK I'M BEGINNING TO UNDER-STAND WHY.
...

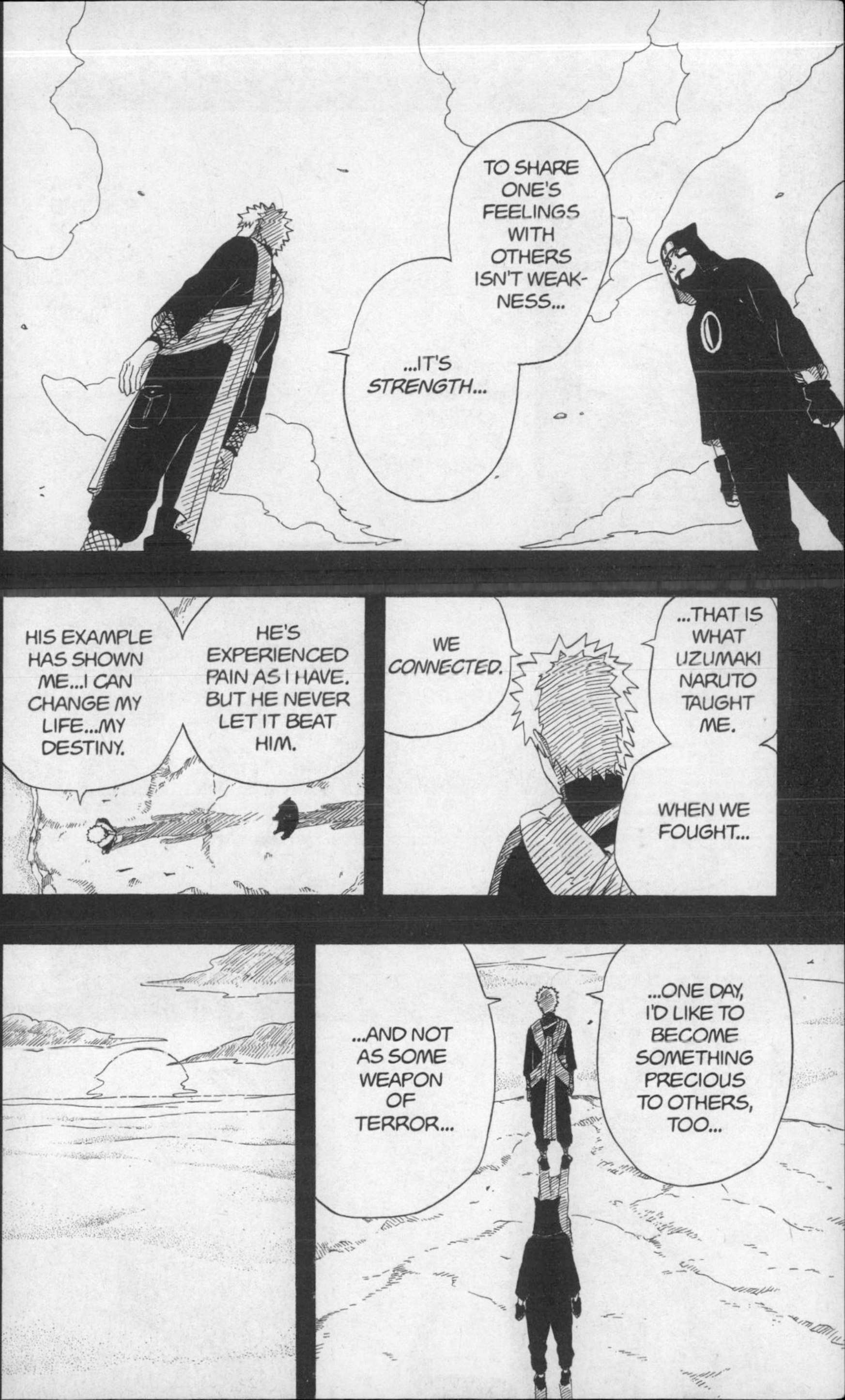
TO SHARE ONE'S FEELINGS WITH OTHERS ISN'T WEAK-NESS...
...IT'S STRENGTH...
...THAT IS WHAT UZUMAKI NARUTO TAUGHT ME.
WHEN WE FOUGHT...
WE CONNECTED.
HE'S EXPERIENCED PAIN AS I HAVE. BUT HE NEVER LET IT BEAT HIM.
HIS EXAMPLE HAS SHOWN ME...I CAN CHANGE MY LIFE...MY DESTINY.
...ONE DAY, I'D LIKE TO BECOME SOMETHING PRECIOUS TO OTHERS, TOO...
...AND NOT AS SOME WEAPON OF TERROR...

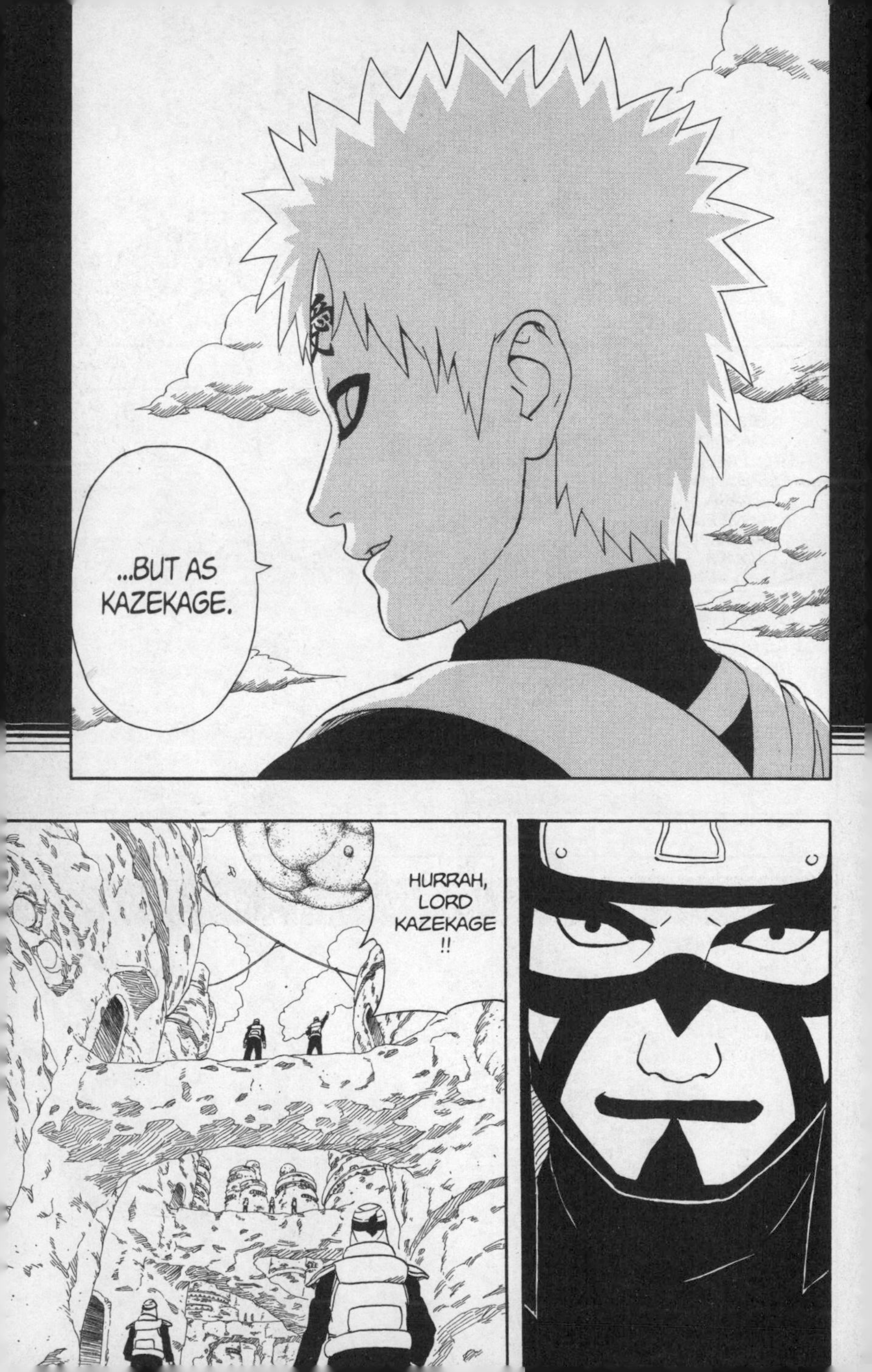
...BUT AS KAZEKAGE.
HURRAH, LORD KAZEKAGE!!

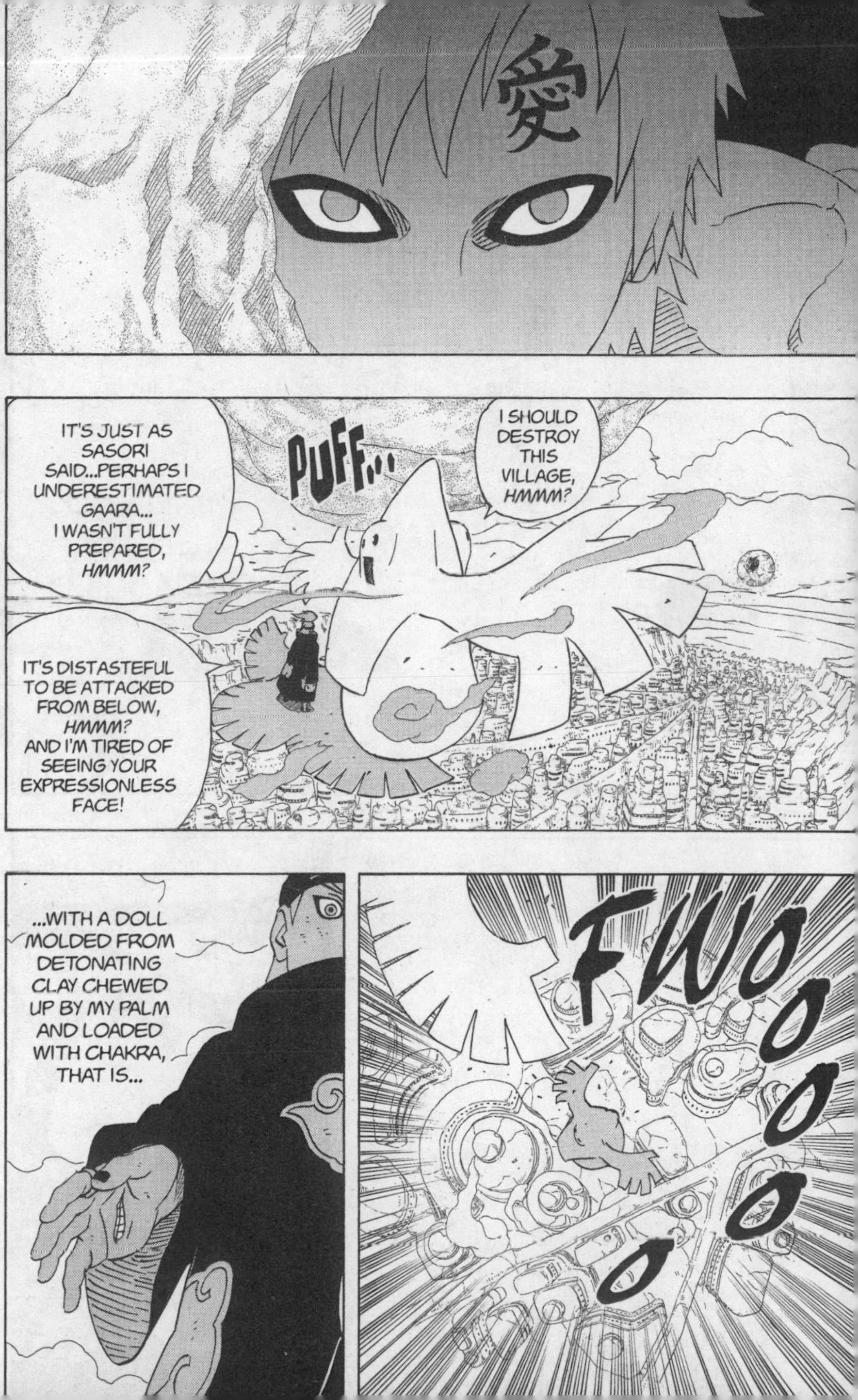
愛
I SHOULD DESTROY THIS VILLAGE, *HMMM?*
PUFF...
IT'S JUST AS SASORI SAID...PERHAPS I UNDERESTIMATED GAARA... I WASN'T FULLY PREPARED, *HMMM?*
IT'S DISTASTEFUL TO BE ATTACKED FROM BELOW, *HMMM?* AND I'M TIRED OF SEEING YOUR EXPRESSIONLESS FACE!
FWOOOOOO
...WITH A DOLL MOLDED FROM DETONATING CLAY CHEWED UP BY MY PALM AND LOADED WITH CHAKRA, THAT IS...

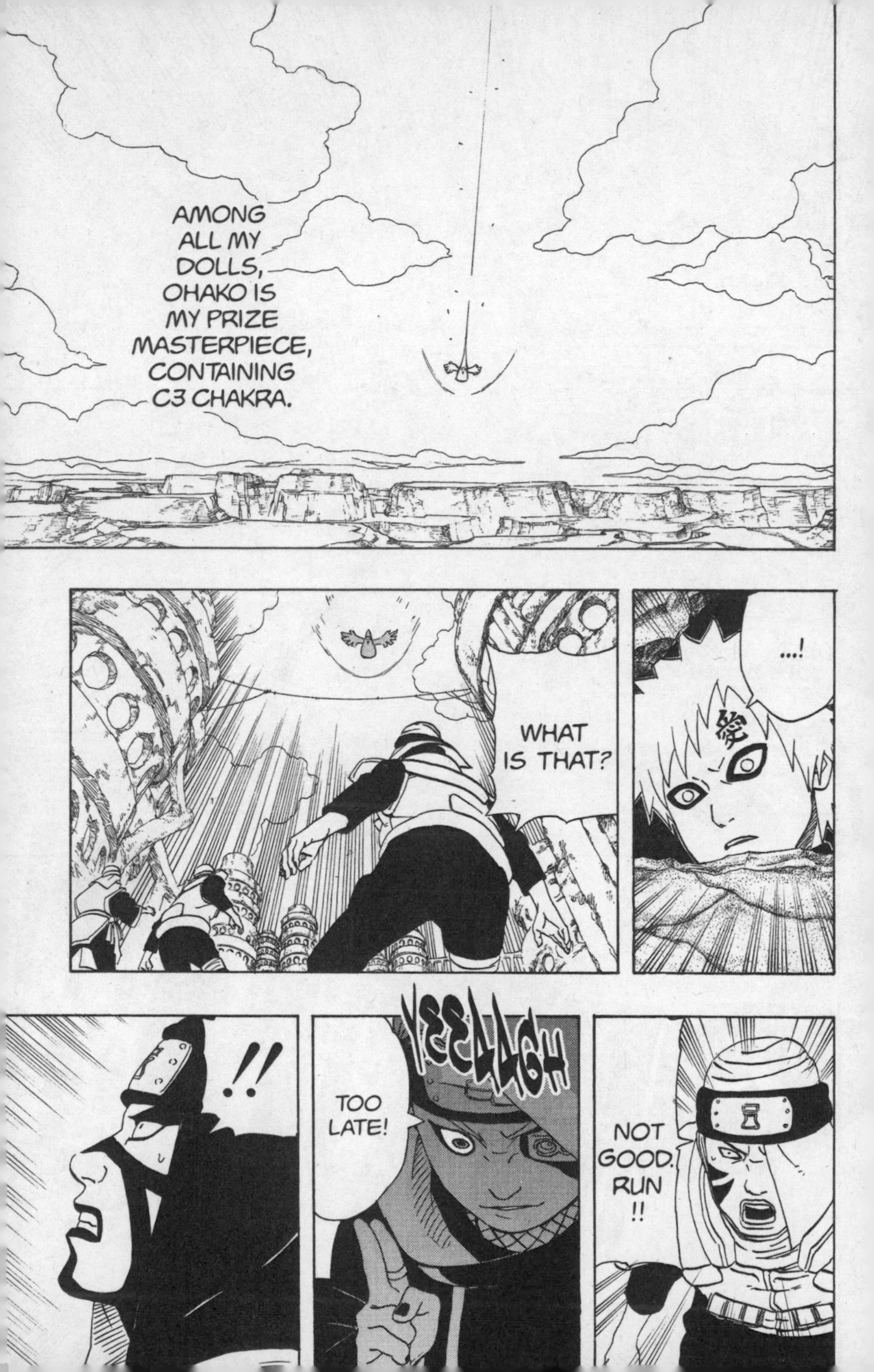
AMONG ALL MY DOLLS, OHAKO IS MY PRIZE MASTERPIECE, CONTAINING C3 CHAKRA.
...!
WHAT IS THAT?
NOT GOOD. RUN!!
YEEAAGH
TOO LATE!
!!

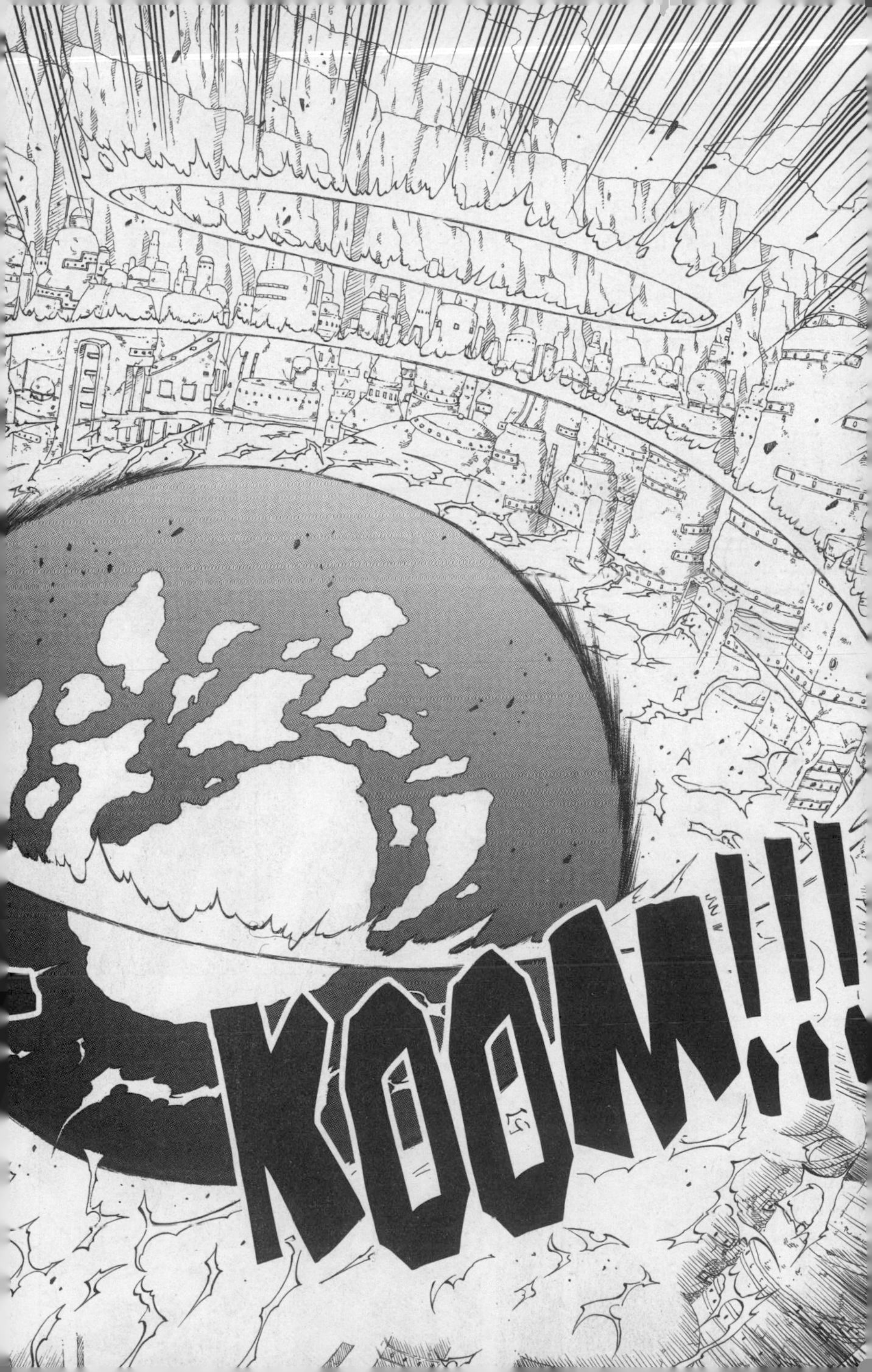
KOOM!!!

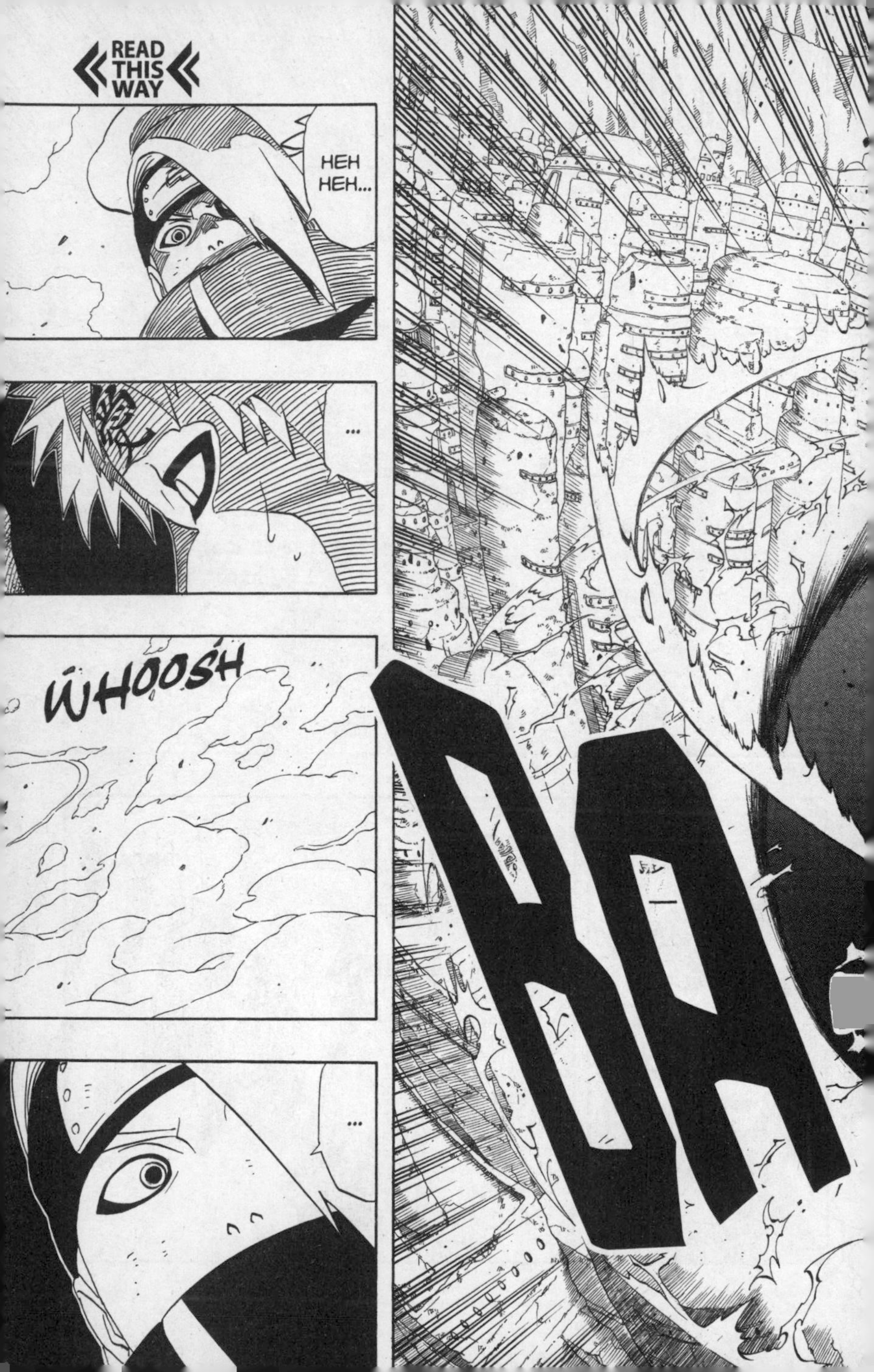
READ THIS WAY
BO
HEH HEH...
...
WHOOSH
...

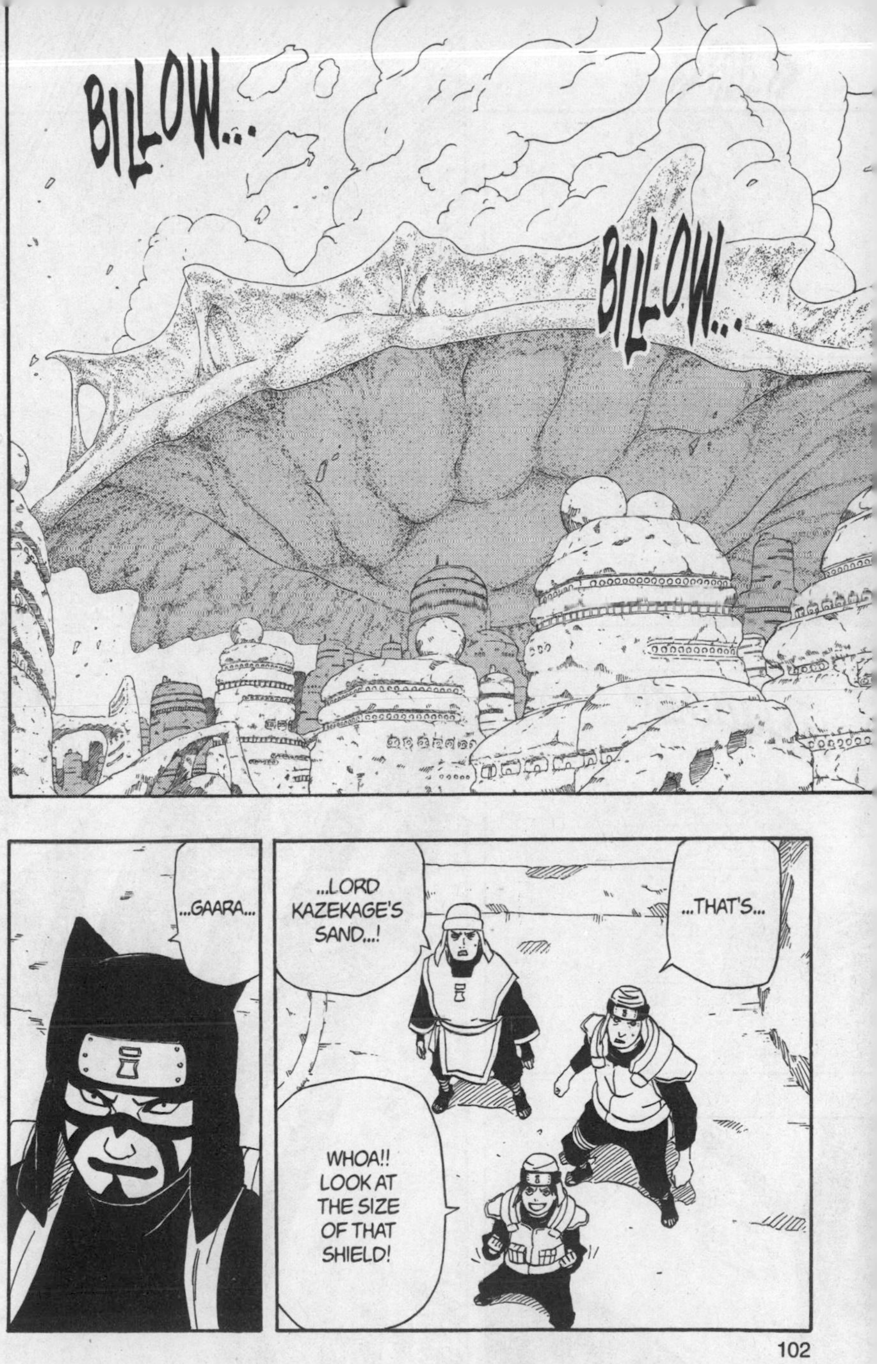
BILLOW...
BILLOW...
...THAT'S...
...LORD KAZEKAGE'S SAND...!
WHOA!! LOOK AT THE SIZE OF THAT SHIELD!
...GAARA...

READ THIS WAY

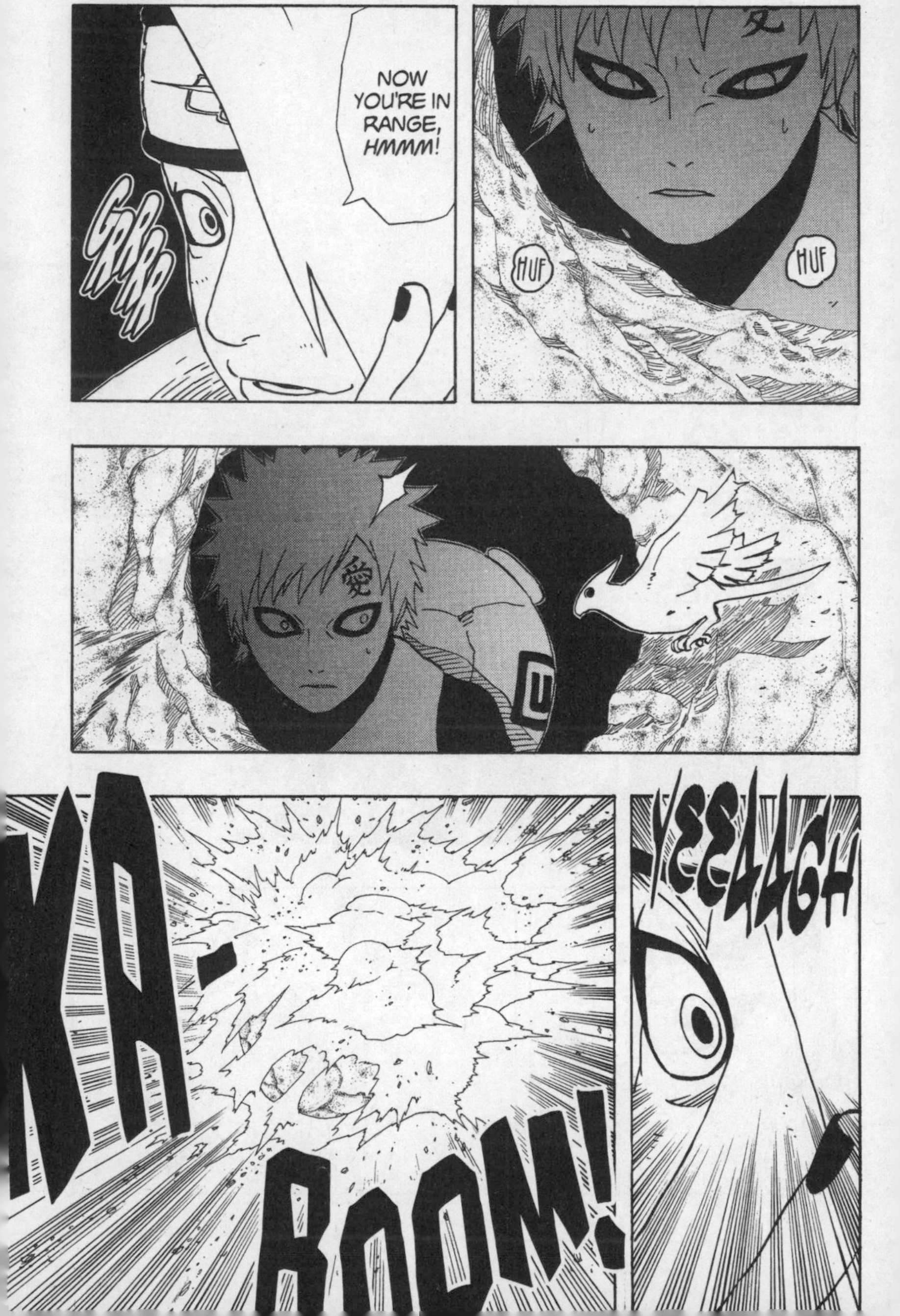
HUF
HUF
NOW YOU'RE IN RANGE, *HMMM!*
GRRR
YEEAAGH
KA-ROOM!

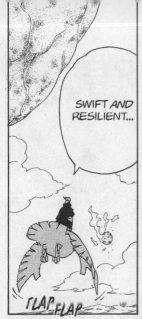

SWIFT AND
RESILIENT...

FLAP FLAP

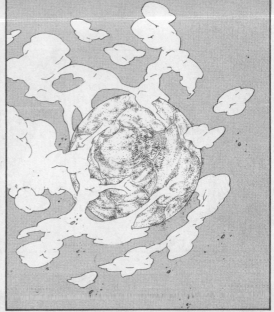

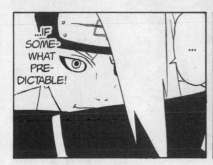

...IF SOMEWHAT PREDICTABLE!

...

HUF HUF

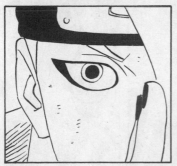

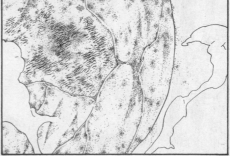

READ THIS WAY

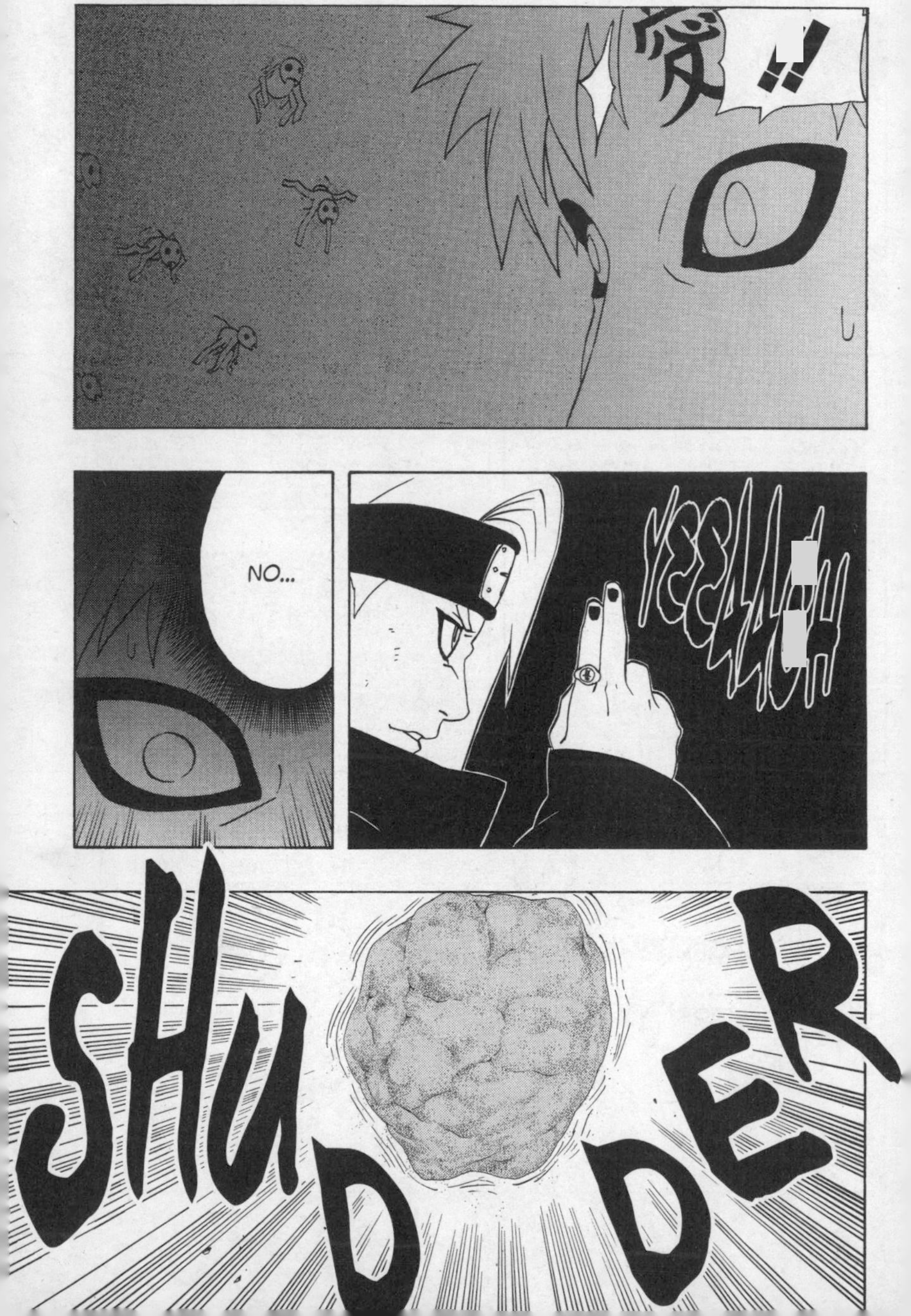
!!
NO...
SHUDDER

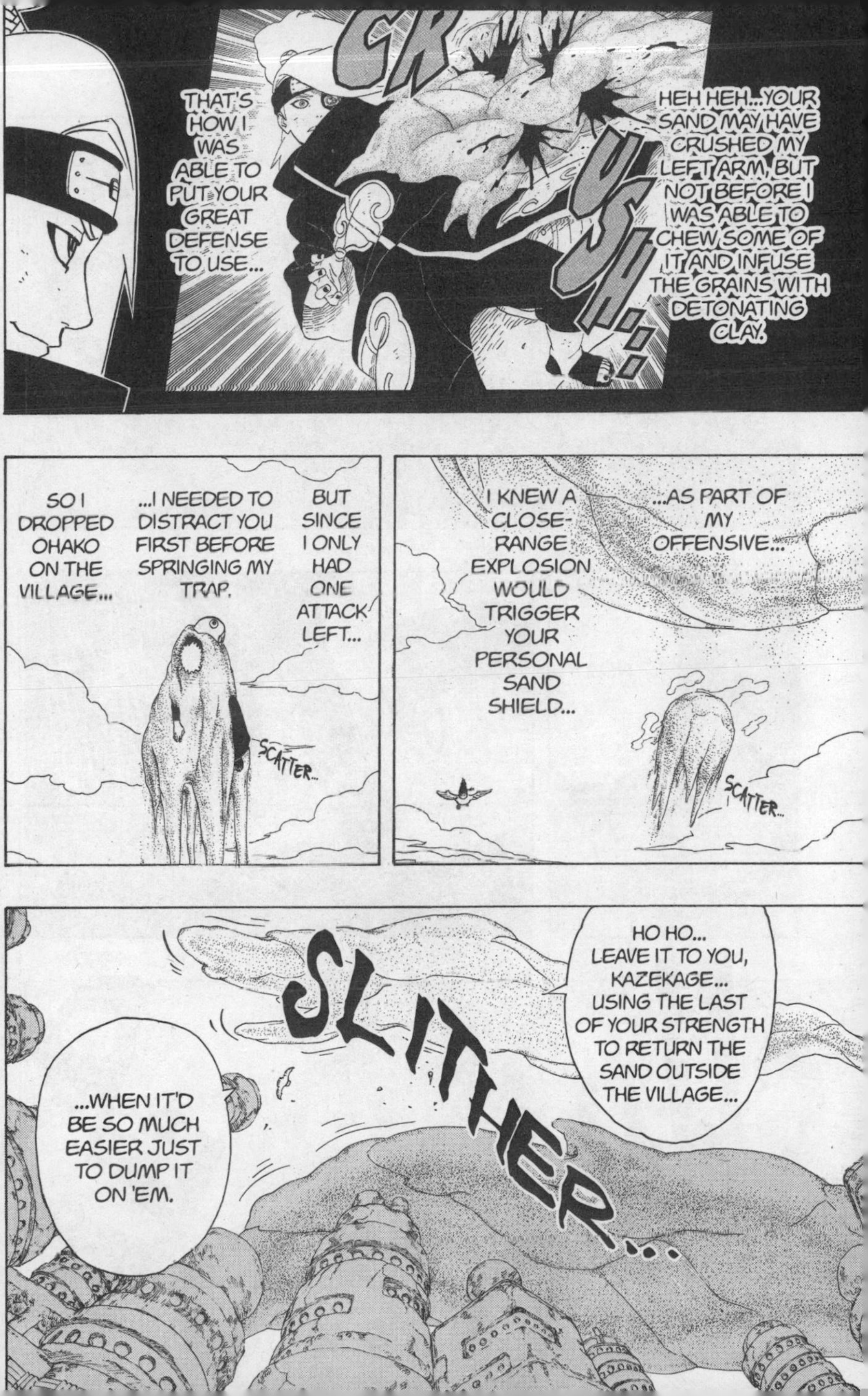
HEH HEH...YOUR SAND MAY HAVE CRUSHED MY LEFT ARM, BUT NOT BEFORE I WAS ABLE TO CHEW SOME OF IT AND INFUSE THE GRAINS WITH DETONATING CLAY.
CRUSH...
THAT'S HOW I WAS ABLE TO PUT YOUR GREAT DEFENSE TO USE...
...AS PART OF MY OFFENSIVE...
I KNEW A CLOSE-RANGE EXPLOSION WOULD TRIGGER YOUR PERSONAL SAND SHIELD...
SCATTER...
BUT SINCE I ONLY HAD ONE ATTACK LEFT...
...I NEEDED TO DISTRACT YOU FIRST BEFORE SPRINGING MY TRAP.
SO I DROPPED OHAKO ON THE VILLAGE...
SCATTER...
HO HO... LEAVE IT TO YOU, KAZEKAGE... USING THE LAST OF YOUR STRENGTH TO RETURN THE SAND OUTSIDE THE VILLAGE...
SLITHER...
...WHEN IT'D BE SO MUCH EASIER JUST TO DUMP IT ON 'EM.

READ THIS WAY

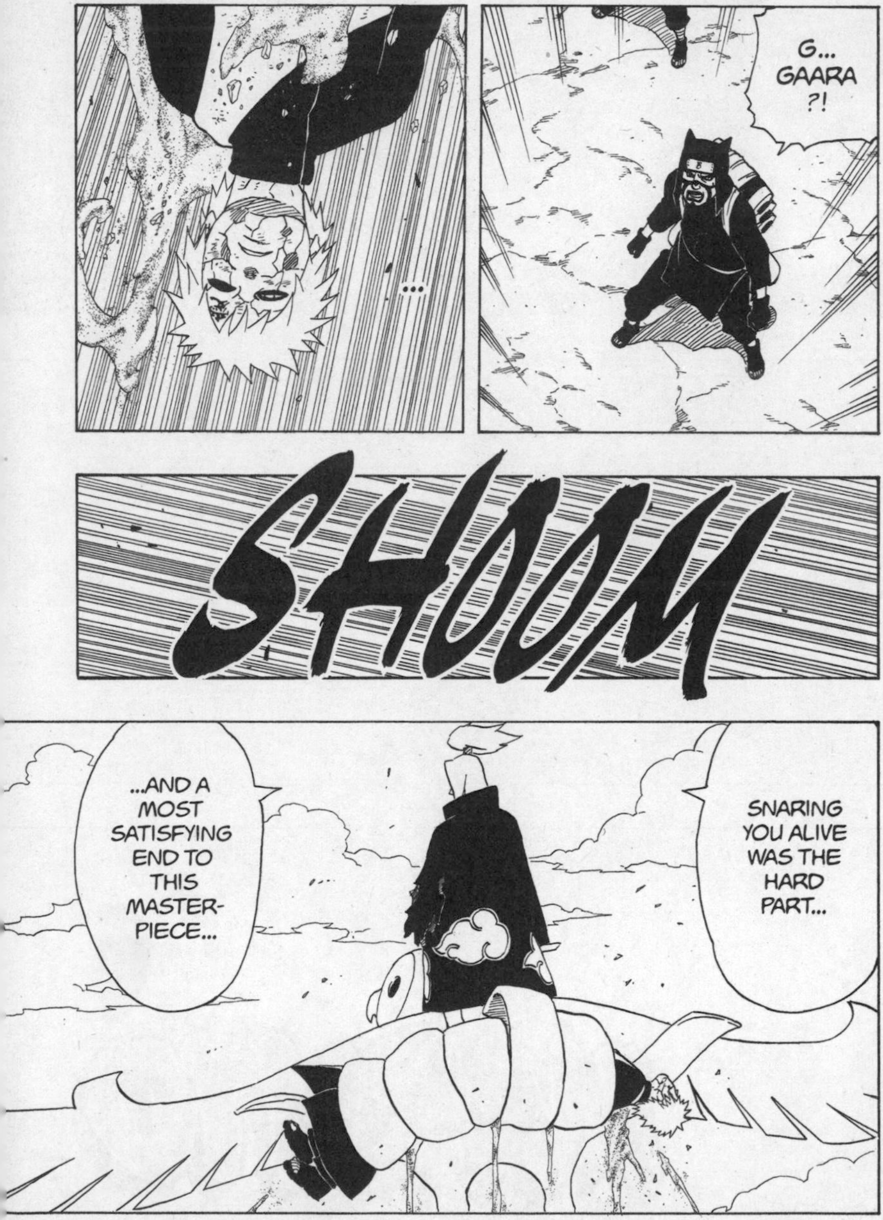
G... GAARA ?!
...
SHOOM
SNARING YOU ALIVE WAS THE HARD PART...
...AND A MOST SATISFYING END TO THIS MASTERPIECE...

NARUTO

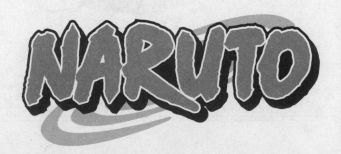

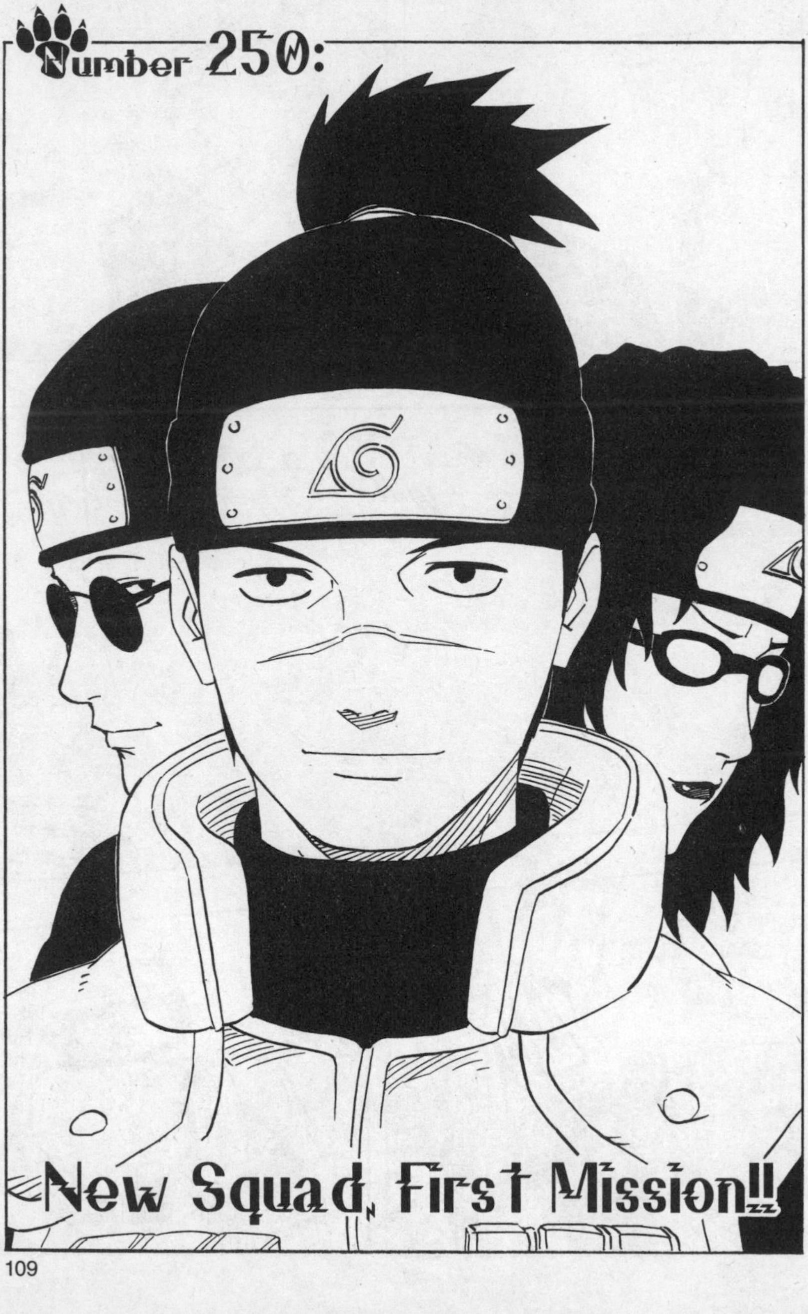
Number 250:
New Squad, First Mission!!

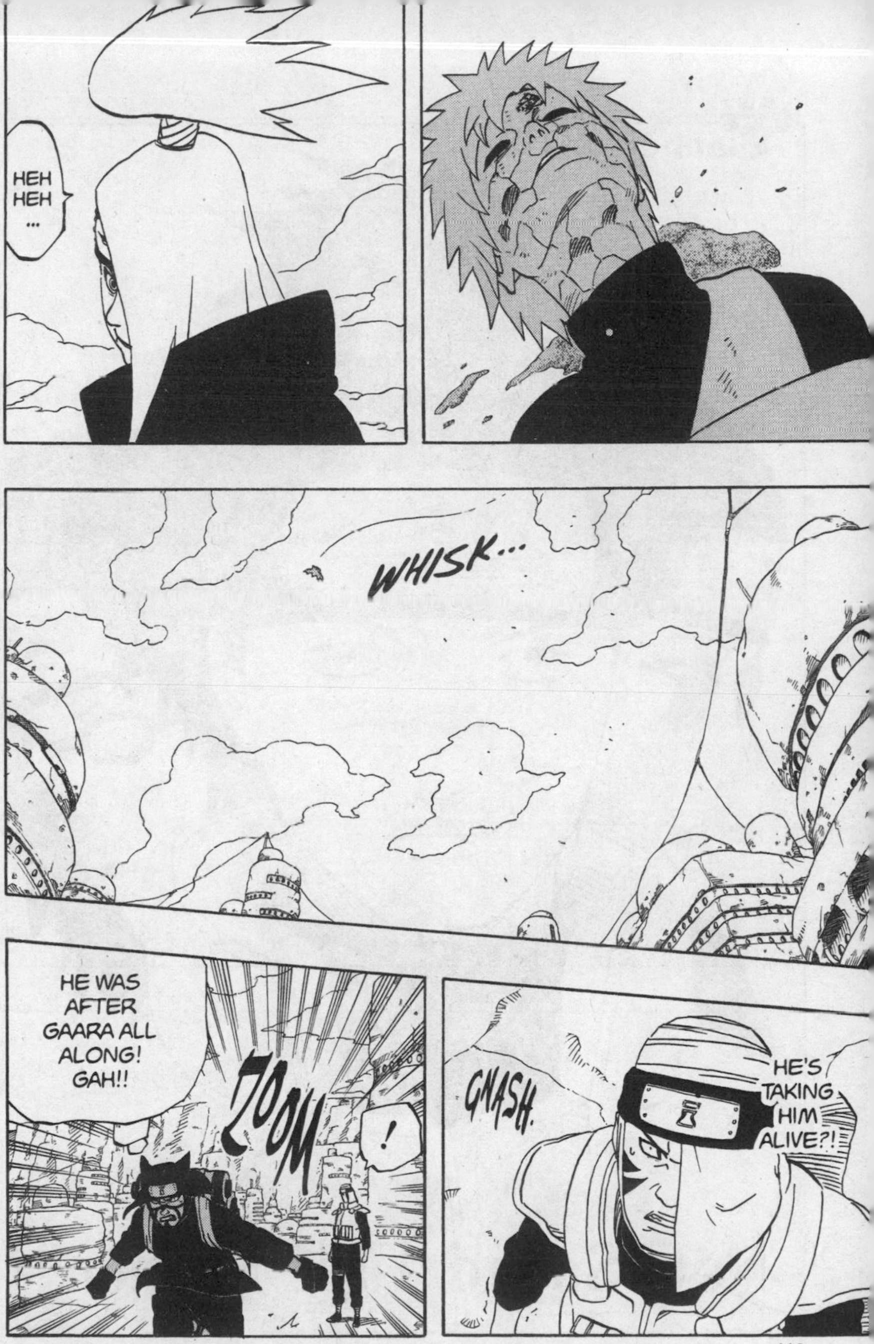
HEH HEH ...
WHISK...
HE'S TAKING HIM ALIVE?!
GNASH.
HE WAS AFTER GAARA ALL ALONG! GAH!!
ZOOM
!

READ THIS WAY

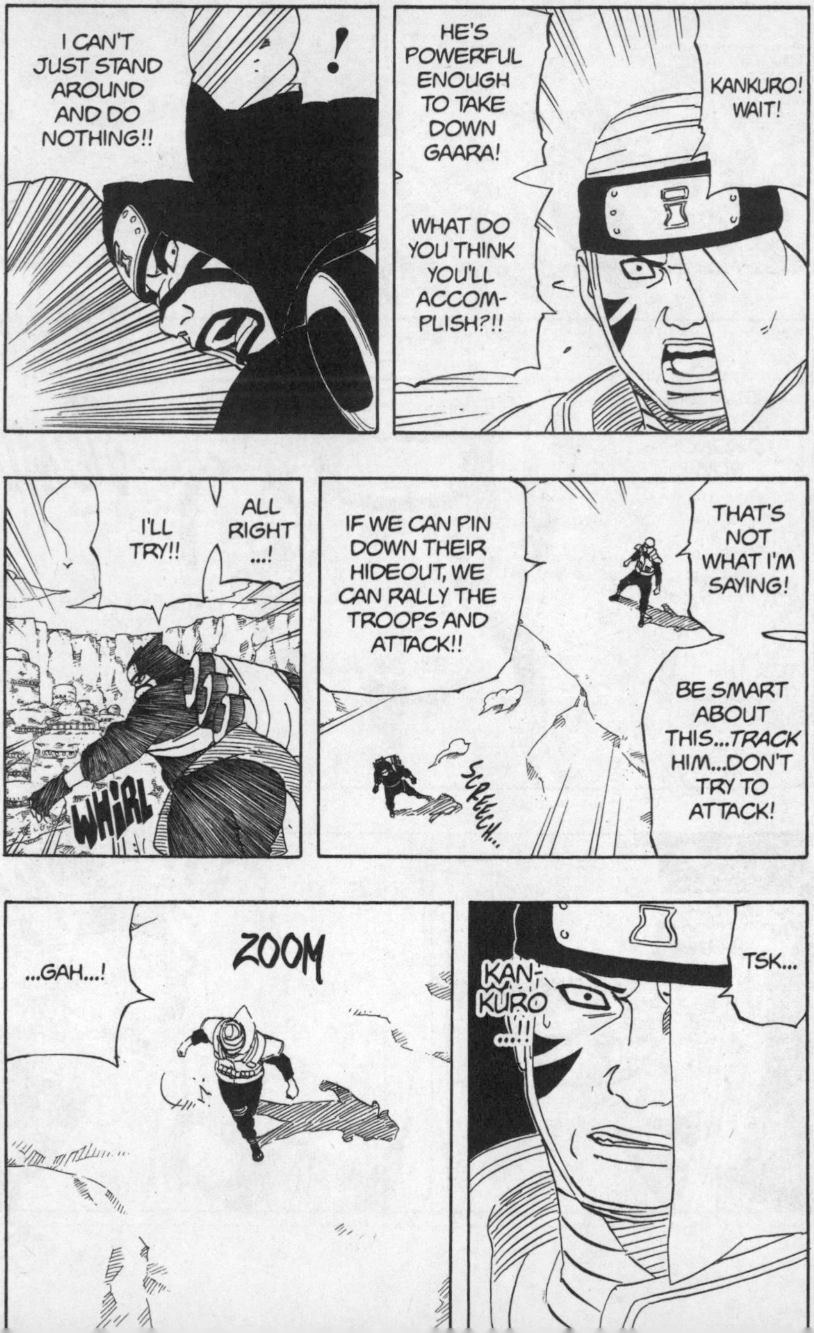
KANKURO! WAIT!
HE'S POWERFUL ENOUGH TO TAKE DOWN GAARA!
WHAT DO YOU THINK YOU'LL ACCOM-PLISH?!!
!
I CAN'T JUST STAND AROUND AND DO NOTHING!!
THAT'S NOT WHAT I'M SAYING!
IF WE CAN PIN DOWN THEIR HIDEOUT, WE CAN RALLY THE TROOPS AND ATTACK!!
BE SMART ABOUT THIS...*TRACK* HIM...DON'T TRY TO ATTACK!
SCREECH...
ALL RIGHT ...!
I'LL TRY!!
WHIRL
TSK...
KAN-KURO ...!!!
ZOOM
...GAH...!

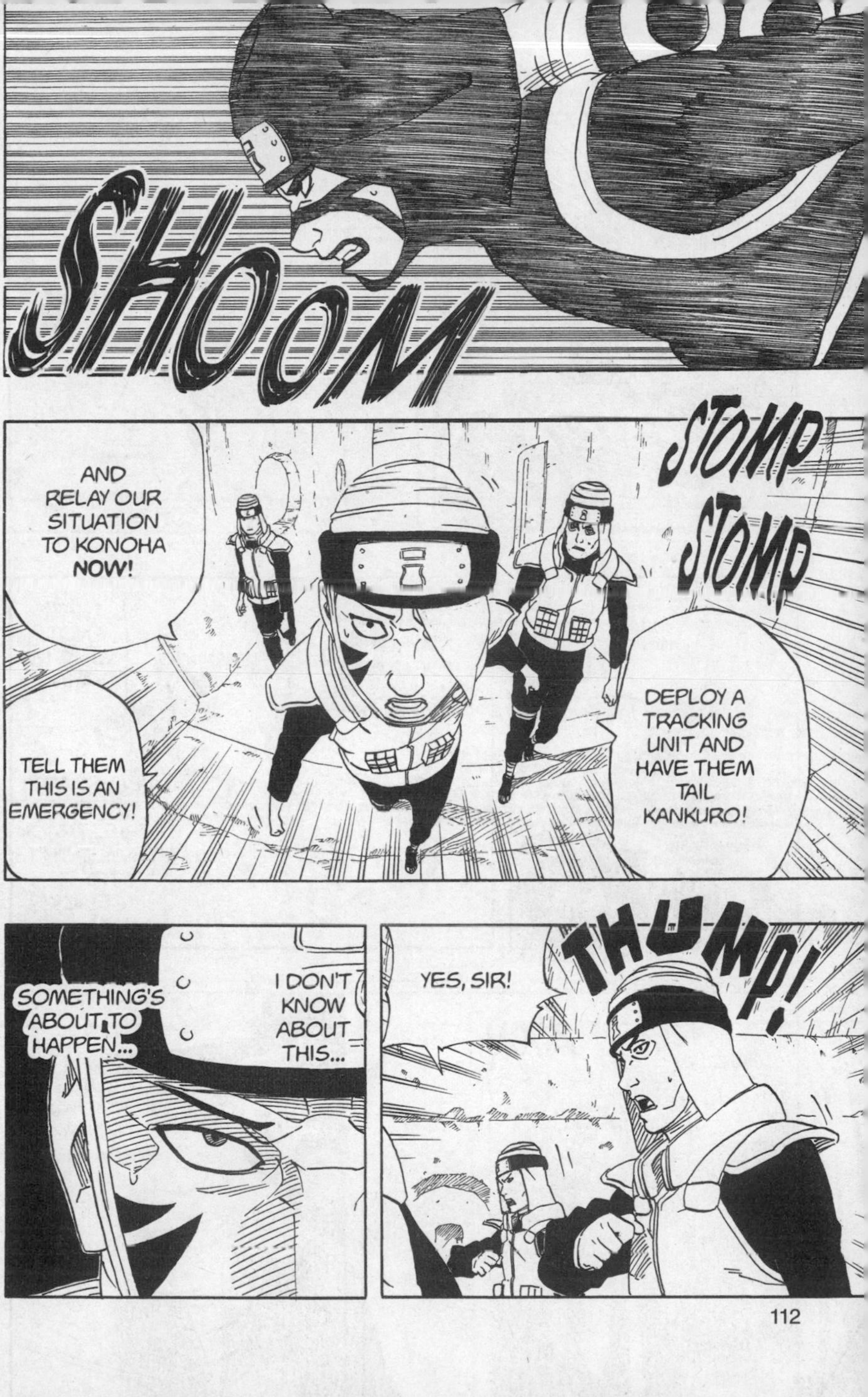
SHOOM
STOMP STOMP
DEPLOY A TRACKING UNIT AND HAVE THEM TAIL KANKURO!
AND RELAY OUR SITUATION TO KONOHA **NOW!**
TELL THEM THIS IS AN EMERGENCY!
THUMP!
YES, SIR!
I DON'T KNOW ABOUT THIS...
SOMETHING'S ABOUT TO HAPPEN...

READ THIS WAY

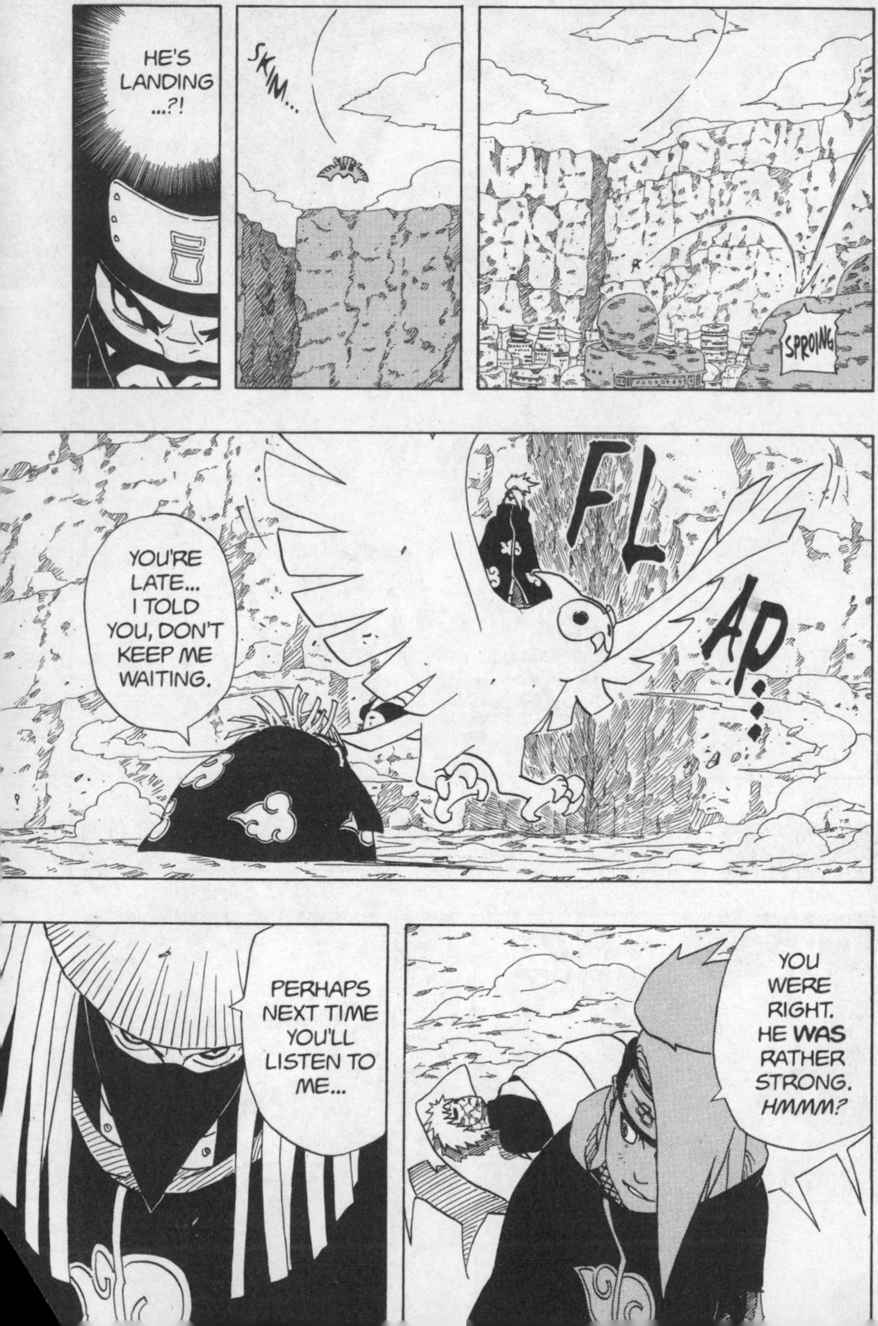
SPROING
SKIM...
HE'S LANDING ...?!
FLAP...
YOU'RE LATE... I TOLD YOU, DON'T KEEP ME WAITING.
YOU WERE RIGHT. HE WAS RATHER STRONG. HMMM?
PERHAPS NEXT TIME YOU'LL LISTEN TO ME...

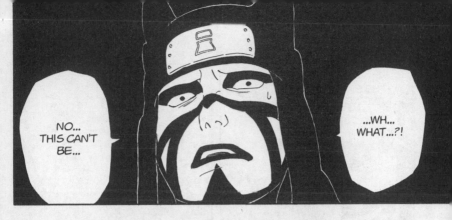

NO...
THIS CAN'T
BE...

...WH...
WHAT...?!

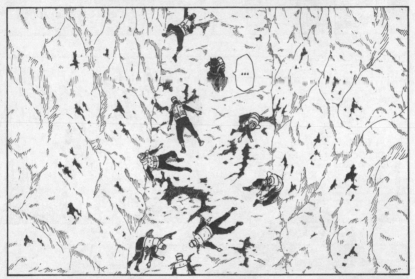

....

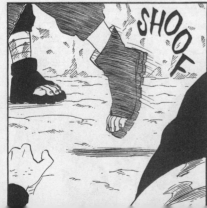

SHOOF

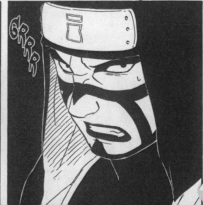

GRRRR

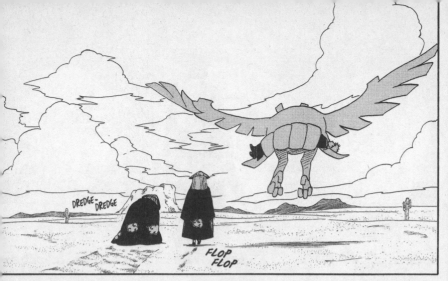

DREDGE-DREDGE

FLOP
FLOP

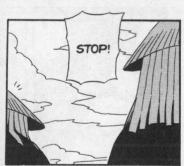

STOP!

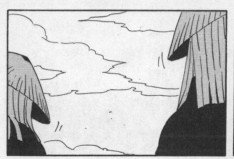

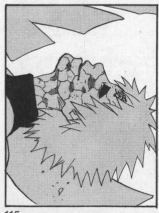

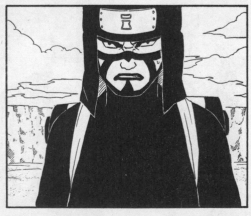

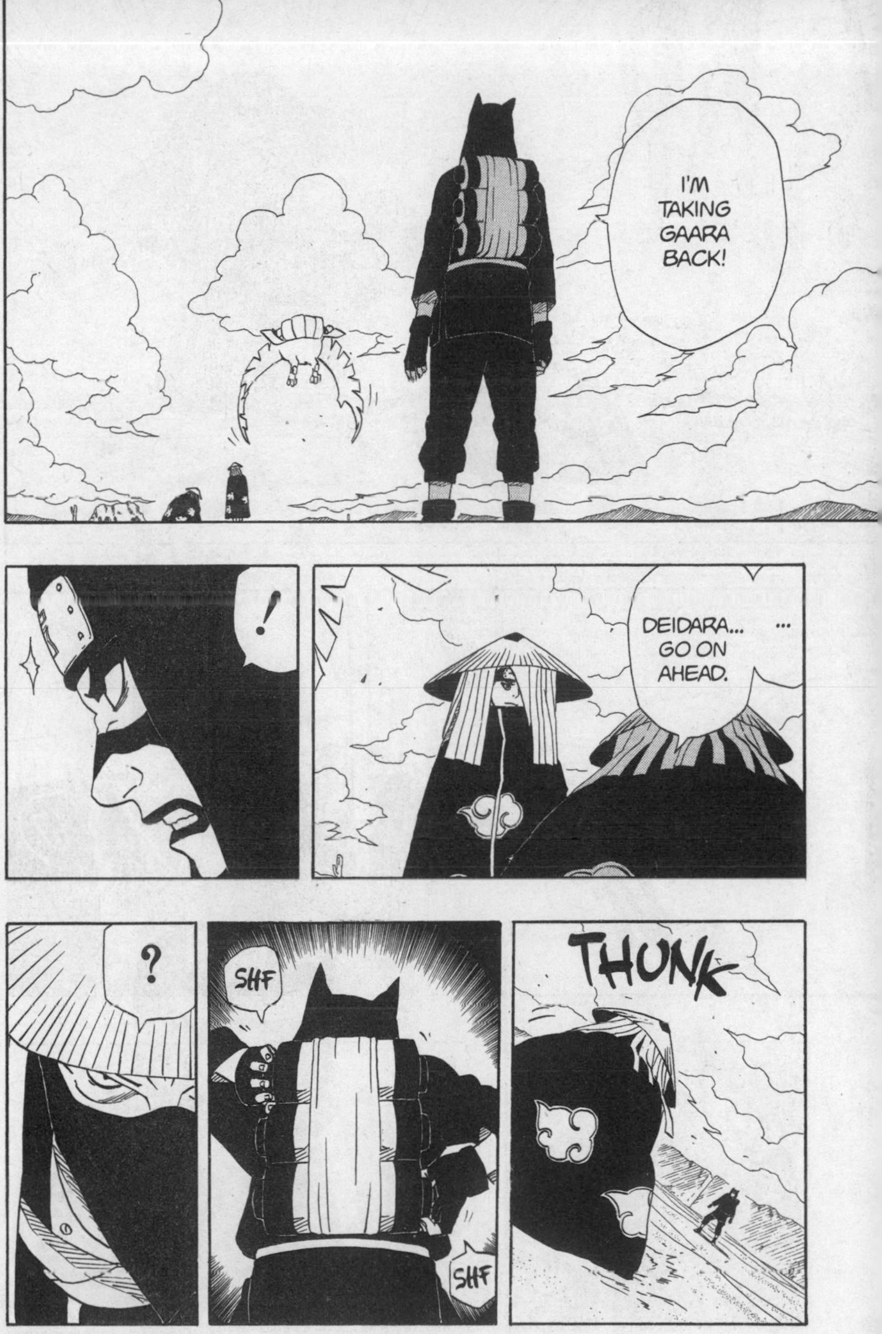
I'M TAKING GAARA BACK!
...
DEIDARA... GO ON AHEAD.
!
THUNK
SHF
SHF
?

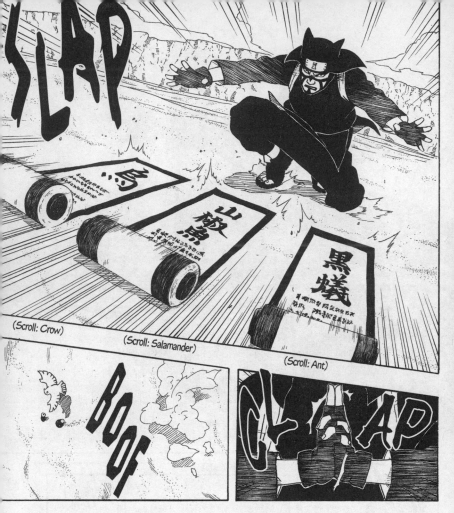

(Scroll: Crow)

(Scroll: Salamander)

(Scroll: Ant)

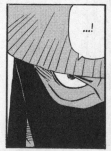

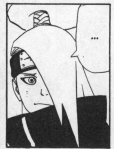

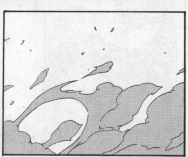

117

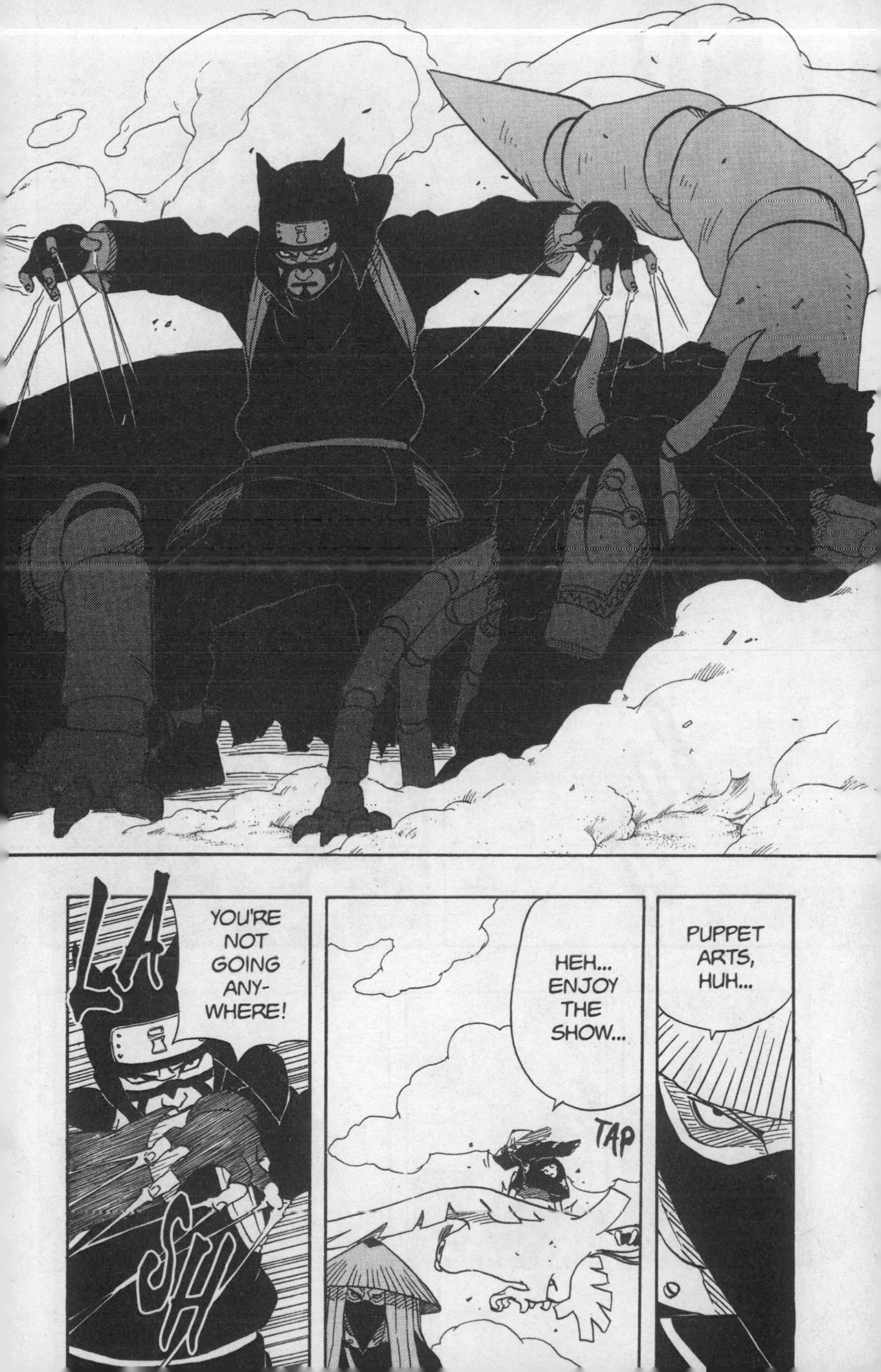
PUPPET ARTS, HUH...
HEH... ENJOY THE SHOW...
TAP
YOU'RE NOT GOING ANYWHERE!
LA
SH

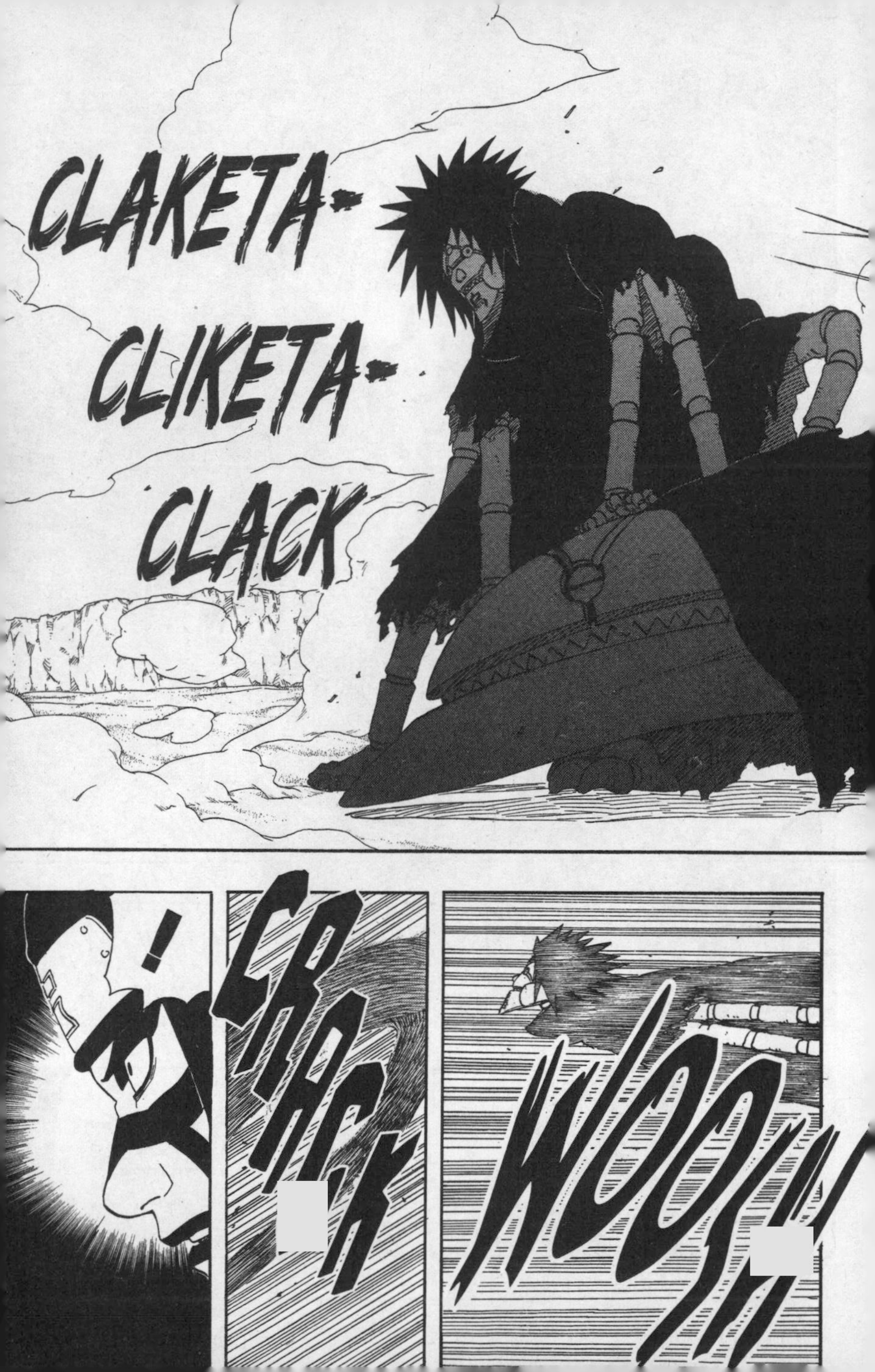
CLAKETA-
CLIKETA-
CLACK
WHOOSH
CRACK
!

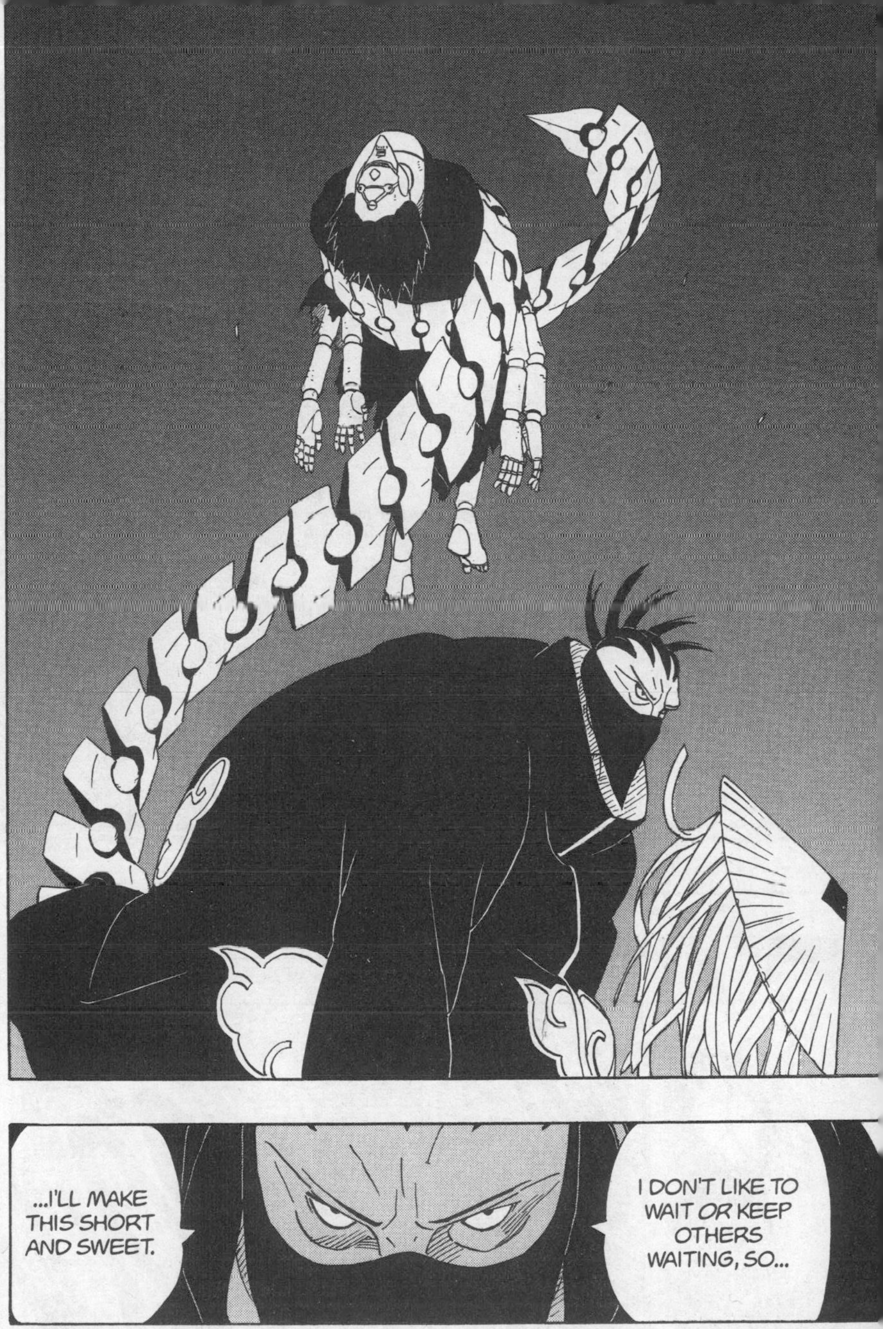
I DON'T LIKE TO WAIT OR KEEP OTHERS WAITING, SO...
...I'LL MAKE THIS SHORT AND SWEET.

READ THIS WAY

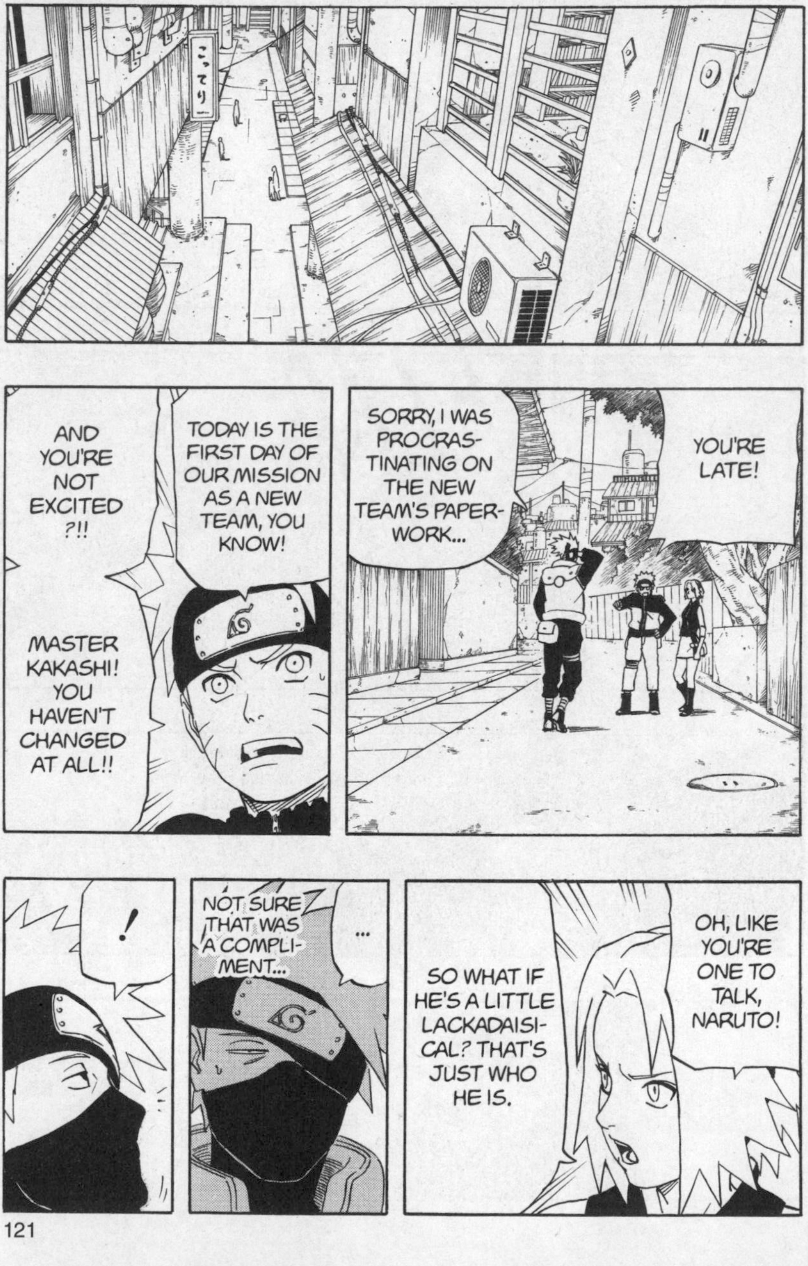
こってり
YOU'RE LATE!
SORRY, I WAS PROCRAS-TINATING ON THE NEW TEAM'S PAPER-WORK...
TODAY IS THE FIRST DAY OF OUR MISSION AS A NEW TEAM, YOU KNOW!
AND YOU'RE NOT EXCITED?!!
MASTER KAKASHI! YOU HAVEN'T CHANGED AT ALL!!
OH, LIKE YOU'RE ONE TO TALK, NARUTO!
SO WHAT IF HE'S A LITTLE LACKADAISI-CAL? THAT'S JUST WHO HE IS.
...
NOT SURE THAT WAS A COMPLI-MENT...
!

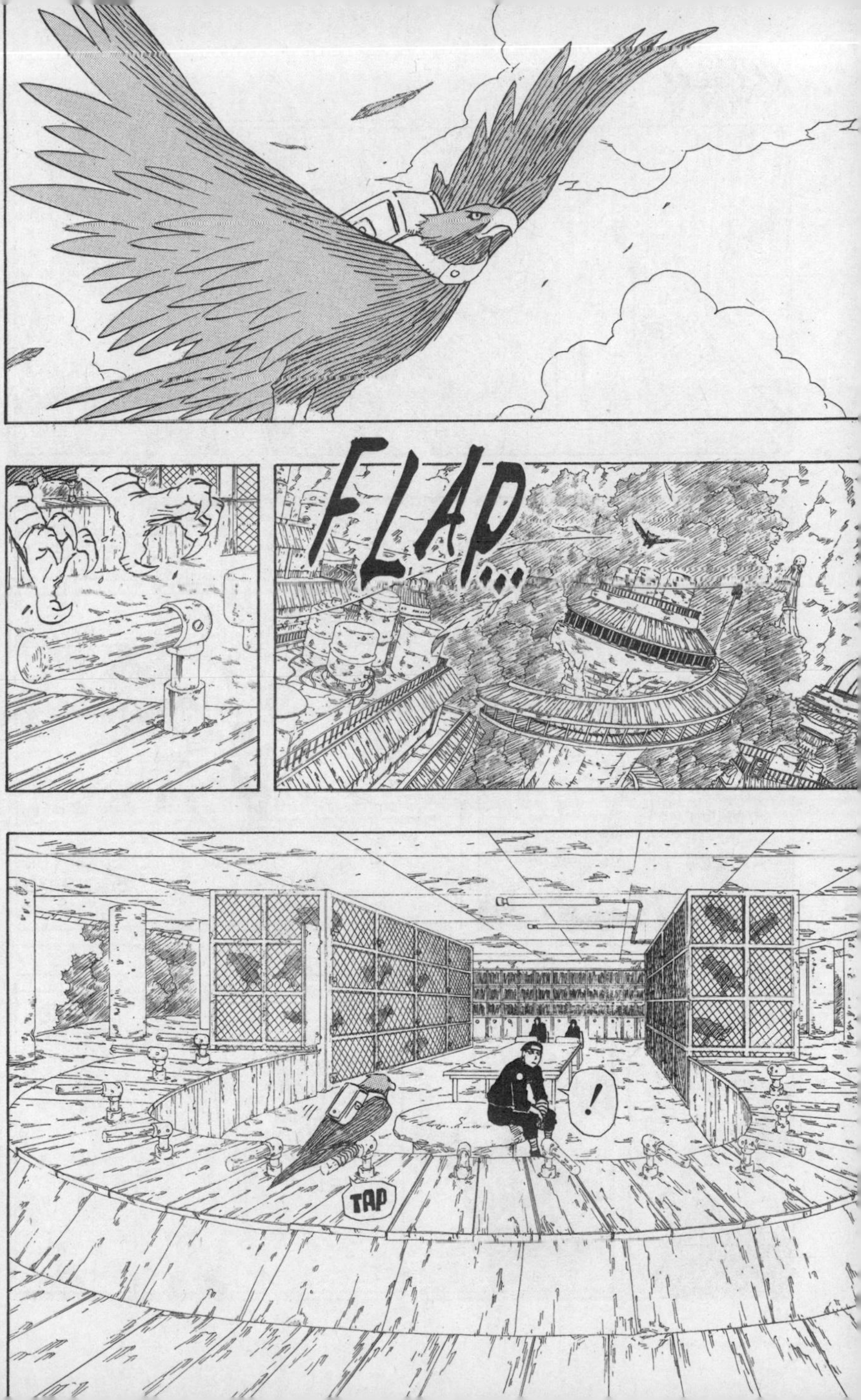
FLAP...
!
TAP

READ THIS WAY

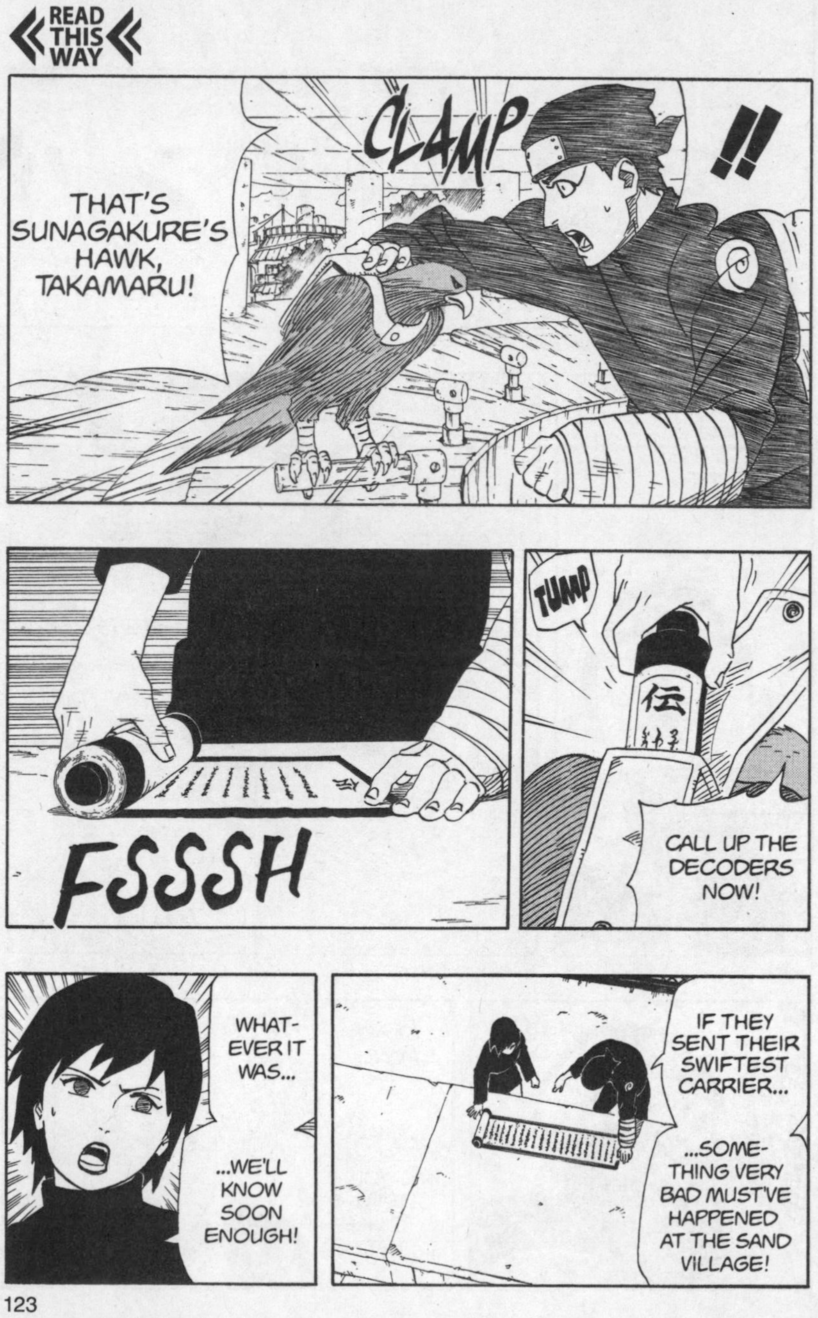
CLAMP
!!
THAT'S SUNAGAKURE'S HAWK, TAKAMARU!
TUMP
CALL UP THE DECODERS NOW!
FSSSH
IF THEY SENT THEIR SWIFTEST CARRIER...
...SOME-THING VERY BAD MUST'VE HAPPENED AT THE SAND VILLAGE!
WHAT-EVER IT WAS...
...WE'LL KNOW SOON ENOUGH!

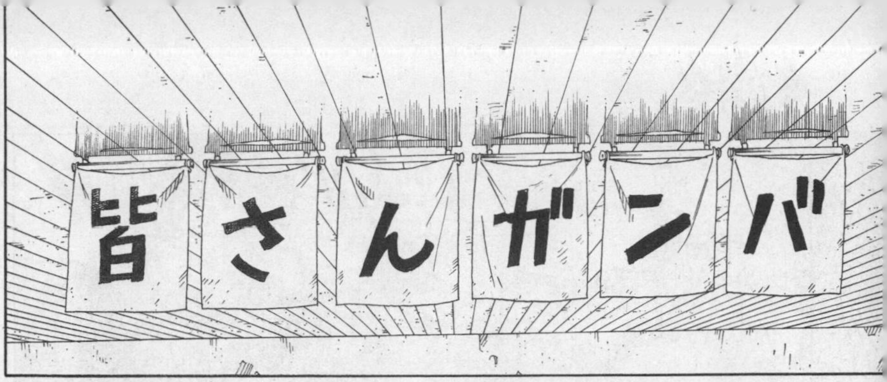

皆さんガンバ

(Banner: Everyone, Good Luck)

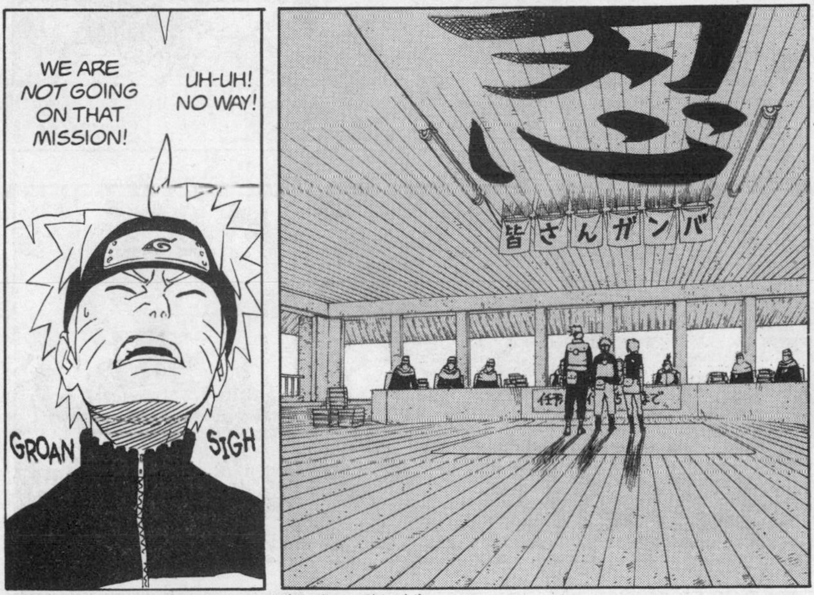

忍
皆さんガンバ
UH-UH! NO WAY!
WE ARE NOT GOING ON THAT MISSION!
SIGH
GROAN

(Ceiling: Shinobi)

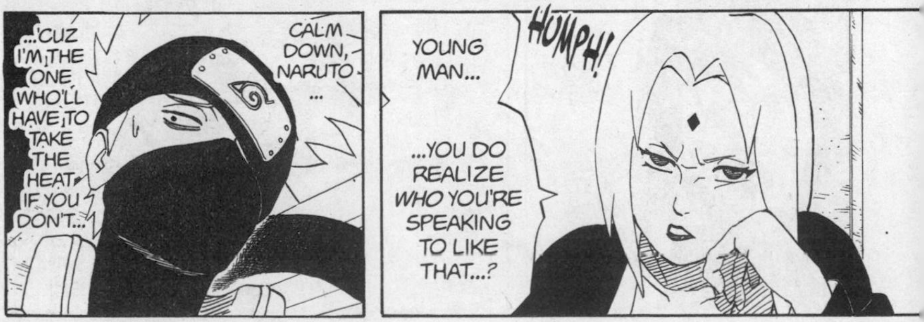

HUMPH!
YOUNG MAN...
...YOU DO REALIZE WHO YOU'RE SPEAKING TO LIKE THAT...?
CALM DOWN, NARUTO...
...'CUZ I'M THE ONE WHO'LL HAVE TO TAKE THE HEAT IF YOU DON'T...

READ THIS WAY

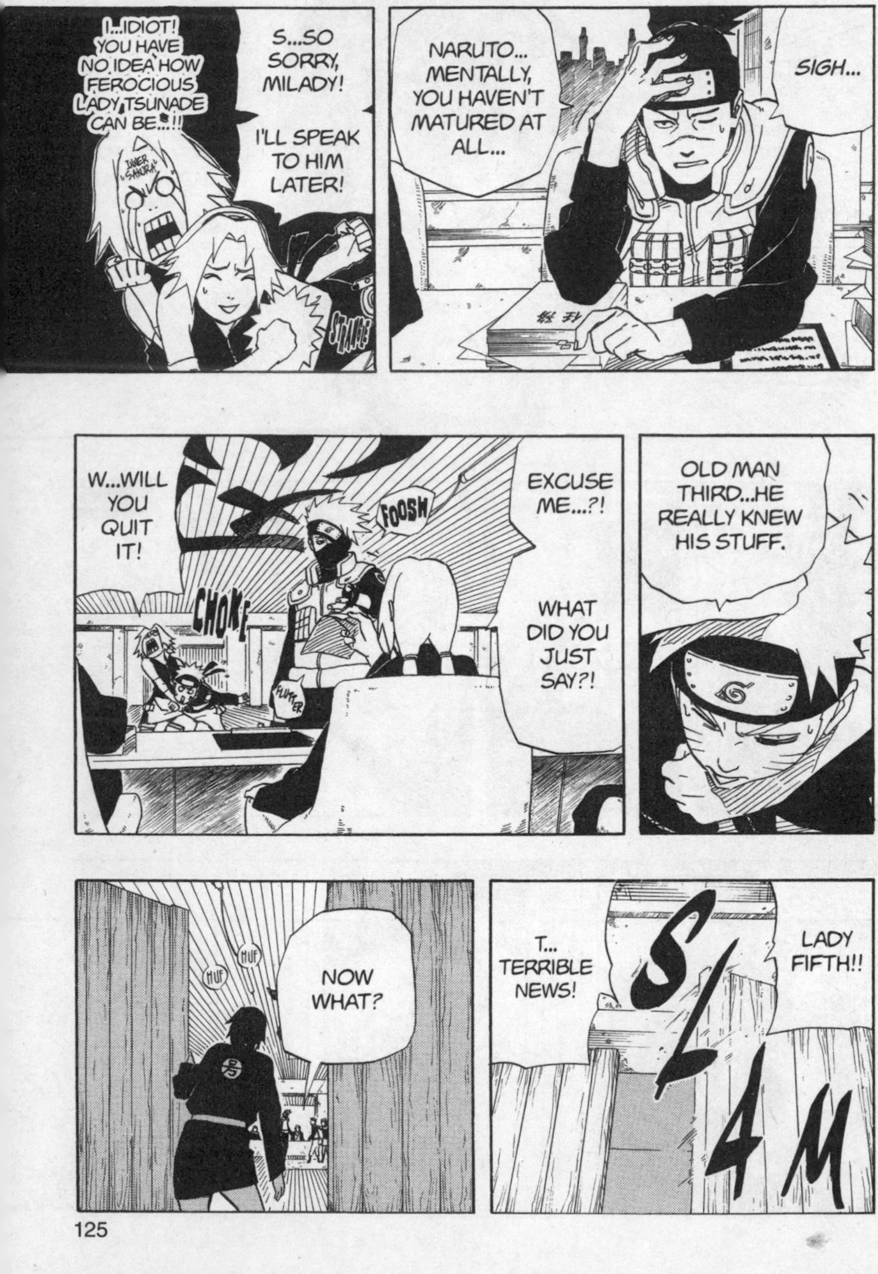
SIGH...
NARUTO... MENTALLY, YOU HAVEN'T MATURED AT ALL...
S...SO SORRY, MILADY!
I'LL SPEAK TO HIM LATER!
I...IDIOT! YOU HAVE NO IDEA HOW FEROCIOUS LADY TSUNADE CAN BE...!!
INNER SAKURA
STRAIN
OLD MAN THIRD...HE REALLY KNEW HIS STUFF.
EXCUSE ME...?!
WHAT DID YOU JUST SAY?!
FOOSH
W...WILL YOU QUIT IT!
CHOKE
FLUTTER
LADY FIFTH!!
SLAM
T... TERRIBLE NEWS!
NOW WHAT?
HUF
HUF

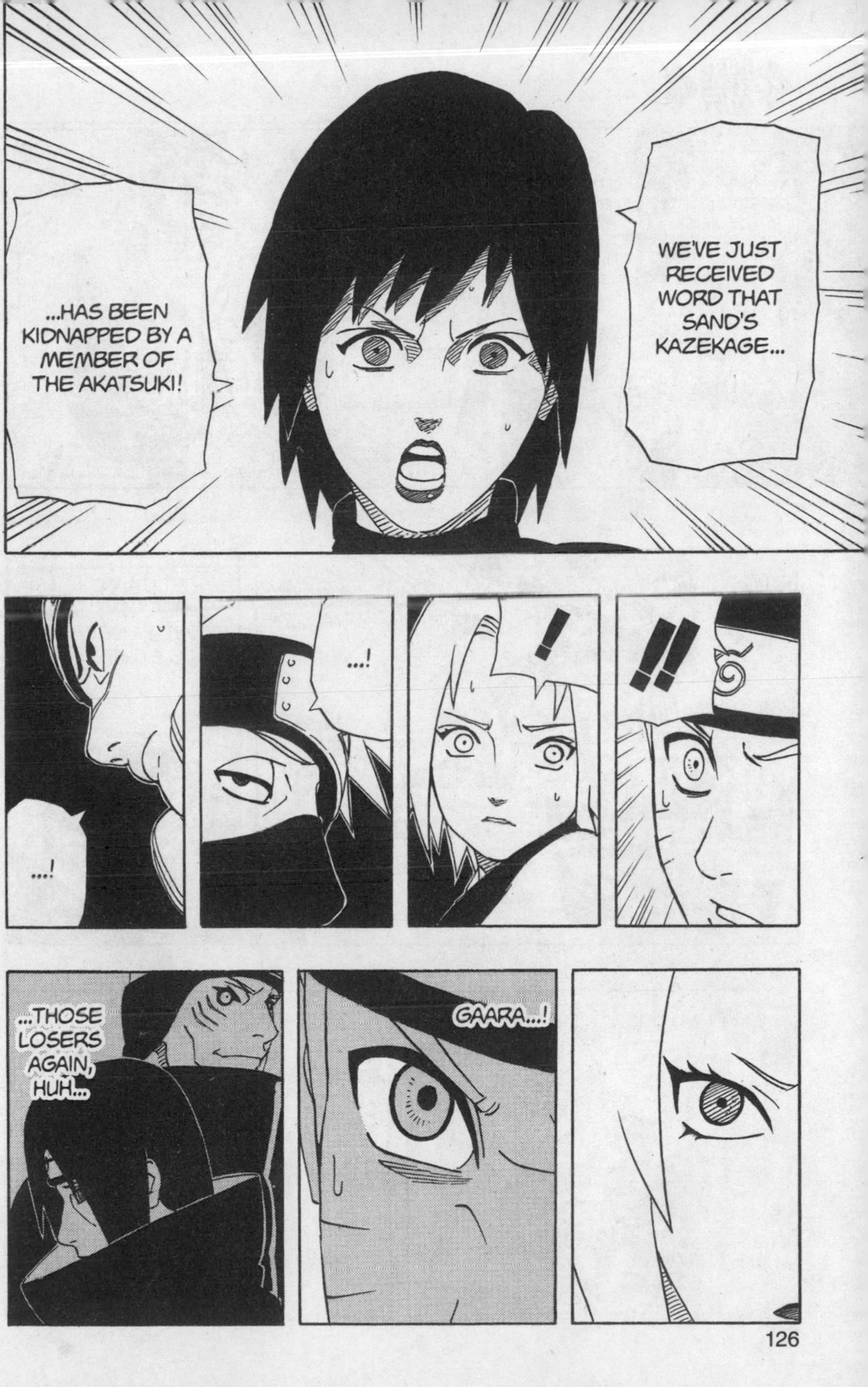
WE'VE JUST RECEIVED WORD THAT SAND'S KAZEKAGE...
...HAS BEEN KIDNAPPED BY A MEMBER OF THE AKATSUKI!
!!
!
...!
...!
GAARA...!
...THOSE LOSERS AGAIN, HUH...

READ THIS WAY

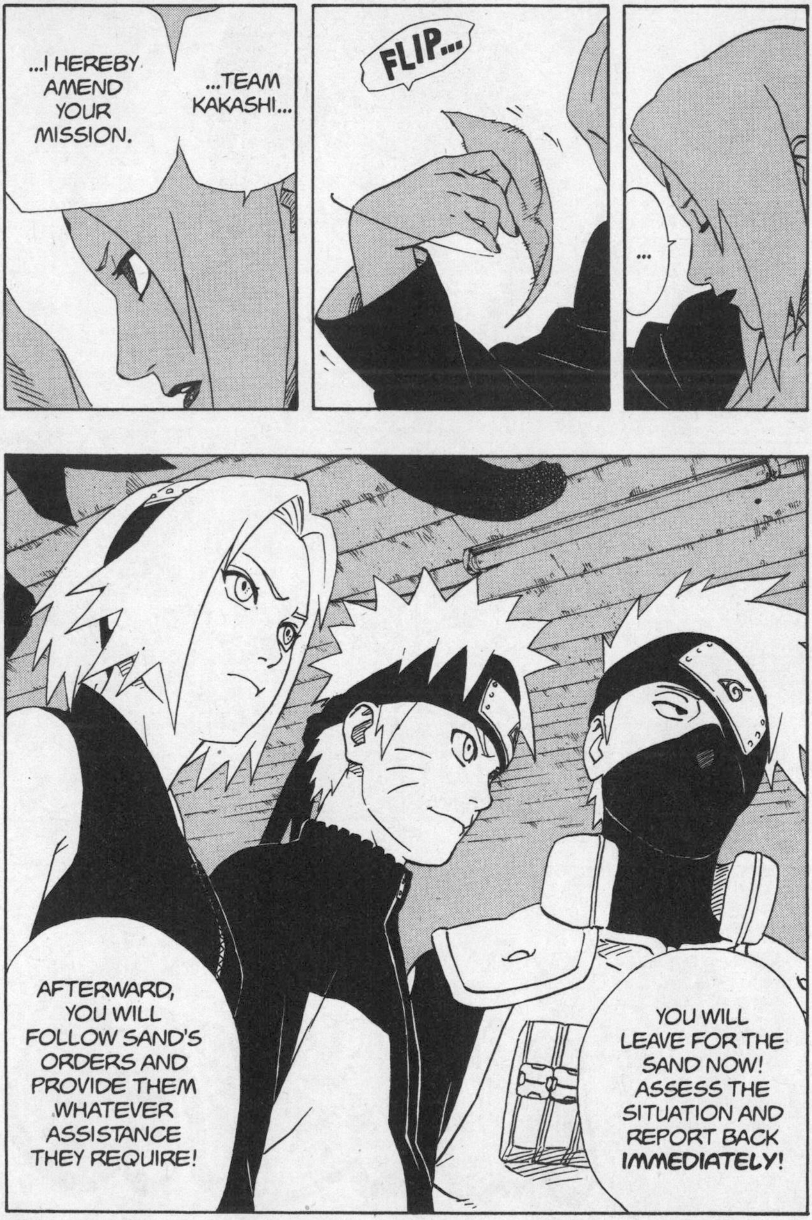
...
FLIP...
...TEAM KAKASHI...
...I HEREBY AMEND YOUR MISSION.
YOU WILL LEAVE FOR THE SAND NOW! ASSESS THE SITUATION AND REPORT BACK **IMMEDIATELY**!
AFTERWARD, YOU WILL FOLLOW SAND'S ORDERS AND PROVIDE THEM WHATEVER ASSISTANCE THEY REQUIRE!

NARUTO

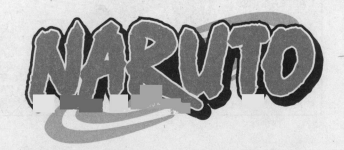

Number 251: To the Sand...!!

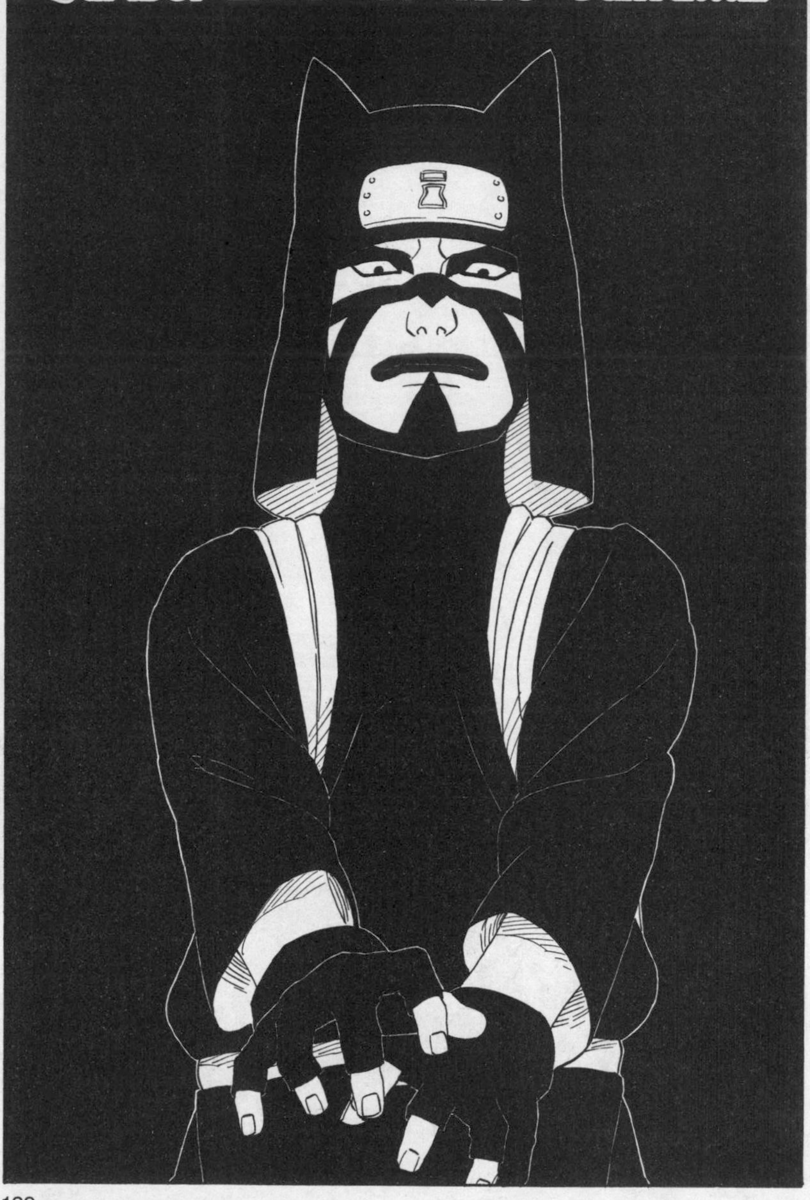

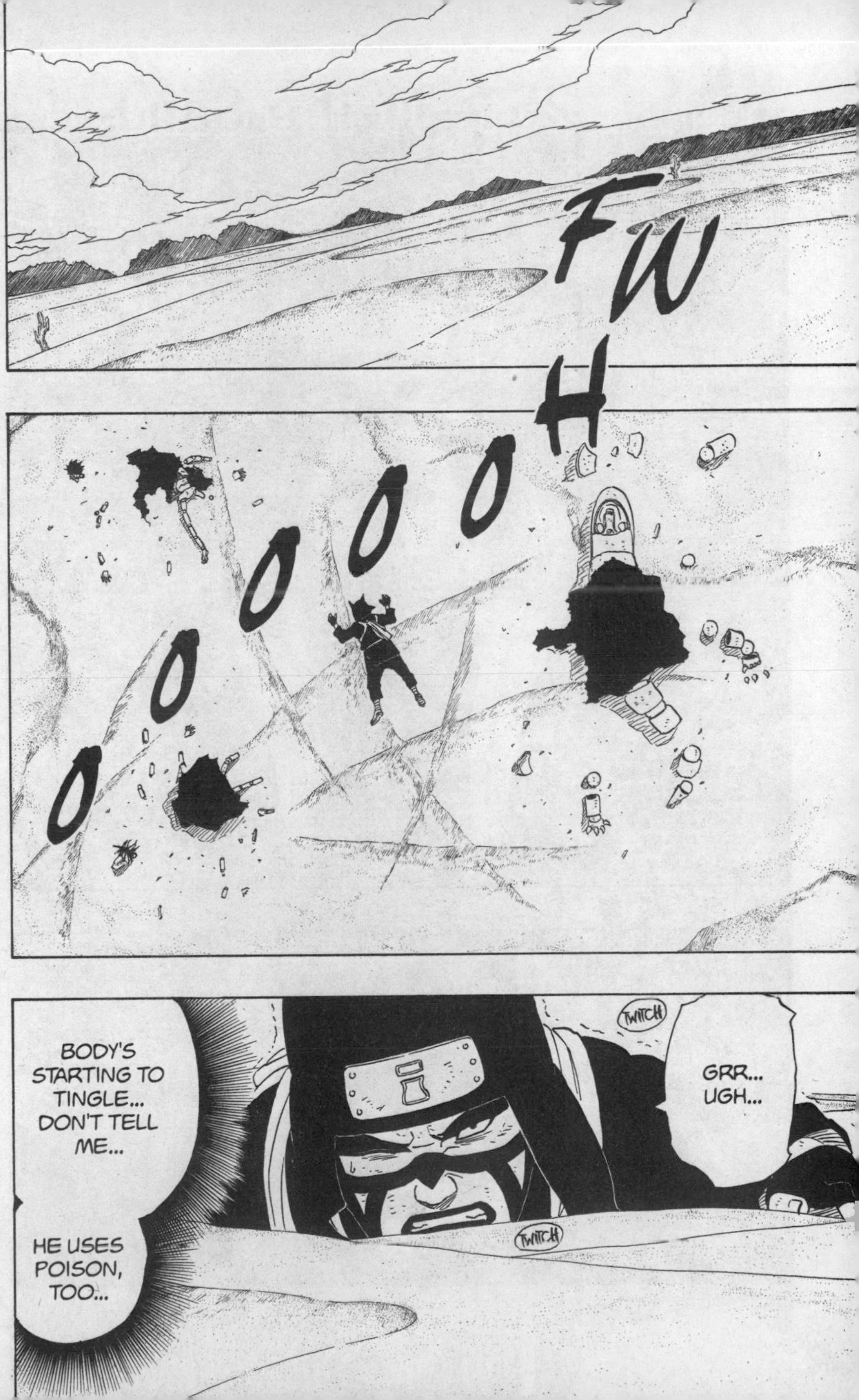
FWOOOOOH
TWITCH
GRR... UGH...
BODY'S STARTING TO TINGLE... DON'T TELL ME...
HE USES POISON, TOO...
TWITCH

READ THIS WAY

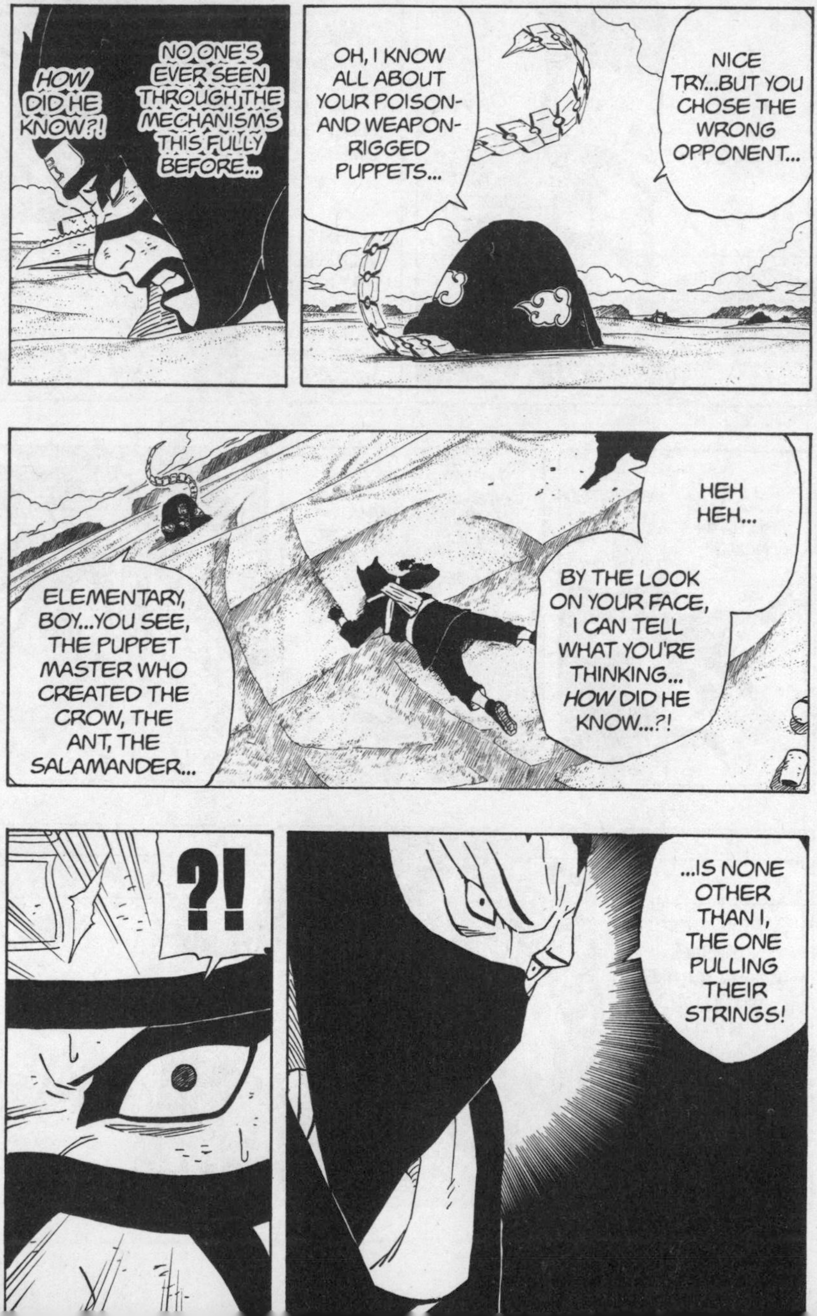
NICE TRY...BUT YOU CHOSE THE WRONG OPPONENT...
OH, I KNOW ALL ABOUT YOUR POISON- AND WEAPON-RIGGED PUPPETS...
NO ONE'S EVER SEEN THROUGH THE MECHANISMS THIS FULLY BEFORE...
HOW DID HE KNOW?!
HEH HEH...
BY THE LOOK ON YOUR FACE, I CAN TELL WHAT YOU'RE THINKING... HOW DID HE KNOW...?!
ELEMENTARY, BOY...YOU SEE, THE PUPPET MASTER WHO CREATED THE CROW, THE ANT, THE SALAMANDER...
...IS NONE OTHER THAN I, THE ONE PULLING THEIR STRINGS!
?!

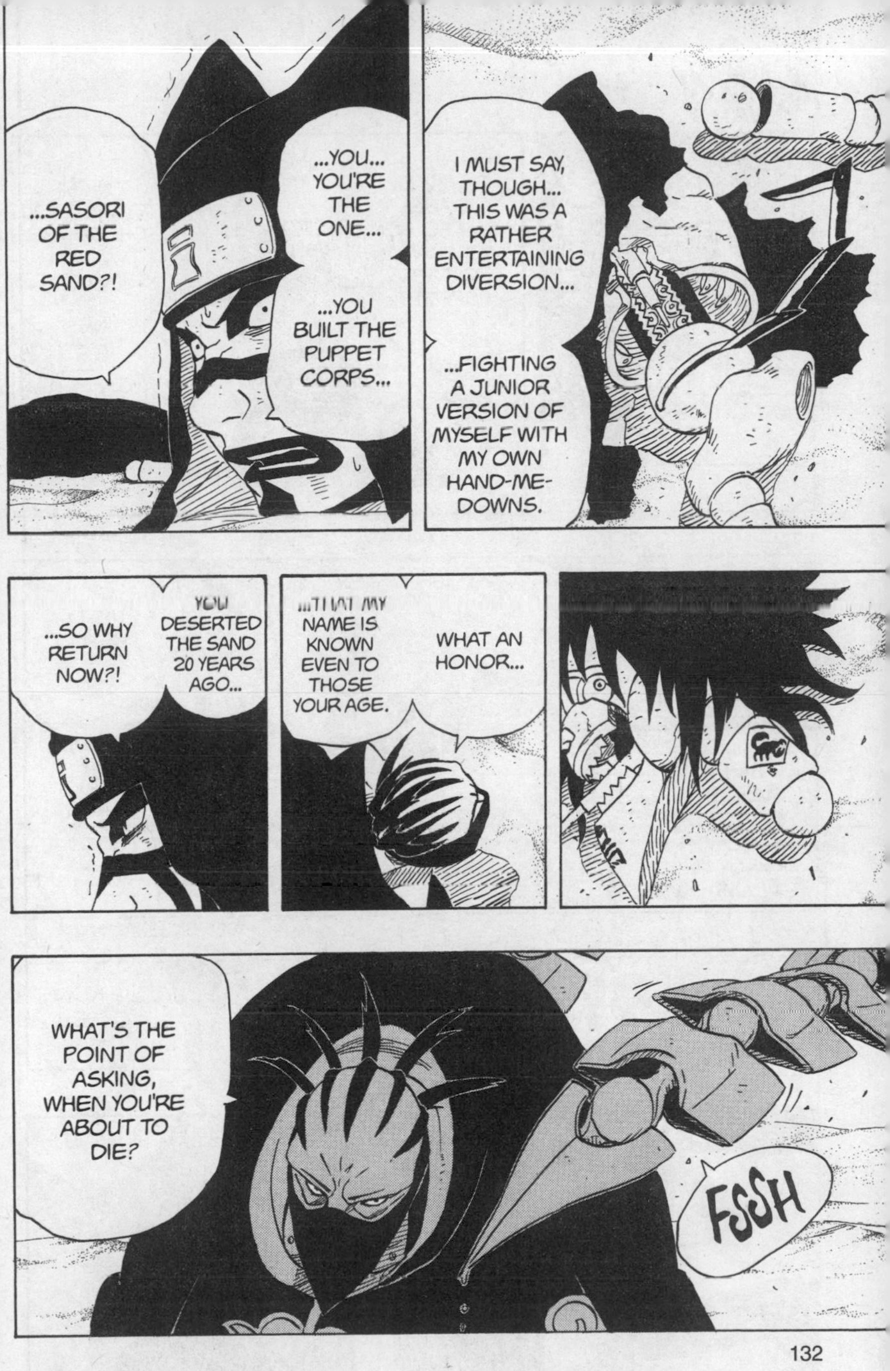
I MUST SAY, THOUGH... THIS WAS A RATHER ENTERTAINING DIVERSION...
...FIGHTING A JUNIOR VERSION OF MYSELF WITH MY OWN HAND-ME-DOWNS.
...YOU... YOU'RE THE ONE...
...YOU BUILT THE PUPPET CORPS...
...SASORI OF THE RED SAND?!
WHAT AN HONOR...
...THAT MY NAME IS KNOWN EVEN TO THOSE YOUR AGE.
YOU DESERTED THE SAND 20 YEARS AGO...
...SO WHY RETURN NOW?!
FSSH
WHAT'S THE POINT OF ASKING, WHEN YOU'RE ABOUT TO DIE?

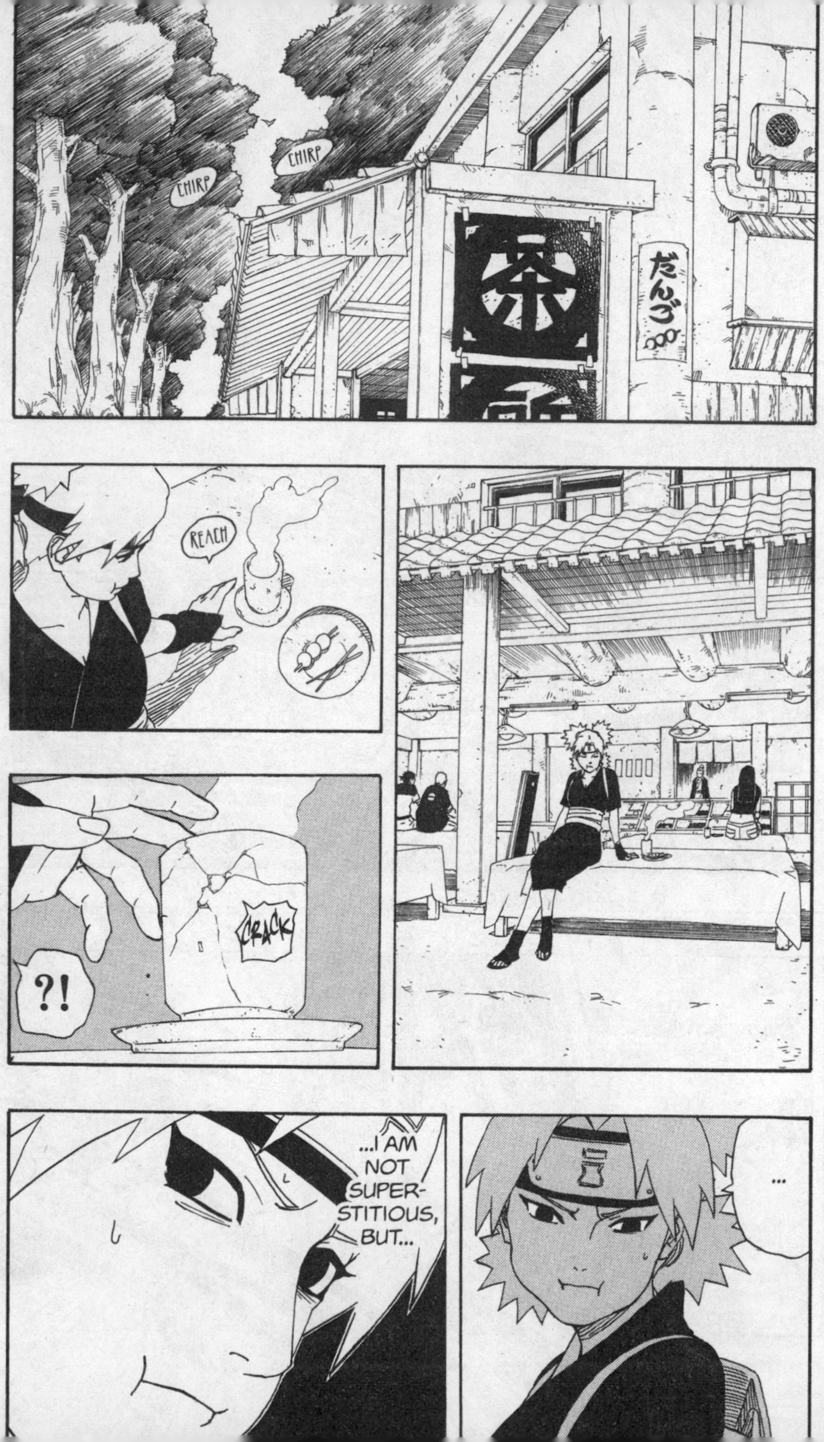
CHIRP
CHIRP
茶
だんご
REACH
CRACK
?!
...
...I AM NOT SUPER-STITIOUS, BUT...

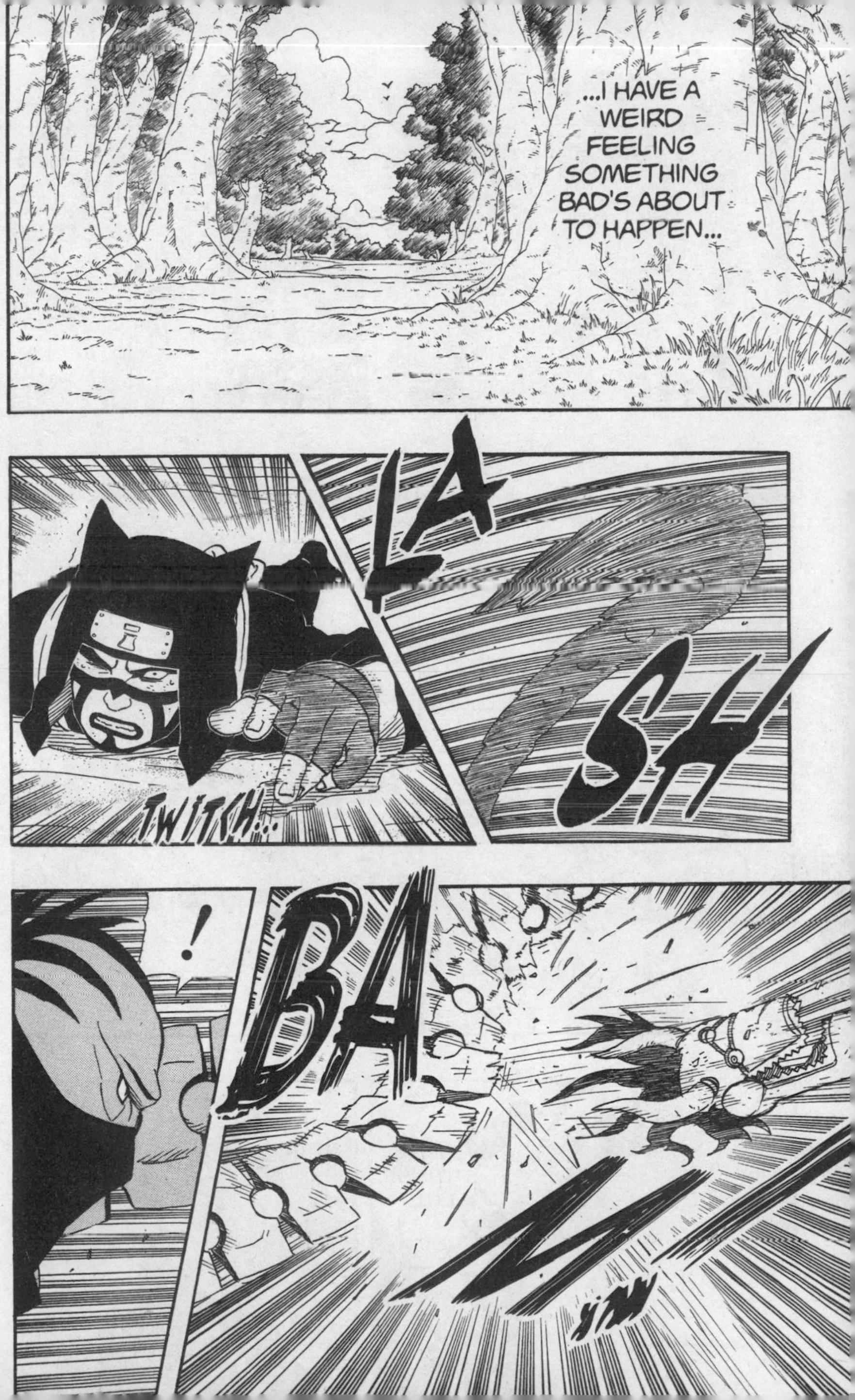
...I HAVE A WEIRD FEELING SOMETHING BAD'S ABOUT TO HAPPEN...
LASH
TWITCH...
BAN
!

READ THIS WAY

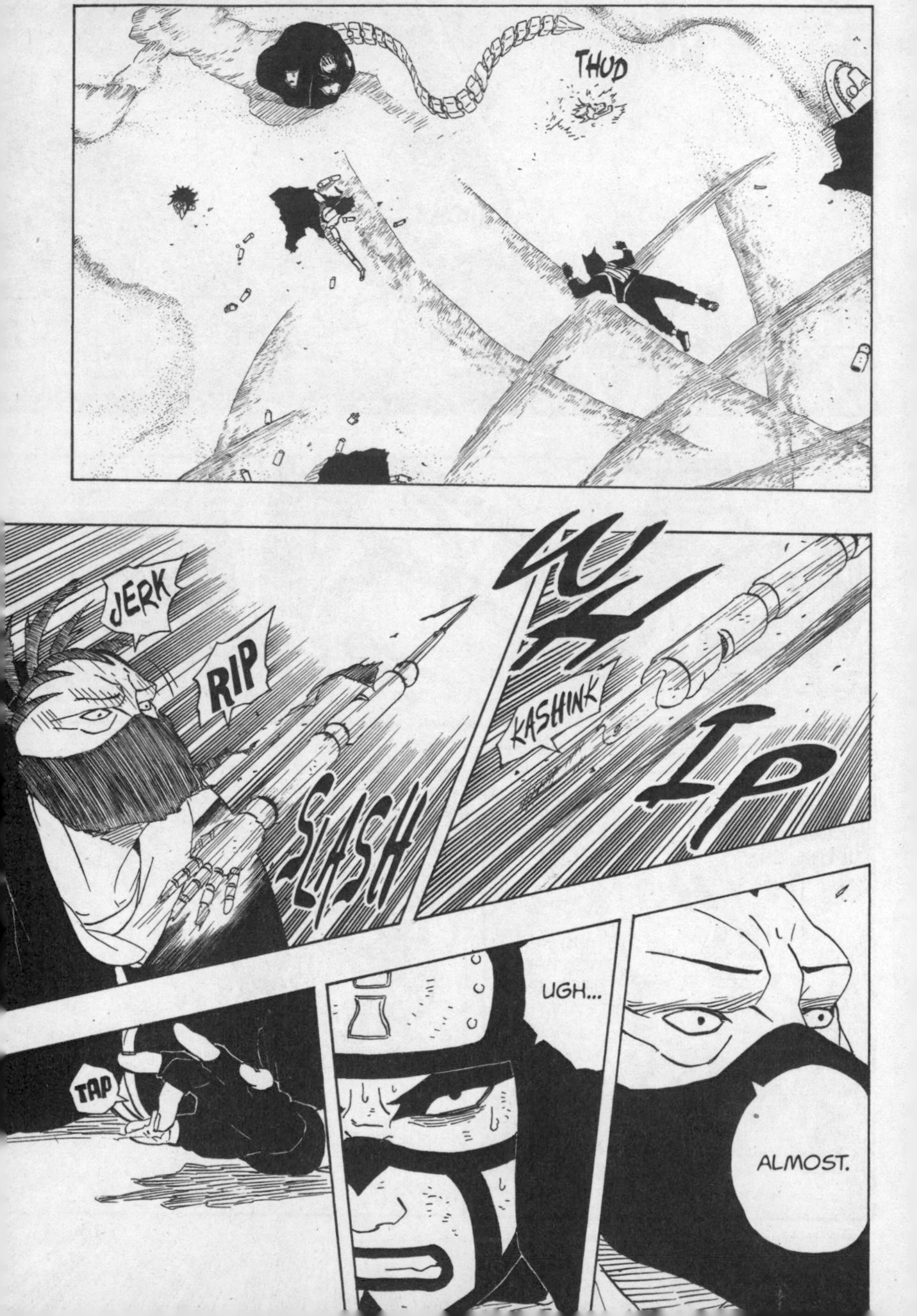
THUD
KASHINK
JERK
RIP
SLASH
ALMOST.
UGH...
TAP

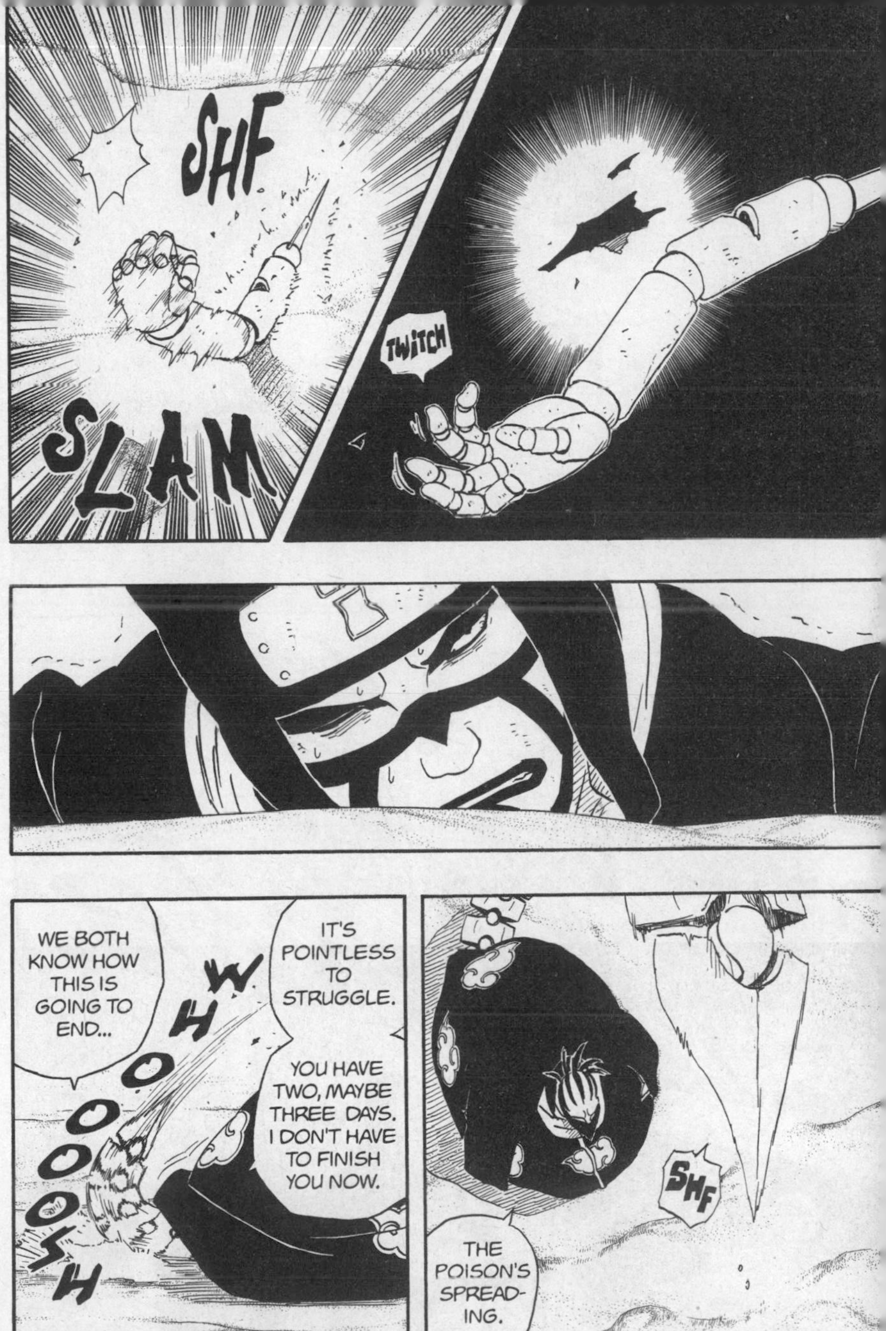
TWITCH
SHF
SLAM
SHF
THE POISON'S SPREADING.
IT'S POINTLESS TO STRUGGLE.
YOU HAVE TWO, MAYBE THREE DAYS. I DON'T HAVE TO FINISH YOU NOW.
WE BOTH KNOW HOW THIS IS GOING TO END...
WHOOOOOSH

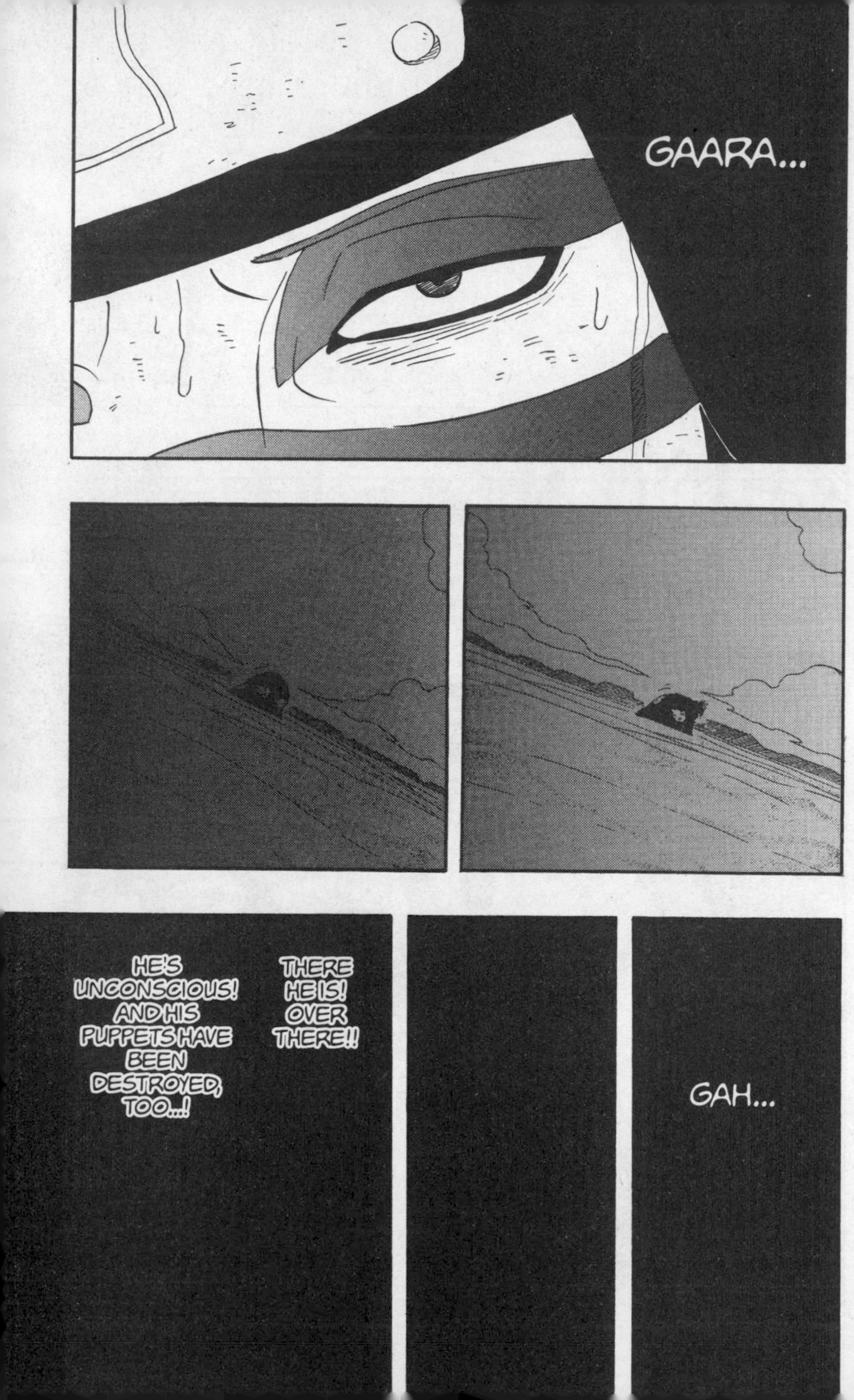
GAARA...
GAH...
THERE HE IS! OVER THERE!!
HE'S UNCONSCIOUS! AND HIS PUPPETS HAVE BEEN DESTROYED, TOO...!

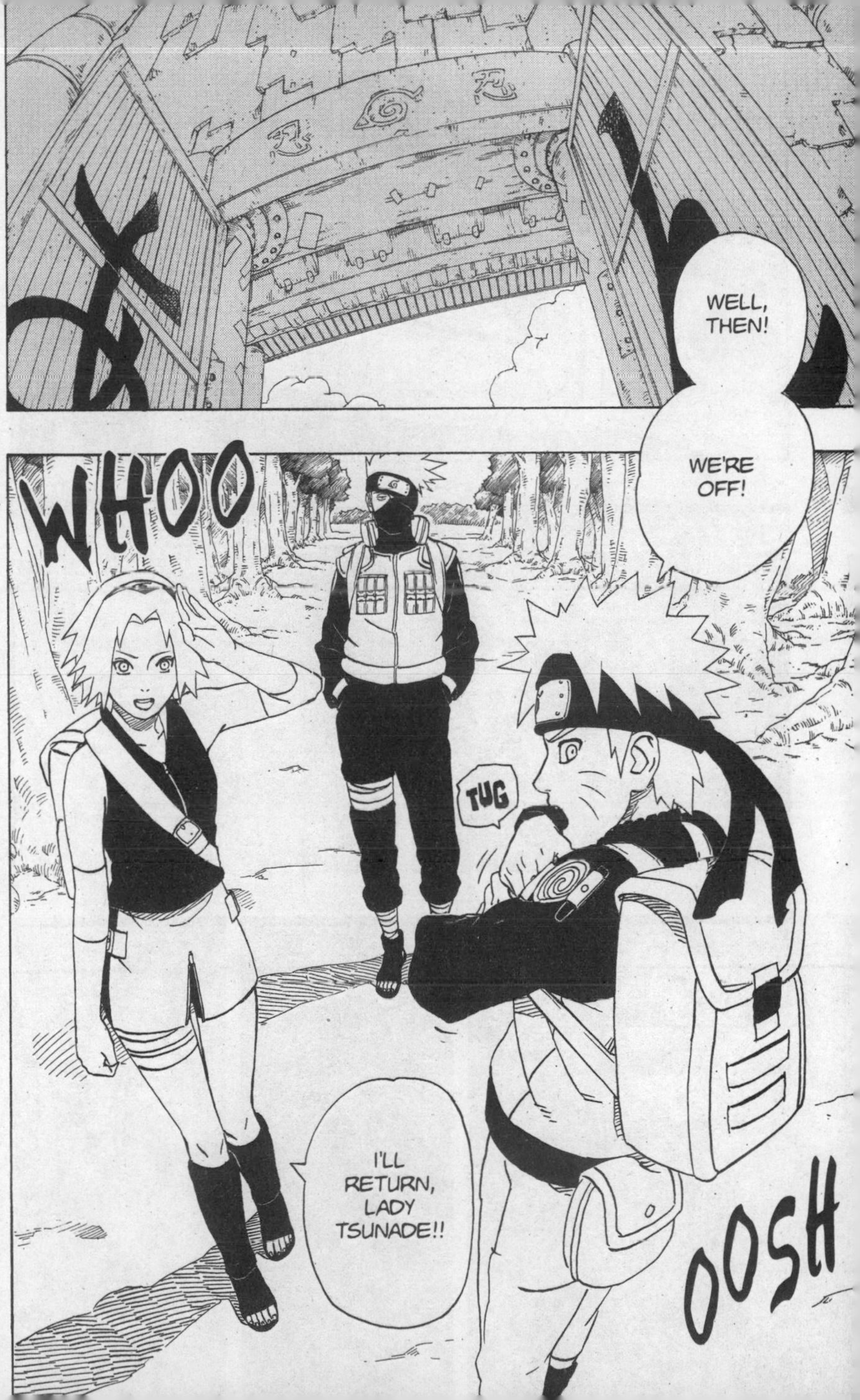
WELL, THEN!
WE'RE OFF!
TUG
WHOO
OOSH
I'LL RETURN, LADY TSUNADE!!

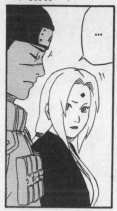

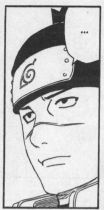

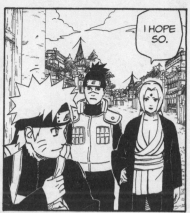

I HOPE SO.

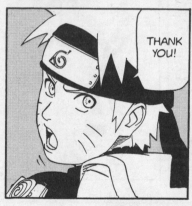

THANK YOU!

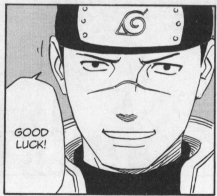

GOOD LUCK!

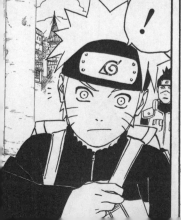

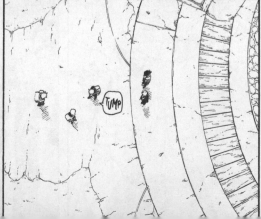

TUMP

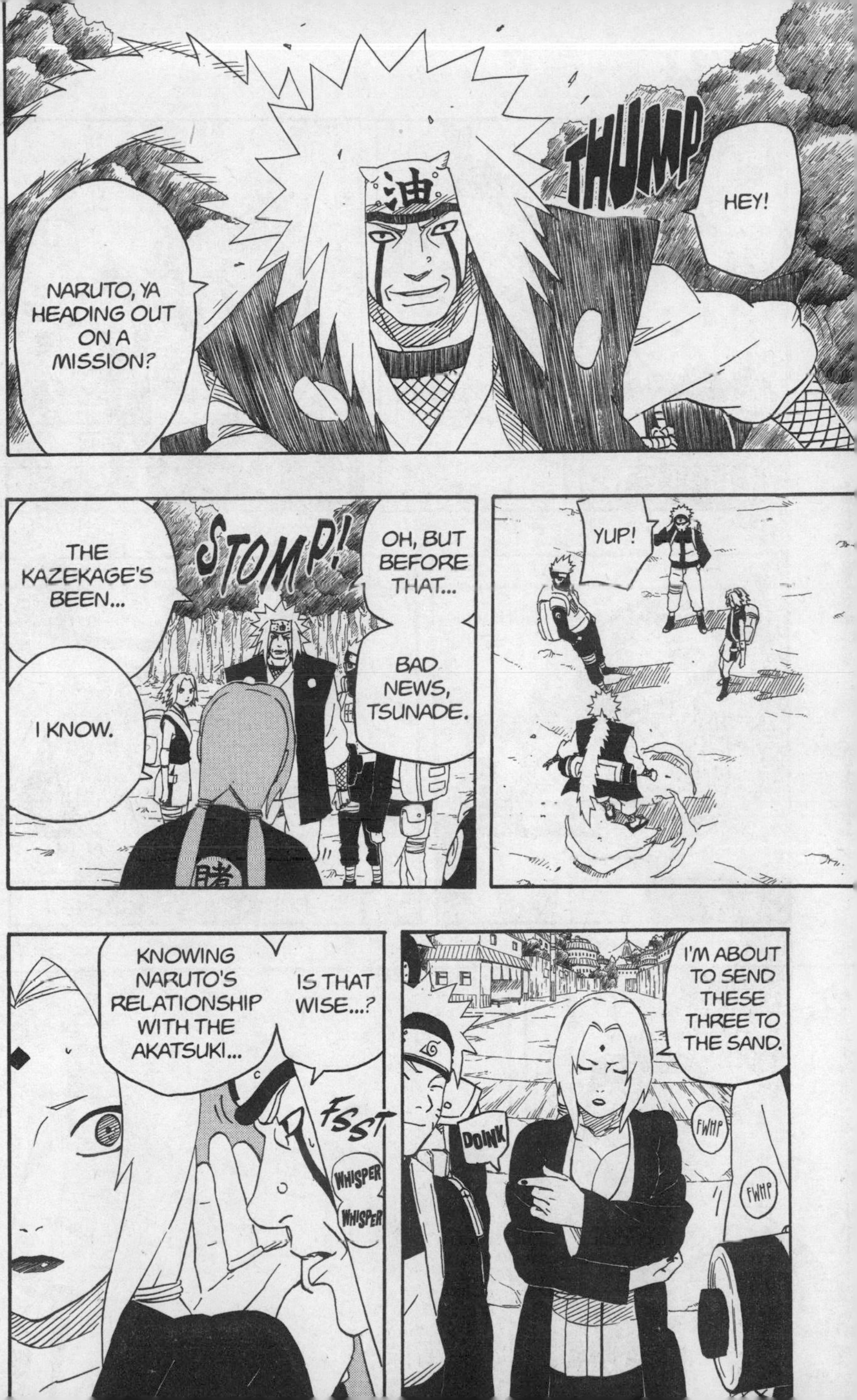
THUMP
HEY!
NARUTO, YA HEADING OUT ON A MISSION?
YUP!
OH, BUT BEFORE THAT...
BAD NEWS, TSUNADE.
STOMP!
THE KAZEKAGE'S BEEN...
I KNOW.
I'M ABOUT TO SEND THESE THREE TO THE SAND.
FWHP
FWHP
DOINK
IS THAT WISE...?
KNOWING NARUTO'S RELATIONSHIP WITH THE AKATSUKI...
FSST
WHISPER
WHISPER

READ THIS WAY

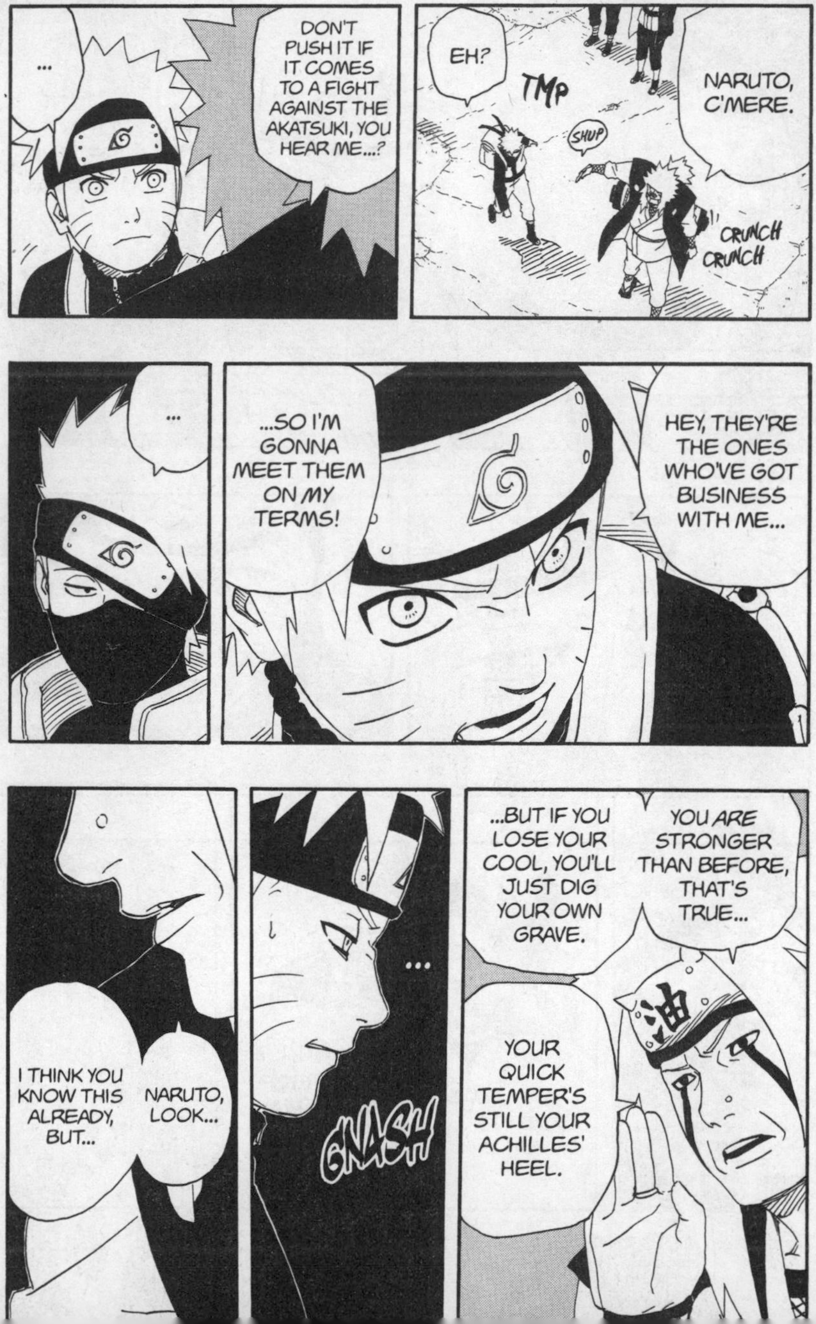
NARUTO, C'MERE.
EH?
TMP
SHUP
CRUNCH CRUNCH
DON'T PUSH IT IF IT COMES TO A FIGHT AGAINST THE AKATSUKI, YOU HEAR ME...?
...
HEY, THEY'RE THE ONES WHO'VE GOT BUSINESS WITH ME...
...SO I'M GONNA MEET THEM ON MY TERMS!
...
YOU ARE STRONGER THAN BEFORE, THAT'S TRUE...
...BUT IF YOU LOSE YOUR COOL, YOU'LL JUST DIG YOUR OWN GRAVE.
YOUR QUICK TEMPER'S STILL YOUR ACHILLES' HEEL.
...
GNASH
NARUTO, LOOK...
I THINK YOU KNOW THIS ALREADY, BUT...

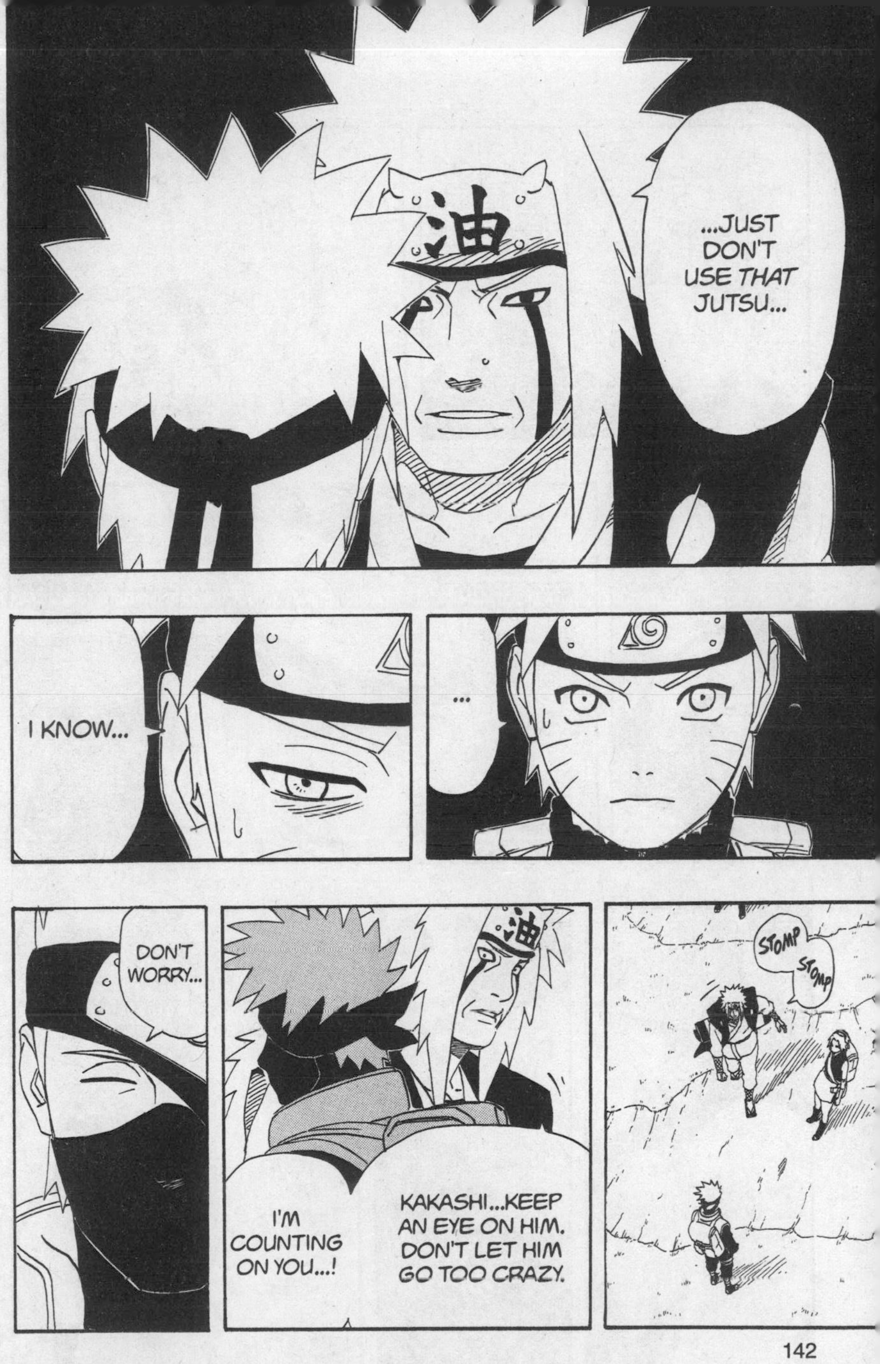
...JUST DON'T USE THAT JUTSU...
...
I KNOW...
STOMP
STOMP
KAKASHI...KEEP AN EYE ON HIM. DON'T LET HIM GO TOO CRAZY.
I'M COUNTING ON YOU...!
DON'T WORRY...

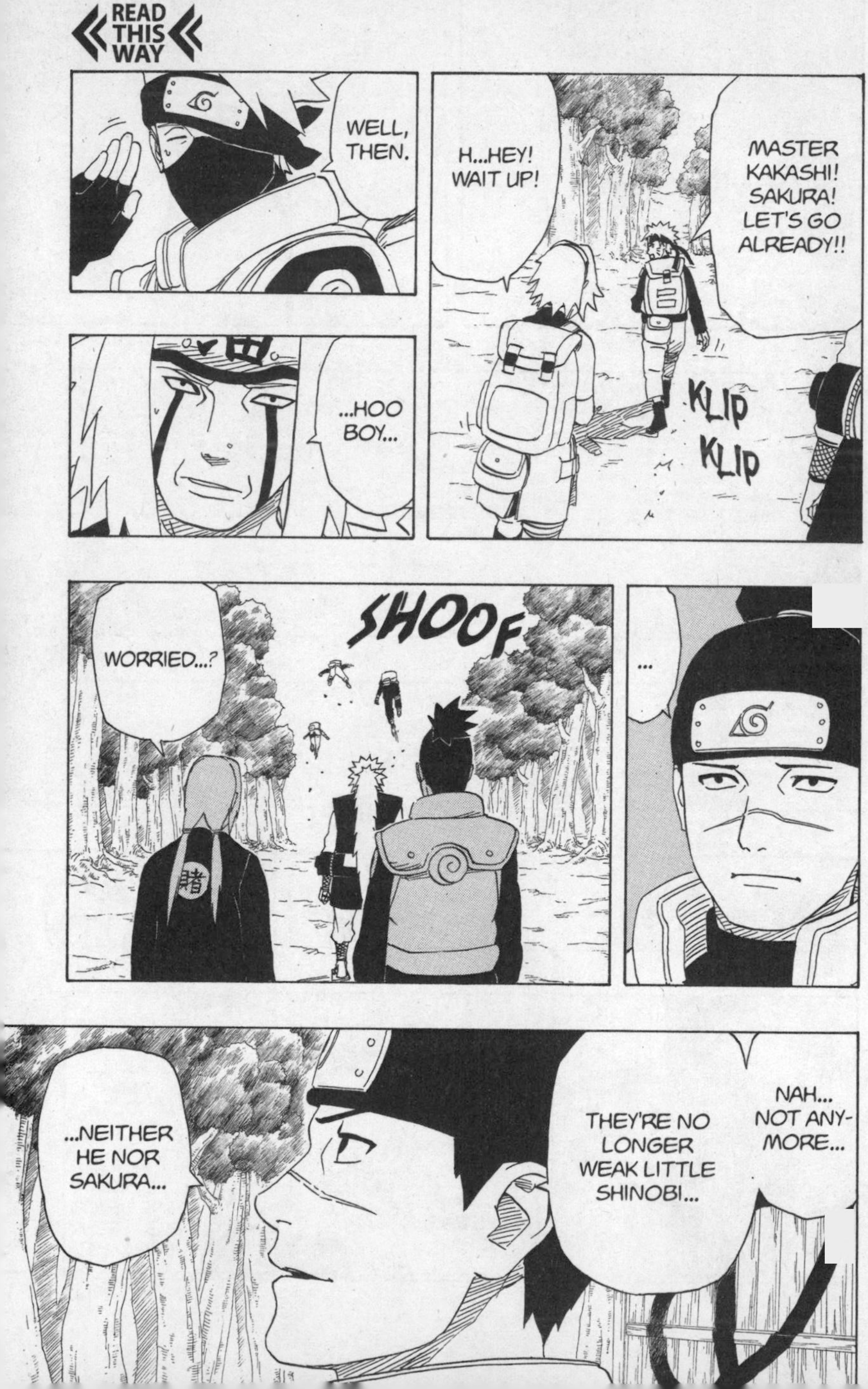
READ THIS WAY
MASTER KAKASHI! SAKURA! LET'S GO ALREADY!!
H...HEY! WAIT UP!
KLIP
KLIP
WELL, THEN.
...HOO BOY...
...
SHOOF
WORRIED...?
NAH... NOT ANY-MORE...
THEY'RE NO LONGER WEAK LITTLE SHINOBI...
...NEITHER HE NOR SAKURA...

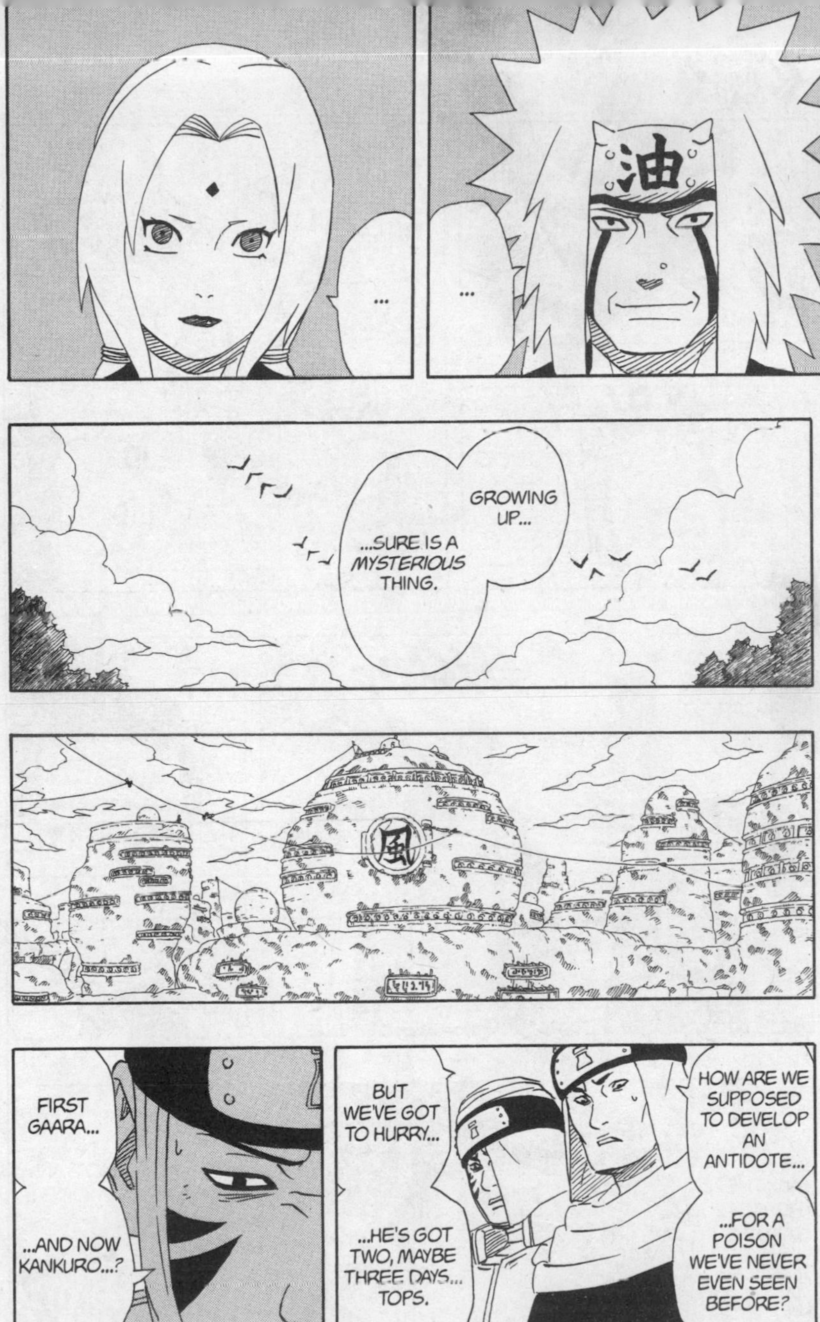
...
...
GROWING UP...
...SURE IS A MYSTERIOUS THING.
HOW ARE WE SUPPOSED TO DEVELOP AN ANTIDOTE...
...FOR A POISON WE'VE NEVER EVEN SEEN BEFORE?
BUT WE'VE GOT TO HURRY...
...HE'S GOT TWO, MAYBE THREE DAYS... TOPS.
FIRST GAARA...
...AND NOW KANKURO...?

READ THIS WAY

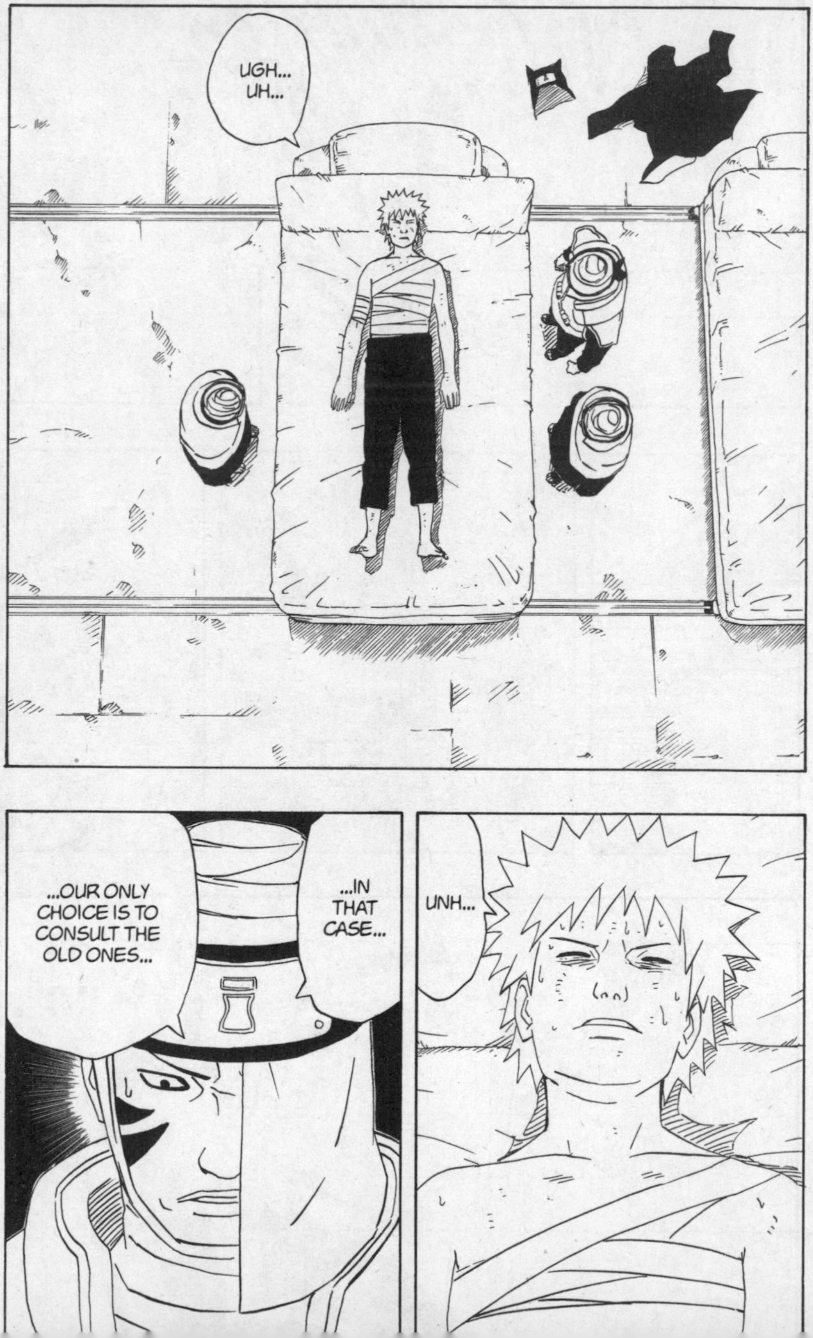
UGH... UH...
UNH...
...IN THAT CASE...
...OUR ONLY CHOICE IS TO CONSULT THE OLD ONES...

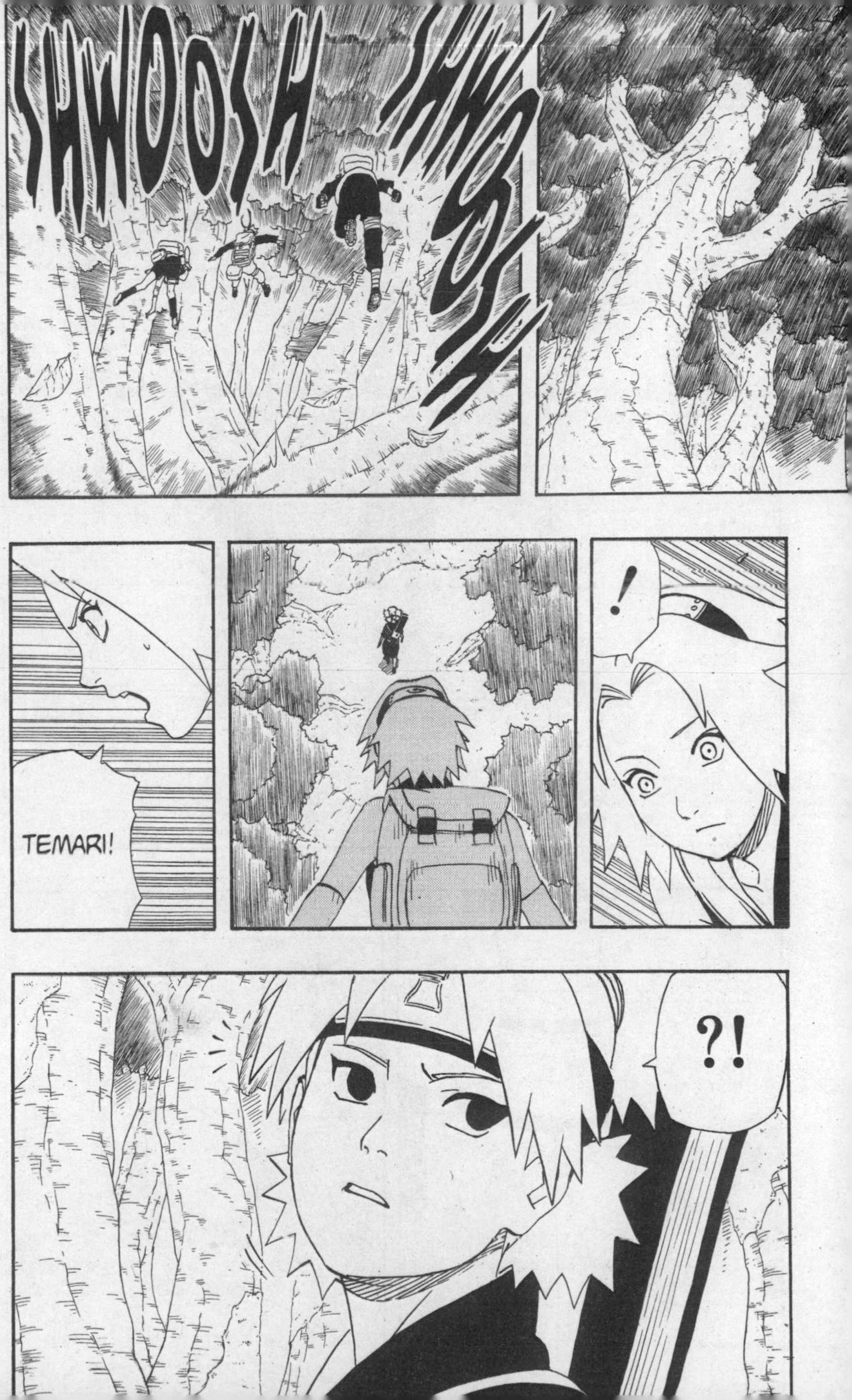
SHWOOSH
SHWOOSH
!
TEMARI!
?!

READ THIS WAY

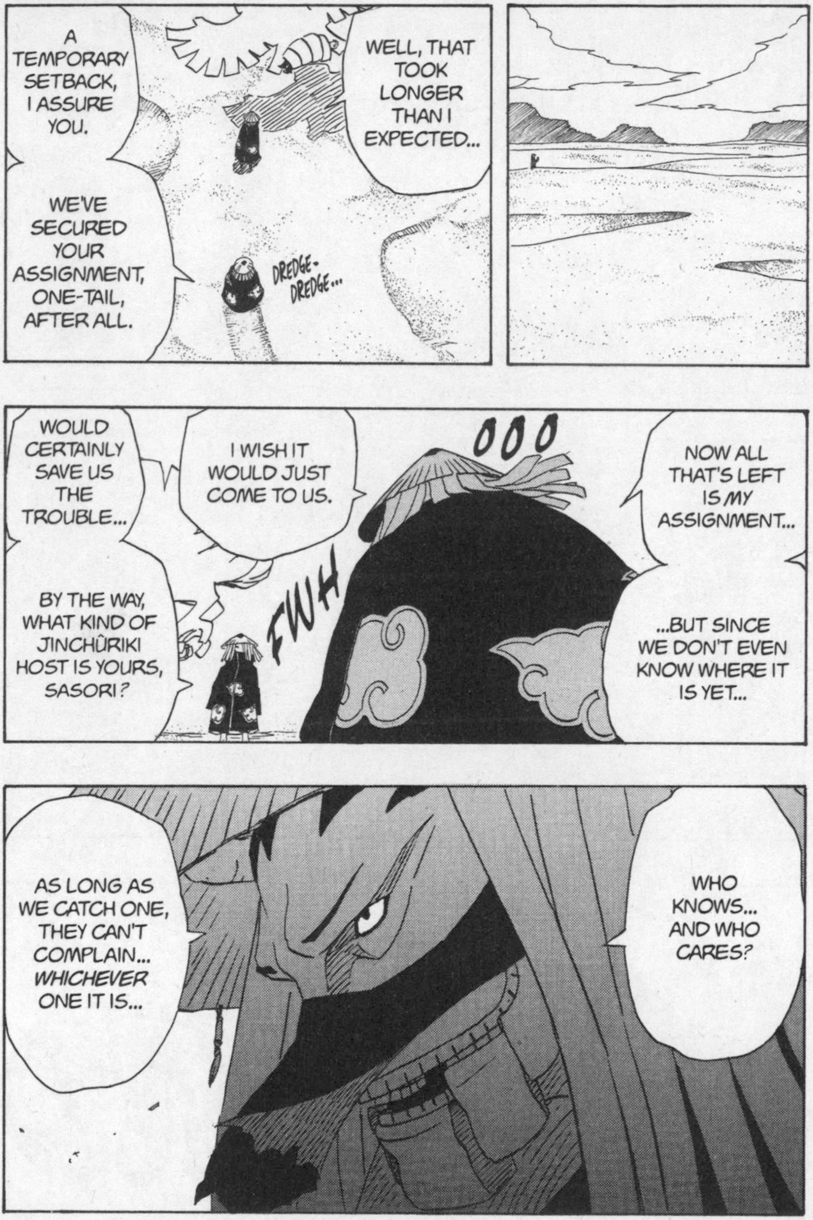
WELL, THAT TOOK LONGER THAN I EXPECTED...
A TEMPORARY SETBACK, I ASSURE YOU.
DREDGE-DREDGE...
WE'VE SECURED YOUR ASSIGNMENT, ONE-TAIL, AFTER ALL.
OOO
NOW ALL THAT'S LEFT IS MY ASSIGNMENT...
...BUT SINCE WE DON'T EVEN KNOW WHERE IT IS YET...
FWH
I WISH IT WOULD JUST COME TO US.
WOULD CERTAINLY SAVE US THE TROUBLE...
BY THE WAY, WHAT KIND OF JINCHÛRIKI HOST IS YOURS, SASORI?
WHO KNOWS... AND WHO CARES?
AS LONG AS WE CATCH ONE, THEY CAN'T COMPLAIN... *WHICHEVER* ONE IT IS...

NARUTO

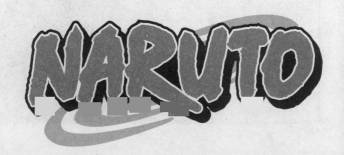

Number 252: Feelings Run Wild...!!

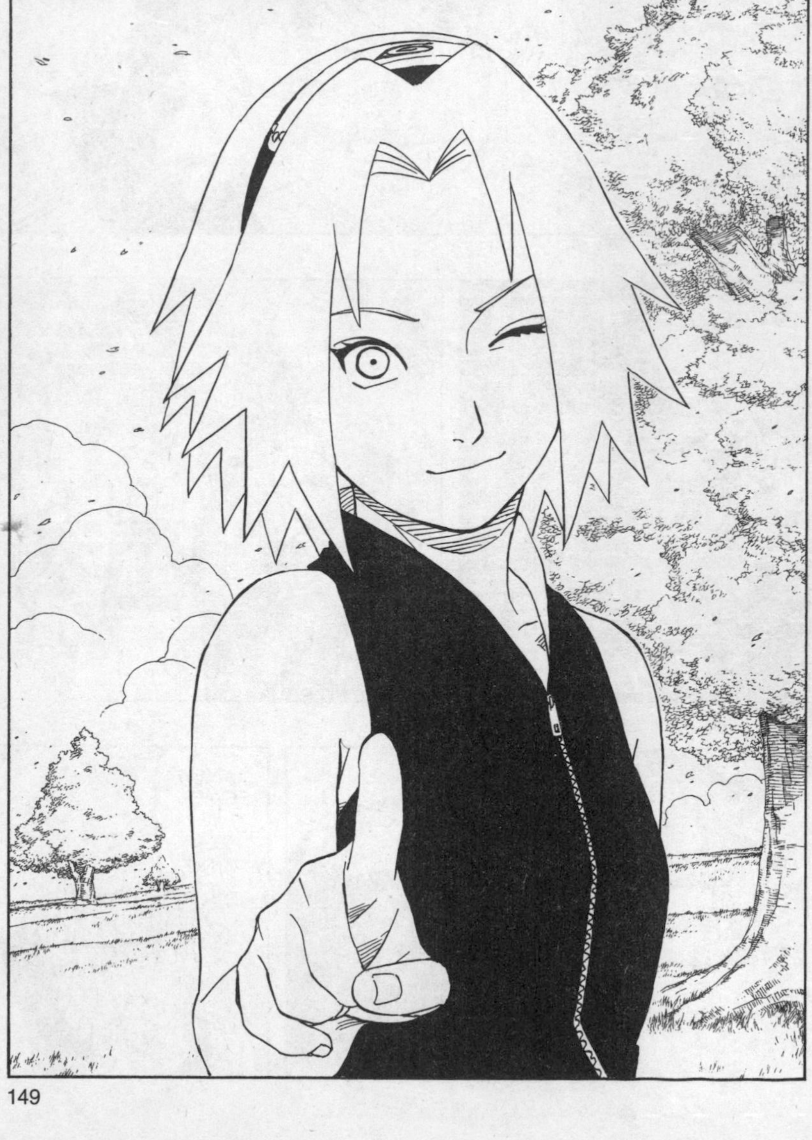

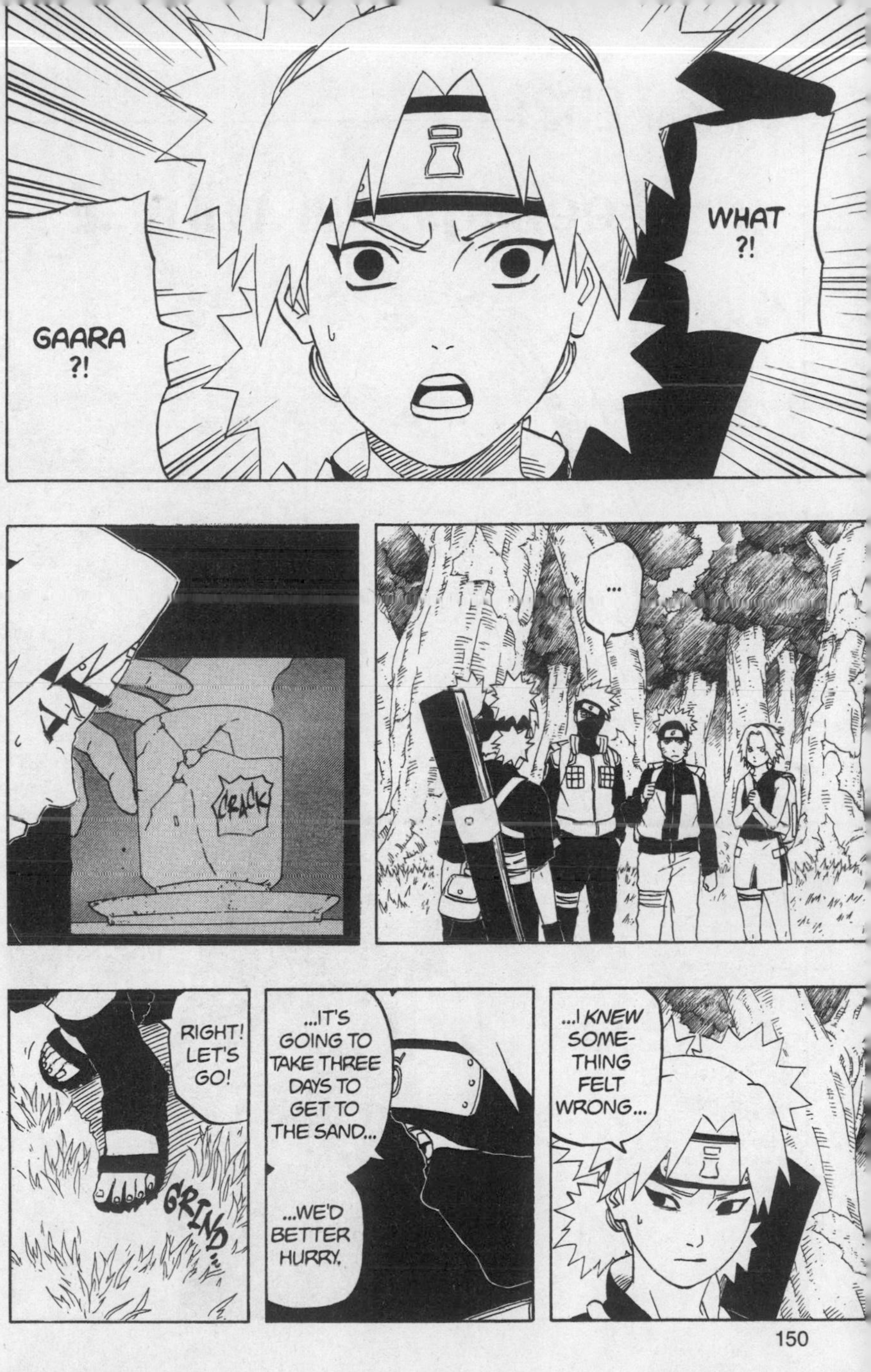
WHAT ?!
GAARA ?!
...
CRACK
...I KNEW SOME-THING FELT WRONG...
...IT'S GOING TO TAKE THREE DAYS TO GET TO THE SAND...
...WE'D BETTER HURRY.
RIGHT! LET'S GO!
GRIND...

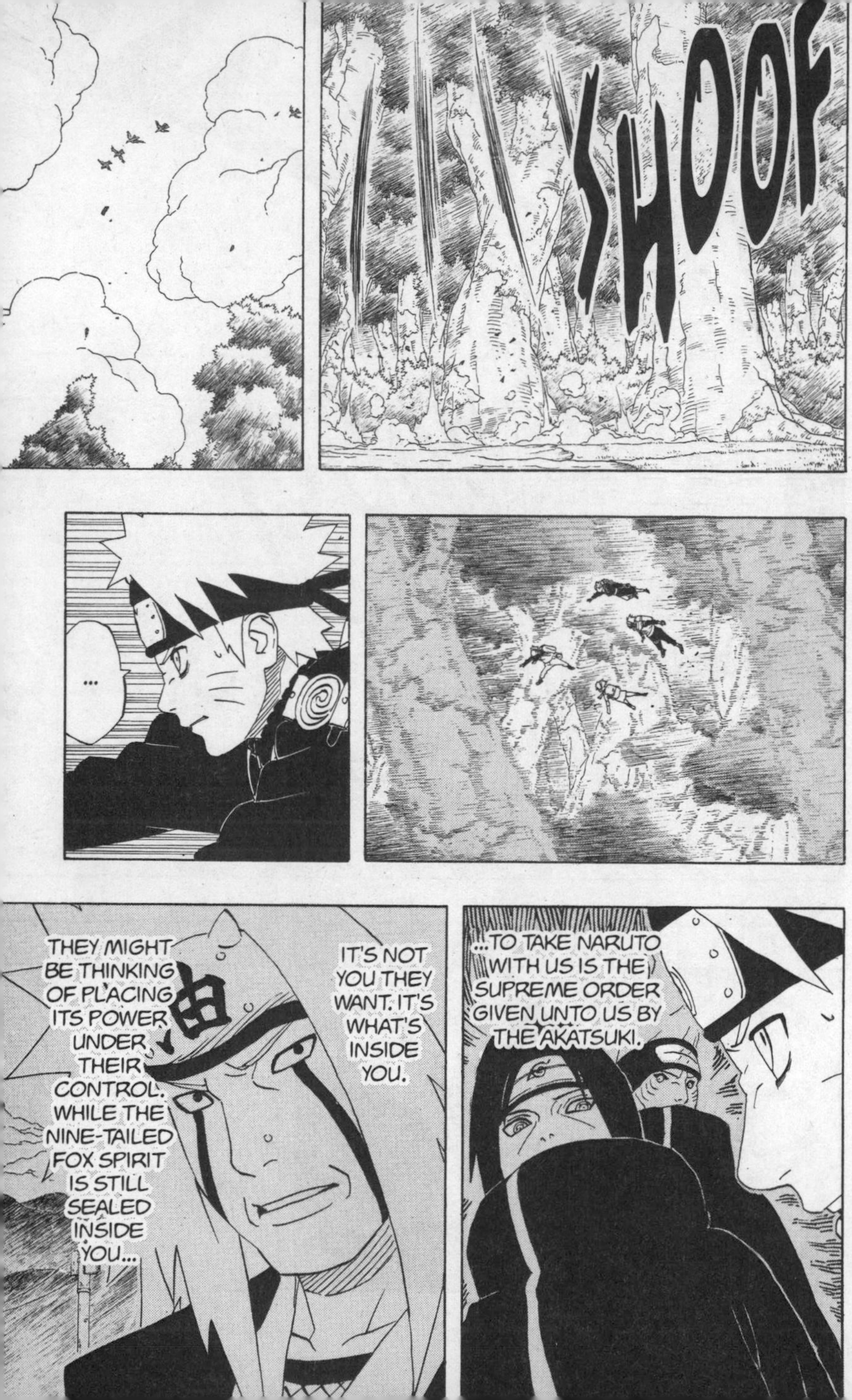
SHOOF
...
...TO TAKE NARUTO WITH US IS THE SUPREME ORDER GIVEN UNTO US BY THE AKATSUKI.
IT'S NOT YOU THEY WANT. IT'S WHAT'S INSIDE YOU.
THEY MIGHT BE THINKING OF PLACING ITS POWER UNDER THEIR CONTROL. WHILE THE NINE-TAILED FOX SPIRIT IS STILL SEALED INSIDE YOU...

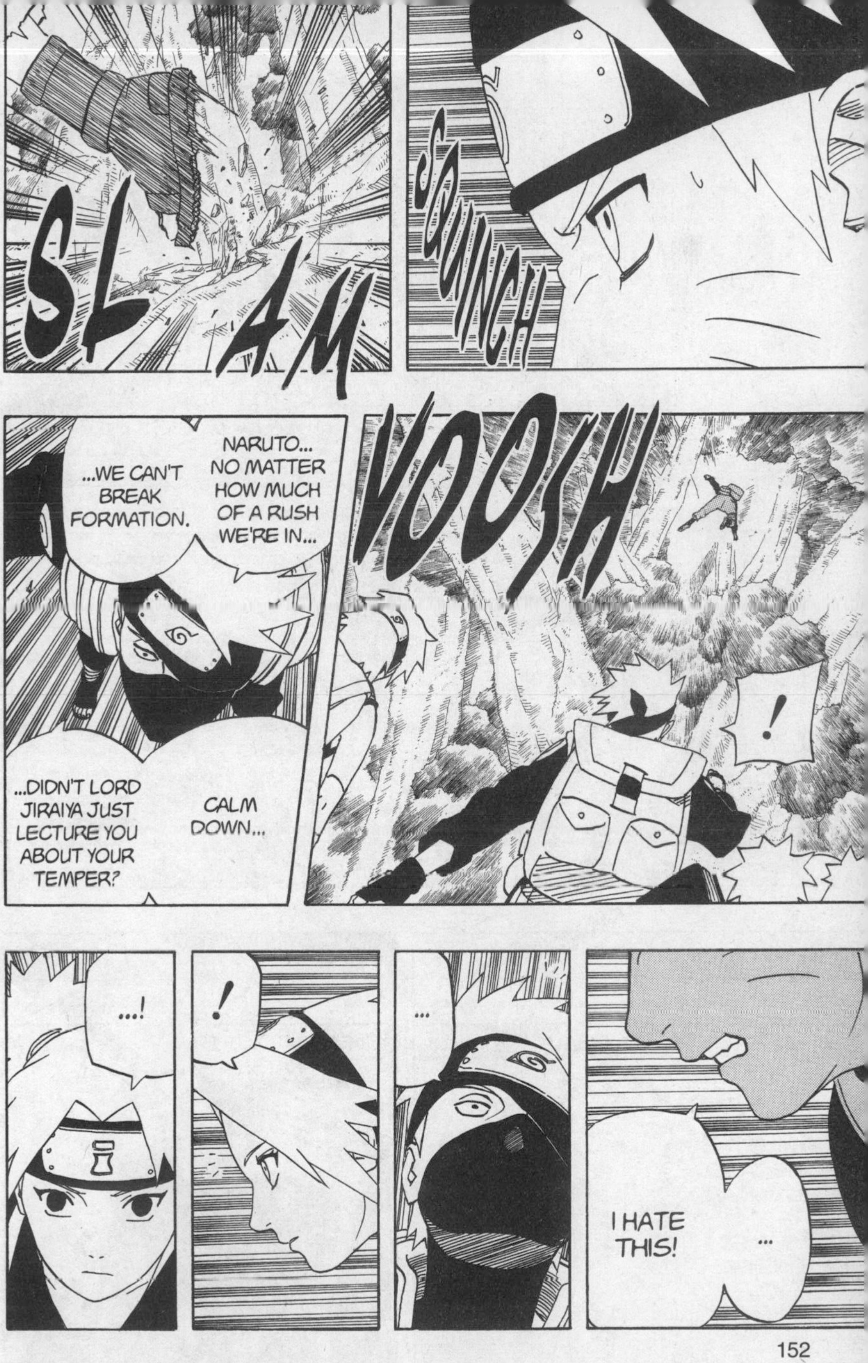
SQUINCH
SLAM
VOOSH
!
NARUTO... NO MATTER HOW MUCH OF A RUSH WE'RE IN...
...WE CAN'T BREAK FORMATION.
CALM DOWN...
...DIDN'T LORD JIRAIYA JUST LECTURE YOU ABOUT YOUR TEMPER?
...
I HATE THIS!
...
!
...!

READ THIS WAY

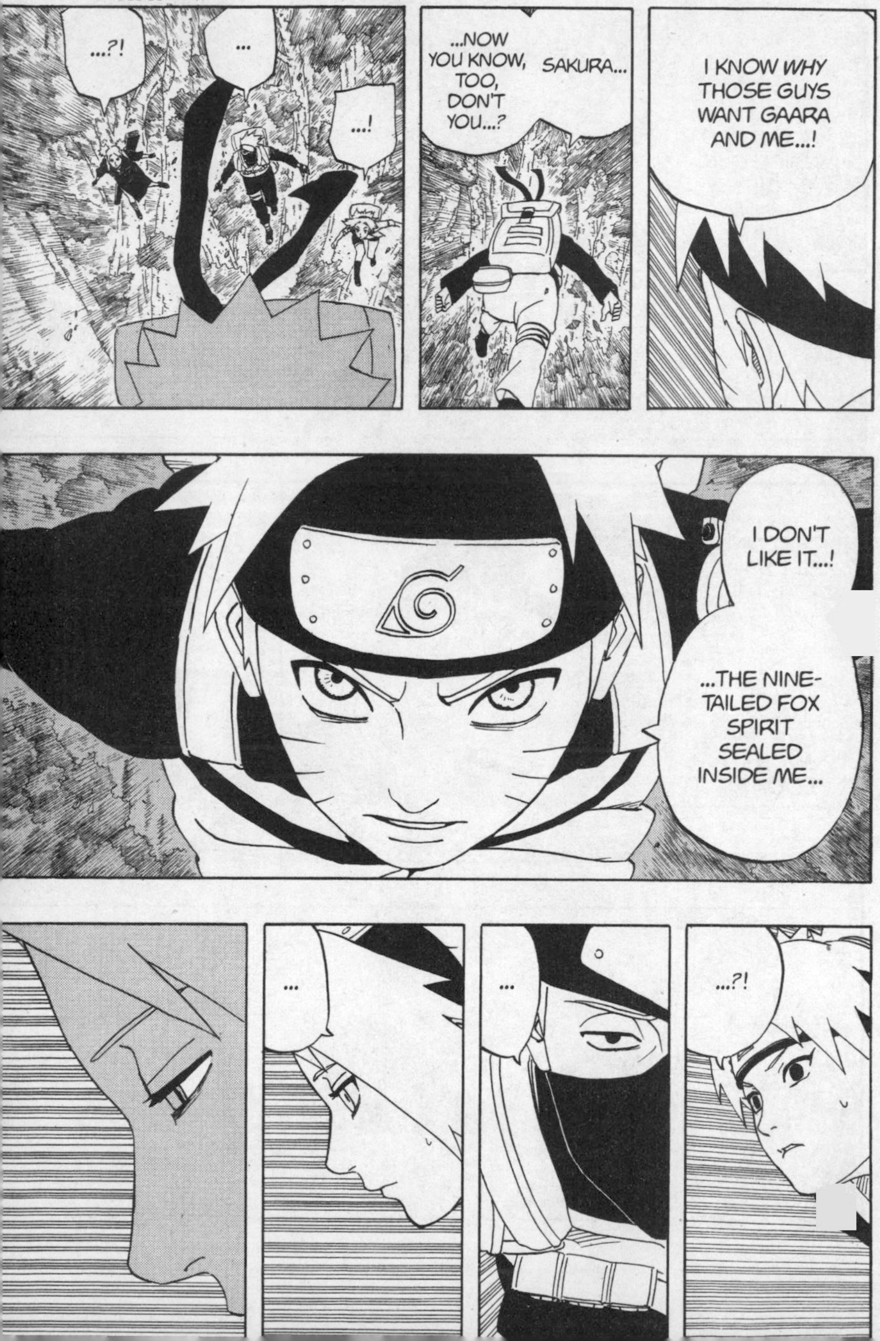

I KNOW WHY THOSE GUYS WANT GAARA AND ME...!
SAKURA...
...NOW YOU KNOW, TOO, DON'T YOU...?
...!
...
...?!
I DON'T LIKE IT...!
...THE NINE-TAILED FOX SPIRIT SEALED INSIDE ME...
...?!
...
...

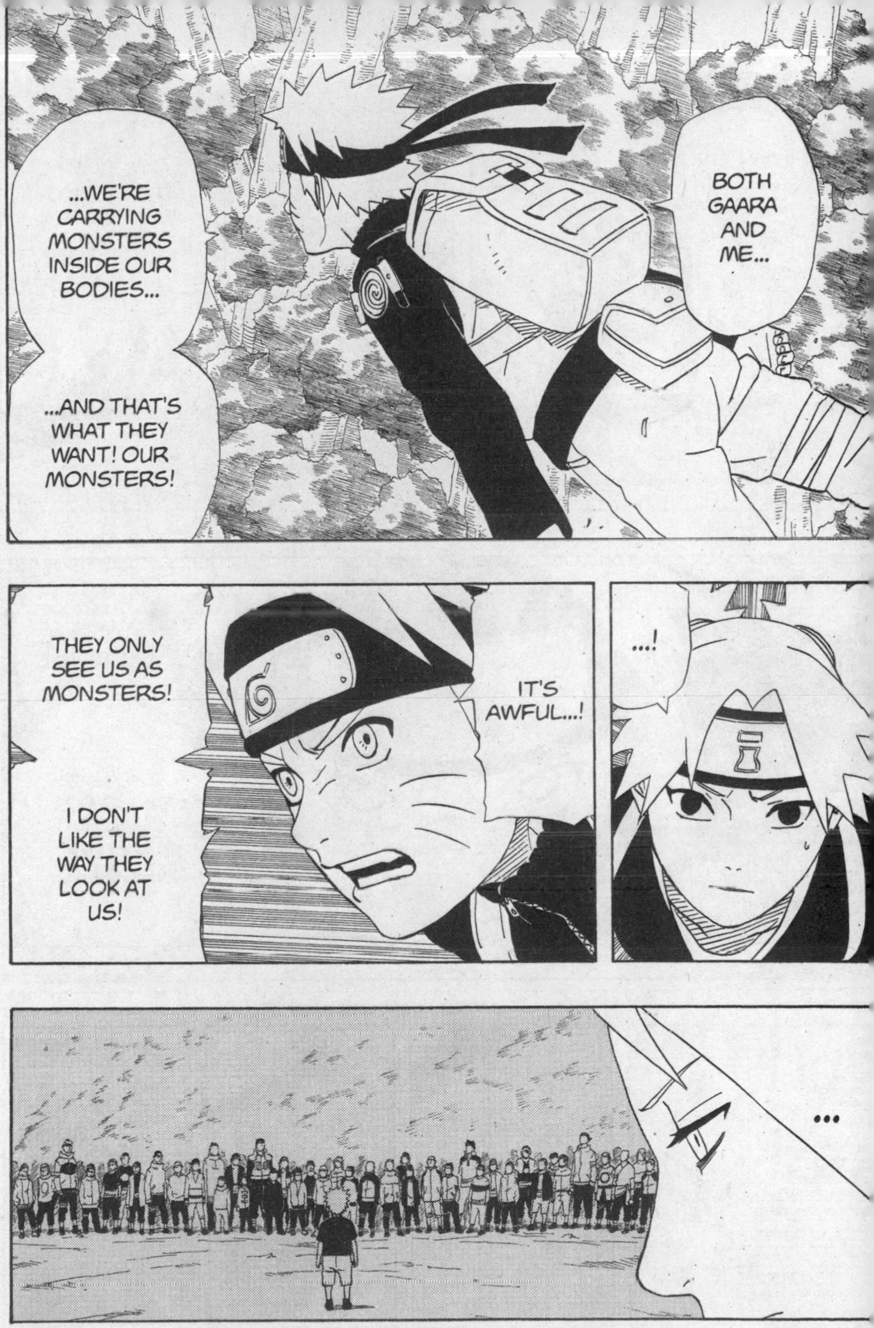
BOTH GAARA AND ME...
...WE'RE CARRYING MONSTERS INSIDE OUR BODIES...
...AND THAT'S WHAT THEY WANT! OUR MONSTERS!
...!
IT'S AWFUL...!
THEY ONLY SEE US AS MONSTERS!
I DON'T LIKE THE WAY THEY LOOK AT US!
...

READ THIS WAY

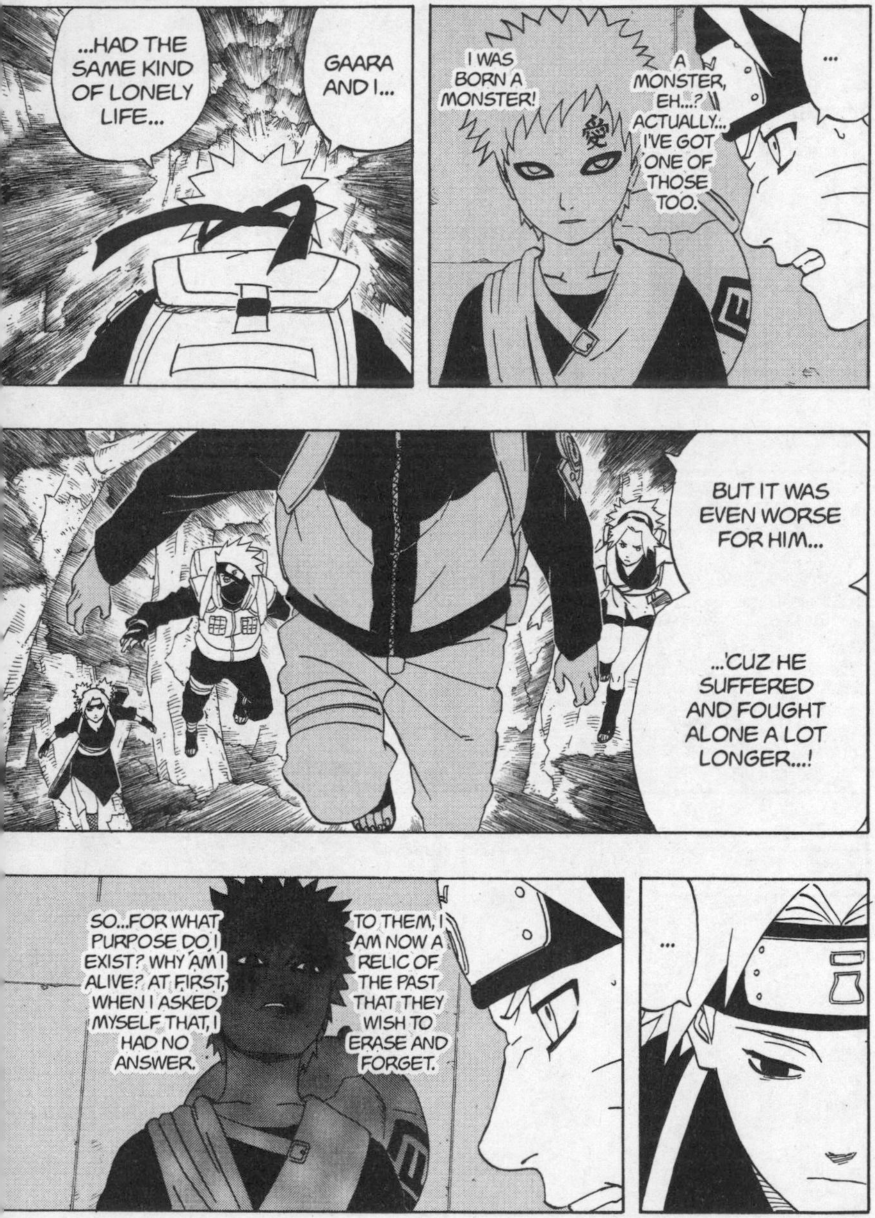
...
A MONSTER, EH...? ACTUALLY... I'VE GOT ONE OF THOSE TOO.
I WAS BORN A MONSTER!
GAARA AND I...
...HAD THE SAME KIND OF LONELY LIFE...
BUT IT WAS EVEN WORSE FOR HIM...
...'CUZ HE SUFFERED AND FOUGHT ALONE A LOT LONGER...!
...
TO THEM, I AM NOW A RELIC OF THE PAST THAT THEY WISH TO ERASE AND FORGET.
SO...FOR WHAT PURPOSE DO I EXIST? WHY AM I ALIVE? AT FIRST, WHEN I ASKED MYSELF THAT, I HAD NO ANSWER.

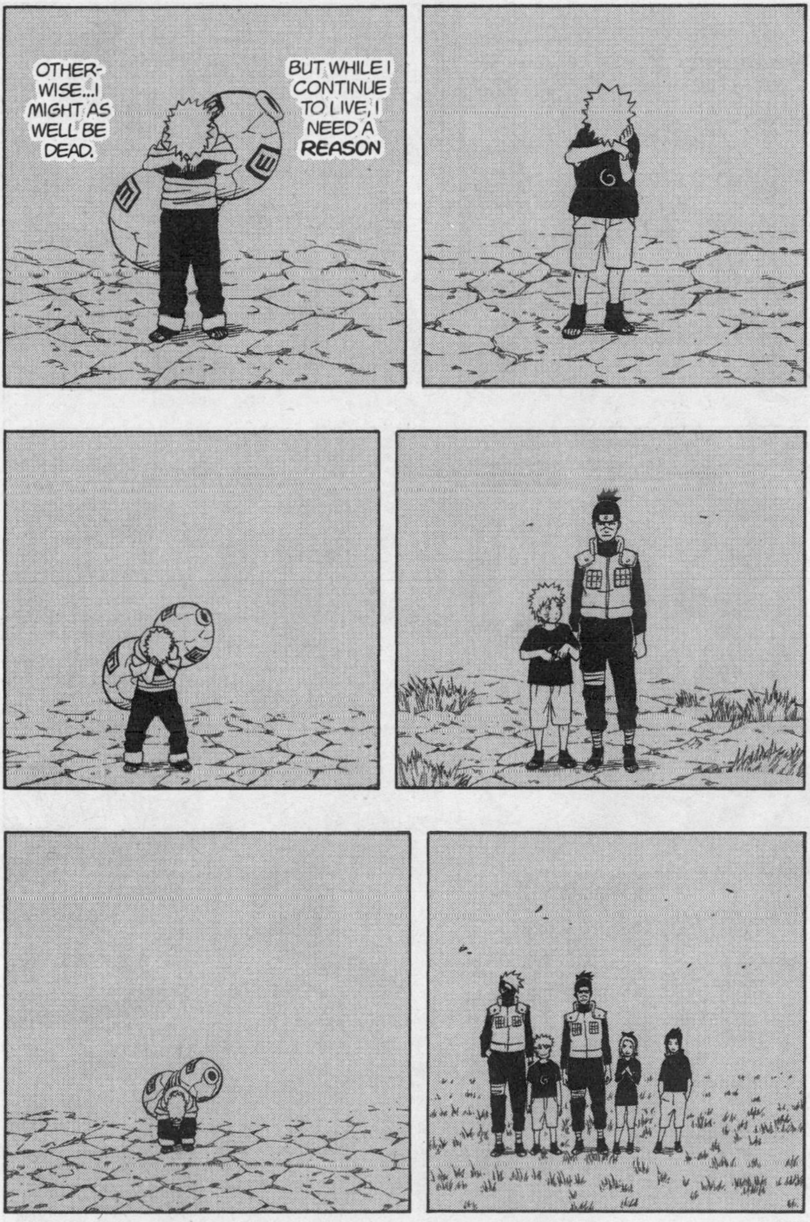
BUT WHILE I CONTINUE TO LIVE, I NEED A **REASON**
OTHER-WISE...I MIGHT AS WELL BE DEAD.

READ THIS WAY

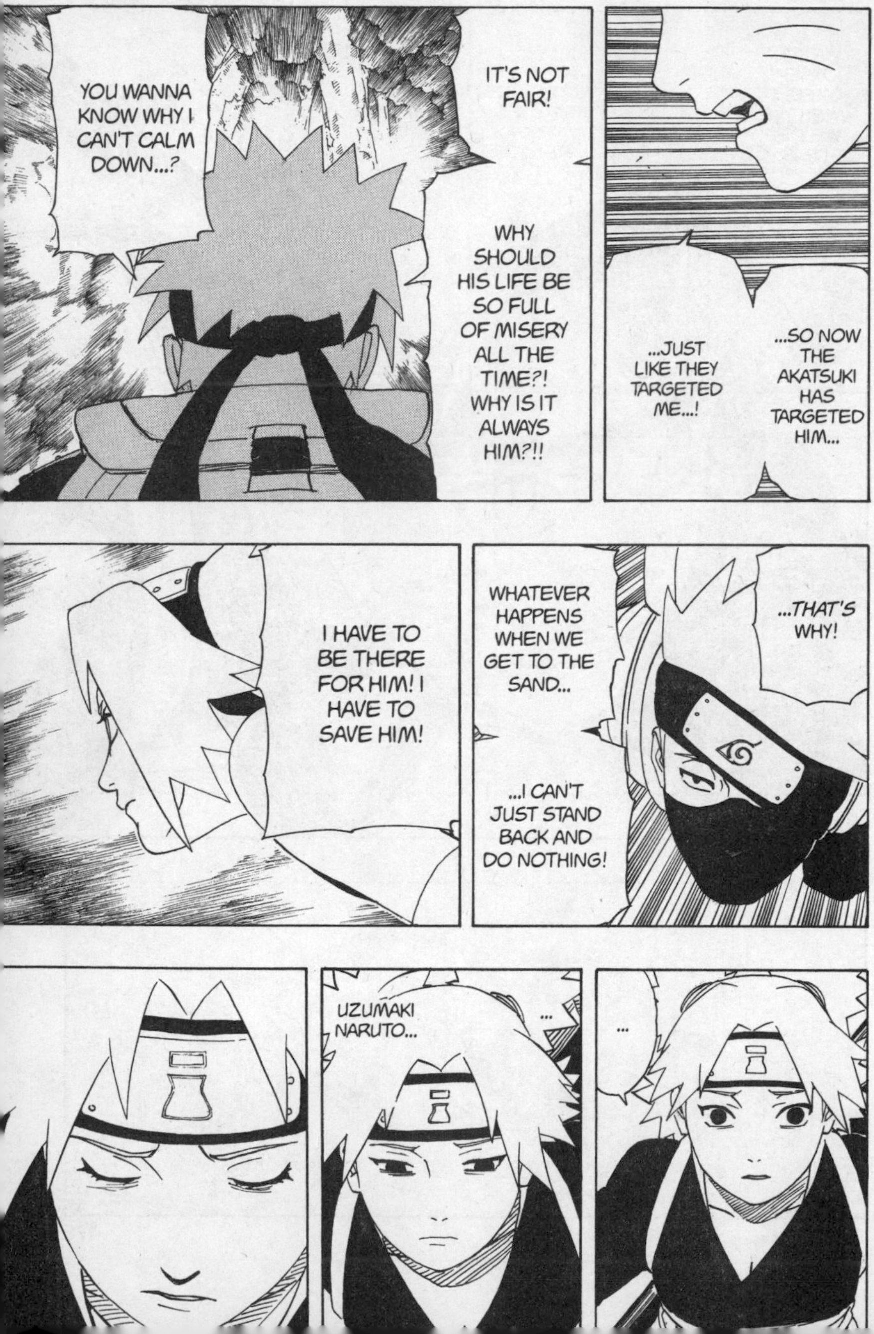
...SO NOW THE AKATSUKI HAS TARGETED HIM...
...JUST LIKE THEY TARGETED ME...!
YOU WANNA KNOW WHY I CAN'T CALM DOWN...?
IT'S NOT FAIR!
WHY SHOULD HIS LIFE BE SO FULL OF MISERY ALL THE TIME?! WHY IS IT ALWAYS HIM?!!
...THAT'S WHY!
WHATEVER HAPPENS WHEN WE GET TO THE SAND...
...I CAN'T JUST STAND BACK AND DO NOTHING!
I HAVE TO BE THERE FOR HIM! I HAVE TO SAVE HIM!
...
...
UZUMAKI NARUTO...

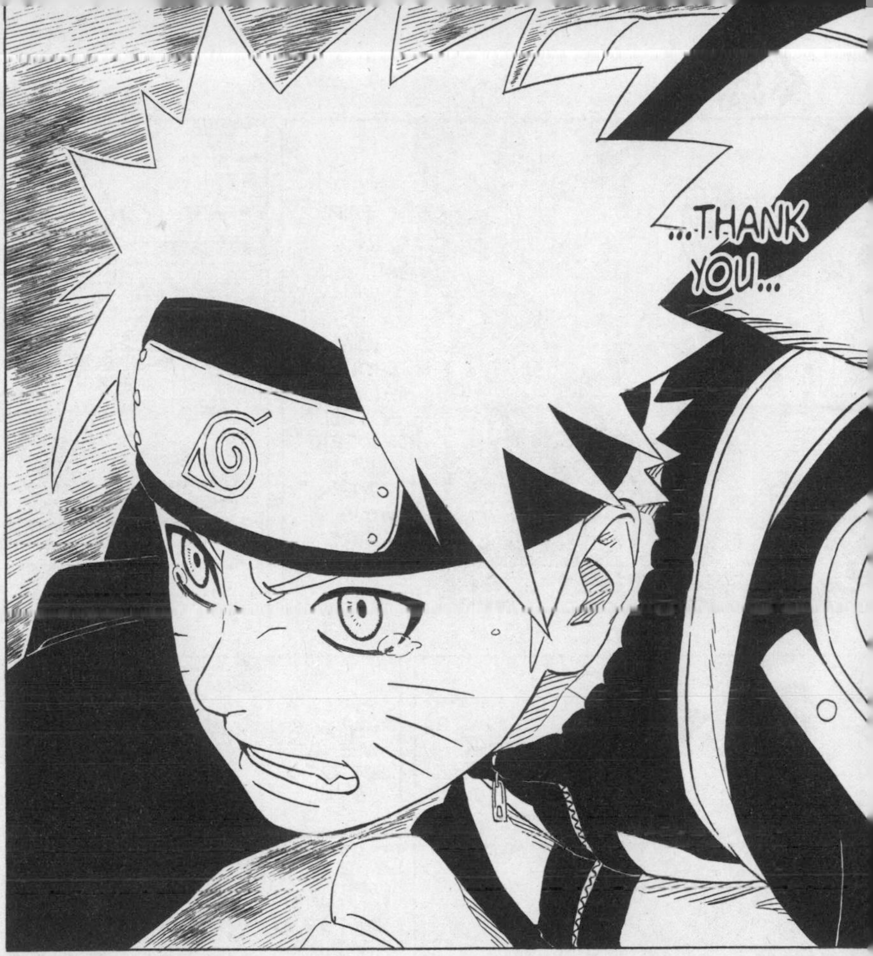
...THANK
YOU...

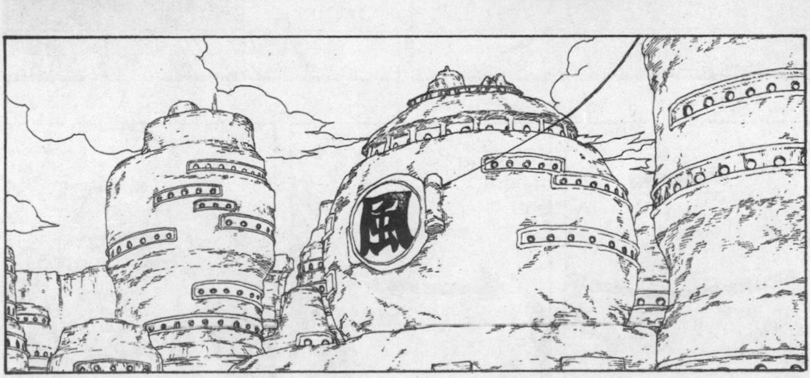

READ THIS WAY

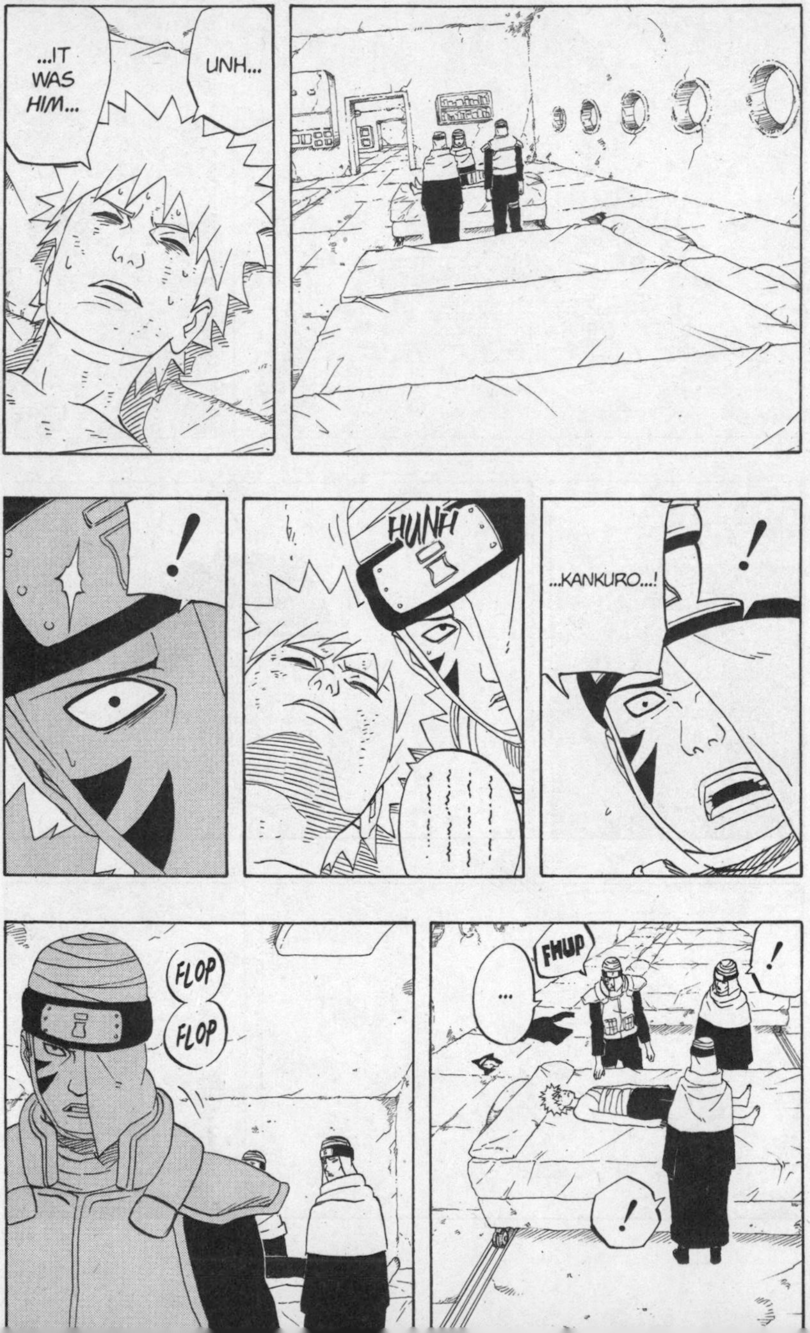
UNH...
...IT WAS HIM...
!
...KANKURO...!
HUNH
!
!
FHUP
...
!
FLOP
FLOP

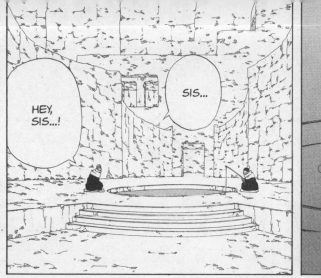

HEY, SIS...!

SIS...

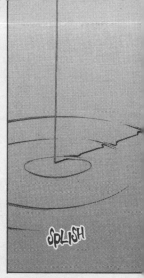

SPLISH

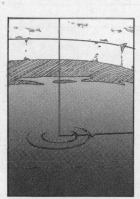

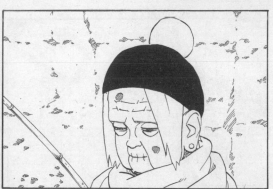

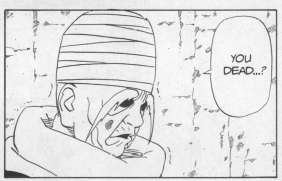

YOU DEAD...?

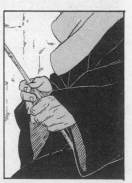

160

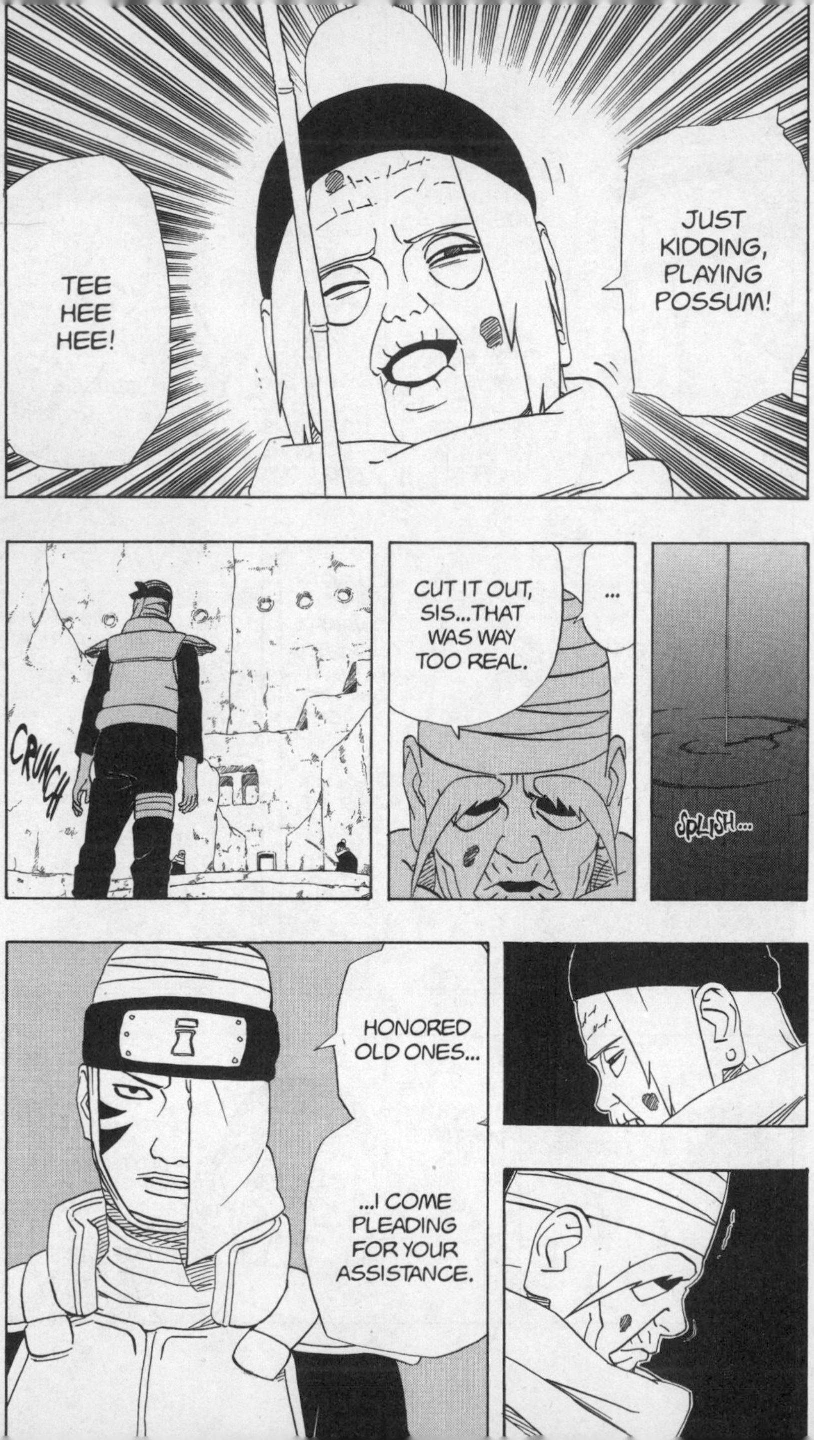
JUST KIDDING, PLAYING POSSUM!
TEE HEE HEE!
SPLISH...
...
CUT IT OUT, SIS...THAT WAS WAY TOO REAL.
CRUNCH
HONORED OLD ONES...
...I COME PLEADING FOR YOUR ASSISTANCE.

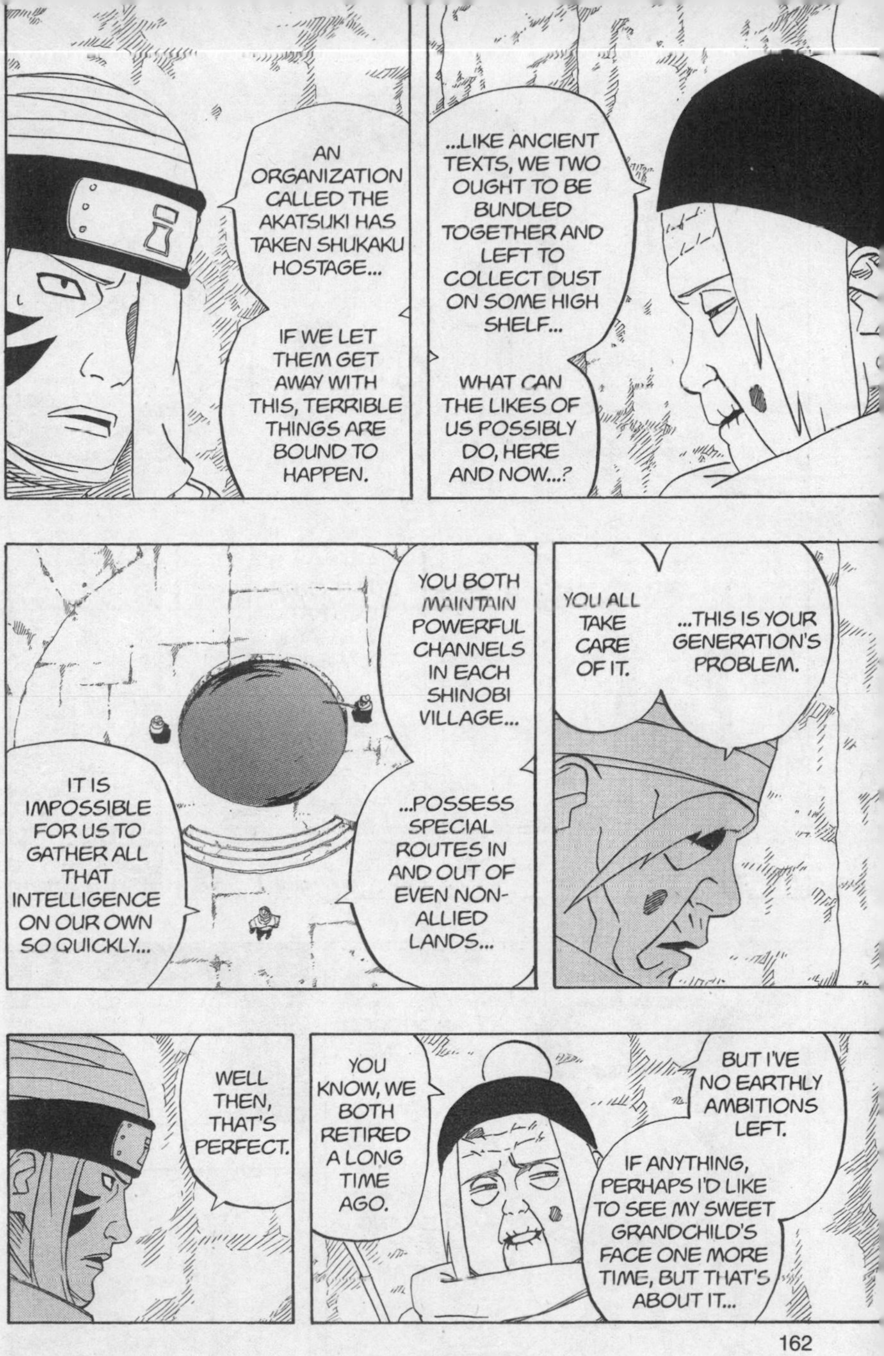
...LIKE ANCIENT TEXTS, WE TWO OUGHT TO BE BUNDLED TOGETHER AND LEFT TO COLLECT DUST ON SOME HIGH SHELF...
WHAT CAN THE LIKES OF US POSSIBLY DO, HERE AND NOW...?
AN ORGANIZATION CALLED THE AKATSUKI HAS TAKEN SHUKAKU HOSTAGE...
IF WE LET THEM GET AWAY WITH THIS, TERRIBLE THINGS ARE BOUND TO HAPPEN.
...THIS IS YOUR GENERATION'S PROBLEM.
YOU ALL TAKE CARE OF IT.
YOU BOTH MAINTAIN POWERFUL CHANNELS IN EACH SHINOBI VILLAGE...
...POSSESS SPECIAL ROUTES IN AND OUT OF EVEN NON-ALLIED LANDS...
IT IS IMPOSSIBLE FOR US TO GATHER ALL THAT INTELLIGENCE ON OUR OWN SO QUICKLY...
YOU KNOW, WE BOTH RETIRED A LONG TIME AGO.
BUT I'VE NO EARTHLY AMBITIONS LEFT.
IF ANYTHING, PERHAPS I'D LIKE TO SEE MY SWEET GRANDCHILD'S FACE ONE MORE TIME, BUT THAT'S ABOUT IT...
WELL THEN, THAT'S PERFECT.

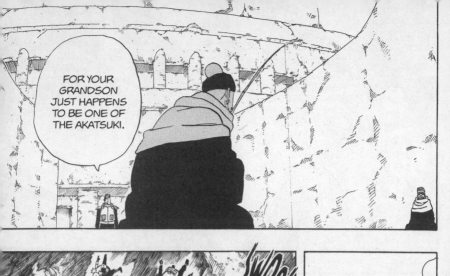

FOR YOUR GRANDSON JUST HAPPENS TO BE ONE OF THE AKATSUKI.

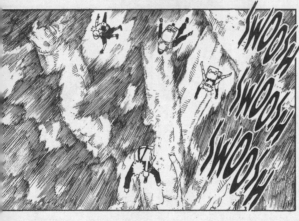

SWOOSH

SWOOSH

SWOOSH

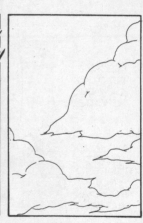

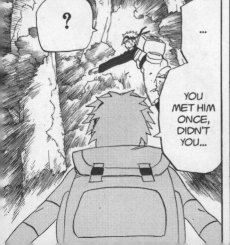

?

...

YOU MET HIM ONCE, DIDN'T YOU...

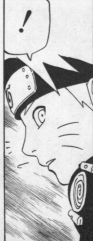

!

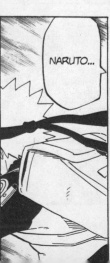

NARUTO...

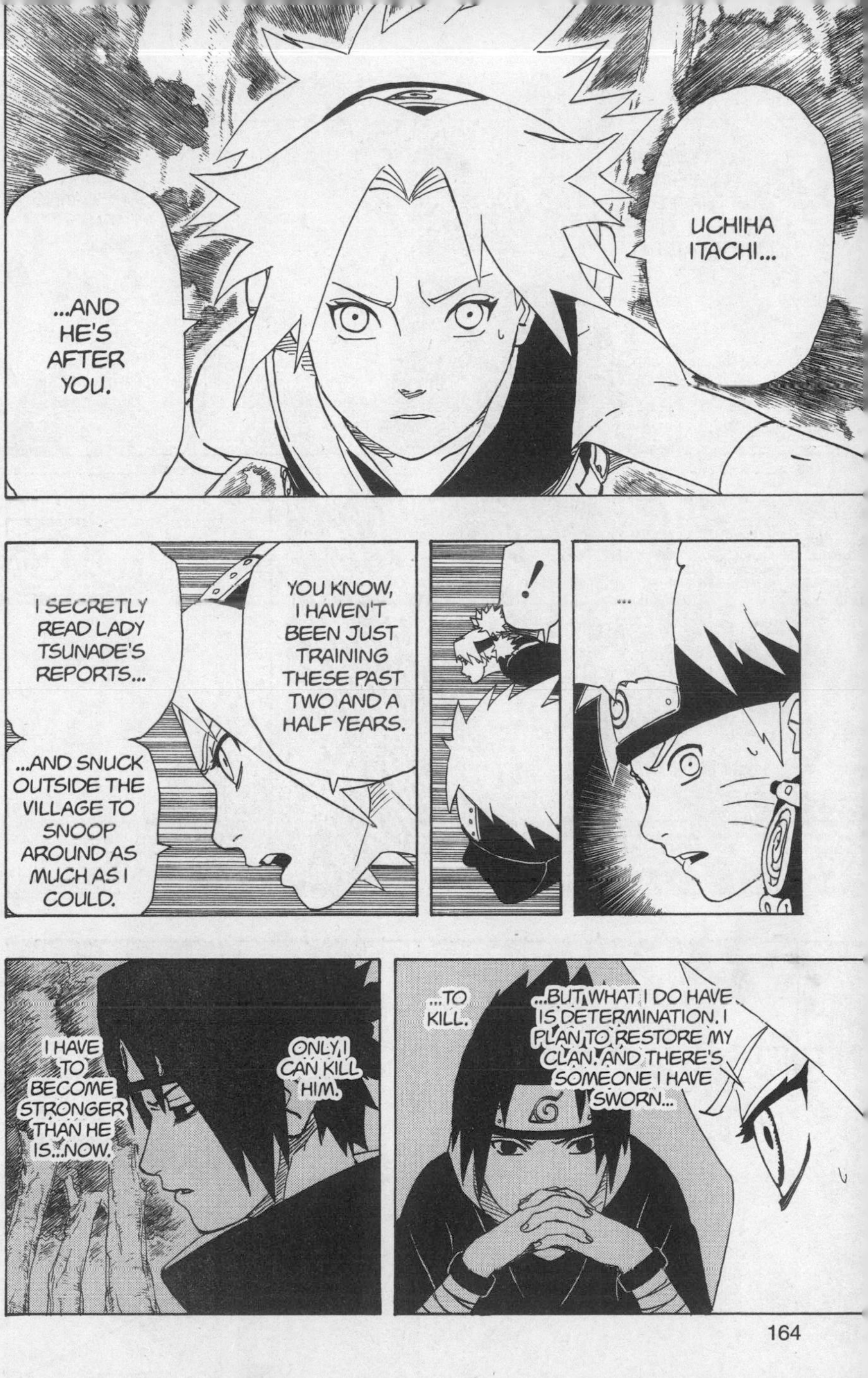
UCHIHA ITACHI...
...AND HE'S AFTER YOU.
...
!
YOU KNOW, I HAVEN'T BEEN JUST TRAINING THESE PAST TWO AND A HALF YEARS.
I SECRETLY READ LADY TSUNADE'S REPORTS...
...AND SNUCK OUTSIDE THE VILLAGE TO SNOOP AROUND AS MUCH AS I COULD.
...BUT WHAT I DO HAVE IS DETERMINATION. I PLAN TO RESTORE MY CLAN. AND THERE'S SOMEONE I HAVE SWORN...
...TO KILL.
ONLY I CAN KILL HIM.
I HAVE TO BECOME STRONGER THAN HE IS...NOW.

READ THIS WAY

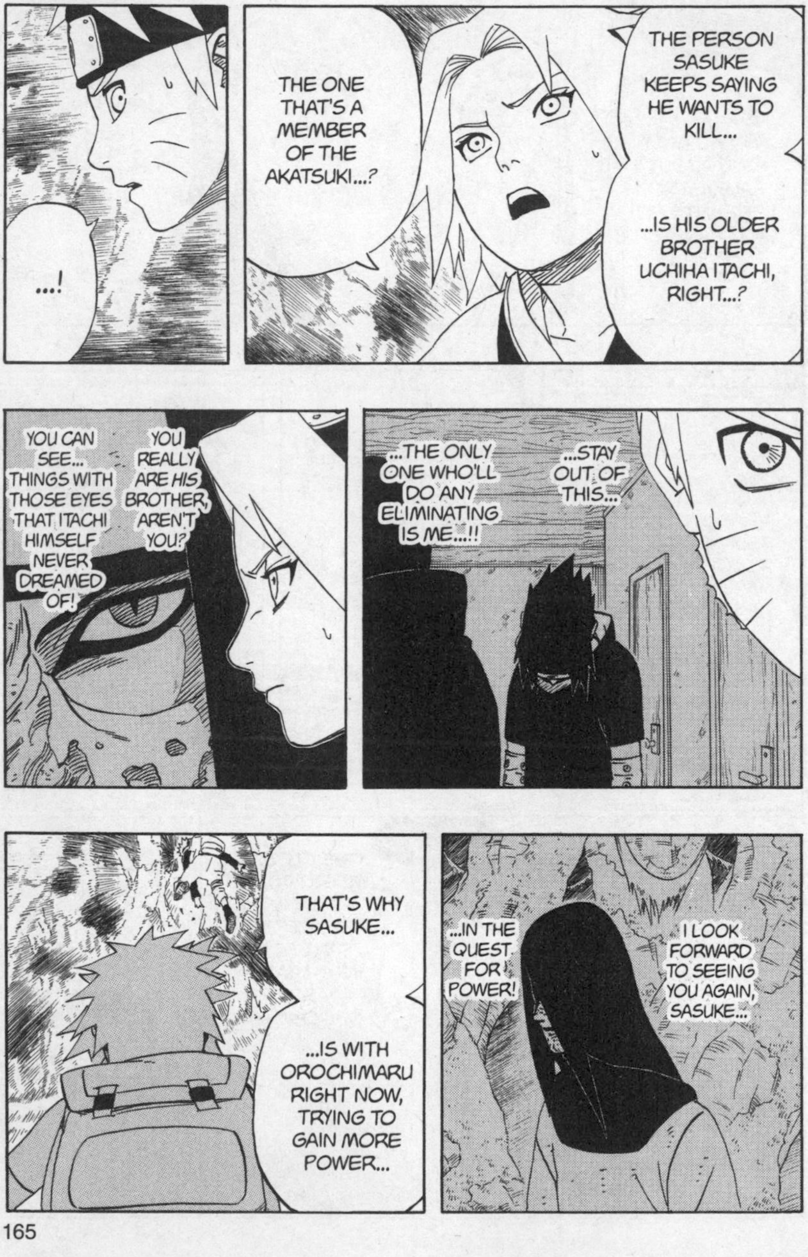
THE PERSON SASUKE KEEPS SAYING HE WANTS TO KILL...
...IS HIS OLDER BROTHER UCHIHA ITACHI, RIGHT...?
THE ONE THAT'S A MEMBER OF THE AKATSUKI...?
...!
...STAY OUT OF THIS...
...THE ONLY ONE WHO'LL DO ANY ELIMINATING IS ME...!!
YOU REALLY ARE *HIS* BROTHER, AREN'T YOU?
YOU CAN SEE... THINGS WITH THOSE EYES THAT ITACHI HIMSELF NEVER DREAMED OF!
I LOOK FORWARD TO SEEING YOU AGAIN, SASUKE...
...IN THE QUEST FOR POWER!
THAT'S WHY SASUKE...
...IS WITH OROCHIMARU RIGHT NOW, TRYING TO GAIN MORE POWER...

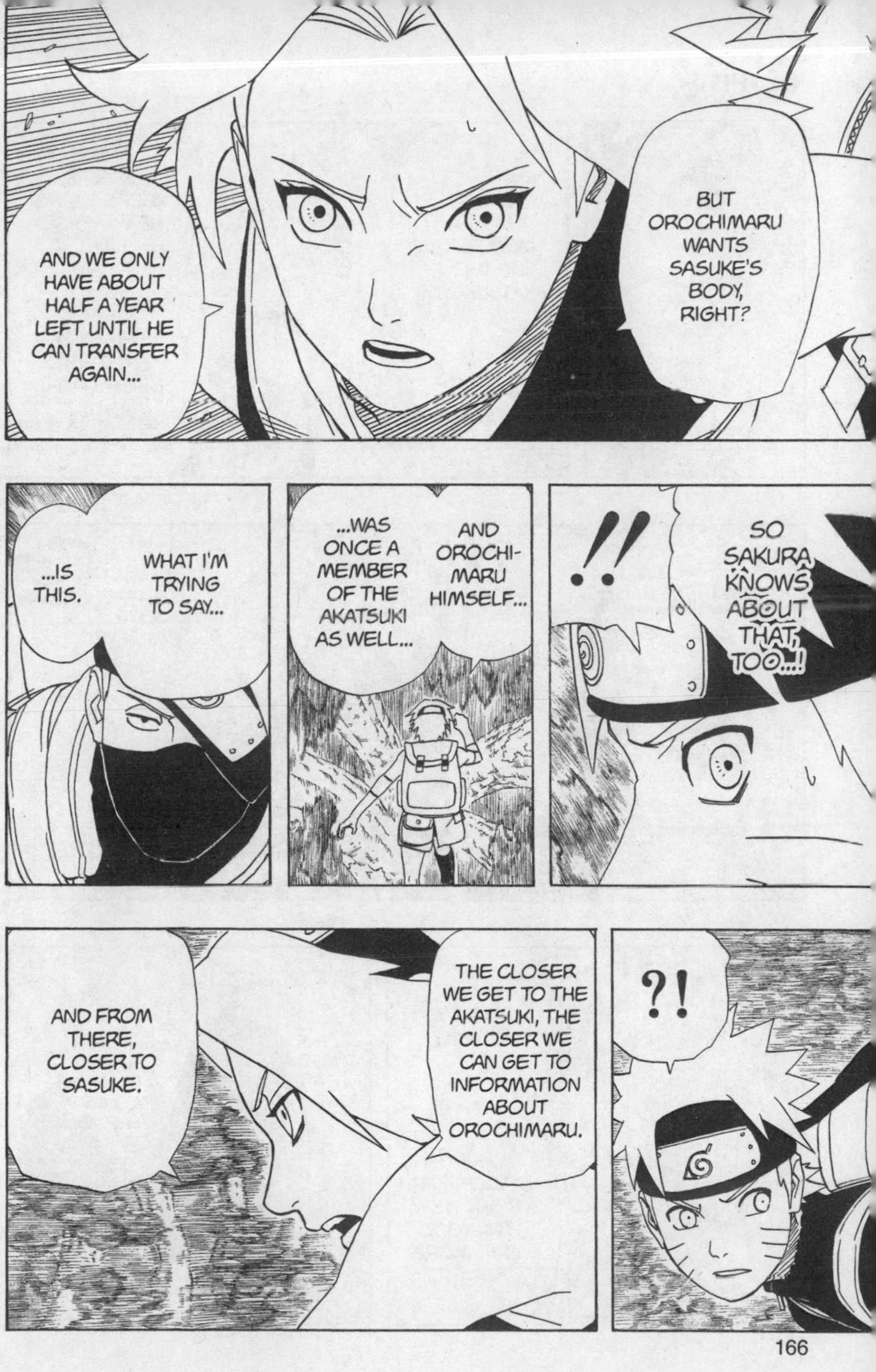
BUT OROCHIMARU WANTS SASUKE'S BODY, RIGHT?
AND WE ONLY HAVE ABOUT HALF A YEAR LEFT UNTIL HE CAN TRANSFER AGAIN...
!!
SO SAKURA KNOWS ABOUT THAT, TOO...!
AND OROCHIMARU HIMSELF...
...WAS ONCE A MEMBER OF THE AKATSUKI AS WELL...
WHAT I'M TRYING TO SAY...
...IS THIS.
?!
THE CLOSER WE GET TO THE AKATSUKI, THE CLOSER WE CAN GET TO INFORMATION ABOUT OROCHIMARU.
AND FROM THERE, CLOSER TO SASUKE.

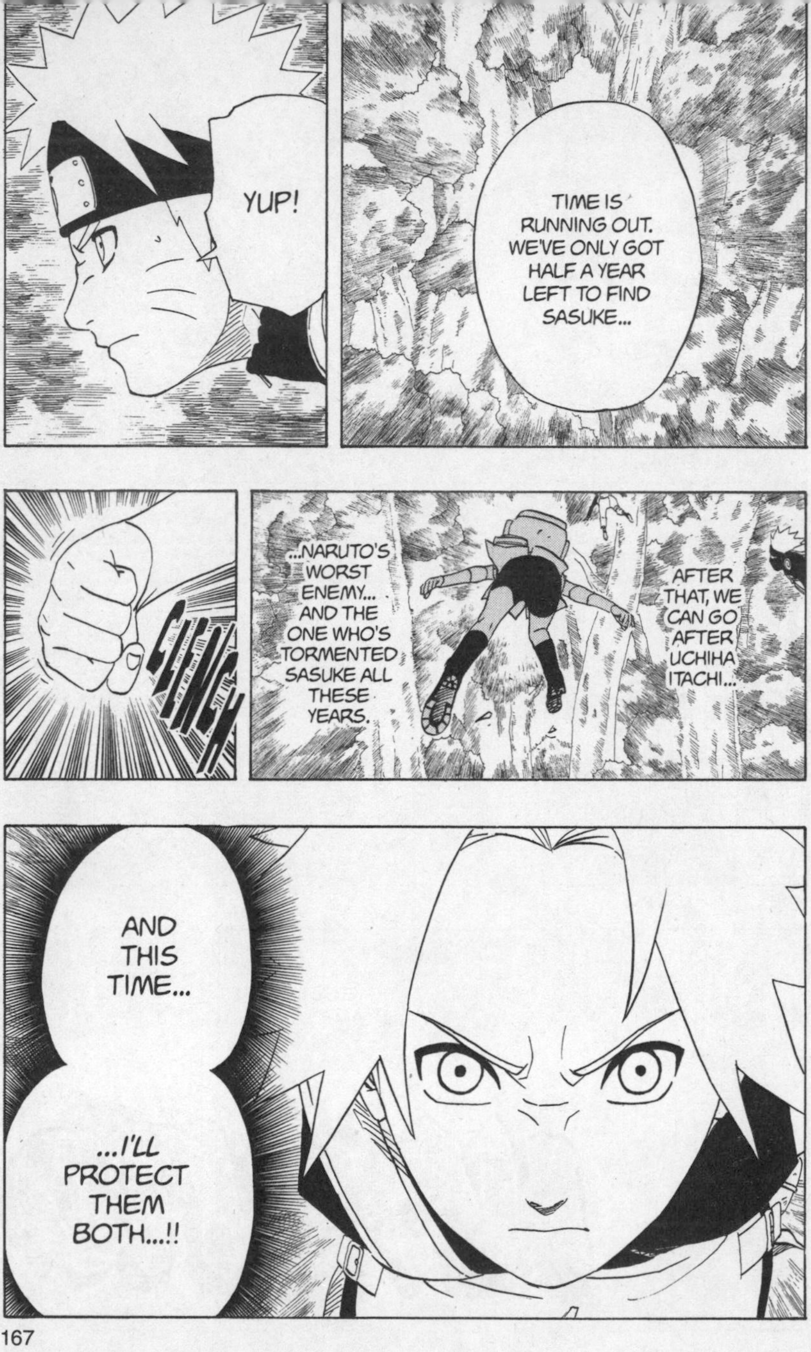
TIME IS RUNNING OUT. WE'VE ONLY GOT HALF A YEAR LEFT TO FIND SASUKE...
YUP!
AFTER THAT, WE CAN GO AFTER UCHIHA ITACHI...
...NARUTO'S WORST ENEMY... AND THE ONE WHO'S TORMENTED SASUKE ALL THESE YEARS.
CLENCH
AND THIS TIME...
...I'LL PROTECT THEM BOTH...!!

NARUTO

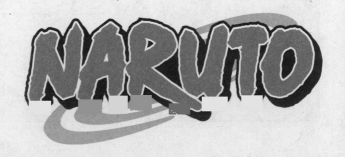

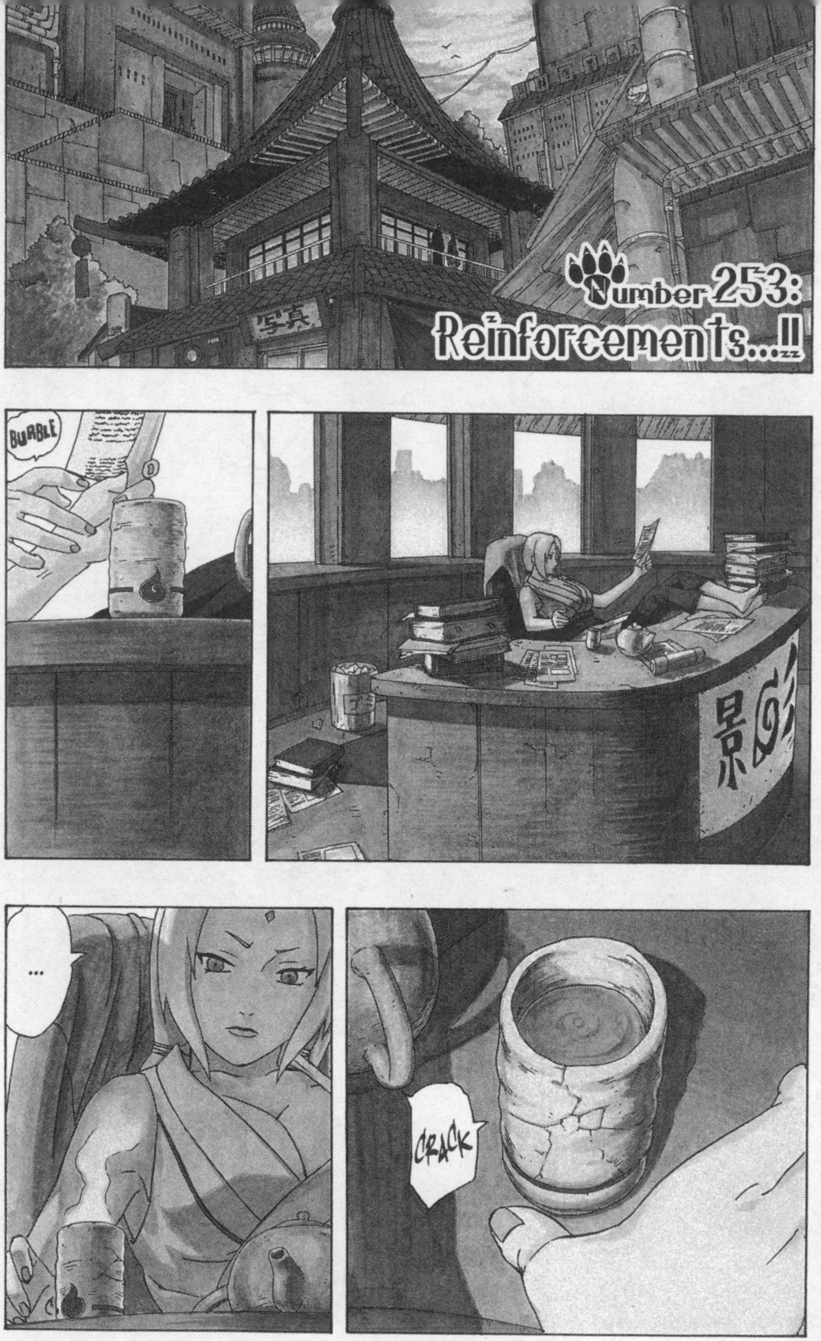
Number 253:
Reinforcements...!!
写真
BURBLE
CRACK
...

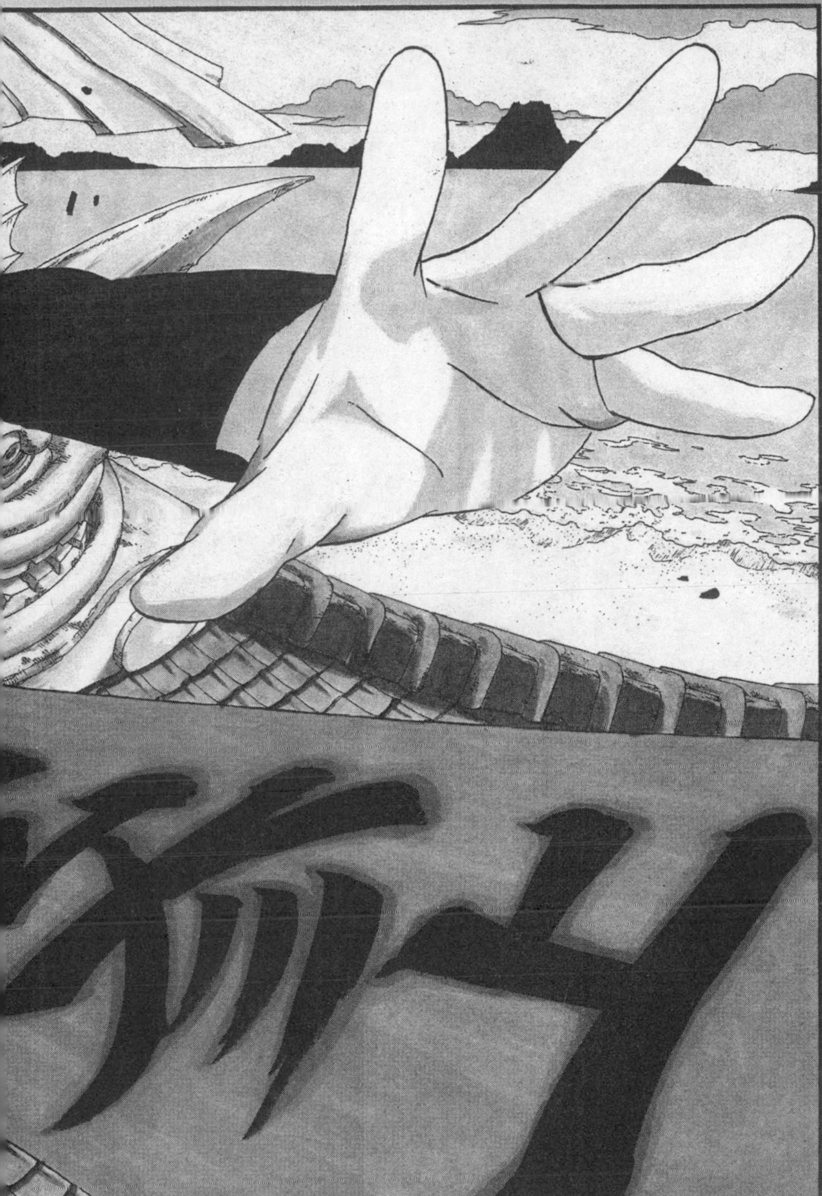

Number 253: Reinforcements...!!

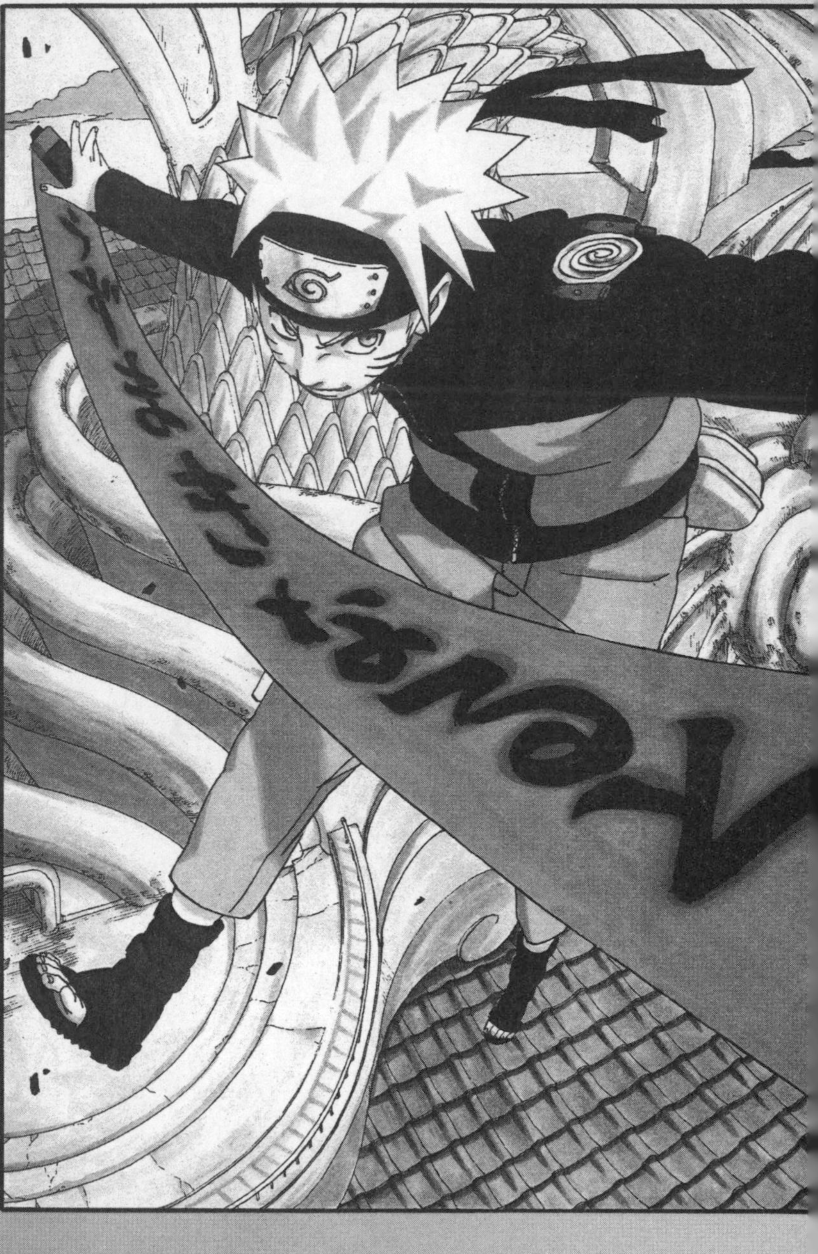

NARUTO -ナルト-

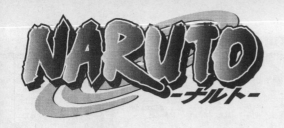

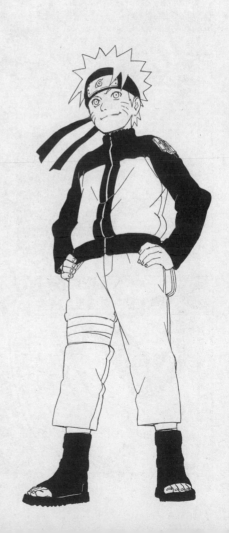

READ THIS WAY

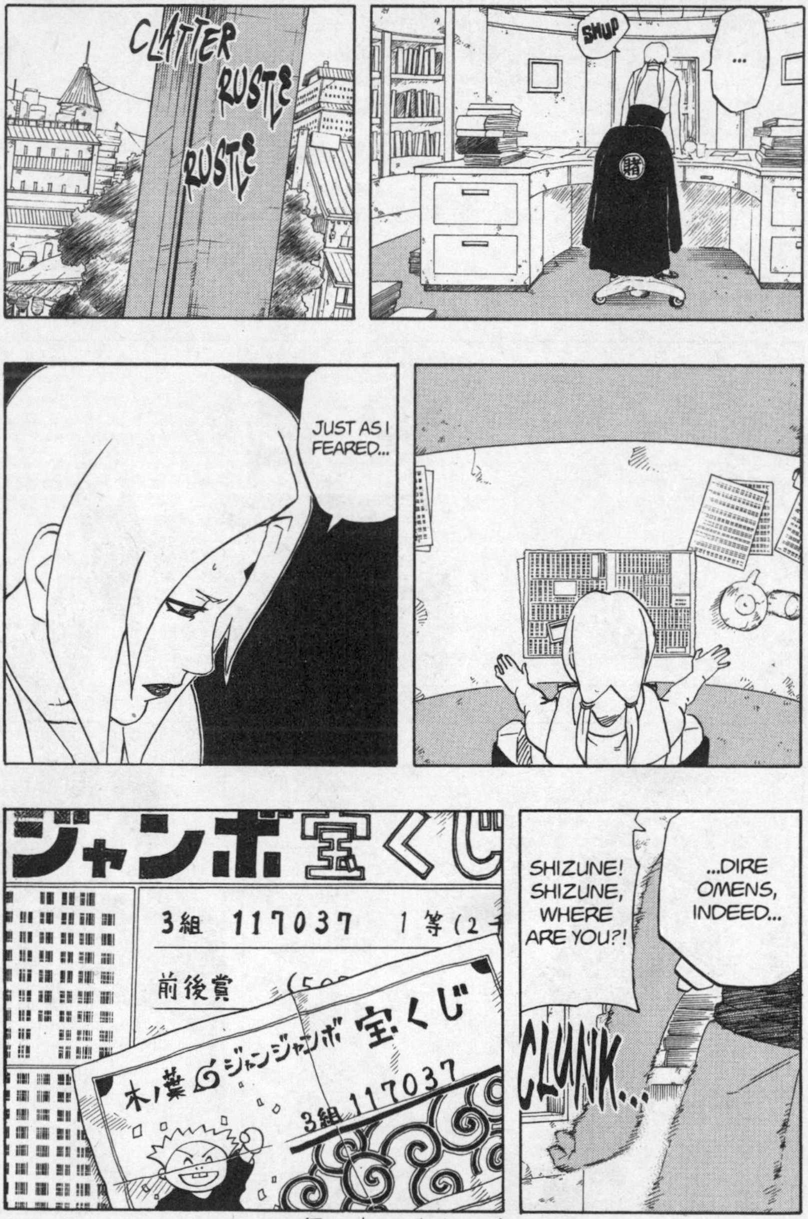
SHUP
...
CLATTER
RUSTLE
RUSTLE
JUST AS I FEARED...
...DIRE OMENS, INDEED...
SHIZUNE! SHIZUNE, WHERE ARE YOU?!
CLUNK...
ジャンボ宝くじ
3組 117037 1等
前後賞
木ノ葉ジャンジャンボ 宝くじ
3組 117037

(Tsunade won the Lottery)

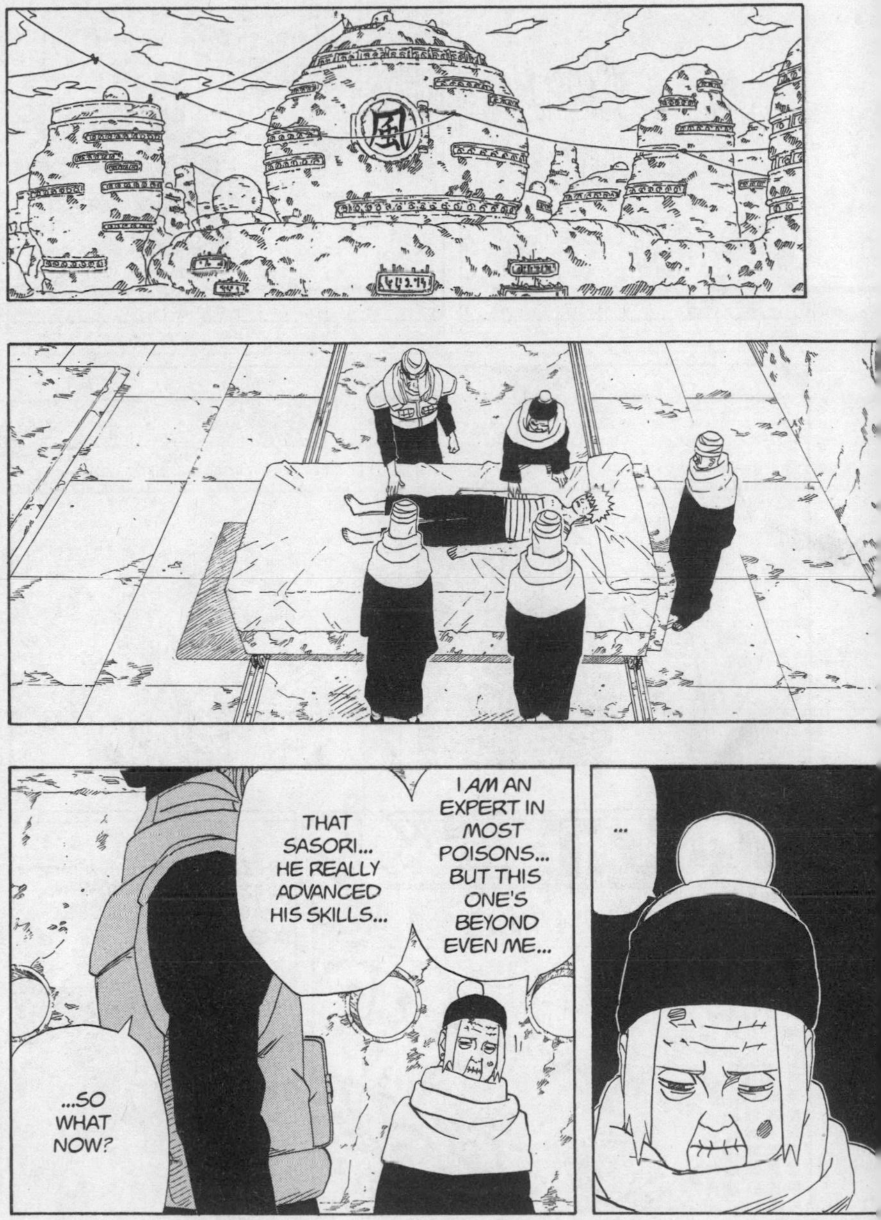
...
I AM AN EXPERT IN MOST POISONS... BUT THIS ONE'S BEYOND EVEN ME...
THAT SASORI... HE REALLY ADVANCED HIS SKILLS...
...SO WHAT NOW?

READ THIS WAY

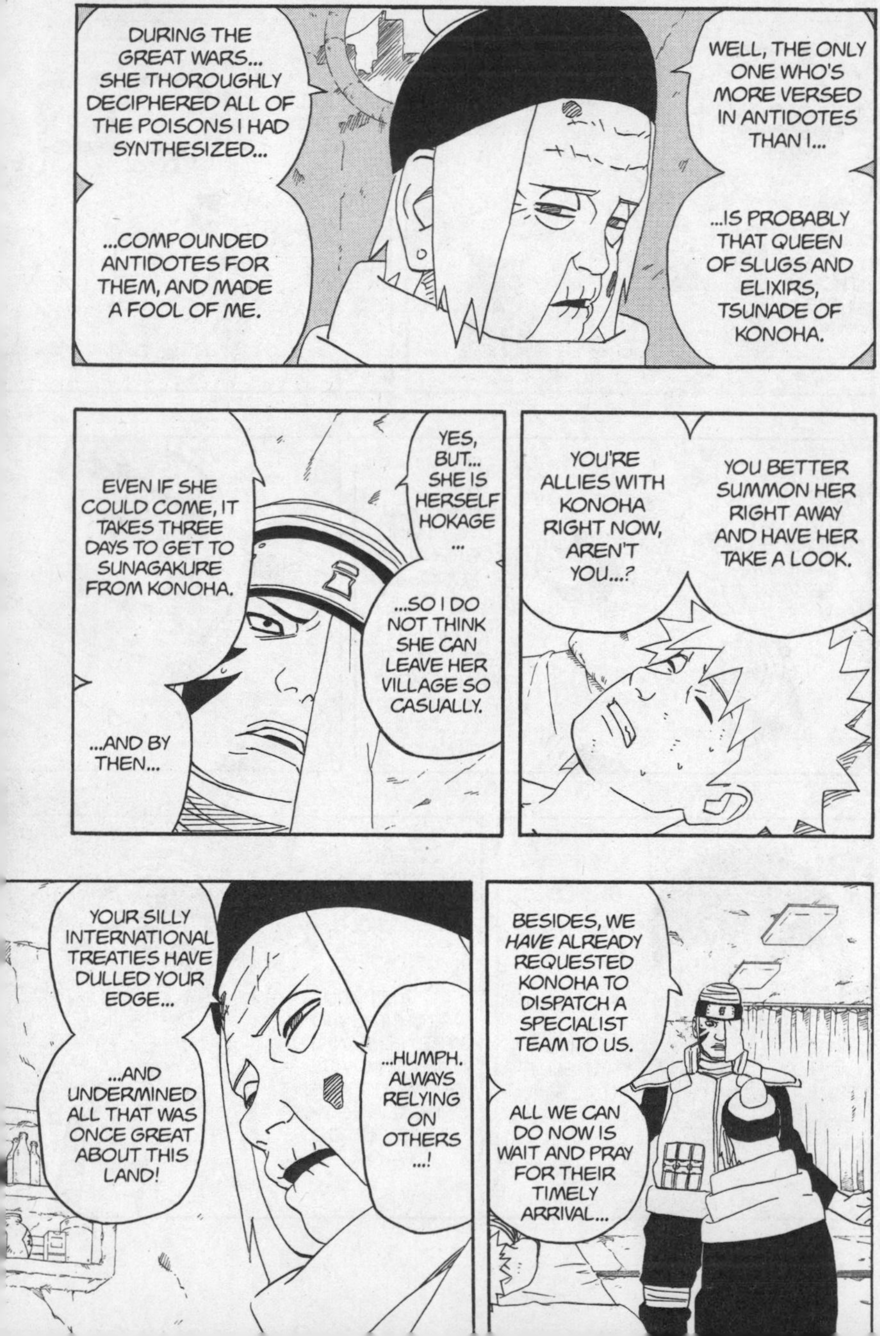
WELL, THE ONLY ONE WHO'S MORE VERSED IN ANTIDOTES THAN I...
...IS PROBABLY THAT QUEEN OF SLUGS AND ELIXIRS, TSUNADE OF KONOHA.
DURING THE GREAT WARS... SHE THOROUGHLY DECIPHERED ALL OF THE POISONS I HAD SYNTHESIZED...
...COMPOUNDED ANTIDOTES FOR THEM, AND MADE A FOOL OF ME.
YOU BETTER SUMMON HER RIGHT AWAY AND HAVE HER TAKE A LOOK.
YOU'RE ALLIES WITH KONOHA RIGHT NOW, AREN'T YOU...?
YES, BUT... SHE IS HERSELF HOKAGE ...
...SO I DO NOT THINK SHE CAN LEAVE HER VILLAGE SO CASUALLY.
EVEN IF SHE COULD COME, IT TAKES THREE DAYS TO GET TO SUNAGAKURE FROM KONOHA.
...AND BY THEN...
BESIDES, WE *HAVE* ALREADY REQUESTED KONOHA TO DISPATCH A SPECIALIST TEAM TO US.
ALL WE CAN DO NOW IS WAIT AND PRAY FOR THEIR TIMELY ARRIVAL...
...HUMPH. ALWAYS RELYING ON OTHERS ...!
YOUR SILLY INTERNATIONAL TREATIES HAVE DULLED YOUR EDGE...
...AND UNDERMINED ALL THAT WAS ONCE GREAT ABOUT THIS LAND!

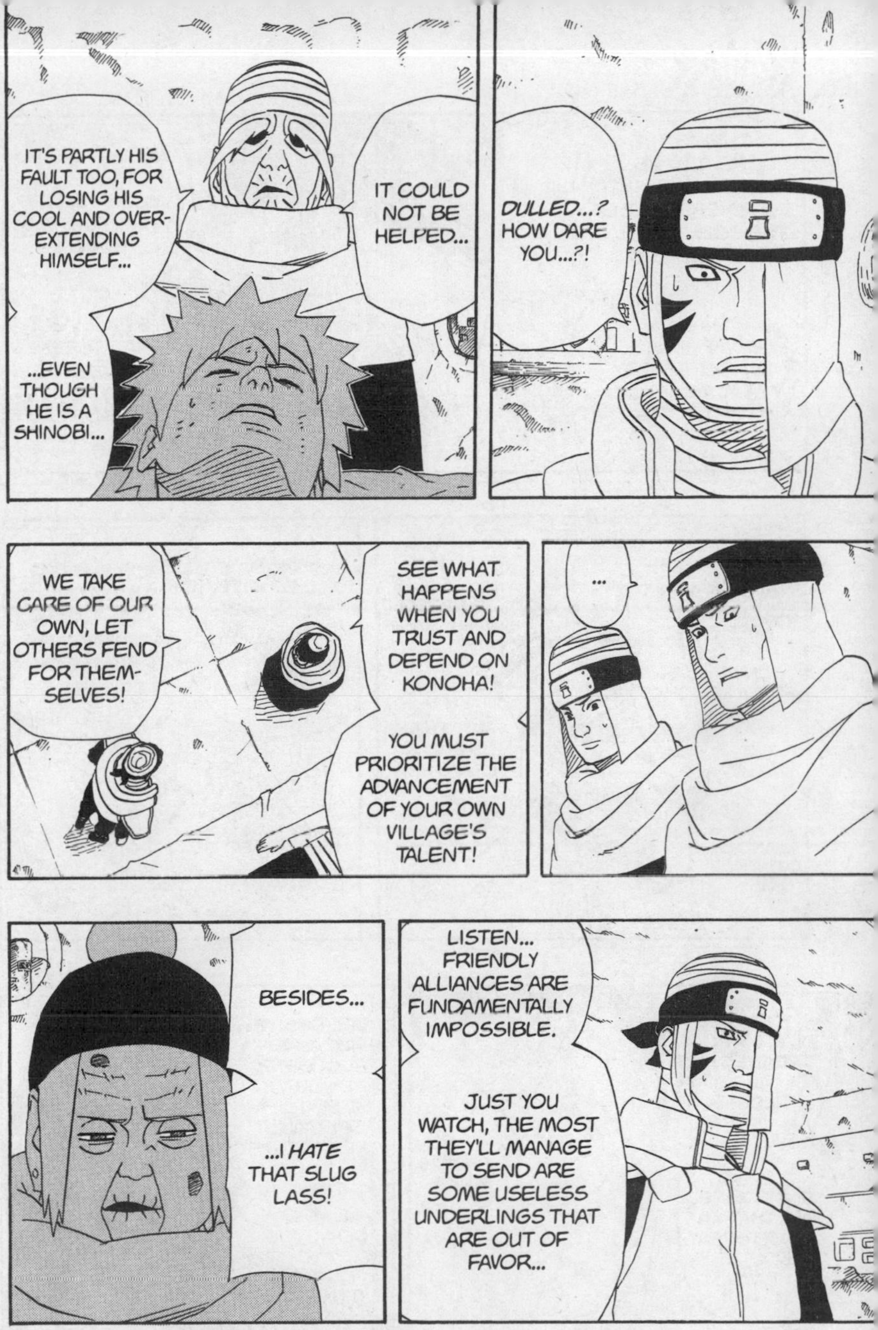
DULLED...? HOW DARE YOU...?!
IT COULD NOT BE HELPED...
IT'S PARTLY HIS FAULT TOO, FOR LOSING HIS COOL AND OVER-EXTENDING HIMSELF...
...EVEN THOUGH HE IS A SHINOBI...
...
SEE WHAT HAPPENS WHEN YOU TRUST AND DEPEND ON KONOHA!
YOU MUST PRIORITIZE THE ADVANCEMENT OF YOUR OWN VILLAGE'S TALENT!
WE TAKE CARE OF OUR OWN, LET OTHERS FEND FOR THEM-SELVES!
LISTEN... FRIENDLY ALLIANCES ARE FUNDAMENTALLY IMPOSSIBLE.
JUST YOU WATCH, THE MOST THEY'LL MANAGE TO SEND ARE SOME USELESS UNDERLINGS THAT ARE OUT OF FAVOR...
BESIDES...
...I *HATE* THAT SLUG LASS!

READ THIS WAY

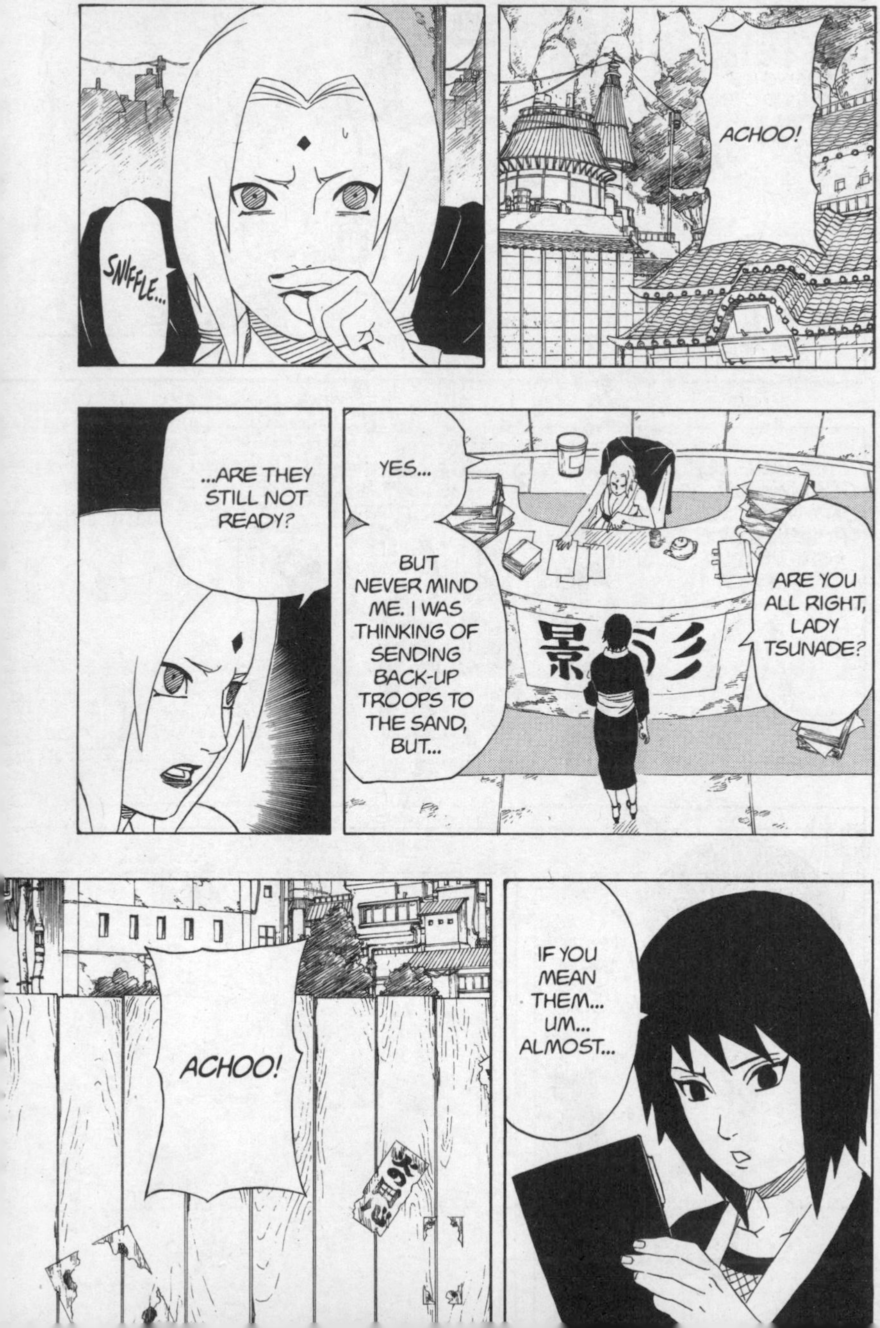
ACHOO!
SNIFFLE...
ARE YOU ALL RIGHT, LADY TSUNADE?
YES...
BUT NEVER MIND ME. I WAS THINKING OF SENDING BACK-UP TROOPS TO THE SAND, BUT...
...ARE THEY STILL NOT READY?
IF YOU MEAN THEM... UM... ALMOST...
ACHOO!

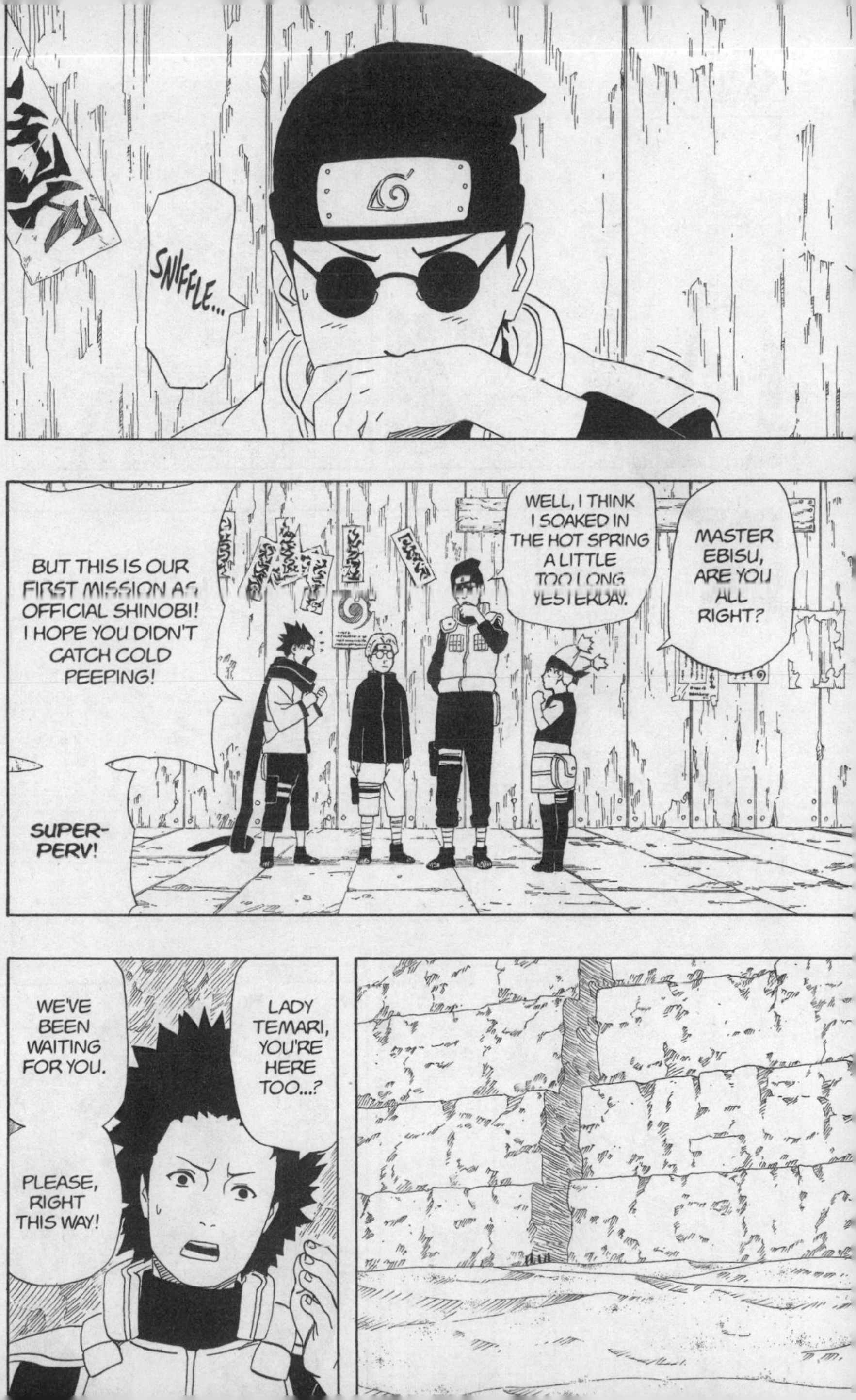
SNIFFLE...
MASTER EBISU, ARE YOU ALL RIGHT?
WELL, I THINK I SOAKED IN THE HOT SPRING A LITTLE TOO LONG YESTERDAY.
BUT THIS IS OUR FIRST MISSION AS OFFICIAL SHINOBI! I HOPE YOU DIDN'T CATCH COLD PEEPING!
SUPER-PERV!
LADY TEMARI, YOU'RE HERE TOO...?
WE'VE BEEN WAITING FOR YOU.
PLEASE, RIGHT THIS WAY!

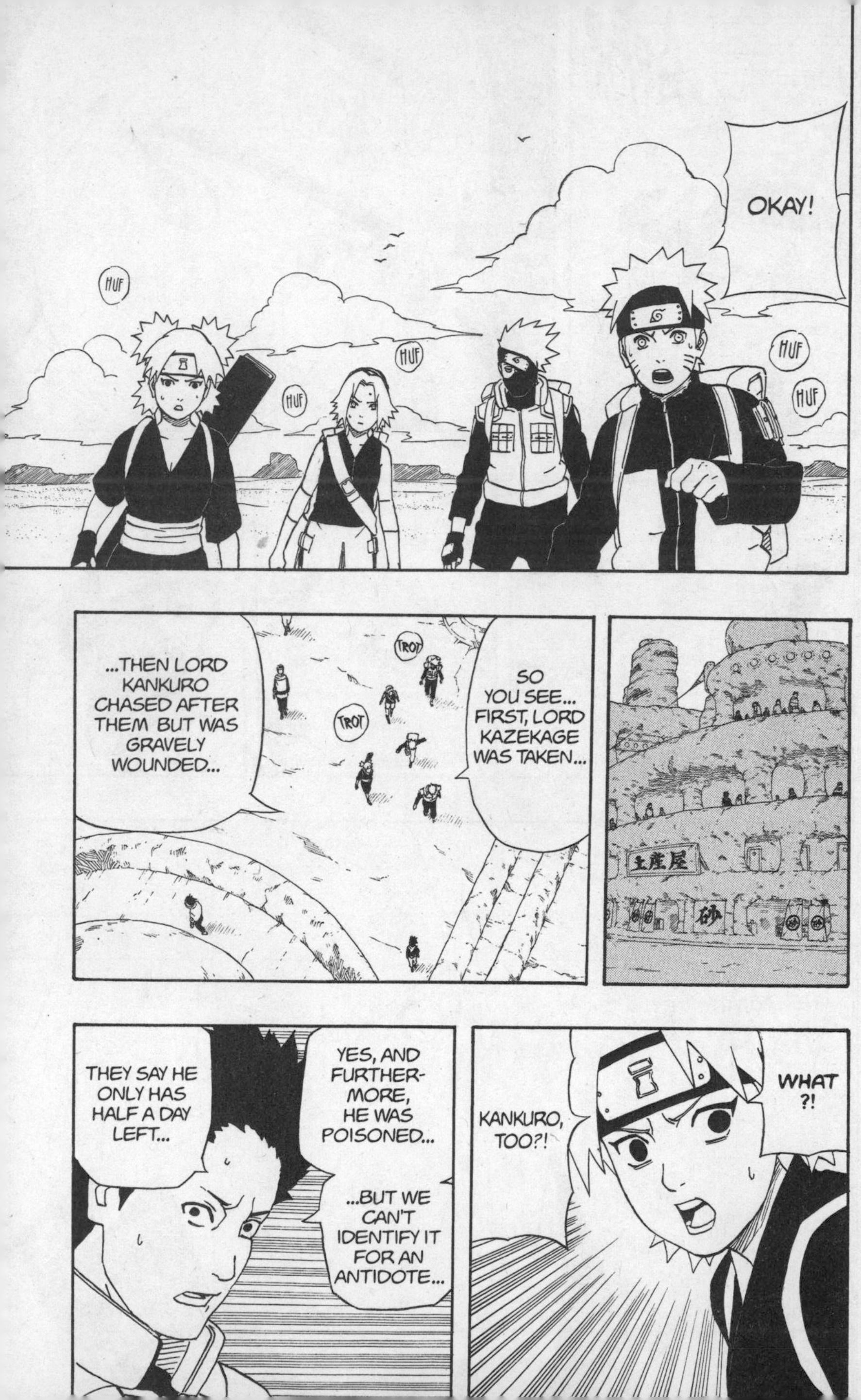
OKAY!
HUF
HUF
HUF
HUF
HUF
土産屋
砂
SO YOU SEE... FIRST, LORD KAZEKAGE WAS TAKEN...
TROT
TROT
...THEN LORD KANKURO CHASED AFTER THEM BUT WAS GRAVELY WOUNDED...
WHAT ?!
KANKURO, TOO?!
YES, AND FURTHER-MORE, HE WAS POISONED...
...BUT WE CAN'T IDENTIFY IT FOR AN ANTIDOTE...
THEY SAY HE ONLY HAS HALF A DAY LEFT...

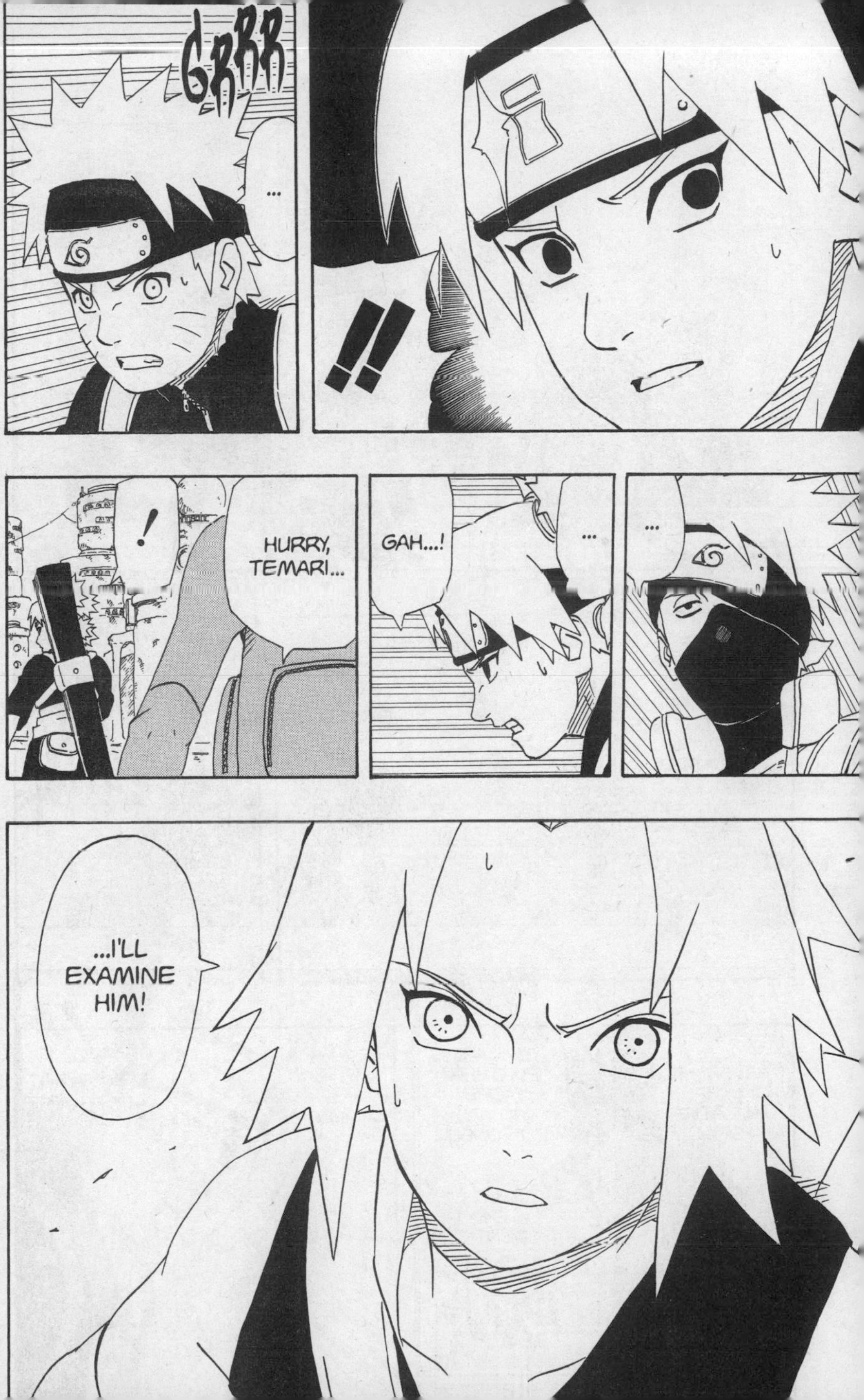
!!
GRRR
...
...
...
GAH...!
HURRY, TEMARI...
!
...I'LL EXAMINE HIM!

READ THIS WAY

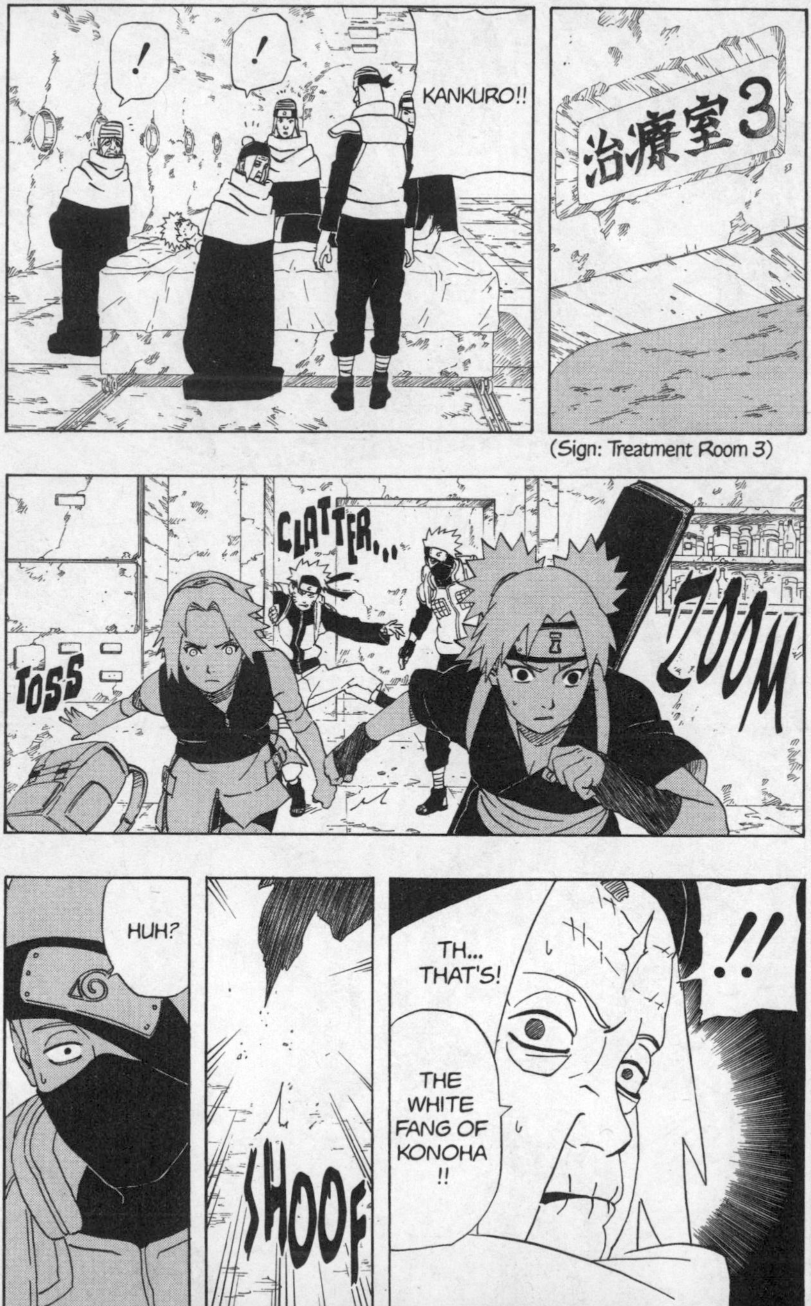
治療室3
(Sign: Treatment Room 3)
KANKURO!!
!
!
ZOOM
CLATTER...
TOSS
!!
TH... THAT'S!
THE WHITE FANG OF KONOHA !!
SHOOF
HUH?

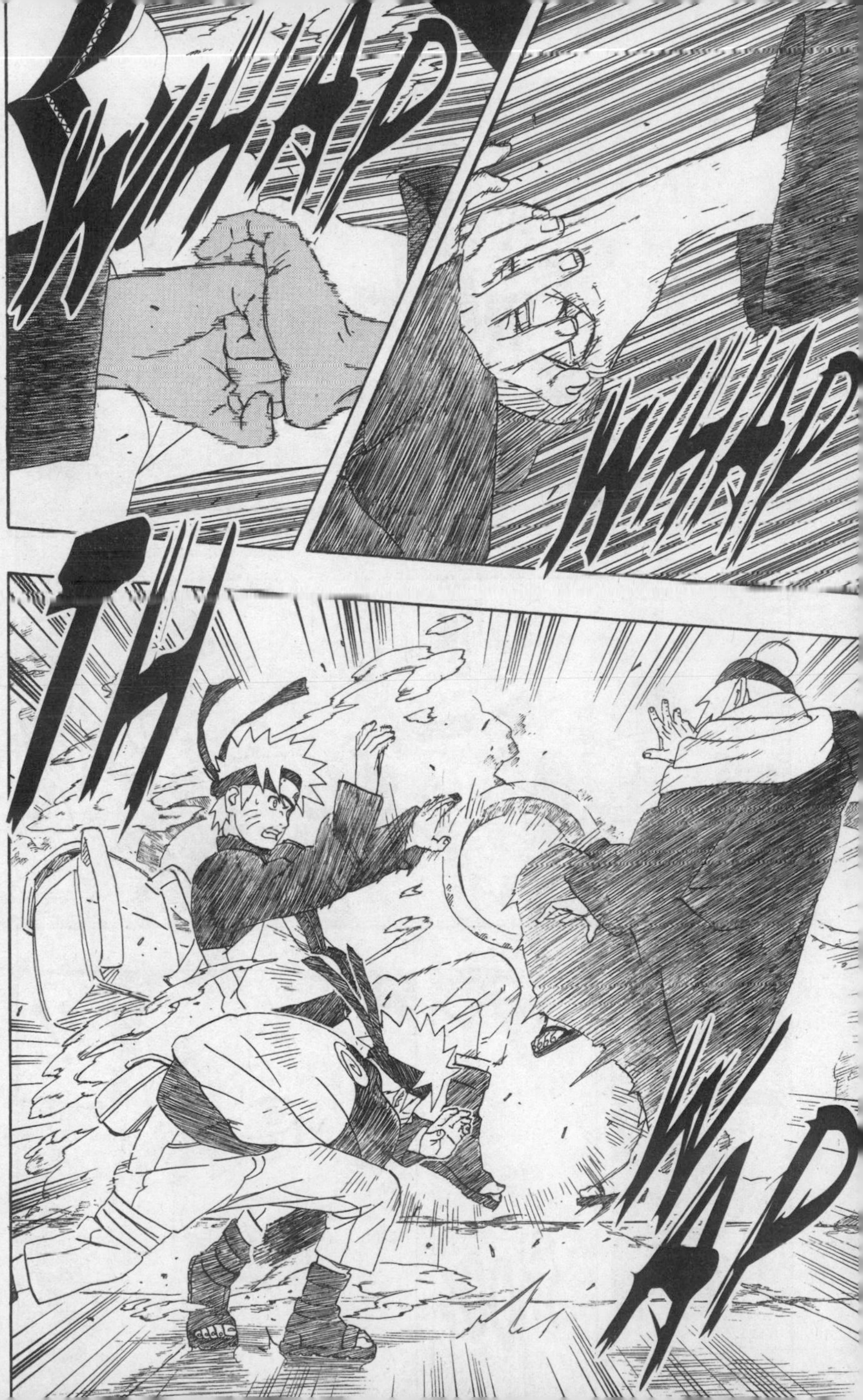
WHAP
SWHAP
THWAP

READ THIS WAY

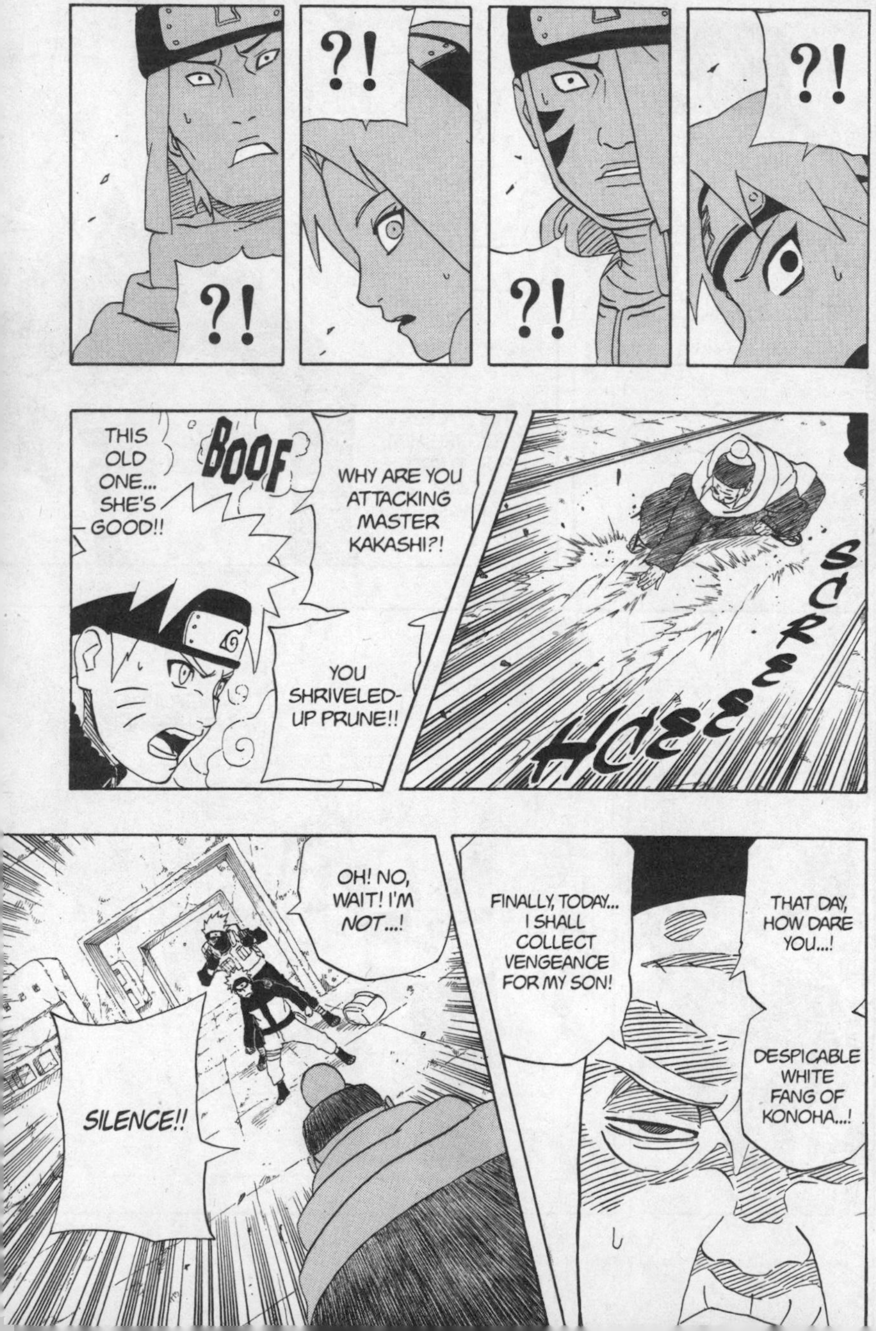
?!
?!
?!
?!
WHY ARE YOU ATTACKING MASTER KAKASHI?!
BOOF
THIS OLD ONE... SHE'S GOOD!!
YOU SHRIVELED-UP PRUNE!!
THAT DAY, HOW DARE YOU...!
FINALLY, TODAY... I SHALL COLLECT VENGEANCE FOR MY SON!
DESPICABLE WHITE FANG OF KONOHA...!
OH! NO, WAIT! I'M *NOT*...!
SILENCE!!

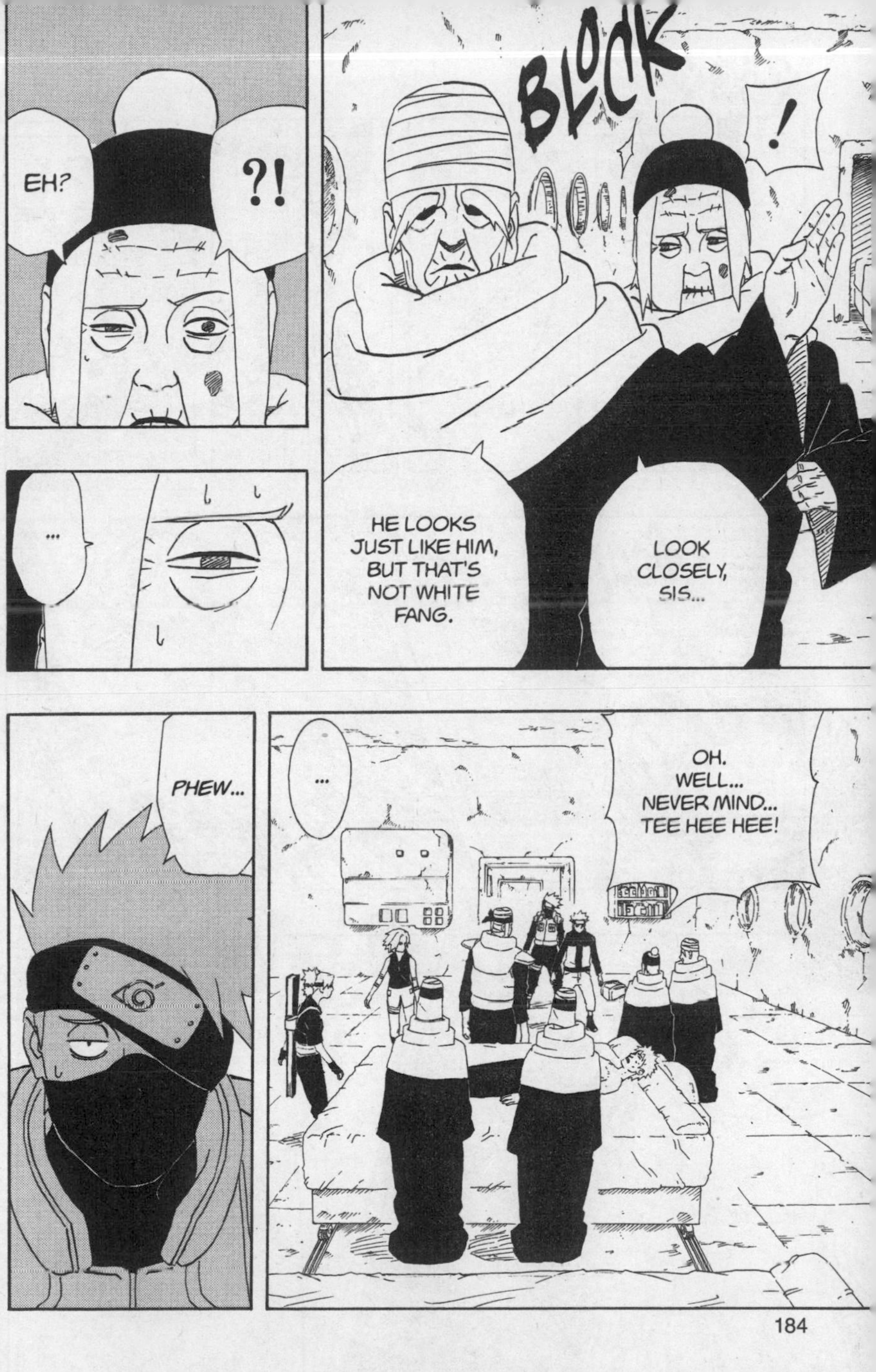
BLOCK
!
LOOK CLOSELY, SIS...
HE LOOKS JUST LIKE HIM, BUT THAT'S NOT WHITE FANG.
?!
EH?
...
OH. WELL... NEVER MIND... TEE HEE HEE!
...
PHEW...

READ THIS WAY

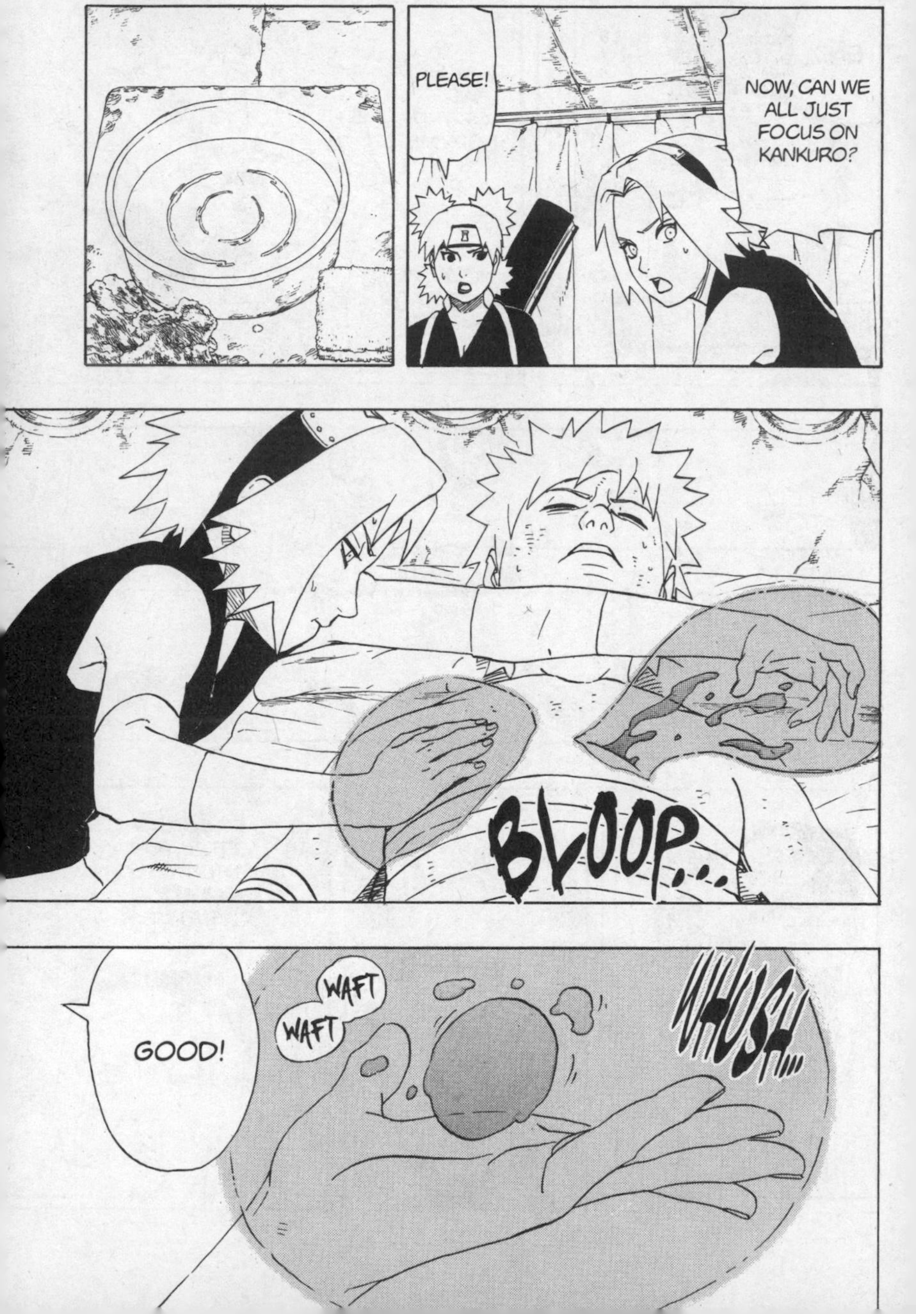
NOW, CAN WE ALL JUST FOCUS ON KANKURO?
PLEASE!
BLOOP...
WHUSH...
WAFT
WAFT
GOOD!

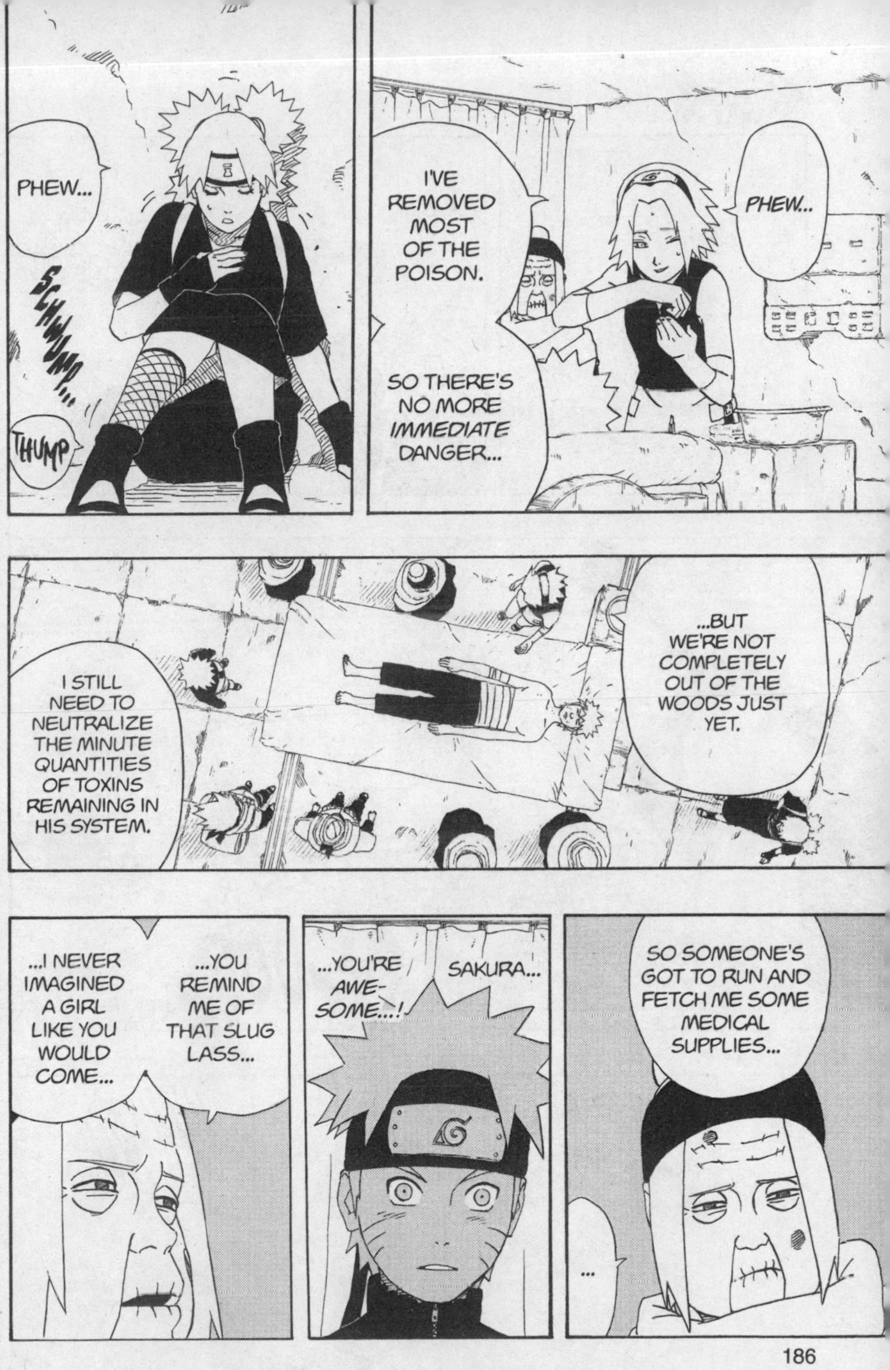
PHEW...
I'VE REMOVED MOST OF THE POISON.
SO THERE'S NO MORE IMMEDIATE DANGER...
PHEW...
SCHWUMP...
THUMP
...BUT WE'RE NOT COMPLETELY OUT OF THE WOODS JUST YET.
I STILL NEED TO NEUTRALIZE THE MINUTE QUANTITIES OF TOXINS REMAINING IN HIS SYSTEM.
SO SOMEONE'S GOT TO RUN AND FETCH ME SOME MEDICAL SUPPLIES...
...
SAKURA...
...YOU'RE AWE-SOME...!
...YOU REMIND ME OF THAT SLUG LASS...
...I NEVER IMAGINED A GIRL LIKE YOU WOULD COME...

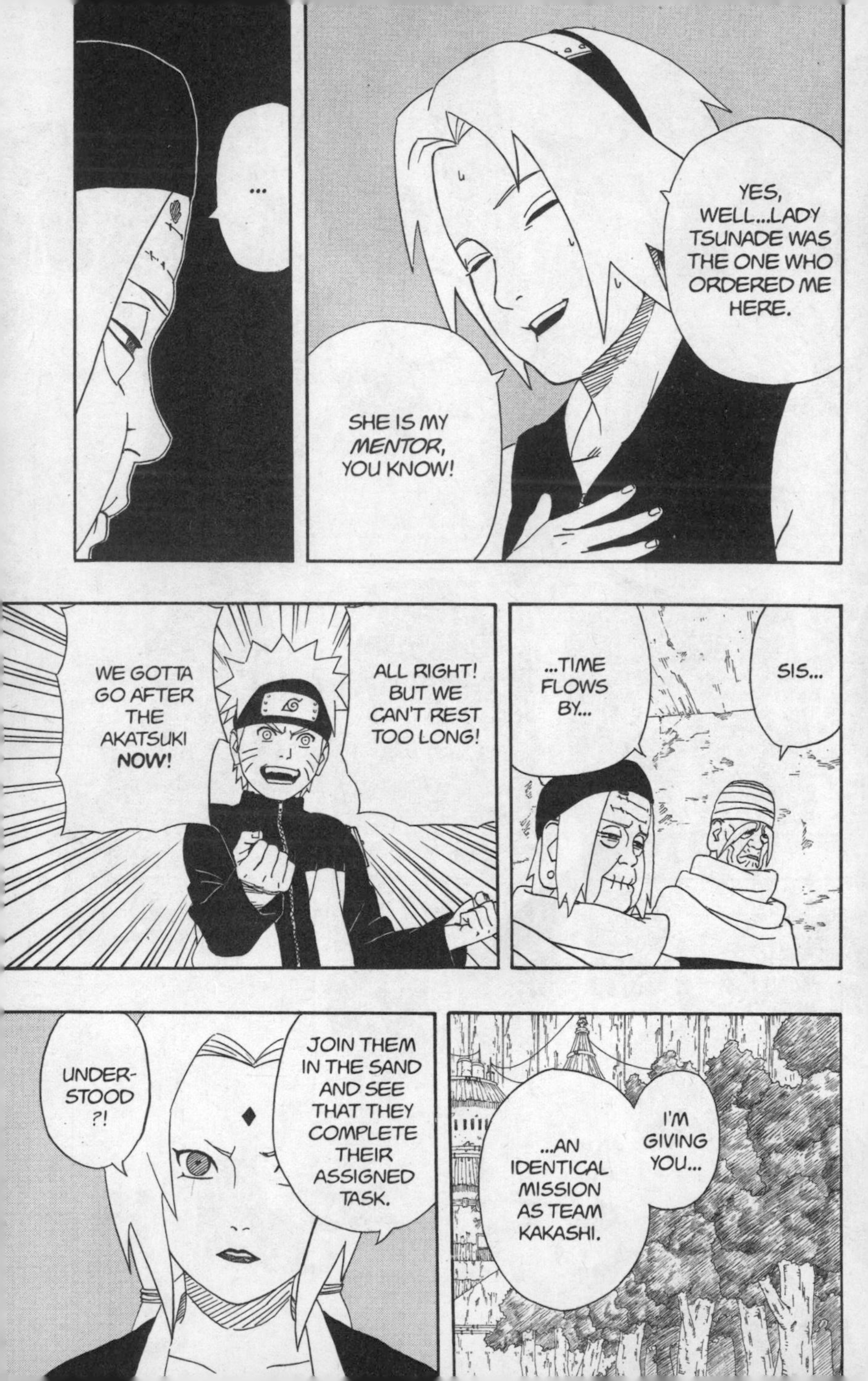
YES, WELL...LADY TSUNADE WAS THE ONE WHO ORDERED ME HERE.
SHE IS MY *MENTOR*, YOU KNOW!
...
SIS...
...TIME FLOWS BY...
ALL RIGHT! BUT WE CAN'T REST TOO LONG!
WE GOTTA GO AFTER THE AKATSUKI **NOW**!
I'M GIVING YOU...
...AN IDENTICAL MISSION AS TEAM KAKASHI.
JOIN THEM IN THE SAND AND SEE THAT THEY COMPLETE THEIR ASSIGNED TASK.
UNDER-STOOD?!

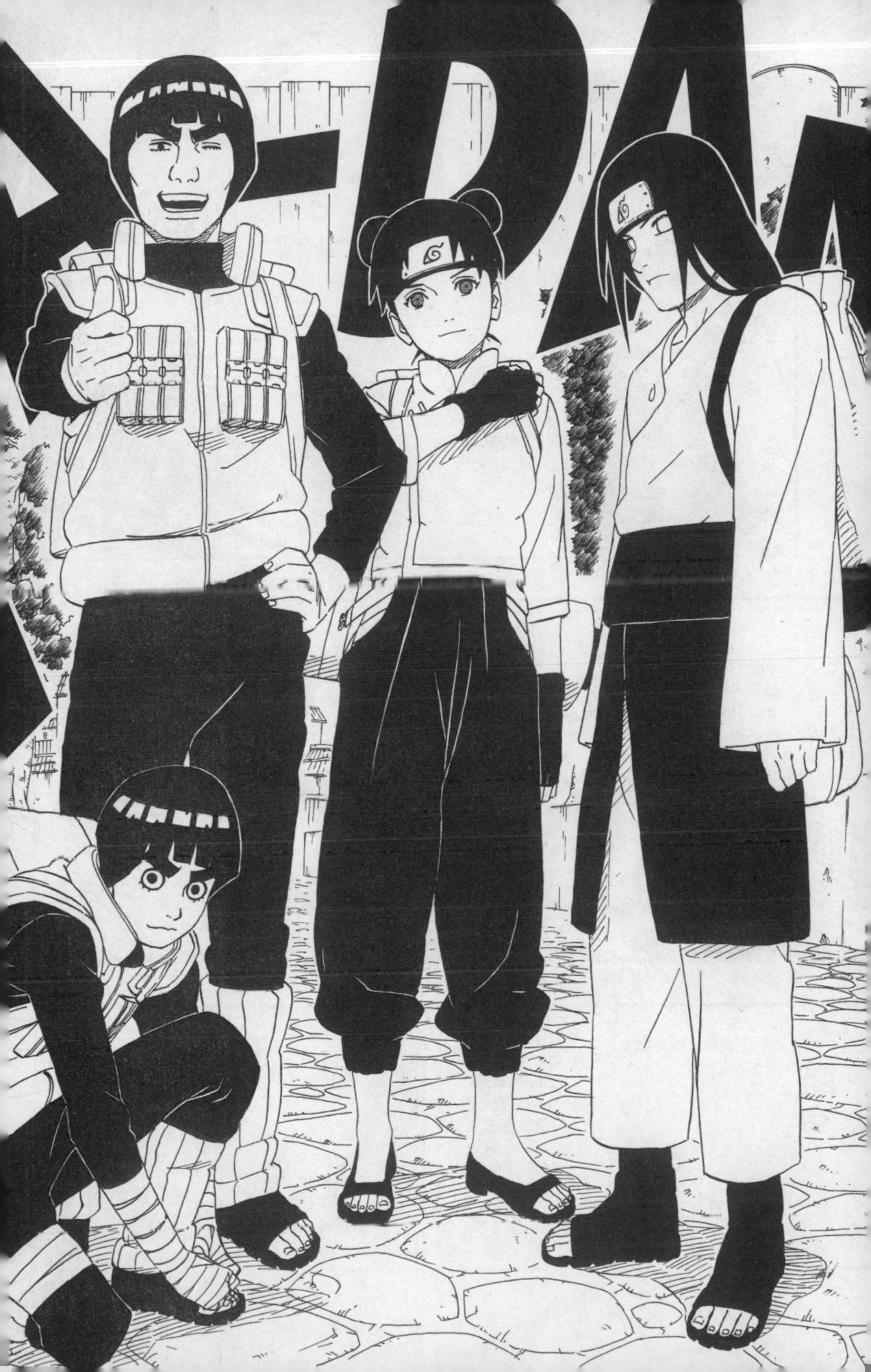
DA

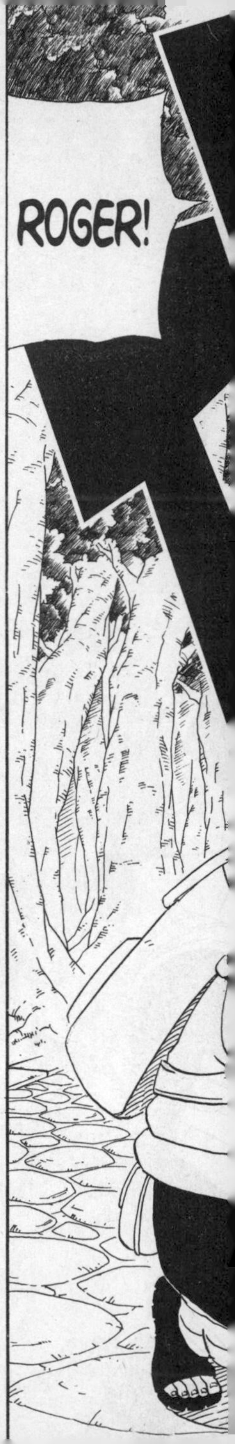
ROGER!

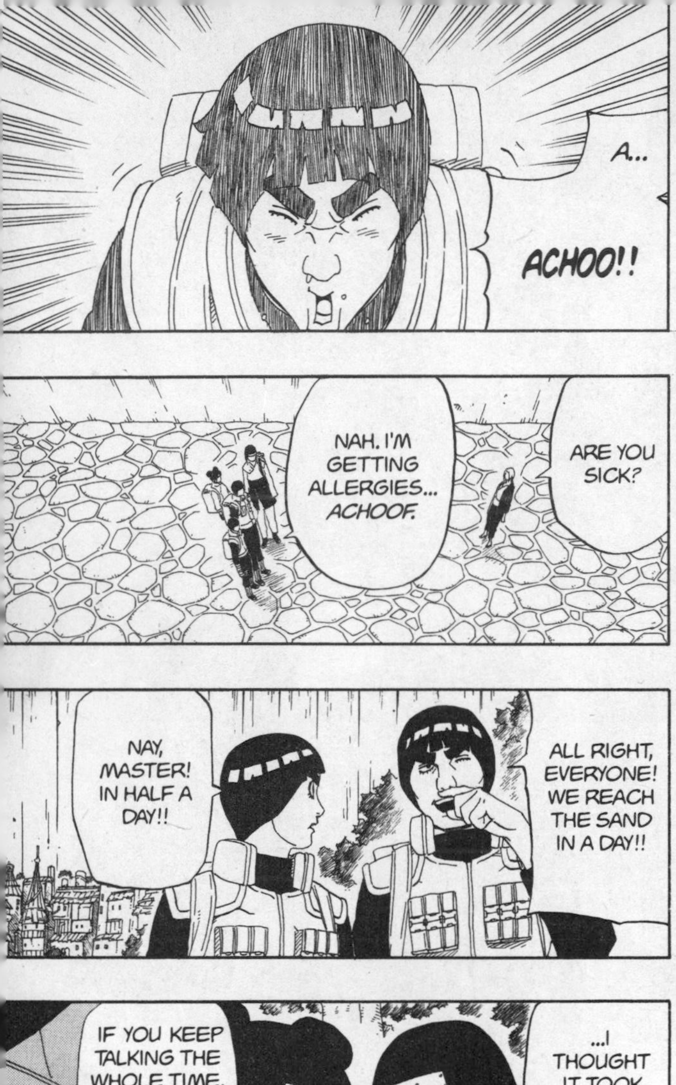
A...
ACHOO!!
ARE YOU SICK?
NAH. I'M GETTING ALLERGIES... *ACHOOF.*
ALL RIGHT, EVERYONE! WE REACH THE SAND IN A DAY!!
NAY, MASTER! IN HALF A DAY!!
...I THOUGHT IT TOOK LIKE *THREE* DAYS...
IF YOU KEEP TALKING THE WHOLE TIME, IT'LL SEEM LIKE FOR-EVER... **CUT IT OUT!**

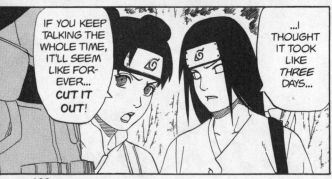

NARUTO

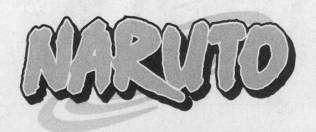

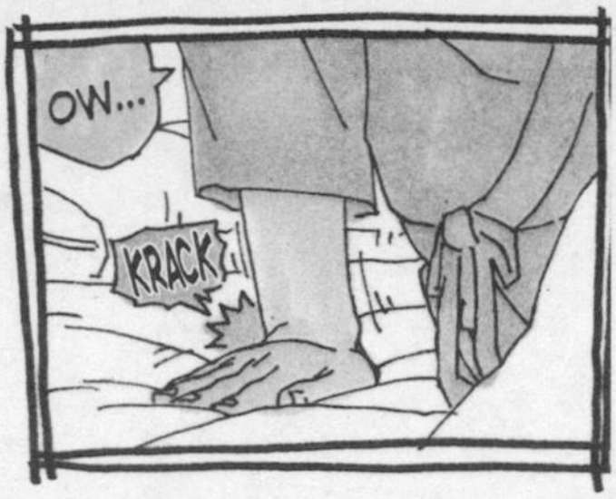
OW...
KRACK

These days, I often hurt my wrists when I wake up in the morning. When I sit up, I put too much weight on one hand and end up twisting it. You're not too aware of things when you've just woken up. So, everyone please be careful when you wake up in the morning.

岸本斉史

—Masashi Kishimoto, 2005

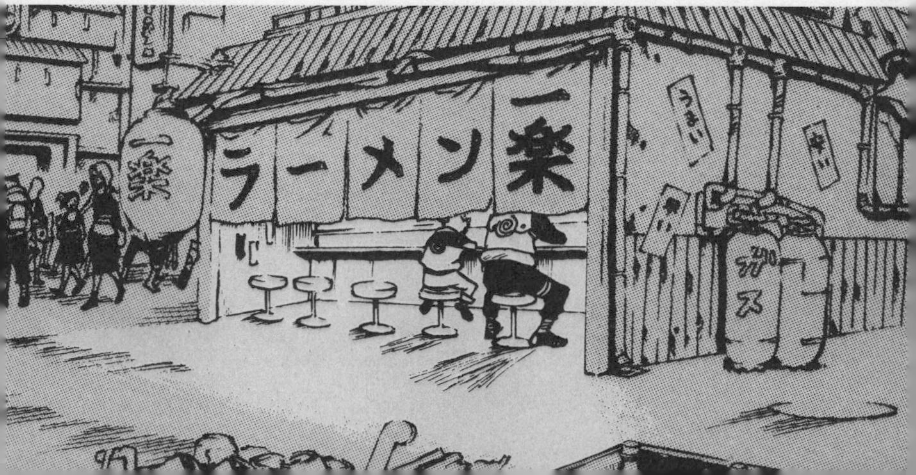
一楽
ラーメン一楽
うまい

NARUTO

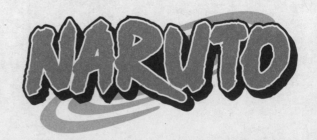

SHONEN JUMP MANGA EDITION

NARUTO

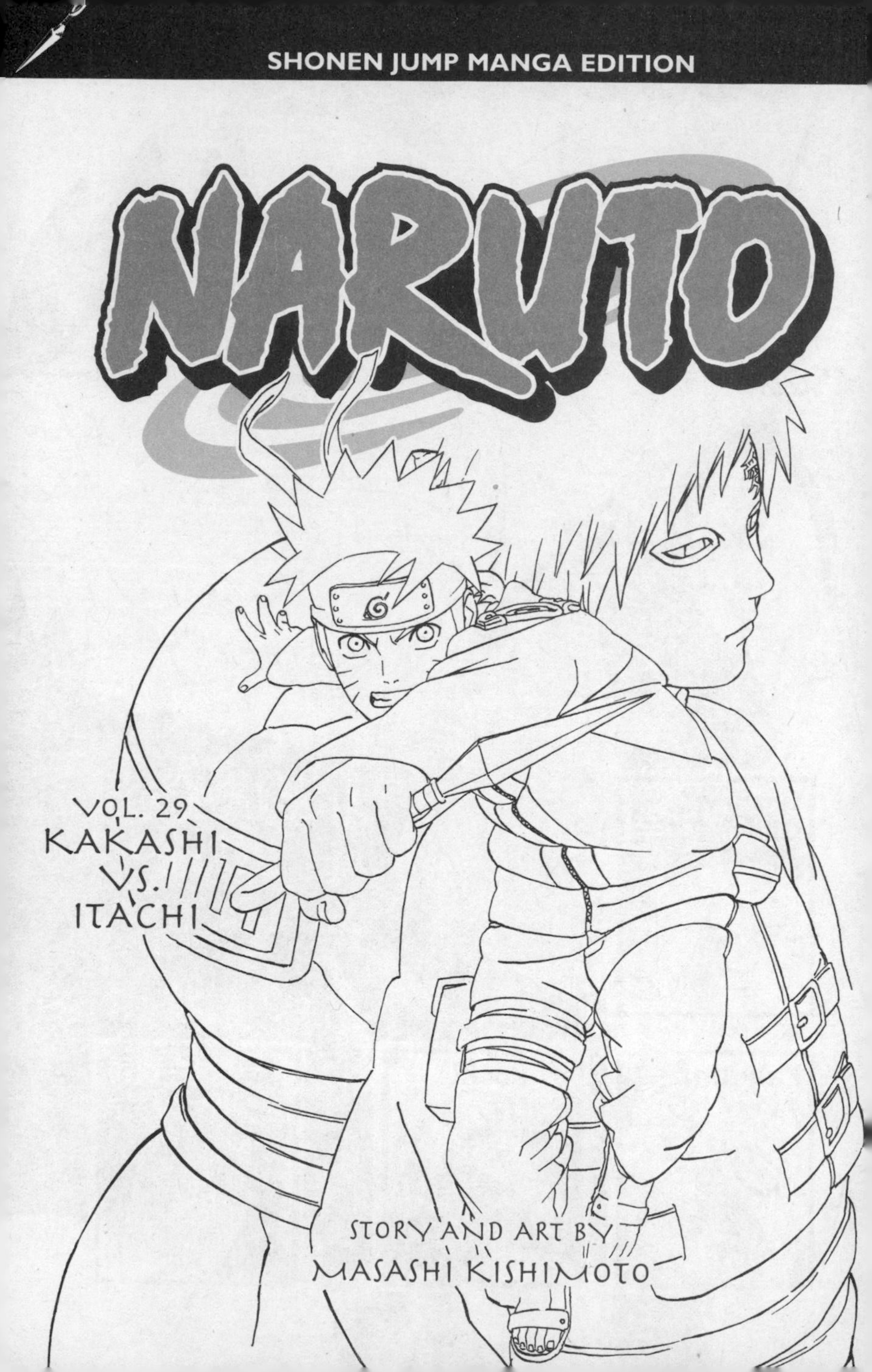

VOL. 29

KAKASHI VS. ITACHI

STORY AND ART BY

MASASHI KISHIMOTO

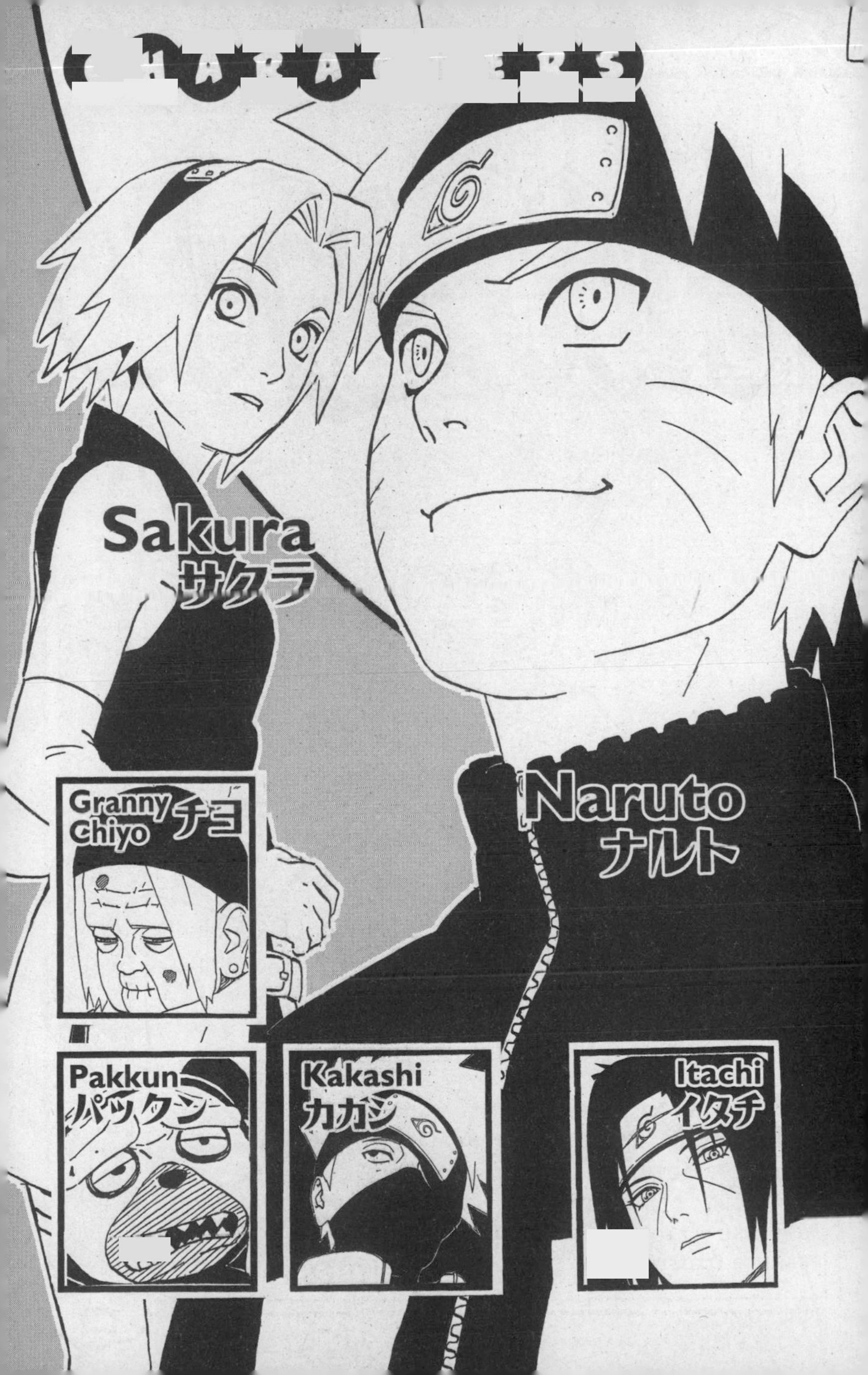
Naruto
ナルト
Sakura
サクラ
Granny Chiyo
チヨ
Itachi
イタチ
Kakashi
カカシ
Pakkun
パックン

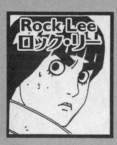

Gaara 我愛羅
Might Guy マイト・ガイ
Rock Lee ロック・リー
Tenten テンテン
Neji ネジ
Kisame 鬼鮫

The Story So Far...

Naruto, the biggest troublemaker at the Ninja Academy in the village of Konohagakure, finally becomes a ninja along with his classmates Sasuke and Sakura. Right in the middle of the Chûnin Selection Exams, Orochimaru and his henchmen launch *Operation Destroy Konoha*, which ends when the revered leader of the village, the Third Hokage, sacrifices his own life to save his people.

Tsunade, one of the Three Great Shinobi of Konoha legend, becomes the Fifth Hokage. Sasuke, succumbing to the allure of Orochimaru's power, leaves the village with the deadly Sound Ninja Four. Naruto fights valiantly against Sasuke, but can't stop him.

Two years pass following that battle, and Naruto and his comrades train and mature. The mysterious Gaara becomes Kazekage and falls into the hands of the secret society of the Akatsuki! Naruto with one team and Lee with another set out for the village of Suna-gakure to save him!!

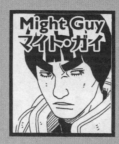

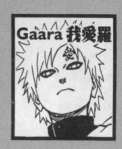

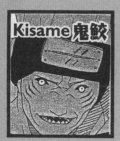

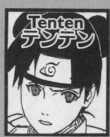

NARUTO

VOL. 29
KAKASHI VS. ITACHI

CONTENTS

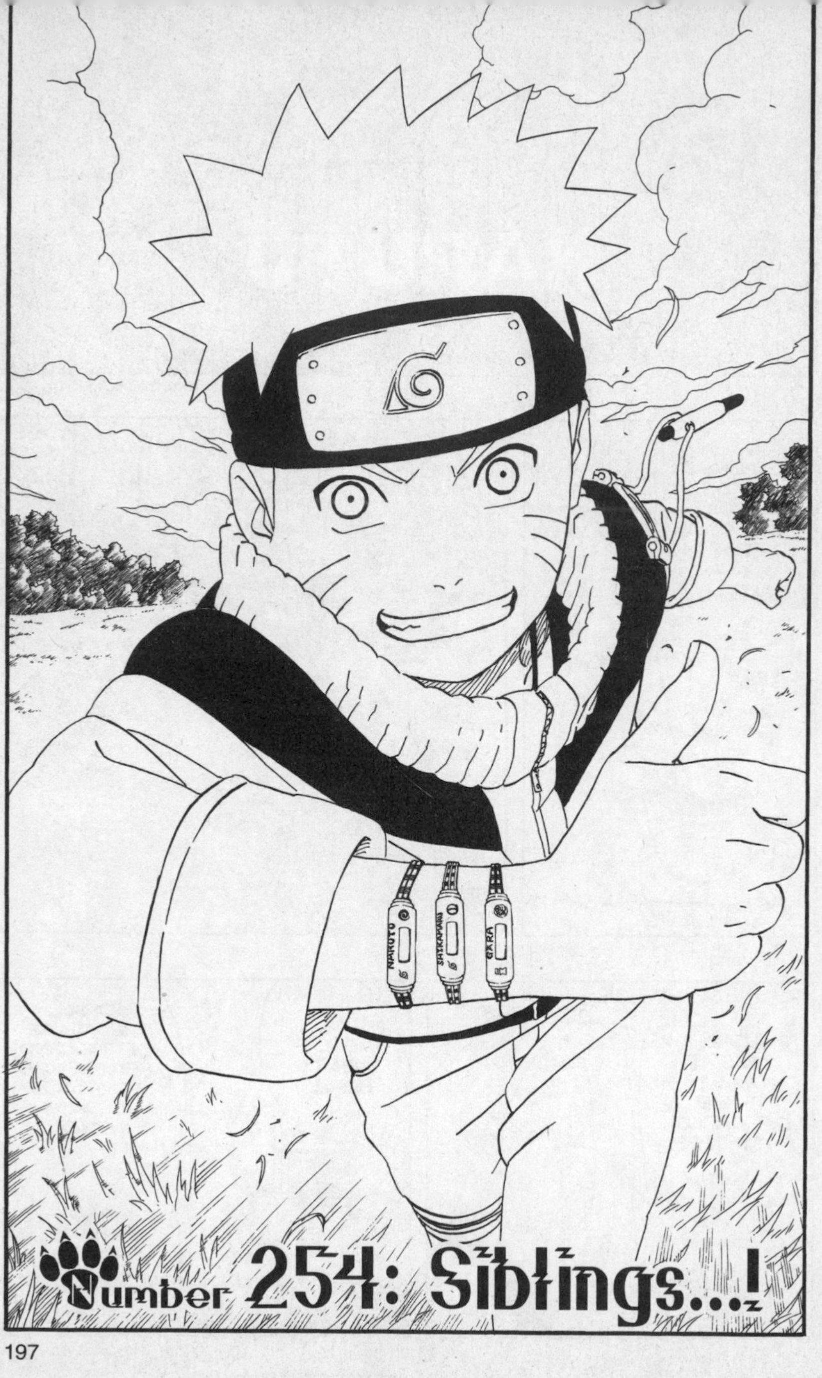
NARUTO
SHIKAMARU
GAARA
Number 254: Siblings...!

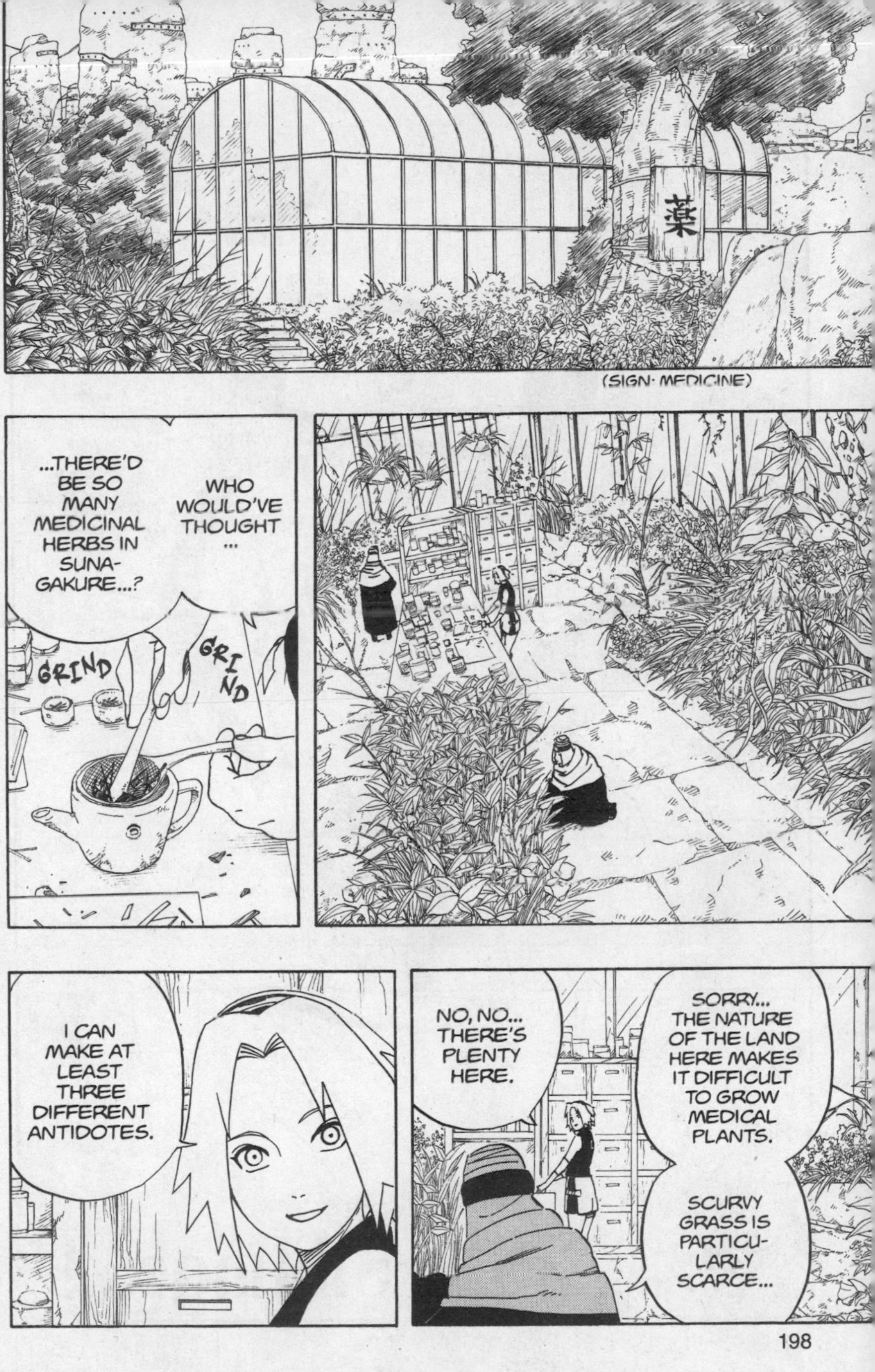
薬
(SIGN: MEDICINE)
WHO WOULD'VE THOUGHT...
...THERE'D BE SO MANY MEDICINAL HERBS IN SUNA-GAKURE...?
GRIND
GRIND
SORRY... THE NATURE OF THE LAND HERE MAKES IT DIFFICULT TO GROW MEDICAL PLANTS.
SCURVY GRASS IS PARTICU-LARLY SCARCE...
NO, NO... THERE'S PLENTY HERE.
I CAN MAKE AT LEAST THREE DIFFERENT ANTIDOTES.

READ THIS WAY

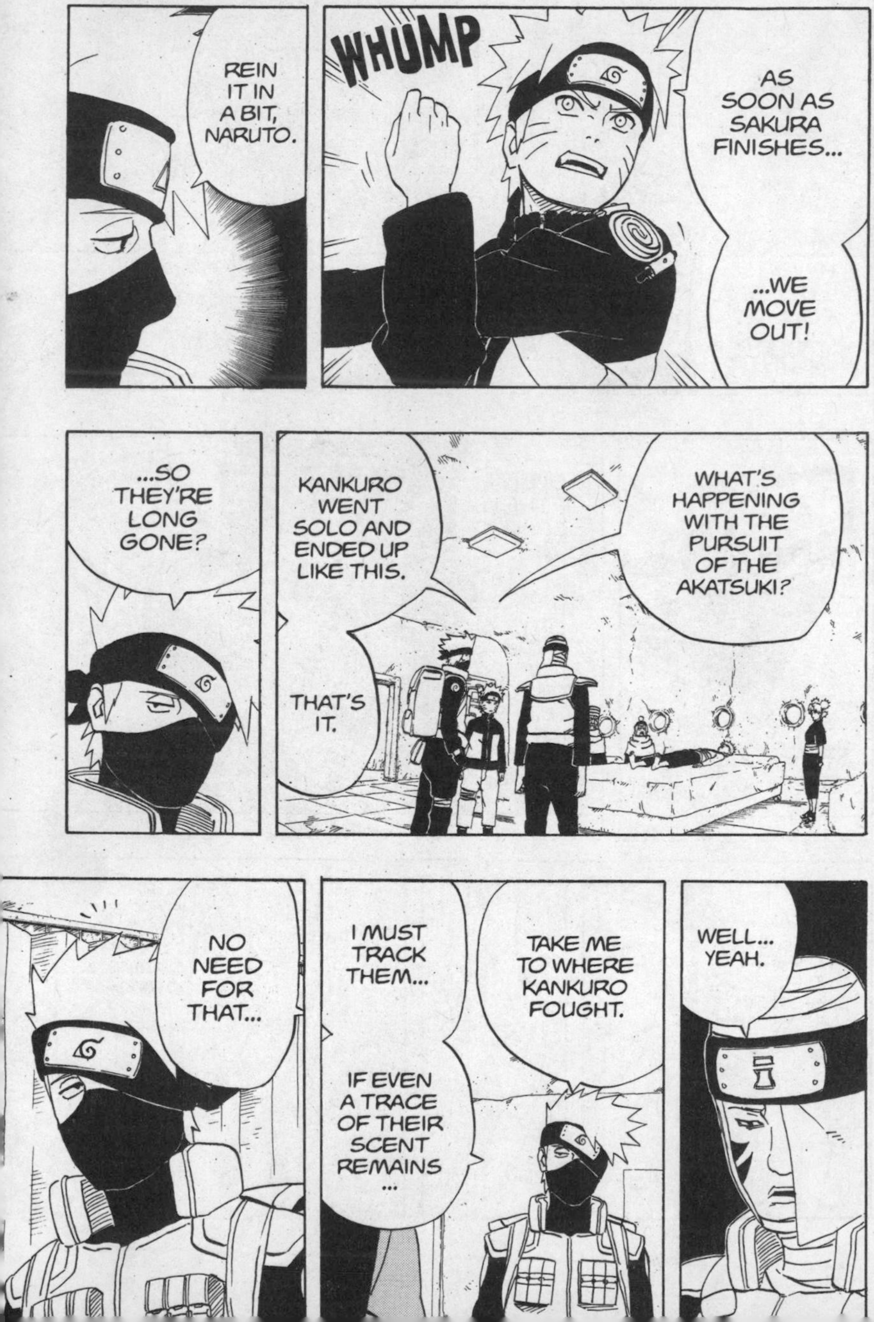
WHUMP
AS SOON AS SAKURA FINISHES...
...WE MOVE OUT!
REIN IT IN A BIT, NARUTO.
WHAT'S HAPPENING WITH THE PURSUIT OF THE AKATSUKI?
KANKURO WENT SOLO AND ENDED UP LIKE THIS.
THAT'S IT.
...SO THEY'RE LONG GONE?
WELL... YEAH.
TAKE ME TO WHERE KANKURO FOUGHT.
I MUST TRACK THEM...
IF EVEN A TRACE OF THEIR SCENT REMAINS...
NO NEED FOR THAT...

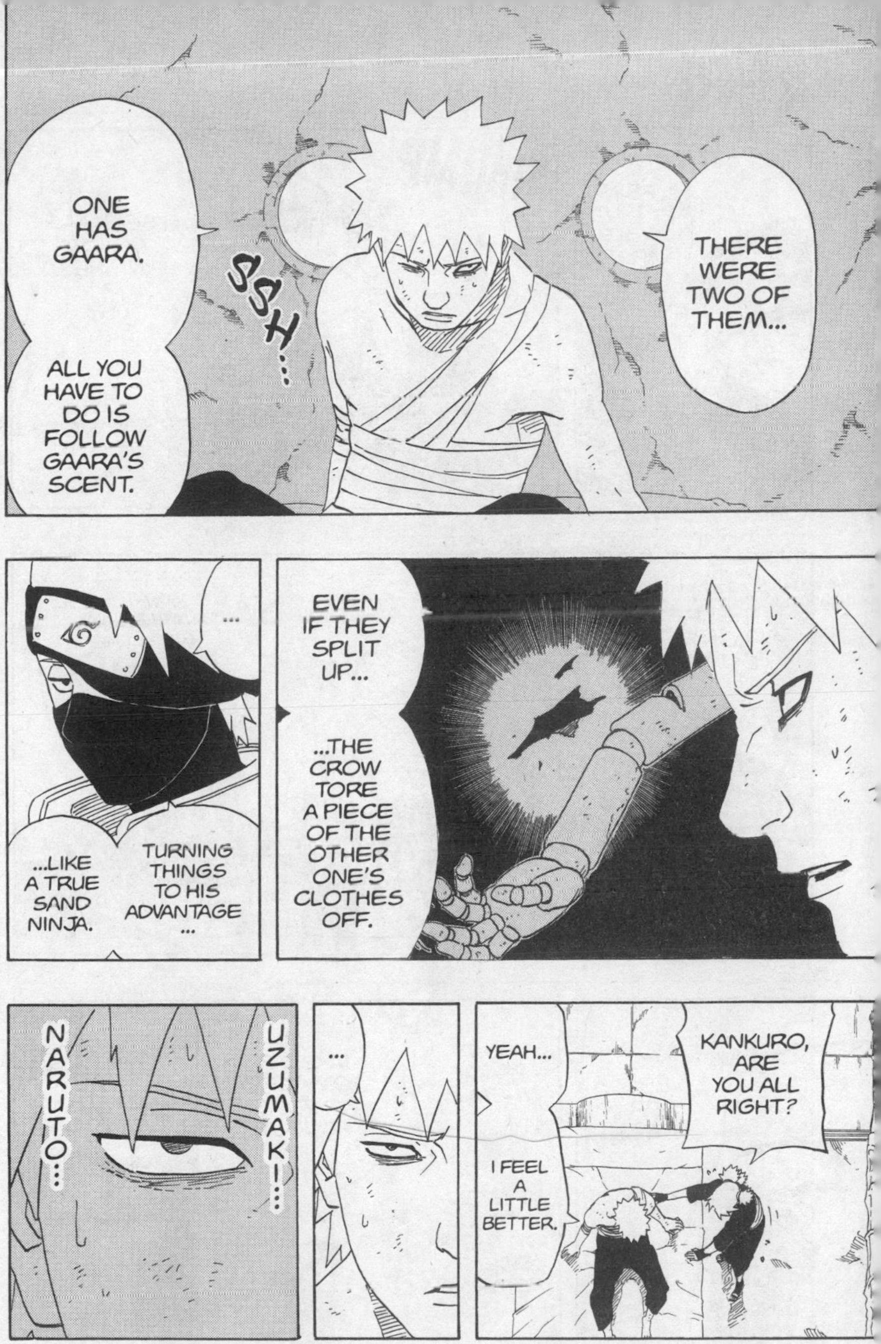
THERE WERE TWO OF THEM...
ONE HAS GAARA.
ALL YOU HAVE TO DO IS FOLLOW GAARA'S SCENT.
SSH...
EVEN IF THEY SPLIT UP...
...THE CROW TORE A PIECE OF THE OTHER ONE'S CLOTHES OFF.
...
TURNING THINGS TO HIS ADVANTAGE...
...LIKE A TRUE SAND NINJA.
KANKURO, ARE YOU ALL RIGHT?
YEAH...
I FEEL A LITTLE BETTER.
...
UZUMAKI...
NARUTO...

READ THIS WAY

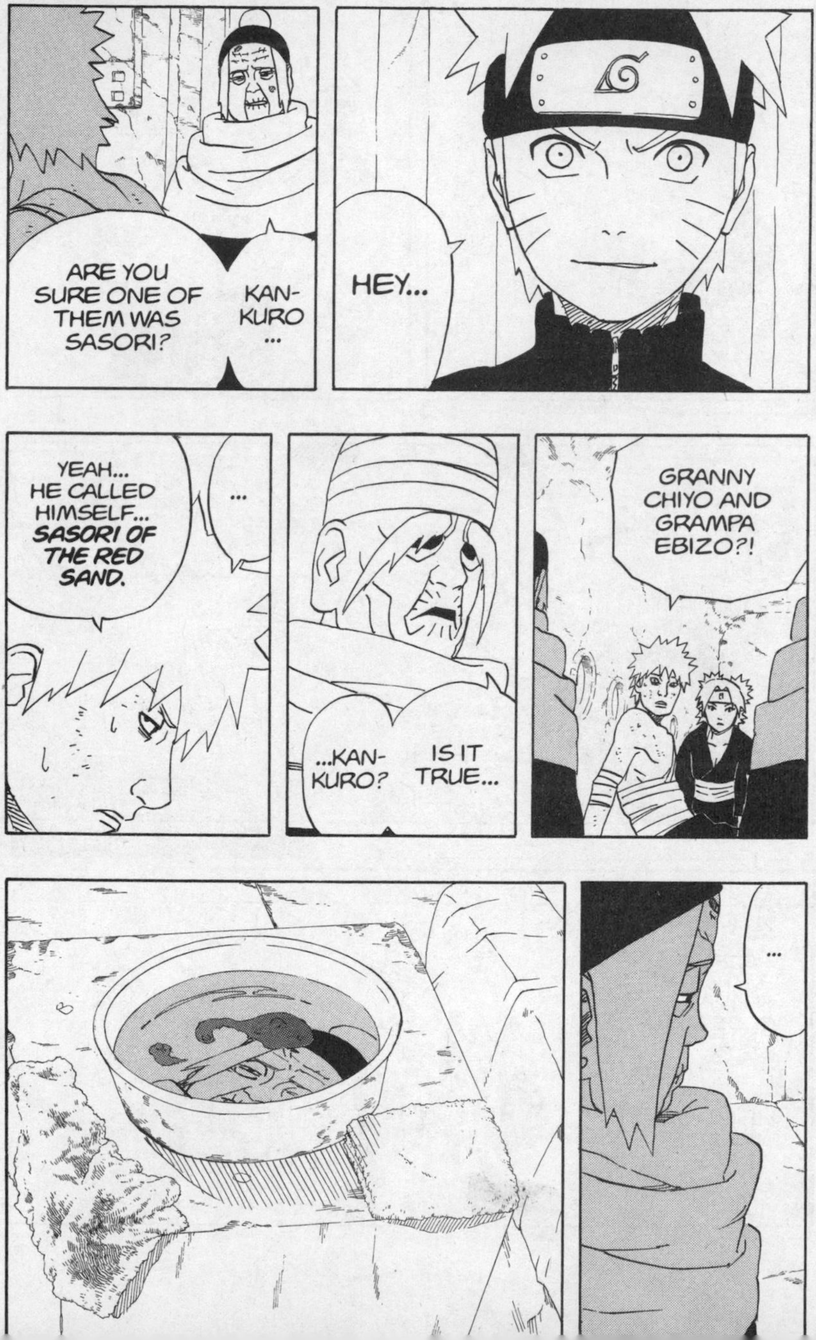
HEY...
KAN-KURO ...
ARE YOU SURE ONE OF THEM WAS SASORI?
GRANNY CHIYO AND GRAMPA EBIZO?!
IS IT TRUE...
...KAN-KURO?
...
YEAH... HE CALLED HIMSELF... *SASORI OF THE RED SAND.*
...

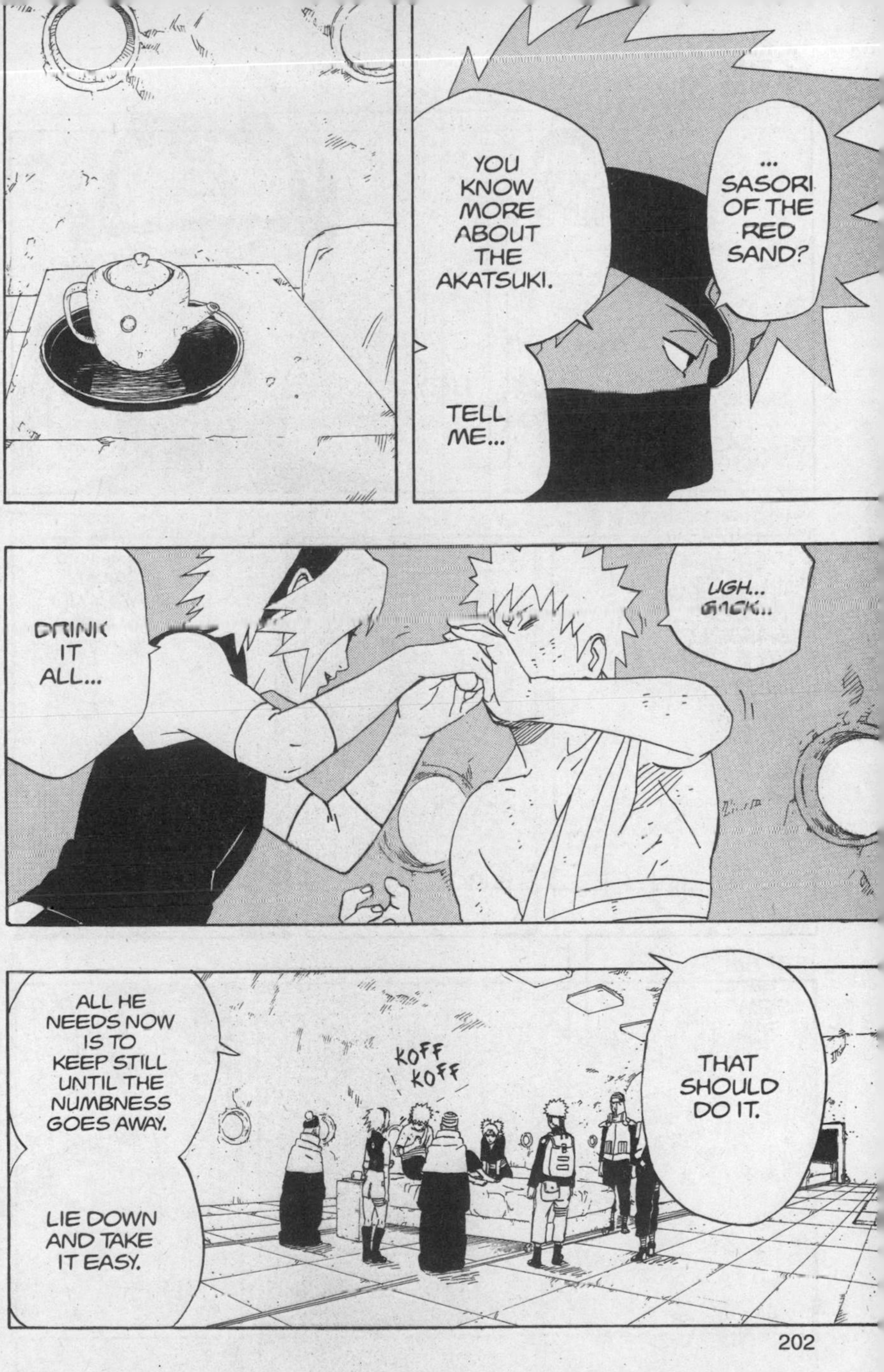
... SASORI OF THE RED SAND?
YOU KNOW MORE ABOUT THE AKATSUKI.
TELL ME...
UGH...
DRINK IT ALL...
THAT SHOULD DO IT.
KOFF KOFF
ALL HE NEEDS NOW IS TO KEEP STILL UNTIL THE NUMBNESS GOES AWAY.
LIE DOWN AND TAKE IT EASY.

READ THIS WAY

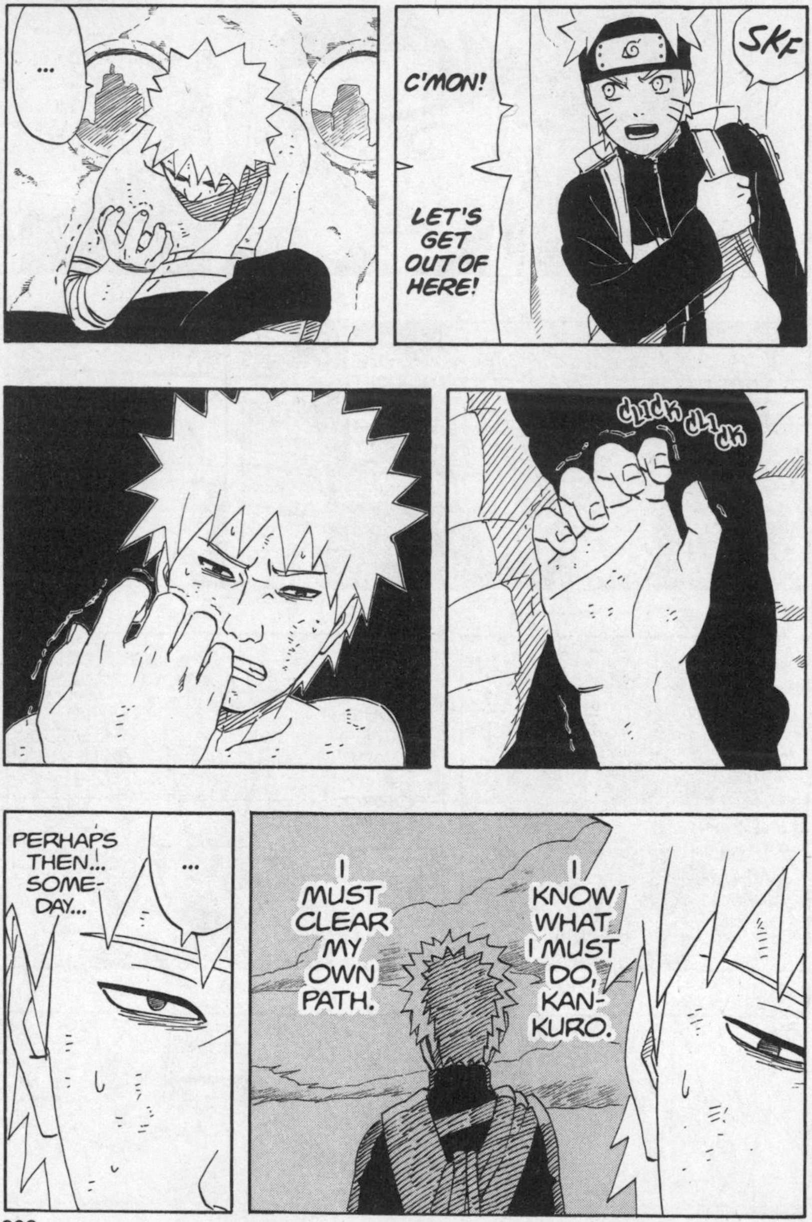
SKF
C'MON!
LET'S GET OUT OF HERE!
...
CLICK CLICK
I KNOW WHAT I MUST DO, KANKURO.
I MUST CLEAR MY OWN PATH.
...
PERHAPS THEN... SOMEDAY...

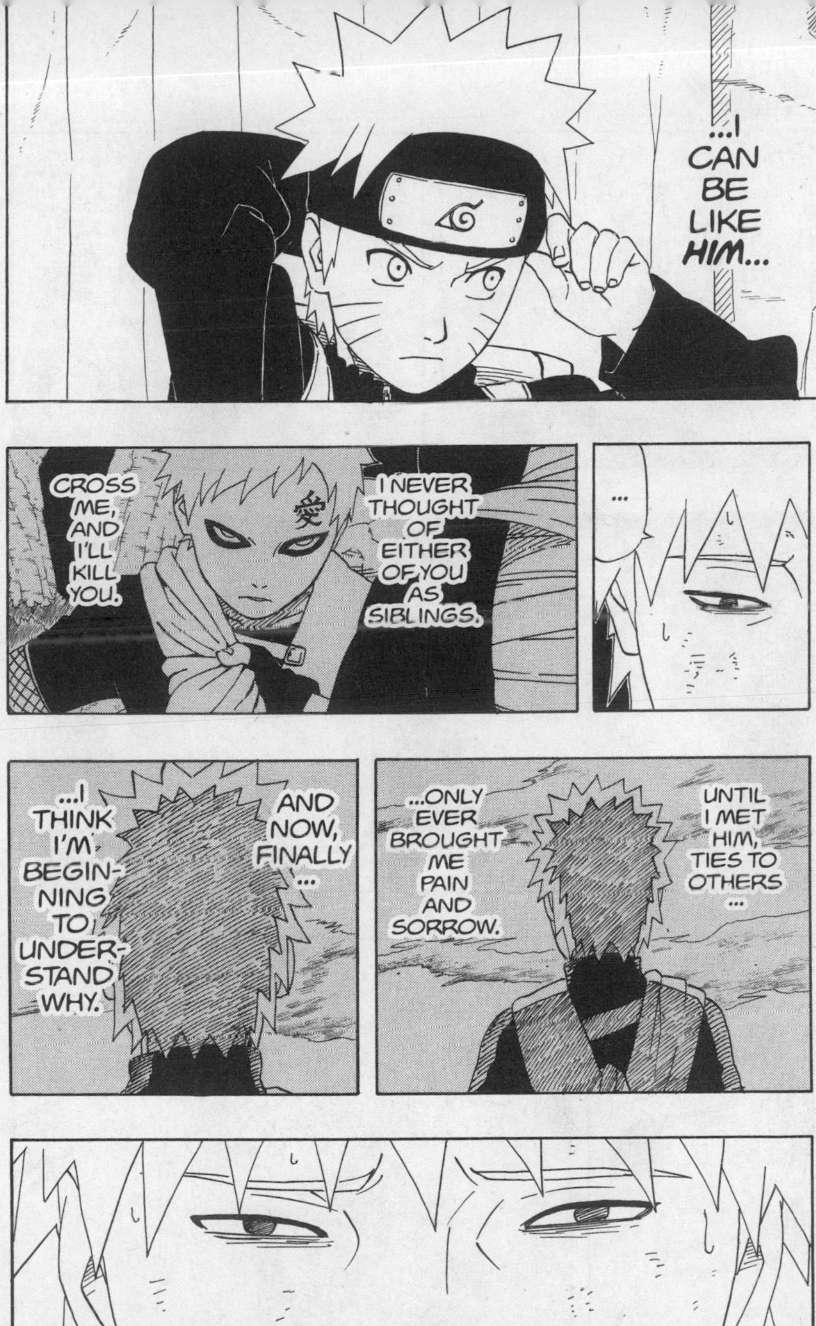
...I CAN BE LIKE HIM...
...
I NEVER THOUGHT OF EITHER OF YOU AS SIBLINGS.
CROSS ME, AND I'LL KILL YOU.
UNTIL I MET HIM, TIES TO OTHERS...
...ONLY EVER BROUGHT ME PAIN AND SORROW.
AND NOW, FINALLY...
...I THINK I'M BEGINNING TO UNDERSTAND WHY.

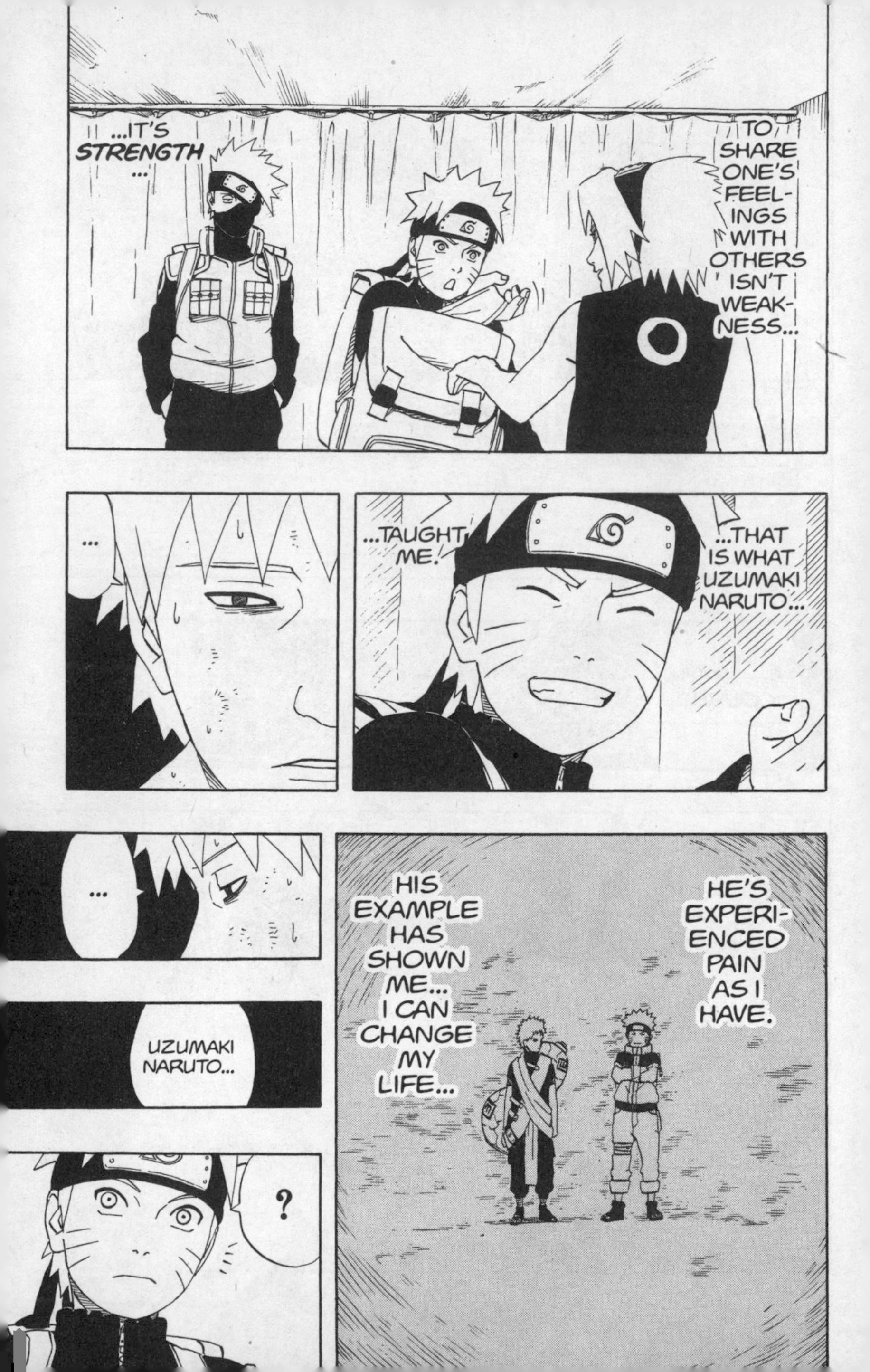
TO SHARE ONE'S FEEL-INGS WITH OTHERS ISN'T WEAK-NESS...
...IT'S **STRENGTH** ...
...THAT IS WHAT UZUMAKI NARUTO...
...TAUGHT ME.
...
HE'S EXPERI-ENCED PAIN AS I HAVE.
HIS EXAMPLE HAS SHOWN ME... I CAN CHANGE MY LIFE...
...
UZUMAKI NARUTO...
?

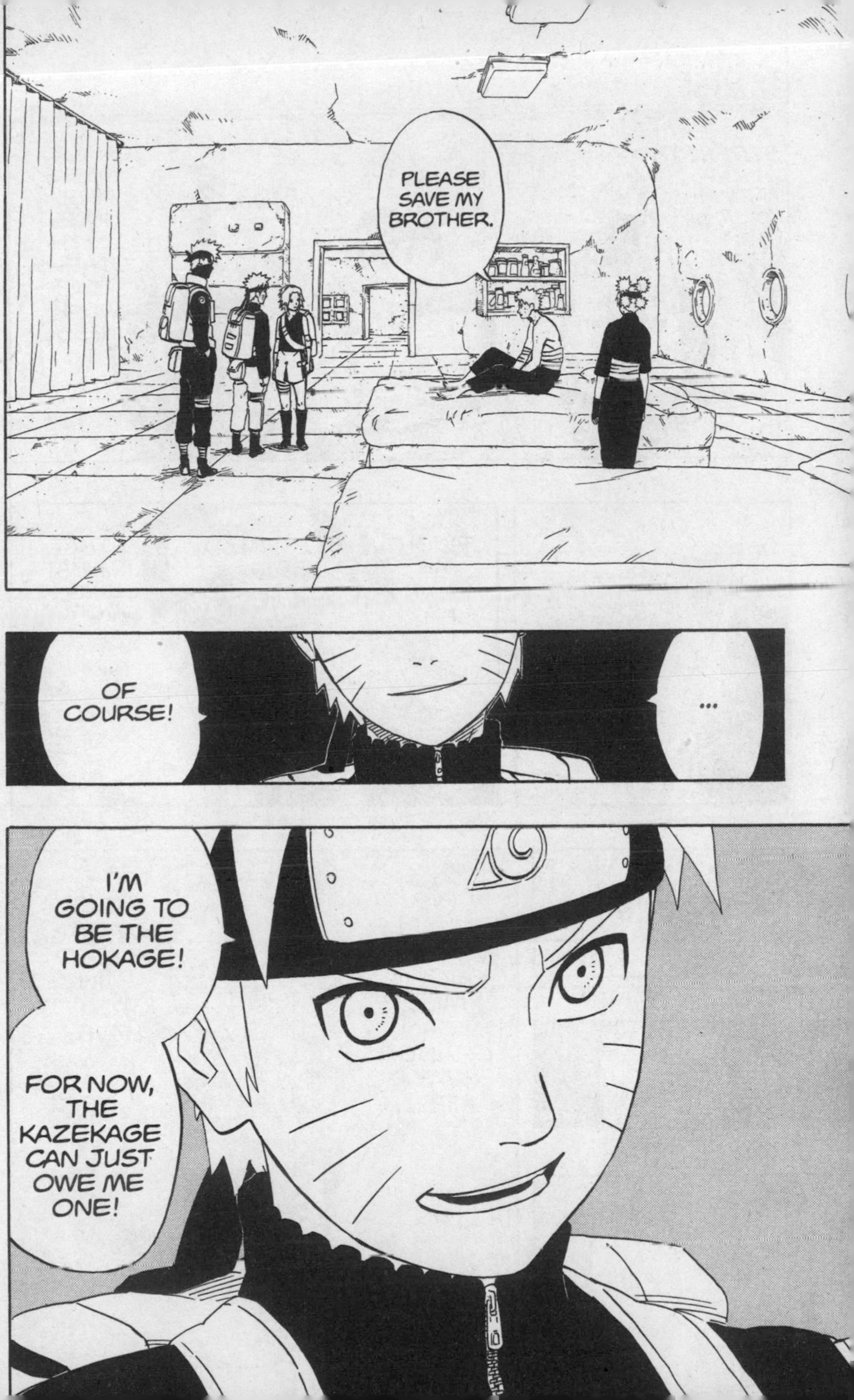
PLEASE SAVE MY BROTHER.
...
OF COURSE!
I'M GOING TO BE THE HOKAGE!
FOR NOW, THE KAZEKAGE CAN JUST OWE ME ONE!

READ THIS WAY

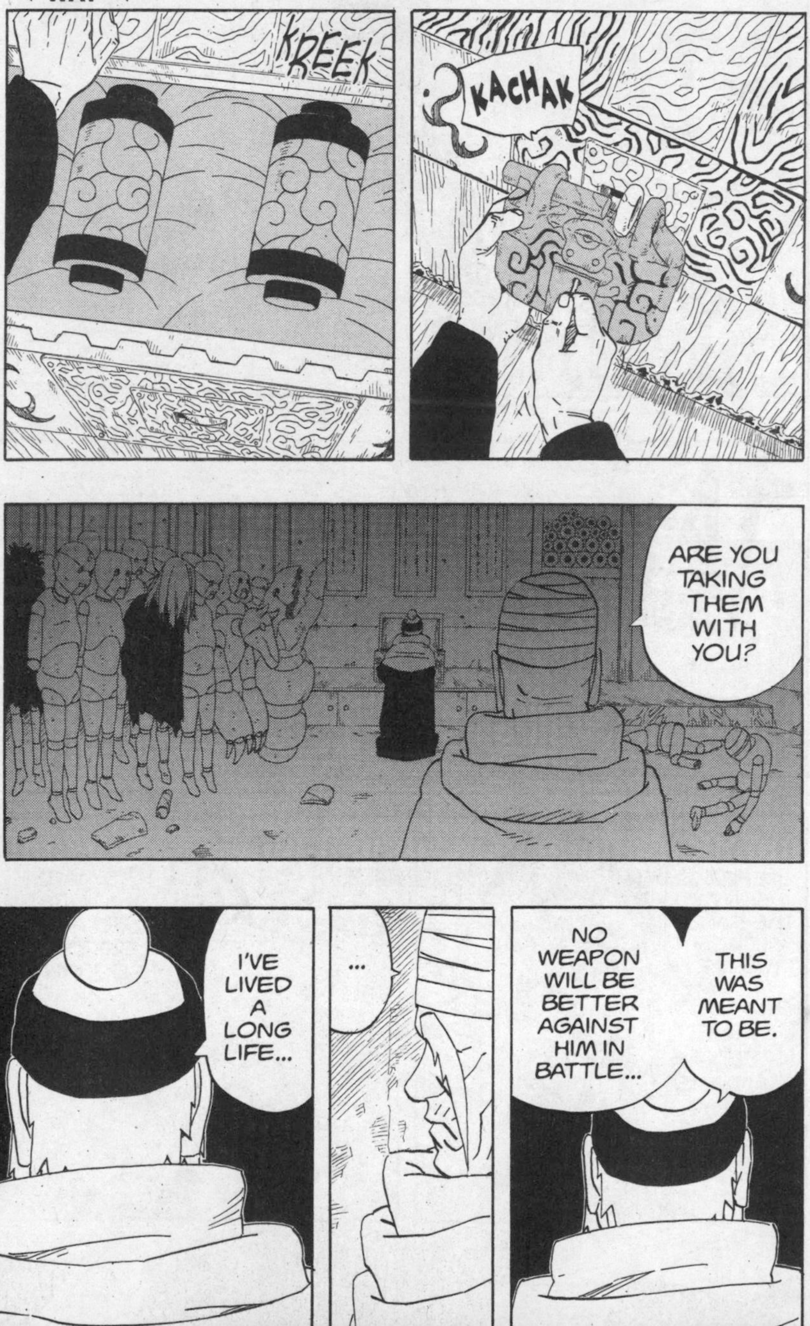
KACHAK
KREEK
ARE YOU TAKING THEM WITH YOU?
THIS WAS MEANT TO BE.
NO WEAPON WILL BE BETTER AGAINST HIM IN BATTLE...
...
I'VE LIVED A LONG LIFE...

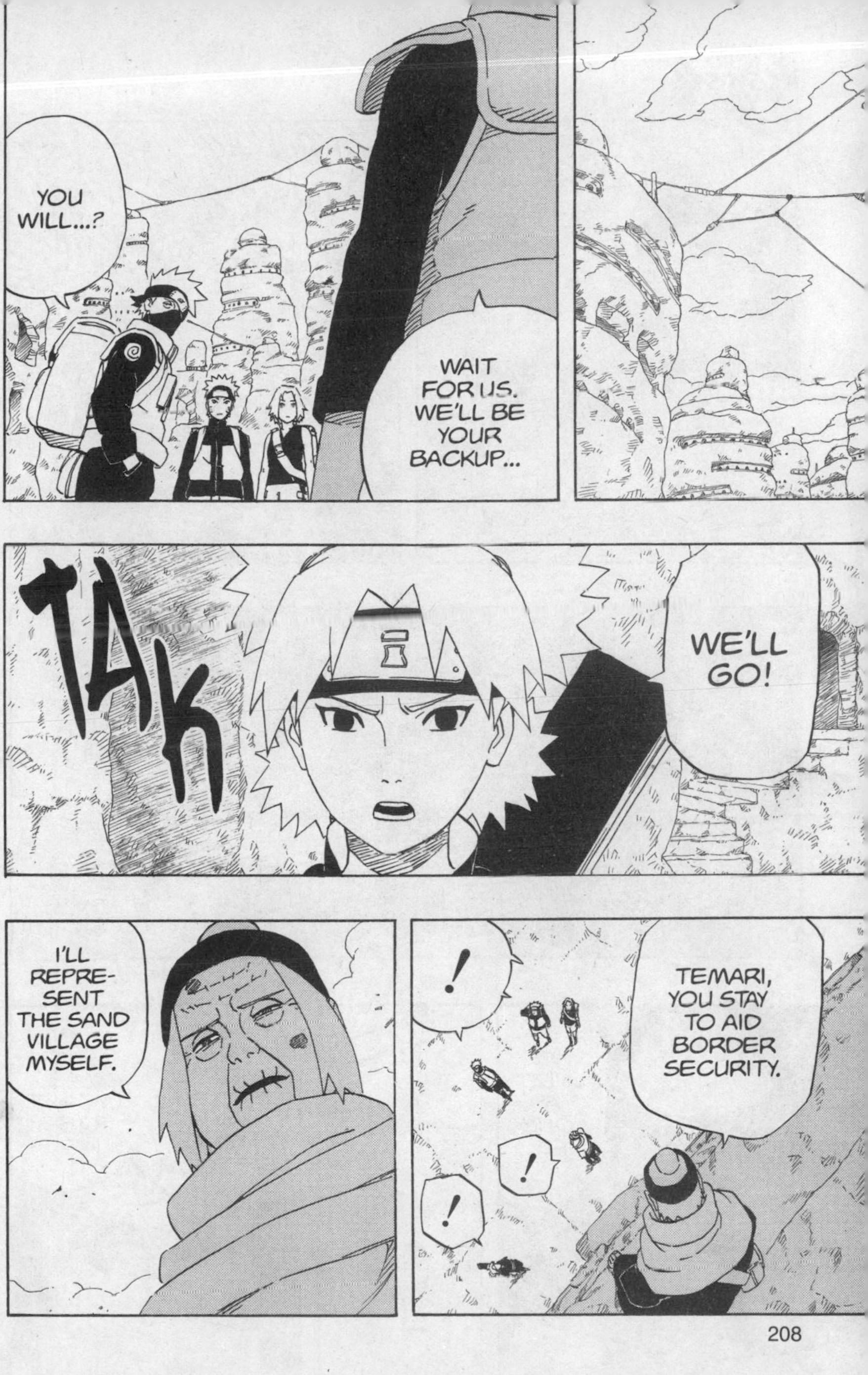
WAIT FOR US. WE'LL BE YOUR BACKUP...
YOU WILL...?
WE'LL GO!
TAK
TEMARI, YOU STAY TO AID BORDER SECURITY.
!
!
!
I'LL REPRESENT THE SAND VILLAGE MYSELF.

READ THIS WAY

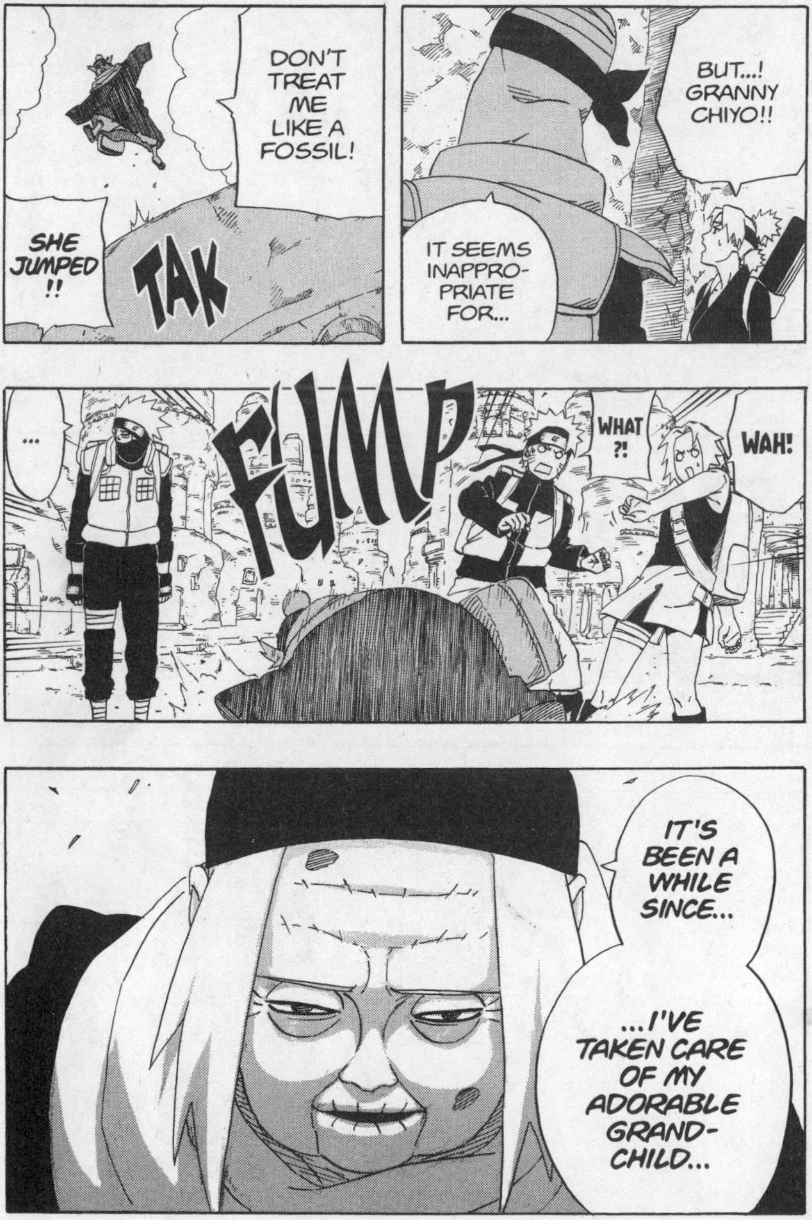

BUT...! GRANNY CHIYO!!
IT SEEMS INAPPROPRIATE FOR...
DON'T TREAT ME LIKE A FOSSIL!
TAK
SHE JUMPED !!
WAH!
WHAT ?!
FUMP
...
IT'S BEEN A WHILE SINCE...
...I'VE TAKEN CARE OF MY ADORABLE GRAND-CHILD...

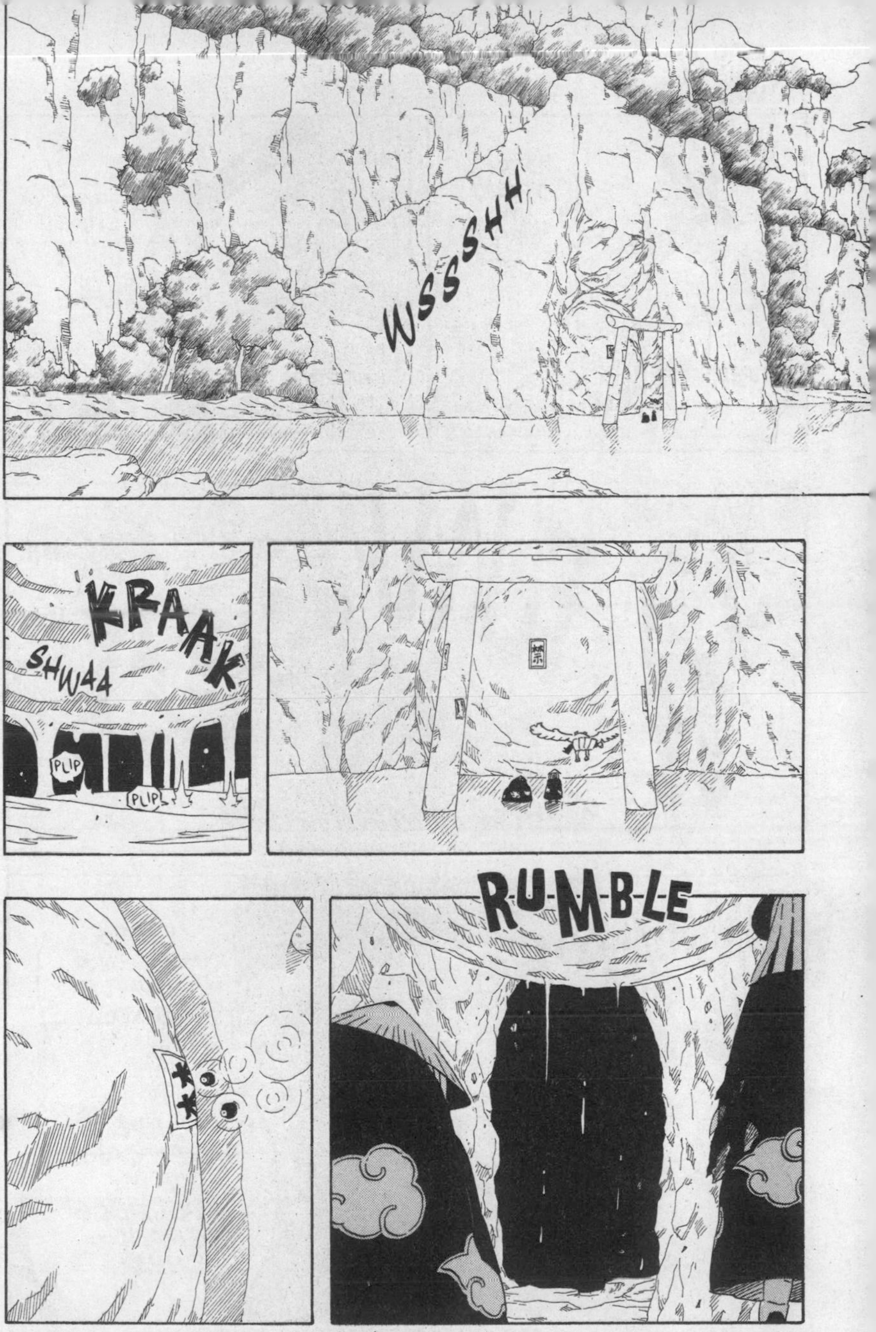
WSSSHH
禁
KRAAAK
SHWAA
PLIP
PLIP
R-U-M-B-L-E

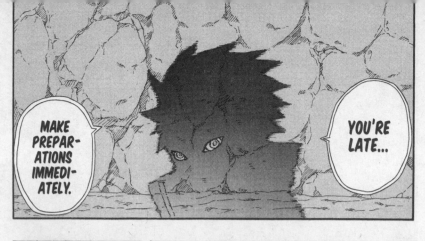

MAKE PREPARATIONS IMMEDIATELY.

YOU'RE LATE...

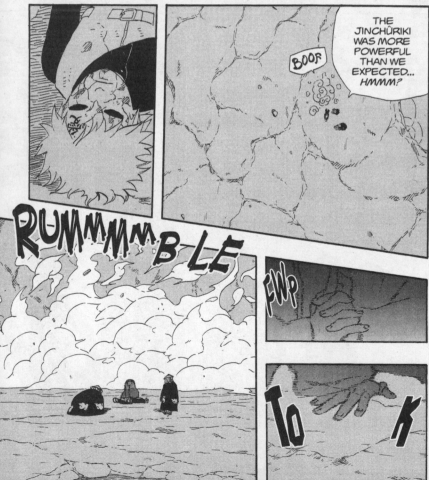

BOOF

THE JINCHÛRIKI WAS MORE POWERFUL THAN WE EXPECTED... HMMM?

RUMMMMBLE

FWP

TO K

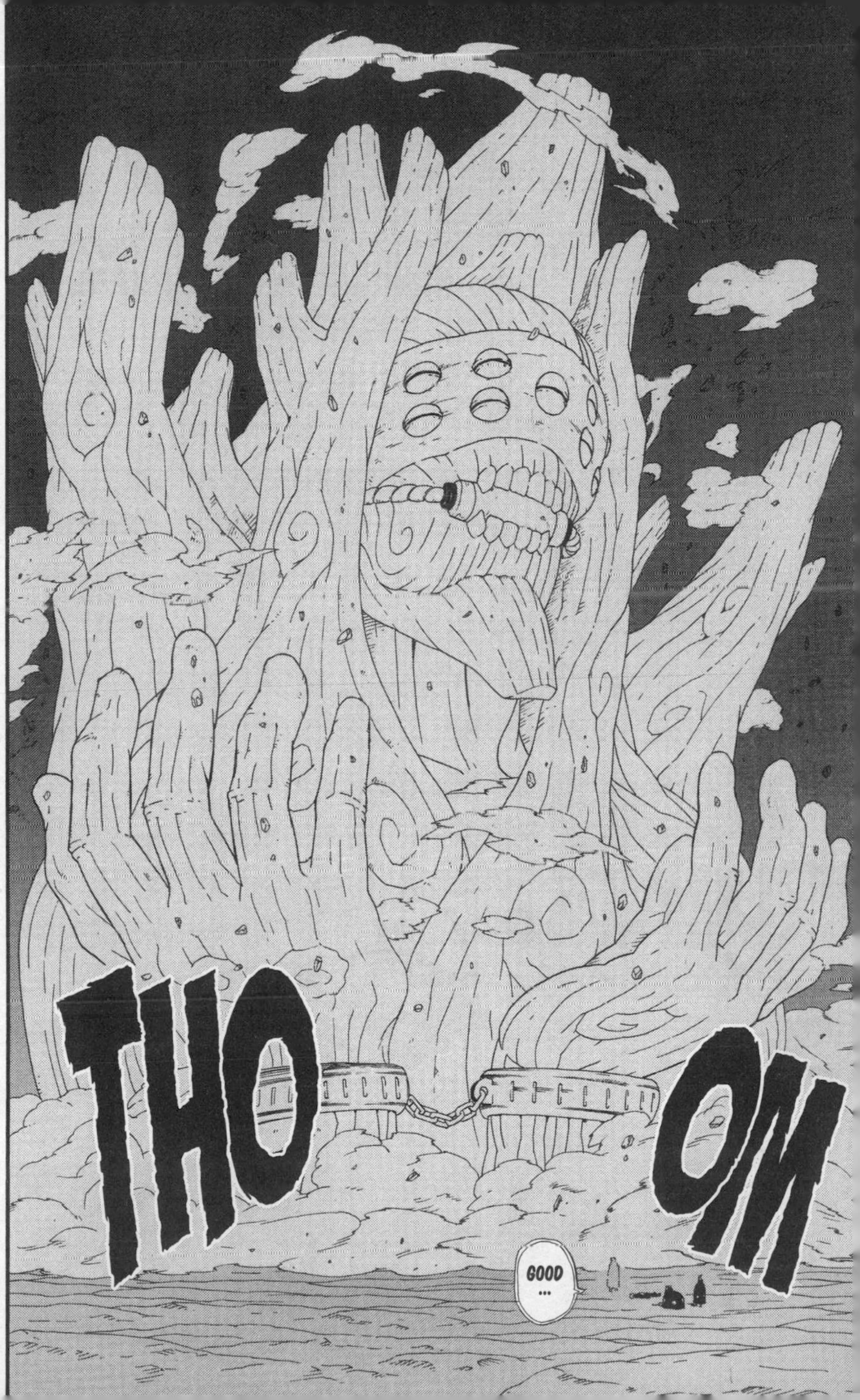
THOOM
GOOD ...

READ THIS WAY

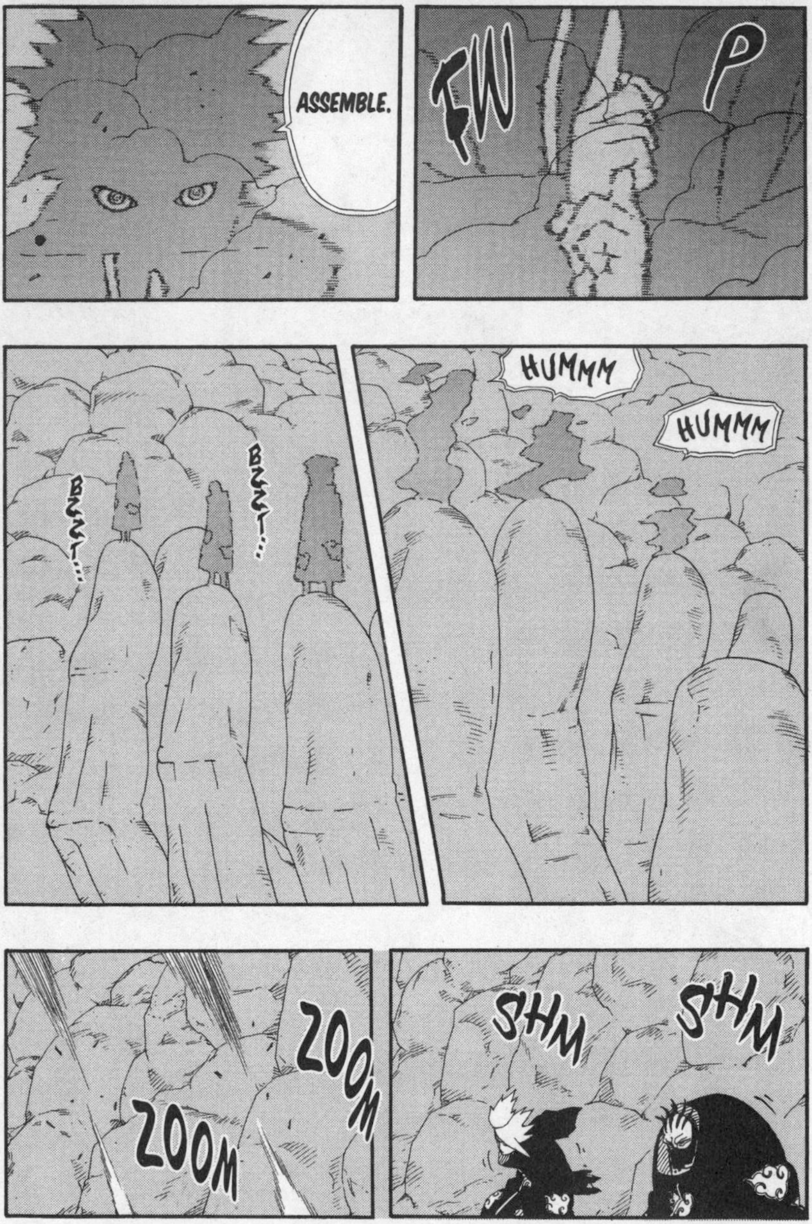
FWP
ASSEMBLE.
HUMMM
HUMMM
BZZT...
BZZT...
SHM
SHM
ZOOM
ZOOM

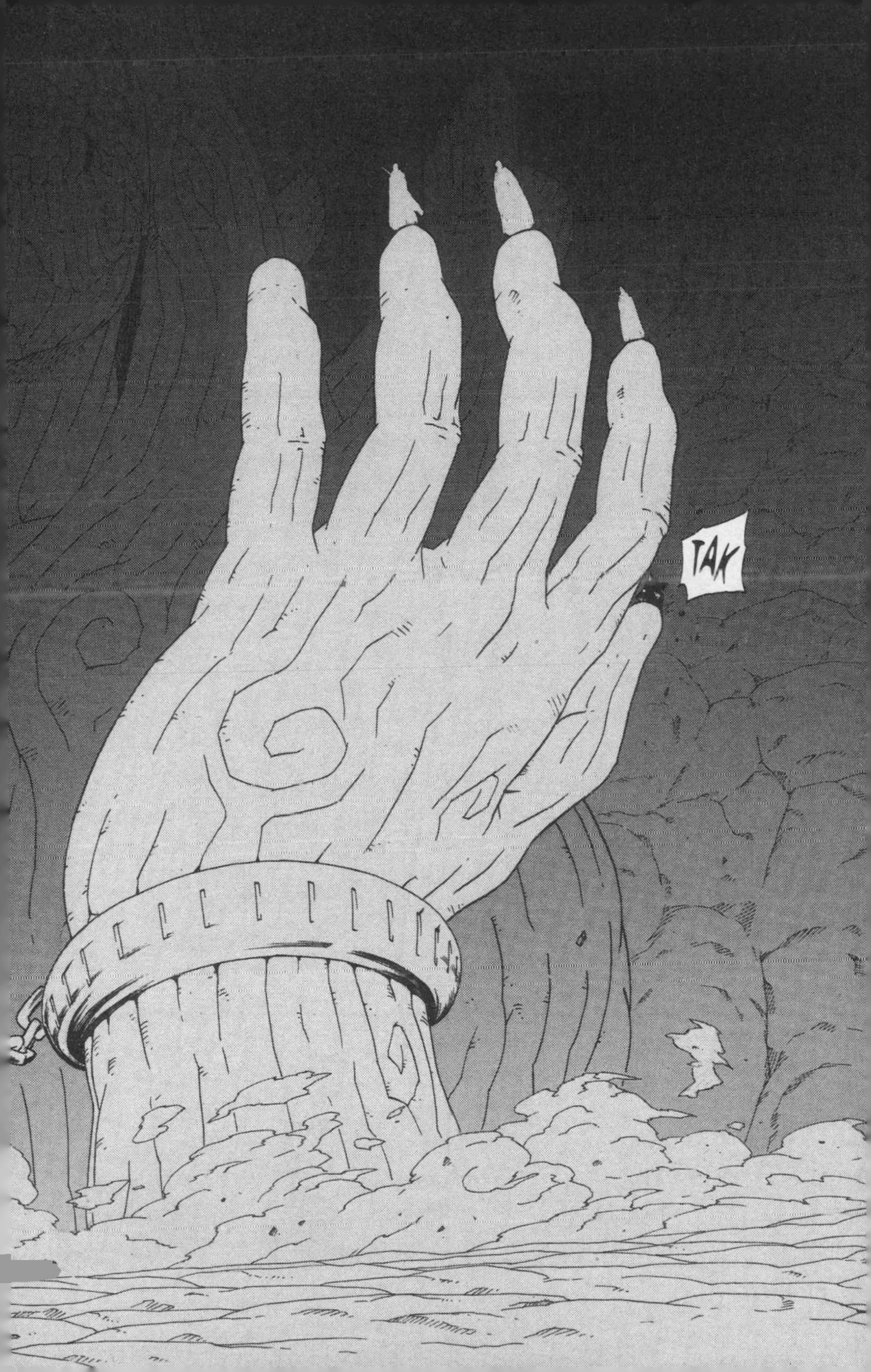
TAK

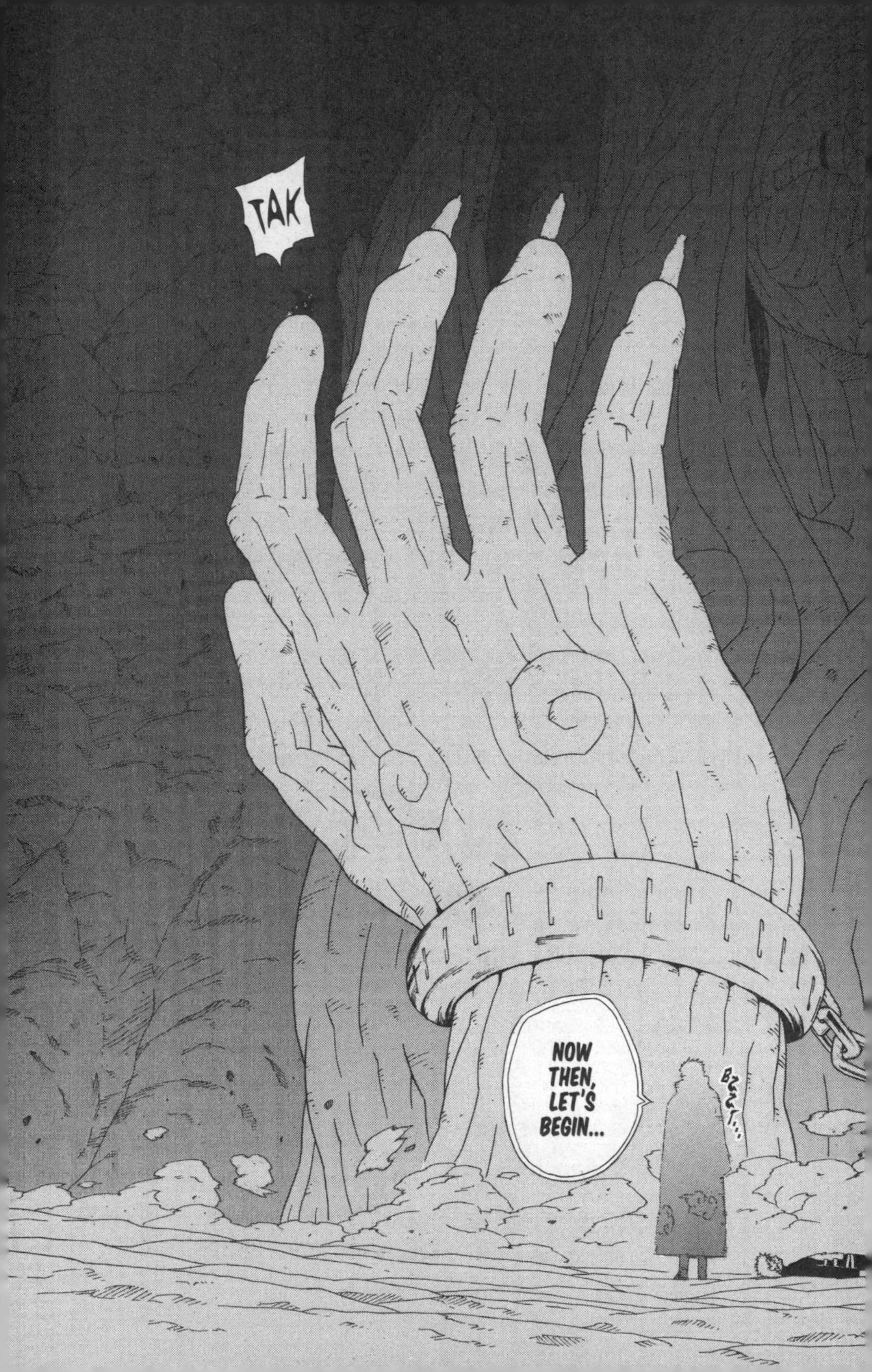
TAK
NOW THEN, LET'S BEGIN...
BZZZT...

THE WORLD OF KISHIMOTO MASASHI
MY PERSONAL HISTORY:
FIGHTING AGAINST CHAOS, PART I

THERE'S ONE THING I HAVE LEARNED FROM MY SIX YEARS' EXPERIENCE CREATING MANGA. WHAT'S THAT, YOU ASK...?

IT IS THAT IF PEOPLE STAY IN ONE PLACE WITH THE SAME PEOPLE WITHOUT SLEEPING FOR A LONG PERIOD OF TIME, THEY WILL SLOWLY GO INSANE. THESE ARE SYMPTOMS THAT APPEAR AMONG MY ASSISTANTS: CRACKING UP OVER AN EXTREMELY LAME JOKE, SPENDING A HALF HOUR TAPE RECORDING FARTS, CONVERSING IN MOANING VOICES, AND SO ON. IN THESE WAYS AND COUNTLESS OTHERS, THINGS START GOING LOOPY.

IN A SENSE, MY ASSISTANTS COME TO BE CONTROLLED BY A KIND OF CHAOS. HOWEVER, THEY AREN'T AWARE OF IT, AND A STATE OF CHAOS BECOMES NORMAL... WHENEVER A NEW PERSON JOINS THE TEAM, THE GAP MY ASSISTANTS FEEL BETWEEN THEMSELVES AND THE NEW GUY MAKES THEM REALIZE JUST HOW WEIRD THEY'VE BECOME. THEN THEY REGRET THE SILLINESS THEY'D BEEN UP TO A LITTLE BIT. BUT... TIME IS A DREADFUL THING, BECAUSE BEFORE YOU KNOW IT THEY'VE ABSORBED THE NEW ASSISTANT AND RETURNED TO THEIR STATE OF CHAOS.

ONE DAY, THE FOLLOWING INCIDENT TOOK PLACE: I GOT STUCK WRITING A MANGA JUST BEFORE THE DEADLINE, SO I LAY DOWN BEHIND MY DESK TO TAKE A SHORT NAP. WHEN I WAS LOOKING FOR SOMETHING TO USE AS A PILLOW, I FOUND A BIG FROG-SHAPED *GAMAGUCHI* CUSHION. (THIS IS A CUSHION MODELED ON THE FROGGIE WALLET THAT NARUTO USES IN THE SERIES. IT WAS MADE AS A PRESENT FOR READERS.)

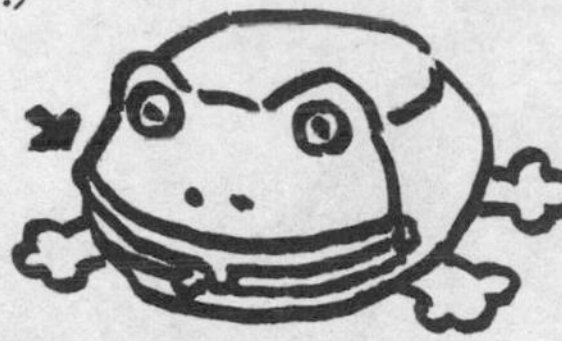

THE CUSHION WAS JUST THE RIGHT SIZE TO LAY MY HEAD ON. THINKING I HAD MADE A GREAT DISCOVERY, I WAS GOING TO TAKE A NAP USING IT AS A PILLOW. ...BUT... THIS COIN PURSE-TYPE CUSHION CAN BE OPENED JUST LIKE A REGULAR COIN PURSE. WHILE GAZING AT IT IN A STUPOR, AN IDEA CROSSED MY MIND. IF IT'S BIG ENOUGH TO LAY MY HEAD ON, WOULDN'T IT BE POSSIBLE TO STICK MY HEAD INSIDE IT? THIS RATHER POINTLESS SUSPICION ENTERED MY HEAD. I SHOULD'VE JUST TAKEN THE NAP IMMEDIATELY; I WAS TIRED, AFTER ALL. BUT FOR SOME REASON, I COULDN'T HELP CONFIRMING MY SUSPICION. SO I PUT MY HEAD IN THE COIN PURSE CUSHION AND FOUND THAT MY HEAD AND NECK JUST BARELY FIT INSIDE IT.

TO THIS DAY, I HAVE NO IDEA WHY I DID THIS. I'M CONVINCED THAT I HAD FALLEN VICTIM TO THE CHAOS. AT THE TIME, I HAD NO IDEA THE DISASTER THAT THIS WOULD LEAD TO. (TO BE CONTINUED...)

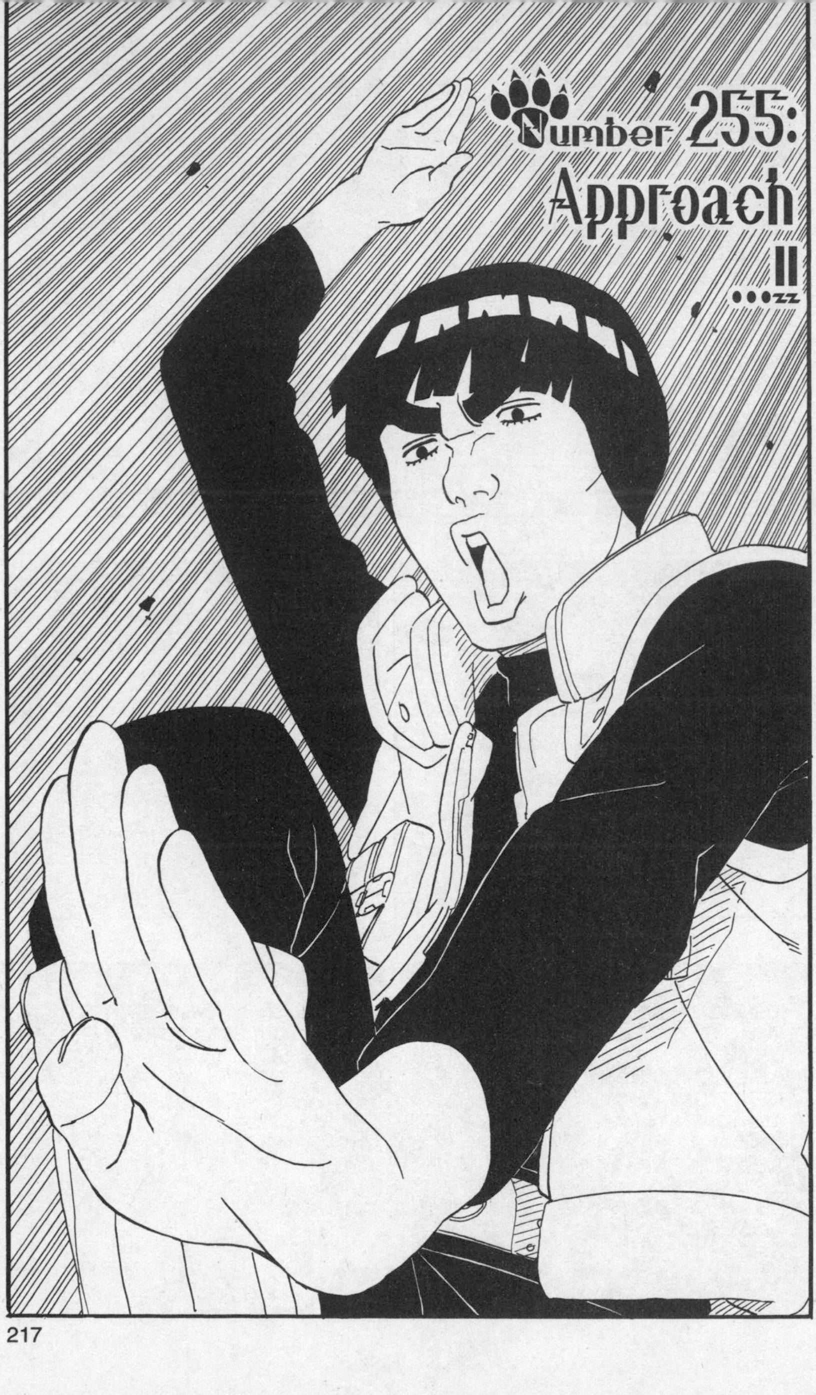
Number 255:
Approach
...!!

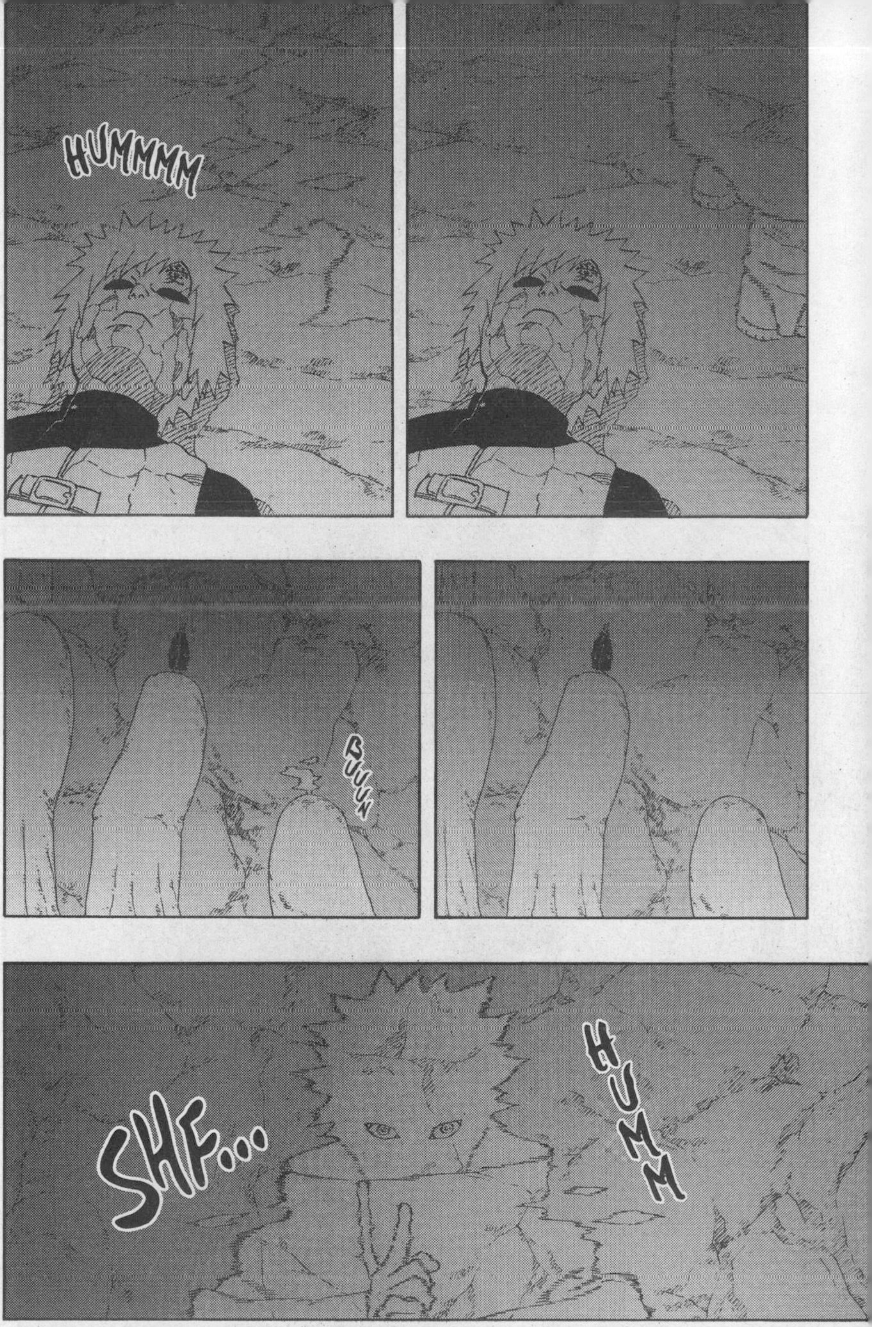
HUMMMM
BUUUN
HUMM
SHF...

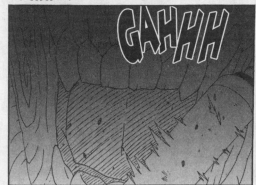

READ THIS WAY

SHUK
GAHHH
THIS IS GOING TO TAKE THREE FULL DAYS.
STAY AWARE OF YOUR PHYSICAL SELVES.
...
AND ZETSU, HAVE YOUR PHYSICAL BODY STAND GUARD OUTSIDE.
USE THE ONE WITH THE GREATEST RANGE, GOT IT?
UNDER-STOOD.

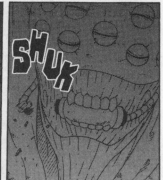

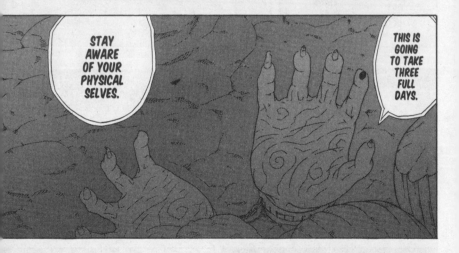

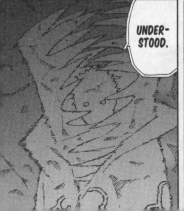

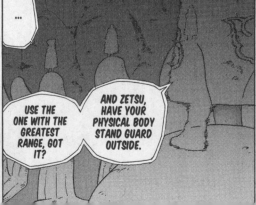

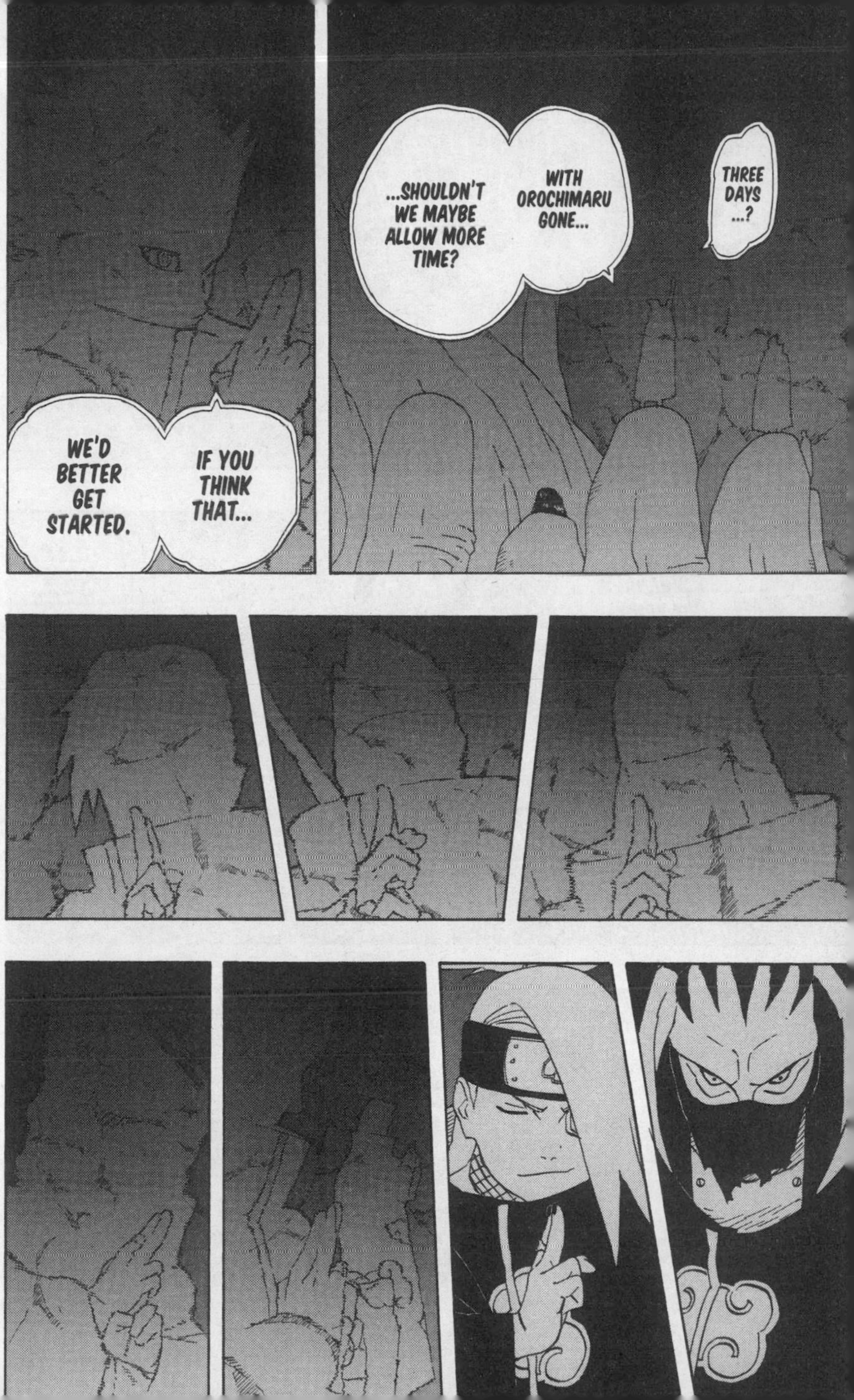
THREE DAYS ...?
WITH OROCHIMARU GONE...
...SHOULDN'T WE MAYBE ALLOW MORE TIME?
IF YOU THINK THAT...
WE'D BETTER GET STARTED.

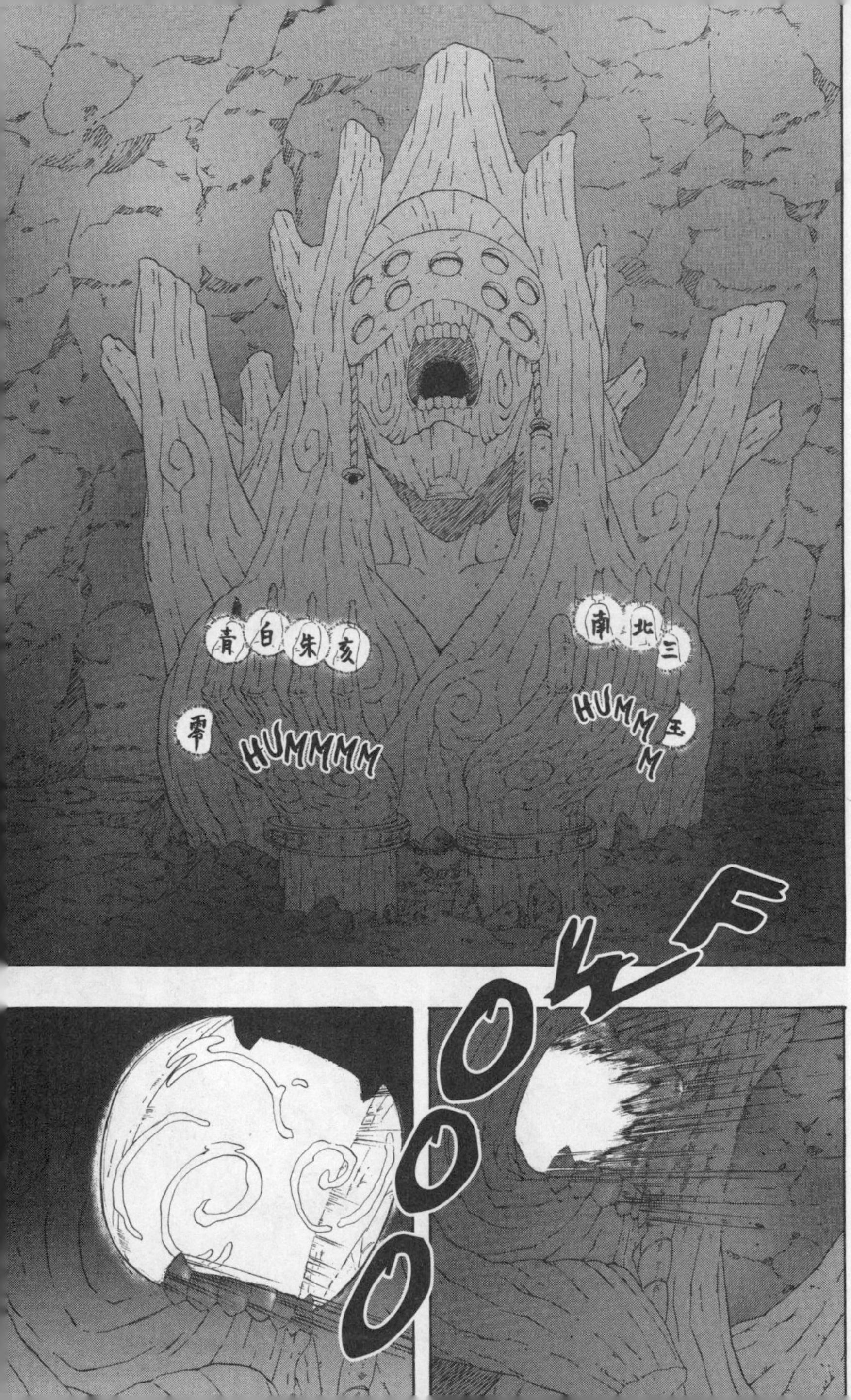

南北三
王
HUMMMM
青白朱亥
零
HUMMMM
FWOOOO

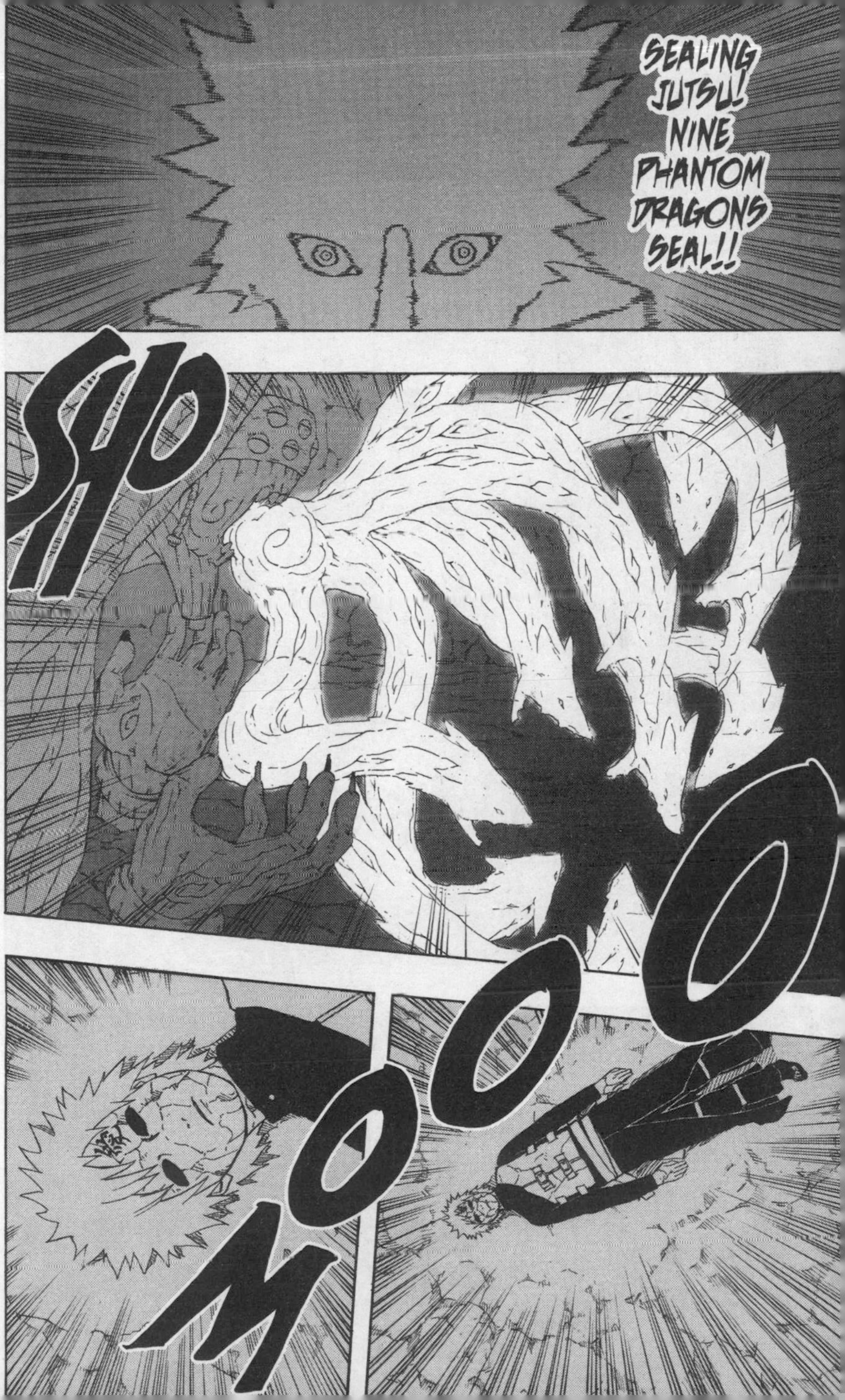
SEALING JUTSU! NINE PHANTOM DRAGONS SEAL!!
SHP
WOOOOO

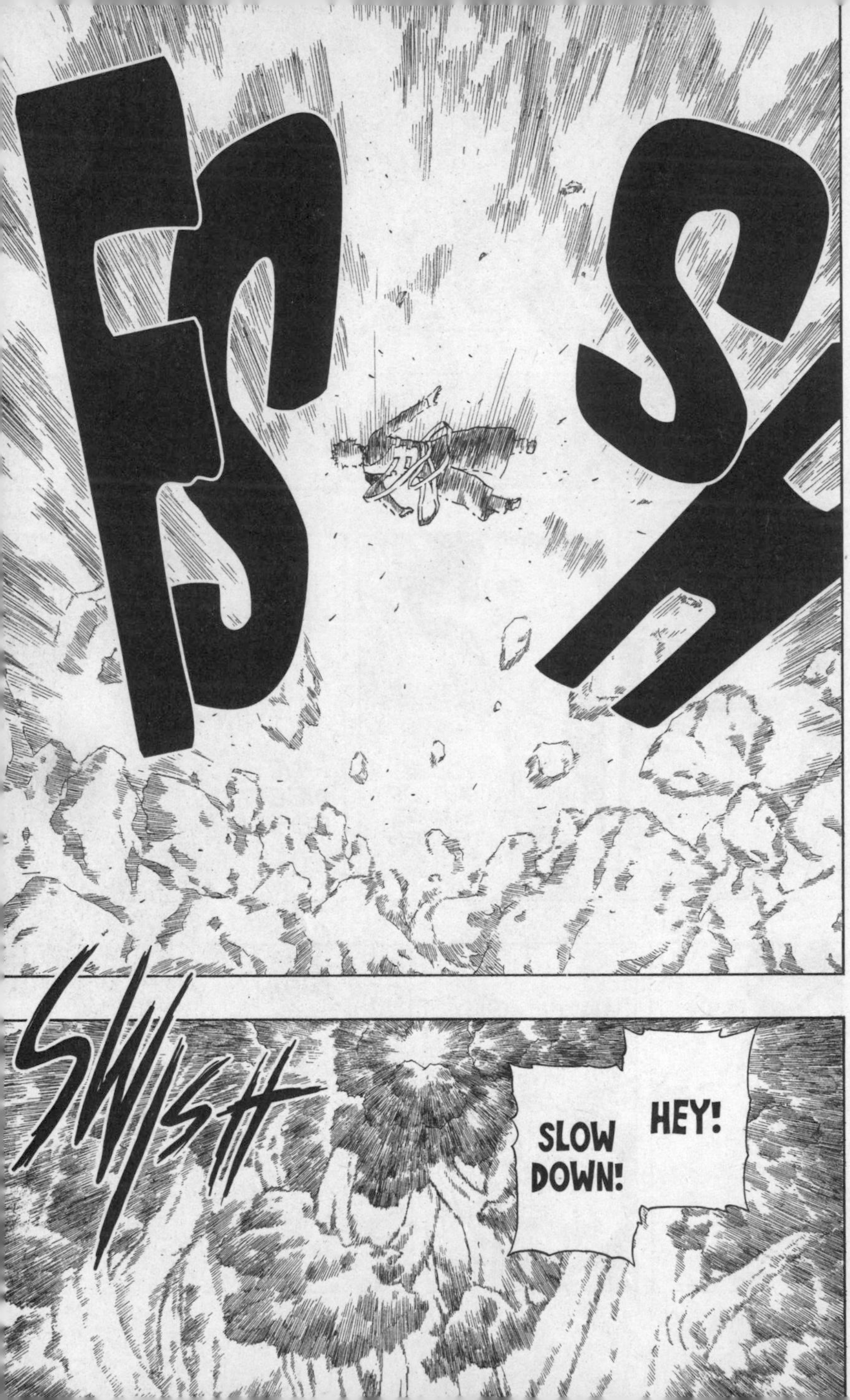
FSSH
HEY! SLOW DOWN!
SWISH

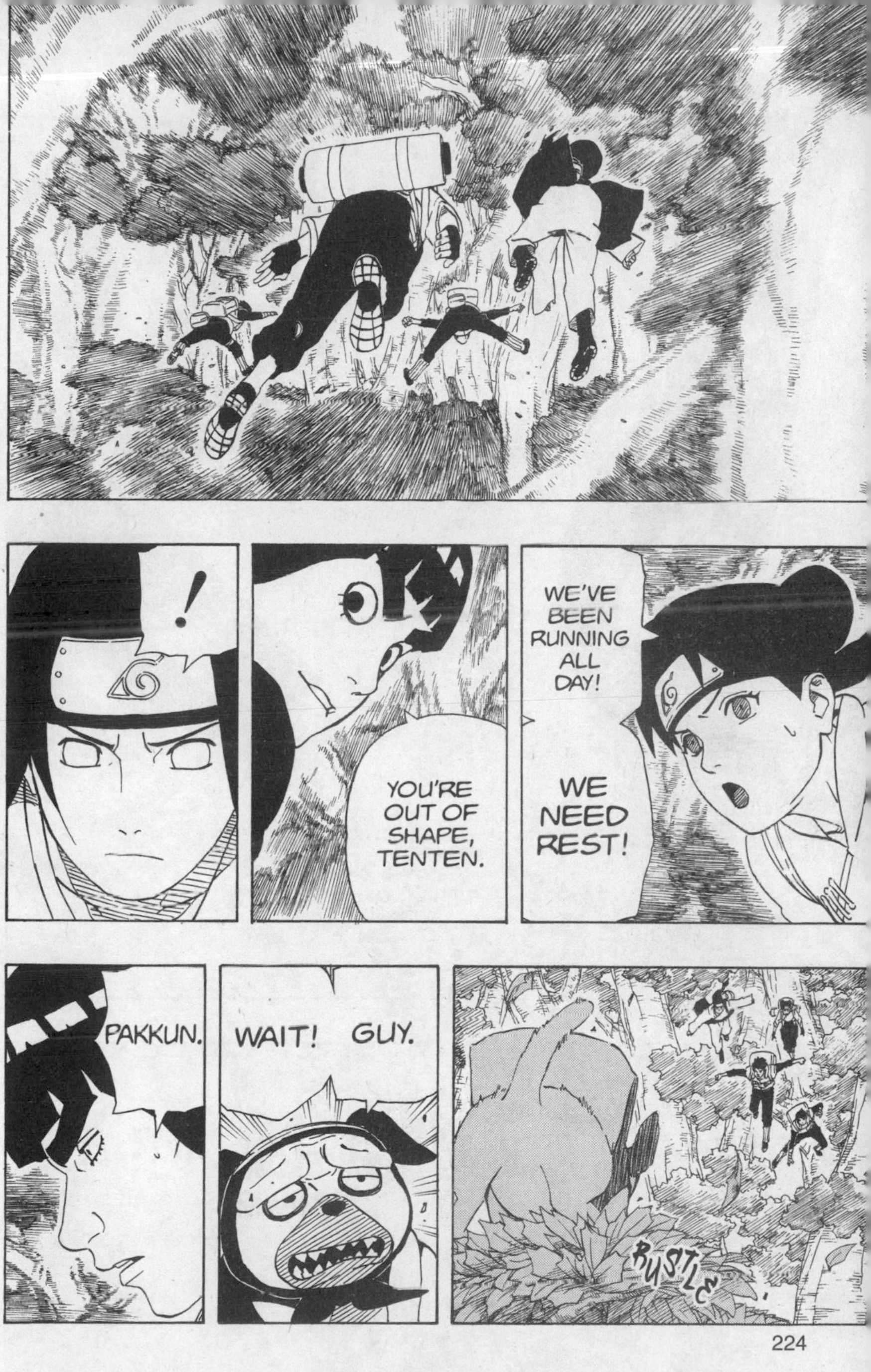
WE'VE BEEN RUNNING ALL DAY!
WE NEED REST!
YOU'RE OUT OF SHAPE, TENTEN.
!
RUSTLE
GUY.
WAIT!
PAKKUN.

READ THIS WAY

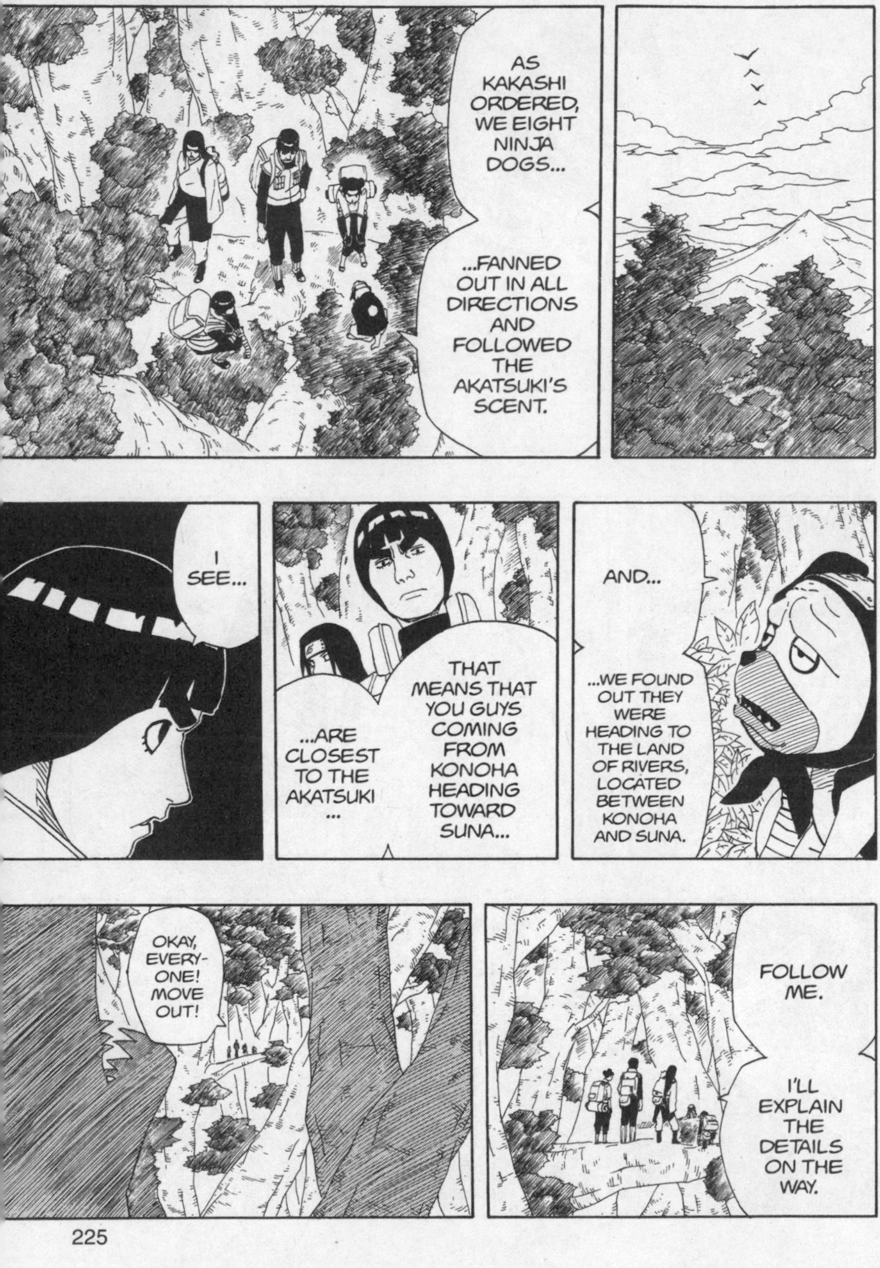
AS KAKASHI ORDERED, WE EIGHT NINJA DOGS...
...FANNED OUT IN ALL DIRECTIONS AND FOLLOWED THE AKATSUKI'S SCENT.
AND...
...WE FOUND OUT THEY WERE HEADING TO THE LAND OF RIVERS, LOCATED BETWEEN KONOHA AND SUNA.
THAT MEANS THAT YOU GUYS COMING FROM KONOHA HEADING TOWARD SUNA...
...ARE CLOSEST TO THE AKATSUKI...
I SEE...
FOLLOW ME.
I'LL EXPLAIN THE DETAILS ON THE WAY.
OKAY, EVERYONE! MOVE OUT!

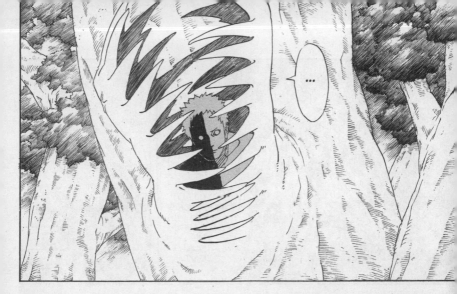

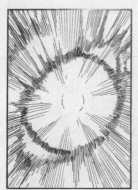

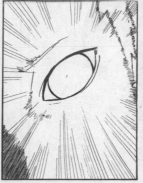

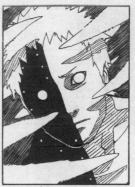

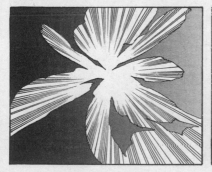

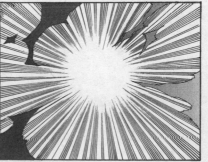

READ THIS WAY

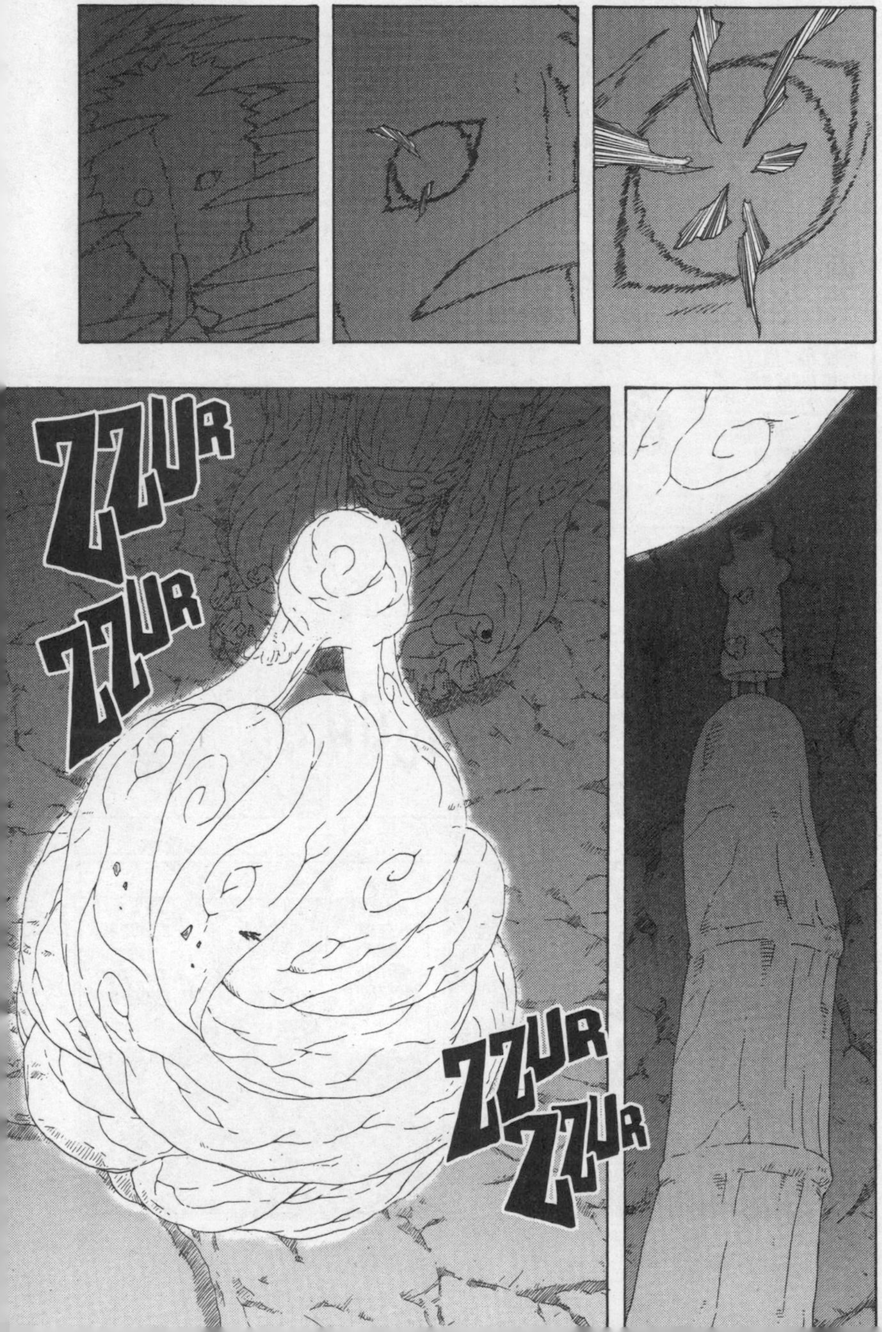
ZZUR
ZZUR
ZZUR
ZZUR

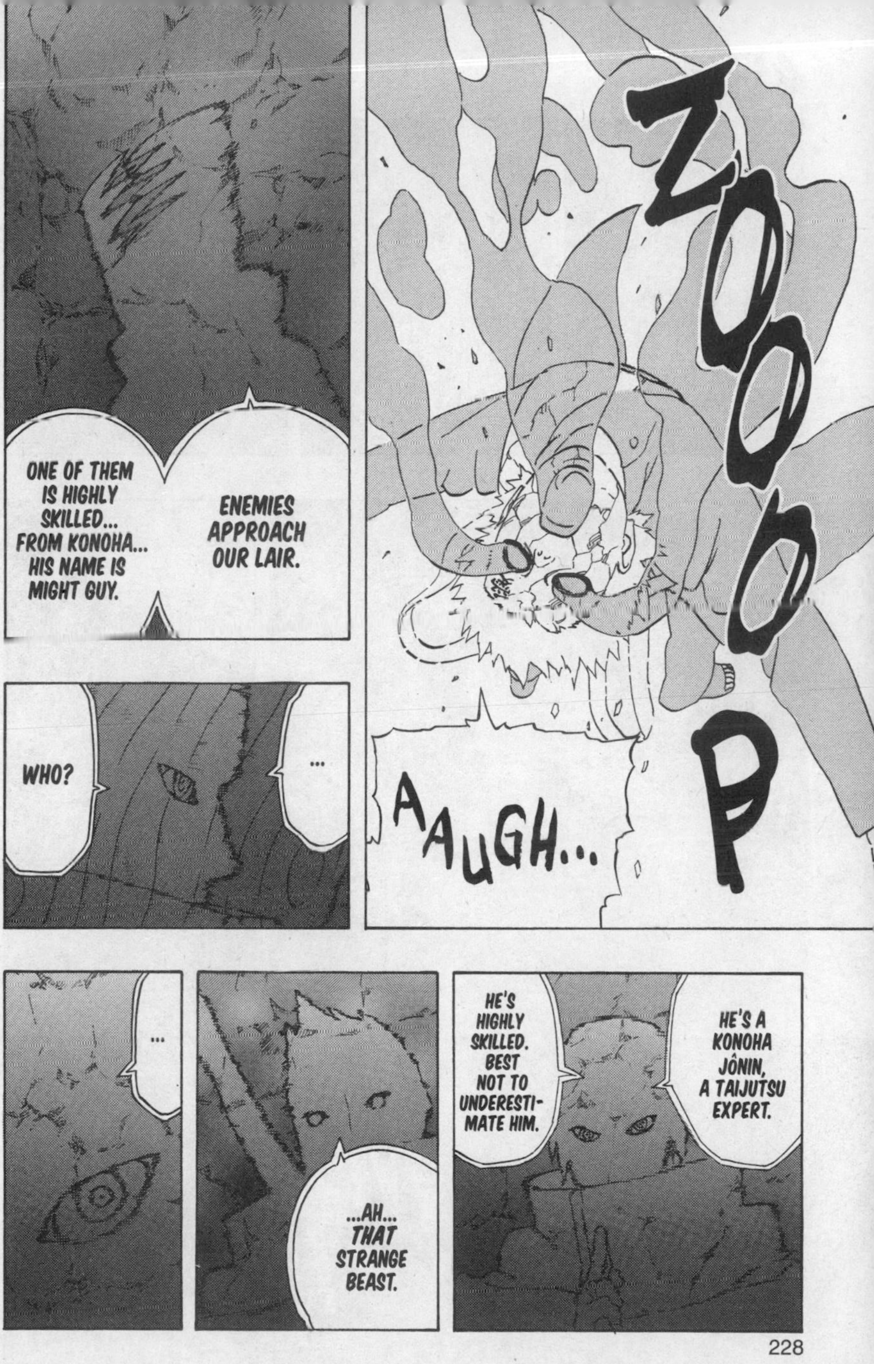
ZOOOOOP
AAUGH...
ENEMIES APPROACH OUR LAIR.
ONE OF THEM IS HIGHLY SKILLED... FROM KONOHA... HIS NAME IS MIGHT GUY.
...
WHO?
HE'S A KONOHA JÔNIN, A TAIJUTSU EXPERT.
HE'S HIGHLY SKILLED. BEST NOT TO UNDERESTI-MATE HIM.
...AH... THAT STRANGE BEAST.
...

READ THIS WAY

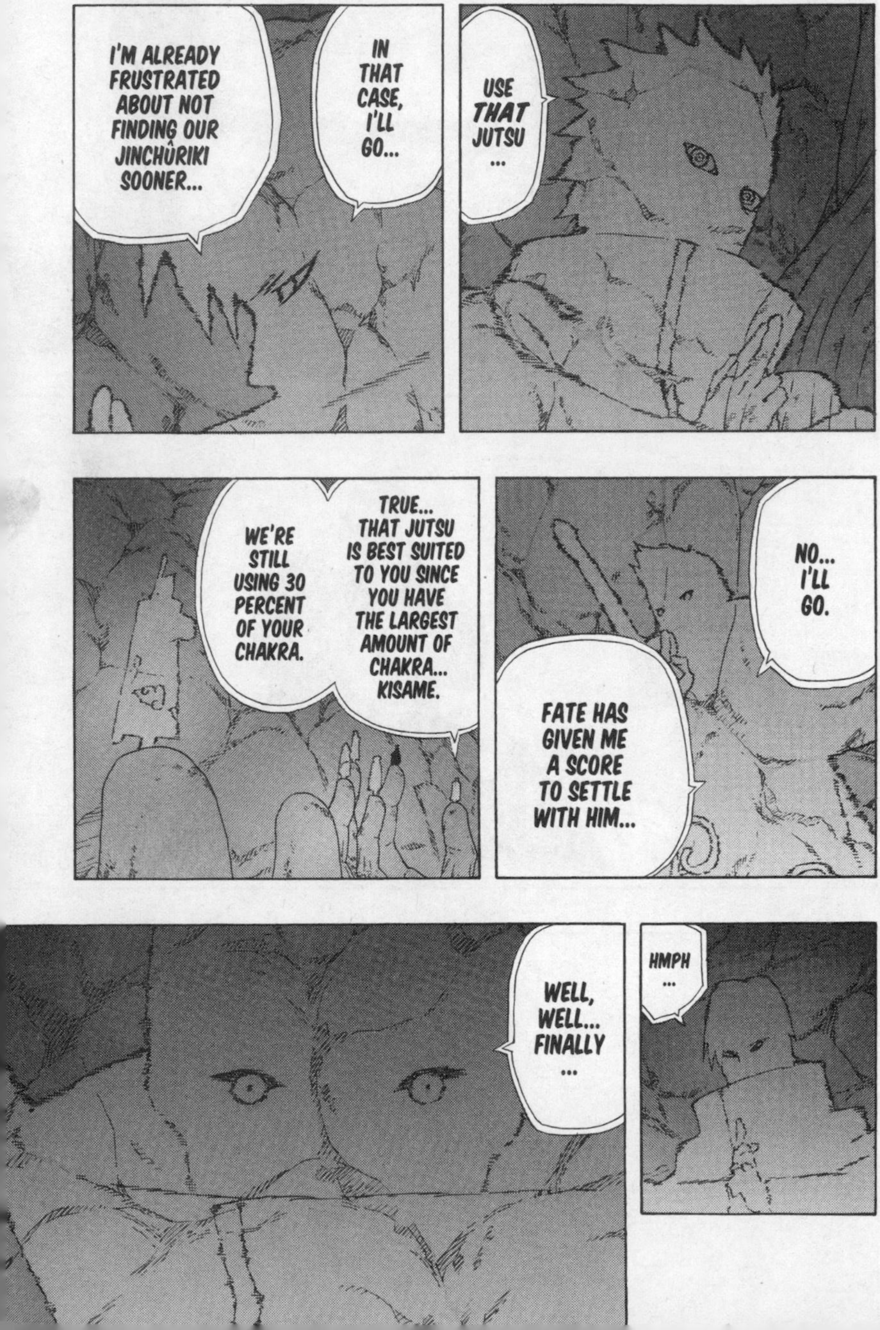
USE THAT JUTSU...
IN THAT CASE, I'LL GO...
I'M ALREADY FRUSTRATED ABOUT NOT FINDING OUR JINCHÛRIKI SOONER...
NO... I'LL GO.
FATE HAS GIVEN ME A SCORE TO SETTLE WITH HIM...
TRUE... THAT JUTSU IS BEST SUITED TO YOU SINCE YOU HAVE THE LARGEST AMOUNT OF CHAKRA... KISAME.
WE'RE STILL USING 30 PERCENT OF YOUR CHAKRA.
HMPH...
WELL, WELL... FINALLY...

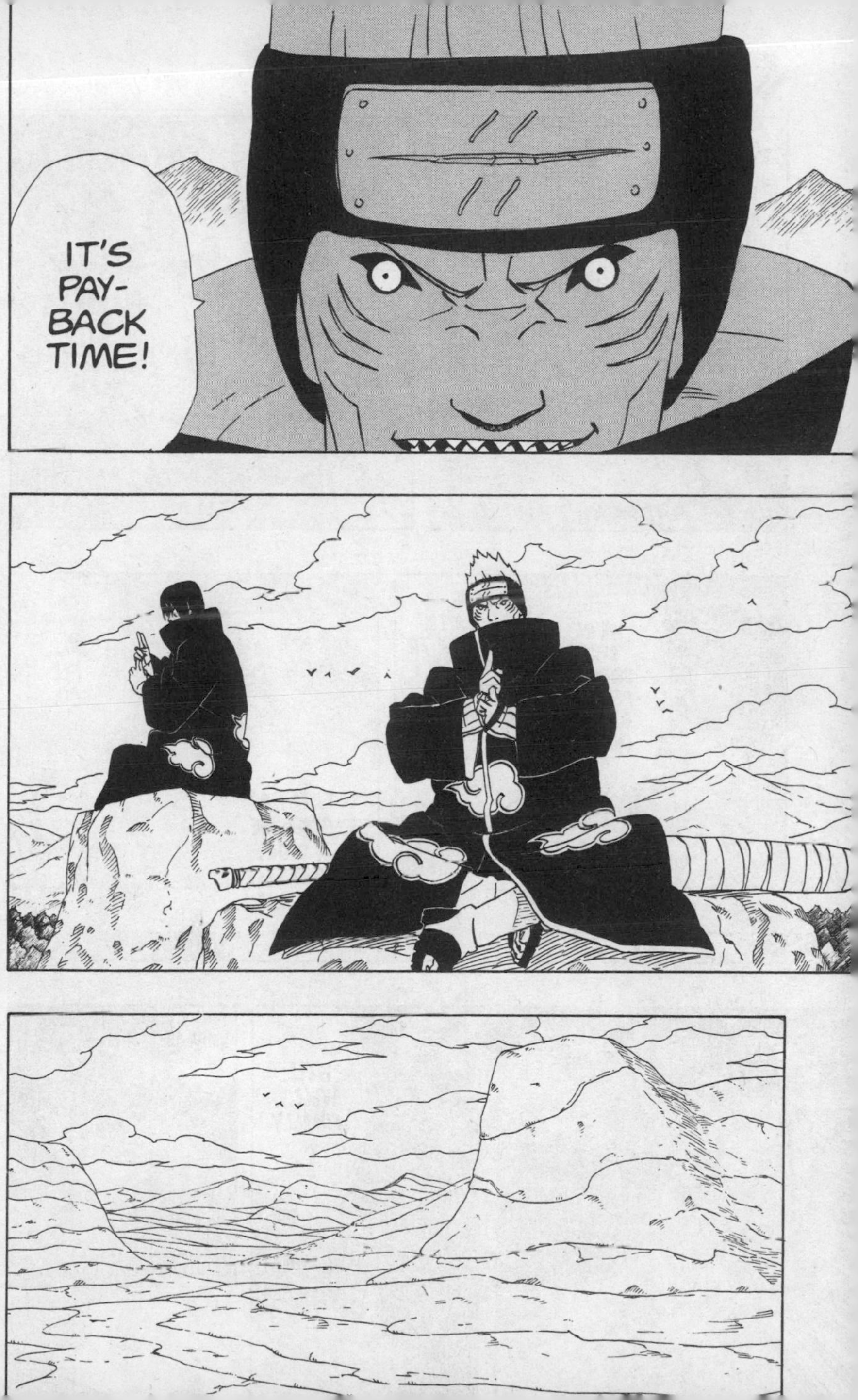
IT'S PAY-BACK TIME!

READ THIS WAY

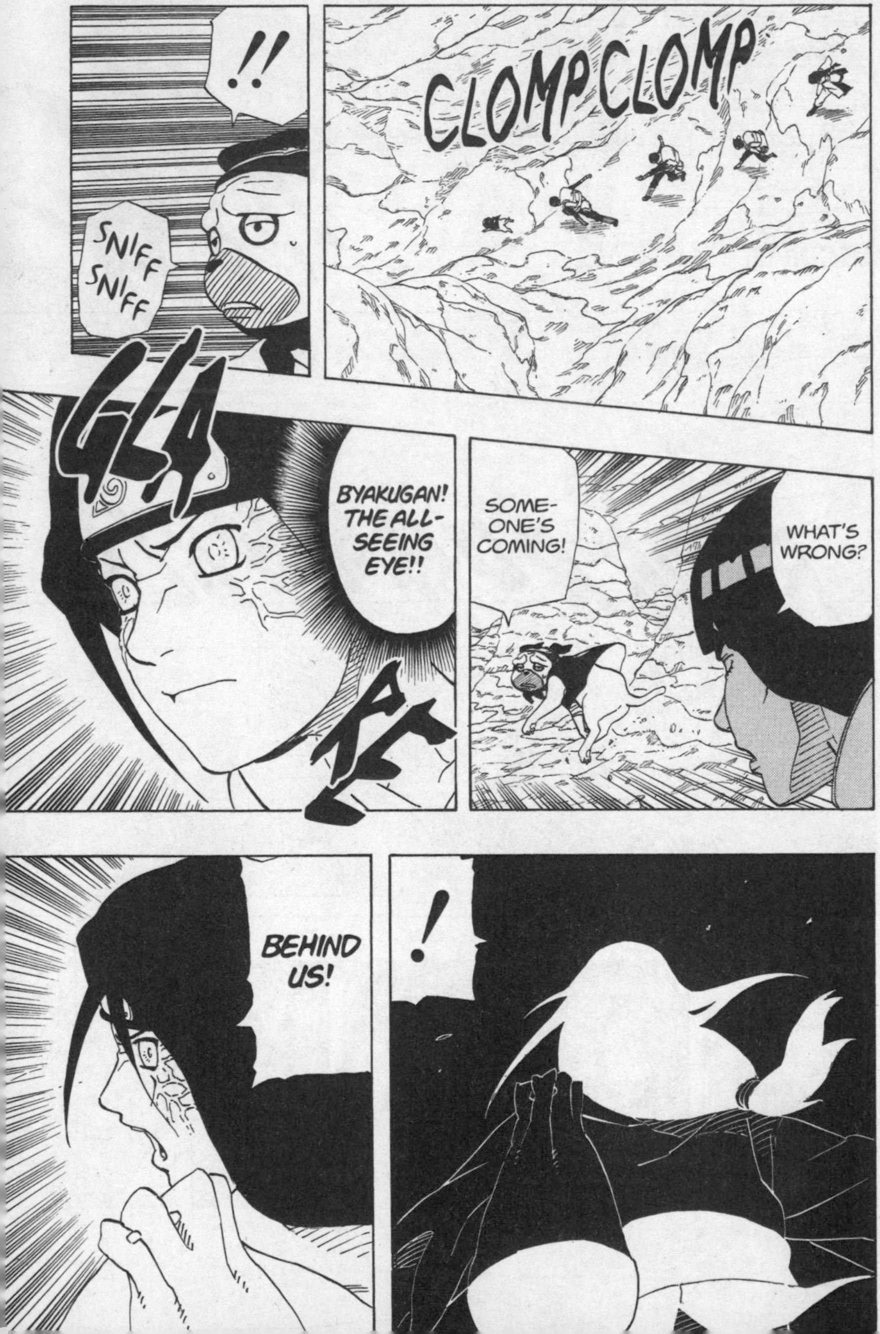
CLOMP CLOMP
!!
SNIFF SNIFF
WHAT'S WRONG?
SOME-ONE'S COMING!
BYAKUGAN! THE ALL-SEEING EYE!!
!
BEHIND US!

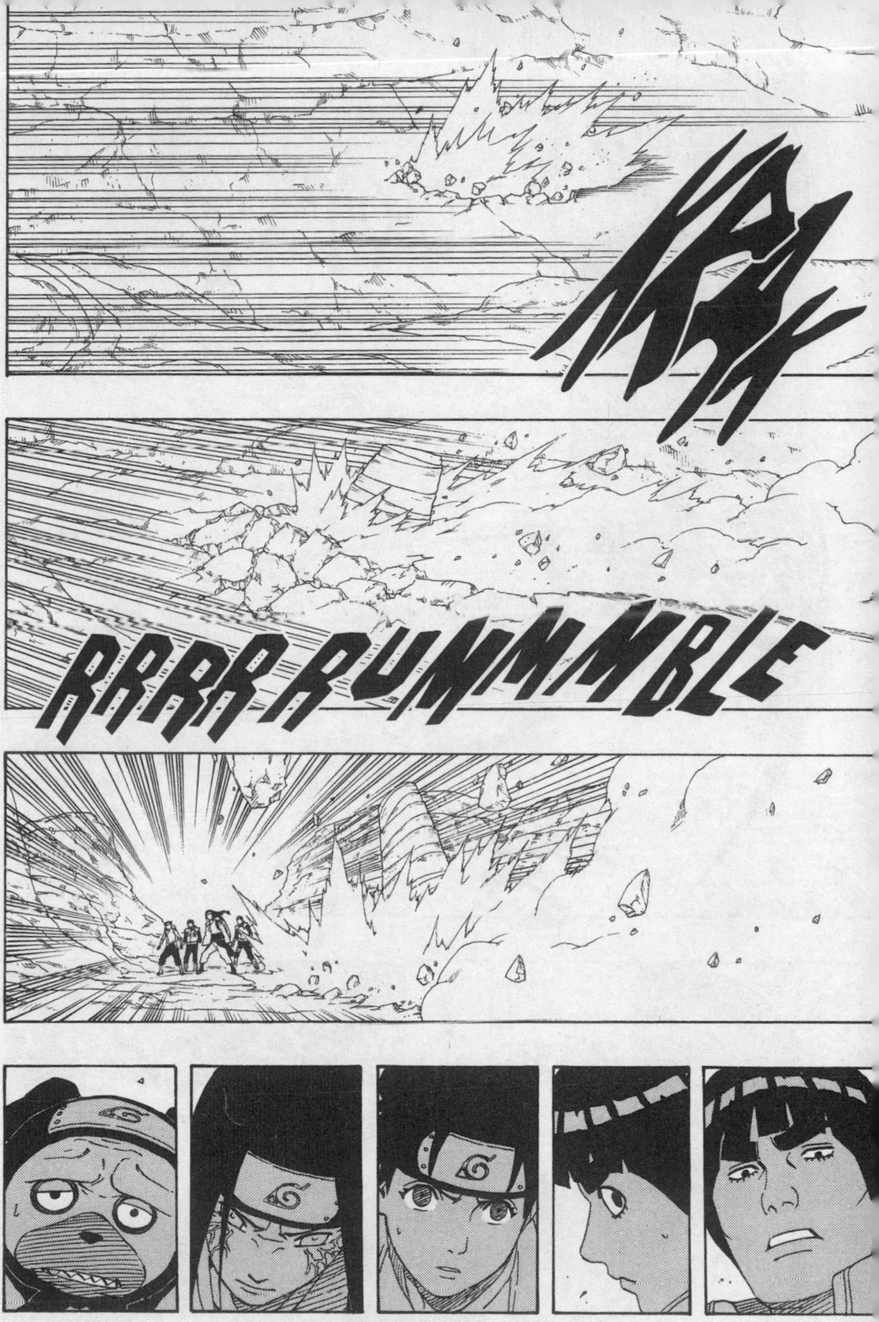
KRAK
RRRR RUMMMBLE

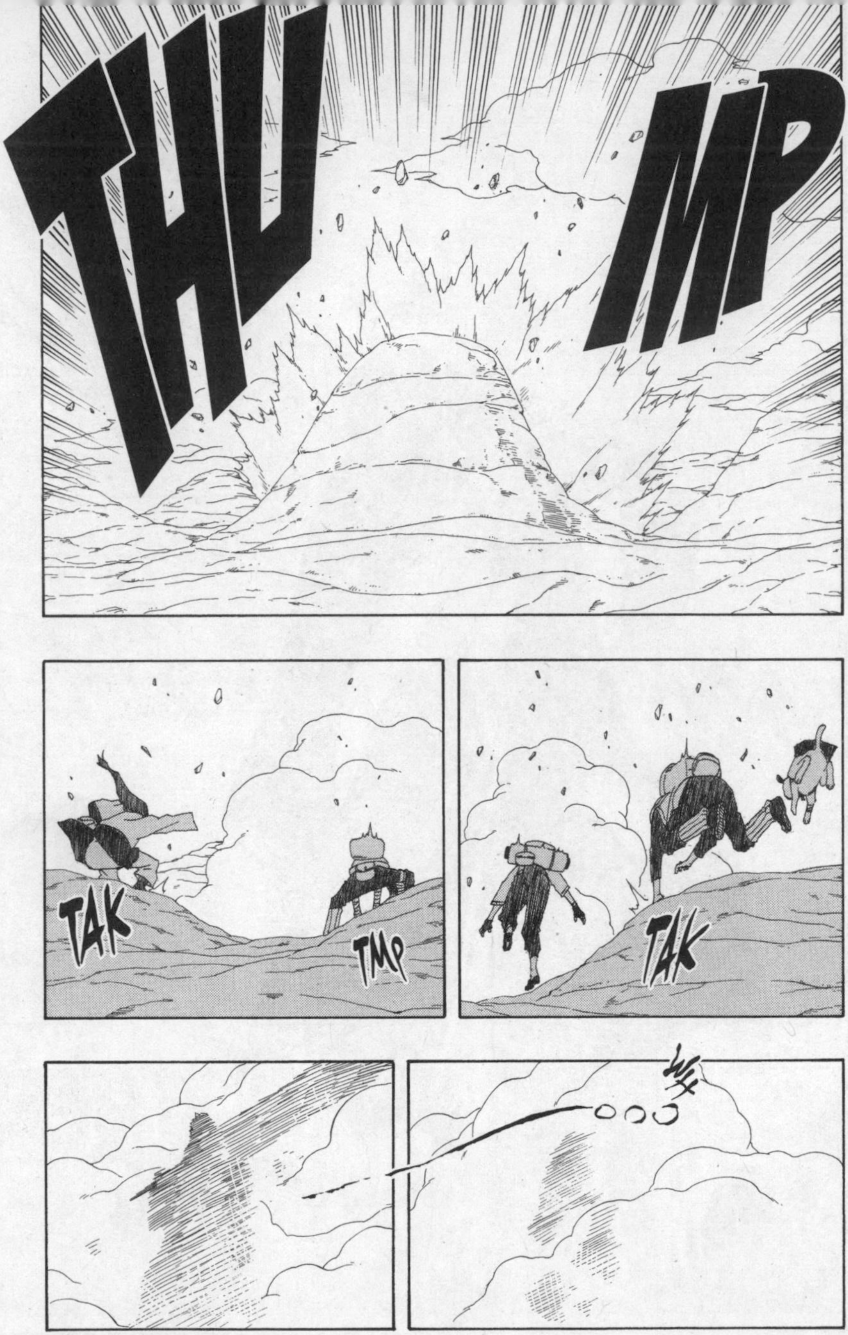
THUMP
TAK
TMP
TAK

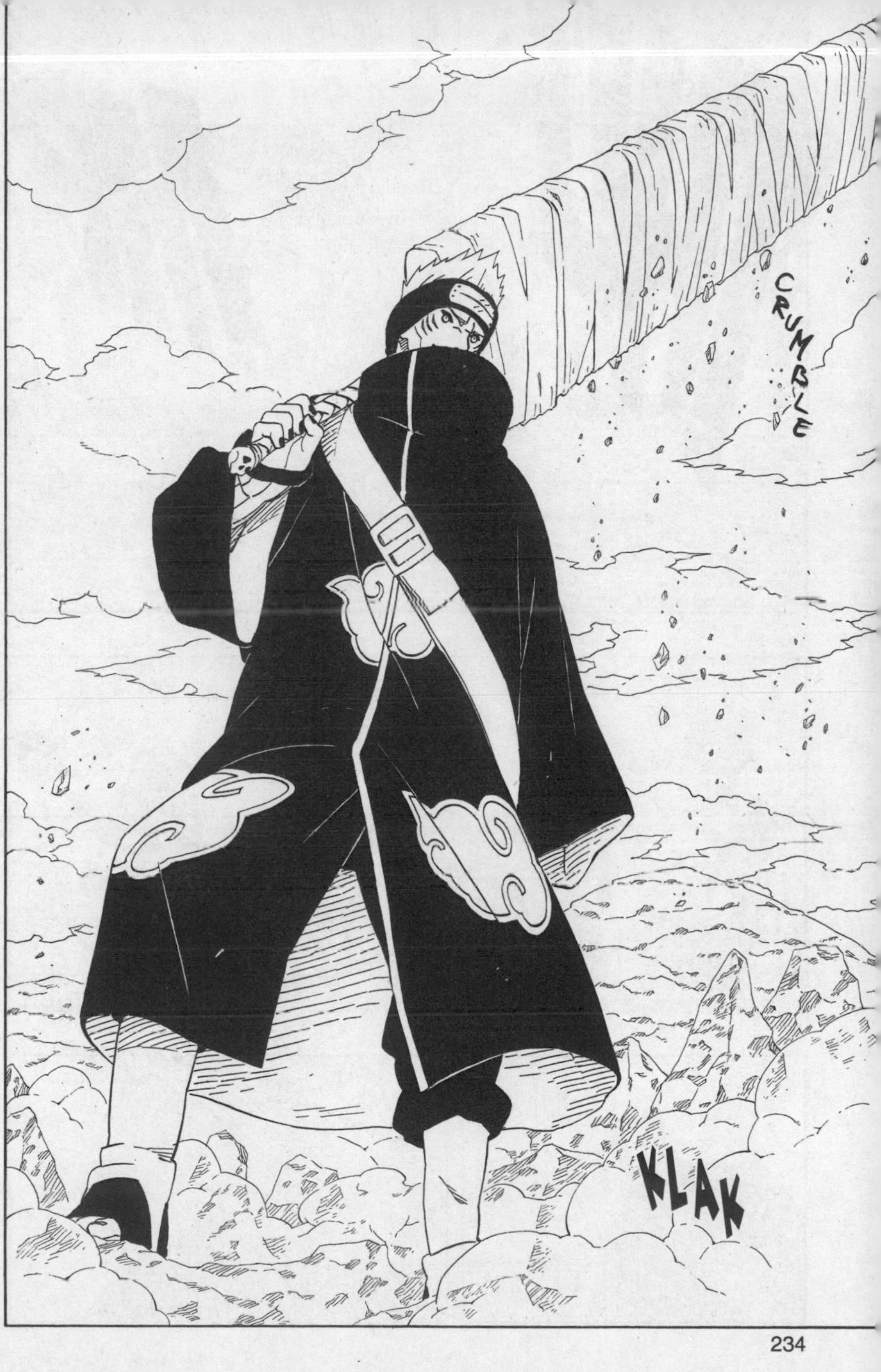
CRUMBLE
KLAK

READ THIS WAY

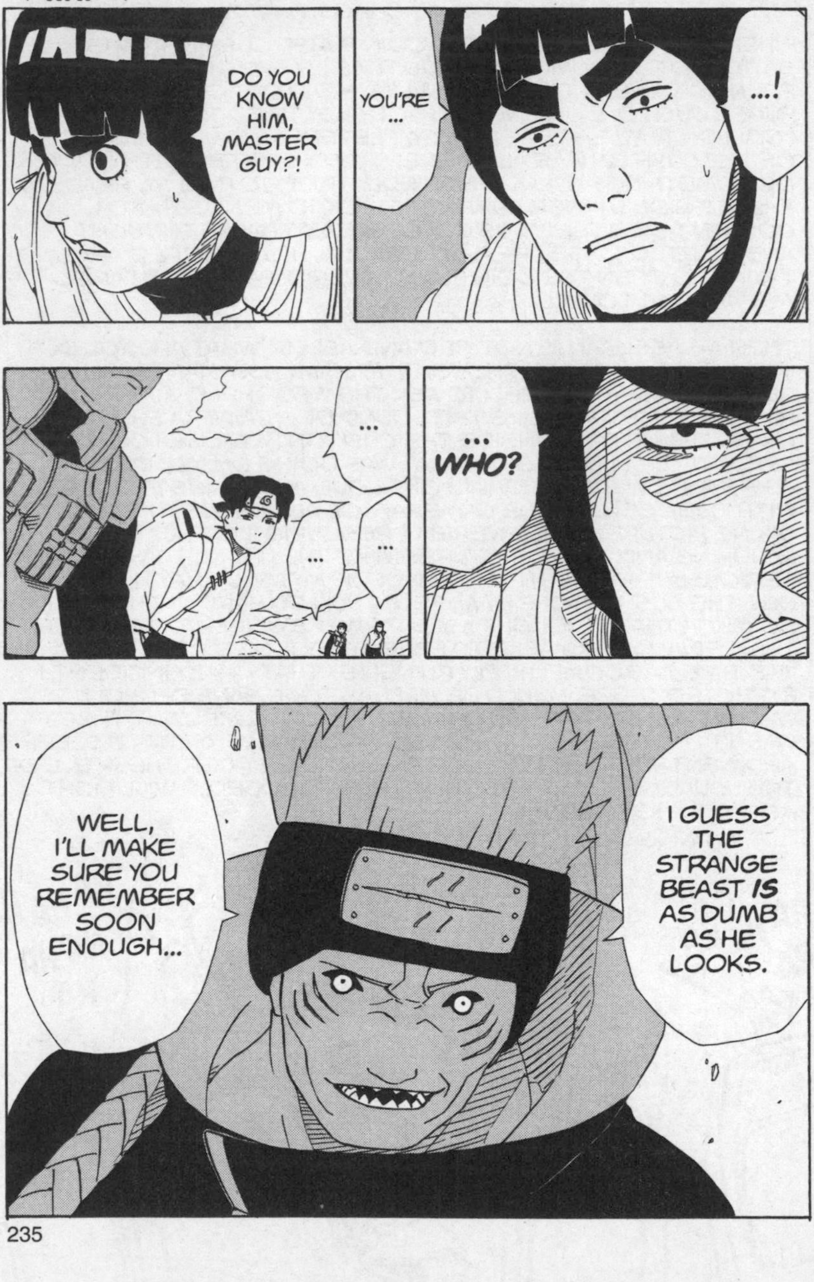
...!
YOU'RE ...
DO YOU KNOW HIM, MASTER GUY?!
... WHO?
...
...
...
I GUESS THE STRANGE BEAST IS AS DUMB AS HE LOOKS.
WELL, I'LL MAKE SURE YOU REMEMBER SOON ENOUGH...

THE WORLD OF KISHIMOTO MASASHI
MY PERSONAL HISTORY:
FIGHTING AGAINST CHAOS, PART 2

WHEN I PUT MY HEAD INTO THE COIN PURSE CUSHION, I WAS SATISFIED TO CONFIRM THAT, JUST AS I SUSPECTED, MY HEAD FIT INSIDE. THEN I TRIED TO PULL MY HEAD OUT OF THE COIN PURSE CUSHION. ...BUT, WHEN I ACTUALLY TRIED TO PULL IT OFF, I COULDN'T! MY EARS WERE COMPLETELY STUCK! THE INSIDE OF THE CUSHION WAS ALMOST ENTIRELY STUFFED WITH COTTON OR SOMETHING AND, AS I HURRIEDLY TRIED TO PULL MY HEAD OUT, THE CUSHION'S INNER SURFACE STUCK TO MY NOSE, AND I COULDN'T BREATHE! "THIS COULD BE VERY BAD!" I THOUGHT AND STARTED TO GET REALLY NERVOUS. I FLOUNDERED AROUND, TRYING TO OPEN THE COIN PURSE CUSHION WITH BOTH ARMS AS HARD AS I COULD.

THEN MY ASSISTANTS NOTICED AND ASKED, "WHAT ARE YOU DOING, MR. KISHIMOTO?" I THOUGHT, "YES!! MY ASSISTANTS WILL RESCUE ME!" AND I TRIED TO ASK THEM FOR HELP. ...JUST THEN I HEARD SOMETHING LIKE THE SOUND OF A CAMERA SHUTTER. I WASN'T SURE FROM INSIDE THE CUSHION BECAUSE I COULDN'T SEE, BUT I COULD IMAGINE WHAT WAS GOING ON. ALL OF MY ASSISTANTS WERE LAUGHING OUT LOUD AND TAKING PICTURES WITH THEIR CELL PHONE CAMERAS! OF ALL THINGS, THEY WERE TAKING PICTURES! THEY WEREN'T RESCUING ME; THEY WERE LAUGHING AND TAKING PICTURES! "NO! THEY'RE NOT TAKING THIS SERIOUSLY!!" I THOUGHT, AND MADE UP MY MIND THAT I HAD TO GET THE CUSHION OFF BY MYSELF. I PULLED HARD AND IT HURT SO MUCH THAT I THOUGHT MY EARS WERE GOING TO TEAR OFF. THEN, FINALLY, I WAS ABLE TO FREE MYSELF. NEEDLESS TO SAY, MY NAP TIME WAS COMPLETELY RUINED BY THAT CRAZY INCIDENT. I EXPECTED THERE WOULD BE AT LEAST ONE SANE PERSON WHO WOULD SAY, "ARE YOU OKAY, MR. KISHIMOTO?!" ...BUT THERE WASN'T. IT'S TRUE THAT THE ASSISTANTS HAD VERY LITTLE SLEEP AND WENT A BIT NUTTY. ALL OF THEM WERE UNDER THE SPELL OF THE USUAL CHAOS. IT WAS THEN THAT I PLEDGED... I WILL FIGHT AGAINST THIS CHAOS!

WARNING: DON'T TRY THIS AT HOME!

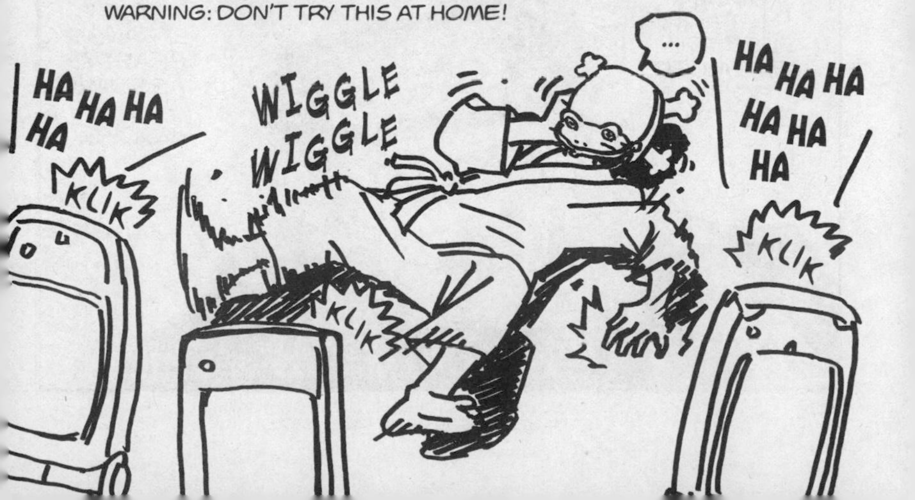
...
HA HA HA HA HA HA
KLIK
WIGGLE WIGGLE
KLIK
HA HA HA HA
KLIK

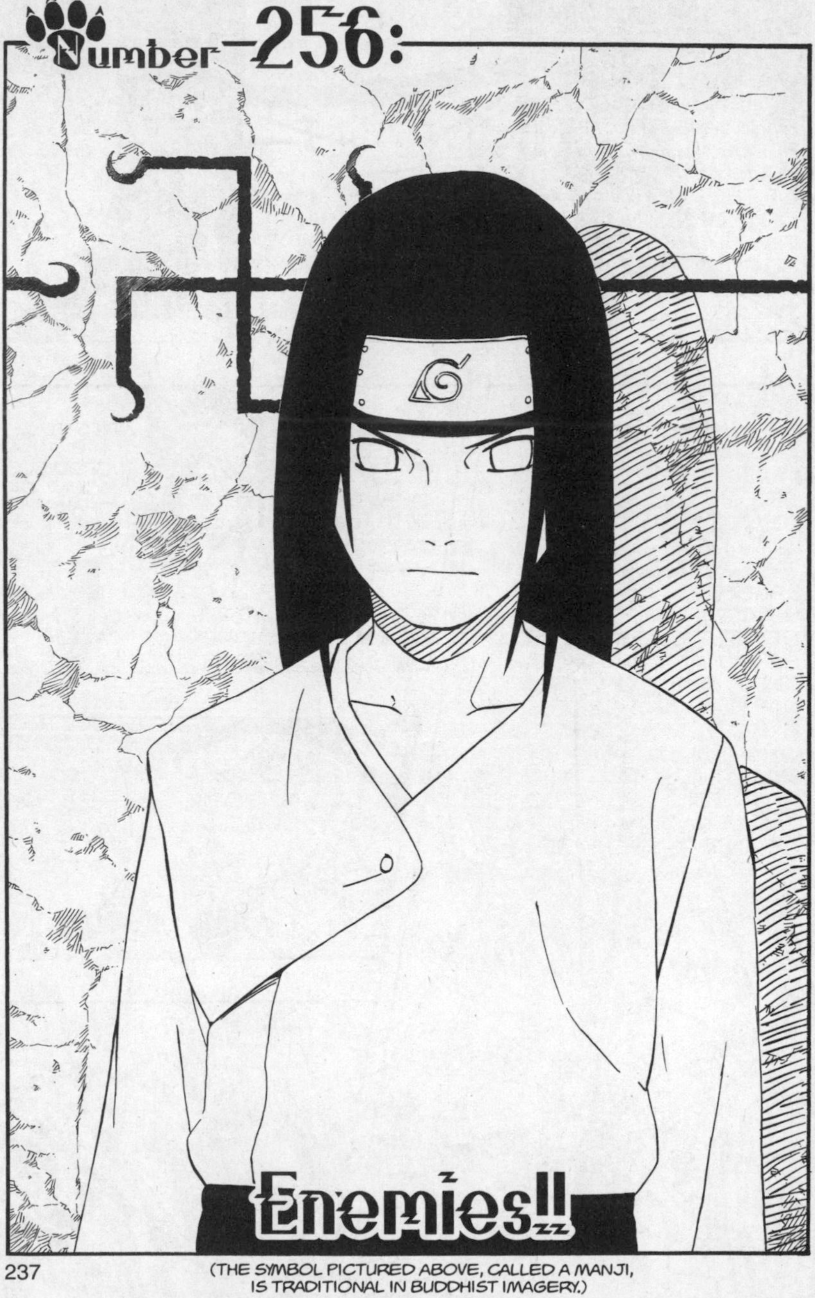
Number 256:
Enemies!!

(THE SYMBOL PICTURED ABOVE, CALLED A MANJI, IS TRADITIONAL IN BUDDHIST IMAGERY.)

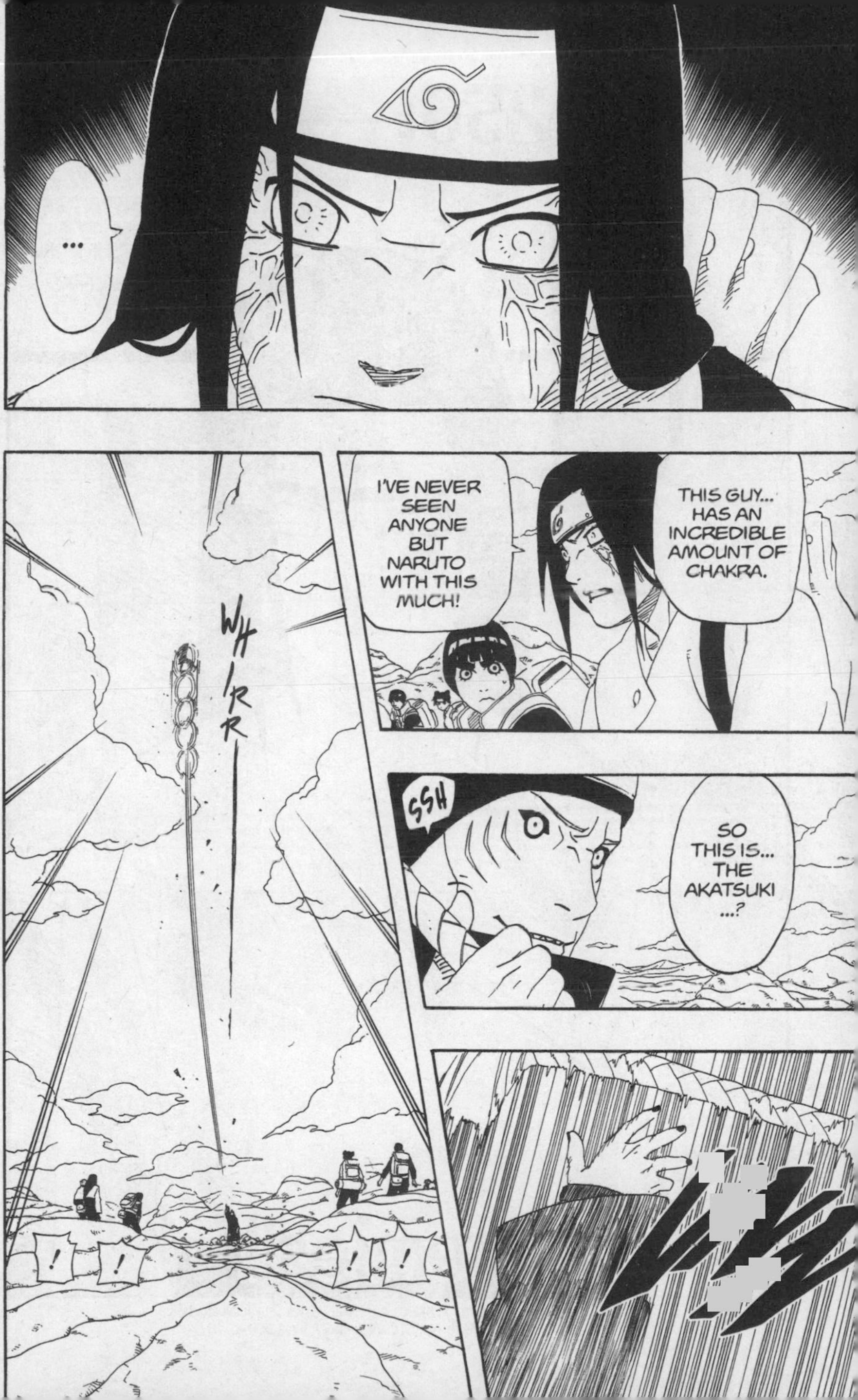
...
THIS GUY... HAS AN INCREDIBLE AMOUNT OF CHAKRA.
I'VE NEVER SEEN ANYONE BUT NARUTO WITH THIS MUCH!
SSH
SO THIS IS... THE AKATSUKI ...?
WHIRR
!
!
!
!

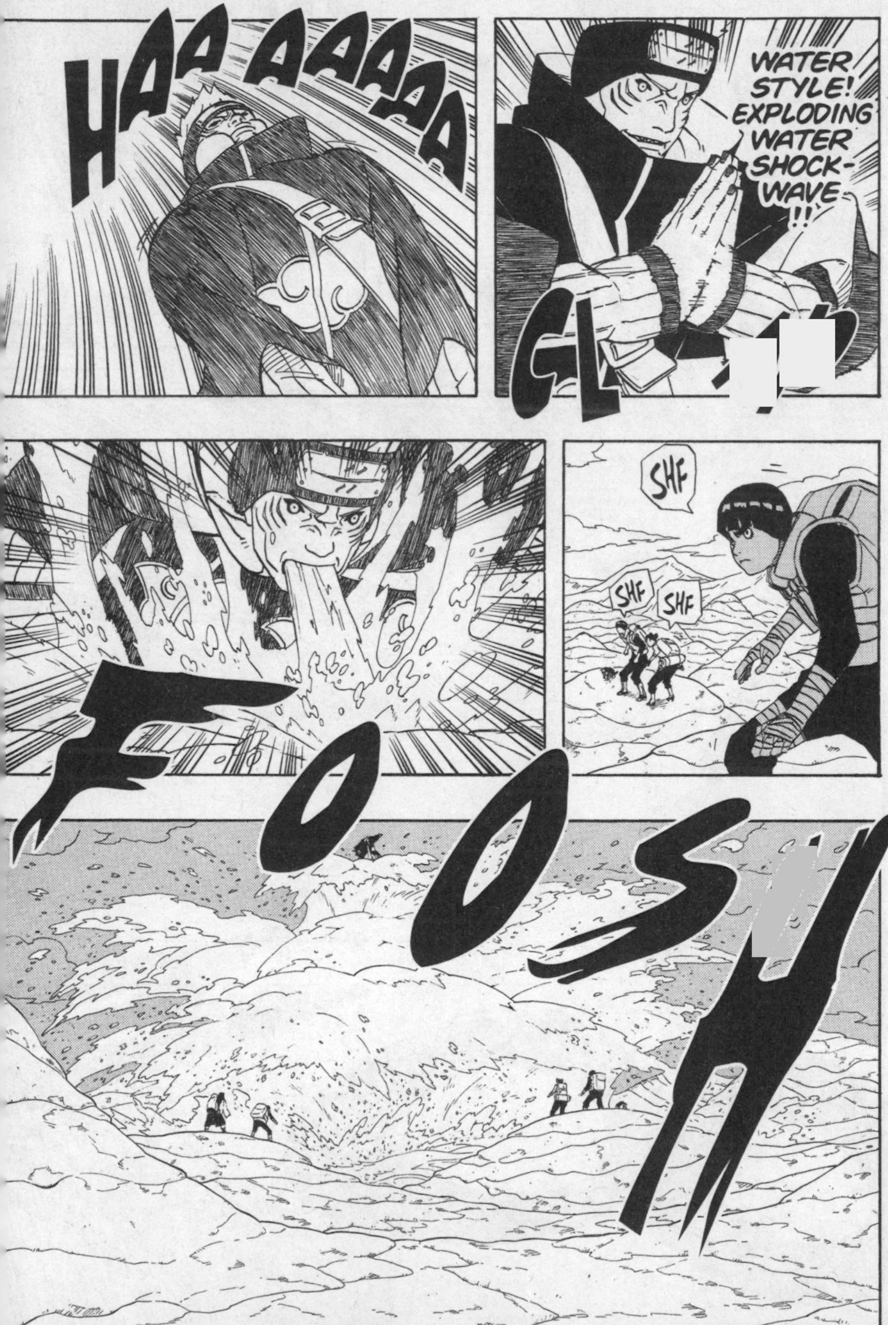
WATER STYLE! EXPLODING WATER SHOCK-WAVE!!
GL
HAAAAAAA
SHF
SHF
SHF
FOOSH

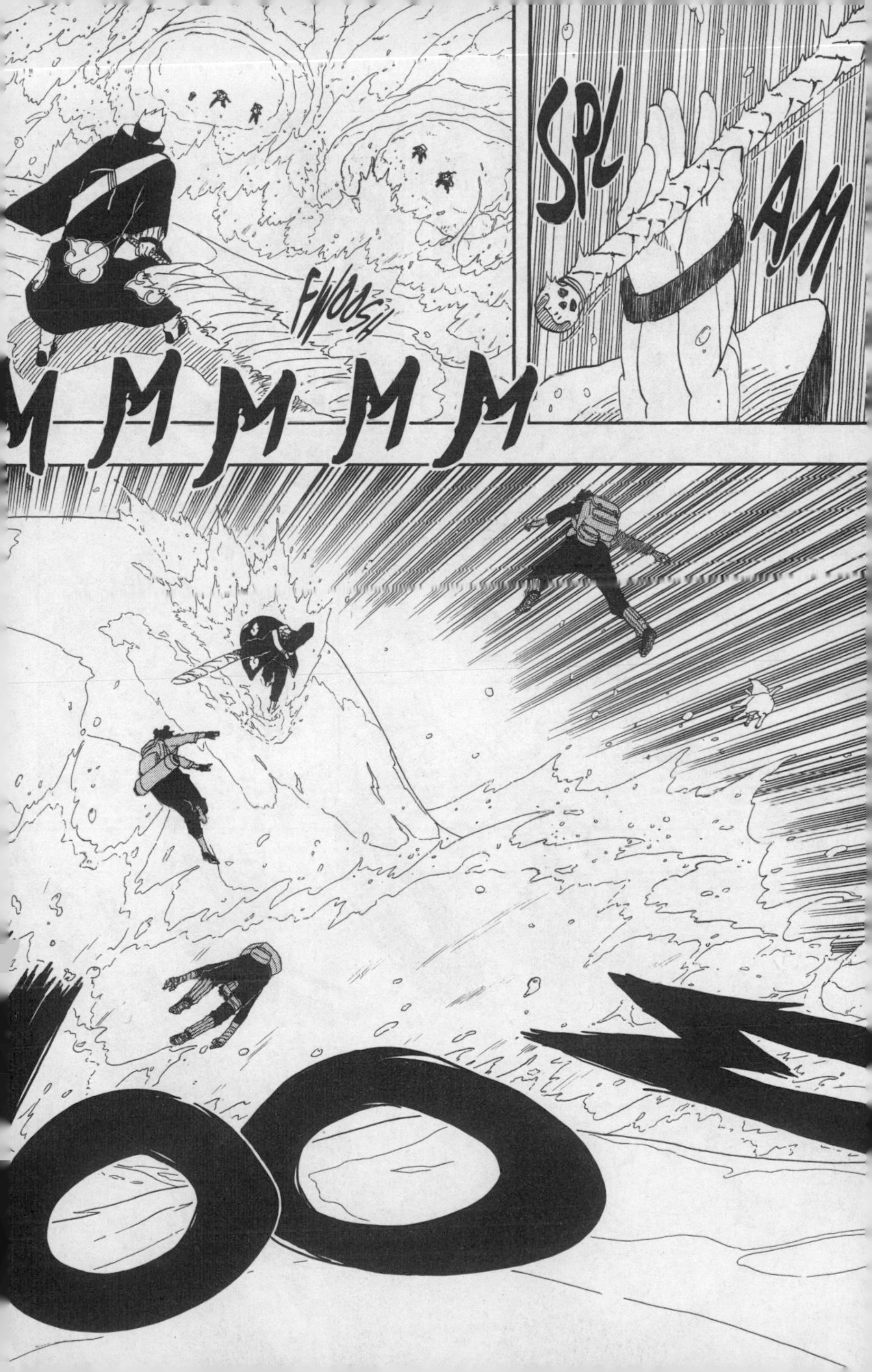
SPLAM
FWOOSH
MMMMM

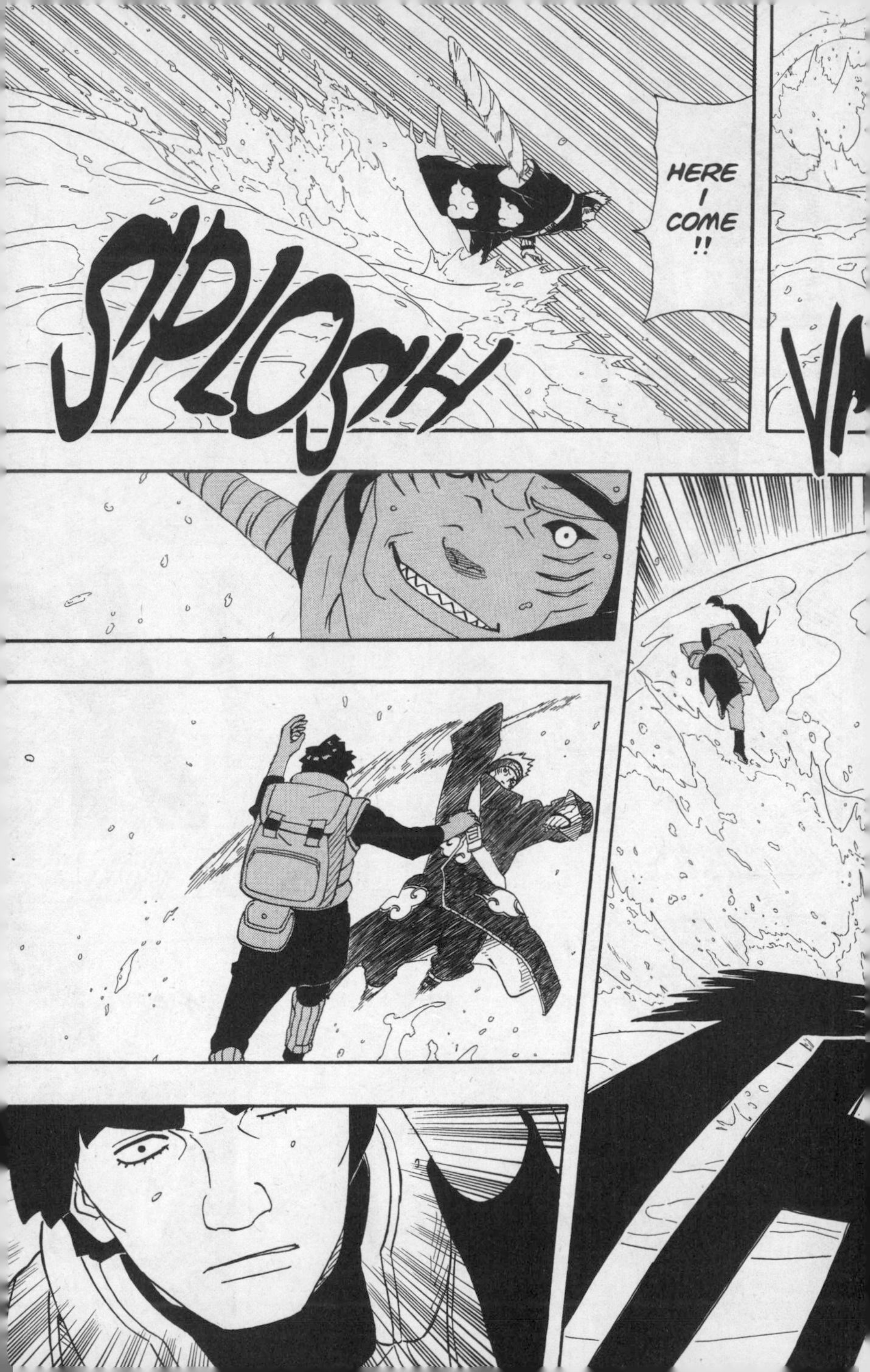
HERE I COME !!
SPLOSH

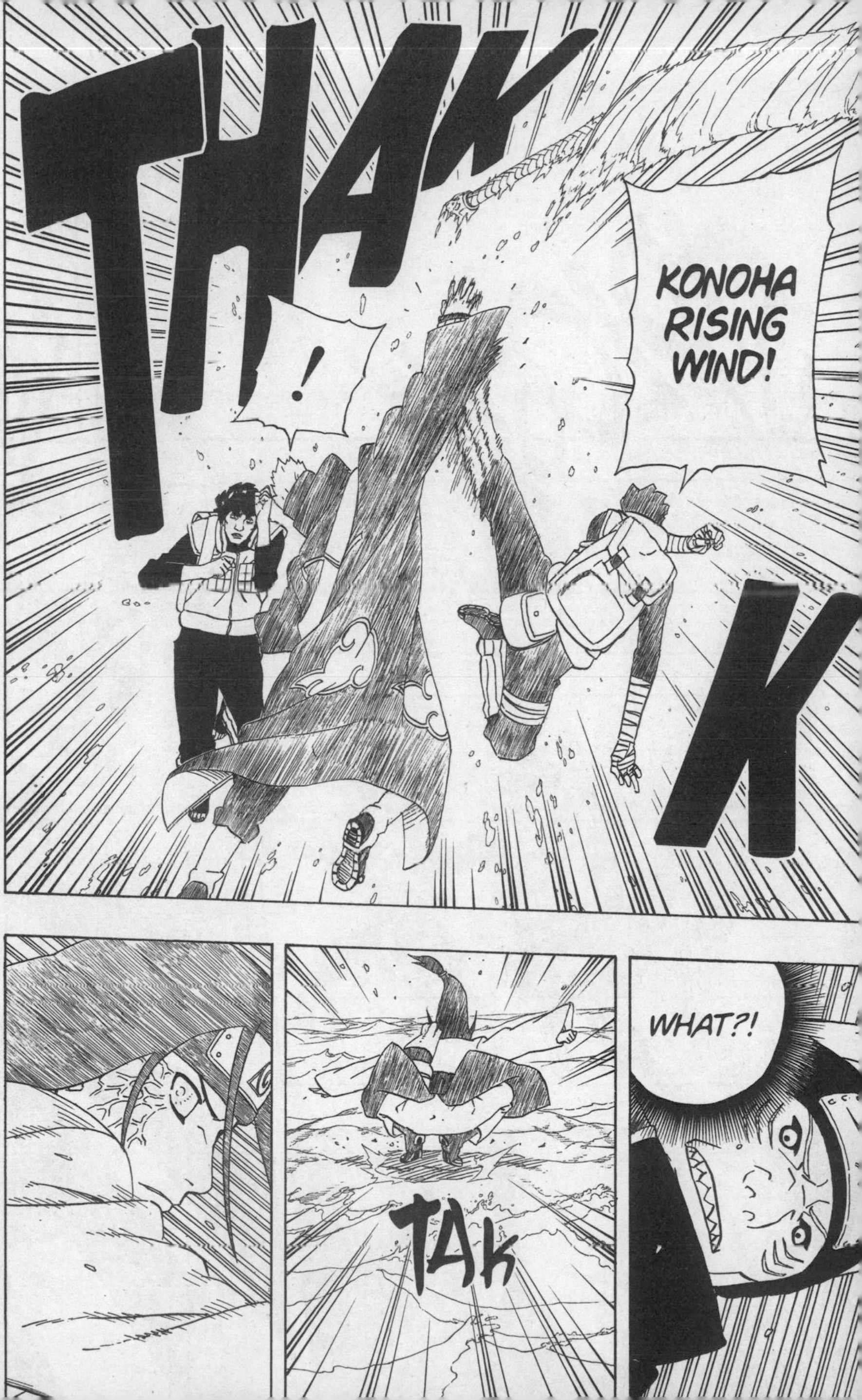
KONOHA RISING WIND!
THAK
!
K
WHAT?!
TAK

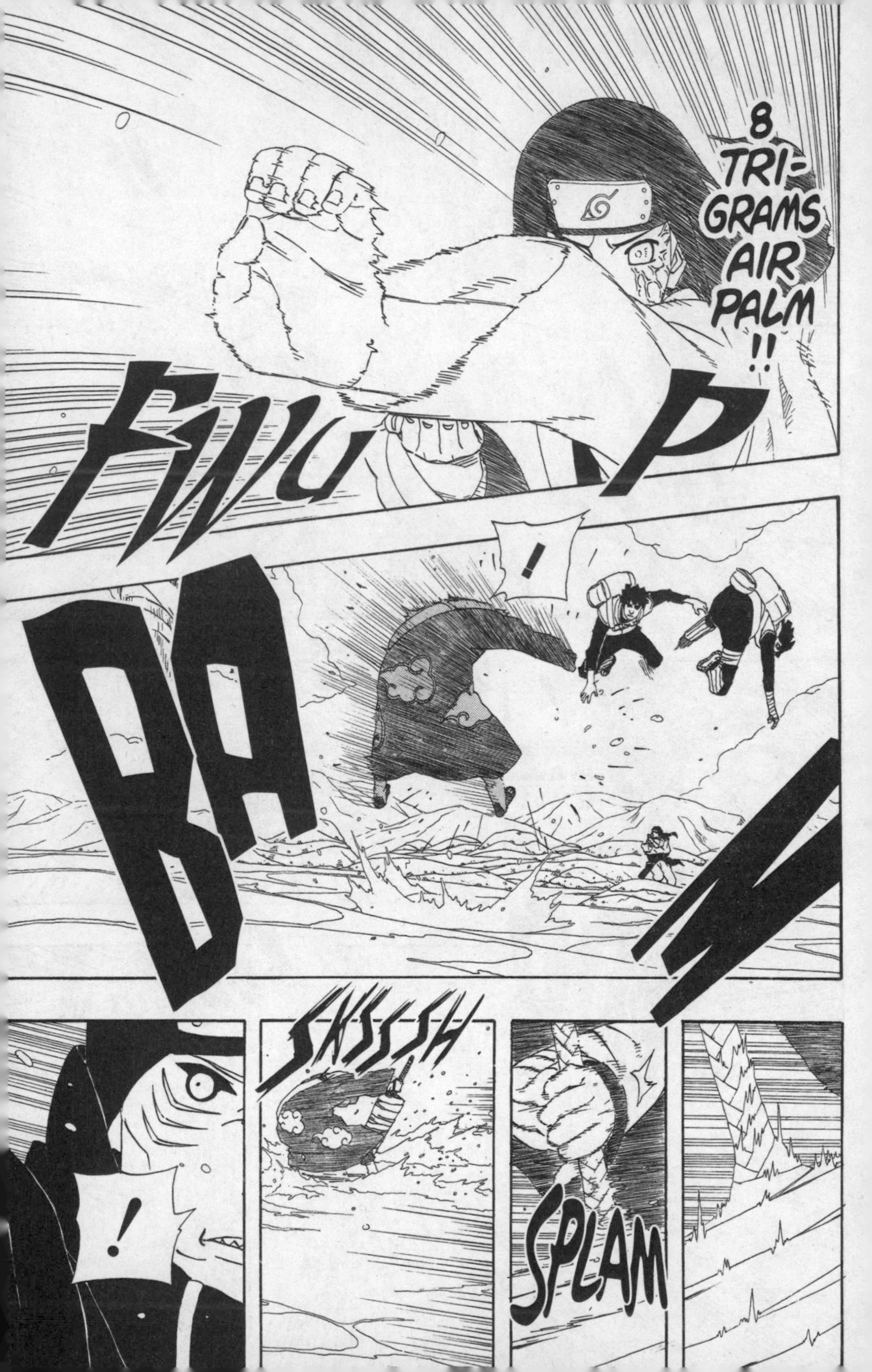
8 TRI-GRAMS AIR PALM!!
FWUMP
!
BABAM
!
SKSSSH
SPLAM

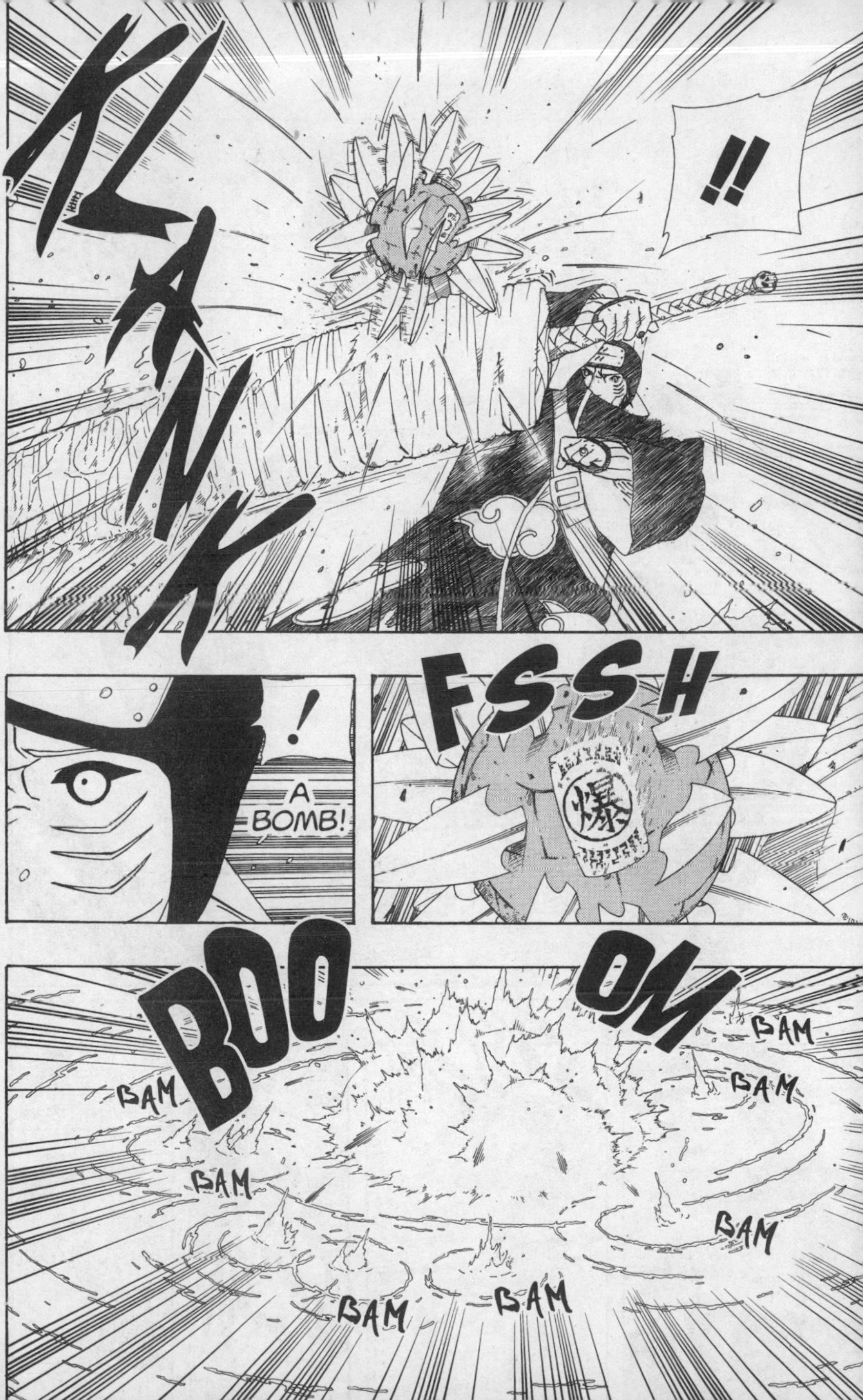
!!
KLANK
FSSH
!
A BOMB!
BOOOM
BAM
BAM
BAM
BAM
BAM
BAM
BAM

READ THIS WAY

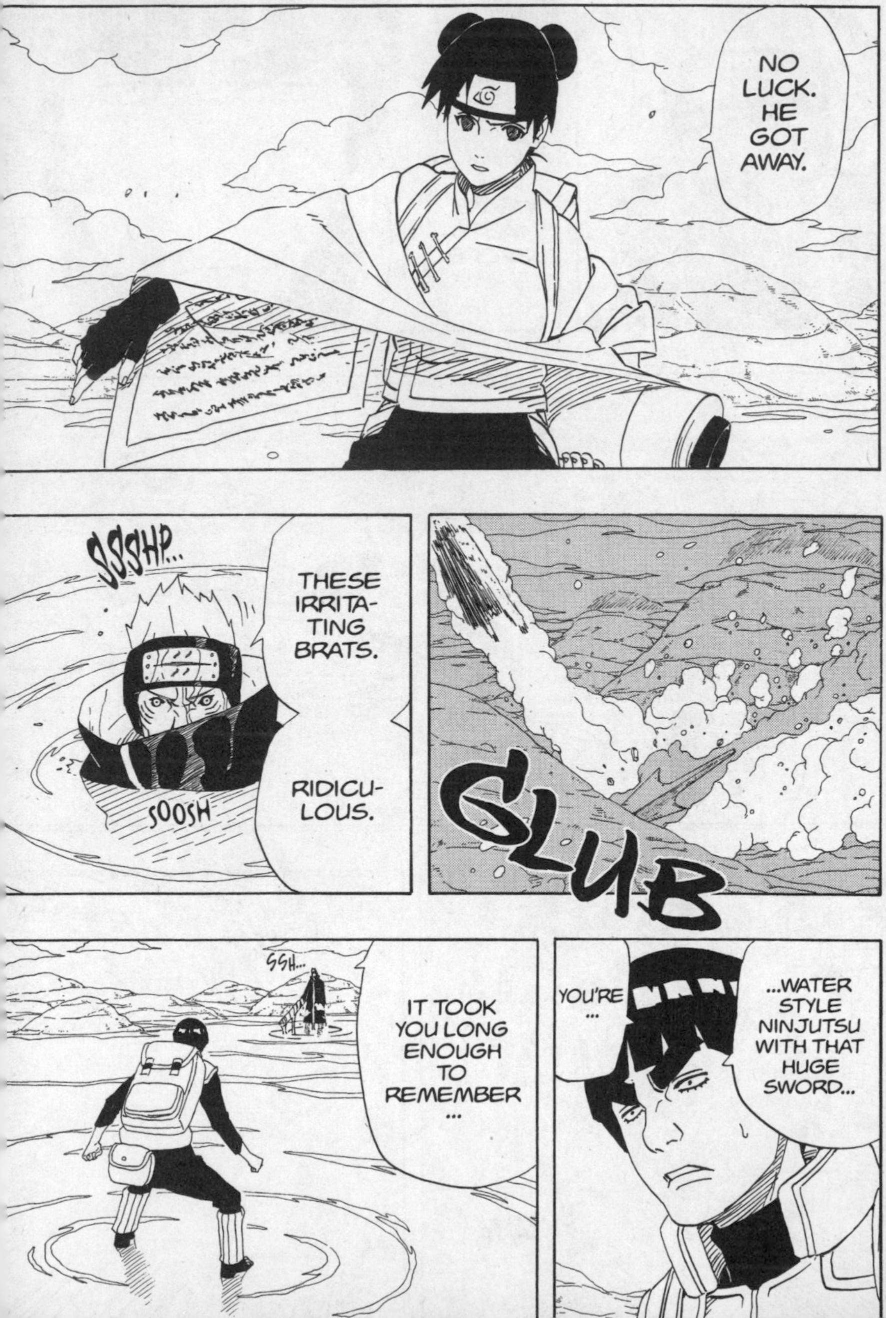
NO LUCK. HE GOT AWAY.
GLUB
THESE IRRITA-TING BRATS.
SSSHP...
RIDICU-LOUS.
SOOSH
...WATER STYLE NINJUTSU WITH THAT HUGE SWORD...
YOU'RE ...
IT TOOK YOU LONG ENOUGH TO REMEMBER ...
SSH...

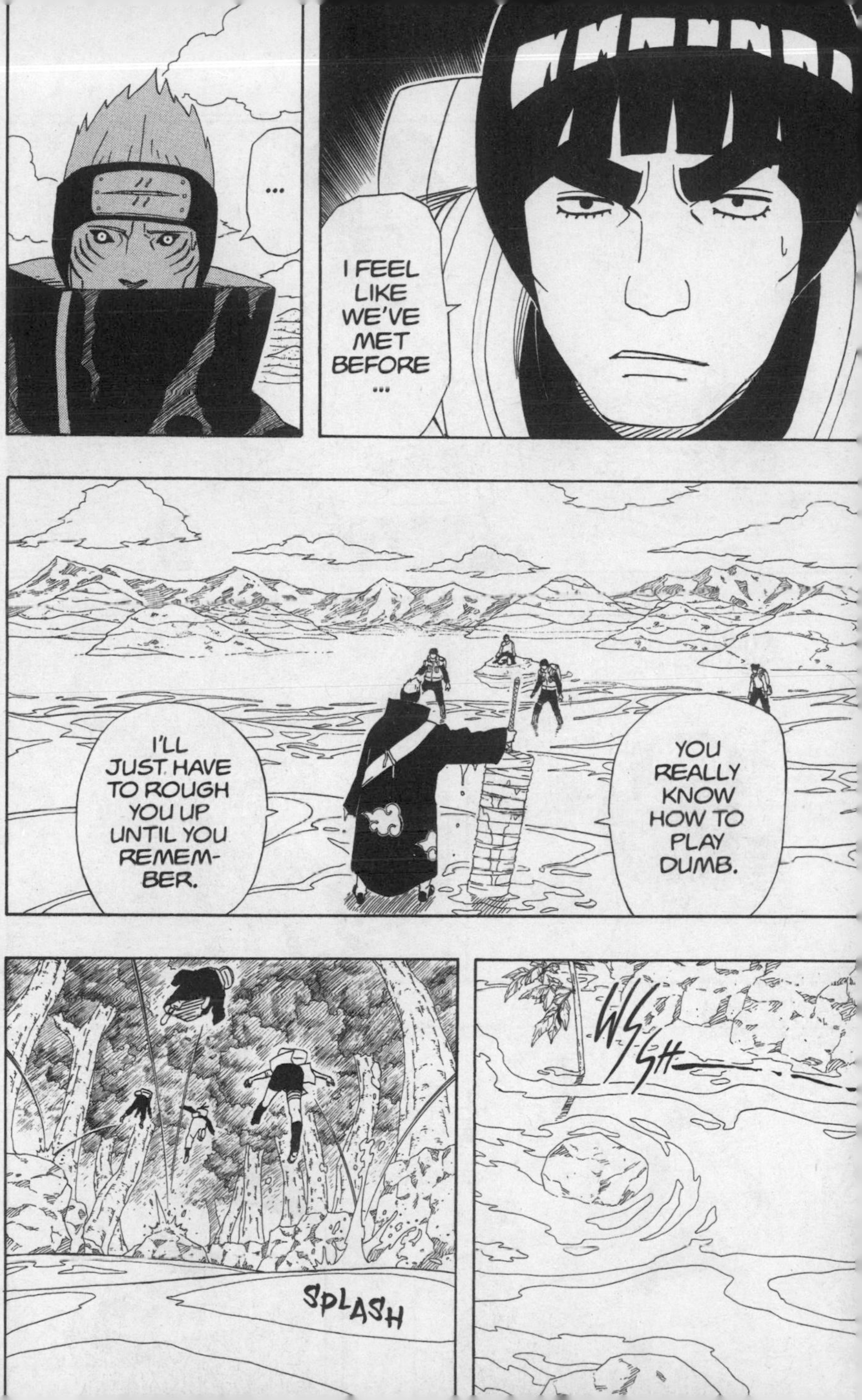
I FEEL LIKE WE'VE MET BEFORE ...
...
YOU REALLY KNOW HOW TO PLAY DUMB.
I'LL JUST HAVE TO ROUGH YOU UP UNTIL YOU REMEM-BER.
WSSH
SPLASH

READ THIS WAY

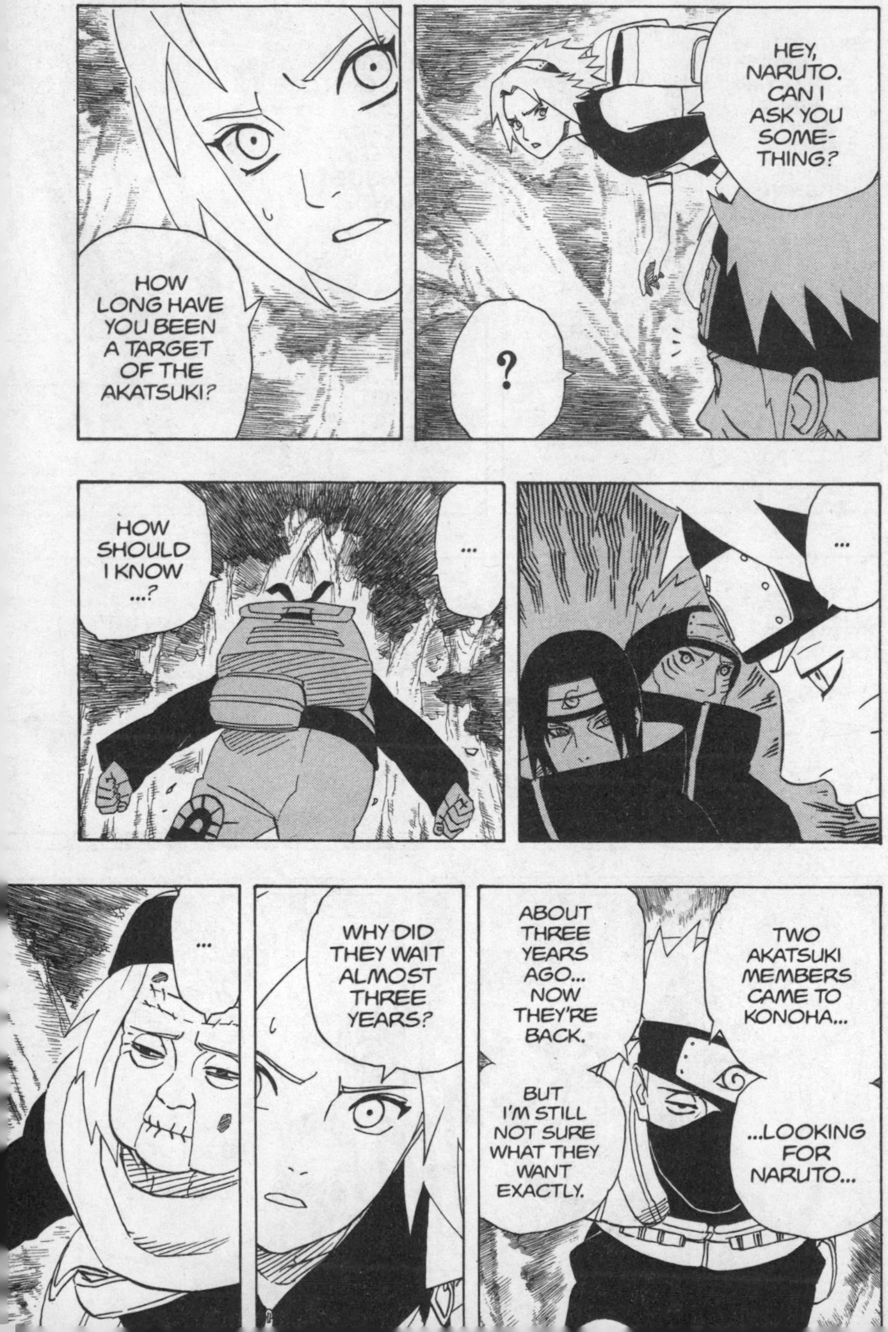
HEY, NARUTO. CAN I ASK YOU SOME-THING?
?
HOW LONG HAVE YOU BEEN A TARGET OF THE AKATSUKI?
...
...
HOW SHOULD I KNOW ...?
TWO AKATSUKI MEMBERS CAME TO KONOHA...
ABOUT THREE YEARS AGO... NOW THEY'RE BACK.
...LOOKING FOR NARUTO...
BUT I'M STILL NOT SURE WHAT THEY WANT EXACTLY.
WHY DID THEY WAIT ALMOST THREE YEARS?
...

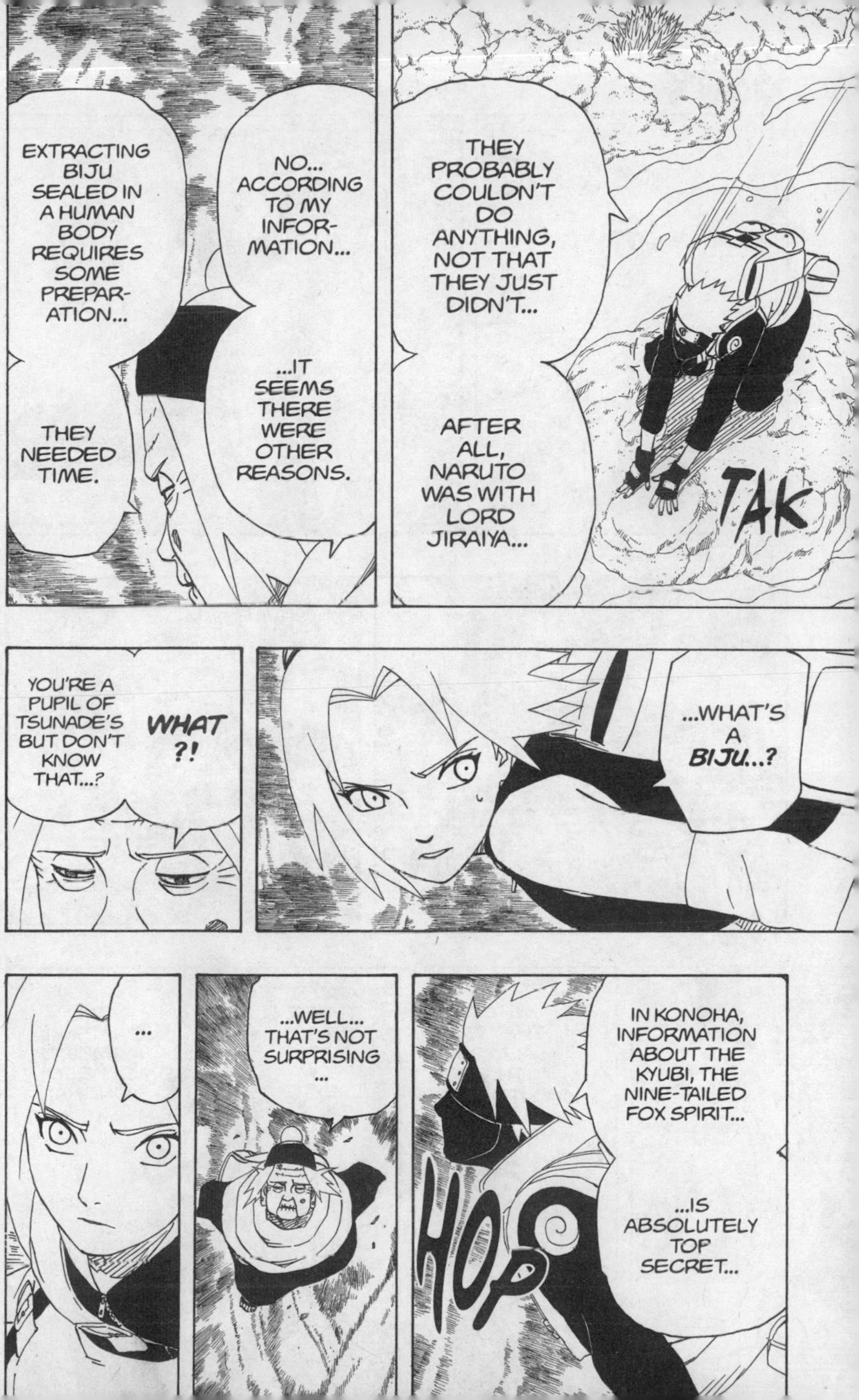
THEY PROBABLY COULDN'T DO ANYTHING, NOT THAT THEY JUST DIDN'T...
AFTER ALL, NARUTO WAS WITH LORD JIRAIYA...
TAK
NO... ACCORDING TO MY INFORMATION...
...IT SEEMS THERE WERE OTHER REASONS.
EXTRACTING BIJU SEALED IN A HUMAN BODY REQUIRES SOME PREPARATION...
THEY NEEDED TIME.
...WHAT'S A BIJU...?
WHAT ?!
YOU'RE A PUPIL OF TSUNADE'S BUT DON'T KNOW THAT...?
IN KONOHA, INFORMATION ABOUT THE KYUBI, THE NINE-TAILED FOX SPIRIT...
...IS ABSOLUTELY TOP SECRET...
HOP
...WELL... THAT'S NOT SURPRISING ...
...

READ THIS WAY

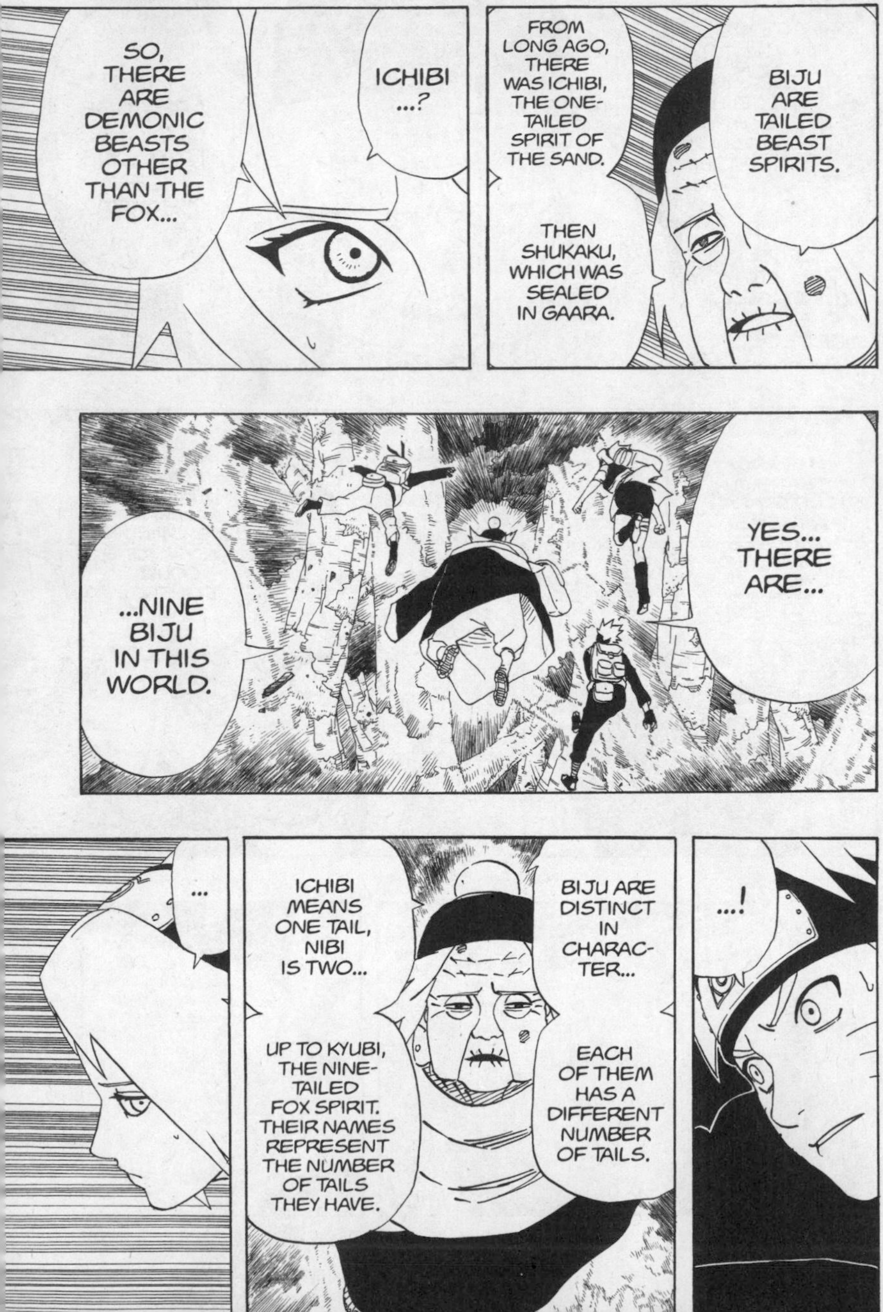
BIJU ARE TAILED BEAST SPIRITS.
FROM LONG AGO, THERE WAS ICHIBI, THE ONE-TAILED SPIRIT OF THE SAND.
THEN SHUKAKU, WHICH WAS SEALED IN GAARA.
ICHIBI ...?
SO, THERE ARE DEMONIC BEASTS OTHER THAN THE FOX...
YES... THERE ARE...
...NINE BIJU IN THIS WORLD.
...!
BIJU ARE DISTINCT IN CHARACTER...
EACH OF THEM HAS A DIFFERENT NUMBER OF TAILS.
ICHIBI MEANS ONE TAIL, NIBI IS TWO...
UP TO KYUBI, THE NINE-TAILED FOX SPIRIT. THEIR NAMES REPRESENT THE NUMBER OF TAILS THEY HAVE.
...

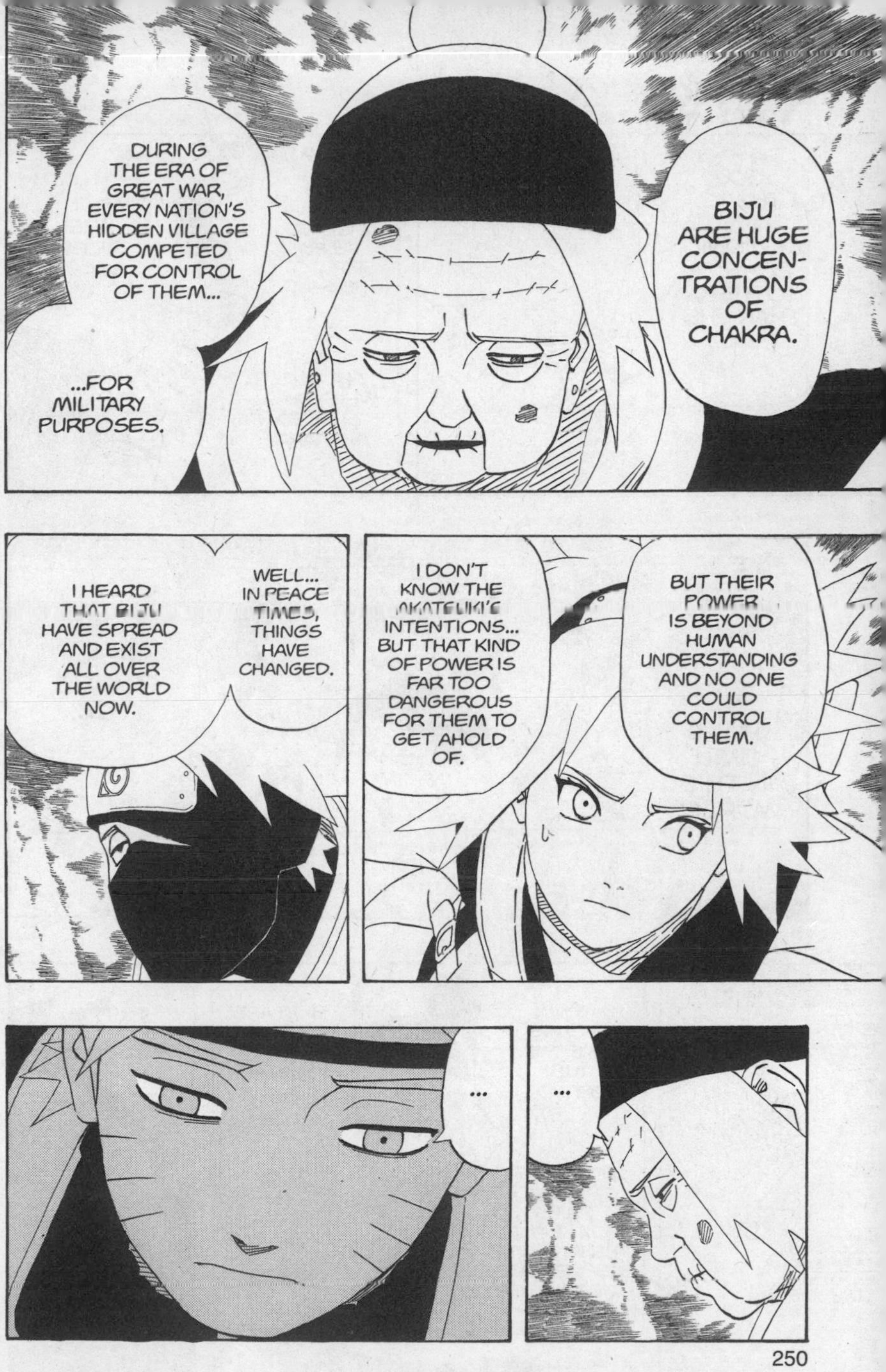
BIJU ARE HUGE CONCENTRATIONS OF CHAKRA.
DURING THE ERA OF GREAT WAR, EVERY NATION'S HIDDEN VILLAGE COMPETED FOR CONTROL OF THEM...
...FOR MILITARY PURPOSES.
BUT THEIR POWER IS BEYOND HUMAN UNDERSTANDING AND NO ONE COULD CONTROL THEM.
I DON'T KNOW THE AKATSUKI'S INTENTIONS... BUT THAT KIND OF POWER IS FAR TOO DANGEROUS FOR THEM TO GET AHOLD OF.
WELL... IN PEACE TIMES, THINGS HAVE CHANGED.
I HEARD THAT BIJU HAVE SPREAD AND EXIST ALL OVER THE WORLD NOW.
...
...

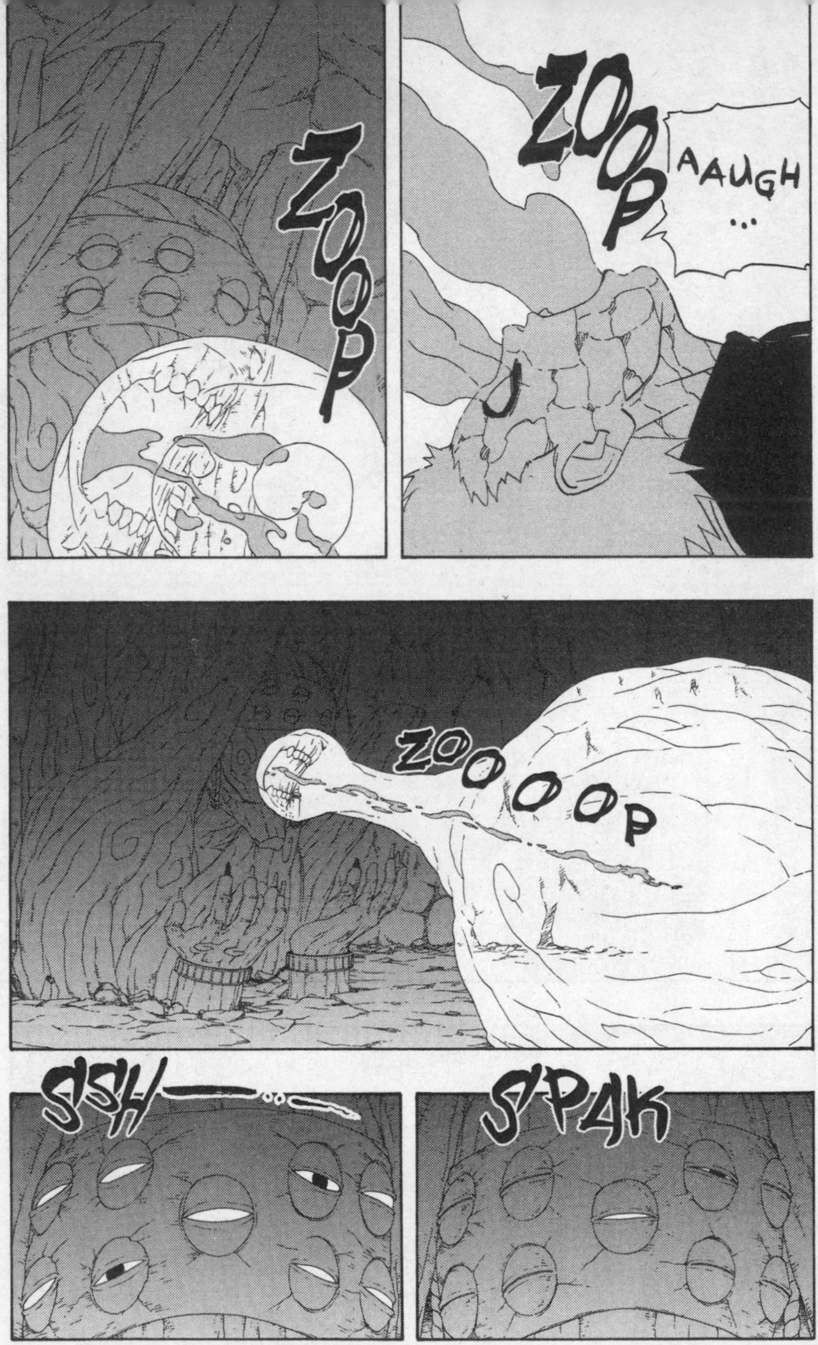
ZOOP
AAUGH ...
ZOOP
ZOOOOOP
SPAK
SISH—..—

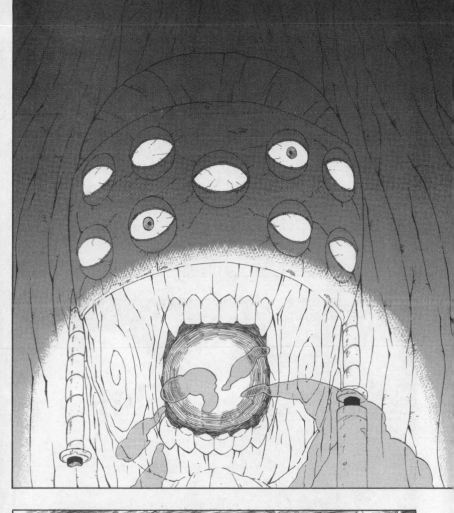

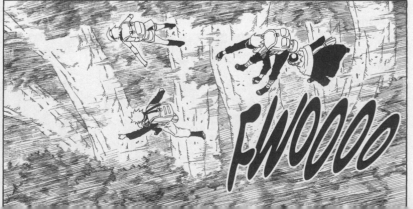

FWOOOO

READ THIS WAY

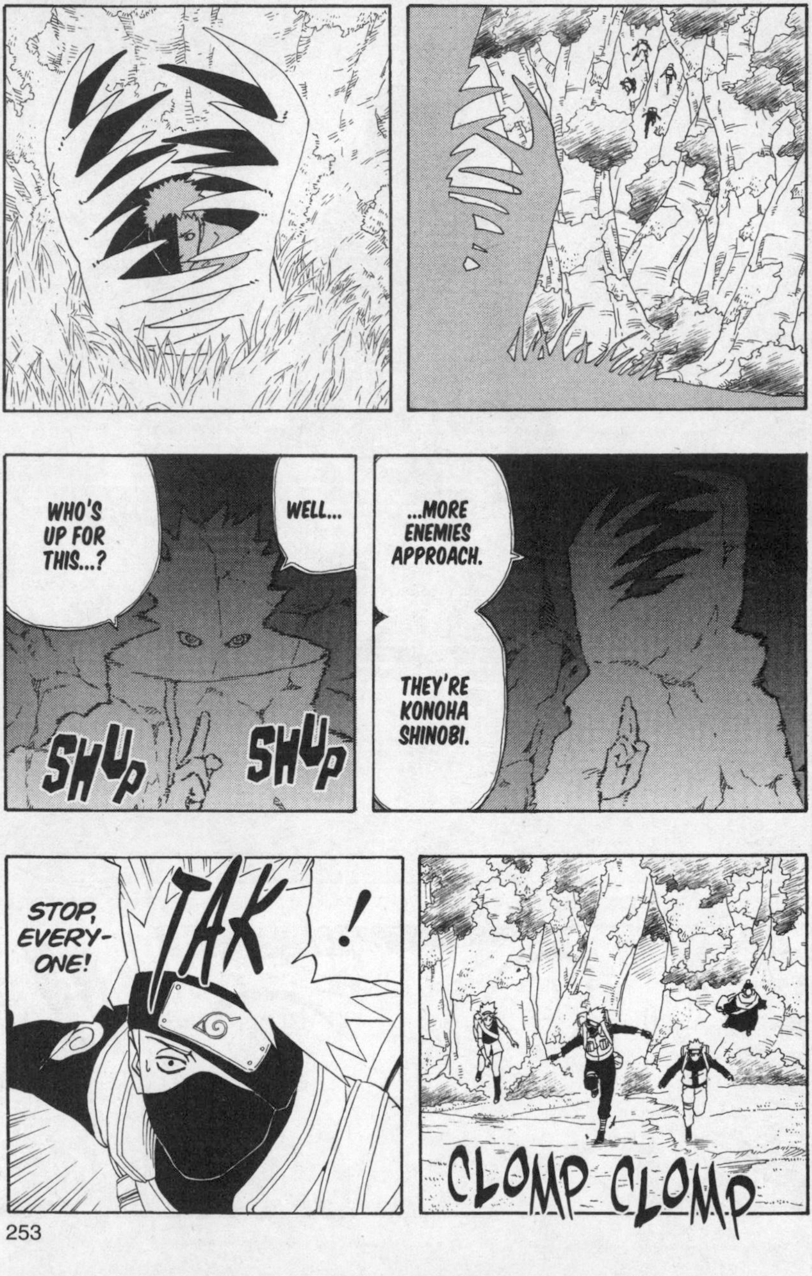
...MORE ENEMIES APPROACH.
THEY'RE KONOHA SHINOBI.
WELL...
WHO'S UP FOR THIS...?
SHUP
SHUP
CLOMP CLOMP
TAK!
STOP, EVERY-ONE!

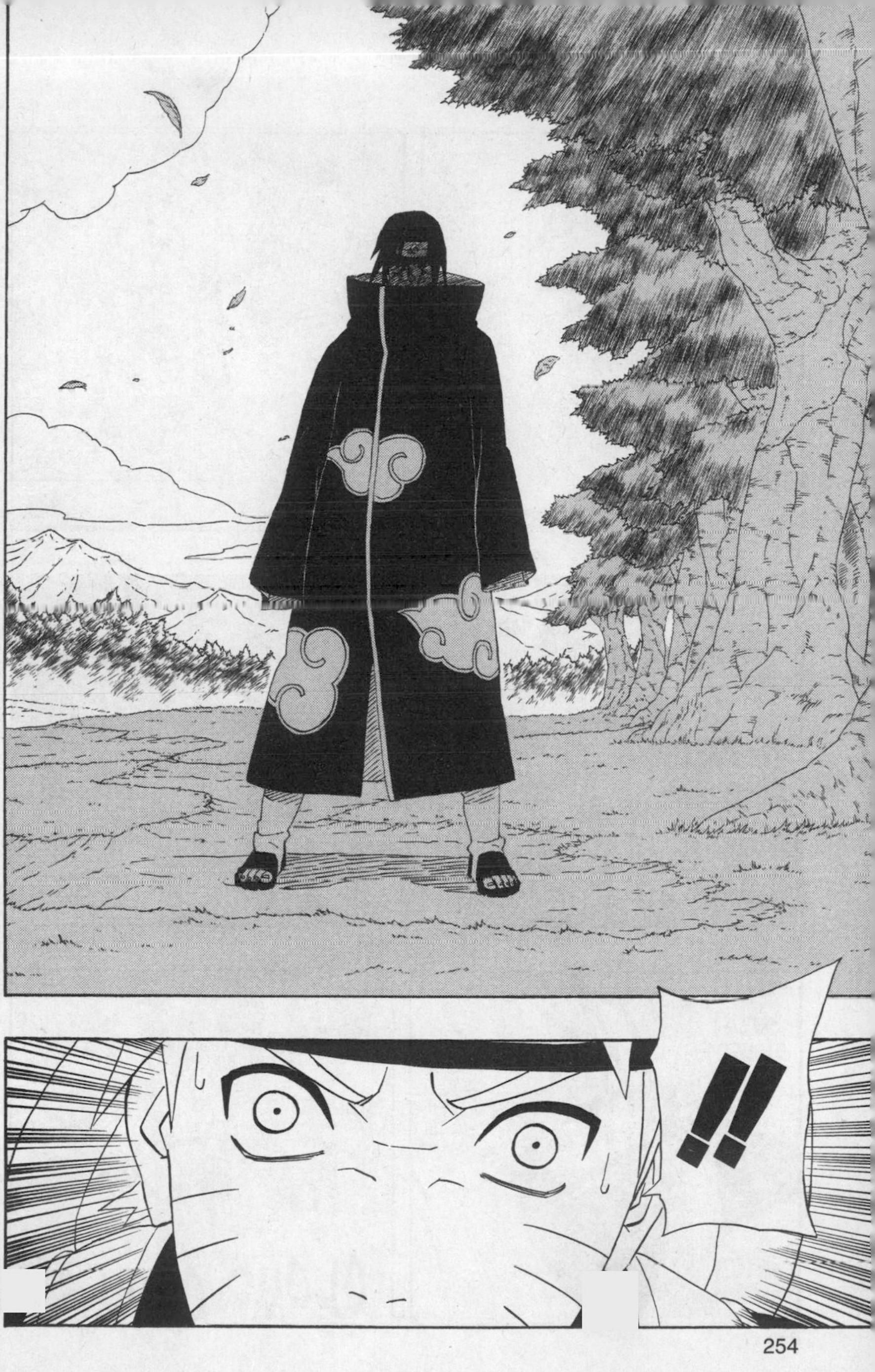
!!

READ THIS WAY

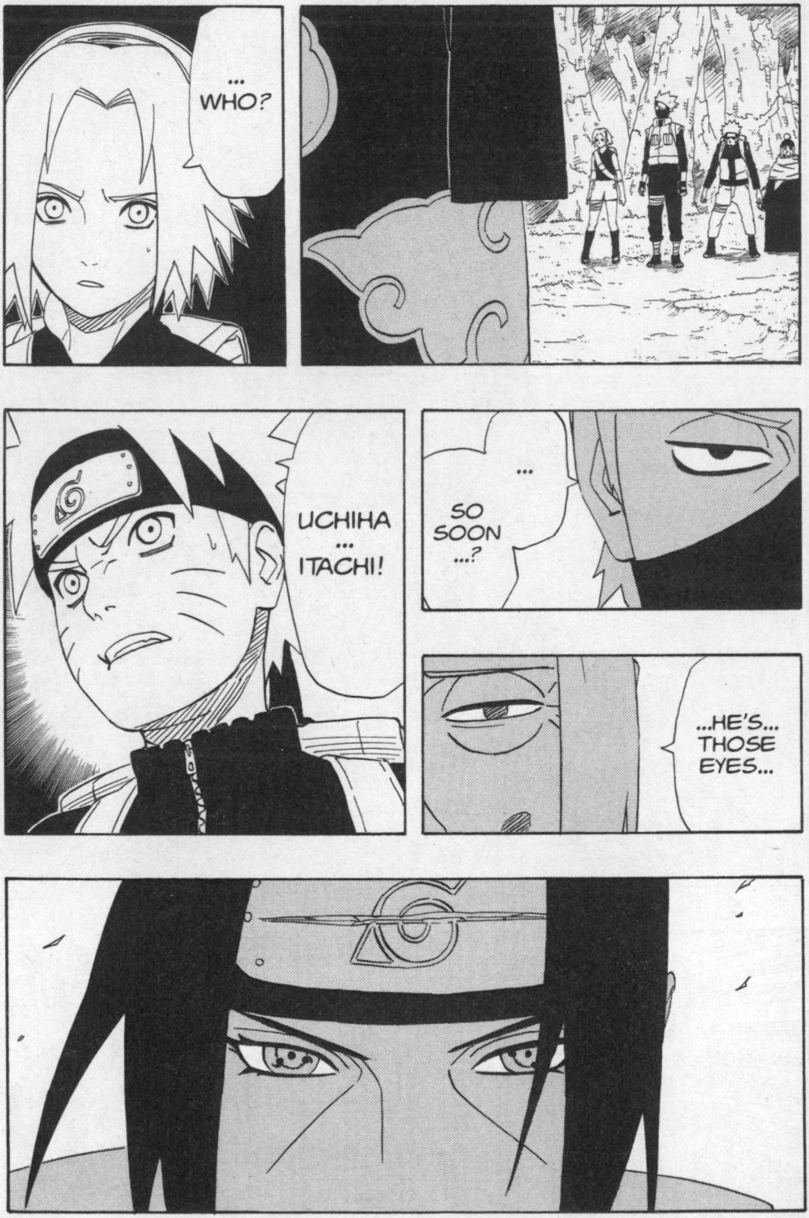
... WHO?
...
SO SOON ...?
...HE'S... THOSE EYES...
UCHIHA ... ITACHI!

NARUTO

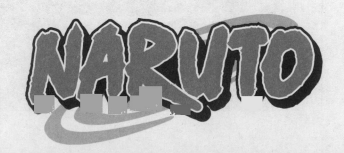

Number 257: Kakashi Comes Through

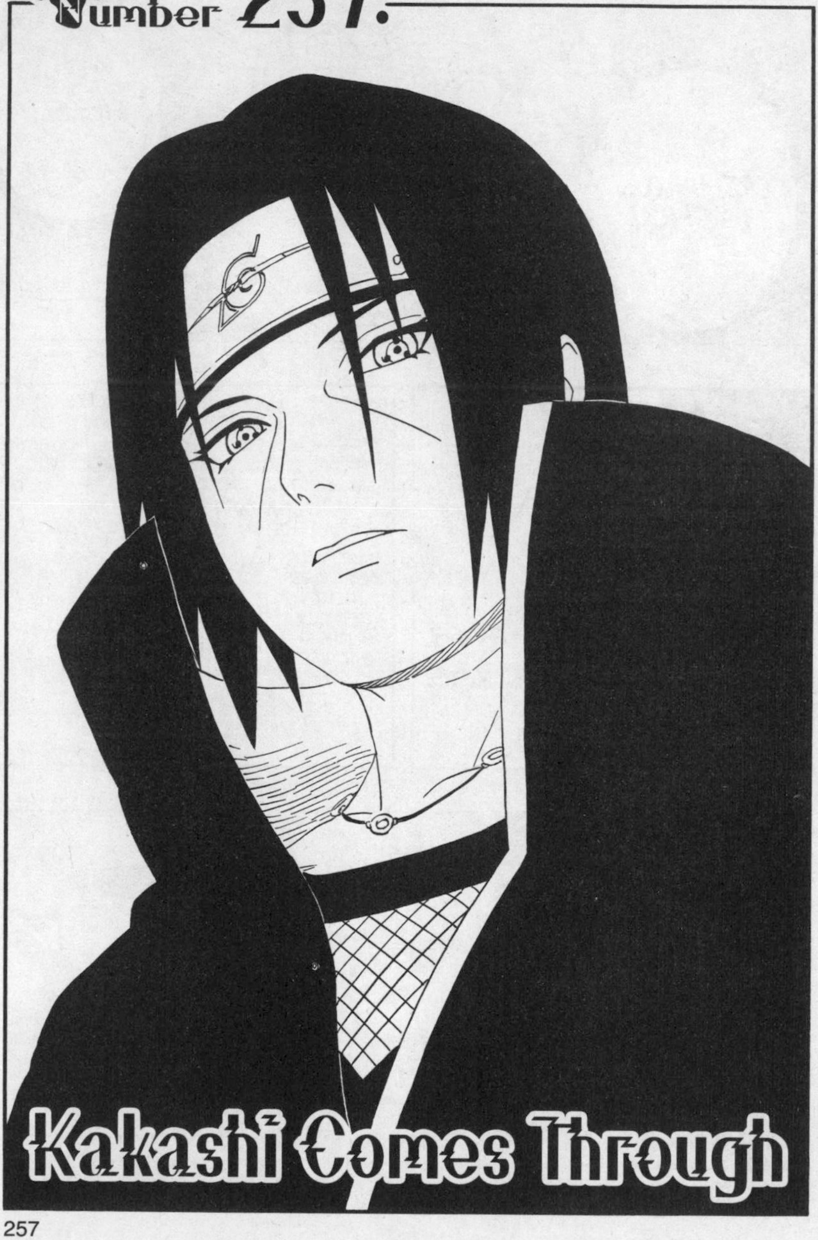

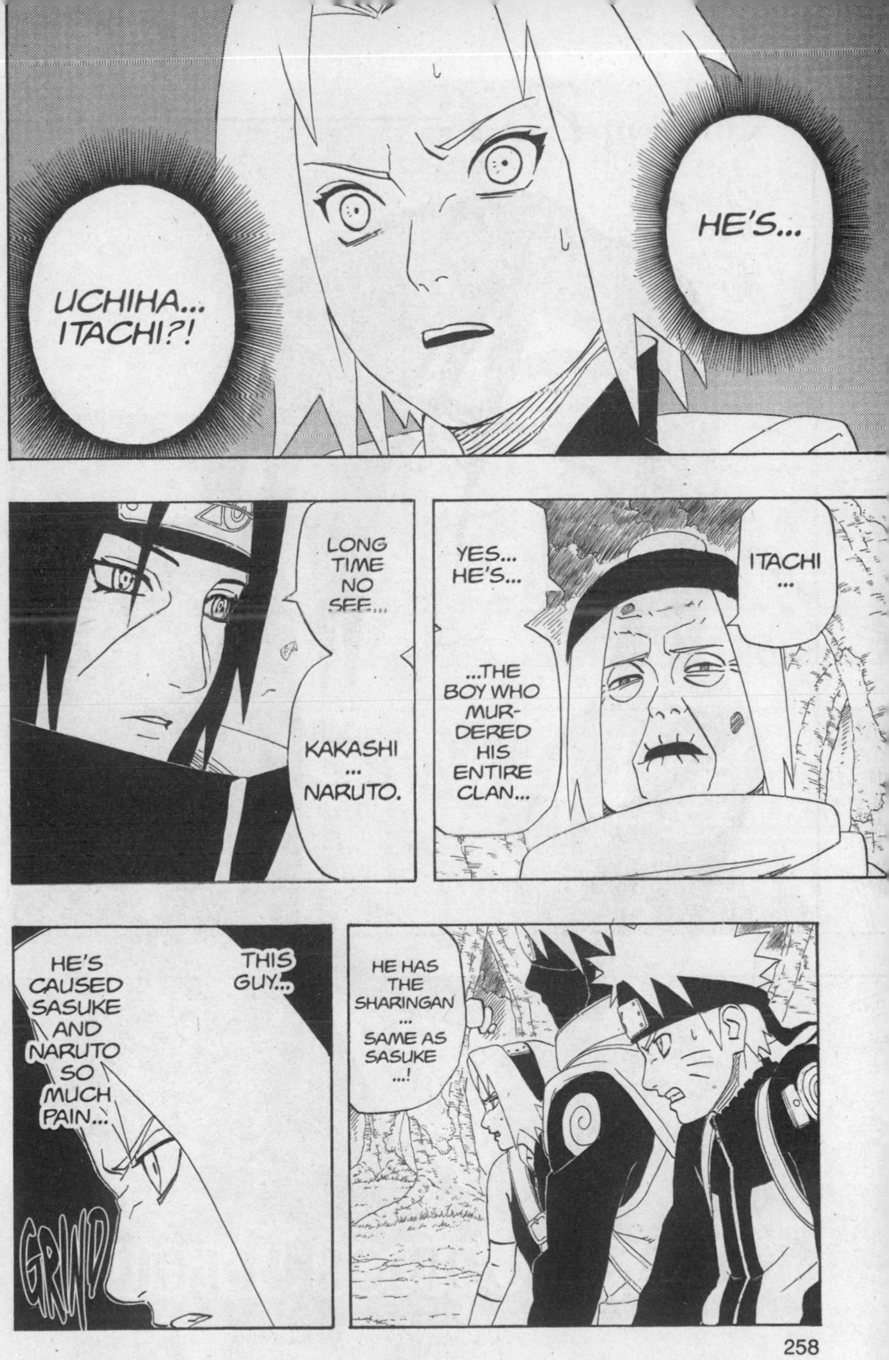
HE'S...
UCHIHA... ITACHI?!
ITACHI ...
YES... HE'S...
...THE BOY WHO MURDERED HIS ENTIRE CLAN...
LONG TIME NO SEE...
KAKASHI ... NARUTO.
HE HAS THE SHARINGAN ... SAME AS SASUKE ...!
THIS GUY...
HE'S CAUSED SASUKE AND NARUTO SO MUCH PAIN...
GRIND

READ THIS WAY

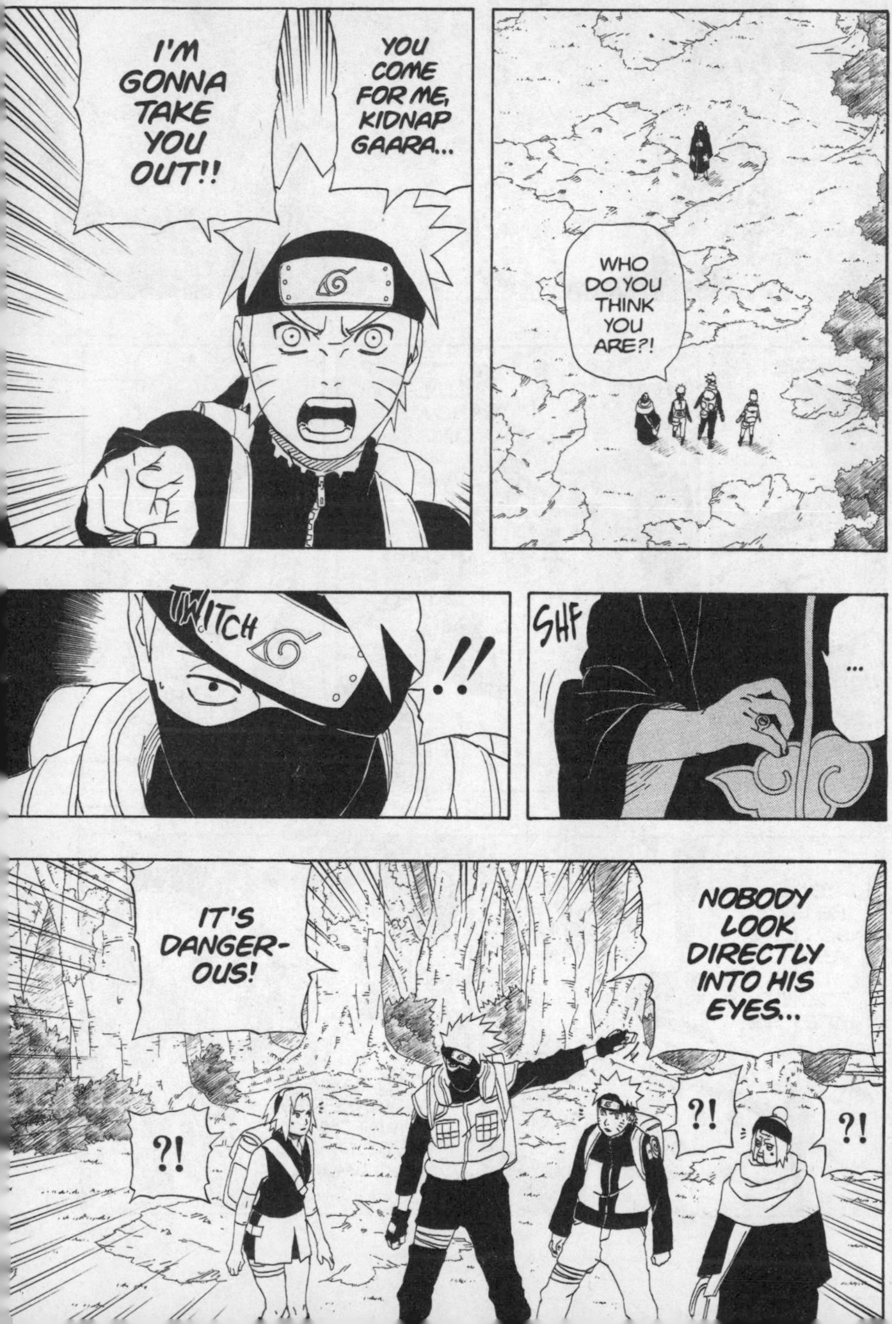

WHO DO YOU THINK YOU ARE?!
YOU COME FOR ME, KIDNAP GAARA...
I'M GONNA TAKE YOU OUT!!
SHF
...
TWITCH
!!
NOBODY LOOK DIRECTLY INTO HIS EYES...
IT'S DANGER-OUS!
?!
?!
?!

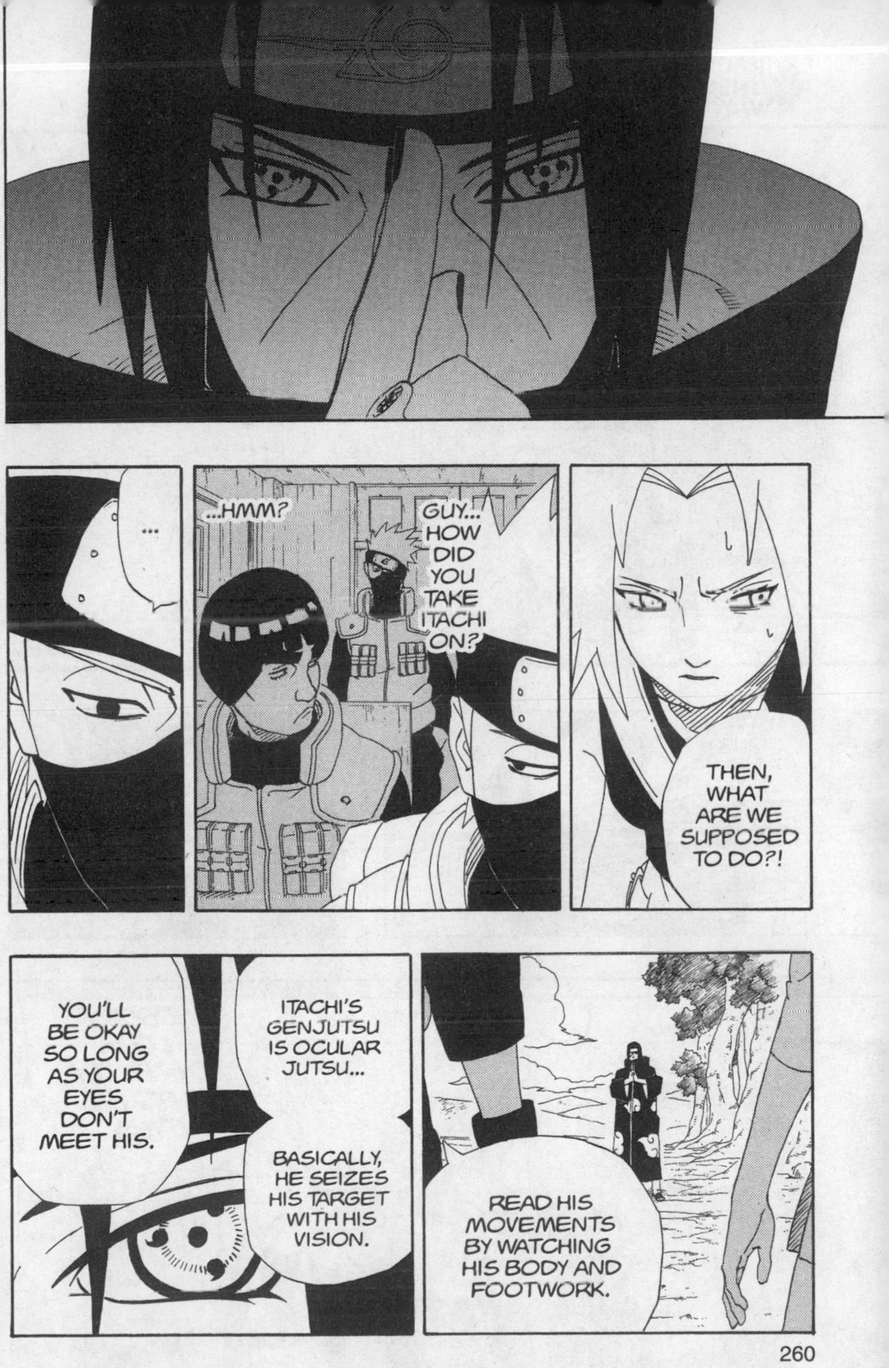
THEN, WHAT ARE WE SUPPOSED TO DO?!
GUY... HOW DID YOU TAKE ITACHI ON?
...HMM?
...
READ HIS MOVEMENTS BY WATCHING HIS BODY AND FOOTWORK.
ITACHI'S GENJUTSU IS OCULAR JUTSU...
BASICALLY, HE SEIZES HIS TARGET WITH HIS VISION.
YOU'LL BE OKAY SO LONG AS YOUR EYES DON'T MEET HIS.

READ THIS WAY

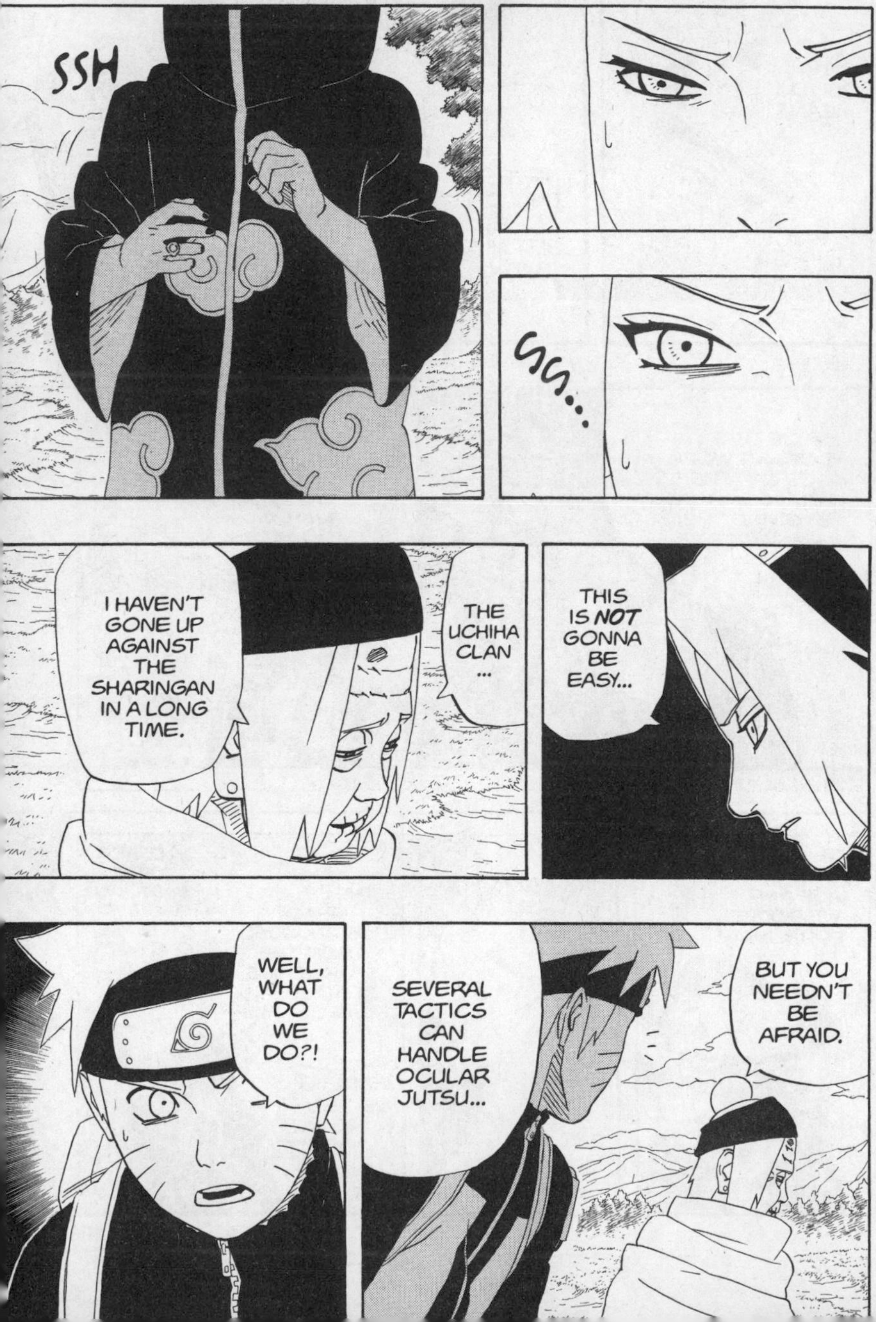
SS...
SSH
THIS IS NOT GONNA BE EASY...
THE UCHIHA CLAN ...
I HAVEN'T GONE UP AGAINST THE SHARINGAN IN A LONG TIME.
BUT YOU NEEDN'T BE AFRAID.
SEVERAL TACTICS CAN HANDLE OCULAR JUTSU...
WELL, WHAT DO WE DO?!

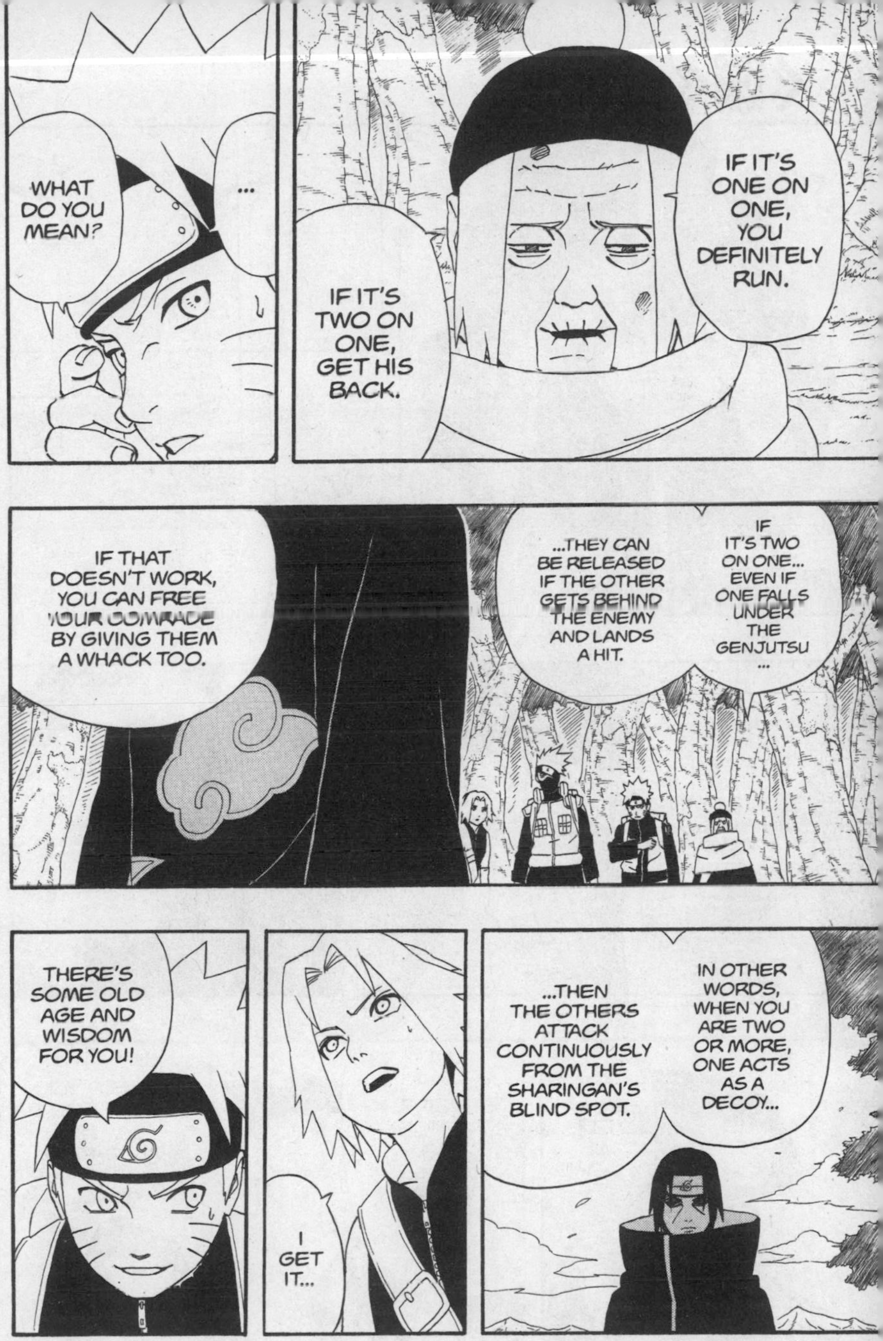
IF IT'S ONE ON ONE, YOU DEFINITELY RUN.
IF IT'S TWO ON ONE, GET HIS BACK.
...
WHAT DO YOU MEAN?
IF IT'S TWO ON ONE... EVEN IF ONE FALLS UNDER THE GENJUTSU ...
...THEY CAN BE RELEASED IF THE OTHER GETS BEHIND THE ENEMY AND LANDS A HIT.
IF THAT DOESN'T WORK, YOU CAN FREE YOUR COMRADE BY GIVING THEM A WHACK TOO.
IN OTHER WORDS, WHEN YOU ARE TWO OR MORE, ONE ACTS AS A DECOY...
...THEN THE OTHERS ATTACK CONTINUOUSLY FROM THE SHARINGAN'S BLIND SPOT.
I GET IT...
THERE'S SOME OLD AGE AND WISDOM FOR YOU!

READ THIS WAY

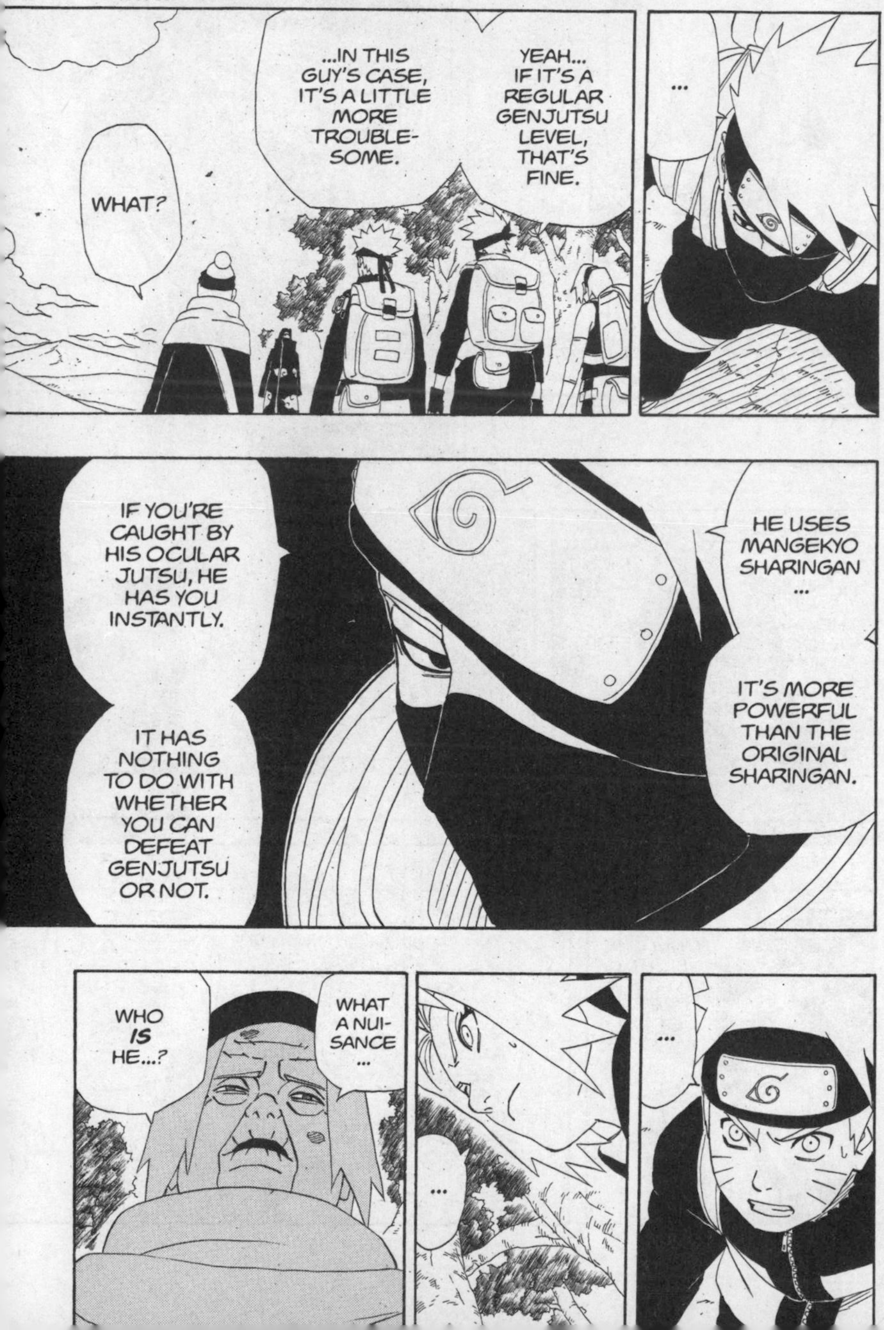
...
YEAH... IF IT'S A REGULAR GENJUTSU LEVEL, THAT'S FINE.
...IN THIS GUY'S CASE, IT'S A LITTLE MORE TROUBLE-SOME.
WHAT?
HE USES MANGEKYO SHARINGAN ...
IT'S MORE POWERFUL THAN THE ORIGINAL SHARINGAN.
IF YOU'RE CAUGHT BY HIS OCULAR JUTSU, HE HAS YOU INSTANTLY.
IT HAS NOTHING TO DO WITH WHETHER YOU CAN DEFEAT GENJUTSU OR NOT.
...
...
WHAT A NUI-SANCE ...
WHO *IS* HE...?

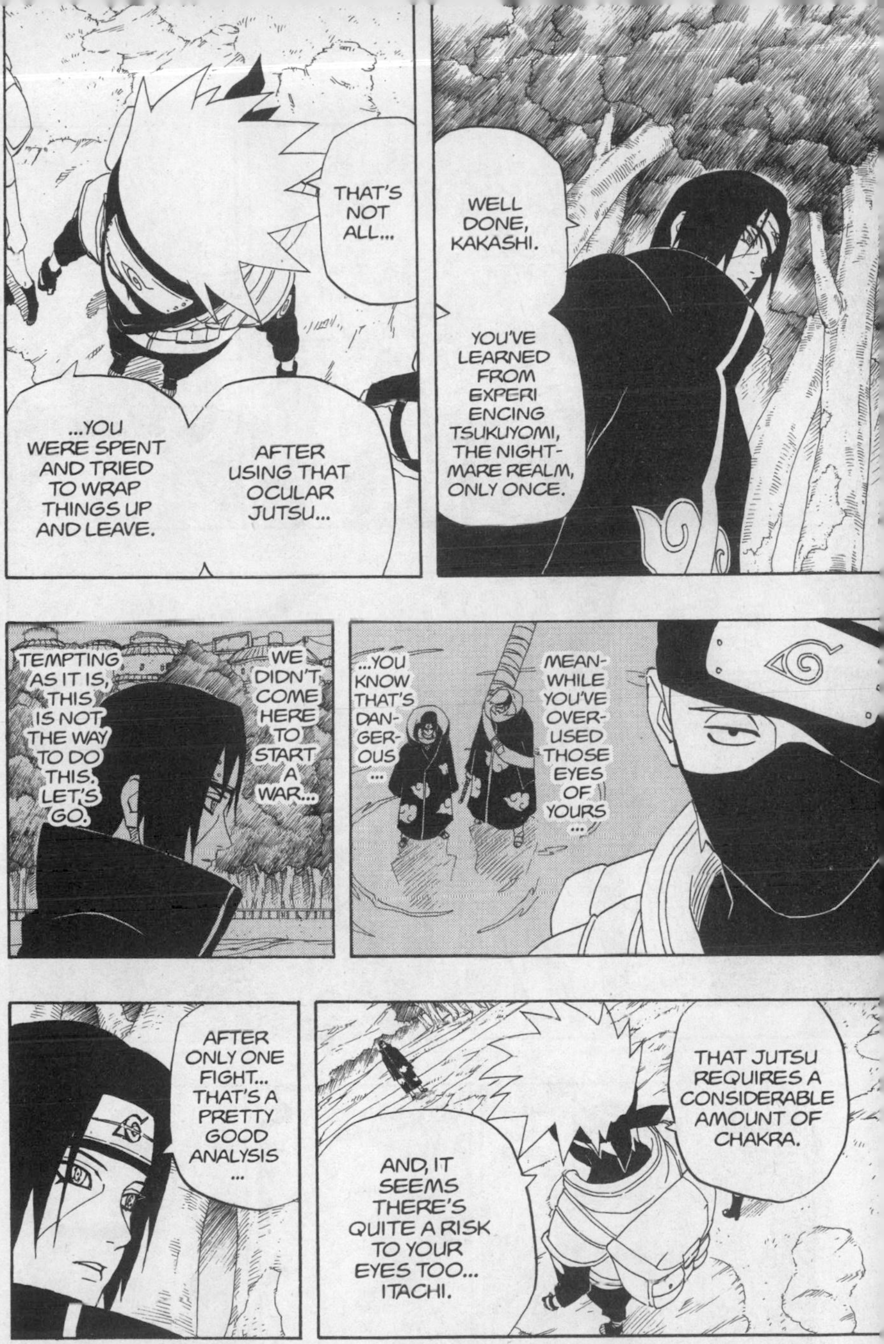
WELL DONE, KAKASHI.
YOU'VE LEARNED FROM EXPERIENCING TSUKUYOMI, THE NIGHTMARE REALM, ONLY ONCE.
THAT'S NOT ALL...
AFTER USING THAT OCULAR JUTSU...
...YOU WERE SPENT AND TRIED TO WRAP THINGS UP AND LEAVE.
MEANWHILE YOU'VE OVERUSED THOSE EYES OF YOURS...
...YOU KNOW THAT'S DANGEROUS...
WE DIDN'T COME HERE TO START A WAR...
TEMPTING AS IT IS, THIS IS NOT THE WAY TO DO THIS. LET'S GO.
THAT JUTSU REQUIRES A CONSIDERABLE AMOUNT OF CHAKRA.
AND, IT SEEMS THERE'S QUITE A RISK TO YOUR EYES TOO... ITACHI.
AFTER ONLY ONE FIGHT... THAT'S A PRETTY GOOD ANALYSIS...

READ THIS WAY

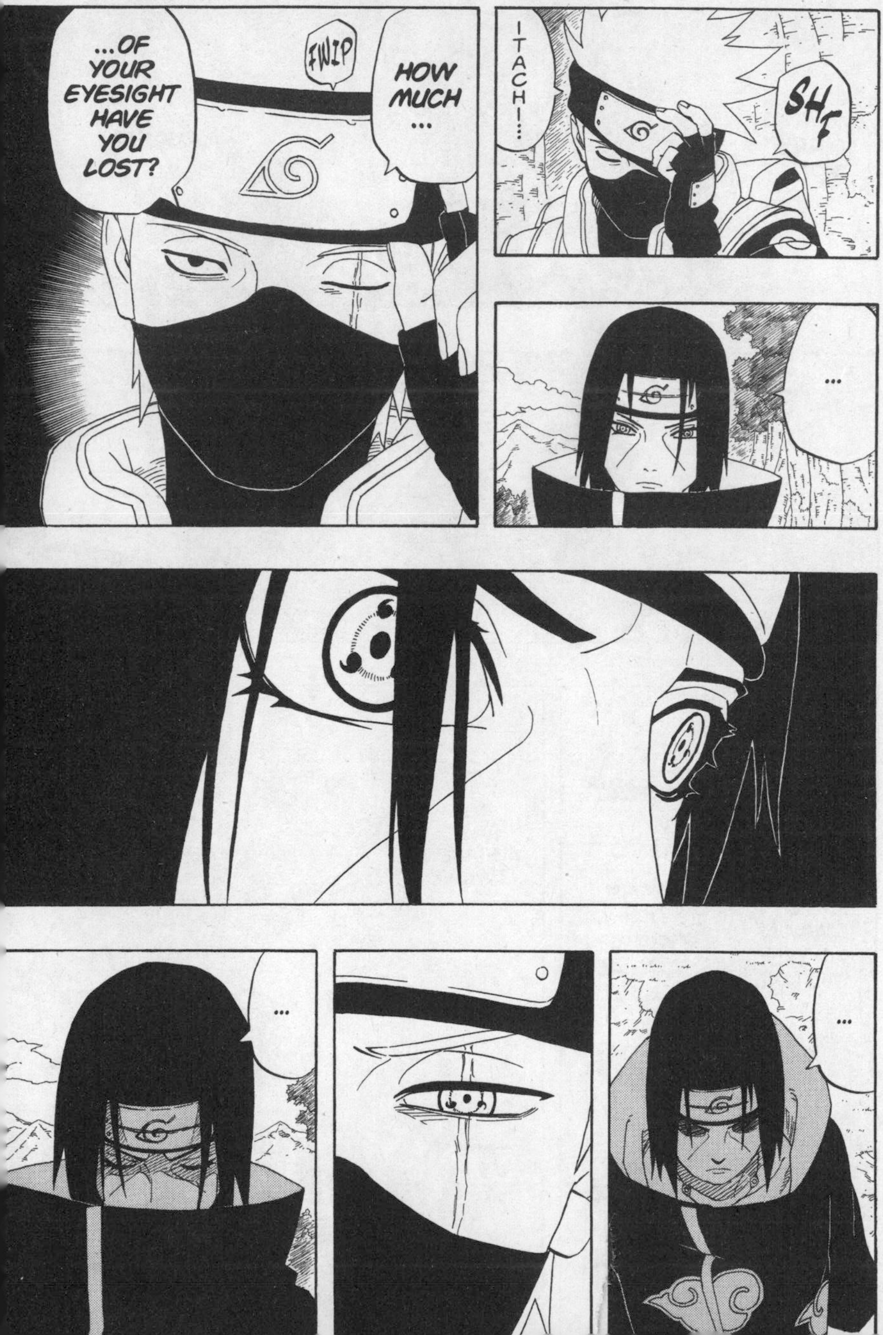
SHF
ITACHI...!!
...
HOW MUCH...
FWIP
...OF YOUR EYESIGHT HAVE YOU LOST?
...
...

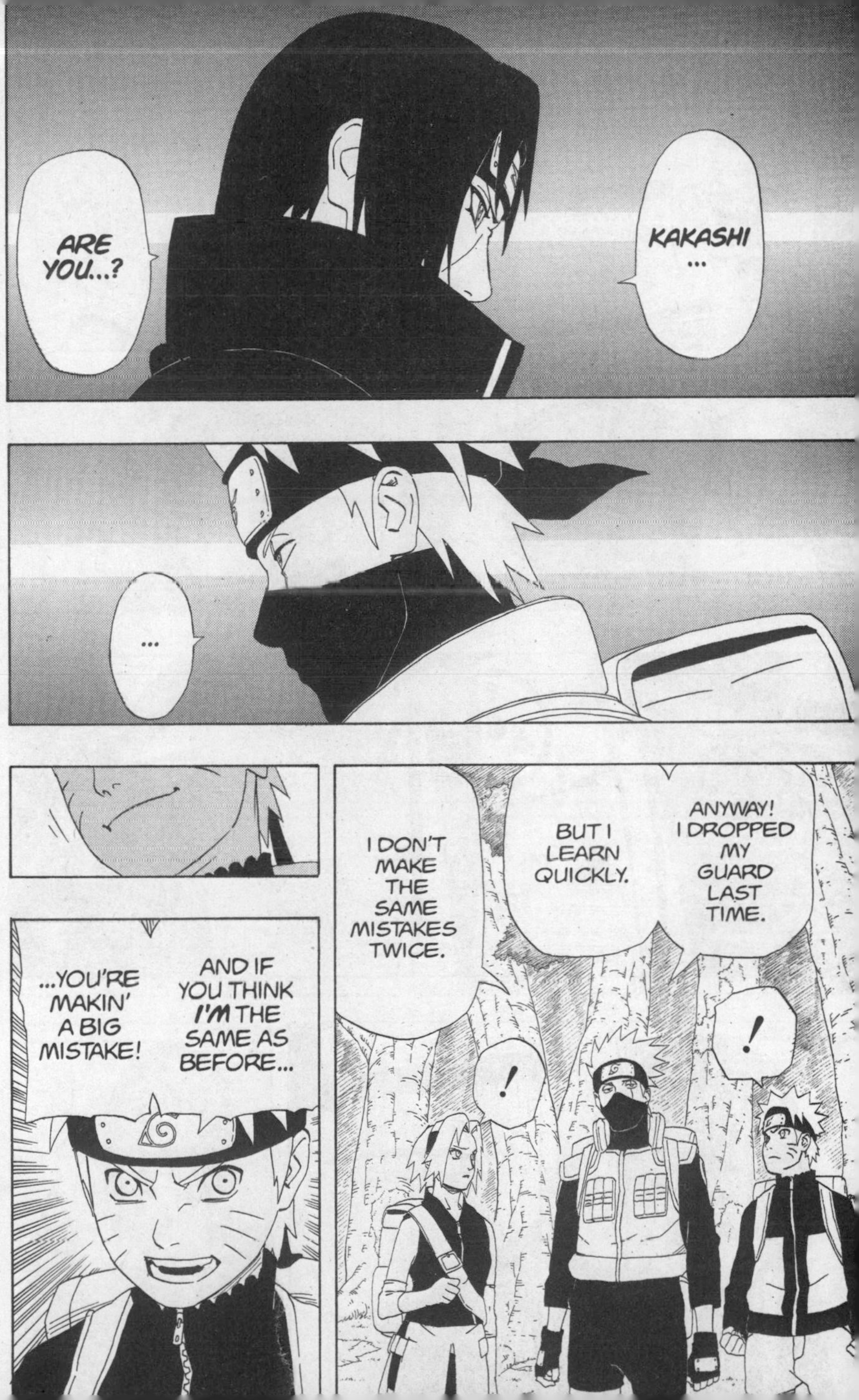

KAKASHI ...
ARE YOU...?
...
ANYWAY! I DROPPED MY GUARD LAST TIME.
BUT I LEARN QUICKLY.
I DON'T MAKE THE SAME MISTAKES TWICE.
!
!
AND IF YOU THINK *I'M* THE SAME AS BEFORE...
...YOU'RE MAKIN' A BIG MISTAKE!

READ THIS WAY

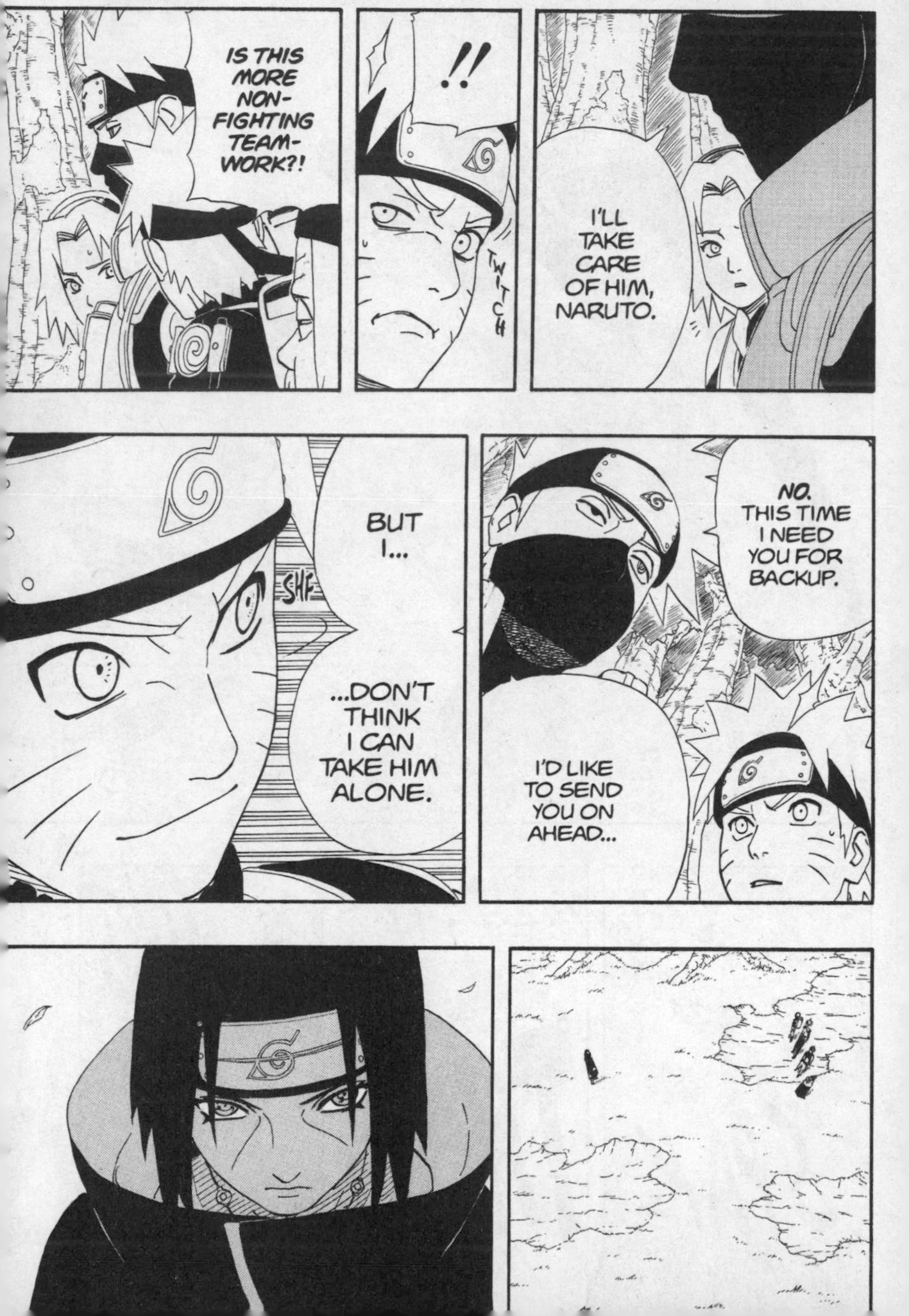
I'LL TAKE CARE OF HIM, NARUTO.
!!
TWITCH
IS THIS MORE NON-FIGHTING TEAM-WORK?!
NO. THIS TIME I NEED YOU FOR BACKUP.
I'D LIKE TO SEND YOU ON AHEAD...
BUT I...
SHF
...DON'T THINK I CAN TAKE HIM ALONE.

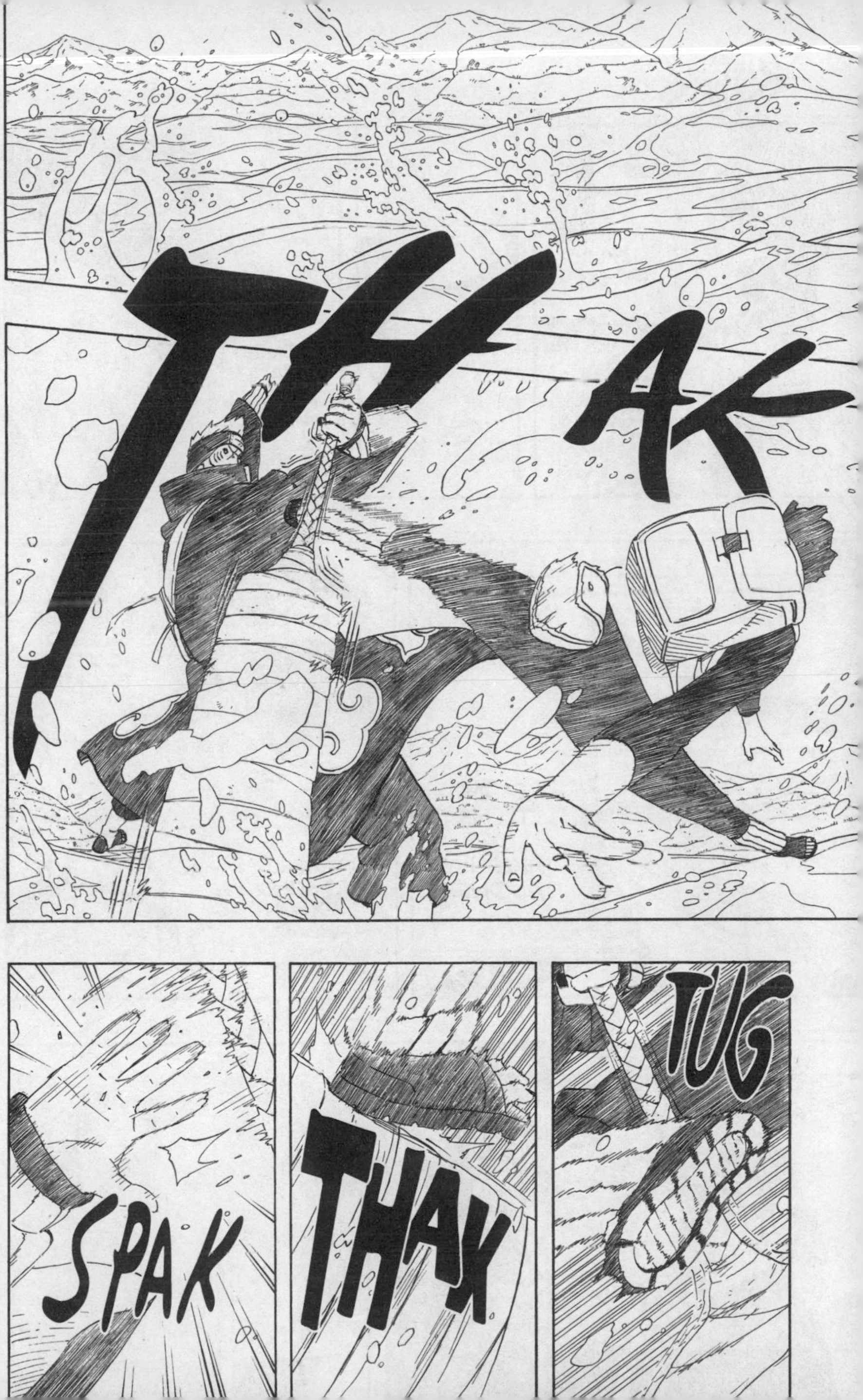
THAK
TUG
THAK
SPAK

READ THIS WAY

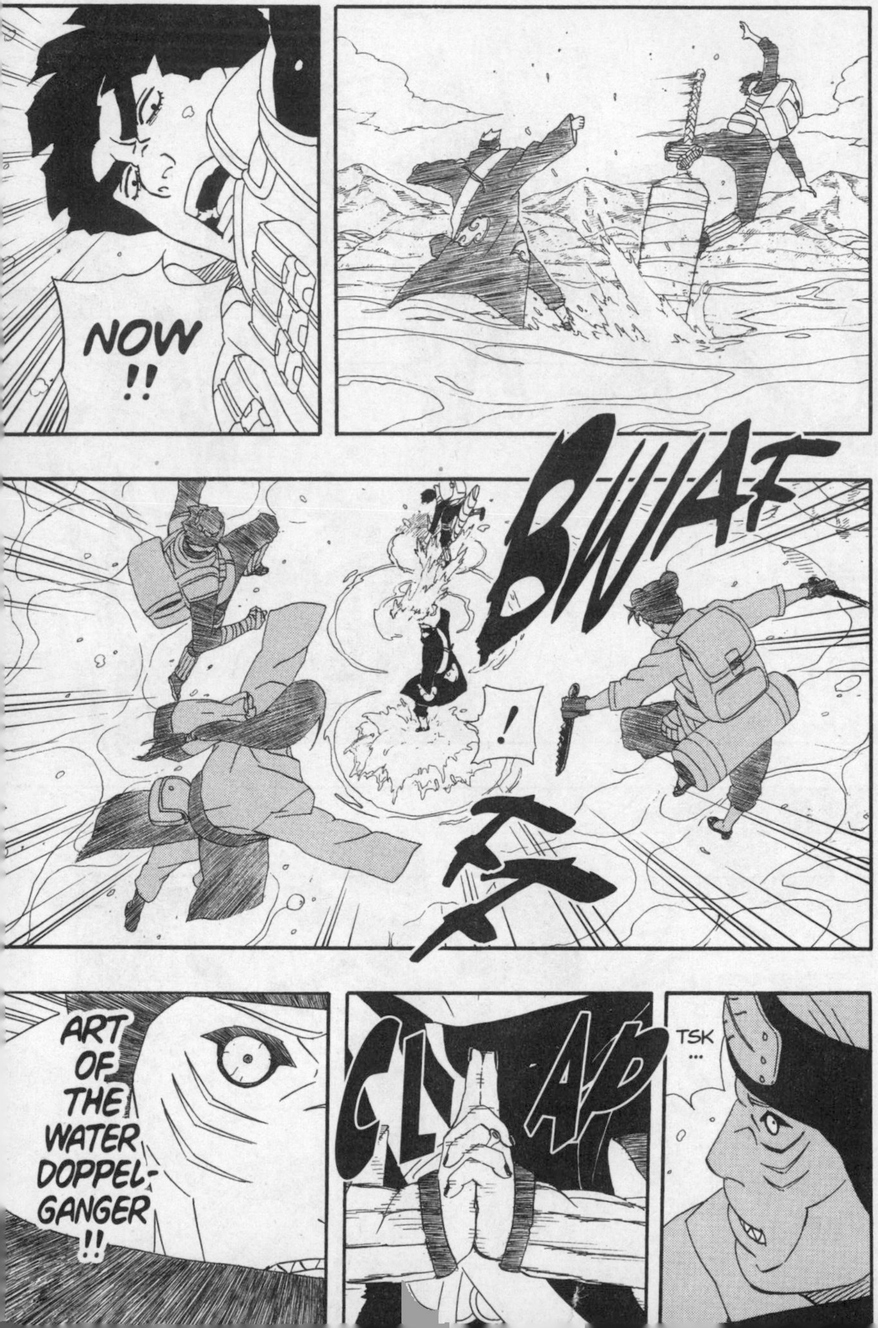
NOW!!
BWAF
!
TSK ...
CLAP
ART OF THE WATER DOPPEL-GANGER!!

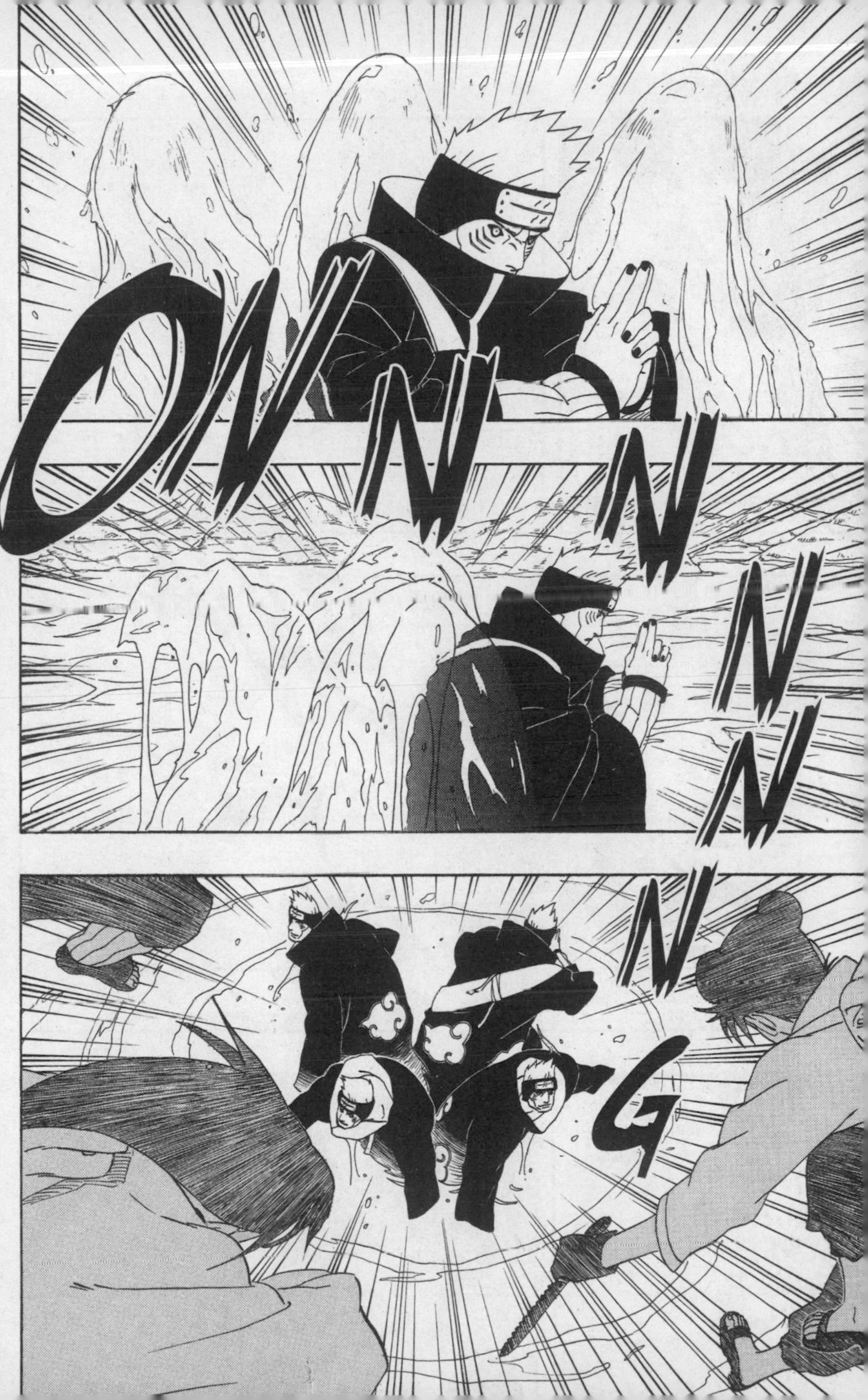

OWNNNNNNG

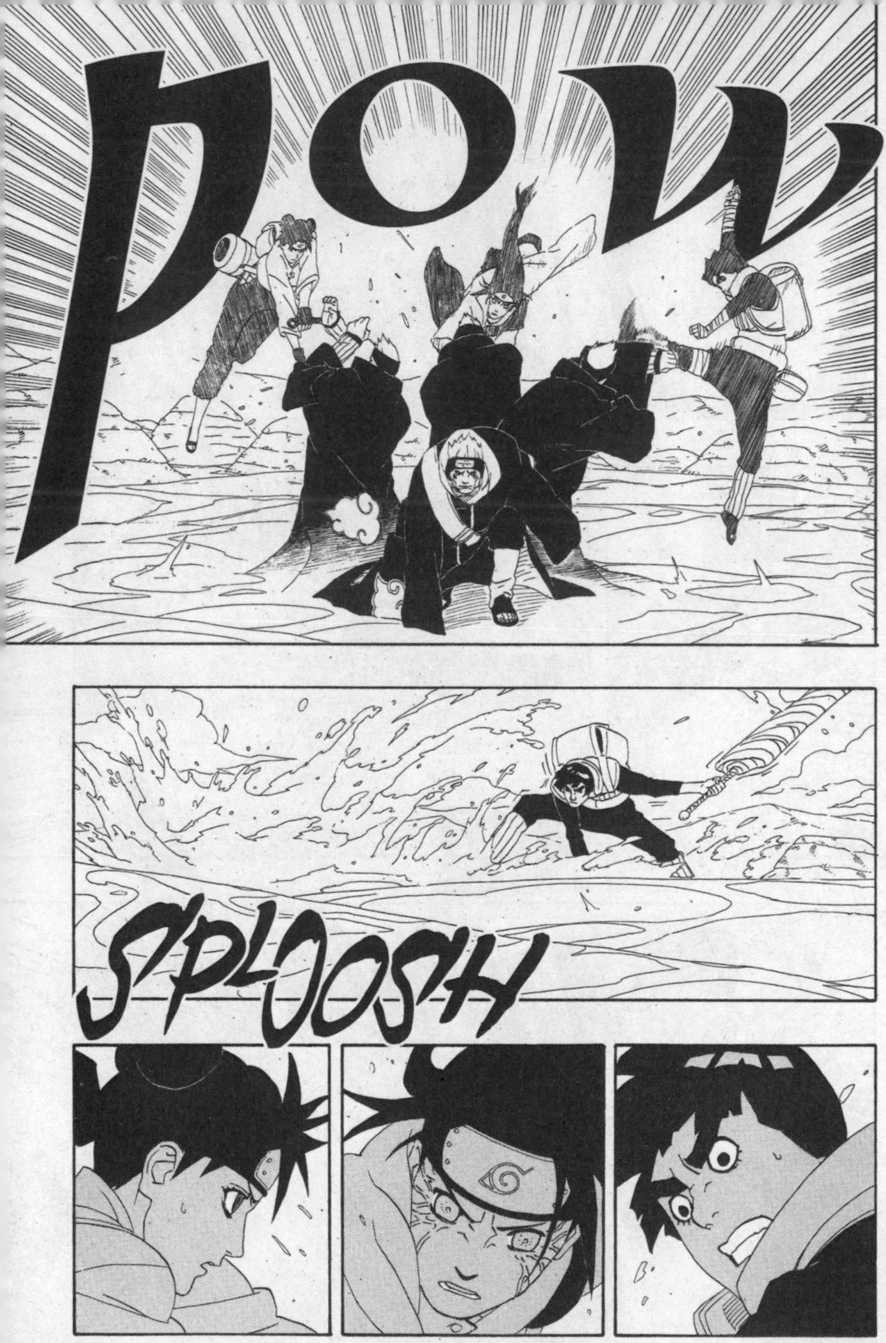
POW
SPLOOSH

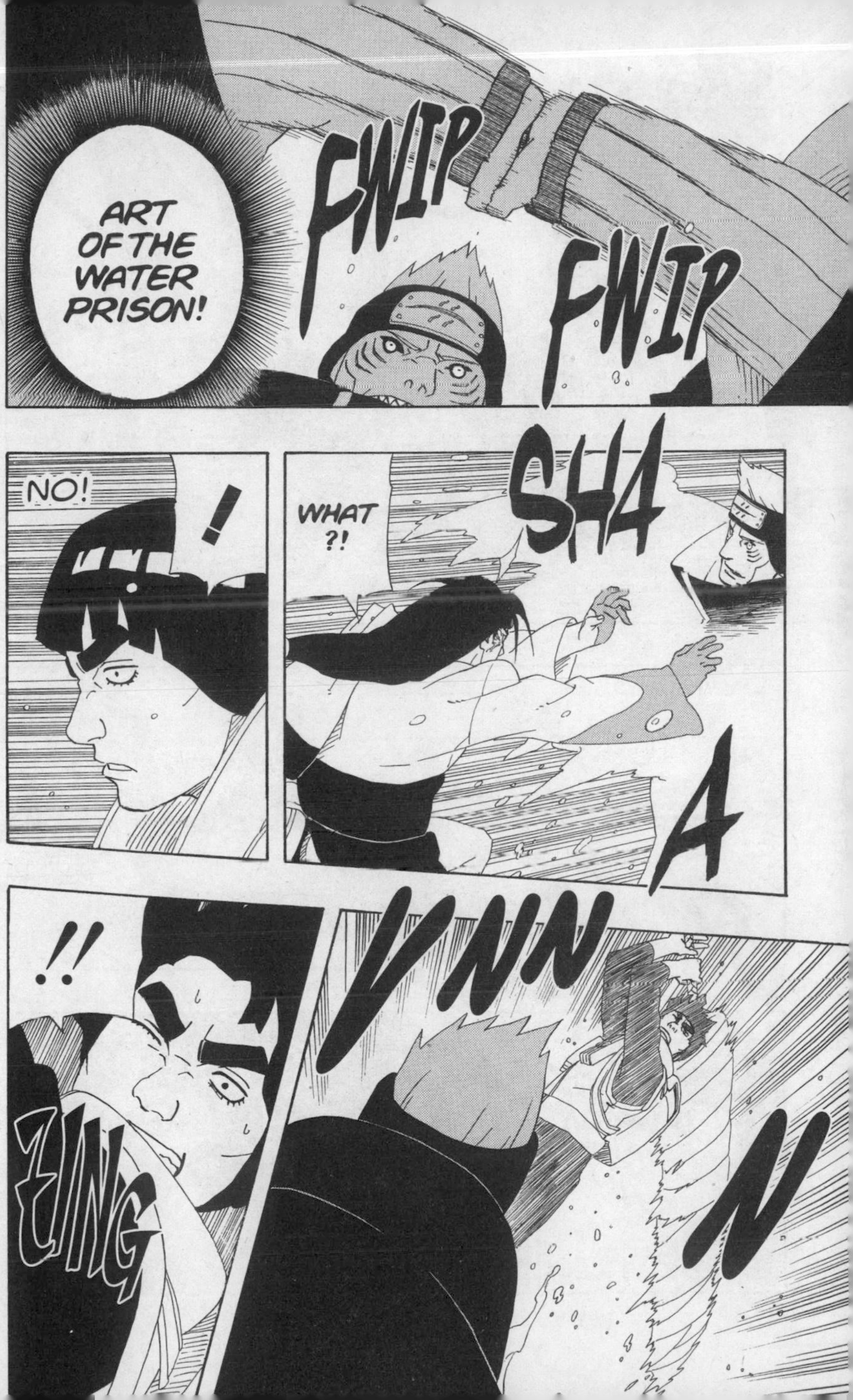
FWIP
FWIP
ART OF THE WATER PRISON!
SHA
A
WHAT ?!
NO!
!
VNN
N
!!
ZING

READ THIS WAY

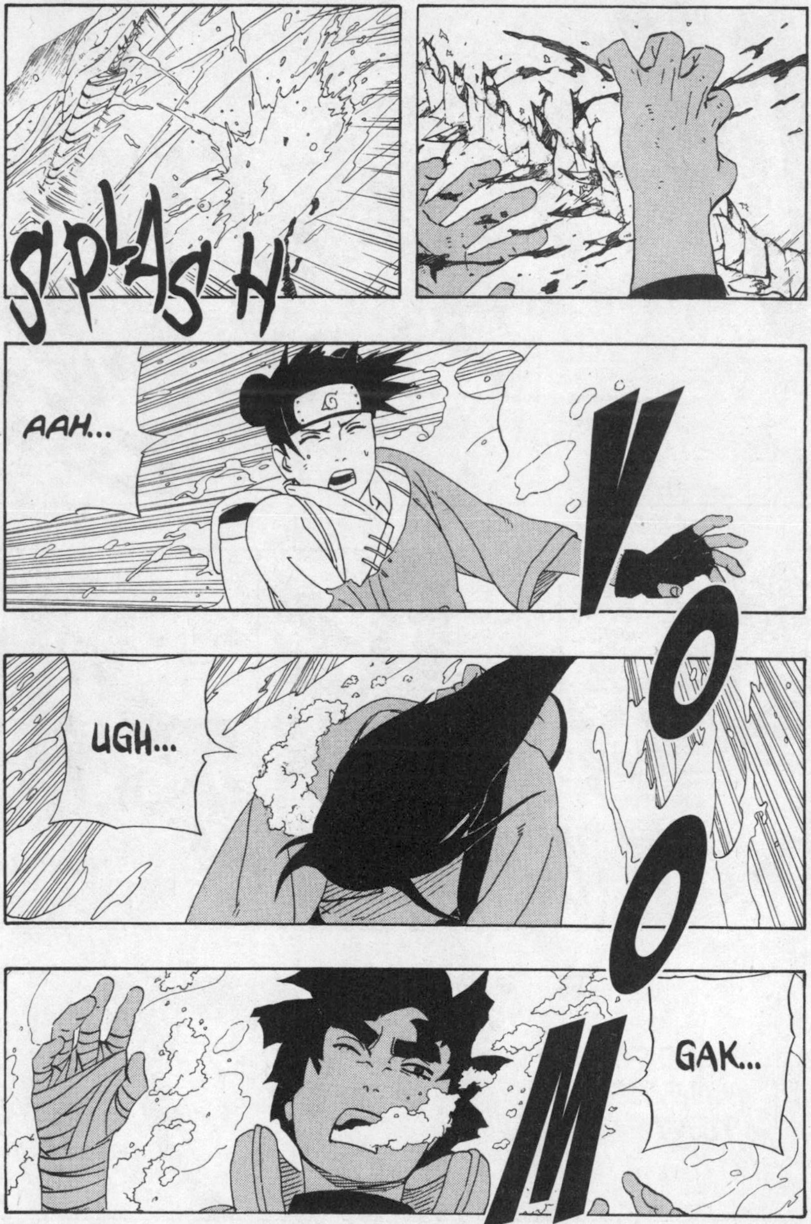
SPLASH
AAH...
VOOM
UGH...
GAK...

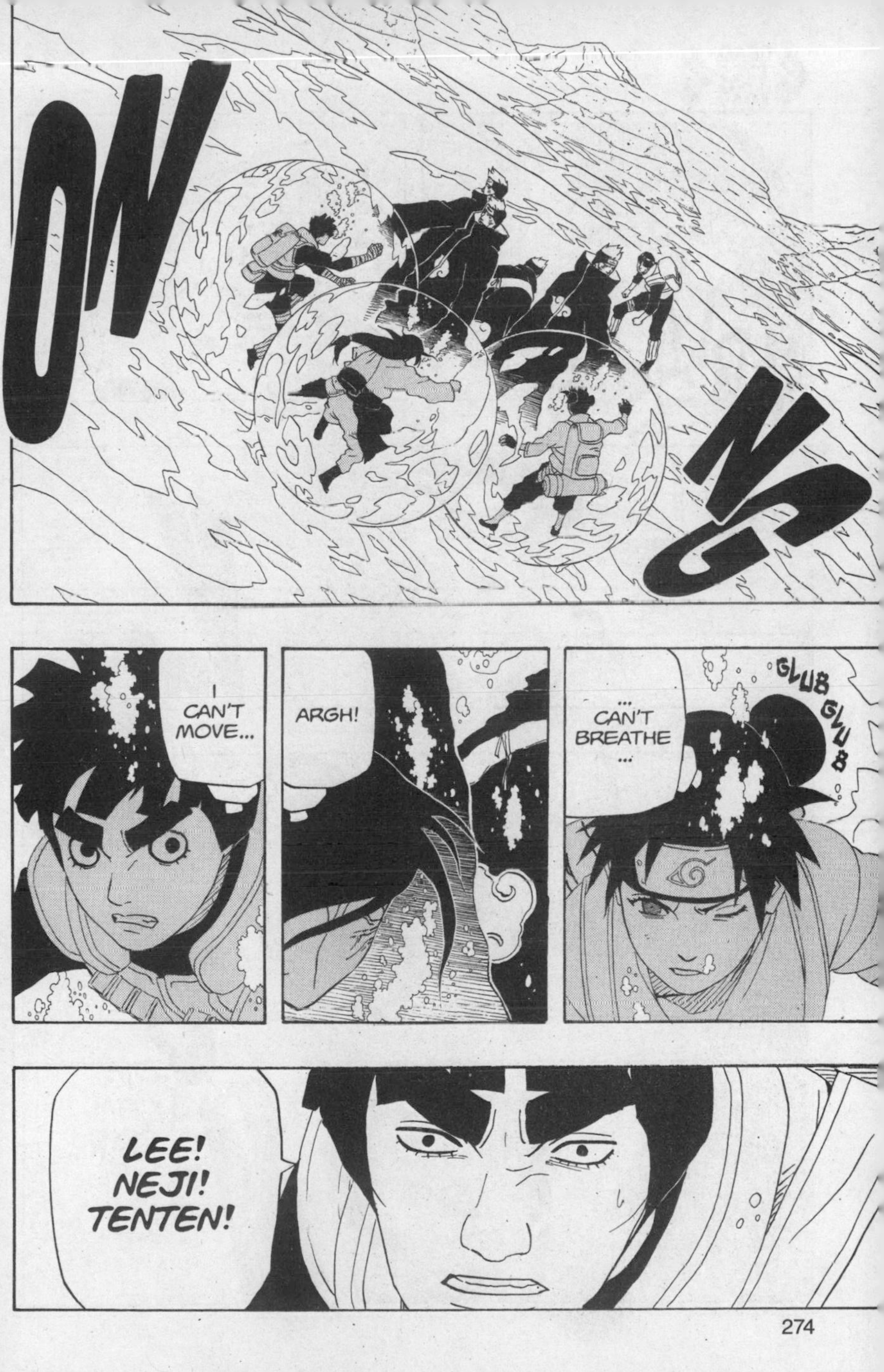
ON
NG
... CAN'T BREATHE ...
GLUB GLUB
ARGH!
I CAN'T MOVE...
LEE! NEJI! TENTEN!

READ THIS WAY

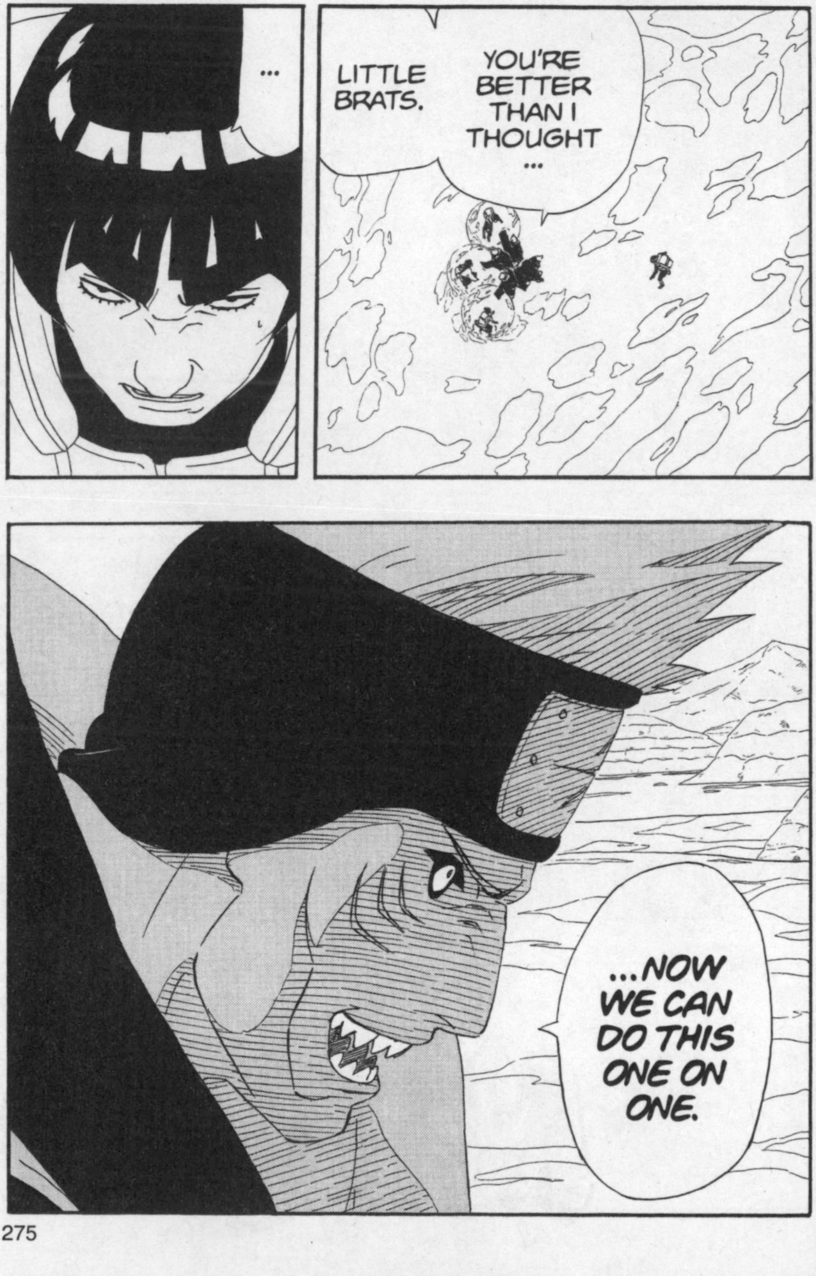
YOU'RE BETTER THAN I THOUGHT ...
LITTLE BRATS.
...
...NOW WE CAN DO THIS ONE ON ONE.

NARUTO

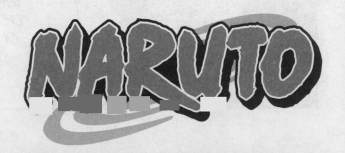

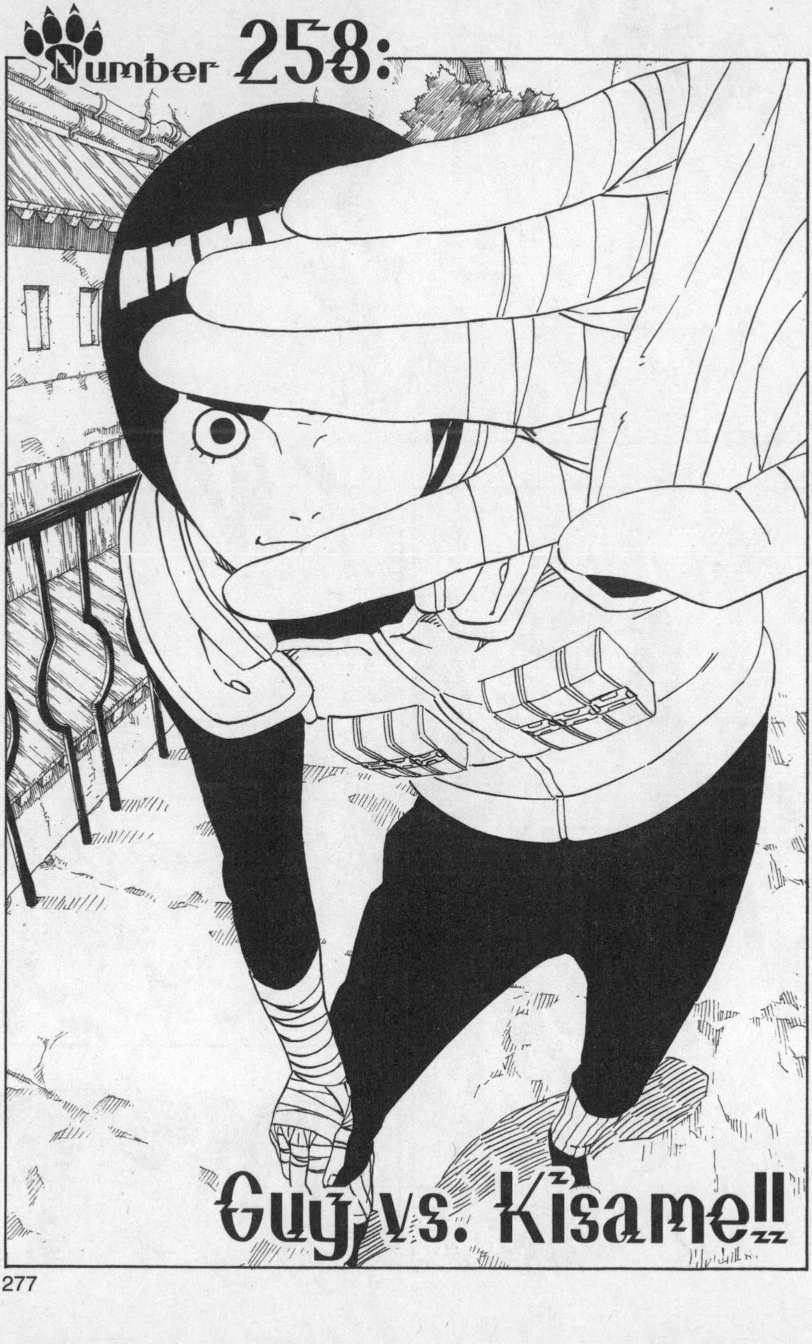
Number 258:
Guy vs. Kisame!!

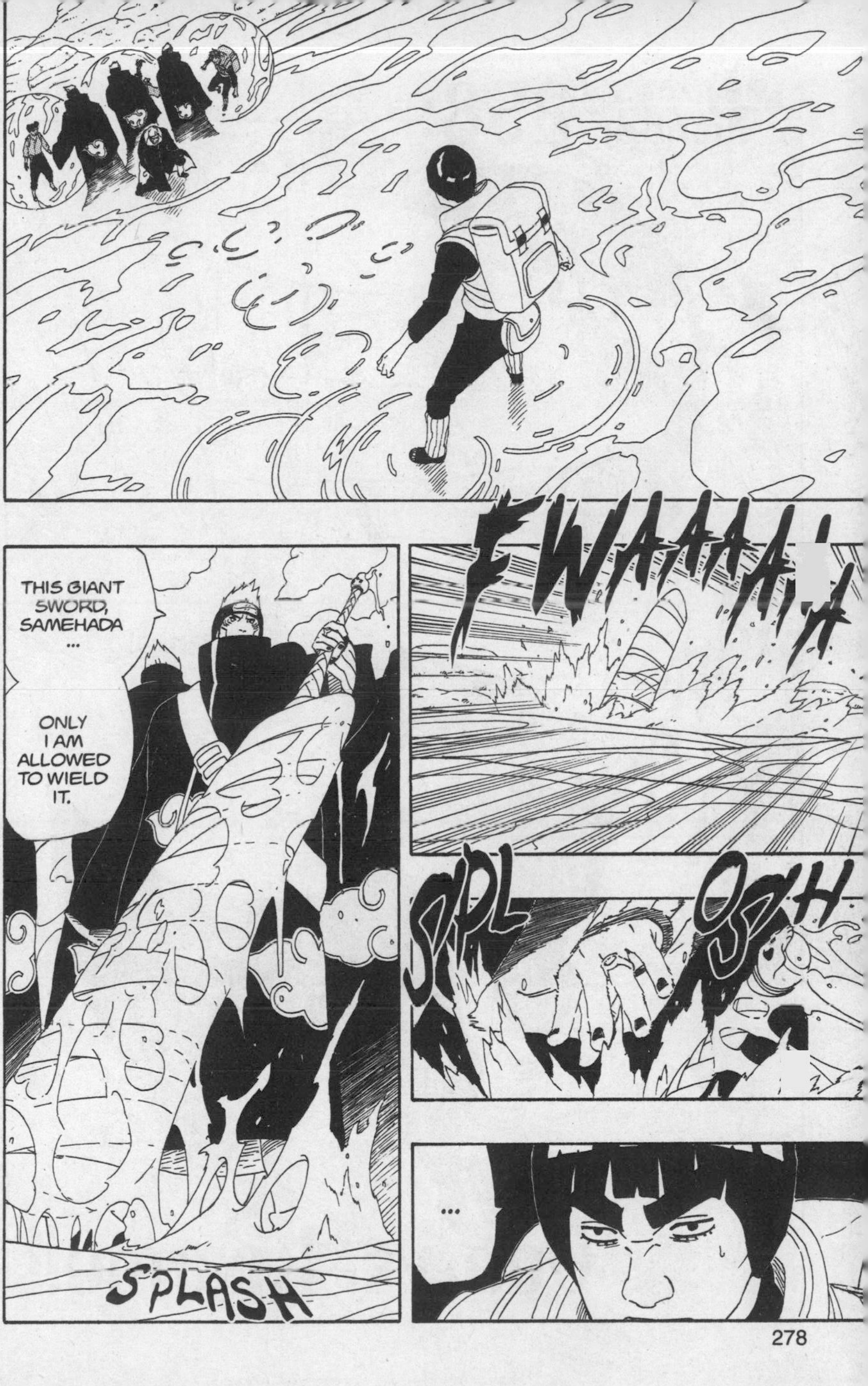
FWAAAAAH
SPLOSH
...
THIS GIANT SWORD, SAMEHADA ...
ONLY I AM ALLOWED TO WIELD IT.
SPLASH

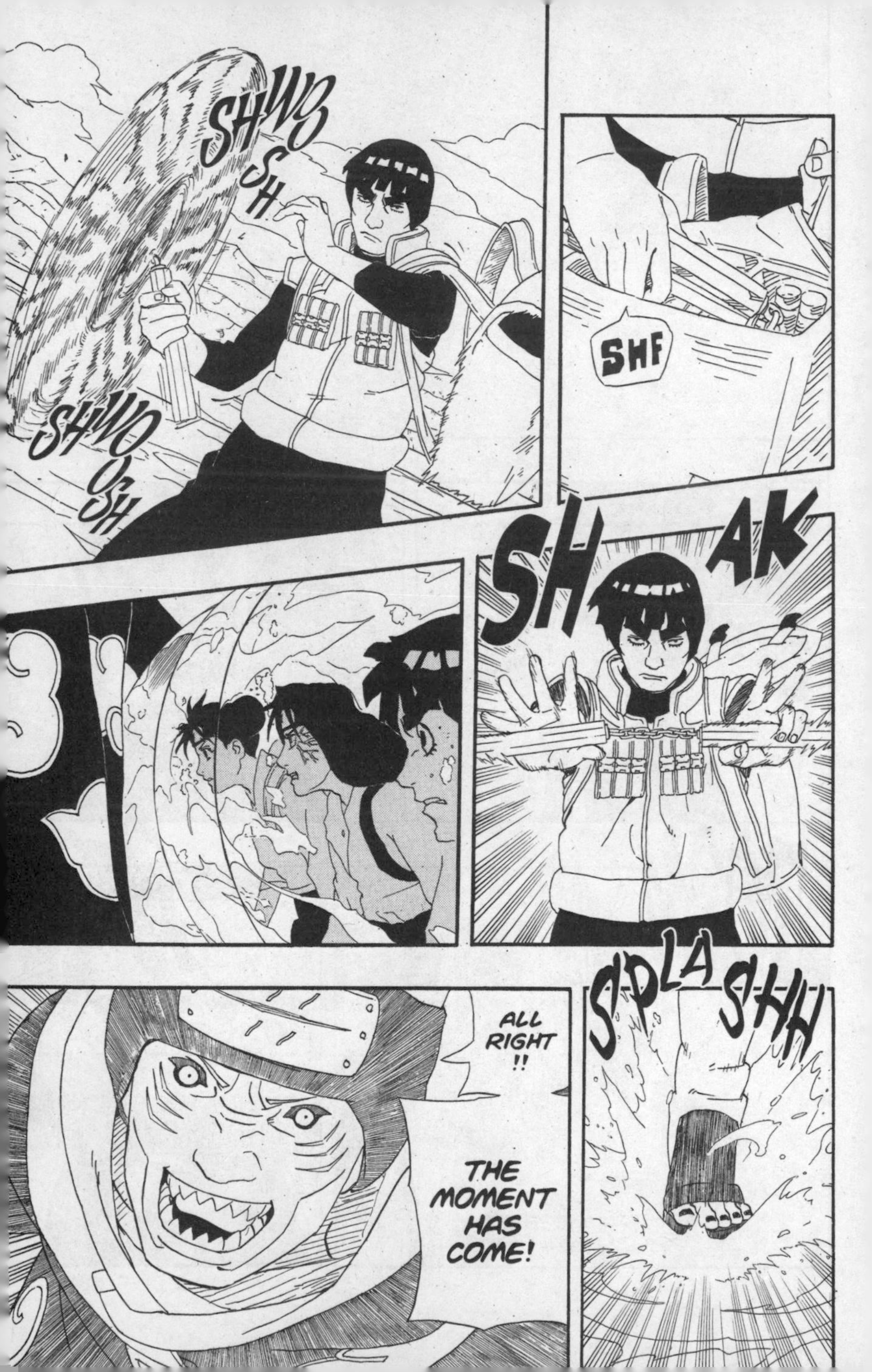
SHF
SHWOSH
SHWOOSH
SHAK
SPLASHH
ALL RIGHT!!
THE MOMENT HAS COME!

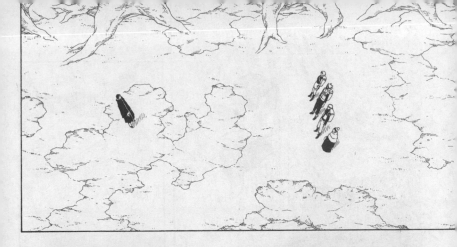

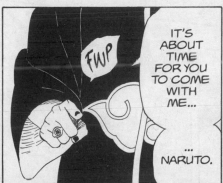

IT'S ABOUT TIME FOR YOU TO COME WITH ME...

... NARUTO.

FWP

SSH

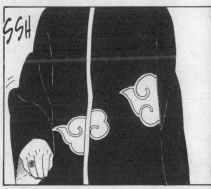

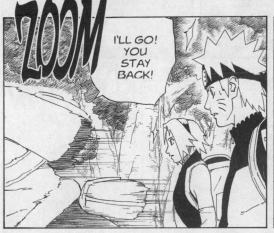

I'LL GO! YOU STAY BACK!

ZOOM

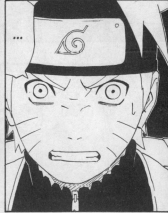

...

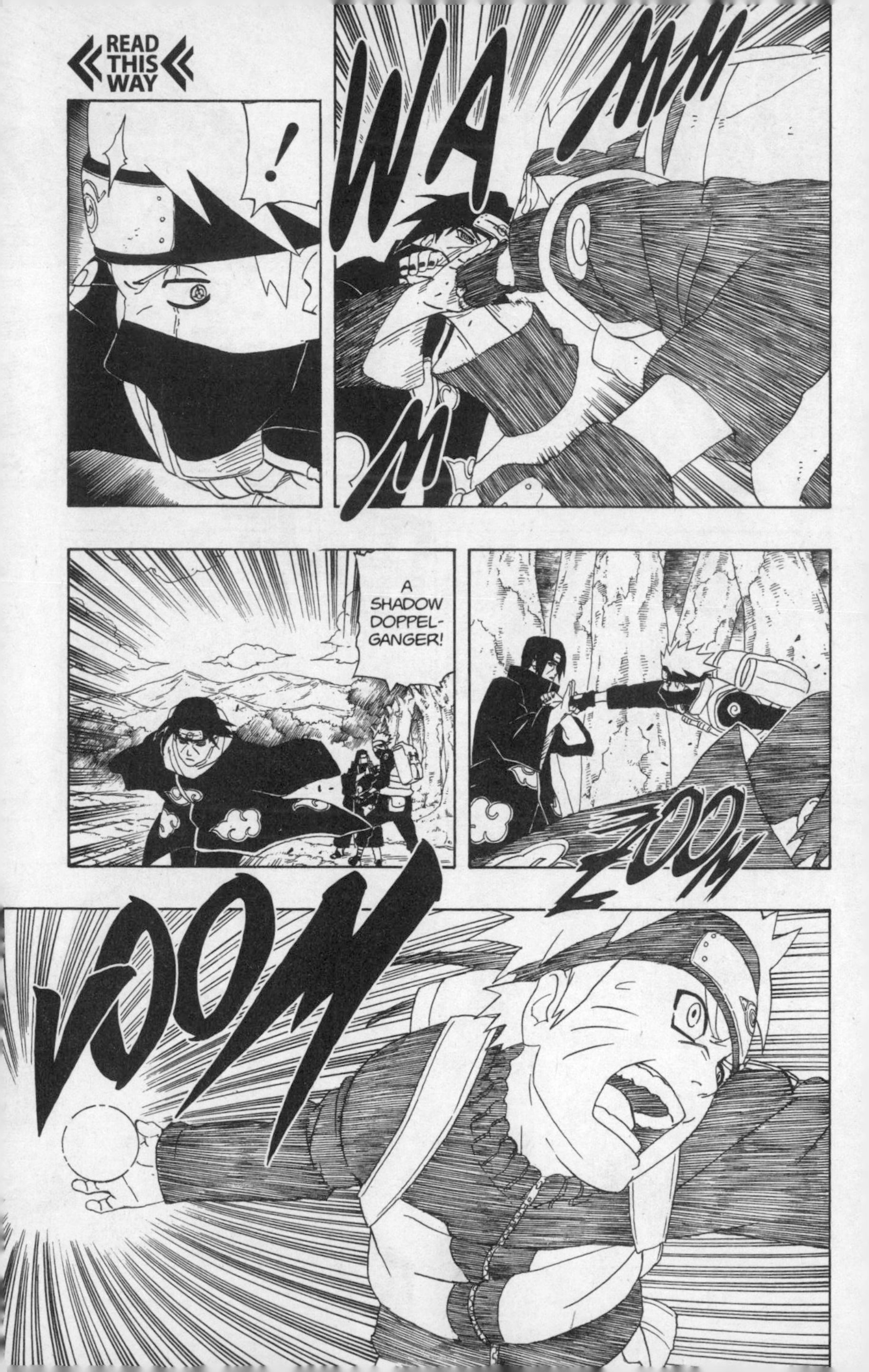
READ THIS WAY
WAMMMM
!
ZOOM
A SHADOW DOPPEL-GANGER!
VOOM

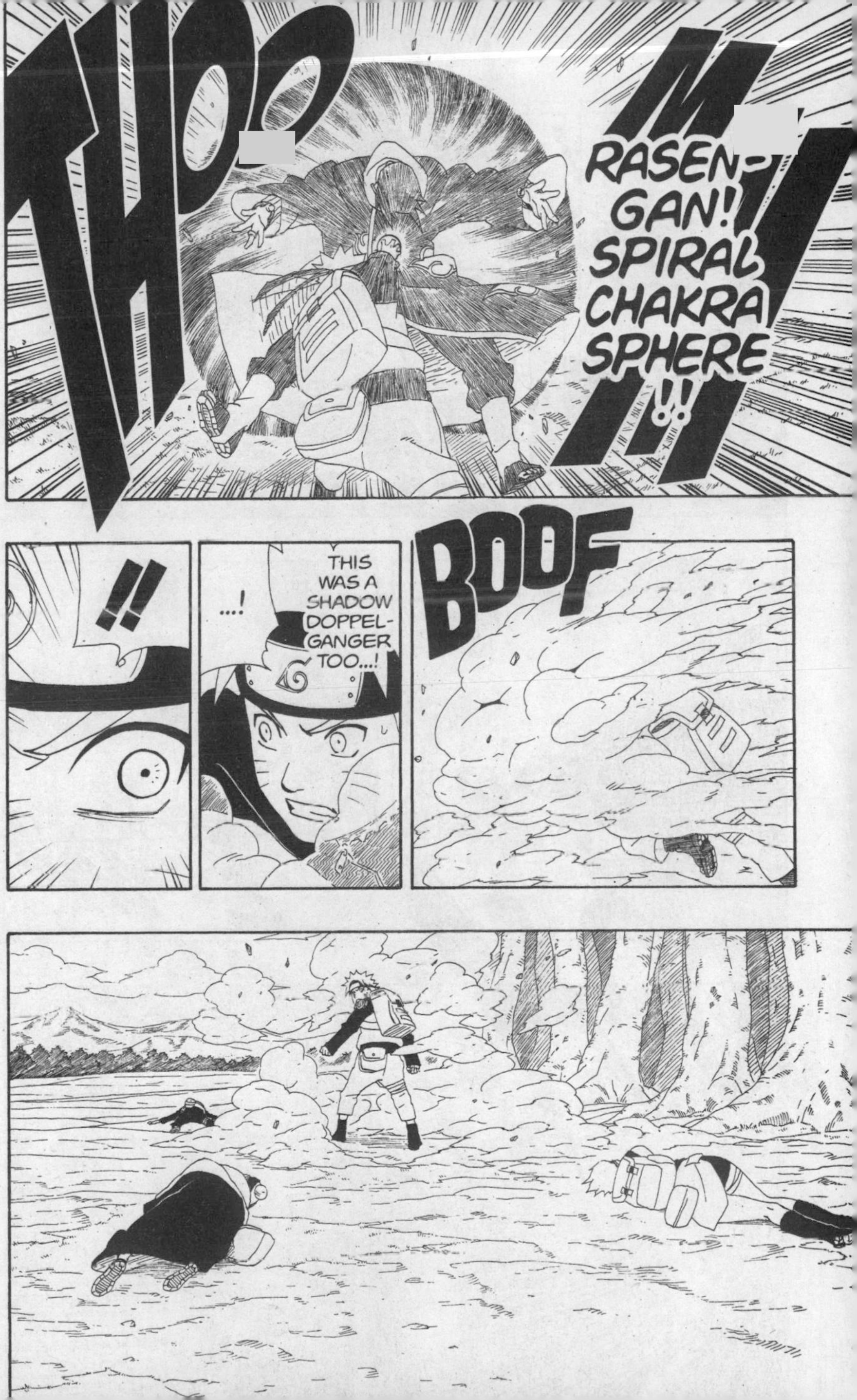
THOOM
RASEN-GAN! SPIRAL CHAKRA SPHERE!!
BOOF
THIS WAS A SHADOW DOPPEL-GANGER TOO...!
...!
!!

READ THIS WAY

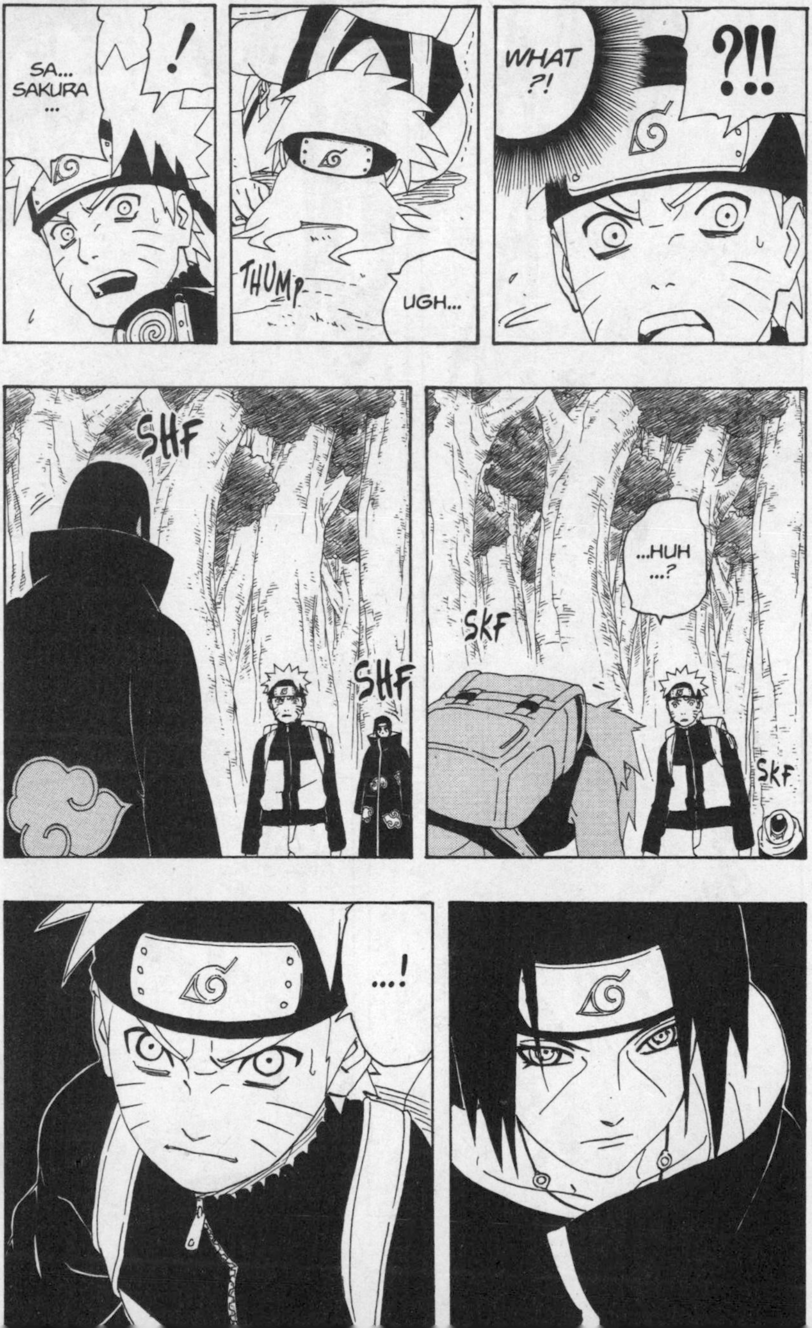
?!!
WHAT ?!
THUMP
UGH...
!
SA... SAKURA ...
...HUH ...?
SKF
SKF
SHF
SHF
...!

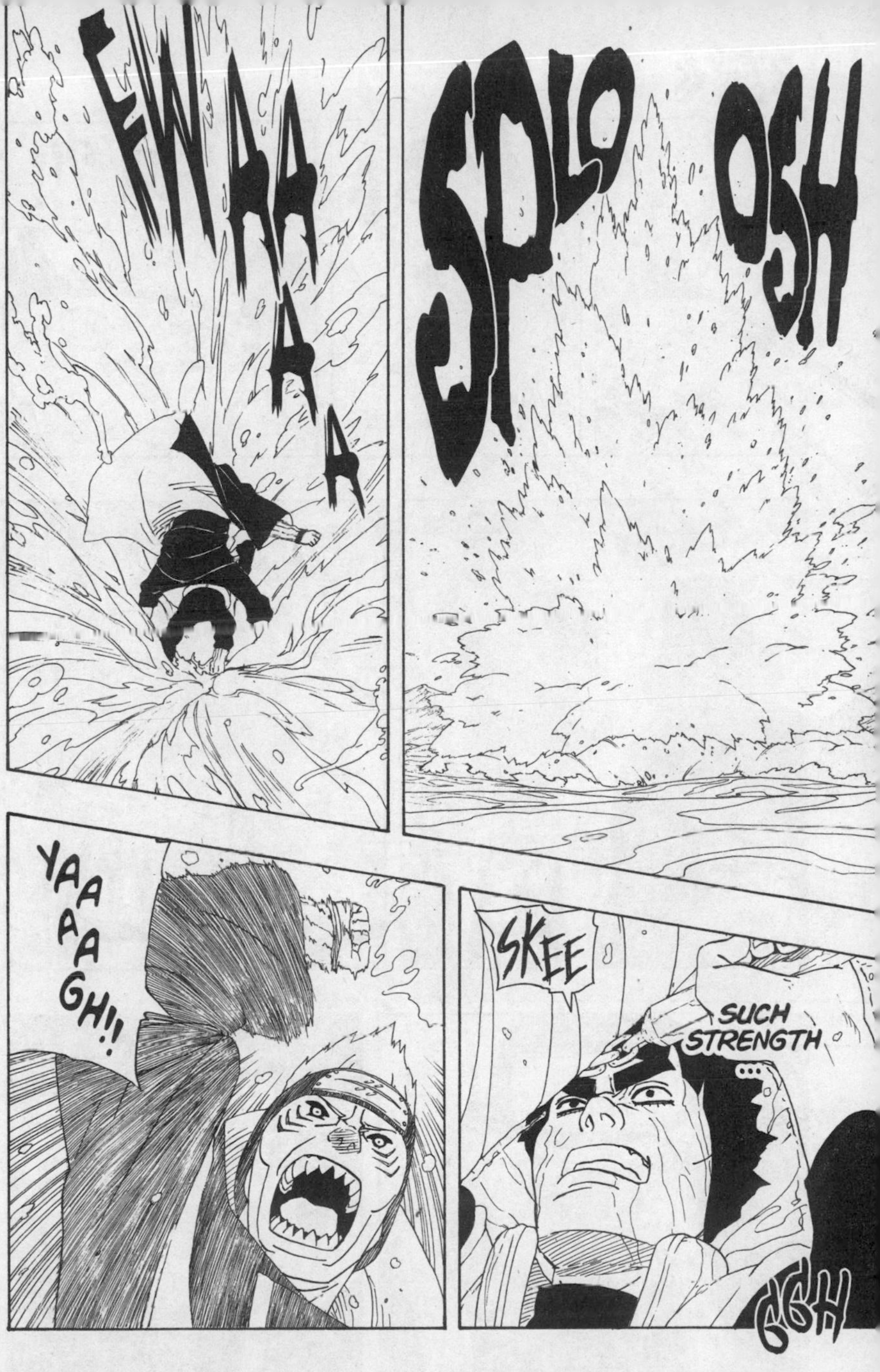
SPLOOSH
FWAAAAA
SKEE
SUCH STRENGTH...
GGH
YAAAAGH!!

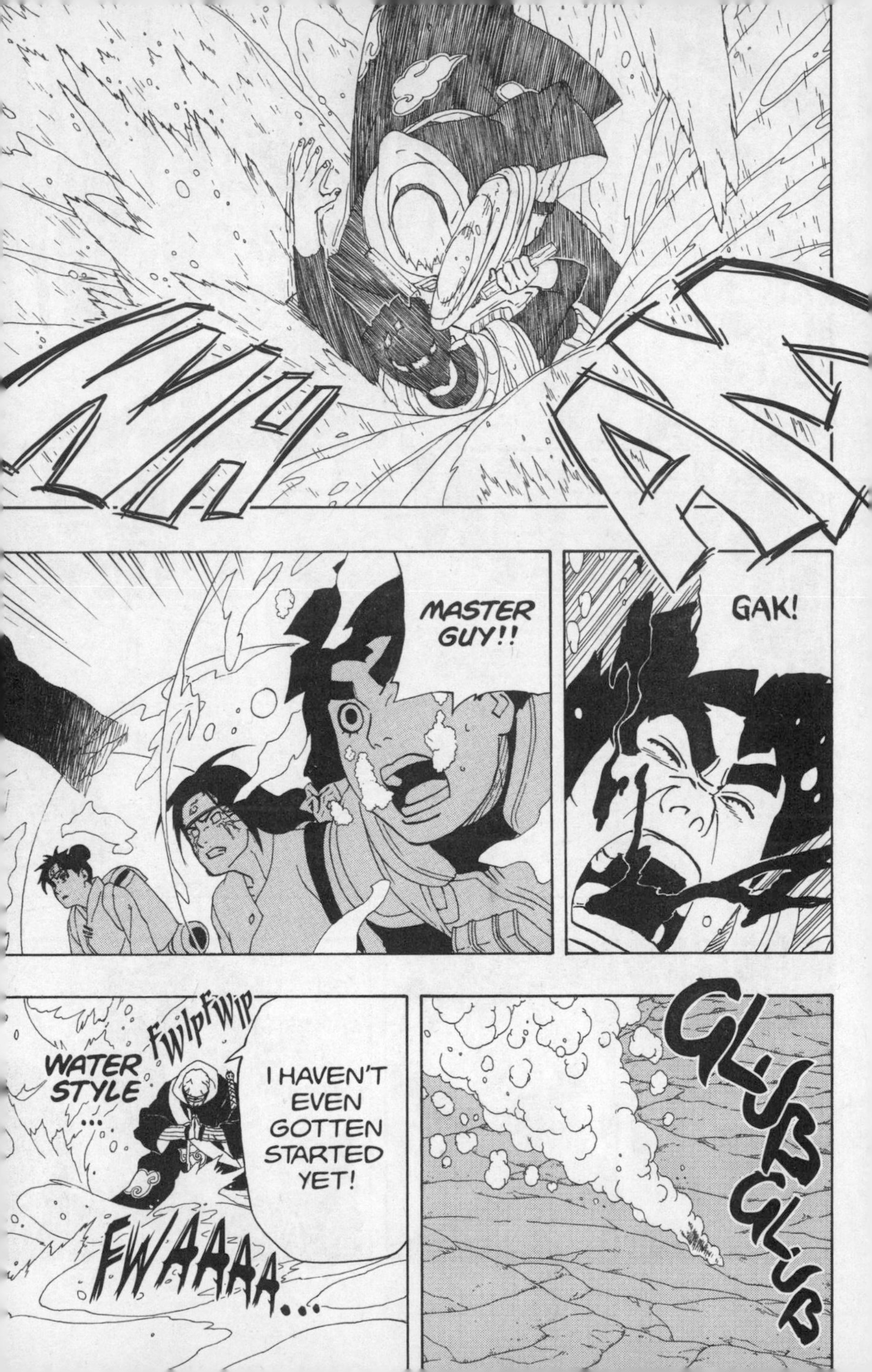
GAK!
MASTER GUY!!
GLUBGLUB
Fwip Fwip
I HAVEN'T EVEN GOTTEN STARTED YET!
WATER STYLE ...
FWAAAA...

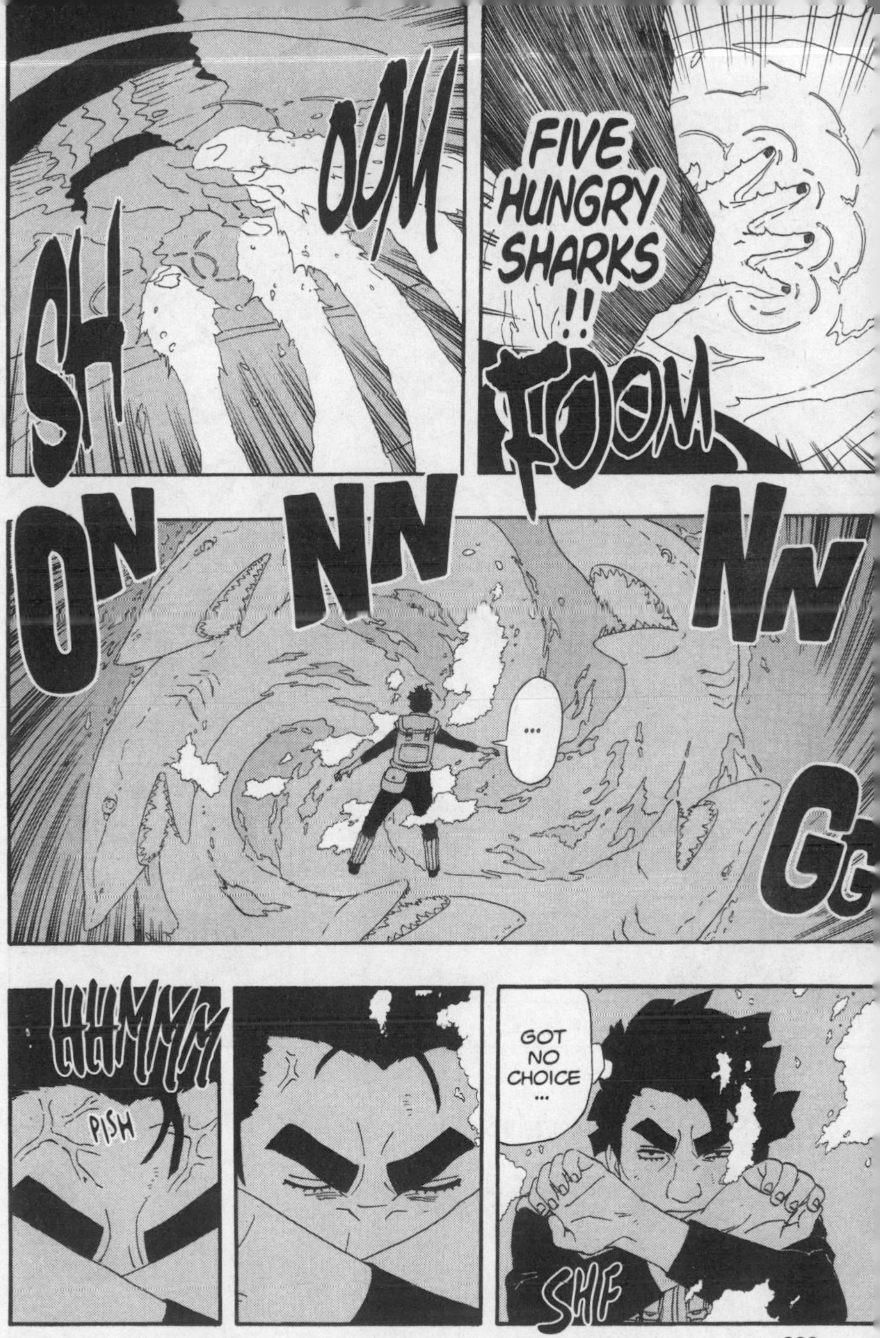
FIVE HUNGRY SHARKS!!
FOOM
SHOOM
ONNNNNNGG
...
GOT NO CHOICE ...
SHF
HHMMM
PISH

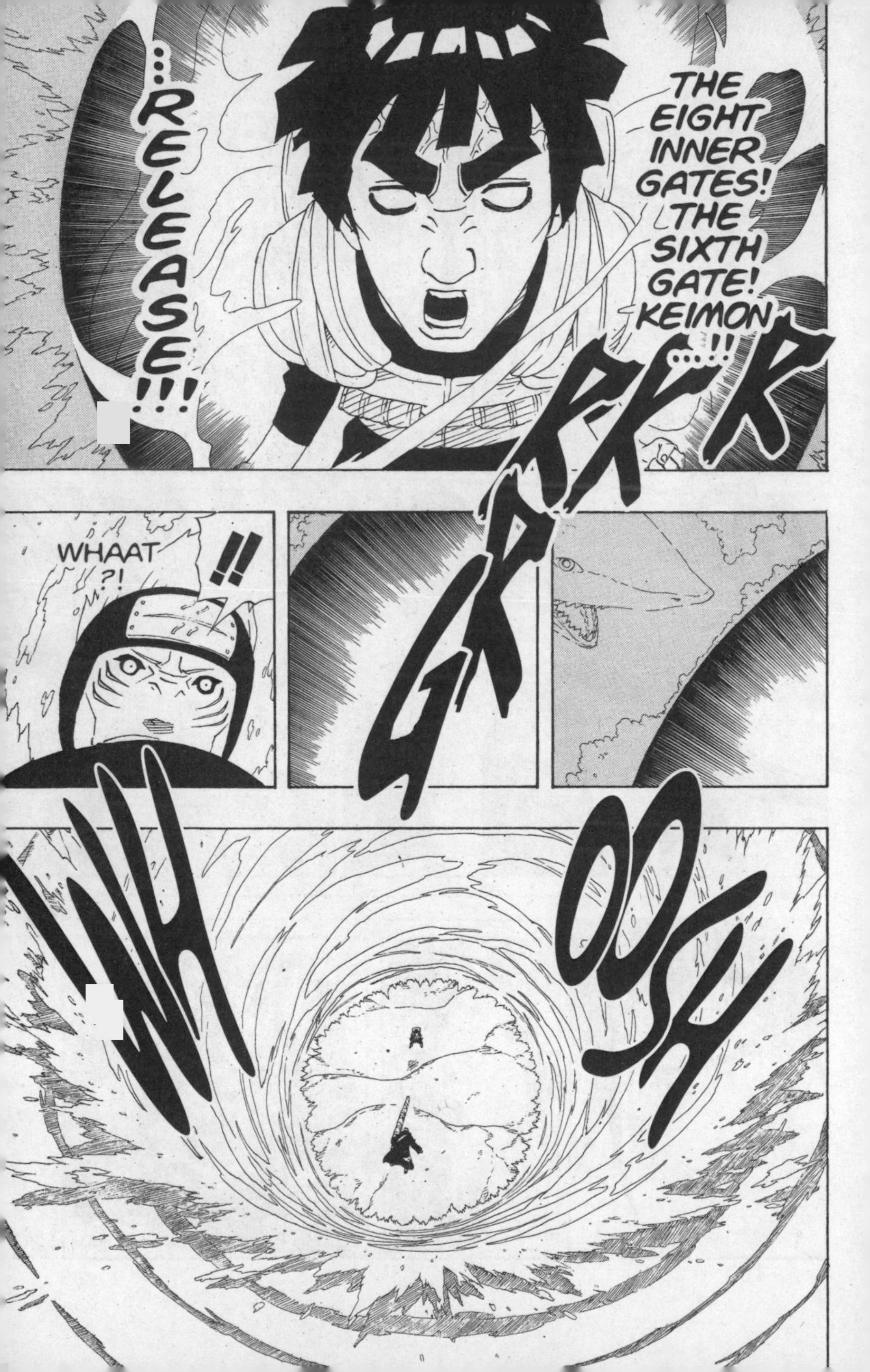
THE EIGHT INNER GATES! THE SIXTH GATE! KEIMON...!!
...RELEASE!!!
!!
WHAAT ?!
WHOOSH

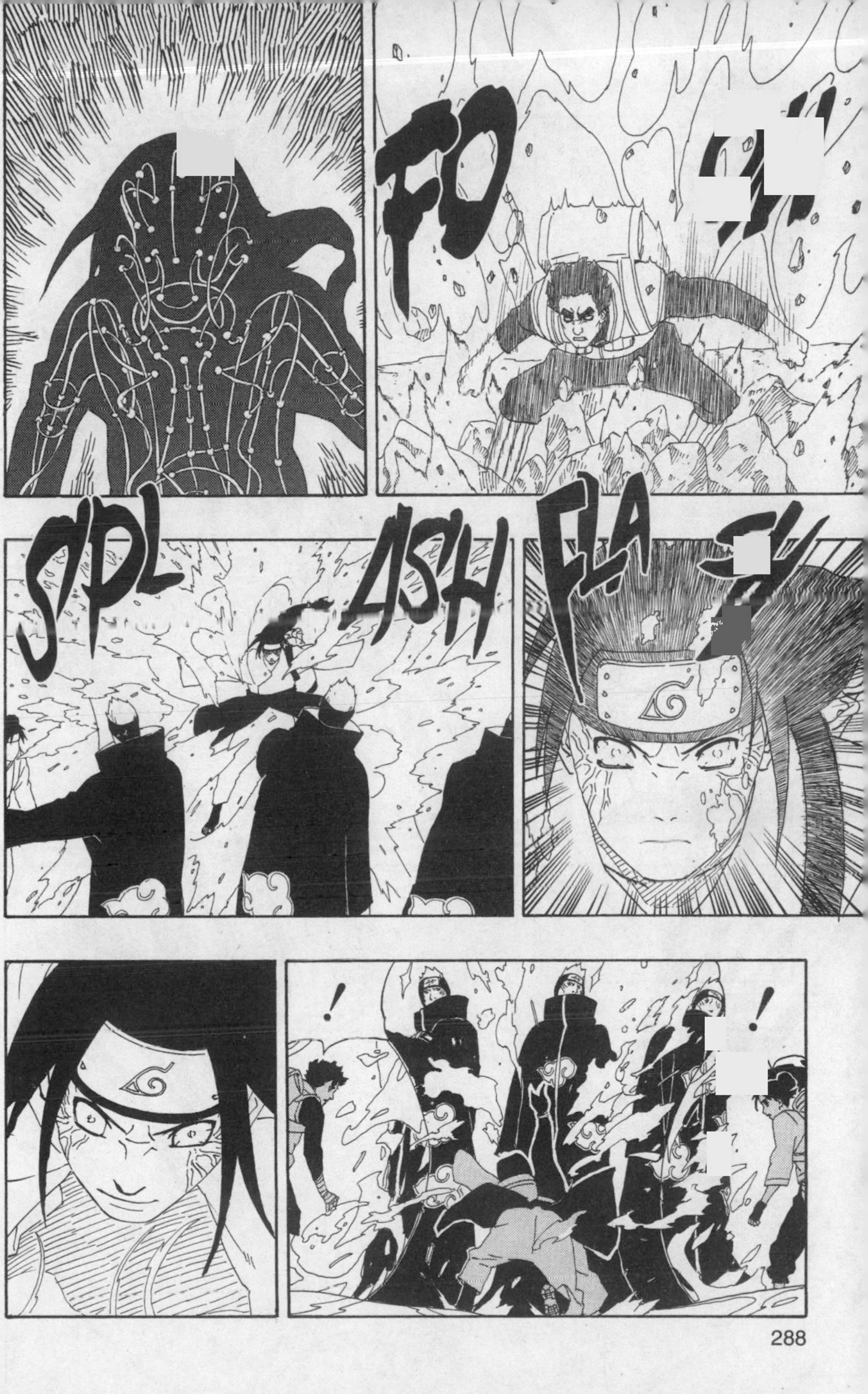
FO
FLA
SPLASH
!
!

READ THIS WAY

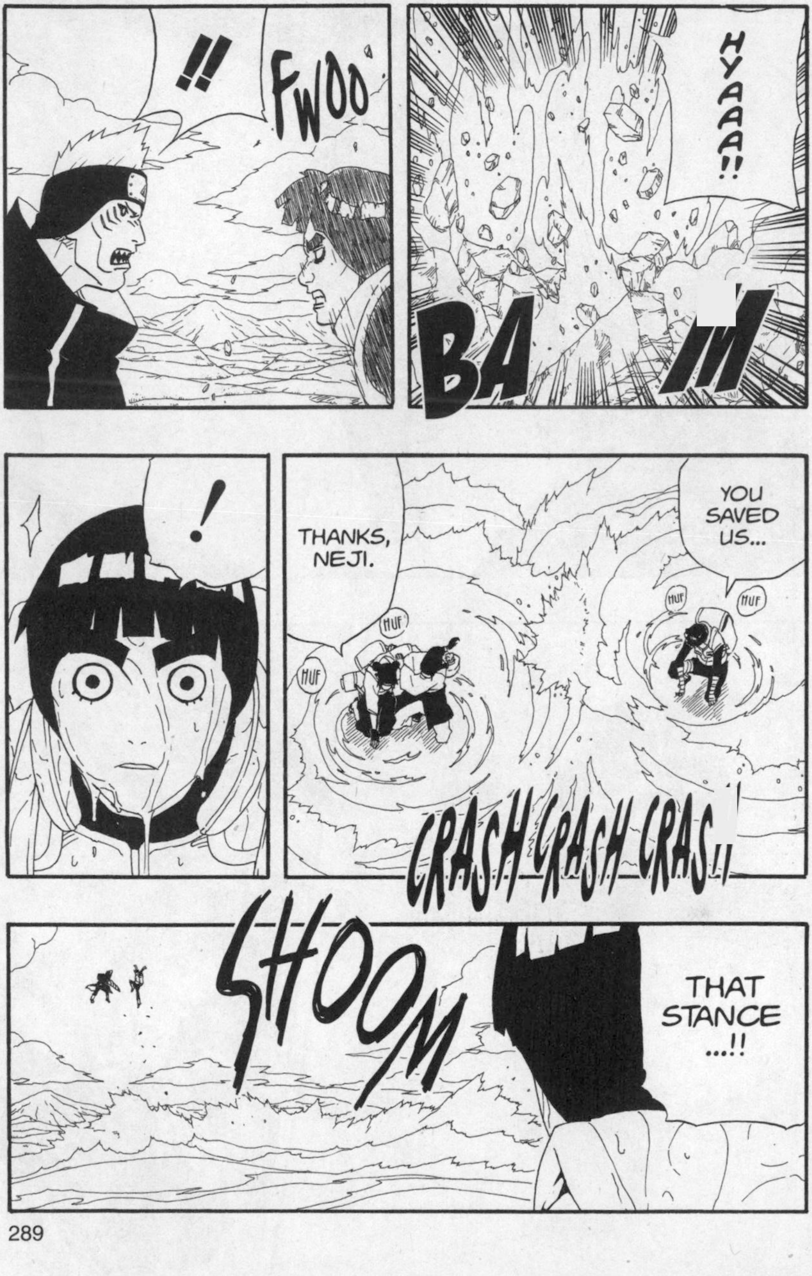

HYAAAA!!
BA
M
!!
FWOO
YOU SAVED US...
HUF
HUF
THANKS, NEJI.
HUF
HUF
CRASH CRASH CRAS !!
!
THAT STANCE ...!!
SHOOM

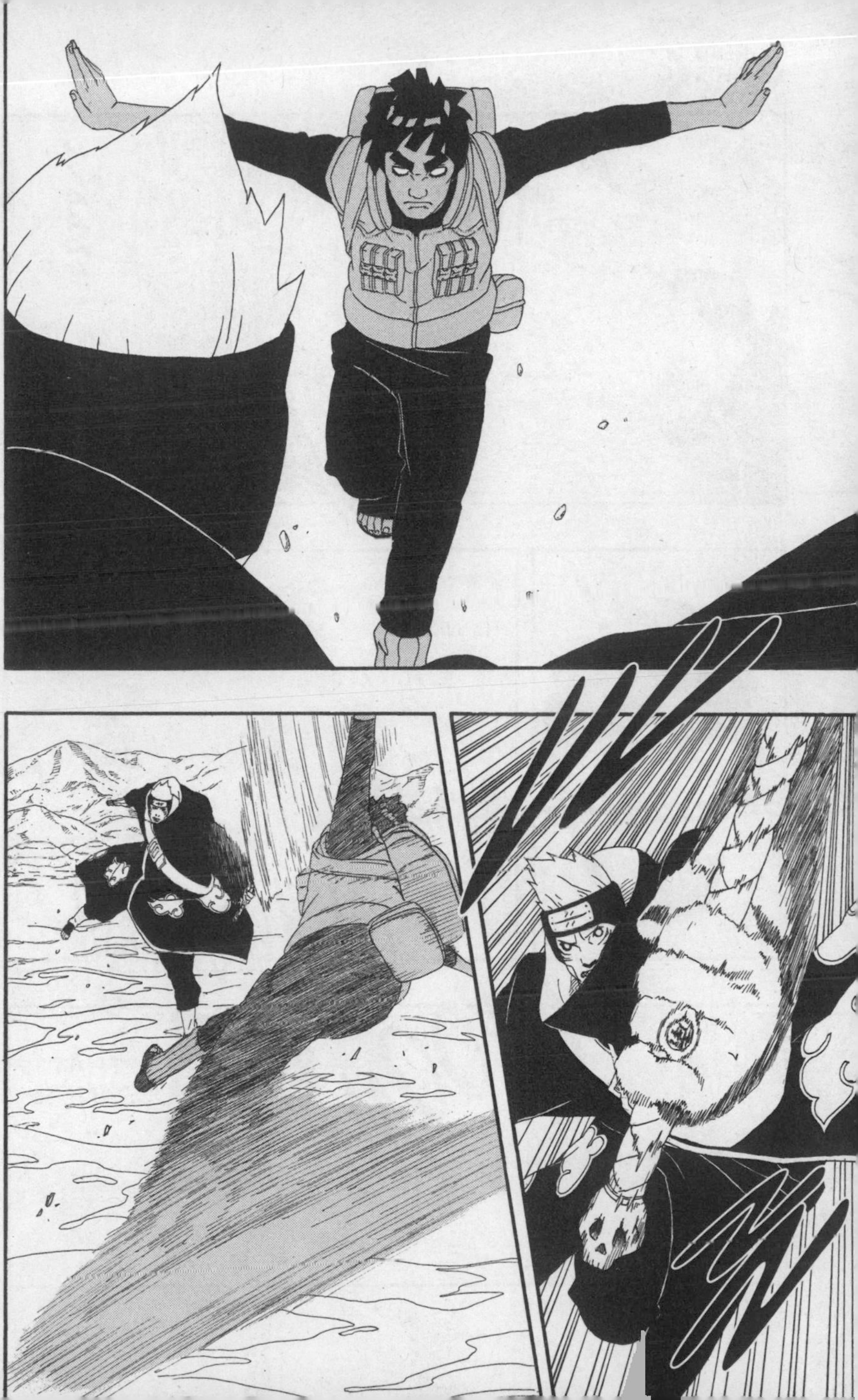

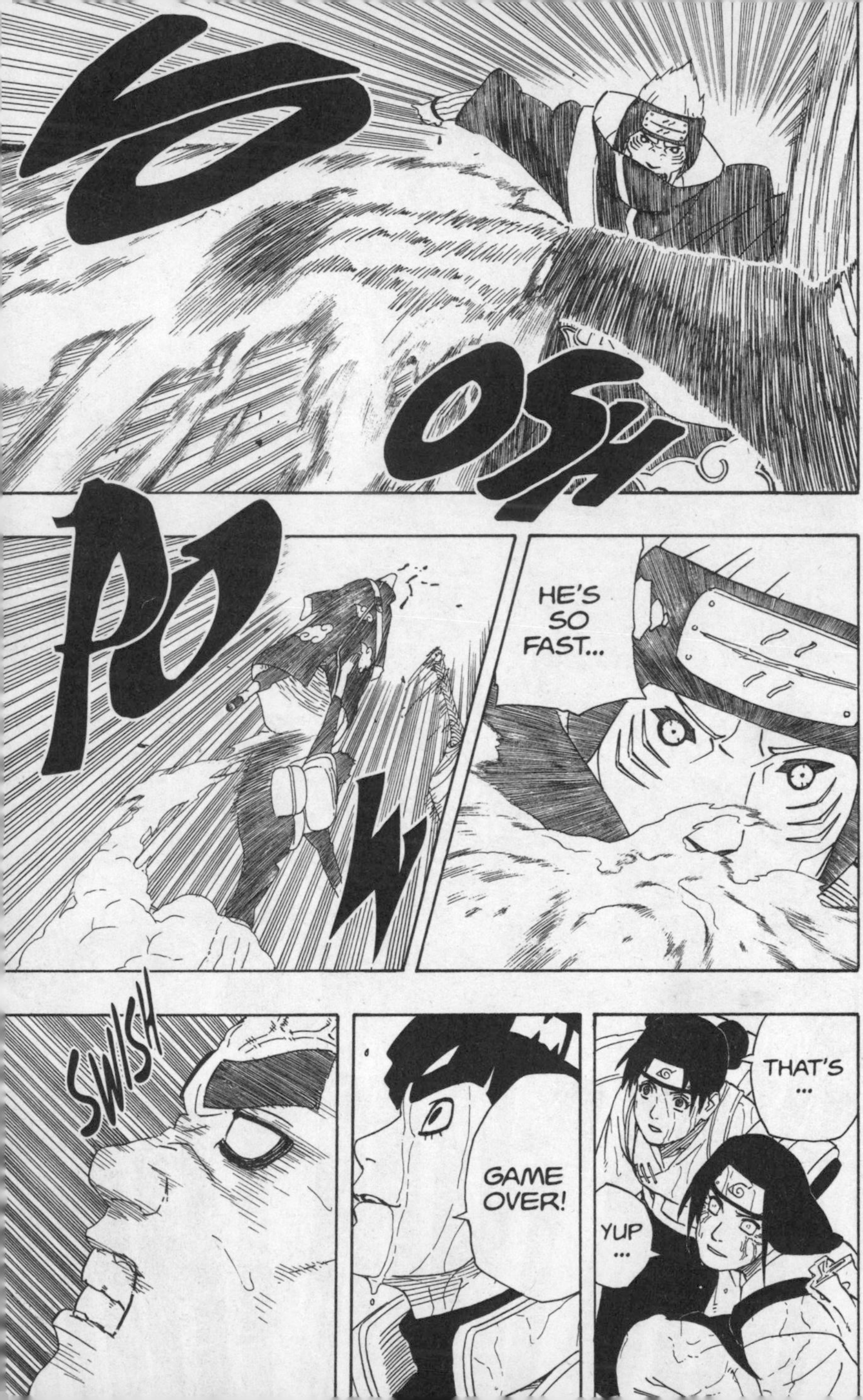
SOSH
HE'S SO FAST...
POW
THAT'S ...
YUP ...
GAME OVER!
SWISH

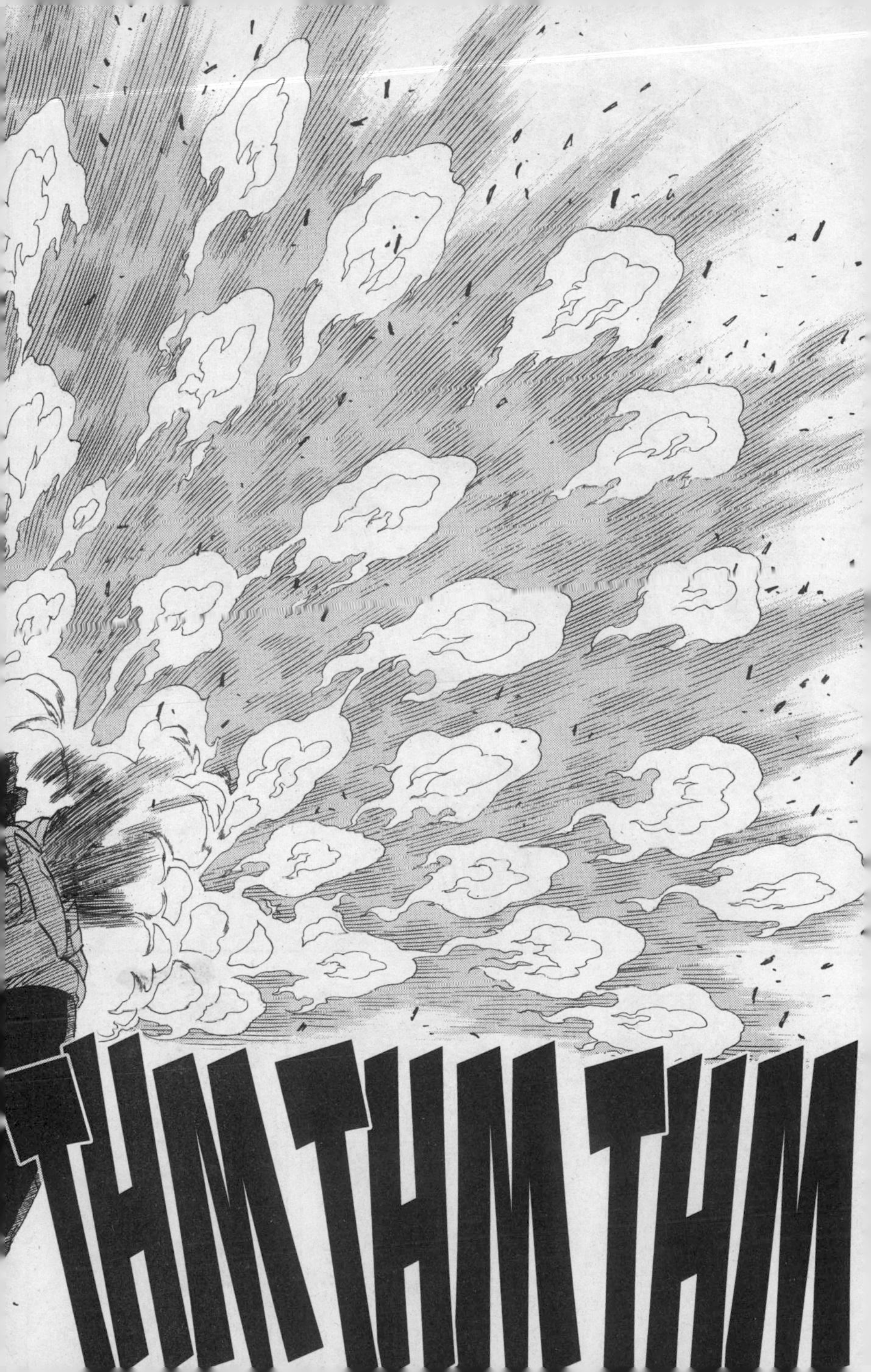
THM THM THM

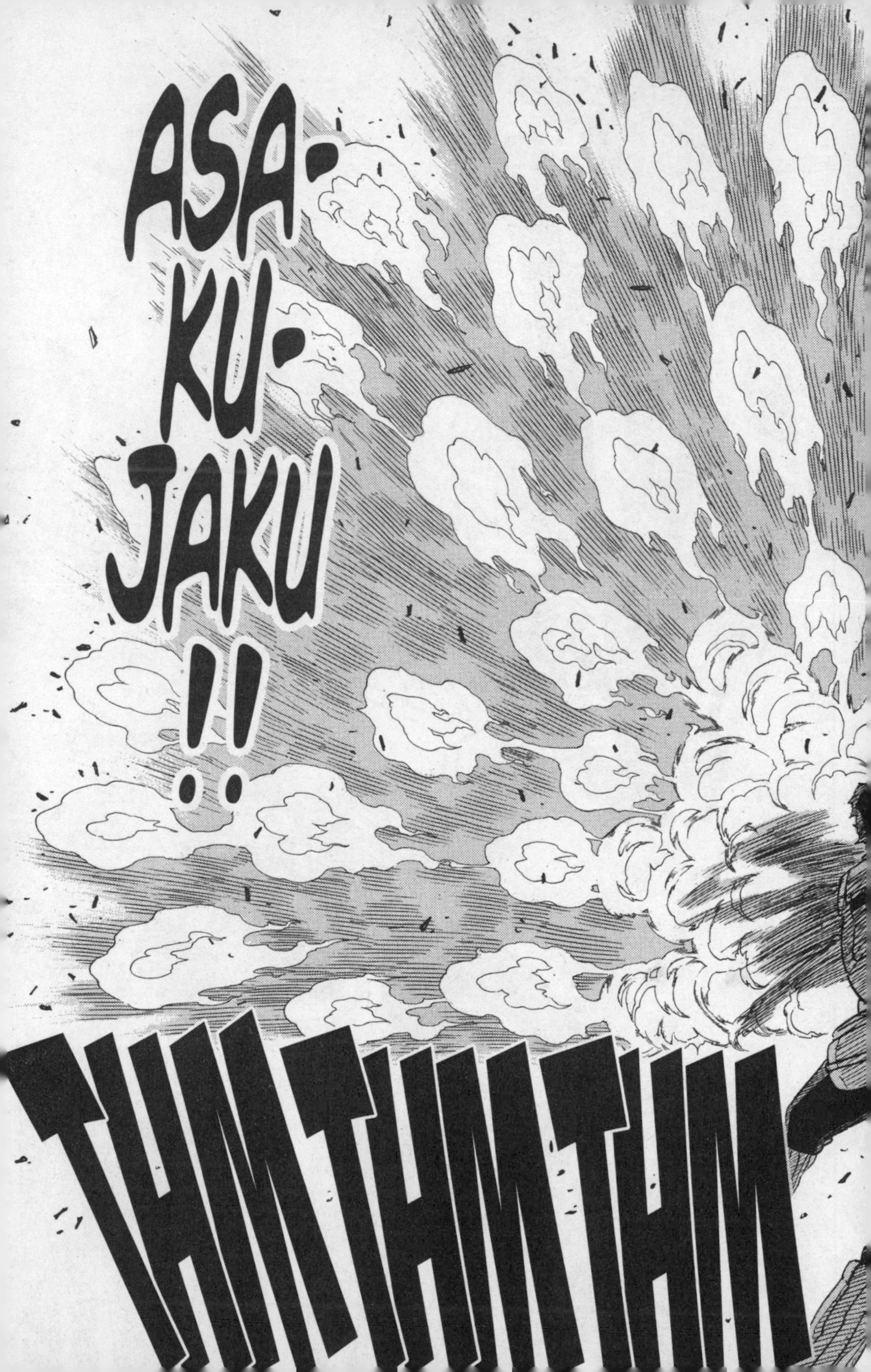
ASA-KU-JAKU!!
THMTHMTHM

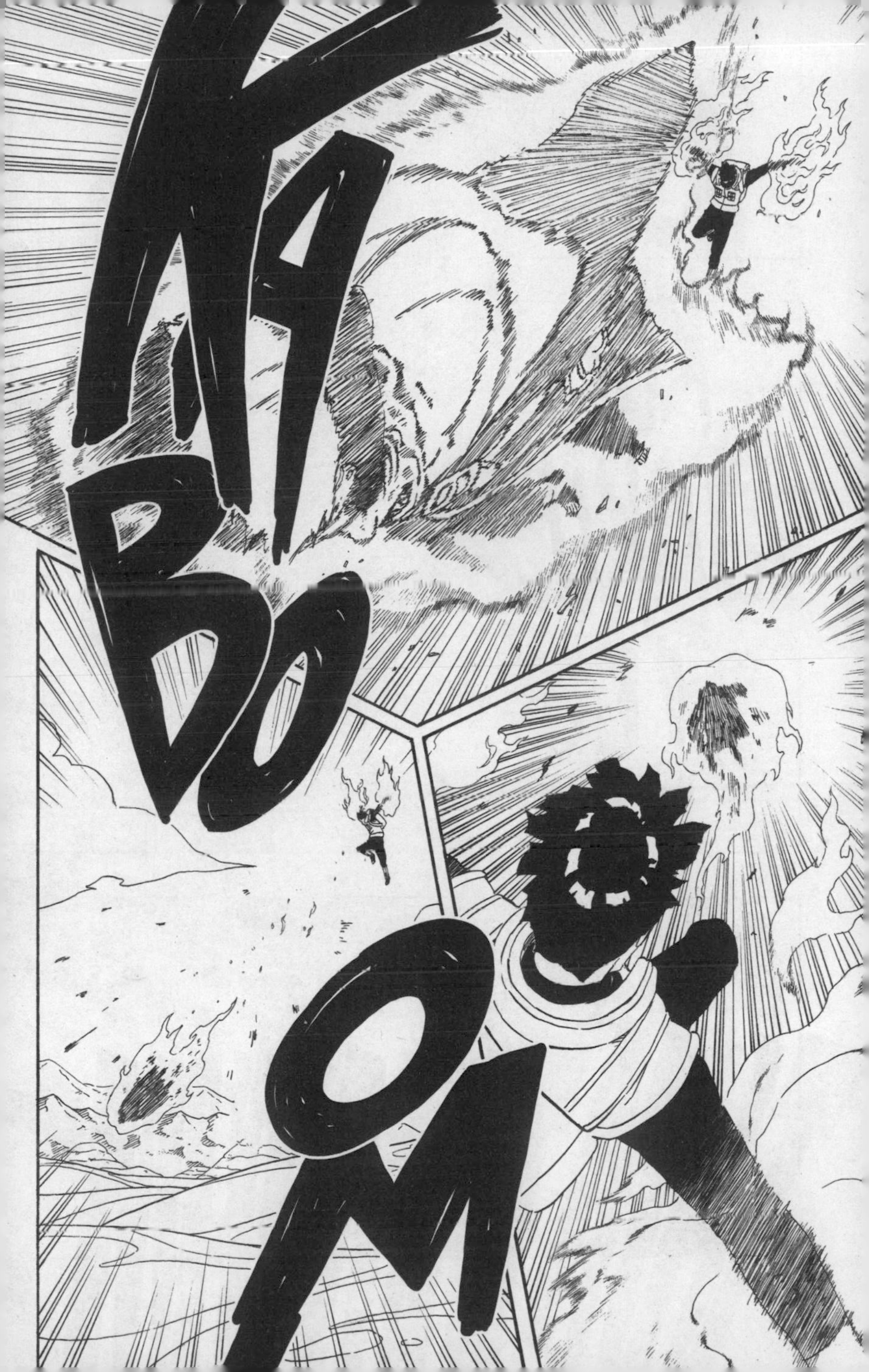
KABOOOM

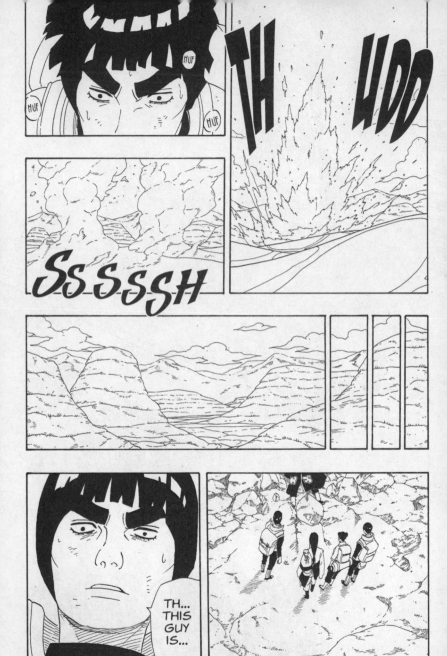

TH

HDD

SSSSSH

TH...
THIS
GUY
IS...

NARUTO

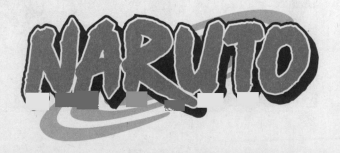

Number 259: The Power of Itachi...!!

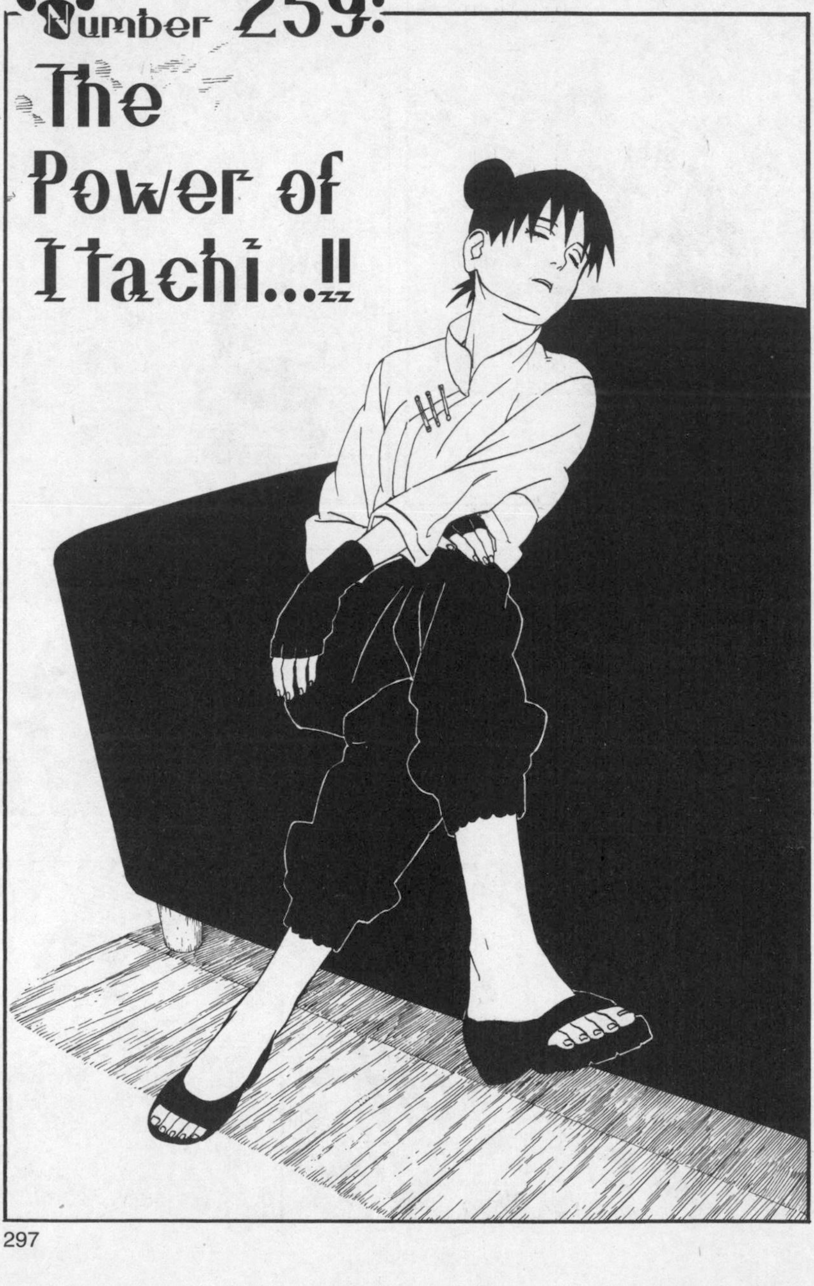

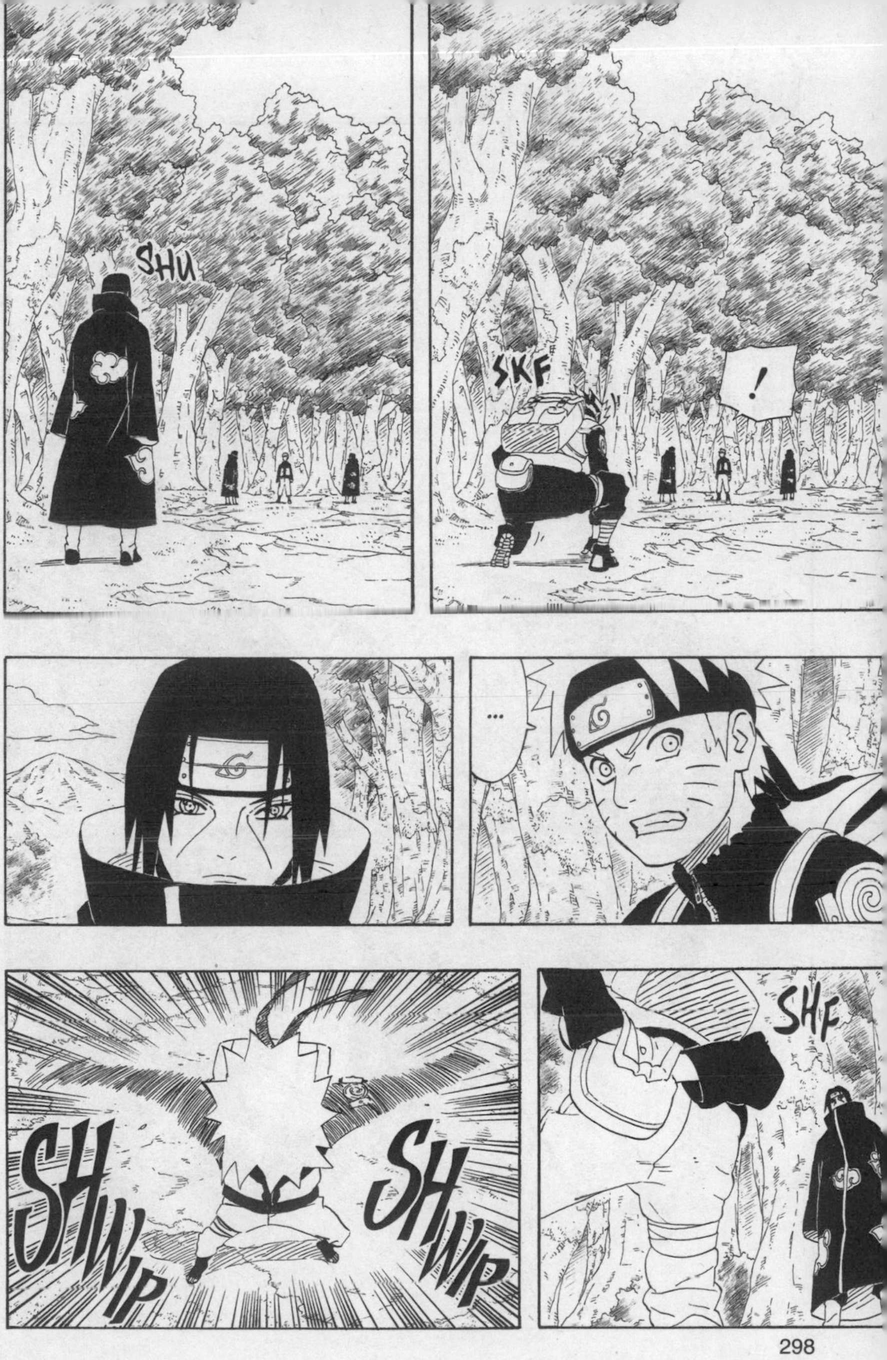
SKF
!
SHU
...
SHF
SHWIP
SHWIP

READ THIS WAY

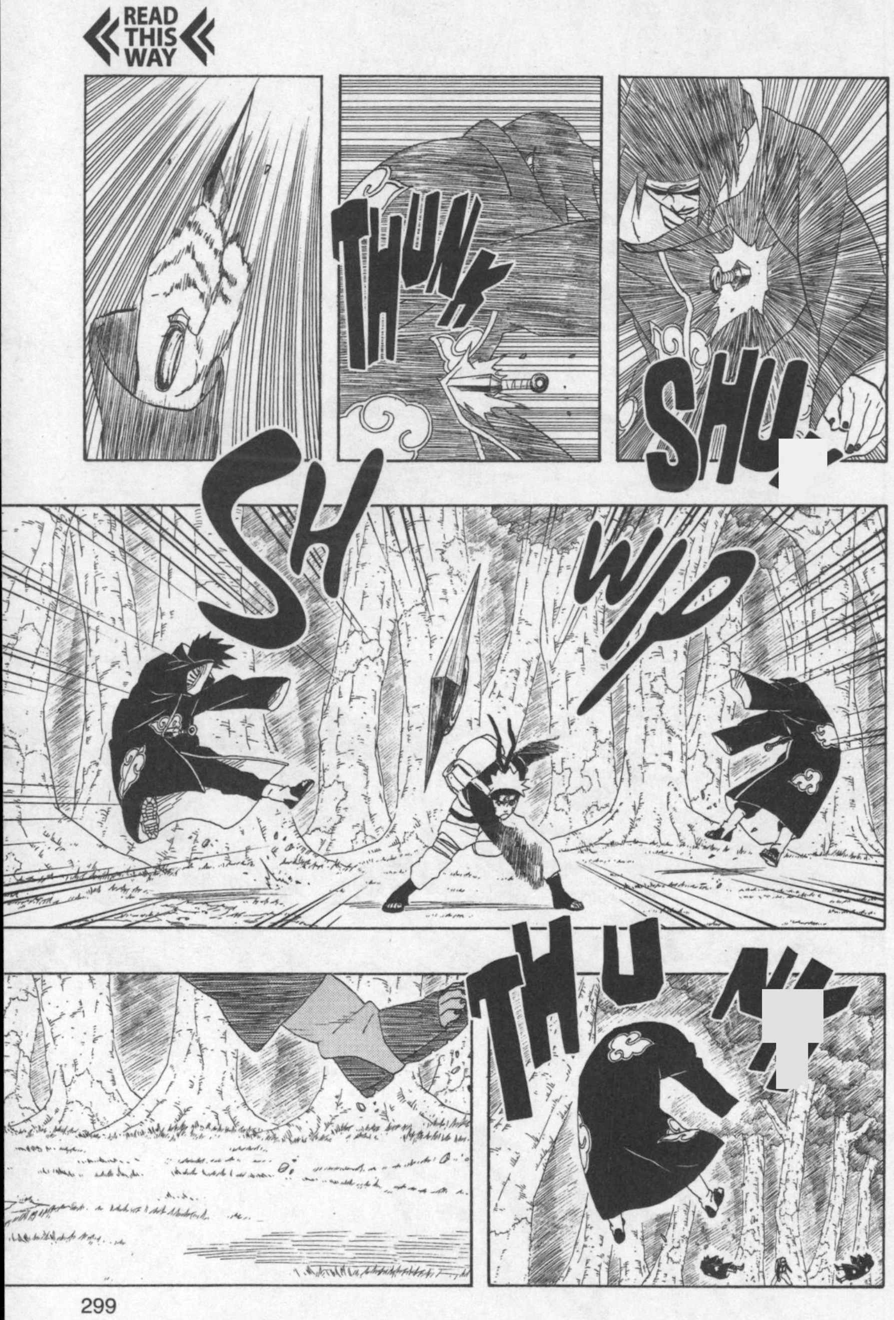
SHU
THUNK
SHWIP
THUN

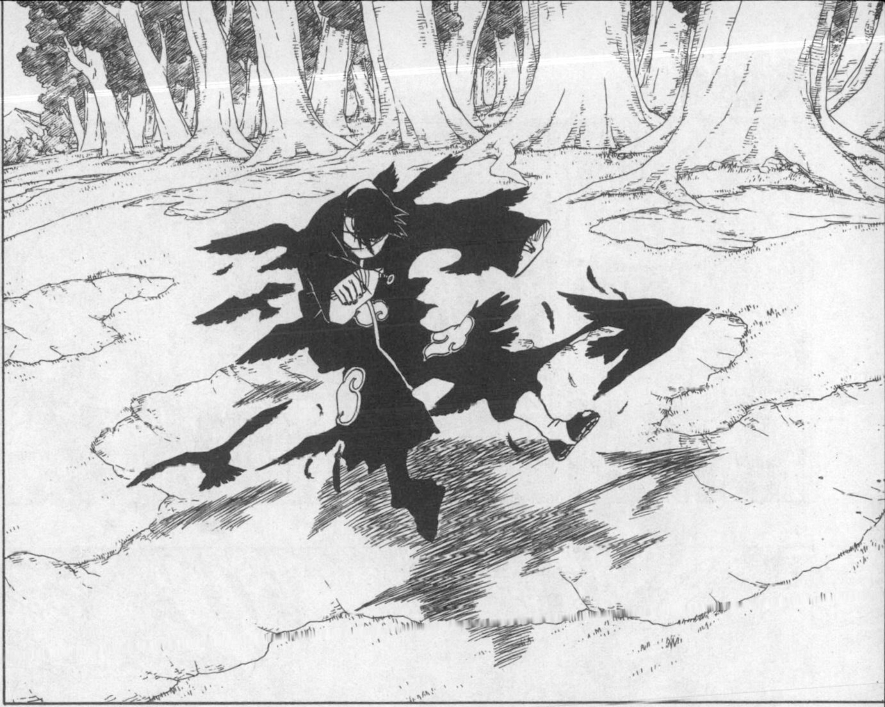

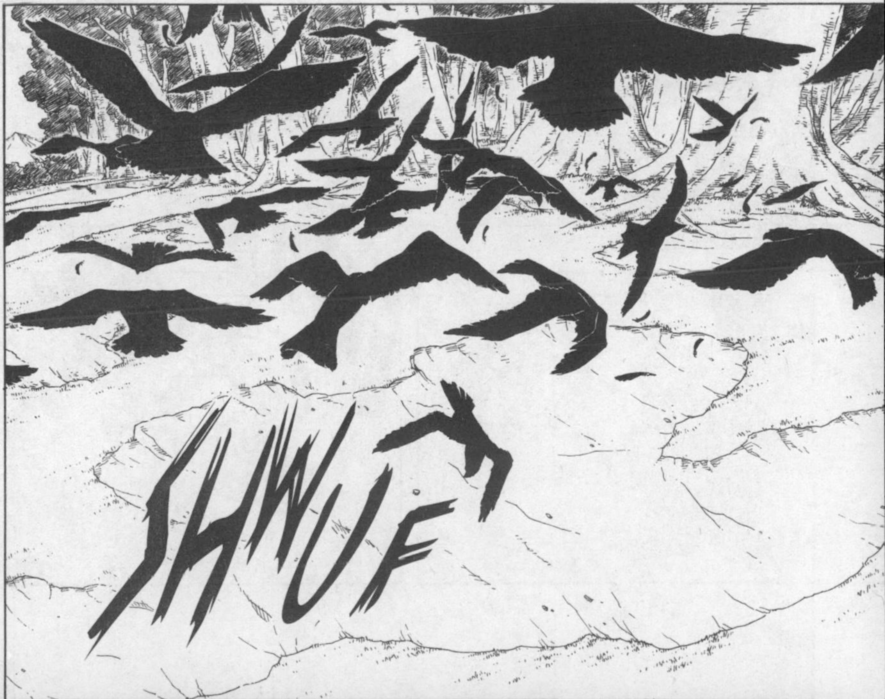
SHWUF

READ THIS WAY

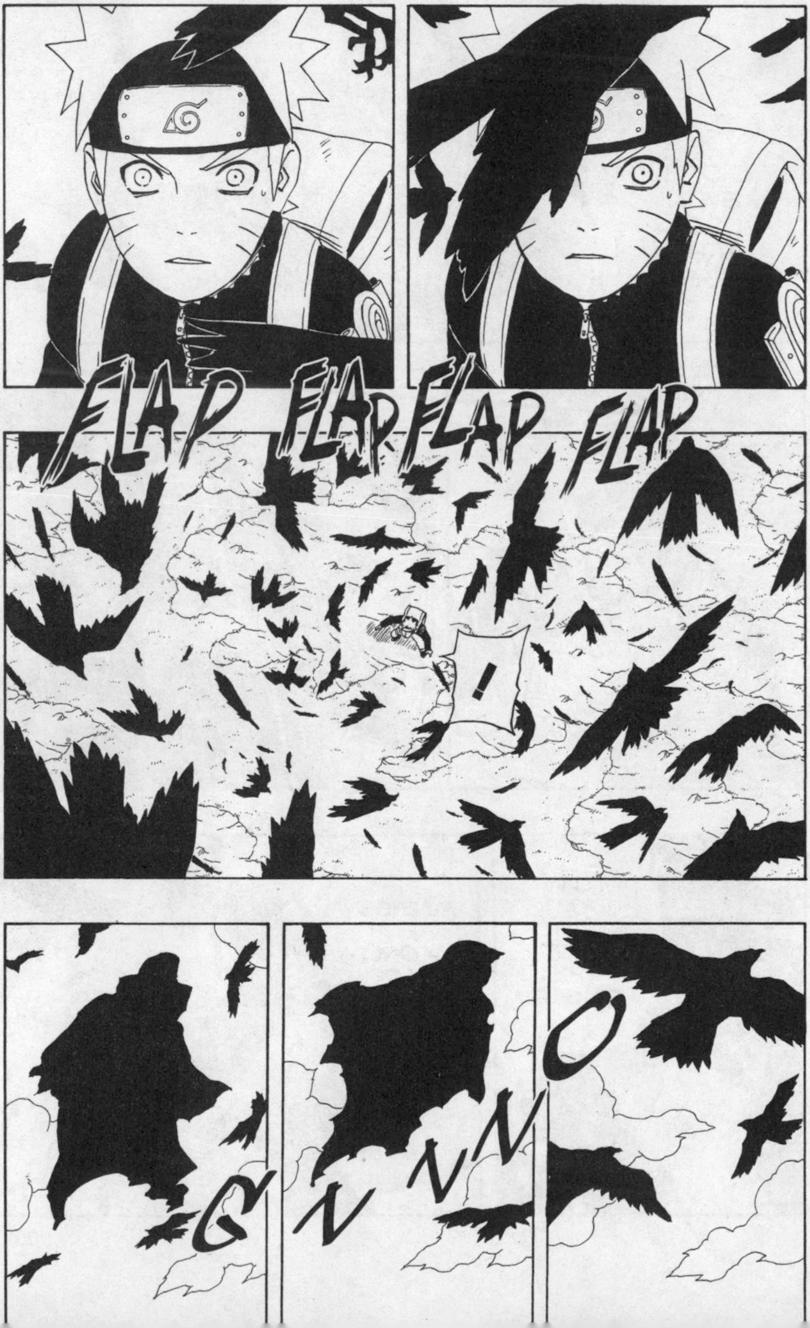
FLAP FLAP FLAP FLAP
!
GNNNO

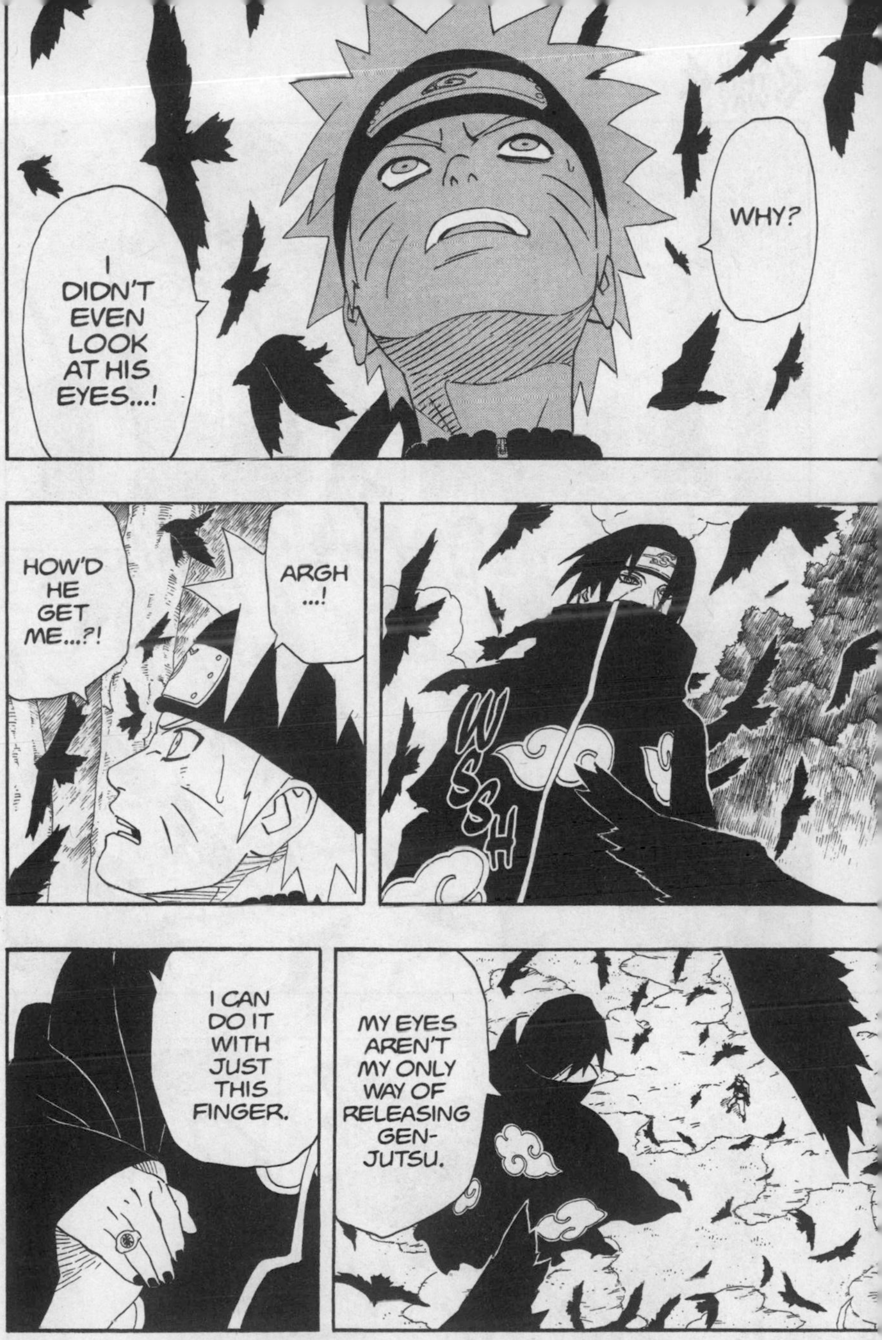
WHY?
I DIDN'T EVEN LOOK AT HIS EYES...!
WSSH
ARGH ...!
HOW'D HE GET ME...?!
MY EYES AREN'T MY ONLY WAY OF RELEASING GEN-JUTSU.
I CAN DO IT WITH JUST THIS FINGER.

READ THIS WAY

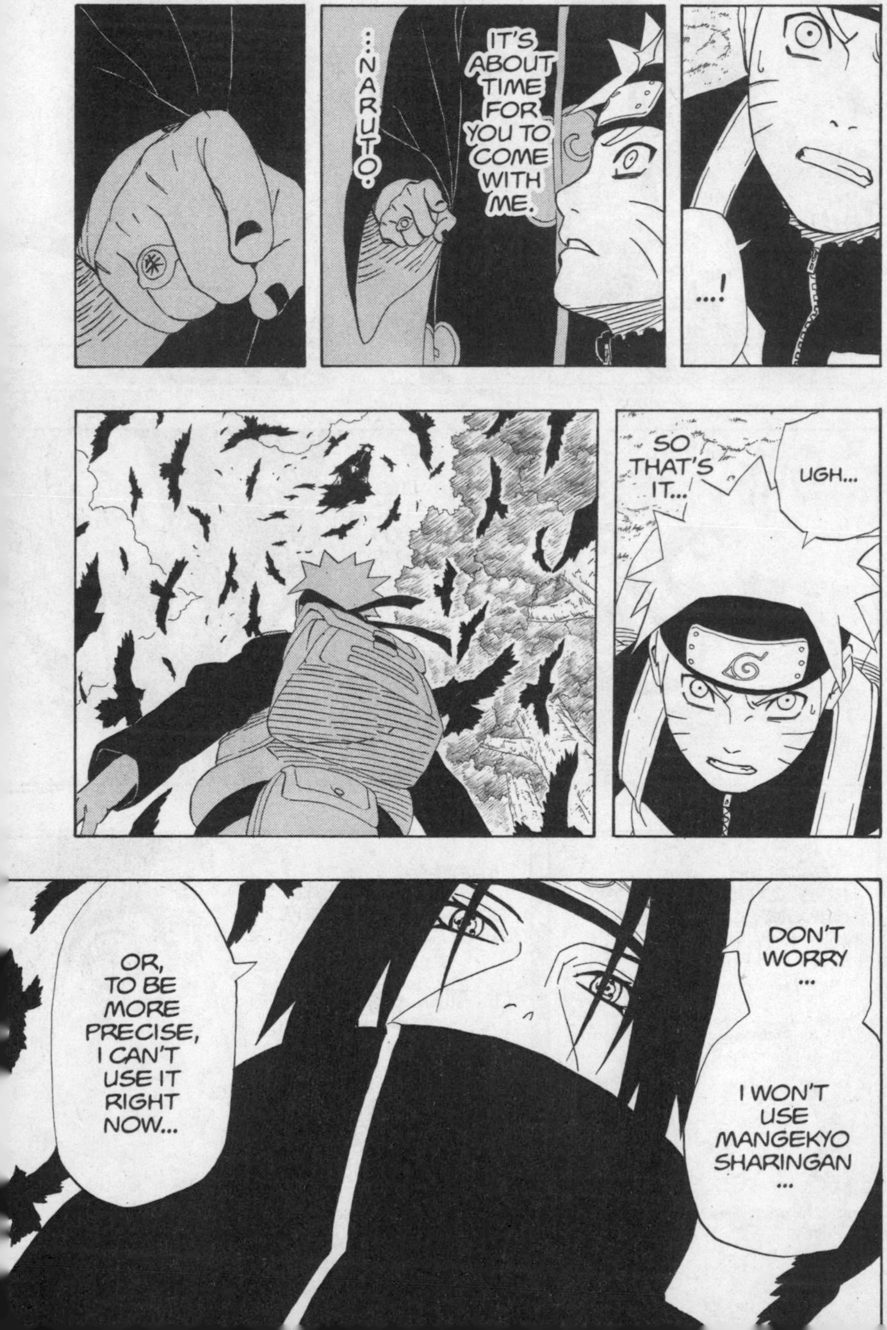
...!
IT'S ABOUT TIME FOR YOU TO COME WITH ME.
...NARUTO.
UGH...
SO THAT'S IT...
DON'T WORRY ...
I WON'T USE MANGEKYO SHARINGAN ...
OR, TO BE MORE PRECISE, I CAN'T USE IT RIGHT NOW...

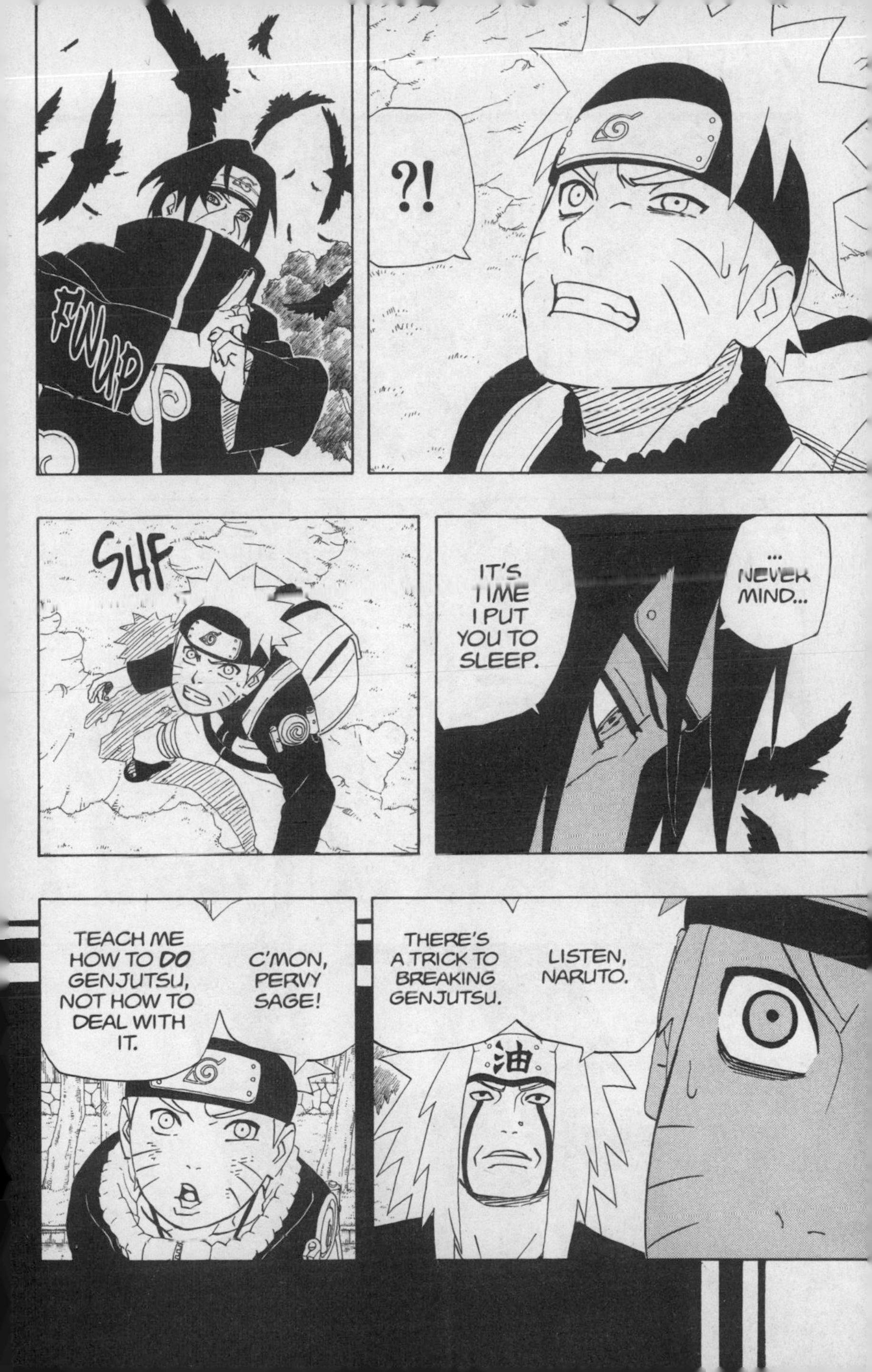
?!
FWUP
...NEVER MIND...
IT'S TIME I PUT YOU TO SLEEP.
SHF
LISTEN, NARUTO.
THERE'S A TRICK TO BREAKING GENJUTSU.
油
C'MON, PERVY SAGE!
TEACH ME HOW TO **DO** GENJUTSU, NOT HOW TO DEAL WITH IT.

READ THIS WAY

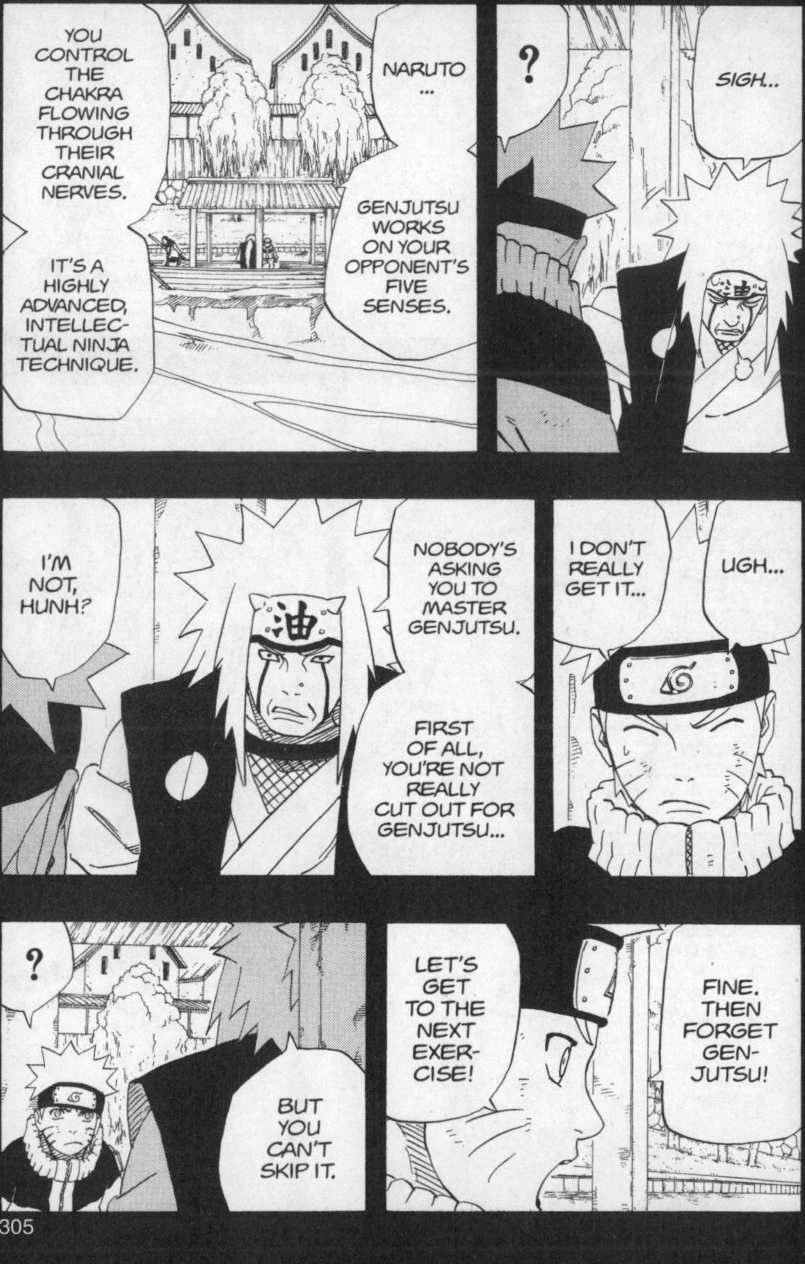
SIGH...
?
NARUTO ...
GENJUTSU WORKS ON YOUR OPPONENT'S FIVE SENSES.
YOU CONTROL THE CHAKRA FLOWING THROUGH THEIR CRANIAL NERVES.
IT'S A HIGHLY ADVANCED, INTELLEC-TUAL NINJA TECHNIQUE.
UGH...
I DON'T REALLY GET IT...
NOBODY'S ASKING YOU TO MASTER GENJUTSU.
FIRST OF ALL, YOU'RE NOT REALLY CUT OUT FOR GENJUTSU...
I'M NOT, HUNH?
FINE. THEN FORGET GEN-JUTSU!
LET'S GET TO THE NEXT EXER-CISE!
BUT YOU CAN'T SKIP IT.
?

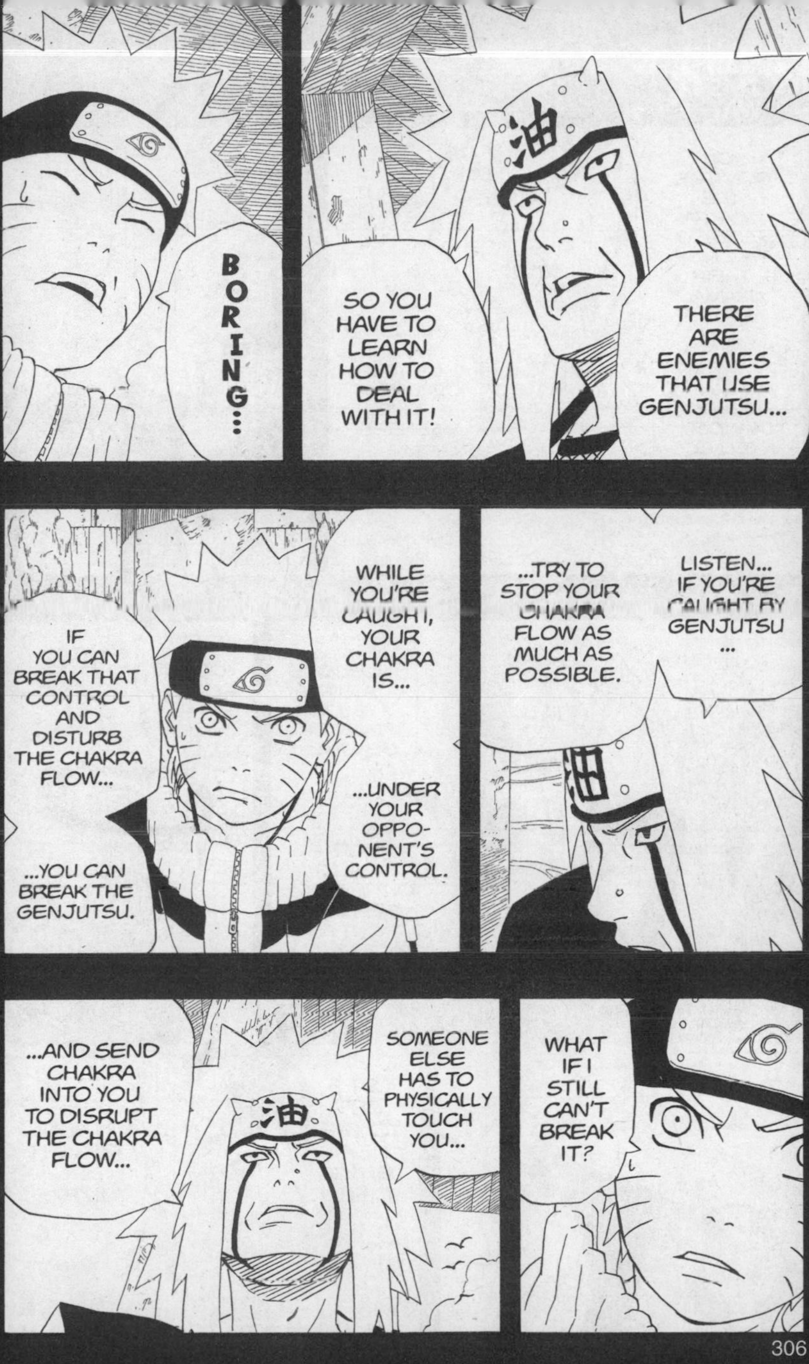

THERE ARE ENEMIES THAT USE GENJUTSU...
SO YOU HAVE TO LEARN HOW TO DEAL WITH IT!
BORING...
LISTEN... IF YOU'RE CAUGHT BY GENJUTSU ...
...TRY TO STOP YOUR CHAKRA FLOW AS MUCH AS POSSIBLE.
WHILE YOU'RE CAUGHT, YOUR CHAKRA IS...
...UNDER YOUR OPPONENT'S CONTROL.
IF YOU CAN BREAK THAT CONTROL AND DISTURB THE CHAKRA FLOW...
...YOU CAN BREAK THE GENJUTSU.
WHAT IF I STILL CAN'T BREAK IT?
SOMEONE ELSE HAS TO PHYSICALLY TOUCH YOU...
...AND SEND CHAKRA INTO YOU TO DISRUPT THE CHAKRA FLOW...

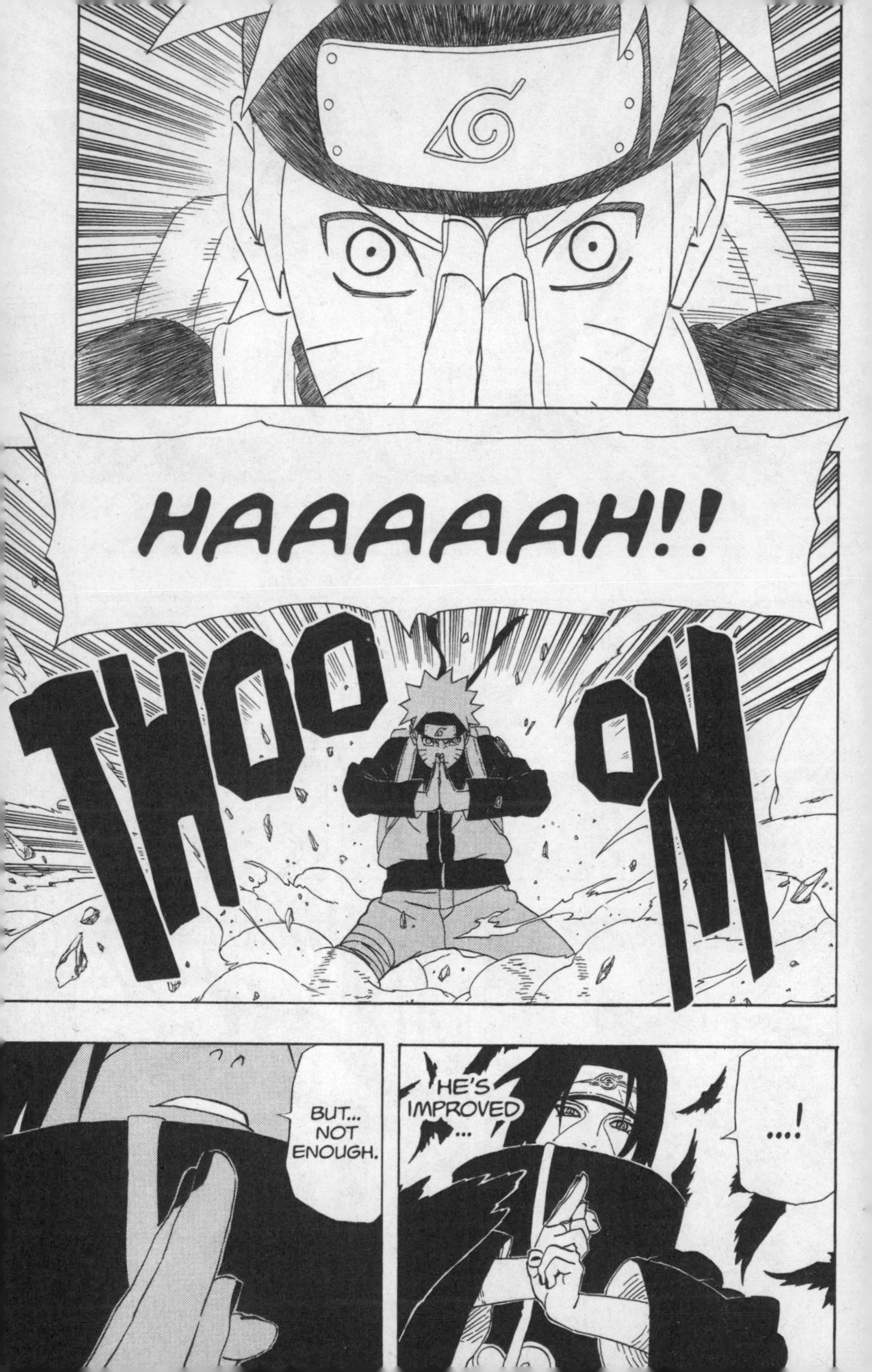
HAAAAAH!!
THOOOM
...!
HE'S IMPROVED...
BUT... NOT ENOUGH.

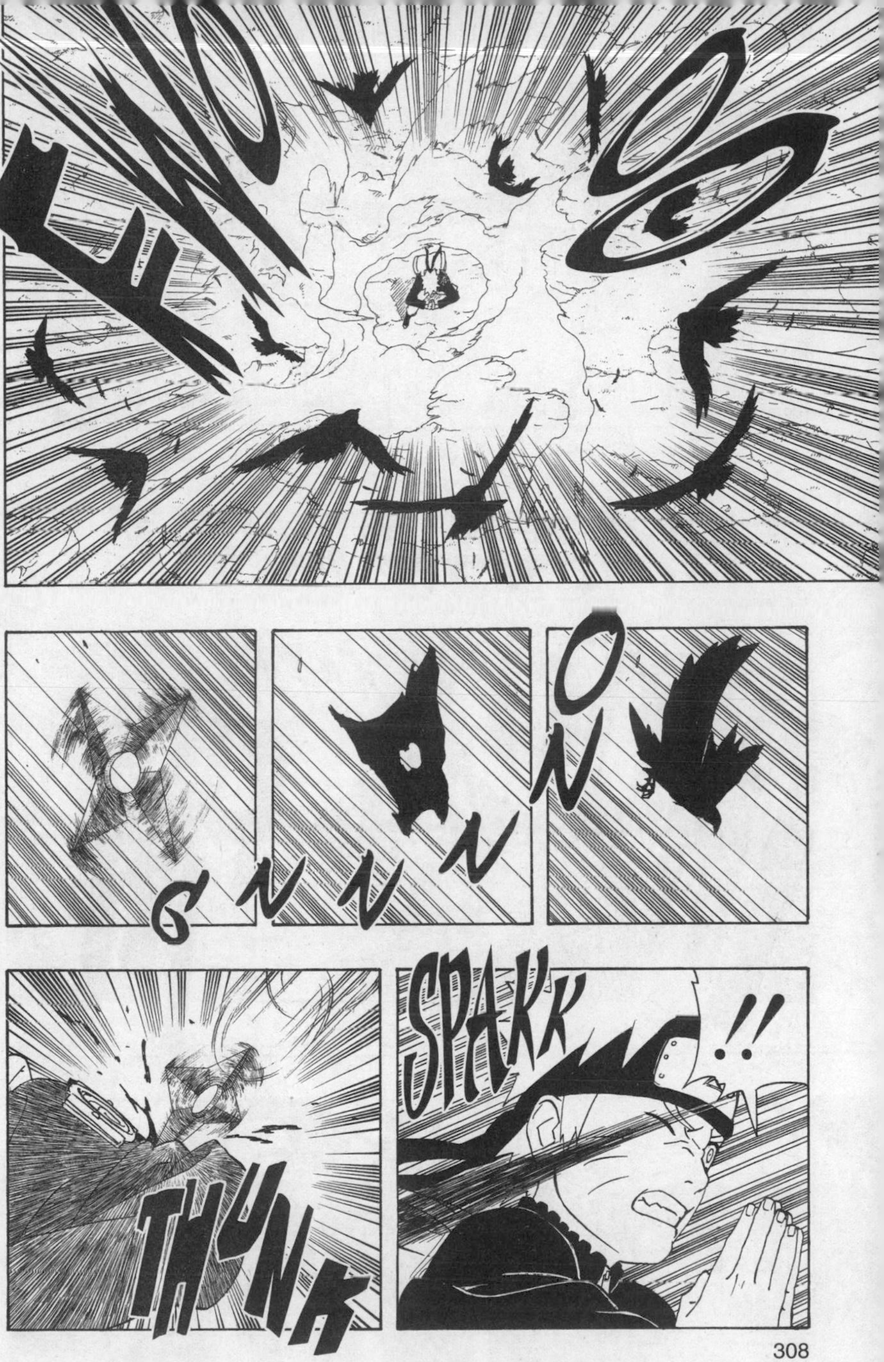
SPAKK
!!
THUNK

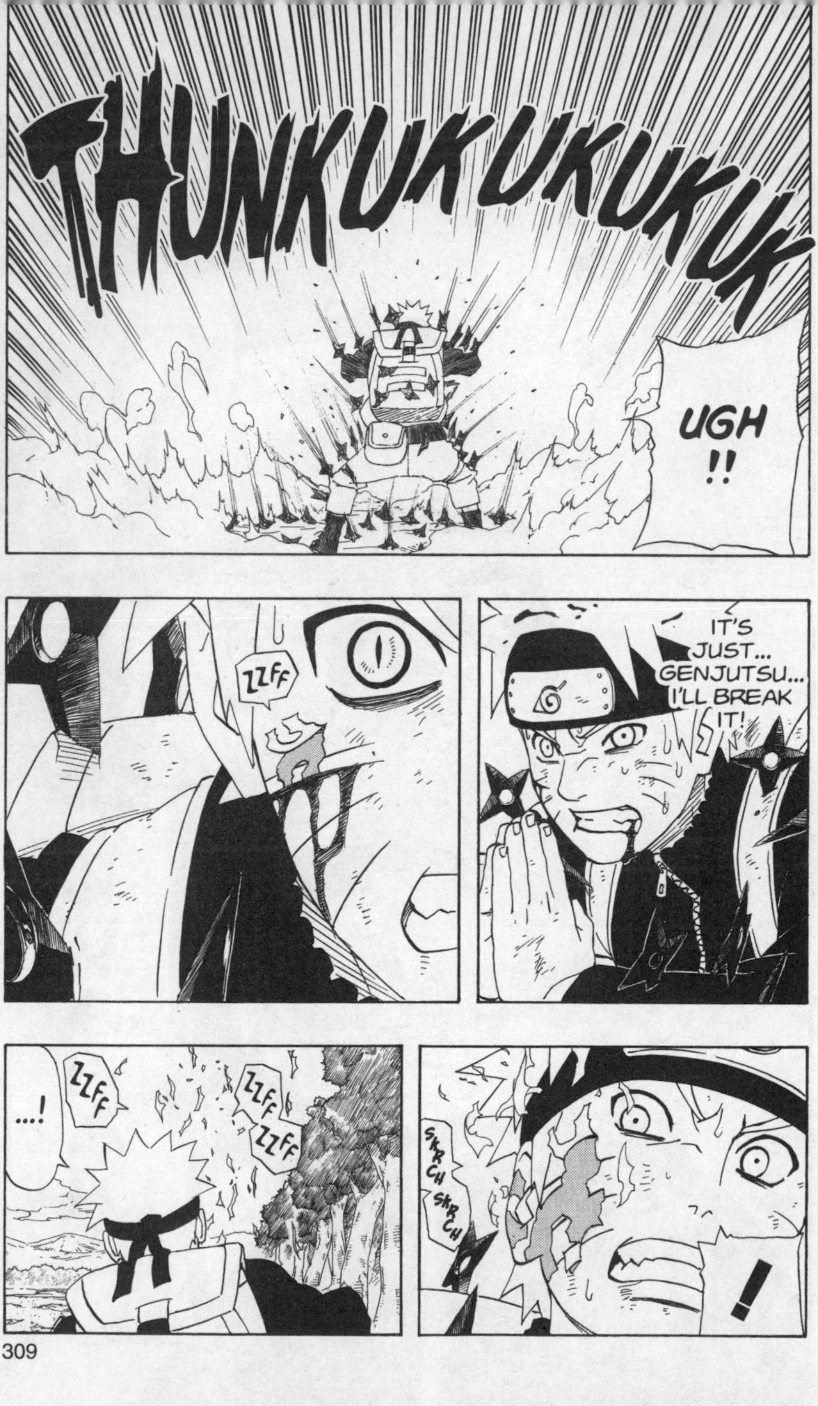
THUNKUKUKUKUKUK
UGH !!
IT'S JUST... GENJUTSU... I'LL BREAK IT!
ZZFF
SKRCH SKRCH
!
ZZFF
ZZFF
...!
ZZFF

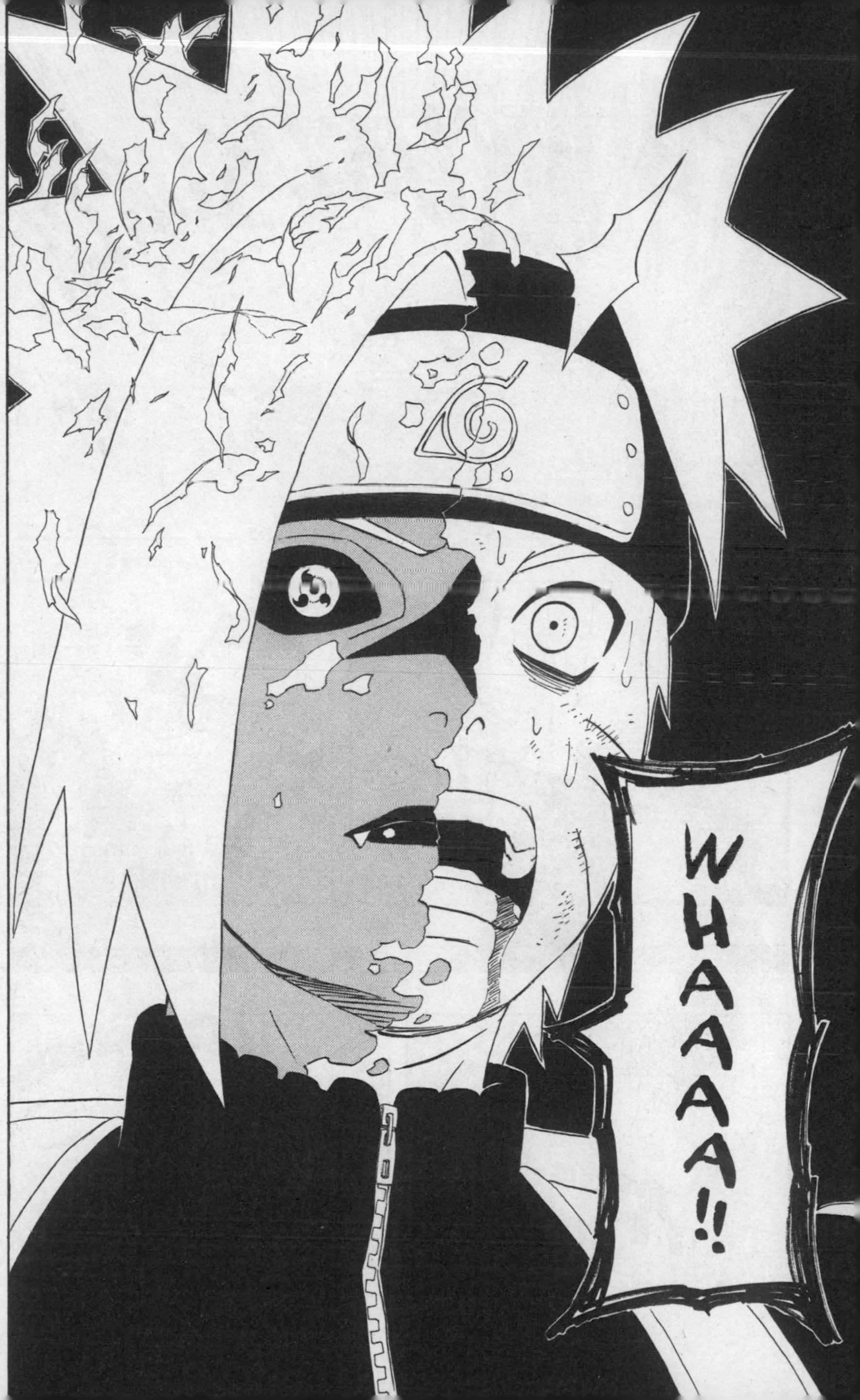
WHAAAA!!

READ THIS WAY

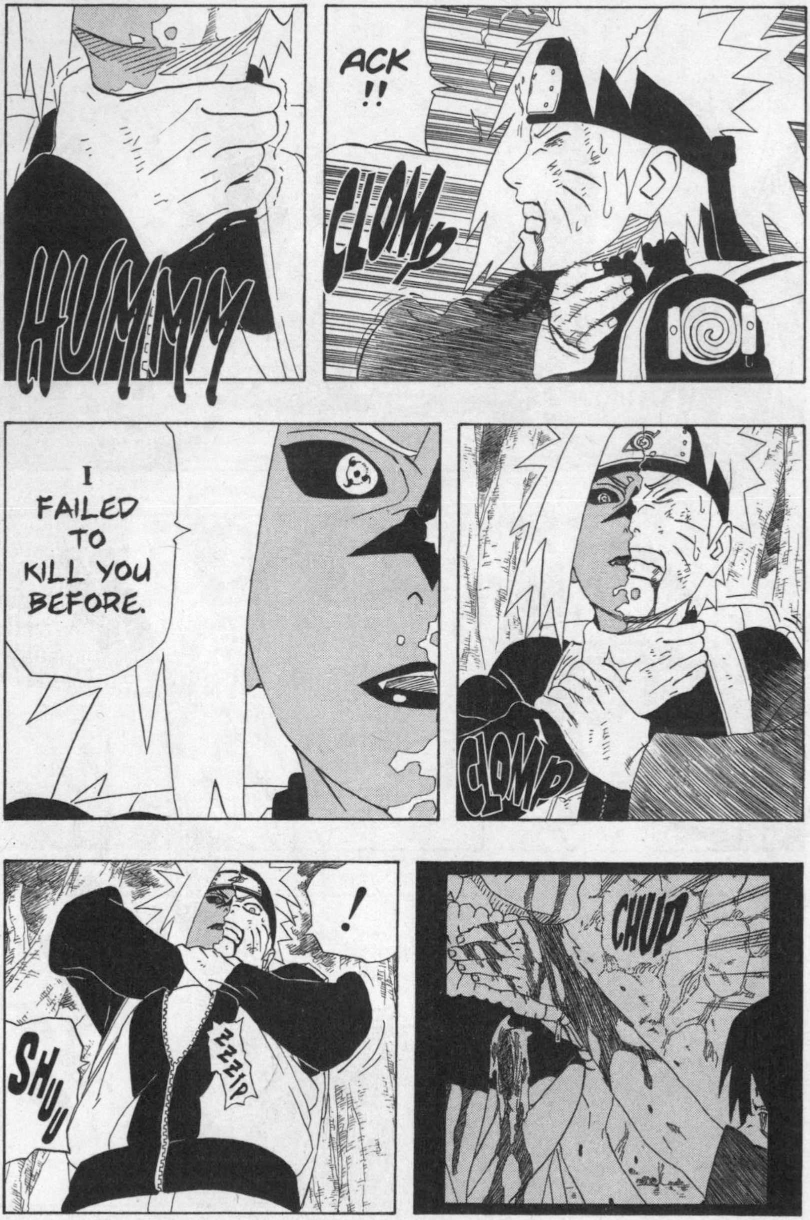
ACK !!
CLOMP
HUMMM
CLOMP
I FAILED TO KILL YOU BEFORE.
CHUP
!
ZZZIP
SHUU

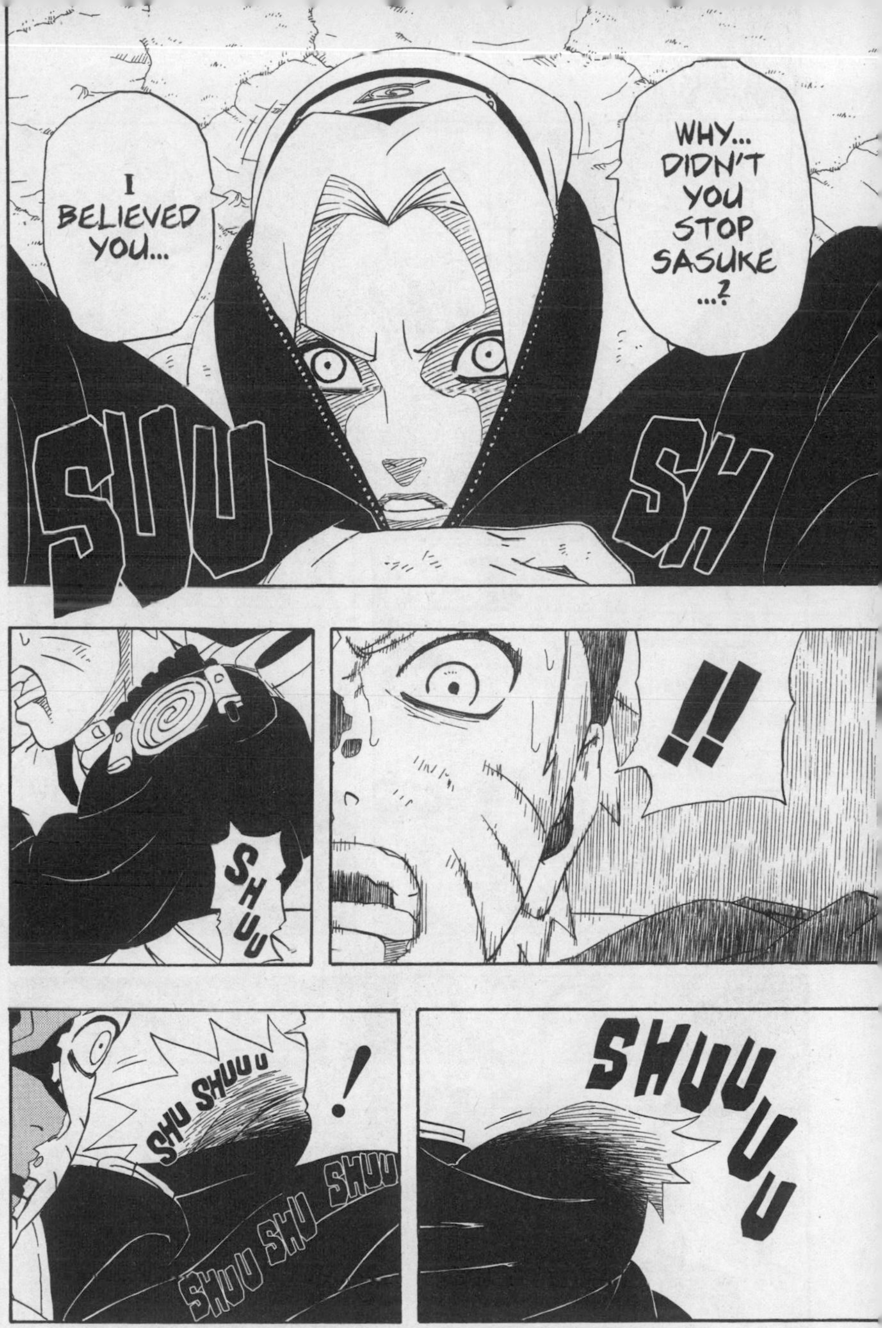
WHY... DIDN'T YOU STOP SASUKE ...?
I BELIEVED YOU...
SH
SUU
!!
SHUU
SHUUUU
!
SHU SHUUU
SHUU SHU SHUU

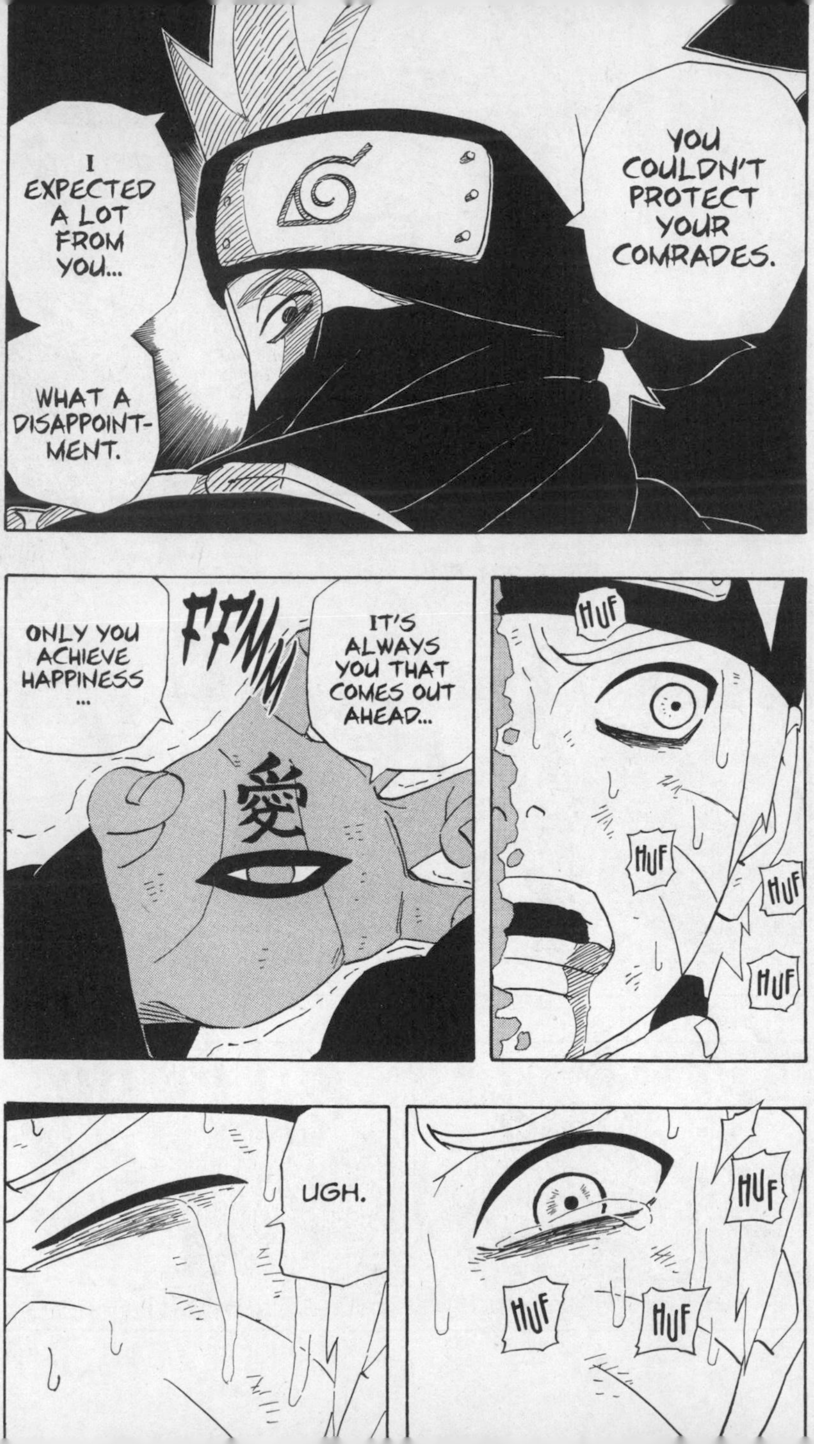
YOU COULDN'T PROTECT YOUR COMRADES.
I EXPECTED A LOT FROM YOU...
WHAT A DISAPPOINT-MENT.
HUF
HUF
HUF
HUF
IT'S ALWAYS YOU THAT COMES OUT AHEAD...
FFMM
ONLY YOU ACHIEVE HAPPINESS ...
HUF
HUF
HUF
UGH.

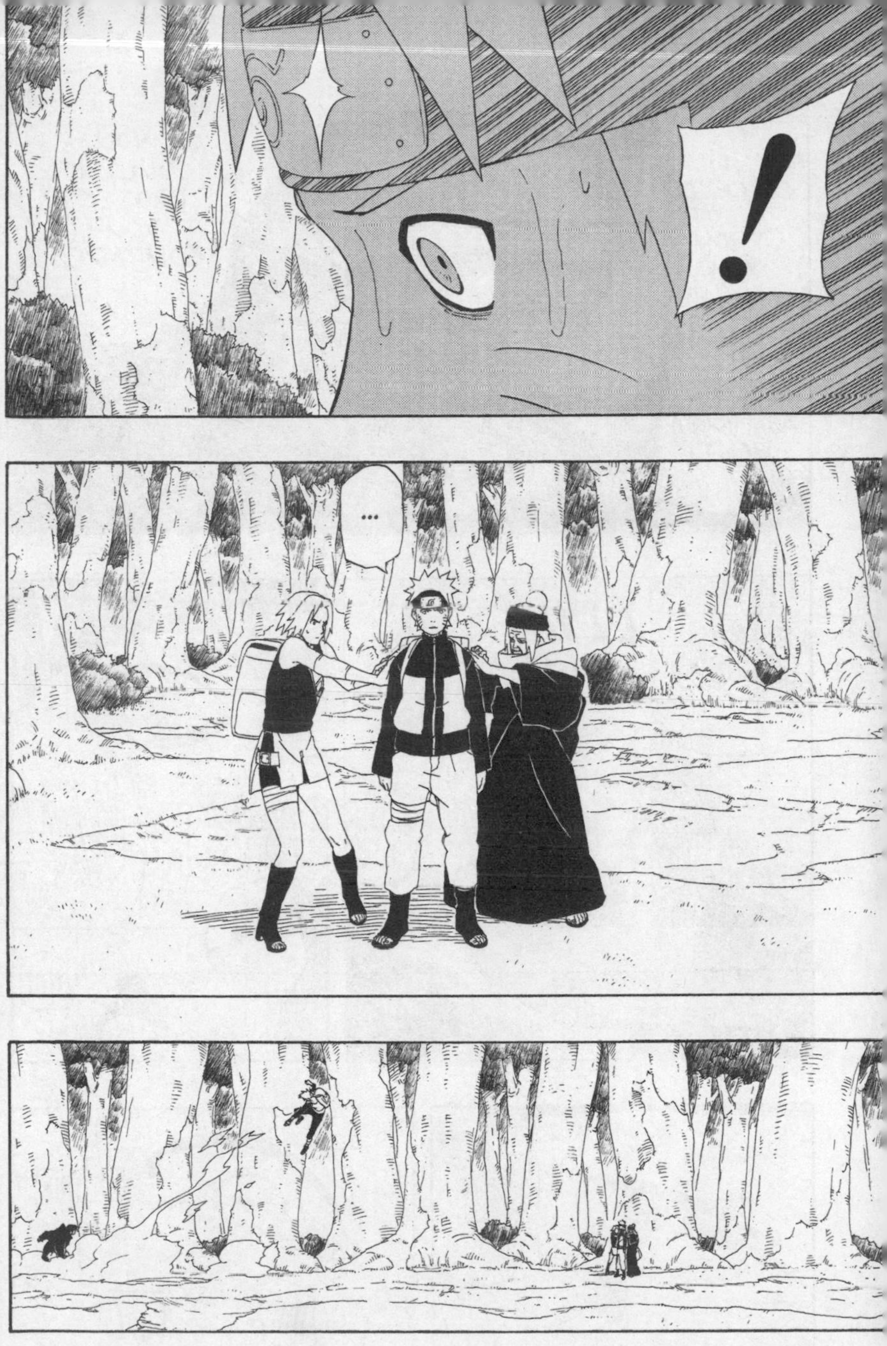
!
...

READ THIS WAY

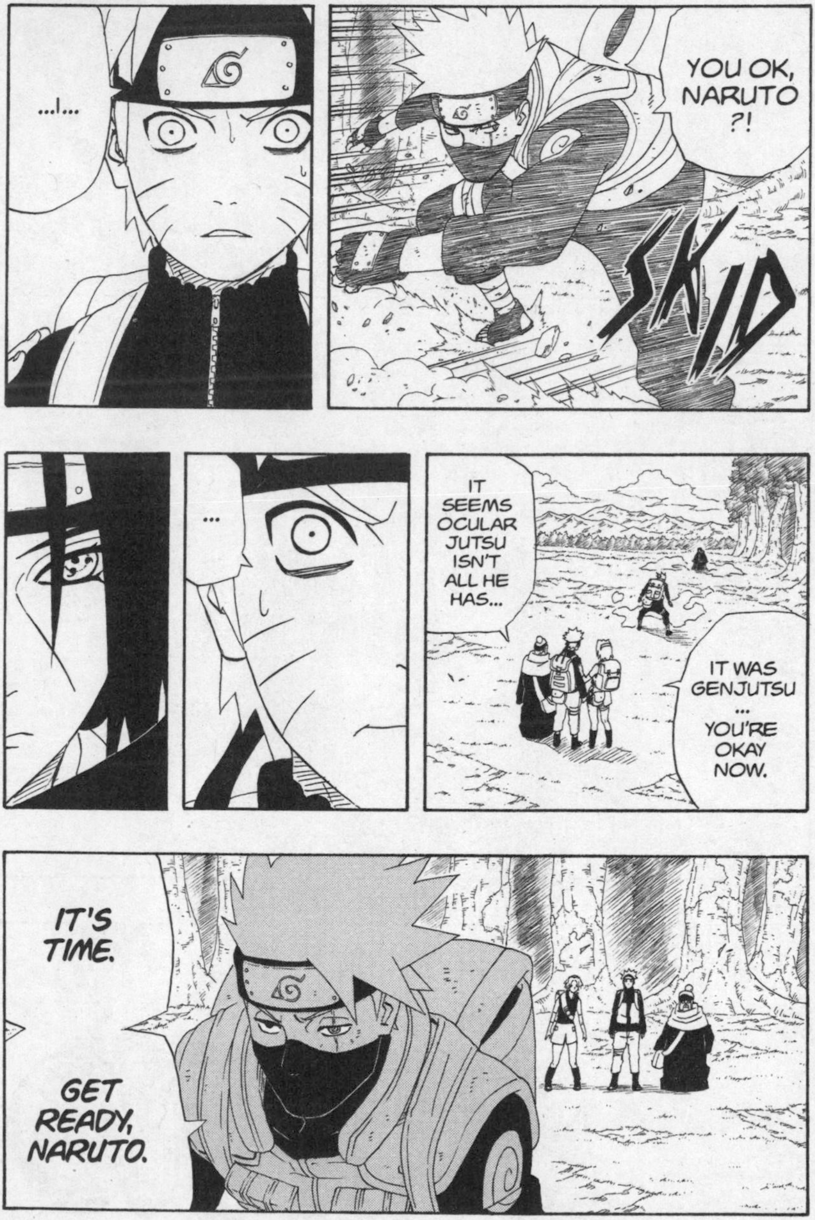

YOU OK, NARUTO ?!
SKID
...I...
IT SEEMS OCULAR JUTSU ISN'T ALL HE HAS...
IT WAS GENJUTSU ... YOU'RE OKAY NOW.
...
IT'S TIME.
GET READY, NARUTO.

NARUTO

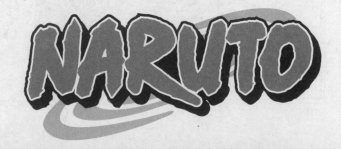

Number 260: Kakashi vs. Itachi!!

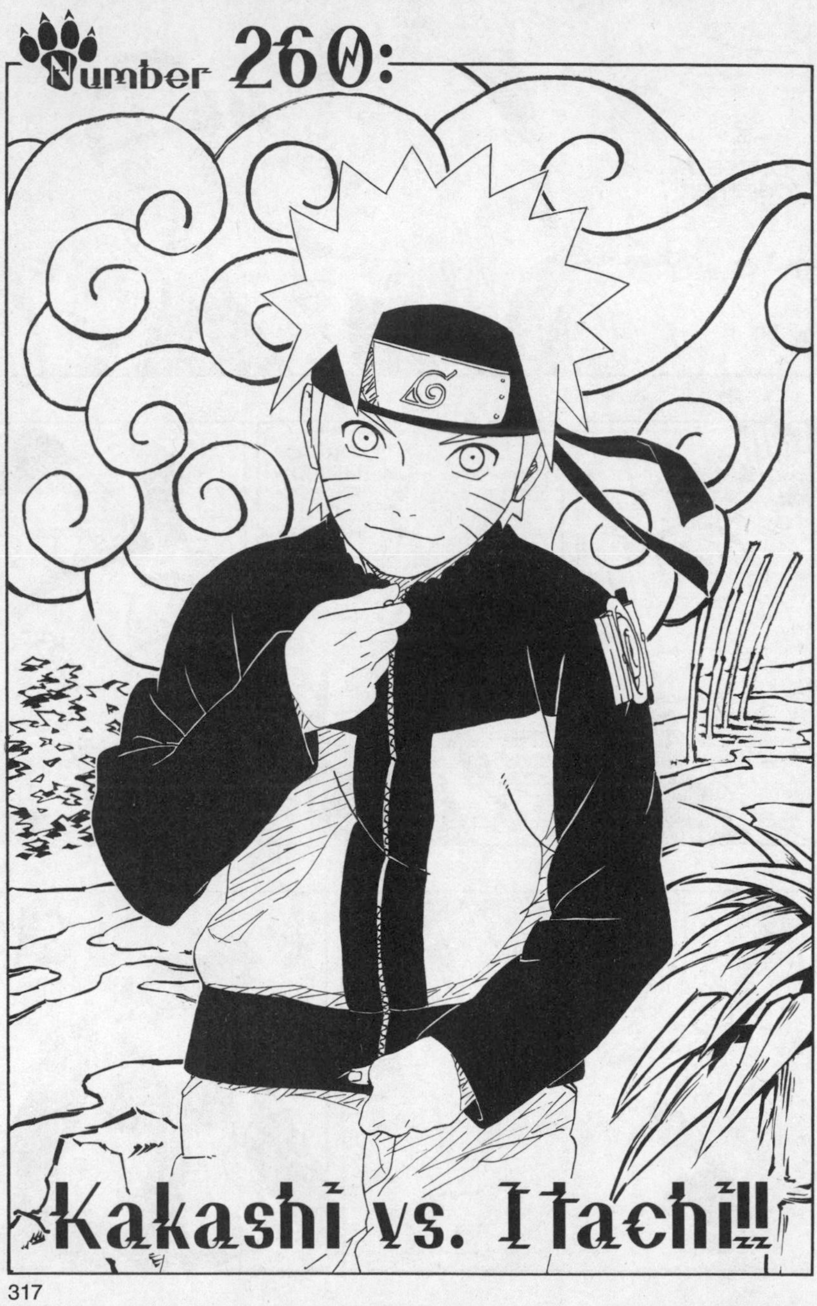

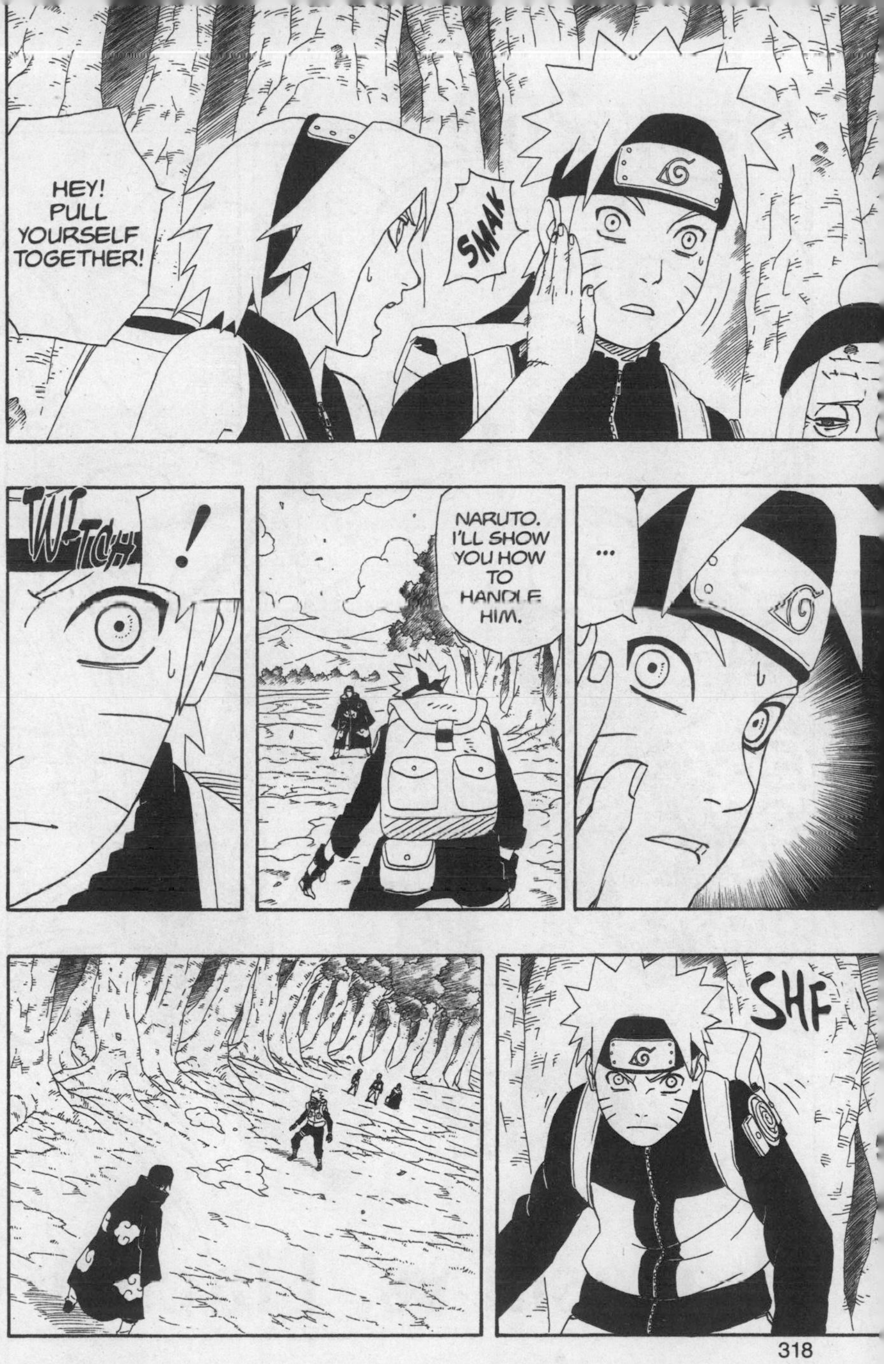
SMAK
HEY! PULL YOURSELF TOGETHER!
...
NARUTO. I'LL SHOW YOU HOW TO HANDLE HIM.
TWI-TCH
!
SHF

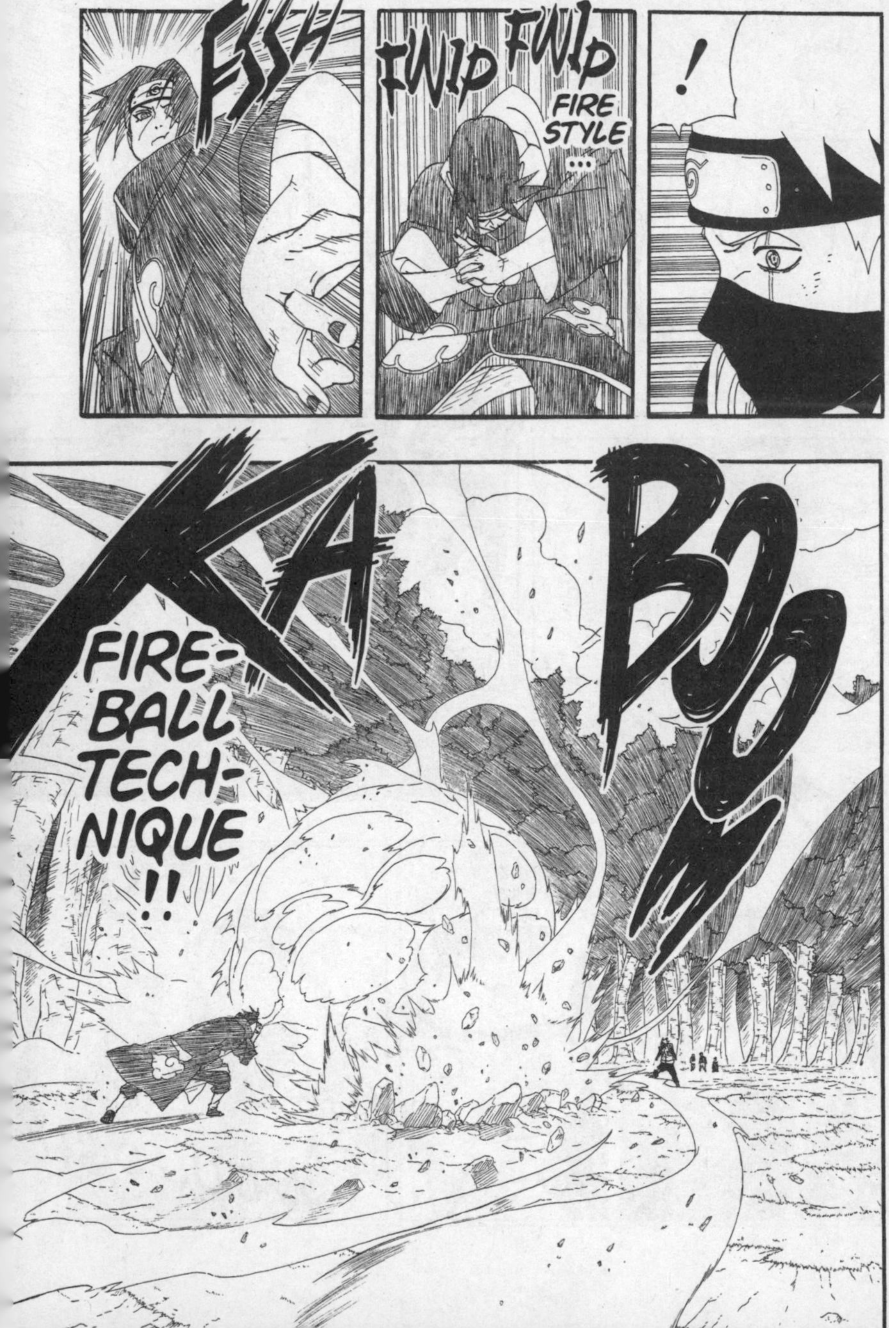
!
FWIP FWIP
FIRE STYLE ...
FSSH
KABOOM
FIRE-BALL TECH-NIQUE!!

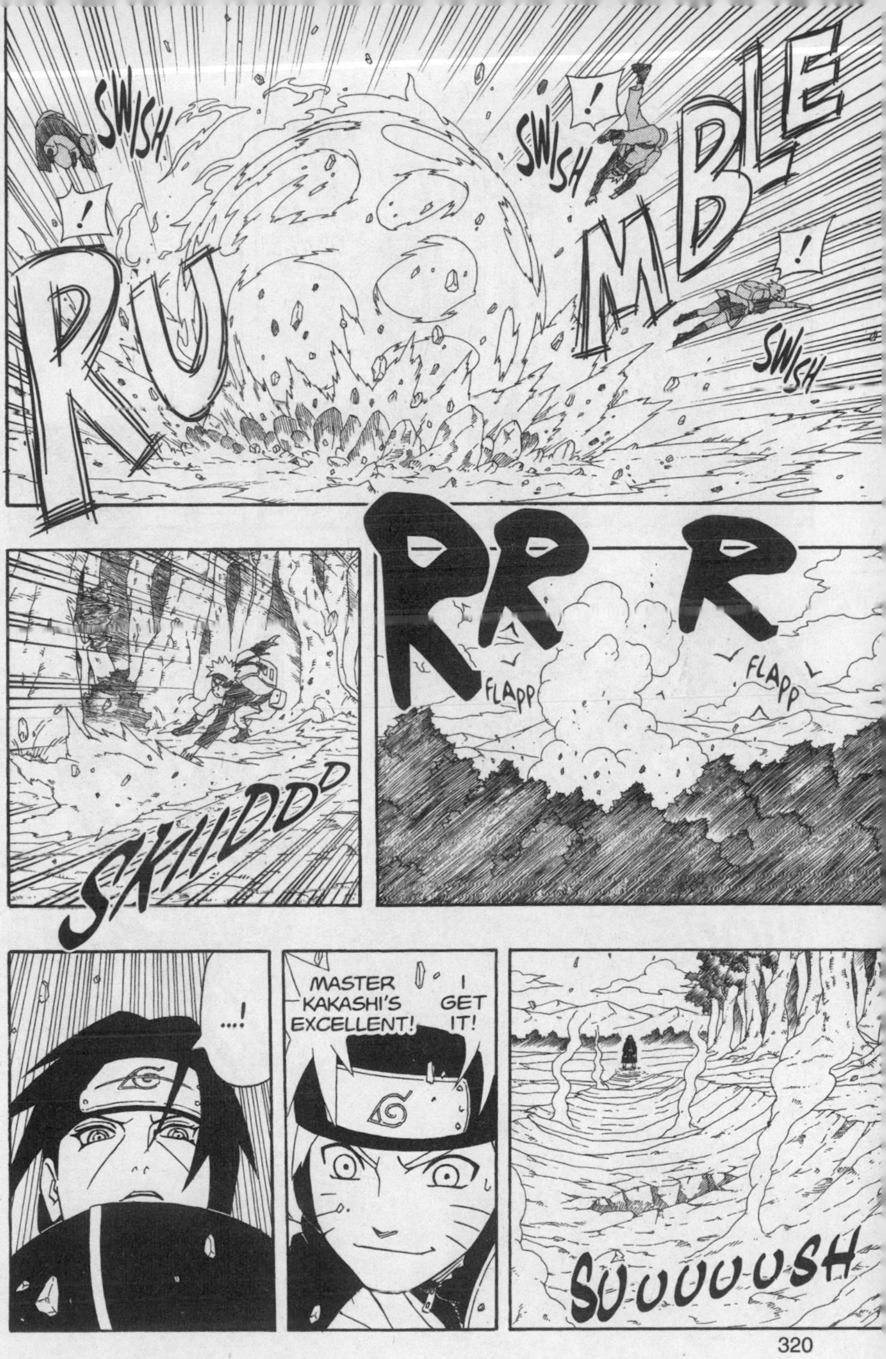
!
SWISH
RUMBLE
!
SWISH
SWISH
!
RRRR
FLAPP
FLAPP
SKIIDDDD
SUUUUUSH
I GET IT!
MASTER KAKASHI'S EXCELLENT!
...!

READ THIS WAY

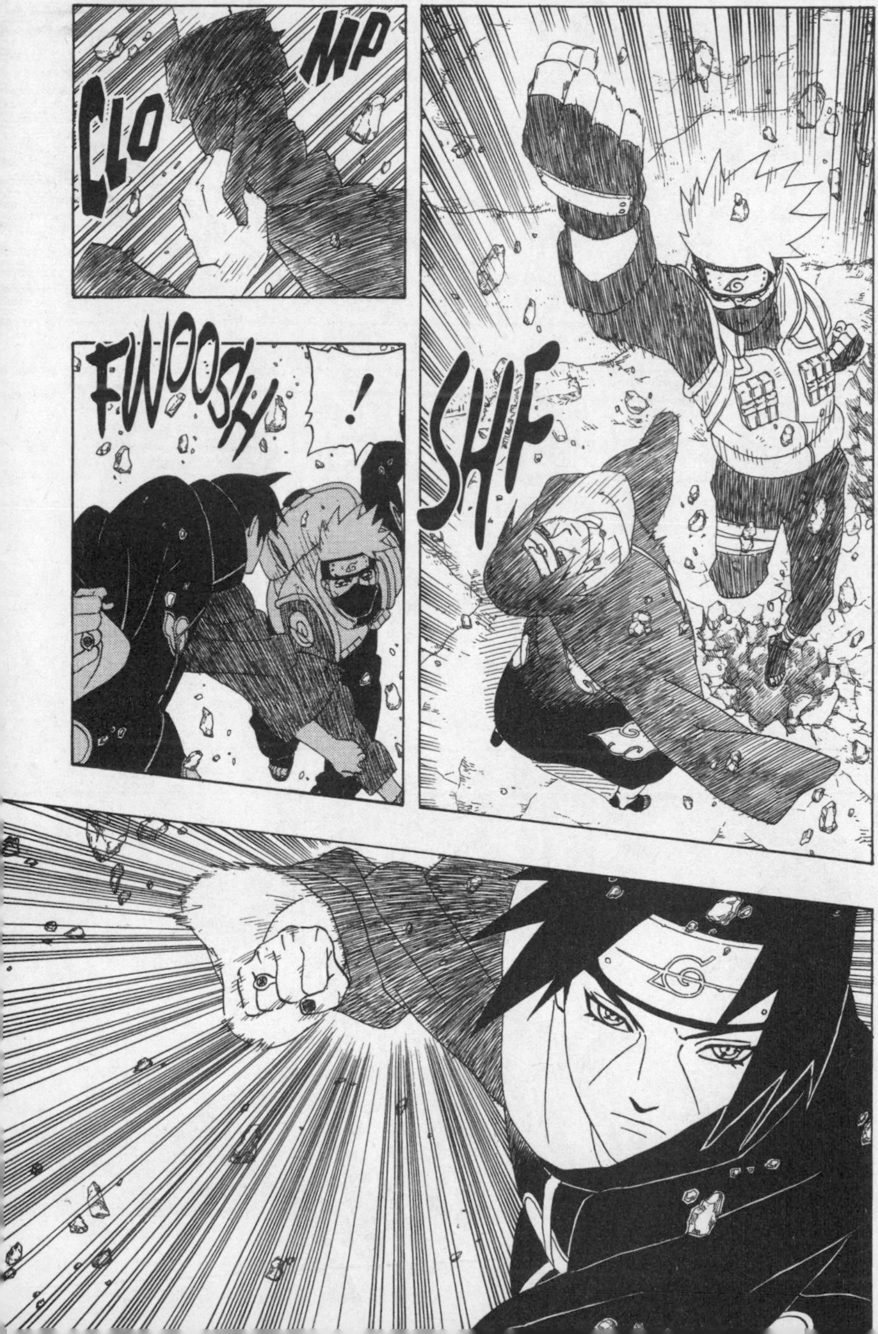
SHF
CLOMP
FWOOSH
!

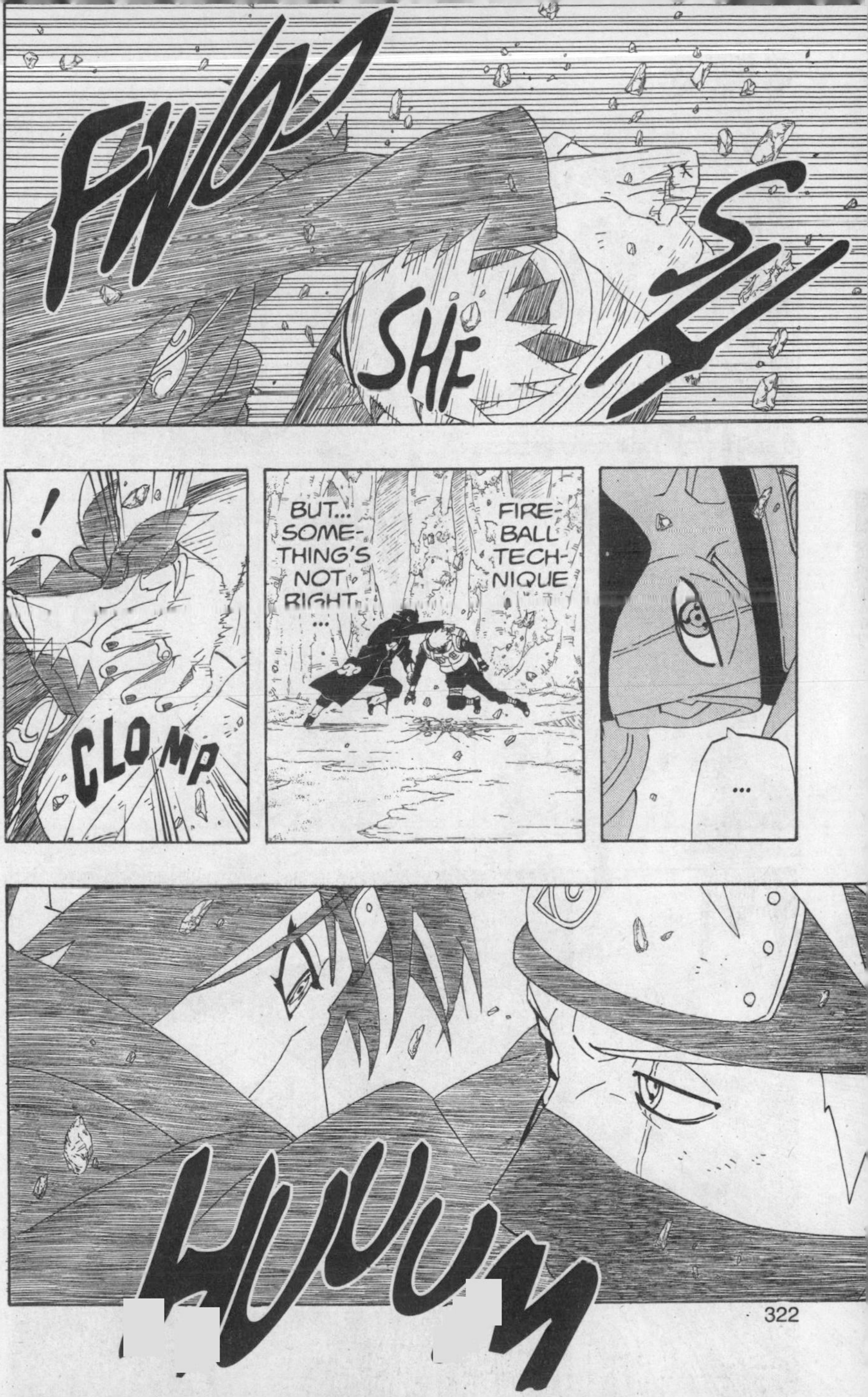
FWOOSH
SHF
...
FIRE-BALL TECHNIQUE
BUT... SOMETHING'S NOT RIGHT...
!
CLOMP
HWUUM

READ THIS WAY

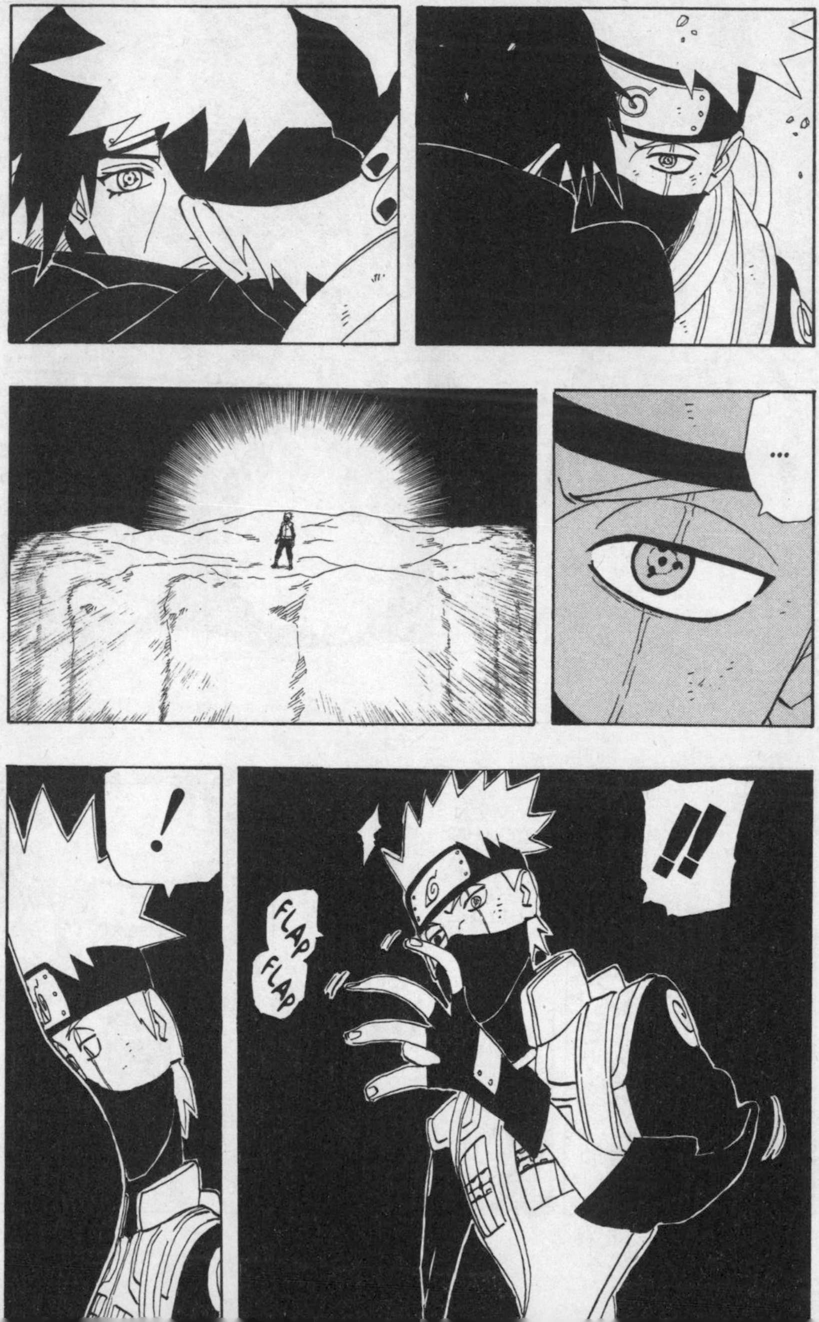
...
!!
FLAP FLAP
!

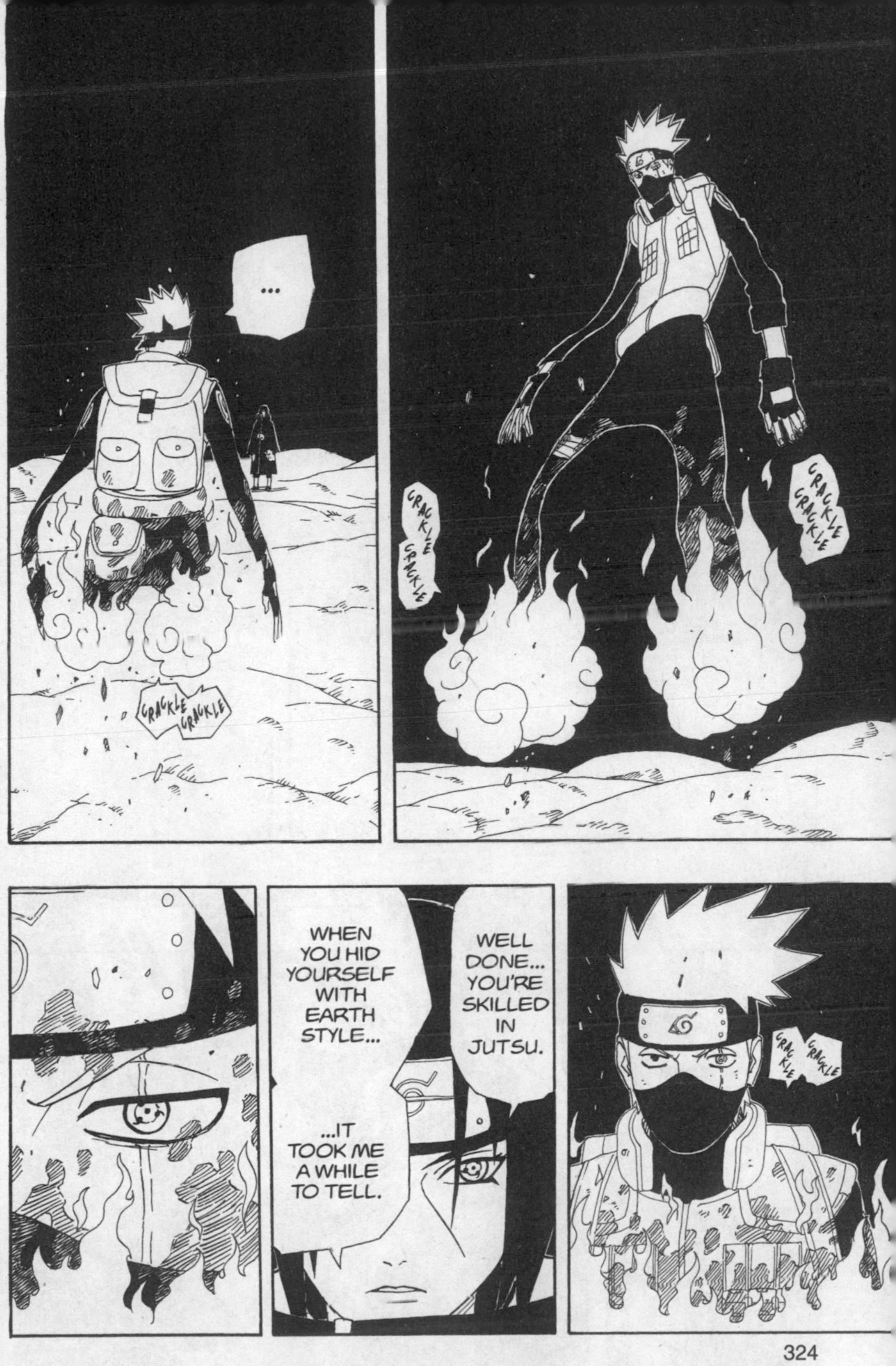
CRACKLE CRACKLE
CRACKLE CRACKLE
...
CRACKLE CRACKLE
CRACKLE CRACKLE
WELL DONE... YOU'RE SKILLED IN JUTSU.
WHEN YOU HID YOURSELF WITH EARTH STYLE...
...IT TOOK ME A WHILE TO TELL.

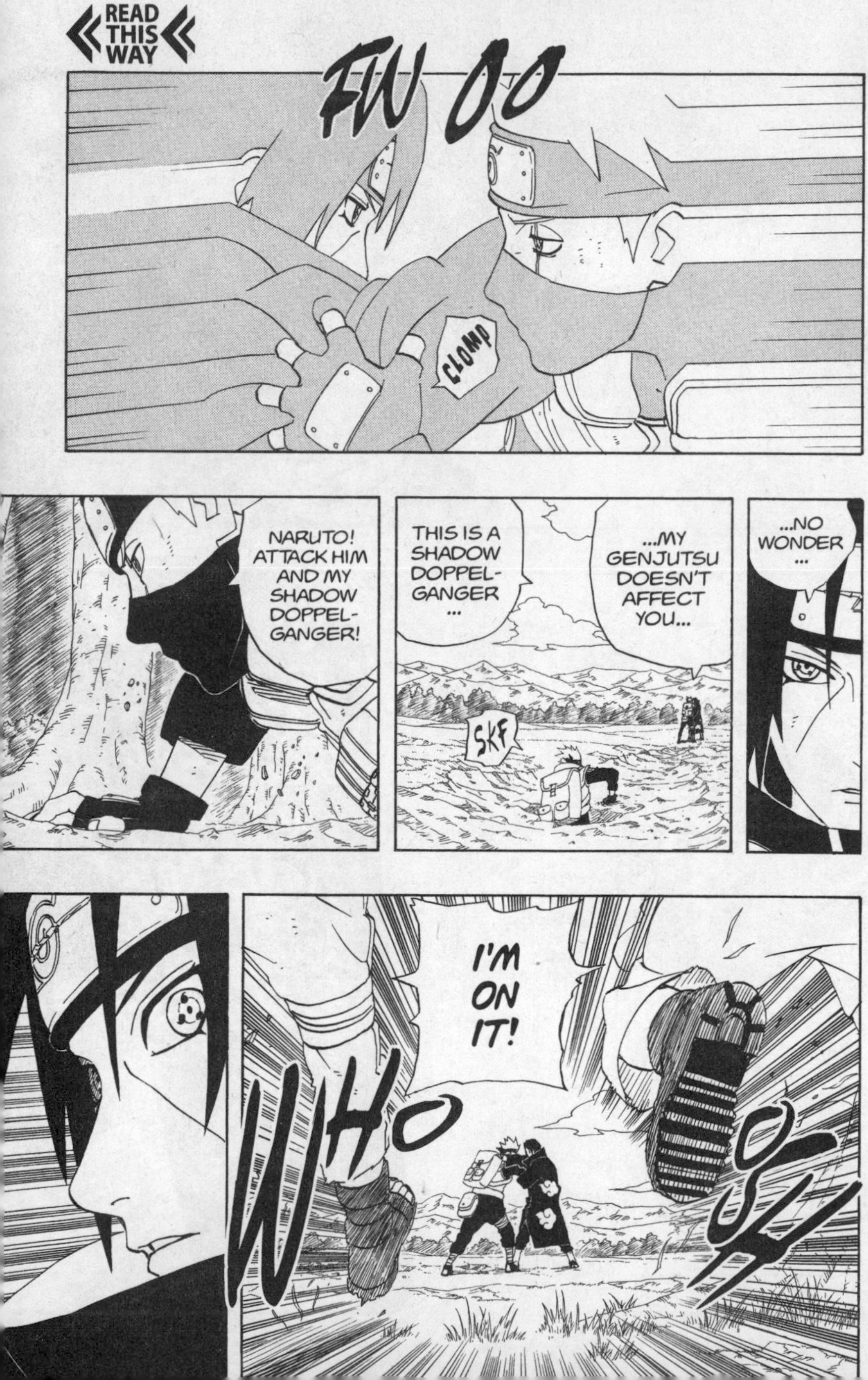
READ THIS WAY
FWOO
CLOMP
...NO WONDER ...
...MY GENJUTSU DOESN'T AFFECT YOU...
THIS IS A SHADOW DOPPEL-GANGER ...
SKF
NARUTO! ATTACK HIM AND MY SHADOW DOPPEL-GANGER!
I'M ON IT!
WHOOSH

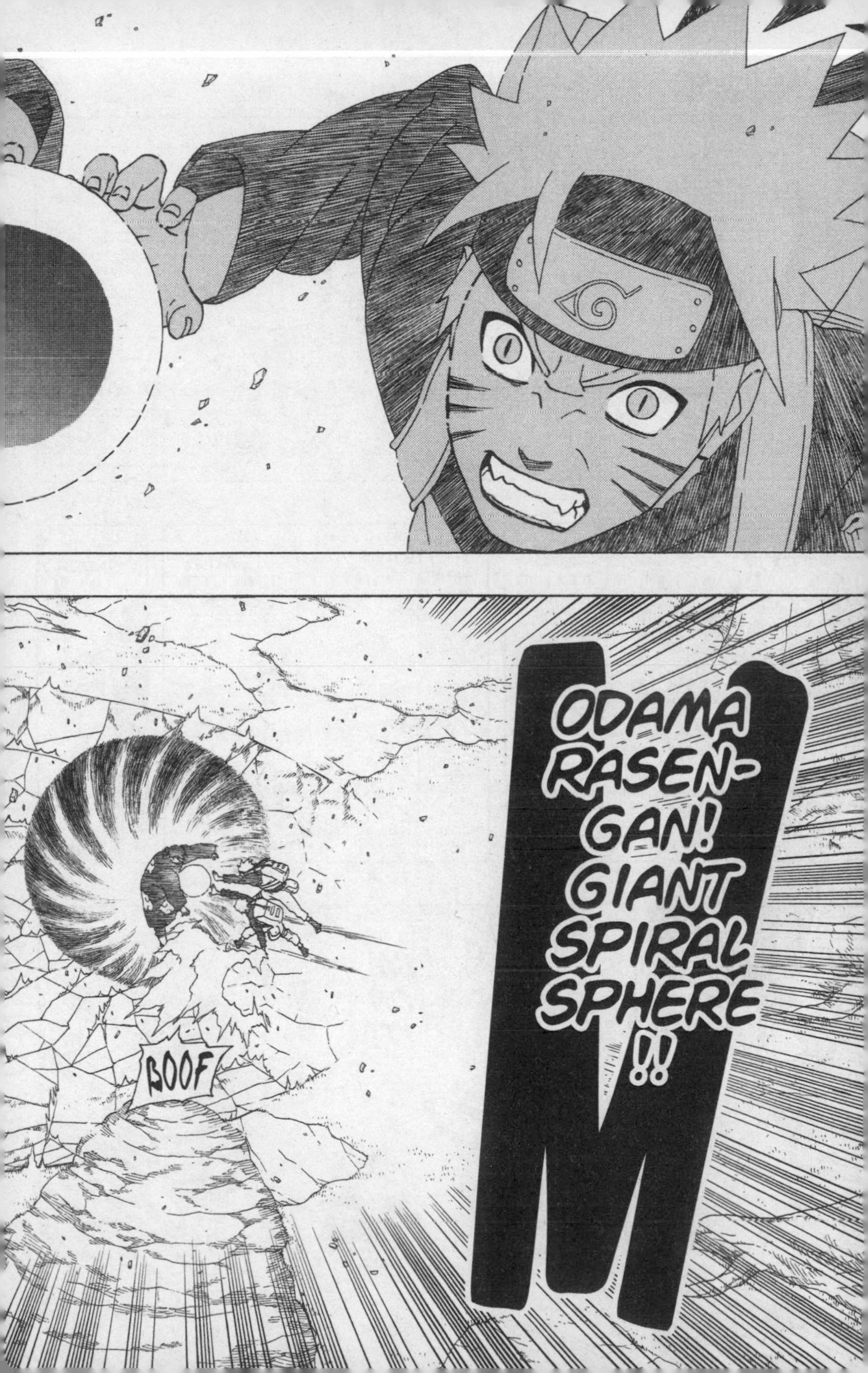
ODAMA RASEN-GAN! GIANT SPIRAL SPHERE!!
BOOF

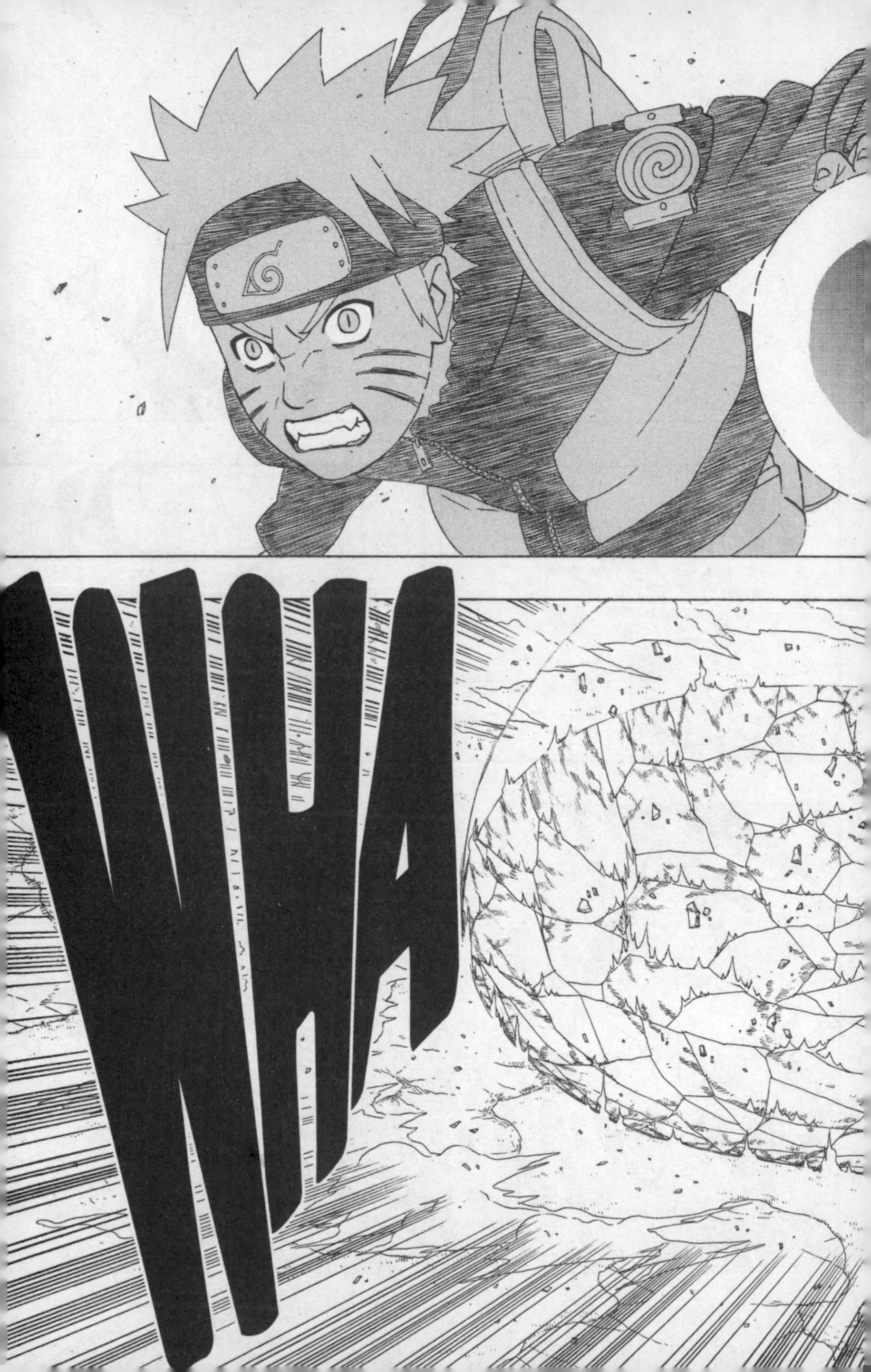
WHA

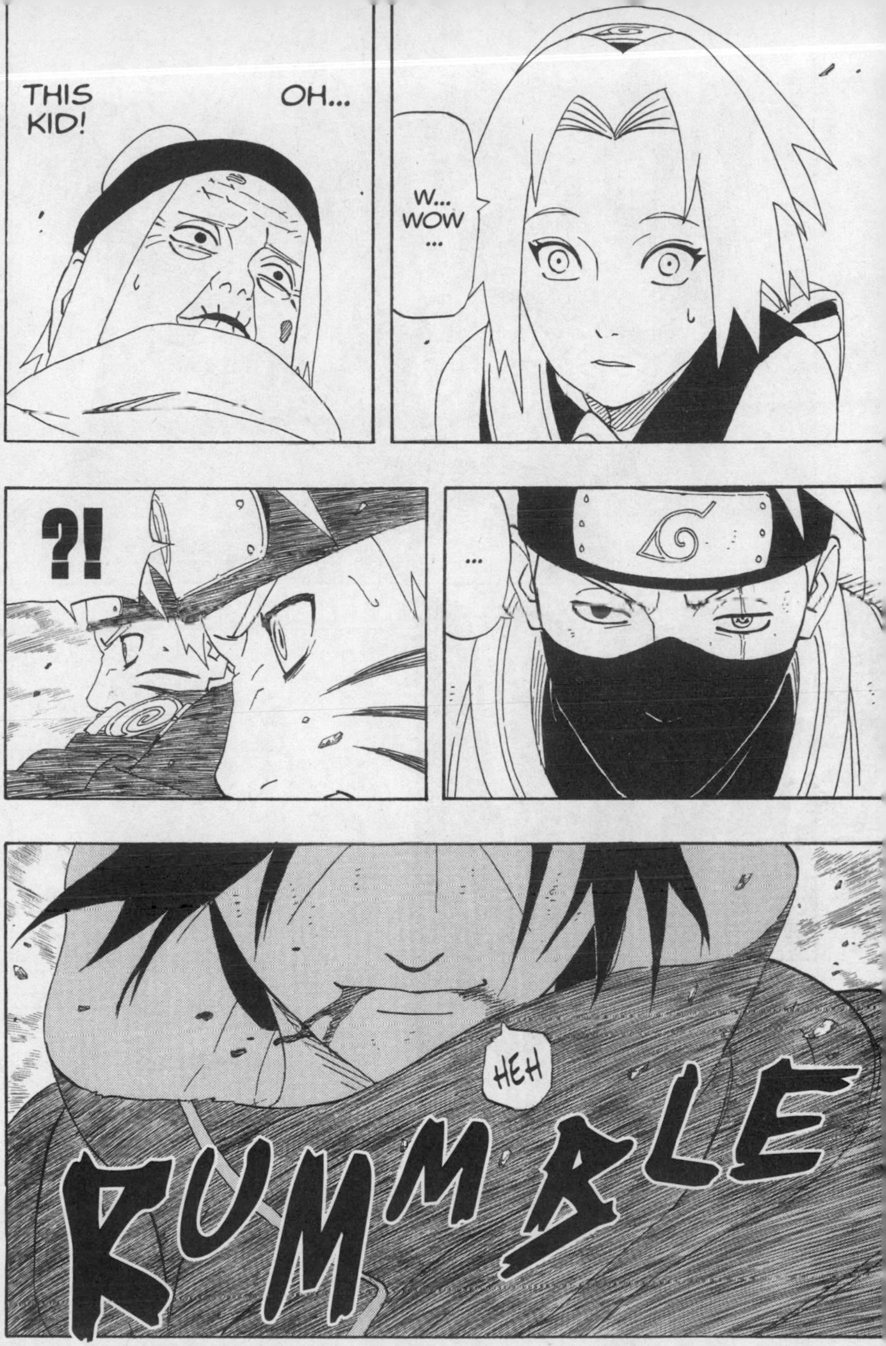
W... WOW ...
OH...
THIS KID!
...
?!
HEH
RUMMBLE

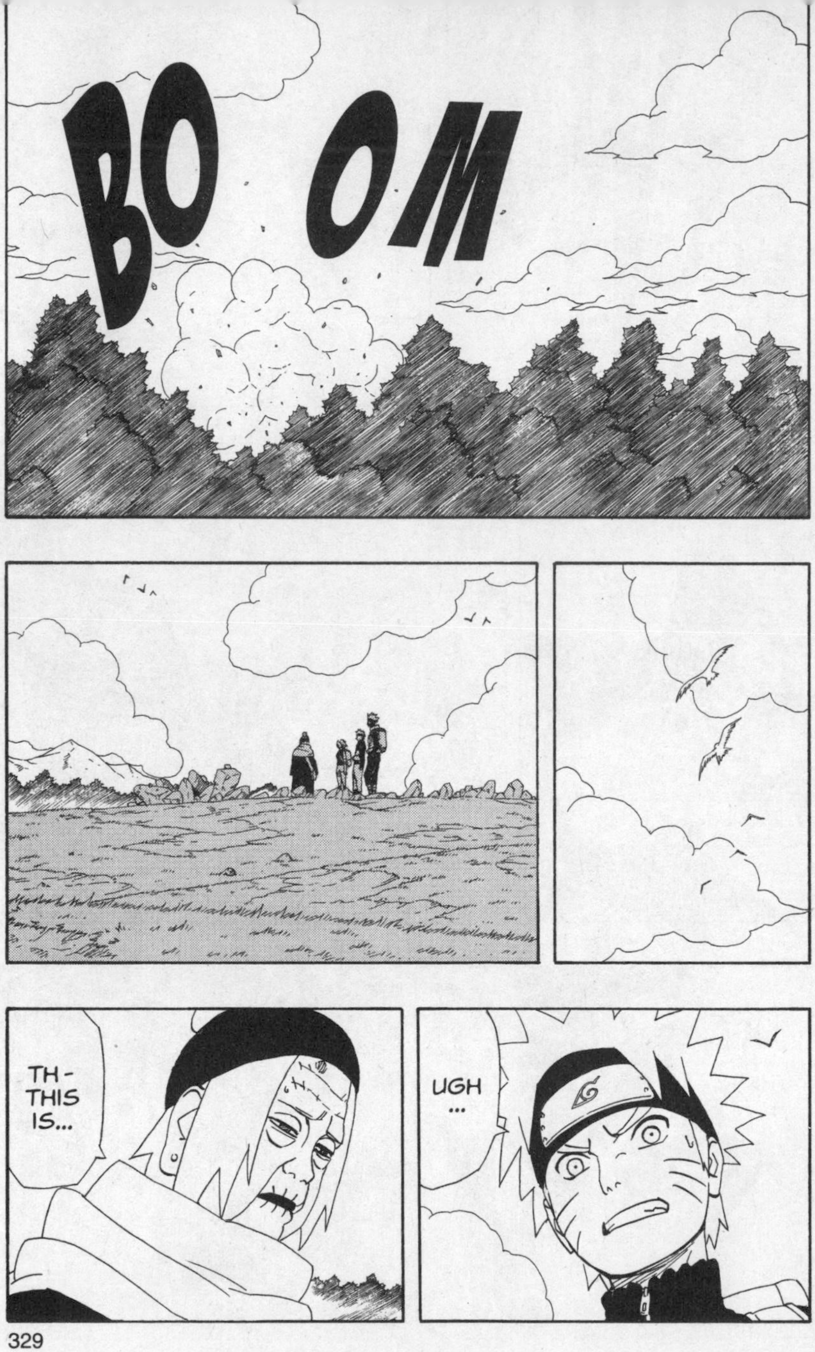
BOOM
UGH ...
TH- THIS IS...

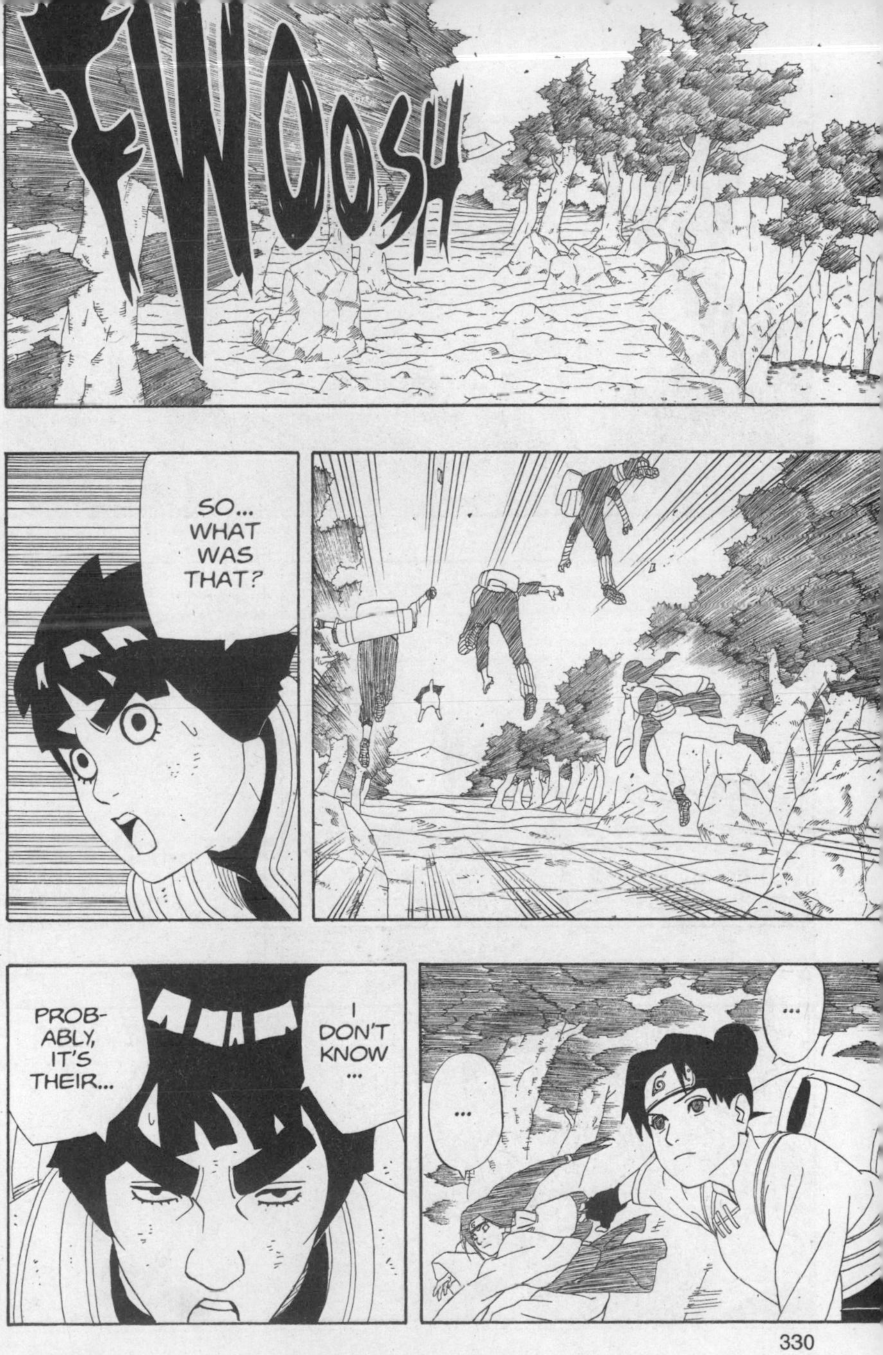
FWOOSH
SO... WHAT WAS THAT?
...
...
I DON'T KNOW ...
PROB-ABLY, IT'S THEIR...

READ THIS WAY

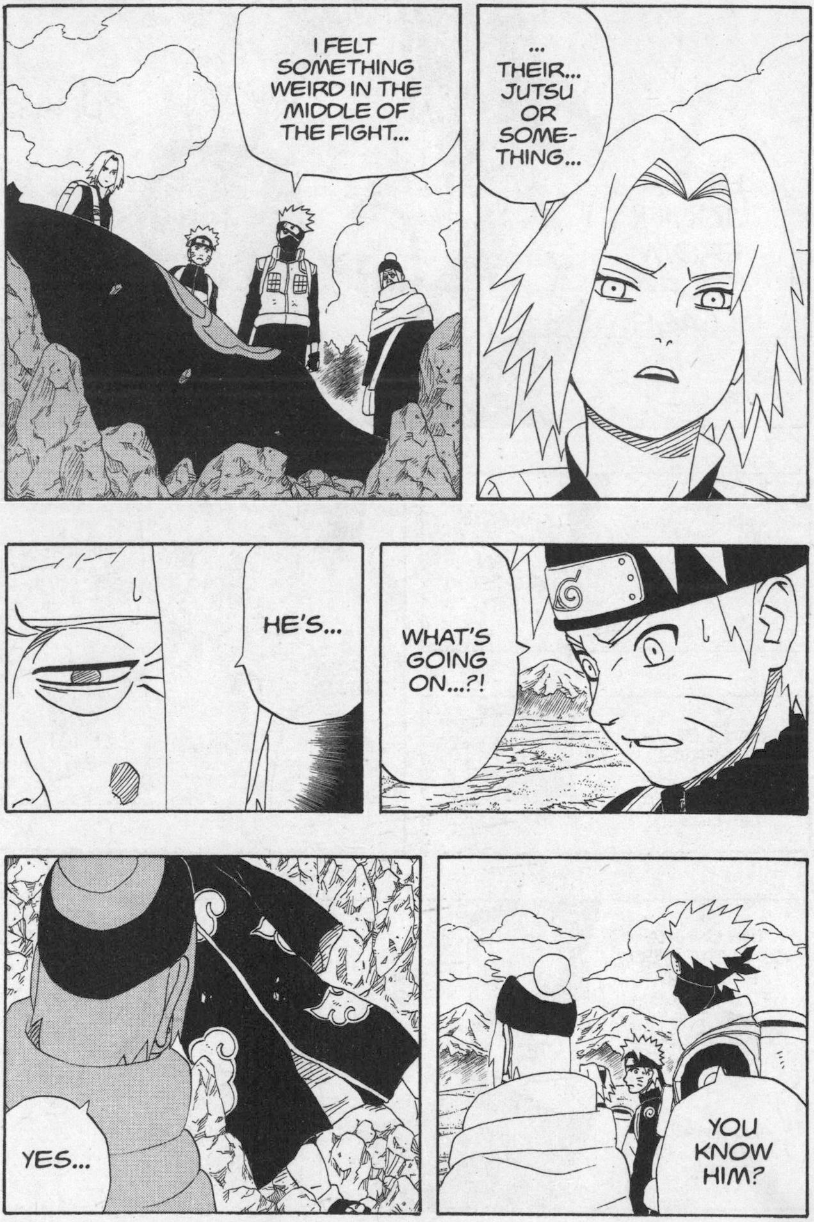

... THEIR... JUTSU OR SOME-THING...
I FELT SOMETHING WEIRD IN THE MIDDLE OF THE FIGHT...
WHAT'S GOING ON...?!
HE'S...
YOU KNOW HIM?
YES...

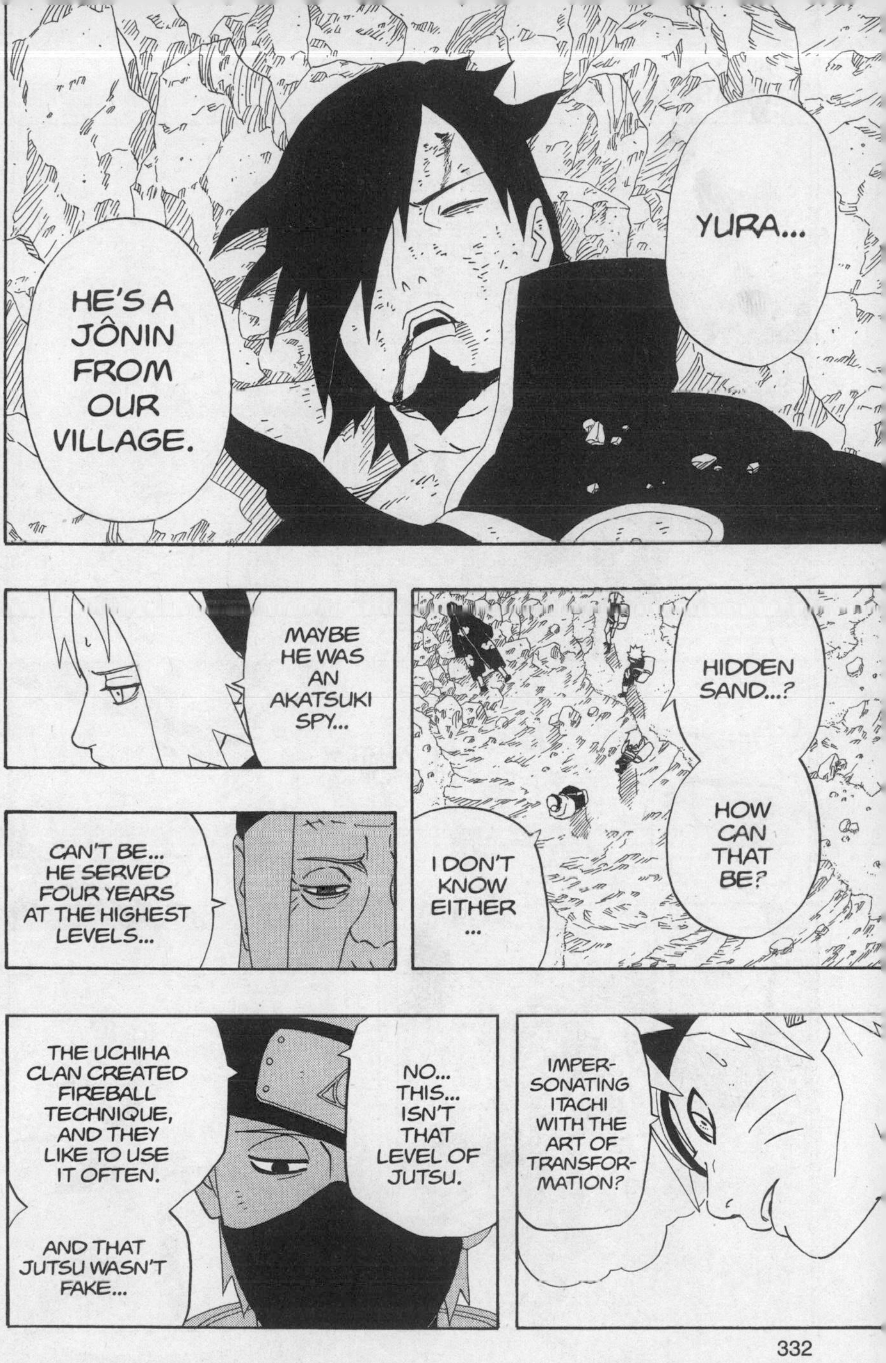
YURA...
HE'S A JÔNIN FROM OUR VILLAGE.
HIDDEN SAND...?
HOW CAN THAT BE?
I DON'T KNOW EITHER ...
MAYBE HE WAS AN AKATSUKI SPY...
CAN'T BE... HE SERVED FOUR YEARS AT THE HIGHEST LEVELS...
IMPER-SONATING ITACHI WITH THE ART OF TRANSFOR-MATION?
NO... THIS... ISN'T THAT LEVEL OF JUTSU.
THE UCHIHA CLAN CREATED FIREBALL TECHNIQUE, AND THEY LIKE TO USE IT OFTEN.
AND THAT JUTSU WASN'T FAKE...

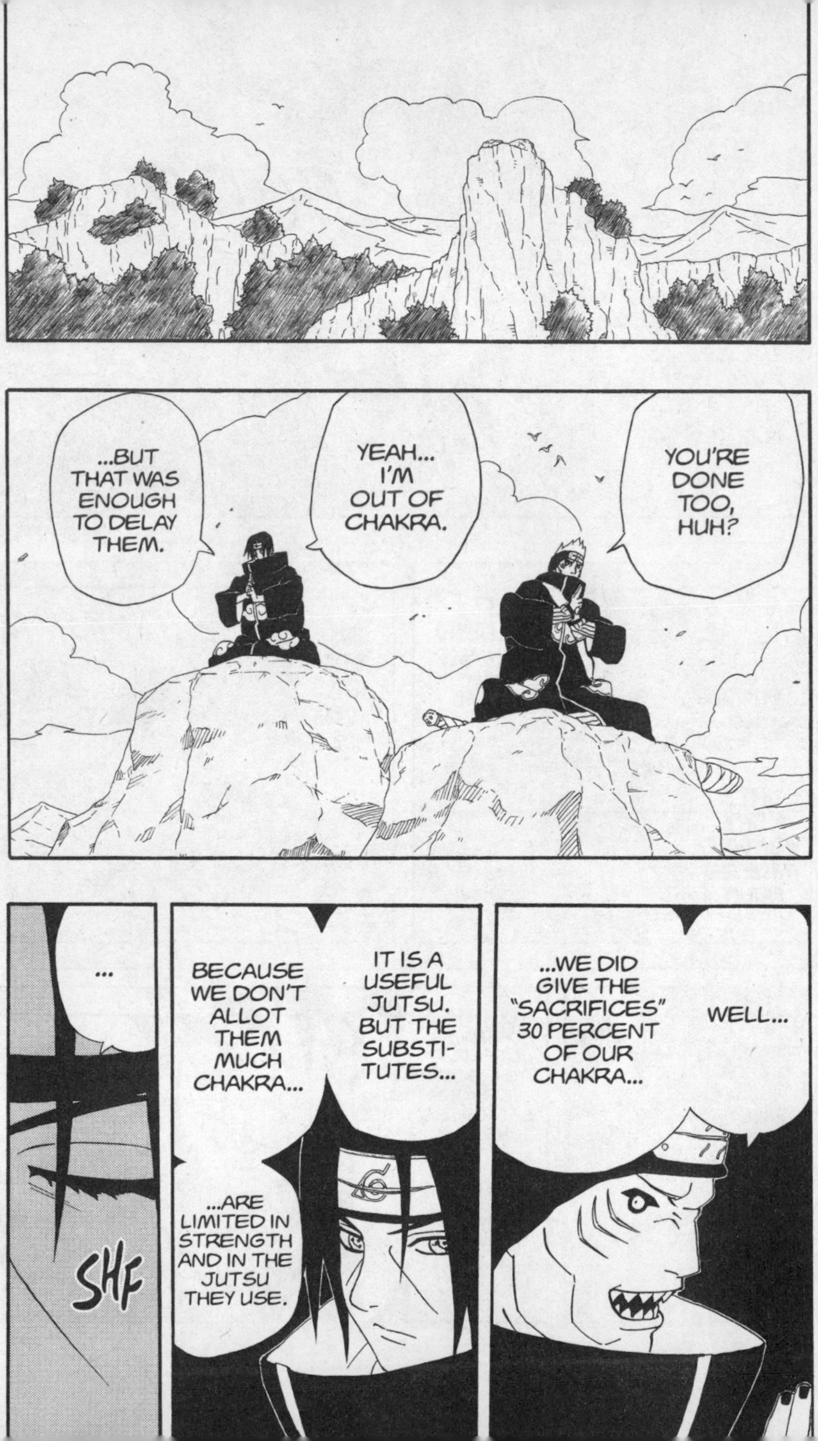
YOU'RE DONE TOO, HUH?
YEAH... I'M OUT OF CHAKRA.
...BUT THAT WAS ENOUGH TO DELAY THEM.
WELL...
...WE DID GIVE THE "SACRIFICES" 30 PERCENT OF OUR CHAKRA...
IT IS A USEFUL JUTSU. BUT THE SUBSTITUTES...
...ARE LIMITED IN STRENGTH AND IN THE JUTSU THEY USE.
BECAUSE WE DON'T ALLOT THEM MUCH CHAKRA...
...
SHF

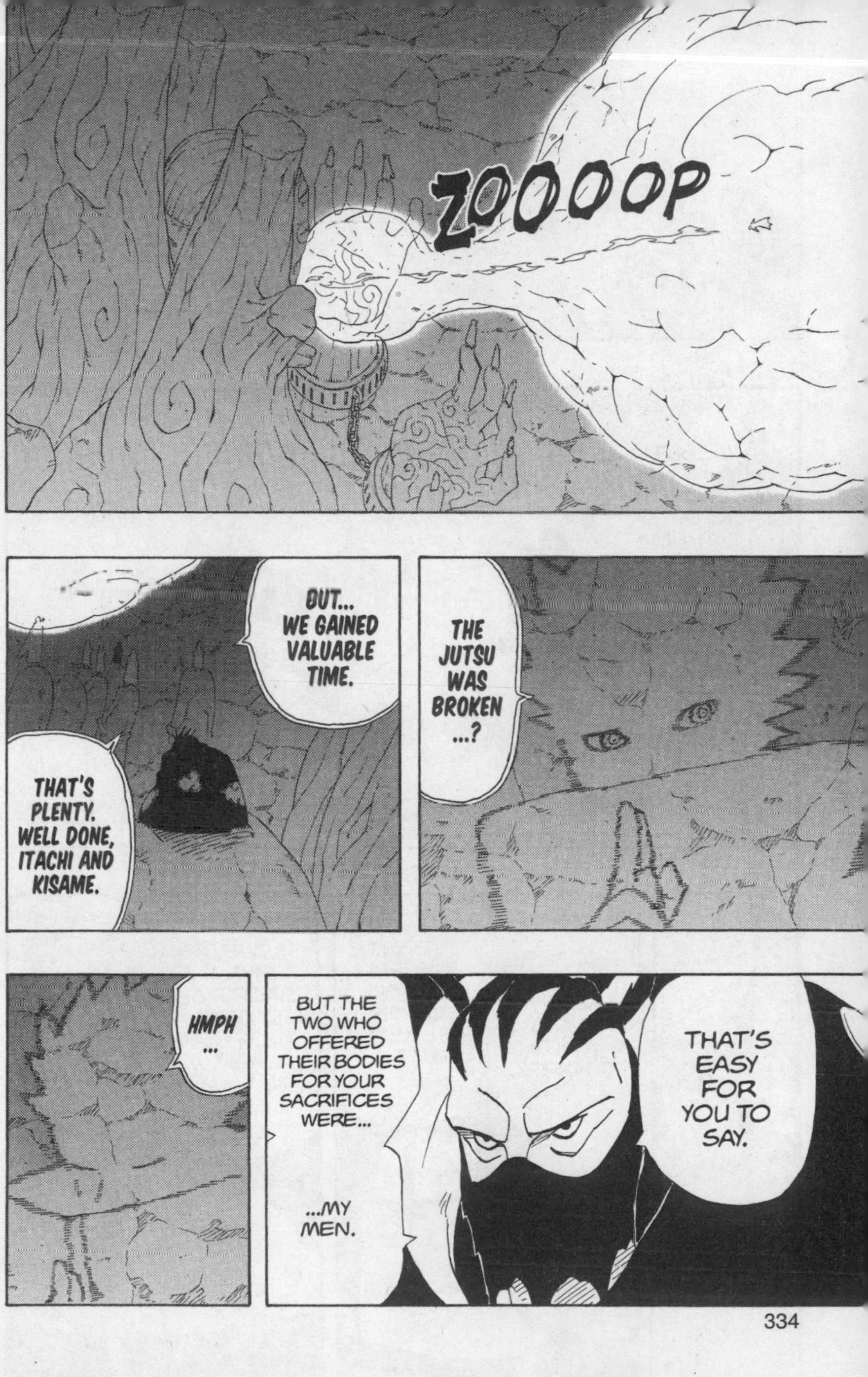
ZOOOOP
THE JUTSU WAS BROKEN ...?
BUT... WE GAINED VALUABLE TIME.
THAT'S PLENTY. WELL DONE, ITACHI AND KISAME.
THAT'S EASY FOR YOU TO SAY.
BUT THE TWO WHO OFFERED THEIR BODIES FOR YOUR SACRIFICES WERE...
...MY MEN.
HMPH ...

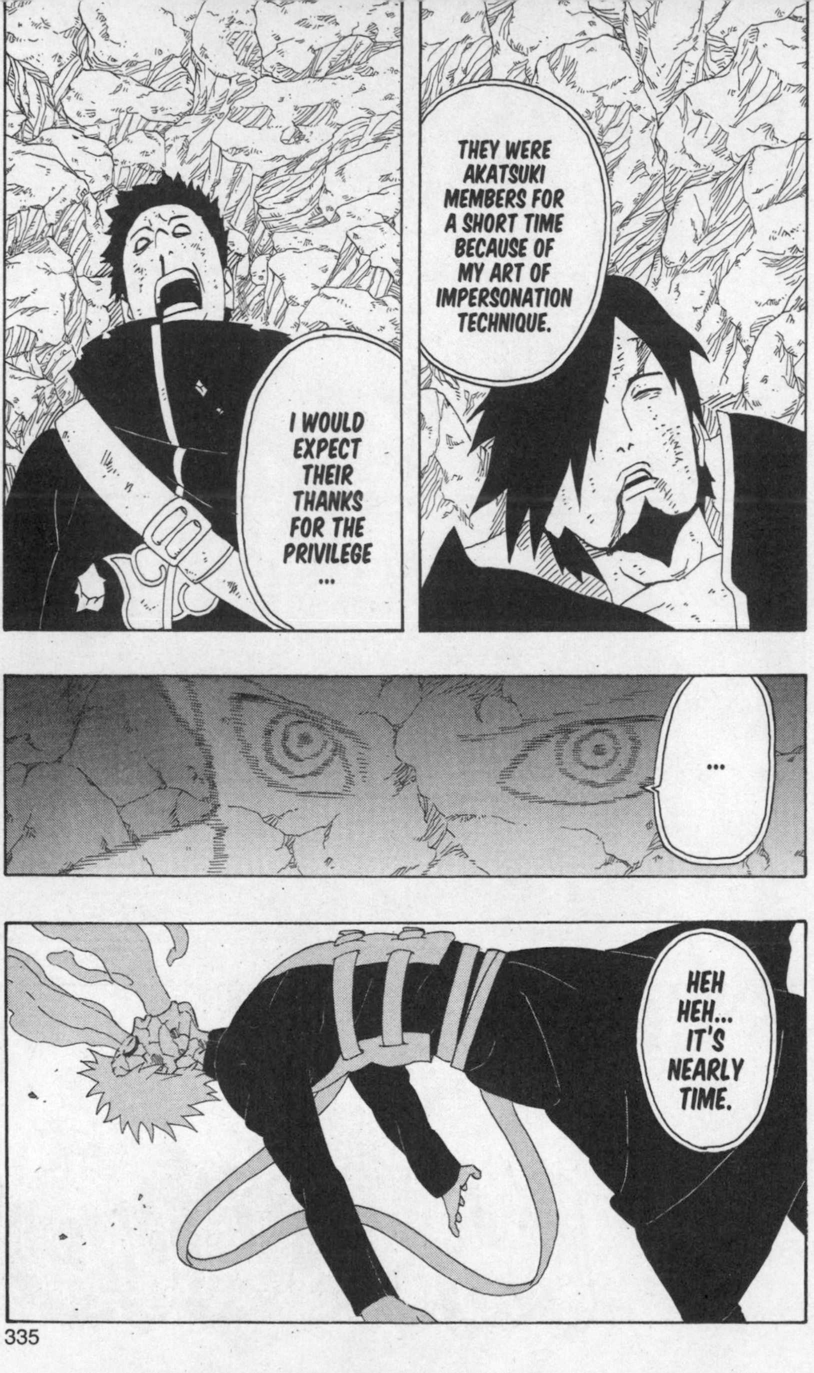
THEY WERE AKATSUKI MEMBERS FOR A SHORT TIME BECAUSE OF MY ART OF IMPERSONATION TECHNIQUE.
I WOULD EXPECT THEIR THANKS FOR THE PRIVILEGE ...
...
HEH HEH... IT'S NEARLY TIME.

NARUTO

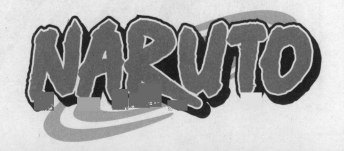

Number 261: Jinchûriki Host...!!

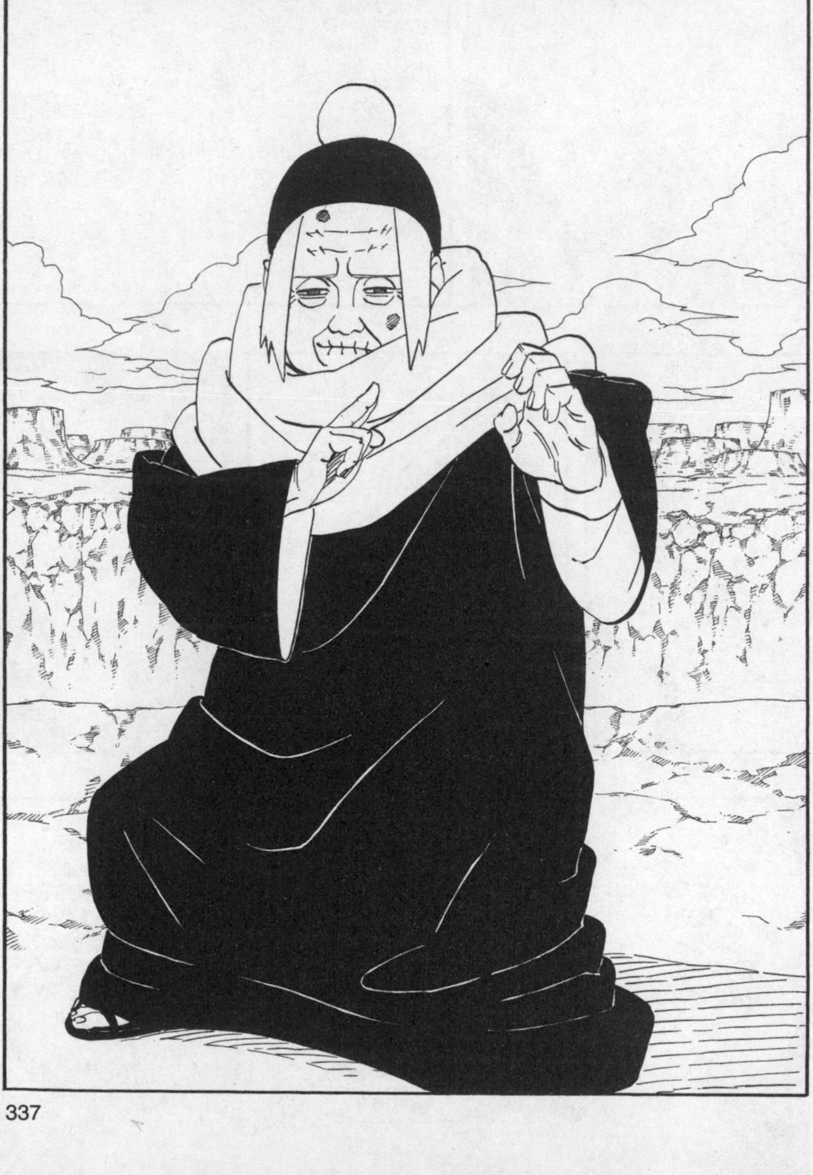

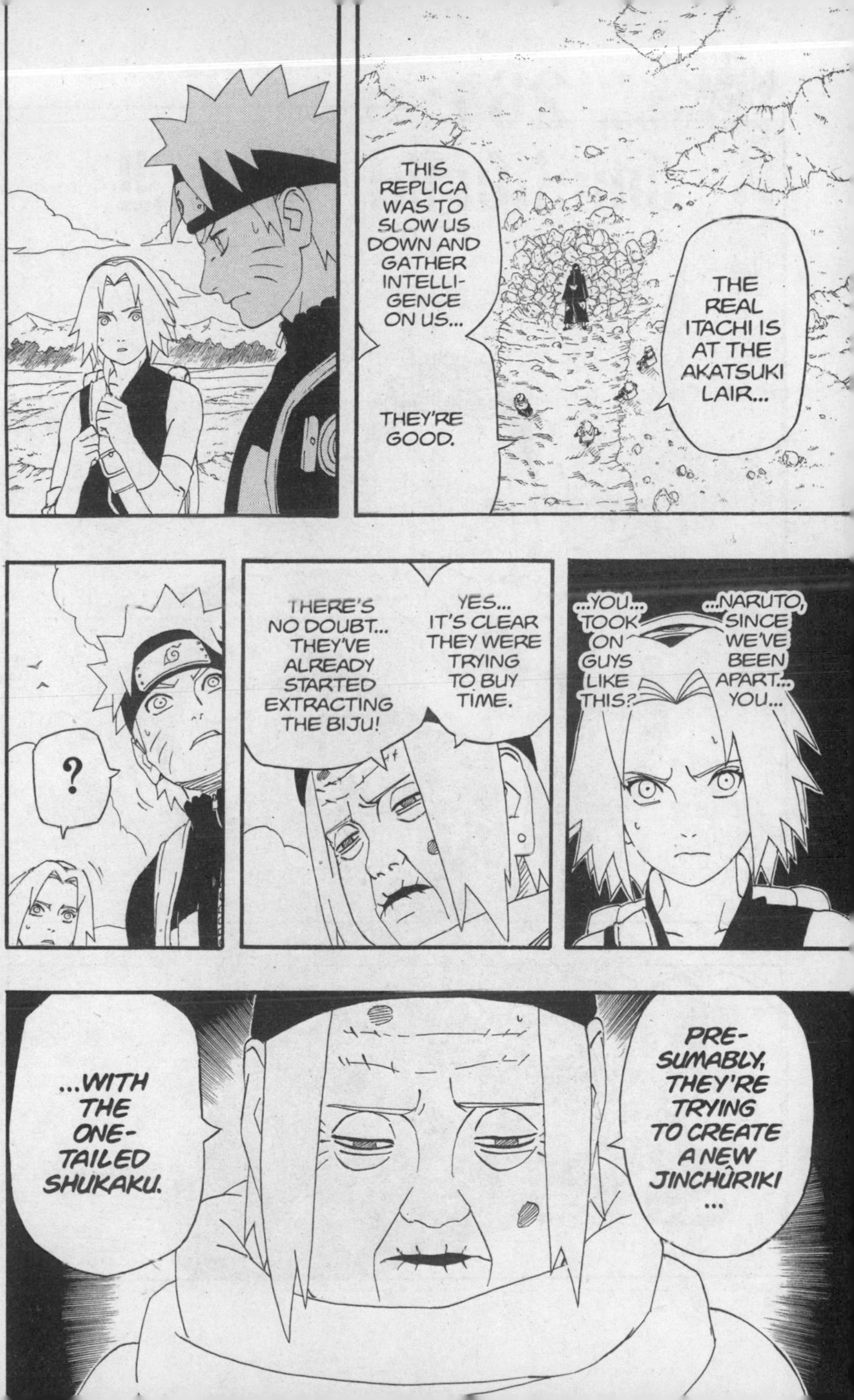
THE REAL ITACHI IS AT THE AKATSUKI LAIR...
THIS REPLICA WAS TO SLOW US DOWN AND GATHER INTELLIGENCE ON US...
THEY'RE GOOD.
...NARUTO, SINCE WE'VE BEEN APART... YOU...
...YOU... TOOK ON GUYS LIKE THIS?
YES... IT'S CLEAR THEY WERE TRYING TO BUY TIME.
THERE'S NO DOUBT... THEY'VE ALREADY STARTED EXTRACTING THE BIJU!
?
PRESUMABLY, THEY'RE TRYING TO CREATE A NEW JINCHÛRIKI ...
...WITH THE ONE-TAILED SHUKAKU.

READ THIS WAY

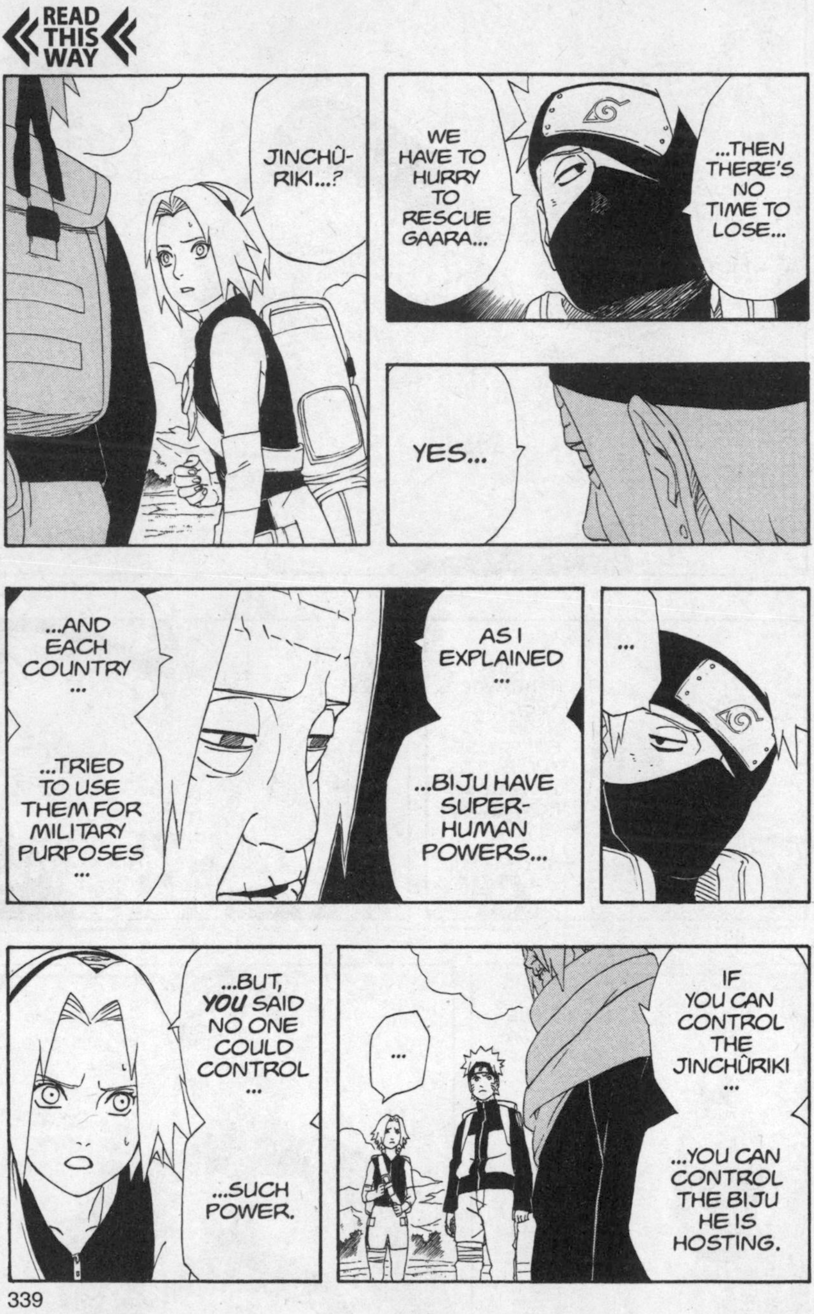
...THEN THERE'S NO TIME TO LOSE...
WE HAVE TO HURRY TO RESCUE GAARA...
YES...
JINCHÛ-RIKI...?
...
AS I EXPLAINED ...
...BIJU HAVE SUPER-HUMAN POWERS...
...AND EACH COUNTRY ...
...TRIED TO USE THEM FOR MILITARY PURPOSES ...
IF YOU CAN CONTROL THE JINCHÛRIKI ...
...YOU CAN CONTROL THE BIJU HE IS HOSTING.
...
...BUT, ***YOU*** SAID NO ONE COULD CONTROL ...
...SUCH POWER.

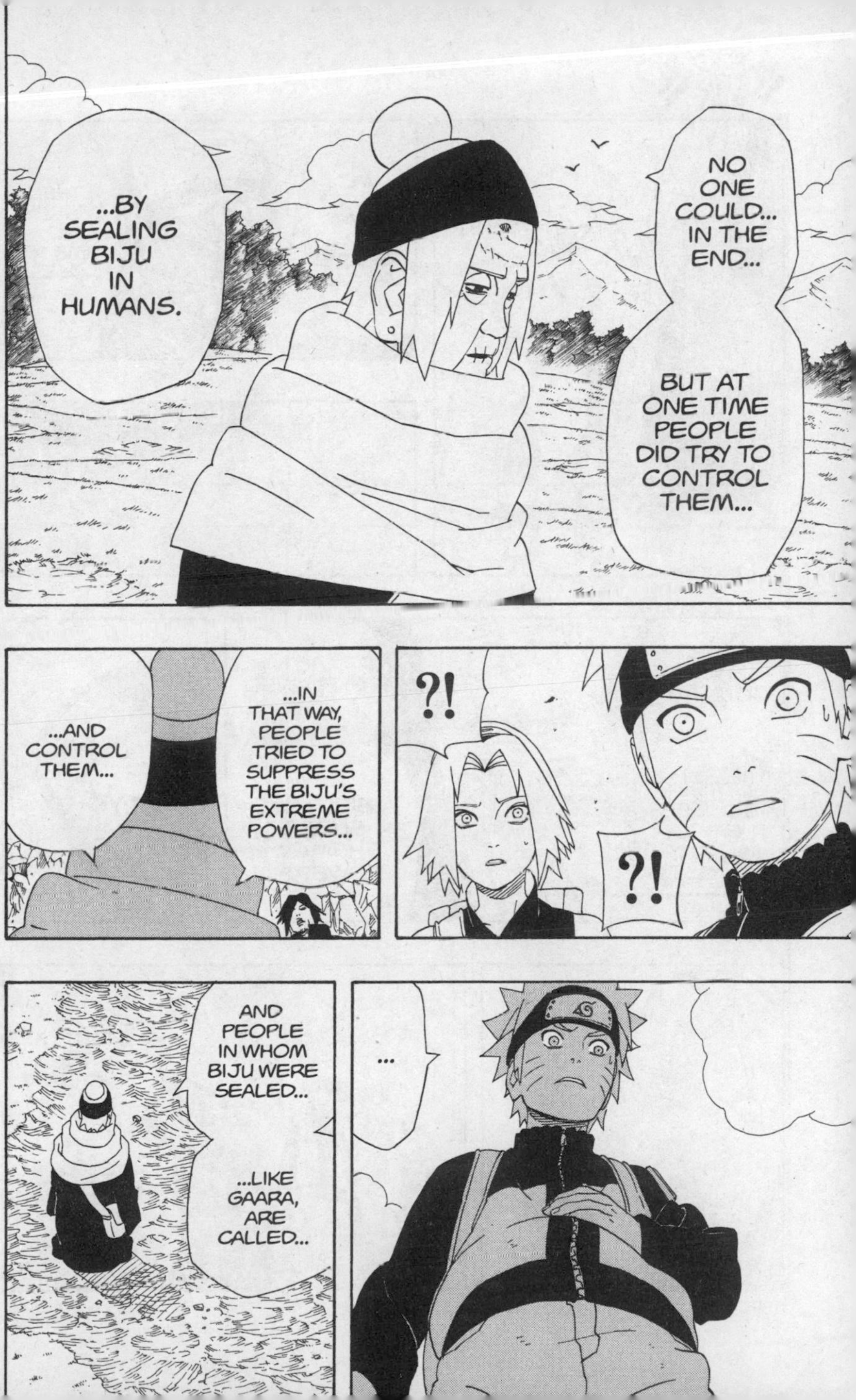
NO ONE COULD... IN THE END...
BUT AT ONE TIME PEOPLE DID TRY TO CONTROL THEM...
...BY SEALING BIJU IN HUMANS.
?!
?!
...IN THAT WAY, PEOPLE TRIED TO SUPPRESS THE BIJU'S EXTREME POWERS...
...AND CONTROL THEM...
...
AND PEOPLE IN WHOM BIJU WERE SEALED...
...LIKE GAARA, ARE CALLED...

READ THIS WAY

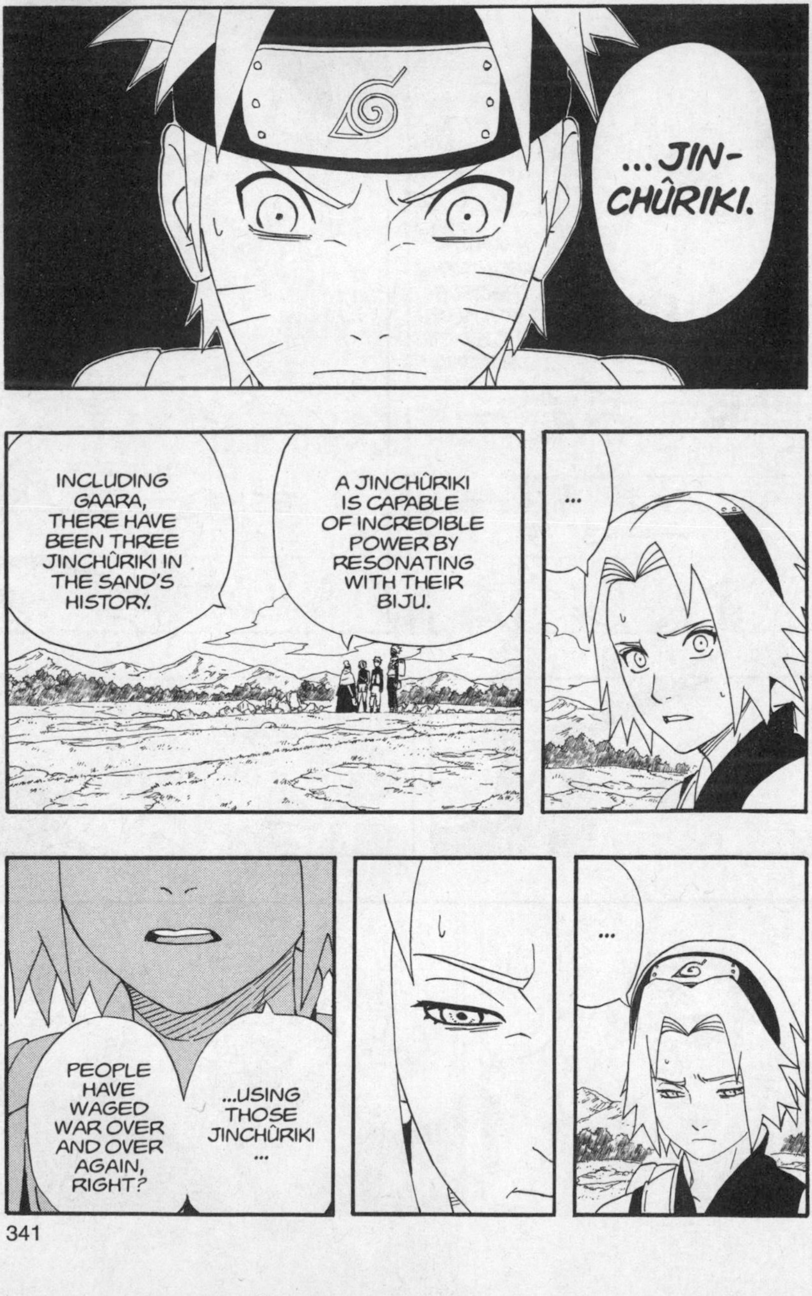

... JIN-CHÛRIKI.
...
A JINCHÛRIKI IS CAPABLE OF INCREDIBLE POWER BY RESONATING WITH THEIR BIJU.
INCLUDING GAARA, THERE HAVE BEEN THREE JINCHÛRIKI IN THE SAND'S HISTORY.
...
...USING THOSE JINCHÛRIKI ...
PEOPLE HAVE WAGED WAR OVER AND OVER AGAIN, RIGHT?

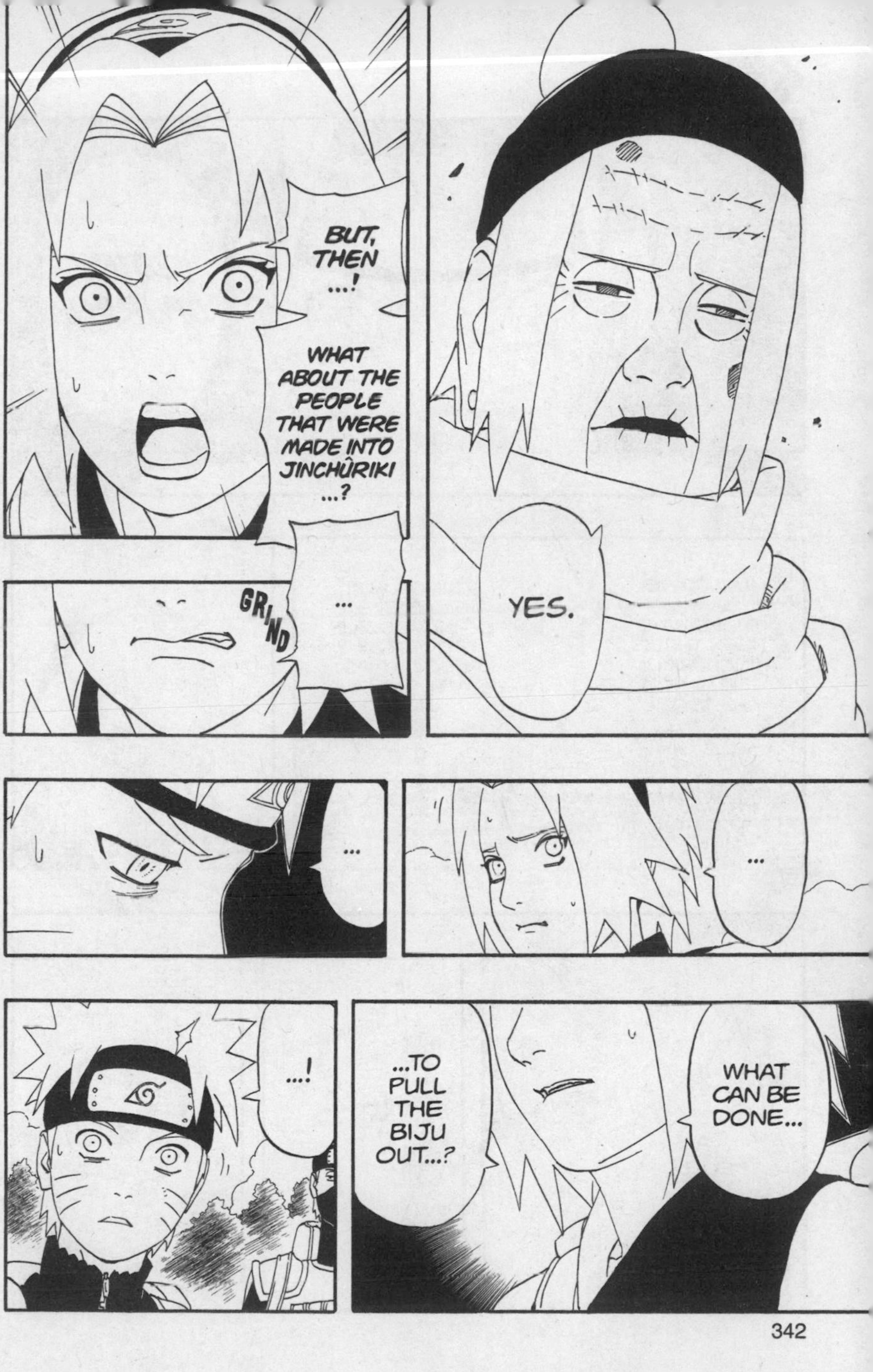
YES.
BUT, THEN ....!
WHAT ABOUT THE PEOPLE THAT WERE MADE INTO JINCHÛRIKI ...?
GRIND
...
...
...
WHAT CAN BE DONE...
...TO PULL THE BIJU OUT...?
....!

READ THIS WAY

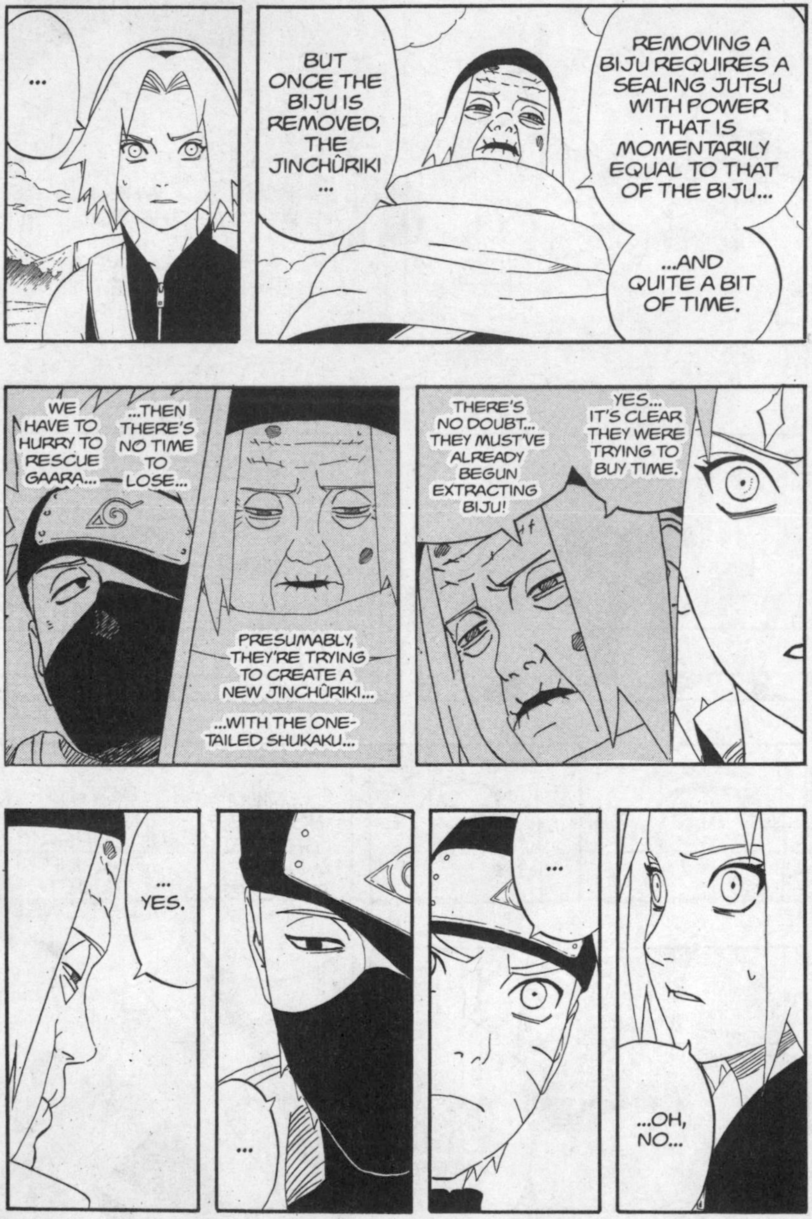
REMOVING A BIJU REQUIRES A SEALING JUTSU WITH POWER THAT IS MOMENTARILY EQUAL TO THAT OF THE BIJU...
...AND QUITE A BIT OF TIME.
BUT ONCE THE BIJU IS REMOVED, THE JINCHÛRIKI ...
...
YES... IT'S CLEAR THEY WERE TRYING TO BUY TIME.
THERE'S NO DOUBT... THEY MUST'VE ALREADY BEGUN EXTRACTING BIJU!
...THEN THERE'S NO TIME TO LOSE...
WE HAVE TO HURRY TO RESCUE GAARA...
PRESUMABLY, THEY'RE TRYING TO CREATE A NEW JINCHÛRIKI...
...WITH THE ONE-TAILED SHUKAKU...
...OH, NO...
...
...
... YES.

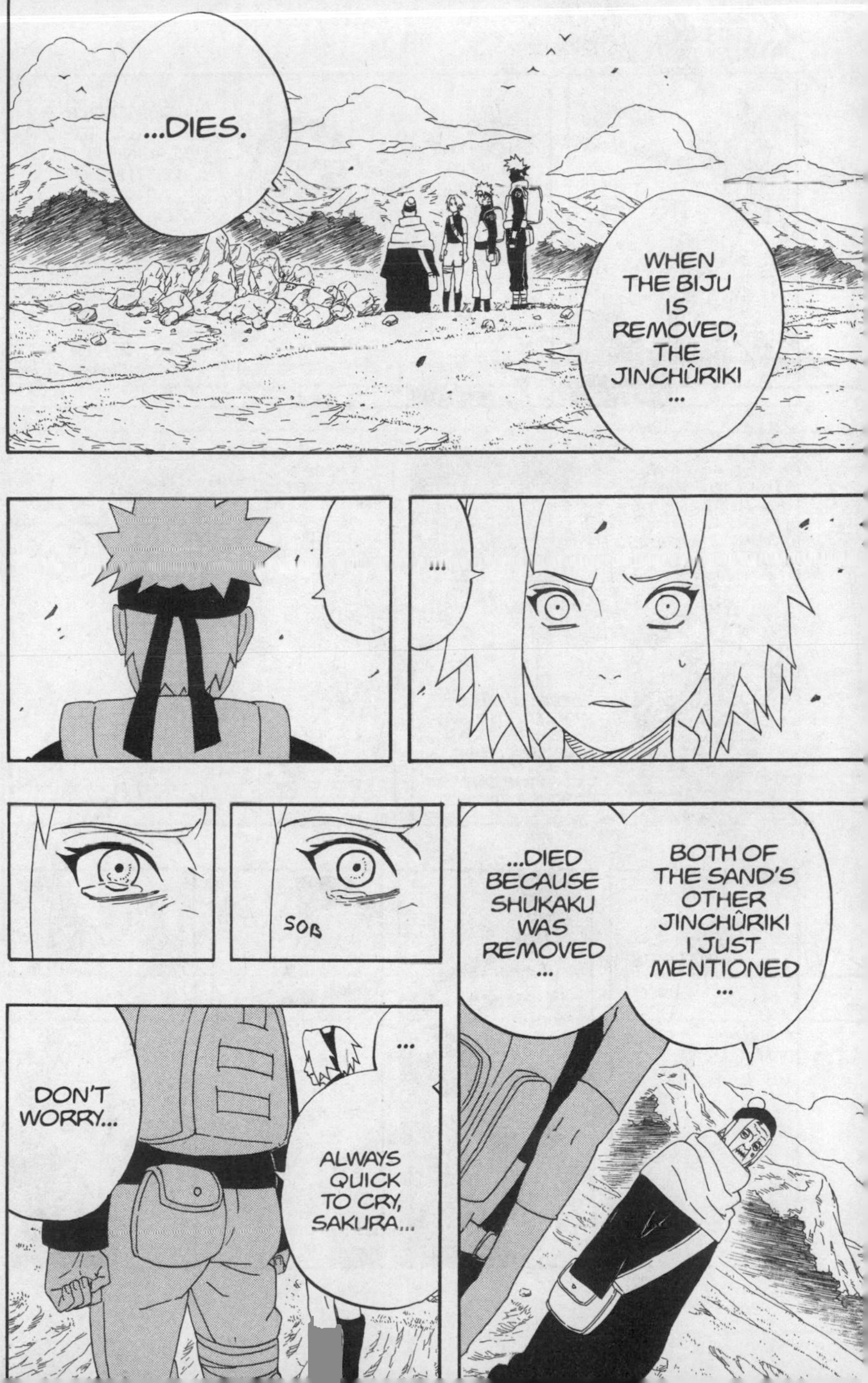
WHEN THE BIJU IS REMOVED, THE JINCHÛRIKI ...
...DIES.
...
BOTH OF THE SAND'S OTHER JINCHÛRIKI I JUST MENTIONED ...
...DIED BECAUSE SHUKAKU WAS REMOVED ...
SOB
...
ALWAYS QUICK TO CRY, SAKURA...
DON'T WORRY...

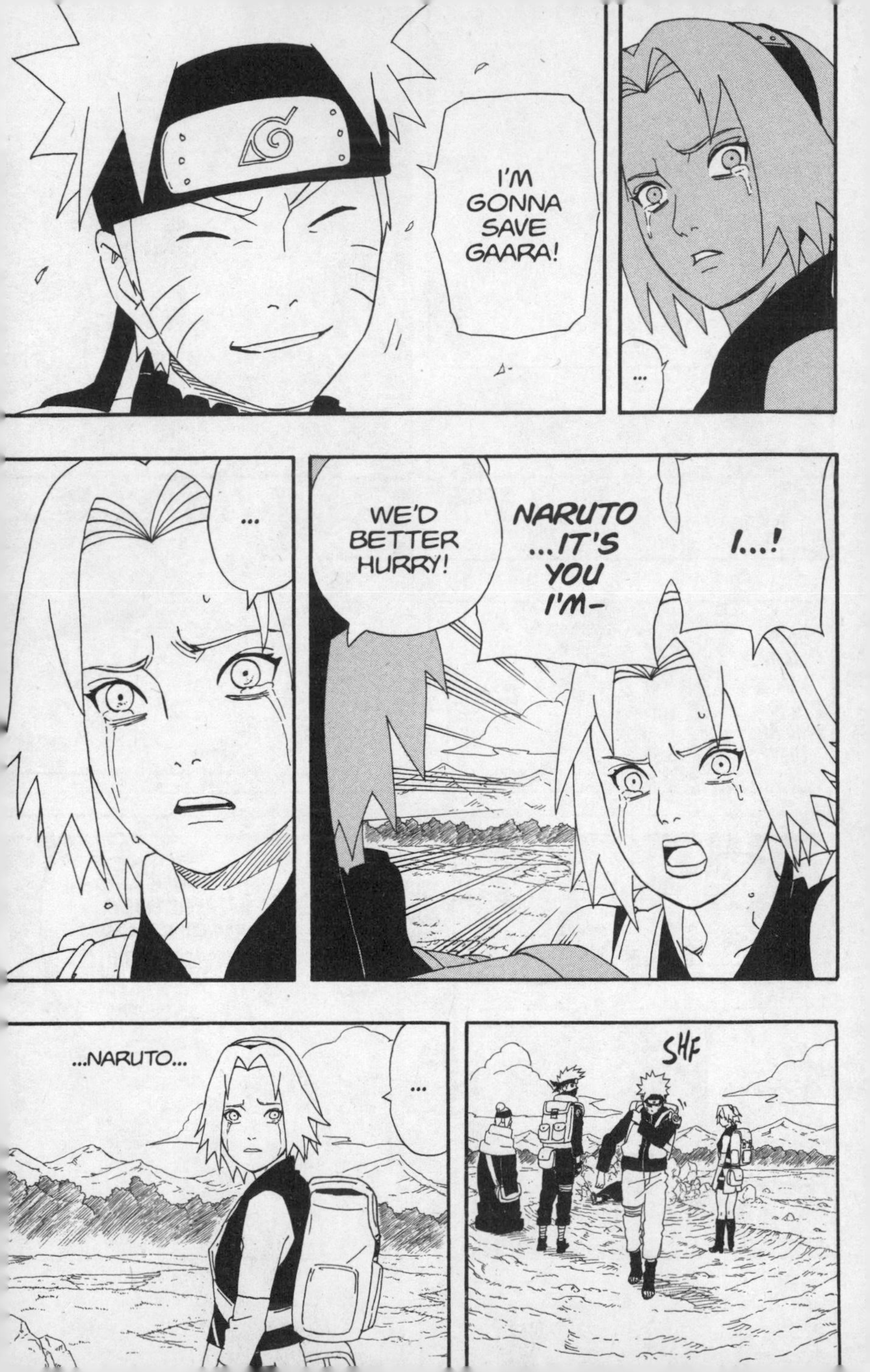
...
I'M GONNA SAVE GAARA!
I...!
NARUTO ...IT'S YOU I'M-
WE'D BETTER HURRY!
...
SHF
...
...NARUTO...

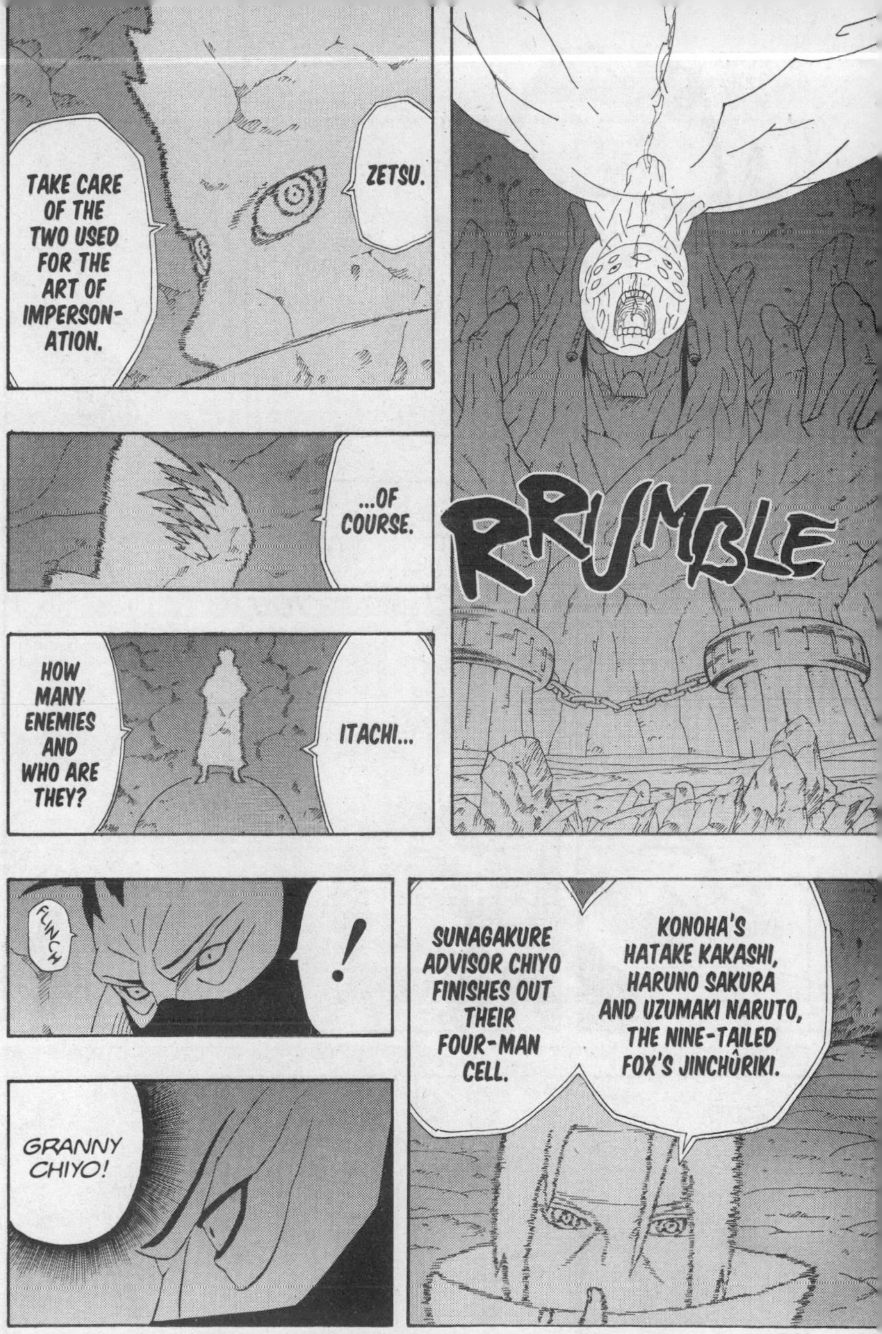
RRUMBLE
ZETSU.
TAKE CARE OF THE TWO USED FOR THE ART OF IMPERSON-ATION.
...OF COURSE.
ITACHI...
HOW MANY ENEMIES AND WHO ARE THEY?
KONOHA'S HATAKE KAKASHI, HARUNO SAKURA AND UZUMAKI NARUTO, THE NINE-TAILED FOX'S JINCHÛRIKI.
SUNAGAKURE ADVISOR CHIYO FINISHES OUT THEIR FOUR-MAN CELL.
!
FLINCH
GRANNY CHIYO!

READ THIS WAY

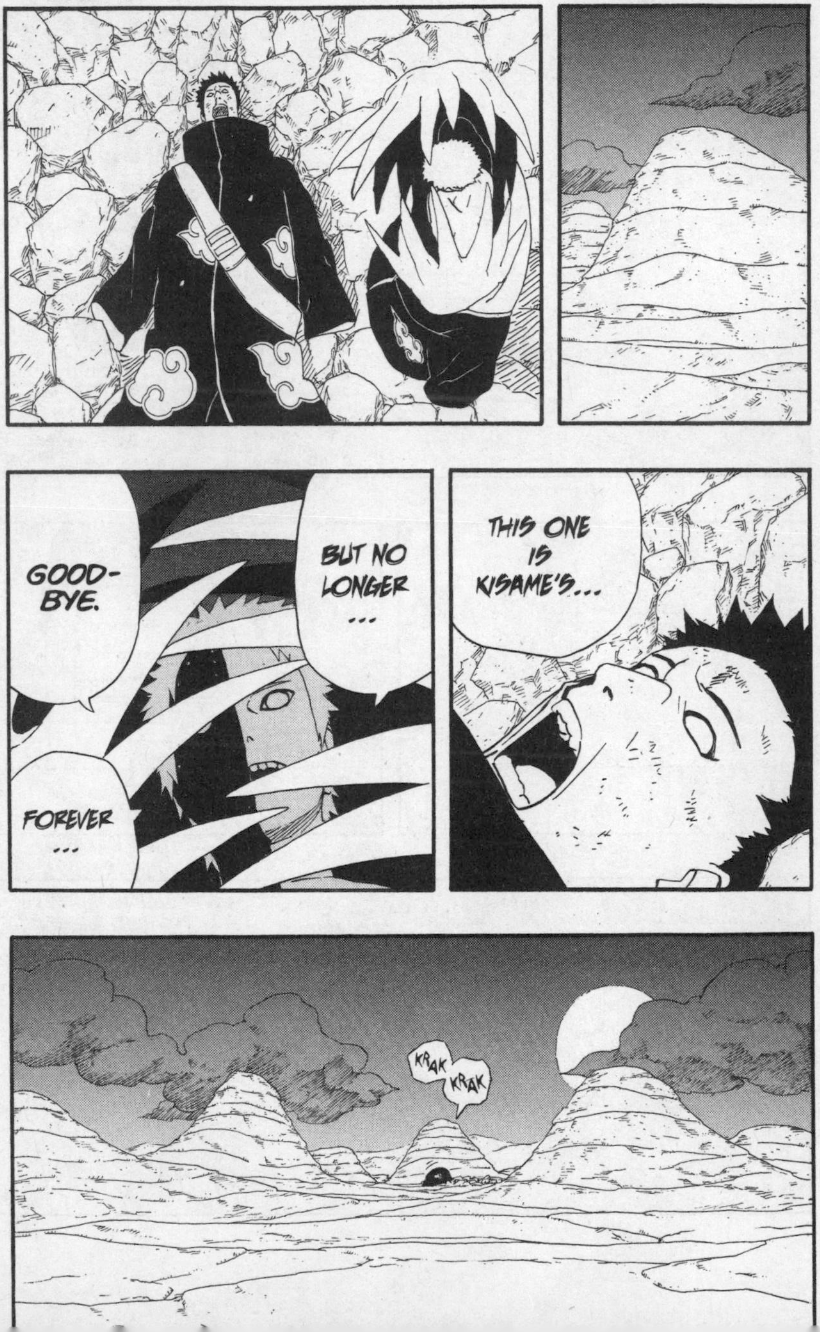
THIS ONE IS KISAME'S...
BUT NO LONGER ...
GOOD-BYE.
FOREVER ...
KRAK KRAK

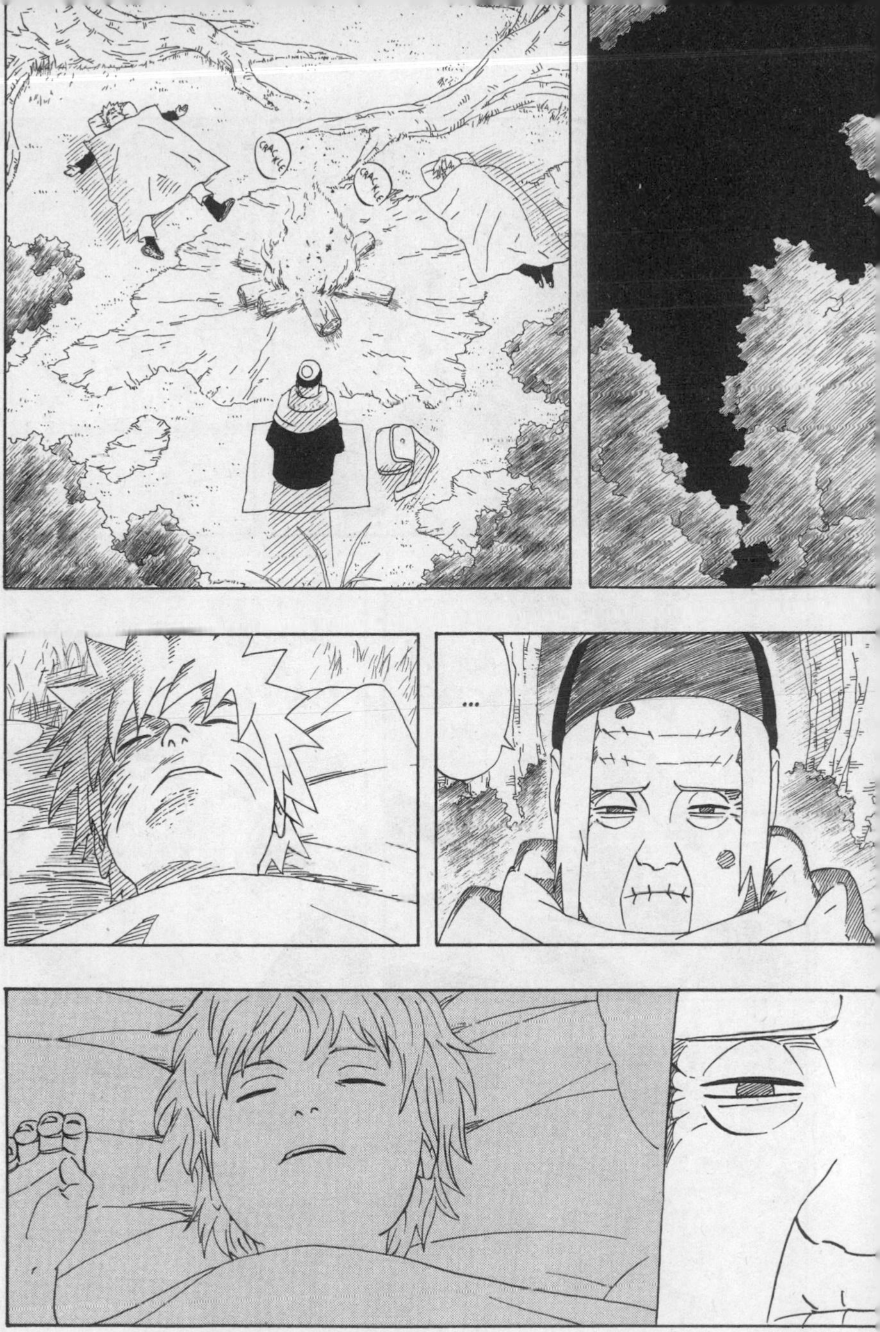
CRACKLE
CRACKLE
...

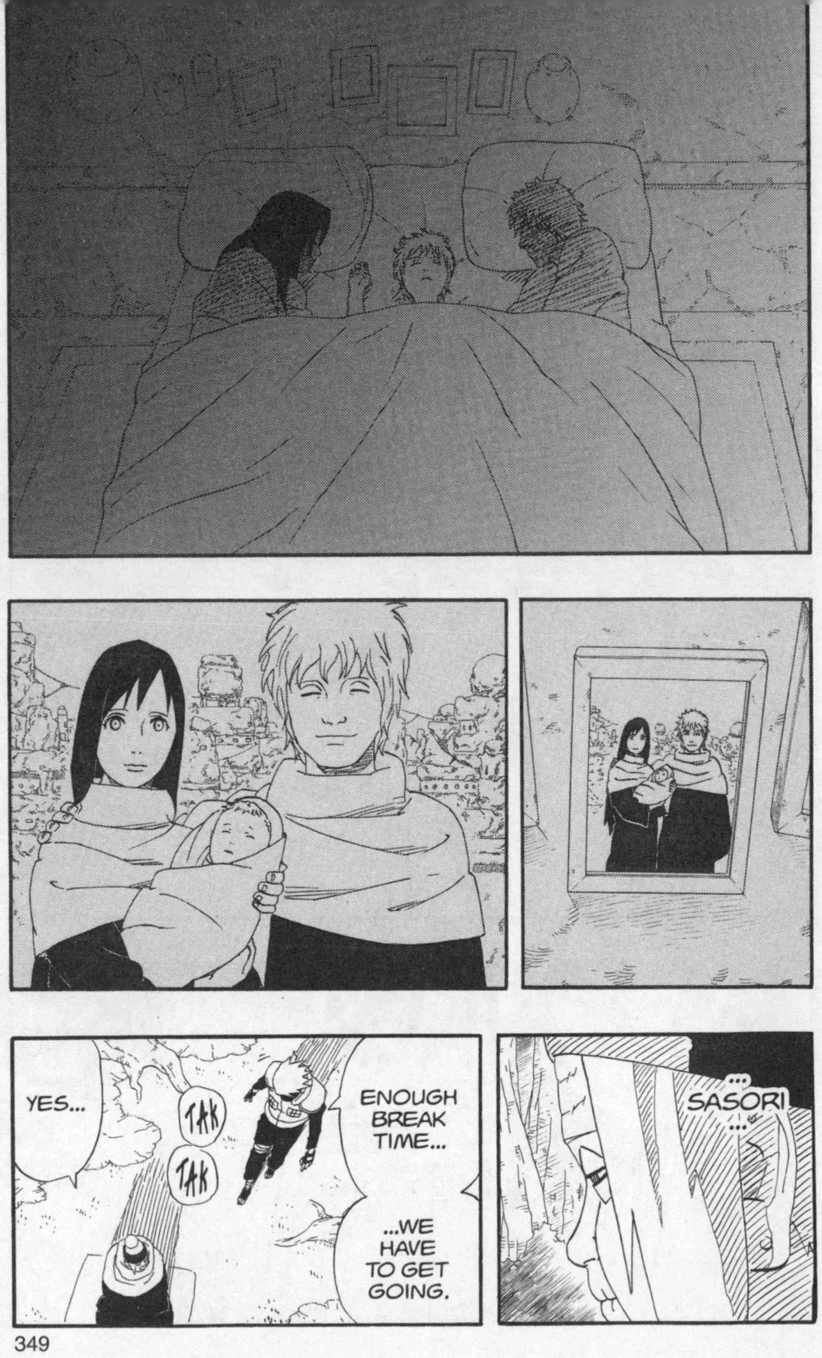
...SASORI...
ENOUGH BREAK TIME...
...WE HAVE TO GET GOING.
TAK
TAK
YES...

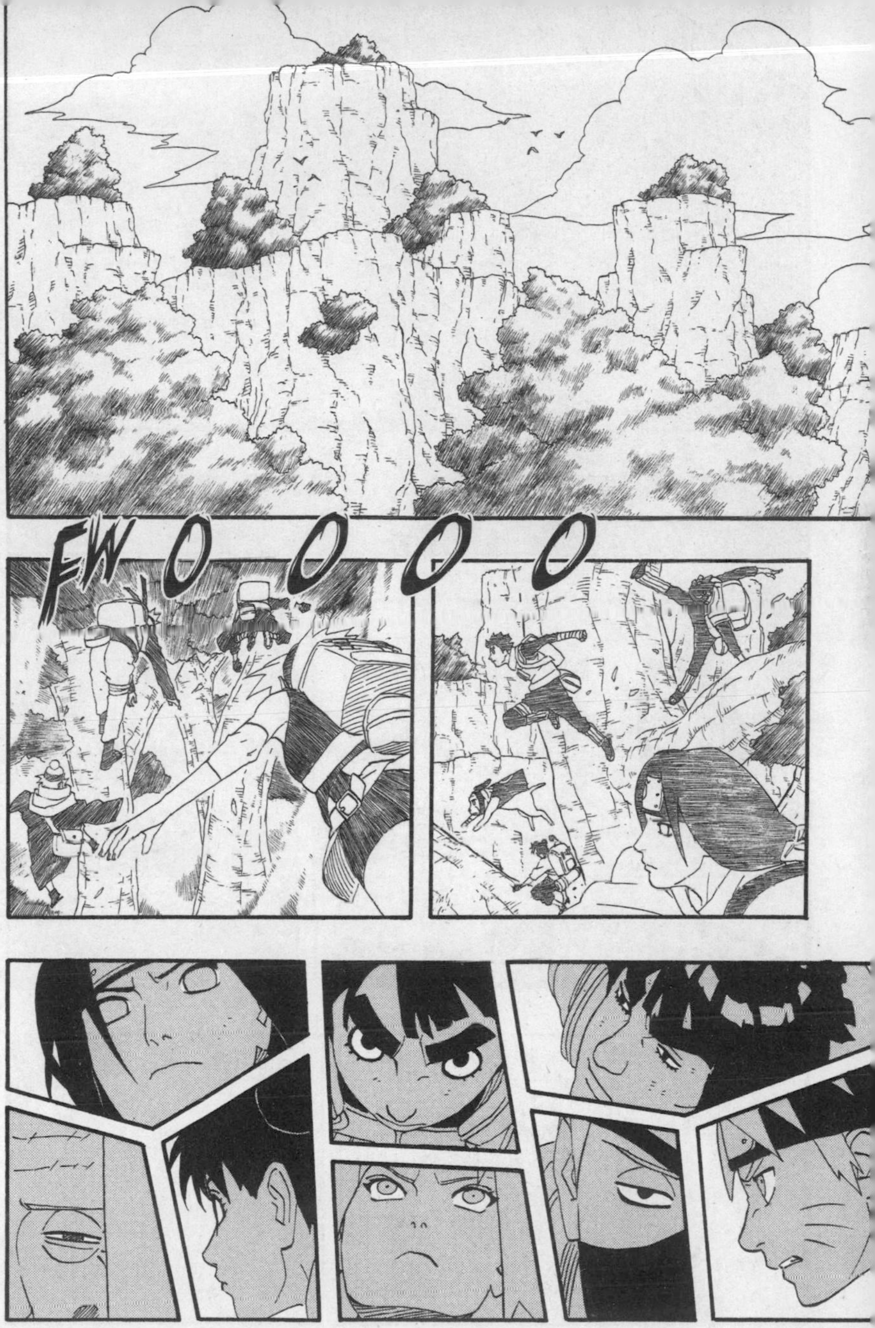
FWOOOOO

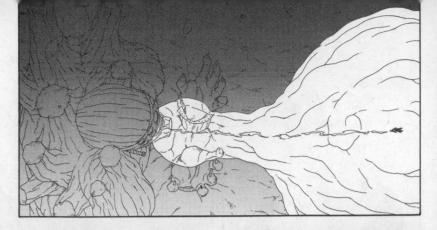

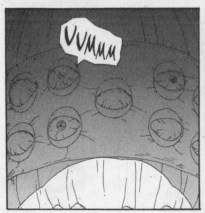

VVMMM

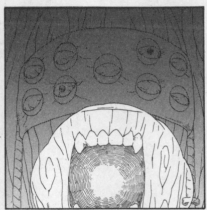

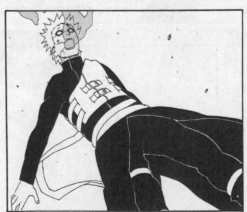

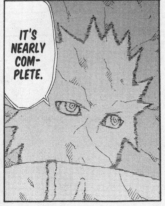

IT'S NEARLY COM-PLETE.

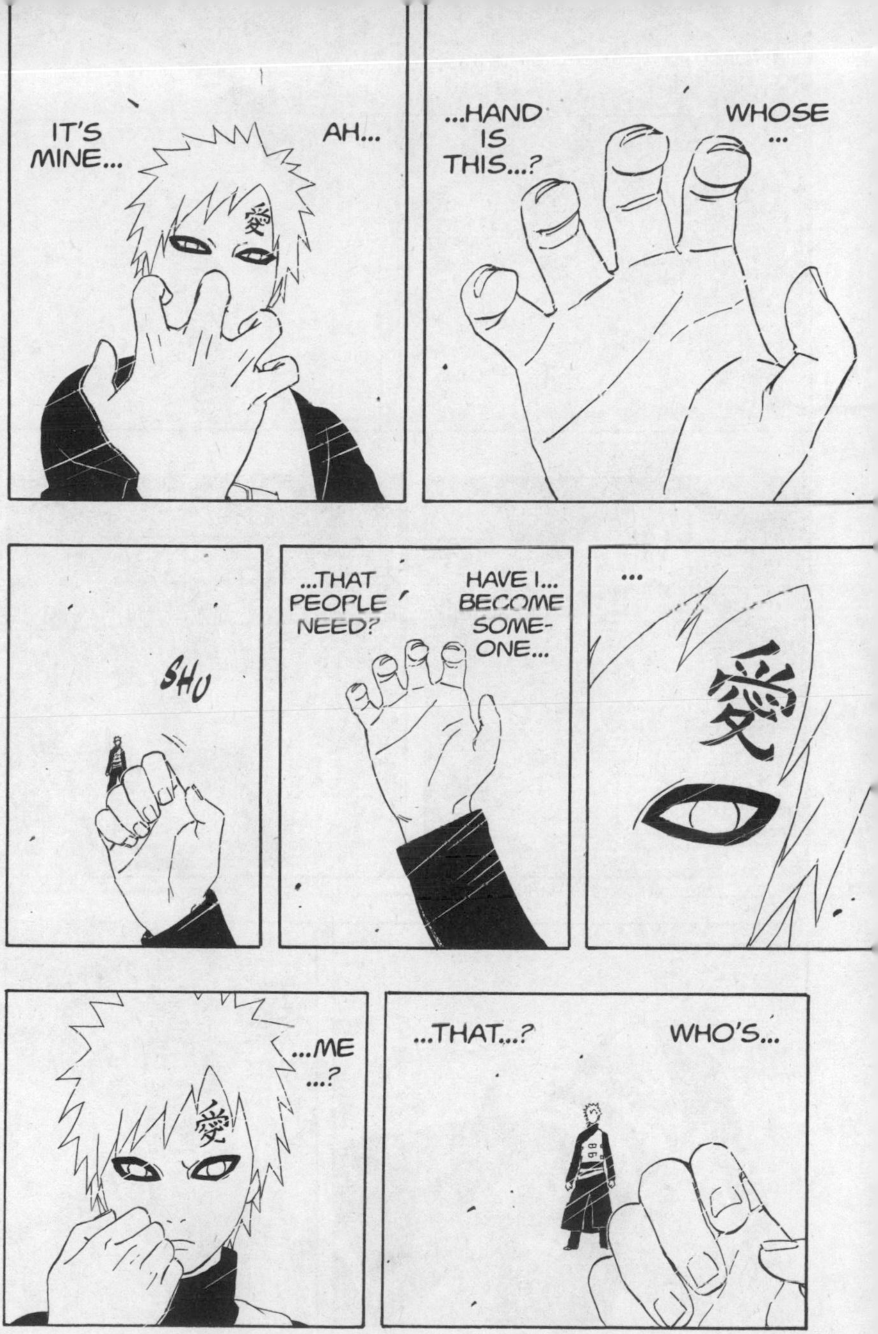
WHOSE ...
...HAND IS THIS...?
AH...
IT'S MINE...
...
HAVE I... BECOME SOME-ONE...
...THAT PEOPLE NEED?
SHU
WHO'S...
...THAT...?
...ME ...?

READ THIS WAY

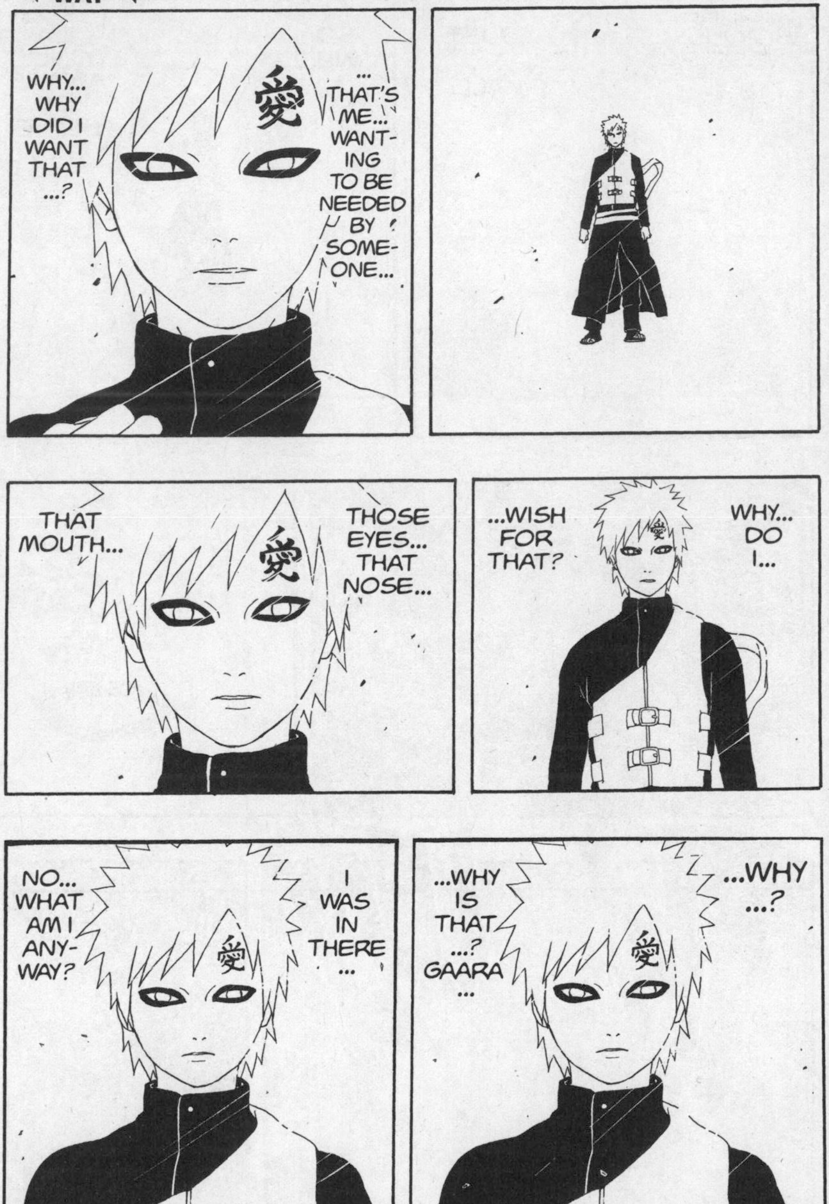
...THAT'S ME... WANTING TO BE NEEDED BY SOMEONE...
WHY... WHY DID I WANT THAT...?
WHY... DO I...
...WISH FOR THAT?
THOSE EYES... THAT NOSE...
THAT MOUTH...
...WHY...?
...WHY IS THAT...? GAARA...
I WAS IN THERE...
NO... WHAT AM I ANYWAY?

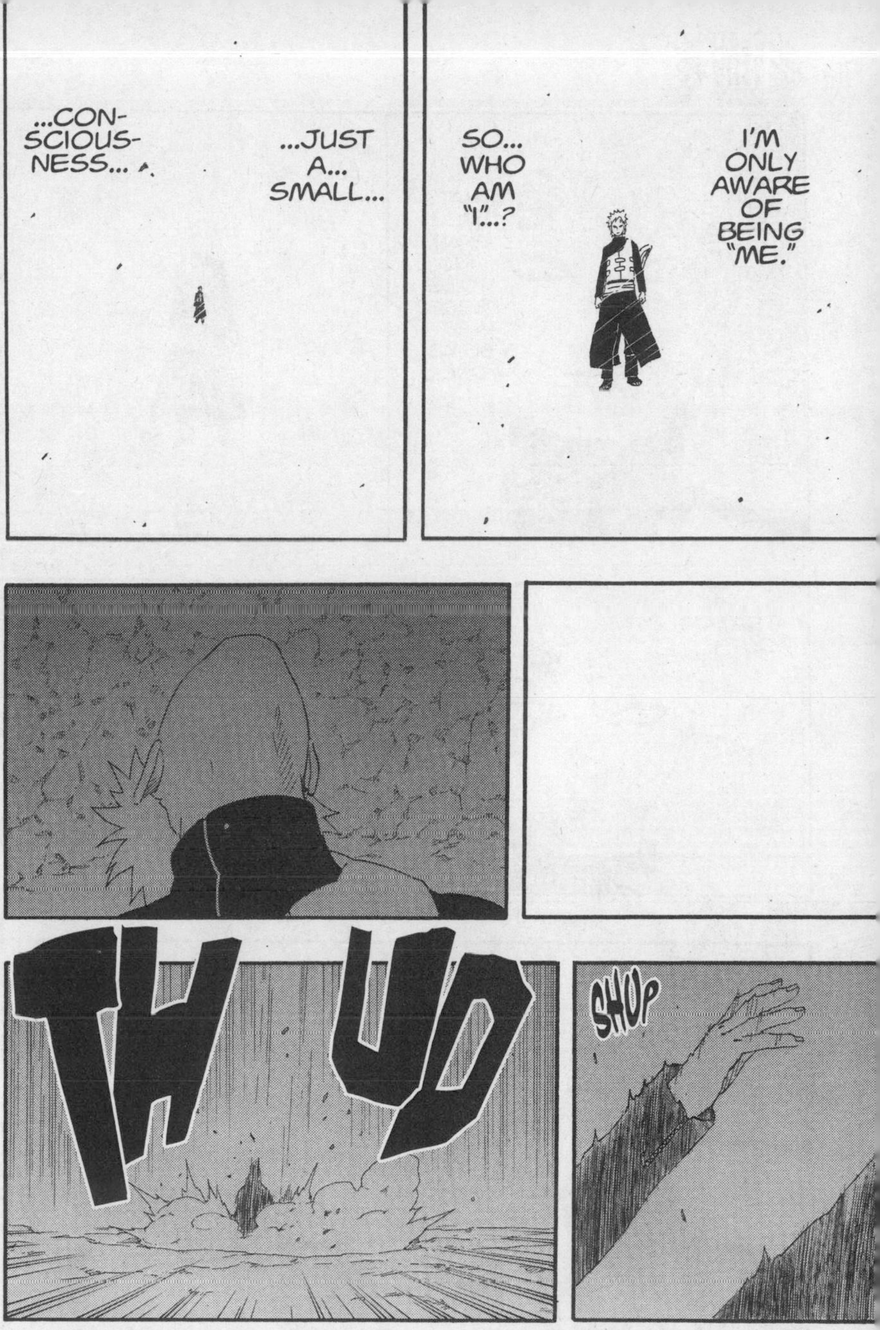
I'M ONLY AWARE OF BEING "ME."
SO... WHO AM "I"...?
...JUST A... SMALL...
...CON-SCIOUS-NESS...
SHUP
THUD

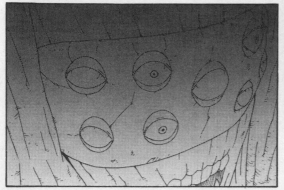

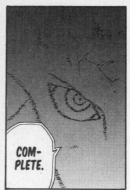

COM-
PLETE.

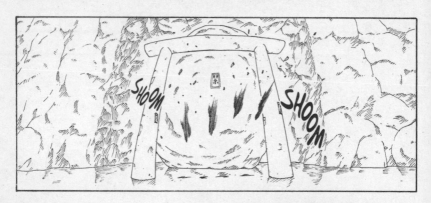

SHOOM

SHOOM

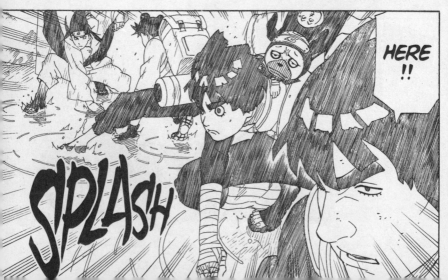

HERE
!!

SPLASH

NARUTO

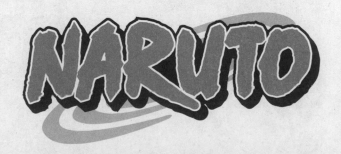

Number 262: Naruto Charges On...!!

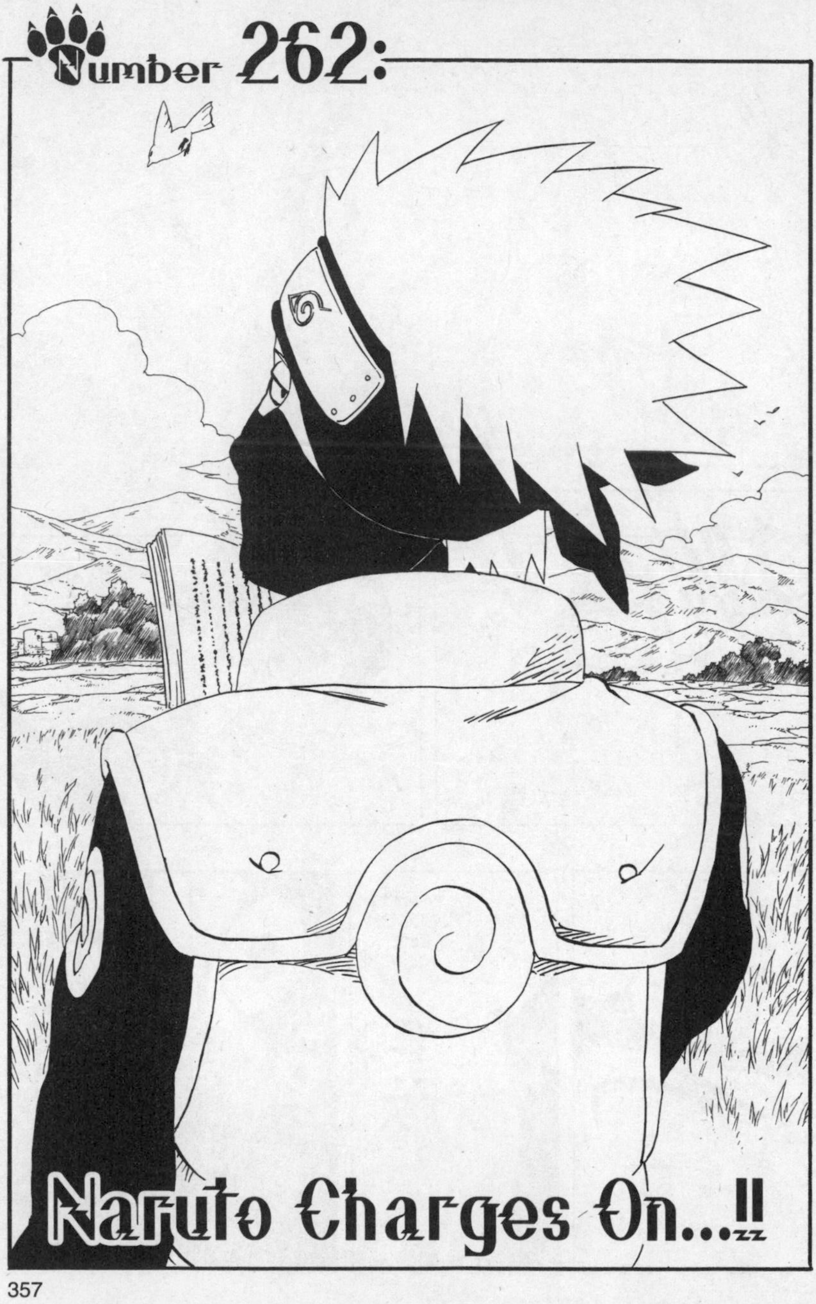

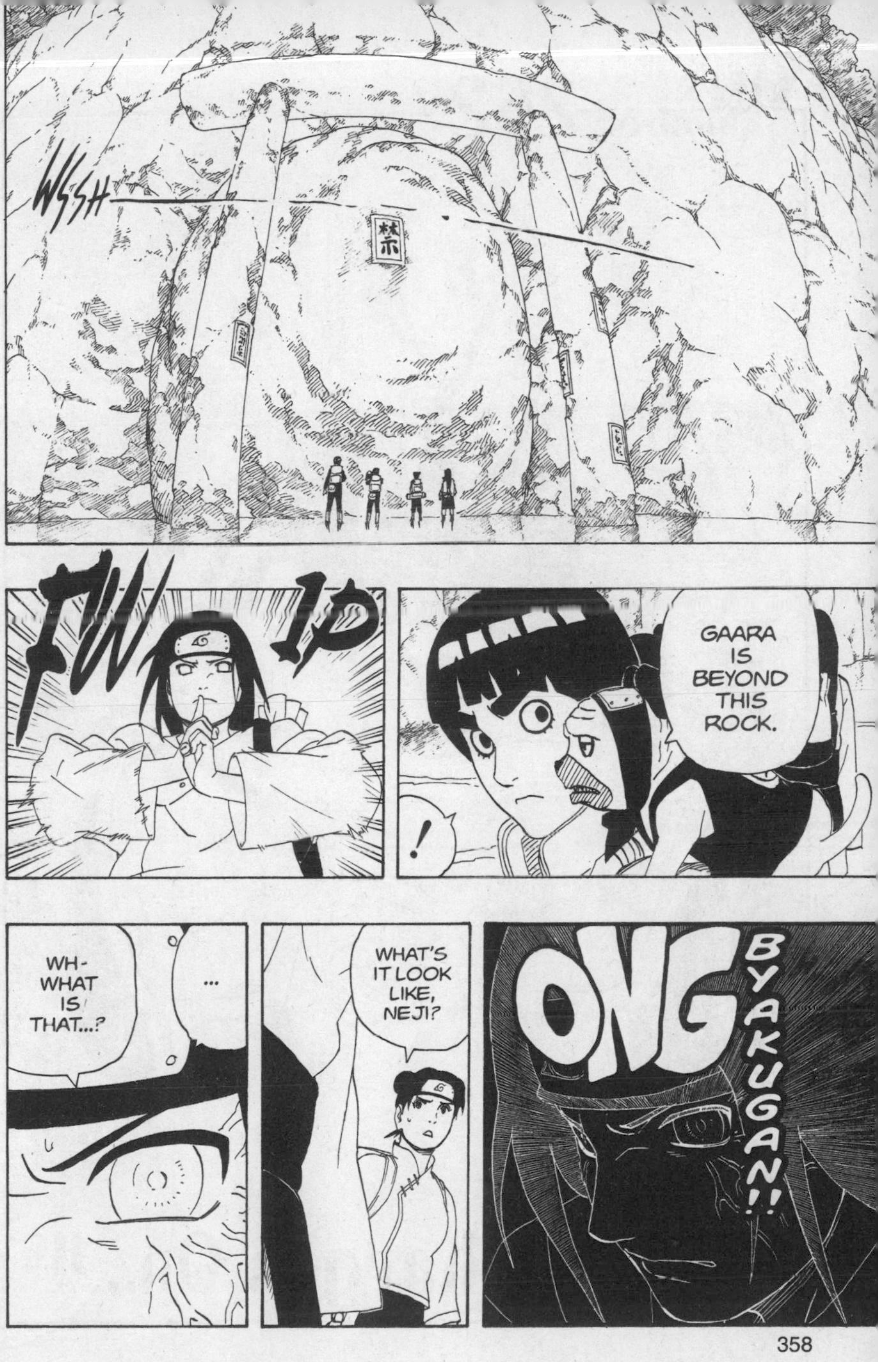
WSSH
!
GAARA IS BEYOND THIS ROCK.
FWIP
ONG
BYAKUGAN!!
WHAT'S IT LOOK LIKE, NEJI?
...
WH- WHAT IS THAT...?

READ THIS WAY

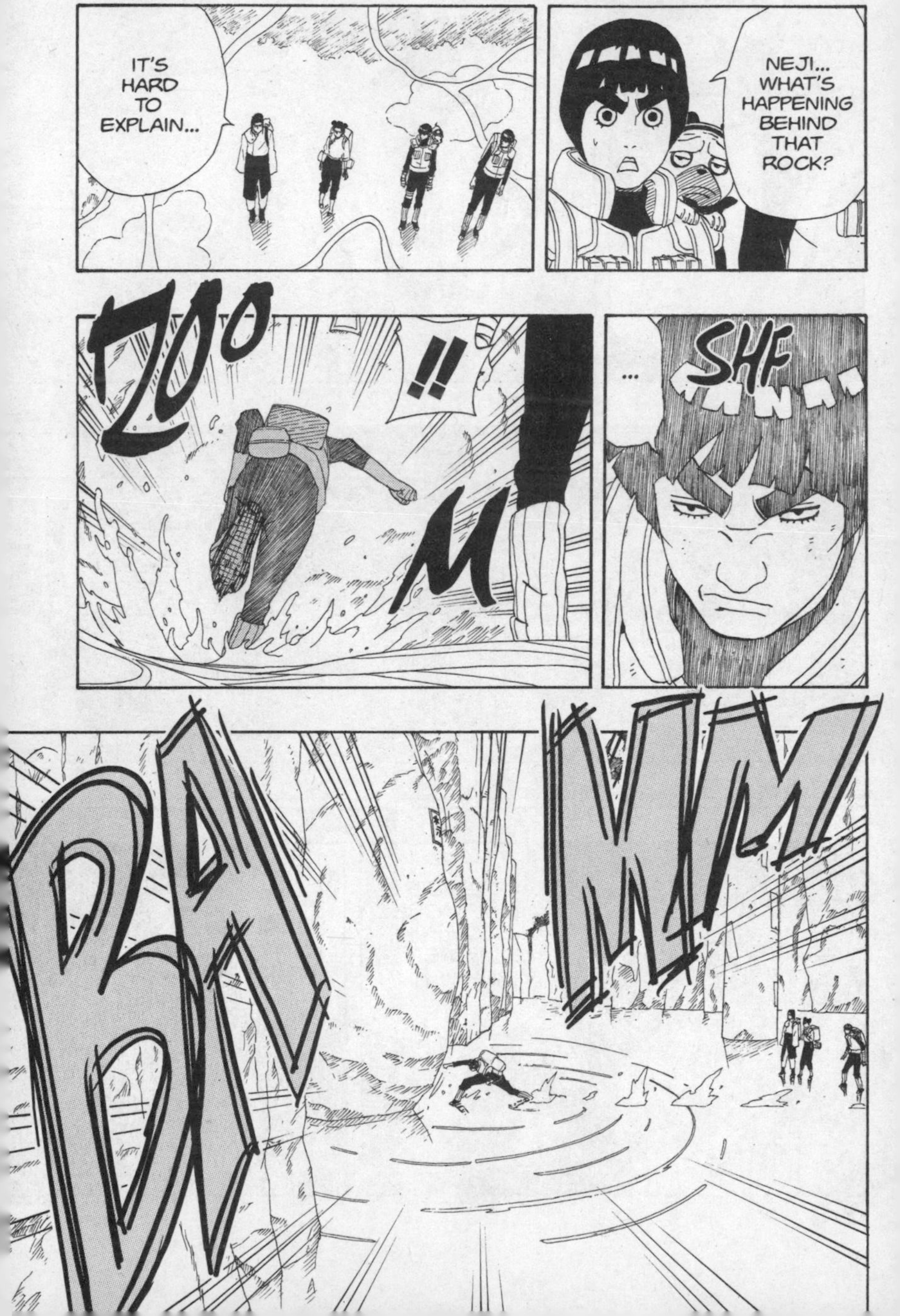
NEJI... WHAT'S HAPPENING BEHIND THAT ROCK?
IT'S HARD TO EXPLAIN...
...
SHF
ZOOM
!!
BAMM

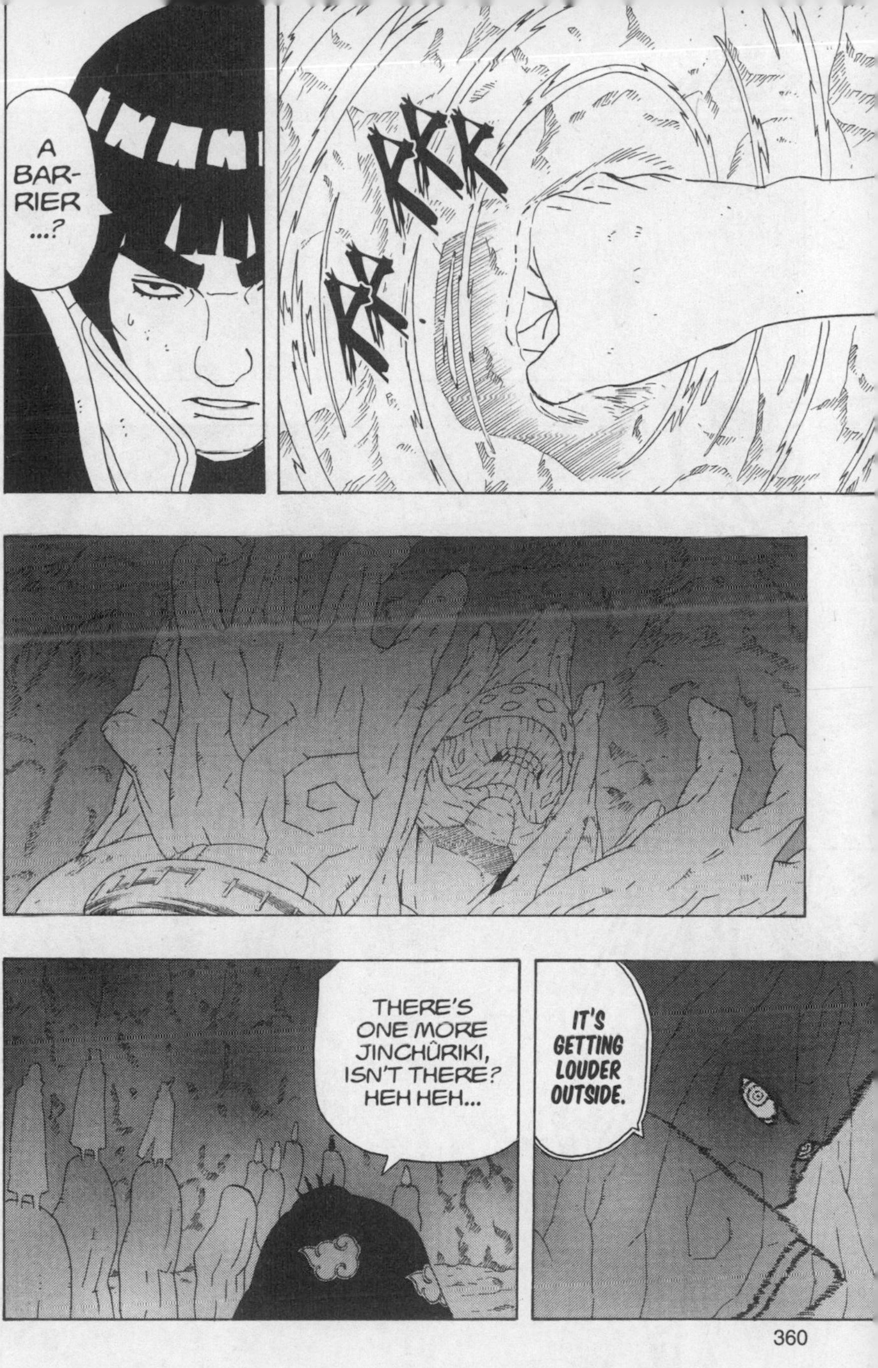
RRR
RR
A BARRIER...?
IT'S GETTING LOUDER OUTSIDE.
THERE'S ONE MORE JINCHŪRIKI, ISN'T THERE? HEH HEH...

READ THIS WAY

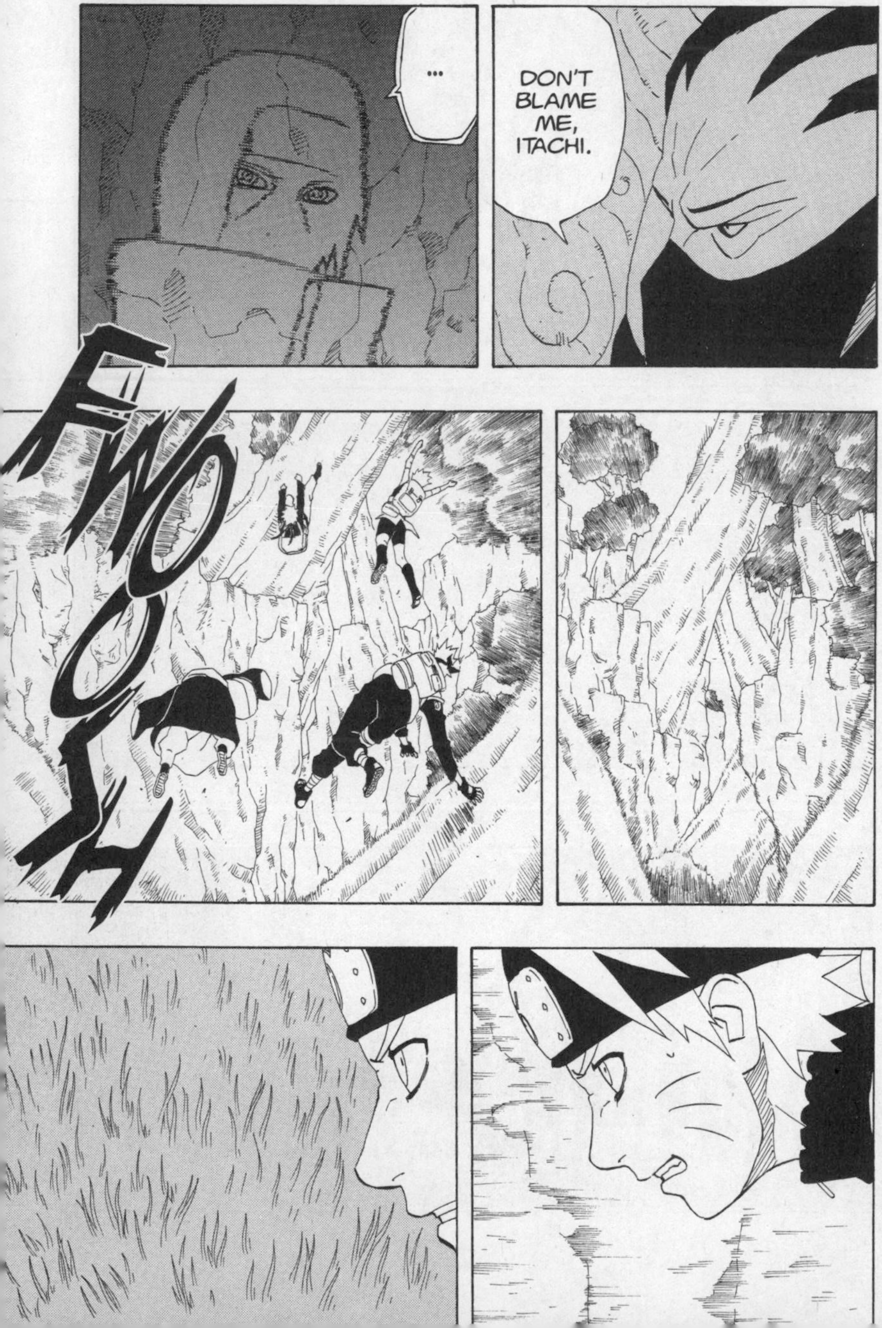
DON'T BLAME ME, ITACHI.
...
FWOOSH

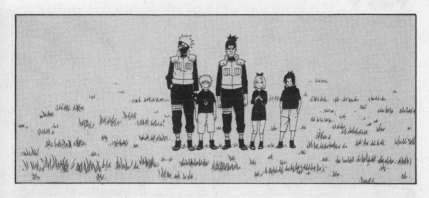

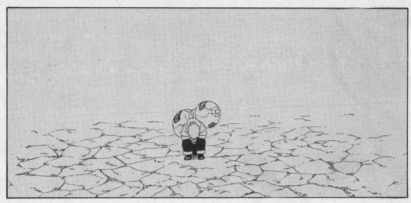

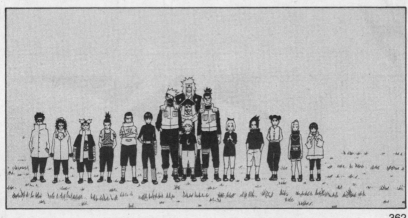

READ THIS WAY

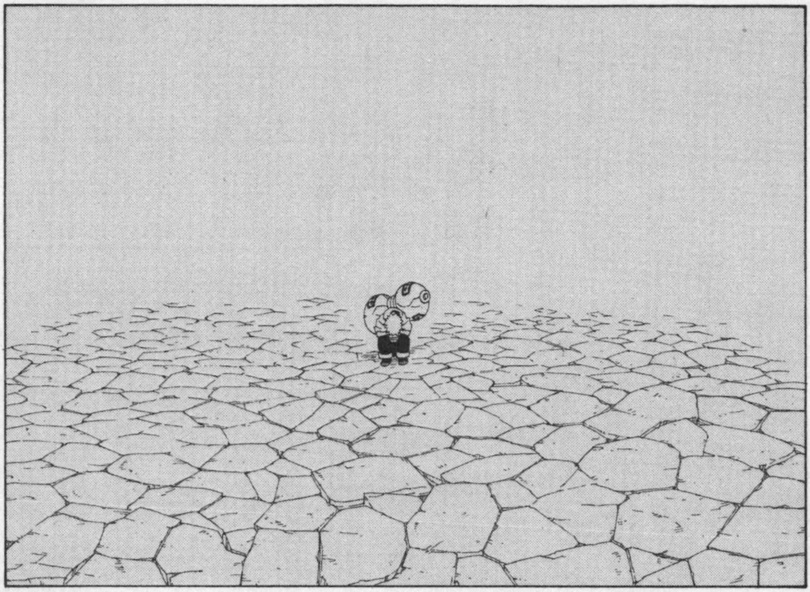

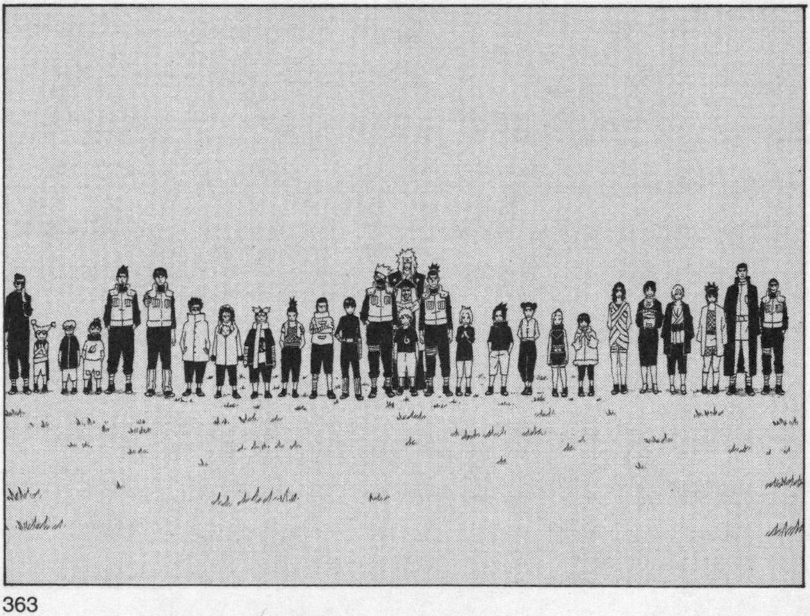

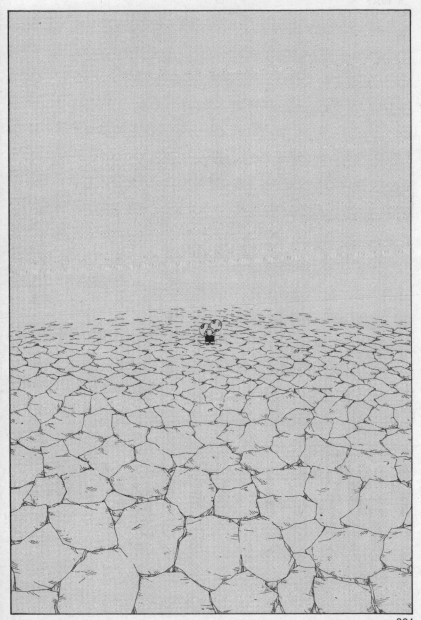

READ THIS WAY

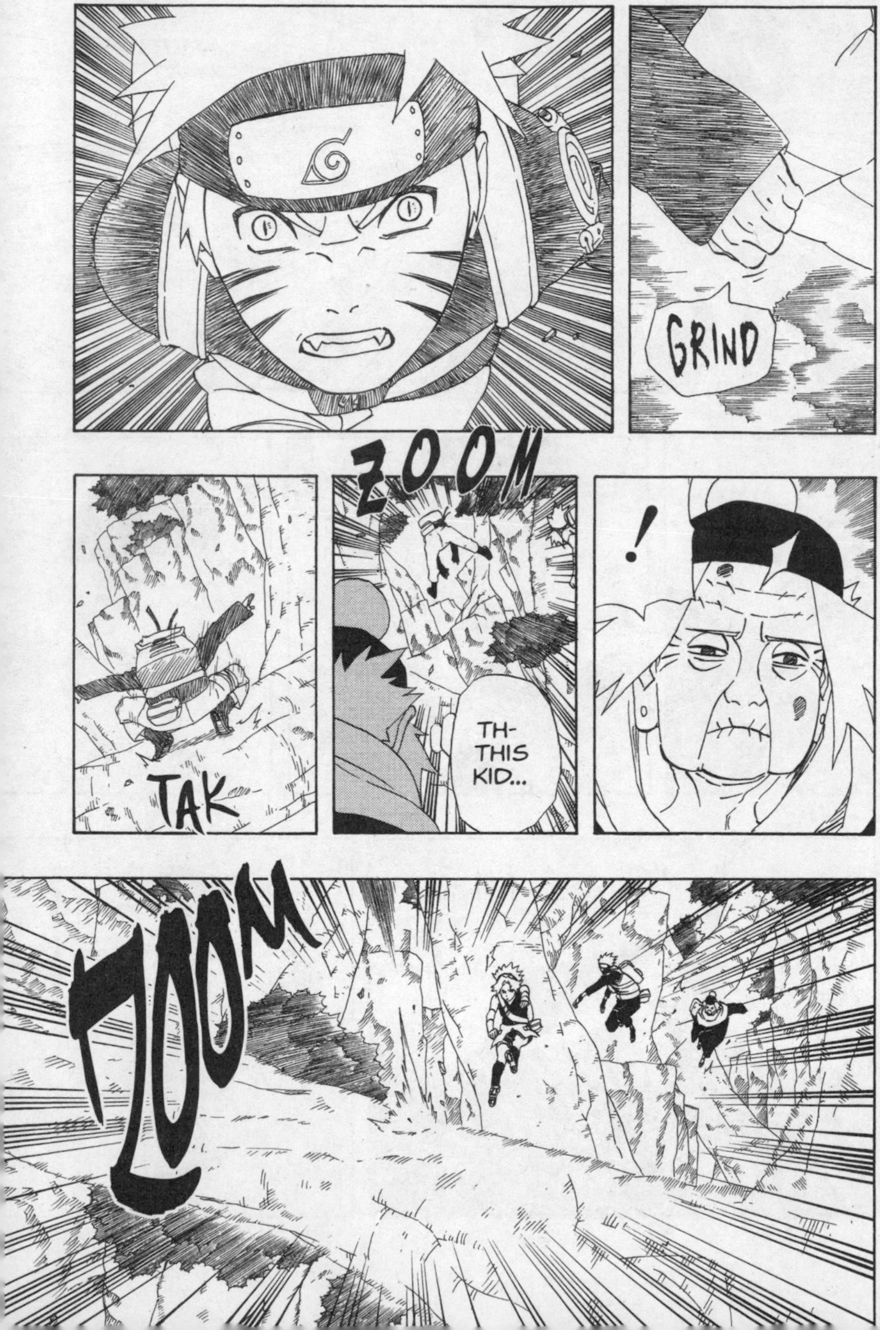
GRIND
!
ZOOM
TH- THIS KID...
TAK
ZOOM

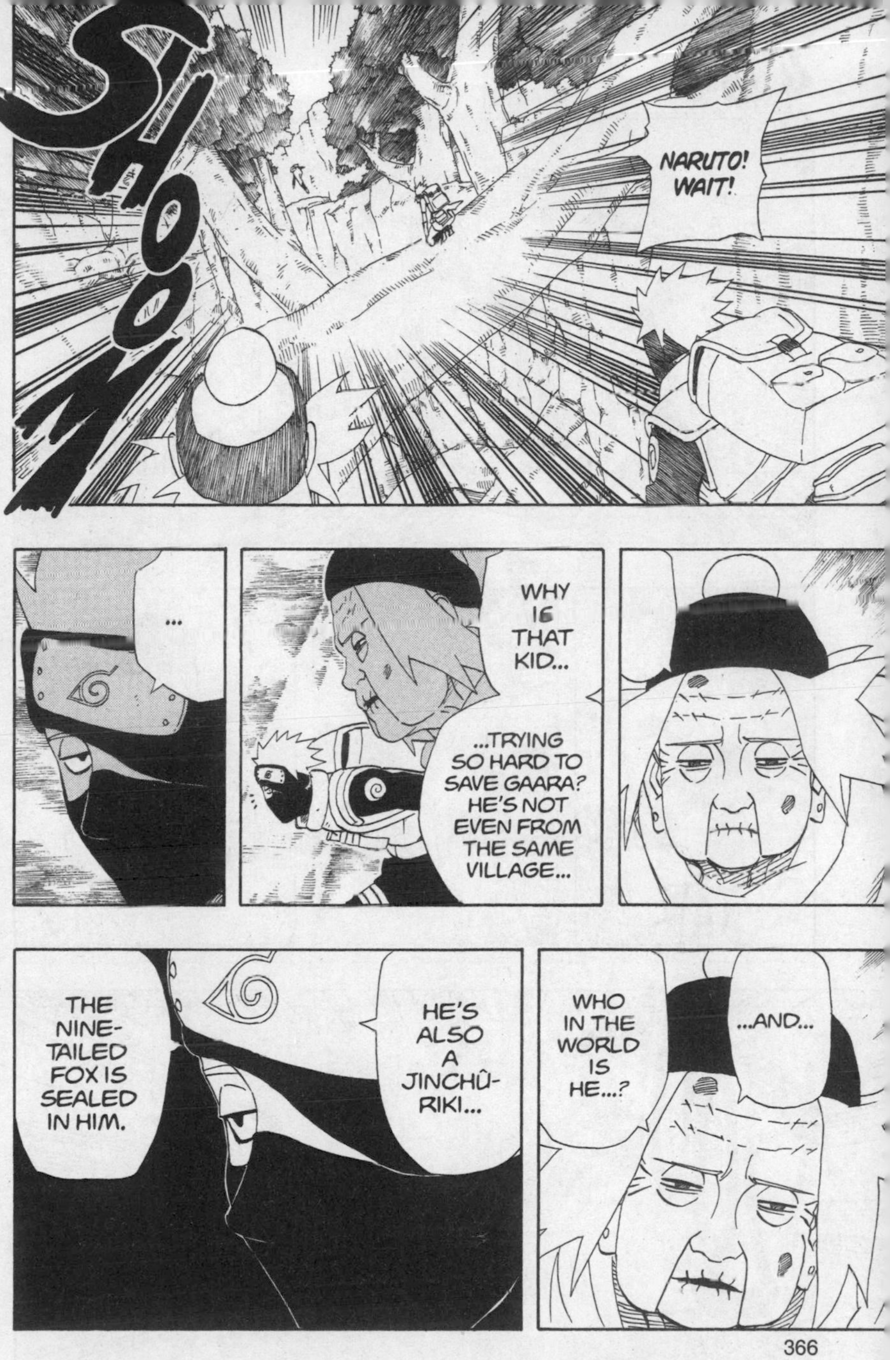
NARUTO! WAIT!
SHOOM
WHY IS THAT KID...
...TRYING SO HARD TO SAVE GAARA? HE'S NOT EVEN FROM THE SAME VILLAGE...
...
...AND...
WHO IN THE WORLD IS HE...?
HE'S ALSO A JINCHÛ-RIKI...
THE NINE-TAILED FOX IS SEALED IN HIM.

READ THIS WAY

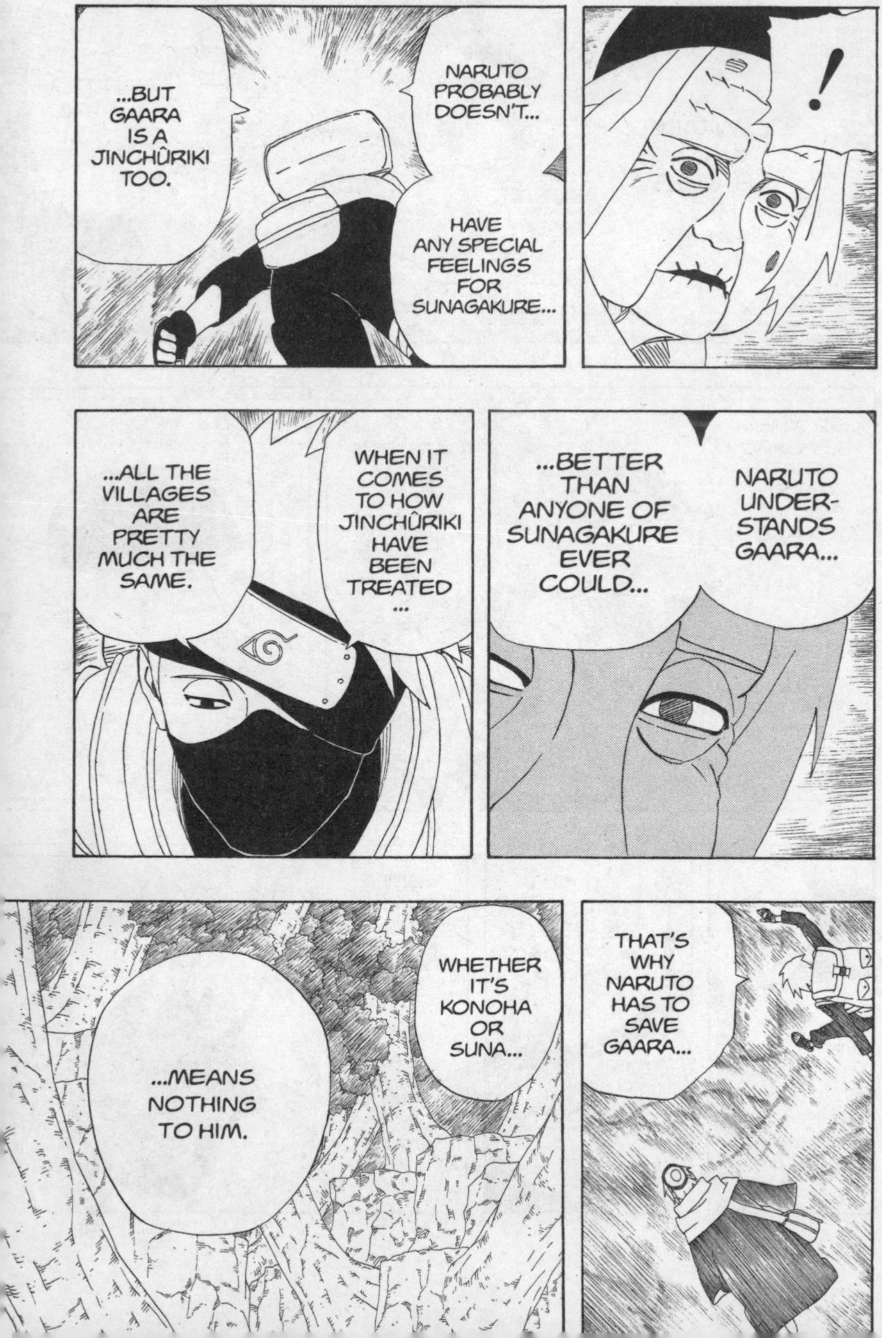
!
NARUTO PROBABLY DOESN'T...
HAVE ANY SPECIAL FEELINGS FOR SUNAGAKURE...
...BUT GAARA IS A JINCHŪRIKI TOO.
NARUTO UNDER-STANDS GAARA...
...BETTER THAN ANYONE OF SUNAGAKURE EVER COULD...
WHEN IT COMES TO HOW JINCHŪRIKI HAVE BEEN TREATED...
...ALL THE VILLAGES ARE PRETTY MUCH THE SAME.
THAT'S WHY NARUTO HAS TO SAVE GAARA...
WHETHER IT'S KONOHA OR SUNA...
...MEANS NOTHING TO HIM.

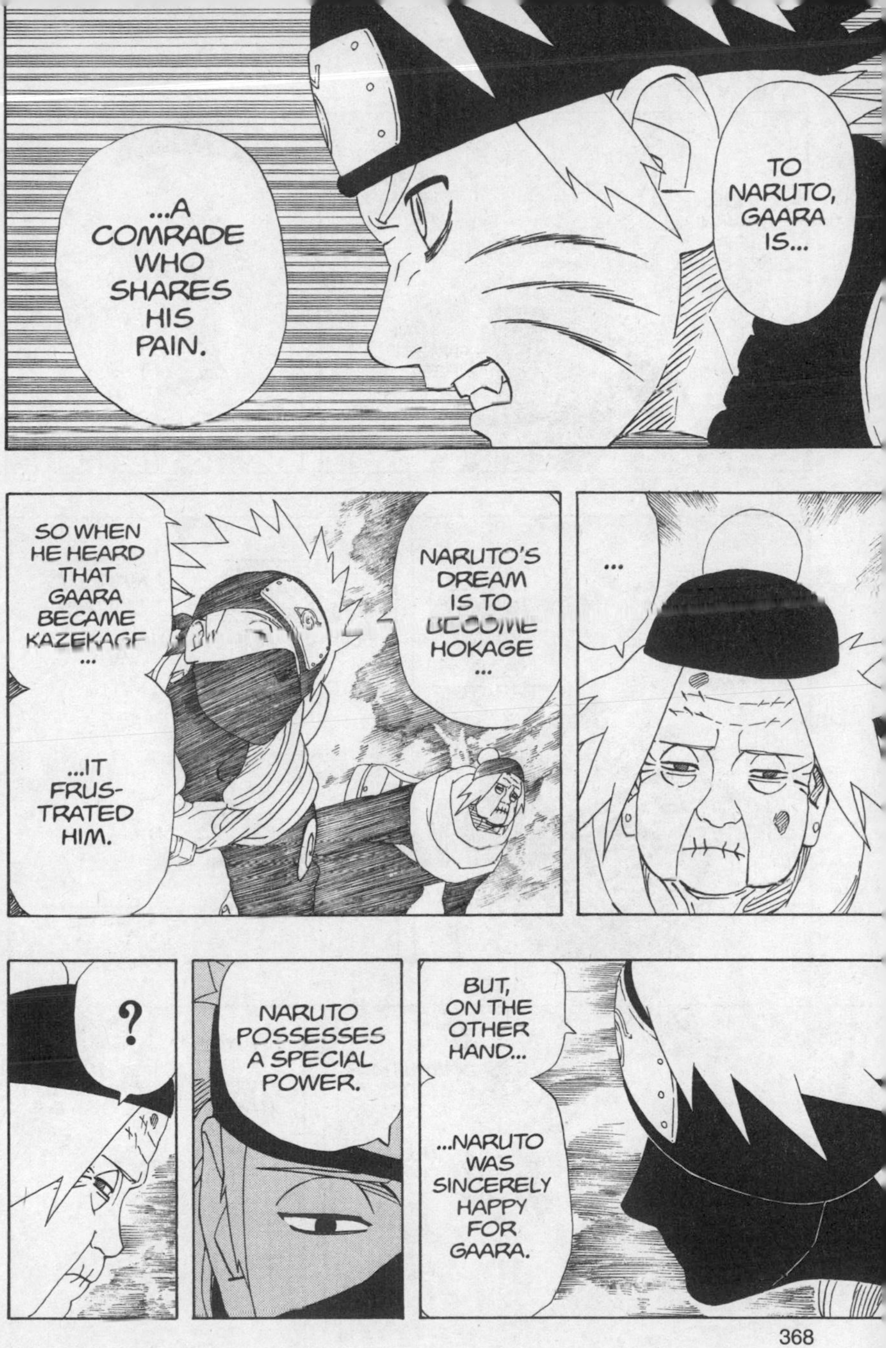
TO NARUTO, GAARA IS...
...A COMRADE WHO SHARES HIS PAIN.
...
NARUTO'S DREAM IS TO BECOME HOKAGE...
SO WHEN HE HEARD THAT GAARA BECAME KAZEKAGE...
...IT FRUS-TRATED HIM.
BUT, ON THE OTHER HAND...
...NARUTO WAS SINCERELY HAPPY FOR GAARA.
NARUTO POSSESSES A SPECIAL POWER.
?

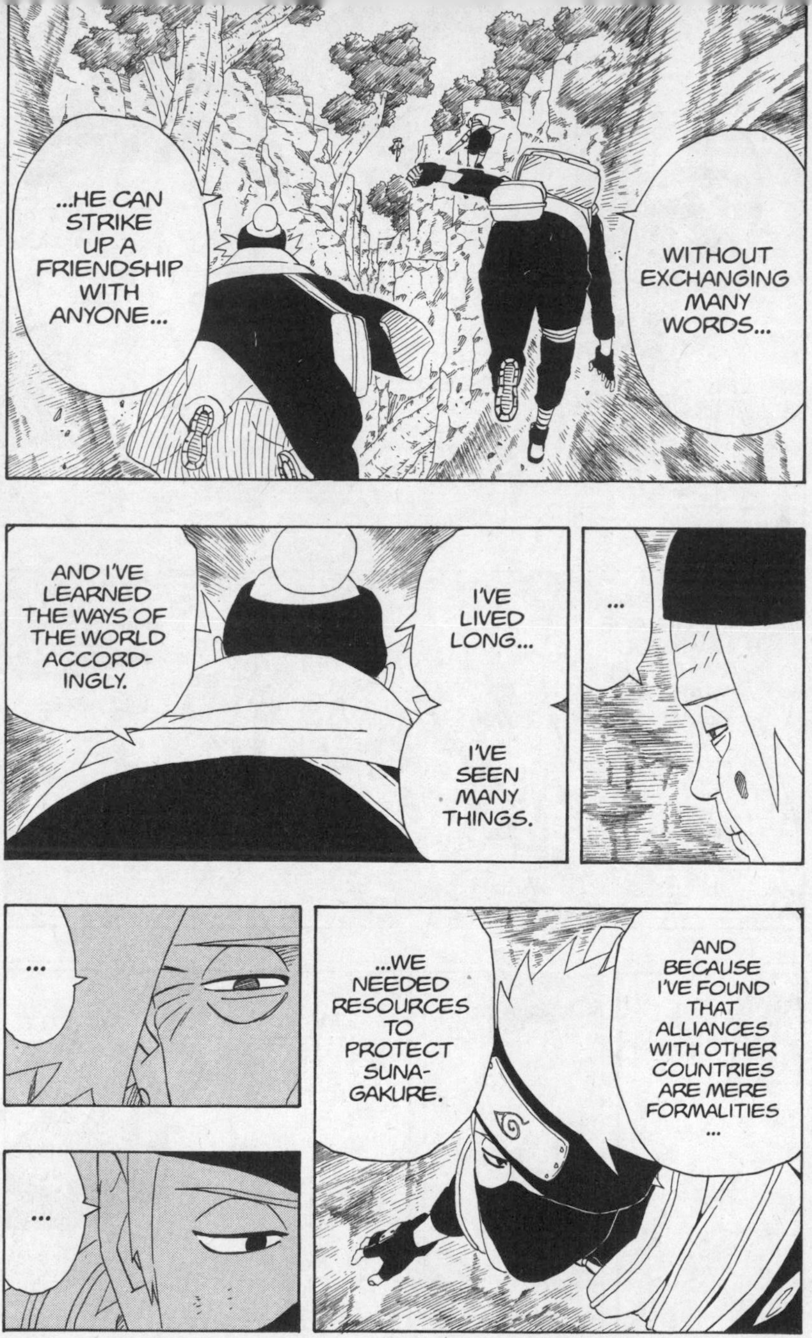
WITHOUT EXCHANGING MANY WORDS...
...HE CAN STRIKE UP A FRIENDSHIP WITH ANYONE...
...
I'VE LIVED LONG...
I'VE SEEN MANY THINGS.
AND I'VE LEARNED THE WAYS OF THE WORLD ACCORD-INGLY.
AND BECAUSE I'VE FOUND THAT ALLIANCES WITH OTHER COUNTRIES ARE MERE FORMALITIES ...
...WE NEEDED RESOURCES TO PROTECT SUNA-GAKURE.
...
...

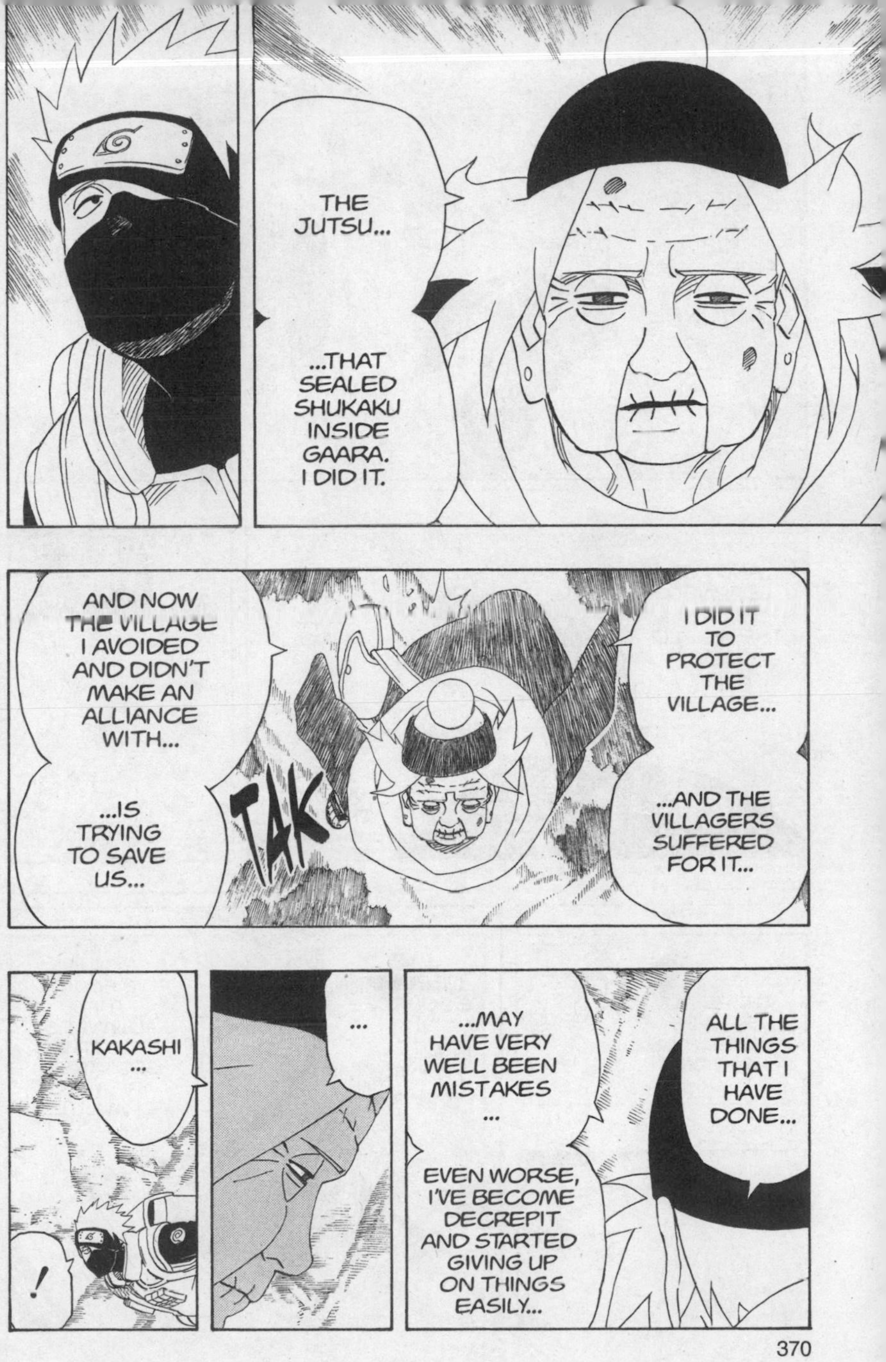
THE JUTSU...
...THAT SEALED SHUKAKU INSIDE GAARA. I DID IT.
I DID IT TO PROTECT THE VILLAGE...
...AND THE VILLAGERS SUFFERED FOR IT...
AND NOW THE VILLAGE I AVOIDED AND DIDN'T MAKE AN ALLIANCE WITH...
...IS TRYING TO SAVE US...
TAK
ALL THE THINGS THAT I HAVE DONE...
...MAY HAVE VERY WELL BEEN MISTAKES...
EVEN WORSE, I'VE BECOME DECREPIT AND STARTED GIVING UP ON THINGS EASILY...
...
KAKASHI...
!

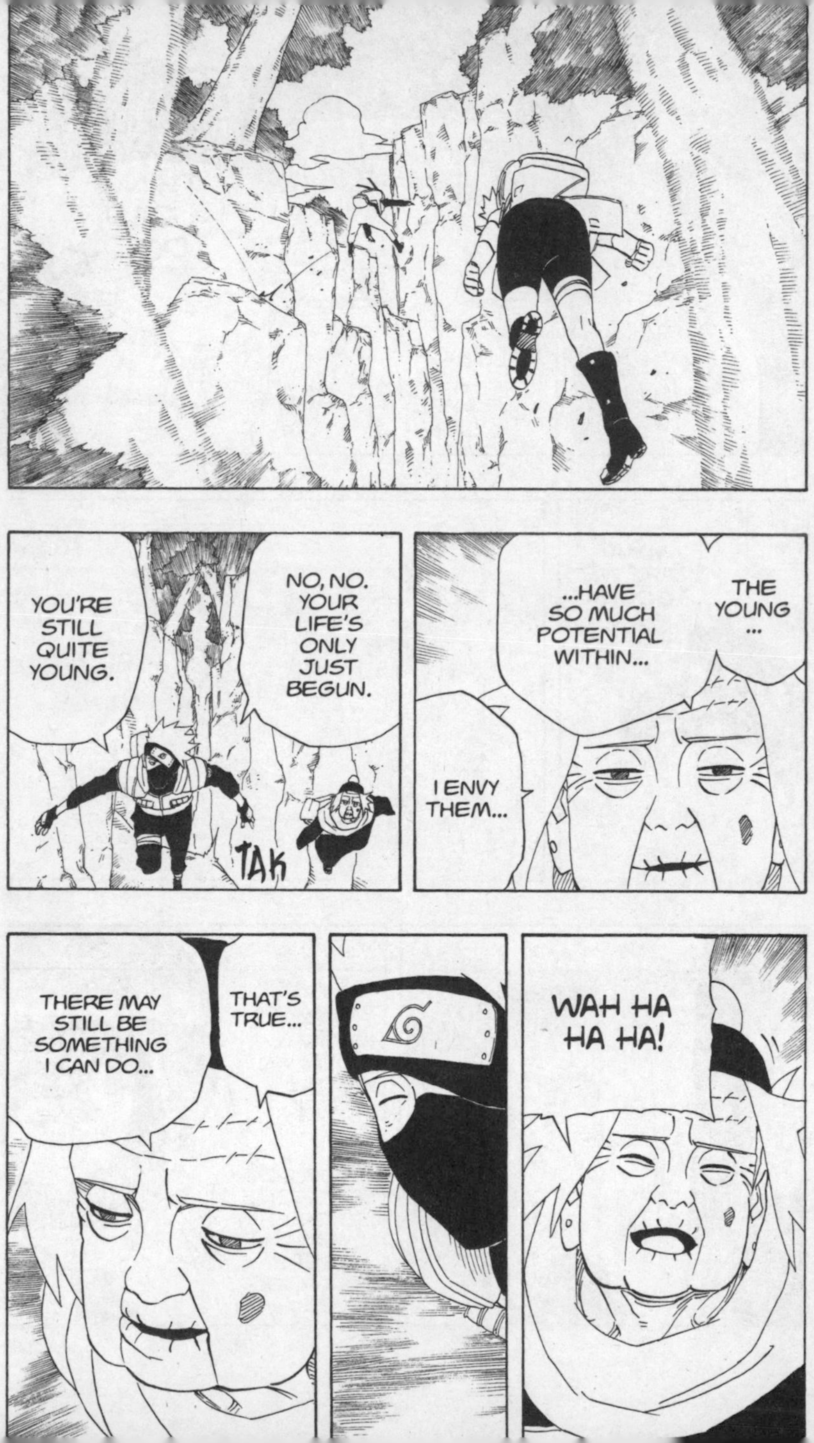
THE YOUNG ...
...HAVE SO MUCH POTENTIAL WITHIN...
I ENVY THEM...
NO, NO. YOUR LIFE'S ONLY JUST BEGUN.
YOU'RE STILL QUITE YOUNG.
TAK
WAH HA HA HA!
THAT'S TRUE...
THERE MAY STILL BE SOMETHING I CAN DO...

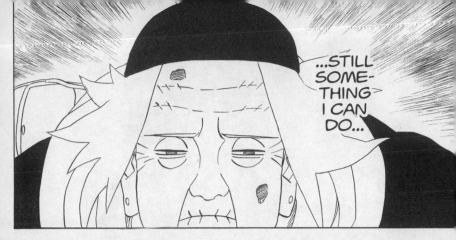

...STILL SOME-THING I CAN DO...

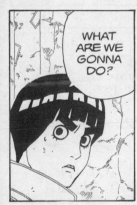

WHAT ARE WE GONNA DO?

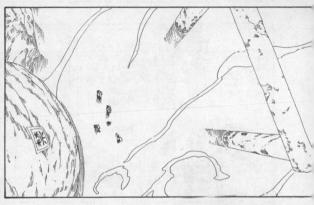

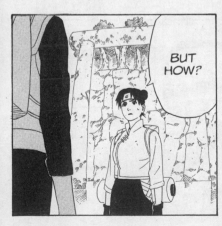

BUT HOW?

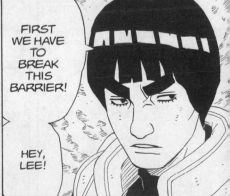

FIRST WE HAVE TO BREAK THIS BARRIER!

HEY, LEE!

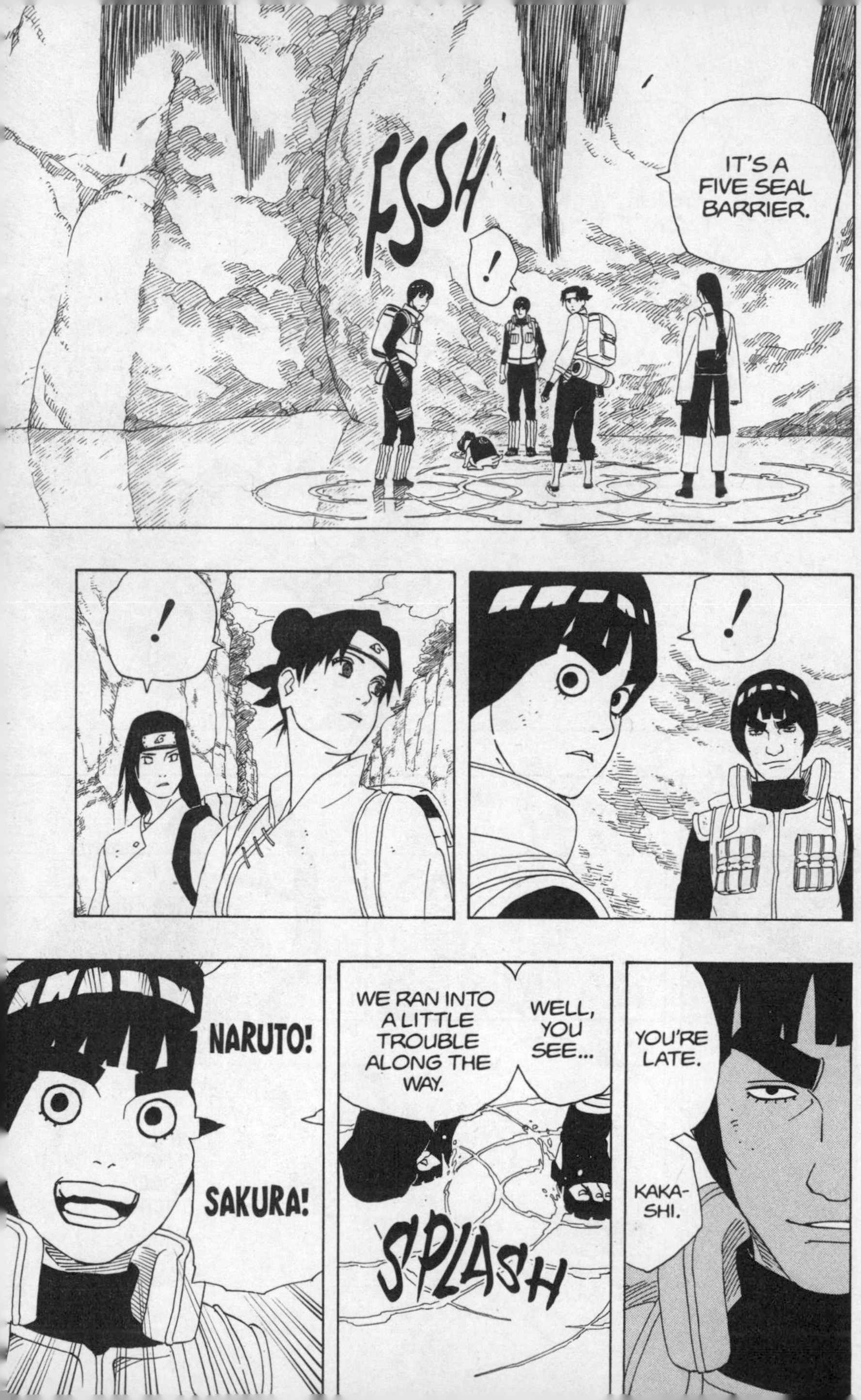
IT'S A FIVE SEAL BARRIER.
FSSH
!
!
!
YOU'RE LATE.
KAKA-SHI.
WELL, YOU SEE...
WE RAN INTO A LITTLE TROUBLE ALONG THE WAY.
SPLASH
NARUTO!
SAKURA!

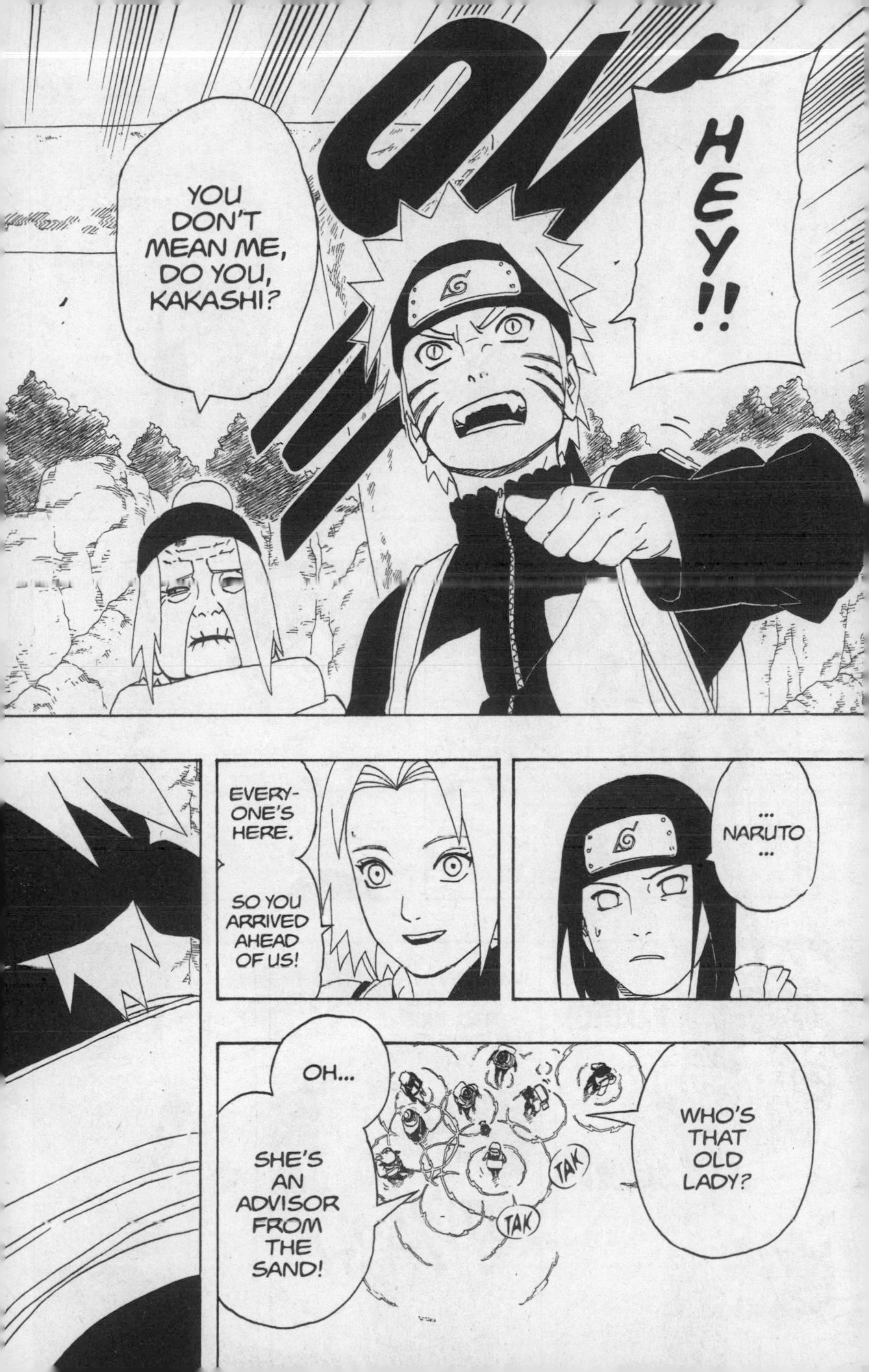
HEY!!
YOU DON'T MEAN ME, DO YOU, KAKASHI?
... NARUTO ...
EVERY-ONE'S HERE.
SO YOU ARRIVED AHEAD OF US!
WHO'S THAT OLD LADY?
TAK
TAK
OH...
SHE'S AN ADVISOR FROM THE SAND!

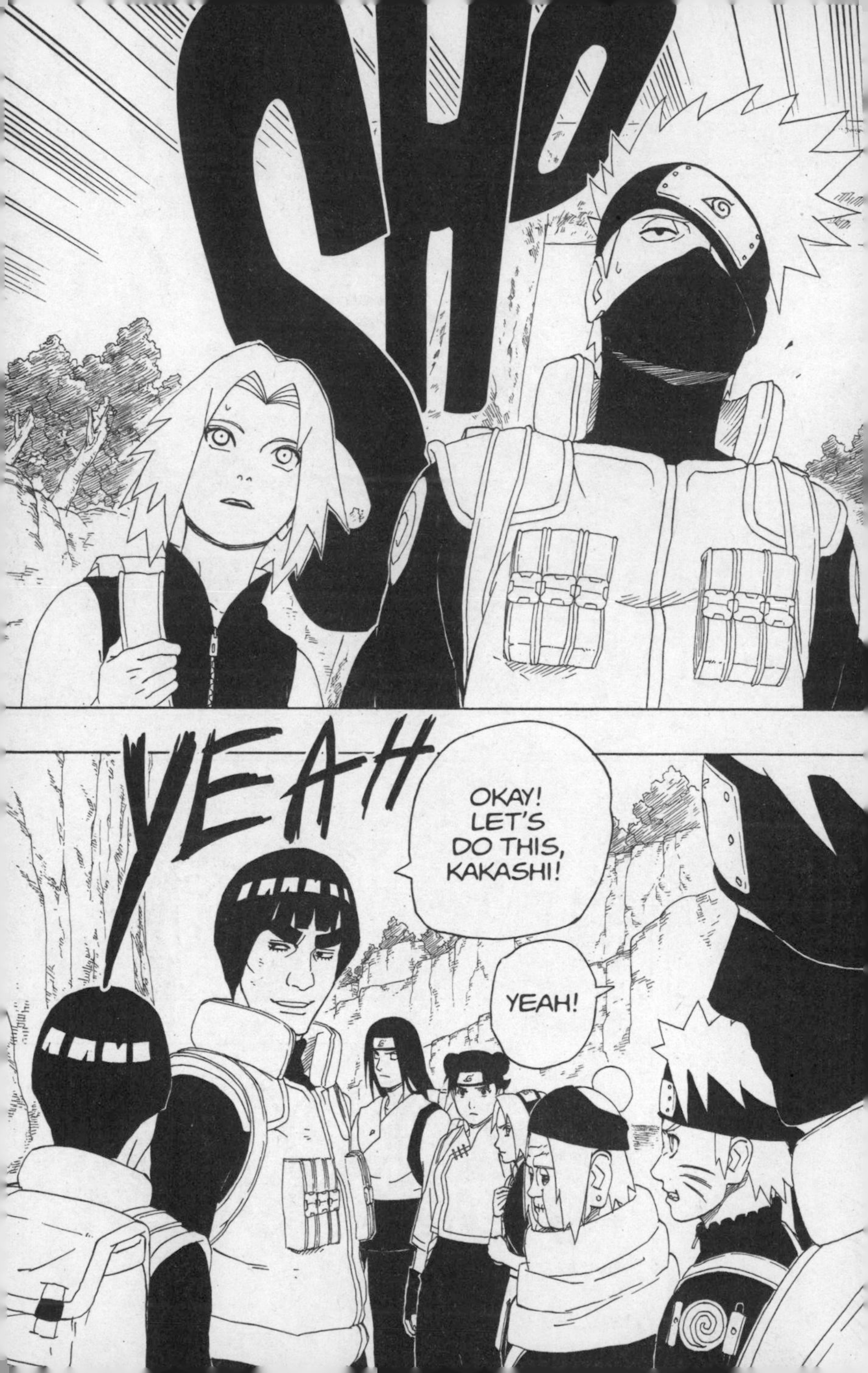
SHP
OKAY! LET'S DO THIS, KAKASHI!
YEAH!
YEAH

NARUTO

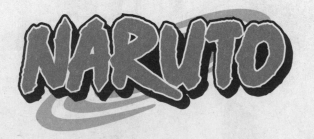

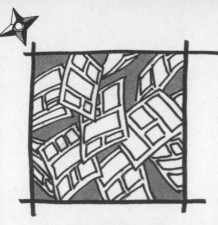

岸本斉史

The movies and games coming out these days look so incredible it stuns me. I'm starting to suspect my readers are so used to rich imagery that manga must feel rather underwhelming by comparison. After all, it's still published in black and white... Remember, though, that manga's strength is in its rapid production. So please overlook its weaknesses.

—Masashi Kishimoto, 2005

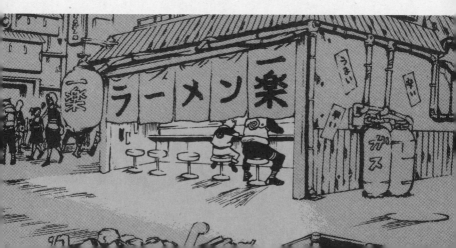

NARUTO

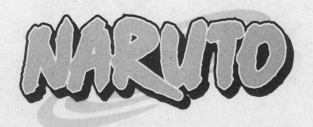

SHONEN JUMP MANGA EDITION

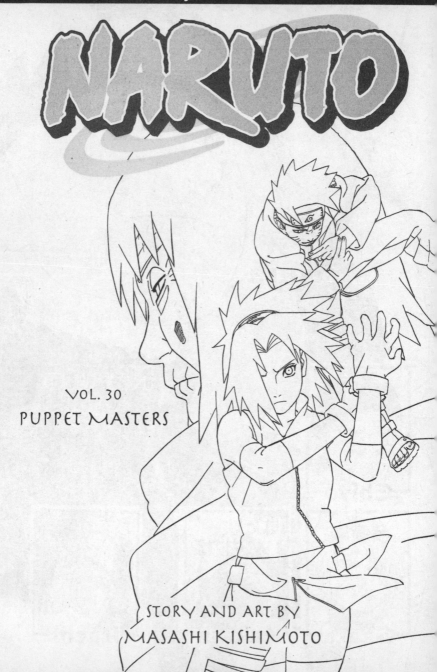

NARUTO

VOL. 30
PUPPET MASTERS

STORY AND ART BY
MASASHI KISHIMOTO

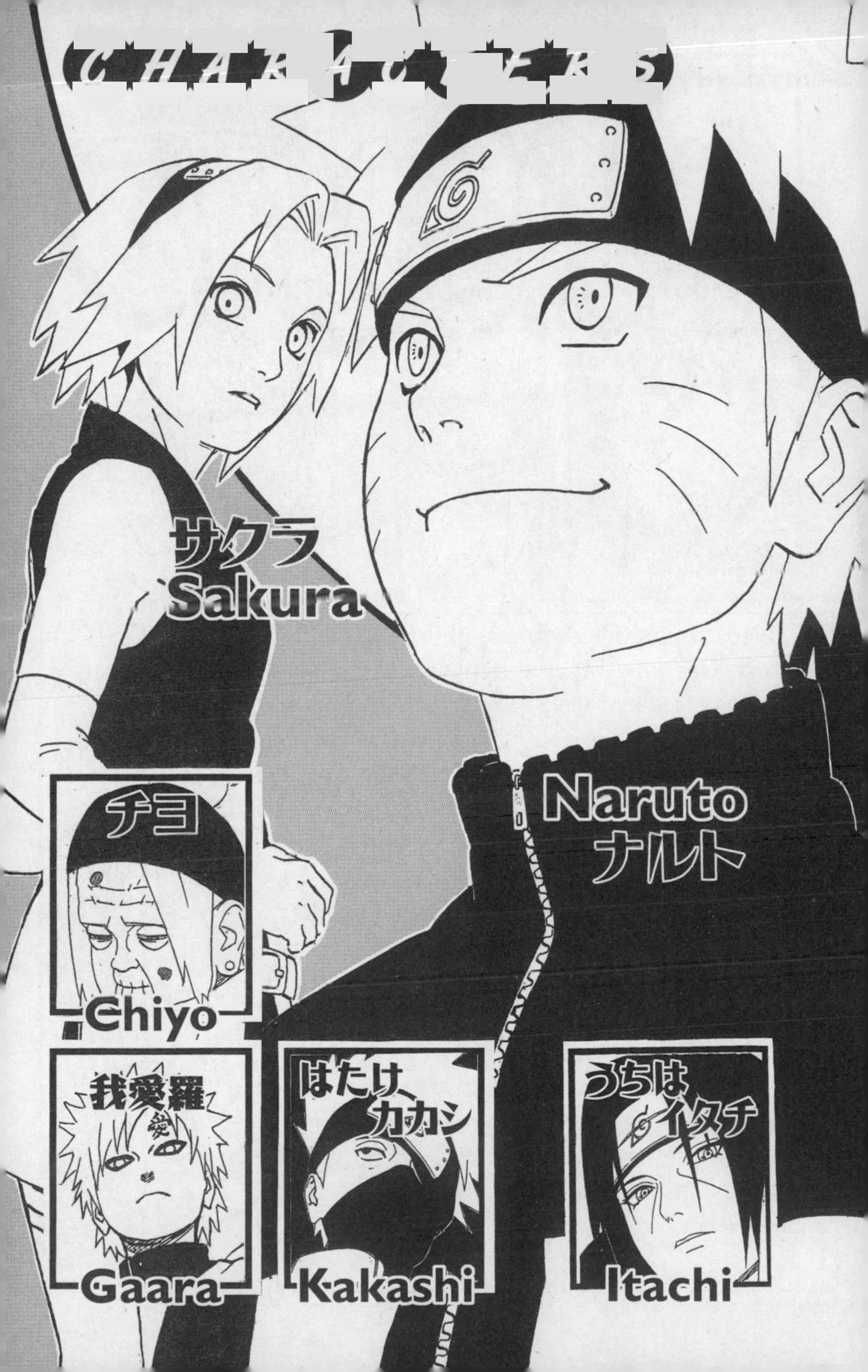
CHARACTERS
Naruto
ナルト
サクラ
Sakura
チヨ
Chiyo
うちは
イタチ
Itachi
はたけ
カカシ
Kakashi
我愛羅
Gaara

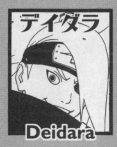

マイト・ガイ
Might Guy
ロック・リー
Rock Lee
デイダラ
Deidara
テンテン
Tenten
ひゅうが
日向ネジ
Neji
サソリ
Sasori

The Story So Far...

Naruto was once the bane of the Konohagakure Ninja Academy. Despite the rough start, he successfully joins the ranks of ninja along with Sasuke and Sakura. During the Chûnin Exam, Orochimaru launches *Operation Destroy Konoha,* an attack thwarted by the Third Hokage's sacrifice of his own life. After the battle, Tsunade steps up to become the Fifth Hokage. Lured by Orochimaru's power, Sasuke leaves Konoha in the company of the Sound Ninja Four. Naruto confronts Sasuke, but no matter how hard he fights, he can't stop his friend.

More than two years pass. Naruto and his friends mature, each undergoing rigorous training. Gaara, who has become Kazekage, is suddenly kidnapped by the dark Akatsuki organization. Naruto and the gang set out for the Akatsuki hideaway on their way to rescue Gaara.

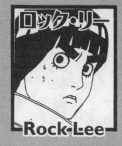

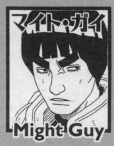

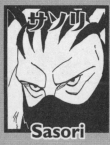

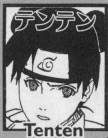

NARUTO

VOL. 30
PUPPET MASTERS

CONTENTS

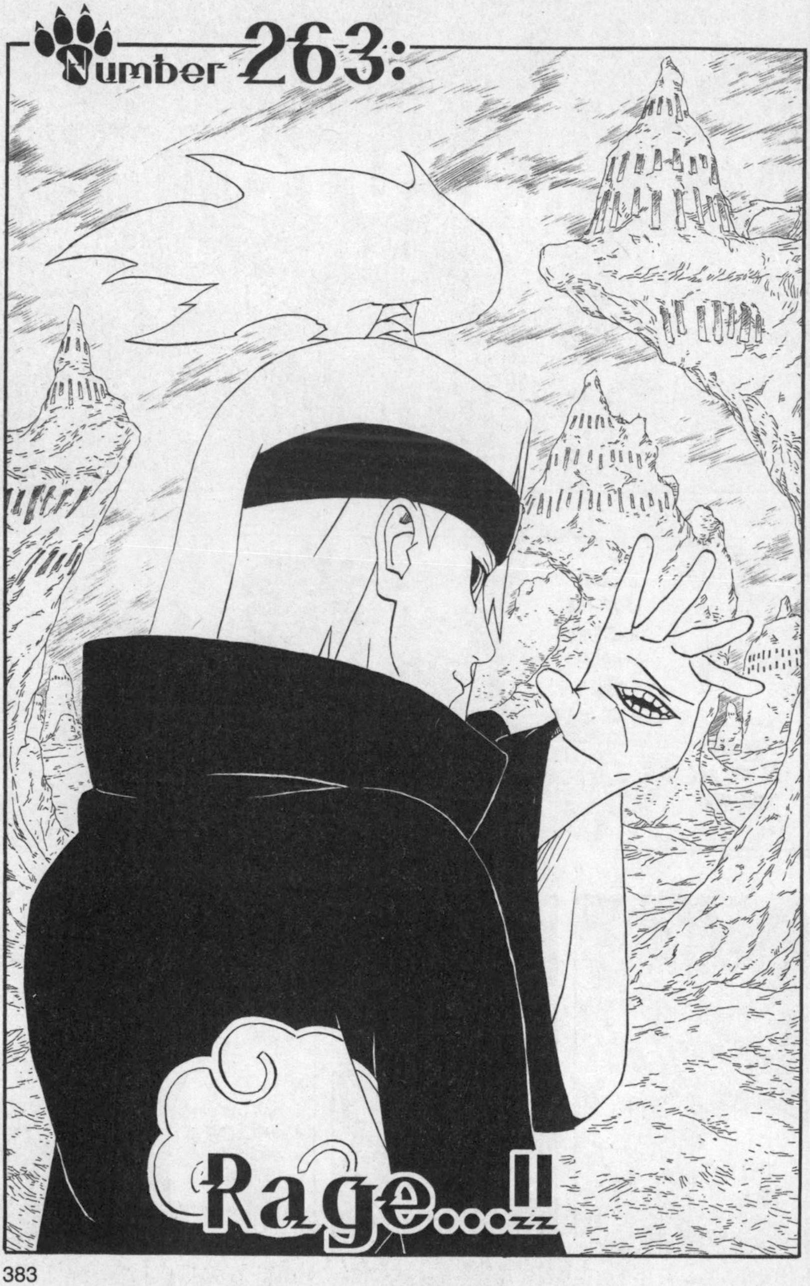
Number 263:
Rage...!!

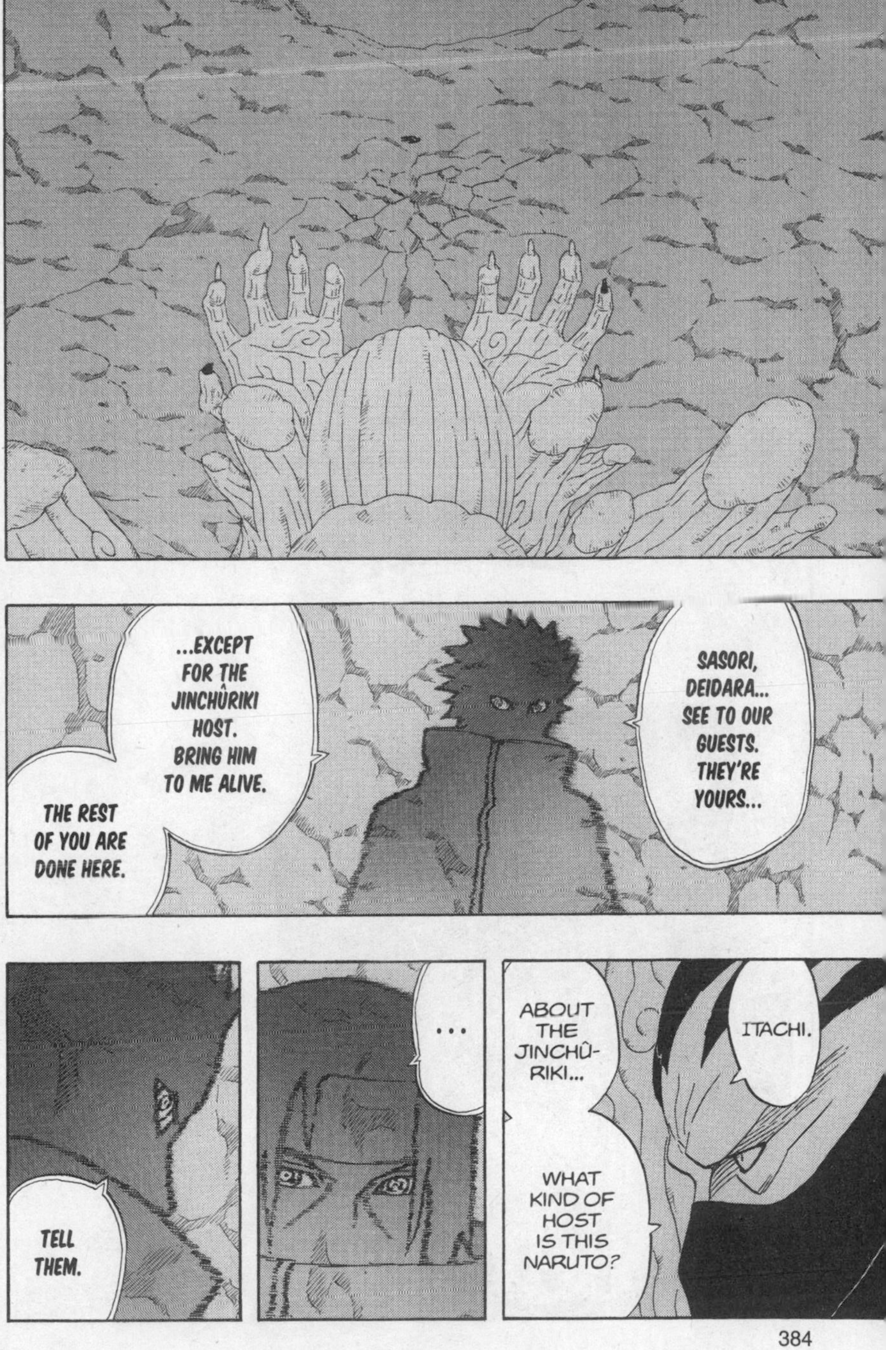
SASORI, DEIDARA... SEE TO OUR GUESTS. THEY'RE YOURS...
...EXCEPT FOR THE JINCHÛRIKI HOST. BRING HIM TO ME ALIVE.
THE REST OF YOU ARE DONE HERE.
ITACHI.
ABOUT THE JINCHÛ-RIKI...
WHAT KIND OF HOST IS THIS NARUTO?
...
TELL THEM.

READ THIS WAY

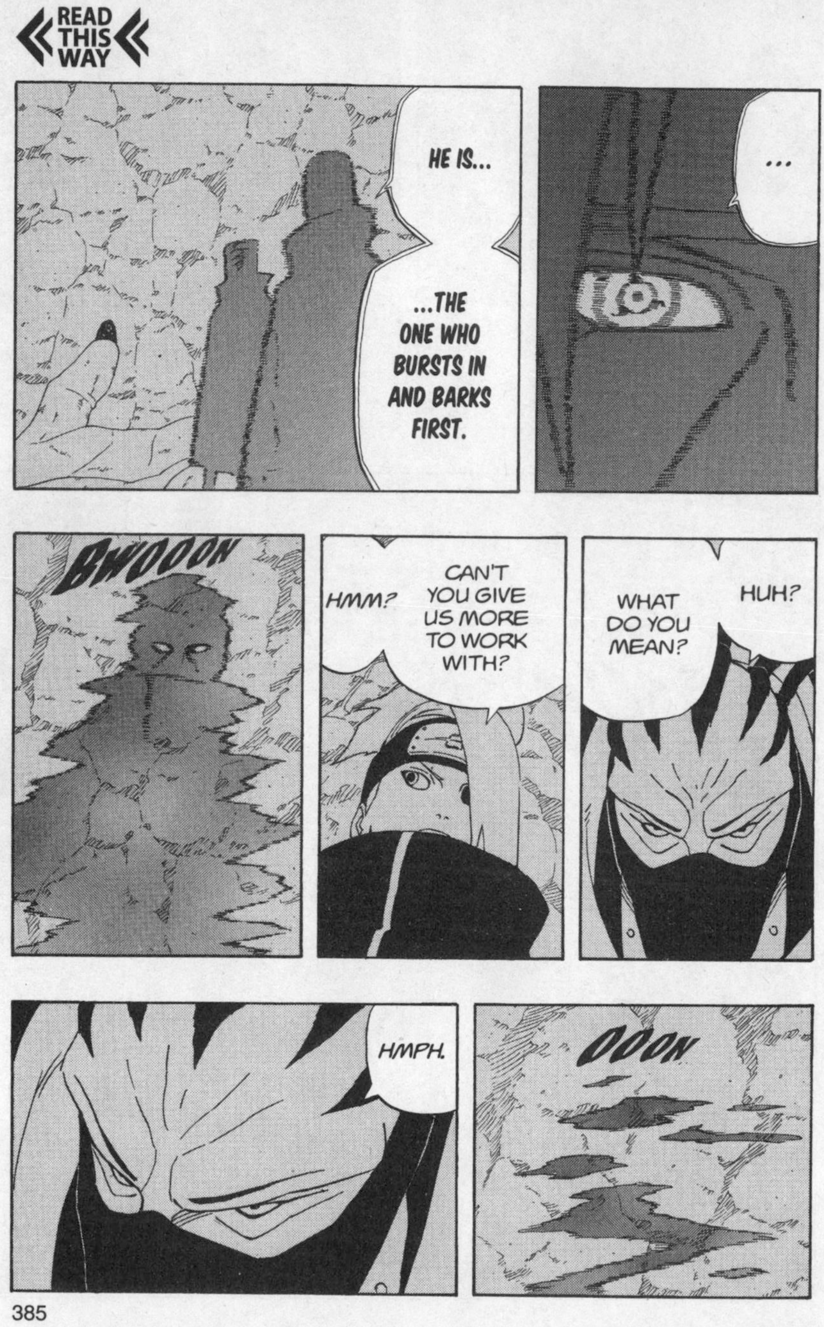

...
HE IS...
...THE ONE WHO BURSTS IN AND BARKS FIRST.
HUH?
WHAT DO YOU MEAN?
CAN'T YOU GIVE US MORE TO WORK WITH?
HMM?
BWOOOON
OOON
HMPH.

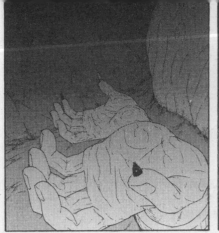
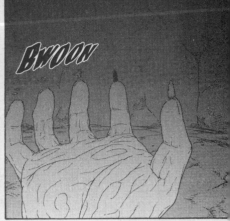

BWOON

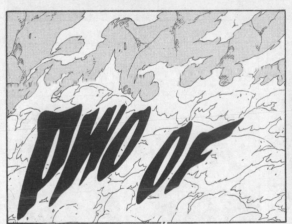

DWOOF

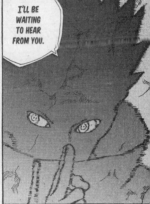

I'LL BE WAITING TO HEAR FROM YOU.

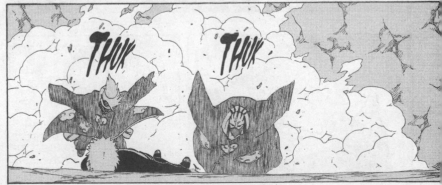

THOK THOK

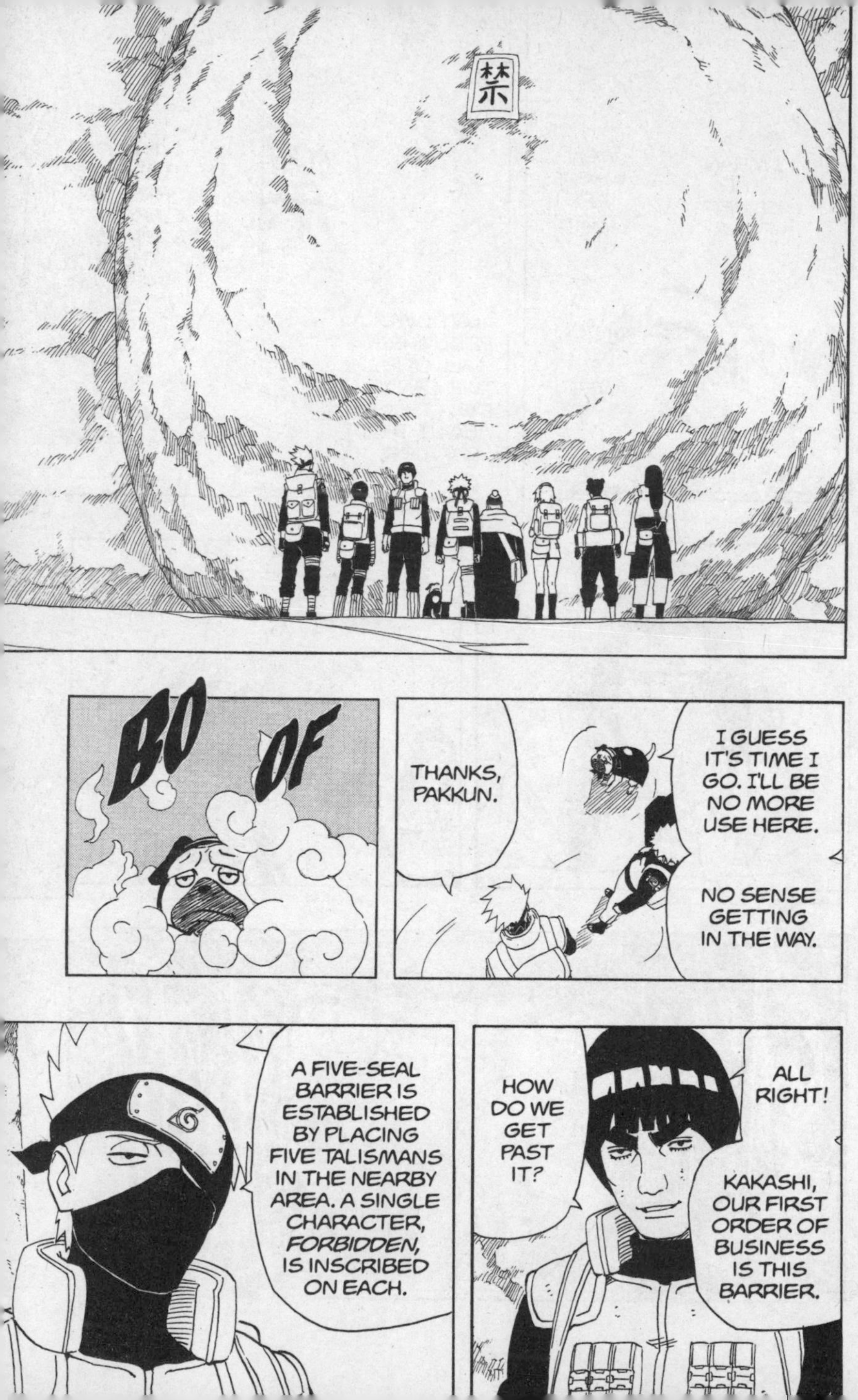
禁
I GUESS IT'S TIME I GO. I'LL BE NO MORE USE HERE.
NO SENSE GETTING IN THE WAY.
THANKS, PAKKUN.
BOOF
ALL RIGHT!
KAKASHI, OUR FIRST ORDER OF BUSINESS IS THIS BARRIER.
HOW DO WE GET PAST IT?
A FIVE-SEAL BARRIER IS ESTABLISHED BY PLACING FIVE TALISMANS IN THE NEARBY AREA. A SINGLE CHARACTER, *FORBIDDEN*, IS INSCRIBED ON EACH.

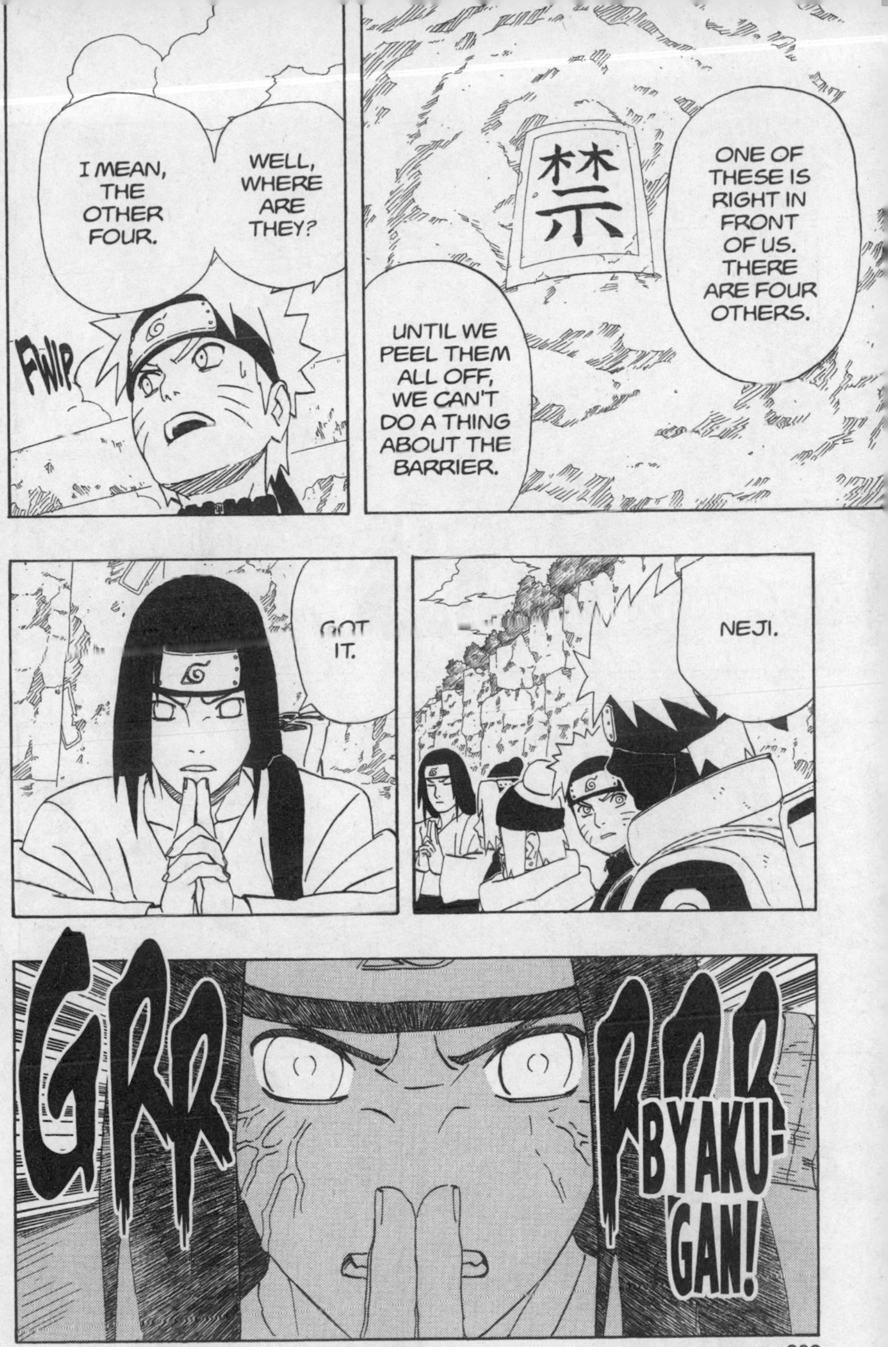
禁
ONE OF THESE IS RIGHT IN FRONT OF US. THERE ARE FOUR OTHERS.
UNTIL WE PEEL THEM ALL OFF, WE CAN'T DO A THING ABOUT THE BARRIER.
WELL, WHERE ARE THEY?
I MEAN, THE OTHER FOUR.
FWIP
NEJI.
GOT IT.
GRR
RRR
BYAKU-GAN!

READ THIS WAY

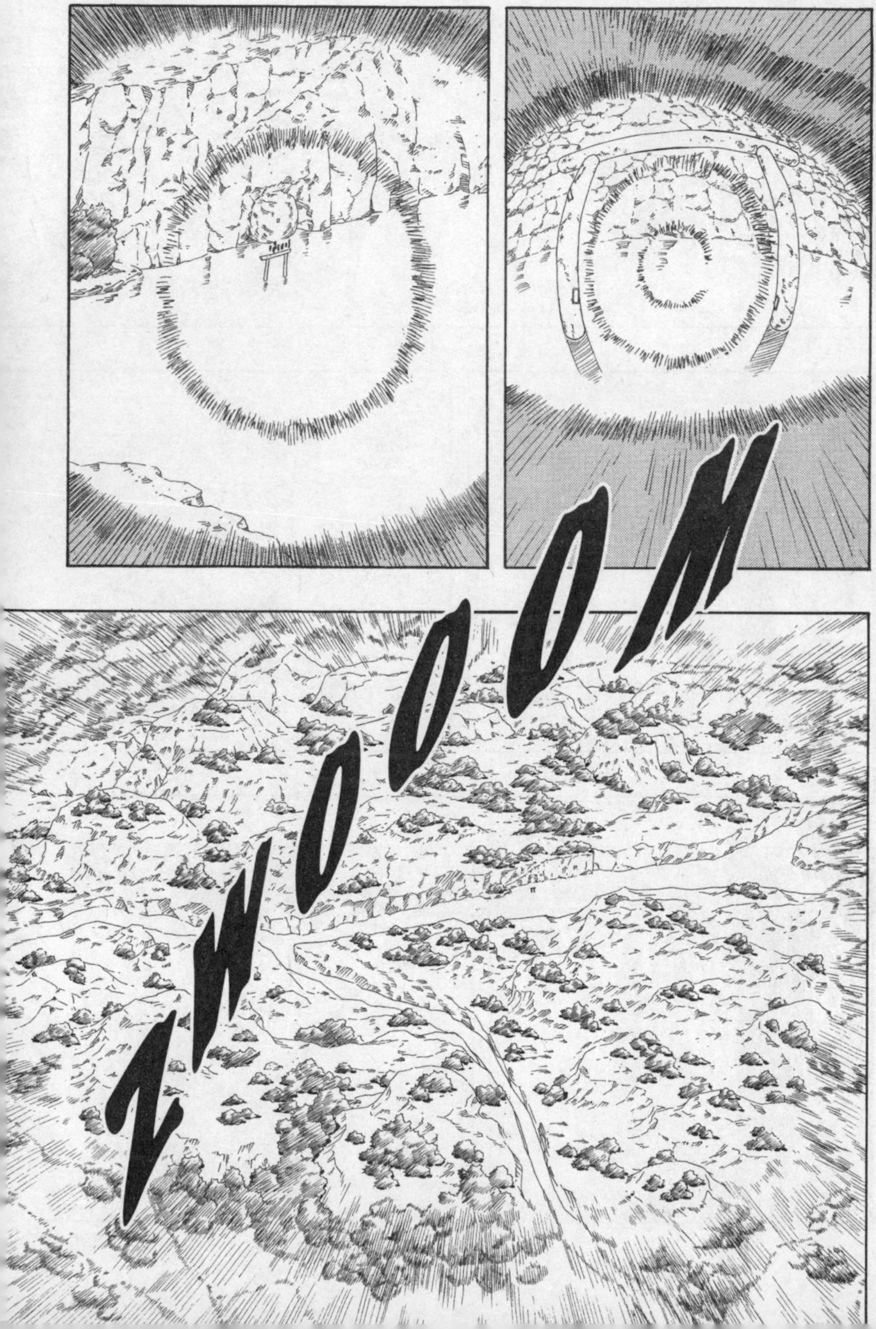
ZWOOOM

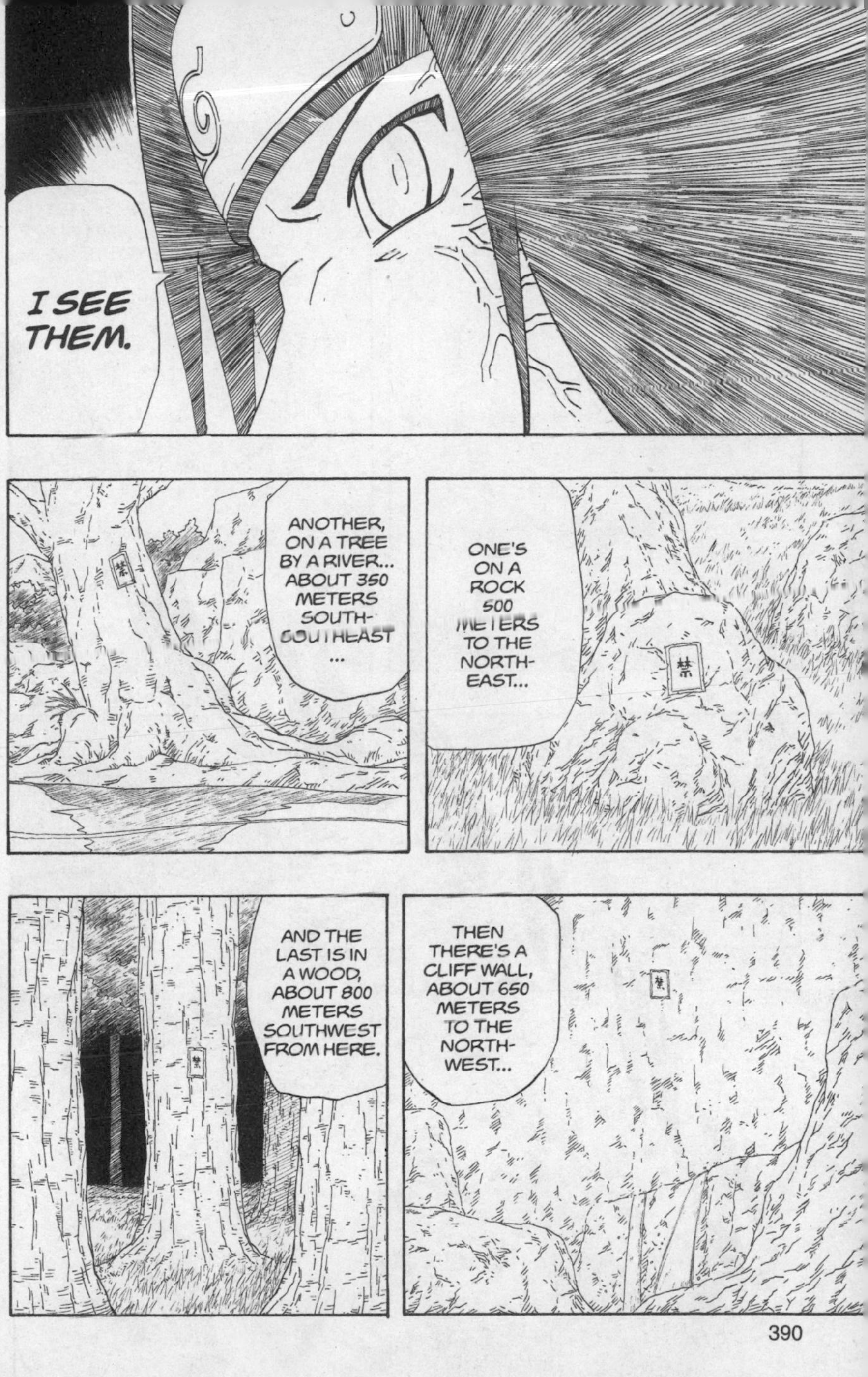
I SEE THEM.
ONE'S ON A ROCK 500 METERS TO THE NORTHEAST...
ANOTHER, ON A TREE BY A RIVER... ABOUT 350 METERS SOUTH-SOUTHEAST...
THEN THERE'S A CLIFF WALL, ABOUT 650 METERS TO THE NORTHWEST...
AND THE LAST IS IN A WOOD, ABOUT 800 METERS SOUTHWEST FROM HERE.

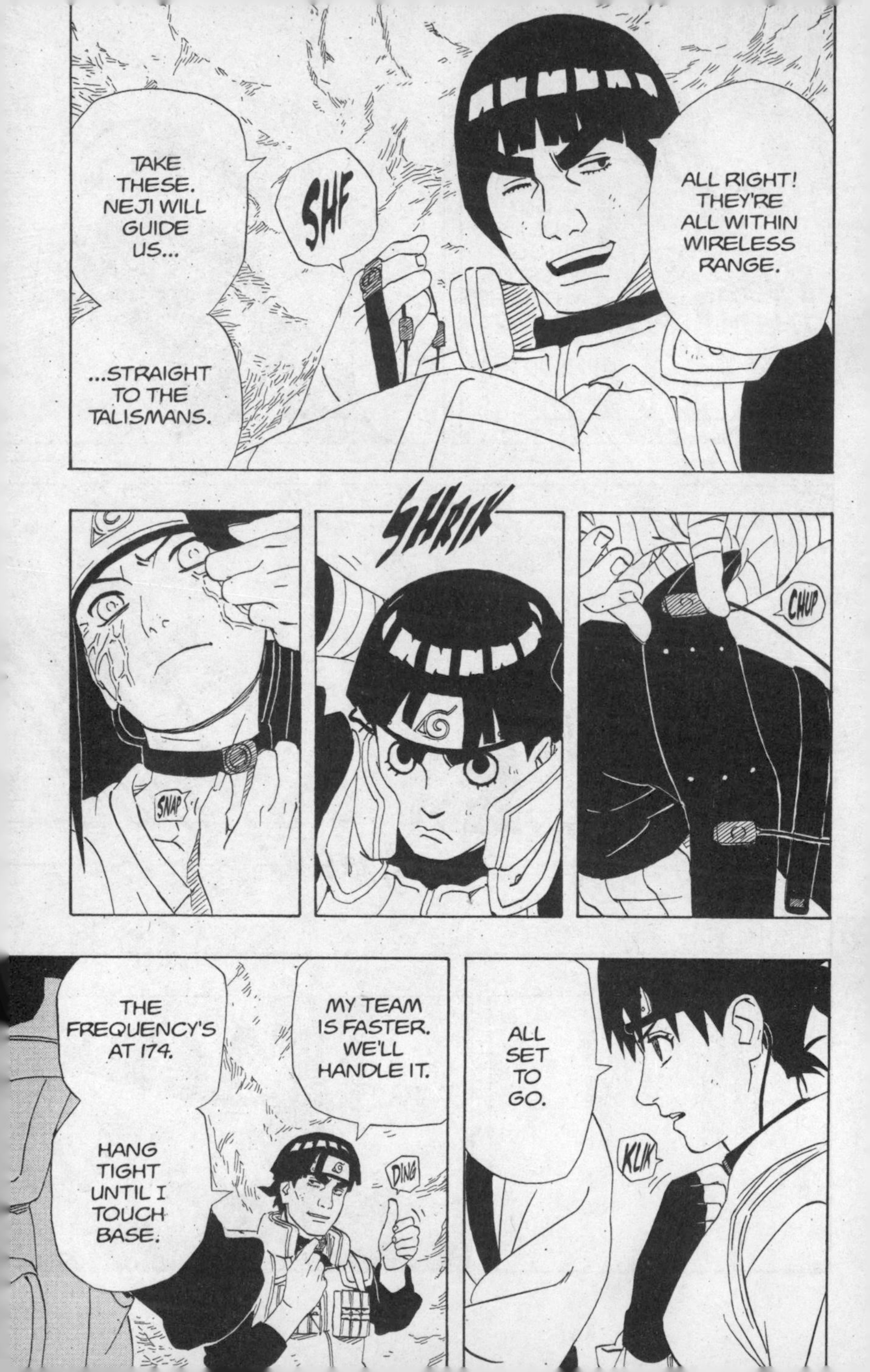
ALL RIGHT! THEY'RE ALL WITHIN WIRELESS RANGE.
SHF
TAKE THESE. NEJI WILL GUIDE US...
...STRAIGHT TO THE TALISMANS.
CHUP
SHRIK
SNAP
ALL SET TO GO.
KLIK
MY TEAM IS FASTER. WE'LL HANDLE IT.
DING
THE FREQUENCY'S AT 174.
HANG TIGHT UNTIL I TOUCH BASE.

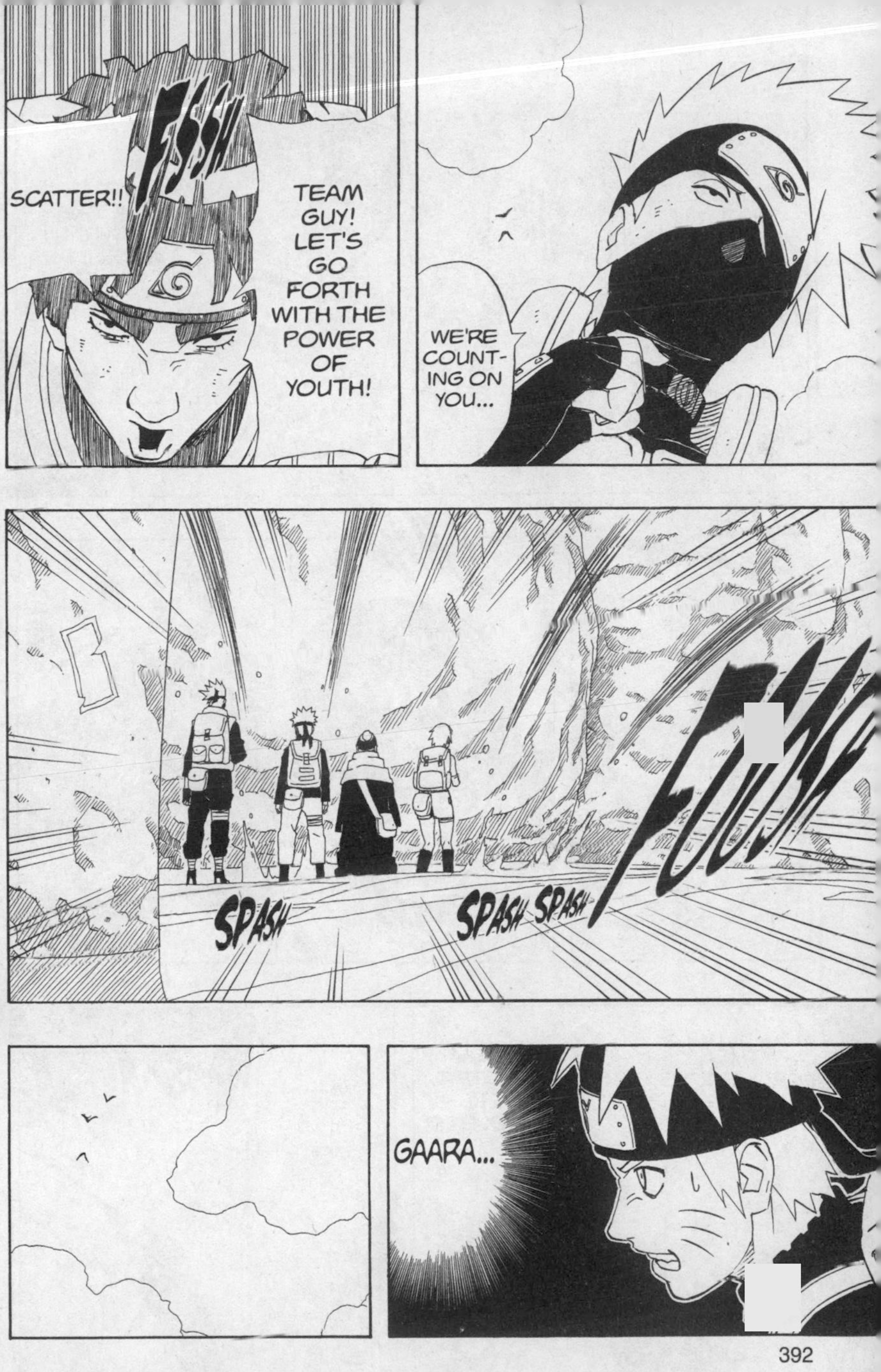
WE'RE COUNTING ON YOU...
TEAM GUY! LET'S GO FORTH WITH THE POWER OF YOUTH!
FSSH
SCATTER!!
FOOSH
SPASH SPASH
SPASH
GAARA...

READ THIS WAY

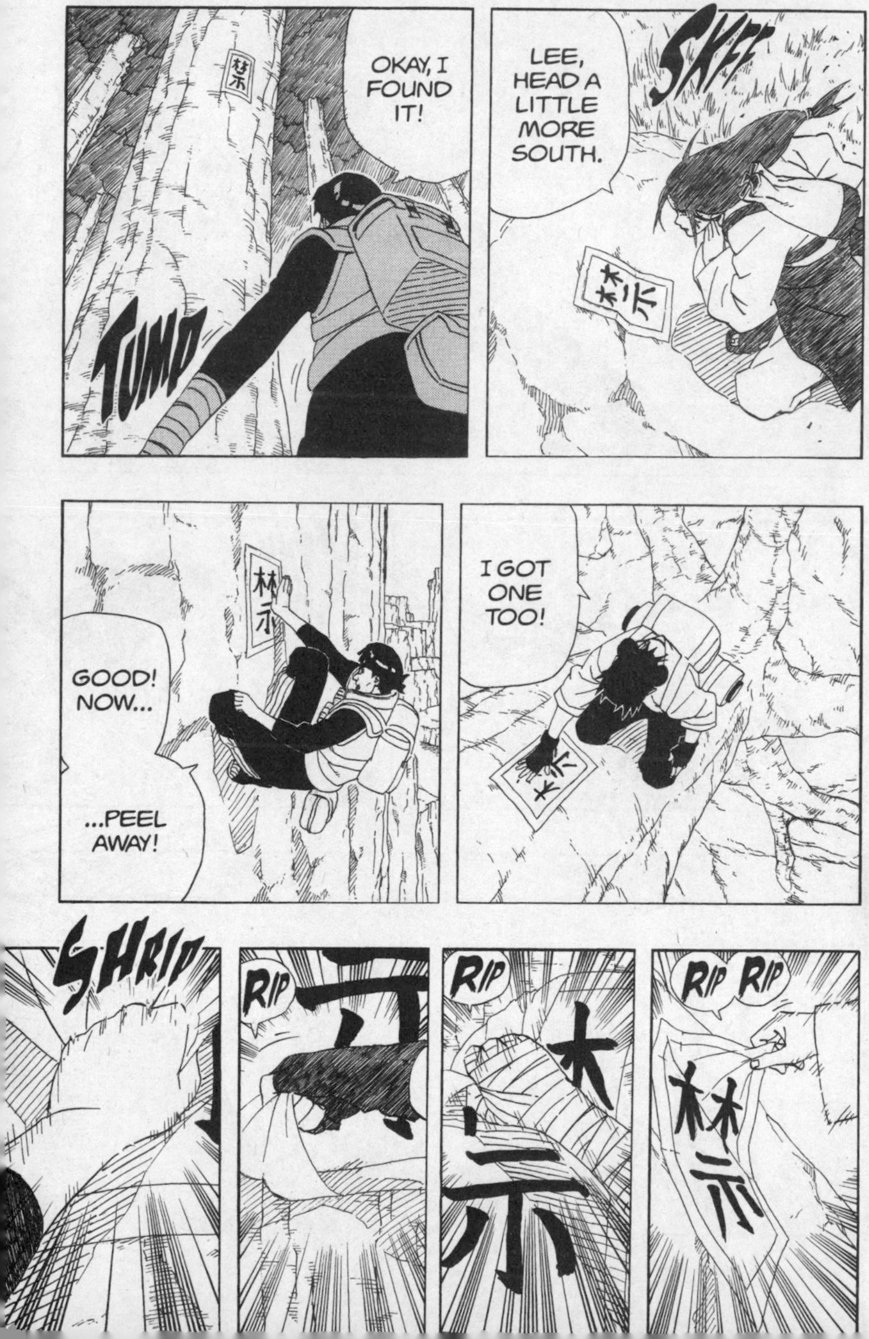
SHFF
LEE, HEAD A LITTLE MORE SOUTH.
OKAY, I FOUND IT!
TUMP
I GOT ONE TOO!
GOOD! NOW...
...PEEL AWAY!
RIP RIP
RIP
RIP
SHRIP

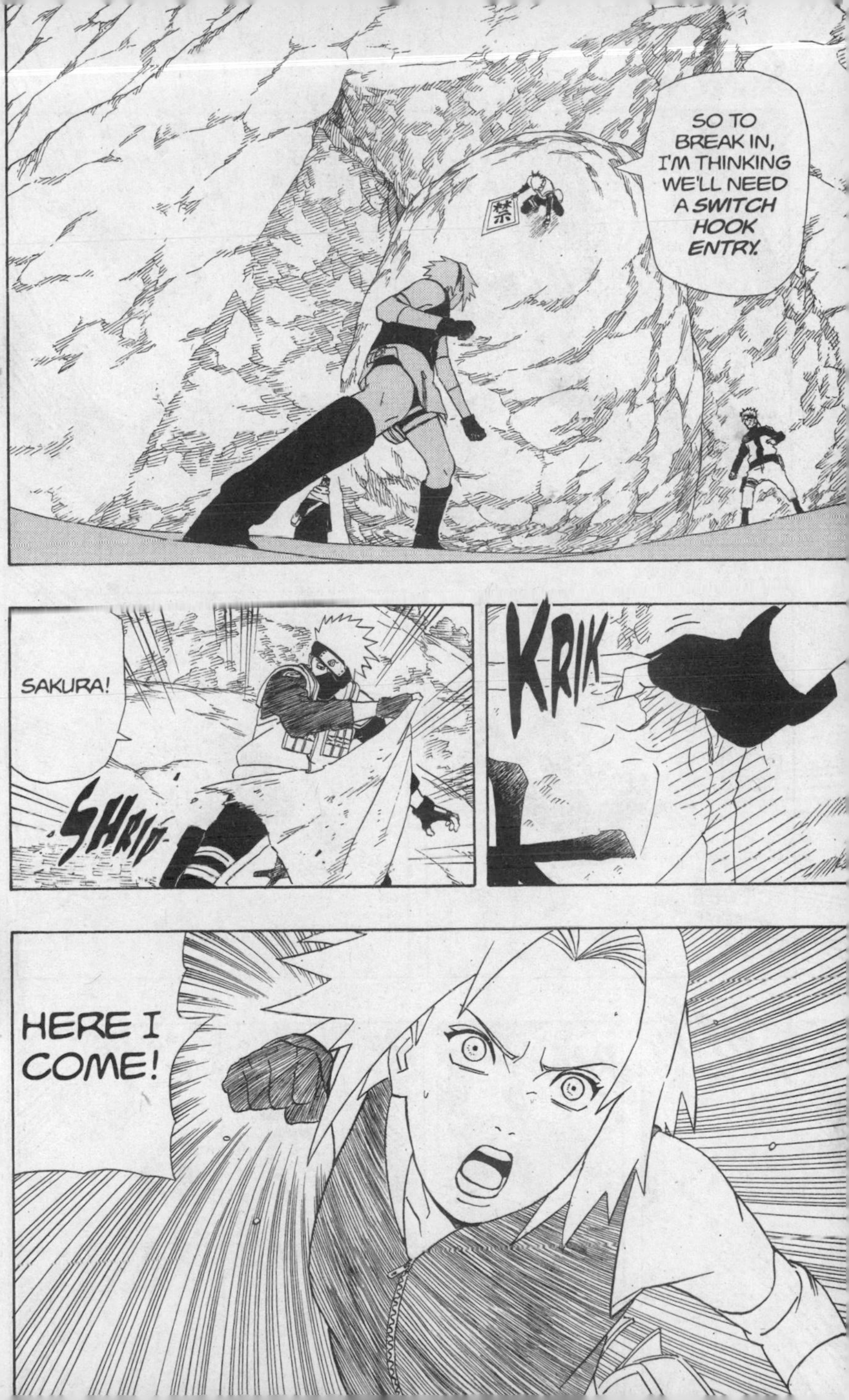
SO TO BREAK IN, I'M THINKING WE'LL NEED A *SWITCH HOOK ENTRY.*
禁
KRIK
SAKURA!
SHRIP
HERE I COME!

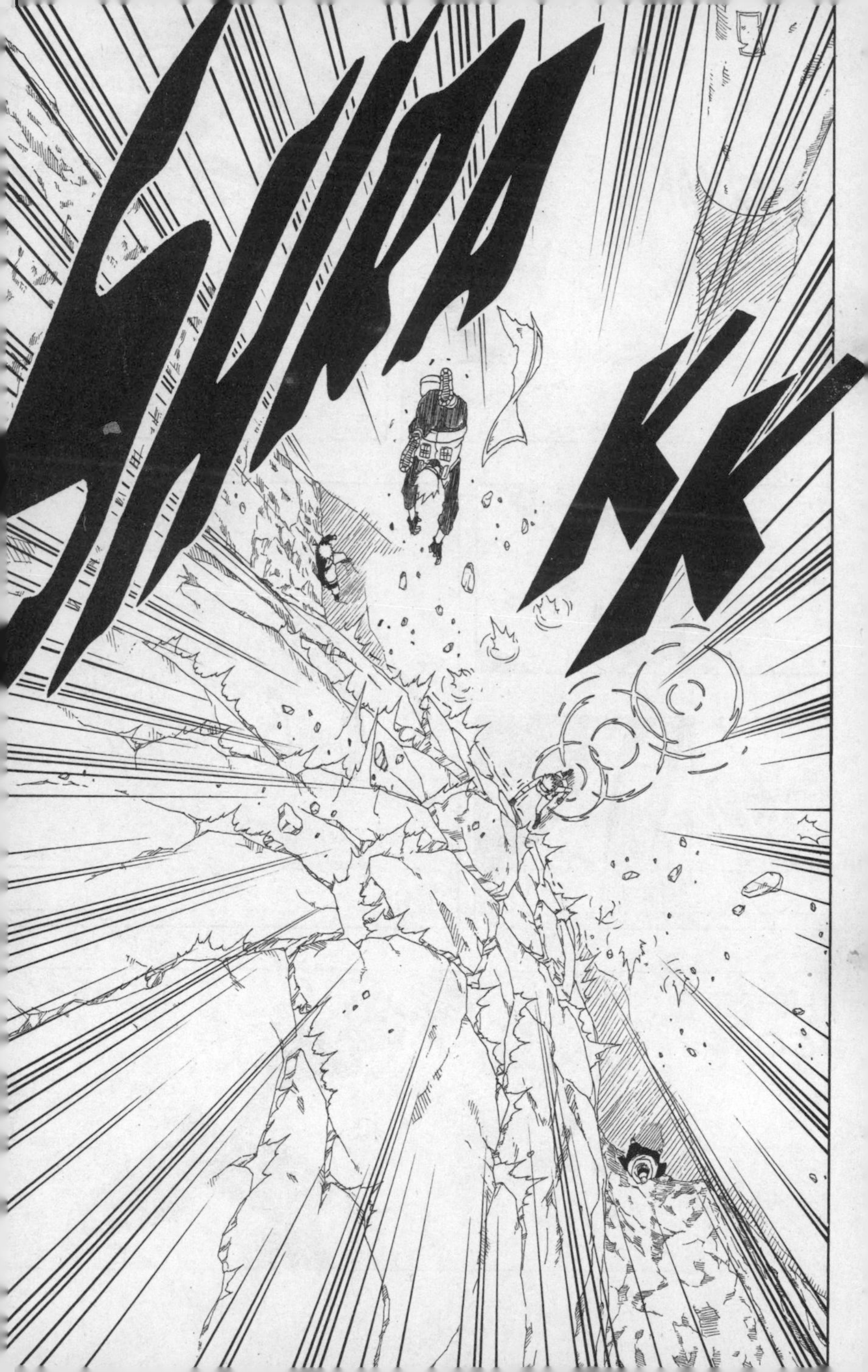

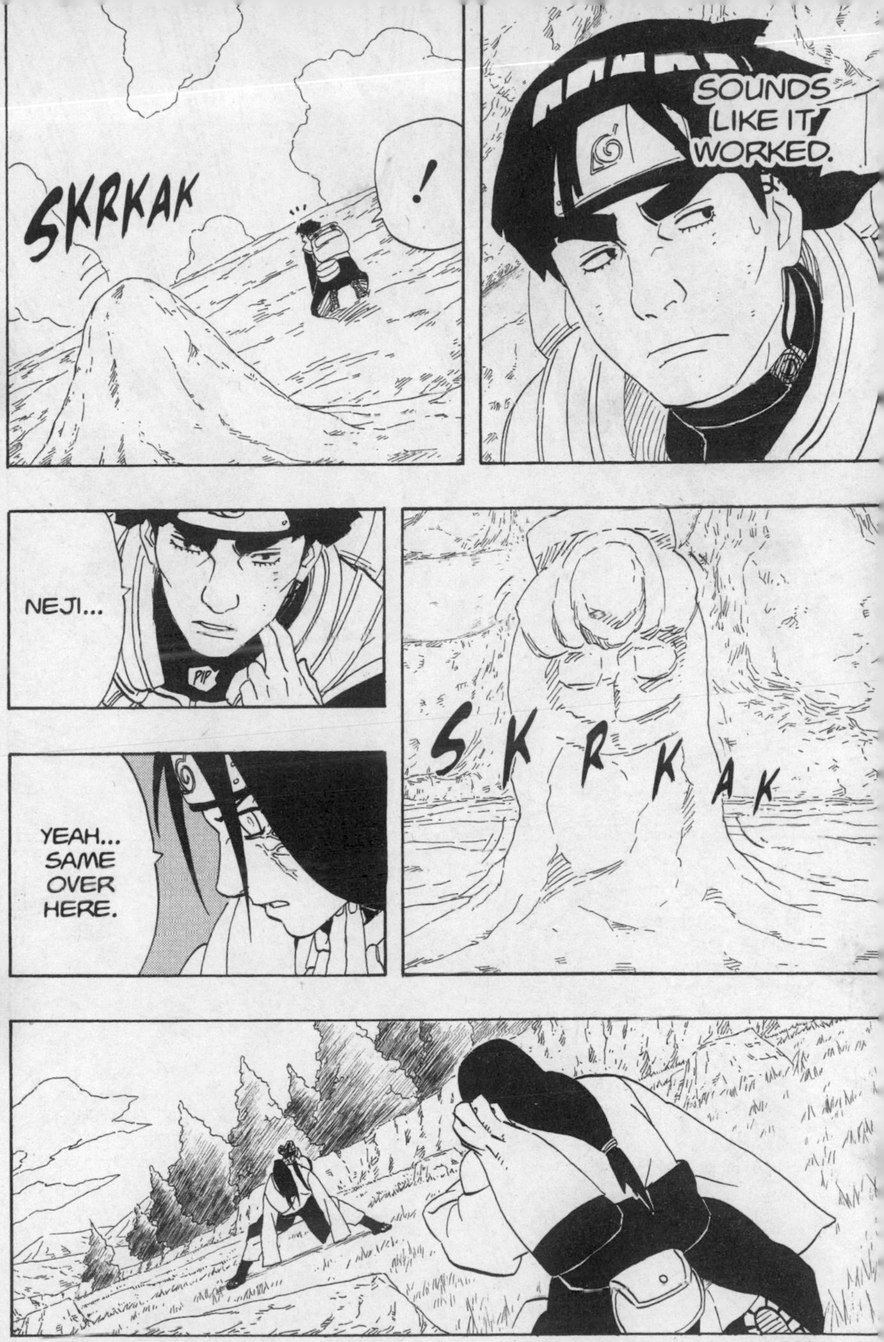
SOUNDS LIKE IT WORKED.
!
SKRKAK
SKRKAK
NEJI...
PIP
YEAH... SAME OVER HERE.

READ THIS WAY

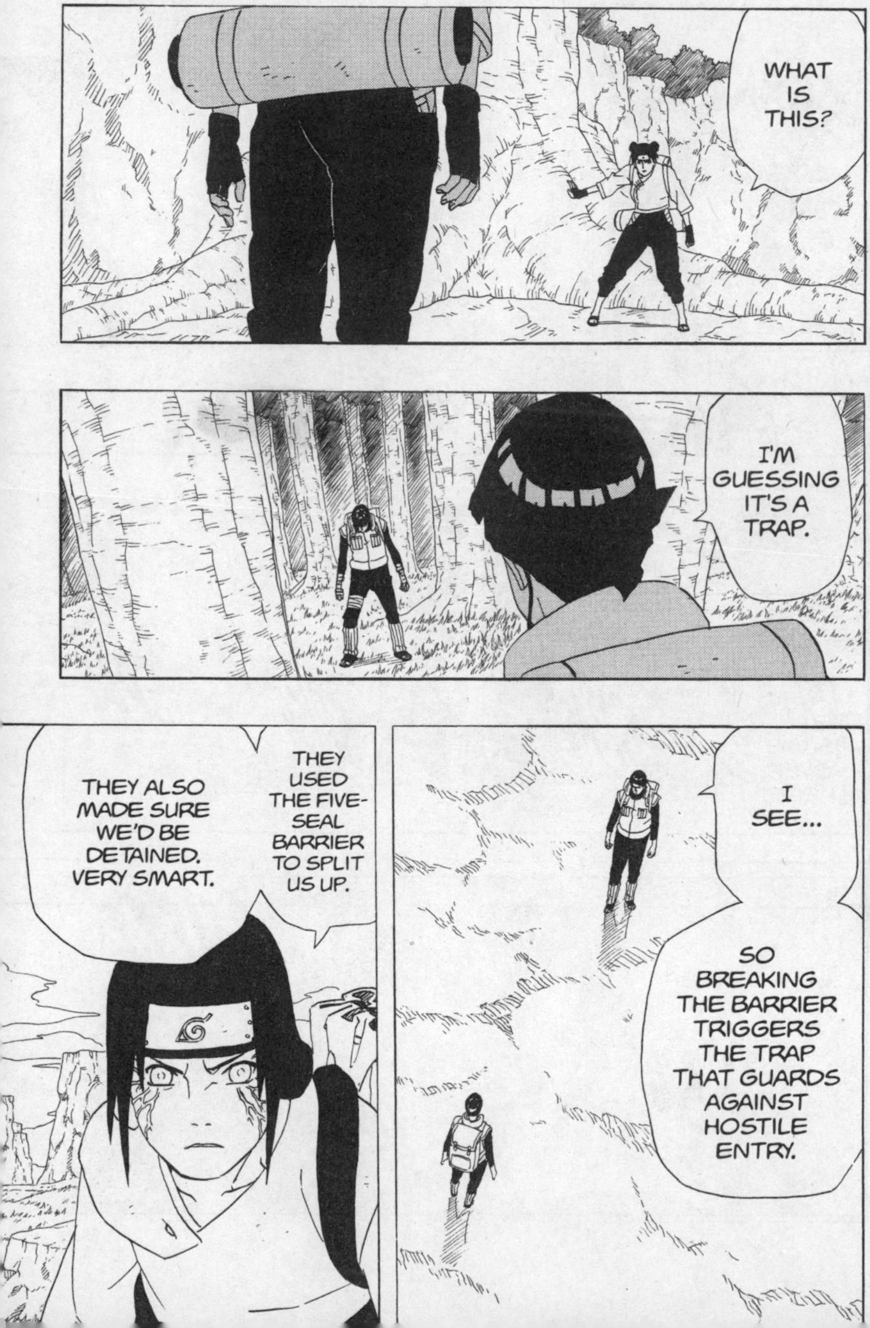

WHAT IS THIS?
I'M GUESSING IT'S A TRAP.
I SEE...
SO BREAKING THE BARRIER TRIGGERS THE TRAP THAT GUARDS AGAINST HOSTILE ENTRY.
THEY USED THE FIVE-SEAL BARRIER TO SPLIT US UP.
THEY ALSO MADE SURE WE'D BE DETAINED. VERY SMART.

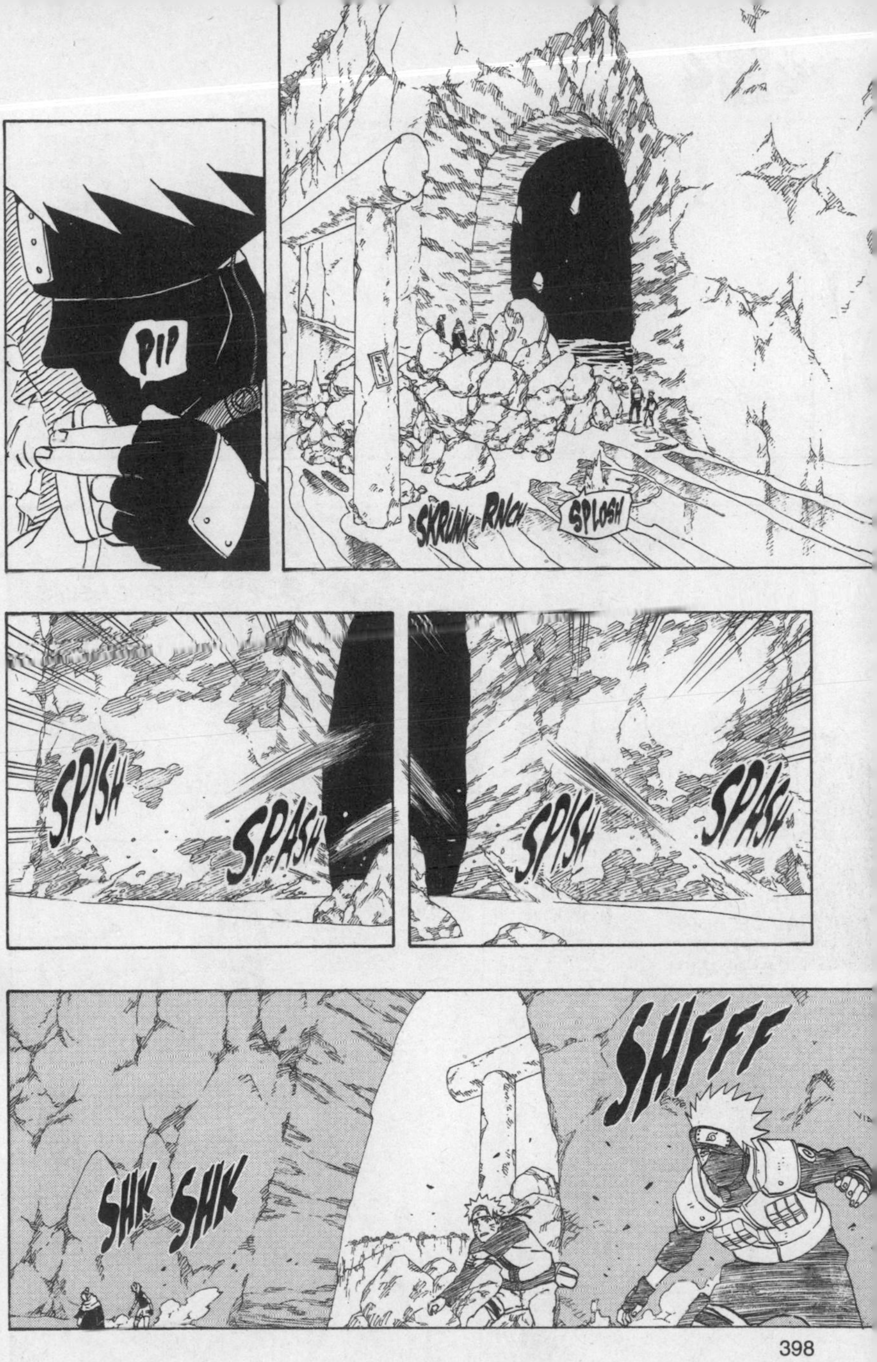
SPLOSH
RNCH
SKRUNK
PIP
SPASH
SPISH
SPASH
SPISH
SHFFF
SHK
SHK

READ THIS WAY

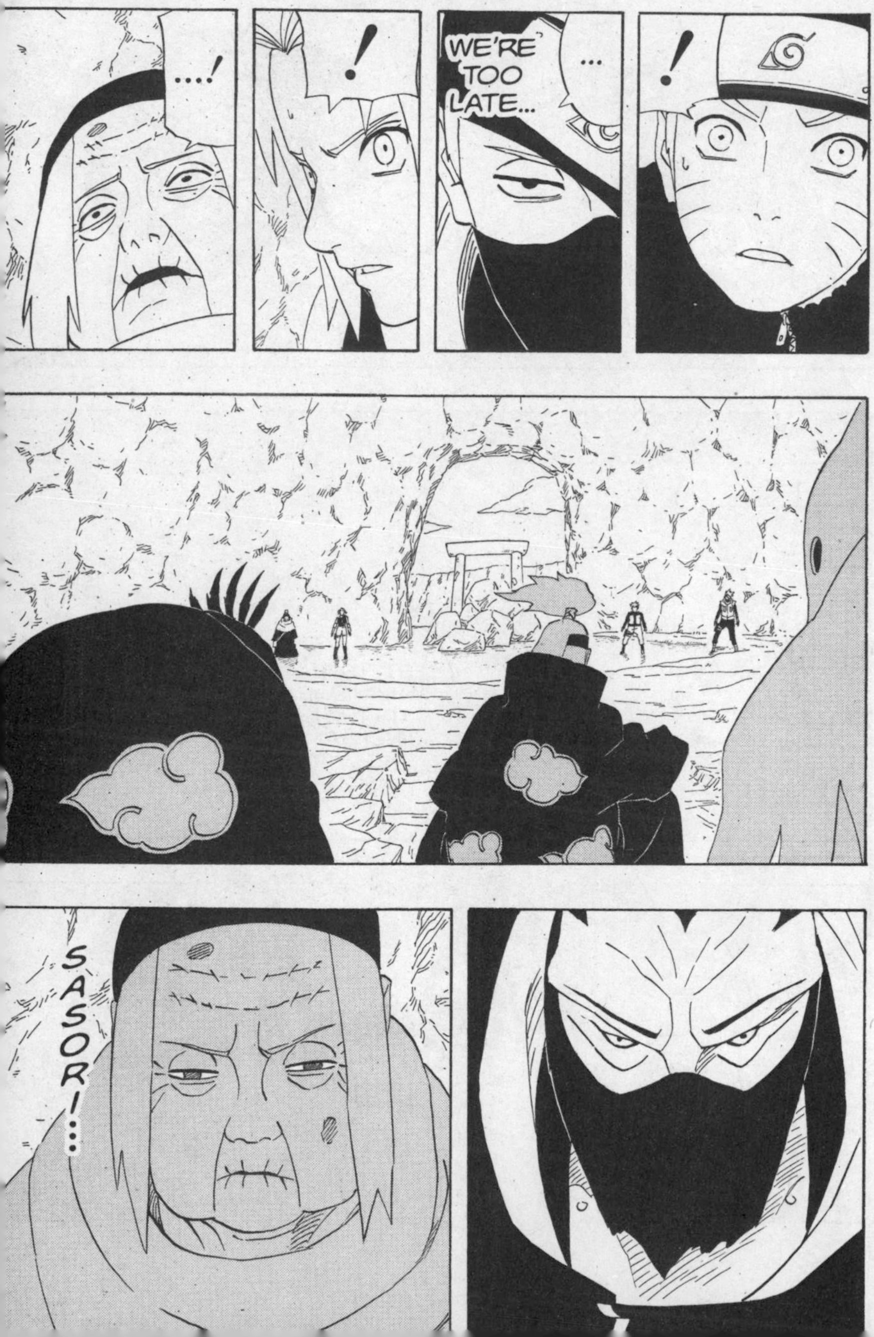
!
WE'RE TOO LATE...
...
!
....!
SASORI...

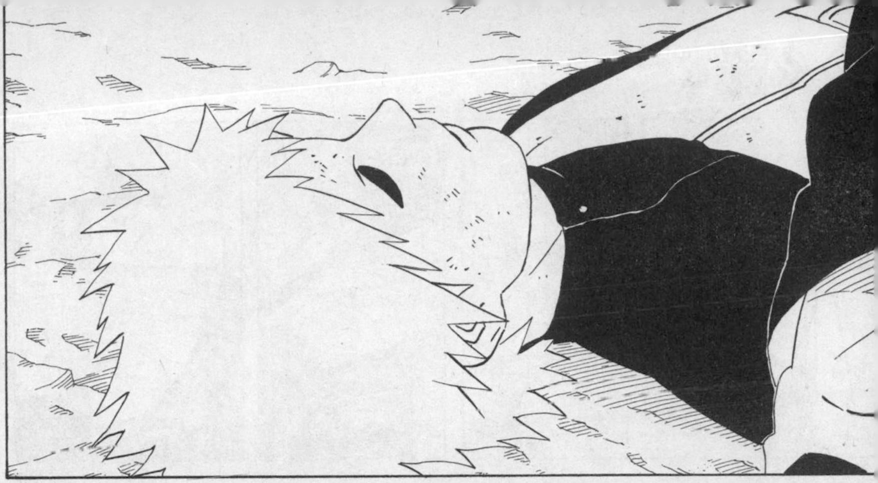

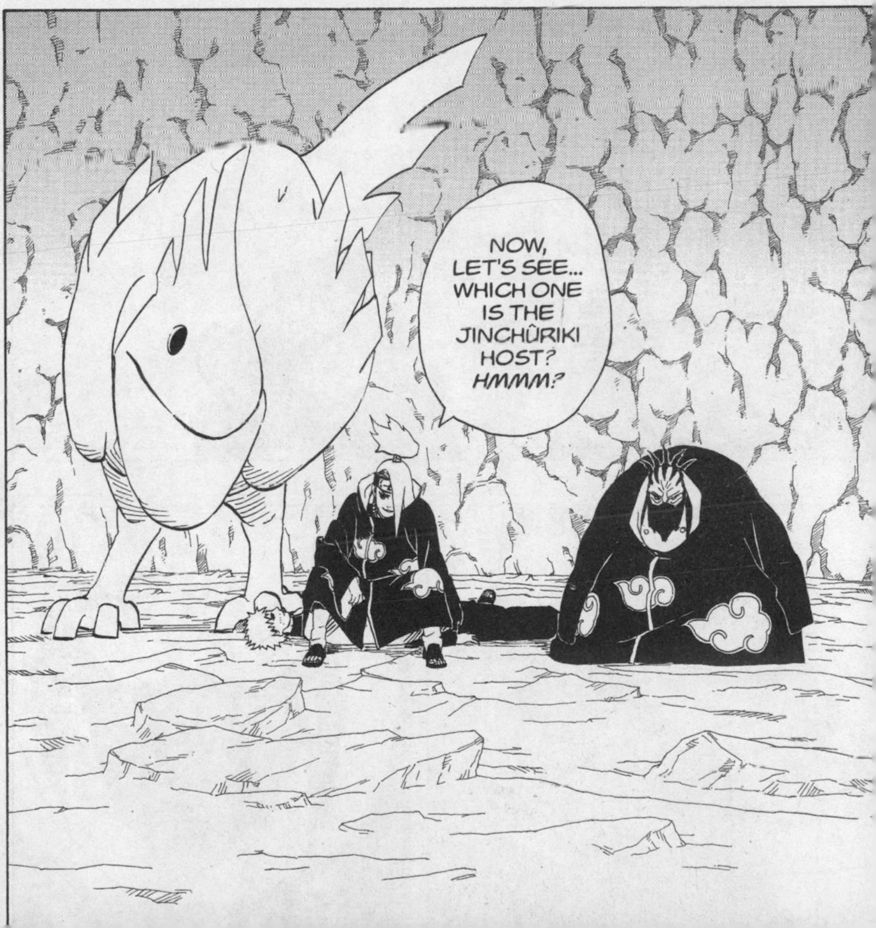
NOW, LET'S SEE... WHICH ONE IS THE JINCHÛRIKI HOST? *HMMM?*

READ THIS WAY

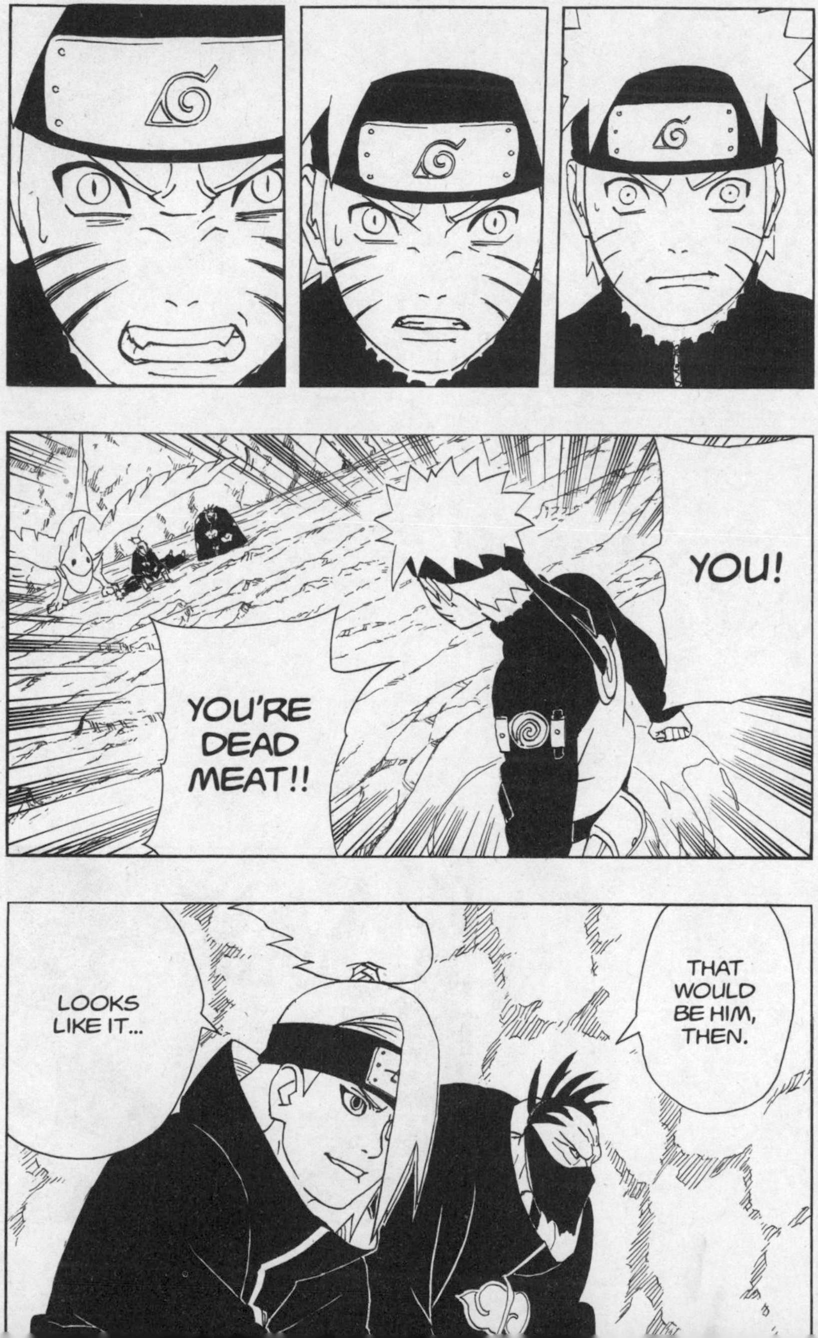
YOU!
YOU'RE DEAD MEAT!!
THAT WOULD BE HIM, THEN.
LOOKS LIKE IT...

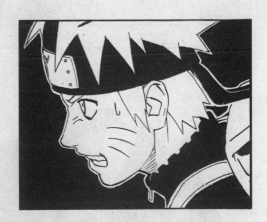

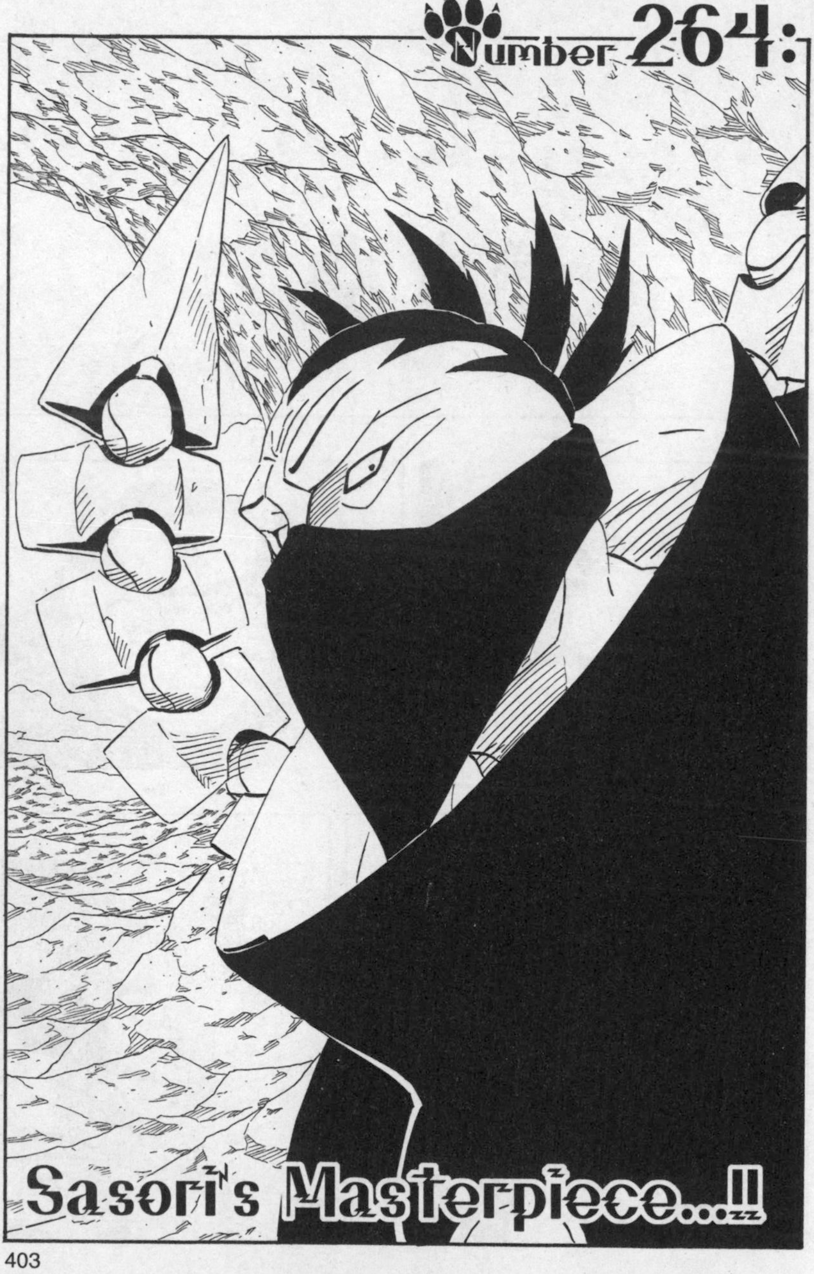
Number 264:
Sasori's Masterpiece...!!

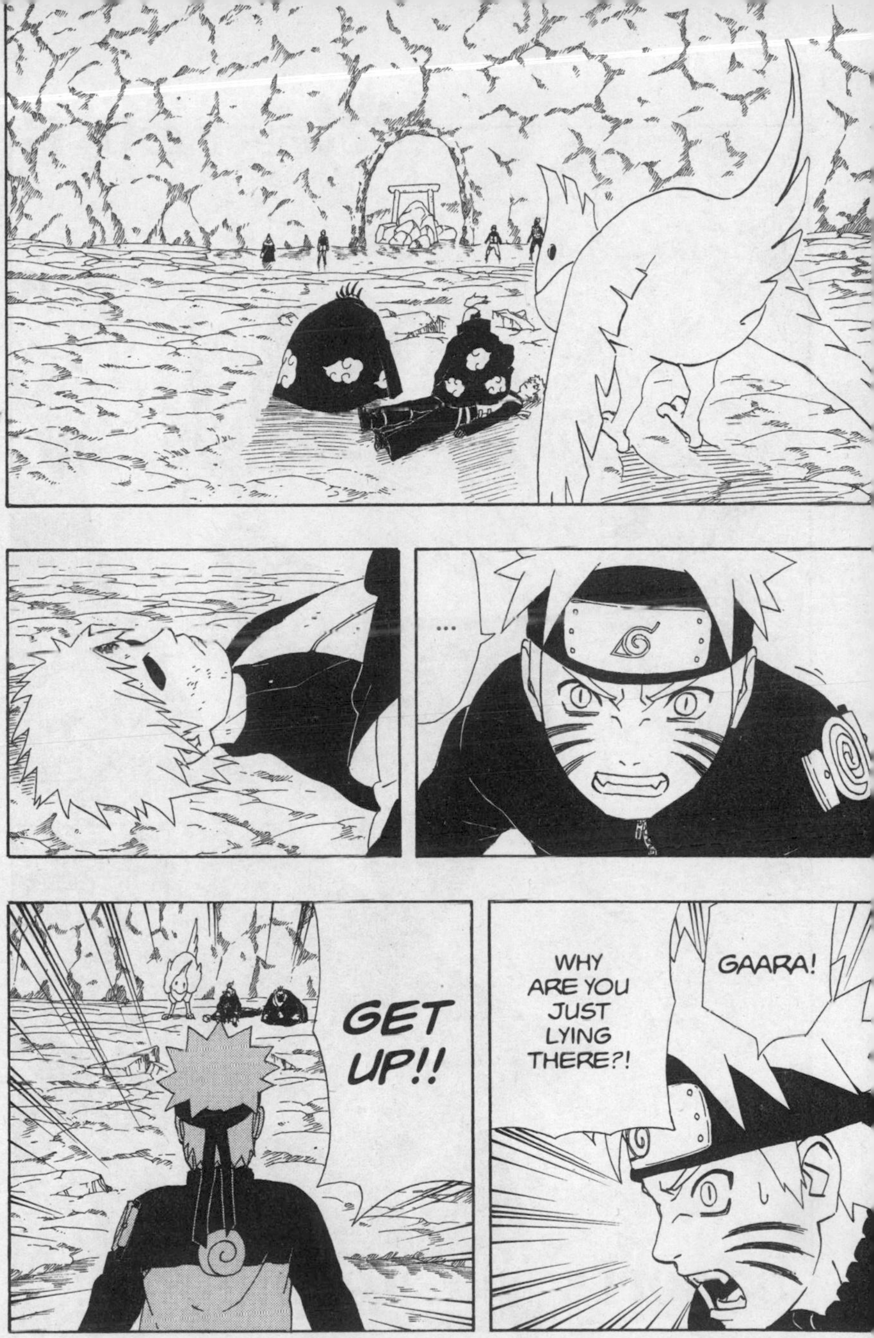
...
GAARA!
WHY ARE YOU JUST LYING THERE?!
GET UP!!

READ THIS WAY

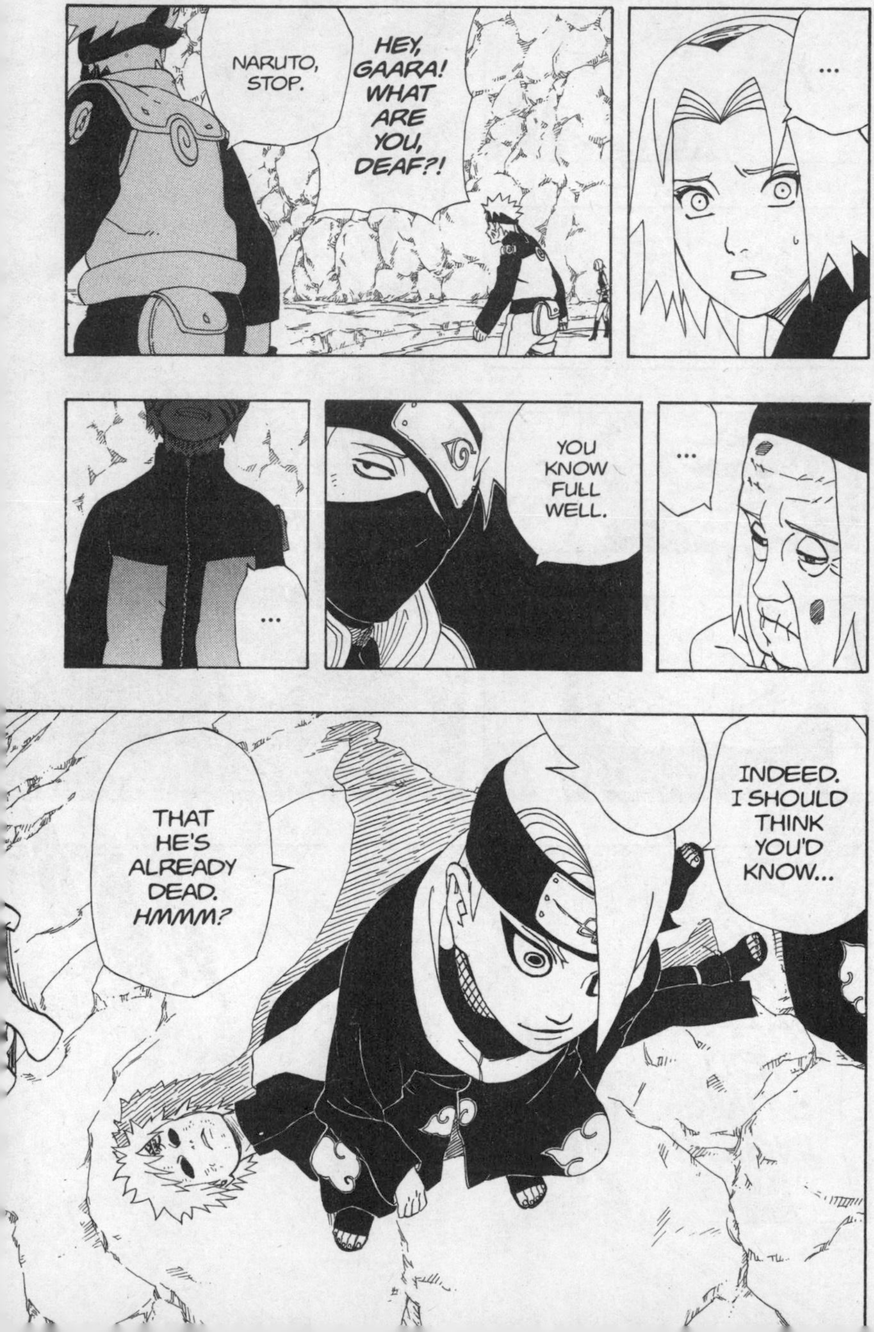
...
HEY, GAARA! WHAT ARE YOU, DEAF?!
NARUTO, STOP.
...
YOU KNOW FULL WELL.
...
INDEED. I SHOULD THINK YOU'D KNOW...
THAT HE'S ALREADY DEAD. HMMM?

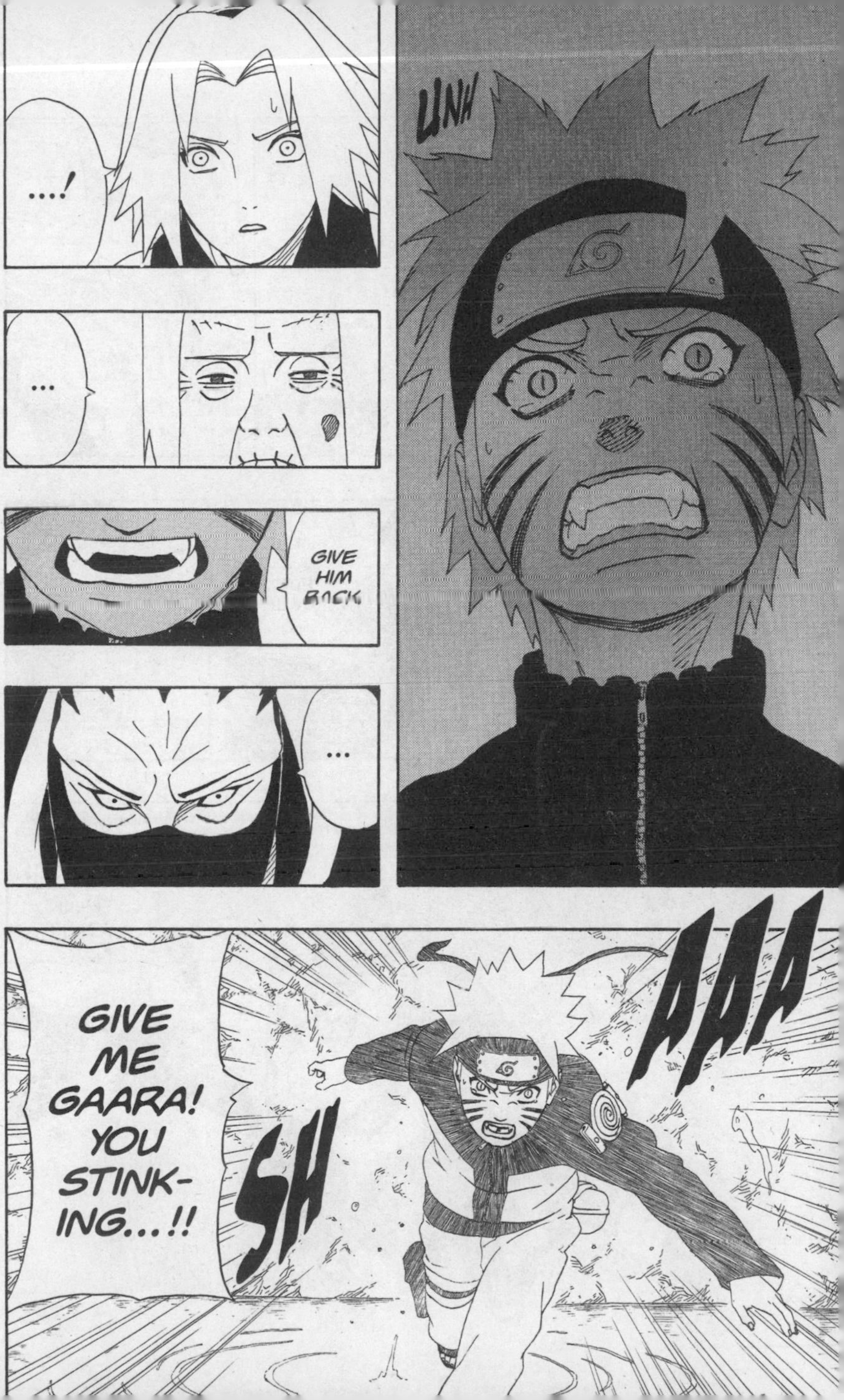
UNH
...!
...
GIVE HIM BACK
...
AAA
GIVE ME GAARA! YOU STINKING...!!
SH

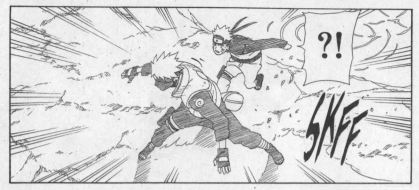

?!

SKFF

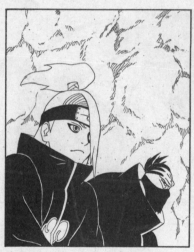

CHARGE IN WITHOUT THINKING, AND YOU'LL GET US ALL KILLED.

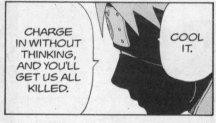

COOL IT.

URK...

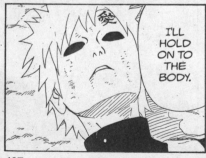

I'LL HOLD ON TO THE BODY.

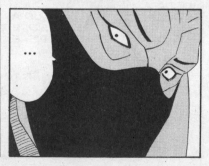

...

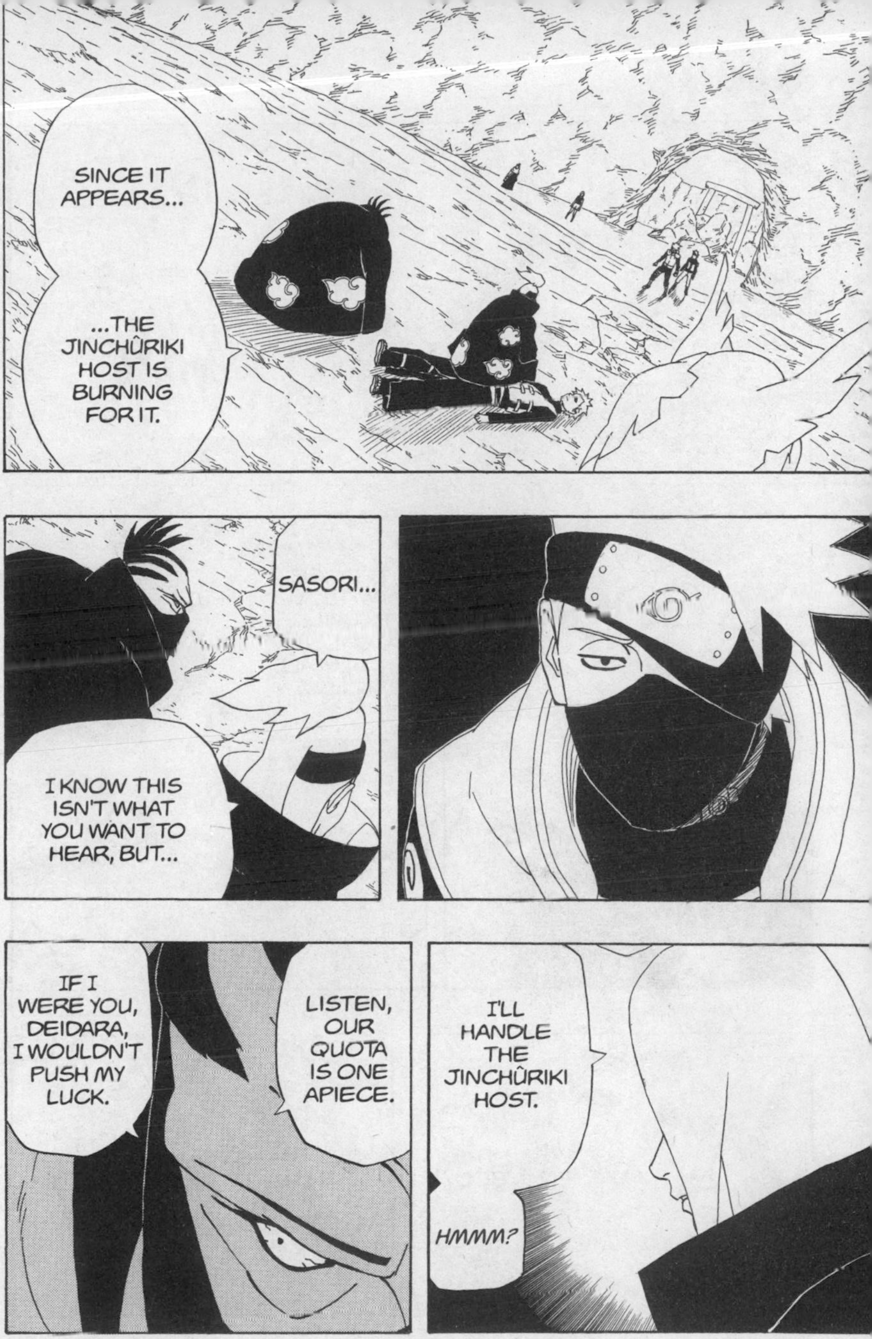
SINCE IT APPEARS...
...THE JINCHÛRIKI HOST IS BURNING FOR IT.
SASORI...
I KNOW THIS ISN'T WHAT YOU WANT TO HEAR, BUT...
I'LL HANDLE THE JINCHÛRIKI HOST.
HMMM?
LISTEN, OUR QUOTA IS ONE APIECE.
IF I WERE YOU, DEIDARA, I WOULDN'T PUSH MY LUCK.

READ THIS WAY

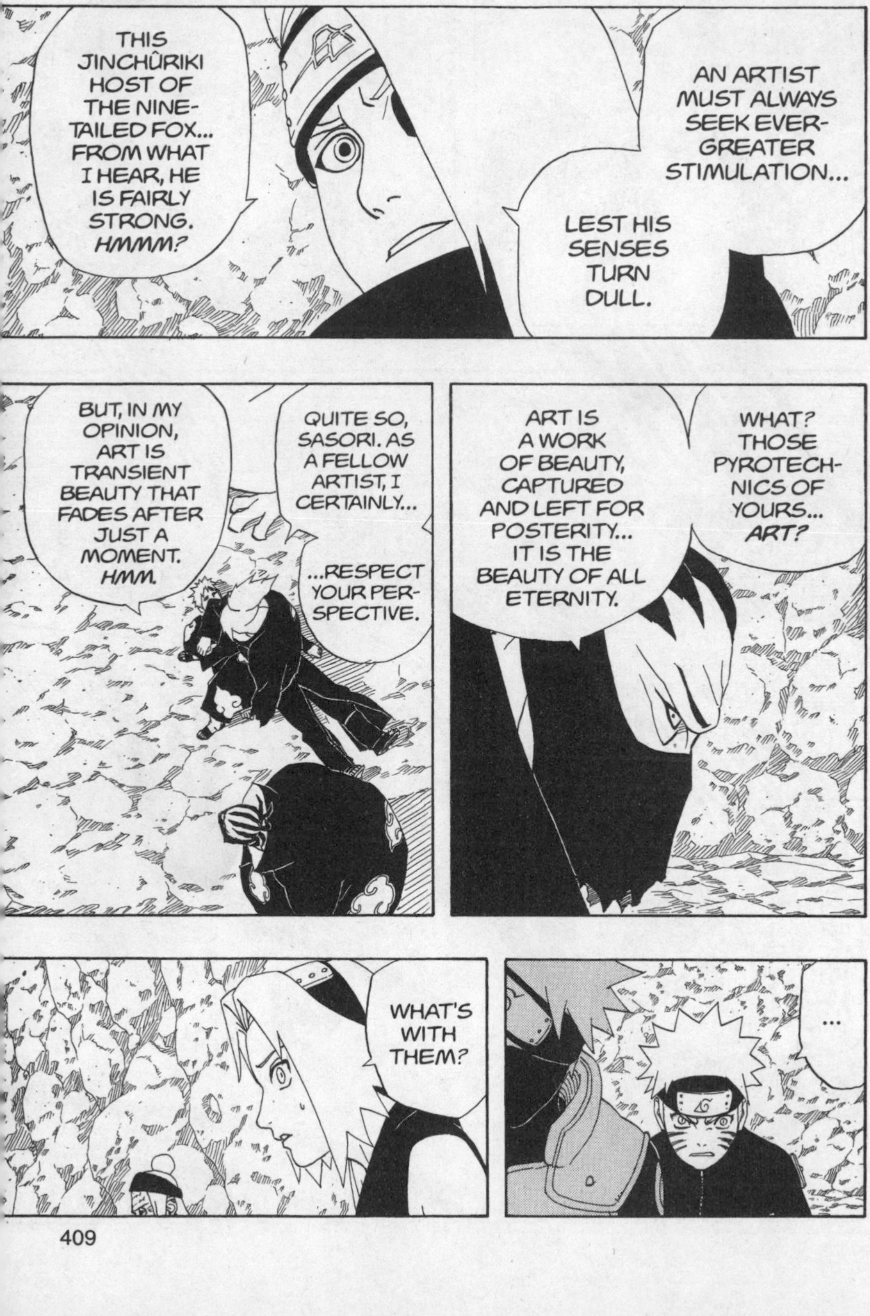
AN ARTIST MUST ALWAYS SEEK EVER-GREATER STIMULATION...
LEST HIS SENSES TURN DULL.
THIS JINCHŪRIKI HOST OF THE NINE-TAILED FOX... FROM WHAT I HEAR, HE IS FAIRLY STRONG. *HMMM?*
WHAT? THOSE PYROTECHNICS OF YOURS... *ART?*
ART IS A WORK OF BEAUTY, CAPTURED AND LEFT FOR POSTERITY... IT IS THE BEAUTY OF ALL ETERNITY.
QUITE SO, SASORI. AS A FELLOW ARTIST, I CERTAINLY...
...RESPECT YOUR PERSPECTIVE.
BUT, IN MY OPINION, ART IS TRANSIENT BEAUTY THAT FADES AFTER JUST A MOMENT. *HMM.*
...
WHAT'S WITH THEM?

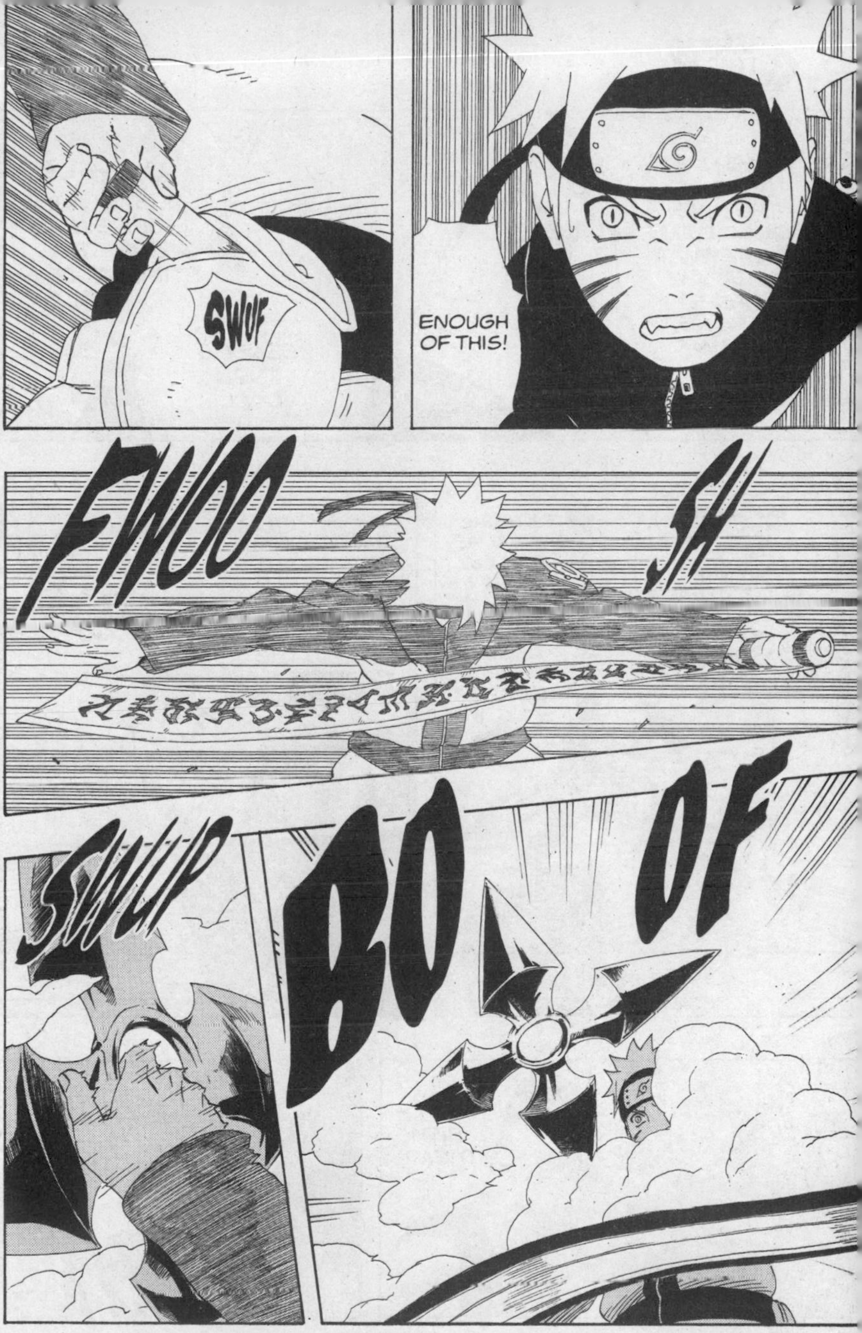
ENOUGH OF THIS!
SWUF
FWOOSH
BOOF
SWUP

READ THIS WAY

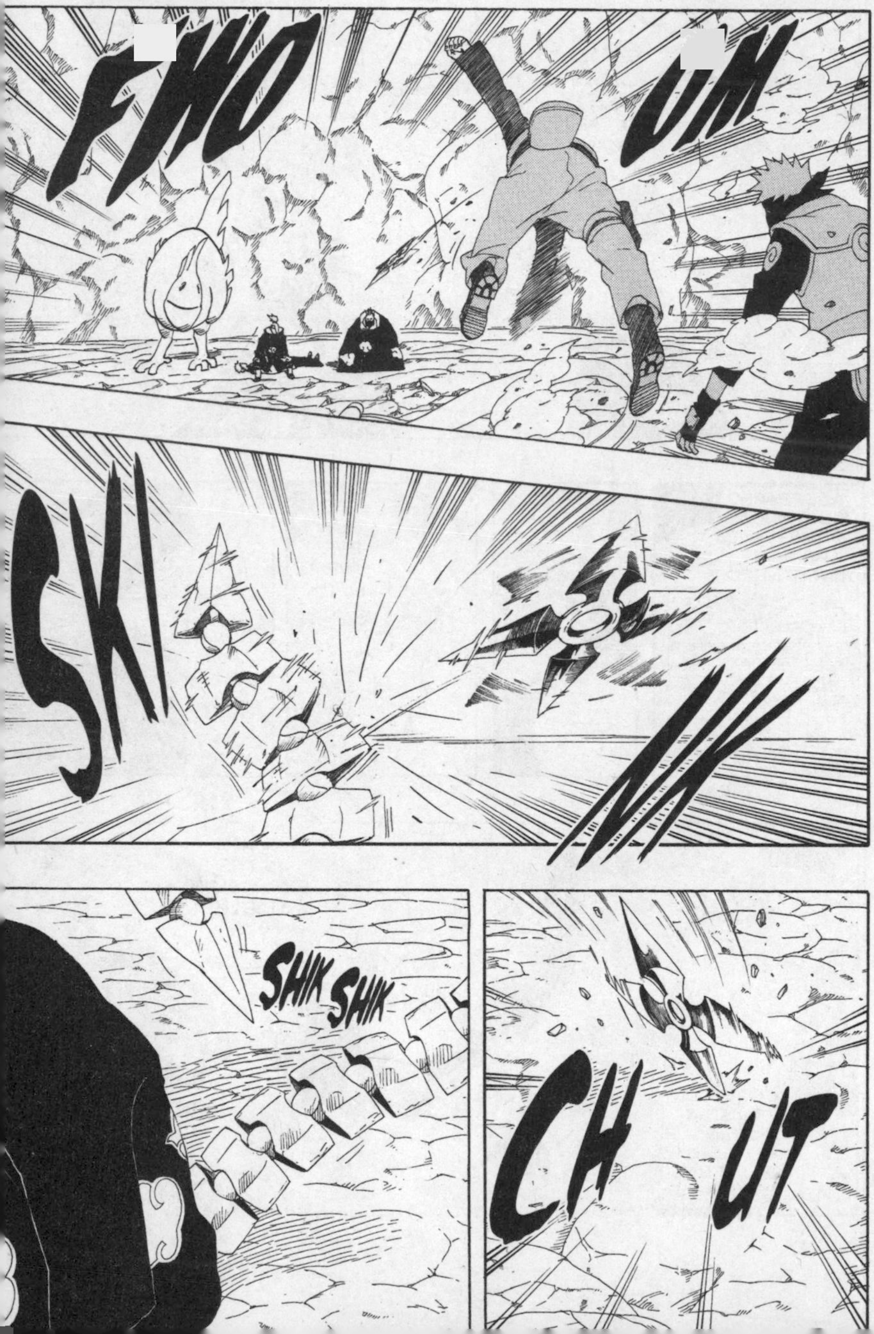
FWOOM
SKIINK
CHUT
SHIK SHIK

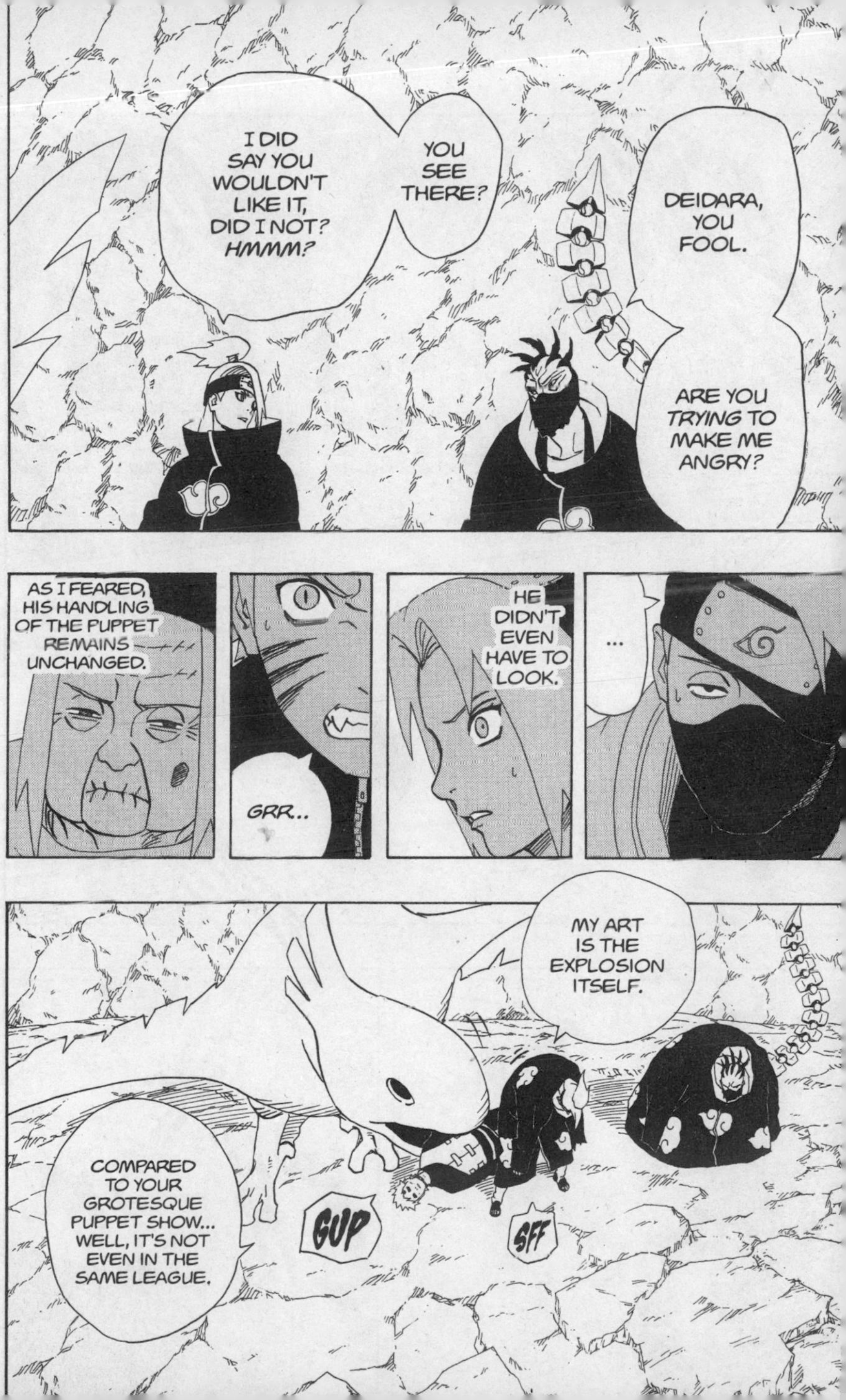
DEIDARA, YOU FOOL.
ARE YOU TRYING TO MAKE ME ANGRY?
YOU SEE THERE?
I DID SAY YOU WOULDN'T LIKE IT, DID I NOT? HMMM?
...
HE DIDN'T EVEN HAVE TO LOOK.
GRR...
AS I FEARED, HIS HANDLING OF THE PUPPET REMAINS UNCHANGED.
MY ART IS THE EXPLOSION ITSELF.
SFF
GUP
COMPARED TO YOUR GROTESQUE PUPPET SHOW... WELL, IT'S NOT EVEN IN THE SAME LEAGUE.

READ THIS WAY

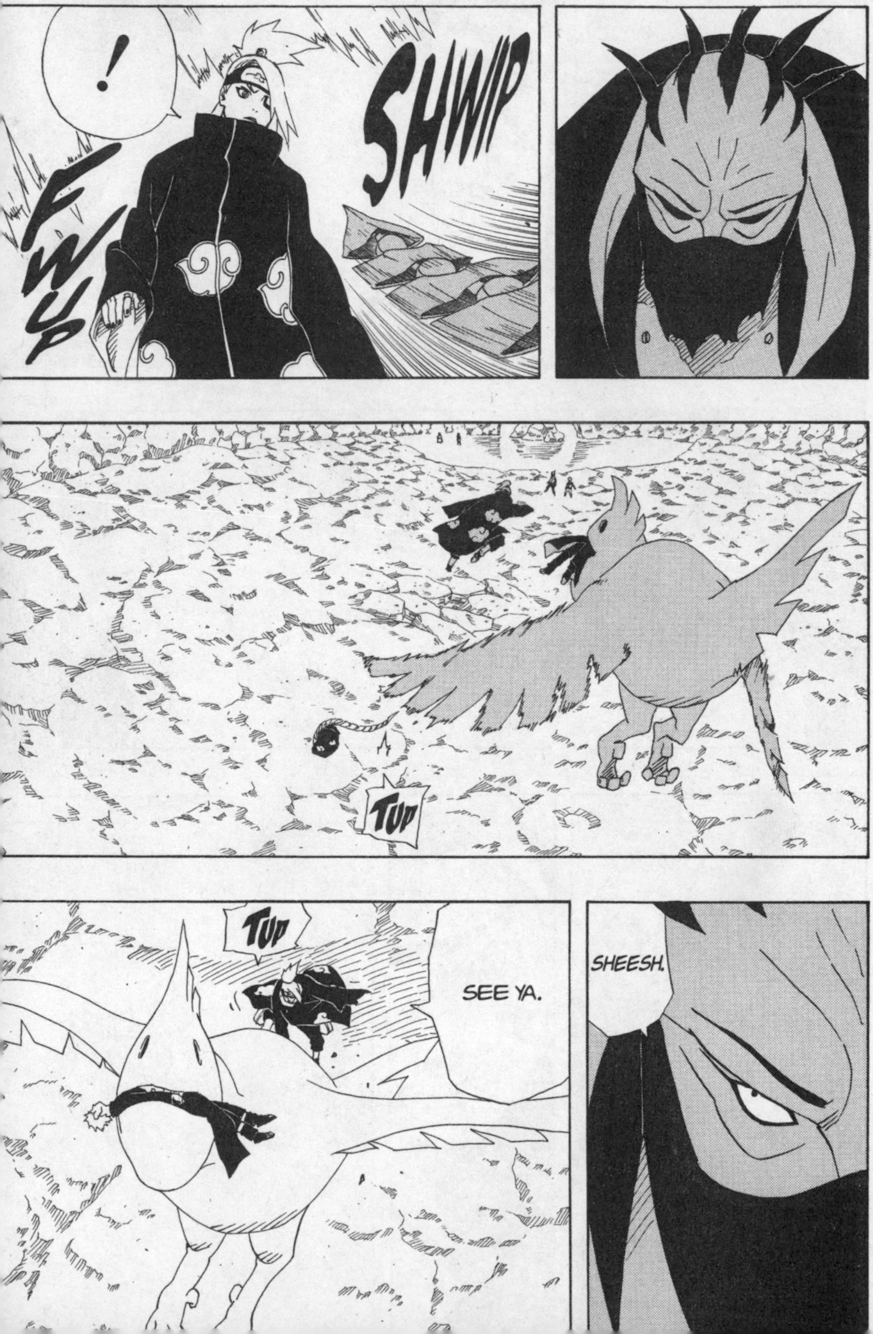
SHWIP
!
FWUP
TUP
SHEESH.
TUP
SEE YA.

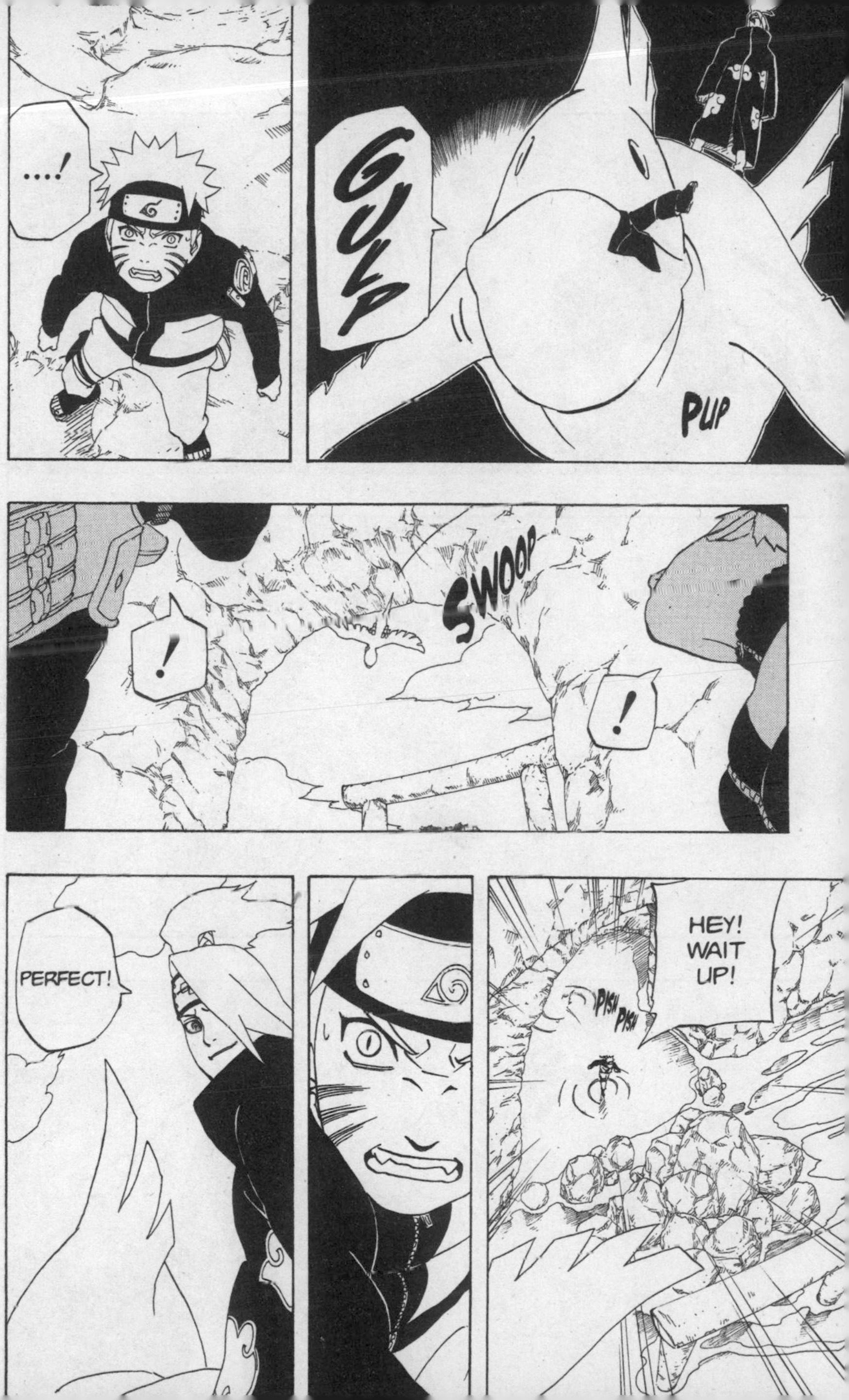
GULP
PUP
....!
SWOOP
!
!
HEY! WAIT UP!
PISH PISH
PERFECT!

READ THIS WAY

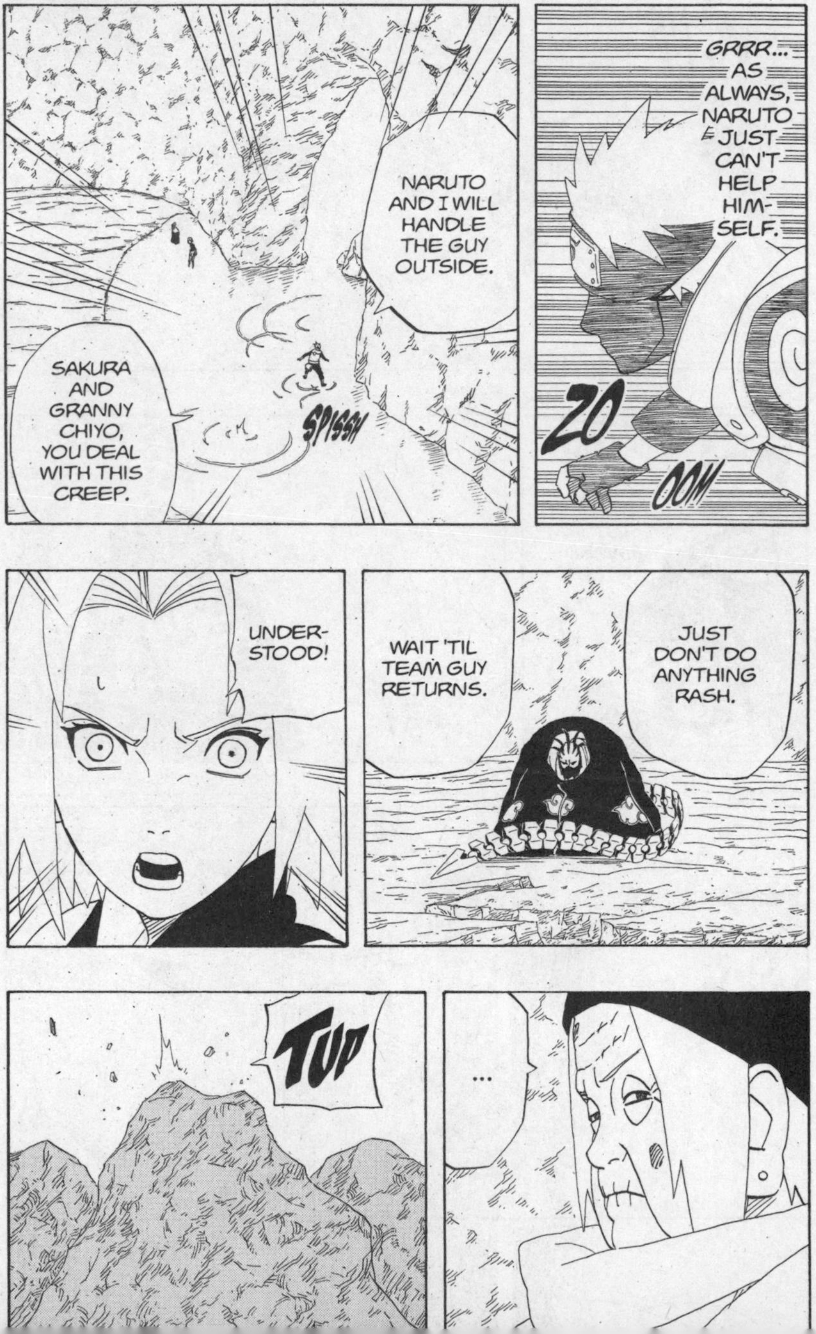
GRRR... AS ALWAYS, NARUTO JUST CAN'T HELP HIM-SELF.
ZOOOM
NARUTO AND I WILL HANDLE THE GUY OUTSIDE.
SPISSH
SAKURA AND GRANNY CHIYO, YOU DEAL WITH THIS CREEP.
JUST DON'T DO ANYTHING RASH.
WAIT 'TIL TEAM GUY RETURNS.
UNDER-STOOD!
...
TUP

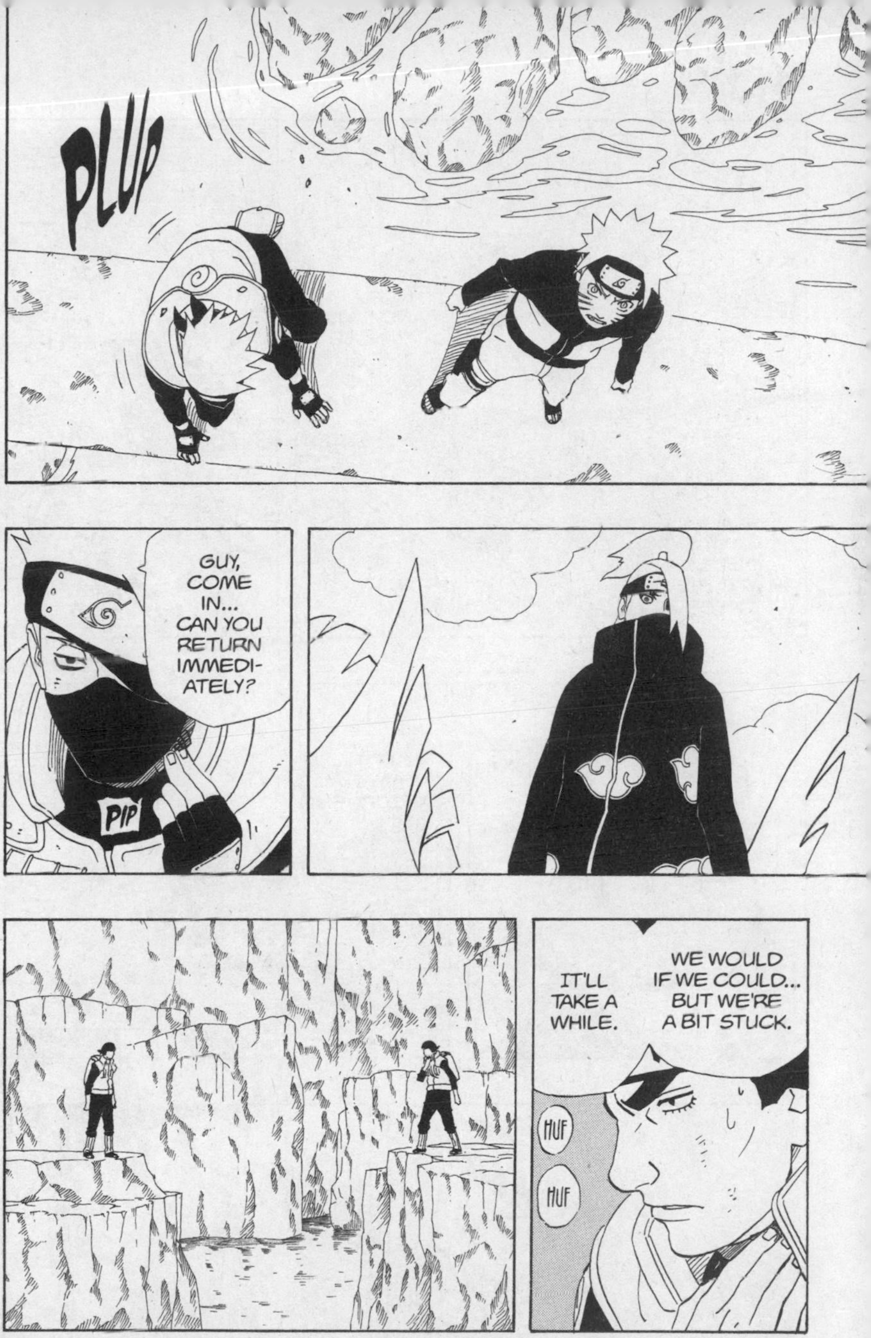
PLUP
GUY, COME IN... CAN YOU RETURN IMMEDIATELY?
PIP
WE WOULD IF WE COULD... BUT WE'RE A BIT STUCK.
IT'LL TAKE A WHILE.
HUF
HUF

READ THIS WAY

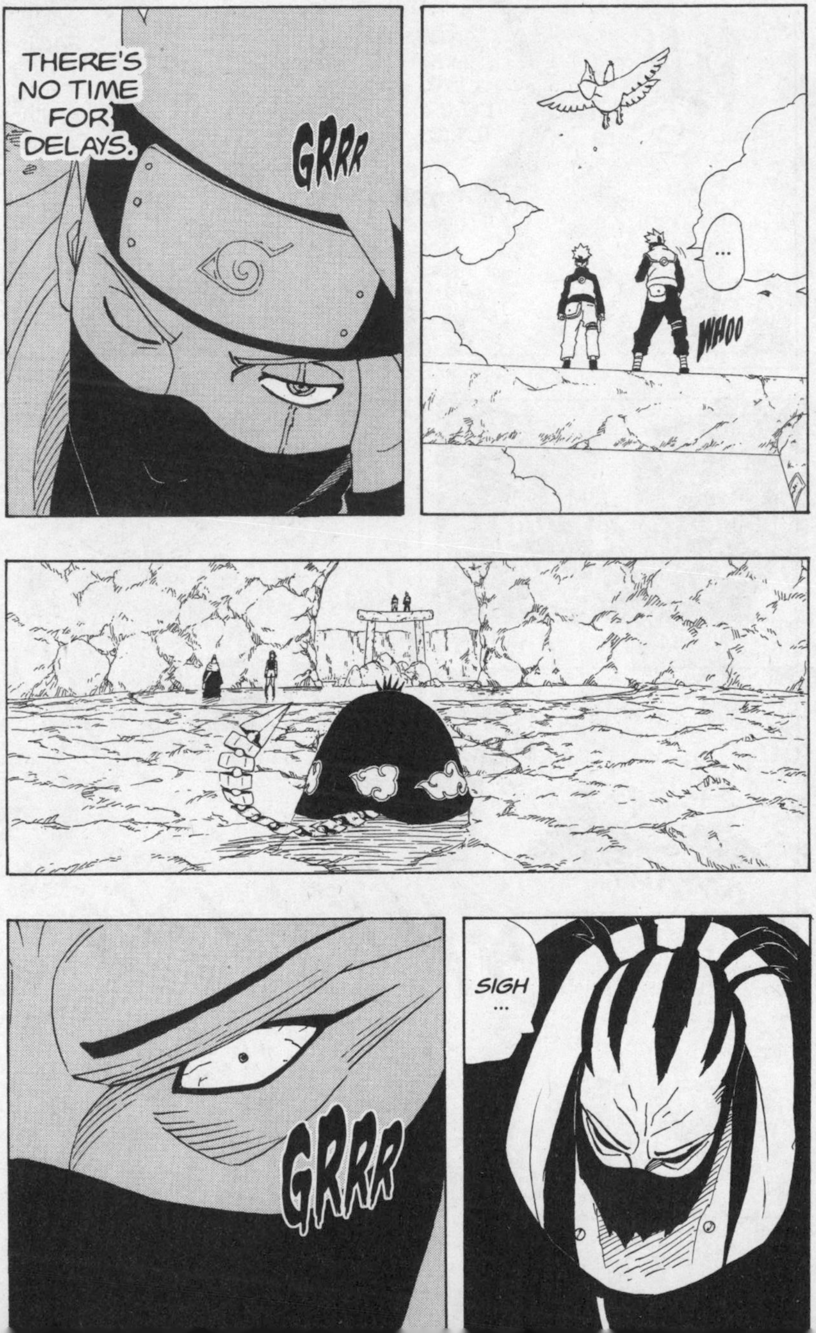
...
WHOO
THERE'S NO TIME FOR DELAYS.
GRRR
SIGH ...
GRRR

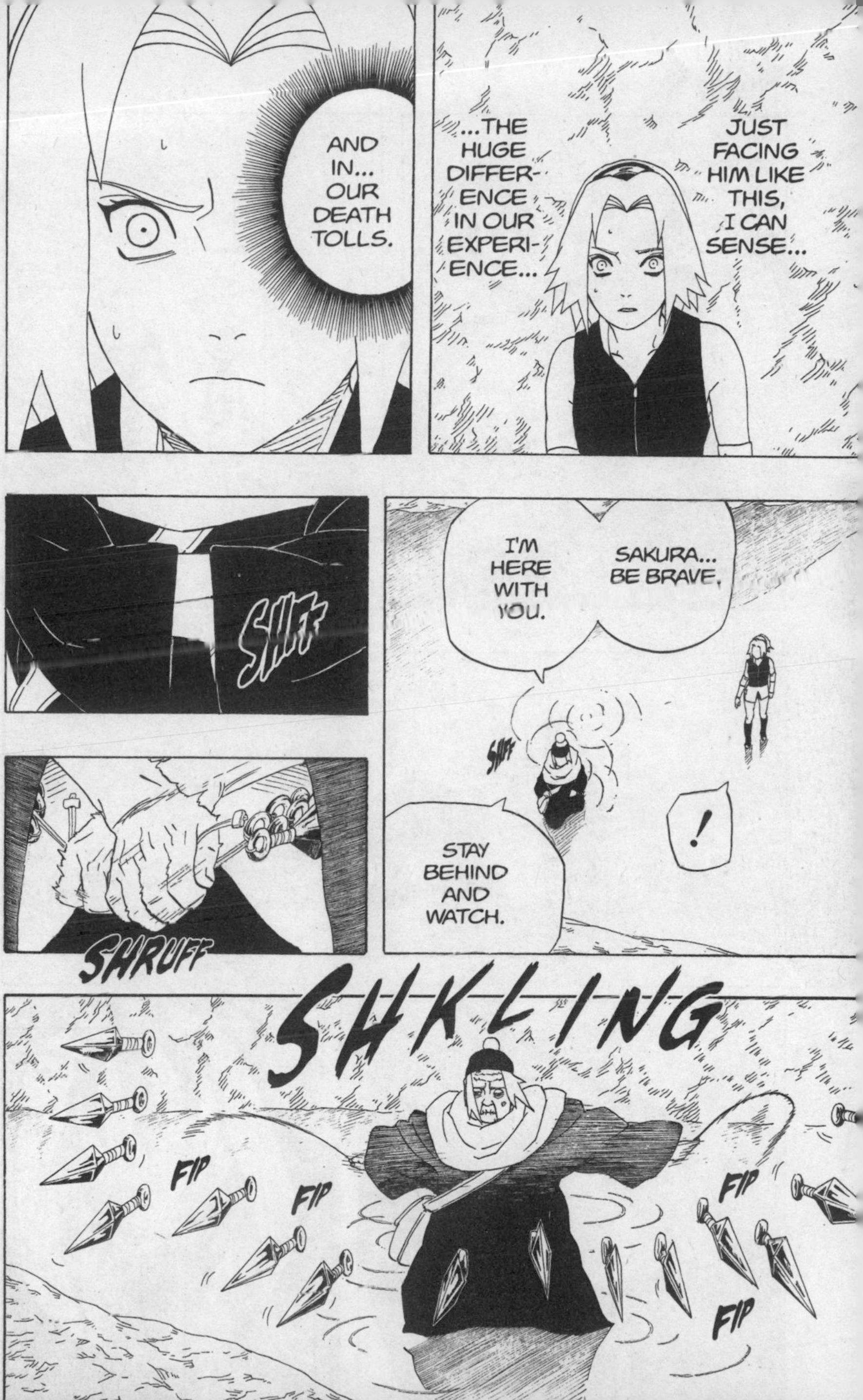
JUST FACING HIM LIKE THIS, I CAN SENSE...
...THE HUGE DIFFER-ENCE IN OUR EXPERI-ENCE...
AND IN... OUR DEATH TOLLS.
SAKURA... BE BRAVE.
I'M HERE WITH YOU.
SHFF
!
STAY BEHIND AND WATCH.
SHFF
SHRUFF
SHKLING
FIP
FIP
FIP
FIP

READ THIS WAY

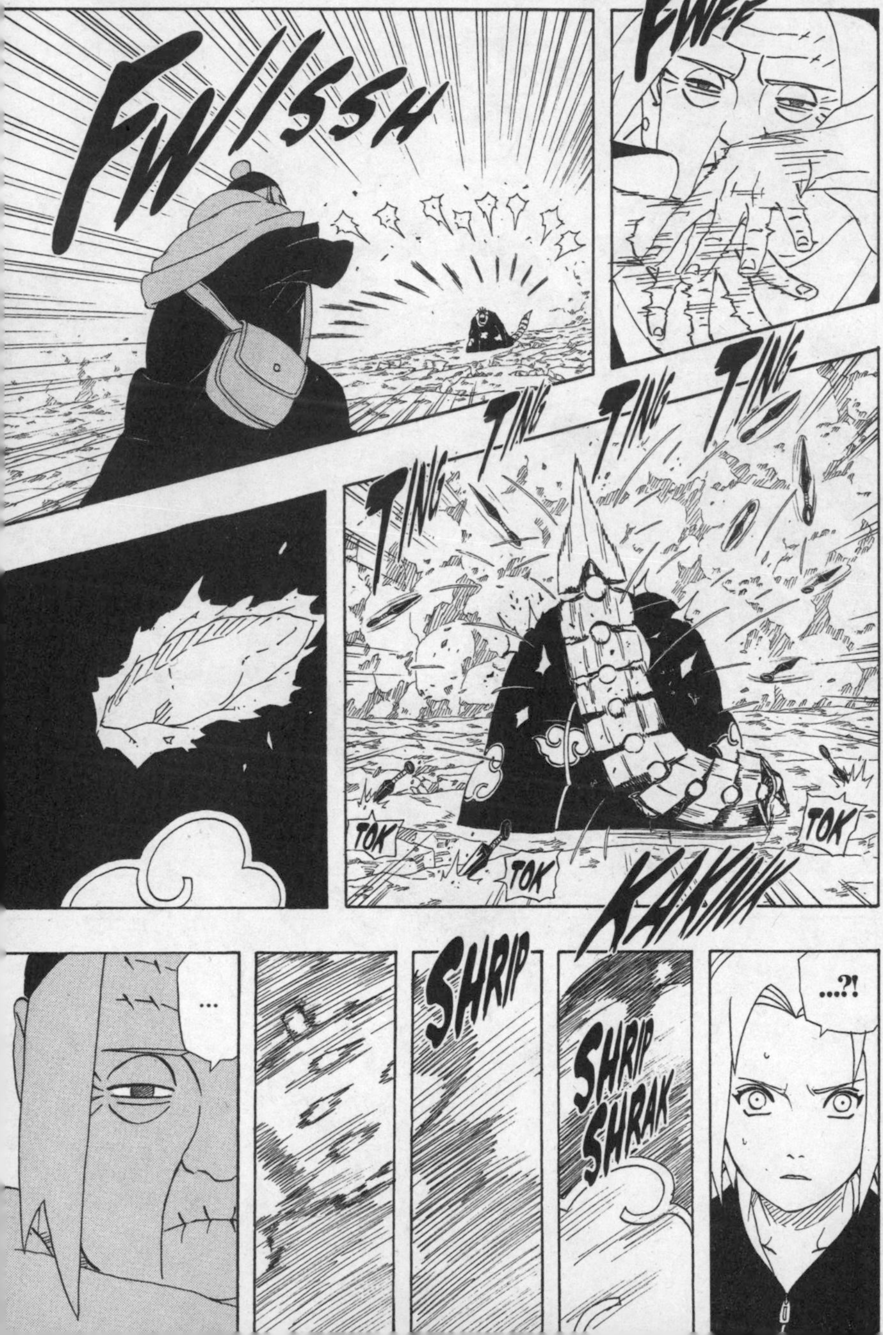
FWFF
FWISSH
TING
TING
TING
TING
TOK
TOK
TOK
KAKINK
...?!
SHRIP
SHRAK
SHRIP
...

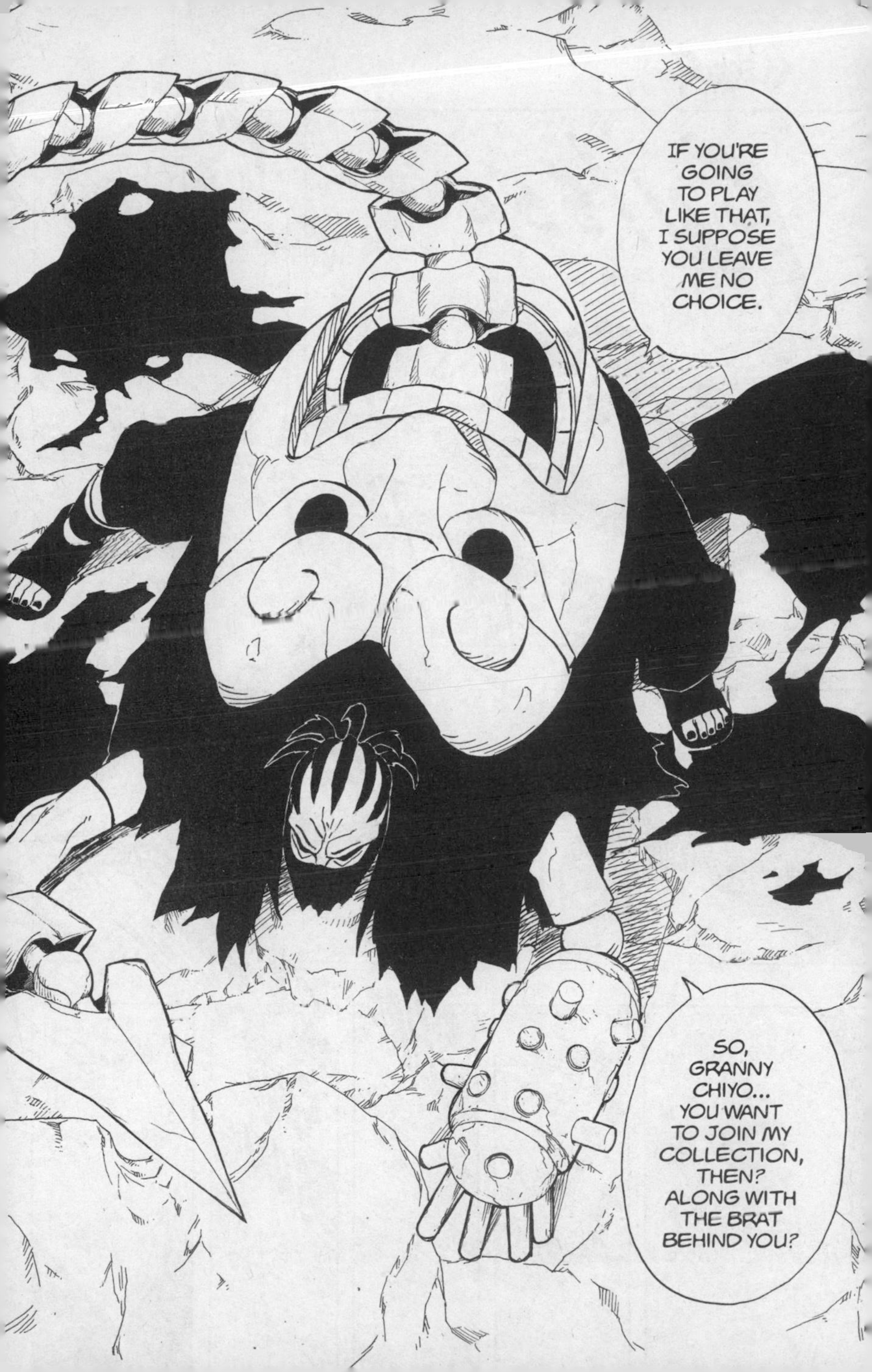
IF YOU'RE GOING TO PLAY LIKE THAT, I SUPPOSE YOU LEAVE ME NO CHOICE.
SO, GRANNY CHIYO... YOU WANT TO JOIN MY COLLECTION, THEN? ALONG WITH THE BRAT BEHIND YOU?

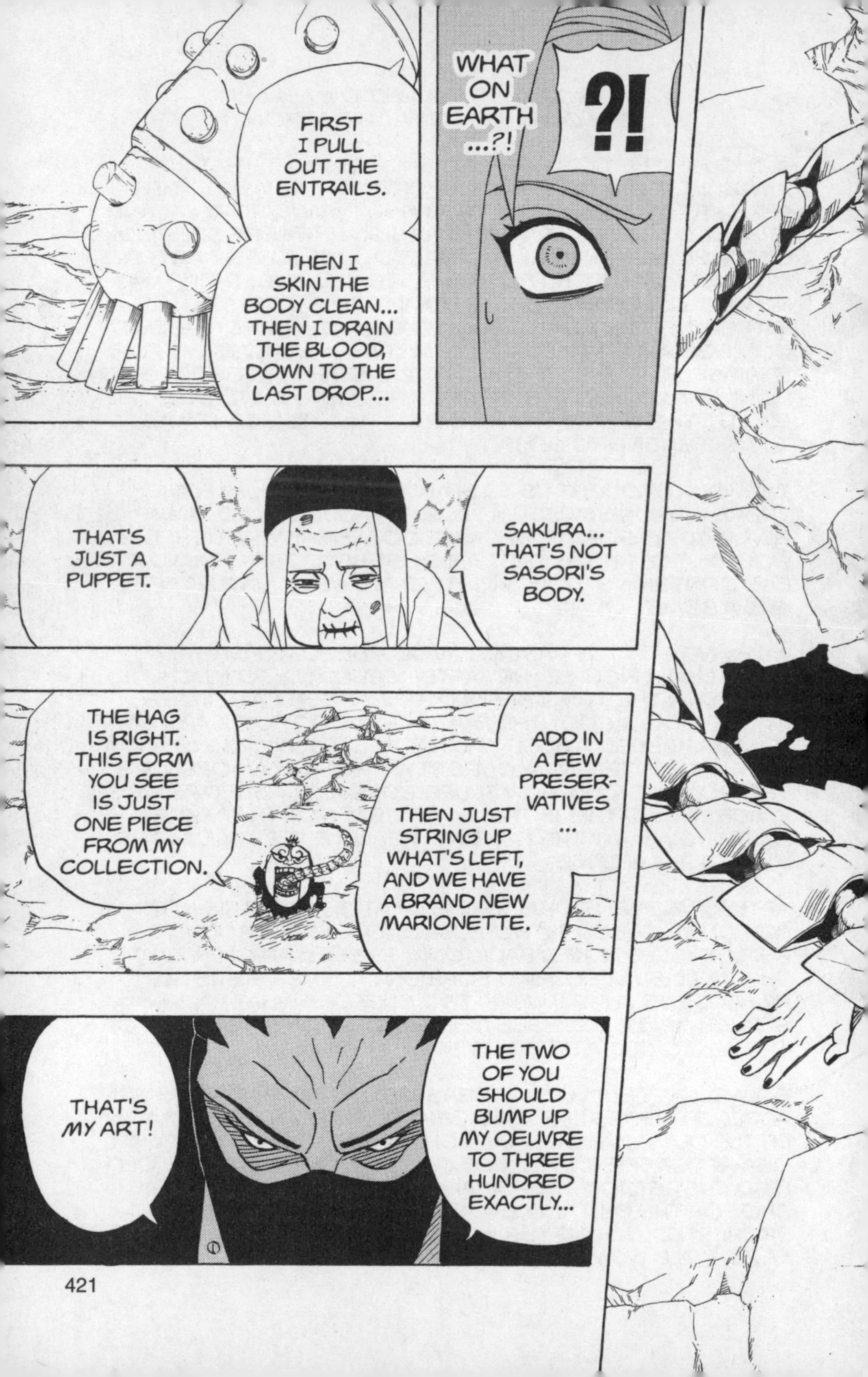

WHAT ON EARTH ...?!
?!
FIRST I PULL OUT THE ENTRAILS.
THEN I SKIN THE BODY CLEAN... THEN I DRAIN THE BLOOD, DOWN TO THE LAST DROP...
SAKURA... THAT'S NOT SASORI'S BODY.
THAT'S JUST A PUPPET.
ADD IN A FEW PRESER-VATIVES ...
THEN JUST STRING UP WHAT'S LEFT, AND WE HAVE A BRAND NEW MARIONETTE.
THE HAG IS RIGHT. THIS FORM YOU SEE IS JUST ONE PIECE FROM MY COLLECTION.
THE TWO OF YOU SHOULD BUMP UP MY OEUVRE TO THREE HUNDRED EXACTLY...
THAT'S MY ART!

THE WORLD OF KISHIMOTO MASASHI
PERSONAL HISTORY: A TRIP ABROAD

ALTHOUGH THE COLLEGE I ATTENDED WASN'T THAT
AMAZING, IT DID OFFER AN OPPORTUNITY TO VISIT OVER-
SEAS ART MUSEUMS. THE TRIP WASN'T MANDATORY OR ANY-
THING, SO I WASN'T PLANNING TO SIGN UP. THERE SEEMED
LITTLE POINT IN TRAVELING ABROAD JUST TO VISIT ART
MUSEUMS. BESIDES, IT WAS SUPER EXPENSIVE. THERE WAS
NO WAY I COULD SWING IT ON A PART-TIME JOB. STILL, MY
FATHER INSISTED THAT I SHOULD GO, RATTLING ON ABOUT
COLLEGE AND TREASURED MEMORIES. HE'D EVEN PAY FOR
IT HIMSELF, HE SAID. IF I HADN'T ACCEPTED, I MIGHT'VE GIVEN
HIM A CONNIPTION. (AS A FATHER HE JUST HAD TO BITE THE
BULLET. THERE'S NO WAY HE COULD TELL HIS SON IT WAS
TOO EXPENSIVE TO GO.)

THE TOUR BROUGHT US TO SPAIN AND FRANCE. IN SPAIN,
THERE WAS ONE MUSEUM I WAS PARTICULARLY LOOKING
FORWARD TO SEEING. WHEN WE GOT THERE, THOUGH, THEY
WOULDN'T LET US IN. THEY TOLD US THEY'D JUST FOUND A
BAG CONTAINING EXPLOSIVES. SO ALL WE WOUND UP SEEING
WAS A BOMB SQUAD.

WHEN WE GOT TO FRANCE, I MADE A BEELINE FOR THE
MONA LISA. I FIGURED, HEY, AFTER SPENDING SO MUCH
MONEY ON THE TRIP, I SHOULD AT LEAST GET A GLIMPSE
OF THE REAL MCCOY. THE PAINTING WAS SO POPULAR THAT
IT HAD AMASSED A HUGE WALL OF PEOPLE, BLOCKING ANY
VIEW. UNDAUNTED IN MY QUEST, I WAITED FOR AN OPENING.
THE MOMENT A PERSON SHUFFLED AWAY, I DASHED FOR HIS
PLACE. "AH, SO THIS IS THE MONA LISA!" NOT THAT I KNEW
ANYTHING ABOUT THE PAINTING, REALLY, BUT I STILL ACTED
LIKE IT TOUCHED ME.

AFTER A MOMENT OF GAWKING UP AT IT, I FELT THIS INTENSE
PAIN ON MY CHEEK. "*YOWCH!*" FALLING TO THE GROUND, I
REFLEXIVELY LOOKED BACK, ONLY TO SEE... AN OLD WOMAN.
THIS WELL-BUILT, ELDERLY FOREIGN LADY, HER FIST STILL
RETRACTING. A FIST! WELL, TWO GUESSES WHAT HAD
STRUCK ME. I GUESS SHE NEEDED THIS GUY'S HEAD OUT OF
THE WAY TO GET A BETTER VIEW.

SO, WELL, IF I SUM UP MY TREASURED MEMORY OF THIS TRIP
ABROAD, IT GOES LIKE THIS: BEING PUNCHED DOWN BY A
LITTLE OLD FOREIGN LADY RIGHT IN FRONT OF THE MONA
LISA AFTER SPENDING A LOT OF MONEY TO SEE IT. THE OLD
BIRD JUST STOOD THERE, TAKING SNAPSHOT AFTER SNAP-
SHOT OF THE PAINTING, EVEN THOUGH CAMERAS WERE
PROHIBITED. NO MATTER WHAT COUNTRY THEY'RE FROM, IT
SEEMS OLD WOMEN ARE ALWAYS FRIGHTENING.

Number 265: Granny Chiyo & Sakura

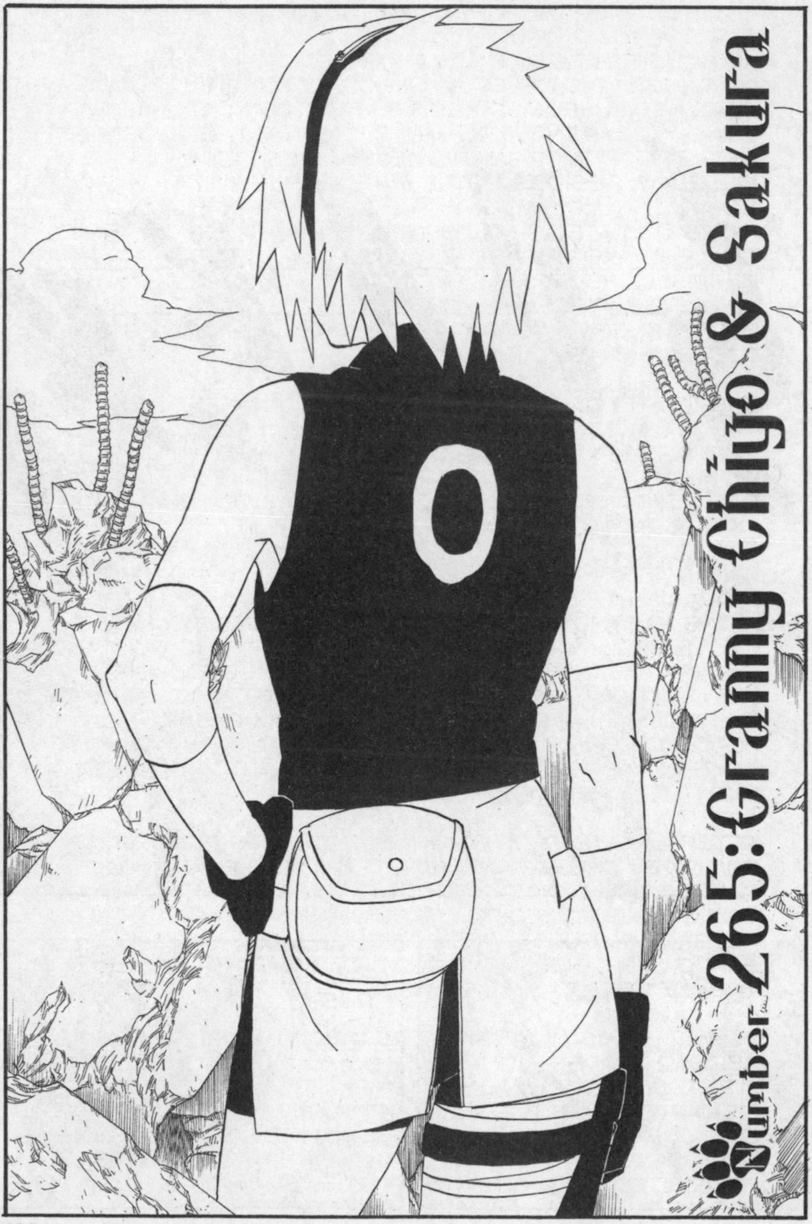

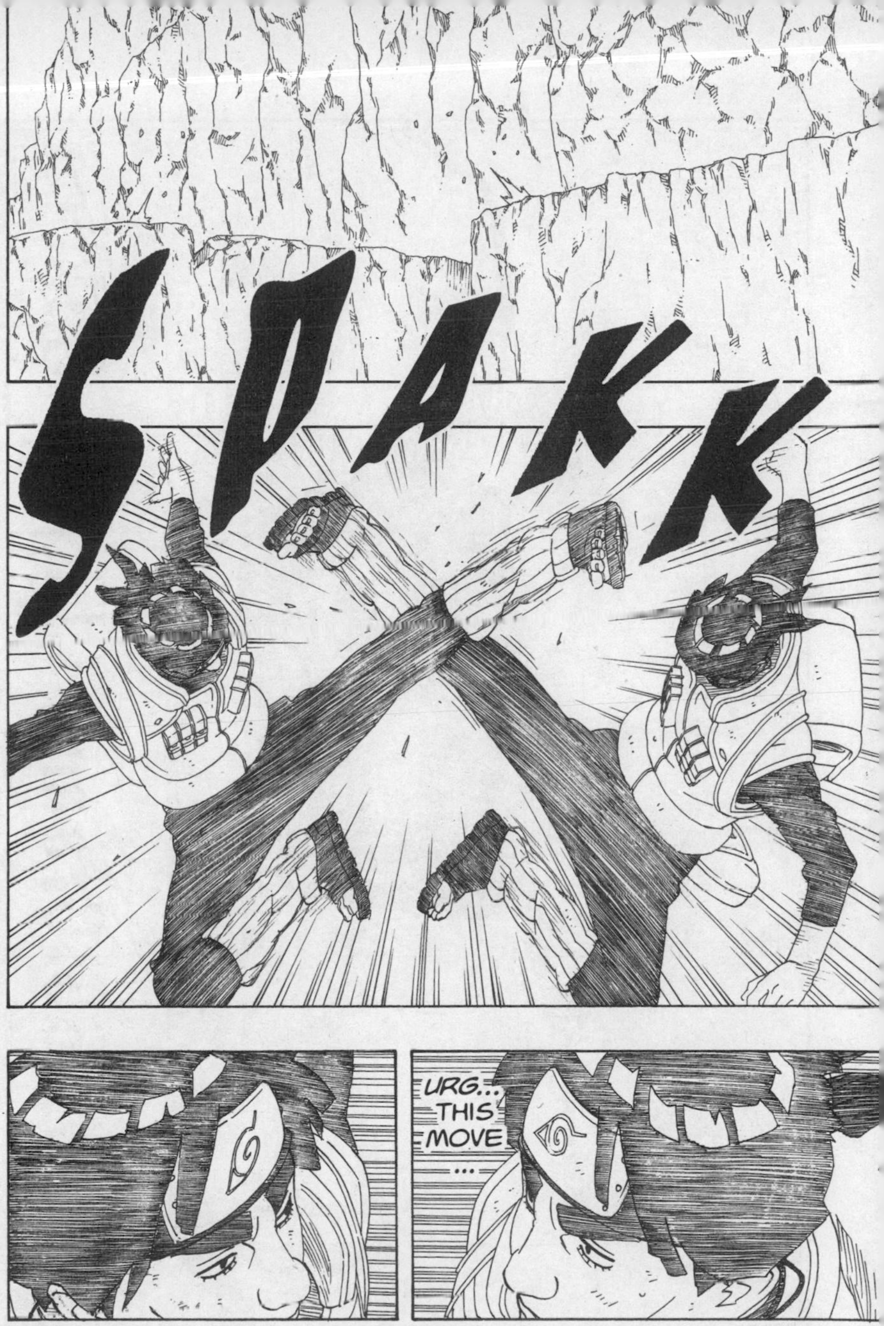
SPAKK
URG... THIS MOVE ...

READ THIS WAY

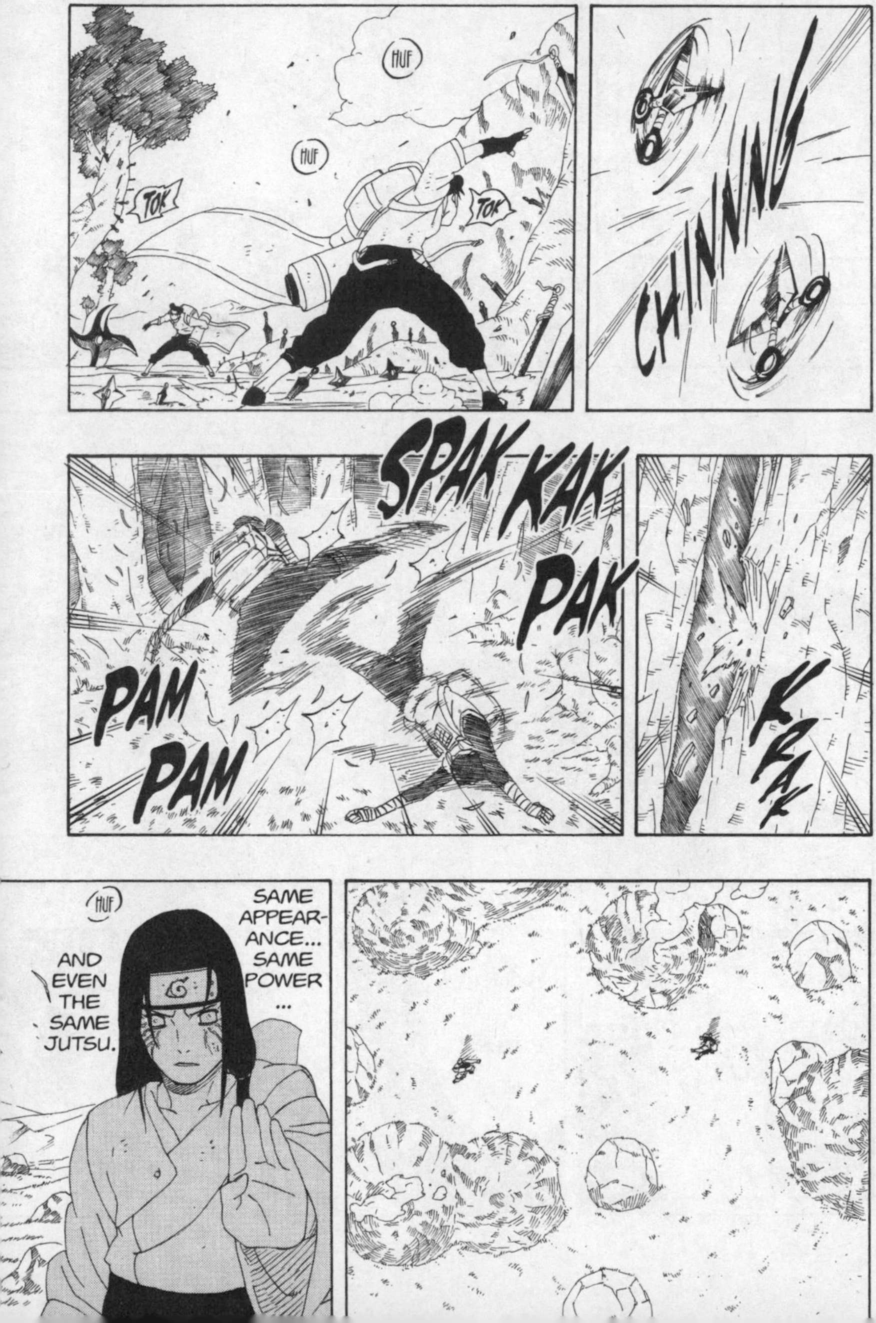
CHINNNG
HUF
HUF
TOK
TOK
KRAK
SPAK
KAK
PAK
PAM PAM
SAME APPEARANCE... SAME POWER...
HUF
AND EVEN THE SAME JUTSU.

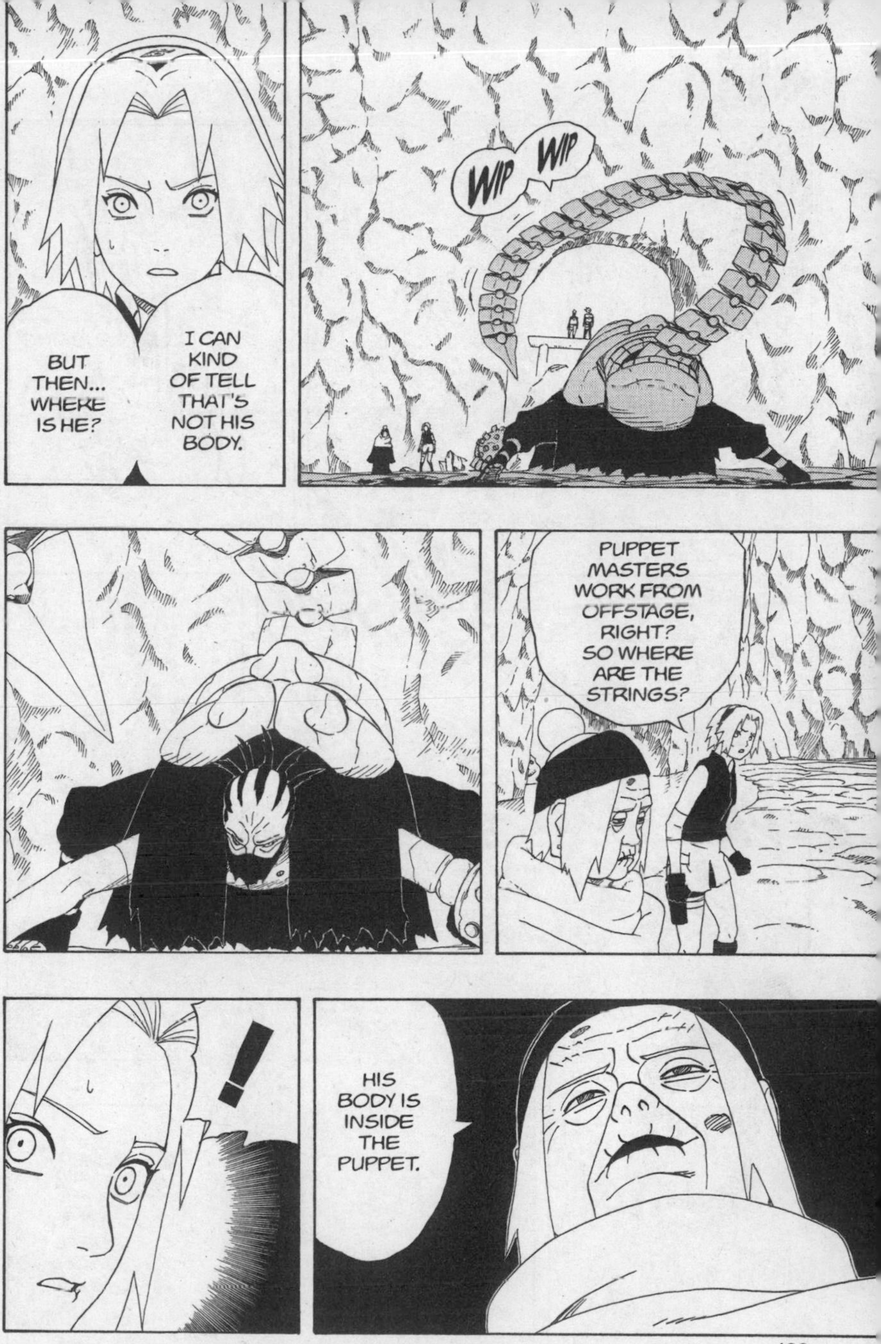

WIP
WIP
I CAN KIND OF TELL THAT'S NOT HIS BODY.
BUT THEN... WHERE IS HE?
PUPPET MASTERS WORK FROM OFFSTAGE, RIGHT? SO WHERE ARE THE STRINGS?
HIS BODY IS INSIDE THE PUPPET.
!

READ THIS WAY

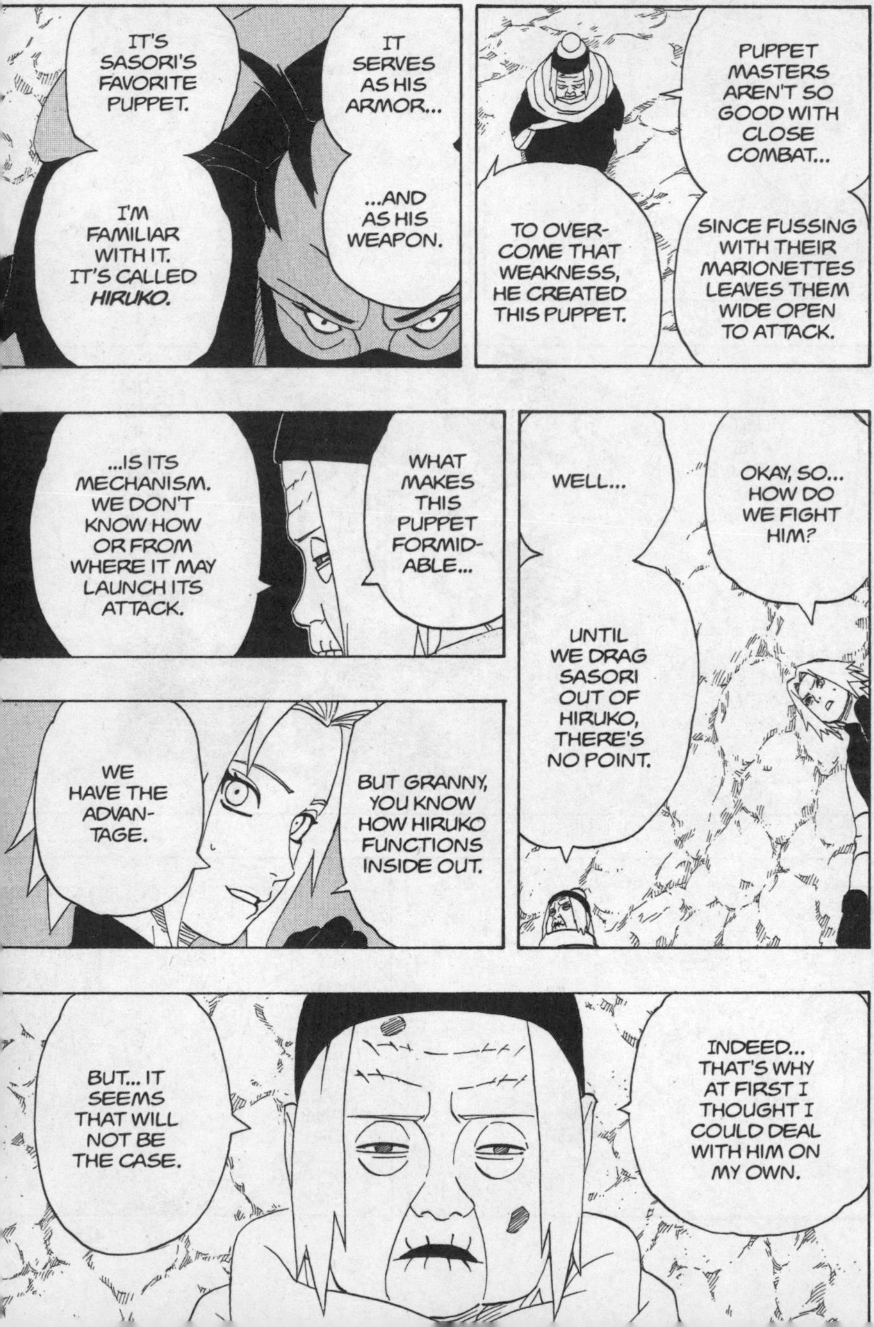
PUPPET MASTERS AREN'T SO GOOD WITH CLOSE COMBAT...
SINCE FUSSING WITH THEIR MARIONETTES LEAVES THEM WIDE OPEN TO ATTACK.
TO OVER-COME THAT WEAKNESS, HE CREATED THIS PUPPET.
IT SERVES AS HIS ARMOR...
...AND AS HIS WEAPON.
IT'S SASORI'S FAVORITE PUPPET.
I'M FAMILIAR WITH IT. IT'S CALLED *HIRUKO*.
OKAY, SO... HOW DO WE FIGHT HIM?
WELL...
UNTIL WE DRAG SASORI OUT OF HIRUKO, THERE'S NO POINT.
WHAT MAKES THIS PUPPET FORMID-ABLE...
...IS ITS MECHANISM. WE DON'T KNOW HOW OR FROM WHERE IT MAY LAUNCH ITS ATTACK.
BUT GRANNY, YOU KNOW HOW HIRUKO FUNCTIONS INSIDE OUT.
WE HAVE THE ADVAN-TAGE.
INDEED... THAT'S WHY AT FIRST I THOUGHT I COULD DEAL WITH HIM ON MY OWN.
BUT... IT SEEMS THAT WILL NOT BE THE CASE.

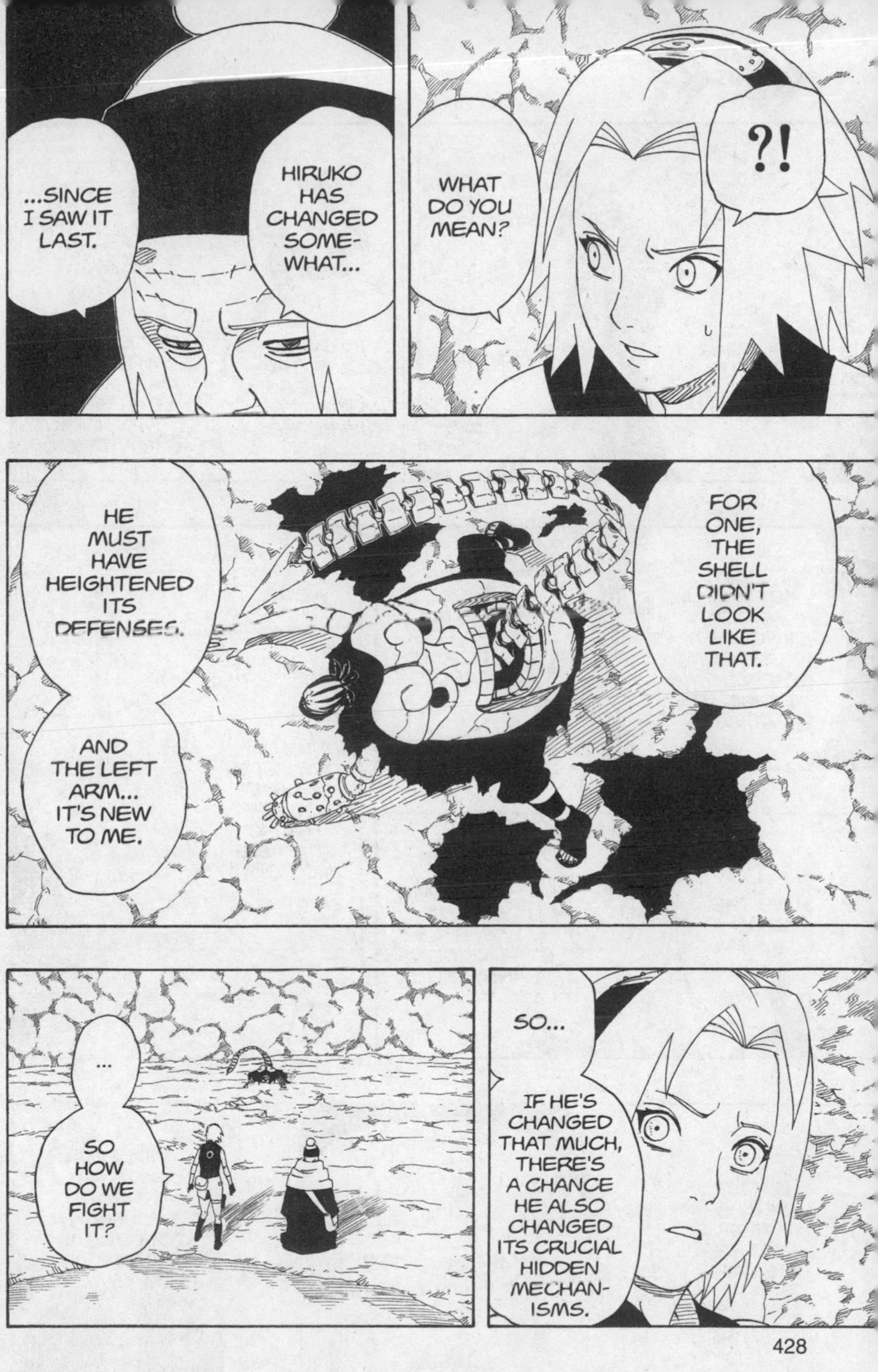
?!
WHAT DO YOU MEAN?
HIRUKO HAS CHANGED SOME-WHAT...
...SINCE I SAW IT LAST.
FOR ONE, THE SHELL DIDN'T LOOK LIKE THAT.
HE MUST HAVE HEIGHTENED ITS DEFENSES.
AND THE LEFT ARM... IT'S NEW TO ME.
SO...
IF HE'S CHANGED THAT MUCH, THERE'S A CHANCE HE ALSO CHANGED ITS CRUCIAL HIDDEN MECHAN-ISMS.
...
SO HOW DO WE FIGHT IT?

READ THIS WAY

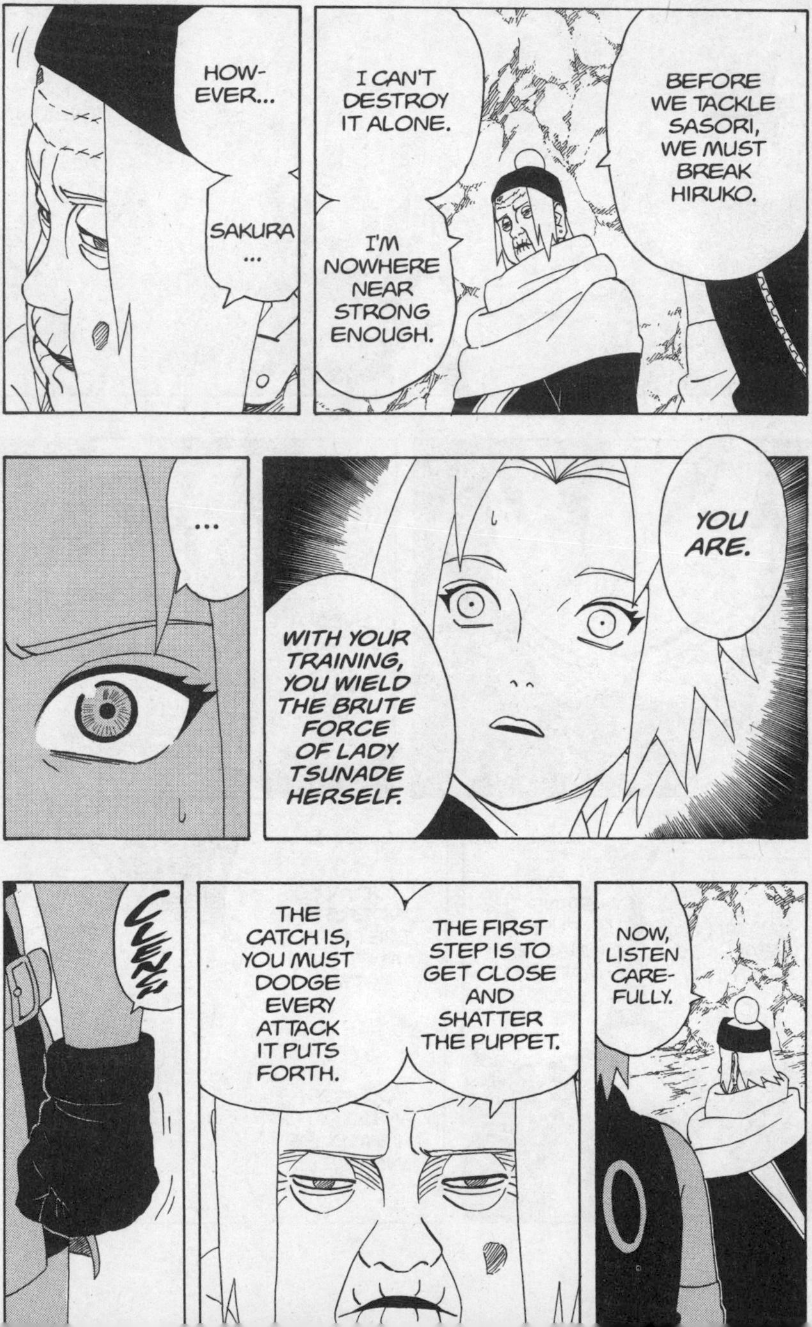
BEFORE WE TACKLE SASORI, WE MUST BREAK HIRUKO.
I CAN'T DESTROY IT ALONE.
I'M NOWHERE NEAR STRONG ENOUGH.
HOW-EVER...
SAKURA ...
YOU ARE.
WITH YOUR TRAINING, YOU WIELD THE BRUTE FORCE OF LADY TSUNADE HERSELF.
...
NOW, LISTEN CARE-FULLY.
THE FIRST STEP IS TO GET CLOSE AND SHATTER THE PUPPET.
THE CATCH IS, YOU MUST DODGE EVERY ATTACK IT PUTS FORTH.
CLENCH

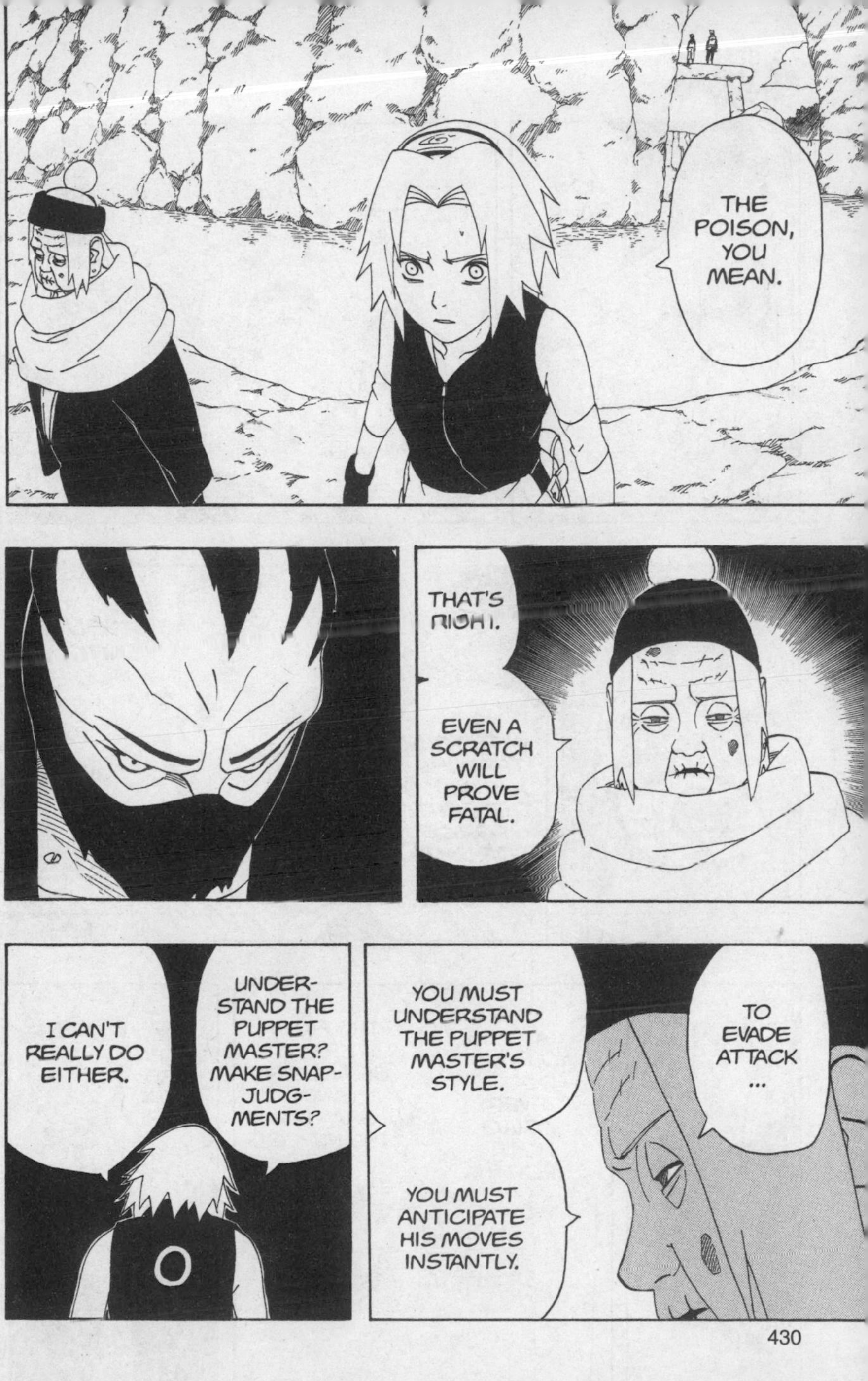
THE POISON, YOU MEAN.
THAT'S RIGHT.
EVEN A SCRATCH WILL PROVE FATAL.
TO EVADE ATTACK ...
YOU MUST UNDERSTAND THE PUPPET MASTER'S STYLE.
YOU MUST ANTICIPATE HIS MOVES INSTANTLY.
UNDERSTAND THE PUPPET MASTER? MAKE SNAP-JUDGMENTS?
I CAN'T REALLY DO EITHER.

READ THIS WAY

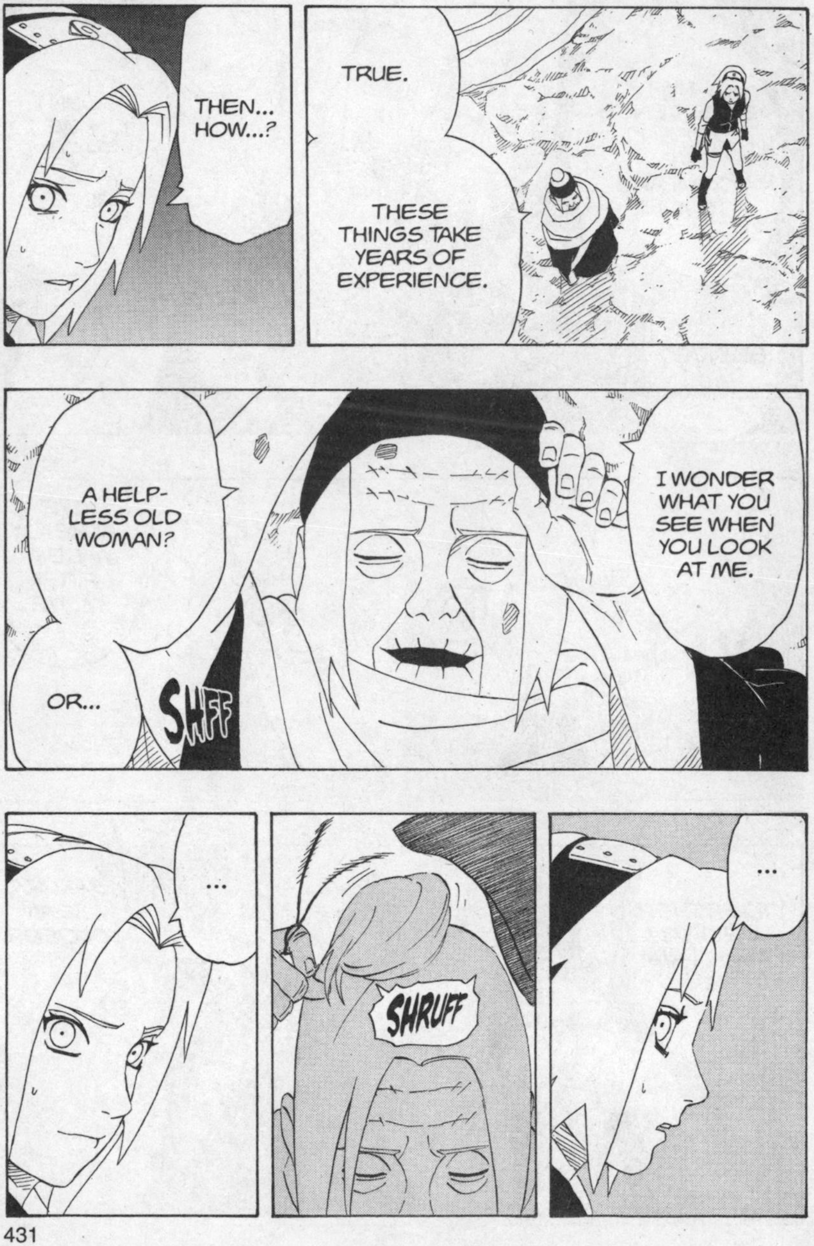
TRUE.
THESE THINGS TAKE YEARS OF EXPERIENCE.
THEN... HOW...?
I WONDER WHAT YOU SEE WHEN YOU LOOK AT ME.
A HELP-LESS OLD WOMAN?
OR...
SHFF
...
SHRUFF
...

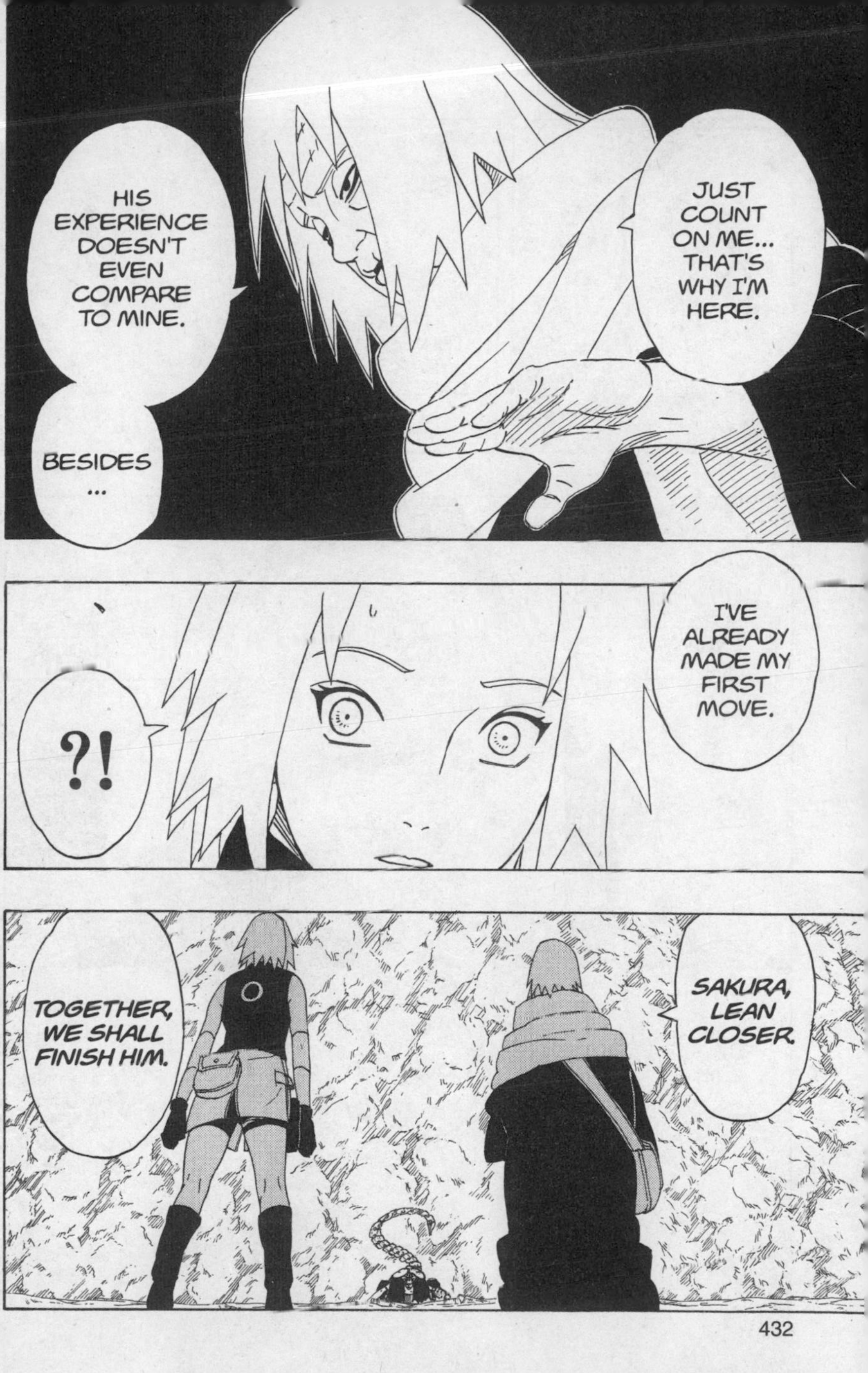
JUST COUNT ON ME... THAT'S WHY I'M HERE.
HIS EXPERIENCE DOESN'T EVEN COMPARE TO MINE.
BESIDES ...
I'VE ALREADY MADE MY FIRST MOVE.
?!
SAKURA, LEAN CLOSER.
TOGETHER, WE SHALL FINISH HIM.

READ THIS WAY

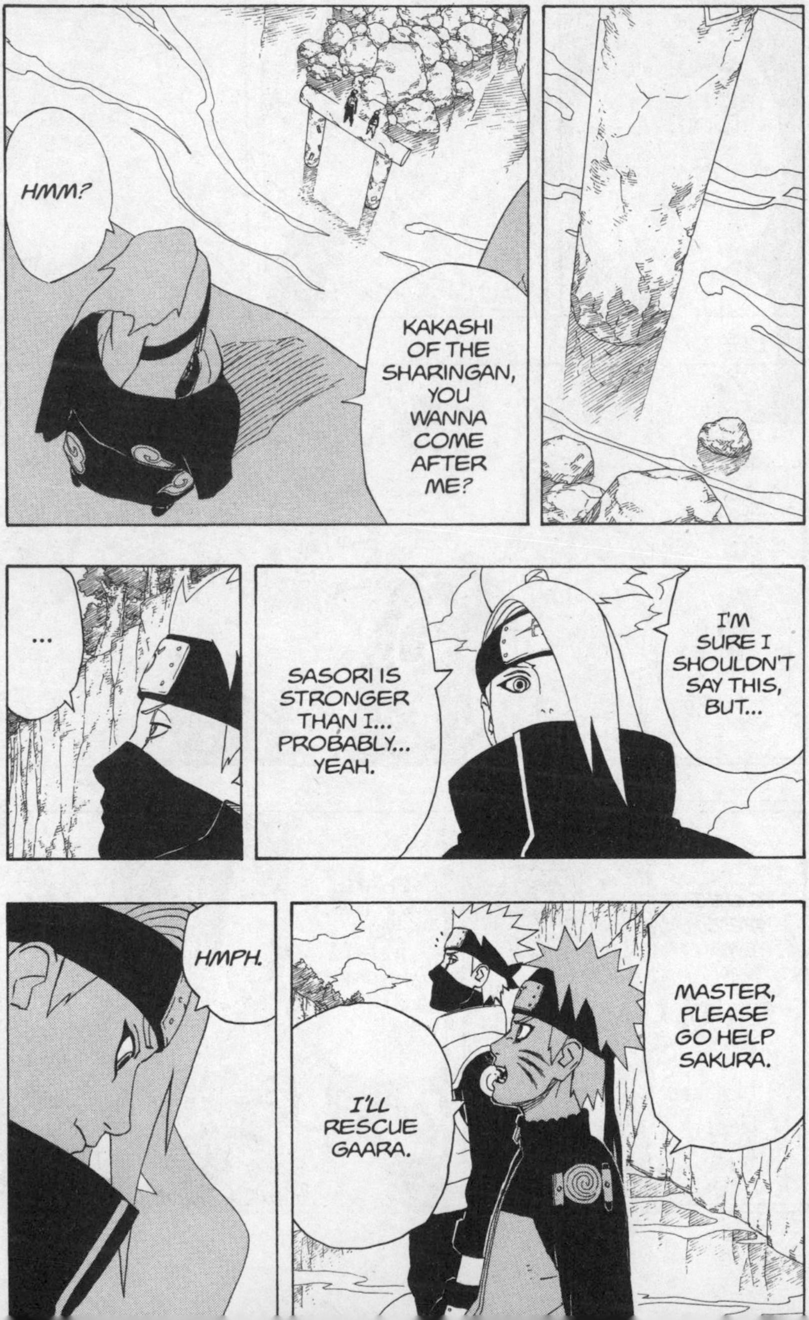
KAKASHI OF THE SHARINGAN, YOU WANNA COME AFTER ME?
HMM?
I'M SURE I SHOULDN'T SAY THIS, BUT...
SASORI IS STRONGER THAN I... PROBABLY... YEAH.
...
MASTER, PLEASE GO HELP SAKURA.
I'LL RESCUE GAARA.
HMPH.

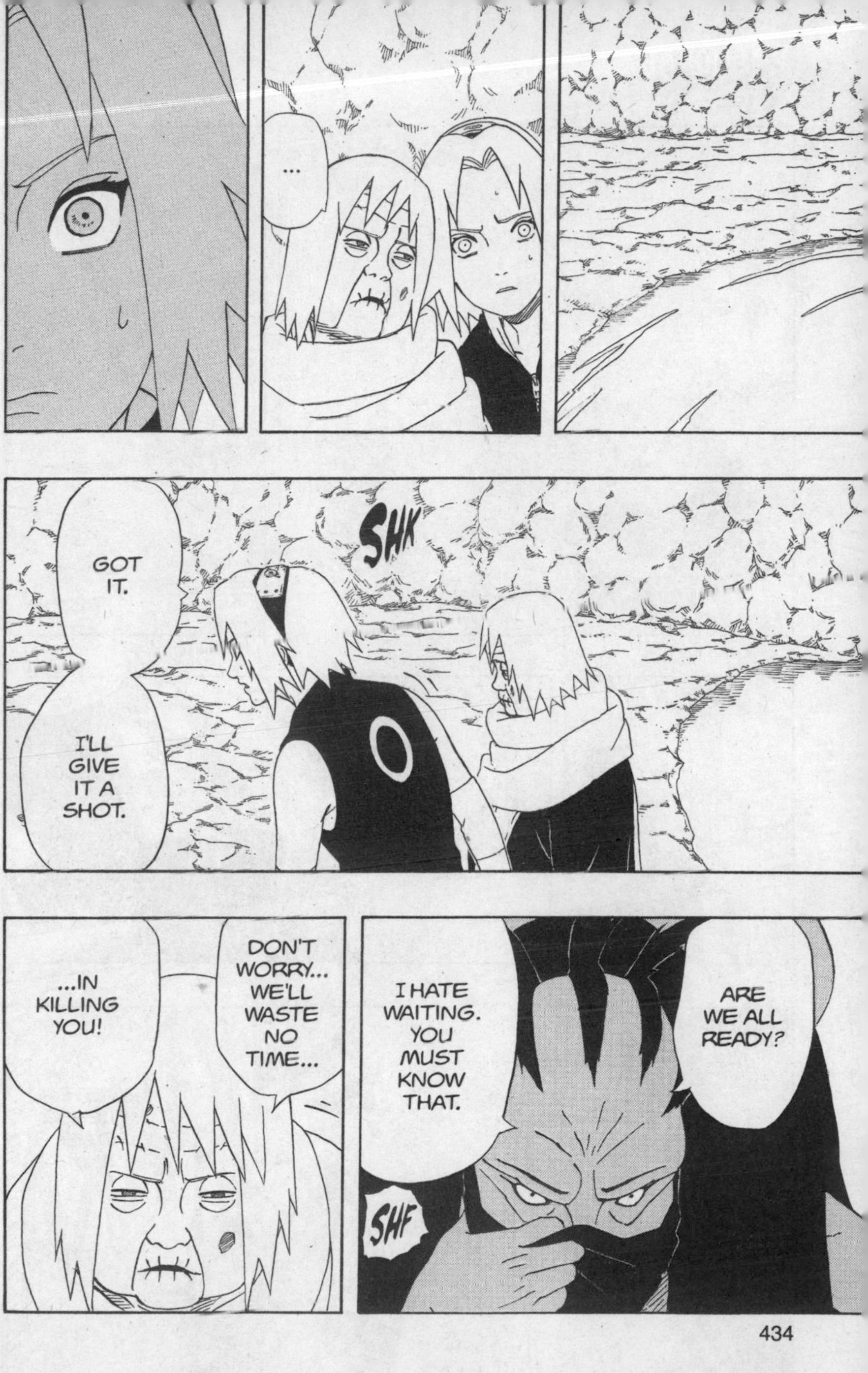
...
SHK
GOT IT.
I'LL GIVE IT A SHOT.
ARE WE ALL READY?
I HATE WAITING. YOU MUST KNOW THAT.
SHF
DON'T WORRY... WE'LL WASTE NO TIME...
...IN KILLING YOU!

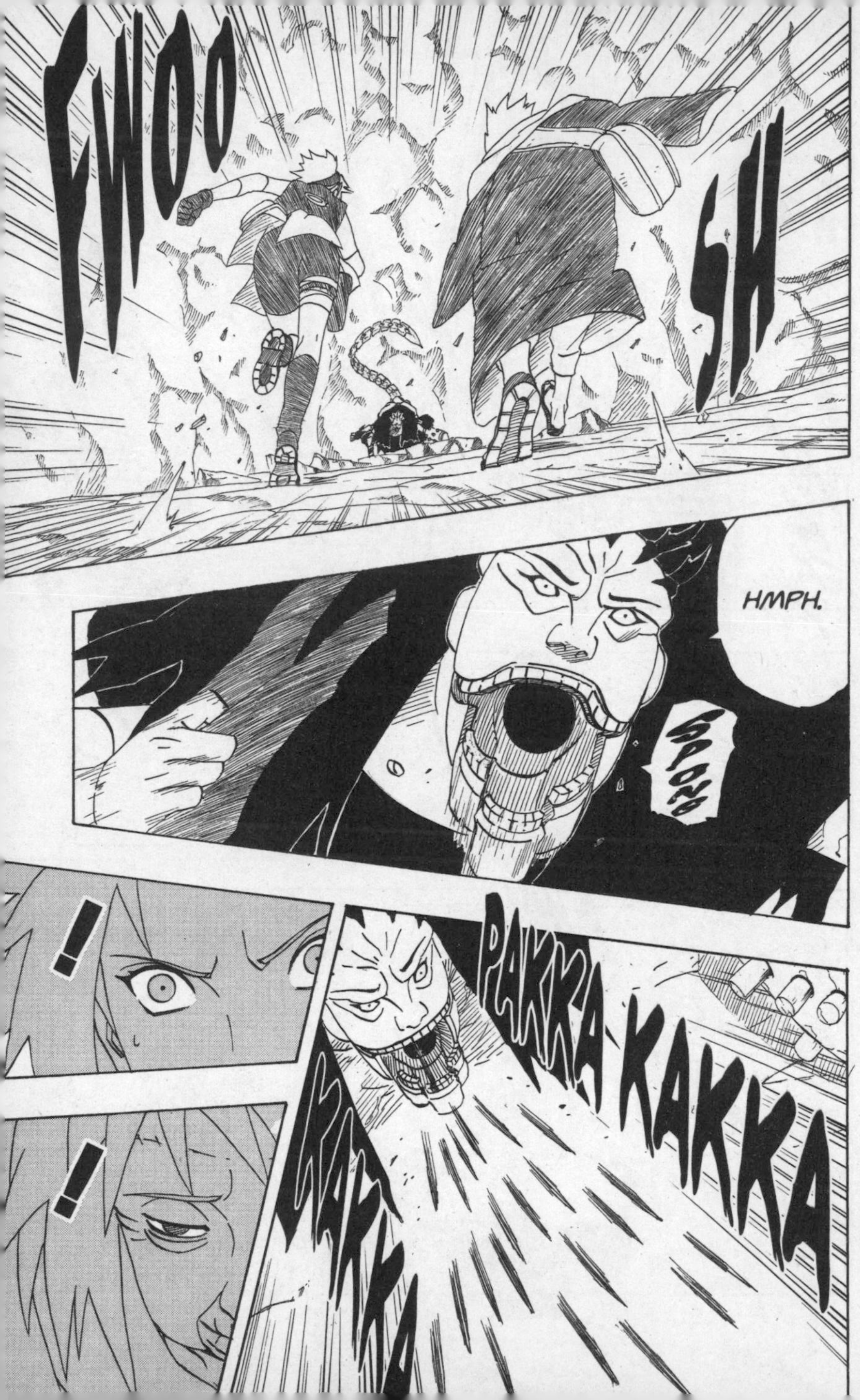
FWOO
SH
HMPH.
SPONG
PAKKA
KAKKA
KAKKA
!
!

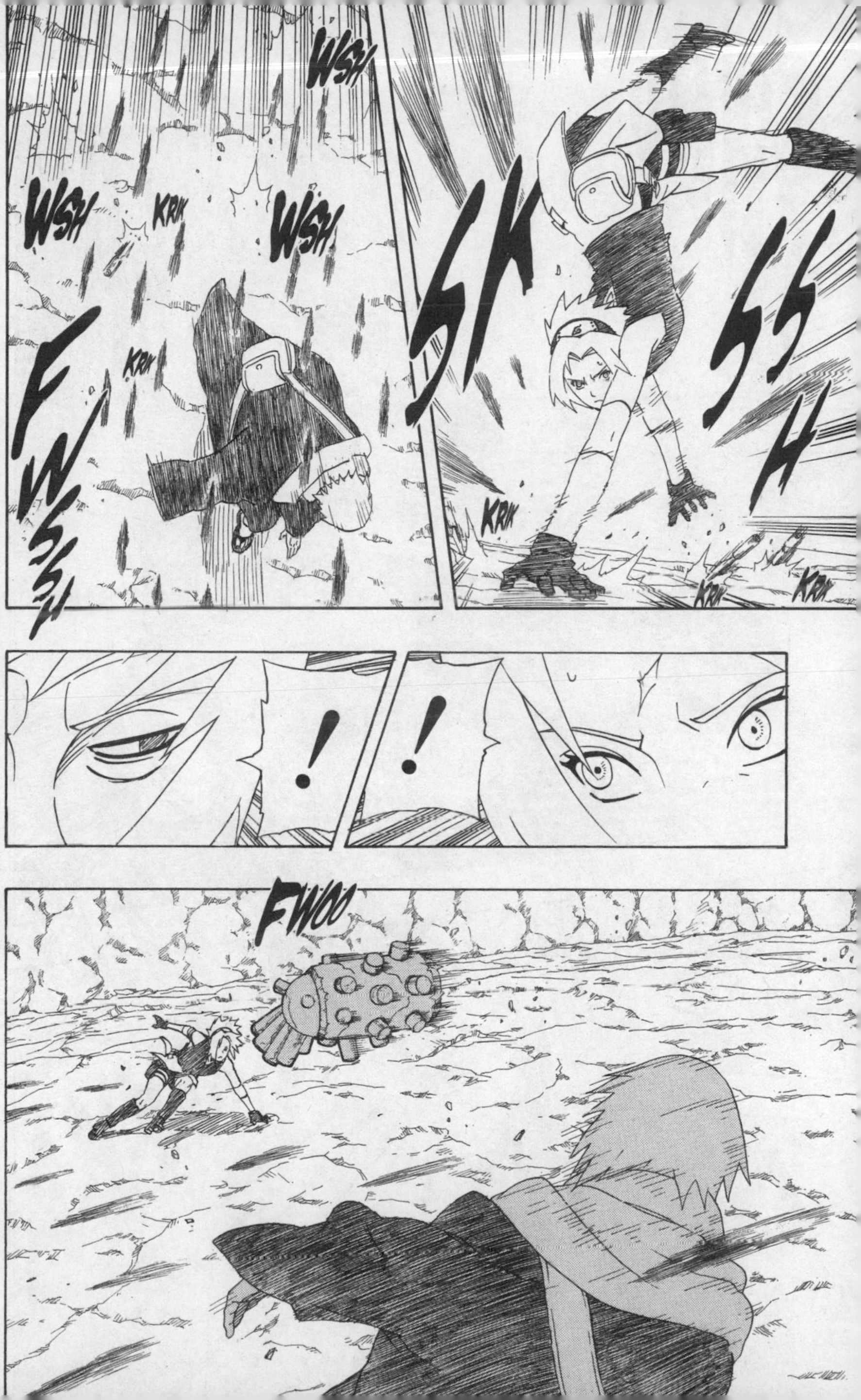
SSH
SK
KRIK
KRIK
KRIK
WSH
WSH
KRIK
WSH
KRIK
FWSSH
!
!
FWOO

READ THIS WAY

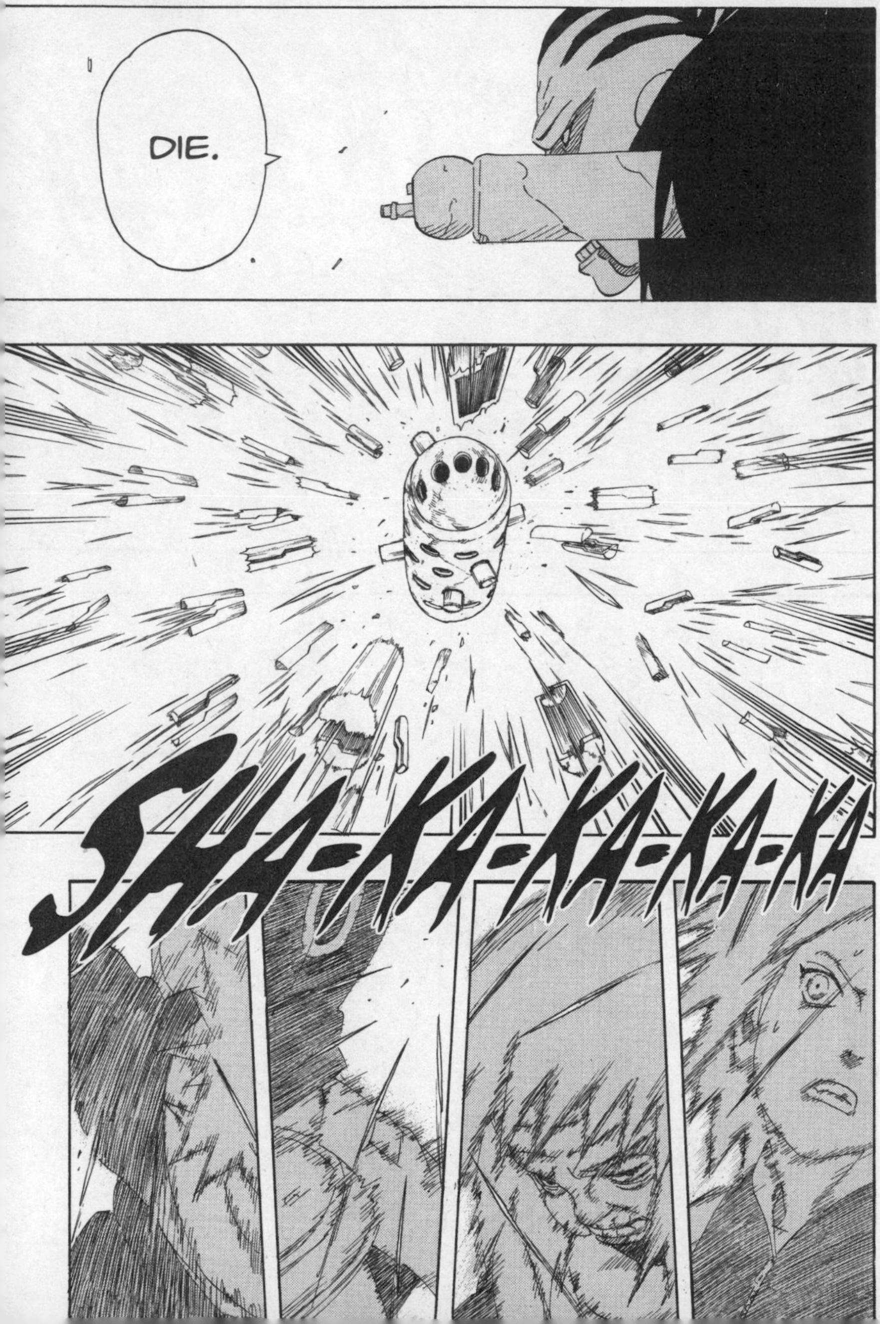
DIE.
SHA-KA-KA-KA-KA-KA

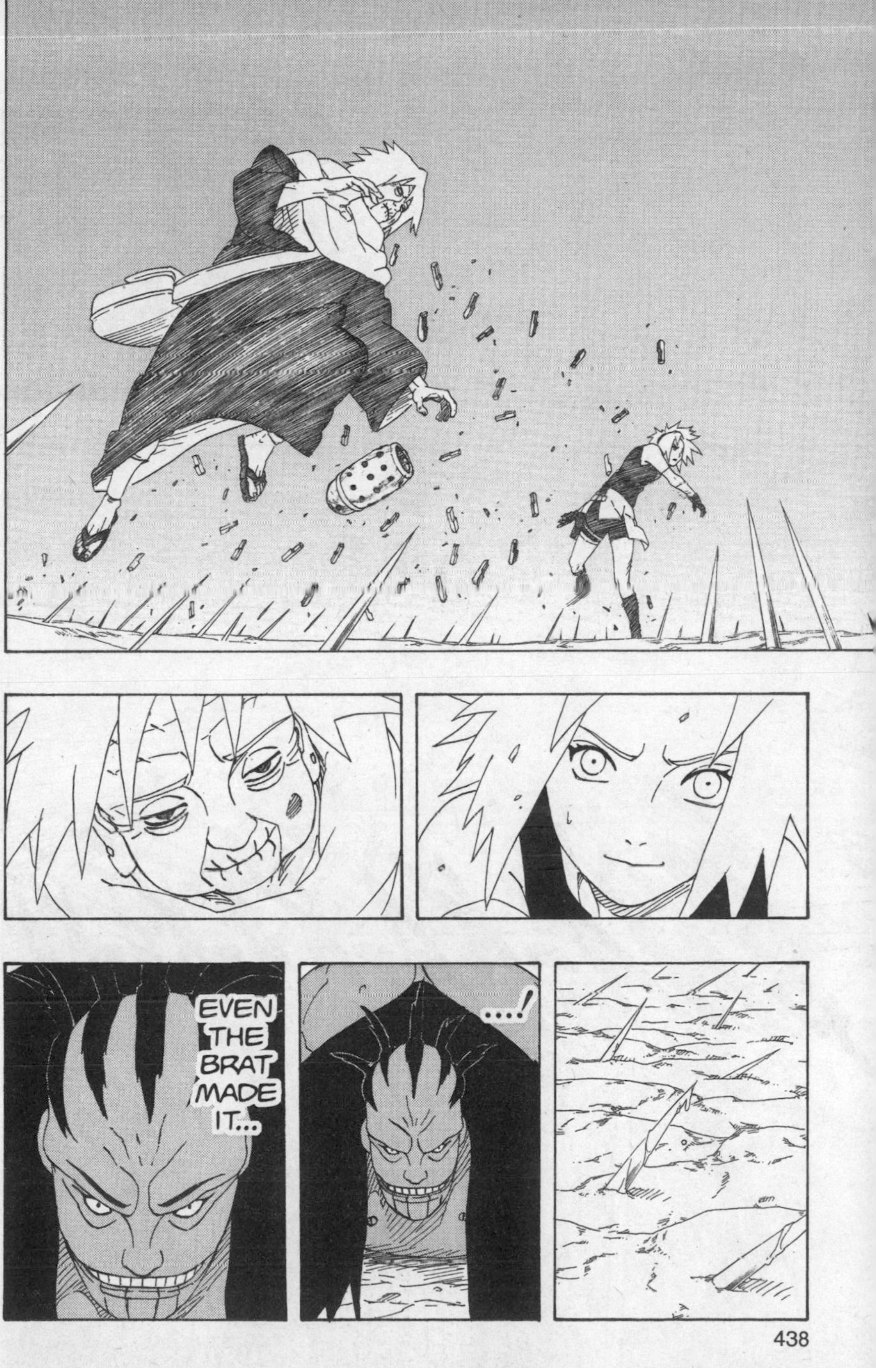
....!
EVEN THE BRAT MADE IT...

READ THIS WAY

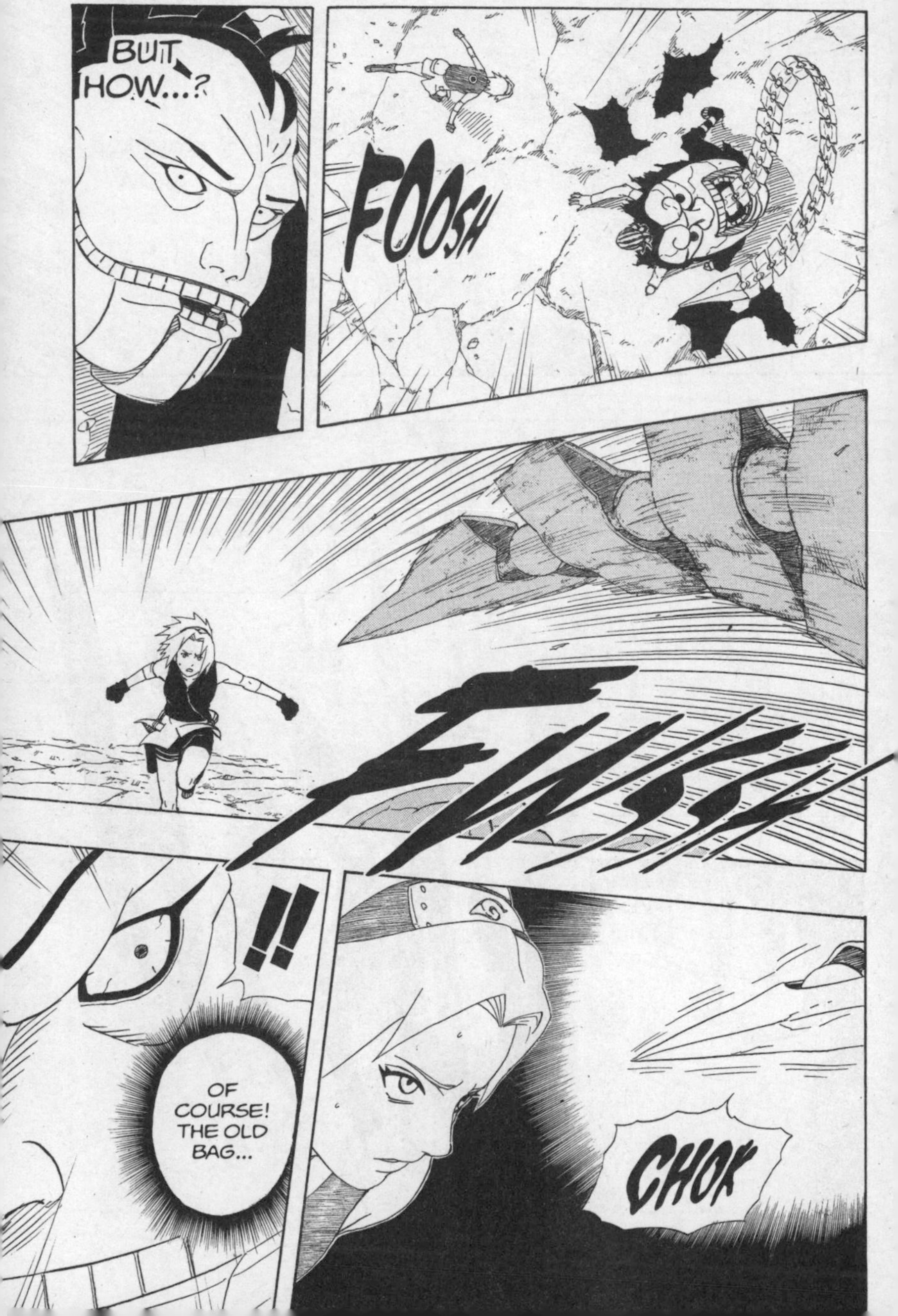
FOOSH
BUT HOW...?
FWSSH
CHOK
!!
OF COURSE! THE OLD BAG...

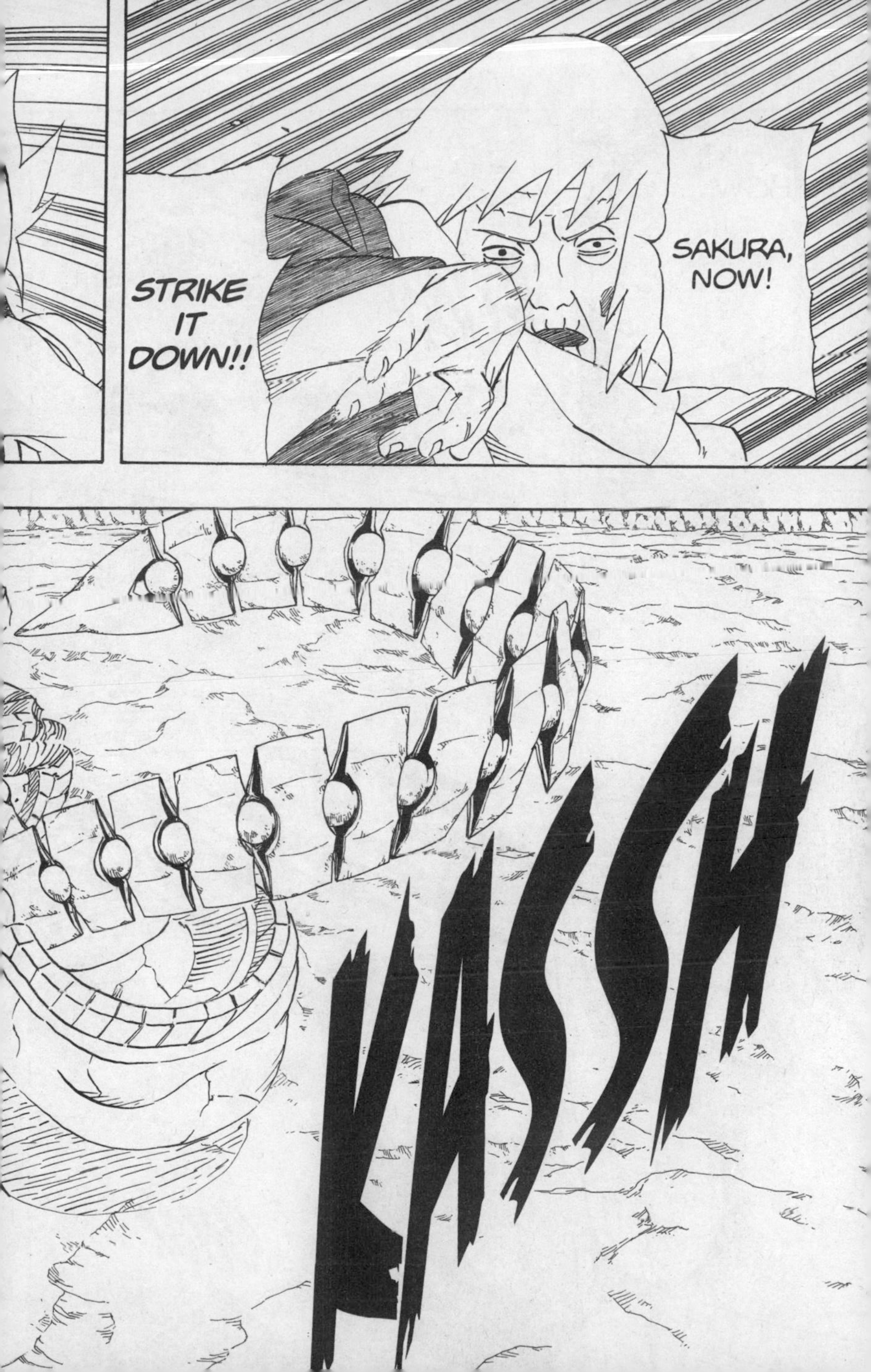
SAKURA, NOW!
STRIKE IT DOWN!!
VASSH

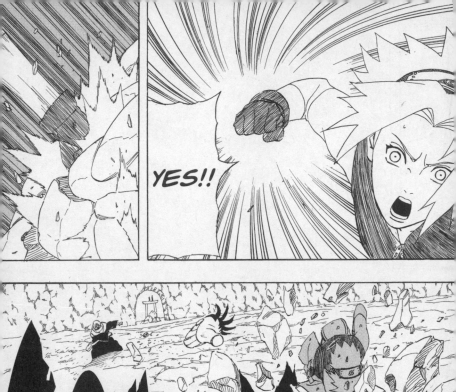

YES!!

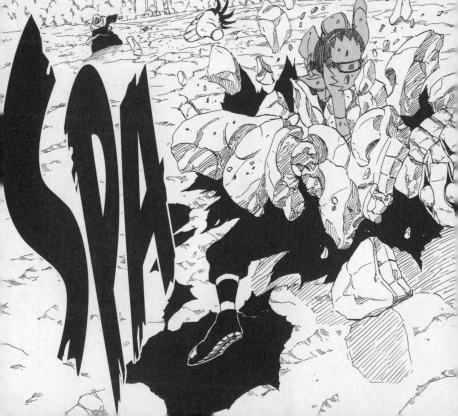

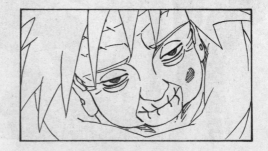

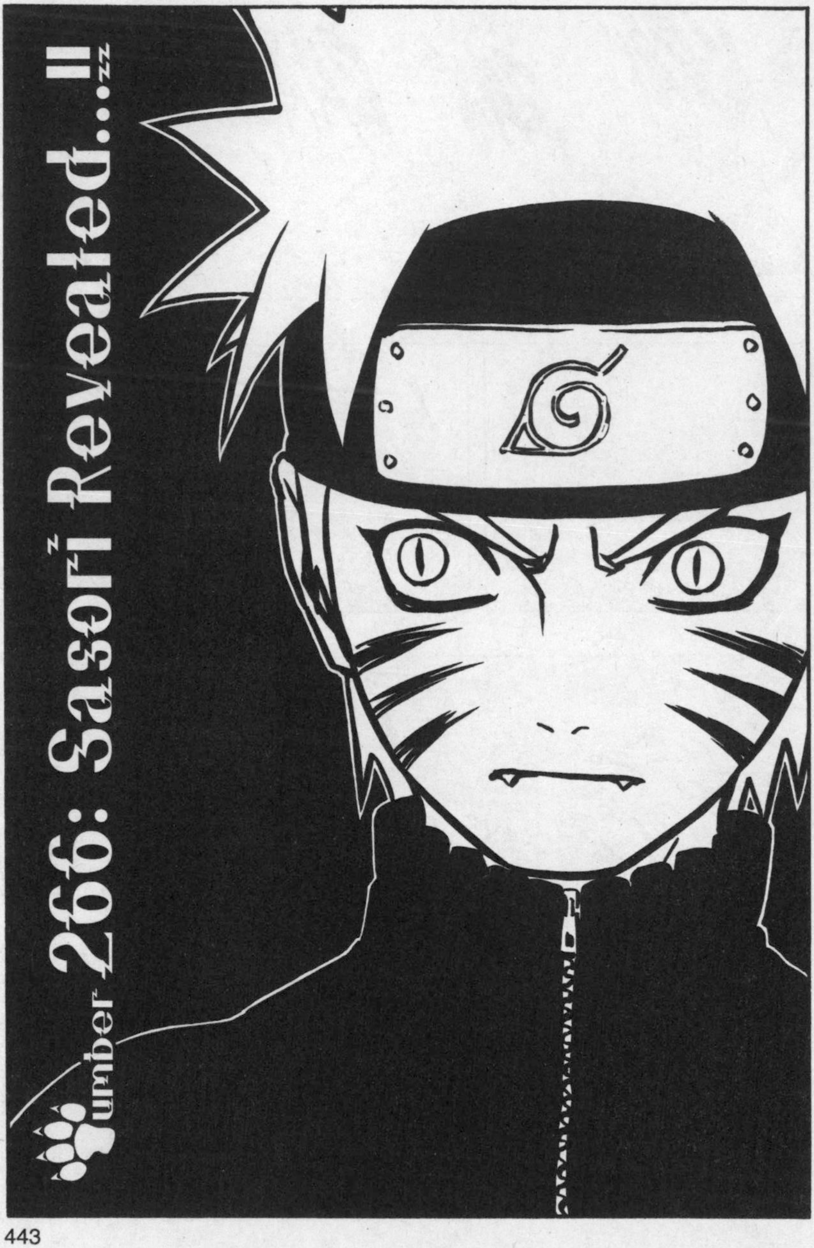
Number 266: Sasori Revealed...!!

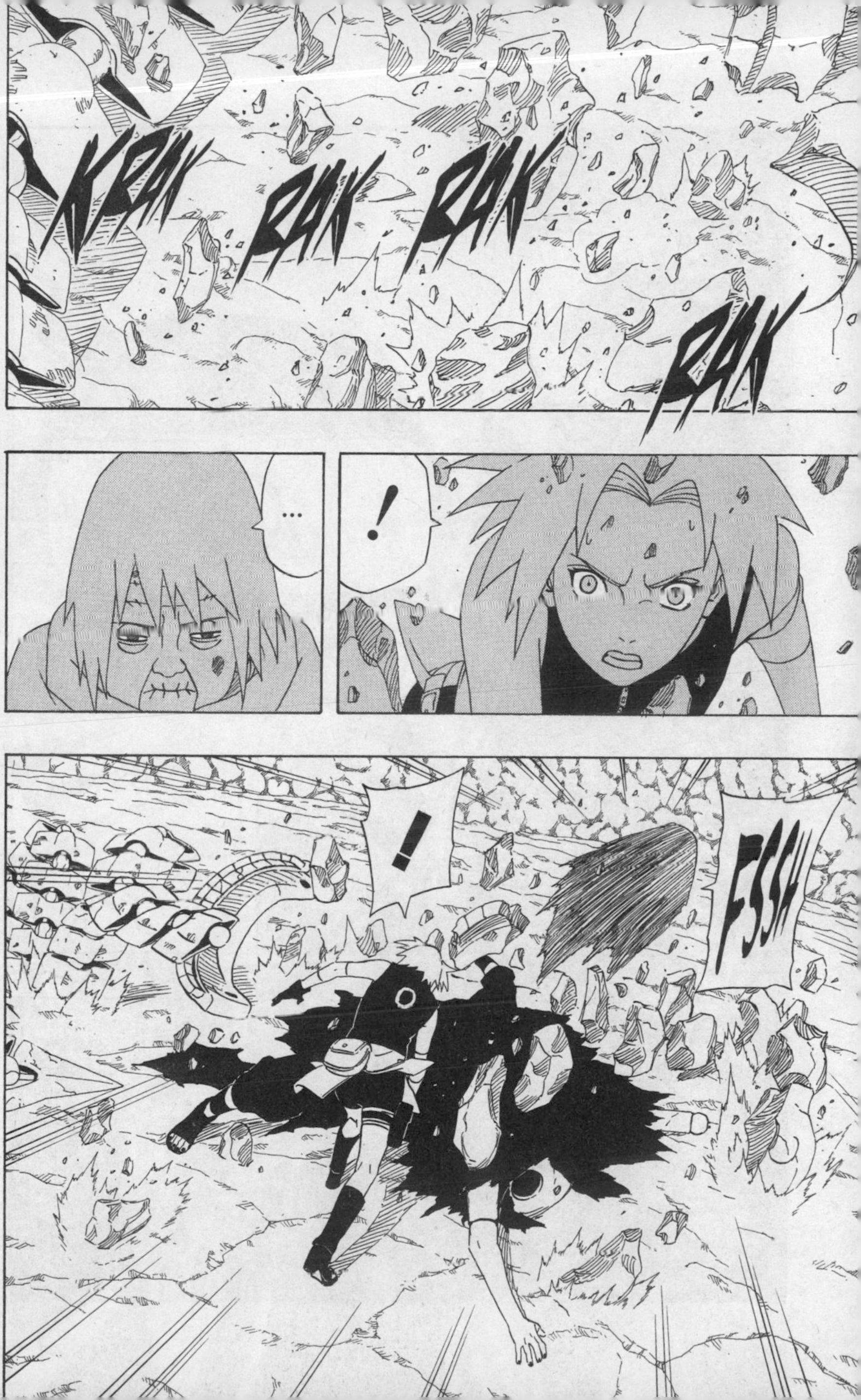
RAK
RAK
RAK
KRAK
!
...
FSSH
!

READ THIS WAY

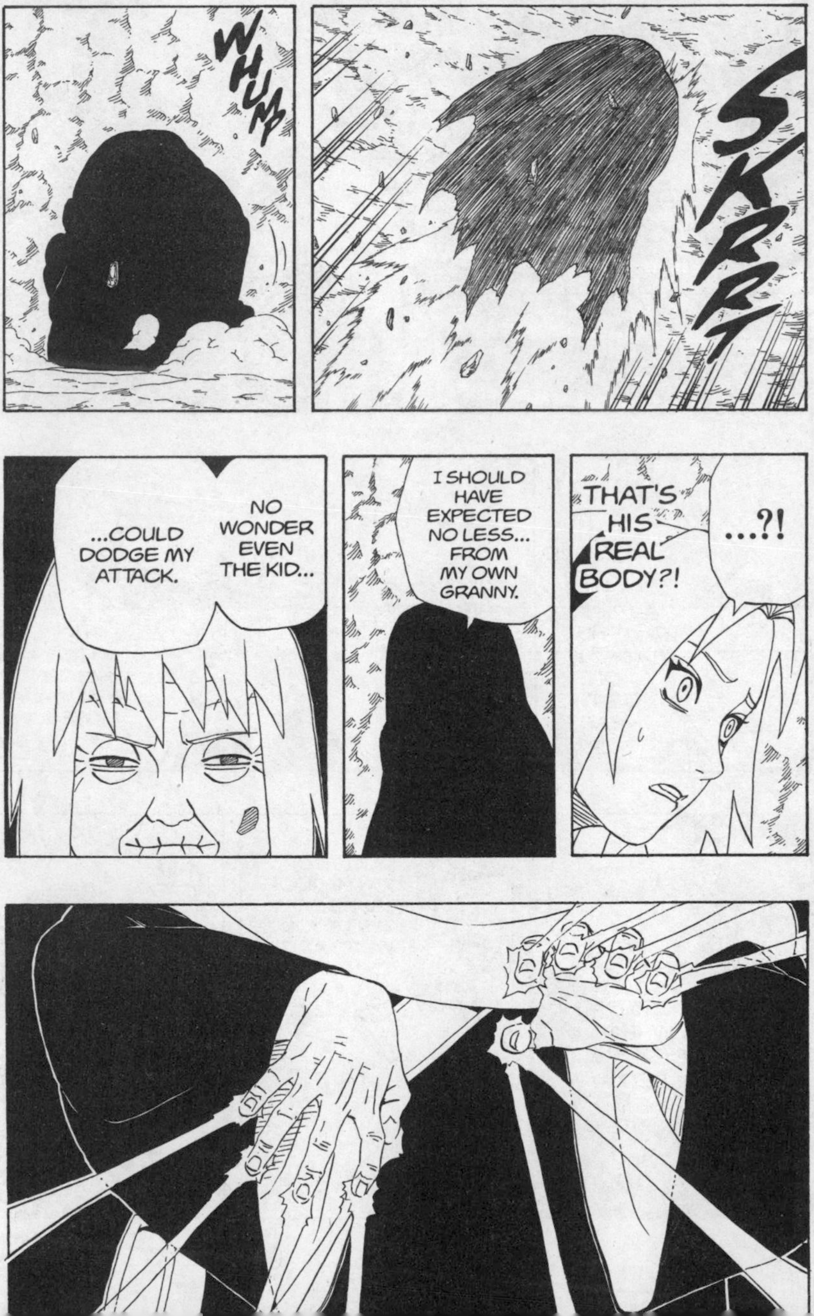
SKRRT
WHUMP
...?!
THAT'S HIS REAL BODY?!
I SHOULD HAVE EXPECTED NO LESS... FROM MY OWN GRANNY.
NO WONDER EVEN THE KID...
...COULD DODGE MY ATTACK.

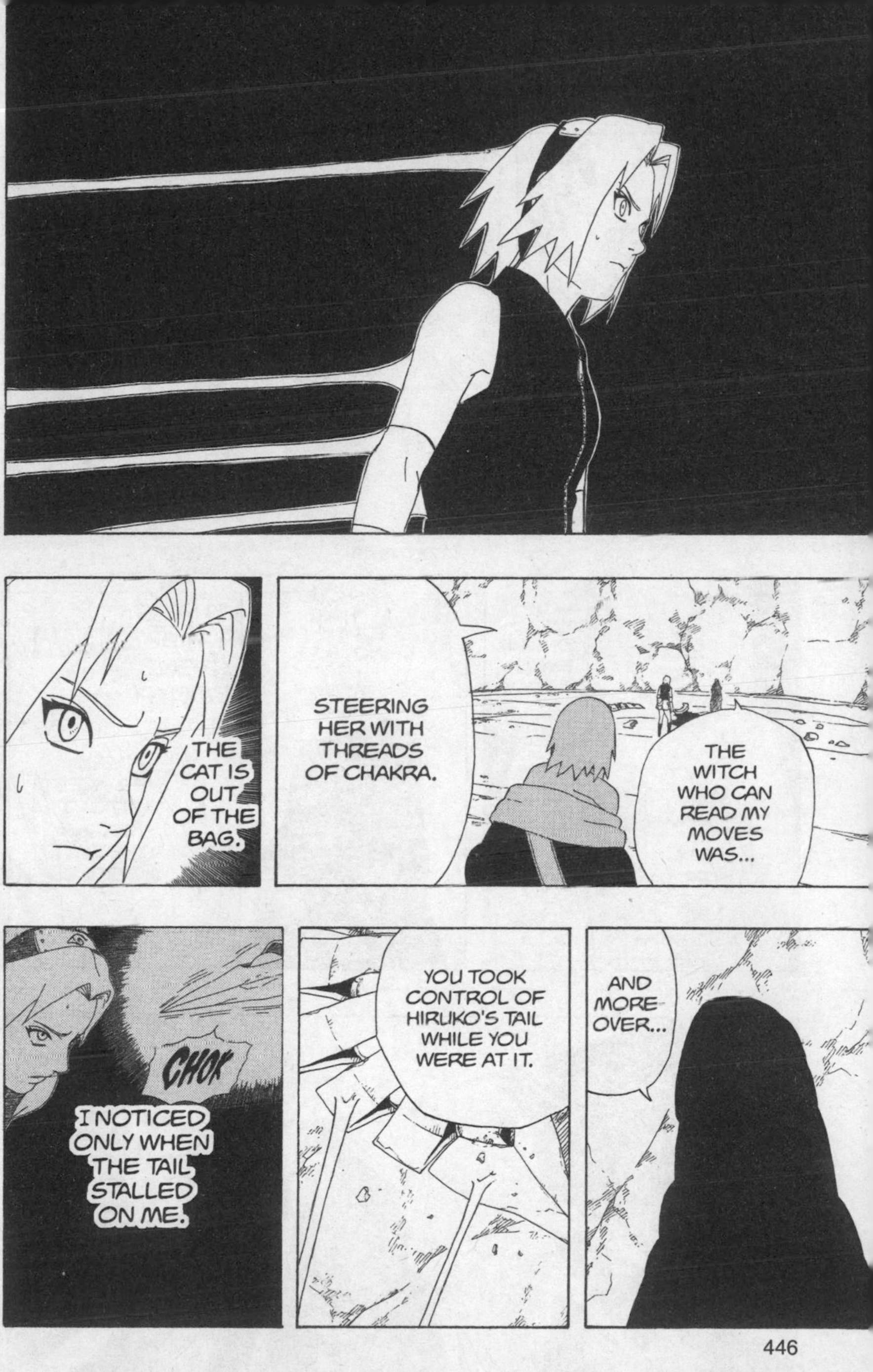
THE WITCH WHO CAN READ MY MOVES WAS...
STEERING HER WITH THREADS OF CHAKRA.
THE CAT IS OUT OF THE BAG.
AND MORE OVER...
YOU TOOK CONTROL OF HIRUKO'S TAIL WHILE YOU WERE AT IT.
CHOK
I NOTICED ONLY WHEN THE TAIL STALLED ON ME.

READ THIS WAY

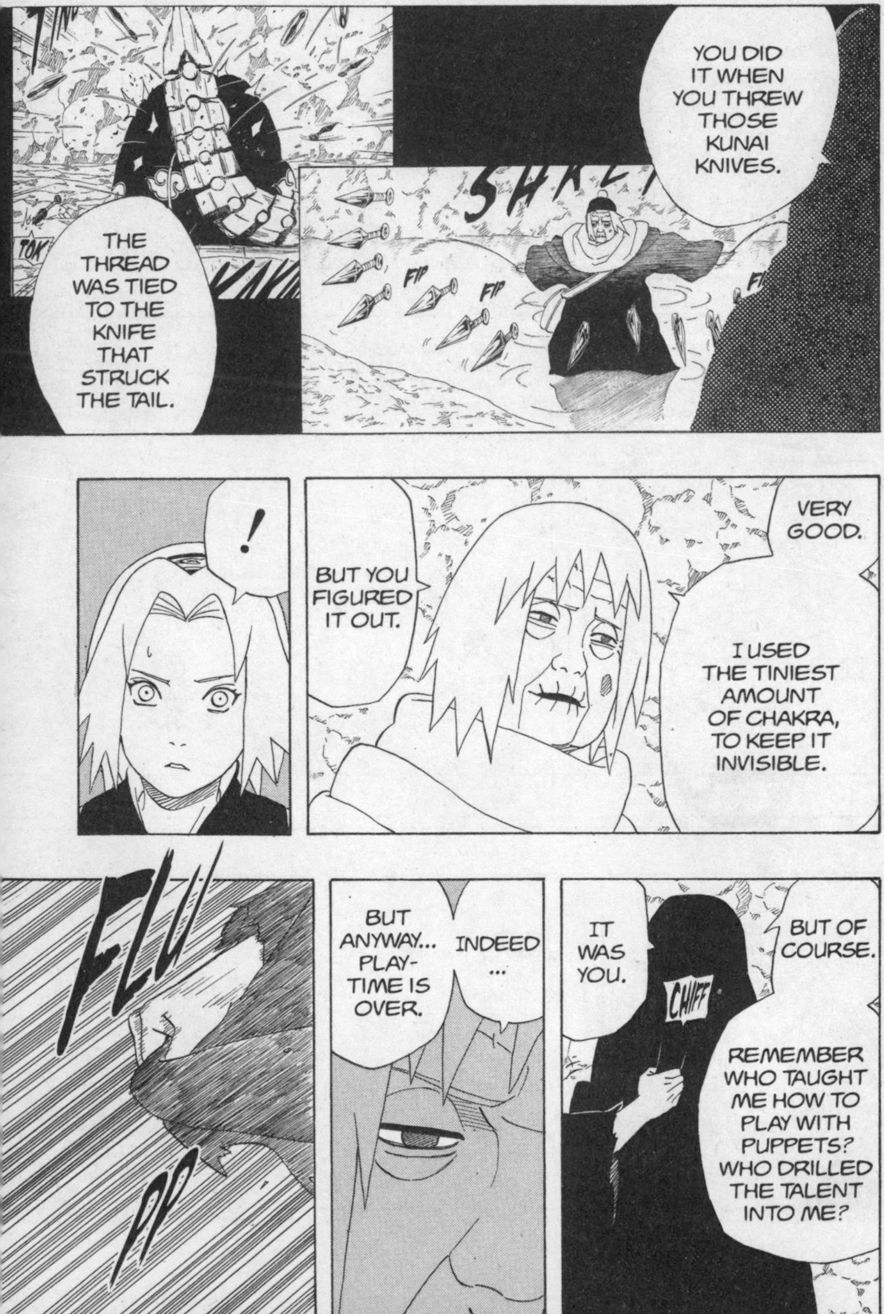
YOU DID IT WHEN YOU THREW THOSE KUNAI KNIVES.
FIP
FIP
TOK
THE THREAD WAS TIED TO THE KNIFE THAT STRUCK THE TAIL.
VERY GOOD.
I USED THE TINIEST AMOUNT OF CHAKRA, TO KEEP IT INVISIBLE.
BUT YOU FIGURED IT OUT.
!
BUT OF COURSE.
IT WAS YOU.
CHIFF
REMEMBER WHO TAUGHT ME HOW TO PLAY WITH PUPPETS? WHO DRILLED THE TALENT INTO ME?
INDEED ...
BUT ANYWAY... PLAY-TIME IS OVER.
FLU
PP

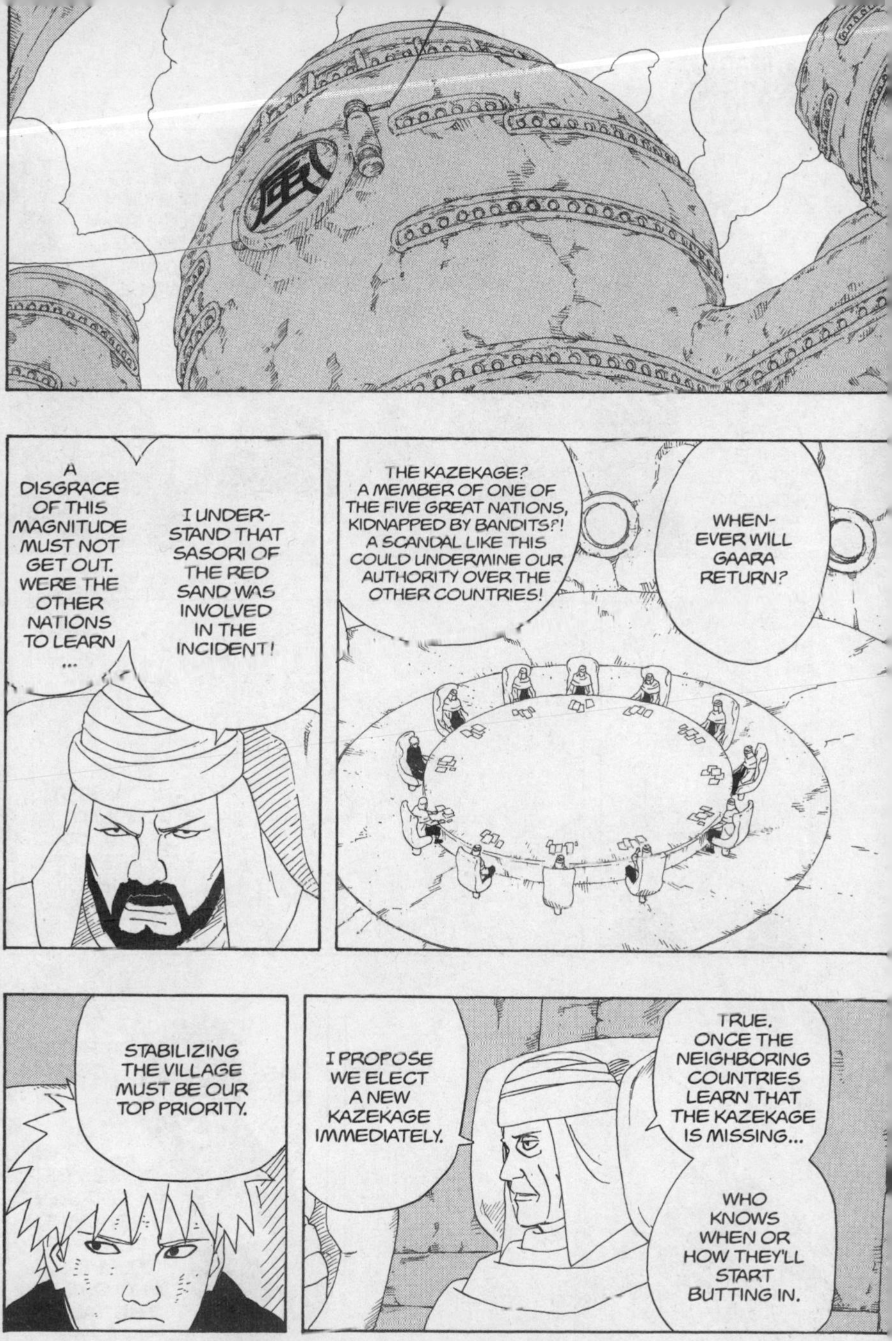
WHEN-EVER WILL GAARA RETURN?
THE KAZEKAGE? A MEMBER OF ONE OF THE FIVE GREAT NATIONS, KIDNAPPED BY BANDITS?! A SCANDAL LIKE THIS COULD UNDERMINE OUR AUTHORITY OVER THE OTHER COUNTRIES!
I UNDER-STAND THAT SASORI OF THE RED SAND WAS INVOLVED IN THE INCIDENT!
A DISGRACE OF THIS MAGNITUDE MUST NOT GET OUT. WERE THE OTHER NATIONS TO LEARN ...
TRUE. ONCE THE NEIGHBORING COUNTRIES LEARN THAT THE KAZEKAGE IS MISSING...
WHO KNOWS WHEN OR HOW THEY'LL START BUTTING IN.
I PROPOSE WE ELECT A NEW KAZEKAGE IMMEDIATELY.
STABILIZING THE VILLAGE MUST BE OUR TOP PRIORITY.

READ THIS WAY

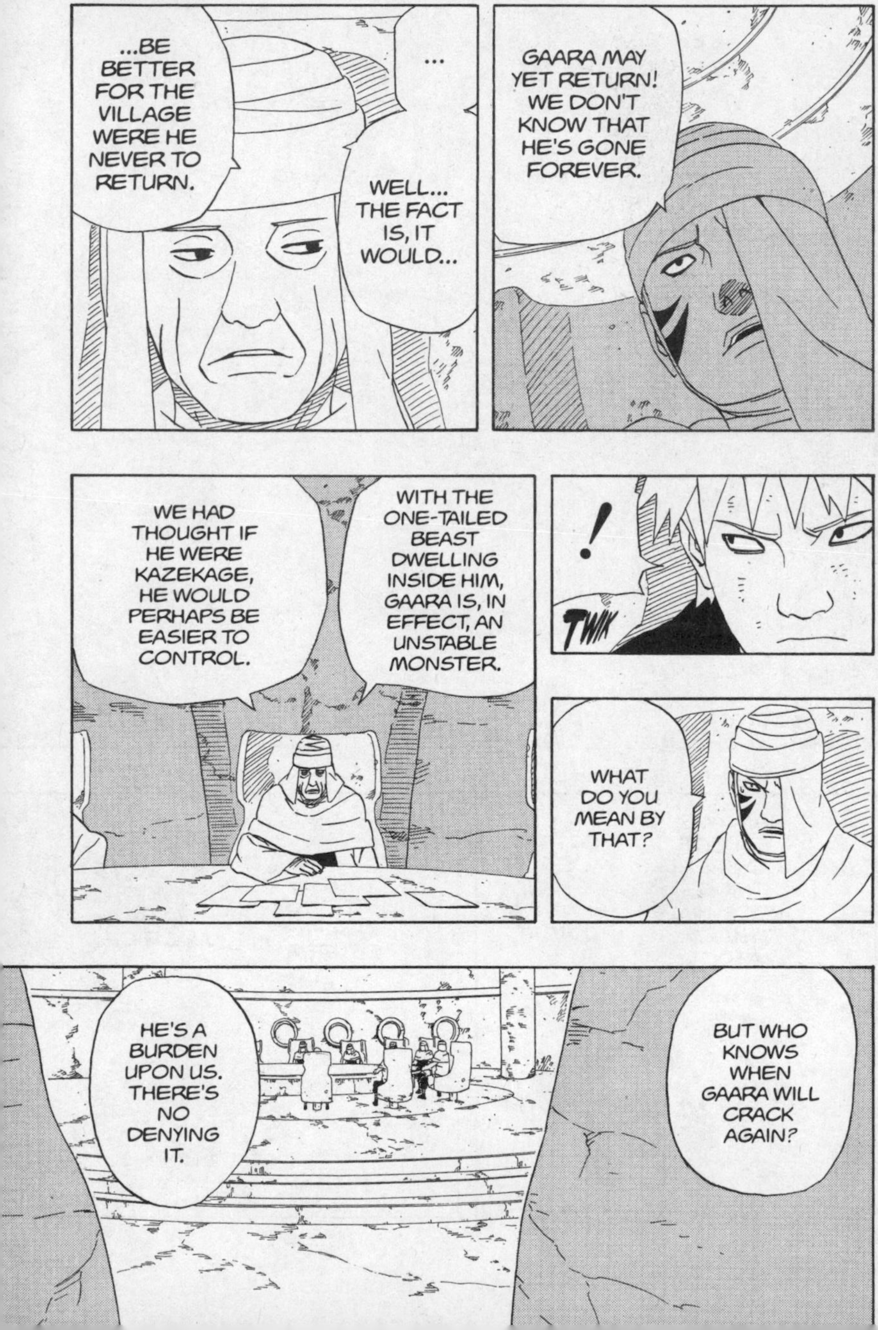
GAARA MAY YET RETURN! WE DON'T KNOW THAT HE'S GONE FOREVER.
...
WELL... THE FACT IS, IT WOULD...
...BE BETTER FOR THE VILLAGE WERE HE NEVER TO RETURN.
!
TWIK
WHAT DO YOU MEAN BY THAT?
WITH THE ONE-TAILED BEAST DWELLING INSIDE HIM, GAARA IS, IN EFFECT, AN UNSTABLE MONSTER.
WE HAD THOUGHT IF HE WERE KAZEKAGE, HE WOULD PERHAPS BE EASIER TO CONTROL.
BUT WHO KNOWS WHEN GAARA WILL CRACK AGAIN?
HE'S A BURDEN UPON US. THERE'S NO DENYING IT.

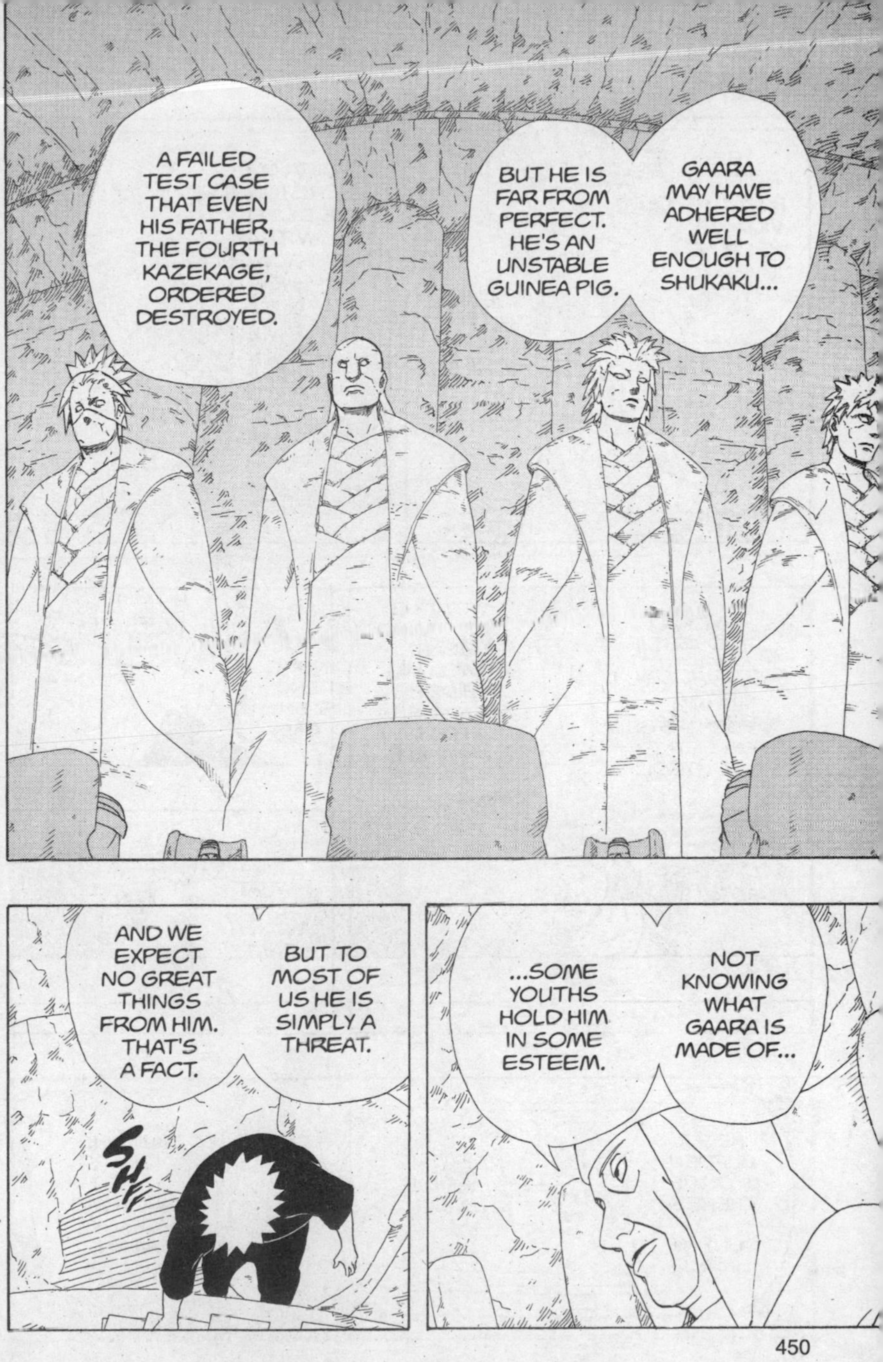
GAARA MAY HAVE ADHERED WELL ENOUGH TO SHUKAKU...
BUT HE IS FAR FROM PERFECT. HE'S AN UNSTABLE GUINEA PIG.
A FAILED TEST CASE THAT EVEN HIS FATHER, THE FOURTH KAZEKAGE, ORDERED DESTROYED.
NOT KNOWING WHAT GAARA IS MADE OF...
...SOME YOUTHS HOLD HIM IN SOME ESTEEM.
BUT TO MOST OF US HE IS SIMPLY A THREAT.
AND WE EXPECT NO GREAT THINGS FROM HIM. THAT'S A FACT.
SHFF

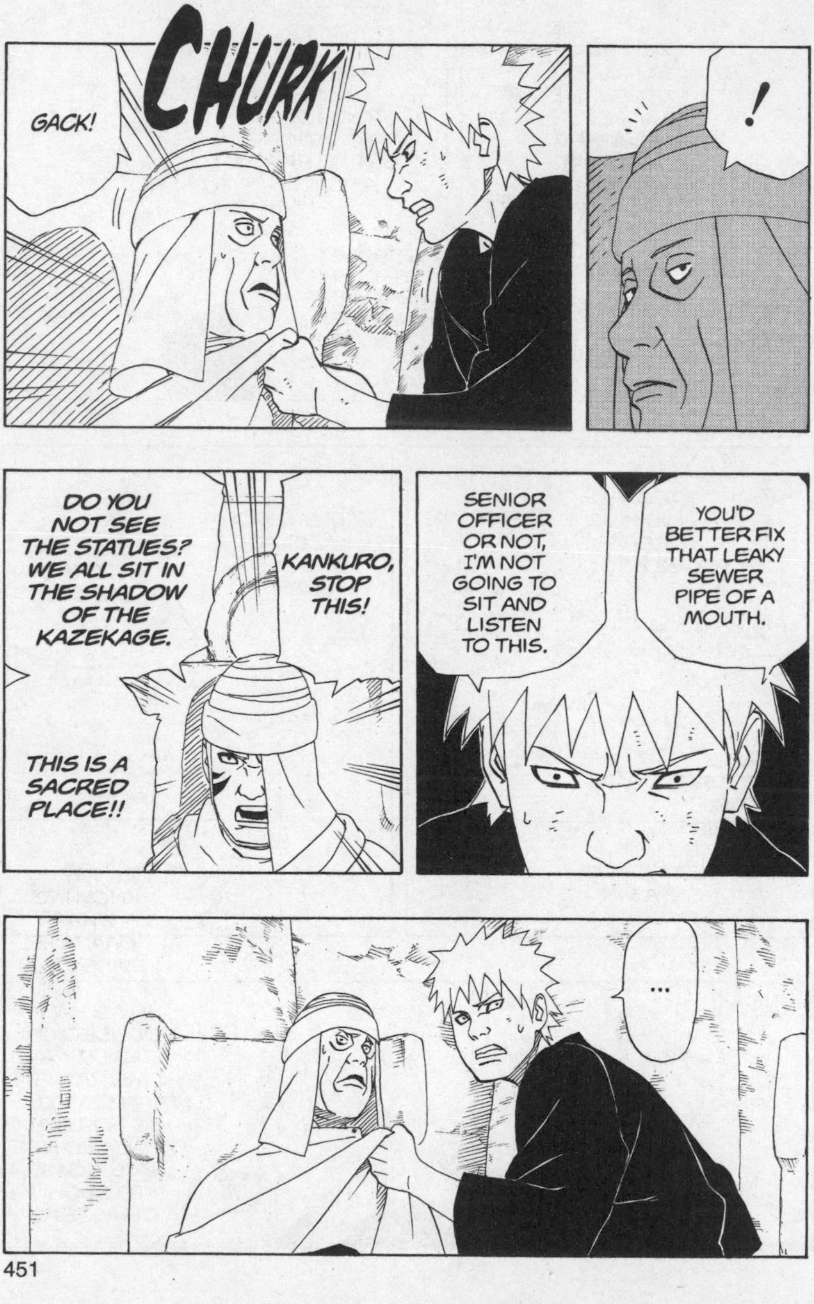
!
CHURK
GACK!
YOU'D BETTER FIX THAT LEAKY SEWER PIPE OF A MOUTH.
SENIOR OFFICER OR NOT, I'M NOT GOING TO SIT AND LISTEN TO THIS.
KANKURO, STOP THIS!
DO YOU NOT SEE THE STATUES? WE ALL SIT IN THE SHADOW OF THE KAZEKAGE.
THIS IS A SACRED PLACE!!
...

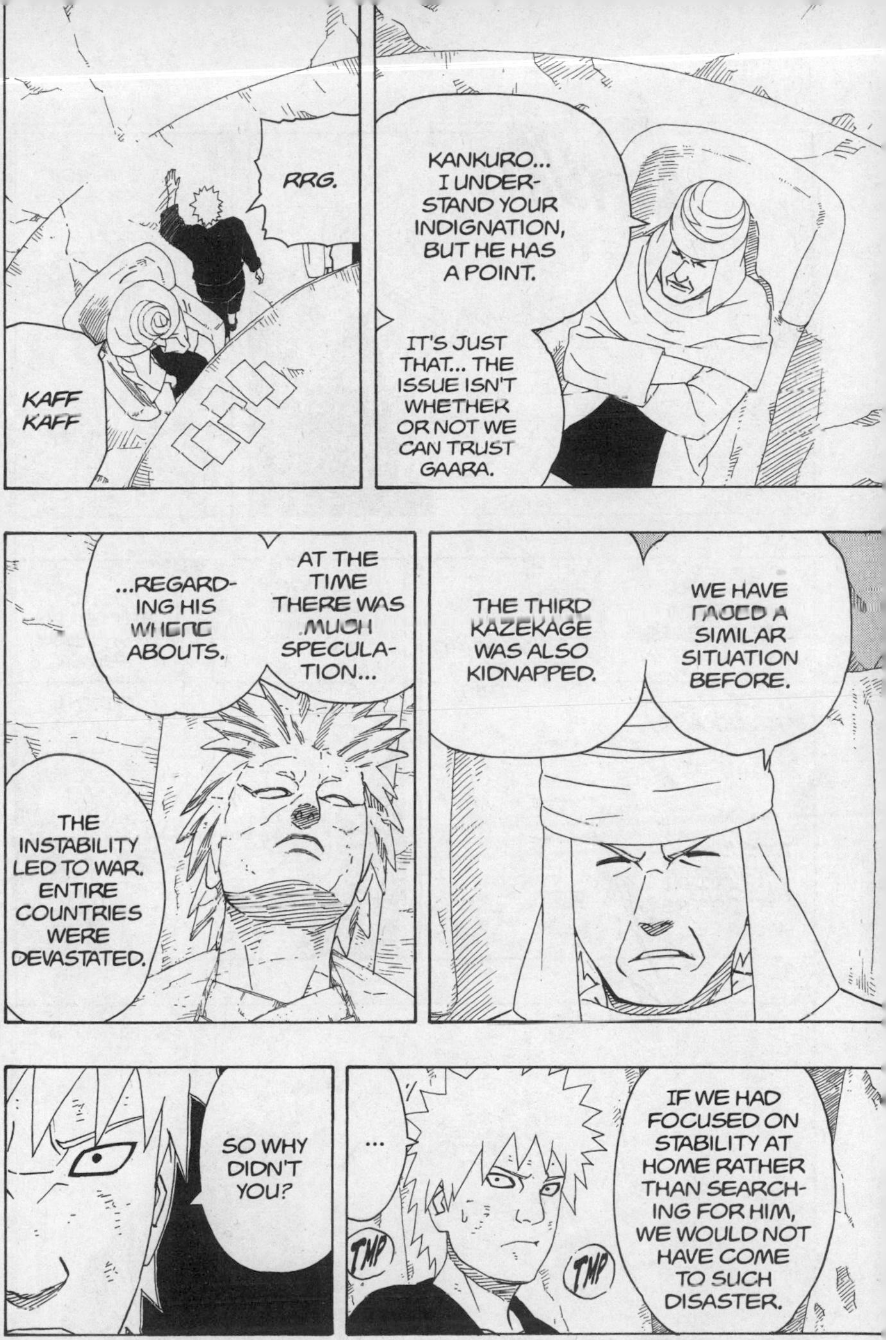
KANKURO... I UNDERSTAND YOUR INDIGNATION, BUT HE HAS A POINT.
IT'S JUST THAT... THE ISSUE ISN'T WHETHER OR NOT WE CAN TRUST GAARA.
RRG.
KAFF KAFF
WE HAVE FACED A SIMILAR SITUATION BEFORE.
THE THIRD KAZEKAGE WAS ALSO KIDNAPPED.
AT THE TIME THERE WAS MUCH SPECULATION...
...REGARDING HIS WHEREABOUTS.
THE INSTABILITY LED TO WAR. ENTIRE COUNTRIES WERE DEVASTATED.
IF WE HAD FOCUSED ON STABILITY AT HOME RATHER THAN SEARCHING FOR HIM, WE WOULD NOT HAVE COME TO SUCH DISASTER.
...
TMP
TMP
SO WHY DIDN'T YOU?

READ THIS WAY

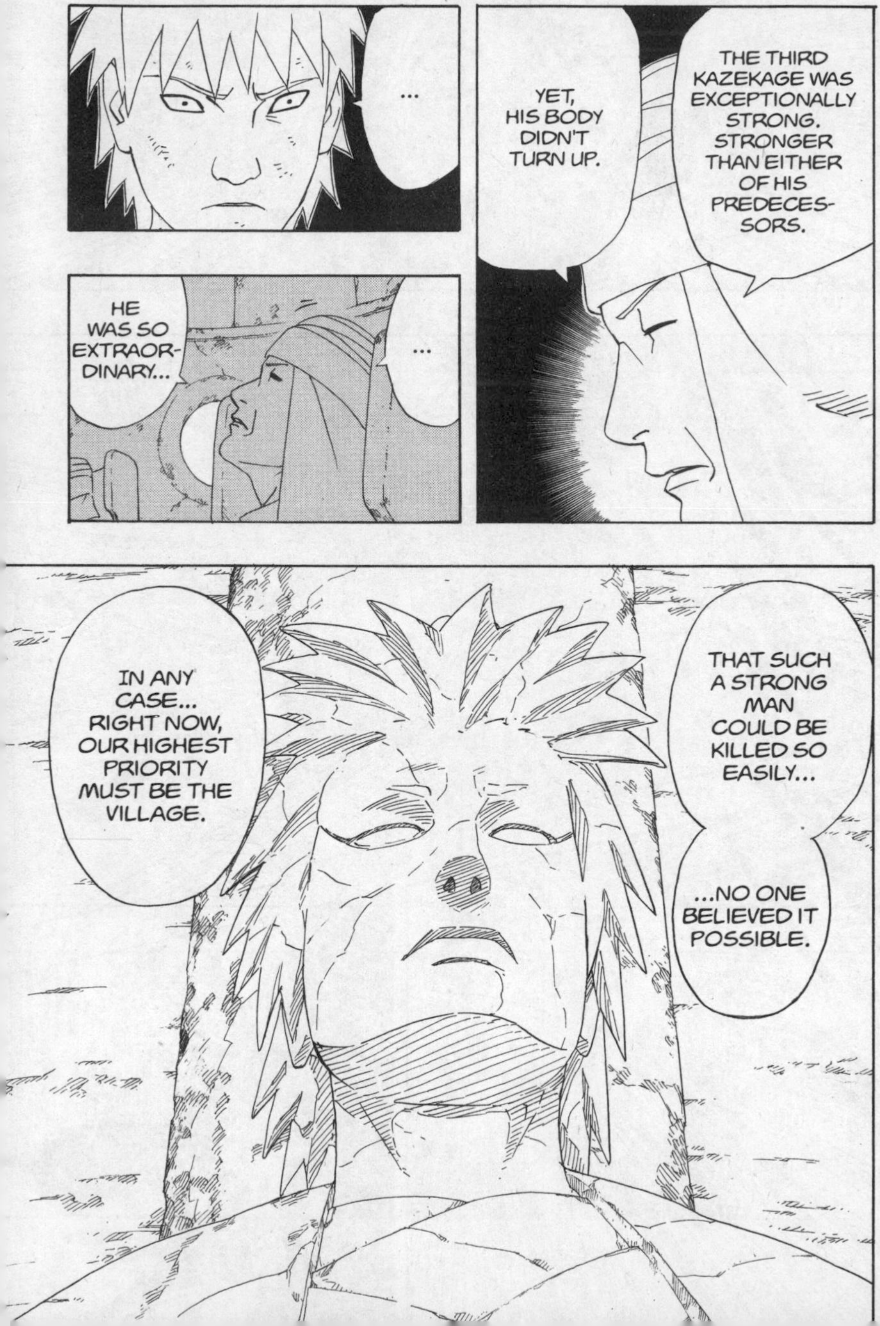
THE THIRD KAZEKAGE WAS EXCEPTIONALLY STRONG. STRONGER THAN EITHER OF HIS PREDECES-SORS.
YET, HIS BODY DIDN'T TURN UP.
...
...
HE WAS SO EXTRAOR-DINARY...
THAT SUCH A STRONG MAN COULD BE KILLED SO EASILY...
...NO ONE BELIEVED IT POSSIBLE.
IN ANY CASE... RIGHT NOW, OUR HIGHEST PRIORITY MUST BE THE VILLAGE.

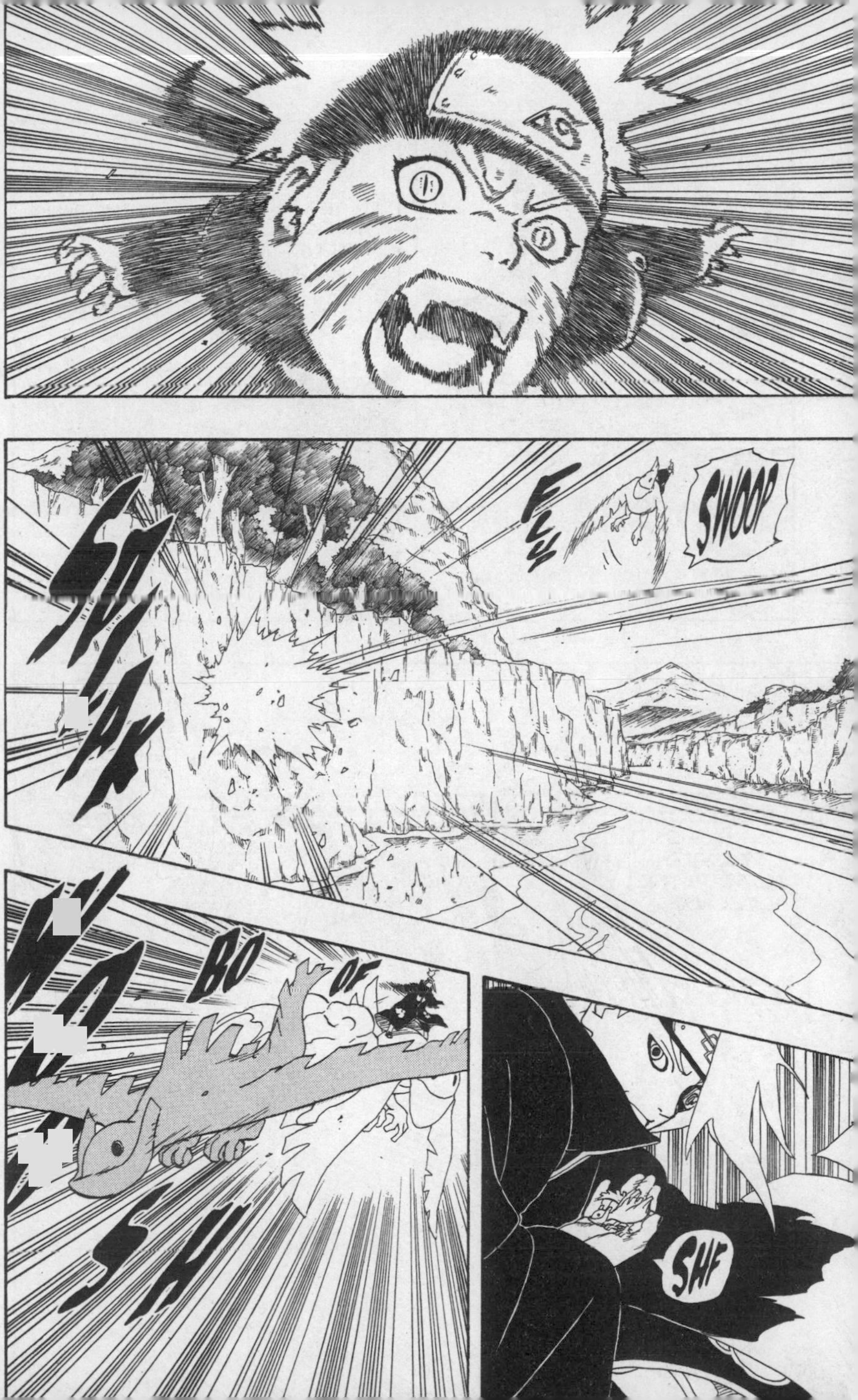
SWOOP
SHF
BO
OF

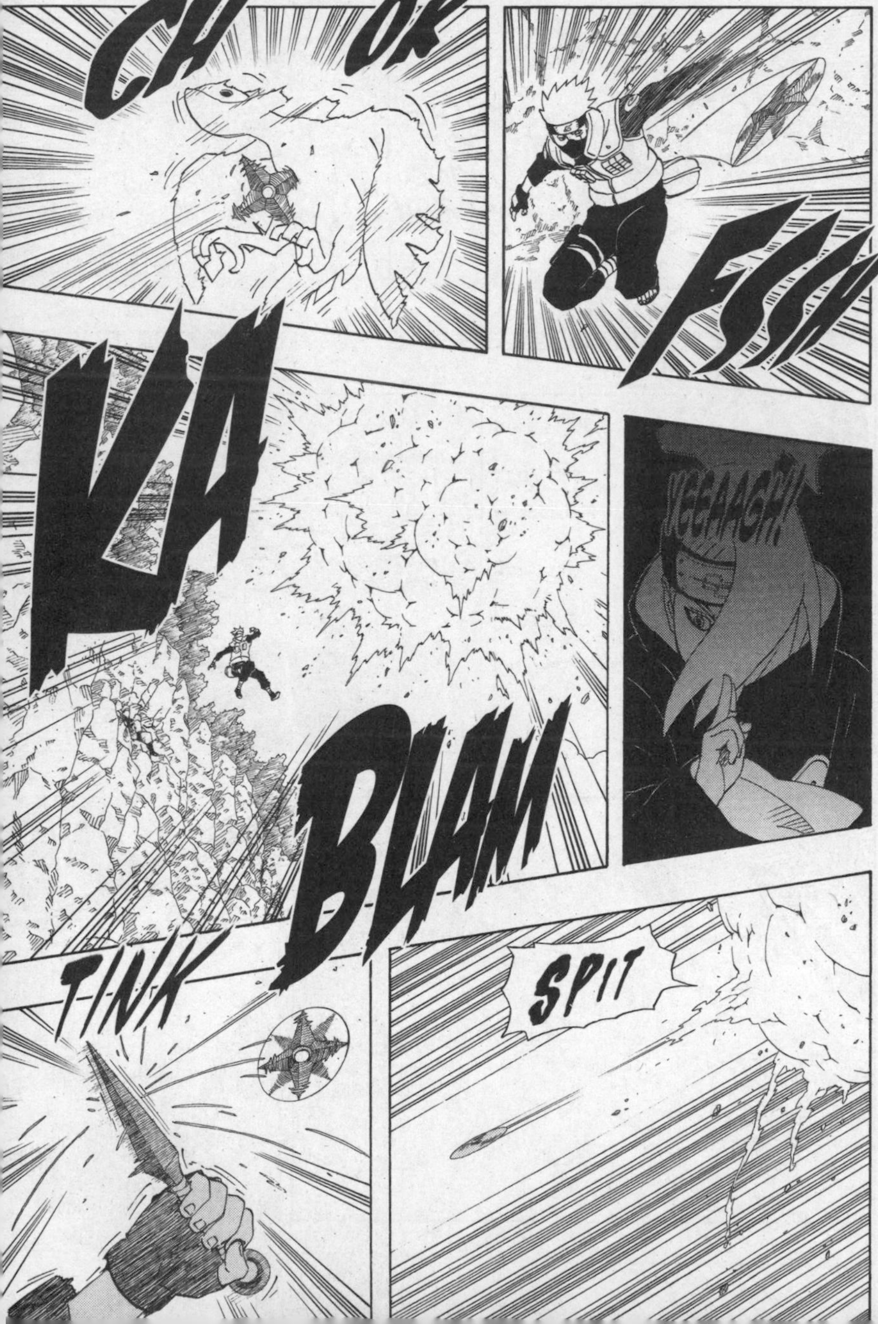
FSSH
CH OK
YEEAAGH!!
VA
BLAM
SPIT
TINK

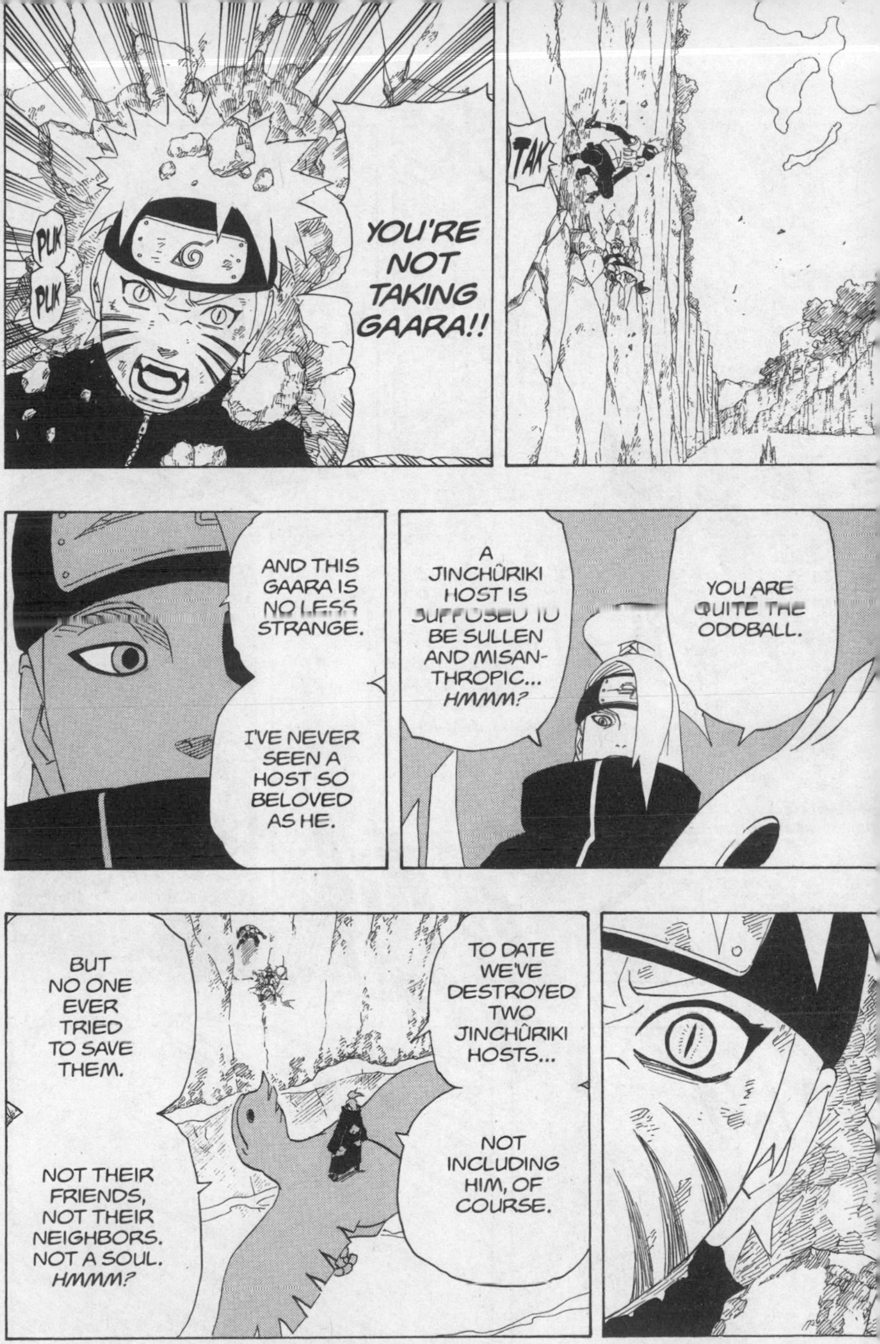
TAK
YOU'RE NOT TAKING GAARA!!
PUK
PUK
YOU ARE QUITE THE ODDBALL.
A JINCHŪRIKI HOST IS SUPPOSED TO BE SULLEN AND MISANTHROPIC... HMMM?
AND THIS GAARA IS NO LESS STRANGE.
I'VE NEVER SEEN A HOST SO BELOVED AS HE.
TO DATE WE'VE DESTROYED TWO JINCHŪRIKI HOSTS...
NOT INCLUDING HIM, OF COURSE.
BUT NO ONE EVER TRIED TO SAVE THEM.
NOT THEIR FRIENDS, NOT THEIR NEIGHBORS. NOT A SOUL. *HMMM?*

READ THIS WAY

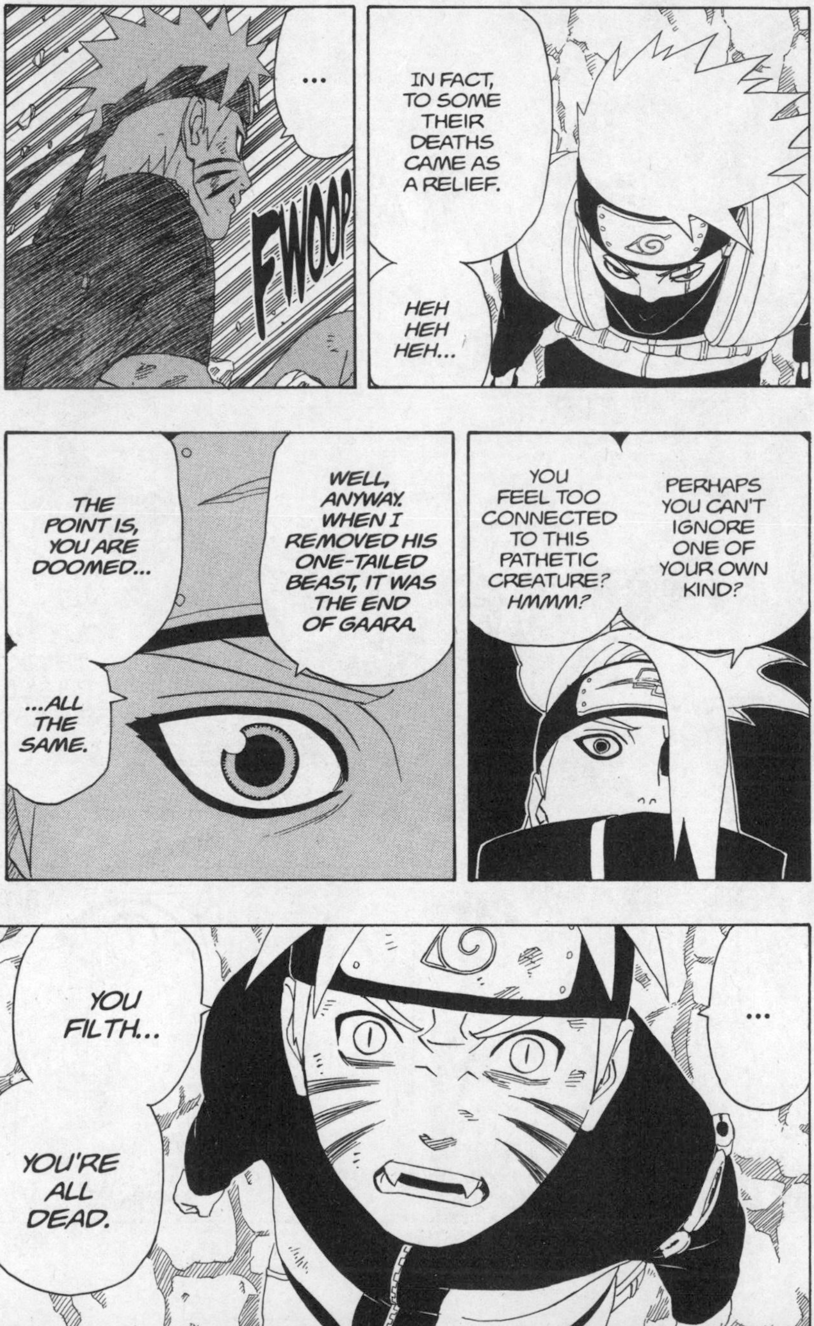

IN FACT, TO SOME THEIR DEATHS CAME AS A RELIEF.
HEH HEH HEH...
...
FWOOP
PERHAPS YOU CAN'T IGNORE ONE OF YOUR OWN KIND?
YOU FEEL TOO CONNECTED TO THIS PATHETIC CREATURE? HMMM?
WELL, ANYWAY. WHEN I REMOVED HIS ONE-TAILED BEAST, IT WAS THE END OF GAARA.
THE POINT IS, YOU ARE DOOMED...
...ALL THE SAME.
...
YOU FILTH...
YOU'RE ALL DEAD.

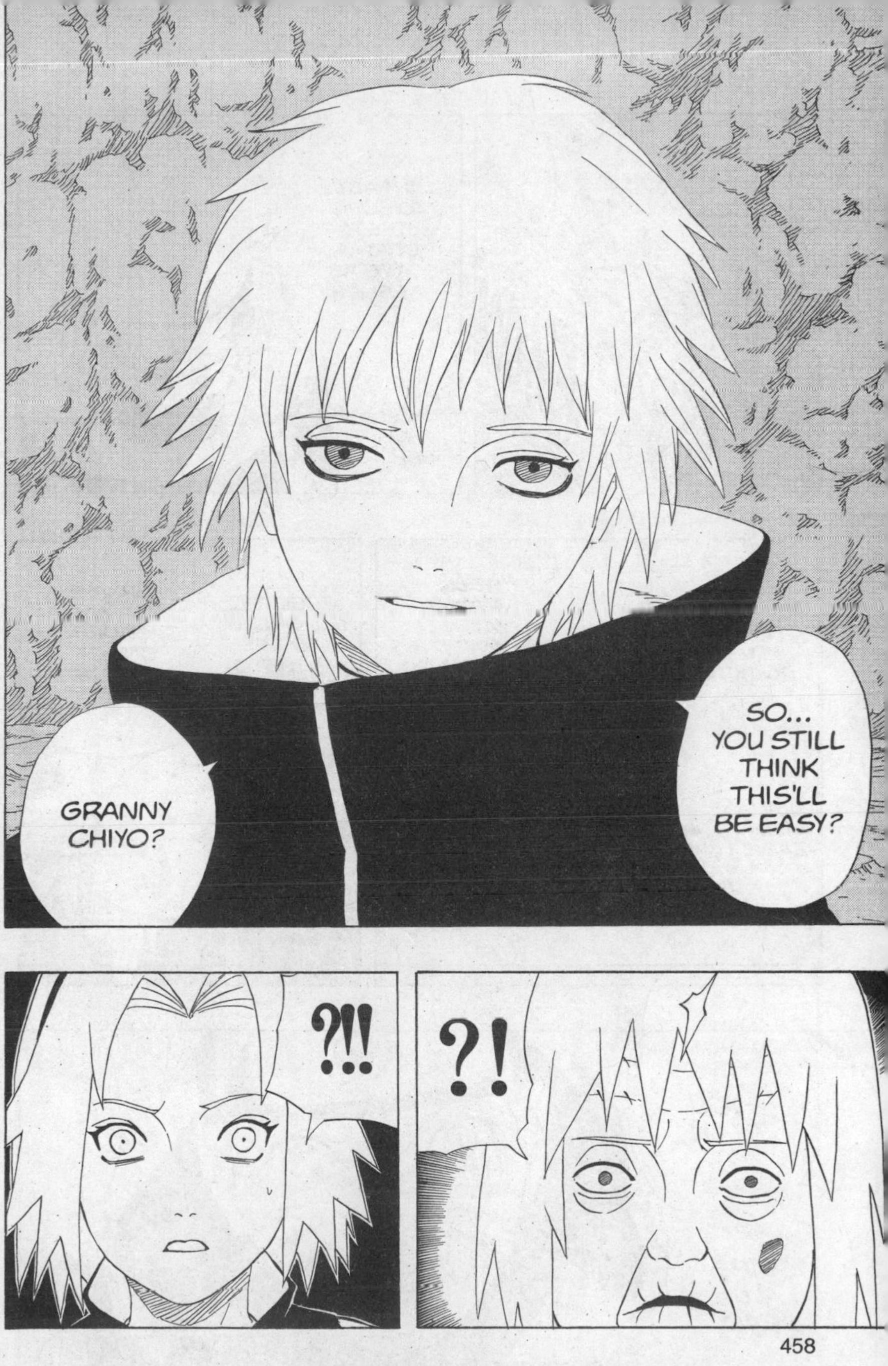
SO... YOU STILL THINK THIS'LL BE EASY?
GRANNY CHIYO?
?!
?!!

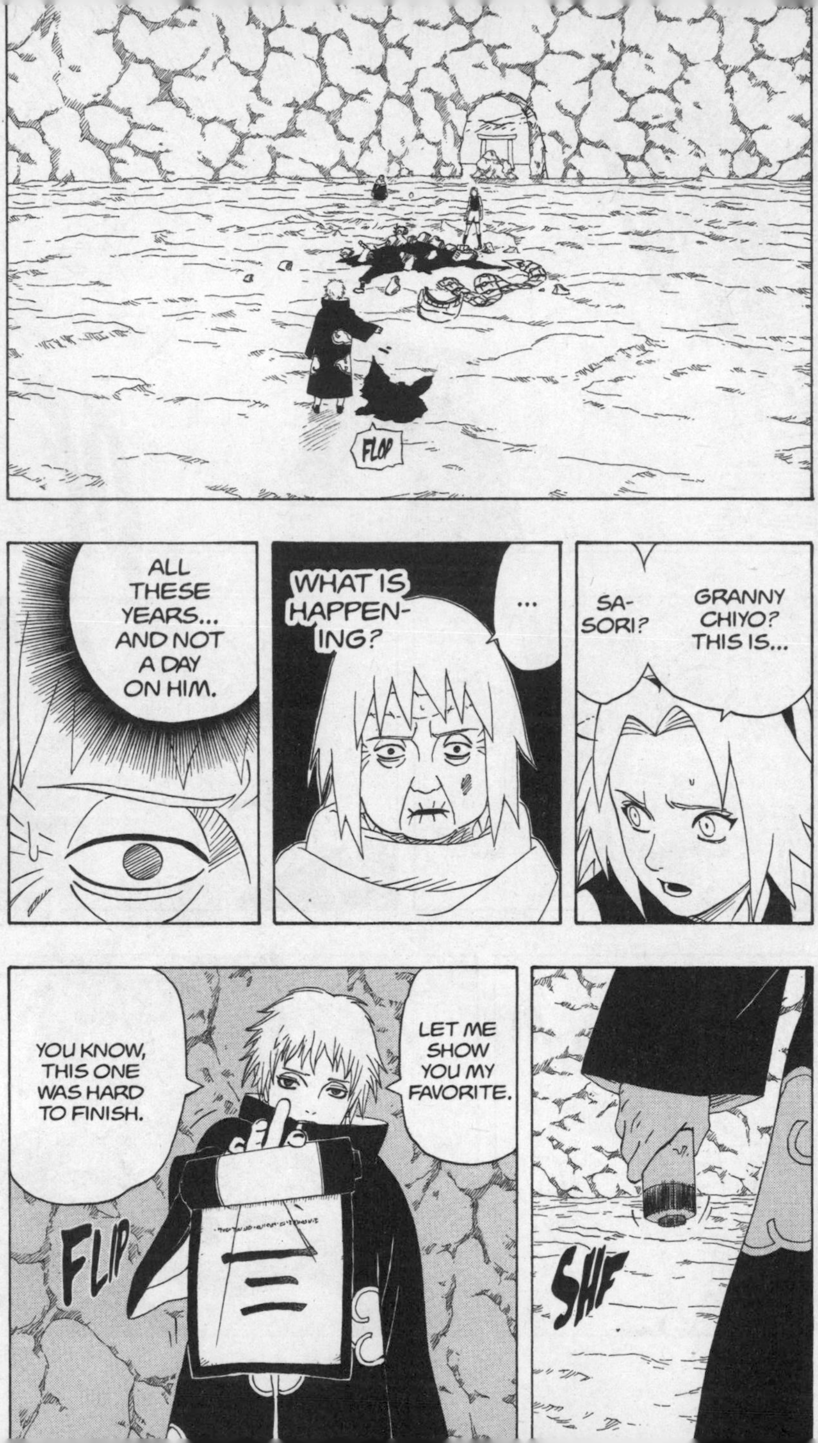
FLOP
GRANNY CHIYO? THIS IS...
SA-SORI?
...
WHAT IS HAPPEN-ING?
ALL THESE YEARS... AND NOT A DAY ON HIM.
SHF
LET ME SHOW YOU MY FAVORITE.
YOU KNOW, THIS ONE WAS HARD TO FINISH.
FLIP

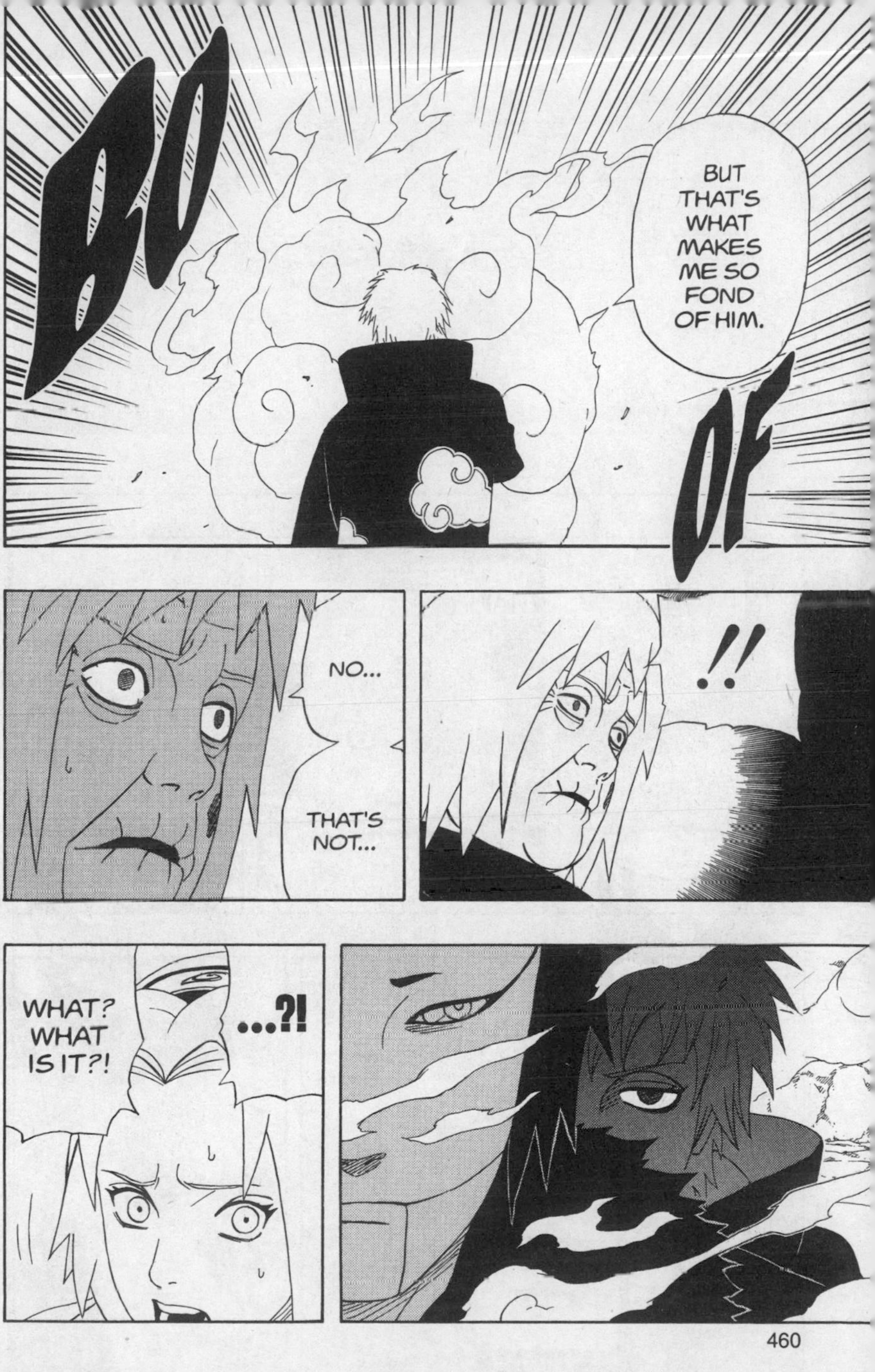
BUT THAT'S WHAT MAKES ME SO FOND OF HIM.
BO
OF
!!
NO...
THAT'S NOT...
...?!
WHAT? WHAT IS IT?!

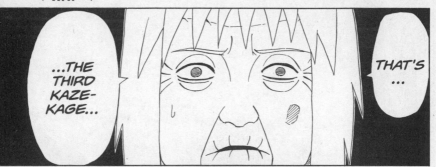

...THE THIRD KAZE-KAGE...

THAT'S...

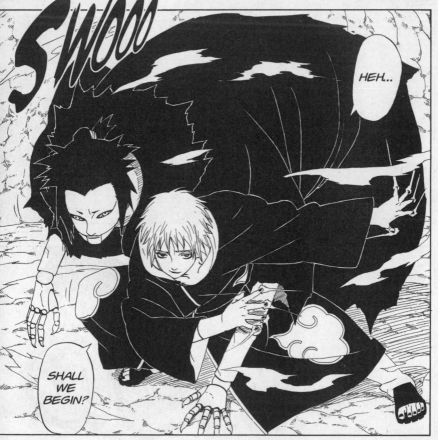

SWOOO

HEH...

SHALL WE BEGIN?

NARUTO

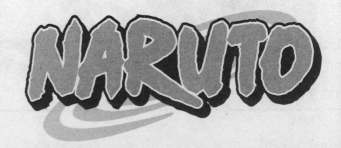

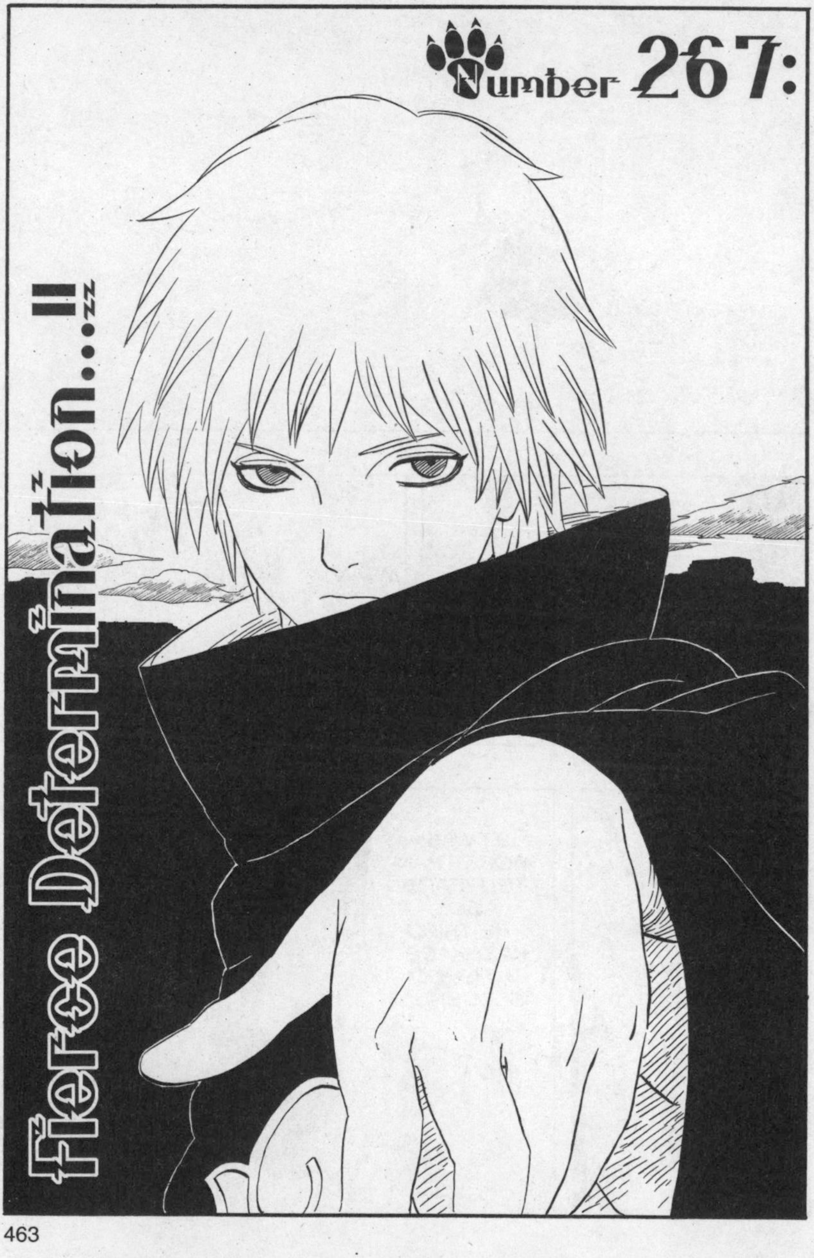
Number 267:
Fierce Determination...!!

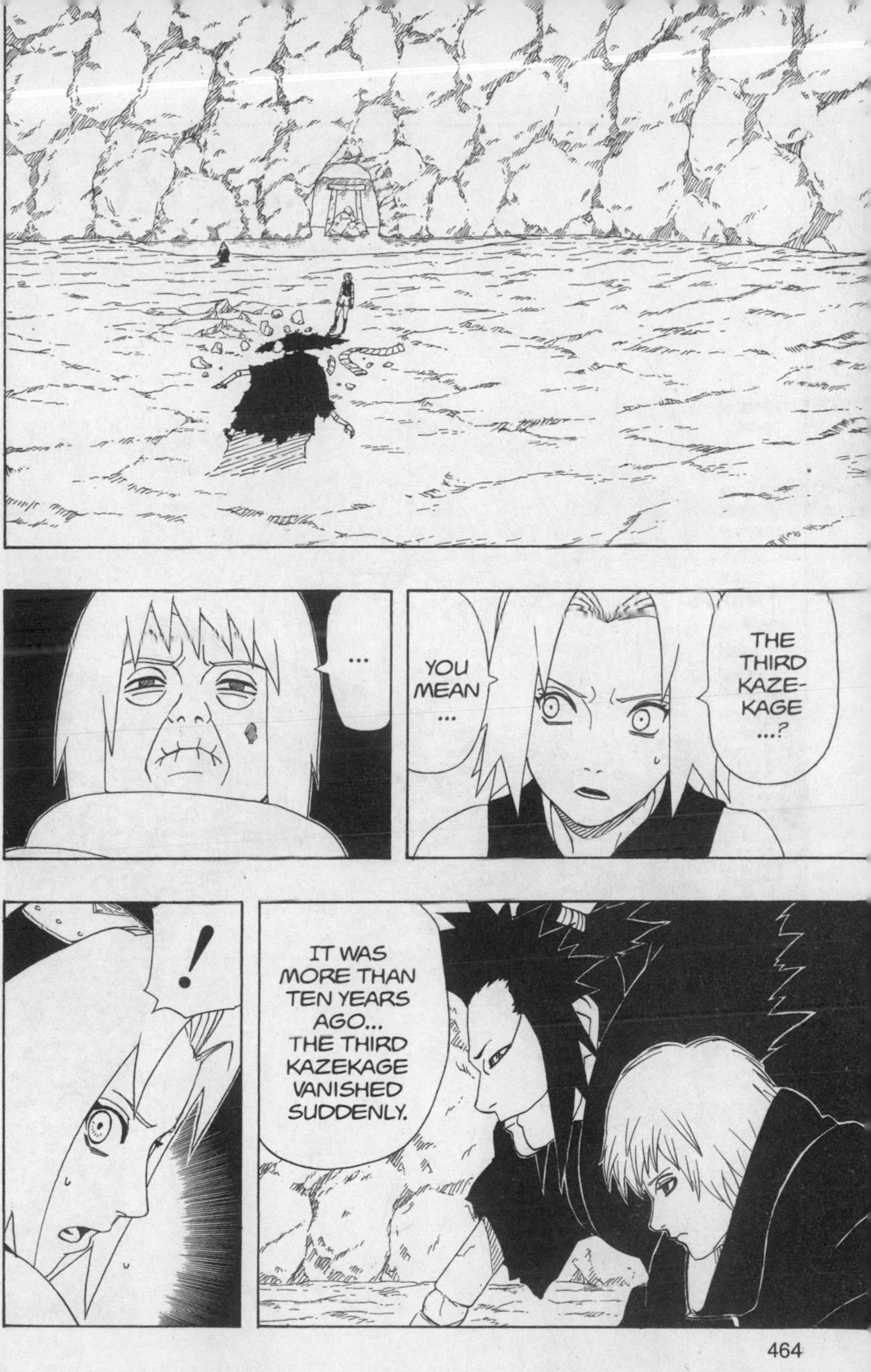
THE THIRD KAZE-KAGE ...?
YOU MEAN ...
...
IT WAS MORE THAN TEN YEARS AGO... THE THIRD KAZEKAGE VANISHED SUDDENLY.
!

READ THIS WAY

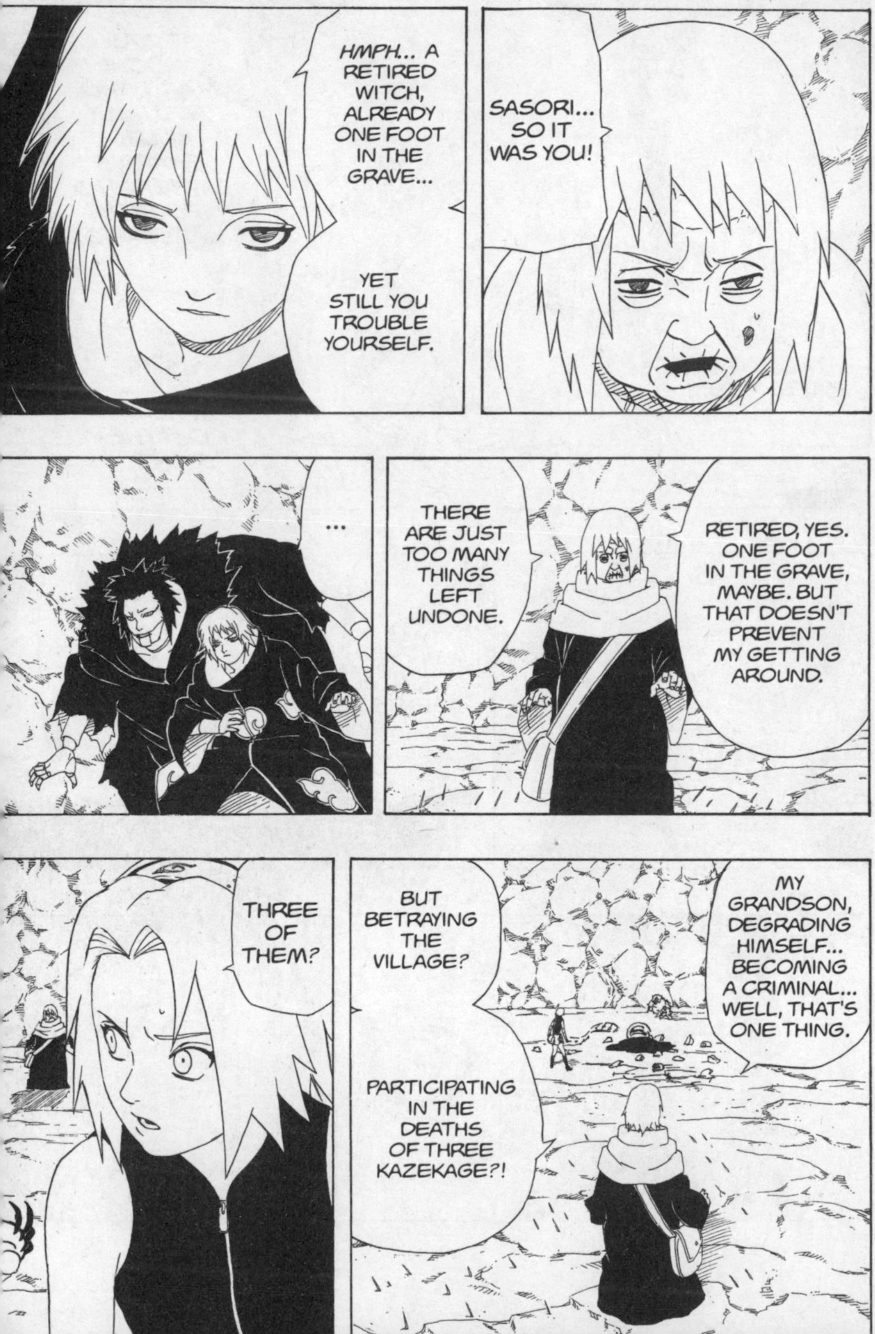
SASORI... SO IT WAS YOU!
HMPH... A RETIRED WITCH, ALREADY ONE FOOT IN THE GRAVE...
YET STILL YOU TROUBLE YOURSELF.
RETIRED, YES. ONE FOOT IN THE GRAVE, MAYBE. BUT THAT DOESN'T PREVENT MY GETTING AROUND.
THERE ARE JUST TOO MANY THINGS LEFT UNDONE.
...
MY GRANDSON, DEGRADING HIMSELF... BECOMING A CRIMINAL... WELL, THAT'S ONE THING.
BUT BETRAYING THE VILLAGE?
PARTICIPATING IN THE DEATHS OF THREE KAZEKAGE?!
THREE OF THEM?

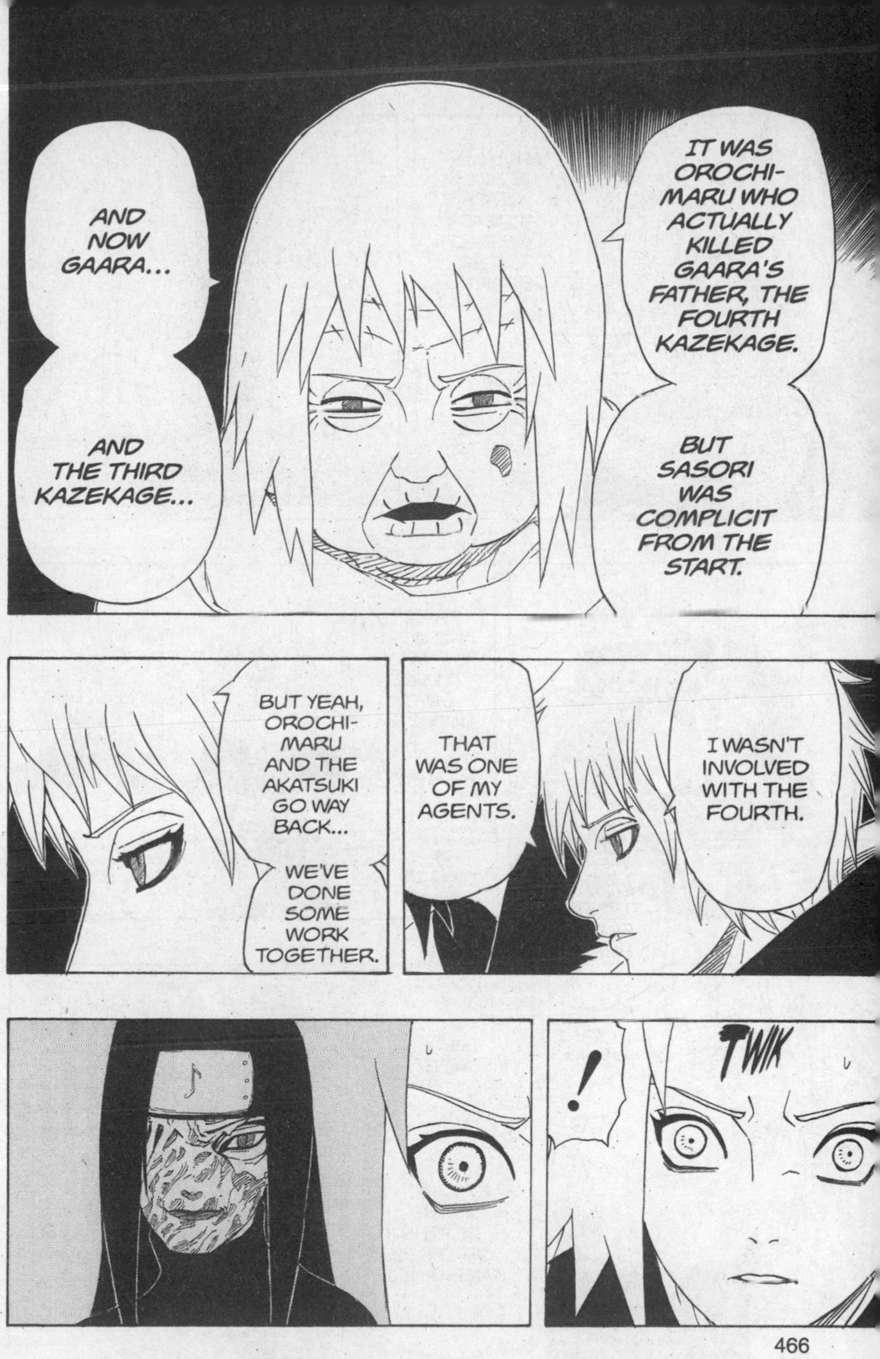
IT WAS OROCHI-MARU WHO ACTUALLY KILLED GAARA'S FATHER, THE FOURTH KAZEKAGE.
BUT SASORI WAS COMPLICIT FROM THE START.
AND NOW GAARA...
AND THE THIRD KAZEKAGE...
I WASN'T INVOLVED WITH THE FOURTH.
THAT WAS ONE OF MY AGENTS.
BUT YEAH, OROCHI-MARU AND THE AKATSUKI GO WAY BACK...
WE'VE DONE SOME WORK TOGETHER.
TWIK
!

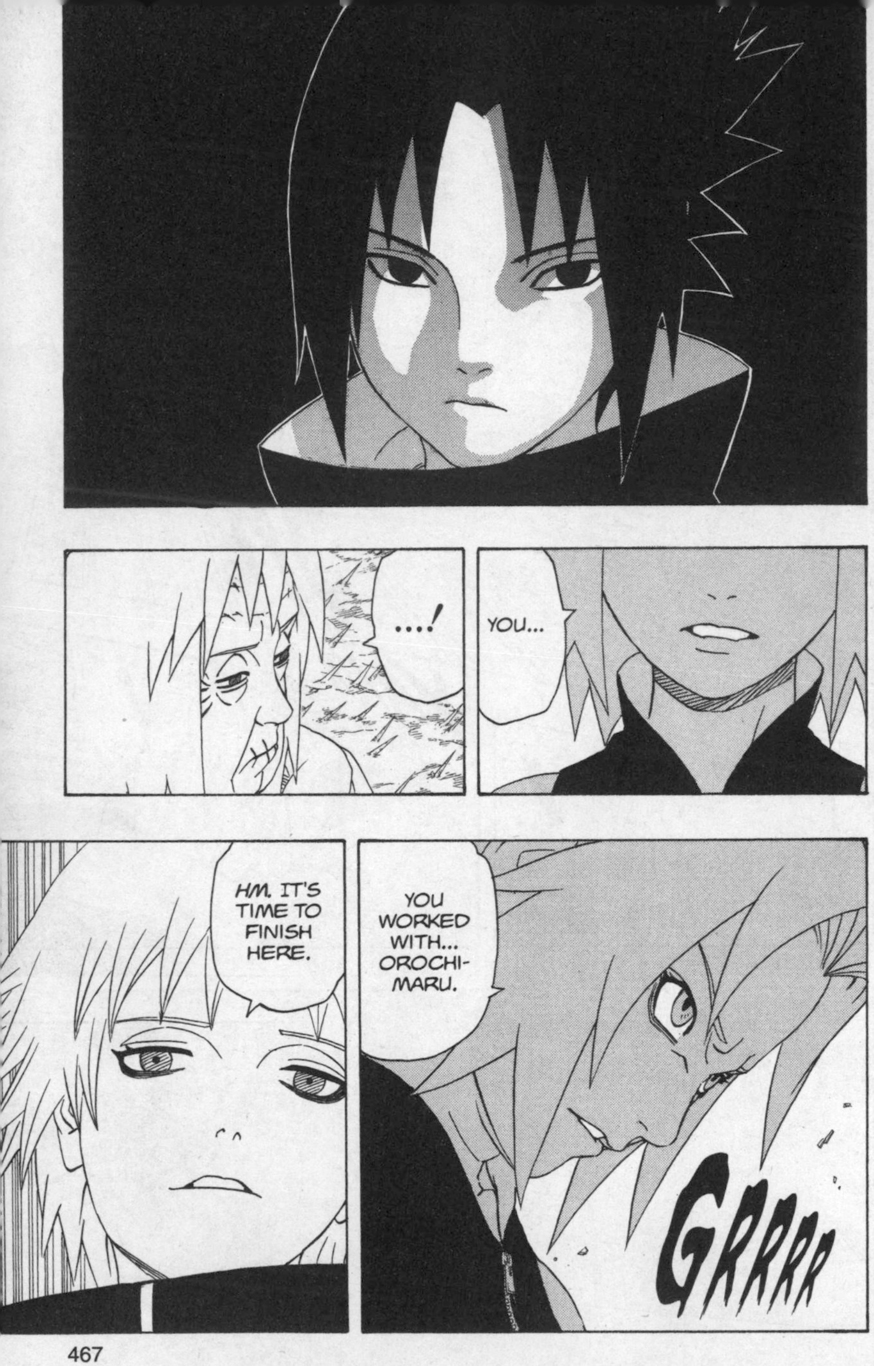
YOU...
...!
YOU WORKED WITH... OROCHIMARU.
GRRRR
HM. IT'S TIME TO FINISH HERE.

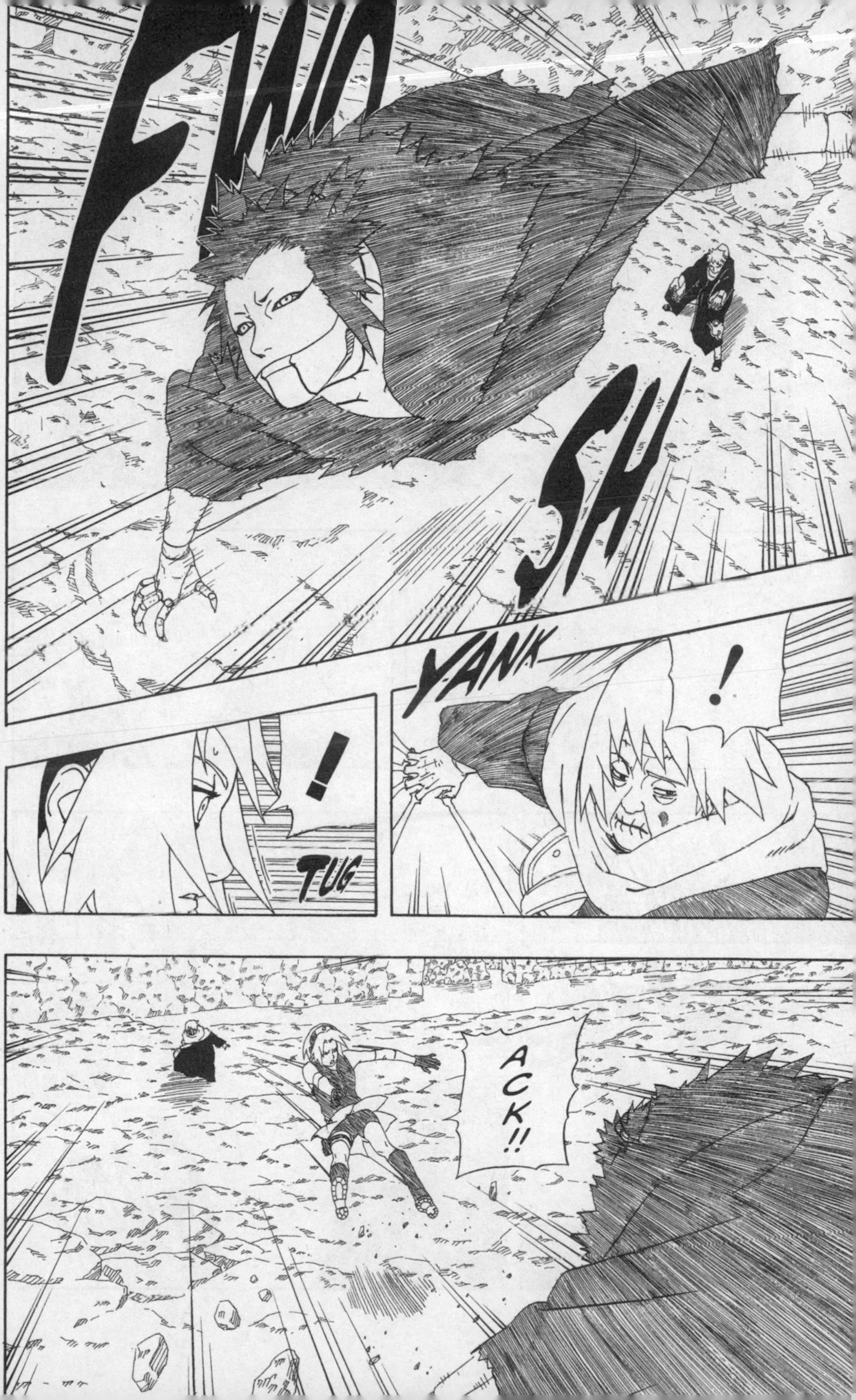
SH
YANK
!
!
TUG
ACK!!

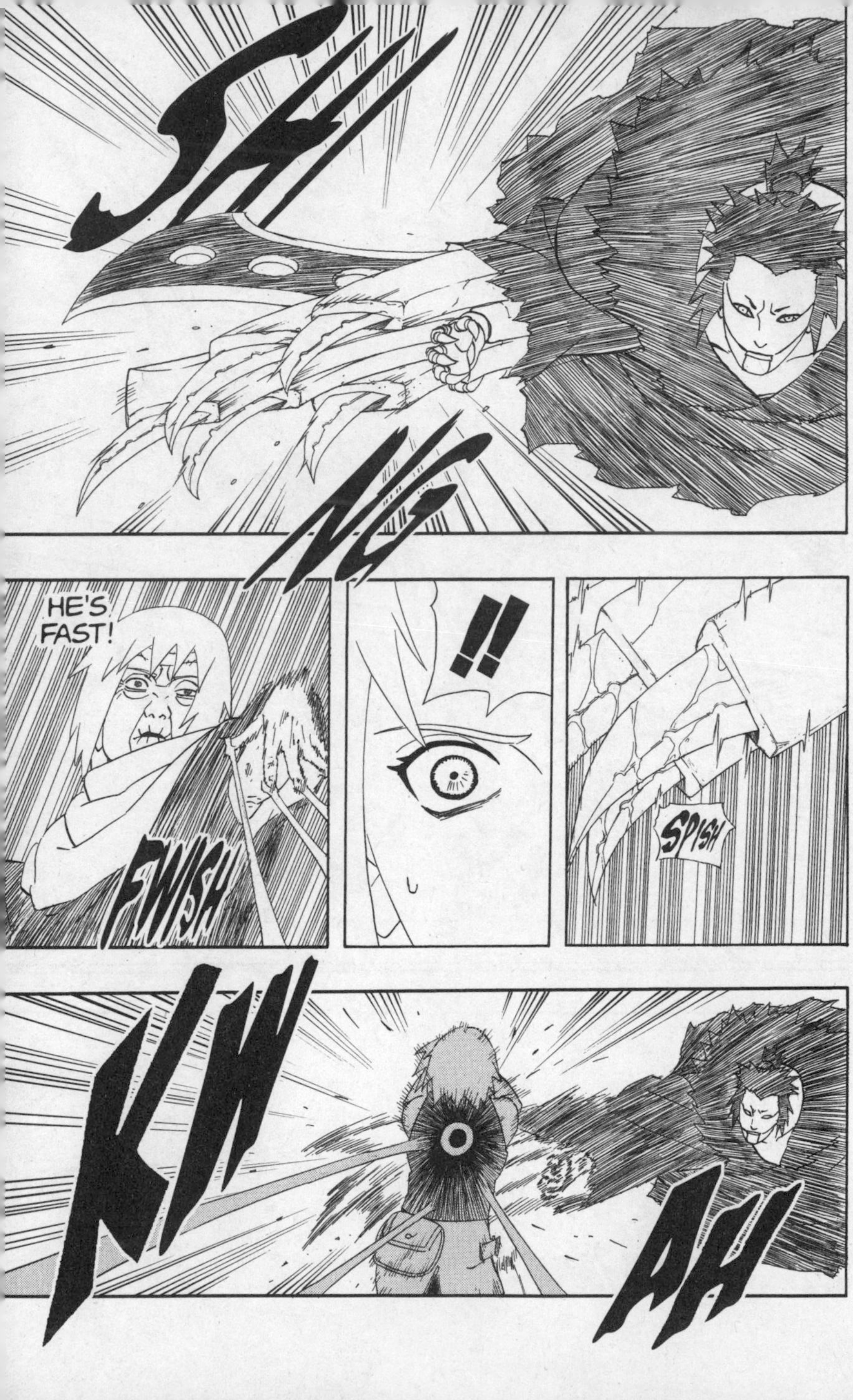
SH
NG
SPISH
!!
HE'S FAST!
FWISH
KH
AH

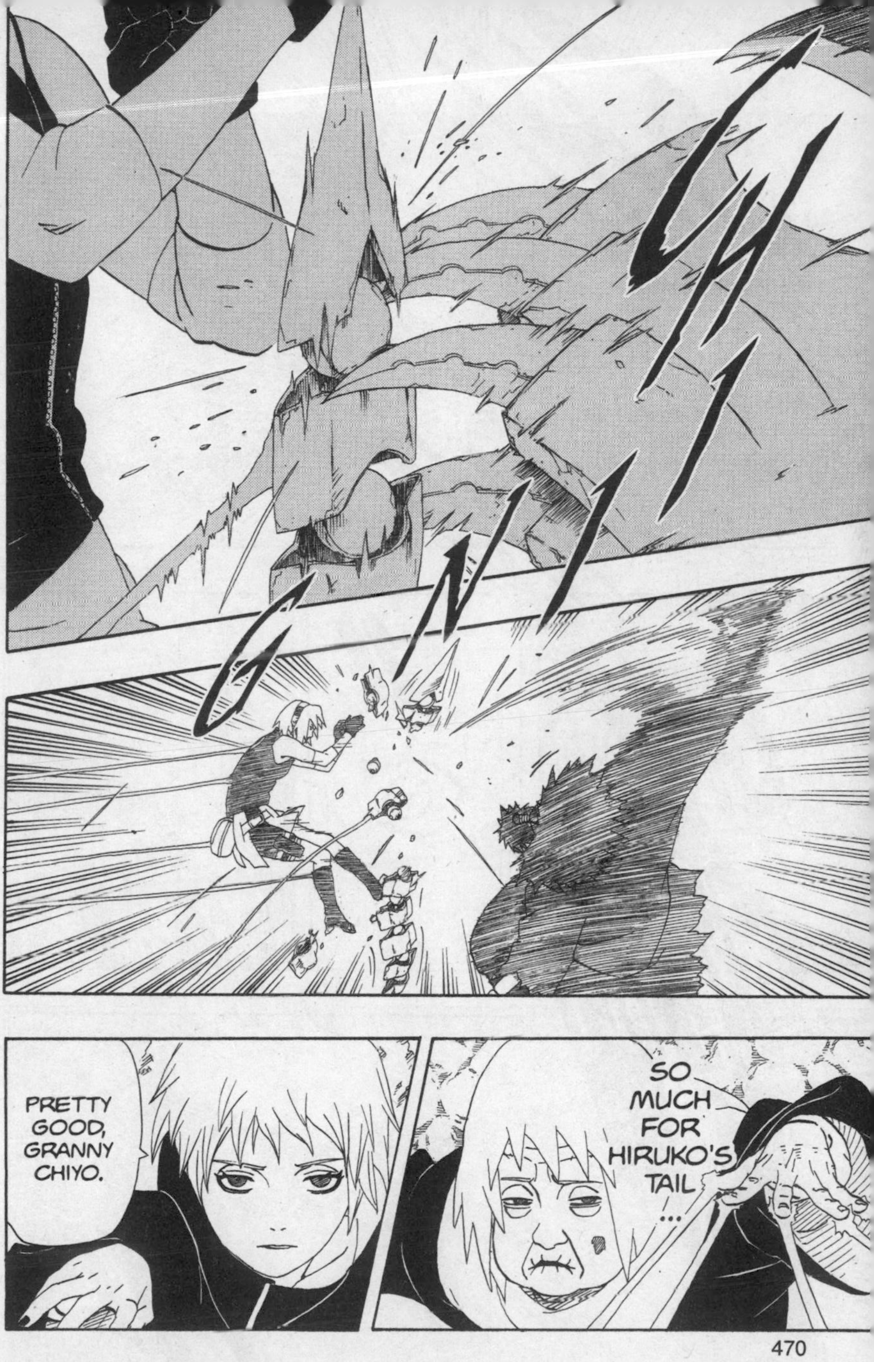
SO MUCH FOR HIRUKO'S TAIL...
PRETTY GOOD, GRANNY CHIYO.

READ THIS WAY

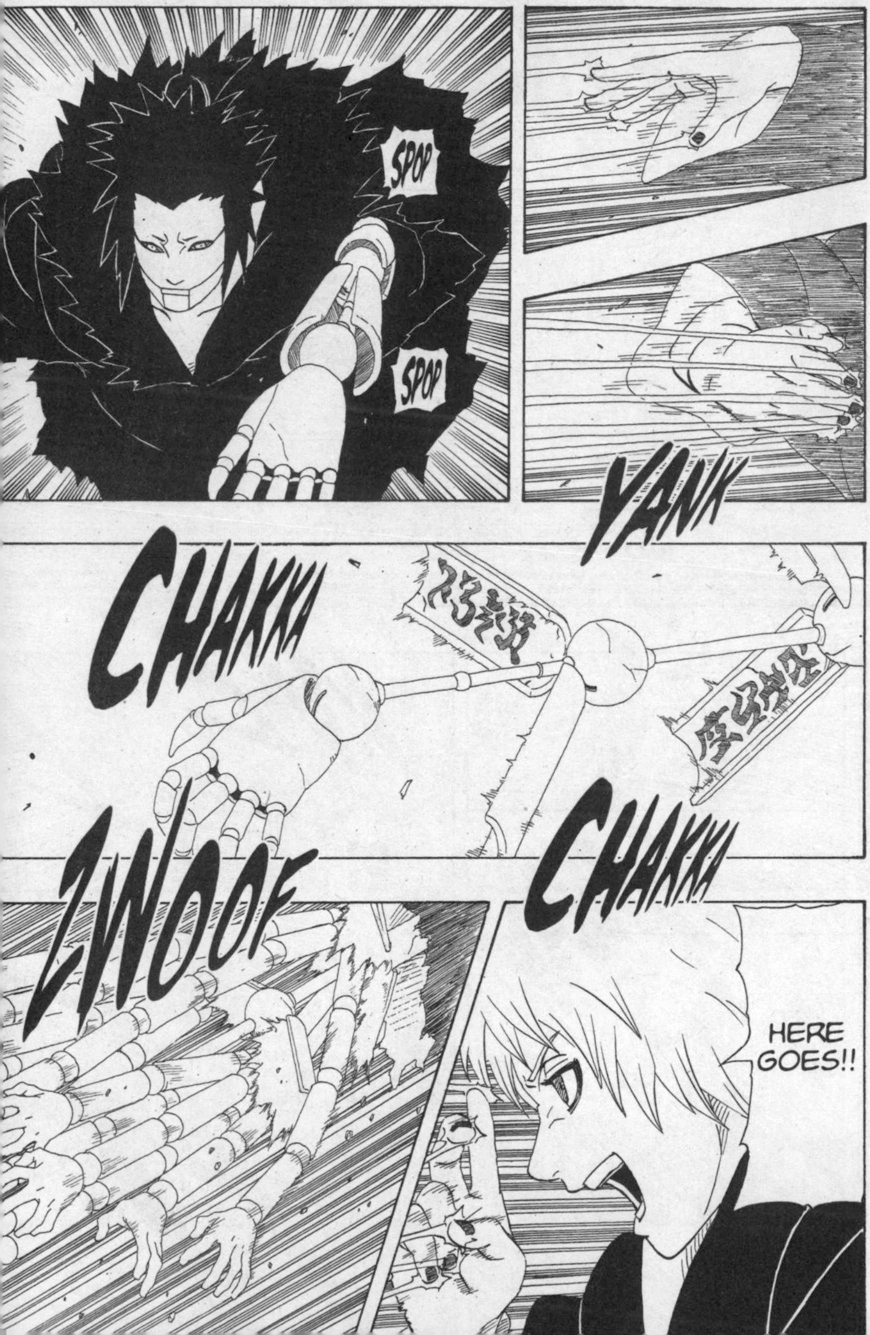
YANK
SPOP
SPOP
CHAKKA
CHAKKA
HERE GOES!!
ZWOOF

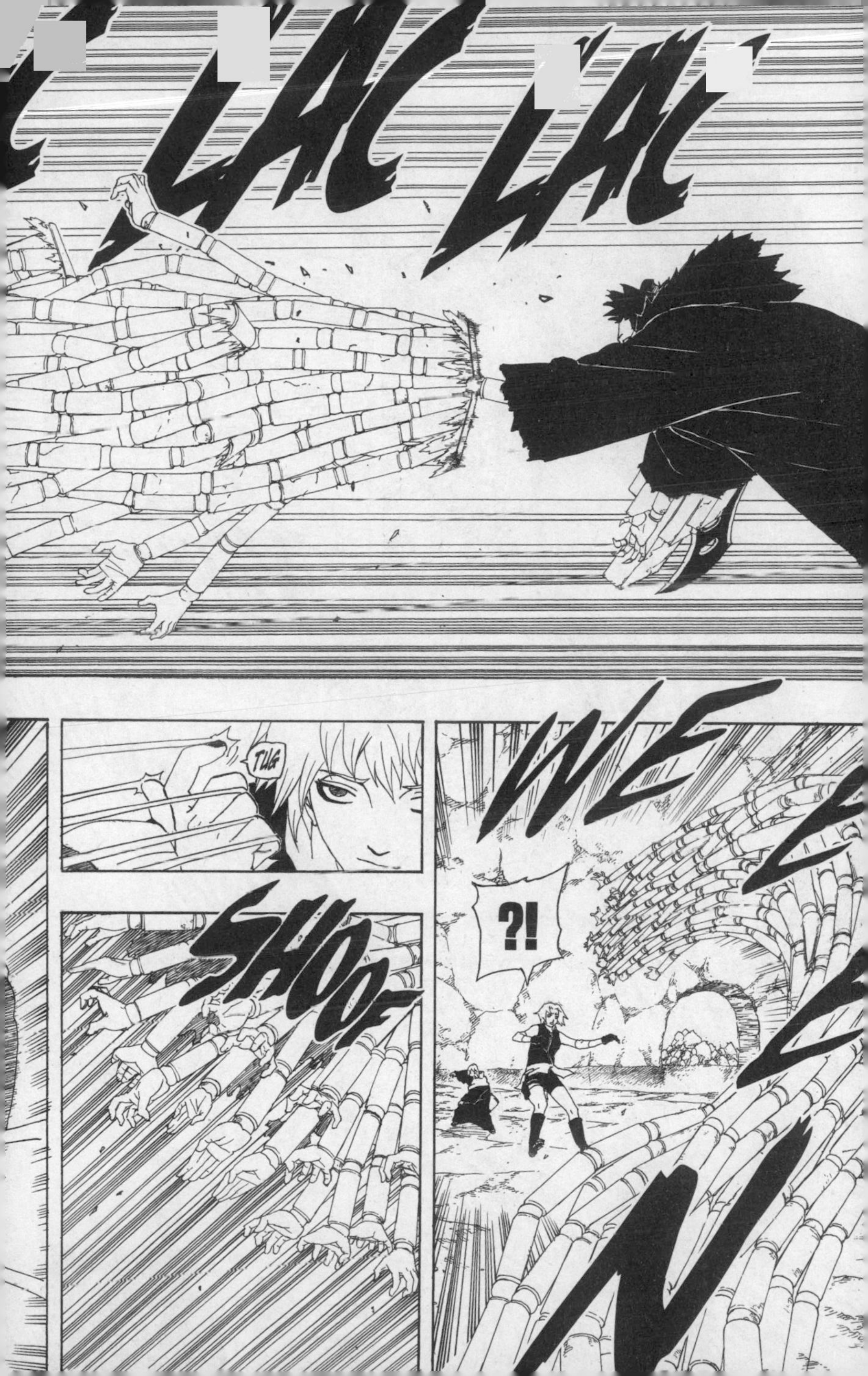
LAC LAC
WE
?!
TUG
SHOOF

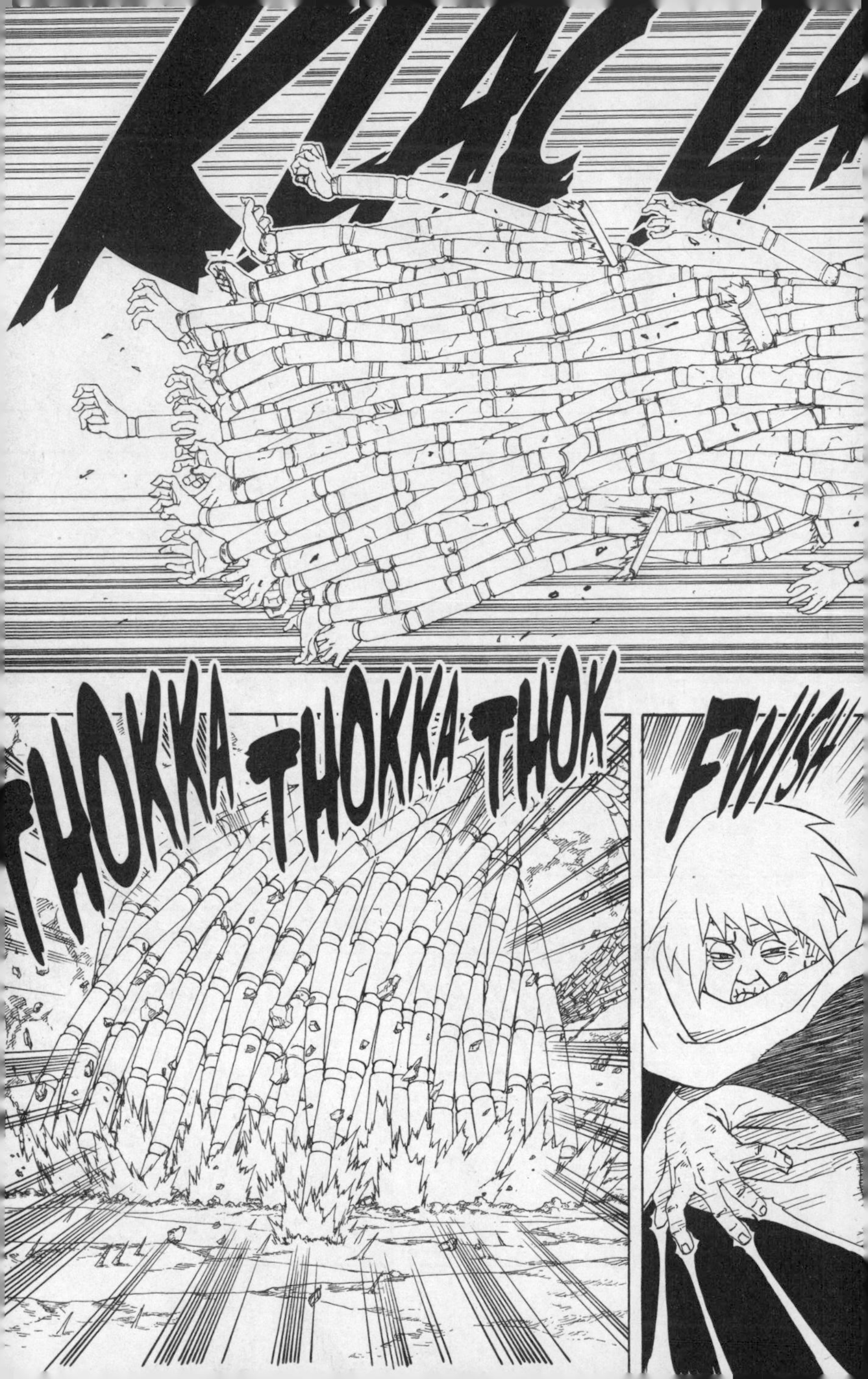
FWISH
THOKKA THOKKA THOK

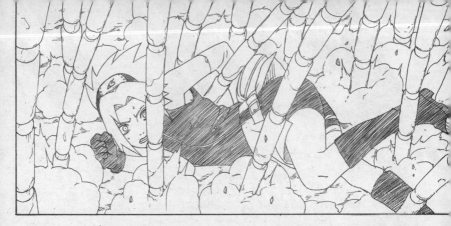

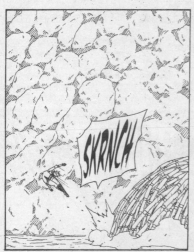

SKRNCH

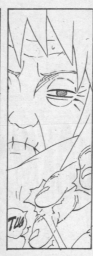

TUG

TUG

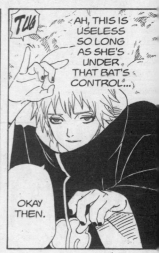

TUG

AH, THIS IS USELESS SO LONG AS SHE'S UNDER THAT BAT'S CONTROL...

OKAY THEN.

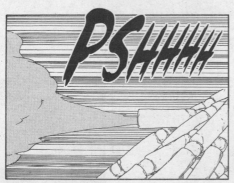

PSHHHH

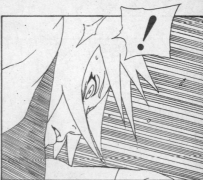

!

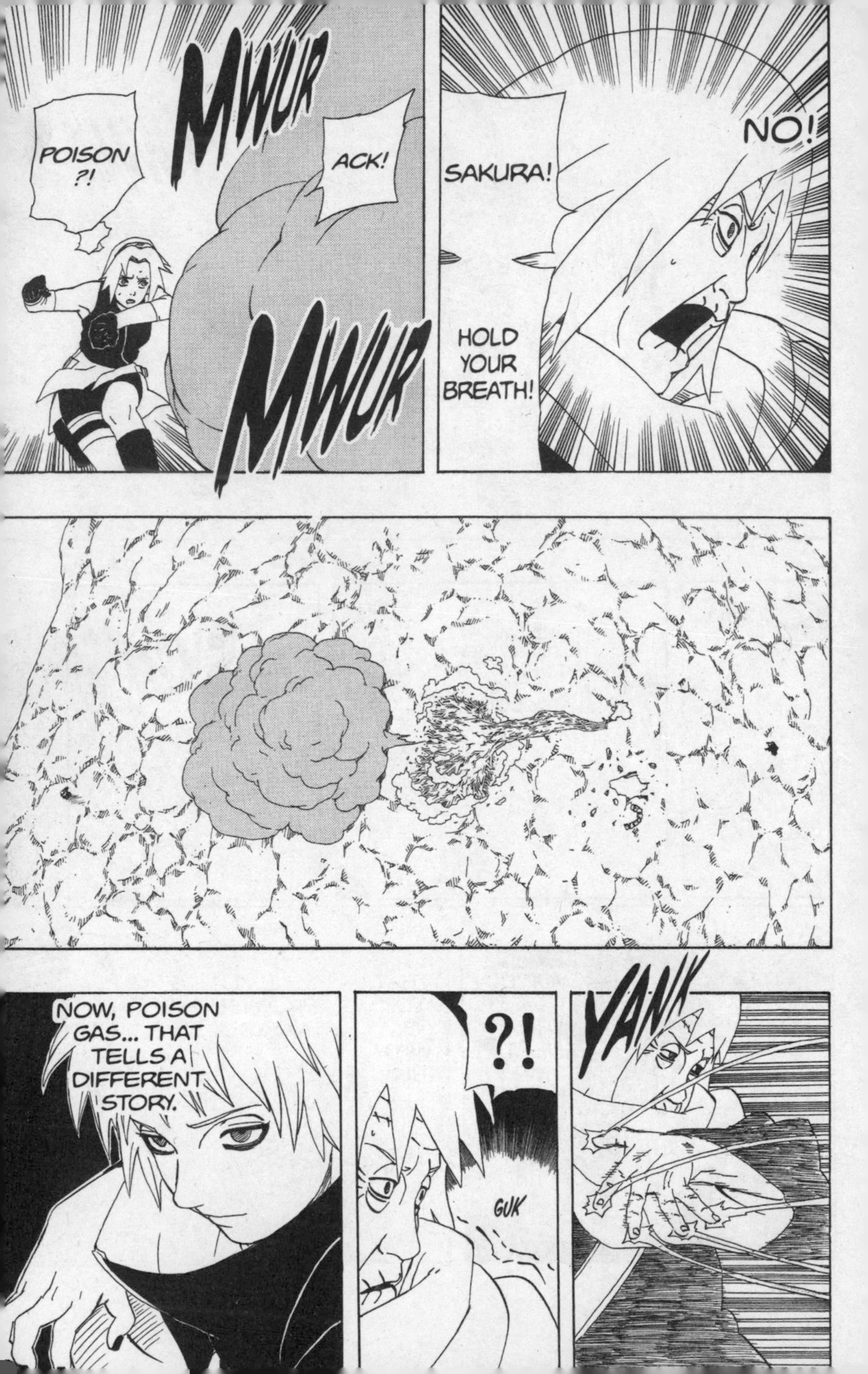
NO!
SAKURA!
HOLD YOUR BREATH!
MWUR
ACK!
POISON ?!
MWUR
YANK
?!
GUK
NOW, POISON GAS... THAT TELLS A DIFFERENT STORY.

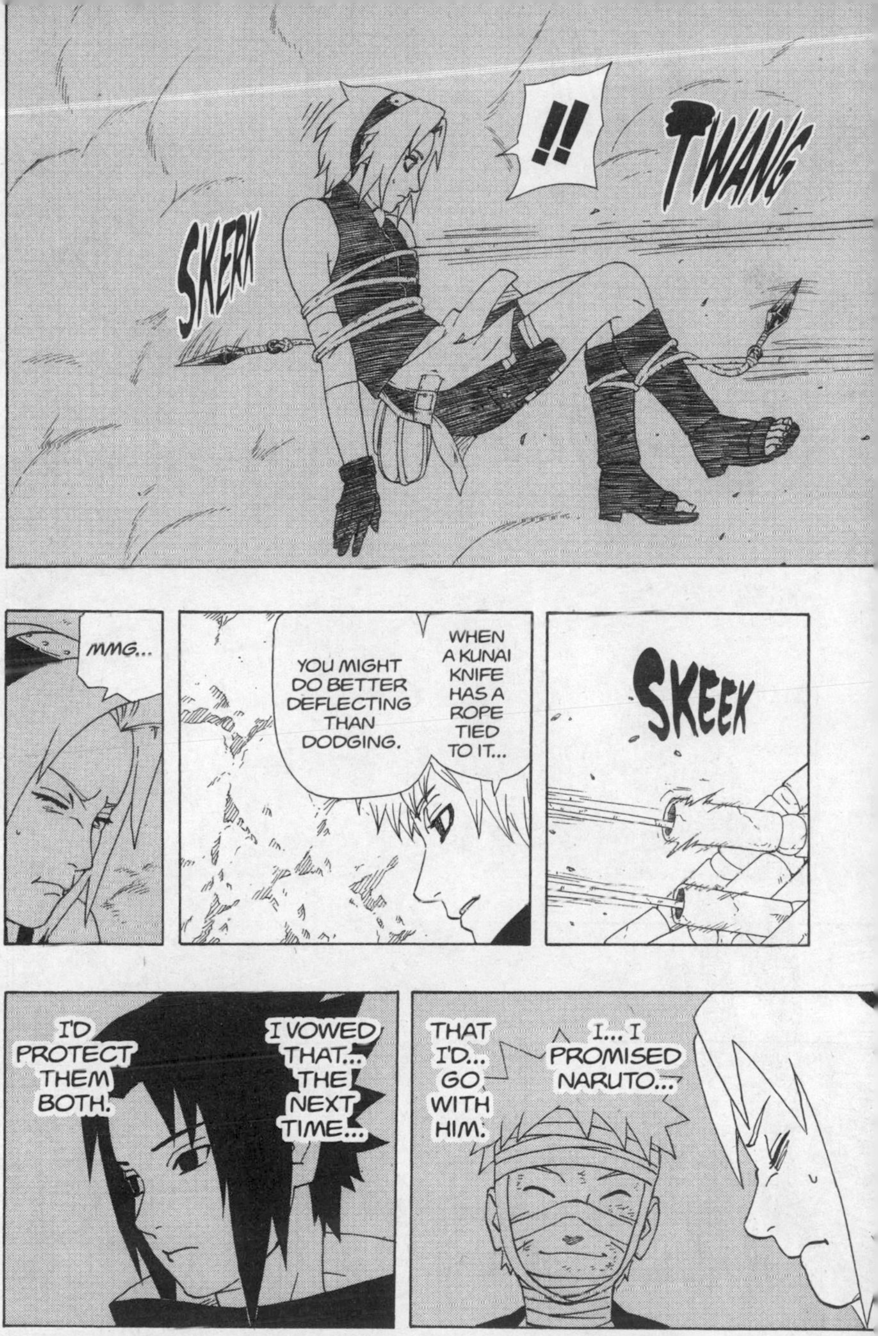
TWANG
!!
SKERK
SKEEK
WHEN A KUNAI KNIFE HAS A ROPE TIED TO IT...
YOU MIGHT DO BETTER DEFLECTING THAN DODGING.
MMG...
I... I PROMISED NARUTO...
THAT I'D... GO WITH HIM.
I VOWED THAT... THE NEXT TIME...
I'D PROTECT THEM BOTH.

READ THIS WAY

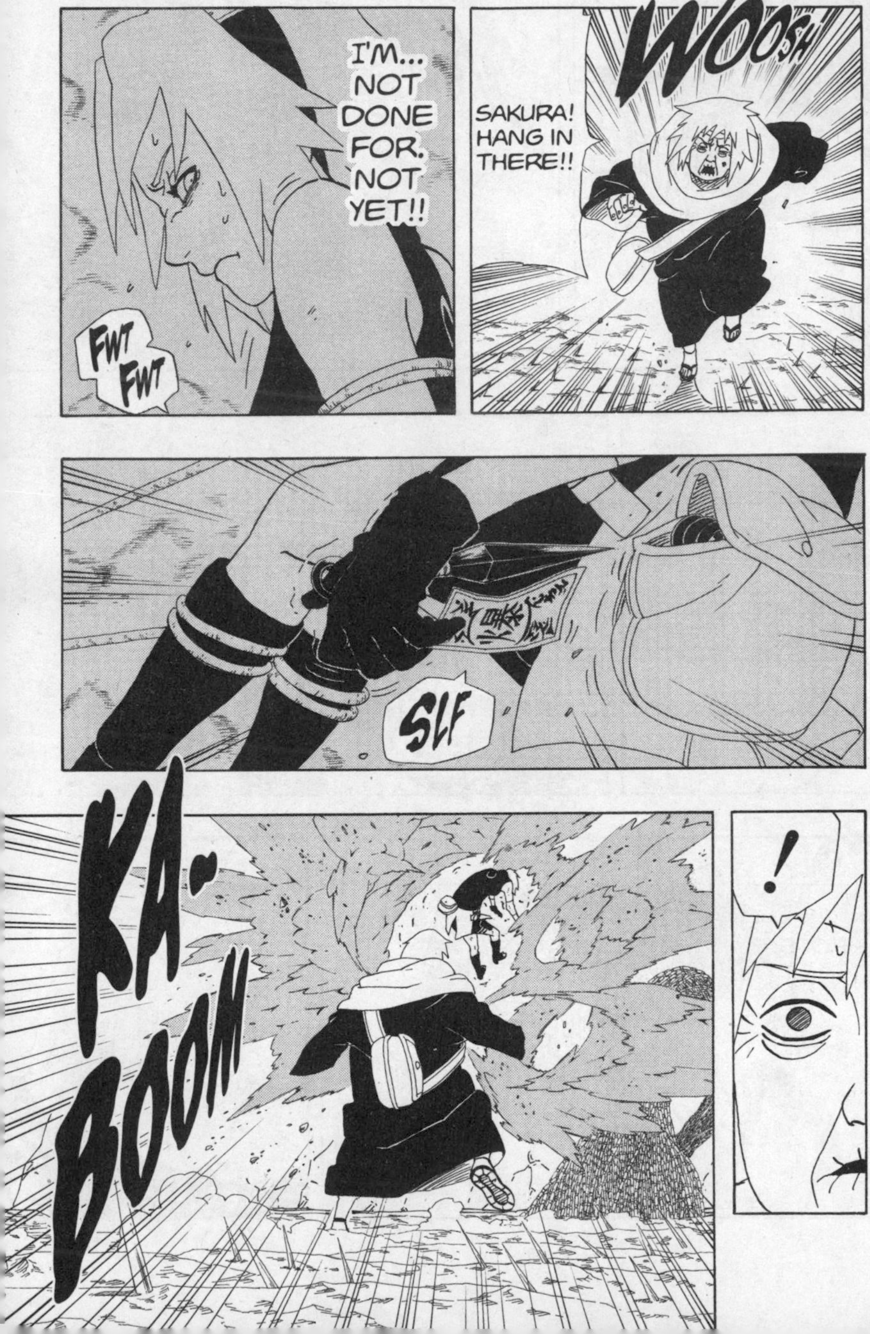
WOOSH
SAKURA! HANG IN THERE!!
I'M... NOT DONE FOR. NOT YET!!
FWT FWT
SLF
!
KA-BOOM

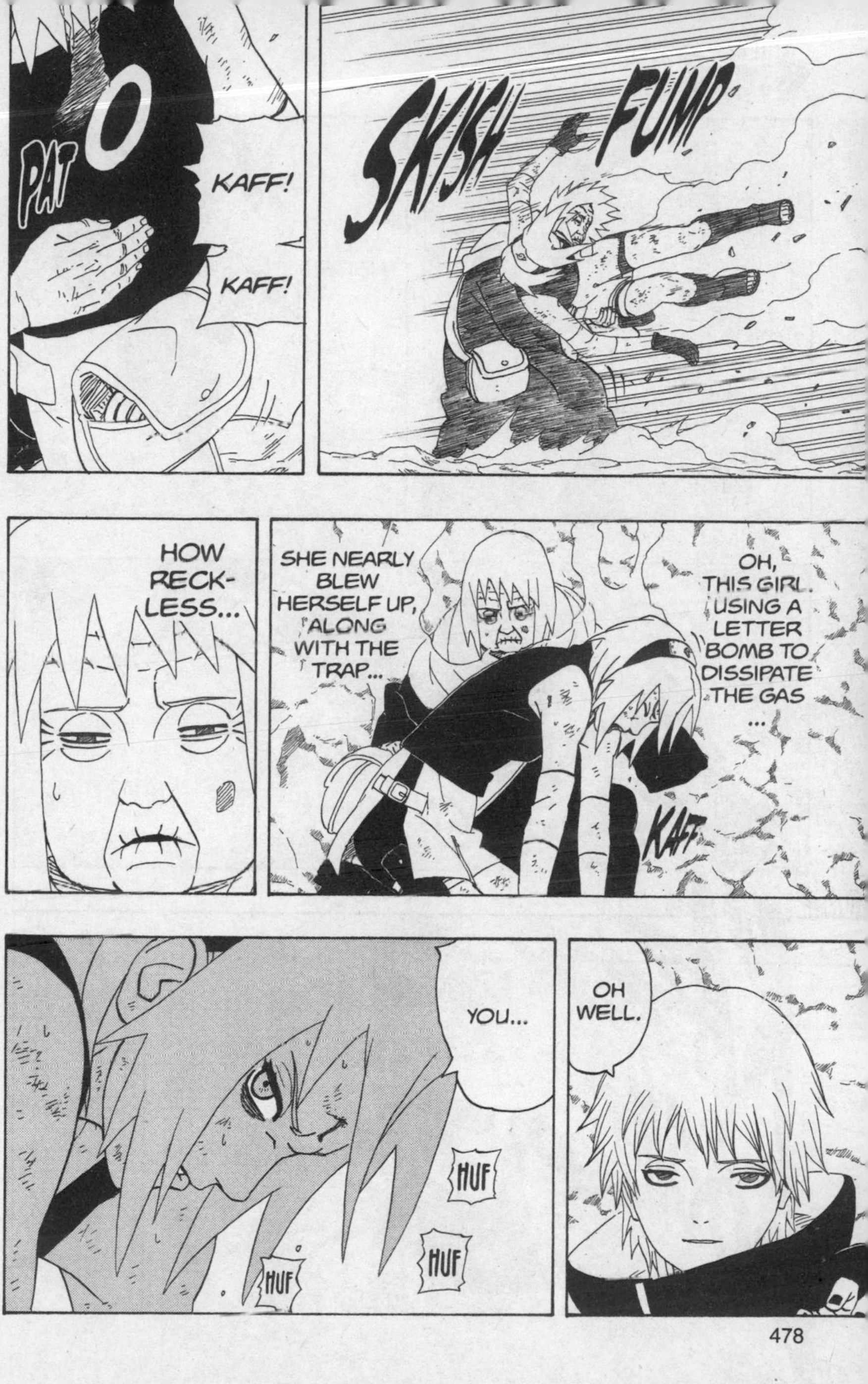
SKISH
FUMP
PAT
KAFF!
KAFF!
OH, THIS GIRL. USING A LETTER BOMB TO DISSIPATE THE GAS ...
SHE NEARLY BLEW HERSELF UP, ALONG WITH THE TRAP...
KAFF
HOW RECK-LESS...
OH WELL.
YOU...
HUF
HUF
HUF

READ THIS WAY

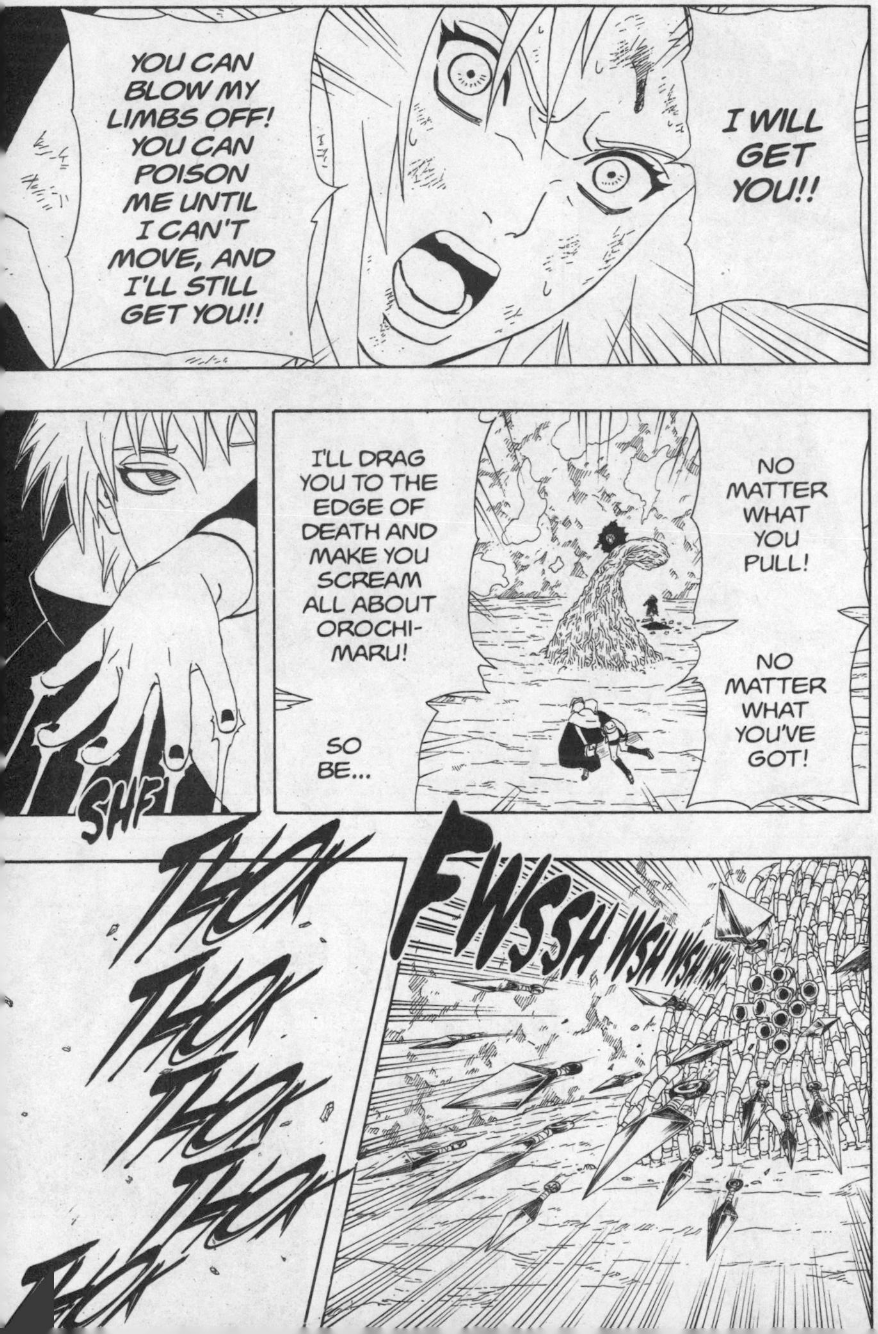
I WILL GET YOU!!
YOU CAN BLOW MY LIMBS OFF! YOU CAN POISON ME UNTIL I CAN'T MOVE, AND I'LL STILL GET YOU!!
NO MATTER WHAT YOU PULL!
NO MATTER WHAT YOU'VE GOT!
I'LL DRAG YOU TO THE EDGE OF DEATH AND MAKE YOU SCREAM ALL ABOUT OROCHI-MARU!
SO BE...
SHF
FWSSH WSH WSH WSH
THOK
THOK
THOK
THOK
THOK

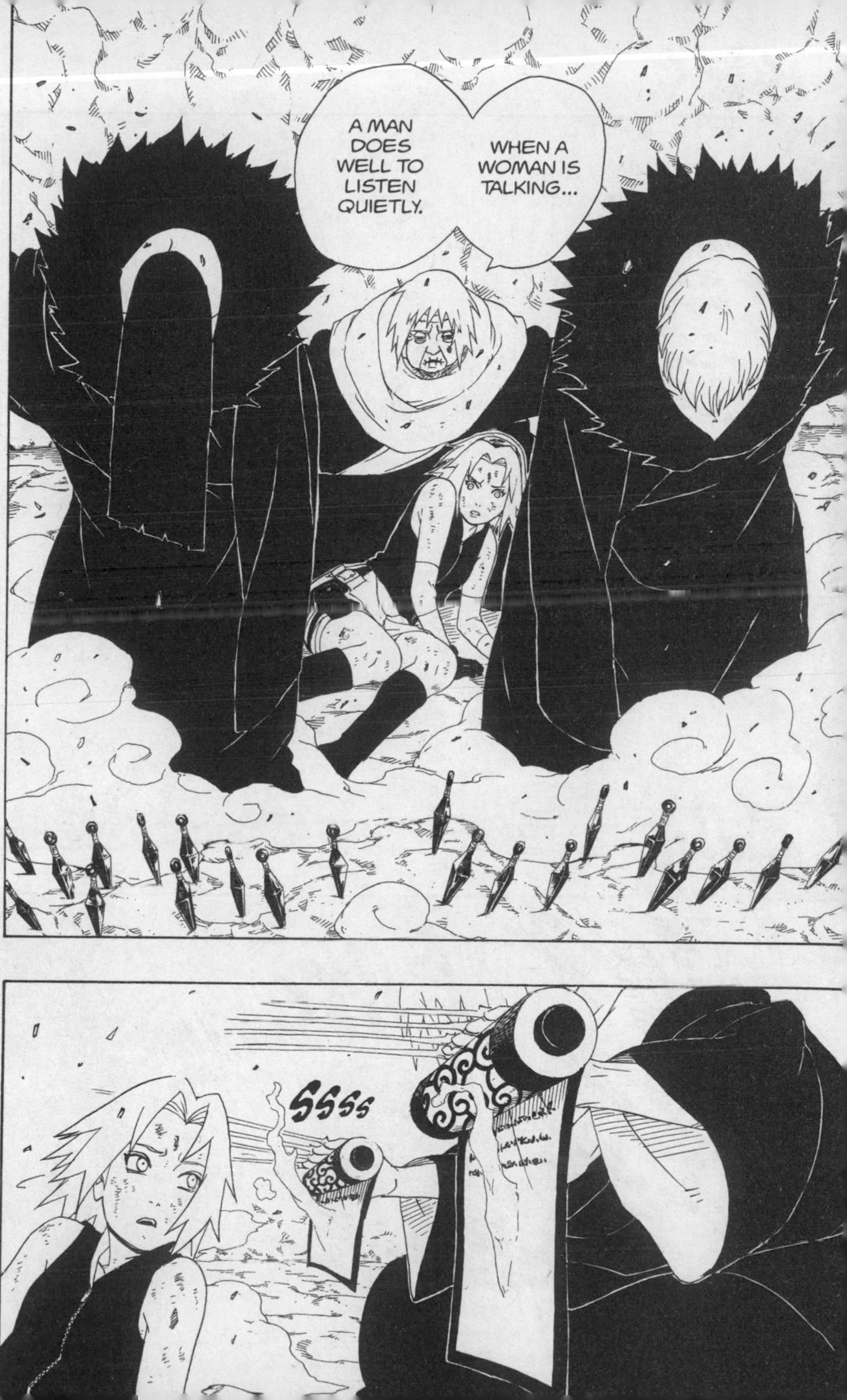

WHEN A WOMAN IS TALKING...
A MAN DOES WELL TO LISTEN QUIETLY.
SSSS

READ THIS WAY

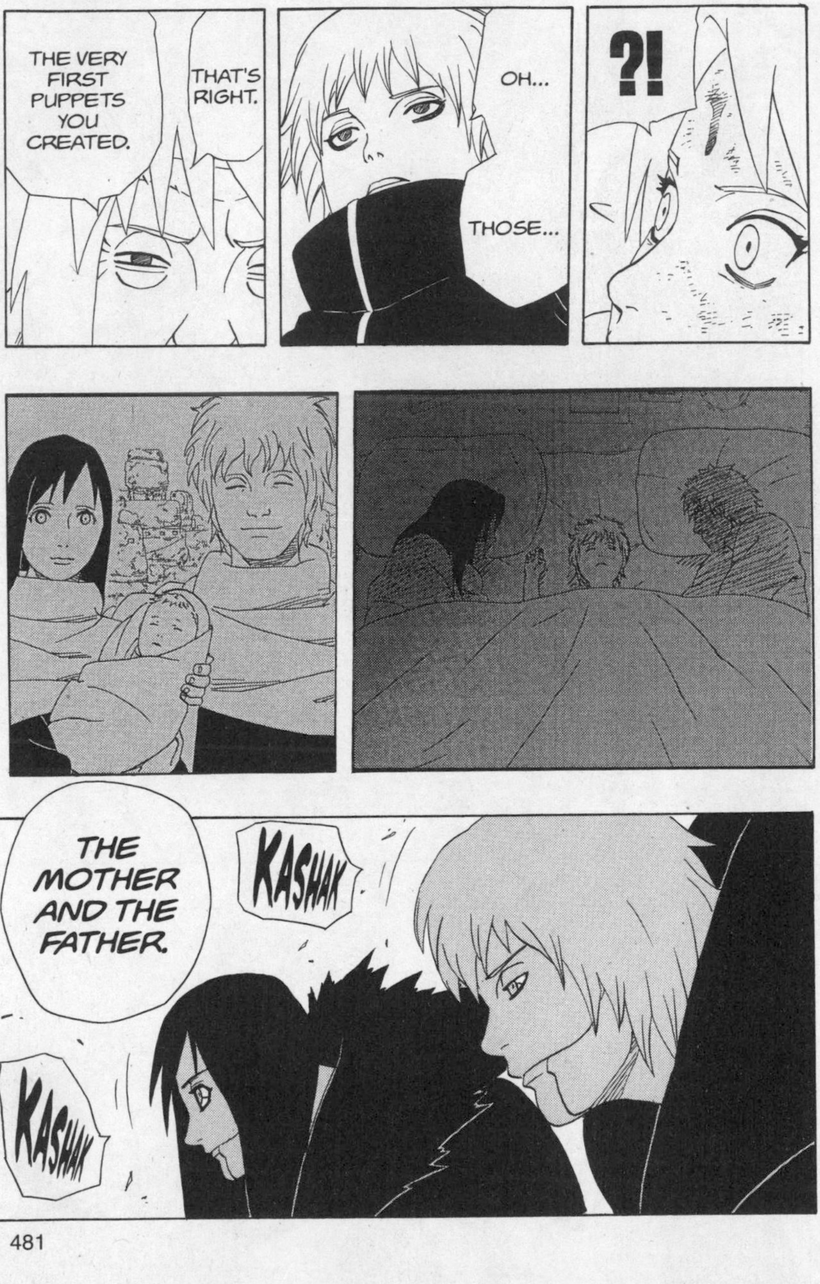
?!
OH...
THOSE...
THAT'S RIGHT.
THE VERY FIRST PUPPETS YOU CREATED.
KASHAK
THE MOTHER AND THE FATHER.
KASHAK

NARUTO

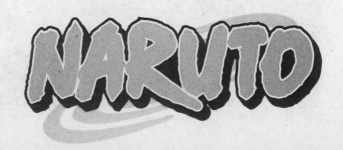

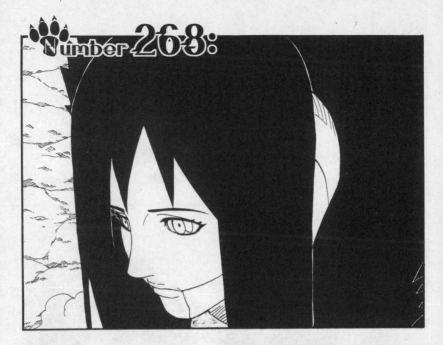

Number 268:

Puppet Masters!!

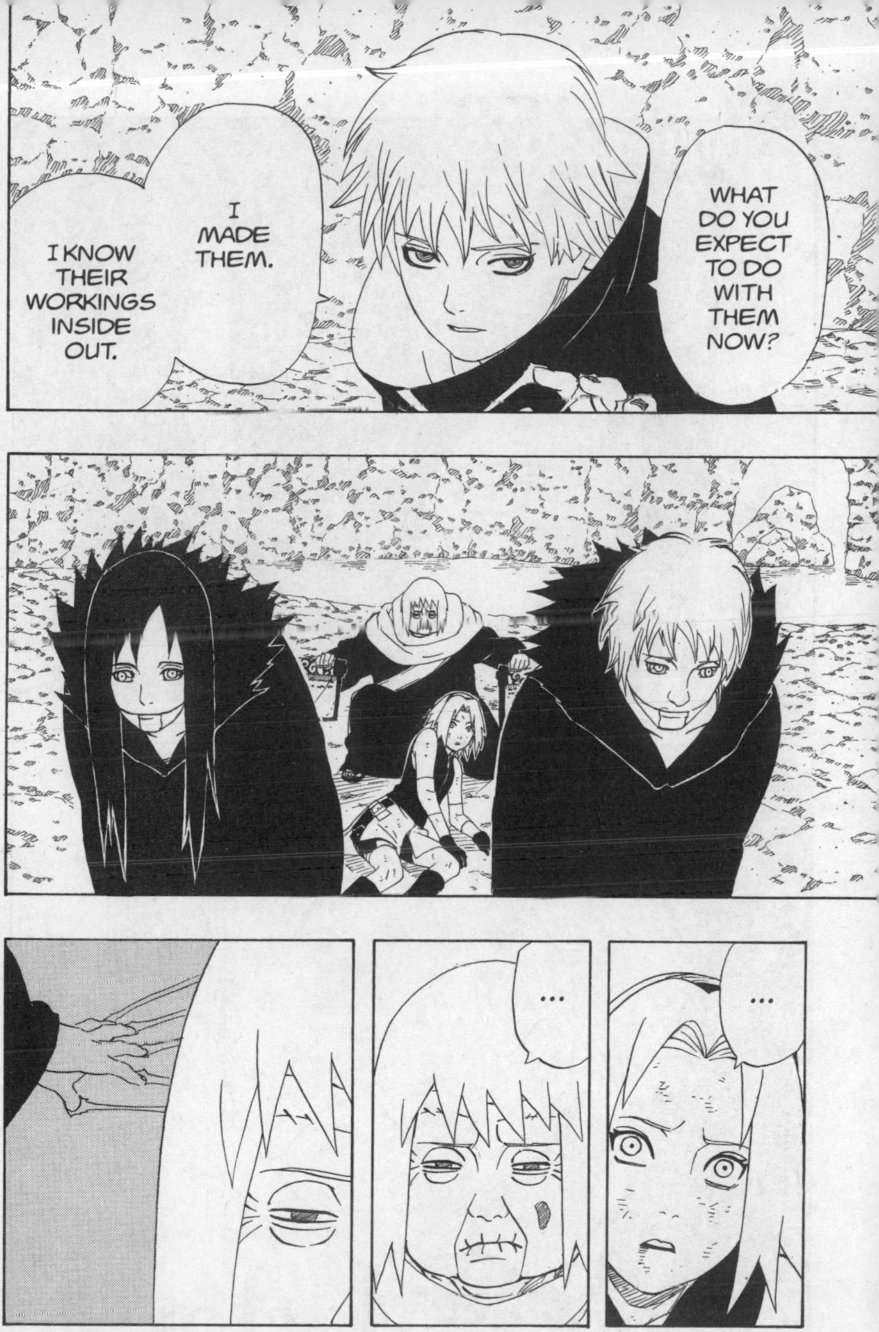
WHAT DO YOU EXPECT TO DO WITH THEM NOW?
I MADE THEM.
I KNOW THEIR WORKINGS INSIDE OUT.
...
...

READ THIS WAY

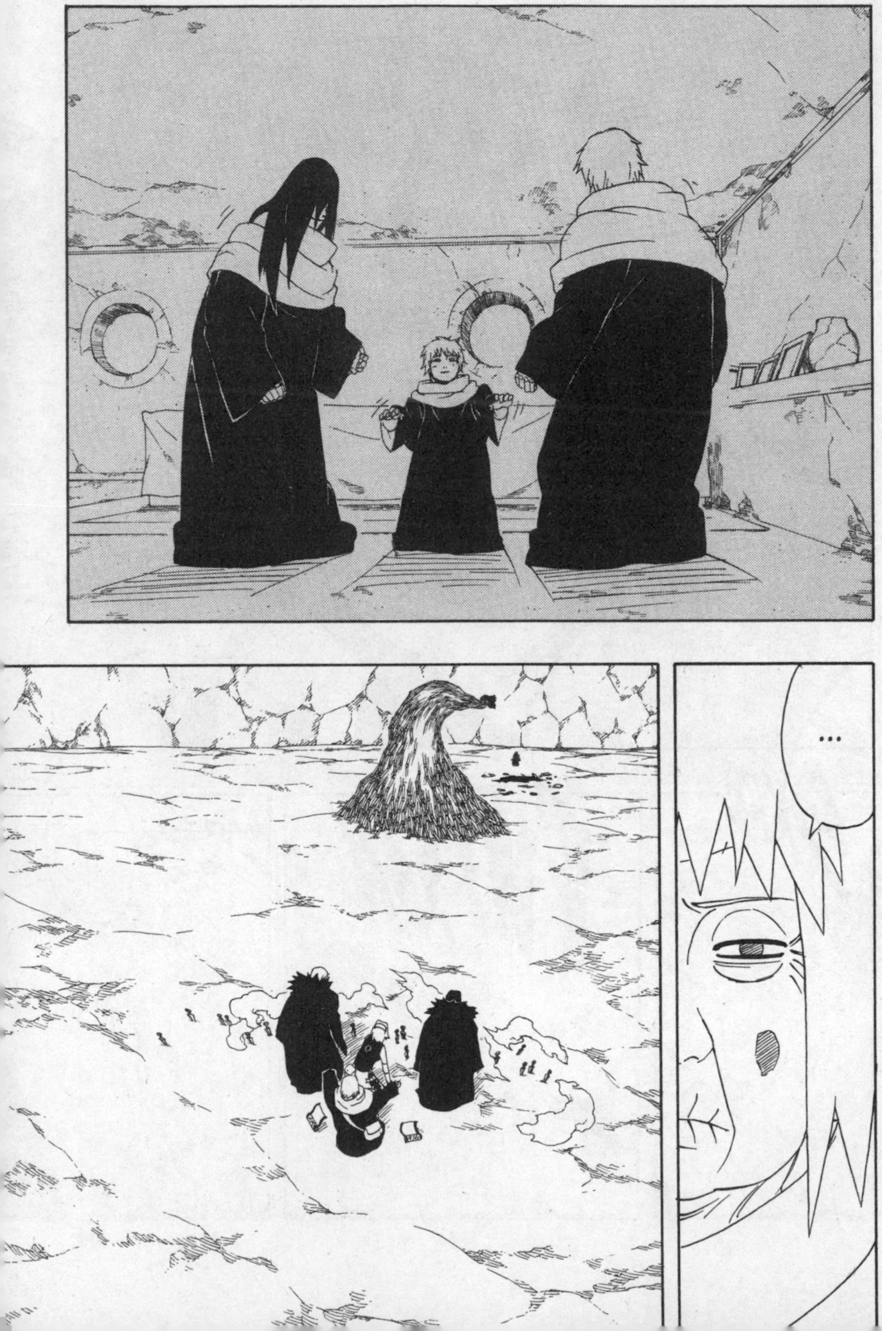
...

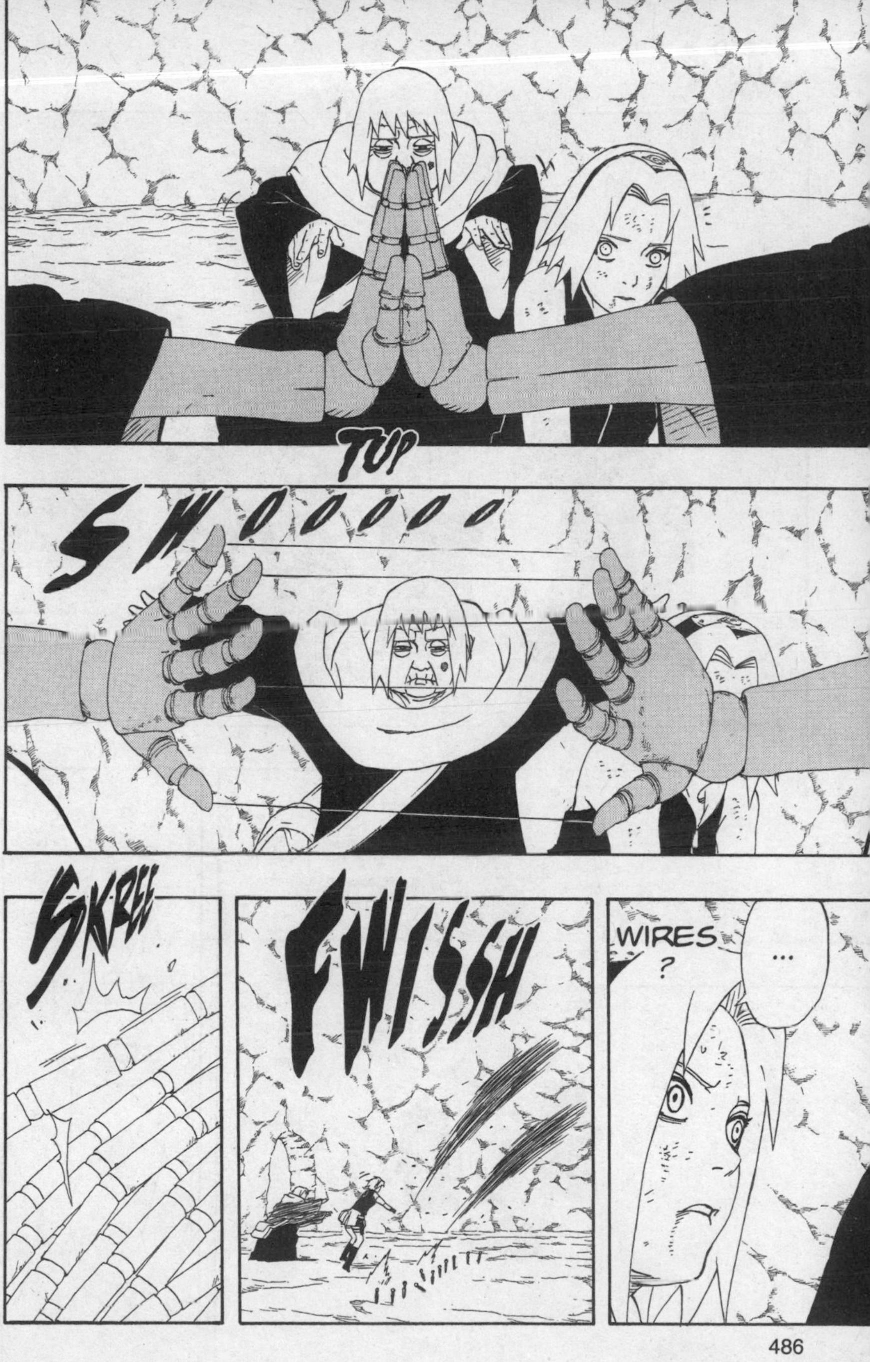
TUP
SWOOOOOO
WIRES ?
...
FWISSH
SKREE

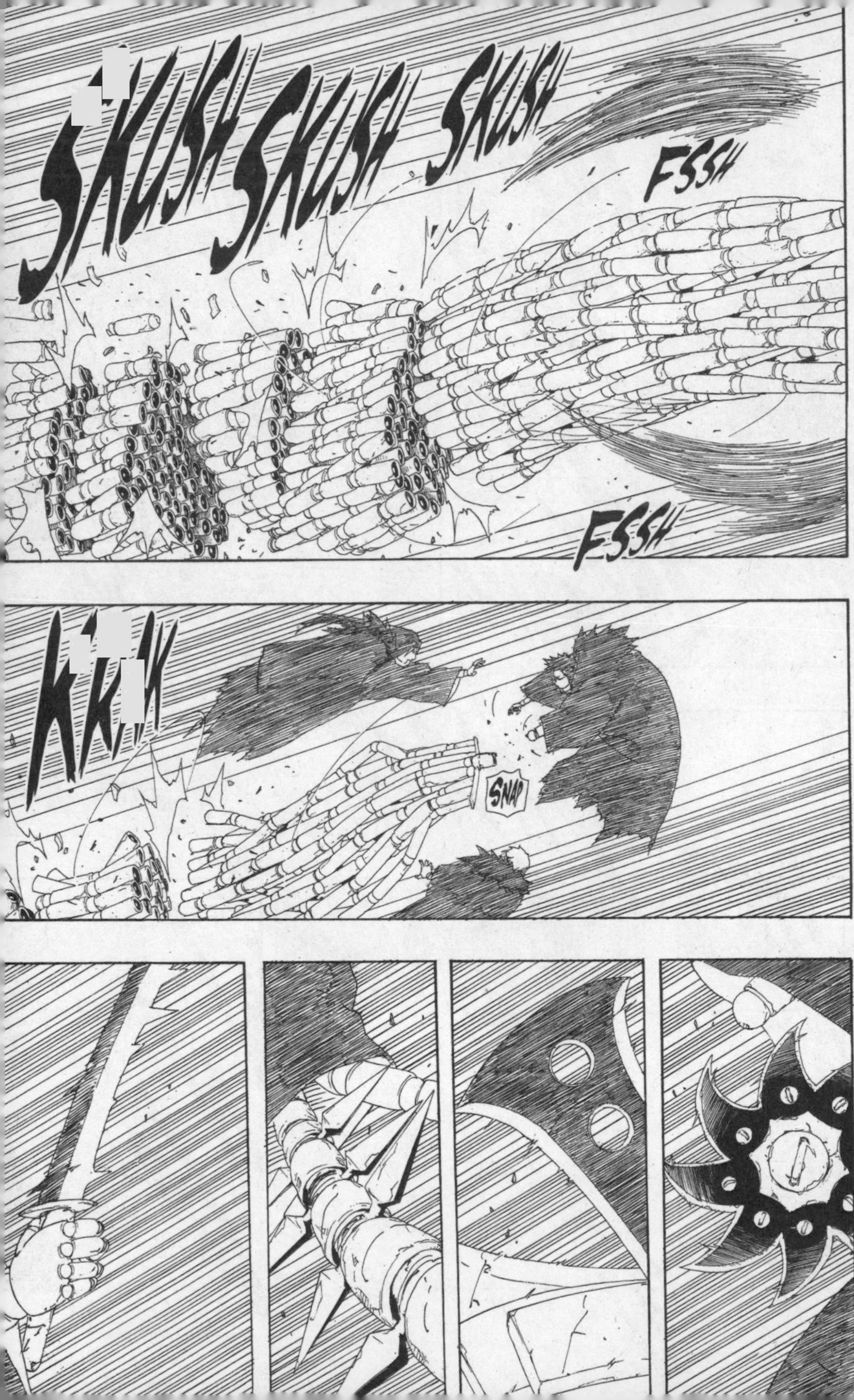
FSSH
SKUSH
SKUSH
SKUSH
FSSH
SNAP

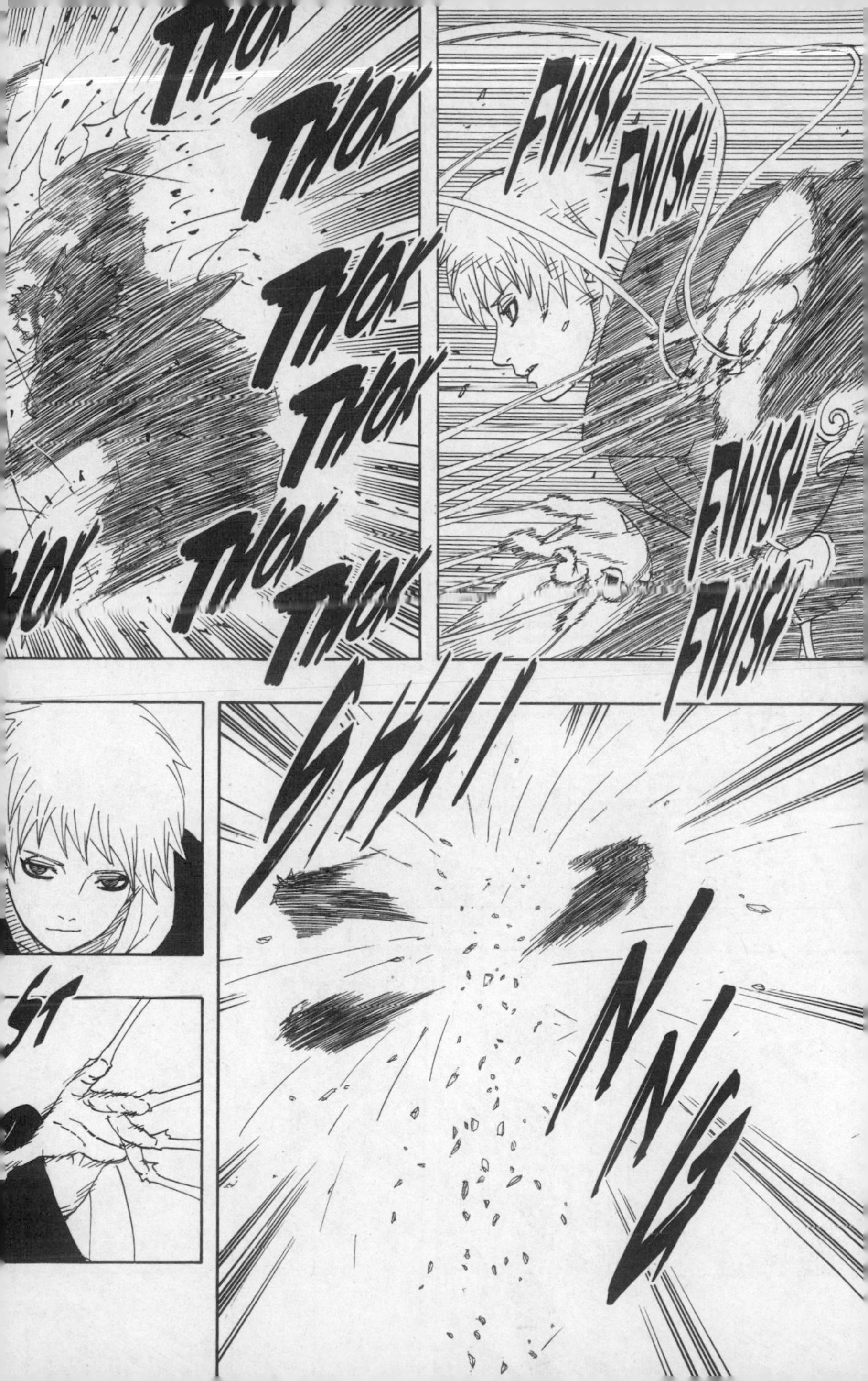
FWISH
FWISH
FWISH
FWISH
THOK
THOK
THOK
THOK
THOK
THOK

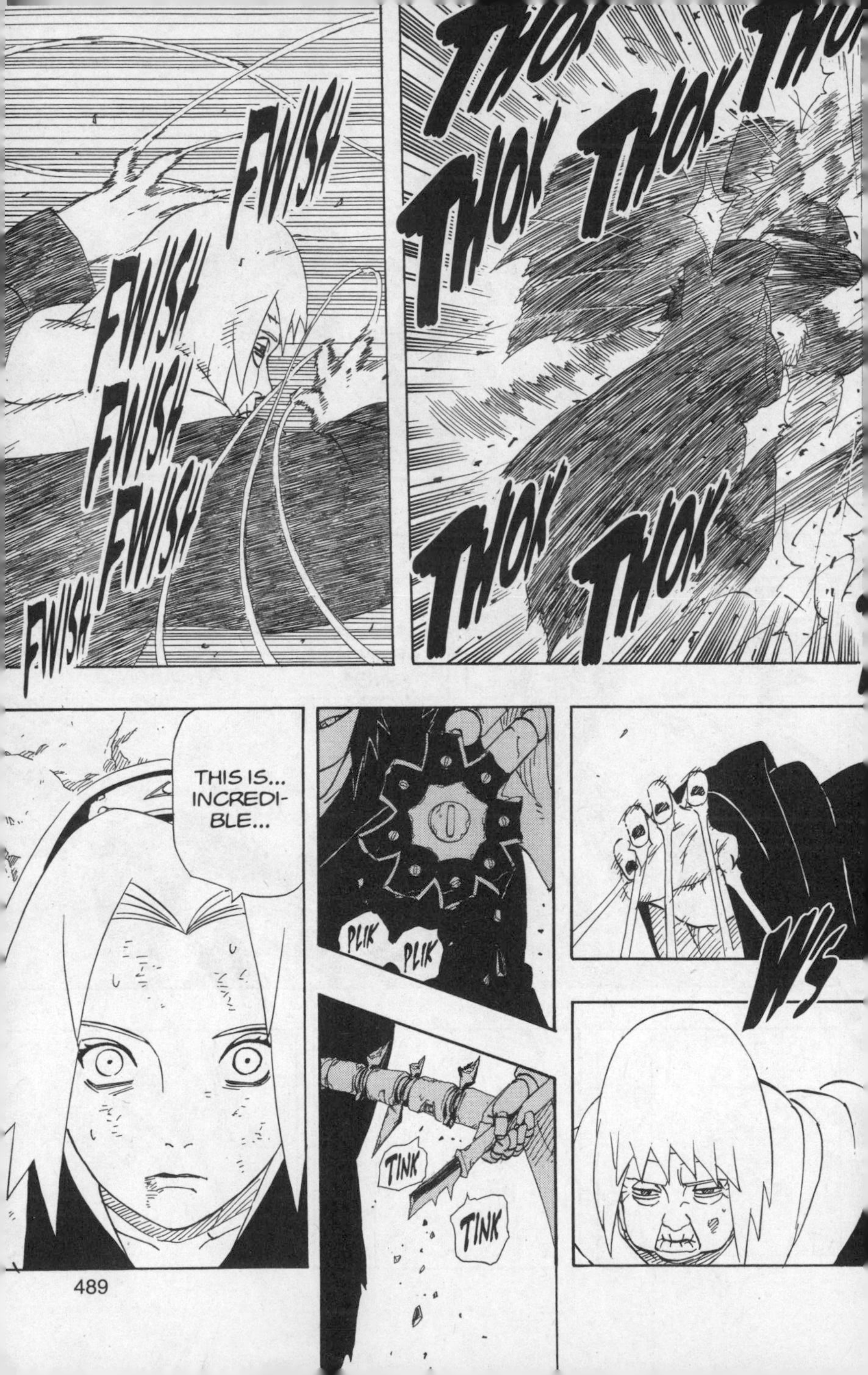
THOK
THOK
THOK
THOK
THOK
THOK
THOK
FWISH
FWISH
FWISH
FWISH
FWISH
WS
PLIK
PLIK
TINK
TINK
THIS IS... INCREDIBLE...

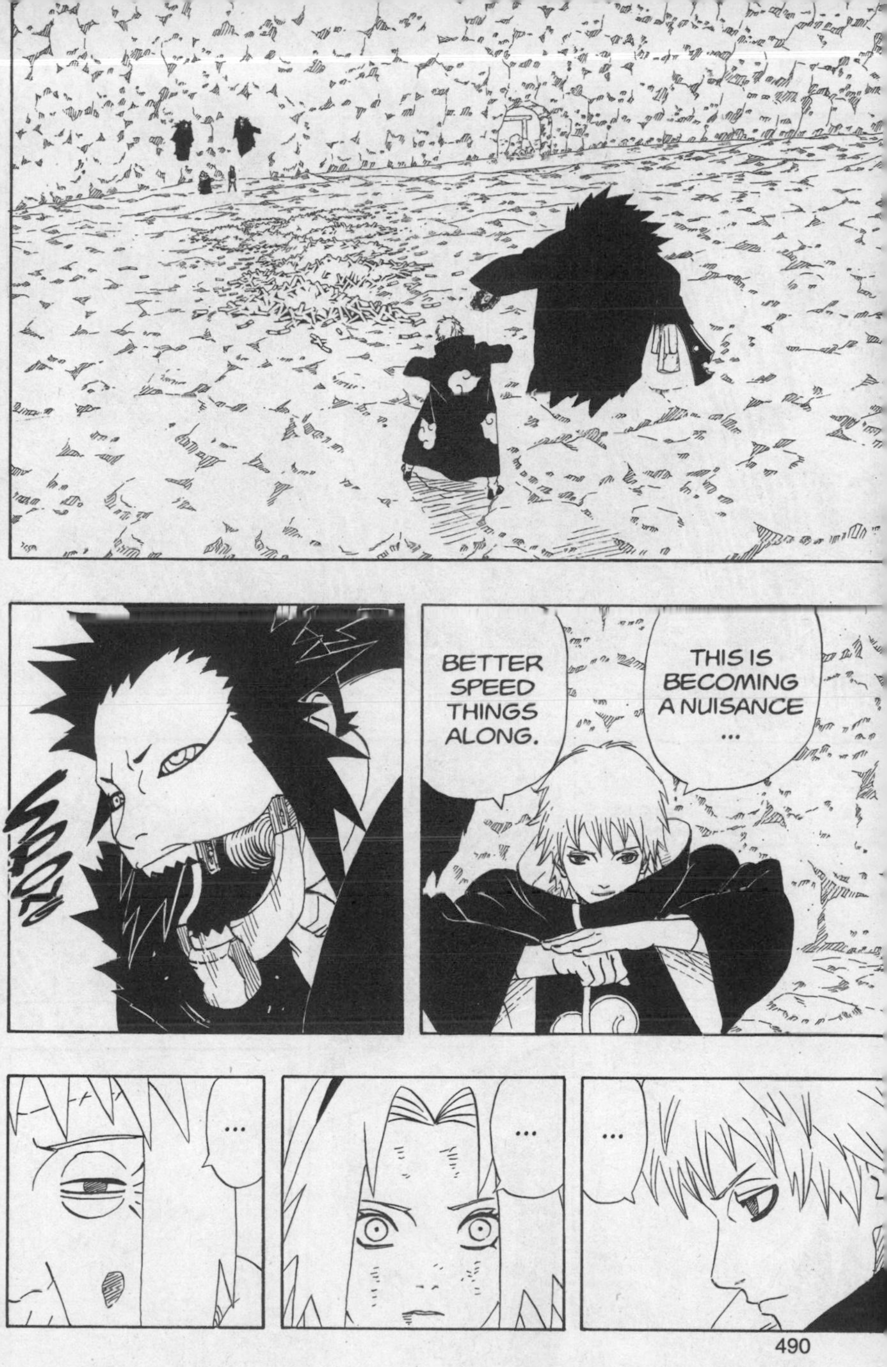
THIS IS BECOMING A NUISANCE ...
BETTER SPEED THINGS ALONG.
...
...
...

READ THIS WAY

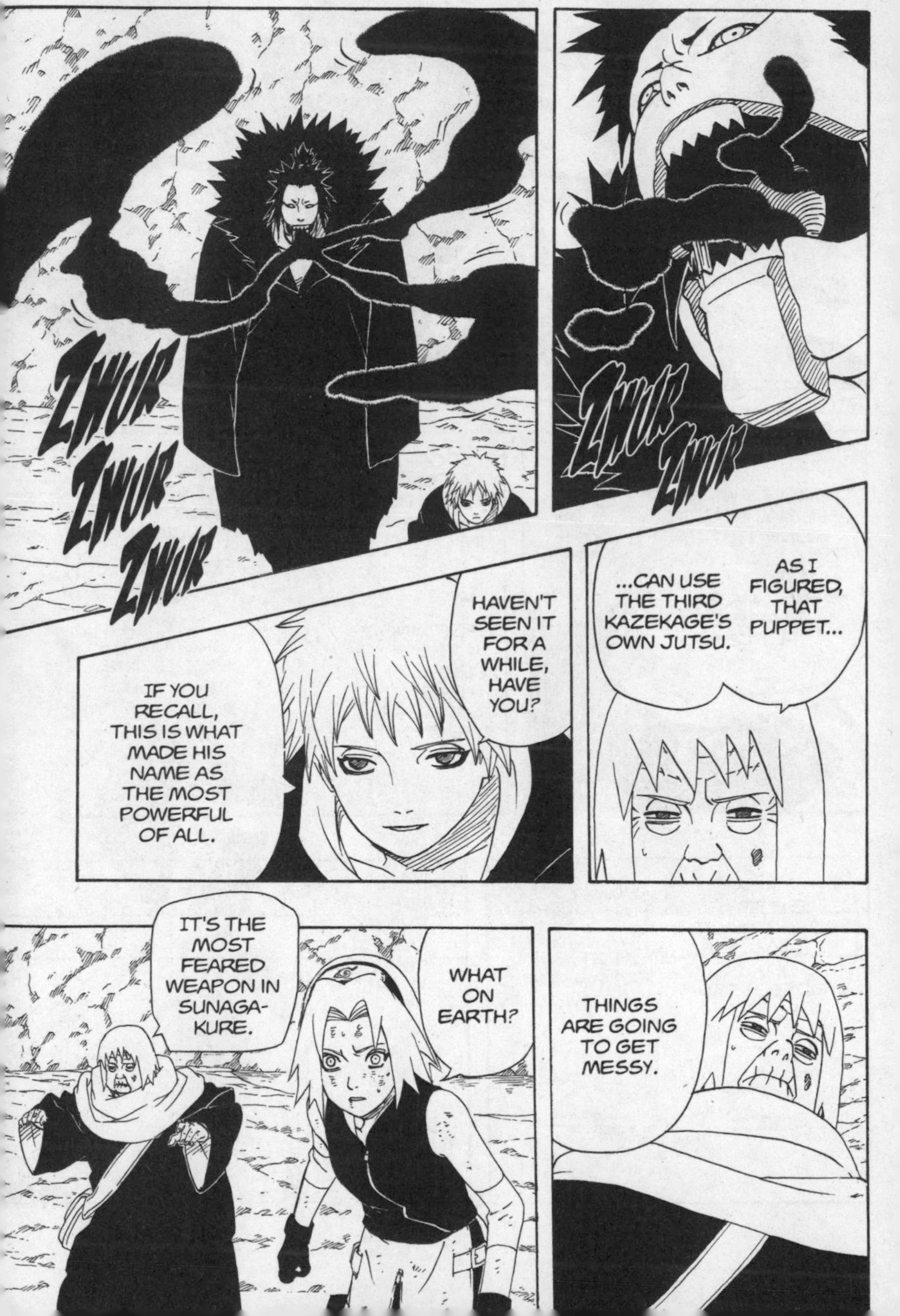
ZWUR ZWUR
ZWUR ZWUR ZWUR
AS I FIGURED, THAT PUPPET...
...CAN USE THE THIRD KAZEKAGE'S OWN JUTSU.
HAVEN'T SEEN IT FOR A WHILE, HAVE YOU?
IF YOU RECALL, THIS IS WHAT MADE HIS NAME AS THE MOST POWERFUL OF ALL.
THINGS ARE GOING TO GET MESSY.
WHAT ON EARTH?
IT'S THE MOST FEARED WEAPON IN SUNAGA-KURE.

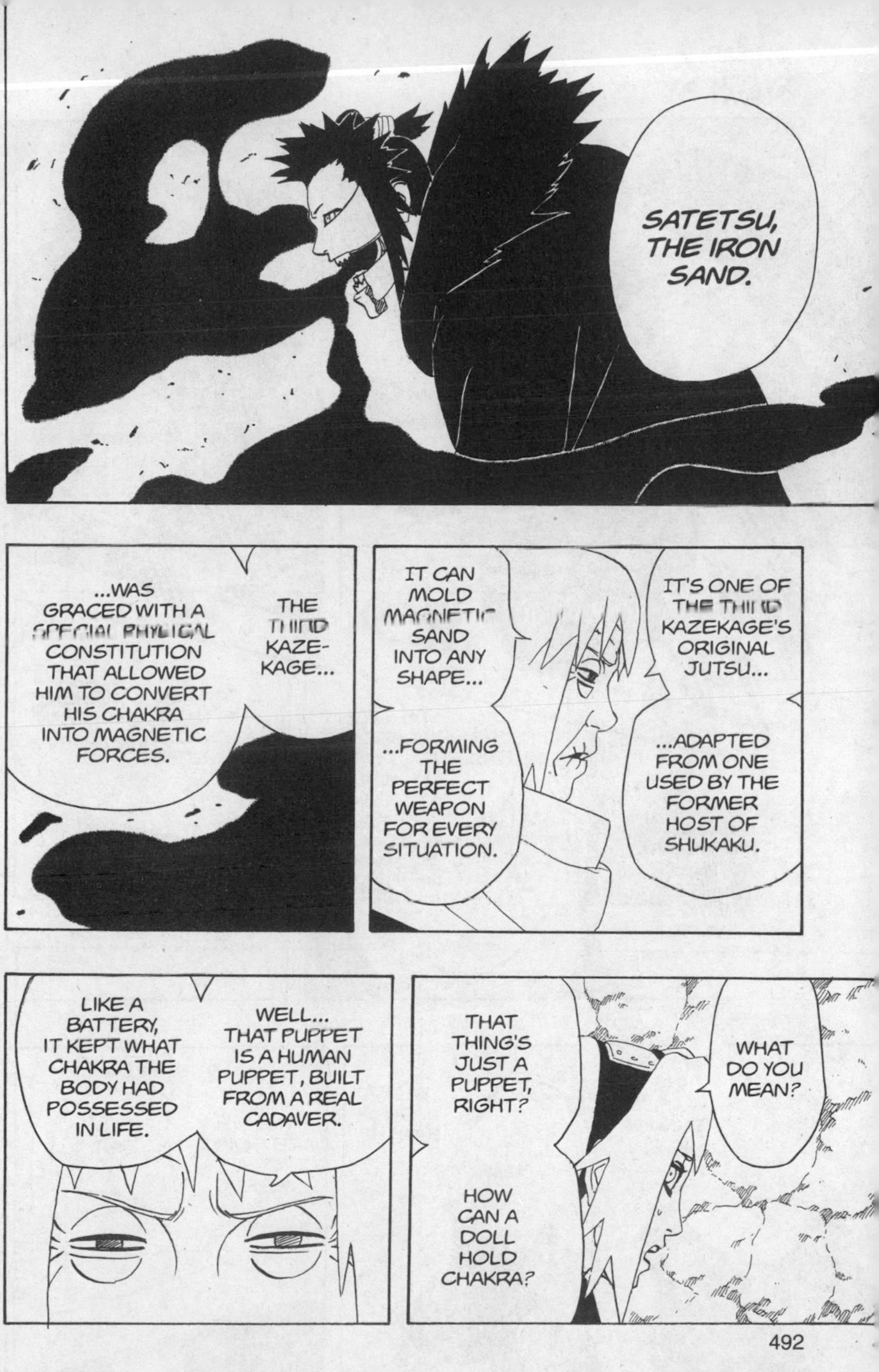
SATETSU, THE IRON SAND.
IT'S ONE OF THE THIRD KAZEKAGE'S ORIGINAL JUTSU...
...ADAPTED FROM ONE USED BY THE FORMER HOST OF SHUKAKU.
IT CAN MOLD MAGNETIC SAND INTO ANY SHAPE...
...FORMING THE PERFECT WEAPON FOR EVERY SITUATION.
THE THIRD KAZE-KAGE...
...WAS GRACED WITH A SPECIAL PHYSICAL CONSTITUTION THAT ALLOWED HIM TO CONVERT HIS CHAKRA INTO MAGNETIC FORCES.
WHAT DO YOU MEAN?
THAT THING'S JUST A PUPPET, RIGHT?
HOW CAN A DOLL HOLD CHAKRA?
WELL... THAT PUPPET IS A HUMAN PUPPET, BUILT FROM A REAL CADAVER.
LIKE A BATTERY, IT KEPT WHAT CHAKRA THE BODY HAD POSSESSED IN LIFE.

READ THIS WAY

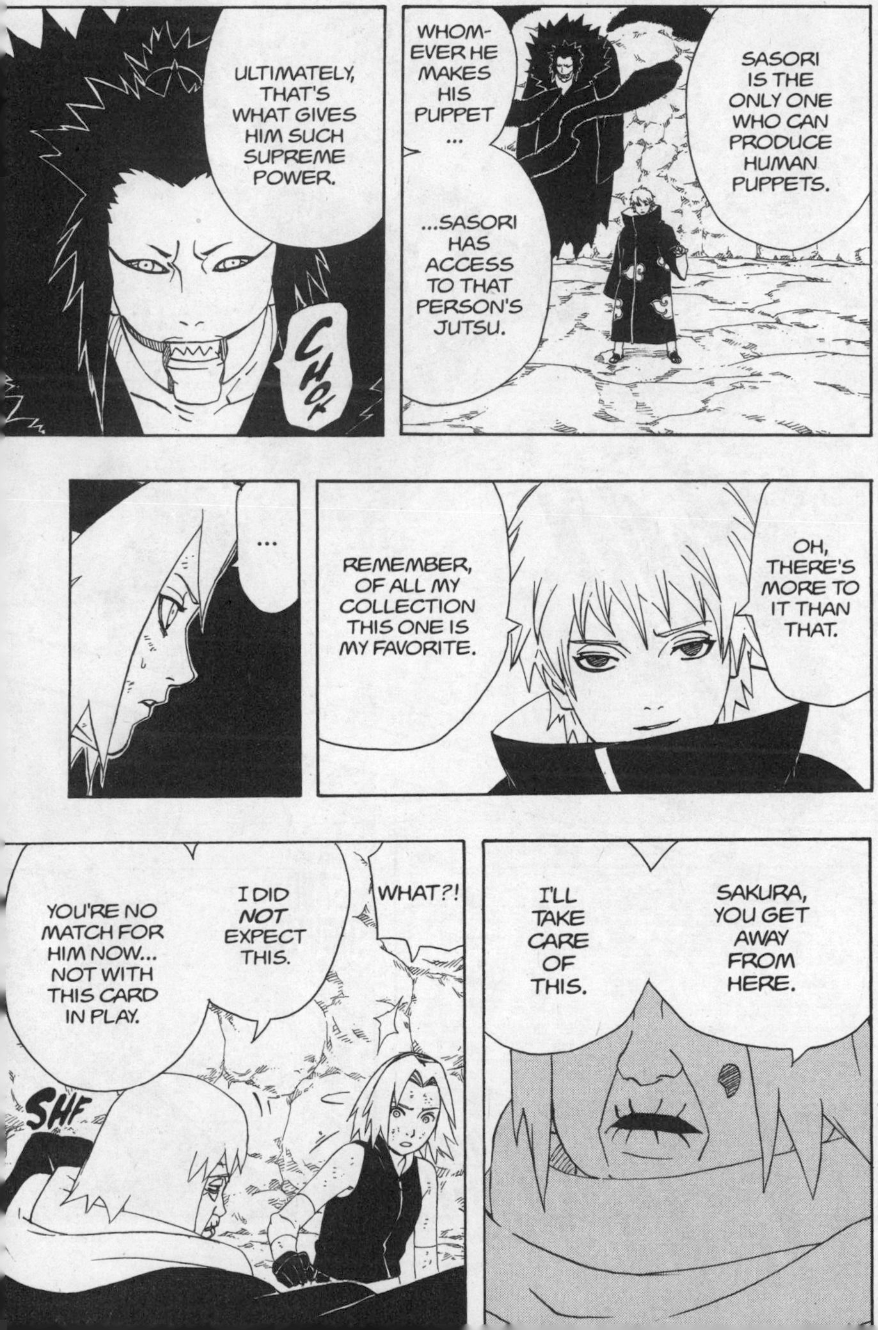
SASORI IS THE ONLY ONE WHO CAN PRODUCE HUMAN PUPPETS.
WHOMEVER HE MAKES HIS PUPPET ...
...SASORI HAS ACCESS TO THAT PERSON'S JUTSU.
ULTIMATELY, THAT'S WHAT GIVES HIM SUCH SUPREME POWER.
CHOK
OH, THERE'S MORE TO IT THAN THAT.
REMEMBER, OF ALL MY COLLECTION THIS ONE IS MY FAVORITE.
...
SAKURA, YOU GET AWAY FROM HERE.
I'LL TAKE CARE OF THIS.
WHAT?!
I DID *NOT* EXPECT THIS.
YOU'RE NO MATCH FOR HIM NOW... NOT WITH THIS CARD IN PLAY.
SHF

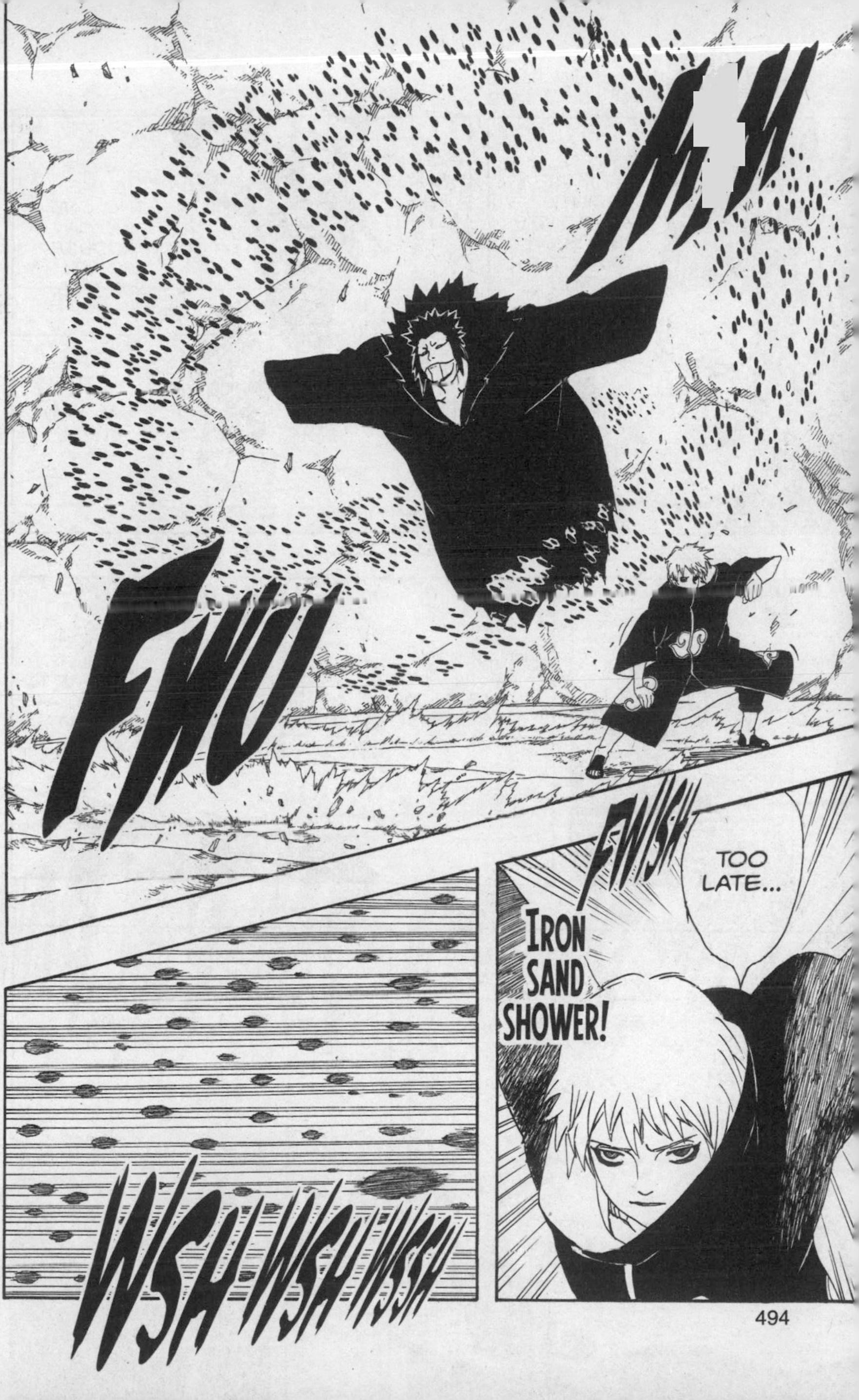

FWU
FWISH
TOO LATE...
IRON SAND SHOWER!
WSH WSH WSH

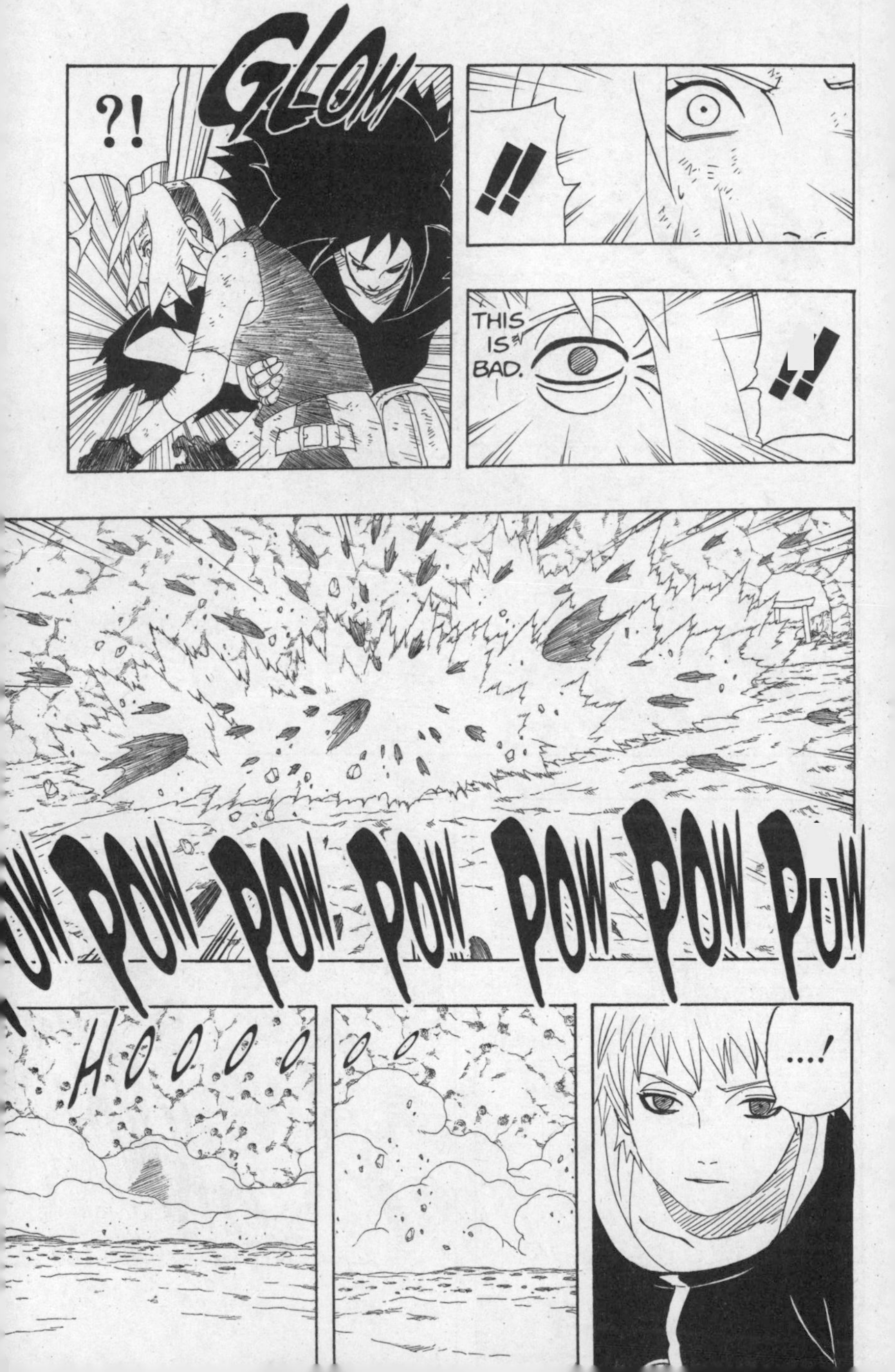
!!
THIS IS BAD.
!!
GLOW
?!
POW POW POW POW POW POW POW
...!
HOOOOOO

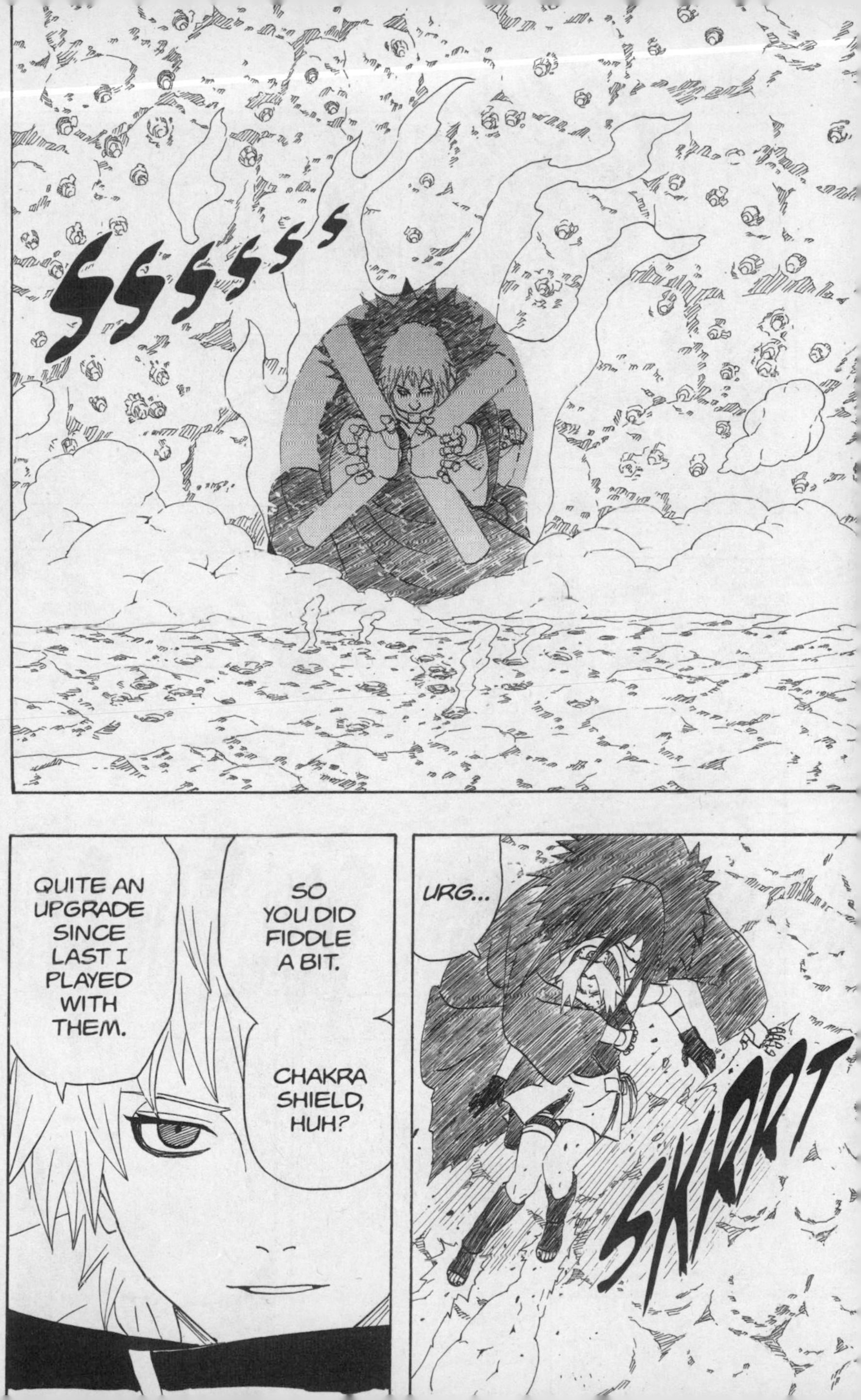
SSSSSS
URG...
SKRRT
SO YOU DID FIDDLE A BIT.
CHAKRA SHIELD, HUH?
QUITE AN UPGRADE SINCE LAST I PLAYED WITH THEM.

READ THIS WAY

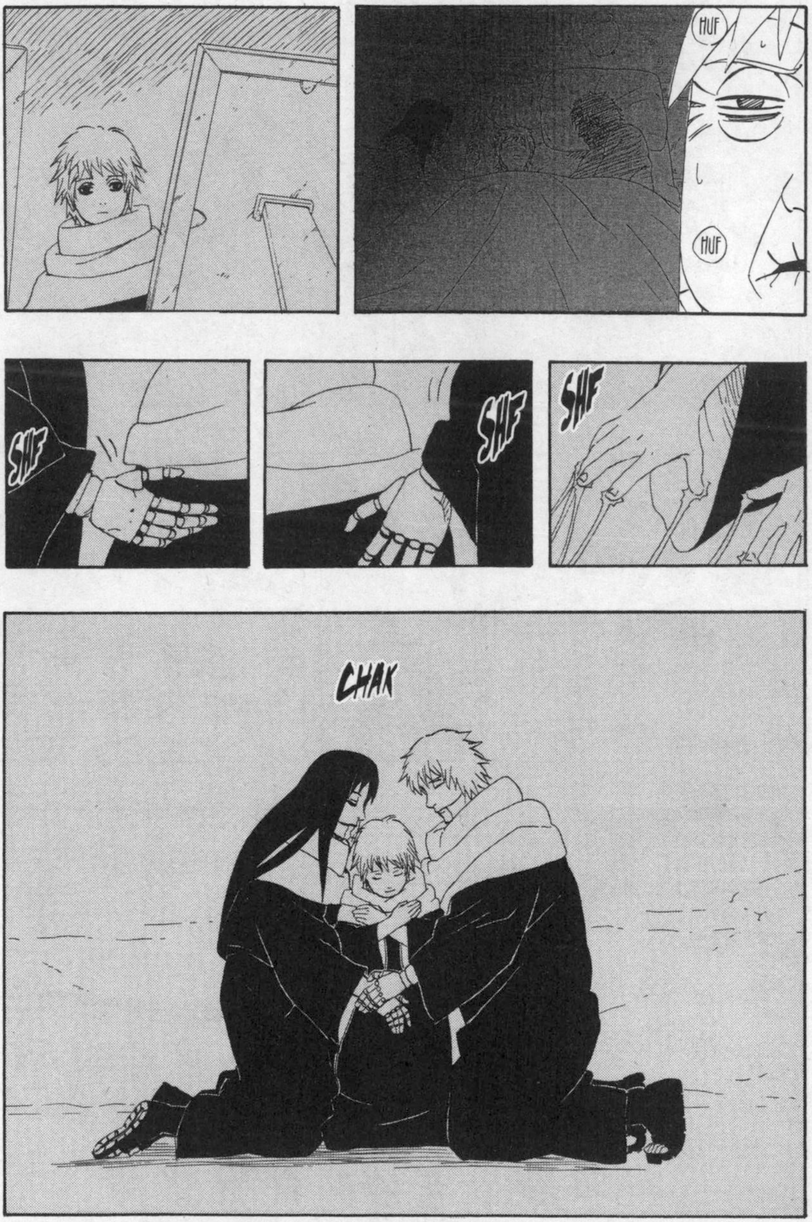

HUF
HUF
SHF
SHF
SHF
CHAK

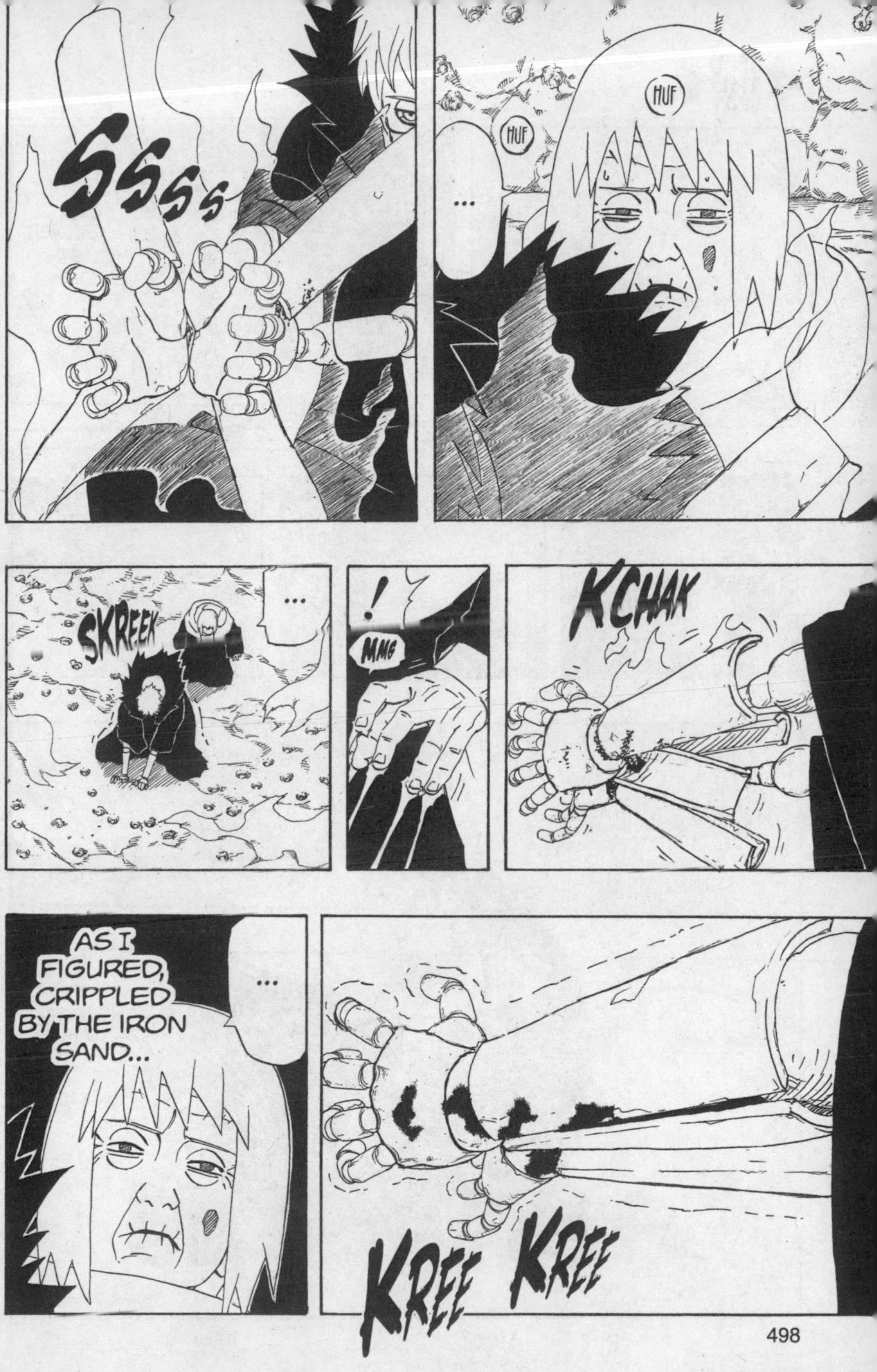
HUF
HUF
...
SSSS
KCHAK
!
MMG
SKREEK
...
KREE KREE
...
AS I FIGURED, CRIPPLED BY THE IRON SAND...

READ THIS WAY

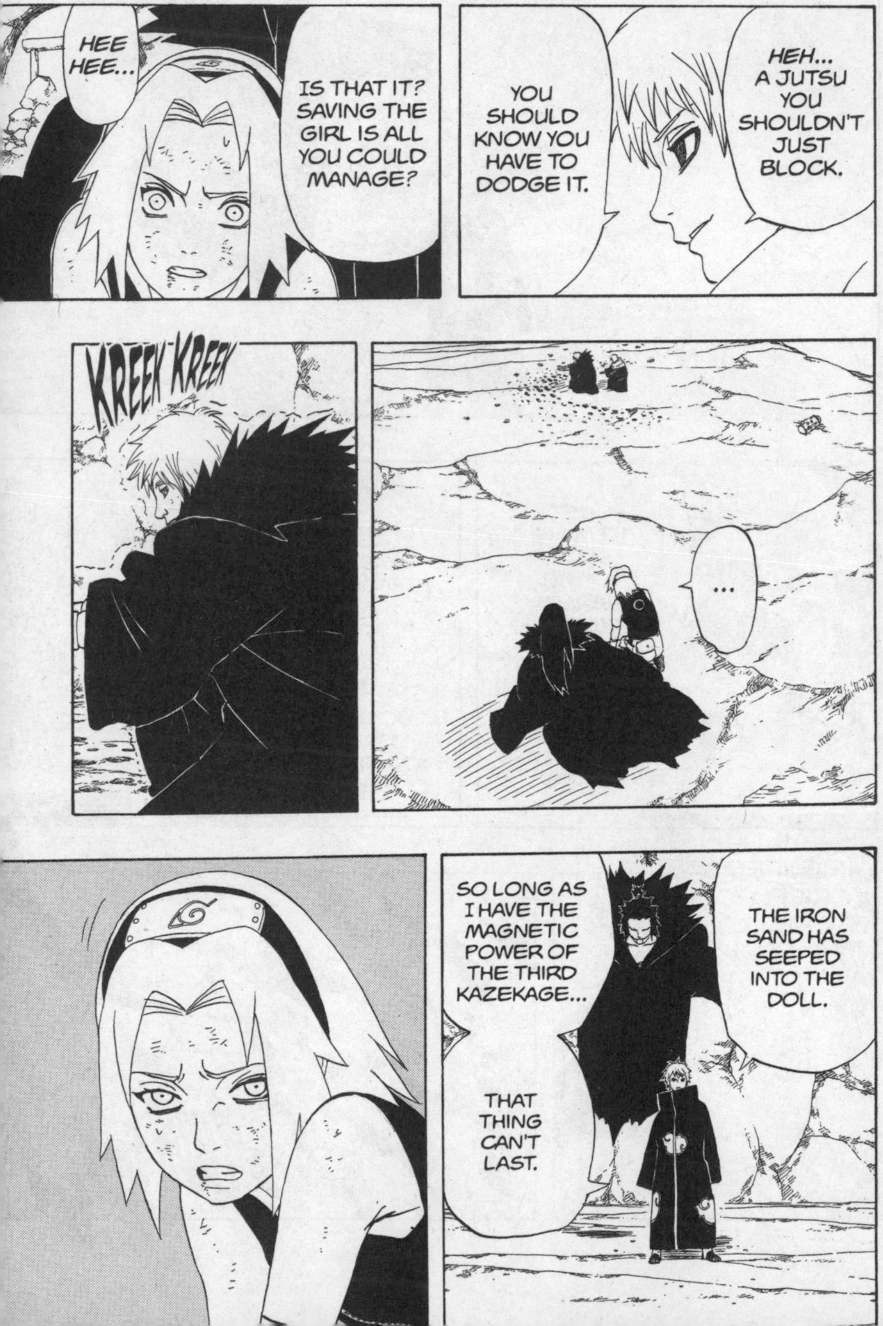
HEH... A JUTSU YOU SHOULDN'T JUST BLOCK.
YOU SHOULD KNOW YOU HAVE TO DODGE IT.
IS THAT IT? SAVING THE GIRL IS ALL YOU COULD MANAGE?
HEE HEE...
...
KREEK KREEK
THE IRON SAND HAS SEEPED INTO THE DOLL.
SO LONG AS I HAVE THE MAGNETIC POWER OF THE THIRD KAZEKAGE...
THAT THING CAN'T LAST.

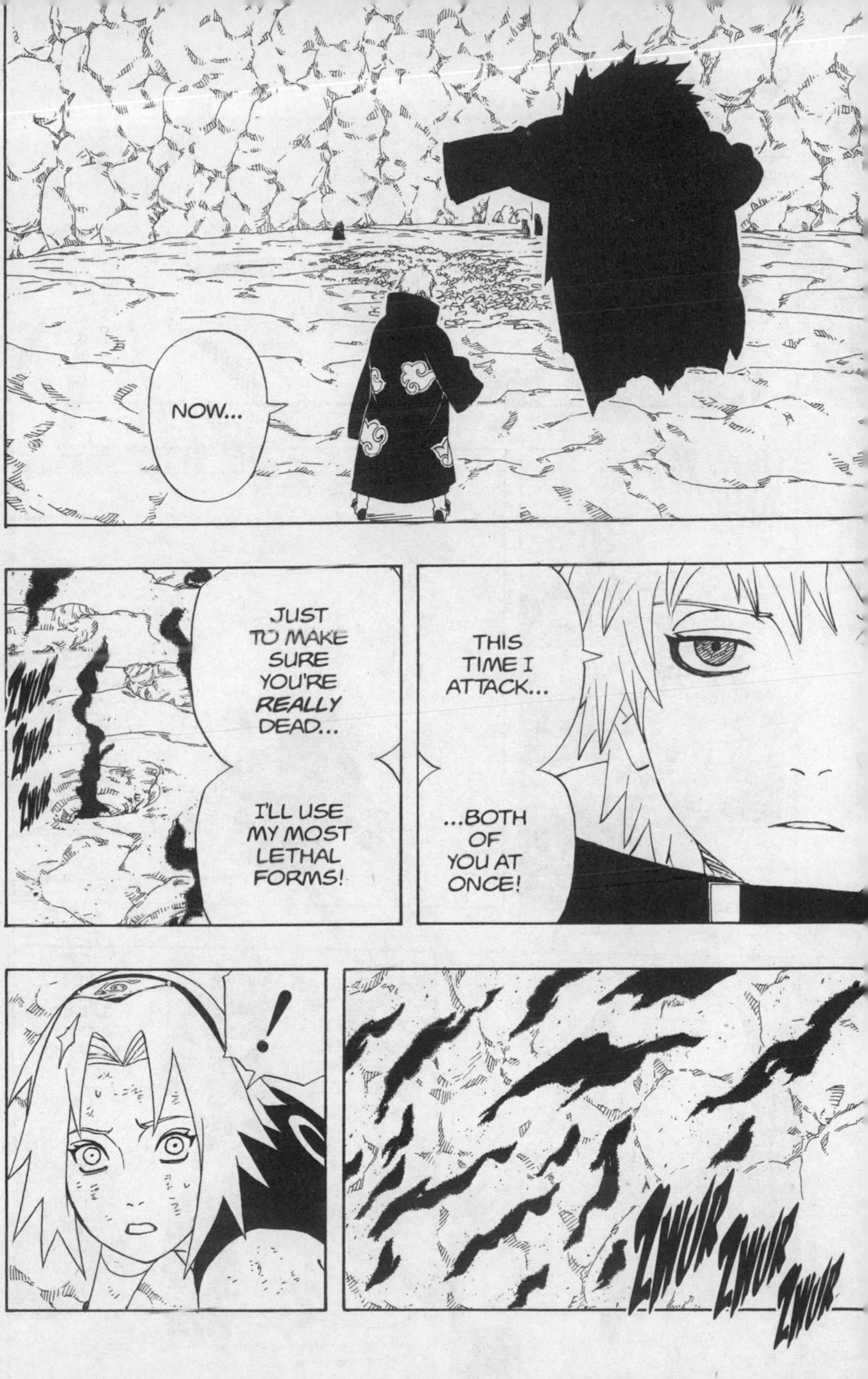
NOW...
THIS TIME I ATTACK...
...BOTH OF YOU AT ONCE!
JUST TO MAKE SURE YOU'RE *REALLY* DEAD...
I'LL USE MY MOST LETHAL FORMS!
ZWUR ZWUR ZWUR
ZWUR ZWUR ZWUR
!

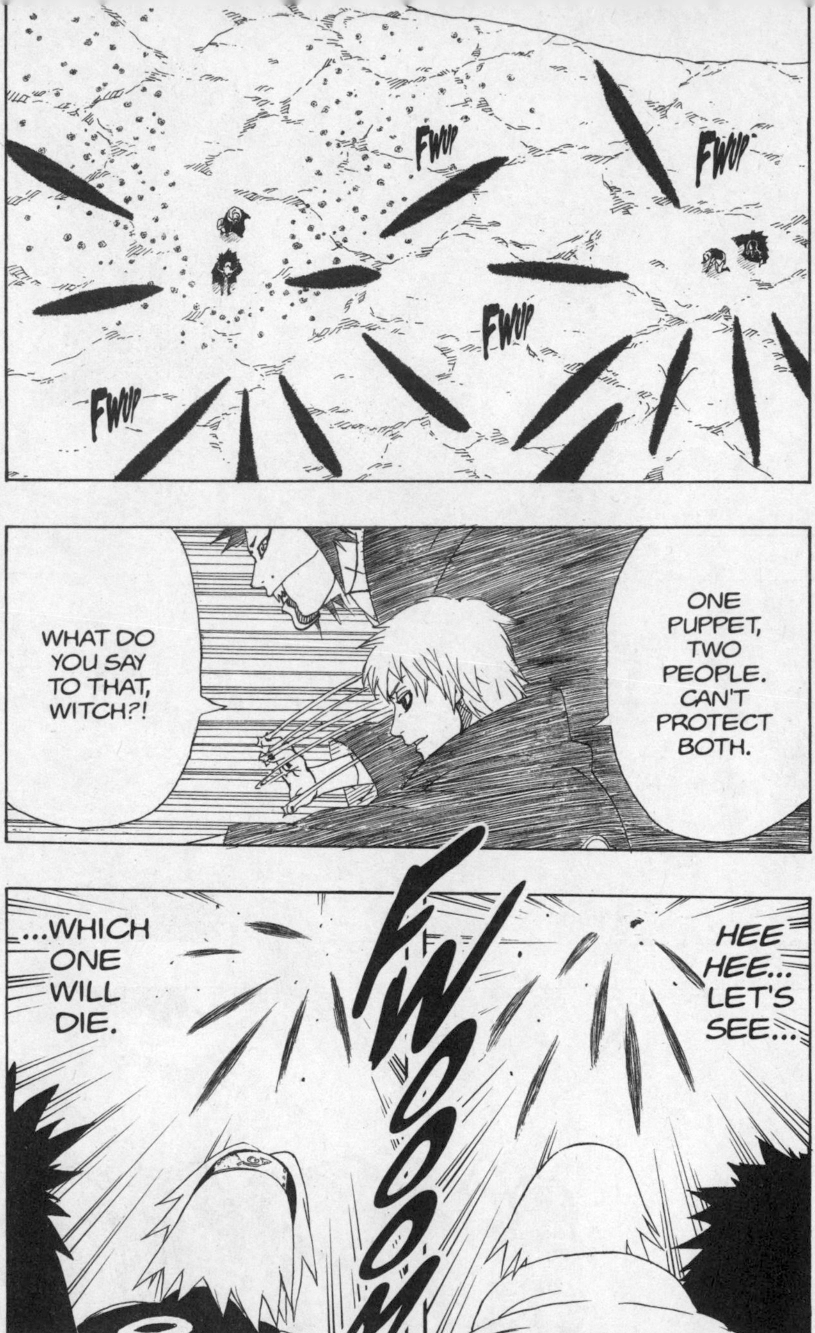
FWUP
FWUP
FWUP
FWUP
ONE PUPPET, TWO PEOPLE. CAN'T PROTECT BOTH.
WHAT DO YOU SAY TO THAT, WITCH?!
HEE HEE... LET'S SEE...
...WHICH ONE WILL DIE.
FWOOOOM

NARUTO

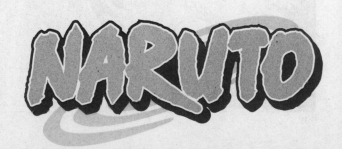

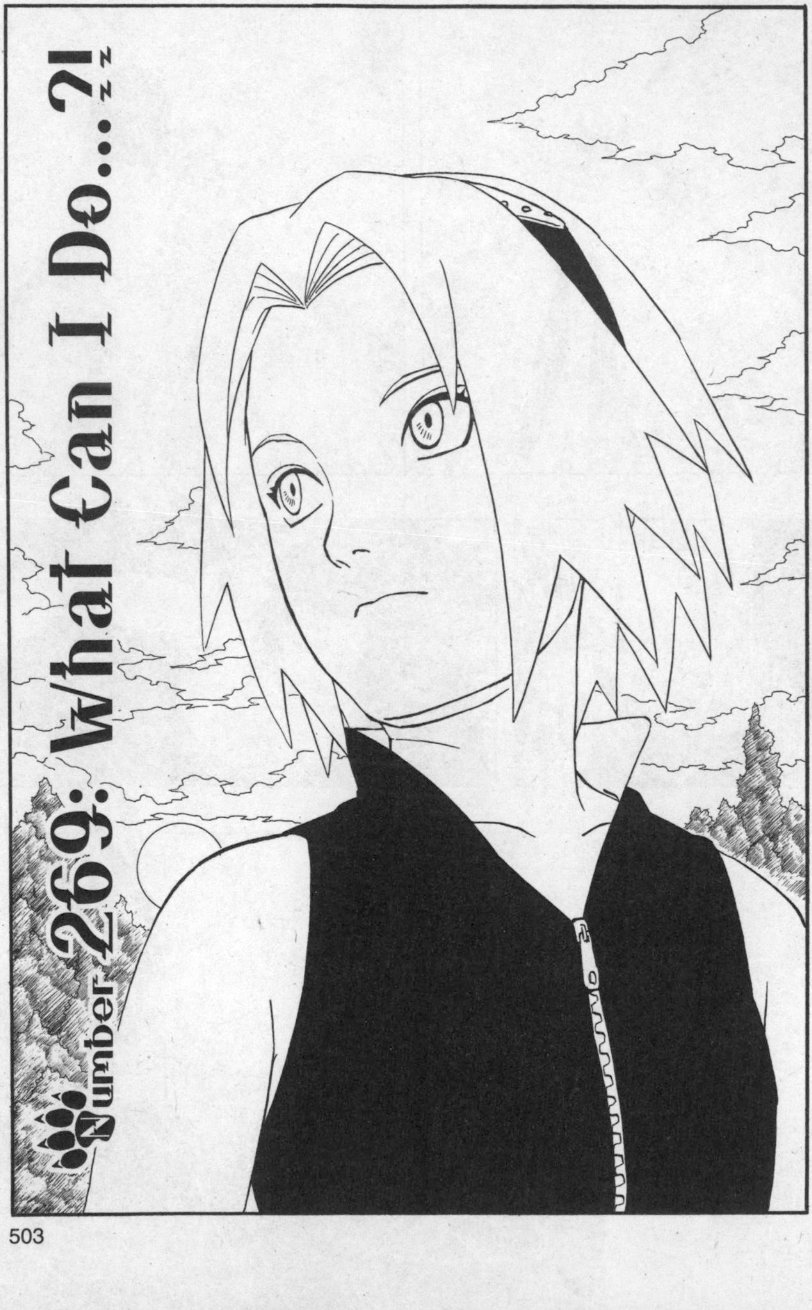
Number 269: What Can I Do...?!

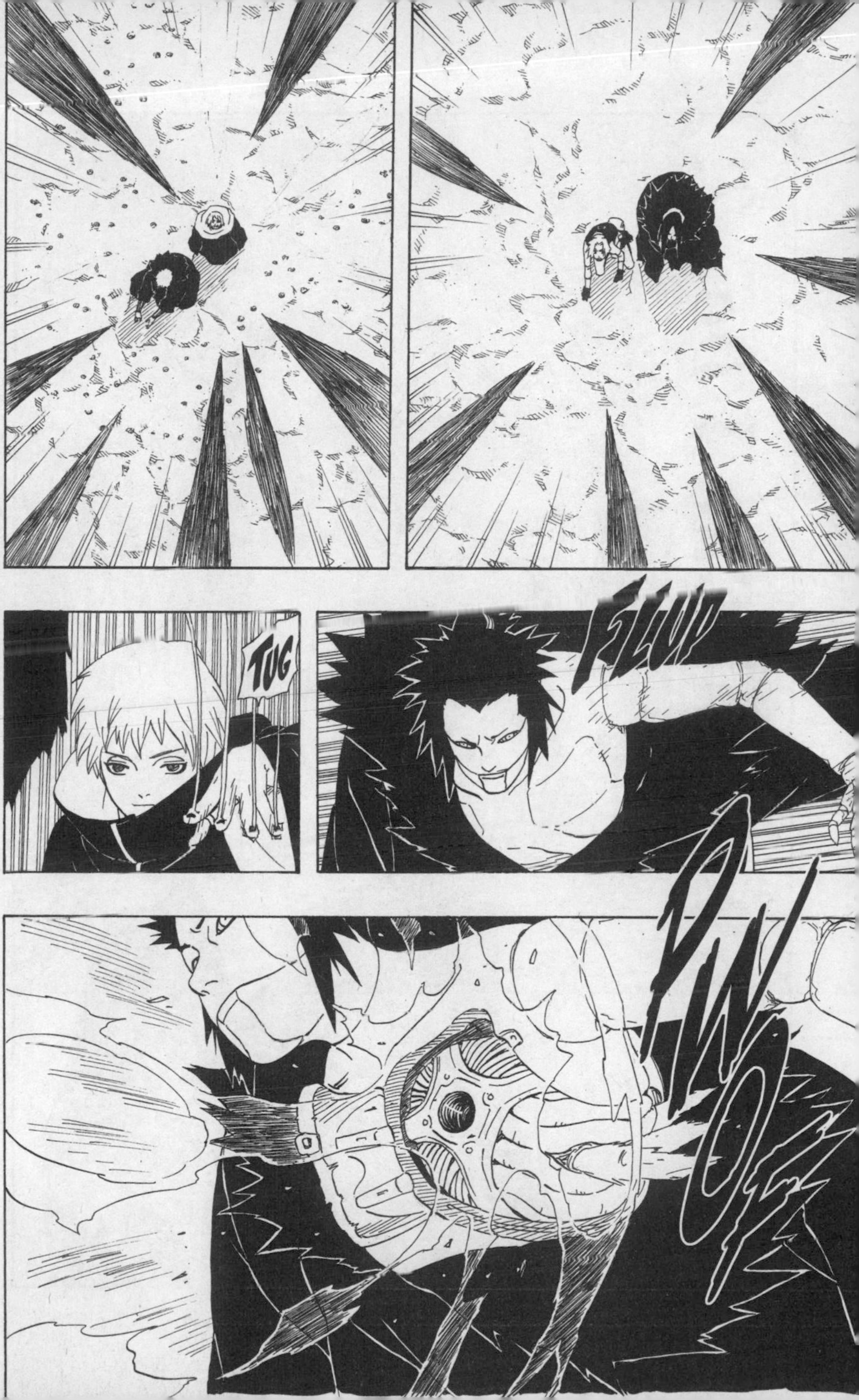
FLUP
TUG

READ THIS WAY

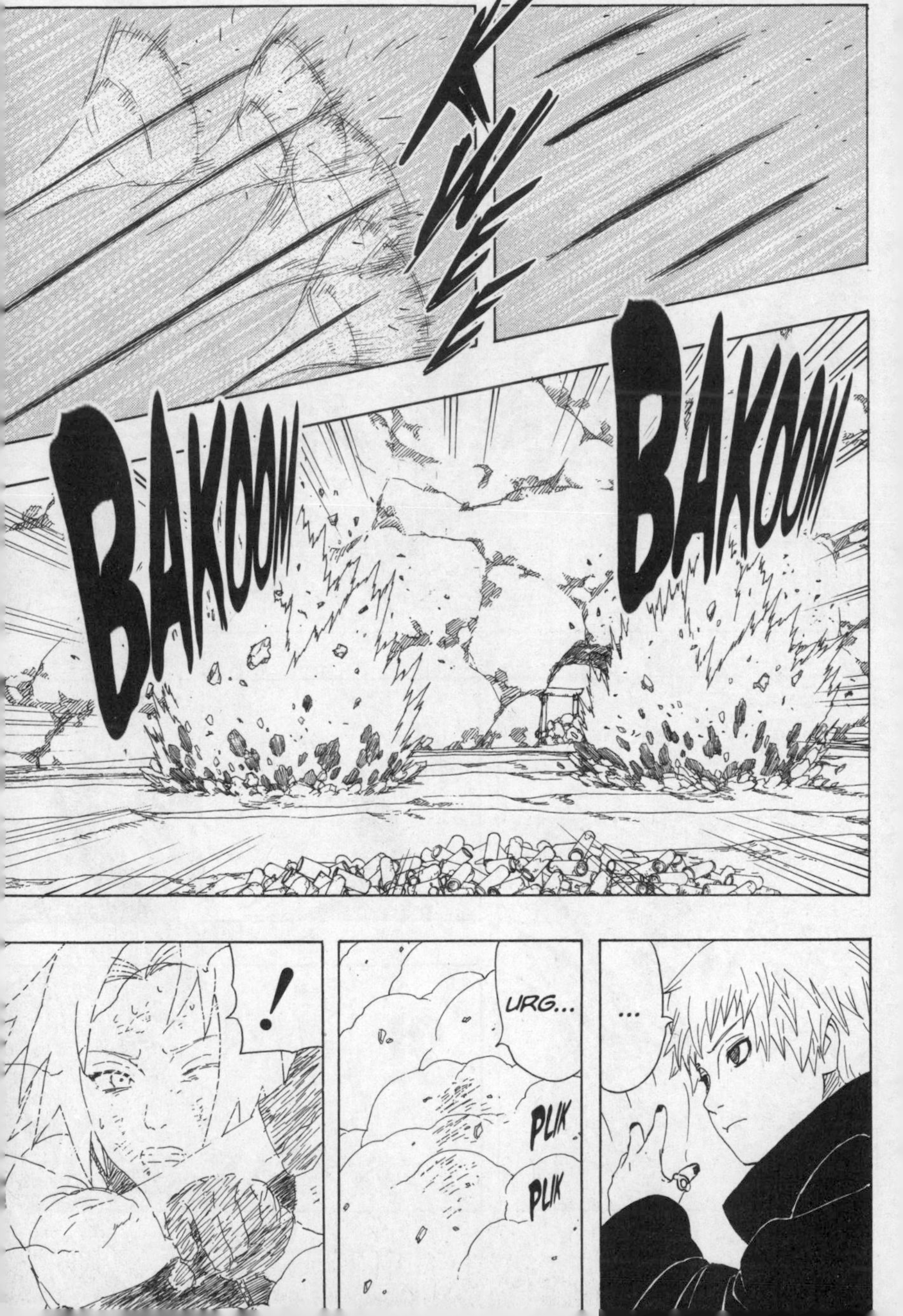
KWEEE
BAKOOM
BAKOOM
...
URG...
PLIK
PLIK
!

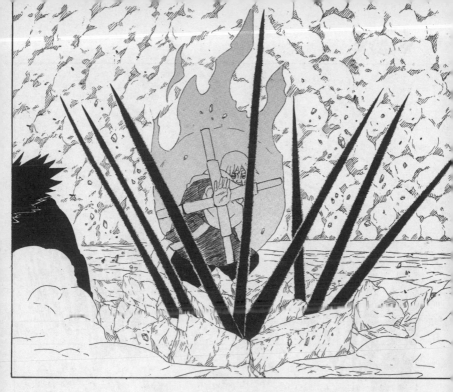

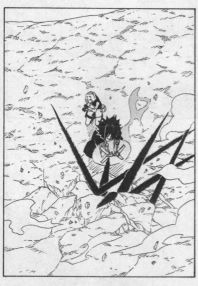

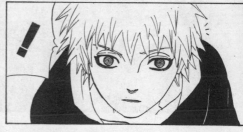

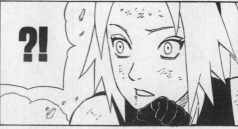

READ THIS WAY

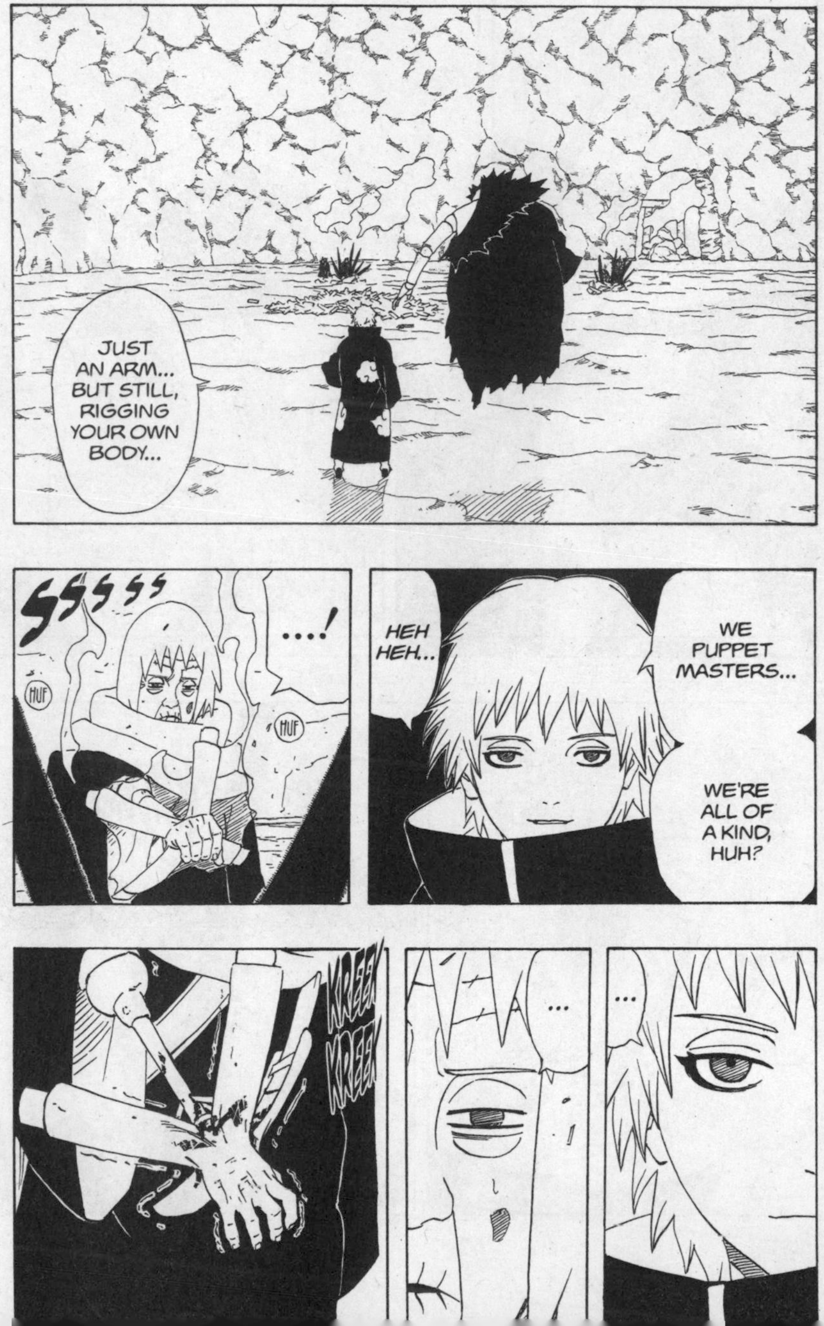
JUST AN ARM... BUT STILL, RIGGING YOUR OWN BODY...
WE PUPPET MASTERS...
HEH HEH...
WE'RE ALL OF A KIND, HUH?
SSSSS
...!
HUF
HUF
...
...
KREEK KREEK

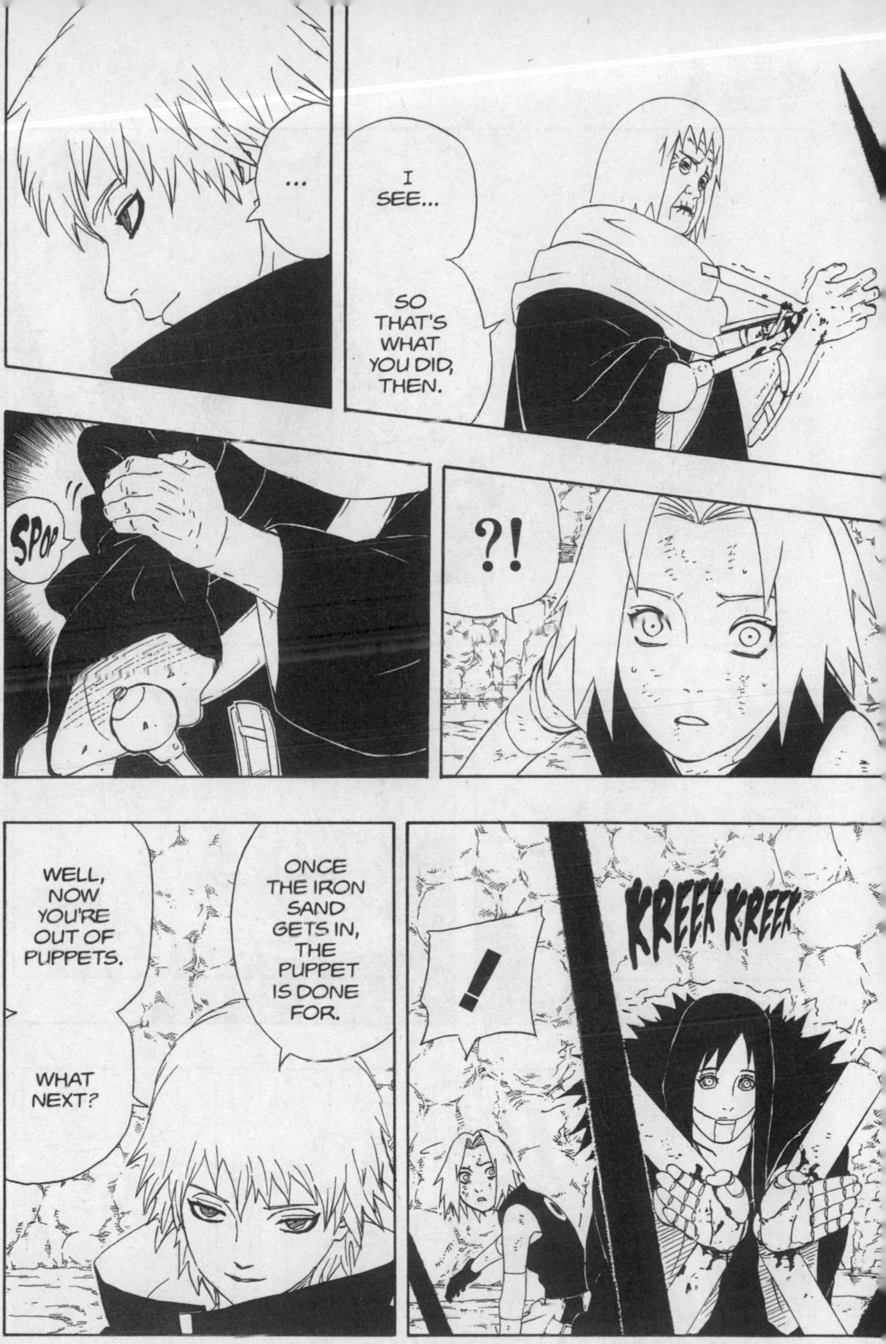
I SEE...
SO THAT'S WHAT YOU DID, THEN.
...
?!
SPOP
KREEK KREEK
!
ONCE THE IRON SAND GETS IN, THE PUPPET IS DONE FOR.
WELL, NOW YOU'RE OUT OF PUPPETS.
WHAT NEXT?

READ THIS WAY

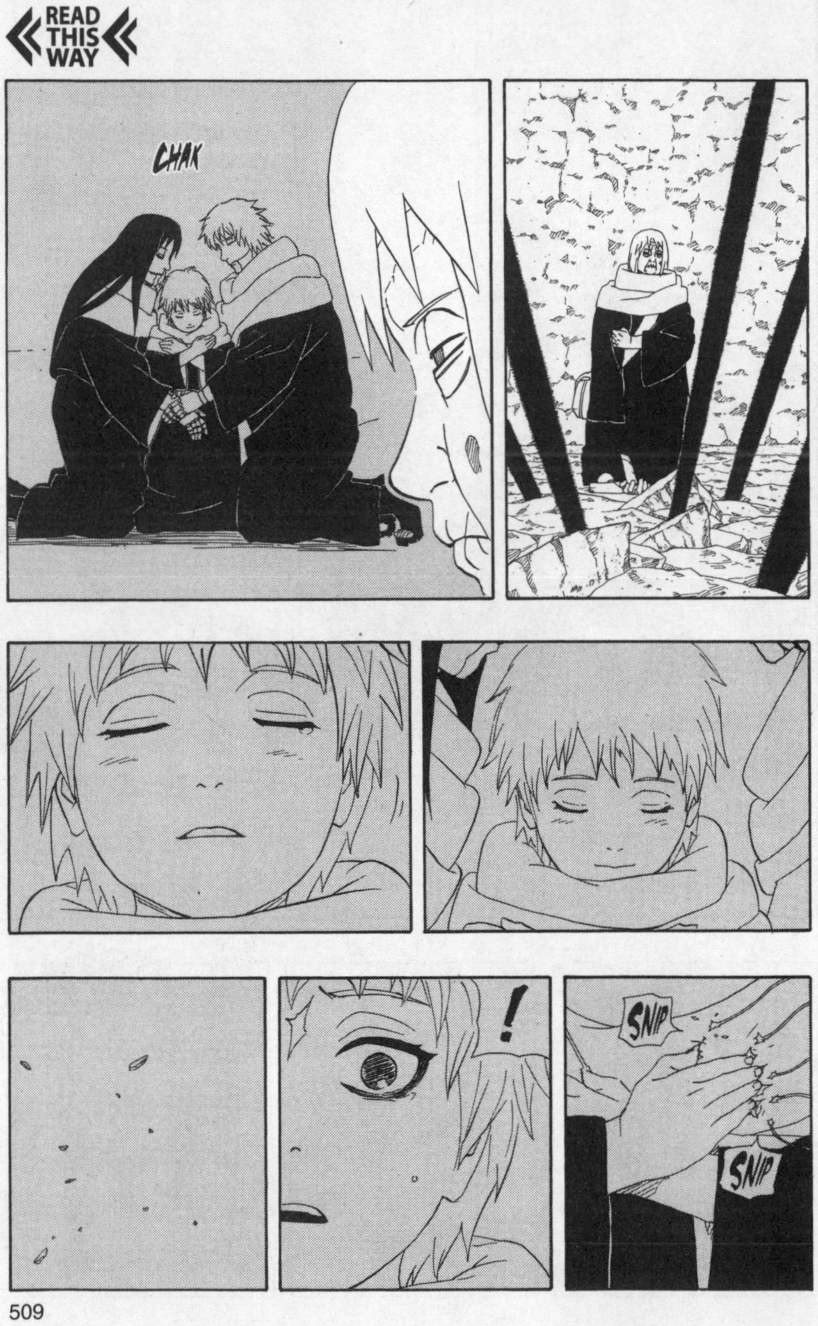
CHAK
SNIP
SNIP
!

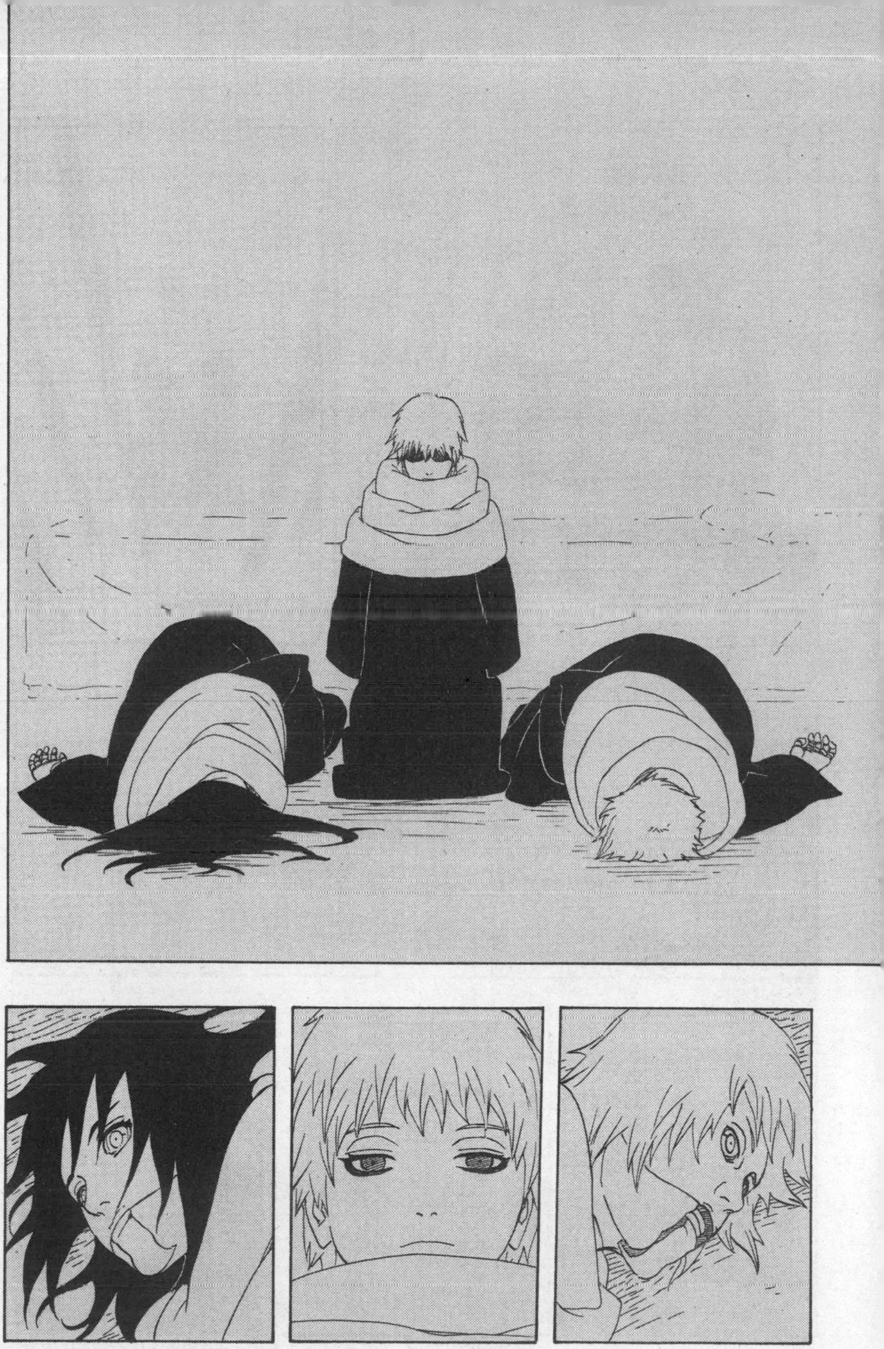

READ THIS WAY

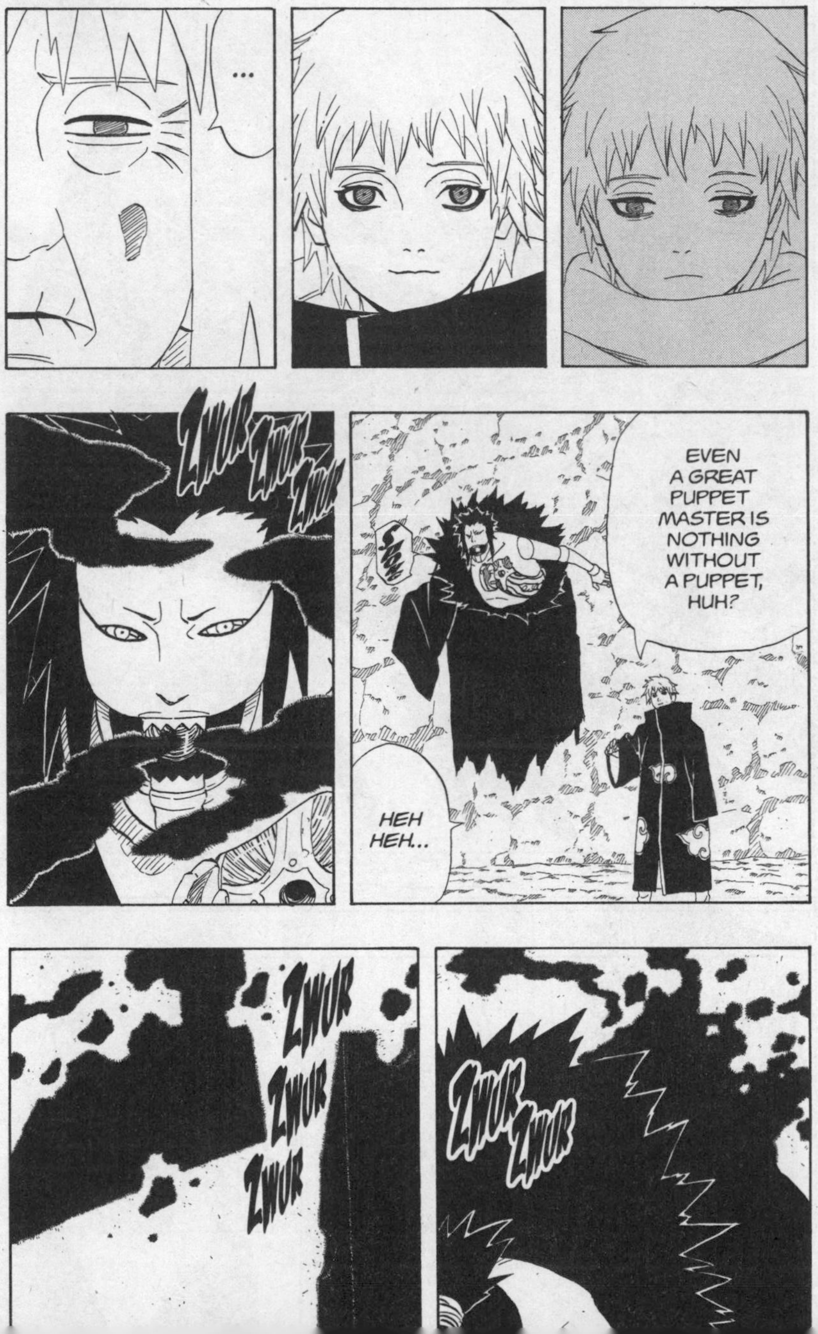
...
EVEN A GREAT PUPPET MASTER IS NOTHING WITHOUT A PUPPET, HUH?
HEH HEH...
ZWUR ZWUR ZWUR
ZWUR ZWUR
ZWUR ZWUR ZWUR ZWUR

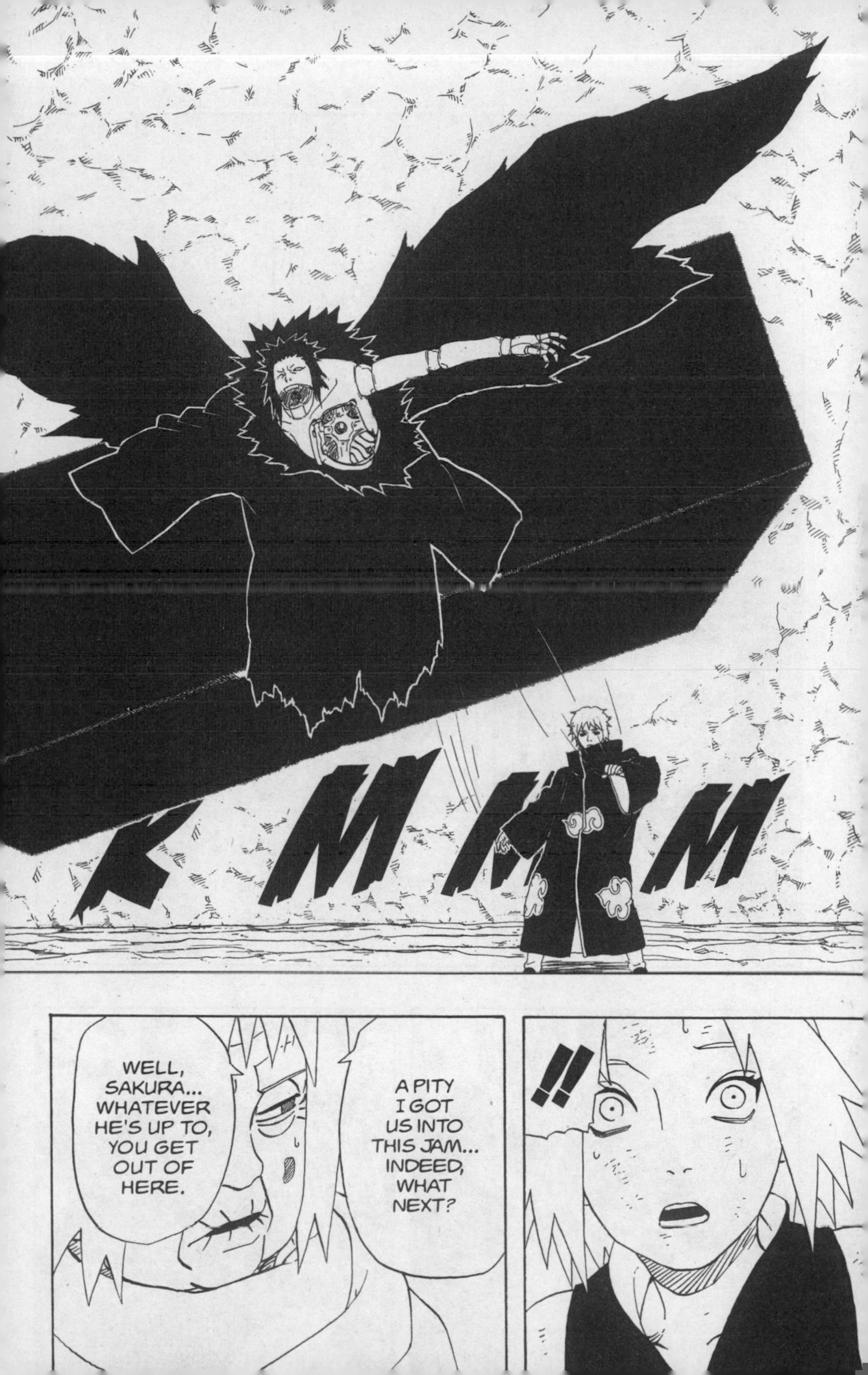
KMMMM
!!
A PITY I GOT US INTO THIS JAM... INDEED, WHAT NEXT?
WELL, SAKURA... WHATEVER HE'S UP TO, YOU GET OUT OF HERE.

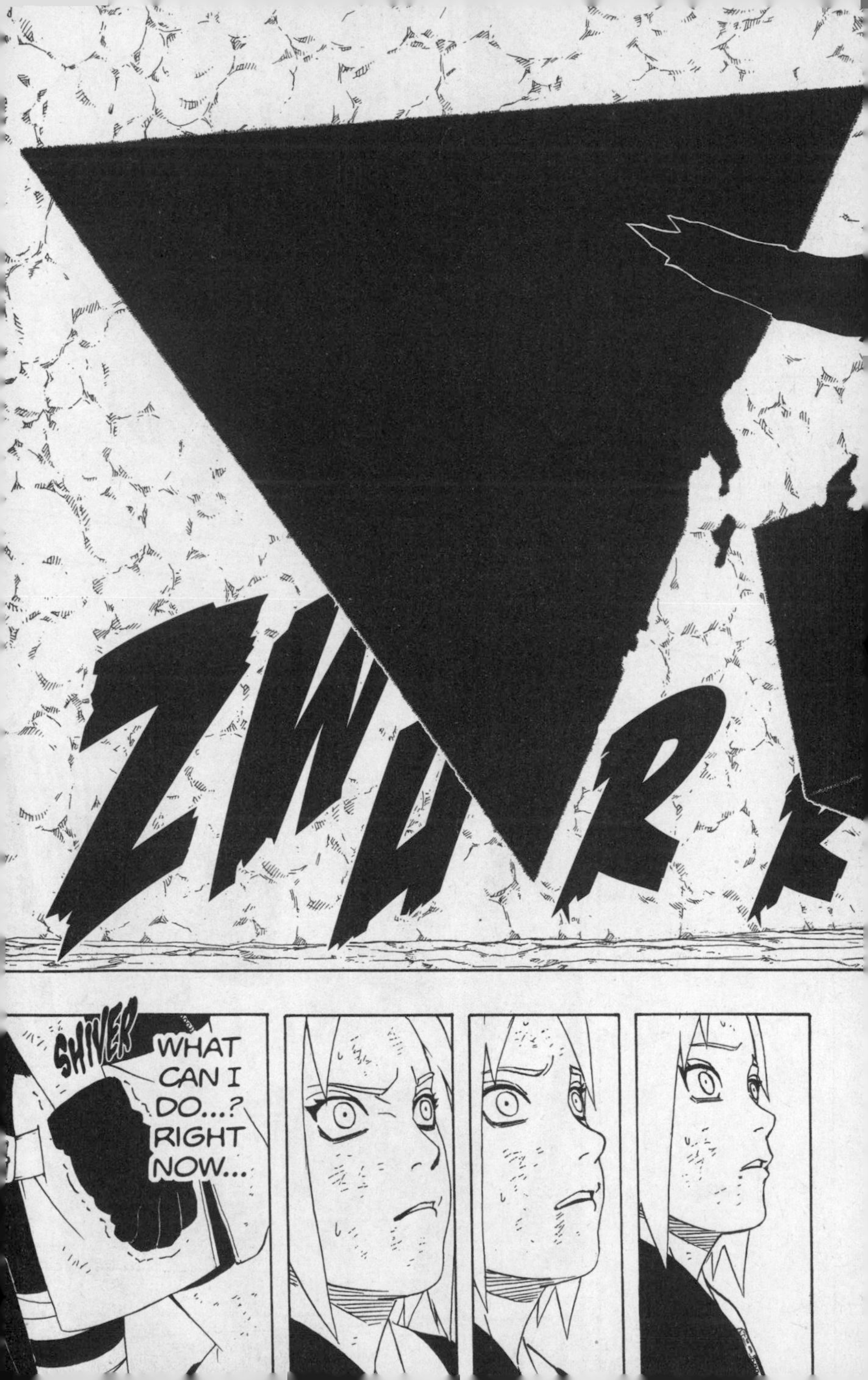
SHIVER
WHAT CAN I DO...? RIGHT NOW...

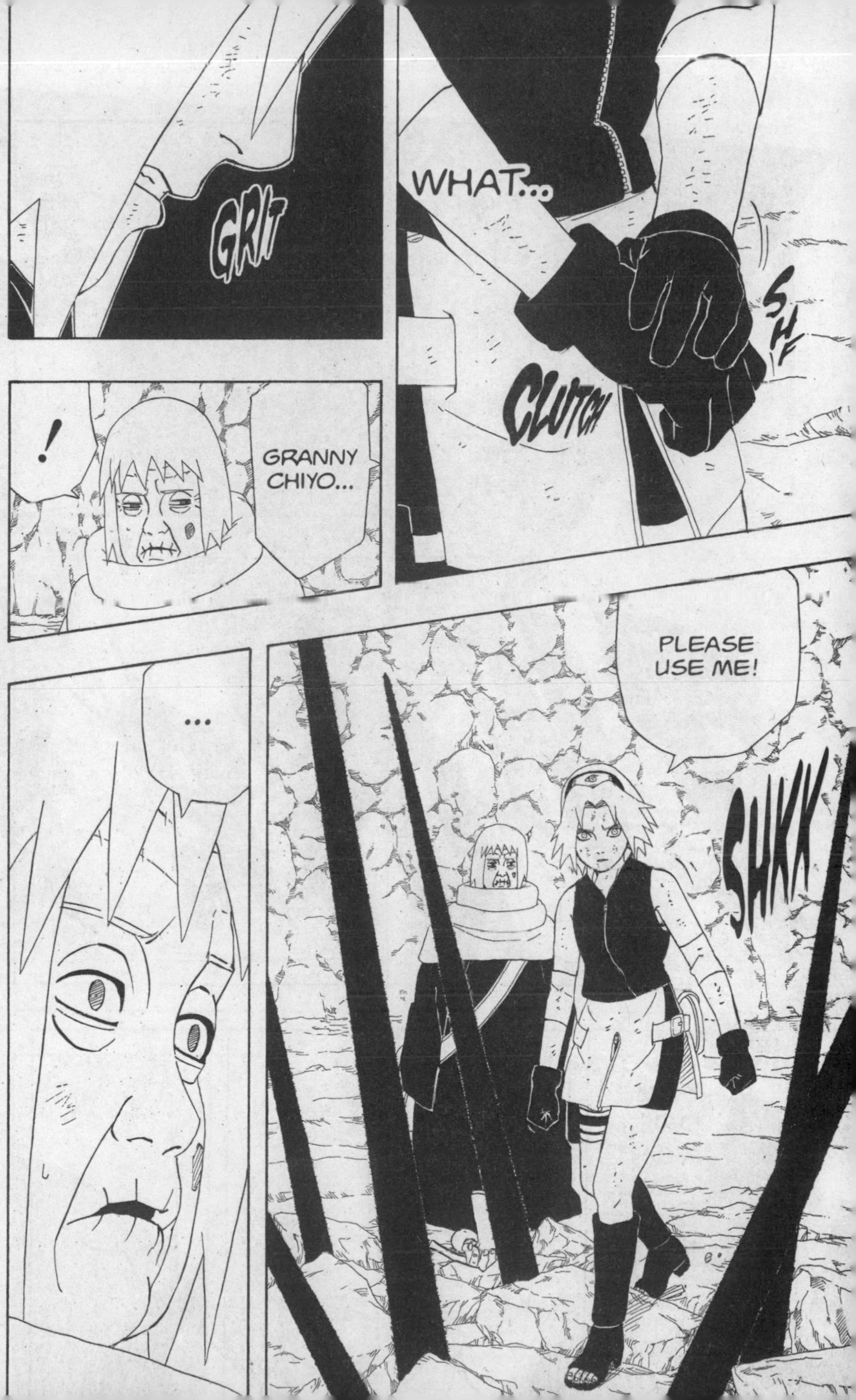
WHAT...
CLUTCH
SHF
GRIT
!
GRANNY CHIYO...
PLEASE USE ME!
SHKK
...

READ THIS WAY

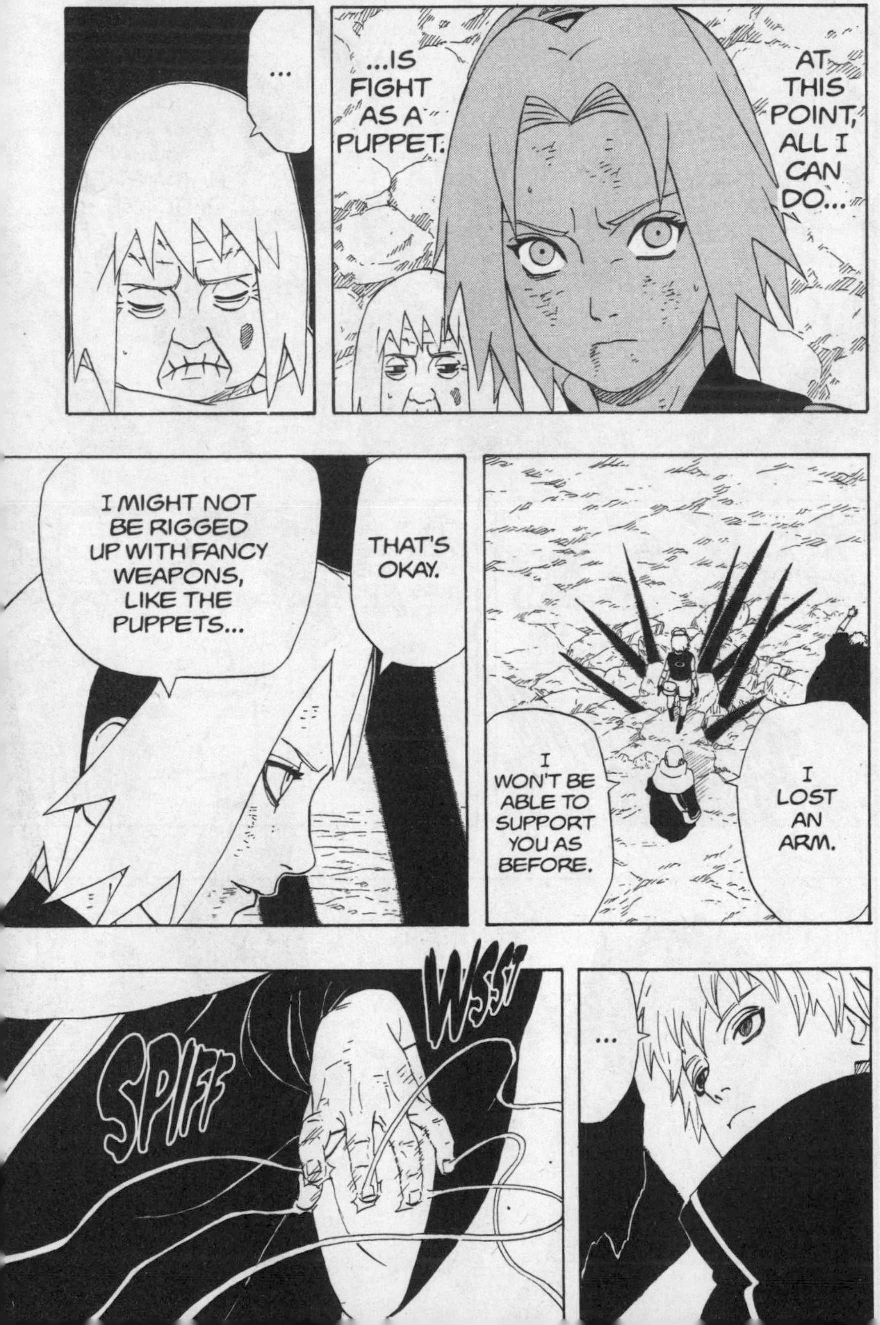

AT THIS POINT, ALL I CAN DO...
...IS FIGHT AS A PUPPET.
...
I LOST AN ARM.
I WON'T BE ABLE TO SUPPORT YOU AS BEFORE.
THAT'S OKAY.
I MIGHT NOT BE RIGGED UP WITH FANCY WEAPONS, LIKE THE PUPPETS...
...
WSST
SPIFF

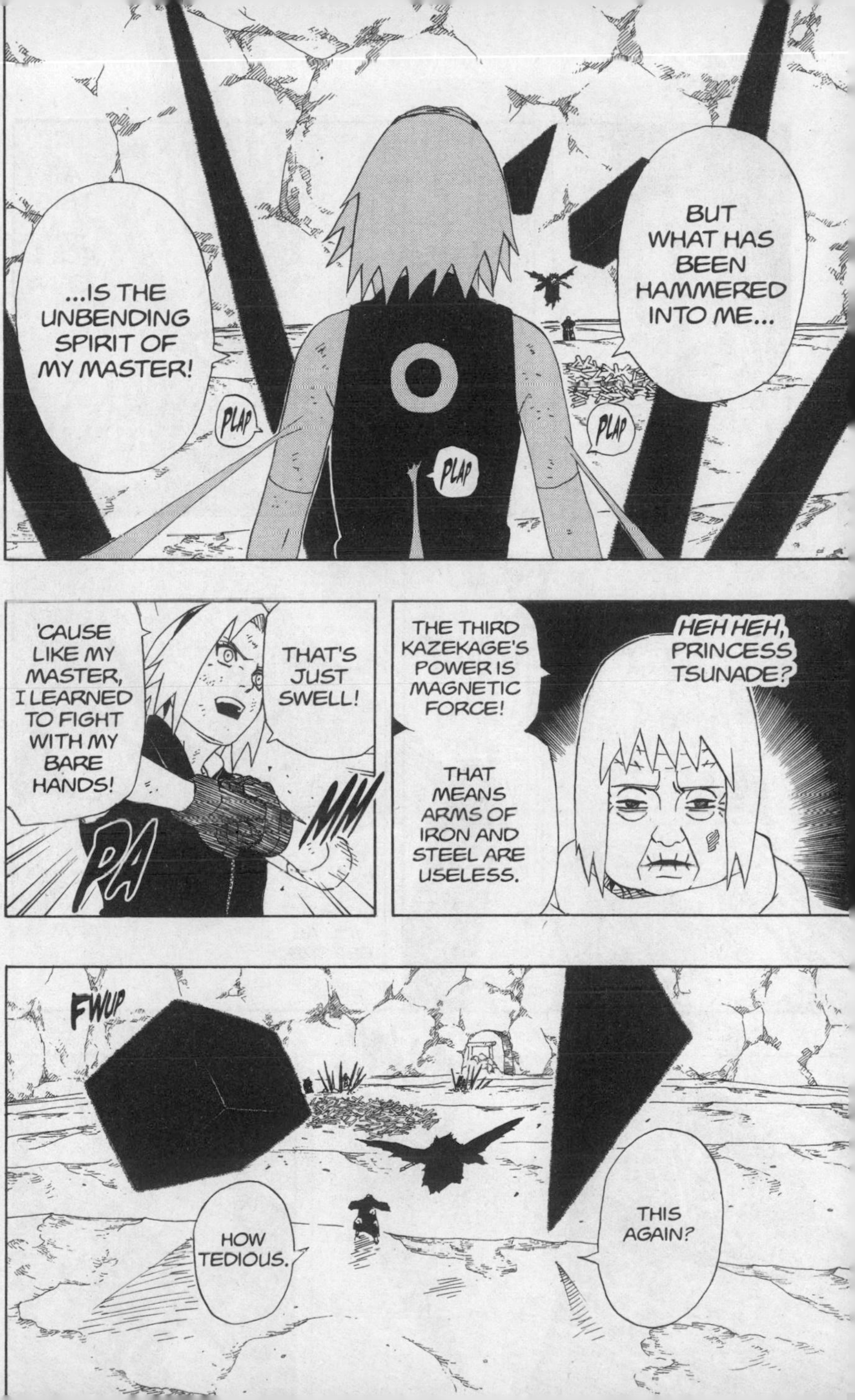
BUT WHAT HAS BEEN HAMMERED INTO ME...
...IS THE UNBENDING SPIRIT OF MY MASTER!
PLAP
PLAP
PLAP
HEH HEH, PRINCESS TSUNADE?
THE THIRD KAZEKAGE'S POWER IS MAGNETIC FORCE!
THAT MEANS ARMS OF IRON AND STEEL ARE USELESS.
THAT'S JUST SWELL!
'CAUSE LIKE MY MASTER, I LEARNED TO FIGHT WITH MY BARE HANDS!
MM
PA
FWUP
THIS AGAIN?
HOW TEDIOUS.

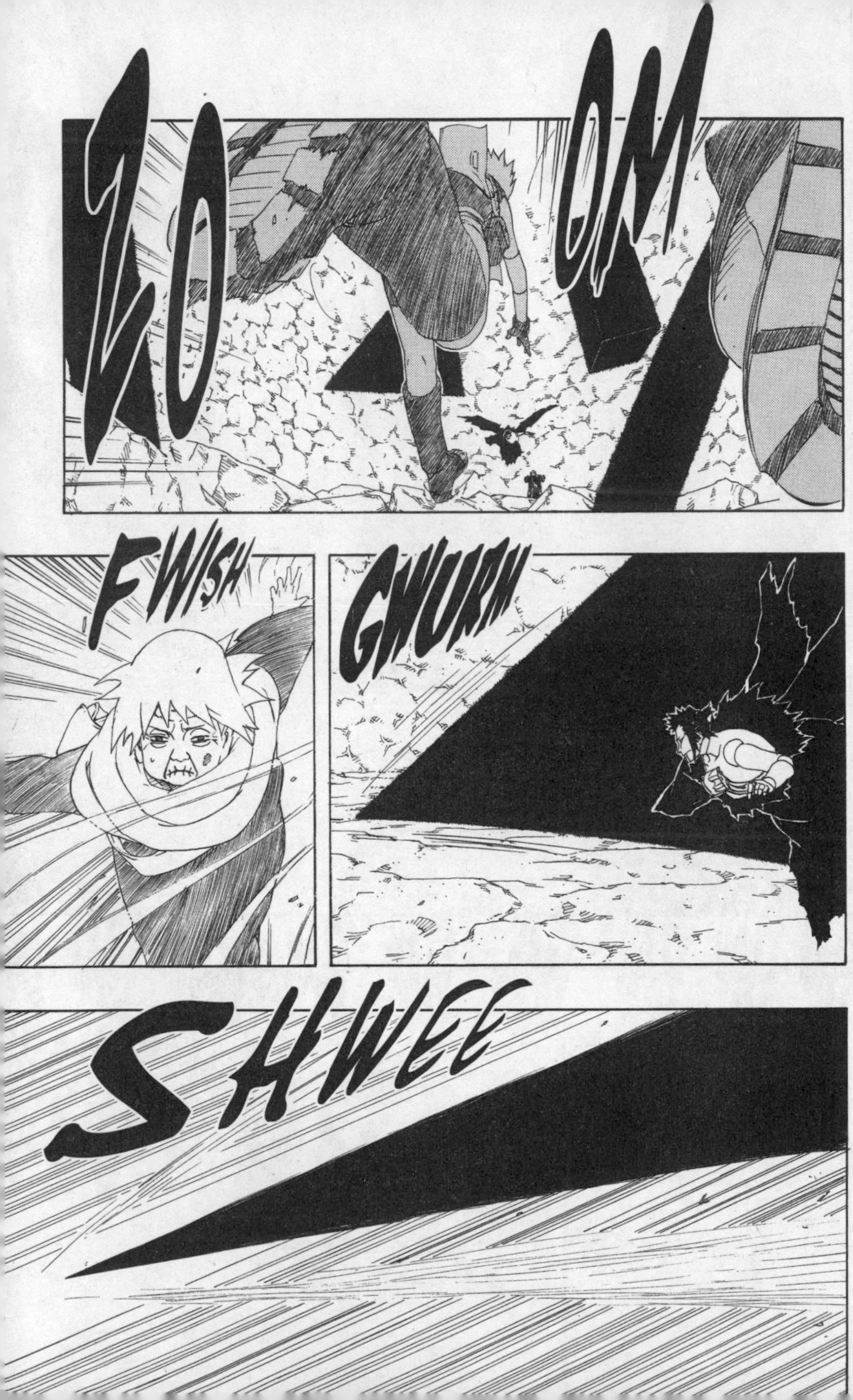
ZOOM
GWURM
FWISH
SHWEE

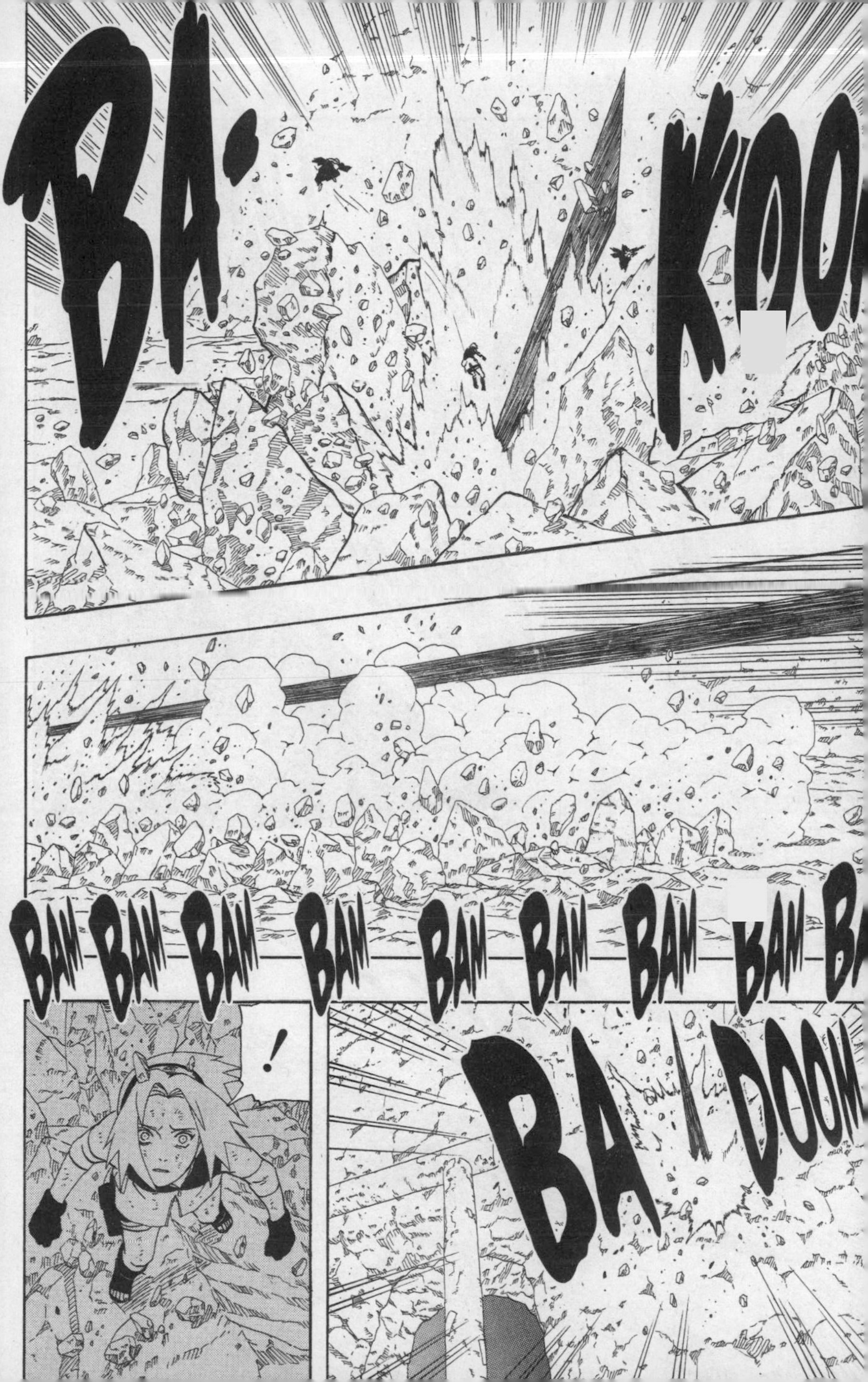
BA-
K'OO
BAM BAM BAM BAM BAM BAM BAM BAM BAM
BA-DOOM
!

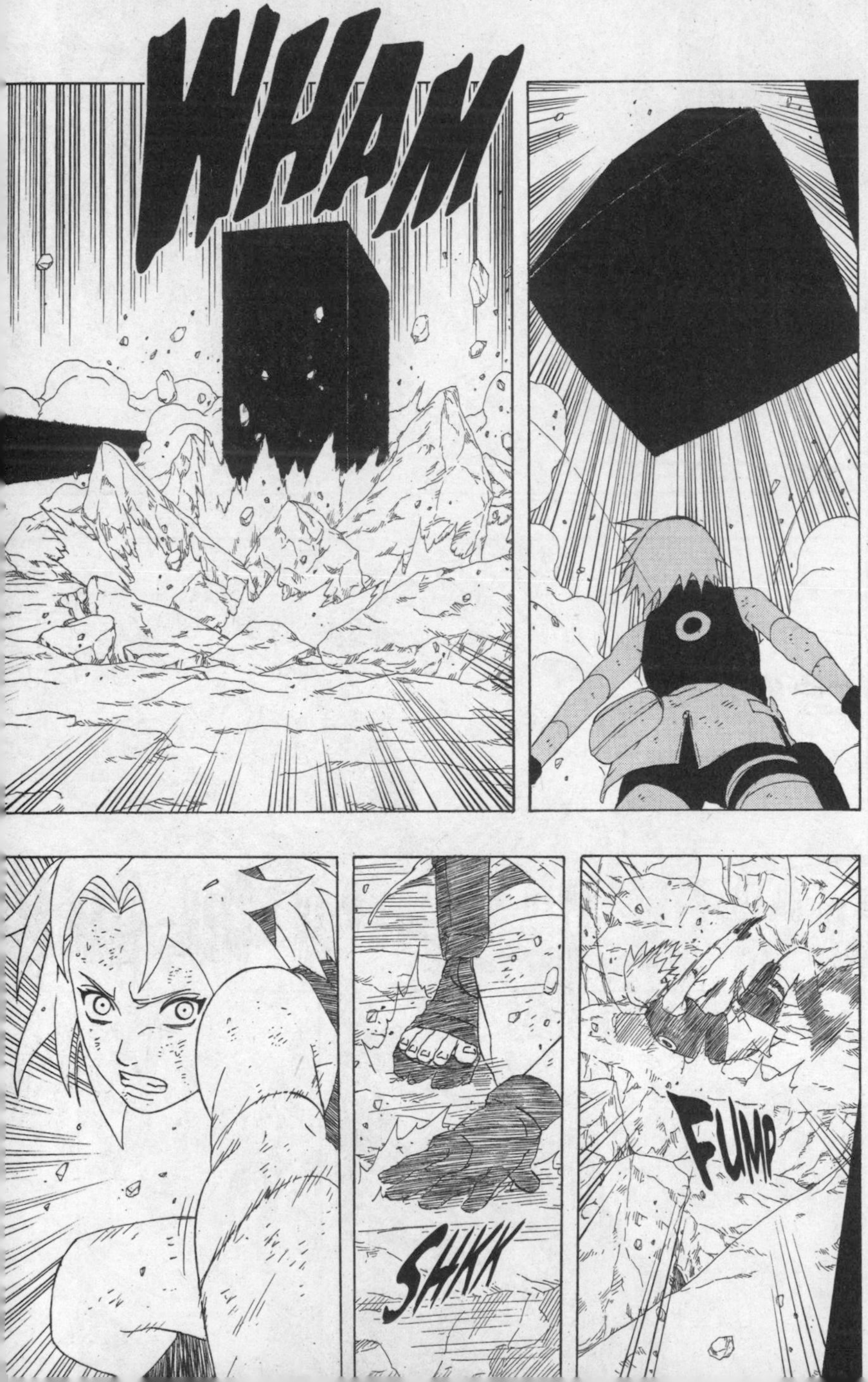
WHAM
FUMP
SHKK

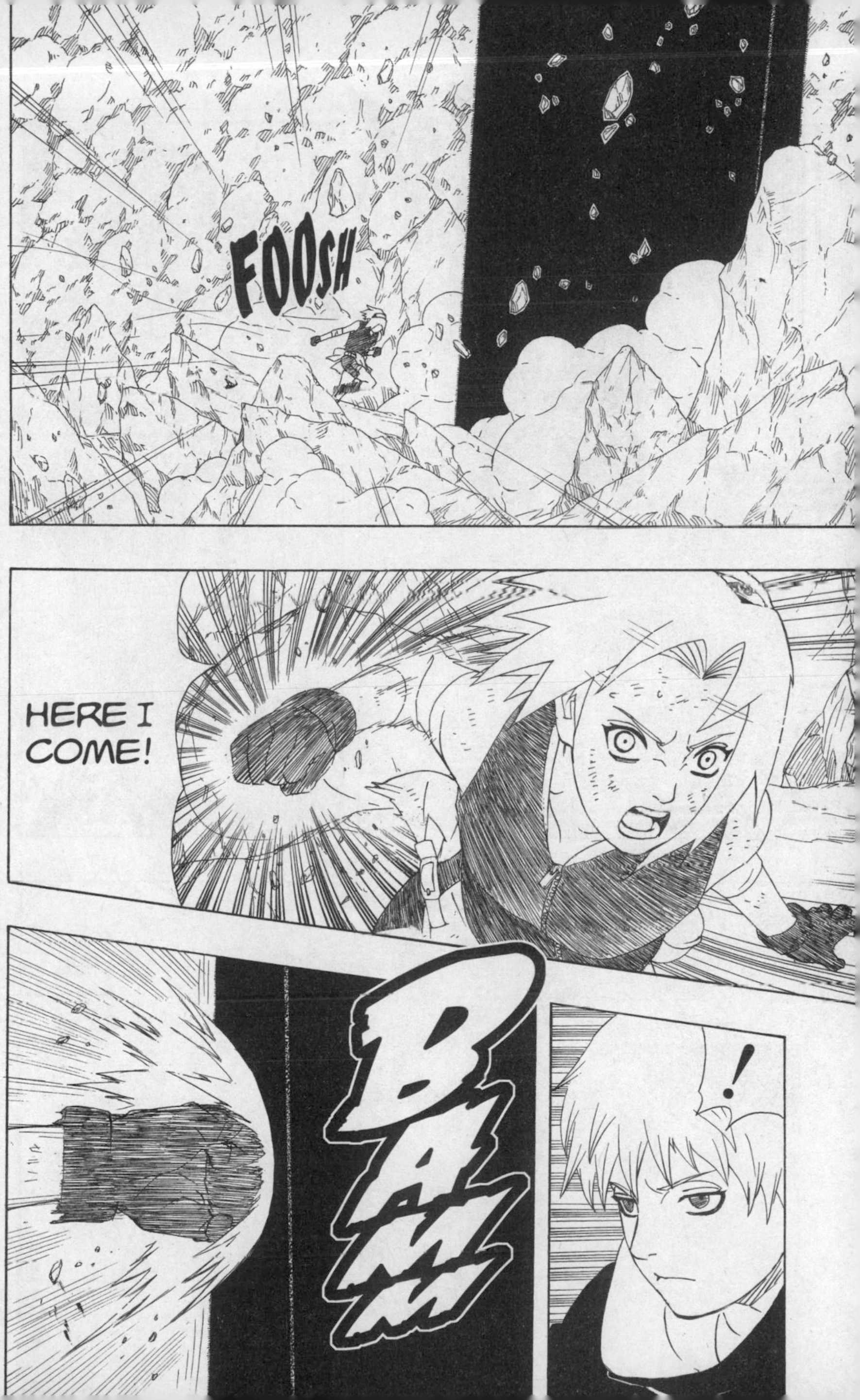
FOOSH
HERE I COME!
!
BAM

READ THIS WAY

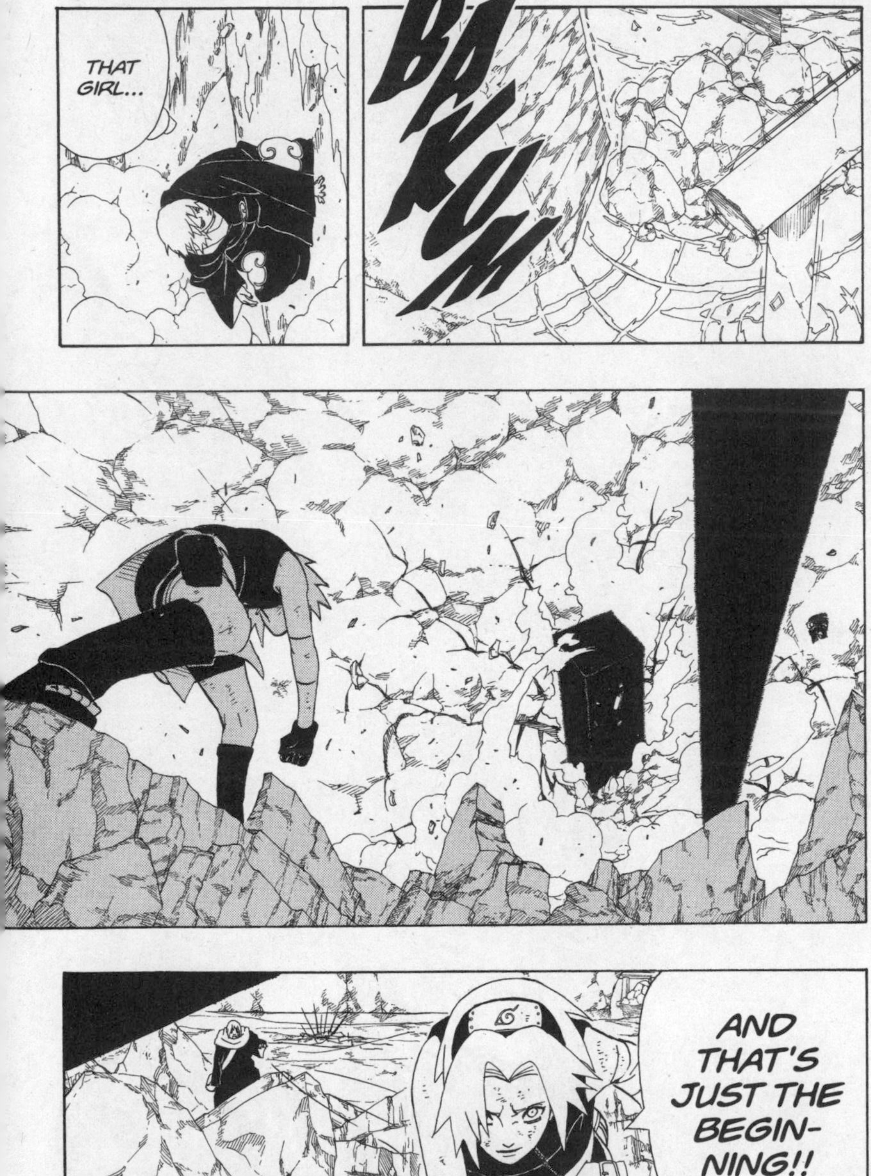
BA-KOOM
THAT GIRL...
AND THAT'S JUST THE BEGIN-NING!!

NARUTO

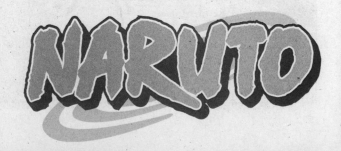

Number 270: Miscalculation...!!

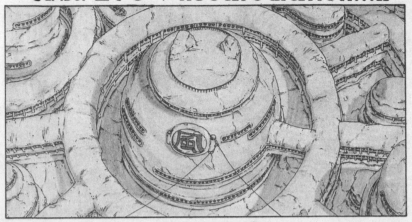

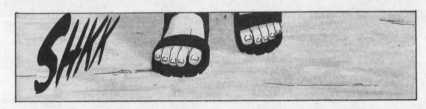

SHKK
HUF
HUF

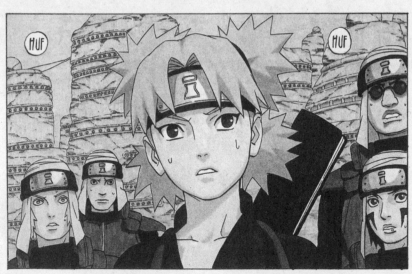

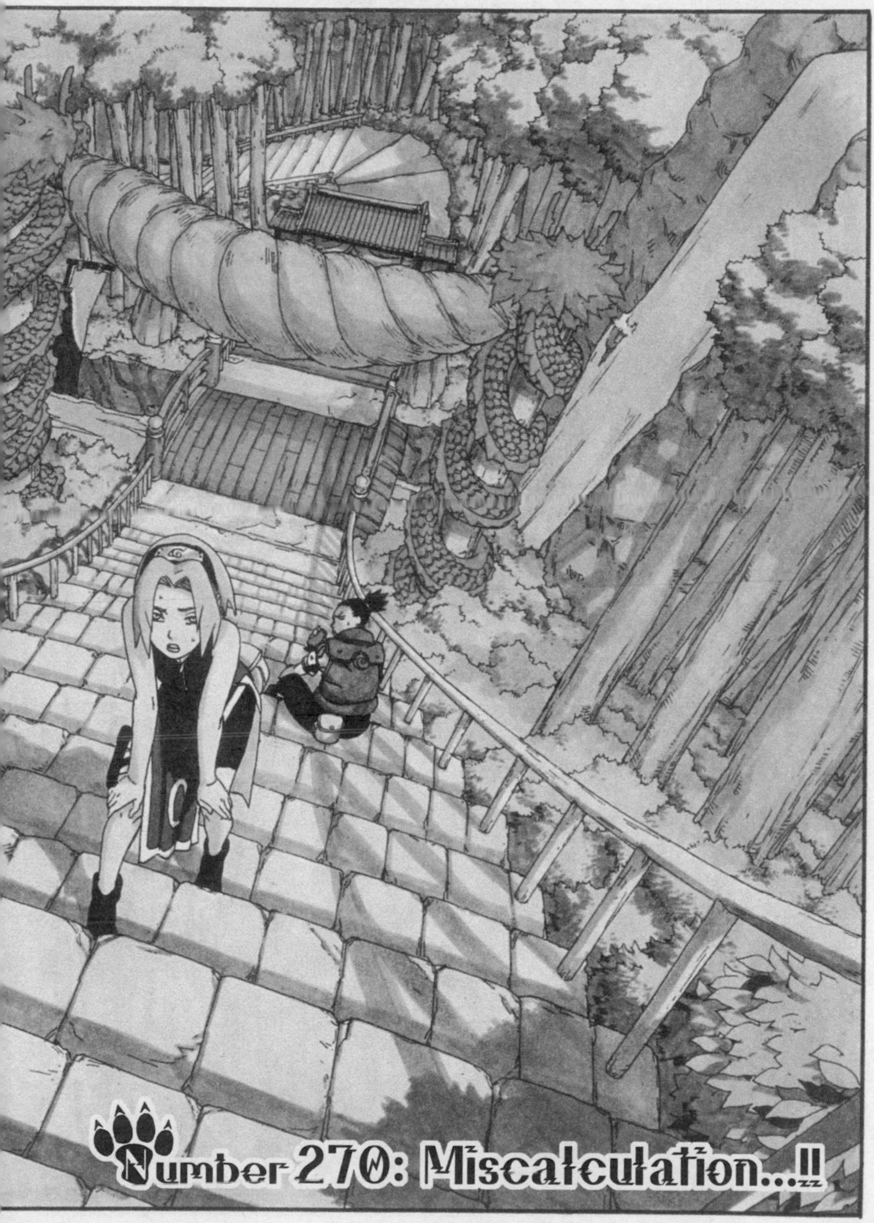
Number 270: Miscalculation...!!

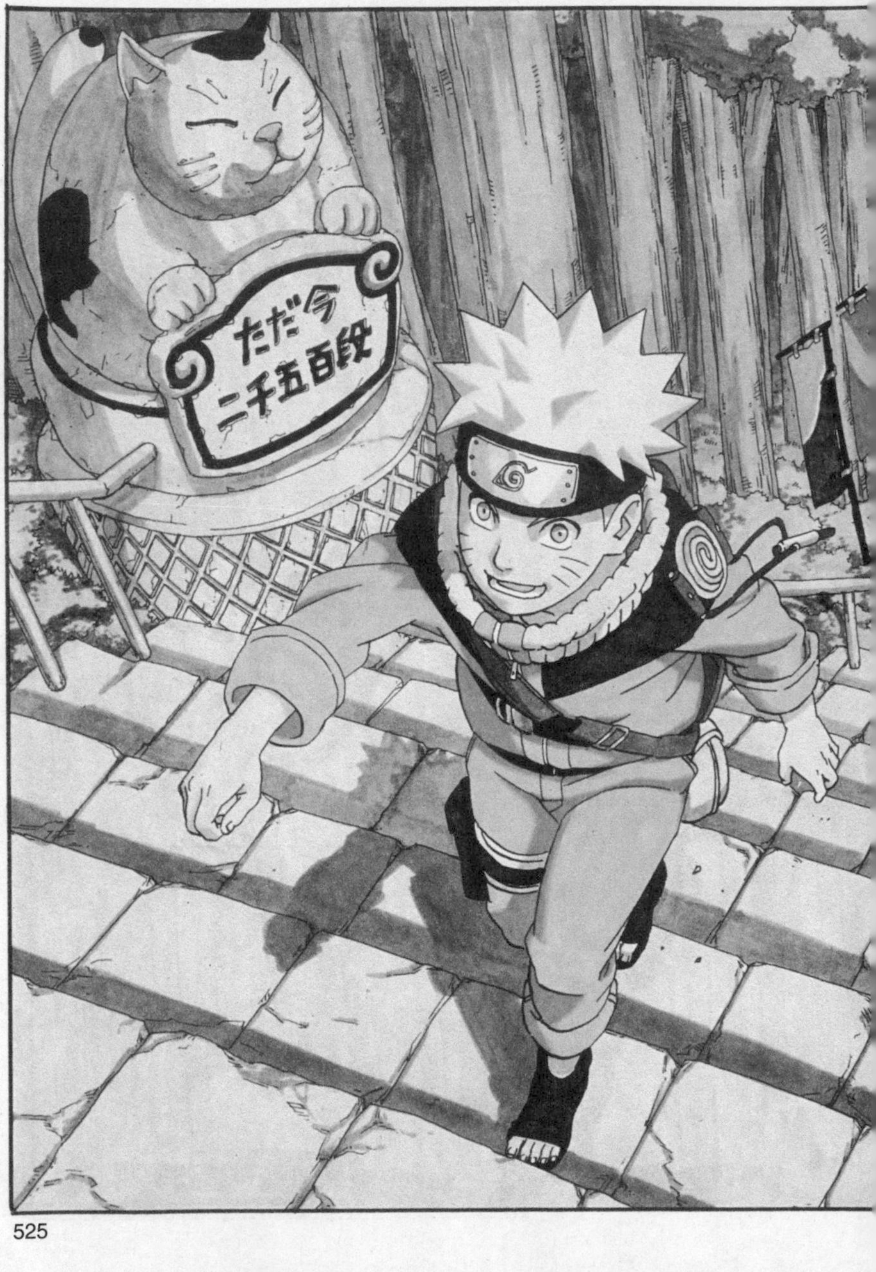
ただ今
二千五百段

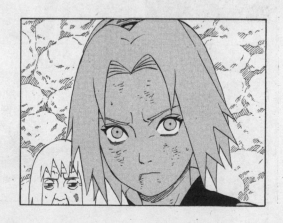

READ THIS WAY

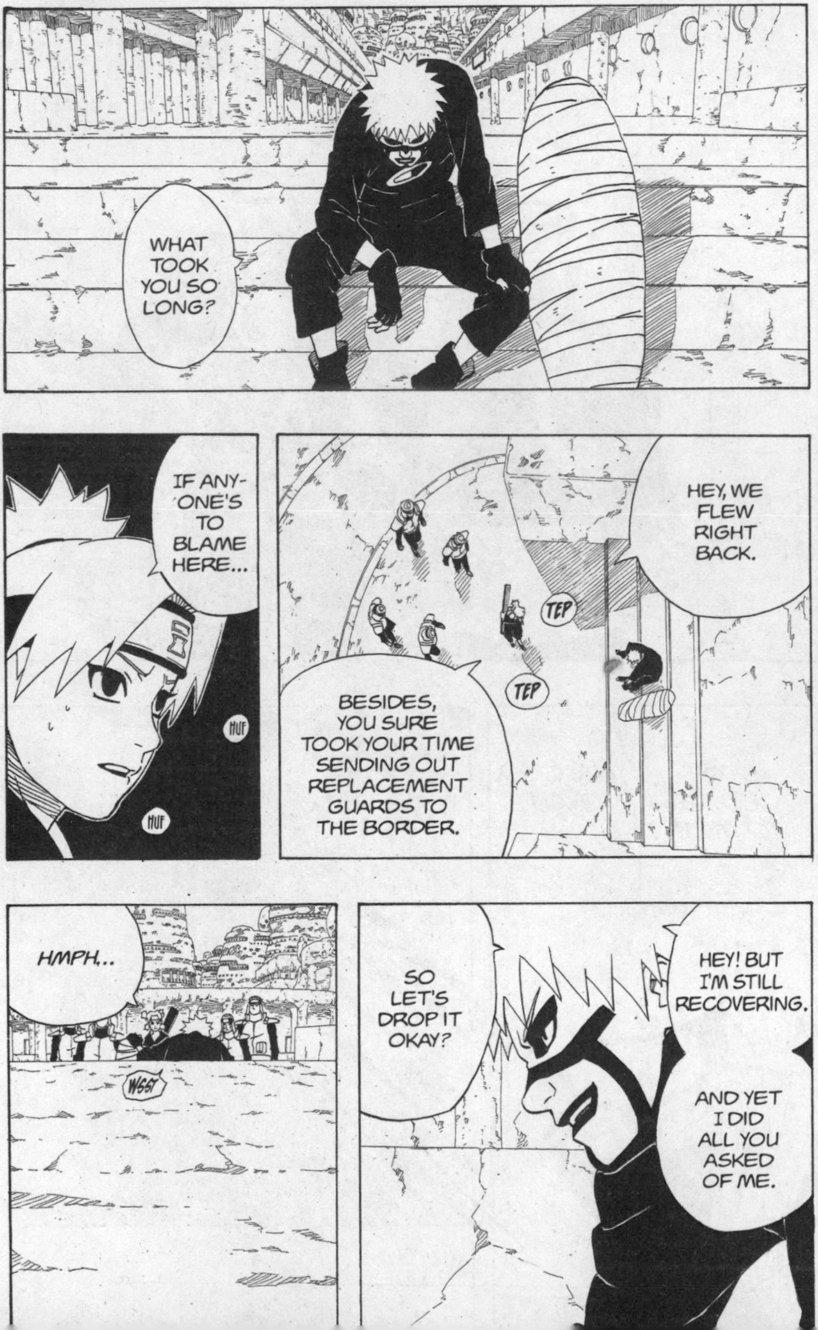
WHAT TOOK YOU SO LONG?
HEY, WE FLEW RIGHT BACK.
TEP
TEP
BESIDES, YOU SURE TOOK YOUR TIME SENDING OUT REPLACEMENT GUARDS TO THE BORDER.
IF ANY-ONE'S TO BLAME HERE...
HUF
HUF
HEY! BUT I'M STILL RECOVERING.
AND YET I DID ALL YOU ASKED OF ME.
SO LET'S DROP IT OKAY?
HMPH...
WSST

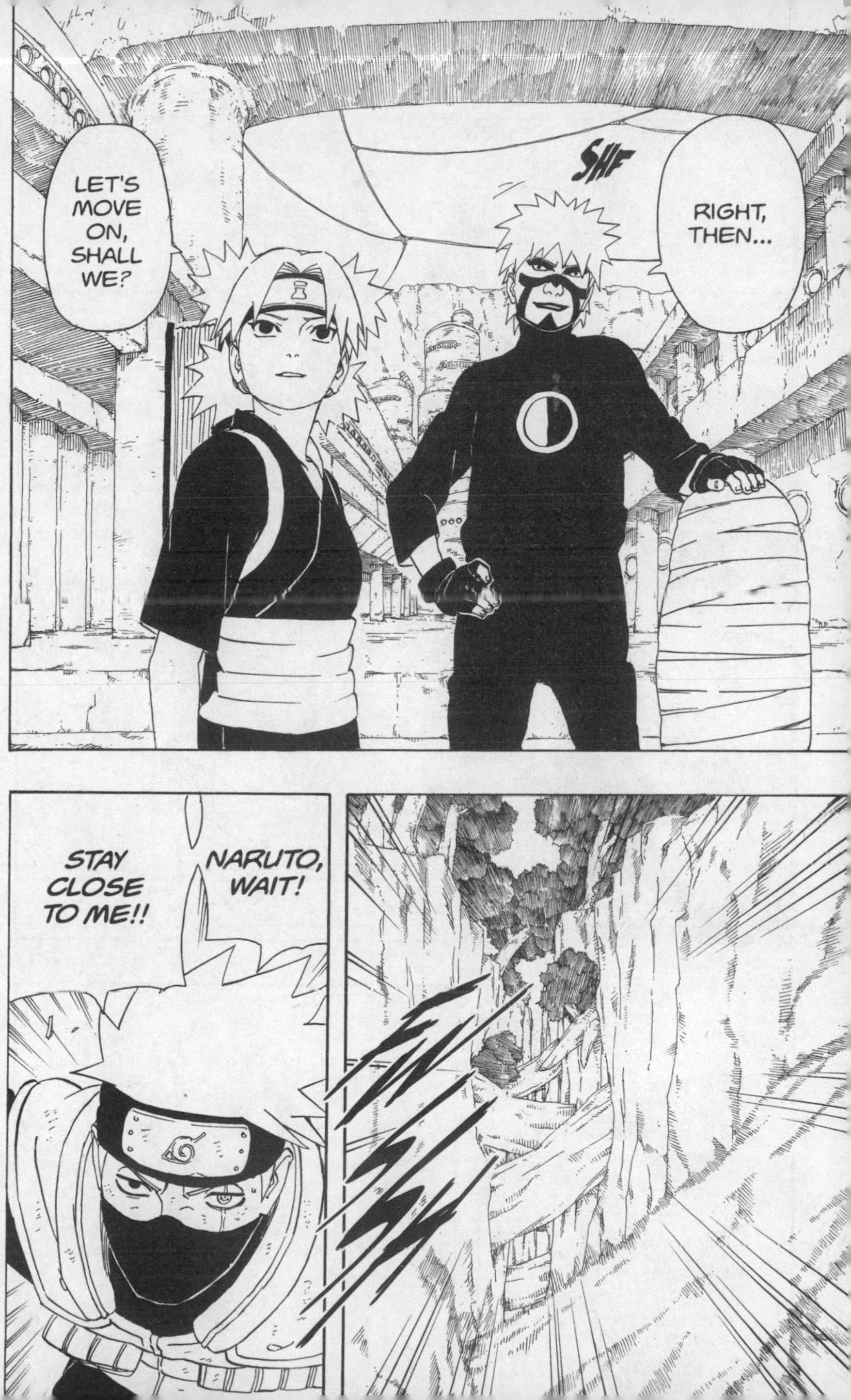
RIGHT, THEN...
SHF
LET'S MOVE ON, SHALL WE?
NARUTO, WAIT!
STAY CLOSE TO ME!!

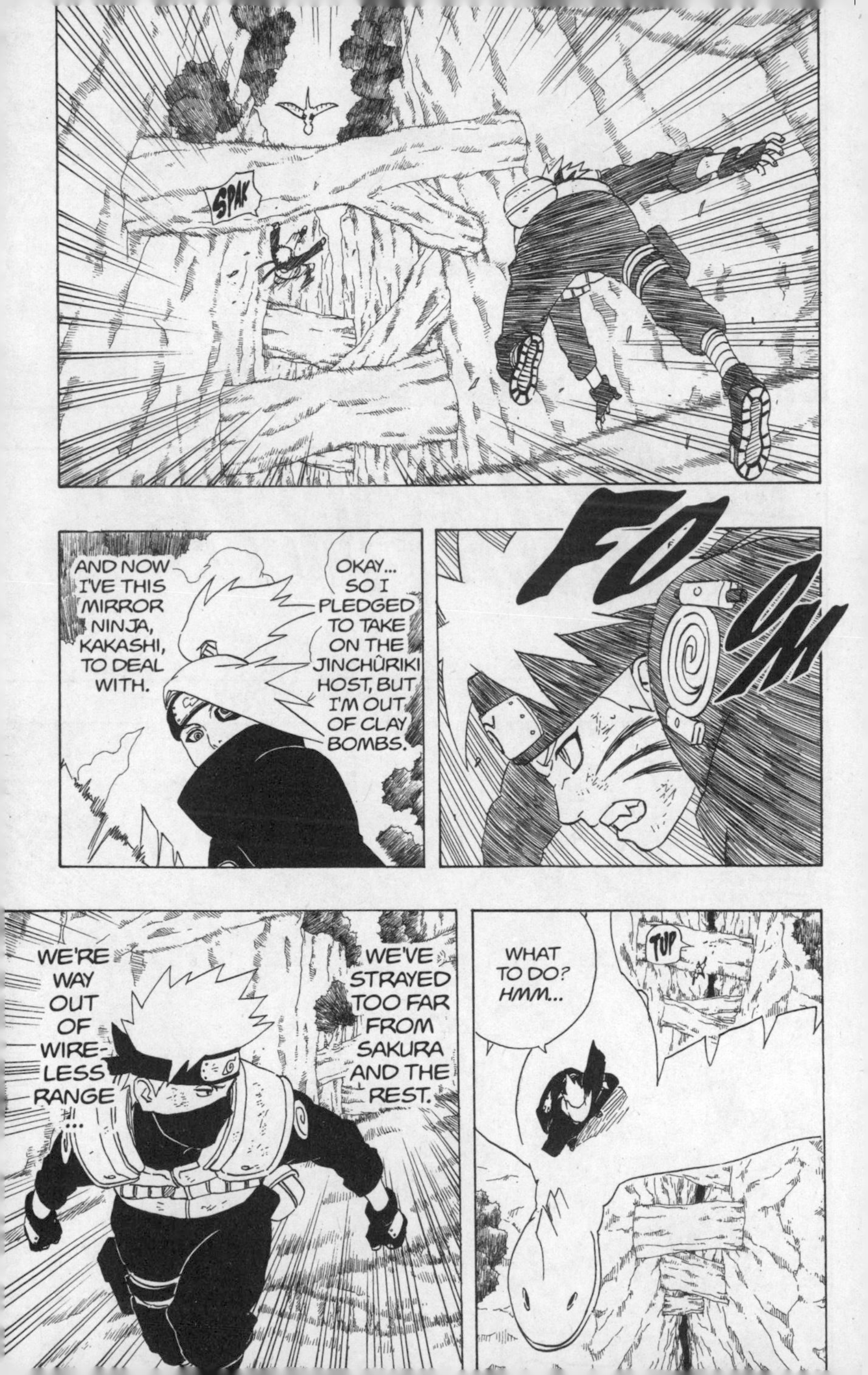
SPAK
FOOM
OKAY... SO I PLEDGED TO TAKE ON THE JINCHÛRIKI HOST, BUT I'M OUT OF CLAY BOMBS.
AND NOW I'VE THIS MIRROR NINJA, KAKASHI, TO DEAL WITH.
TUP
WHAT TO DO? HMM...
WE'VE STRAYED TOO FAR FROM SAKURA AND THE REST.
WE'RE WAY OUT OF WIRE-LESS RANGE...

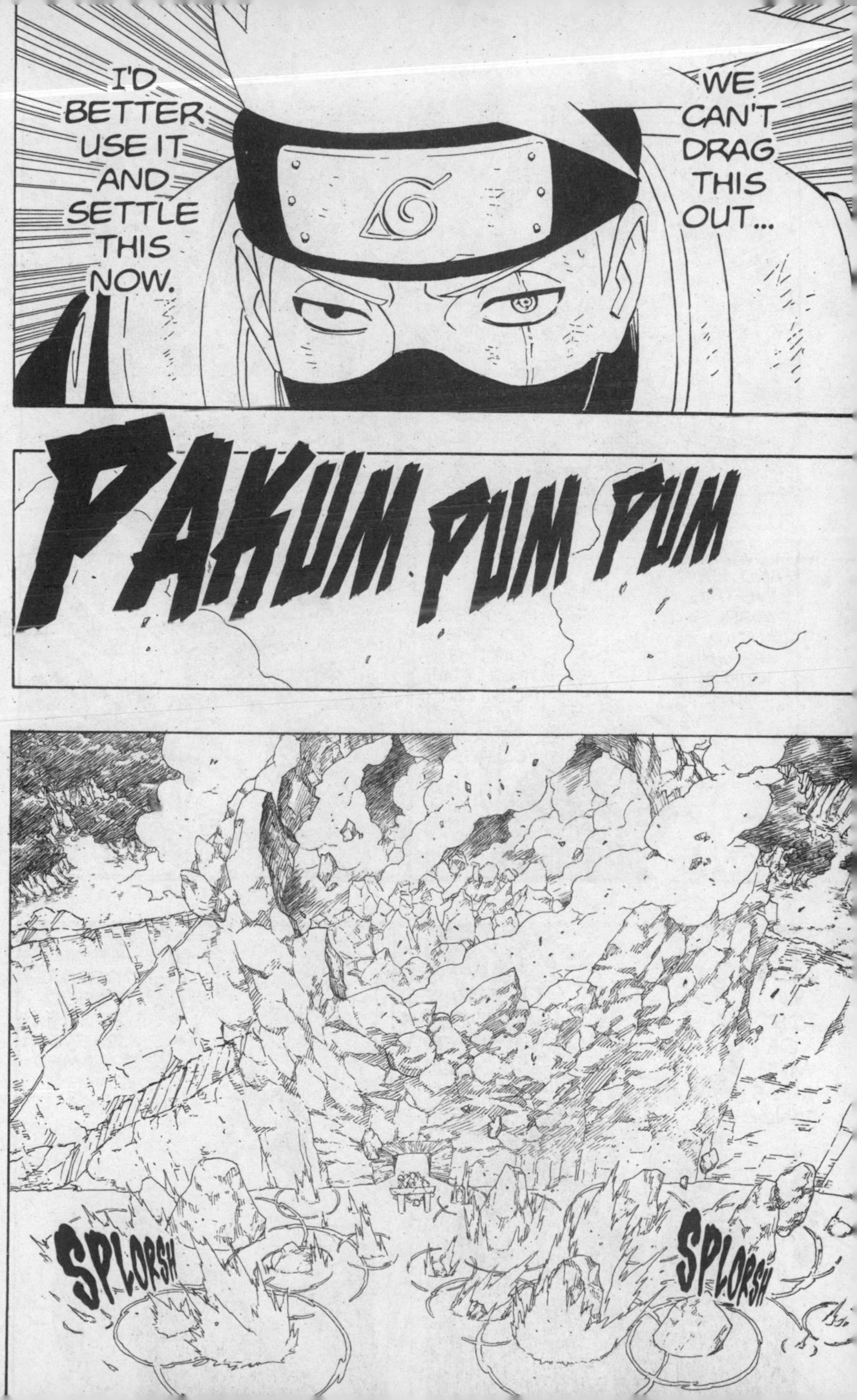
WE CAN'T DRAG THIS OUT...
I'D BETTER USE IT AND SETTLE THIS NOW.
PAKUM PUM PUM
SPLORSH
SPLORSH

READ THIS WAY

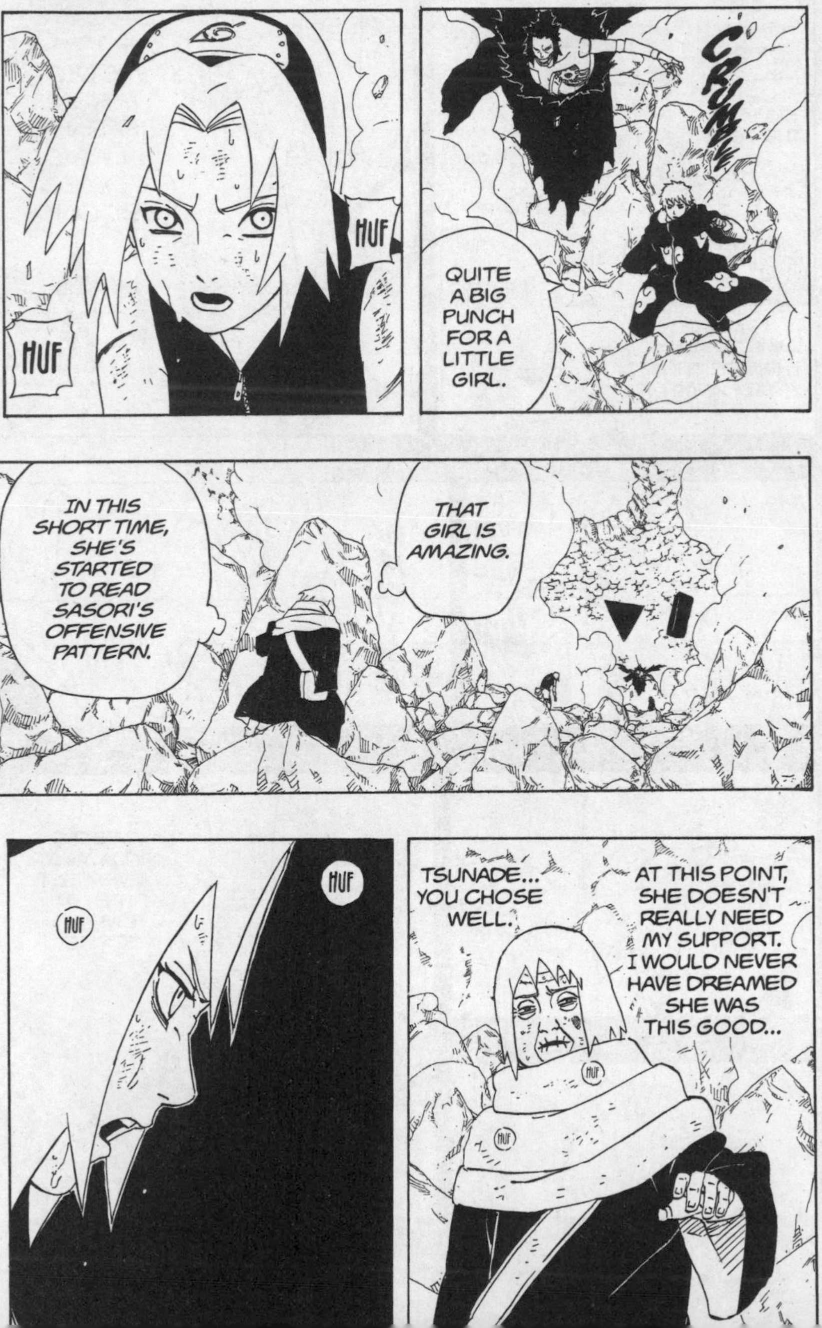
CRUMBLE
QUITE A BIG PUNCH FOR A LITTLE GIRL.
HUF
HUF
THAT GIRL IS AMAZING.
IN THIS SHORT TIME, SHE'S STARTED TO READ SASORI'S OFFENSIVE PATTERN.
AT THIS POINT, SHE DOESN'T REALLY NEED MY SUPPORT. I WOULD NEVER HAVE DREAMED SHE WAS THIS GOOD...
TSUNADE... YOU CHOSE WELL.
HUF
HUF
HUF
HUF

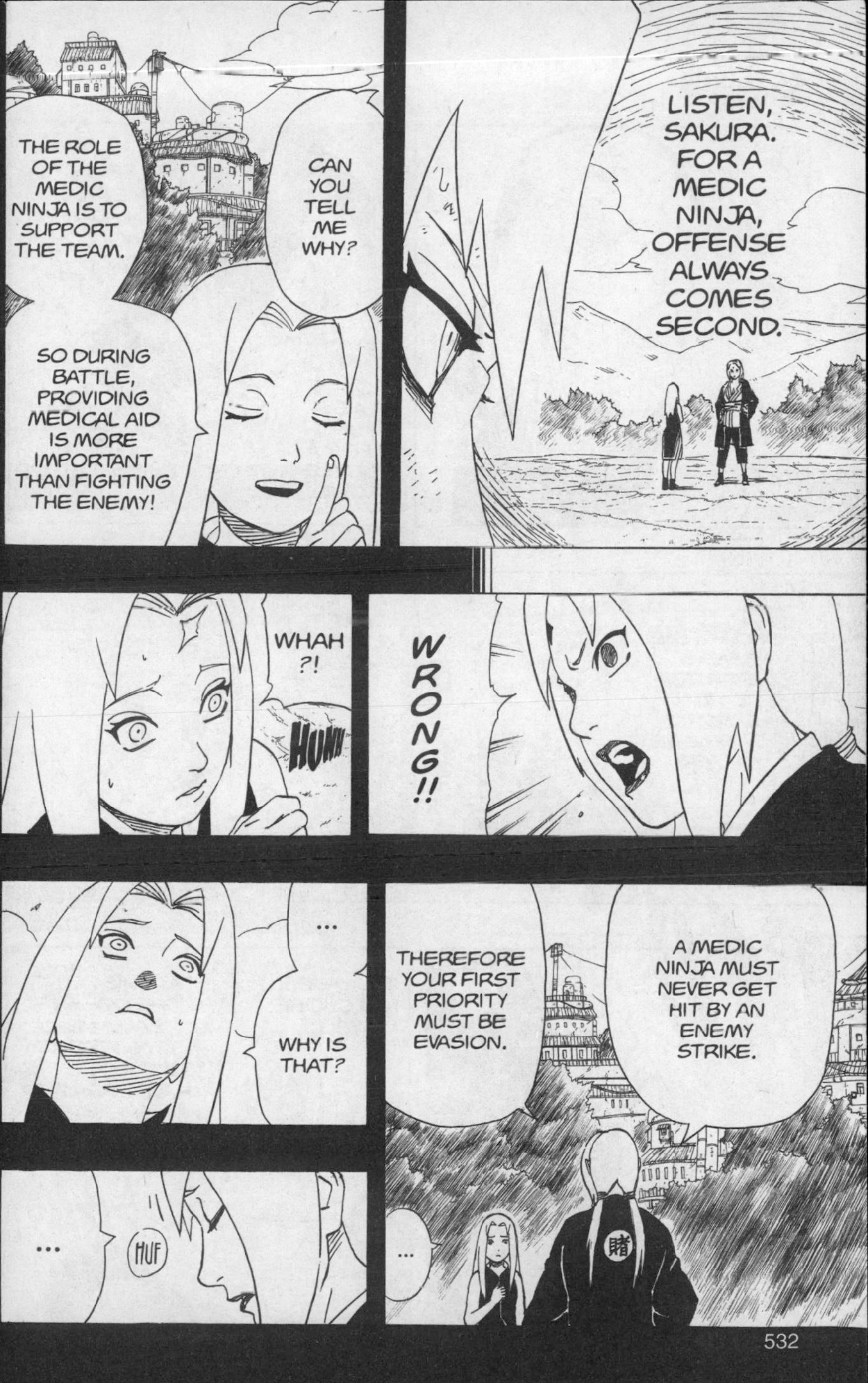
LISTEN, SAKURA. FOR A MEDIC NINJA, OFFENSE ALWAYS COMES SECOND.
CAN YOU TELL ME WHY?
THE ROLE OF THE MEDIC NINJA IS TO SUPPORT THE TEAM.
SO DURING BATTLE, PROVIDING MEDICAL AID IS MORE IMPORTANT THAN FIGHTING THE ENEMY!
WRONG!!
WHAH ?!
HUMM
A MEDIC NINJA MUST NEVER GET HIT BY AN ENEMY STRIKE.
THEREFORE YOUR FIRST PRIORITY MUST BE EVASION.
...
...
WHY IS THAT?
HUF
...

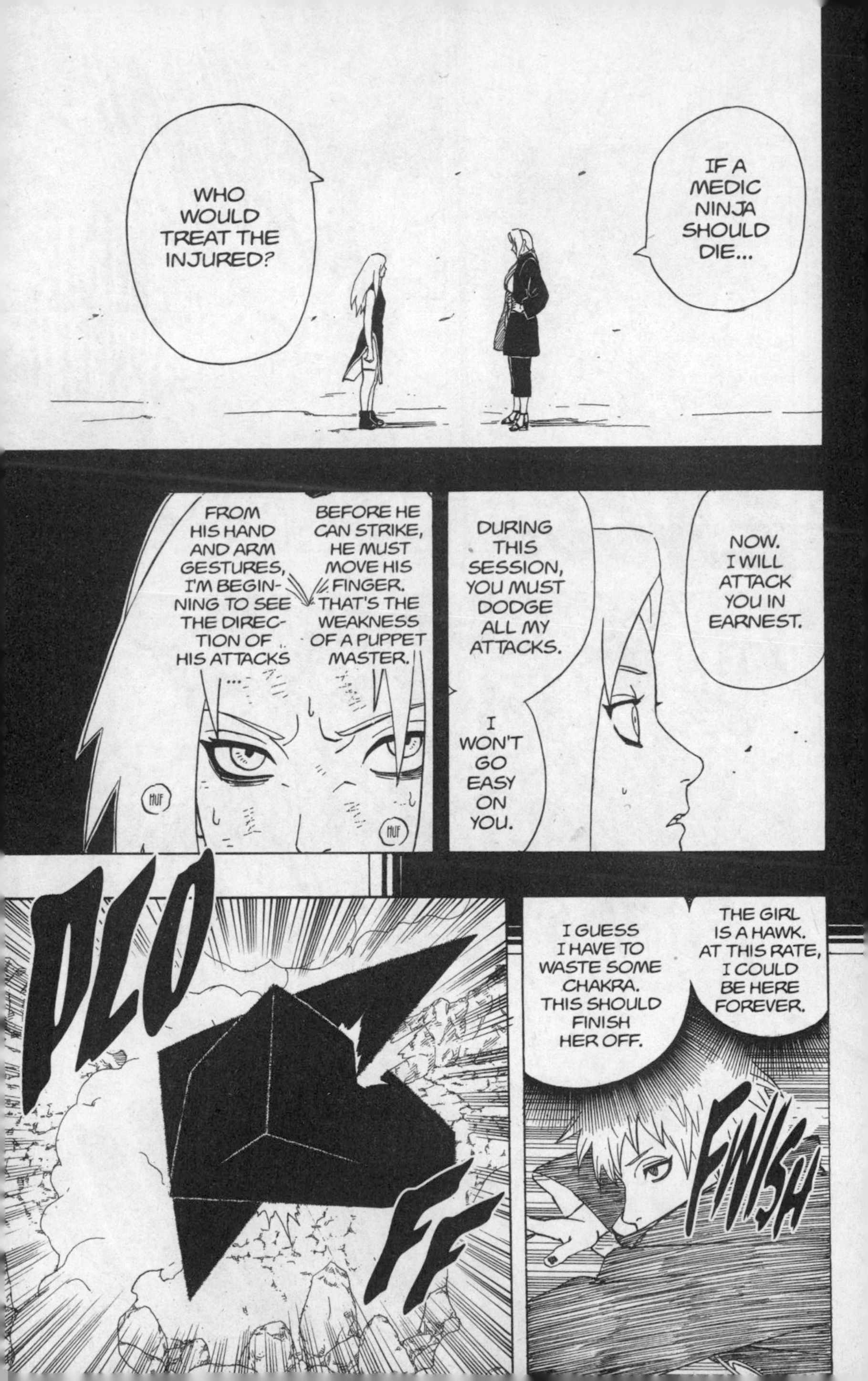
IF A MEDIC NINJA SHOULD DIE...
WHO WOULD TREAT THE INJURED?
NOW. I WILL ATTACK YOU IN EARNEST.
DURING THIS SESSION, YOU MUST DODGE ALL MY ATTACKS.
I WON'T GO EASY ON YOU.
BEFORE HE CAN STRIKE, HE MUST MOVE HIS FINGER. THAT'S THE WEAKNESS OF A PUPPET MASTER.
FROM HIS HAND AND ARM GESTURES, I'M BEGIN-NING TO SEE THE DIREC-TION OF HIS ATTACKS...
HUF
HUF
THE GIRL IS A HAWK. AT THIS RATE, I COULD BE HERE FOREVER.
I GUESS I HAVE TO WASTE SOME CHAKRA. THIS SHOULD FINISH HER OFF.
FWISH
DLOFF

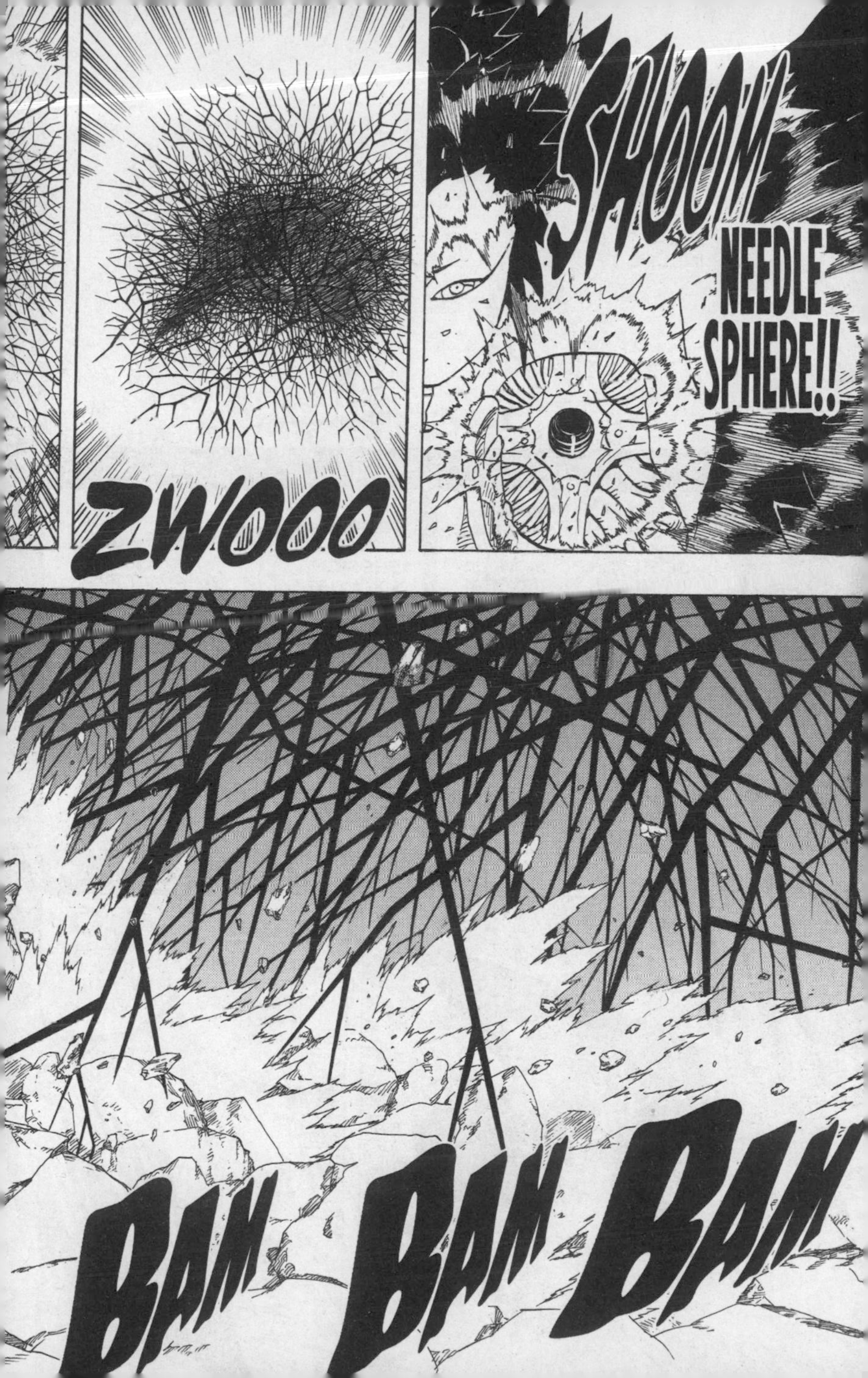
SHOOM
NEEDLE SPHERE!!
ZWOOO
BAM BAM BAM

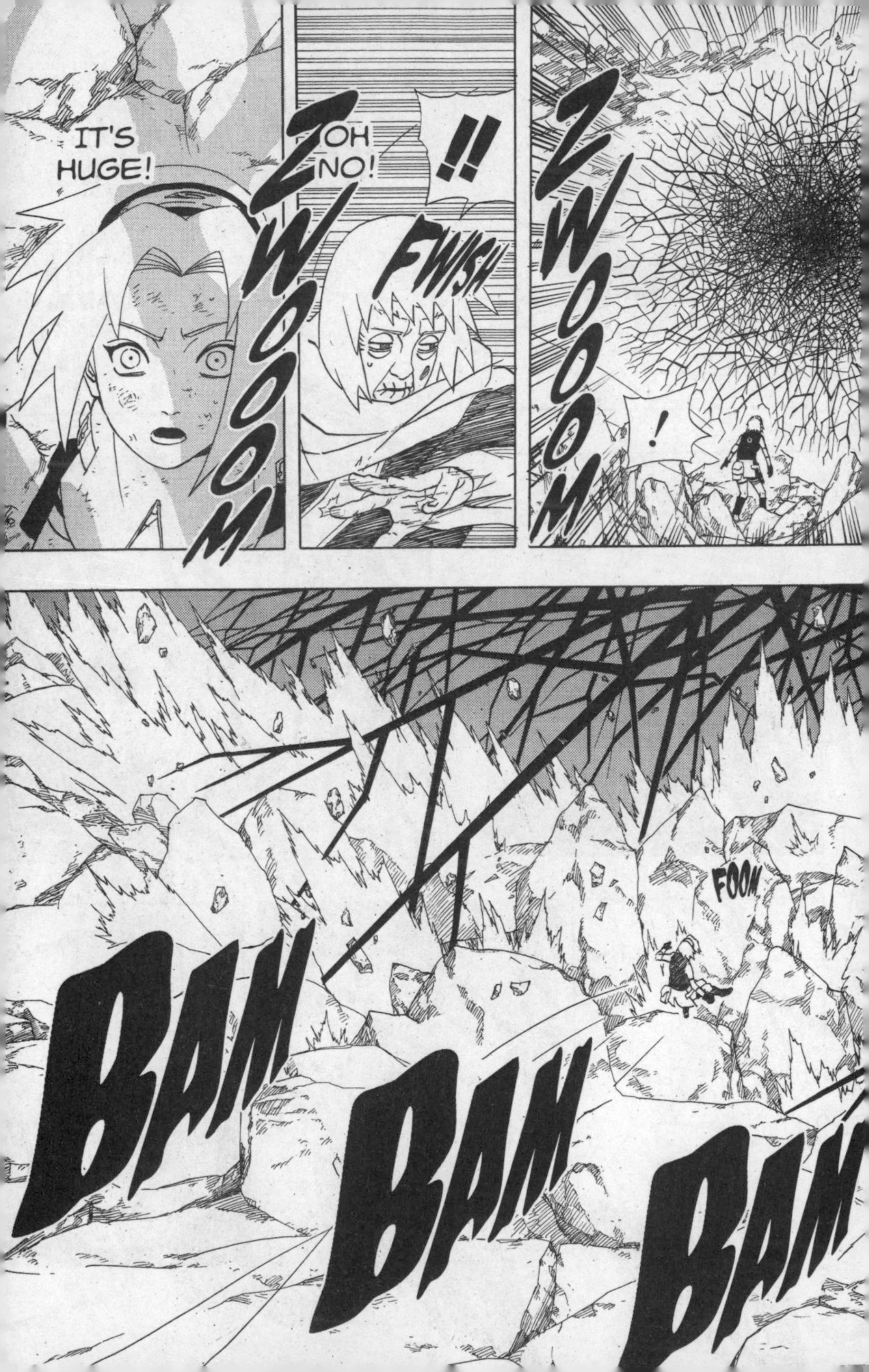
ZWOOOOM
!
OH NO!
!!
FWISH
IT'S HUGE!
ZWOOOOM
FOOM
BAM
BAM
BAM

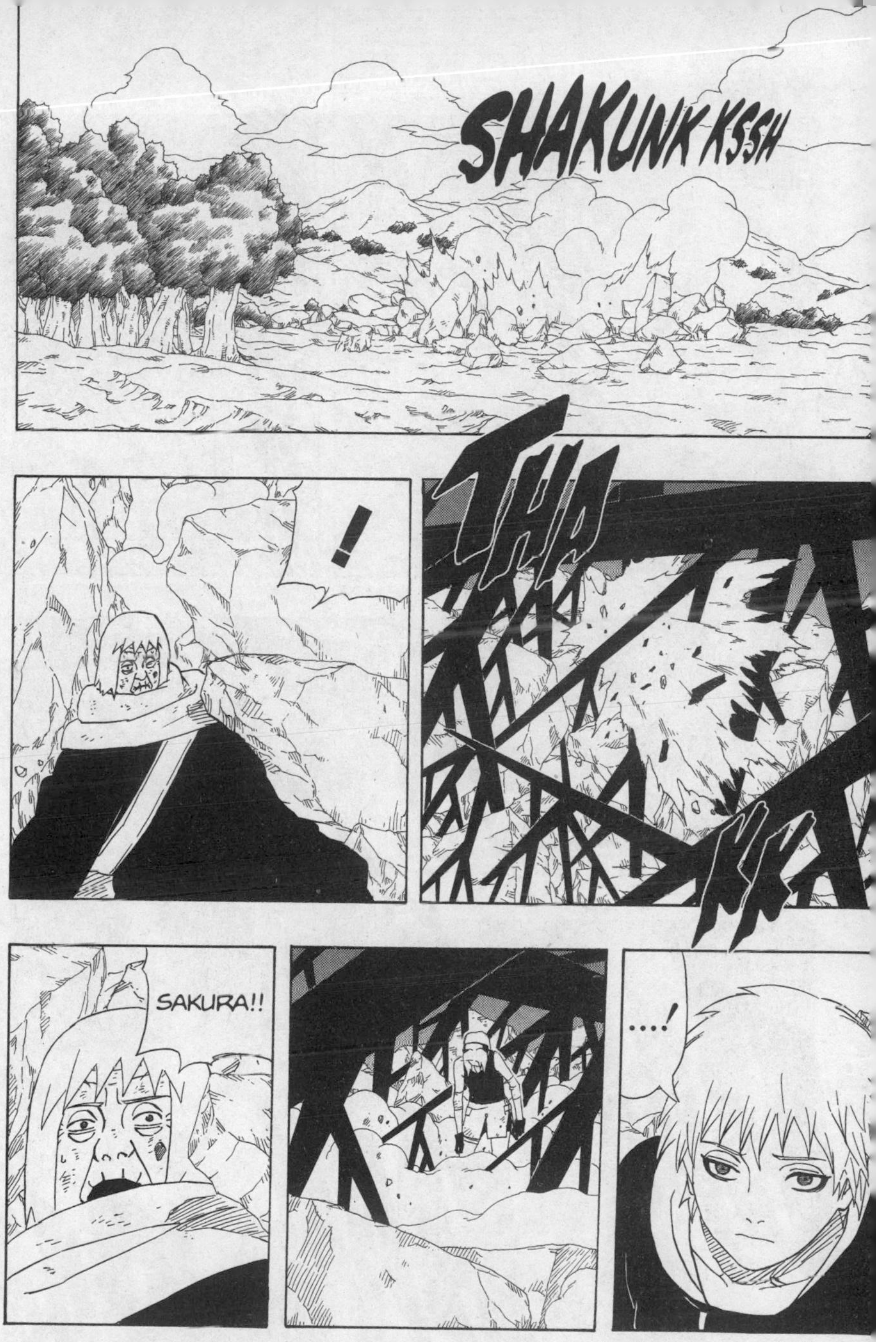
SHAKUNK KSSH
!
...!
SAKURA!!

READ THIS WAY

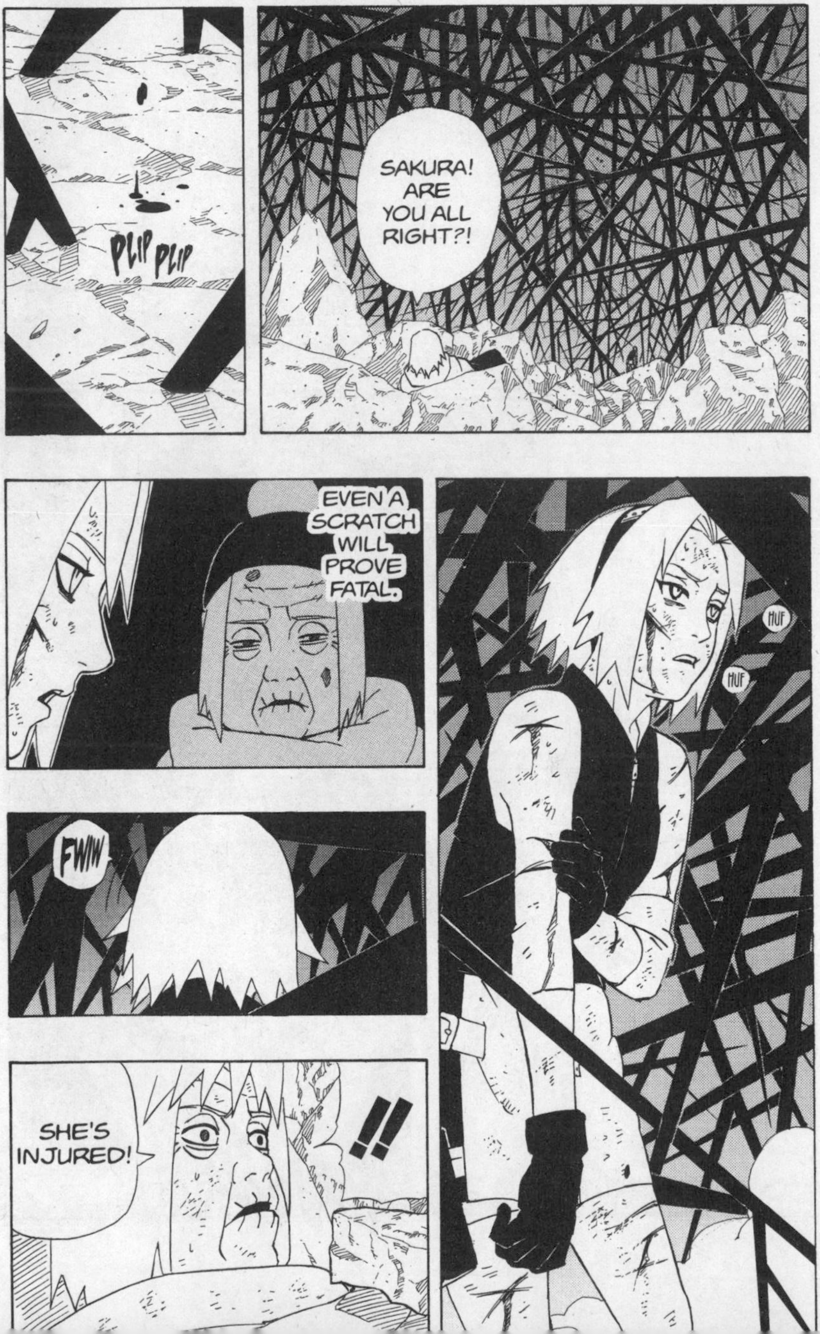
SAKURA! ARE YOU ALL RIGHT?!
PLIP PLIP
HUF
HUF
EVEN A SCRATCH WILL PROVE FATAL.
FWIW
SHE'S INJURED!
!!

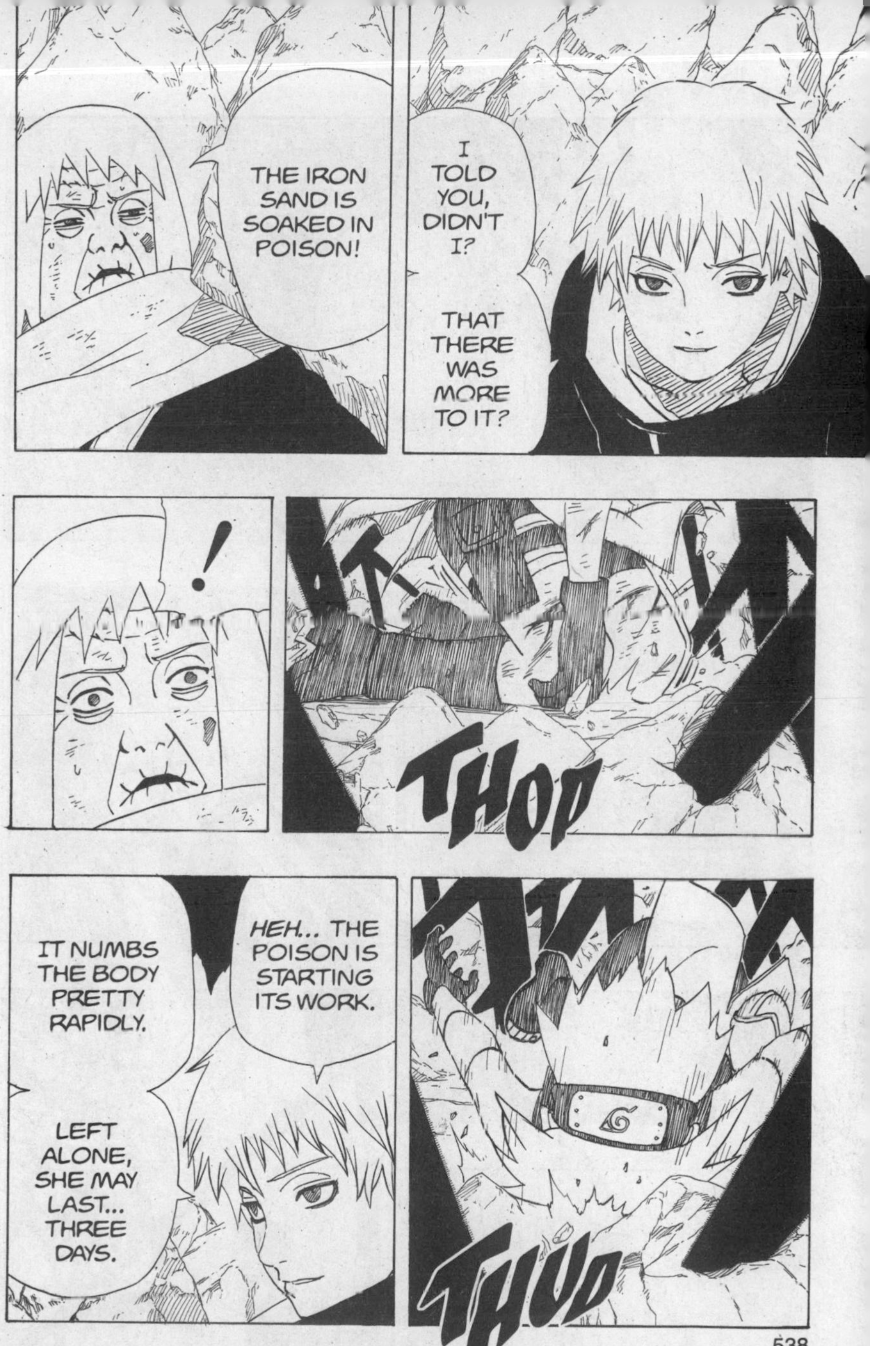
I TOLD YOU, DIDN'T I?
THAT THERE WAS MORE TO IT?
THE IRON SAND IS SOAKED IN POISON!
THOP
!
THUD
HEH... THE POISON IS STARTING ITS WORK.
IT NUMBS THE BODY PRETTY RAPIDLY.
LEFT ALONE, SHE MAY LAST... THREE DAYS.

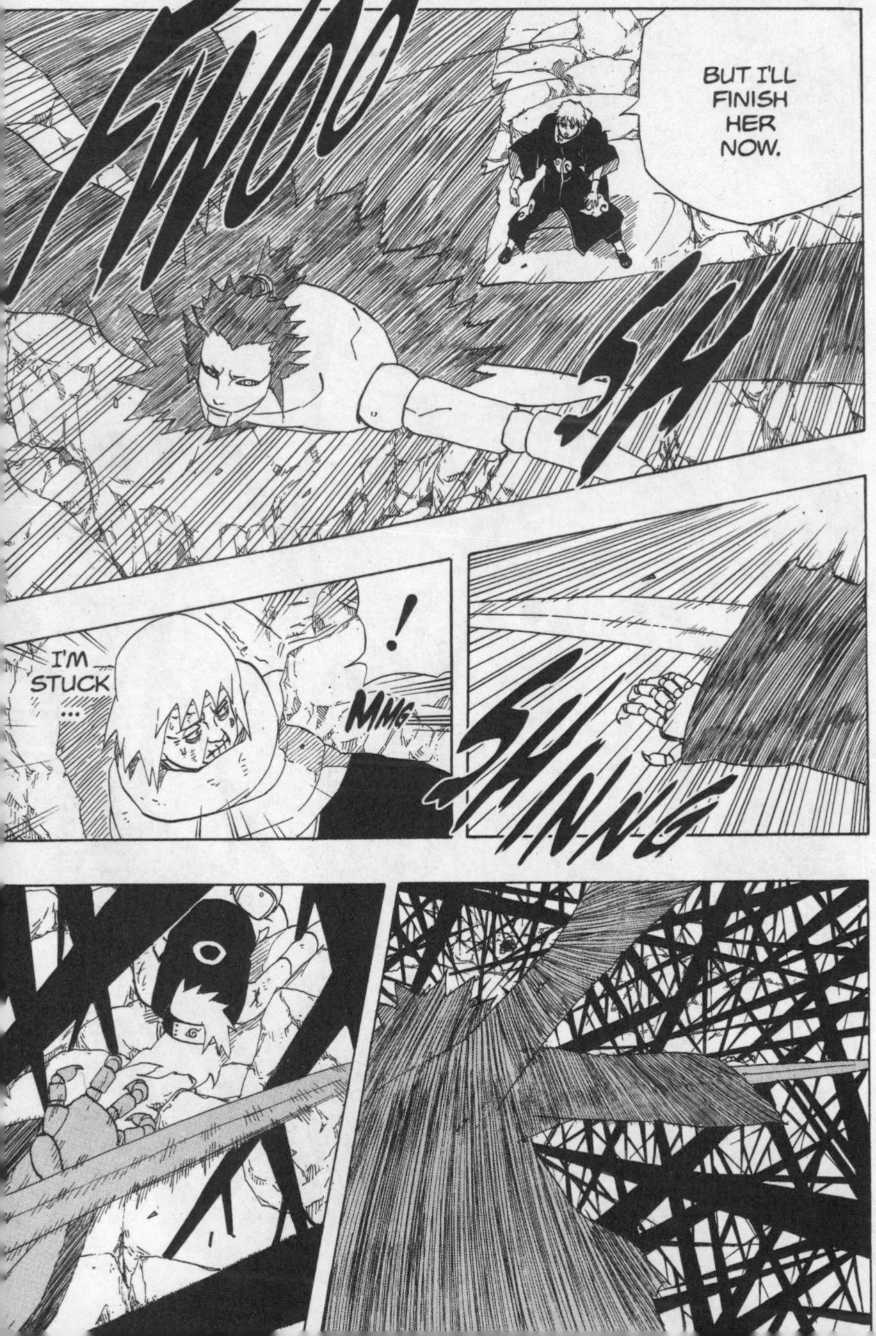
BUT I'LL FINISH HER NOW.
FWOOO
SH
SHING
!
MMG
I'M STUCK ...

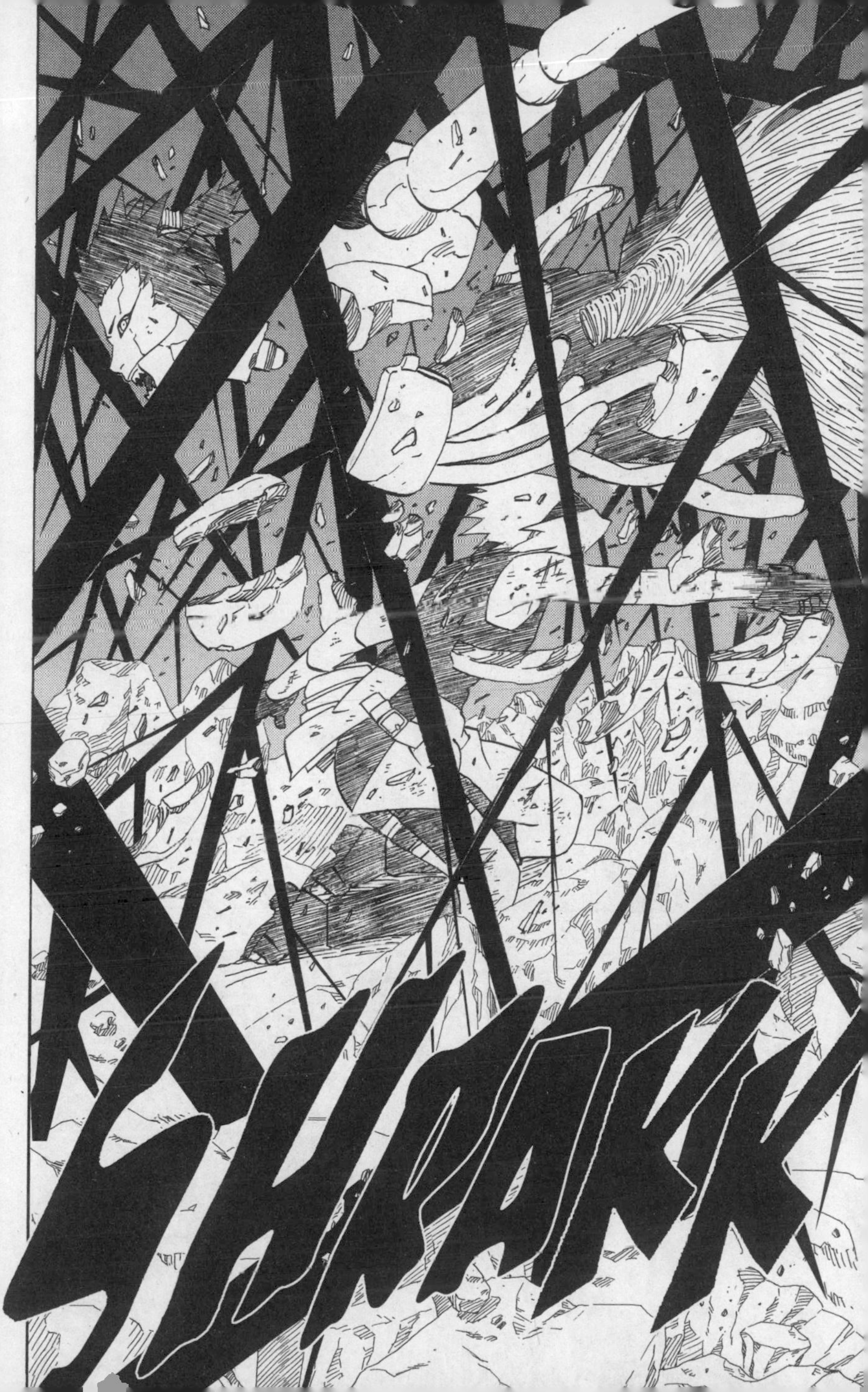
SHRAKK

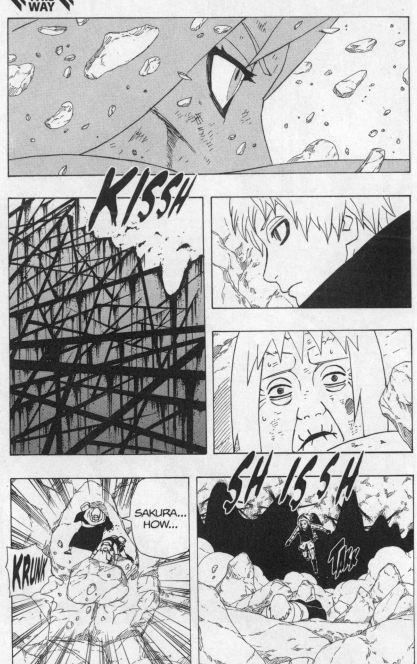

KISSH

SAKURA...
HOW...

KRUNK

SH ISSH

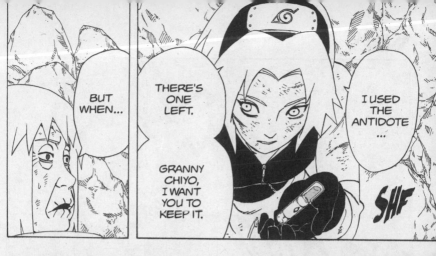

I USED THE ANTIDOTE ...
SHF
THERE'S ONE LEFT.
GRANNY CHIYO, I WANT YOU TO KEEP IT.
BUT WHEN...
I CAN MAKE AT LEAST THREE DIFFERENT ANTIDOTES.
GRIND
GRIND
BACK WHEN I CONCOCTED IT FOR KANKURO...
I HAD ENOUGH FOR THREE DOSES.
I KNEW OUR ADVERSARY USED POISON...
I BROUGHT ALONG THE REST, IN HYPODERMIC FORM.
OH... I SEE...
THE CATCH IS, THE ANTIDOTE IS ONLY REALLY POTENT FOR ABOUT THREE MINUTES.
WHILE IT'S WORKING, WHATEVER POISON YOU'RE EXPOSED TO GETS CONVERTED INTO A HARMLESS PROTEIN.

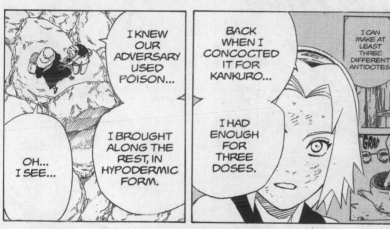

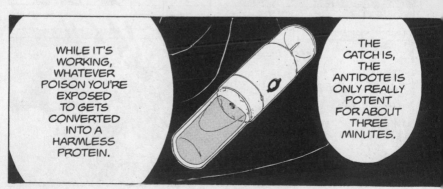

READ THIS WAY

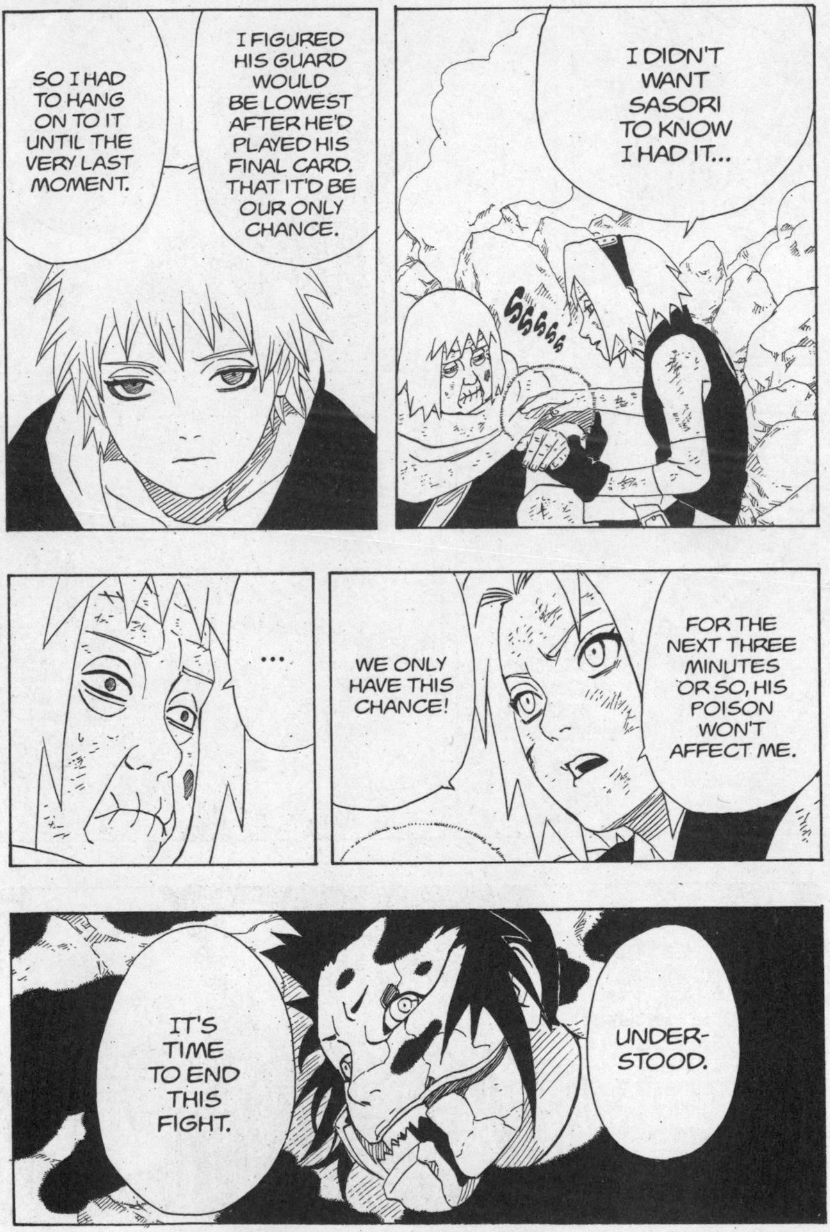
I DIDN'T WANT SASORI TO KNOW I HAD IT...
I FIGURED HIS GUARD WOULD BE LOWEST AFTER HE'D PLAYED HIS FINAL CARD. THAT IT'D BE OUR ONLY CHANCE.
SO I HAD TO HANG ON TO IT UNTIL THE VERY LAST MOMENT.
FOR THE NEXT THREE MINUTES OR SO, HIS POISON WON'T AFFECT ME.
WE ONLY HAVE THIS CHANCE!
...
UNDER-STOOD.
IT'S TIME TO END THIS FIGHT.

NARUTO

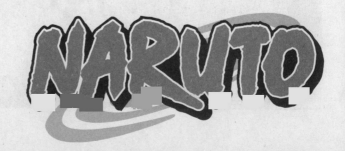

Number 271: Unknown Power...!!

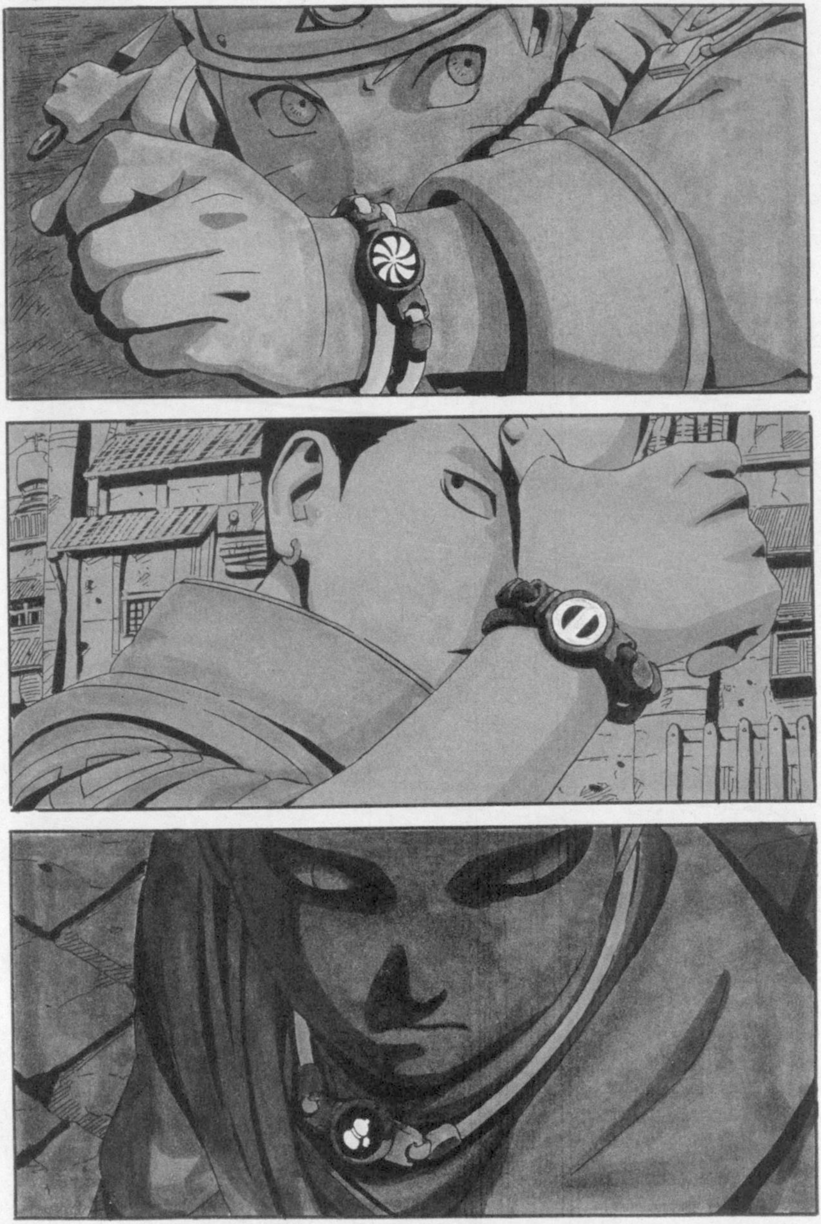

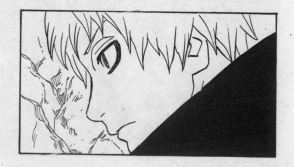

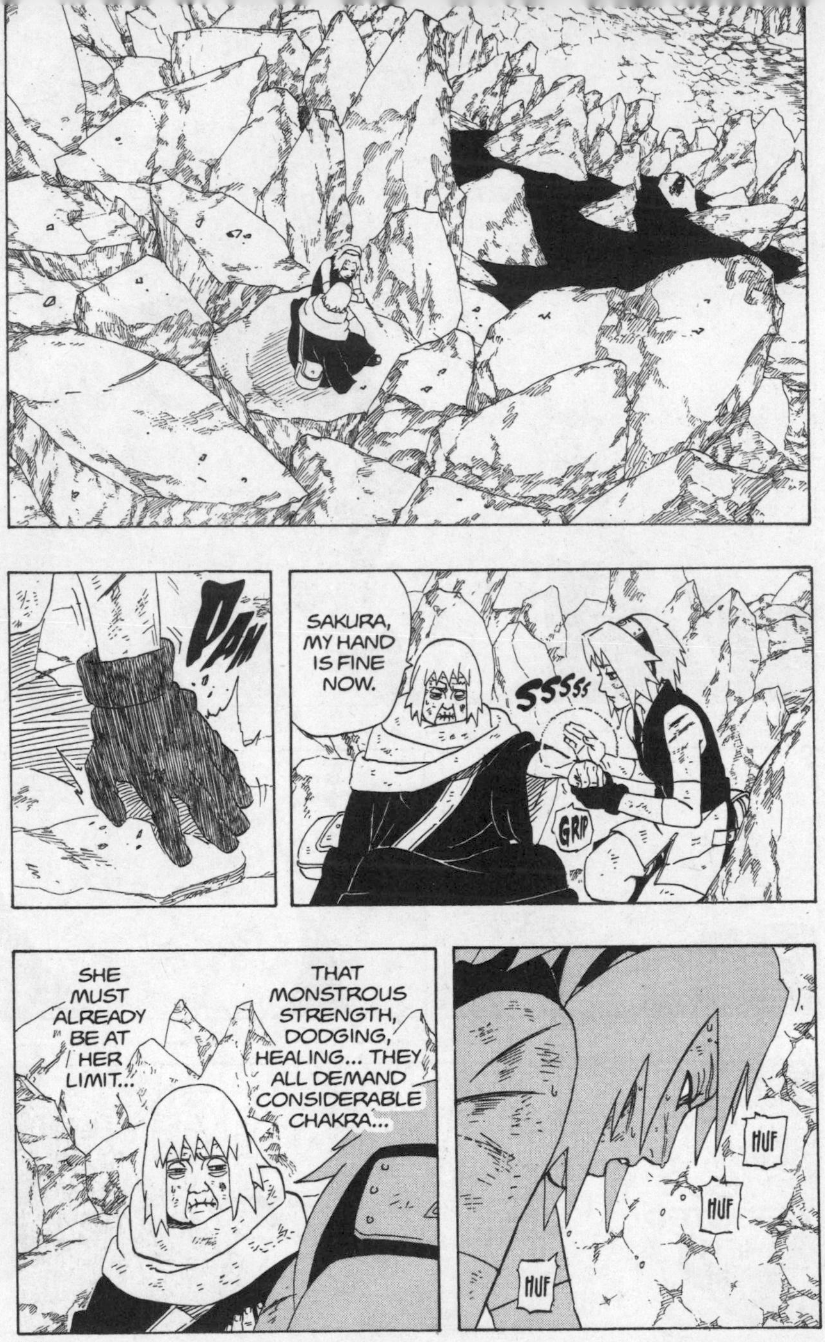
SAKURA, MY HAND IS FINE NOW.
SSSSS
GRIP
DAH
HUF
HUF
HUF
THAT MONSTROUS STRENGTH, DODGING, HEALING... THEY ALL DEMAND CONSIDERABLE CHAKRA...
SHE MUST ALREADY BE AT HER LIMIT...

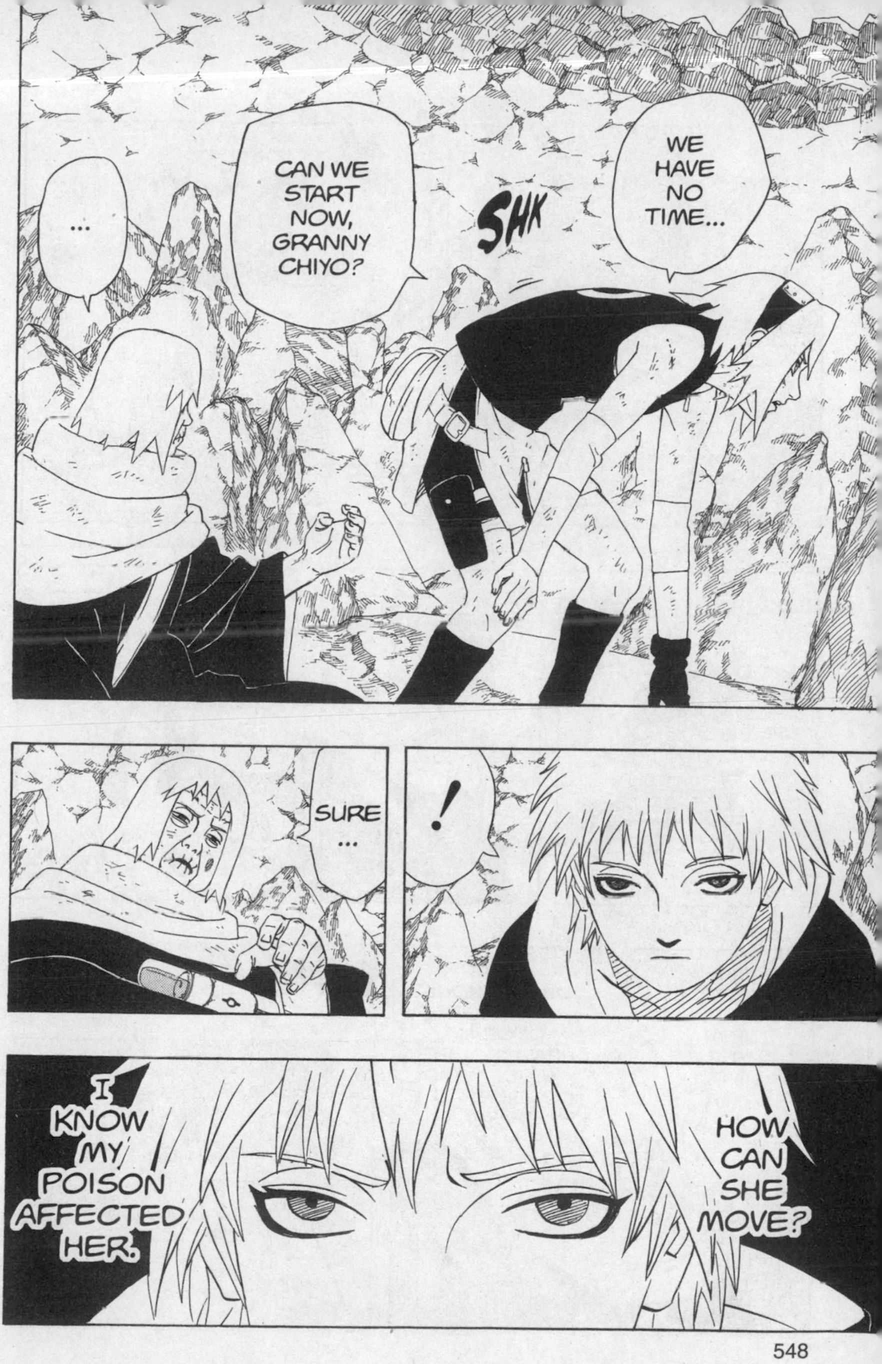
WE HAVE NO TIME...
SHK
CAN WE START NOW, GRANNY CHIYO?
...
!
SURE ...
HOW CAN SHE MOVE?
I KNOW MY POISON AFFECTED HER.

READ THIS WAY

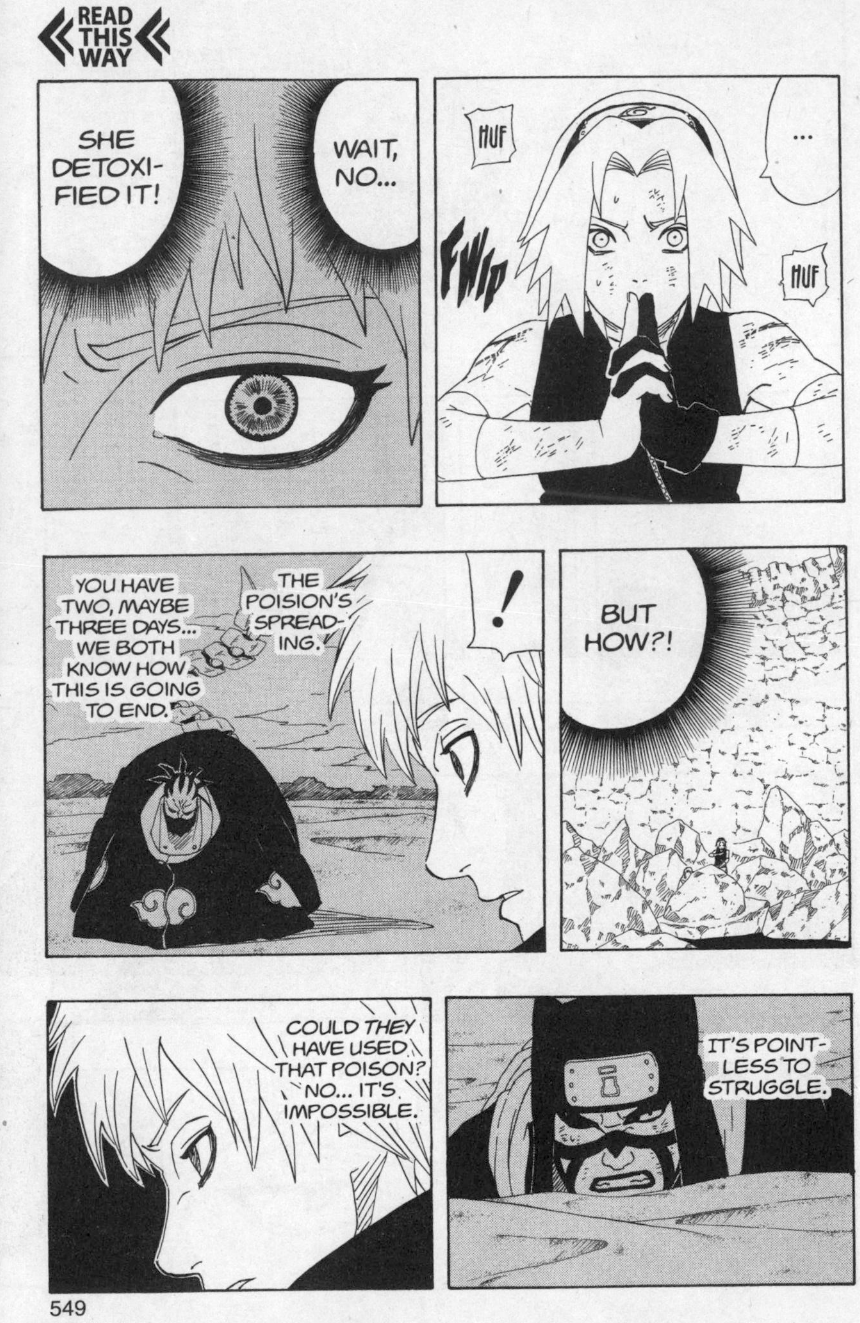

...
HUF
FWIP
HUF
WAIT, NO...
SHE DETOXIFIED IT!
BUT HOW?!
!
THE POISION'S SPREADING.
YOU HAVE TWO, MAYBE THREE DAYS... WE BOTH KNOW HOW THIS IS GOING TO END.
IT'S POINTLESS TO STRUGGLE.
COULD THEY HAVE USED THAT POISON? NO... IT'S IMPOSSIBLE.

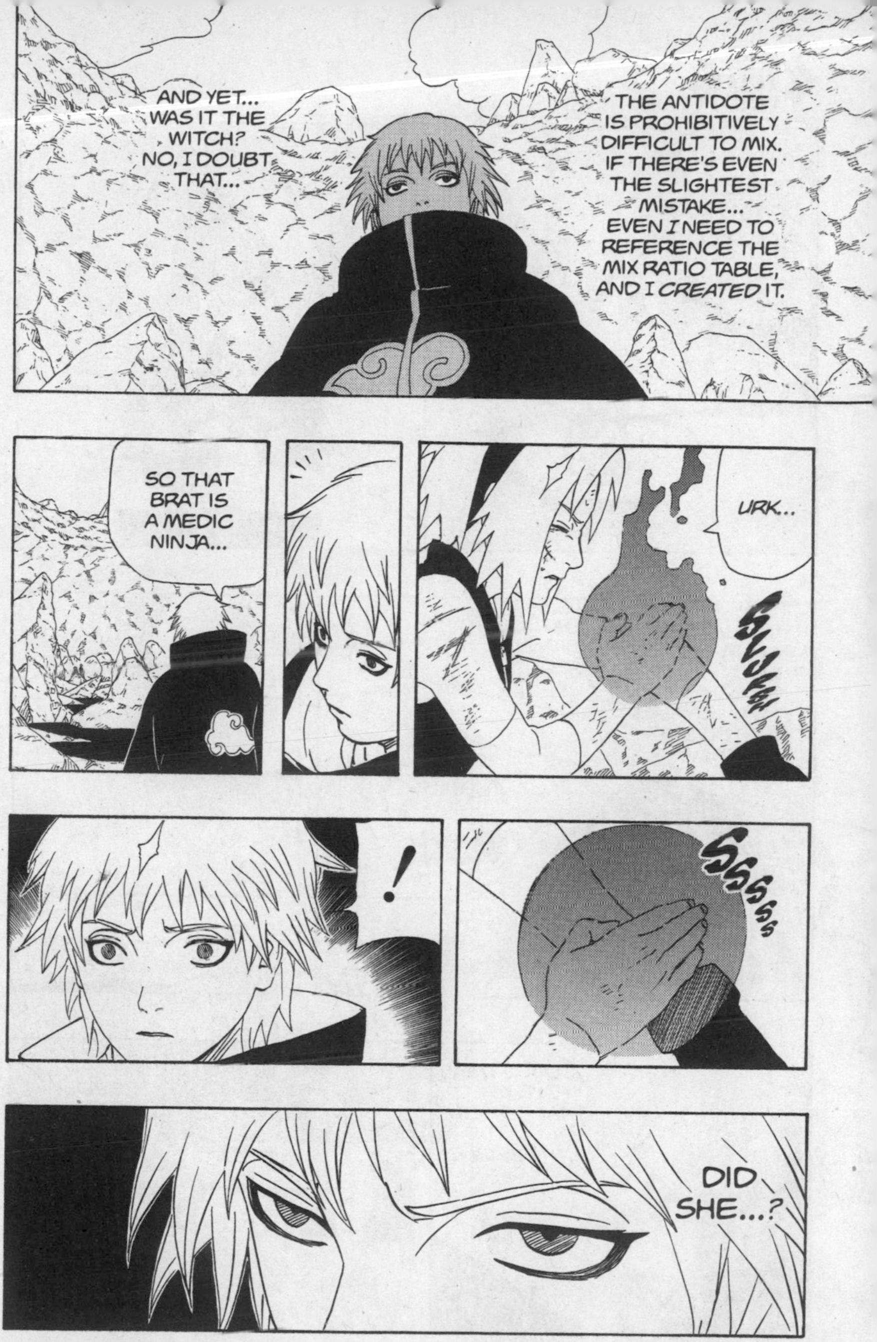
THE ANTIDOTE IS PROHIBITIVELY DIFFICULT TO MIX. IF THERE'S EVEN THE SLIGHTEST MISTAKE... EVEN I NEED TO REFERENCE THE MIX RATIO TABLE, AND I CREATED IT.
AND YET... WAS IT THE WITCH? NO, I DOUBT THAT...
URK...
SO THAT BRAT IS A MEDIC NINJA...
SSSSS
!
DID SHE...?

READ THIS WAY

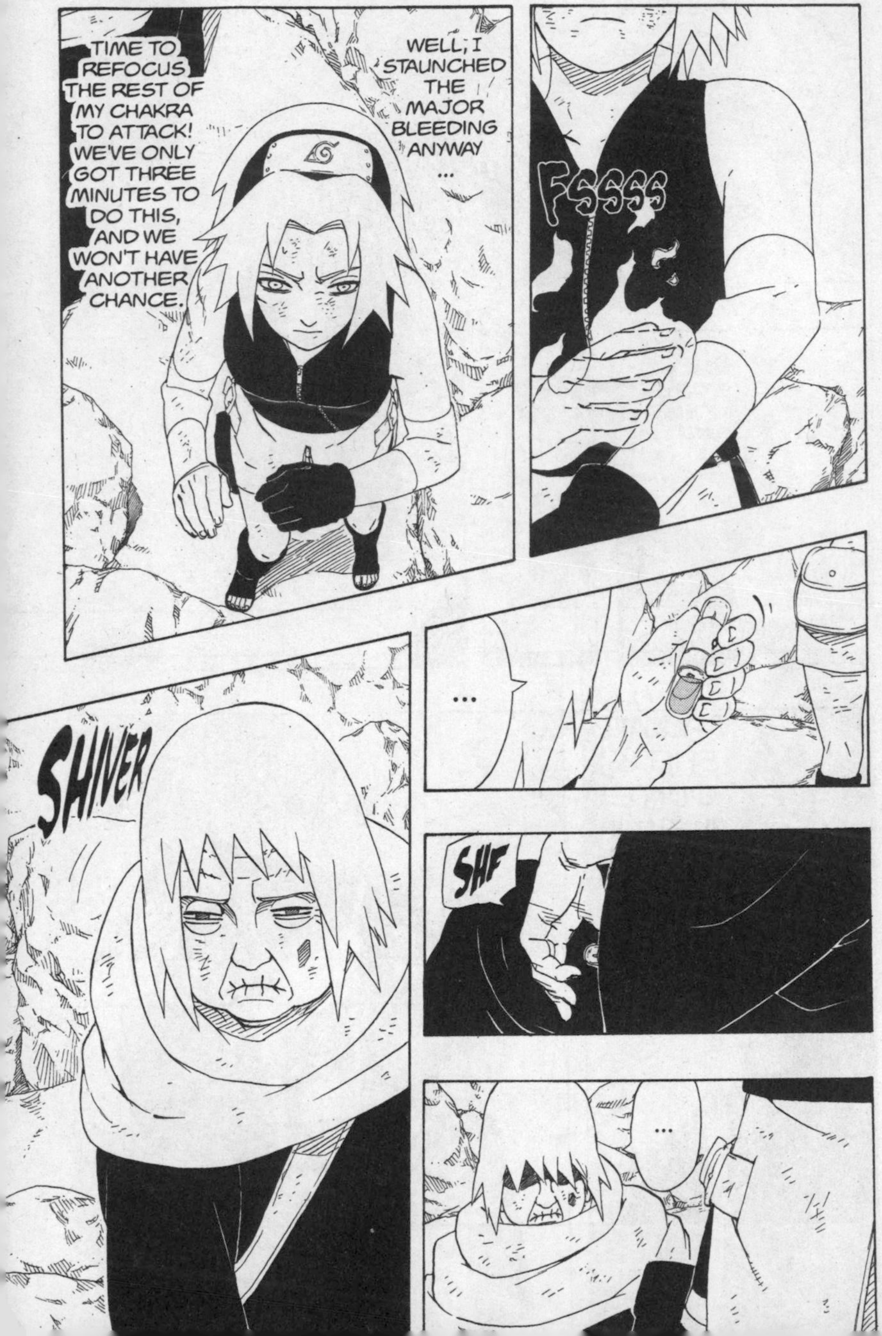
FSSSS
WELL, I STAUNCHED THE MAJOR BLEEDING ANYWAY ...
TIME TO REFOCUS THE REST OF MY CHAKRA TO ATTACK! WE'VE ONLY GOT THREE MINUTES TO DO THIS, AND WE WON'T HAVE ANOTHER CHANCE.
...
SHF
...
SHIVER

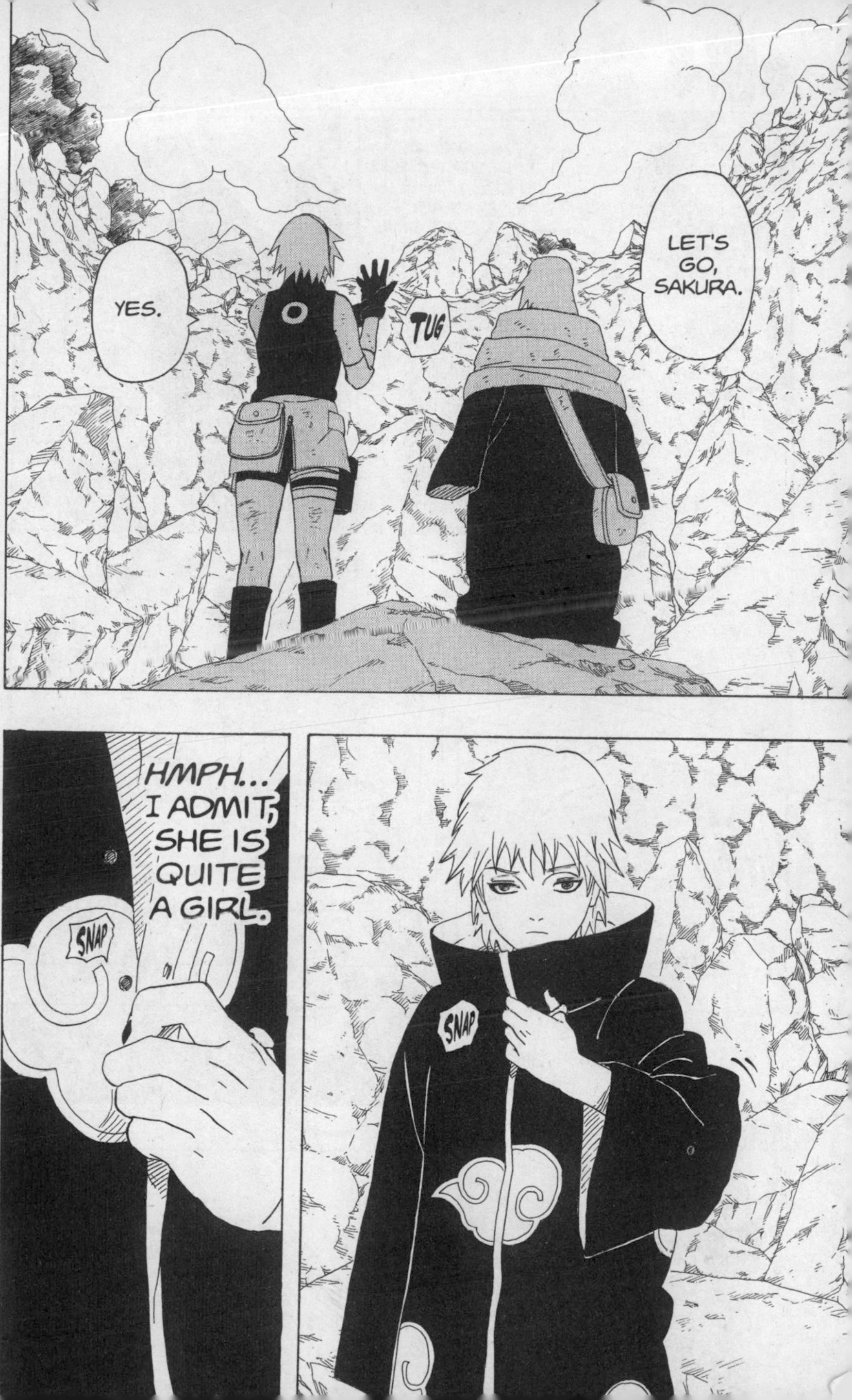
LET'S GO, SAKURA.
YES.
TUG
SNAP
HMPH... I ADMIT, SHE IS QUITE A GIRL.
SNAP

READ THIS WAY

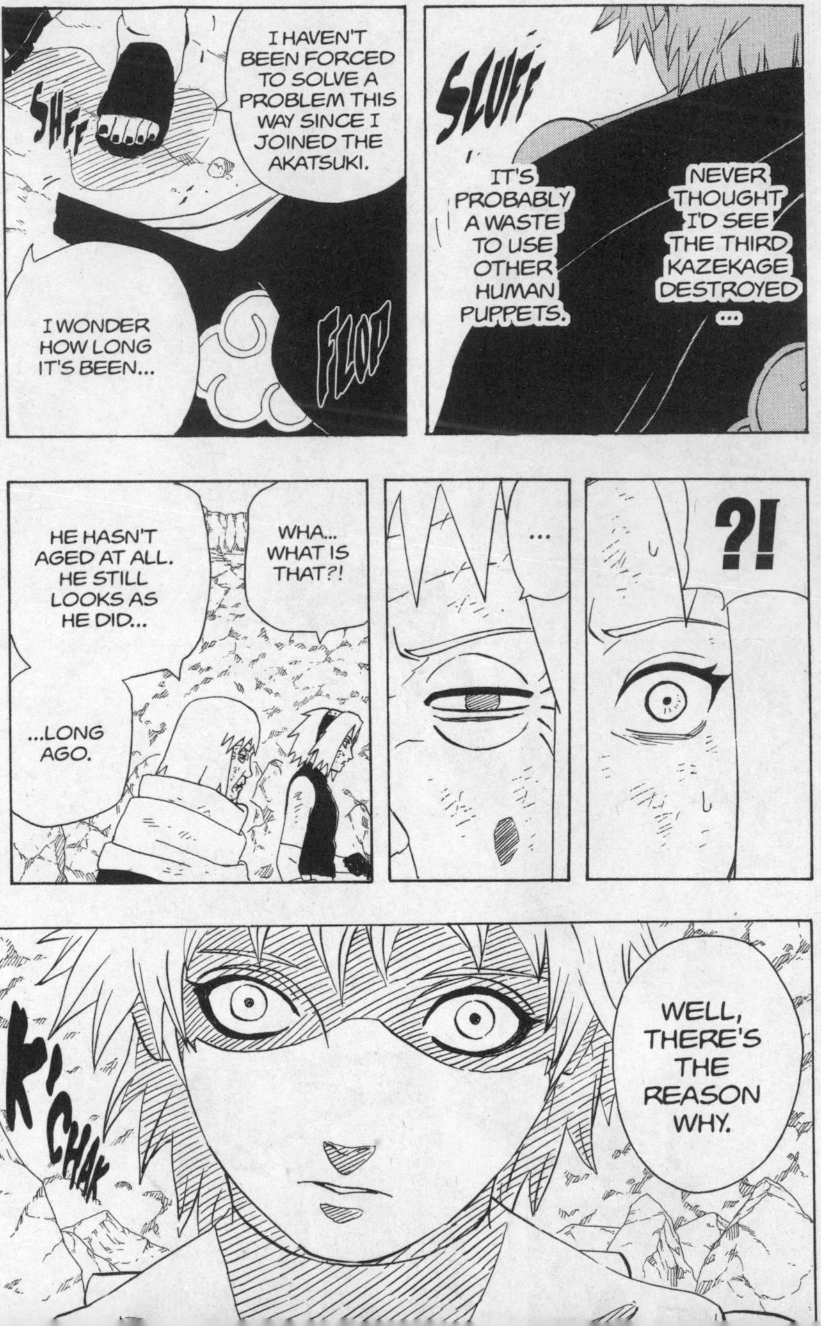
SLUFF
NEVER THOUGHT I'D SEE THE THIRD KAZEKAGE DESTROYED...
IT'S PROBABLY A WASTE TO USE OTHER HUMAN PUPPETS.
I HAVEN'T BEEN FORCED TO SOLVE A PROBLEM THIS WAY SINCE I JOINED THE AKATSUKI.
SHFF
FLOP
I WONDER HOW LONG IT'S BEEN...
?!
...
WHA... WHAT IS THAT?!
HE HASN'T AGED AT ALL. HE STILL LOOKS AS HE DID...
...LONG AGO.
WELL, THERE'S THE REASON WHY.
K'CHAK

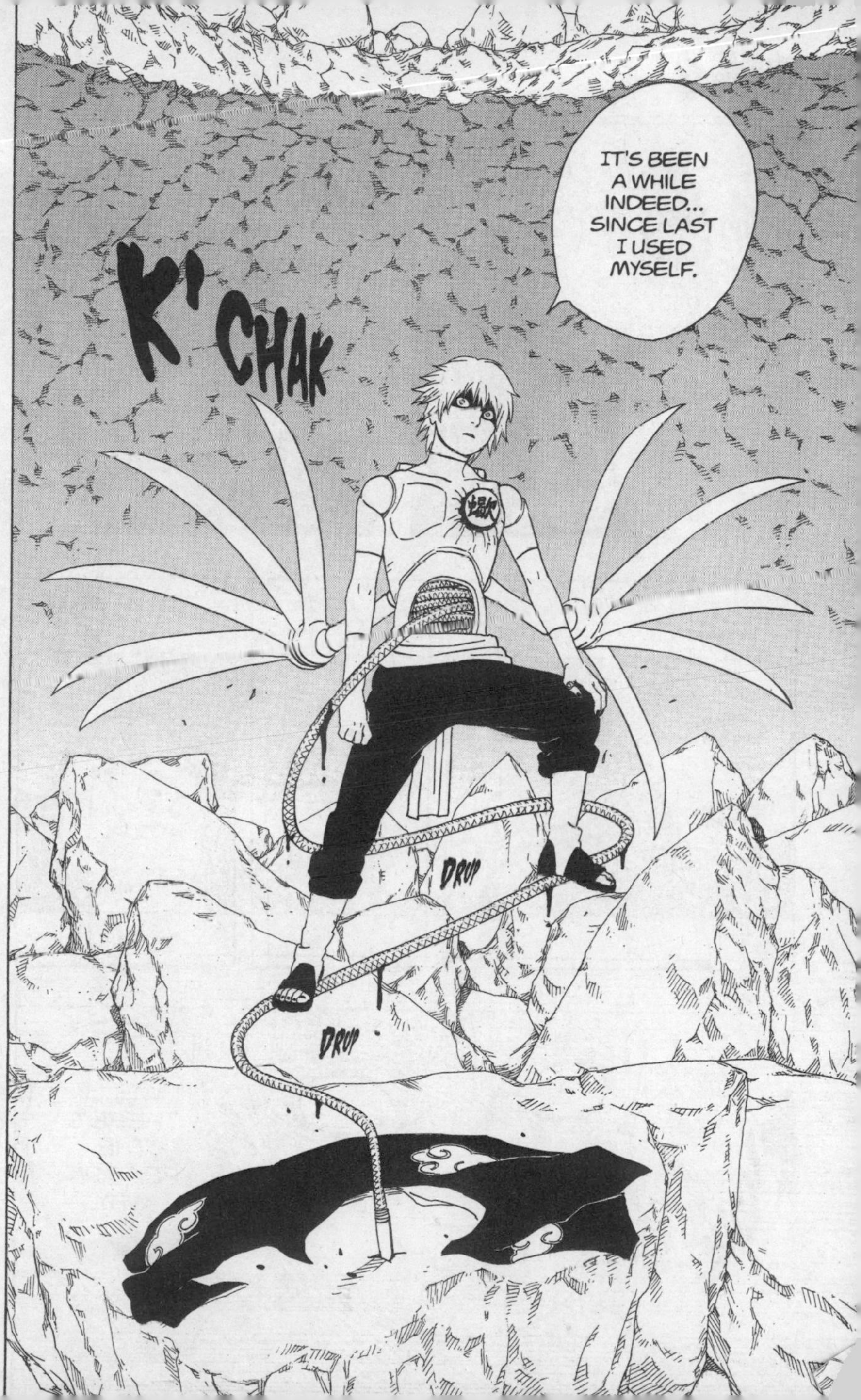
IT'S BEEN A WHILE INDEED... SINCE LAST I USED MYSELF.
K'CHAK
DRIP
DRIP

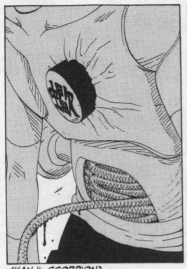

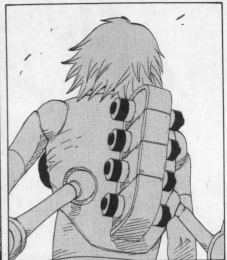

(KANJI: SCORPION)

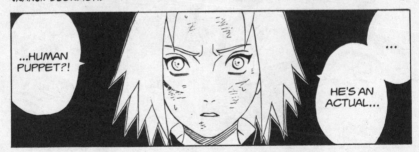

...HUMAN PUPPET?!

...

HE'S AN ACTUAL...

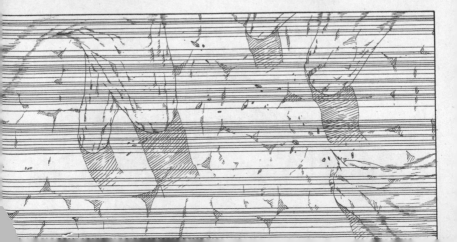

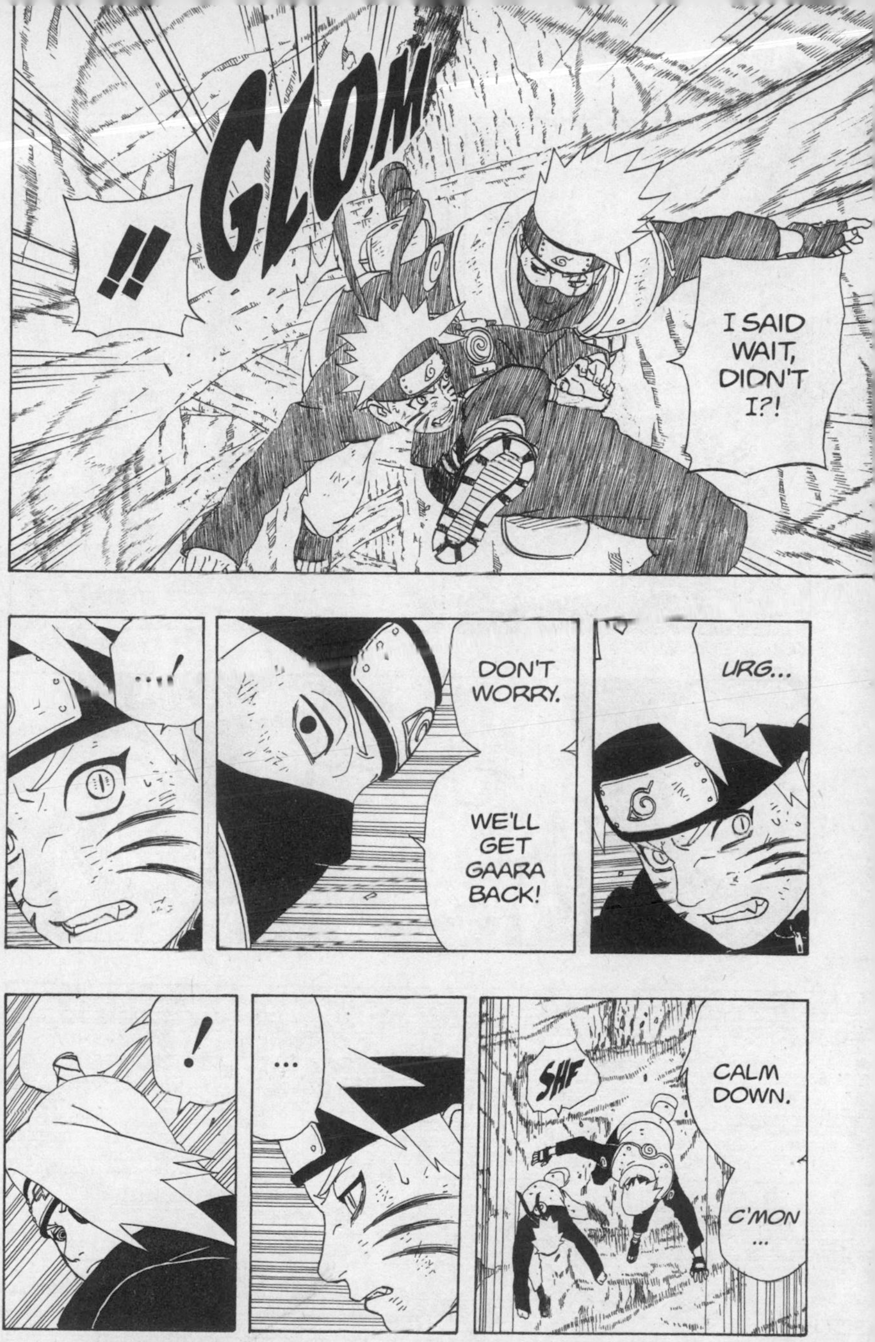
I SAID WAIT, DIDN'T I?!
GLOM
!!
URG...
DON'T WORRY.
WE'LL GET GAARA BACK!
...!
CALM DOWN.
SHF
C'MON ...
...
!

READ THIS WAY

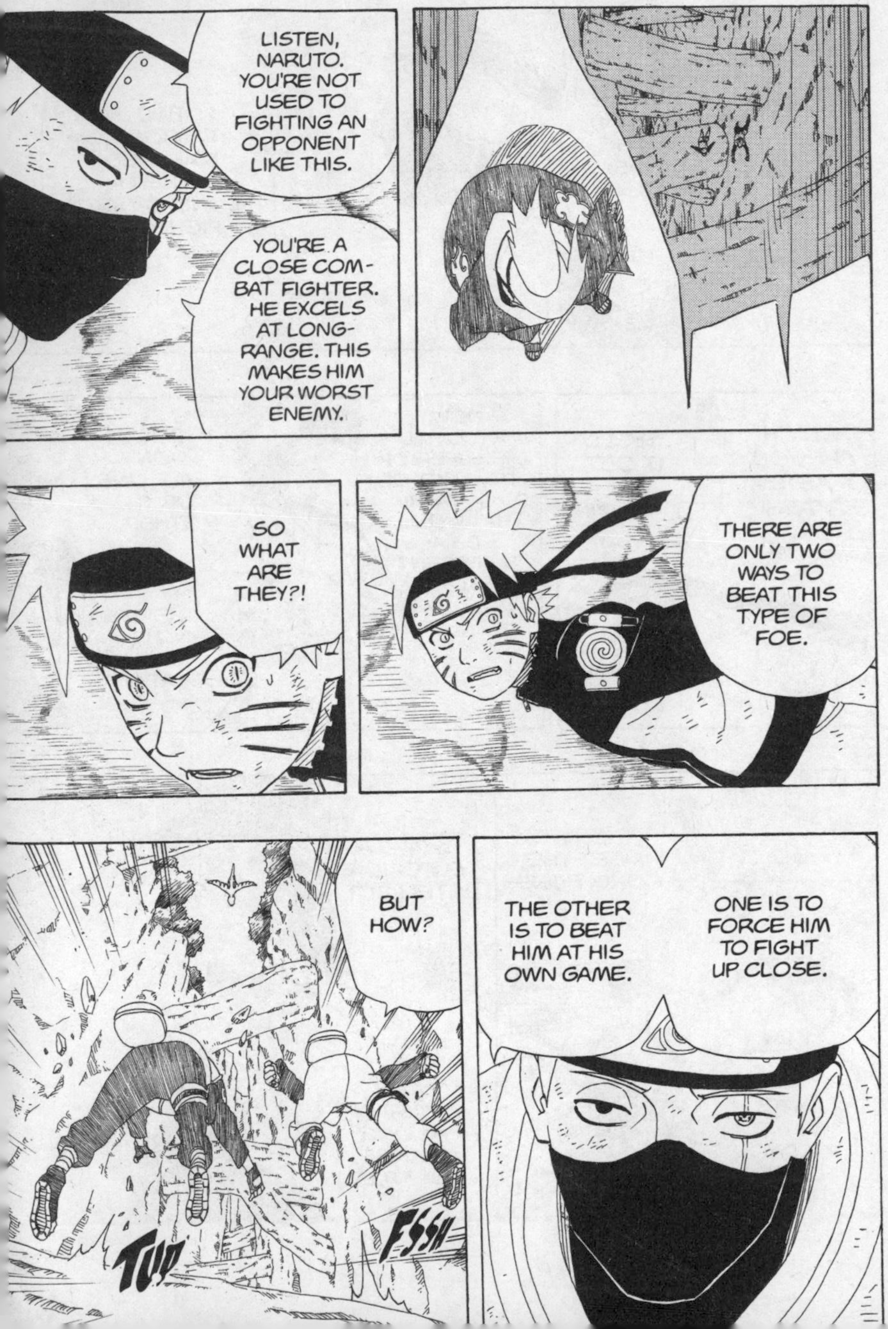
LISTEN, NARUTO. YOU'RE NOT USED TO FIGHTING AN OPPONENT LIKE THIS.
YOU'RE A CLOSE COMBAT FIGHTER. HE EXCELS AT LONG-RANGE. THIS MAKES HIM YOUR WORST ENEMY.
THERE ARE ONLY TWO WAYS TO BEAT THIS TYPE OF FOE.
SO WHAT ARE THEY?!
ONE IS TO FORCE HIM TO FIGHT UP CLOSE.
THE OTHER IS TO BEAT HIM AT HIS OWN GAME.
BUT HOW?
FSSH
TUD

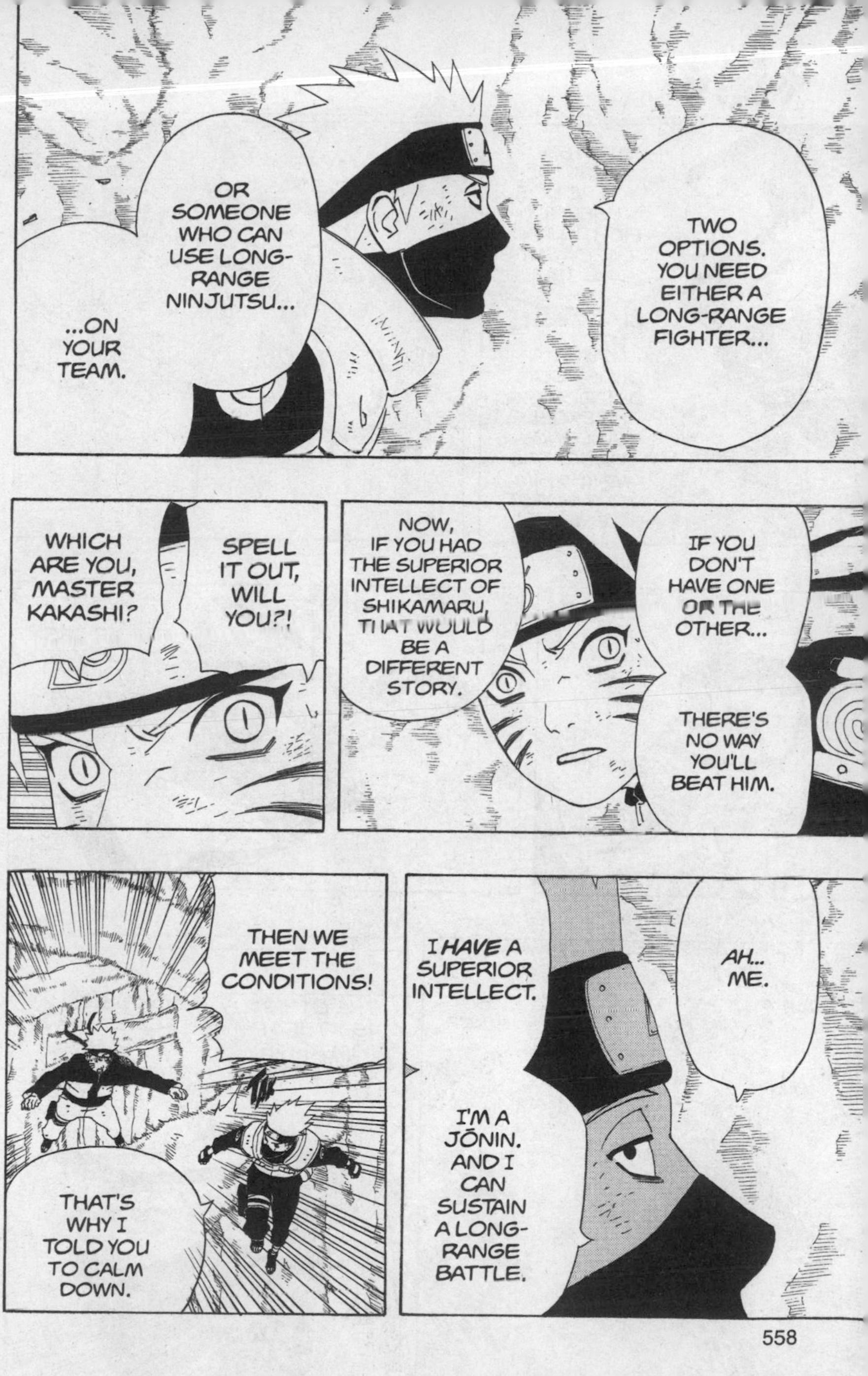
TWO OPTIONS. YOU NEED EITHER A LONG-RANGE FIGHTER...
OR SOMEONE WHO CAN USE LONG-RANGE NINJUTSU...
...ON YOUR TEAM.
IF YOU DON'T HAVE ONE OR THE OTHER...
THERE'S NO WAY YOU'LL BEAT HIM.
NOW, IF YOU HAD THE SUPERIOR INTELLECT OF SHIKAMARU, THAT WOULD BE A DIFFERENT STORY.
SPELL IT OUT, WILL YOU?!
WHICH ARE YOU, MASTER KAKASHI?
AH... ME.
I *HAVE* A SUPERIOR INTELLECT.
I'M A JŌNIN. AND I CAN SUSTAIN A LONG-RANGE BATTLE.
THEN WE MEET THE CONDITIONS!
THAT'S WHY I TOLD YOU TO CALM DOWN.

READ THIS WAY

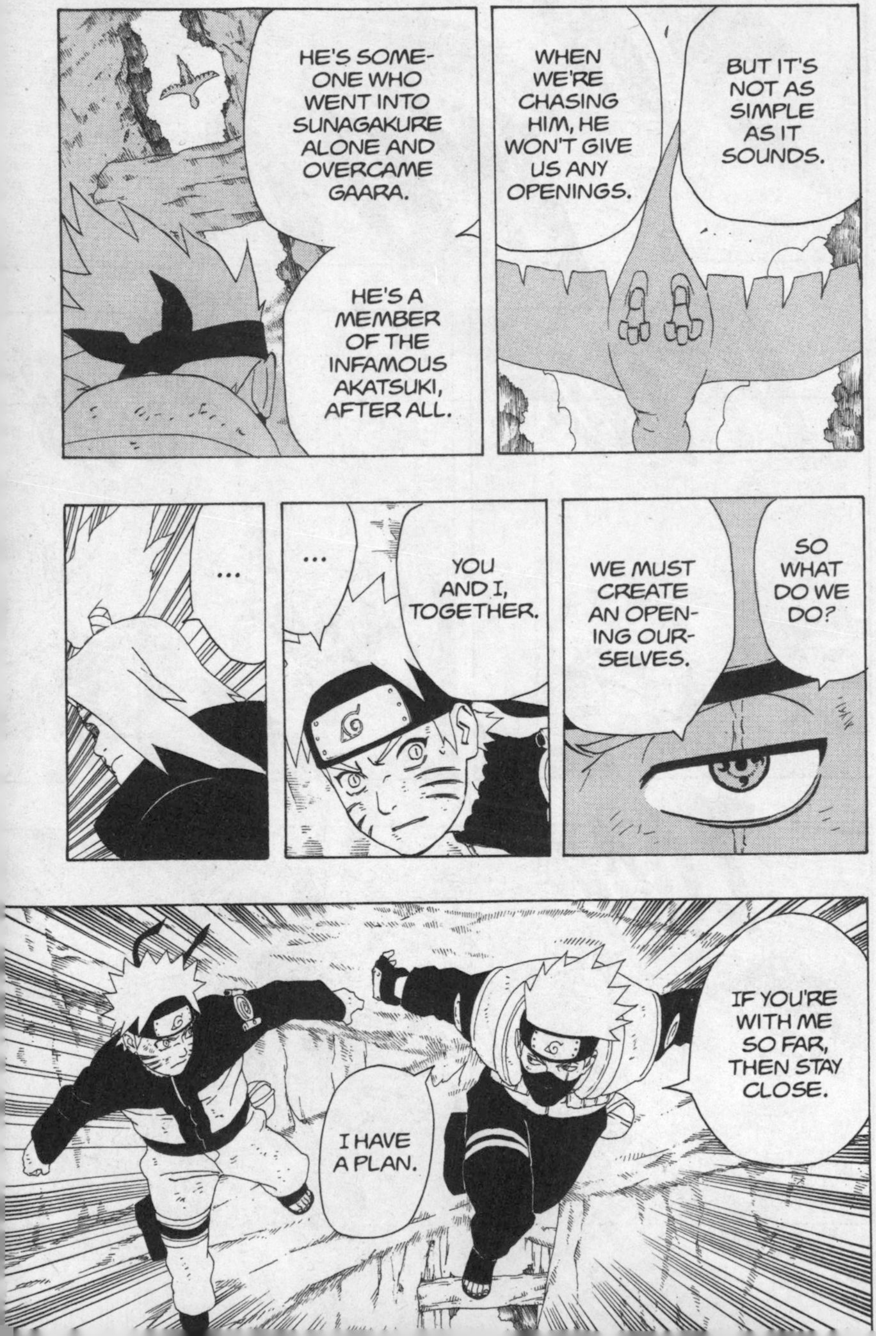
BUT IT'S NOT AS SIMPLE AS IT SOUNDS.
WHEN WE'RE CHASING HIM, HE WON'T GIVE US ANY OPENINGS.
HE'S SOME-ONE WHO WENT INTO SUNAGAKURE ALONE AND OVERCAME GAARA.
HE'S A MEMBER OF THE INFAMOUS AKATSUKI, AFTER ALL.
SO WHAT DO WE DO?
WE MUST CREATE AN OPEN-ING OUR-SELVES.
YOU AND I, TOGETHER.
...
...
IF YOU'RE WITH ME SO FAR, THEN STAY CLOSE.
I HAVE A PLAN.

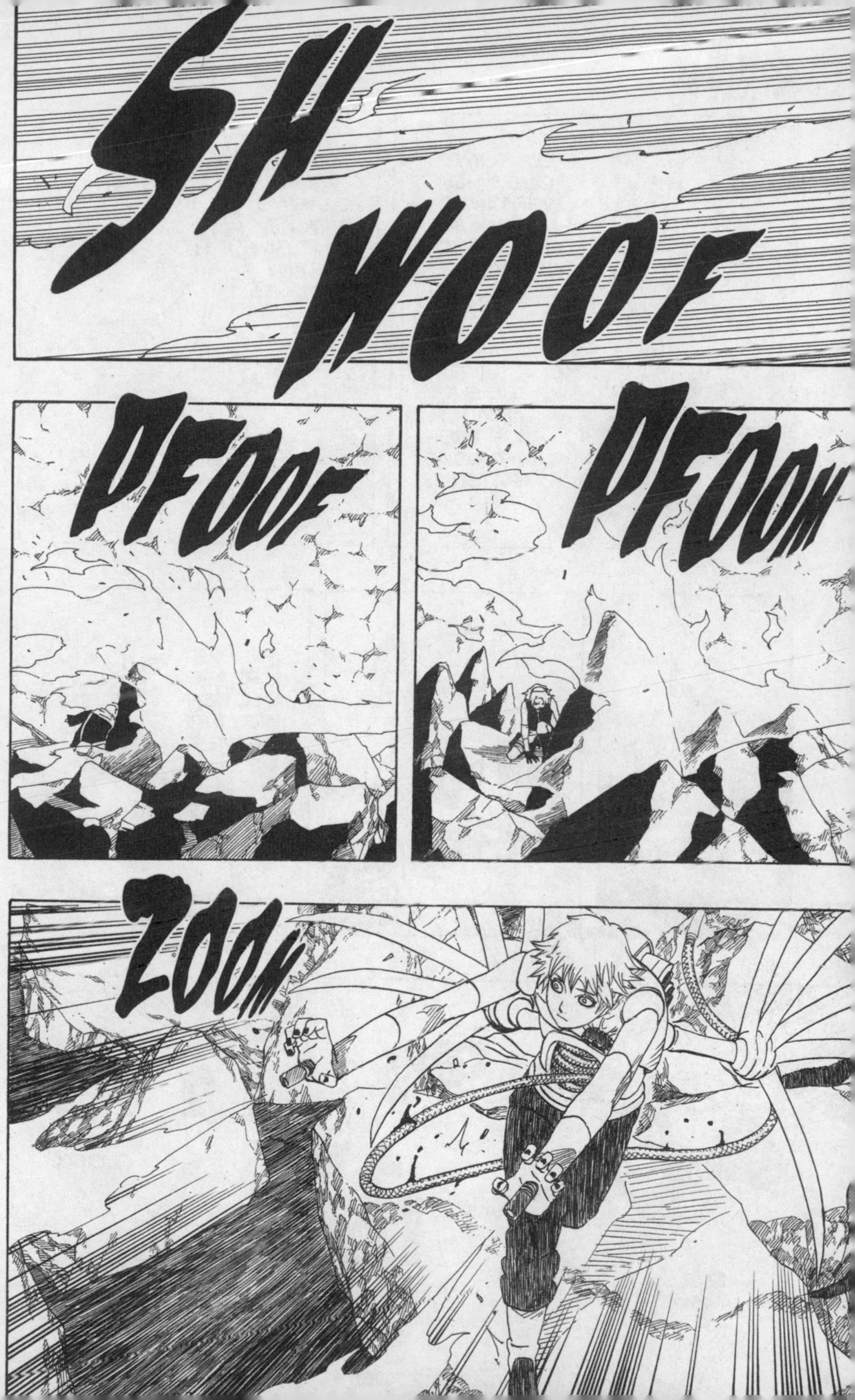
SHWOOF
PFOOM
PFOOF
ZOOM

READ THIS WAY

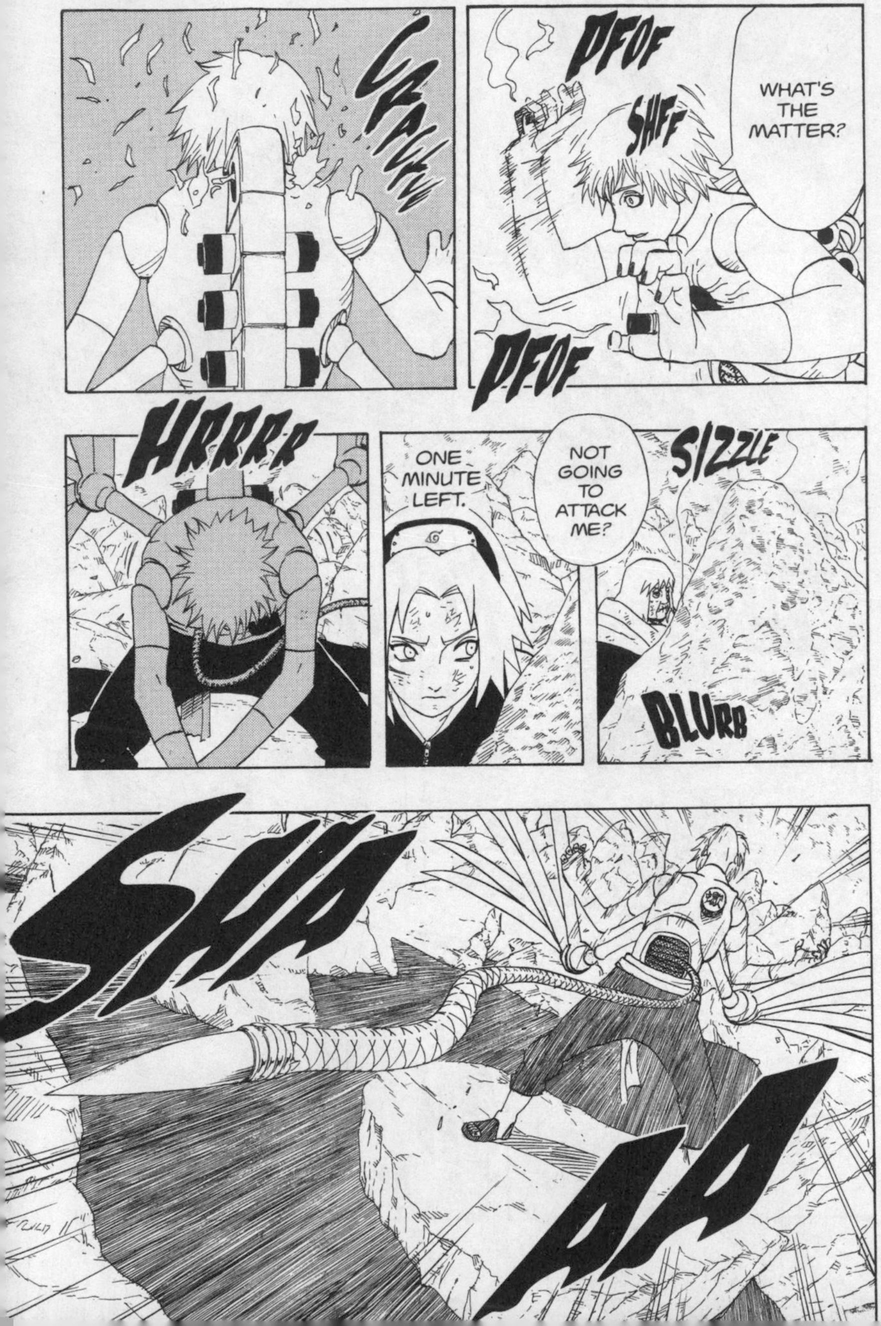
PFOF
SHFF
WHAT'S THE MATTER?
PFOF
SIZZLE
NOT GOING TO ATTACK ME?
BLURB
ONE MINUTE LEFT.
HRRRR
SHA
AA

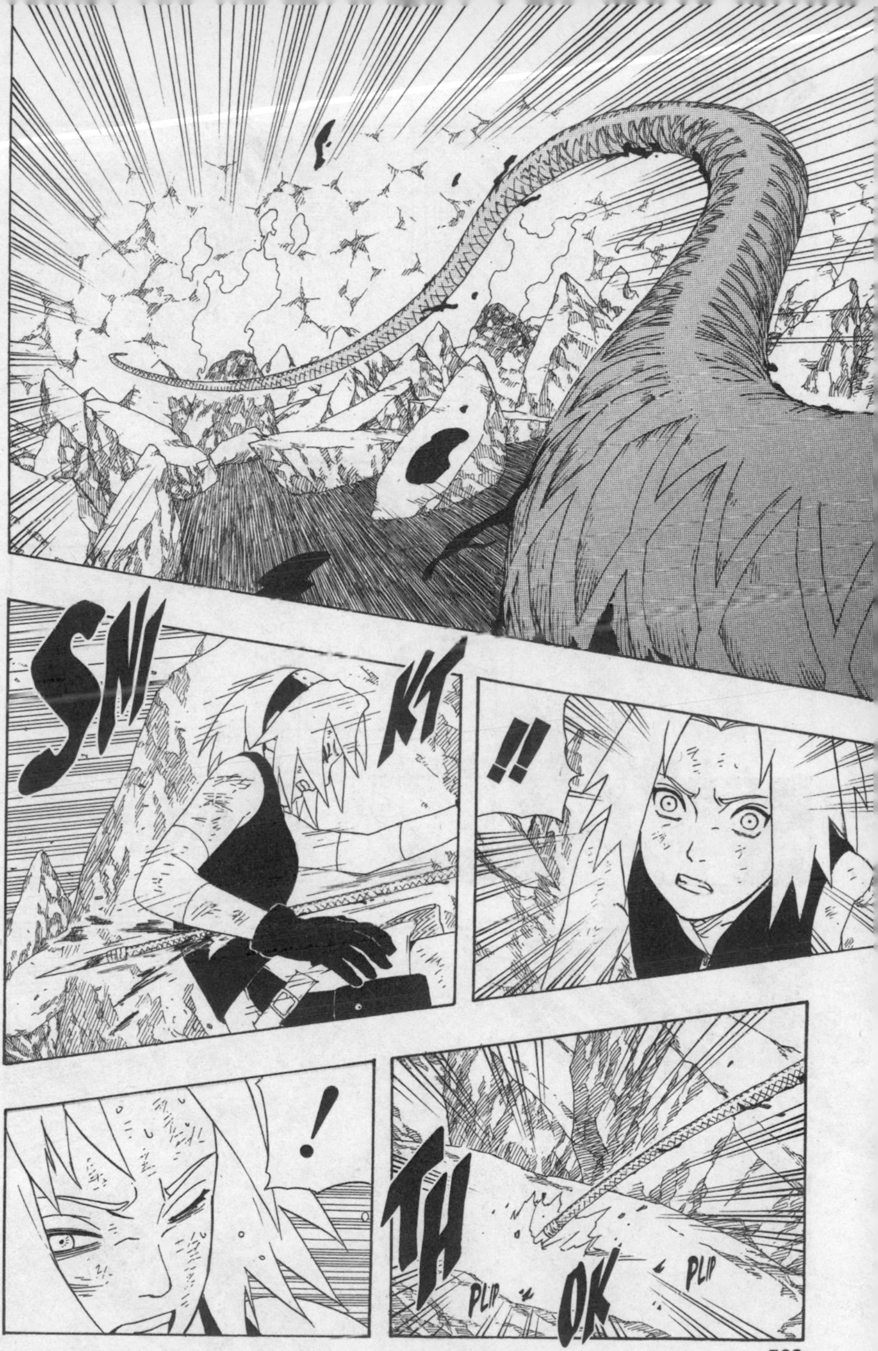
!!
SNIKT
PLIP
PLIP
THOK
!

READ THIS WAY

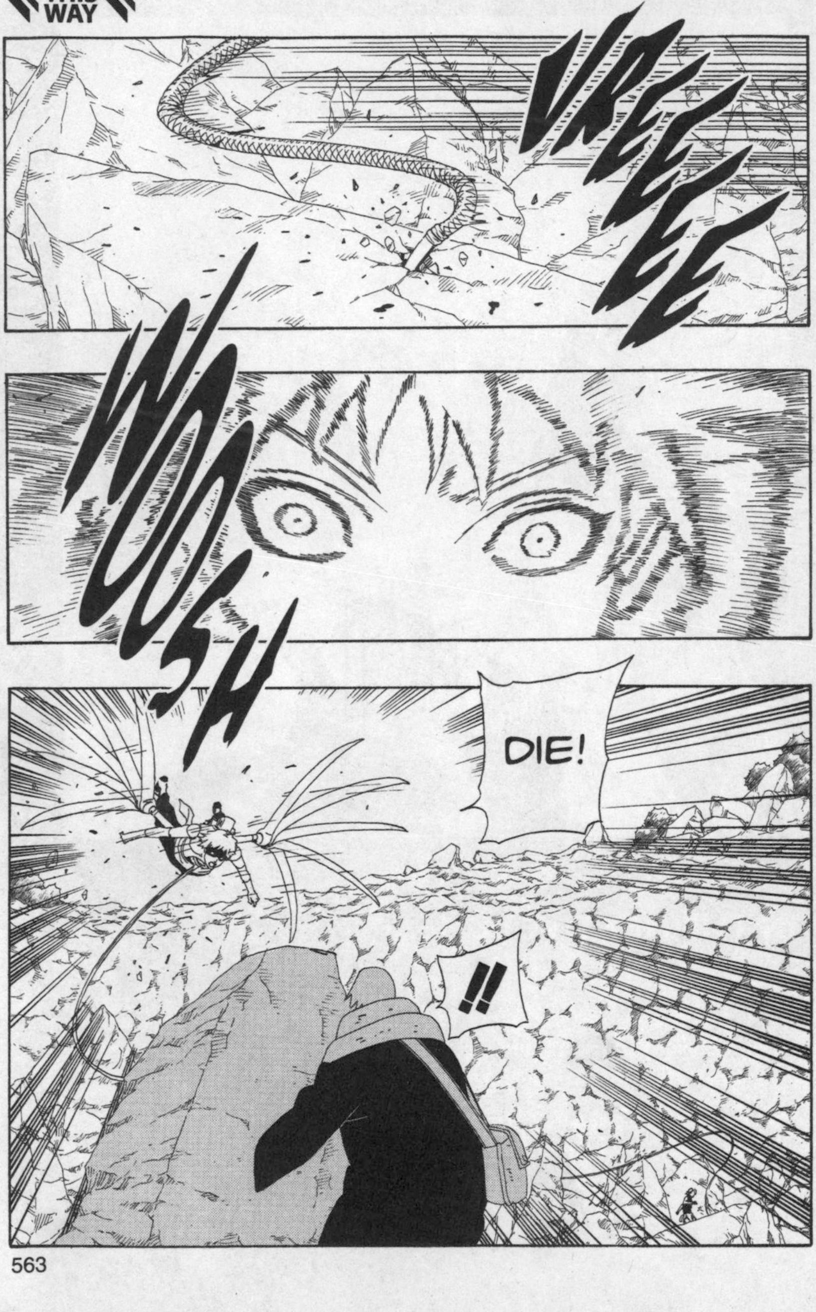
VREEEE
WOOSH
DIE!
!!

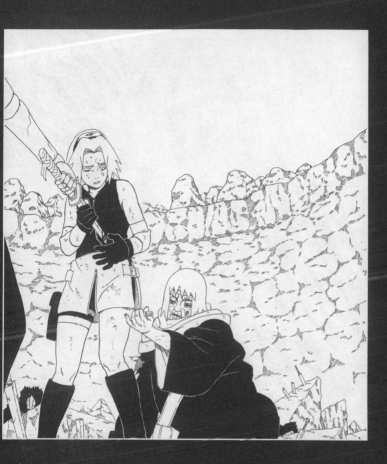

IN THE NEXT VOLUME...

CONSEQUENCES

Stakes are high as Naruto, Sakura, Granny Chiyo and Kakashi engage in deadly conflict with Sasori and Deidara. One wrong decision, and one of Naruto's closest friends could pay the ultimate price.

Upon returning from battle, Team Kakashi is rankled by new member Sai, whose secrets may be disastrous for Naruto.

NARUTO 3-IN-1 EDITION VOLUME 11 AVAILABLE MAY 2015!

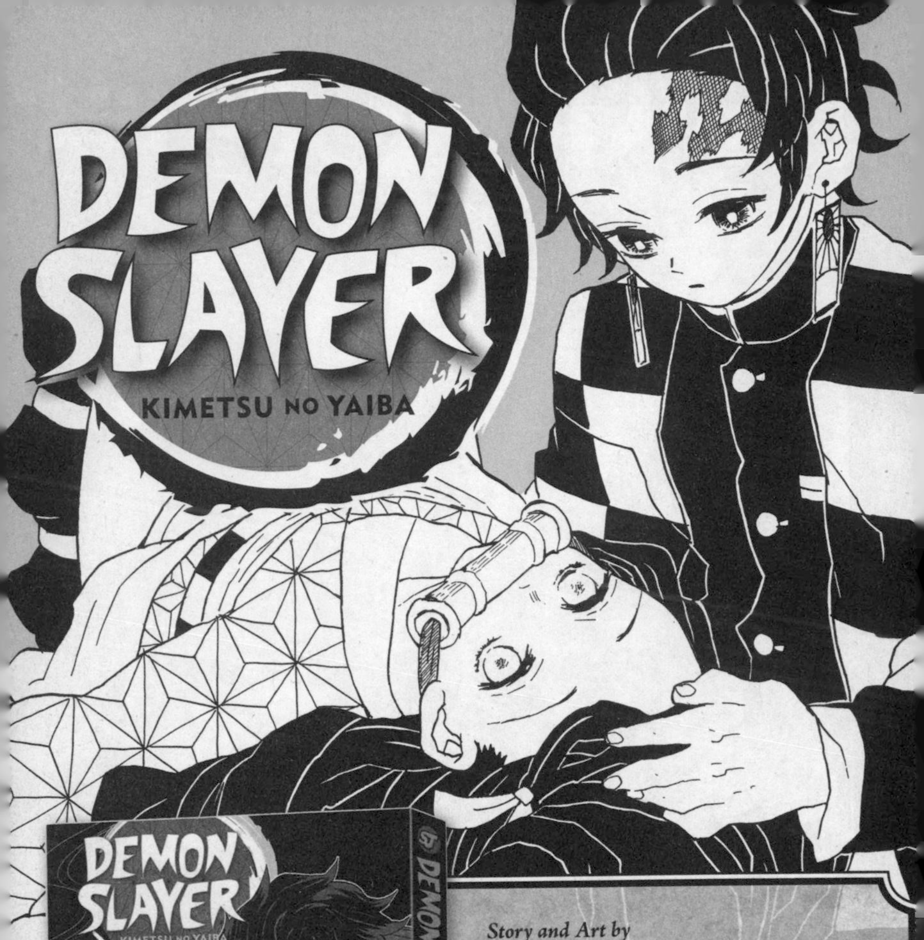

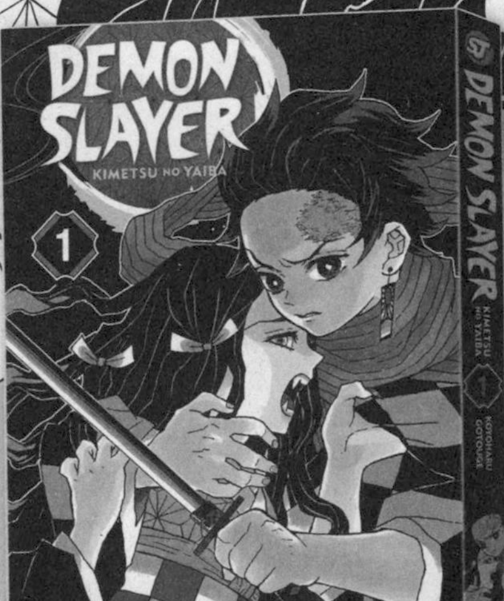

DEMON SLAYER

KIMETSU NO YAIBA

DEMON SLAYER

KIMETSU NO YAIBA

1

Story and Art by
KOYOHARU GOTOUGE

In Taisho-era Japan, kindhearted Tanjiro Kamado makes a living selling charcoal. But his peaceful life is shattered when a demon slaughters his entire family. His little sister Nezuko is the only survivor, but she has been transformed into a demon herself! Tanjiro sets out on a dangerous journey to find a way to return his sister to normal and destroy the demon who ruined his life.

Story and Art by
KOYOHARU GOTOUGE

Black Clover

STORY & ART BY YŪKI TABATA

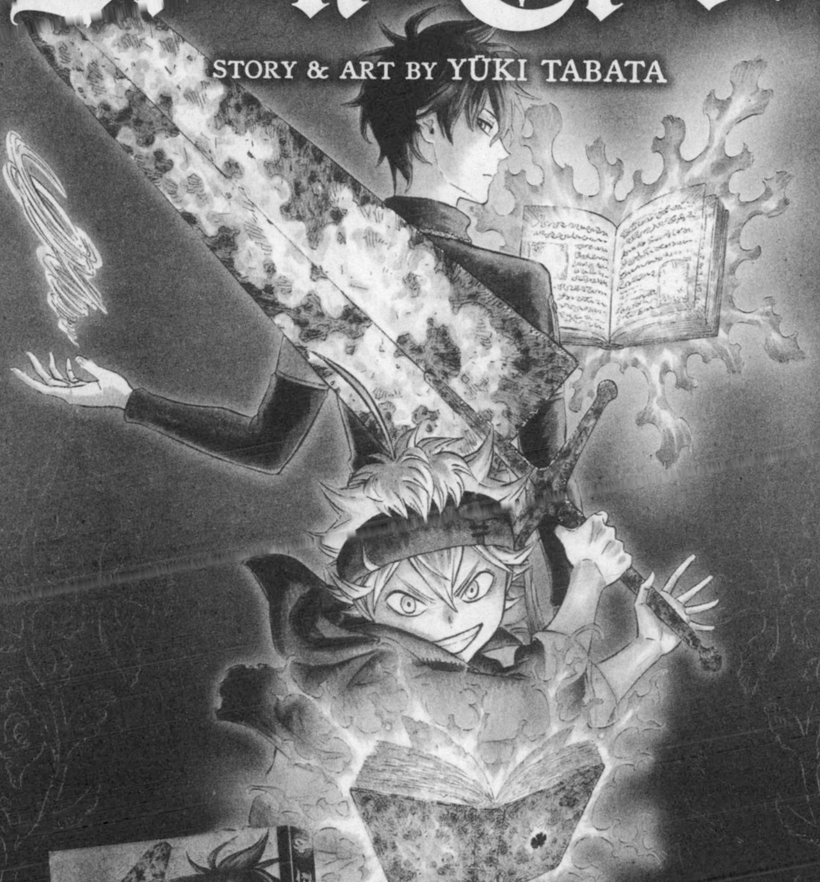

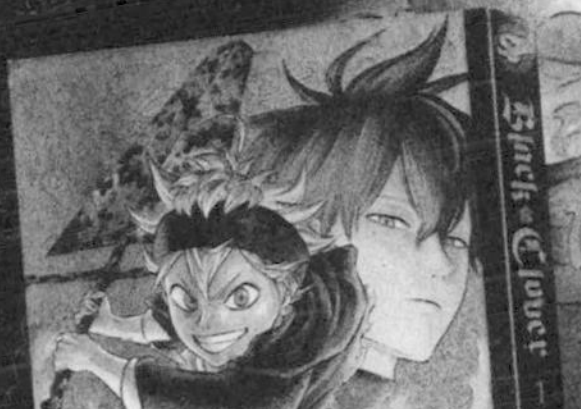
Black Clover
1
YUKI TABATA
STORY & ART BY YUKI TABATA
SHONEN JUMP MANGA

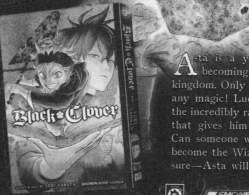

Asta is a young boy who dreams of becoming the greatest mage in the kingdom. Only one problem—he can't use any magic! Luckily for Asta, he receives the incredibly rare five-leaf clover grimoire that gives him the power of anti-magic. Can someone who can't use magic really become the Wizard King? One thing's for sure—Asta will never give up!

RATED T TEEN ratings.viz.com

SHONEN JUMP

VIZ media

www.viz.com

BAKUMAN.

STORY BY TSUGUMI OHBA
ART BY TAKESHI OBATA

From the creators of *Death Note*

The mystery behind manga making REVEALED!

Average student Moritaka Mashiro enjoys drawing for fun. When his classmate and aspiring writer Akito Takagi discovers his talent, he begs to team up. But what exactly does it take to make it in the manga-publishing world?

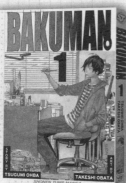

Bakuman., Vol. 1
ISBN: 978-1-4215-3513-5
$9.99 US / $12.99 CAN *

Manga on sale at store.viz.com
Also available at your local bookstore or comic store

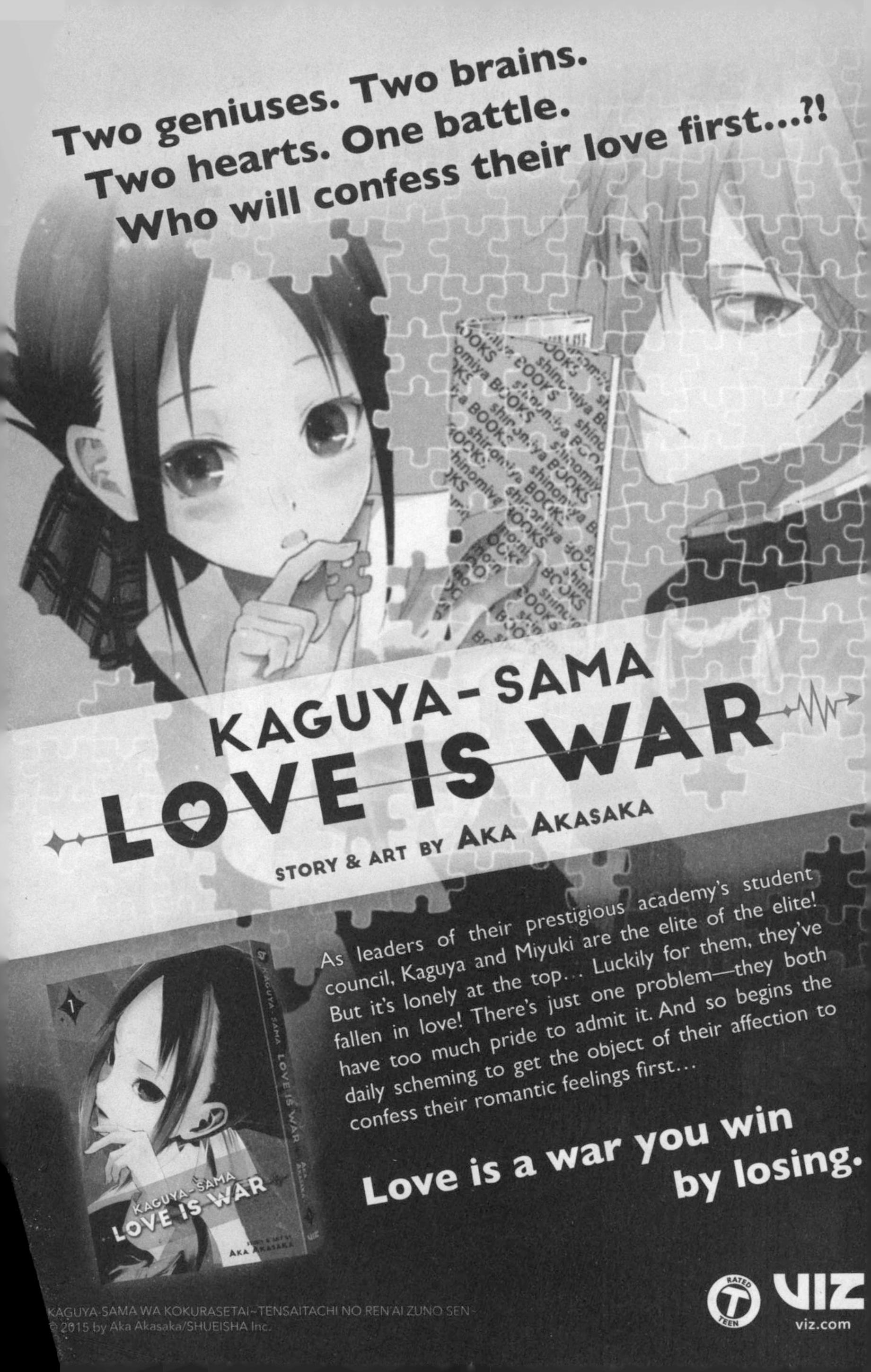
Two geniuses. Two brains.
Two hearts. One battle.
Who will confess their love first...?!
KAGUYA-SAMA
LOVE IS WAR
STORY & ART BY AKA AKASAKA
As leaders of their prestigious academy's student council, Kaguya and Miyuki are the elite of the elite! But it's lonely at the top… Luckily for them, they've fallen in love! There's just one problem—they both have too much pride to admit it. And so begins the daily scheming to get the object of their affection to confess their romantic feelings first…
Love is a war you win by losing.
KAGUYA-SAMA LOVE IS WAR
AKA AKASAKA
RATED T TEEN
VIZ
viz.com
KAGUYA-SAMA WA KOKURASETAI~TENSAITACHI NO REN'AI ZUNO SEN~
© 2015 by Aka Akasaka/SHUEISHA Inc.

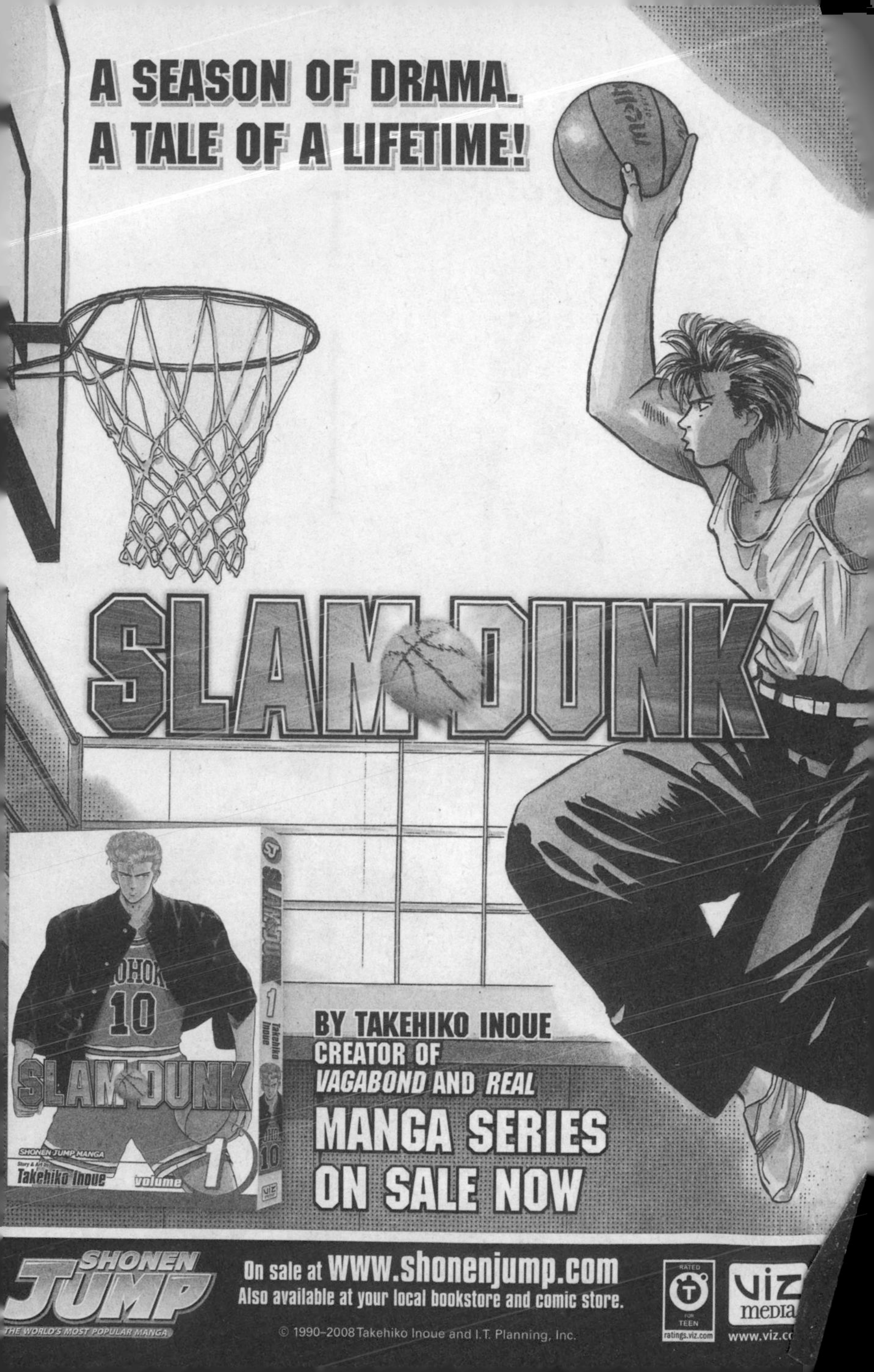
A SEASON OF DRAMA.
A TALE OF A LIFETIME!
SLAM DUNK
SHOHOKU
10
SLAM DUNK
SHONEN JUMP MANGA
Takehiko Inoue
volume 1
BY TAKEHIKO INOUE
CREATOR OF
VAGABOND AND REAL
MANGA SERIES
ON SALE NOW
SHONEN JUMP
THE WORLD'S MOST POPULAR MANGA
On sale at www.shonenjump.com
Also available at your local bookstore and comic store.
© 1990–2008 Takehiko Inoue and I.T. Planning, Inc.
RATED T FOR TEEN
ratings.viz.com
viz media
www.viz.co

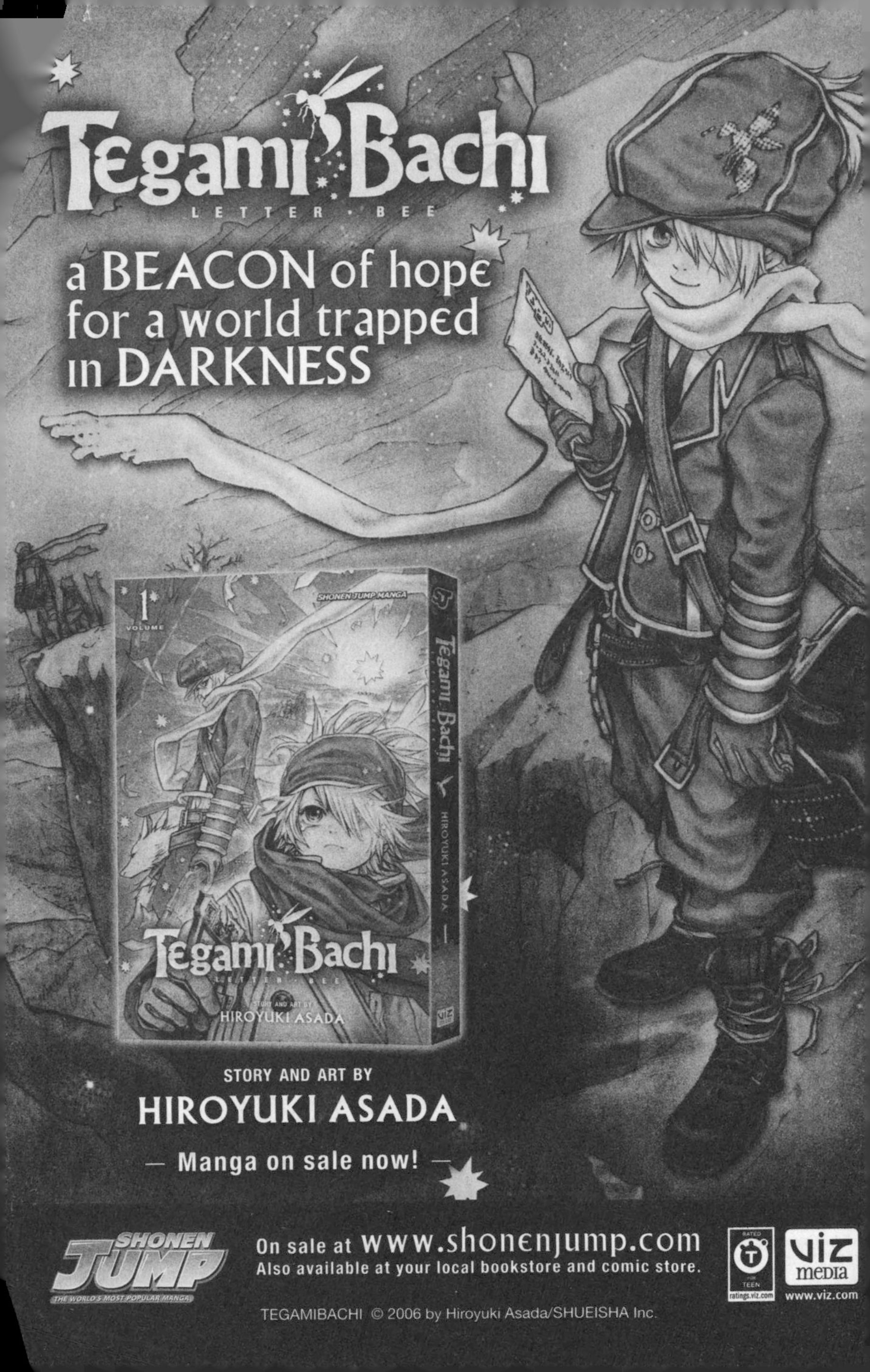
TEGAMI BACHI
LETTER BEE
a BEACON of hope for a world trapped in DARKNESS
SHONEN JUMP MANGA
1 VOLUME
TEGAMI BACHI
LETTER BEE
STORY AND ART BY
HIROYUKI ASADA
STORY AND ART BY
HIROYUKI ASADA
— Manga on sale now! —
SHONEN JUMP
THE WORLD'S MOST POPULAR MANGA
On sale at www.shonenjump.com
Also available at your local bookstore and comic store.
RATED T FOR TEEN
ratings.viz.com
VIZ MEDIA
www.viz.com
TEGAMIBACHI © 2006 by Hiroyuki Asada/SHUEISHA Inc.

Gorgeous color art from Eiichiro Oda's **ONE PIECE**!
The first three **COLOR WALK** art books collected into one beautiful compendium.

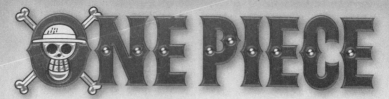

ONE PIECE

EAST BLUE TO SKYPIEA COLOR WALK COMPENDIUM

BY EIICHIRO ODA

Color images and special illustrations from the world's most popular manga, *One Piece*! This compendium features **over 300 pages** of beautiful color art as well as interviews between the creator and other famous manga artists, including **Akira Toriyama**, the creator of *Dragon Ball*.

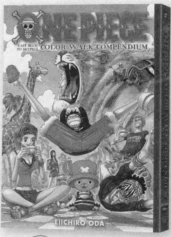

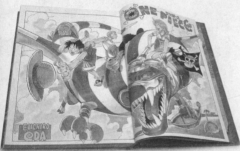

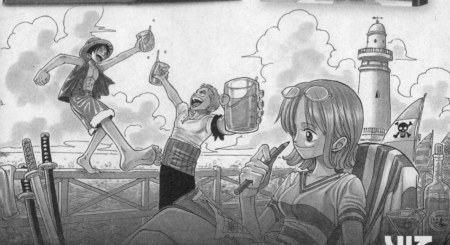

VIZ

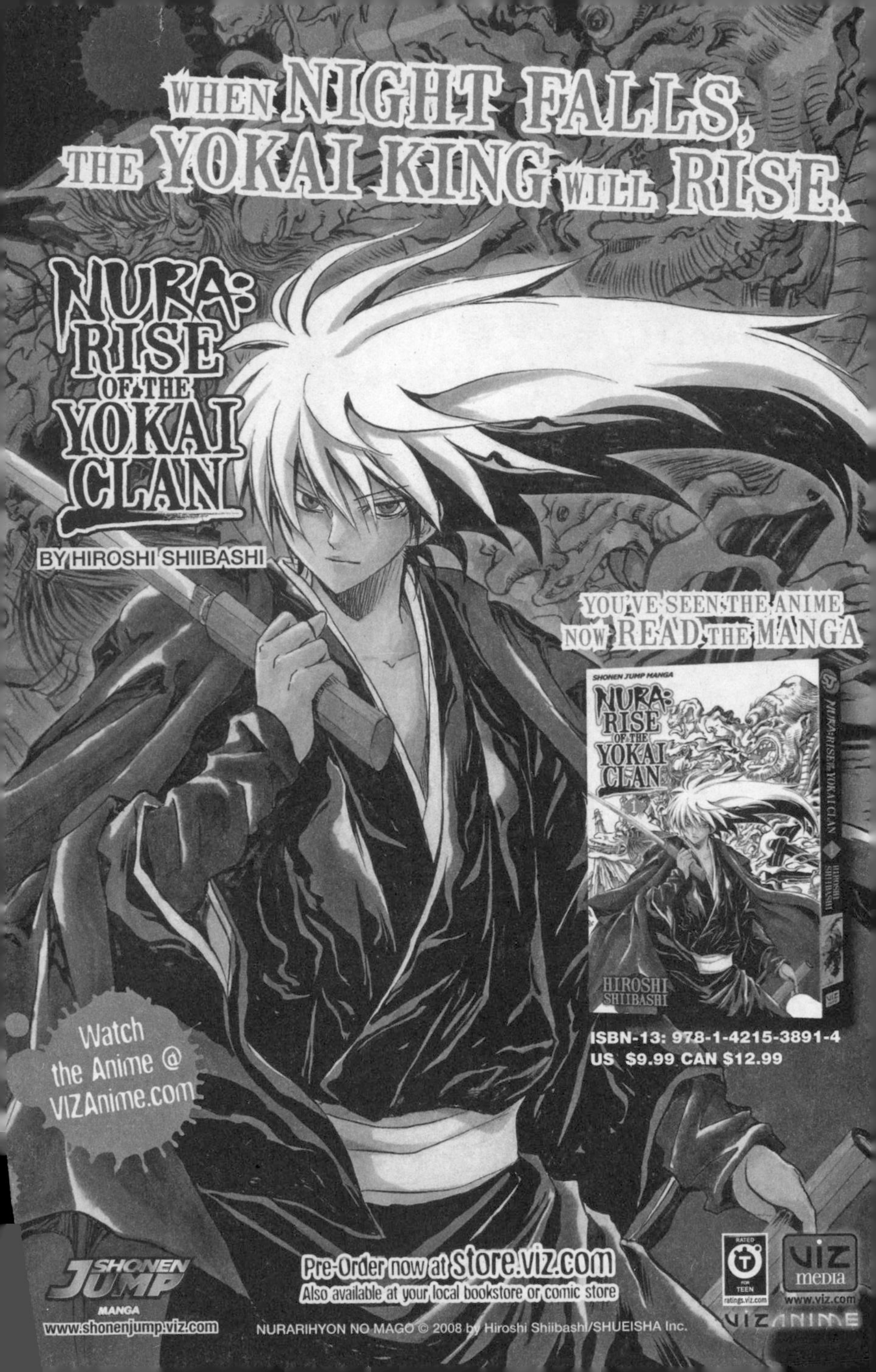

WHEN NIGHT FALLS, THE YOKAI KING WILL RISE.
NURA: RISE OF THE YOKAI CLAN
BY HIROSHI SHIIBASHI
YOU'VE SEEN THE ANIME NOW READ THE MANGA
SHONEN JUMP MANGA
NURA: RISE OF THE YOKAI CLAN
1
HIROSHI SHIIBASHI
ISBN-13: 978-1-4215-3891-4
US $9.99 CAN $12.99
Watch the Anime @ VIZAnime.com
SHONEN JUMP MANGA
www.shonenjump.viz.com
Pre-Order now at store.viz.com
Also available at your local bookstore or comic store
RATED T FOR TEEN
ratings.viz.com
VIZ media
www.viz.com
VIZANIME
NURARIHYON NO MAGO © 2008 by Hiroshi Shiibashi/SHUEISHA Inc.

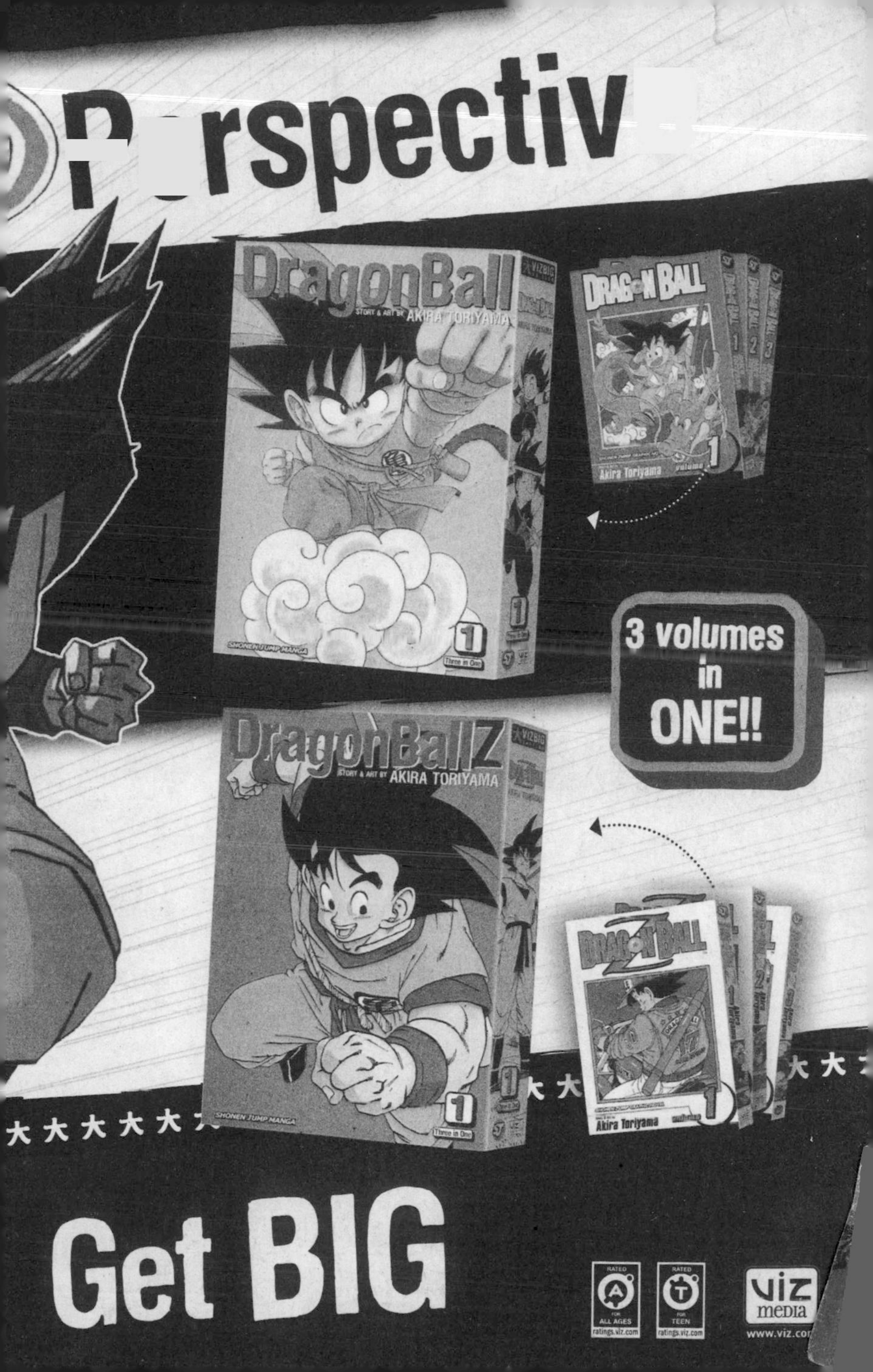
P rspectiv
Dragon Ball
STORY & ART BY AKIRA TORIYAMA
Three in One
SHONEN JUMP MANGA
Akira Toriyama
3 volumes in ONE!!
Dragon Ball Z
STORY & ART BY AKIRA TORIYAMA
Get BIG
RATED A FOR ALL AGES ratings.viz.com
RATED T FOR TEEN ratings.viz.com
VIZ media

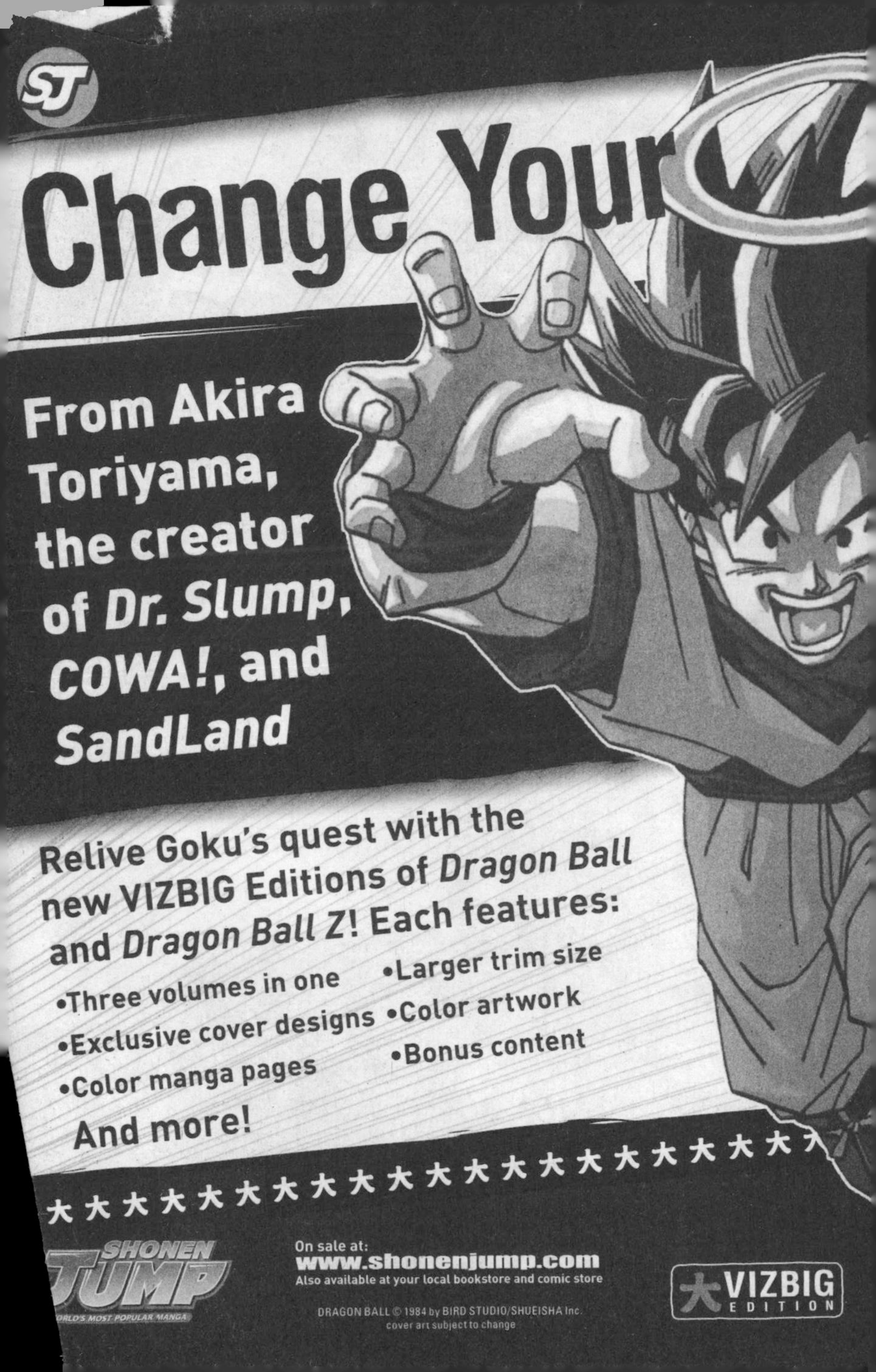
SJ
Change Your
From Akira Toriyama, the creator of Dr. Slump, COWA!, and SandLand
Relive Goku's quest with the new VIZBIG Editions of Dragon Ball and Dragon Ball Z! Each features:
•Three volumes in one
•Exclusive cover designs
•Color manga pages
•Larger trim size
•Color artwork
•Bonus content
And more!
SHONEN JUMP
ORLD'S MOST POPULAR MANGA
On sale at:
www.shonenjump.com
Also available at your local bookstore and comic store
DRAGON BALL © 1984 by BIRD STUDIO/SHUEISHA Inc.
cover art subject to change
大 VIZBIG EDITION

S0-AYT-431

Hey! You're Reading in the Wrong Direction!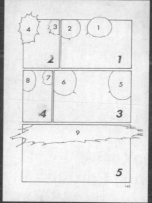

This is the **end** of this graphic novel!

To properly enjoy this VIZ graphic novel, please turn it around and begin reading from **right to left**. Unlike English, Japanese is read right to left, so Japanese comics are read in reverse order from the way English comics are typically read.

Follow the action this way

This book has been printed in the original Japanese format in order to preserve the orientation of the original artwork. Have fun with it!